TROUBLESHOOTING, MAINTAINING & REPAIRING NETWORKS

About the Author

Stephen J. Bigelow is the founder and president of Dynamic Learning Systems—a technical writing, research, and small publishing company specializing in electronic and PC service topics. Bigelow is the author of 15 feature-length books for TAB/McGraw-Hill, and over 100 major articles for mainstream electronics magazines such as *Popular Electronics, Electronics NOW, Circuit Cellar INK*, and *Electronic Service & Technology*. Bigelow is a contributing editor at *CNET* (the "PC Mechanic" column and feature articles) and a regular contributor with *SmartComputing*. Bigelow is also the editor and publisher of *The PC Toolbox*™—a premier PC service newsletter for computer enthusiasts and technicians. He is an Electrical Engineer with a BS EE from Central New England College in Worcester, MA. You may contact the author at **www.dlspubs.com**.

About the Technical Editors

Gary C. Kessler is an Associate Professor and program director of the Computer Networking major at Champlain College in Burlington, VT, where he also is the director of the Vermont Information Technology Center security projects. He is also an independent consultant specializing in issues related to computer and network security, Internet and TCP/IP protocols and applications, e-commerce, and telecommunications technologies and applications. Gary is a frequent speaker at industry conferences and has written two books and over 60 articles on a variety of technology topics. Gary has two children in college and lives in Colchester, VT. More information can be found at **http://www.garykessler.net/**.

Richard Carrara, CCIE (# 7288), CISSP (technical review Chapters 2, 3, 5, 6, 7, 8, 13, 14, 15, and 26) is currently a Senior Network Architect at Data Return, Inc., based in Irving, TX. He is a CCIE and CISSP with over eight years of Information Technology experience. He specializes in the design and architecture of secure, large-scale IP networks. Richard can be reached via email at **rcarrara@hotmail.com**.

About the Contributing Authors

L.J. Zacker (Chapter 2) began working with mainframe and personal computers in the mid 1980s and has since been employed as a network administrator, programmer, and security consultant for mainframe systems and PC LANs. Now a full-time author and editor, L.J. has contributed to numerous books and articles for various publishers including Microsoft Press and Windows 2000 Magazine.

Glen Carty, CCIE (Chapter 3), author of *Broadband Networking* (McGraw Hill/Osborne), has been designing and building local and wide area networking solutions since the early 1980s. He was a senior manager responsible for global design and design standards for the networking solutions offered by IBM Global Network.

Toby J. Velte, Ph.D., CCNA, CCDA, MCSE+I (Chapters 5 and 26), is a respected industry leader in the field of data networking. Dr. Velte has started four high-tech companies and co-authored eight books with McGraw-Hill/Osborne.

Robert C. Elsenpeter (Chapters 5 and 26) is an author, Web content writer, and award-winning journalist. His is co-author of *eBusiness: A Beginner's Guide, Optical Networking: A Beginner's Guide,* and *Windows XP Professional Network Administration* all by McGraw-Hill/Osborne.

Gilbert Held (Chapter 6) is an award-winning author and lecturer. Gil is the author of over 50 books and 450 technical articles, and he represented the United States at technical conferences in Moscow and Jerusalem. Gil can be contacted via email at **gil_held@yahoo.com**.

Cormac Long, CCSI (Chapter 7), is an independent consultant with more than 14 years of engineering experience in local and wide area internetworking. He has designed and installed several major LAN and WAN networks for customers in the United States and Europe. He holds a Bachelor's Degree in Electronic Engineering and a Master's Degree in Telecommunications. He is the author of two internetworking books both published by McGraw-Hill/Osborne: *Cisco Internetworking and Troubleshooting* and *IP Network Design*. As an internationally recognized data and telecommunications expert, he is a frequent conference speaker and has given live Webcasts on advanced IP networking topics.

Jared M. Nussbaum (Chapters 8, 13, and 14) has been involved in the data networking and telecommunications industries for the past 14 years, specializing in systems architecture and data network design, operations, and security. He presently holds a Bachelors of Business Administration from Hofstra University. In April 1997, Mr. Nussbaum was a founding member of building-centric telecommunications provider OnSite Access, Inc. There he was key in designing the network infrastructure that is the basis of OnSite Access' data services. Mr. Nussbaum was also responsible for the development and management of the company's data products, as well as the systems architecture and administration teams. In May 1995, Mr. Nussbaum founded American DataNet, Inc., which specialized in providing high-speed Internet access and Wide Area Networking services to the academic and corporate communities.

Keith Strassberg (Chapter 15) is an experienced information systems security consultant who holds a B.S. in Accounting from Binghamton University. Mr. Strassberg earned his CPA while working in the Computer Risk Management Group of Arthur Andersen, LLP, where he aided clients by identifying and minimizing operational, technological, and business-related risks in their IT systems. Mr. Strassberg joined Greenwich Technology Partners (GTP) in June 1999. Working in their computer security practice, Mr. Strassberg has helped numerous clients improve their network security postures by recommending and implementing best practice firewall configurations. He has previously published, authoring *Firewalls: The Complete Reference* and contributing a chapter to the RSA Press book *Security Architecture, Design, Deployment, and Operations*. You can reach Keith at **kstrassberg@yahoo.com**.

TROUBLESHOOTING, MAINTAINING & REPAIRING NETWORKS

STEPHEN J. BIGELOW

McGraw-Hill/Osborne

New York   Chicago   San Francisco
Lisbon   London   Madrid   Mexico City
Milan   New Delhi   San Juan
Seoul   Singapore   Sydney   Toronto

McGraw-Hill/Osborne
2600 Tenth Street
Berkeley, California 94710
U.S.A.

To arrange bulk purchase discounts for sales promotions, premiums, or fund-raisers, please contact **McGraw-Hill**/Osborne at the above address. For information on translations or book distributors outside the U.S.A., please see the International Contact Information page immediately following the index of this book.

Troubleshooting, Maintaining & Repairing Networks

234567890 DOC DOC 0198765432

ISBN 0-07-222257-3

Publisher
Brandon A. Nordin

Vice President & Associate Publisher
Scott Rogers

Editorial Director
Tracy Dunkelberger

Acquisitions Editor
Lisa McClain

Project Editor
Mark Karmendy

Acquisitions Coordinator
Emma Acker

Technical Editors
Gary Kessler
Richard Carrara

Copy Editor
Dennis Weaver

Proofreader
Pat Mannion

Indexer
Jack Lewis

Computer Designers
Michelle Galicia
Melinda Moore Lytle

Illustrators
Michael Mueller
Lyssa Wald

Series Design
Michelle Galicia

Cover Photos: Stephen Bigelow (cable tester), Paul Eekhoff/Masterfile (network server), GettyImages (man with network server)

This book was composed with Corel VENTURA™ Publisher.

CONTENTS AT A GLANCE

CONTENTS

DISCLAIMER AND CAUTIONS

It is IMPORTANT that you read and understand the following information. Please read it carefully!

PERSONAL RISK AND LIMITS OF LIABILITY

The repair of personal computers, peripherals, and networks involves some amount of personal risk. Use extreme caution when working with AC and high-voltage power sources. Every reasonable effort has been made to identify and reduce areas of personal risk. You are instructed to read this book carefully *before* attempting the procedures discussed. If you are uncomfortable following the procedures that are outlined in this book, do NOT attempt them—refer your service to qualified service personnel.

NEITHER THE AUTHOR, THE PUBLISHER, NOR ANYONE DIRECTLY OR INDIRECTLY CONNECTED WITH THE PUBLICATION OF THIS BOOK SHALL MAKE ANY WARRANTY EITHER EXPRESSED OR IMPLIED, WITH REGARD TO THIS MATERIAL, INCLUDING, BUT NOT LIMITED TO, THE IMPLIED WARRANTIES OF QUALITY, MERCHANTABILITY, AND FITNESS FOR ANY PARTICULAR PURPOSE. Further, neither the author, publisher, nor anyone directly or indirectly connected with the publication of this book shall be liable for errors or omissions contained herein, or for incidental or consequential damages, injuries, or financial or material losses resulting from the use, or inability to use, the material and software contained herein. This material and software is provided AS-IS, and the reader bears all responsibilities and risks connected with its use.

VENDOR WARNING

The Web sites, products, materials, equipment, manufacturers, service providers, and distributors listed and presented in this book are shown for reference purposes only. Their mention and use in this book shall not be construed as an endorsement of any individual or organization, nor the quality of their products or services, nor their performance or business integrity. The author, publisher, and anyone directly or indirectly associated with the production of this book expressly disclaim all liability whatsoever for any financial or material losses or incidental or consequential damages that might occur from contacting or doing business with any such organization or individual.

ACKNOWLEDGMENTS

It is impossible to create a book like this without a generous helping of enthusiastic support and encouragement. I'd like to take a moment and thank those that helped me to develop and refine this title:

- I'd first like to thank Tracy Dunkelberger, Emma Acker, Mark Karmendy, Michelle Galicia, Jean Butterfield, and the rest of the staff at McGraw-Hill/Osborne for their unwavering patience and persistence.

- Thanks also to Gary Kessler for his brutally honest comments and criticisms. I hope that I've ultimately created a title worthy of his extensive time and effort.

- Thanks to Diane Gunderson at Network Instruments for their Observer Suite protocol analyzer (see them at **www.networkinstruments.com**).

- Thanks to Jon Toor at Maxtor for their NAS 3000 network storage device (see them at **www.maxtor.com**).

- Thanks to Diana Ying at Linksys for the use of their wireless Internet router, USB wireless NIC, PCMCIA wireless NIC, KVM switch, GigaCD Server, Cable/DSL voice enabler, and Gigabit Ethernet NIC/switch (see their entire line of networking devices at **www.linksys.com**).

- Thanks to Raymond Jones at SonicWall for the use of their SOHO2 firewall (see them at **www.sonicwall.com**).

- Thanks to Juli Dexter at APCC for the use of their SmartUPS 700 (see them at **www.apcc.com**).

- And a very special thanks to Al Kirts at Gateway for the extremely generous use of their 7400 server platform—this made an incredible difference in the scope and detail of the book (see them at **www.gateway.com**).

Finally, I want to send along a special thank you to my wonderful wife who selflessly endured more than her share of lonely nights while I toiled through this challenging project. Without her loving patience and encouragement, this book would not have been worth the effort.

INTRODUCTION: A BOOK FOR CHANGING TIMES

Years ago, PCs used to be independent—little islands of processing power that populated the desktops of homes and offices alike. The fact that each PC often ran unique versions of an operating system or applications seemed little more than a nuisance. The notion that Bill in accounting was still using a DOS spreadsheet that wasn't compatible with your early Windows version of Excel was simply a fact of life. You'd just resave your Excel file in a format that Bill could read, then tote it up to accounting on diskette. Sure it was a pain, but what else could you do?

As the years passed, a funny thing started to happen. Networking technology took hold for the PC, and users began to realize that they could work together. Allowing PCs to communicate with each other opened tremendous possibilities for cooperation and collaboration. For example, a single version of your Excel file could be made readable by a set of authorized users, and writable by a select few—ensuring immediate access to the latest data. Today, networks are essential to the operation of all business types, and are even found in home environments with multiple PCs. When properly implemented and configured, networks can provide fast and reliable performance.

However, networks do fail—and they fail in ways that continue to exhaust even the most patient mind. When trouble strikes, you will need to take decisive action to identify and correct the problem. Once you realize that many networks can involve hundreds (perhaps thousands) of PCs—in addition to the cabling, hubs, routers, switches, and other network devices—you can see that *effective* troubleshooting requires more than simply an arbitrary swapping of PCs and other network devices. Now, more than ever, efficient and cost-effective troubleshooting requires an understanding of network hardware and operating systems, along with a keen knowledge of symptoms and diagnostics. Setting up, optimizing, and upgrading a network are three other important areas that demand the attention of today's technician.

IN THIS EDITION

This book is intended for the modern network enthusiast and working technician tasked with implementing or fixing their organization's network. It is *not* intended to provide extensive network theory—there are already plenty of theory books out there. Instead, this book is designed to be a hands-on desktop (or workbench) reference for network repair, maintenance, and upgrading. This book concentrates on the symptoms and problem areas that occur in every area of the modern PC, as well as proper *diagnosis* of problems. Online resources are included for almost every chapter making the book ideal for classroom or home study. This book is meant to be a lifeline and a resource to help you repair your network, keep it running, and get the most out of it. You'll find hundreds of problems fully detailed and explained. There are references to hundreds more POST and diagnostic codes to help you identify even the most obscure problems.

SUBSCRIBE TO THE PC TOOLBOX

Many readers also complain that computer books suffer from a limited "life-span". All too often, a book is dated as soon as it gets on bookstore shelves. You can avoid this kind of technical obsolescence by subscribing to our #1 newsletter; *The PC Toolbox*™—stay informed of the latest hands-on service articles, optimization techniques, and find the answers to your computing questions. Even if you don't fix networks for a living, a subscription can save you hundreds of dollars in shop costs. You can learn more about *The PC Toolbox*™ and enter your subscription at **www.dlspubs.com**.

TEST YOUR KNOWLEDGE

Worried about keeping yourself employable? Go for the Dynamic Learning Systems Network Technician's Certificate. As the purchaser of this book, you can take the *DLS Network Technician's Certificate Exam* included in Appendix C. Those readers who pass will receive a high-quality certificate showing your mastery of the material in this book. But the certificate is not just for framing—readers who successfully complete the examination are much better prepared to tackle the industry-recognized Net+ and Server+ examinations.

I'M INTERESTED IN YOUR SUCCESS

I've taken a lot of time and effort to see that this edition is the most comprehensive and understandable book on network troubleshooting available. If you have any questions or comments about the book, please don't hesitate to contact me through Dynamic Learning Systems at **www.dlspubs.com**.

—*Stephen J. Bigelow*

SYMPTOMS AT A GLANCE

1

INTRODUCTION TO NETWORKING

While individual computers can be quite powerful, they still operate alone. Sharing files and resources typically means copying a file to a diskette (or CD-RW disc), then manually walking that diskette to other systems—for example, working on a document after work, then returning that updated document to work the next day in order to print it. Obviously, this is a cumbersome and time-consuming process. If there were a means of "connecting" two or more computers, you could access your work from another location (such as a computer in your home), finish the work that night, and then send the work to a printer located back at the office. This is the underlying premise behind a *network*—two or more computers connected together in order to share files, resources, and even applications. This chapter introduces you to the basic concepts and terminology needed to understand the tangible elements of common networks and servers, highlights the basics of network documentation, then explains the essential guidelines used in network troubleshooting.

A Network Primer

A networked computer that provides resources is called a *server*. The computer accessing those resources is referred to as a *workstation* or *client*. Servers are usually the most powerful computers on the network because they require the added processing power to service the many requests of other computers sharing their resources. By comparison, workstations or clients are usually PCs that are cheaper and less powerful. As a rule, a computer may be a server *or* a workstation, but rarely both (this separation greatly simplifies the management and administration of the network). Small networks with relatively few users may turn to *peer-to-peer* networking where each PC can share information, but this book will focus on the client/server computing scheme. Of course, all of the computers on a network must be physically connected, and such connections are typically established with network interface card (NIC) adapters, and copper cabling (or alternative connections such as fiber-optic or wireless).

ADVANTAGES OF A NETWORK

With individual computers, applications and resources (such as printers or scanners) must be duplicated between PCs. For example, if two data analysts want to work on an Excel spreadsheet and print their results each day, both computers will need a copy of Excel and a printer. If the users needed to share data, it would have to be shuttled between the PCs on diskette or CD-RW. And if users needed to share computers, they would have to wade through the other user's system—each with its own desktop setup, applications, folder arrangement, and so on. In short, it would be a wasteful, frustrating, and error-prone process. As more users become involved, it wouldn't take long before the whole process would be impossible to handle. However, if those two computers in our example were networked together, both users could use Excel across the network (though it's often more common today for each workstation to run its own application, such as Excel, and share the data), access the same raw data, and then output their results to a single "common" printer attached to the network. If more users were then added to the network, all users could share the application, data, and resources in a uniform fashion. More specifically, computers that are part of a network can share

- Documents (memos, spreadsheets, invoices, and so on)
- E-mail messages
- Word-processing software
- Project-tracking software
- Illustrations, photographs, videos, and audio files
- Live audio and video broadcasts
- Printers
- Fax machines
- Modems
- CD-ROM drives and other removable media drives (such as Zip and Jaz drives)
- Hard drives

Since many computers can operate on one network, the entire network can be efficiently managed from a central point (a *network administrator*). Consider our example above and suppose that a new version of Excel became available to our data analysts. With individual computers, each system would have to be upgraded and checked separately. That's not such a big deal with only two systems, but when there are dozens (even hundreds) of PCs in the company, individual upgrades can quickly become costly and inefficient. With a network, an application only needs to be updated on its server once—then all of the network's workstations can use the updated software immediately. Centralized administration also allows security and system monitoring to take place from one location.

But networks allow other benefits in addition to sharing information. With a network, information can be preserved and protected. For example, it is very difficult to coordinate and manage a backup process across a large number of independent PCs. Systems on a network can automatically back up to a central location (such as a tape drive on a network server). If local information is lost, it can be efficiently located and restored from that centralized backup. Data is also more secure. Accessing an individual PC usually means accessing all of the information on that PC. But the security features present in a network also prevent unauthorized users from accessing or deleting sensitive information. For example, each network user has a logon name and password that permits access to only a limited number of network resources. Finally, networks are ideal mediums for communication between users. Rather than exchanging memos and messages on paper, electronic mail (or simply *e-mail*) allows users to send messages, reports, images—virtually any file types—between locations on the network. This also saves the expense of printing and the delays associated with interdepartmental correspondence. E-mail is such a powerful tool that Internet users can exchange messages virtually anywhere in the world almost instantly.

Network Sizes

Computer networks typically fit into one of three groups depending on their size and function. A *local area network* (LAN) is the most fundamental classification of any computer network. LAN architecture can range from simple (two computers connected by a cable) to complex (hundreds of connected computers and peripherals throughout a major corporation). The distinguishing feature of a LAN is that it is confined to a limited geographic area such as a single building or department (typically stated at <5km in diameter). If the computers are connected over several buildings across a large metropolitan area, the network is sometimes termed a *metropolitan area network* (or MAN, usually from 5–50km). By comparison, a *wide area network* (WAN) has no geographical limit. It can connect computers and peripheral devices on opposite sides of the world. In most cases, a WAN is made up of a number of interconnected LANs—perhaps the ultimate WAN is the Internet.

DETERMINING THE NEED

In today's busy business environment, it seems that every vendor offers a network solution intended to bolster sales, improve productivity, and even enhance income. In many cases, businesses are coaxed into network investments without a thorough consideration of the expense and talent involved. If you're an IS manager or decision maker, you may be wondering if the technical and logistical hassles of a new network will be worthwhile. The following issues may help you determine whether your business may benefit from a network:

■ *Your company or department is investing in redundant hardware or software.* Networks allow for an astonishing amount of sharing, so redundant hardware purchases such as printers, drives, and application software may actually be more expensive (in the long run) than establishing a network to share those resources. For example, buying or upgrading ten new printers may be more expensive than implementing one network printer. Not only is the installation and maintenance of one network printer easier and quicker, but *many* networked users can employ the printer.

■ *There are errors and lost productivity due to software incompatibility.* This commonly happens when various users are using different versions of important software. Files developed on an older version may be portable to a later version, but not vice versa. For example, a document developed on Word 6 may open fine in Word 2000, but not vice versa—and not in Word for DOS. This would limit the users that can use each document. This can also happen when different users employ applications from different manufacturers (such as Word versus WordPerfect). A system of networked users can all use the same application version, and are assured of file compatibility. Also, a technician can upgrade the networked application *once* rather than deal with multiple upgrades for individual users.

■ *Training and support costs are significant.* Training costs are increasing steadily, and even manufacturers that have not charged in the past are imposing fees for new training and support. When multiple hardware and software versions are being used, the costs can become prohibitive. Using a network with "standardized" software versions reduces the number of applications being used throughout the organization, and this in turn reduces the variety of support services needed for your users. If training is needed for a given application, a larger number of users can be exposed to the training (reducing the per-user cost).

■ *Productivity is lost waiting for resources.* A great deal of productivity can be lost when users must wait to access other systems. For example, one user must log off their PC so that another user can load their data in order to print a document or report. As another example, customer service representatives on one PC may not have access to a customer's account history, payment information, ordering trends, and other information located on other systems throughout the organization. Customers must then be placed on hold while information is requested from other departments. A networked system can allow one department to access relevant information about a customer. When Internet capabilities are included, customers can even access critical information and make their ordering or support time more productive.

Of course, there are many other signs that may suggest the need for a network. For example, data is lost because some users aren't making backups consistently (if at all). Lost time and productivity due to manual file transfers (aka "sneaker-net") by disk or CD may also be alleviated with a network. Networks can replace important messages on notepads or scraps of paper, and keep messages from being ignored or overlooked. A network can be operated by itself within the confines of your company, or connected to other networks (or even the Internet) for data sharing and communications on a global scale.

Network Types

Networks are generally divided into two distinct categories: *peer to peer* and *server based*. This is an important distinction because these two categories are vastly different and offer different capabilities to the users. Peer-to-peer networks are simpler and less expensive networks that appear in small organizations such as small office/home office (SOHO) or small workgroup applications. Server-based networks are found in midsized and larger organizations where security, centralized administration, and high traffic capacity are important. Let's look a bit closer at these network types.

PEER-TO-PEER NETWORKS

This is a simple and straightforward networking approach that simply connects computers to allow basic file sharing. There are no dedicated servers, and there is no hierarchy among the computers. Since all of the computers are equal, they are known as *peers*. Each computer serves as both a client and a server, and there is no administrator responsible for the entire network—the user at each computer determines what data on that computer is shared on the network. All users can share any of their resources in any manner they choose. This includes data in shared directories, printers, fax cards, and so on. Peer-to-peer networks are also commonly called *workgroups* (which implies a small group of people) because there are typically ten or fewer computers in a peer-to-peer network. As a result of this simplicity, peer-to-peer networks are often less expensive than server-based networks.

In a peer-to-peer network, the networking software does not require the same standard of performance or security as the networking software designed for dedicated server systems. In fact, peer-to-peer networking capability is built into many popular operating systems (such as Windows 98/ME, MacOS, and UNIX/Linux). This means you can set up a peer-to-peer network without any additional network operating system.

Security is a real weakness in peer-to-peer environments. Generally speaking, *security* (i.e., making computers—and the data stored on them—safe from harm or unauthorized access) on a peer-to-peer network consists of setting a password on a resource (i.e., a directory) that is shared on the network. All peer-to-peer network users set their own security, and shared resources can exist on any computer, so centralized control is very difficult to maintain. This has a big impact on network security because some users may not implement any security measures at all. In summary, a peer-to-peer network is often the best choice when

■ There are just a few users—designers usually place the limit at ten users, though there may certainly be more.

■ Users share resources (such as files and printers) but no specialized servers exist.

■ Security is not considered to be an issue.

■ The organization (and the network) is expected to experience only limited growth.

 Since every computer in a peer-to-peer environment can act as both a server and a client, users generally need additional training before they can act as both users and administrators of their computers.

SERVER-BASED NETWORKS

In most network situations, the duality of peer-to-peer networks is simply not adequate. Limited traffic capability and security/management issues often mean that networks need to use dedicated servers (such as the Gateway 7400 in Figure 1-1). A *dedicated* server is a computer that functions only as a server to provide files and manage resources—it is *not* used as a client or workstation. Servers are optimized to handle requests from numerous network clients quickly, and ensure the security of files and directories. Consequently, server-based networks have become the standard models for modern business networking. Server-based networks are also known as *client/server* networks (sometimes denoted as *two-tier* architectures). Keep in mind that it is the operating system and other network software that define a client/server or peer-to-peer network—the hardware and physical network connections are identical.

 Servers provide specific resources and services to the network, and there may be several (perhaps many) servers available in a given network.

Server Types

As networks increase in size (i.e., as the number of connected computers increases, and the physical distance and traffic between them grows), more than one server is usually needed. Spreading the networking

FIGURE 1-1   The Gateway 7400 is a versatile workgroup/departmental server. (Courtesy of Gateway)

tasks among several servers ensures that each task will be performed as efficiently as possible. Servers must perform varied and complex tasks, and servers for large networks have become specialized to accommodate the expanding needs of users. Some examples of different server types included on many large networks are listed below.

File and Print Servers   File and print servers manage the user's overall access and use of file and printer resources. For example, when you're running a word-processing application (such as Microsoft Word), that application runs on your workstation. The document stored on the file and print server is loaded into your workstation's memory so that you can edit or use it locally. In other words, file and print servers are used for file and data storage. If you wish to print the document, the file and print server manages the transfer of that file to the network printer.

Database Servers   In most cases, a database server is a server that runs a SQL-based database management system (DBMS). Client computers send the SQL requests to the database server. The server accesses the stored database to process the request, then returns the results to the client computer. When referring to a database server, the term "server" may refer to the computer itself or the DBMS software that manages the database (such as Microsoft SQL Server).

Application Servers   Where file and print servers will download a file to the requesting client PC, an application server does not—only the results of a request are sent to the client PC. For example, you might search the employee database for all employees who were born in November. Instead of the entire database being downloaded to your PC so that you can search it, the search is performed on the application server itself, and only the result of your query is sent from the server to your computer. This subtle but powerful difference makes application servers (such as Lotus Domino) ideal for maintaining vast quantities of data and efficiently providing that data to clients.

Mail Servers   E-mail is an important part of modern communication, so mail servers (such as Microsoft Exchange Server or Sendmail) handle the flow of e-mail and messaging between network users. In most cases, mail servers are similar to application servers because the e-mail typically remains on that server. When you check your e-mail, you only see the e-mail intended for your screen name. Storing e-mail in a central fashion such as this allows for better security and e-mail management (i.e., old e-mails can be purged after so many days in a system-wide fashion).

A variation of this is the *mailing list* server (aka, a *list server*), which is needed for creating, managing, and serving mailing lists. List servers (such as Majordomo) generally offer more features and better performance than their integrated counterparts. Uses for mailing lists and list servers include the distribution of e-zines, newsletters, product updates, technical support documents, classroom schedules, and product brochures, along with discussion forums for clubs and groups, electronic memos, and so on.

Fax and Communication Servers   Networks rarely exist in a vacuum, and there are generally several ways to access the network from outside. Two popular means of external network access are faxes and dial-up. A fax server (such as FaxMaker) manages fax traffic into and out of the network using one or more fax/modem cards. This allows network users to send faxes outside of the network (and vice versa) without the need for stand-alone fax devices. Communication servers handle data file and e-mail transfers between your own networks and other networks, mainframe computers, or remote users who dial in to the servers over modems and telephone lines. For example, a network user may access the Internet through a communication server.

Audio/Video Servers   Audio and video servers deliver multimedia capabilities to Web sites by giving users the ability to listen to sound or music and watch movie clips through Web browser plug-ins. While the use of traditional formats like **.WAV**, **.MIDI**, **.MOV**, or **.AVI** on Web sites doesn't really demand a specialized server, the recent emergence of streaming audio and video content has made the audio/video server a necessity in many cases (with tools such as RealServer Plus). New streaming technologies mark an important transition for multimedia on the Web, and will undoubtedly become one of the Internet's most exciting technologies as it evolves.

Chat Servers   It is common practice for two or more users to exchange real-time messages. This is called a *chat*, and chat servers (using tools like MeetingPoint) provide the management for real-time discussion capabilities for a large number of users. Potential chat uses include teleconferences, private meeting areas, help support forums, and employee recreational get-togethers. The three major types of communications servers are Internet Relay Chat (IRC), conferencing, and community servers. The most advanced chat servers have recently started augmenting the text-based medium of conversation with dynamic voice (and even video) support. It is not uncommon for IRC-based chat to use dedicated IRC servers (with software like IRCPlus).

FTP Servers   From downloading the newest software to transferring corporate documents, a significant percentage of Internet traffic consists of file transfers. File Transfer Protocol (FTP) servers make it possible to move one or more files between computers with security and data integrity controls appropriate for the Internet (using tools like ZBServer Pro). FTP is a typical client/server arrangement. The FTP server does the main work of file security, file organization, and transfer control. The client (sometimes part of a browser and sometimes a specialized program such as FTP Voyager) receives the files and places them onto the local hard disk.

News Servers   News servers function as a distribution and delivery source for over 20,000 public newsgroups currently accessible over the Usenet news network (the largest news and discussion group-based network on the Internet). News servers use tools (like INN News Server) that employ the Network News Transport Protocol (NNTP) to interface with other USENET news servers and distribute news to anyone using a standard NNTP newsreader (such as Agent or Outlook Express). News servers also make it possible to serve your own news and discussion groups publicly over the Internet—or privately over your own local network.

Gateway Servers   A *gateway* is a translator that allows differing networks to communicate. One common use for gateways is to act as translators between personal computers and minicomputer or mainframe systems. For example, an e-mail gateway may allow translation between GroupWise and SMTP mail systems. In a LAN environment, one computer is usually designated as the gateway computer. Special application programs in the desktop computers access the mainframe by communicating with the mainframe environment through the gateway computer, and users can access resources on the mainframe just as if those resources were on their own desktop computers.

Firewalls and Proxy Servers   Simply stated, a *firewall* is a feature designed to prevent unauthorized access to or from a private network (i.e., a corporation's LAN), and is generally considered to be a first line of defense in protecting private information. Firewalls can be implemented in both hardware and software (and often involve a combination of both). When properly implemented, firewalls prevent unauthorized Internet users from accessing private networks that are connected to the Internet—especially intranets. In large corporate environments, firewalls are also used to prevent unauthorized access within the same LAN or intranet. All messages entering or leaving the intranet pass through the firewall, which examines each message and blocks those that do not meet the required security criteria. There are numerous firewall techniques, including packet filters, application gateways, circuit-level gateways, and proxy servers. The *proxy server* is perhaps the most popular form of firewall. In actual practice, a proxy server sits between a client program (i.e., a Web browser) and some external server (usually another server on the Web). The proxy server effectively hides the true network address, then monitors and intercepts any requests being sent to the external server, or that come in from the Internet connection. This allows the proxy server to filter messages, improve performance, and share connections.

Web Servers   Web servers allow you to provide content over the Internet using the Hypertext Markup Language (HTML). A Web server (using software like Microsoft IIS or Apache) accepts requests from browsers like Netscape and Internet Explorer, and then returns the appropriate HTML document(s) to the requesting computer. A number of server technologies can be used to increase the power of the server beyond its ability to simply deliver standard HTML pages—these include CGI scripts, SSL security, and Active Server Pages (ASPs).

Telnet/WAIS Servers   Telnet servers give users the ability to log on to a host computer and perform tasks as if they're actually working on the remote computer itself. Users can access the host system through the Telnet server from anywhere in the world using a Telnet client application. Before the arrival of the Web, Wide Area Information Server (or "WAIS") servers were critical for allowing users to perform searches for keywords in files. While WAIS is really not that popular today, network developers looking to broaden their selection of Internet services may consider supporting Telnet or WAIS services.

Server Software

One major issue that separates servers from peer computers is the use of software. No matter how powerful a server may be, it requires an operating system (i.e., Windows NT/2000 Server, Novell NetWare, or UNIX/Linux) that can take advantage of the server's resources. Servers also require their specific server applications in order to provide their services to the network. For example, a Web server may use Windows NT and Microsoft IIS. It's not important for you to fully understand software issues at this point. Subsequent chapters will cover network protocols and operating systems in more detail.

Client/Server Advantages   There is little doubt that server-based networks are more complicated to install and configure, but there are some compelling advantages over peer-to-peer networks:

- **Sharing**   Servers allow for better resource organization and sharing. A server is intended to provide access to many files and printers while maintaining performance and security for the user. A server's data and resources can be centrally administered and controlled. This centralized approach makes it easier to find files and support resources than would otherwise be possible on individual computers.

- **Security**   In a server-based environment, one administrator can manage network security by setting network policies and applying them to every user and resource.

- **Backups**   Backup routines are also simplified because only servers need to be backed up (client/workstation PCs do not, though they certainly could be). Server backups can be scheduled to occur automatically (according to a predetermined schedule) even if the servers are located on different parts of the physical network.

- **Fault tolerance**   Since data is mainly held on servers, fault-tolerant data storage (i.e., RAID) can be added to the servers to prevent data loss due to drive failures or system crashes. This creates a more reliable server subject to less downtime.

- **Users**   A server-based network can support thousands of users. Such a large network would be impossible to manage as a peer-to-peer network, but current monitoring and network-management utilities make it possible to operate a server-based network for large numbers of users.

Server Reliability

Reliability is basically the notion of dependable and consistent operation—the probability that a component or system will perform a task for a specified period of time. This includes the server as well as the network, and is often measured as a function of the time between system failures using the term *MTBF* (mean time between failure). Data integrity and the ability to warn of impending hardware failures before they happen are two other aspects of reliability. Servers frequently include reliability features such as redundant power supplies and fans, predictive failure analysis for hard drives (called self-monitoring analysis and reporting technology, or SMART), and RAID (redundant array of independent disks) systems to ensure that a server continues to function and protect its data even when trouble occurs. Other reliability features include the memory self-test at boot time where the system detects and isolates bad memory blocks, as well as ECC (error checking and correcting) memory to improve data integrity.

Reliability is a critical server issue, and is absolutely vital to long-term network operation. Large networks typically strive for 99.999-percent reliability or better.

Server High Availability

A server must constantly be "up" and ready for immediate use, allowing a user to access the resources they need in real time. This is the issue of *high availability*. Another aspect of highly available servers is the capability to quickly recover from a system failure (i.e., use a "hot spare" RAID disk to recover data from a failed drive). Highly available systems may or may not use redundant components (such as redundant power supplies), but they should support the hot swapping of key components. *Hot swapping* is the ability to pull out a failed component and plug in a new one while the power is still on and the system is operating. A highly available system has the ability to detect a potential failure and transparently redirect or *failover* the questionable processes to other devices or subsystems. For example, some SCSI drives can automatically move data from marginal sectors (i.e., sectors that produce occasional read errors) to spare sectors without the operating system or the user being aware of the change.

In general, availability is measured as the percentage of time that a system is functioning and usable. For instance, a system that provides 99-percent availability on a 24 hours/day, 7 days/week basis would actually experience the loss of 88 processing hours a year (unacceptable to many users). However, a 99.999 percent level of availability translates to about 5.25 minutes of unscheduled downtime per year (though this level of availability may be quite costly to achieve).

Server Scalability

Computer customers of the past often bought mainframes twice the size they needed in anticipation of future growth, knowing that they would eventually "grow into" the machine. Today it's possible to select computers to fit the task now, then add more equipment as needs demand—this is known as *scalability*. A scalable PC has the ability to grow in size (capacity) and speed. Some machines offer limited scalability by design, while some can grow to virtually any size needed. Scalability includes the ability to add memory (RAM), add additional processors (i.e., for multiprocessing platforms), and add storage (hard drives), and still work within the limitations of the network operating system.

There is a subtle difference between upgrading and scaling. An upgrade is the replacement of an existing component with a faster or better component. Scaling a PC is the addition of more components for added capacity. For example, an ordinary PC may use a single processor. It may be possible to upgrade that processor to a faster model, but it is not possible to scale up the processing capacity with more processors—you'd need a server with a multiprocessing motherboard for that. By contrast, virtually all PCs can scale memory (RAM) simply by adding more DIMMs or RIMMs to the system. The same concept holds true for your disk space—you can upgrade to a larger or faster disk, or you could scale up the drive capacity by adding additional hard drives.

SMP and Parallel Processing

Since processors are a key element of server performance and scalability, it is a good time to cover multiprocessing in a little more detail. A symmetric multiprocessing (SMP) machine is a computer that utilizes two or more processors. Each processor shares memory and uses only one copy of the operating system. SMP machines can scale by starting small (with only two processors), then adding more processors as business needs and applications grow. Beyond CPUs, such computers typically have the ability to scale memory, cache, and disks. Currently, SMP machines are designed to scale from 2–32 processors.

There are limiting factors to consider when dealing with SMP systems. While it may seem possible to scale far more than 32 processors, that is often not the case. If you were to start with two processors and add two more, a near 100-percent improvement may result, but because there is only one operating system and all memory is shared, a diminishing return on performance will be realized as more processors are added. Most SMP systems will show worthwhile improvements until they scale above eight processors (the diminishing return also varies based on the operating system and the applications in use). While UNIX systems with 16 or more processors are not uncommon today, Windows NT scalability is commonly thought to be limited to about four CPUs. In addition, many operating systems or database applications can only utilize the first 2GB of memory.

By comparison, some of the largest and most scalable systems in the world utilize parallel processing technology. *Parallel processing* takes SMP a step further by combining multiple SMP nodes. These nodes can work in parallel on a single application—usually a database that is fully parallel capable. Because each node has its own copy of the operating system, and the nodes communicate through a specialized interconnection scheme, adding additional nodes does not increasingly tax a single OS. This means parallel processing can scale to much higher levels than SMP alone.

Server Clustering

Years ago, only a single processor was needed to run a server and operate all its applications. With the advent of multiprocessing, two or more processors shared a pool of memory, and the server could handle more and larger applications. Later, multiple servers were organized into groups with each server performing a specific task (i.e., file server, application server, and so on). Today, many high-end networks employ *server clusters*, where two or more server PCs act like a single server—providing higher availability and performance than a single could handle. Applications can move from one server to another, or run on several servers at once, and all transactions are transparent to the users.

Clustering provides higher availability and scalability than would be possible if the computers worked separately. Each node in the cluster typically has its own resources (processors, I/O, memory, OS, storage, and so on), and is responsible for its own set of users. The high availability of a server cluster is provided by failover capability. When one node fails, its resources can *failover* to one or more other nodes in the cluster. Once the original node is restored to normal operation, its resources can be manually (or automatically) switched back. Server clusters are also easily scalable without an interruption of service. Upgrades can be performed by proactively failing over the functions of a server to others in the cluster, bringing that server down to add components, then bringing the server back up into the cluster and switching back its functions from the other servers.

Server clustering is not really a new idea, but it has generally been proprietary in both hardware and software. IS managers are looking at clusters more seriously now as they become more accessible using mass-produced, standards-based hardware like RAID, SMP systems, network and I/O adapters, and other peripherals. While clusters are poised to gain more sophistication in the future, a growing number of cluster options are available today, and formal standards for clustering are still being developed.

Network Hardware

Now that you've had a chance to learn a bit about networks and server types, it's time to learn a bit more about the various hardware elements involved with the implementation of a network. Network hardware has a profound impact on the speed, quality, and overall performance of the network. For the purposes of this book, *network hardware* includes hubs, repeaters, bridges, routers, gateways, network interface cards, and cabling.

REPEATERS

As electrical signals travel along a cable, they degrade and become distorted. This effect is called *attenuation*. As cable lengths increase, the effects of attenuation worsen. If a cable is long enough, attenuation will finally make a signal unrecognizable, and this will cause data errors in the network. Installing a repeater enables signals to travel farther by regenerating the network's signals and sending them out again on other cable lengths. The repeater takes a weak signal from one cable, regenerates it, and passes it to the next cable. As you saw above, active hubs frequently act as repeaters, but stand-alone repeaters may be needed to support very long cable lengths.

It is important to realize that repeaters are simply signal amplifiers (or signal regenerators). They do not translate or filter the network signals from one cable to another. For a repeater to work properly, both cables joined by the repeater must use the same frames, logical protocols, and access method. The two most common access methods are carrier sense multiple access with collision detection (CSMA/CD) and token passing. A repeater cannot connect a segment using CSMA/CD to a segment using the token-passing access method. In effect, a repeater will not allow an Ethernet network to talk to a token ring network—there are other more sophisticated devices used for that type of translation. However, repeaters *can* move packets from one kind of physical media to another. For example, a repeater can take an Ethernet frame coming from a thin coaxial cable and pass it on to a fiber-optic cable (provided that the repeater is capable of accepting the physical connections).

Since repeaters simply pass data back and forth between cables, you should realize that problem data (such as malformed packets) will also be processed by the repeater. Bad data will not be filtered out, and excessive network traffic will not be managed. As a rule, avoid the use of repeaters when there is heavy network traffic or when data filtering features are needed.

HUBS

Simply stated, a *hub* is a central connection device that joins computers in a star topography. A variation of the hub is a Multistation Access Unit (or MAU, sometimes called a token ring hub) used to connect PCs in a token ring topology. Hubs are now standard equipment in modern networks, and are typically classified as *passive* or *active*. A passive hub does not process data at all—it's just a connection panel. By comparison, active hubs (sometimes called repeaters) regenerate the data in order to maintain adequate signal strength. Some hubs also have the ability to handle additional tasks such as bridging, routing, and switching. Hub-based systems are versatile, and offer several advantages over systems that do not use hubs. For example, with an ordinary bus topology, a break in the cable will take the network down. But with hubs, a break in any of the cables attached to the hub affects only that limited segment of the network.

Most hubs are active—that is, they regenerate and retransmit signals in the same way that a repeater does. Since hubs usually have eight to twelve ports for network computers to connect to, they are sometimes called *multiport repeaters*. Active hubs always require electrical power to run. Some hubs are passive (examples include wiring panels or punch-down blocks). They act only as connection points, and do not amplify or regenerate the signal. The signal just passes through the hub. Passive hubs do not require electrical power to run. An emerging generation of hubs will accommodate several different types of cables. These are called *hybrid hubs*.

BRIDGES

A *bridge* offers more features for a busy network. A bridge can act like a repeater to extend the effective length of a network cable. However, a bridge has more "intelligence," and can divide a network to isolate excessive traffic or problem data. For example, if the volume of traffic from one or two computers (or a single department) is flooding the network with data and slowing the entire operation, a bridge could isolate those computers (or departments) by putting them on their own cable segment. Rather than distinguish between one protocol and another, bridges simply pass all protocols along the network. Since all protocols pass across bridges, it is up to the individual computers to determine which protocols they can recognize. Bridges can also link different physical media such as twisted-pair cable and thin coaxial cable.

Routing Data

A bridge also offers superior data-handling capabilities not provided by hubs and repeaters. Bridges "listen" to all traffic, check the source and destination address of each frame, and build a routing table (as information becomes available) so that they can sort data to different parts of the network efficiently. Bridges actually have the ability to learn how to forward data. As traffic passes through the bridge, information about the computer hardware addresses is stored in the bridge's memory. The bridge uses this information to build a routing table based on source addresses. Initially, the bridge's memory is empty, and so is the routing table. As packets are transmitted, the source address is copied to the routing table. With this address information, the bridge eventually learns which computers are on which segment of the network.

When the bridge receives a frame, the source address is compared to the routing table. If the source address is not there, it is added to the table. The bridge then compares the destination address with the routing table database. If the destination address is in the routing table and is on the same network segment as the source address, the frame is discarded (because it's assumed that another PC on the same part of the network has received the data). This filtering helps to reduce network traffic and isolate different parts of the network. If the destination address is in the routing table and not in the same segment as the source address, the bridge forwards the frame out of the appropriate port to reach the destination address. If the destination address is not in the routing table, the bridge forwards the frame to all its ports except the one on which it originated.

Reducing Traffic

Remember that many PCs on a network may need to send data, but not all PCs may need to receive that data. Often, all PCs must receive data to see whether the information is intended for that workstation, then each must wait for an opportunity to send data itself. In a large network, this can significantly reduce network performance. However, large networks often group PCs into departments, and the data sent between departments is often far less than the traffic sent between PCs within the same department. By using bridges to separate the overall company network into several smaller departmental groups, it is possible to reduce the traffic going out to the entire network, and thus improve the overall network's performance.

Let's look at an example. Consider a company with five major departments: Sales, Accounting, Shipping, Manufacturing, and Design. In an "open" network, traffic sent from a PC in Sales would eventually reach every other PC on the network (i.e., Accounting, Shipping, and so on). Since traffic from one department is most commonly intended for other PCs in the same department, it's often a waste of network time to have all of those other PCs check all of that traffic. If a bridge is used to segregate the network into five different areas, traffic sent from one PC in Design to another PC in Design would *not* go out to the other areas of the network. This would reduce traffic because all of the other PCs would not need to check that traffic to see if it was intended for them. If a PC in Design wanted to send traffic to another PC in Sales, the bridge would know (through its routing table) which segment to relay that traffic to, and the other segments would not need to deal with that traffic. This controlling (or restricting) of the flow of network traffic is known as *segmenting* network traffic. A large network is not limited to one bridge. Multiple bridges can be used to combine several small networks into one large network.

Remote Connections

Bridges are often used to join smaller networks that are separated by large physical distances. For example, when two separate LANs are located at a great distance from each other, they can be joined into a single network using two remote bridges connected with synchronous modems to a dedicated data-grade telephone line.

ROUTERS AND BROUTERS

When you're working in more complex network environments that use several different network segments—each with different protocols and architectures—a bridge is often inadequate to handle fast and efficient communication between diverse segments. Such a complex network demands a sophisticated device that knows the address of each segment, determines the best path for sending data, and filters broadcast traffic to the local segment. This type of device is called a *router*. As with a bridge, routers can filter and isolate network traffic, and also connect network segments. Further, routers can switch and route packets across multiple networks. They do this by exchanging specific protocol information between separate networks. Routers have access to more packet information than bridges, and routers use this additional information to improve packet deliveries. Routers are used in complex networks because they provide better traffic management. For example, routers can share status and routing information with one another, and use this information to bypass slow or malfunctioning connections.

There are two principle router protocols: static and dynamic. A "static router" is sometimes called a "manual router" because all routes must be configured manually by the network administrator. Routing tables are fixed, so the static router always uses the same route (even if network activity changes). This means there's no guarantee that the router is using the shortest routes. By comparison, "dynamic routers" must be configured initially, but they will adapt to changing network conditions automatically—using lower-cost or lower-traffic routes as needed.

Routing Data

Routers maintain their own routing tables, which usually consist of network addresses (though host addresses can also be kept if the network needs it). To determine the destination address for incoming data, the routing table includes all known network addresses, logical instructions for connection to other networks, knowledge of the possible paths between routers, and even the costs of sending data over each path. Thus, a router uses its routing table to select the *best* route for data transmission based on costs and available paths. You should understand that the "routing tables" used for bridges and routers are *not* the same thing.

When routers receive packets destined for a remote network, they send them to the router that manages the destination network. The use of routers allows designers to separate large networks into smaller ones, and offer an element of security between the segments. Unfortunately, routers must perform complex functions on each packet, so they are slower than most bridges. For example, as packets are passed from router to router, source and destination addresses are stripped off and then re-created. This enables a router to route a packet from a TCP/IP Ethernet network to a server on a TCP/IP token ring network—a feature unattainable with a bridge.

Reducing Traffic

Routers look at the destination address in the packet and pass information accordingly. If the network address is unknown, packets *are* passed to the default gateway—no router knows every other network address, so all use the default route for unknown networks. Routers will not allow corrupted data to be passed onto the network. This ability to control the data passing through the router reduces the amount of traffic between networks, and allows routers to use these links more efficiently than bridges. Consequently, routers can greatly reduce the amount of traffic on the network and the wait time experienced by users. Remember that not all protocols are routable (you'll see more about protocols in Chapter 2). Typical routable protocols include DECnet, Internet Protocol (IP), and Internetwork Packet Exchange (IPX), while protocols such as Local Area Transport Protocol (LATP) or NetBIOS Extended User Interface (NetBEUI) are not routable. Routers are available that can accommodate multiple protocols (such as IP and DECnet) in the same network.

Selecting a Route

One distinct advantage enjoyed by routers is that they can support numerous active paths between LAN segments—and select redundant paths if necessary. Since routers can link segments that use completely different data packaging and access schemes, there are usually several possible paths available for a router to use. For example, if one router does not function, data can still be sent using alternate routes. This also applies to network traffic. If one path is very busy, the router identifies an alternative path and sends data over that one instead. Routers use powerful algorithms such as OSPF (Open Shortest Path First), RIP (Routing Information Protocol), or NLSP (NetWare Link Services Protocol) to determine an appropriate transmission path for a data packet.

Brouters

The functional distinctions between bridges and routers are blurring as technology advances. Some bridges have advanced intelligence that allows them to handle tasks that would normally require a router. These advanced bridges are called *brouters*. A brouter can act as a "router" for one protocol and "bridge" for all the others. A brouter can route selected routable protocols, bridge nonroutable protocols, and provide more cost-effective and more manageable internetworking than separate bridges and routers.

GATEWAYS

A *gateway* acts as a powerful interpreter designed to connect radically different networks. Although slower than a bridge or router, a gateway can perform complex functions such as translating between networks that speak different languages (using techniques such as protocol and bandwidth conversion). For example, a gateway can convert applications such as cc:Mail to SMTP (and vice versa). Gateways enable communication between entirely different architectures and environments. They effectively repackage and convert data going from one type of network to another so that each can understand the other's data. A gateway repackages information to match the requirements of the destination system, and changes the format of a message so that it conforms to the application running at the receiving end of the transfer. In most cases, gateways are task-specific, which means that they are dedicated to a particular type of transfer. They are often referred to by their task (i.e., "Windows NT Server-to-SNA Gateway").

NETWORK INTERFACE CARDS

The *network interface card* (NIC, also known as a LAN adapter) functions as an interface between the individual computer (server or client) and the network cabling (see Figure 1-2). Internally, the NIC must identify the PC on the network and buffer data between the computer and the cable. When sending data, the NIC must convert the data from parallel bytes into serial bits (then back again during reception). On the network side, a NIC must generate the electrical signals that travel over the network, manage access to the network, and make the physical connection to the cable. Every computer on the network must have at least one NIC port installed. Modern NICs increase their effective throughput using advanced techniques of *adapter teaming* such as *adapter fault tolerance* (AFT), which provides automatic redundancy for your adapter. If the primary adapter fails, the secondary takes over. *Adaptive load balancing* (ALB) allows

FIGURE 1-2   The Symbios SYM22915 network interface card.
(Courtesy LSI Logic Corp.)

balancing the transmission data flow between two to four adapters. You'll see much more about NICs later in the book.

CABLING

Finally, networks of all sizes and configurations depend on the physical *cabling* that connects all of the PCs and other hardware together. Cabling (also referred to as *network media*) comes in many different configurations, but common cabling used for everyday networking includes unshielded twisted pair (UTP), coaxial cable, shielded twisted pair (STP), and fiber-optic (FO) cable. As a technician, you should understand the three main considerations for cabling:

- Resistance to *crosstalk* (electrical currents between pairs of wires in the same cable)
- Resistance to interference from outside electrical fields (noise created by electric motors, power lines, relays, and transmitters)
- Ease of installation

These are important issues because cables resistant to crosstalk and interference can be run longer and support higher data transmission rates. For example, coaxial and shielded twisted-pair cable have a thin metal foil outer layer that offers good resistance to electrical noise, but the extra foil creates a larger, thicker cable that is more difficult to pull through conduit and walls during installation. Unshielded twisted pair is thinner and easier to install, but offers less resistance to electrical noise. By comparison, fiber-optic cable carries light signals instead of electrical pulses, so it is impervious to electrical interference. This allows fiber-optic cable to carry signals faster and farther than any other type of cable. Unfortunately, FO cable is often far more expensive than other cable types, and proper installation demands specialized tools and training.

Network Personnel

In stand-alone computer environments, each individual user is ultimately responsible for the performance of their machine. Some users are simply more talented or skilled than others, and these users are often called on for support when things go awry. The inefficiency and underutilization of stand-alone resources simply become a part of everyday office routine. In a network environment, the management and maintenance of a network is vested with a core of trained professionals. If you're new to networking, there are several network support roles that you should be familiar with in an organization.

NETWORK ADMINISTRATOR

Regardless of need, networks don't simply materialize out of the ether. They are crafted into being through the work of talented and experienced individuals such as a *network administrator*. A network administrator must have good training and be able to draw from detailed information about every aspect of the network. A computer network requires daily maintenance and supervision for it to function as needed and keep its vast data store secure. The network administrator is certainly the most critical part of any network—getting the most out of a system that may be less than state-of-the-art.

If you're making the switch from stand-alone PCs to a networked environment, the best place to begin is by assigning your network administrator. An administrator should be brought on board first and should become involved in every aspect of the system's design, selection, and implementation. As a rule, the search for a suitable administrator should be done deliberately. Interview fully, check references carefully, and hire only that candidate with a proven track record and credentials. You can also make an investment in training an existing employee who has demonstrated the appropriate aptitude. Such an employee should seek to achieve real-world results, look for ways to get best results from existing technology, and avoid the often money-wasting impulsive acquisition of new technologies.

OTHER PERSONNEL

While a single network administrator may be adequate for small to midsized networks, larger or specialized network implementations may demand one or more additional personnel to handle databases, perform physical network maintenance, design Web pages, and so on.

Security Administrator

The administrator may not be able to handle the busy security issues often encountered in very large organizations, so a *security administrator* may be added to track security logs, enforce password policies, investigate and prosecute intrusion, and deal with physical access to hardware.

Database Administrator

A *database administrator* is generally responsible for programming and maintaining a large multi- relational database in a networked environment, and facilitating direct access to the database by individuals on the network.

Workgroup Manager

The workgroup manager is normally responsible for system problem-solving, implementing standards and solutions, reviewing network performance, and optimizing the efficiency of a specific group of individuals who are connected (as a group) to a larger network environment.

Support Staff

As a rule, members of a network support staff provide technical assistance to the system administrator in large, complex network environments. Support personnel provide routine troubleshooting, problem solving, and on-demand personalized training to network end users.

Maintenance Contractor

Maintenance contractors are responsible for hardware repairs and upgrades (for example, wiring a building for network implementation or upgrading workstation drives system-wide). In many cases, this type of position is filled by contracting with a third-party service provider or system vendor.

Webmaster

A Webmaster is responsible for implementing and maintaining the content and style of a company's Internet site. This includes keeping the information accurate, up-to-date, and interesting/appealing to the user.

Network Documentation Basics

If you're planning a trip to a strange place, chances are that you'll use a map. No reasonable person would prevent you from using a map, or ask you to believe that a map isn't necessary to find what you're looking for. Still, network technicians are frequently asked to work with little (or no) meaningful documentation on the physical and logical setups of their network. Over time, even simple networks can evolve into complicated arrangements of servers, workstations, and media. While the individual workstation and server PC hardware may be well understood, the interconnections and setup of various hardware and software components may become obscured over time. The problem is easy to understand—documentation is time-consuming to produce and update, and the task of documenting a network is often abandoned because of time pressure to install, update, and troubleshoot pressing problems. Unfortunately, the layout and configuration of a network is left in the head of an administrator or other personnel, and many experienced technicians can relate tales of woe when their *last* resident network guru left the company.

To prevent such problems, all technicians should have access to a comprehensive collection of network documentation. The actual documents can vary quite a bit between companies, but at its core up-to-date documentation provides information about how the network should look and perform, as well as where to seek help if there are problems. Documentation provides those "need to know" details that show you where to find solutions to the problems that may occur, and will always pay off when you need to repair or update a network. Network documentation should generally contain the following pieces of information:

- A physical map of the entire network, including the locations of all hardware and cabling. This may be accompanied by a logical layout of the network (i.e., a star topology), though that is not always necessary.

- Complete information on each server, such as the make, model, and included hardware devices. This should also include the schedule and locations of all backups. Similar information on each workstation is also helpful, but often does not require the same level of detail.

- Complete information on each repeater, hub, bridge, and router. Often, this merely involves denoting their locations in the network map and including a copy of their respective user manuals.

- Complete network OS and application software information, including versions, licensing, and support details (as well as the location of all installation CDs).

- A complete index of vendors, suppliers, contractors, and other related contacts. If equipment is maintained by manufacturers or outside organizations, be sure to have a current copy of each respective service agreement.

- A detailed repair record of all problems, including symptoms and solutions, event dates, contacts, troubleshooting procedures, and overall results.

LOGICAL MAPS

Logical (or *functional*) maps are usually the type of documentation that you'll create and refer to most often (see Figure 1-3). They serve as an organizational chart of your network, and they clearly indicate which device (or server) is responsible for each major function. Logical maps also show which devices depend upon other devices in order to work. Details are not terribly important here, but you need to see the flow or interconnecting relationship between devices. A logical map can help you to discern important relationships across the network (such as why department A can't talk to the server, but department B can).

You don't need to include every PC or printer on a logical map, but every device that the network relies on (such as servers and routers) *will* need to be included. Devices such as hubs and switches may be included if necessary. Hubs and switches are often presented on their own, but there may be network configurations (for example, a switch may connect two distinctly different areas of the network) where it's better to show them separately. If you have a large or complex network, go ahead and use multiple sheets of paper—don't try to cram everything on one page. With large networks, it's common to draw a "high-level" view on one page, then detail each area of the high-level view on subsequent pages. For example, a high-level view may show each of the network's main areas represented by a box that refers to a separate detail map.

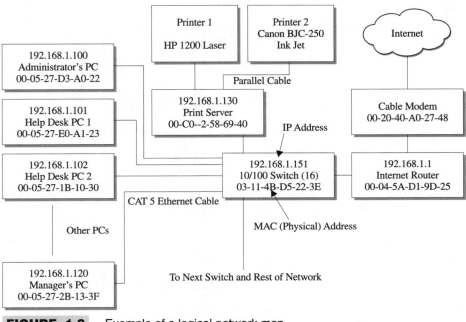

FIGURE 1-3   Example of a logical network map

PHYSICAL MAPS

Physical maps refer to the physical implementation of the network—how things are really interconnected. Since physical maps are often far more detailed than logical maps, you'll generally want to present them in small well-organized chunks (such as the example in Figure 1-4). Some smaller networks (usually fewer than 50 PCs) can get away with just one physical map. Larger networks usually need a physical map for each floor of the building. This is usually a good breakdown for most sites, because it shows each and every wire running to each and every PC, printer, switch, and hub—and this can get rather large. For simpler sites, it's handy to obtain the architectural floor plan of your building and add the network wiring and wire closet layout to it. A more complex site might also need additional documentation in the form of a physical segment map.

A physical *segment* of a network is often considered a group of hubs that are connected without a router or switch. Any hubs that are connected via a switch or router are always considered separate physical segments, and large ones can need their own maps.

In general, you'll want a physical map to get as detailed as possible. Remember to update your maps as they change. Make this a standard procedure with your consultant, network provider, and PC support staff—particularly if you add or change things on your own (rather than having a consultant or other outside staff handle it). Also, make it a point to date your maps. As the network evolves, you'll end up with multiple maps of the same general area. With a date on each map, it's much easier to determine which map is the most current.

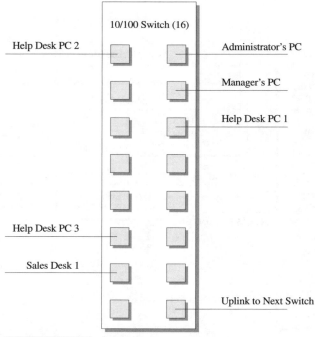

FIGURE 1-4   Example of a physical network map

Avoid the use of color in your maps. Color can be helpful, but is easily lost if photocopies are made or faxes are sent. Use symbols rather than colors to highlight important ideas in the physical map.

LABELING AND DETAILS

Of course, a map does no good at all if you can't find the devices that are shown on the map to begin with. If you're driving along and reading a road map, you wouldn't know which road you're on without signs posted periodically along the way. The same thing is true for networks. There have been cases where the router couldn't be rebooted because no one knew where the router was or what it looked like. A good technician will make it a point to *label* each device clearly and concisely before trouble strikes. Inadequate or incorrect labeling can significantly increase downtime (even when current detailed documentation is available).

If you find that your network cabling and devices have not yet been labeled, and you cannot oblige your installer(s) to go back and apply the appropriate labeling, you'll need to start labeling things as you go. For example, each time you discover a cable or network device, go ahead and apply a label to it. Labeling alleviates the need to rely on memory, and allows others to perform routine maintenance, upgrades, and troubleshooting tasks without the need for your direct supervision. In many cases, a basic Dymo-type label maker is more than adequate for most labeling chores—and the heavy plastic labels won't tear or become obscured by dirt or dust.

Place labels 12-18" from the connector. This may seem like a long way, but remember that there are often *many* cables in close proximity to one another. Putting labels right at the connector will make them hard to see when many other cables are cluttering the area. Also be sure to label *both* ends of a cable.

Finally, be sure to update the labeling (along with the documentation) as your network evolves. This requires a little extra work, but can save you hours of wasted time and confusion. Suppose that you mark a router with an IP address, but that IP address is later changed. If a problem occurs, a technician may waste time (and jeopardize their sanity) vainly trying to locate the router using the old IP address still marked on the device. That little detail alone can make the difference between 10 minutes of downtime versus 2 hours.

Further Study

3Com Technology Information:
   www.3com.com/solutions/en_US/technology.jsp?techid=0&solutiontype=1000003
Google: **groups.google.com**
Microsoft Knowledge Base: **search.support.microsoft.com/kb/c.asp**
Microsoft TechNet: **www.microsoft.com/technet/**

NETWORK ARCHITECTURES AND ACCESS

This chapter covers the basics of network topologies, cabling, and the data link layer protocols. Network topologies, signals, and cabling are the three components that make up the physical layer of the OSI model. The physical layer lies at the bottom of the OSI model and is used to define the nature of the network's hardware elements, such as the nature of the signal that is used to transmit binary data across the wire, the type of network interface card (NIC) that must be installed in each computer on the network, and the type of hub to use. Other options of the physical layer include various types of copper or fiber-optic cable and a number of different wireless solutions. On a local access network (LAN), the physical layer specifications are directly related to the data link layer protocol. This means that when you select a data link layer protocol, you must use one of the physical layer specifications used by that data link protocol.

A data link layer protocol is the channel between each computer's networking hardware and its networking software. The data link protocol that you choose when you design a LAN is the most important factor in determining the hardware that you purchase and how you install it. The most popular data link layer LAN protocol in use today is Ethernet. Other data link layer LAN protocols include token ring and Fiber Distributed Data Interface (FDDI). This chapter begins with a discussion of a component of the physical layer—network topologies.

Network Topologies

The term "topology" refers to the way that the computers and other devices are cabled together on a network. The particular type of cable you use determines the topology of your network. You cannot install a particular type of cable using just any topology you choose. You must use the correct topology to install each particular type of cable. The three primary LAN topologies are bus, star, and ring. The seven topologies discussed here are bus, star, star bus, hierarchical star, ring, mesh, and wireless.

BUS TOPOLOGY

When you select a bus topology for your network, the computers and other devices are connected in a single line with each system cabled to the next system. This configuration is often referred to as a daisy chain. All of the signals transmitted by the systems on the network travel along the bus in both directions through all of the other systems to reach their destination. A bus topology always has two open ends, as shown in Figure 2-1. The two ends of the bus must be terminated with electrical resistors so that the signals do not reflect back in the other direction, which results in interference with newer signals being transmitted. Lack of termination at either or both ends can prevent the computers that are connected to the bus from communicating properly.

Cabling on a bus topology can take two forms: thick and thin Ethernet. Thick Ethernet networks use a single length of coaxial cable. The computers in the network connect to this cable using smaller individual lengths of cable, named attachment unit interface (AUI) cables (also known as transceiver cables). Thin Ethernet networks use a narrower type of coaxial cable cut into individual lengths. Each length of cable connects one computer to the next.

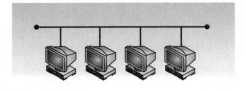

FIGURE 2-1   Bus topology

Each computer on the network has a transceiver that is responsible for both transmitting and receiving data over the network wire. Except for thick Ethernet, all of the Ethernet physical layer standards have their transceivers integrated into the NIC. Thick Ethernet is the only form of Ethernet network that uses an interface separate from the NIC. The transceiver connects to the coaxial cable using a vampire tap device. The transceiver then connects to the NIC in the computer by using the AUI cable. See Figure 2-2.

The main drawback of the bus topology is that a fault anywhere in the cable, a faulty terminator, or a faulty connector affects the network functionality. The network becomes split in two, which prevents systems on opposite sides of the break from communicating. Additionally, when a component failure causes a split in the network each half of the network becomes unterminated, resulting in signal reflection that scrambles the data.

STAR TOPOLOGY

The *star topology* uses a central cabling device called a hub or concentrator. Each computer is connected to the hub using a separate cable, as shown in Figure 2-3. The star topology uses twisted-pair cable, such as 10BaseT and 100BaseT. Most Ethernet LANs and many LANs using other protocols use the star topology.

Even though each computer is connected to the hub by a separate cable, the hub propagates all signals entering through any one of its ports to all other ports. In this manner, all signals transmitted by each computer on the network reach all of the other computers.

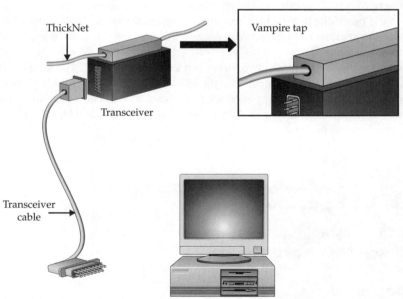

FIGURE 2-2   Vampire tap/transceiver unit used to connect an AUI cable to thick Ethernet

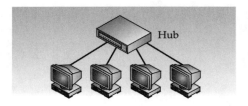

FIGURE 2-3   Star topology

Because each computer has its own dedicated connection to the hub, the star topology is more fault tolerant than the bus topology in that a break in one of the cables does not affect the rest of the network. Only that particular computer connected to the hub by a faulty cable is affected. The disadvantage to using the star topology is that an additional piece of hardware—a hub—must be used to implement it. If the hub fails, it affects the entire network, causing the entire network to go down.

STAR BUS TOPOLOGY

The star bus topology is a method that you can use to expand the size of a LAN beyond one star. You expand the LAN by joining a number of star networks with a separate bus cable segment to connect their hubs together, as shown in Figure 2-4. Each hub transmits its incoming traffic out through the bus port as well as the other star port, enabling all of the computers on the LAN to communicate with one another. This topology was originally designed to expand 10BaseT Ethernet networks, but due to the degradation of network performance attributed to the slowness of coaxial bus networks, it's rarely in use today.

HIERARCHICAL STAR TOPOLOGY

When you need to expand a star network beyond the capacity of the original hub, you implement the hierarchical star topology (also known as a branching tree network), as shown in Figure 2-5. To expand the star network, you simply connect the original hub to a second hub using a standard cable plugged into a special port, called an uplink port, designated for this very purpose. Traffic arriving at either hub is propa-

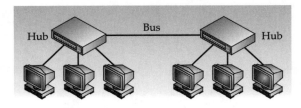

FIGURE 2-4   Star bus topology

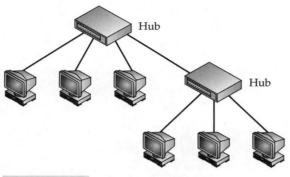

FIGURE 2-5   Hierarchical star topology

gated to both hubs as well as the connected network computers. The protocol that the LAN uses dictates the number of hubs that a single LAN can support. For example, Fast Ethernet networks can usually only support two hubs.

RING TOPOLOGY

A ring topology is like a bus topology in that each computer is connected to the next one. However, instead of the two ends being terminated, they are connected together to form a ring as shown in Figure 2-6. This connection causes the signals to travel from one computer to the next in a circular fashion, eventually returning to their starting point. In most cases, the ring topology is strictly a logical construction and not a physical one because the cables in a ring topology connect to a hub and take the form of a star. You can use several different types of cable in a ring topology. FDDI networks use the ring topology with fiber-optic cable, while token ring networks use twisted-pair cables.

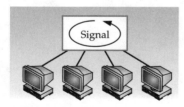

FIGURE 2-6   Ring topology

Token ring networks use a special type of hub called a multistation access unit (MAU). The MAU receives each incoming signal through one port and transmits it out through each of the others in turn. This process is not performed simultaneously as with an Ethernet hub, but one at a time. For example, when a computer that is connected to port number 7 in a 16-port MAU transmits a data packet, the MAU receives and then transmits the packet out through port 8 only. When the computer connected to port 8 receives the packet, the computer immediately returns it to the MAU, which then transmits it out through port number 9, and so forth. The MAU continues this process until it has transmitted the packet to each computer included on the ring. When the computer that originally generated the packet receives it back again, that computer is responsible for removing the packet from the ring.

The design of this topology makes it possible for the network to function even when a cable or a connector fails because the MAU contains special circuitry that will remove a faulty workstation from the ring. The MAU continues to preserve the logical topology and the network is able to function without the faulty workstation's inclusion in the ring.

MESH TOPOLOGY

Using the mesh topology on a LAN is impractical, to say the least. Each computer has a dedicated connection to every other computer on a mesh LAN. This topology is only practical on a two-node network. A mesh network with three or more computers would require a separate NIC for every other computer on the network. For example, a seven-node network would require that each computer on the mesh network have six NICs installed. Although using this topology on a LAN is impractical, it does provide excellent fault tolerance. A single point of failure can only affect one computer, not the entire LAN.

A scheme that you would be able to use the mesh topology on is internetworking. The multiple paths between two destinations that the mesh topology provides can make possible the use of redundant routers, shown in Figure 2-7. This topology is common on large networks because it enables the network to tolerate possible malfunctions, such as cable, hub, and router failures.

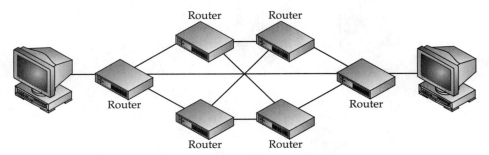

FIGURE 2-7   Mesh topology

WIRELESS TOPOLOGY

Although the term "topology" usually refers to the arrangement of cables in a network, it doesn't have to. Wireless networks use what are called unbound media, which are a form of radio or light waves that form specific patterns that the computers use to communicate with each other. There are two basic wireless topologies: the infrastructure topology and the ad hoc topology. An infrastructure network is comprised of wireless-equipped computers that communicate with the network by wireless transceivers (called network access points) that are themselves connected to the network by standard cables, shown in Figure 2-8. In this topology, the computers do not communicate with each other, but rather with the cabled network via the wireless transceivers. This topology is best suited for a larger network that utilizes only a few wireless computers that don't need to communicate with other computers, such as a laptop belonging to a traveling salesman. These types of users usually do not need to communicate with other workstations on the network, but rather they use the wireless connection to access servers and resources on the network.

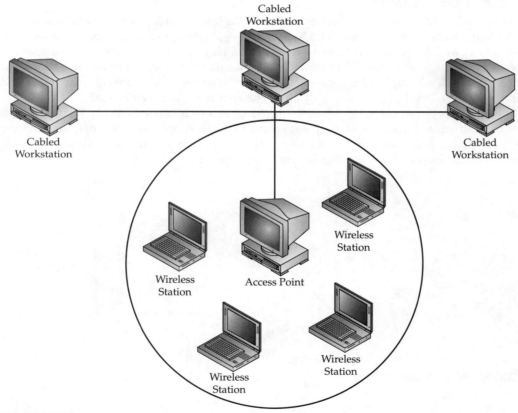

FIGURE 2-8   Wireless topology

The ad hoc topology consists of a group of computers that are all equipped with wireless NICs and that are able to communicate with each other. The downside for both of these wireless topologies is that the computers must remain within the communication range of the wireless technology. This topology is better suited for home or small office networks where the installation of cables is impractical.

Cabling Basics

Because of incompatibility issues that arose between manufacturers of networking products in the early days of networking, the industry recognized the need for a standard to define cabling systems that would support a number of different network technologies. Three organizations rose to the challenge. The American National Standards Institute (ANSI), the Electronic Industry Association (EIA), and the Telecommunications Industry Association (TIA), along with a team of telecommunications companies, developed ANSI/EIA/TIA-568-1991 Commercial Building Telecommunications Cabling Standard. After a number of revisions, the document was renamed to ANSI/TIA/EIA-568-A, with the latest revision occurring in March of 2002 (ANSI/TIA/EIA-568-B). The 568 standard defines cabling specifications used in the United States. There is a separate standard that defines cabling specifications used in Europe. It was based on the 568 standard and developed by the International Organization for Standardization (ISO), and was named the ISO 11801 1995.

The 568 standard defines both voice and data cabling systems that support products for multiple technology vendors and that have a usable lifespan of at least ten years. Specifically, the standard defines the specifications for the installation of the cable within the building site, the elements for the topology and cable segment length specifications, the cable connector specifications, the cable characteristics, and criteria that determine the performance level for each cable type. The cable types discussed are

- Single-mode optical fiber
- Multimode optical fiber
- Unshielded twisted pair (UTP)
- Shielded twisted pair (STP)

Additional standards that you or the contractor that you hire to wire your building should be familiar with are as follows:

- **TIA/EIA-569**   Commercial Building Standard for Telecommunications Pathways and Spaces
- **TIA/EIA-606**   Administration Standard for the Telecommunications Infrastructure of Commercial Buildings
- **TIA/EIA-607**   Ground and Bonding Requirements for Telecommunications in Commercial Building

CABLE TYPES

As mentioned earlier, data link layer protocols are connected with specific types of cable. These protocols include such guidelines as the maximum segment lengths for cables. When you consider which protocol is best for your network, you need to understand the associated cable types and their suitability for your particular network site. During the selection process, you should consider the cost of the cable itself as well as the components associated with the cable, such as NICs for the computers, the connectors for the cable, and the labor required for installation of all the components. You also should consider which grade of cable is best for your site. The grade of the cable depends upon such things as the category rating, whether the cable is shielded or unshielded, and the thickness of the conductor gauge. When you decide on a grade of cable to use for your network, you must also make certain that all wall plates, patch panels, and connectors you use are specifically rated for the same category as the cable to ensure a more stable network environment.

There are three primary types of cable to choose from: coaxial, twisted pair, and fiber optic. Coaxial and twisted-pair cables carry electrical signals and are copper-based. Fiber-optic cables carry light signals and consist of glass or plastic fibers.

Coaxial Cable

Coaxial cable derives its name from the fact that it contains two conductors within the sheath that encases it. Most two-conductor cables have conductors that run side by side within an insulating sheath that separates and protects them. Not so with coaxial cable. Coaxial cable is round with one conductor inside the other, as shown in Figure 2-9. The first conductor, located at the center of the cable, is made up of a copper core that actually carries the electrical signals. The copper core can be either solid copper or braided strands of copper. Surrounding the core is a layer of dielectric foam insulation, meant to protect the core from the second conductor, which is generally made of braided copper mesh and acts as the cable's ground. This entire assembly is encased with an insulating sheath that is made of either PVC or Teflon.

It is important to note here that because the outer insulating sheath of the cable is made of different types of materials, you need make sure that the sheath that is used in your building is correct for the type of

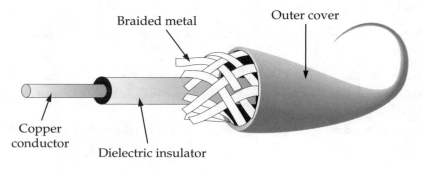

FIGURE 2-9   Coaxial cable

TABLE 2-1   SPECIFICATIONS FOR COAXIAL CABLE

	RG-8/U	RG-58/U OR RG-58A/U	RG-62A/U	RG-59/U
Cable Diameter	.405 inches	.195 inches	.242 inches	.242 inches
Impedance	50 ohms	50 ohms	93 ohms	75 ohms
Attenuation (dB/100' @ 100 MHz)	1.9	4.5	2.7	3.4
Connectors Used	N	BNC	BNC	F
Protocols Supported	Thick Ethernet	Thin Ethernet	ARCnet	Cable TV

cabling you are planning. For example, if you need to run cable through your building's plenums (air spaces), the cable must have a sheath made of a material that won't release toxic gases into the building when it burns. Plenum cable is more expensive than the standard PVC-sheathed cable, but it's a necessary expense when running cable through your building's air spaces.

Table 2-1 lists the types of coaxial cable and their properties. The two types of coaxial cable used in networks are RG-58, known as thin Ethernet (or 10Base2), and RG-8, known as thick Ethernet (or 10Base5). The abbreviations used for these cables (10Base2 and 10Base5) indicate that they are limited to a speed of 10 Mbps, use baseband transmissions, and are limited to maximum cable segments of (approximately) 200 and 500 meters.

Both of these types of cables are used in conjunction with the bus topology. As you can see in the table, the two cables differ primarily in thickness and in the type of connectors they use. RG-8 uses N connectors (shown in Figure 2-10), and RG-58 uses bayonet-Neill-Concelman (BNC) connectors (shown in Figure 2-11).

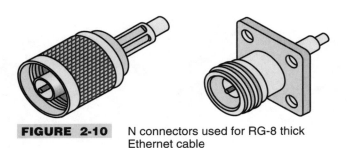

FIGURE 2-10   N connectors used for RG-8 thick Ethernet cable

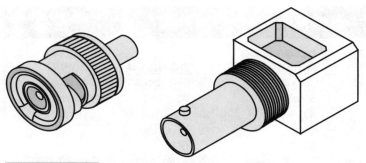

FIGURE 2-11   BNC connectors used for RG-58 thin
Ethernet cable

   Because coaxial cable is limited to a speed of 10 Mbps, it is rather inefficient for data networking—especially in the corporate environment. Although this type of cable is still used today for many applications such as cable television networks, it is becoming obsolete in the data networking environment. Coaxial cable is not the cable of choice in most new Ethernet networks.

Twisted-Pair Cable

Currently, the most common type of cable used in LAN communications is twisted-pair cable wired in a star topology. There are two types of twisted-pair cable available: unshielded twisted pair (UTP), which is in wide use for most new LANs, and shielded twisted pair (STP), which is used in environments that are prone to eletromagnetic interference. Twisted-pair cable contains eight individual insulated copper conductors in the form of wires. These eight wires are arranged in four pairs of twisted wires and each pair is color coded in compliance with the 568 standard, as listed in Table 2-2. The twisted wires are twisted at different rates in order to prevent crosstalk (interference amongst themselves) as well as to prevent interference from outside sources. Finally, these four pairs of wire are encased in a single sheath. Figure 2-12 illustrates a cross-section of a twisted-pair cable.

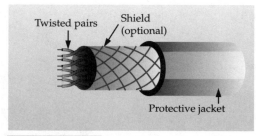

FIGURE 2-12   Twisted-pair cable

PAIR	COLOR
TABLE 2-2	**COLOR CODING FOR TWISTED-PAIR CABLE**
PAIR	**COLOR**
Pair 1	Solid blue, and white with blue stripe
Pair 2	Solid orange, and white with orange stripe
Pair 3	Solid green, and white with green stripe
Pair 4	Solid brown, and white with brown stripe
Note: The solid color carries the signal and the white-striped wire is the ground.	

If the connector on twisted-pair cable looks familiar, that's because the RJ-45 modular connector is very similar to the RJ-11 connector that has been used on standard telephone cables for years (RJ is the acronym for registered jack). The difference between the two is that the RJ-45 connector has eight electrical contacts (shown in Figure 2-13) instead of the four or six that make up the RJ11 connector. The TIA/EIA-568-A standard defines the pinout for the twisted-pair RJ-45 cable connector, shown in Figure 2-14.

There are advantages to using twisted pair rather than coaxial cable. Because twisted-pair cable has been used in the telephone industry for years, there are many contractors already familiar with its installation procedure. This makes it easier for the contractor to simultaneously install the telephone and network cables. Another advantage is that twisted-pair cables are much more flexible, and therefore easier to install, than coaxial cable.

Unshielded Twisted Pair (UTP)   The Telecommunications Industry Association (TIA) and Electronics Industry Association (EIA) developed the TIA/EIA-568 standard that defines the different grades (referred to as categories) of UTP cables. The higher the category rating, the more efficient and faster the cable is able to transmit data. The difference between categories lies in the tightness of each wire pair's twisting. With the exception of 100BaseT4 and 100BaseVG-AnyLAN protocols, Ethernet networks generally use only two of the four wire pairs in the UTP cable—one for receiving and one for transmitting data. Even though all four wire pairs may not be in use, you are not free to use the other two pairs for another application, such as telecommunications traffic. The introduction of signals on the two unused wire pairs would most likely lead to an increase in the amount of crosstalk across the wire, which greatly increases the potential for data loss and a compromise to the signal.

FIGURE 2-13   An RJ-45 connector

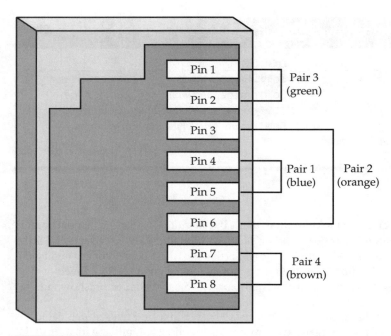

FIGURE 2-14 The pinout for a 568A twisted-pair cable connector

The two most important UTP grades for LANs are Category 3 and Category 5 (also known as Cat5). Most new UTP cable installations for networks today use at least a Category 5 cable. Category 3 cable generally is not used for Fast Ethernet, but is sufficient for 10-Mbps Ethernet networks (where the cable is referred to as 10BaseT). The 100BaseT4 Fast Ethernet protocol is an exception in that it uses Category 3 UTP cable and is designed to run at 100 Mbps. It is possible for this protocol to run at a higher rate because 100BaseT4 uses all four wire pairs in the cable, instead of the usual two pairs in use by other cable systems. See Table 2-3 for a list of UTP categories.

Category 5 UTP is suitable for Ethernet networks running at 100 Mbps as well as for slower protocols. It also can run 1000BaseT if it meets the additional testing parameters in TIA/EIA TSB-95. The Category 5e standard increases the performance levels for use on 1000BaseT networks (also known as Gigabit Ethernet). The Category 5e cable standard is designed to run on 100-meter segment UTP cable with a frequency of 100 MHz.

TABLE 2-3   UTP CABLE TIA/EIA CATEGORY RATINGS

CATEGORY	FREQUENCY	PURPOSE
1	= 100 KHz	Voice-grade telephone and alarm systems only; not meant for data network transmissions
2	< 4 MHz	Voice-grade telephone, as well as connections to IBM dumb terminals for mainframes and minicomputers, ARCnet, and LocalTalk
3	Up to 16 MHz	Voice-grade telephone, 10-Mbps Ethernet (10BaseT Ethernet), 4-Mbps token ring, 100BaseT4 (Fast Ethernet), and 100BaseVG-AnyLAN, viable for a telecommunications network (100BaseT4 and 100BaseVG-AnyLAN use all four wire pairs rather than the usual two pairs)
4	Up to 20 MHz	16-Mbps token ring networks, viable for a telecommunications network
5	Up to 100 MHz, can run 1000BaseT if it meets the additional testing parameters in TIA/EIA TSB-95	100BaseTX (Fast Ethernet), Synchronous Optical Network (SONET), and Optical Carrier (OC-3) Asynchronous Transfer Mode (ATM), viable for a telecommunications network
5e	Up to 100 MHz	1000BaseT (Gigabit Ethernet) networks, viable for a telecommunications network

Shielded Twisted Pair (STP)   IBM, which developed the Token Ring protocol that used shielded twisted pair, was also responsible for standardizing the various types of STP cable listed in Table 2-4. (The TIA/EIA-T568-A standard only recognizes two of these STP cable types: Type 1A and Type 6A.) STP is still used primarily in token ring networks, and also is used in installations where the cable requires

TABLE 2-4   STP CABLE TYPES

CABLE TYPE	WIRES	OUTER SHEATH MATERIAL
Type 1A	Two pairs of 22-gauge solid wires with foil shielding, with a shield layer (foil or braid) around both pairs, used in backbones and horizontal wiring	Either PVC or plenum-rated
Type 2A	Two pairs of 22-gauge solid wires with foil shielding, with a shield layer (foil or braid) around both pairs, plus four additional pairs of 22-gauge solid wires for voice communications	Either PVC or plenum-rated
Type 6A	Two pairs of 26-gauge stranded wires with foil or mesh shielding around both pairs, used for patch cables	Either PVC or plenum-rated
Type 9A	Two pairs of 26-gauge stranded wires with foil or mesh shielding around both pairs	Either PVC or plenum-rated

additional shielding to protect against the electromagnetic interference that is often caused by the proximity of electrical equipment. STP differs in construction from UTP in that is has only two pairs of twisted wires with an additional foil or mesh shielding around each pair. The additional metallic shielding is as conductive as the copper in the twisted-pair wires. When this sheath is properly grounded, it converts the ambient noise into a current, which is carried to the wires that it encases. Once it reaches the encased wires, the current creates an opposite and equal current flowing within the twisted pairs. The result is that the opposite currents cancel each other out, thus eliminating the ambient noise that would otherwise disturb the signals passing over the wires.

Fiber-Optic Cable

Fiber-optic cable is comprised of a clear glass or clear plastic core that carries light pulses. The core is surrounded by a reflective layer that is called the cladding; surrounding the cladding is a plastic spacer layer; next comes a protective layer made of woven Kevlar fibers; and, finally, it is all covered by an outer sheath made out of Teflon or PVC, as shown in Figure 2-15.

Fiber-optic cable is a completely different type of cable than coaxial or twisted-pair cable. This is because, instead of carrying signals in the form of electrical voltages over copper conductors, the

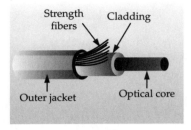

FIGURE 2-15   Fiber-optic cable

fiber-optic cable uses pulses of light (photons) to transmit the binary signals generated by computers over a glass or plastic filament. Because fiber-optic cable uses light instead of electricity to transmit signals, it is resistant to any electromagnetic interference, as well as to crosstalk, and is less subject to attenuation (the tendency of a signal to weaken as it travels over the wire) than are copper cables. Some fiber-optic cables can span a distance of up to 120 kilometers without noticeable signal degradation. Compare this to traditional copper cable, for which signal degradation occurs to the point of unreadability after 100 to 500 meters, depending upon the type of cable you use. If you need to install cable that spans long distances or that connects buildings, fiber-optic cable is the best choice. An additional advantage is that fiber-optic cables are much more secure than copper cables because when a fiber-optic link is tapped into, normal communication over that link is affected.

The two primary types of fiber-optic cable are single mode and multimode. The main difference between the two is the thickness of the core and of the cladding. You can identify the type of of fiber-optic cable by the optical-fiber size (the total thickness of the core/cladding). Single-mode fiber generally has a core diameter of 8.3 microns, and the total thickness of the core plus the cladding together is 125 microns. Single-mode cable, therefore, is usually referred to as 8.3/125 single-mode fiber. In comparison, multimode fiber has a core diameter of 62.5 and the thickness of the core and the cladding is 125 microns. Multimode fiber is referred to as 62.5/125 multimode fiber.

The signal carried by single-mode fiber uses a single-wavelength laser as a light source as opposed to multimode fiber, which uses a light-emitting diode (LED) as a light source and is able to carry multiple wavelengths. Because single-mode fiber uses a single-wavelength laser, it can carry signals for extremely long distances and so is generally used in outdoor installations such as cable television networks. This type of cable is much more expensive than multimode cable and has a higher bend radius, and so is not very well suited to network installations. Multimode cable is better suited for LAN installation because, although it cannot span distances as long as single-mode cable, it is less expensive and is able to bend around corners better. The most common connectors used are the subscriber connector (SC) or the straight tip (ST), shown in Figure 2-16.

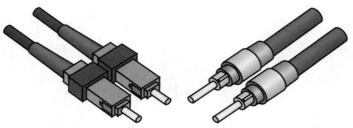

FIGURE 2-16   Fiber optic cable connectors

Data Link Layer Protocols

The data link layer protocol provides the link between the physical and the protocol stack on the computer. It typically consists of three elements:

- The format for the frame
- The mechanism that regulates access to the shared network
- The network's physical layer guidelines

ETHERNET

For the most part, when people refer to a LAN they are referring to an Ethernet LAN. Since its development, it's been upgraded a number of times to satisfy the changing requirements of the marketplace. The early Ethernet networks ran at speeds of 10 Mbps, and today run at speeds of 100 Mbps, 1,000 Mbps, and even 10 Gbps, enabling networks to fulfill the needs of the smallest home networks, on up to high-capacity backbones.

Ethernet Basics

Ethernet was first designed in the 1970s and eventually came to be known as thick Ethernet due to the size of the cable, which was approximately 1 cm wide. The first of two standards, titled "The Ethernet, a Local Area Network: Data Link Layer and Physical Layer Specifications," was first published in 1980 and was developed by by Digital Equipment Corporation, Intel, and Xerox, and become known as DIX Ethernet. This standard defined a network using RG-8 coaxial cable running at 10 Mbps in a bus topology, and came to be known as thick Ethernet, thickNet, or 10Base5. They updated their standard in 1982, named the DIX Ethernet II standard, to add a second physical layer option to the protocol using a thinner type of coaxial cable (RG-58), which came to be referred to as thin Ethernet, or thinnet, or 10Base2.

Meanwhile, an international standards-making body named the Institute of Electrical and Electronic Engineers (IEEE) began working on an international standard defining Ethernet-like networks for public use. To this end, the IEEE established a working group and gave it a designation of IEEE 802.3. Because Xerox had trademarked the Ethernet name, the working group could not call their network Ethernet, so in 1985 they published "IEEE 802.3 Carrier Sense Multiple Access with Collision Detection (CSMA/CD) Access Method and Physical Layer Specifications." In addition to the two same coaxial cable options used in DIX Ethernet, they also added a standard for unshielded twisted-pair cable, otherwise known as 10BaseT. The IEEE 802.3 working group published additional documents in 1995 named IEEE 802.3u that define the 100-Mbps Fast Ethernet specifications, and IEEE 802.3z and IEEE 802.ab, which are standards for 1000-Mbps Gigabit Ethernet.

The main differences between the IEEE 802.3 standard and the DIX Ethernet standard are that the IEEE standard contains additional physical layer options, mentioned in the above paragraphs, and some differences in the frame format. Even though the industry uses the name "Ethernet" to describe this standard, the protocol that networks use today is actually IEEE 802.3 because this standard provides the additional physical layer as well and standards for Fast Ethernet and Gigabit Ethernet. The only element of the DIX Ethernet standard that is still in use today is the Ethernet II frame format. The Ethernet II frame format contains the Ethertype field used to identify the network layer protocol that generated the data contained in each packet. Table 2-5 summarizes the different between the DIX Ethernet II standard and the IEEE 802.3 standard.

Both the DIX and the IEEE 802.3 Ethernet standards consist of the following components:

- Physical layer specifications that define wiring restrictions, cable types, and signaling methods
- Frame format that defines the functions and order of the bits transmitted in a packet
- Media Access Control (MAC) mechanism called Carrier Sense Multiple Access with Collision Detection (CSMA/CD) that enables the computers on the network access to the network medium

Ethernet Types and the Physical Layer

The Ethernet standards physical layer specifications describe such things as the topology, maximum cable lengths, and the types of cables you can use to build your network. The basic specifications for the Ethernet physical layer options are listed in Table 2-6. It is important to observe the guidelines of these specifications to limit the effects of problems like crosstalk and attenuation. You should also check the manufacturer's specifications for a particular technology because there will be some variations from manufacturer to manufacturer on the exact numbers.

TABLE 2-5 SUMMARY OF DIFFERENCES BETWEEN DIX ETHERNET II AND IEEE 802.3 STANDARDS

STANDARD	PHYSICAL LAYER OPTIONS	BITS 13-14 OF FRAME HEADER	EXTERNAL TRANSCEIVER TEST
DIX Ethernet II	Coaxial only	Ethertype	Collision presence test
IEEE 802.3	Coaxial, UTP, fiber optic	Length of data field	SQE Test

TABLE 2-6   ETHERNET SPECIFICATIONS

DESIGNATION	SPEED	TOPOLOGY	CABLE TYPE	MAXIMUM SEGMENT LENGTH	ETHERNET TYPE
10Base5	10 Mbps	Bus	RG-8 coaxial	500 meters	Ethernet
10Base2	10 Mbps	Bus	RG-58 coaxial	185 meters	Ethernet
10BaseT	10 Mbps	Star	Category 3 UTP	100 meters	Ethernet
Fiber-Optic Inter-Repeater Link (FOIRL)	10 Mbps	Star	62.5/125 multimode fiber optic	1,000 meters	Ethernet
10BaseFL	10 Mbps	Star	62.5/125 multimode fiber optic	2,000 meters	Ethernet
10Base-FB	10 Mbps	Star	62.5/125 multimode fiber optic	2,000 meters	Ethernet
10BaseFP	10 Mbps	Star	62.5/125 multimode fiber optic	500 meters	Ethernet
100BaseTX	100 Mbps	Star	Category 5 UTP	100 meters	Fast Ethernet
100BaseT4	100 Mbps	Star	Category 3 UTP	100 meters	Fast Ethernet
100BaseFX	100 Mbps	Star	62.5/125 multimode fiber optic	412 meters at half duplex and/or 2,000 meters at full duplex	Fast Ethernet
1000BaseLX	1,000 Mbps	Star	9/125 single-mode fiber optic	5,000 meters	Gigabit Ethernet
1000BaseLX	1,000 Mbps	Star	50/125 or 62.5/125 multimode fiber optic	550 meters	Gigabit Ethernet
1000BaseSX	1,000 Mbps	Star	50/125 multimode fiber optic (400 MHz)	500 meters	Gigabit Ethernet
1000BaseSX	1,000 Mbps	Star	50/125 multimode fiber optic (500 MHz)	550 meters	Gigabit Ethernet
1000BaseSX	1,000 Mbps	Star	62.5/125 multimode fiber optic (160 MHz)	220 meters	Gigabit Ethernet
1000BaseSX	1,000 Mbps	Star	62.5/125 multimode fiber optic (200 MHz)	275 meters	Gigabit Ethernet
1000BaseLH	1,000 Mbps	Star	9/125 single-mode fiber optic	10 km	Gigabit Ethernet
1000BaseZX	1,000 Mbps	Star	9/125 single-mode fiber optic	100 km	Gigabit Ethernet
1000BaseCX	1,000 Mbps	Star	150-ohm shielded copper cable	25 meters	Gigabit Ethernet
1000BaseT	1,000 Mbps	Star	Category 5 (or 5E) UTP	100 meters	Gigabit Ethernet

Ethernet   The Ethernet standard (IEEE 802.3) includes four cable specifications, summarized in Table 2-7. Thick Ethernet is limited to a transmission rate of 10 Mbps, which makes it impossible to use as a backbone medium. It is still a good illustration, though, of the components that make up the physical layer of an Ethernet network.

First off, the coaxial cable segment is more efficient when it is a single unbroken length of cable. If that isn't possible, the next best option is to piece together the segment from the same spool or cable lot using an N connector on each cable end and an N barrel connector between them, with as few breaks as possible. If your only choice turns out to be using cable from different lots, you should measure the individual pieces to be 23.4, 70.2, or 117 meters long. These lengths will minimize the signal reflections that may occur. Finally, you must terminate both ends of the bus with a 50-ohm resistor that is built into an N terminator, and ground only one end using a grounding connector attached to the N terminator.

Except for using RG-58 coaxial cable that is more flexible and thinner in diameter (5 millimeters), thin Ethernet is similar to thick Ethernet. Thin Ethernet uses BNC connectors in conjunction with a T connector (see Figure 2-17). The T connector is used to connect coaxial cable to both the computer itself and then to the next system. Thin Ethernet must be terminated and grounded, too. The two computers at both ends of the network must have a terminator containing a 50-ohm resistor on one end of their T's to terminate the bus. One end (only one of the two computers) should be connected to a ground.

Unlike coaxial cable, twisted-pair Ethernet requires the use of a hub (with one exception). A hub functions both as a signal repeater and as a wiring nexus. Although the specified maximum length for each cable segment is 100 meters, if an intervening hub that repeats the signal is used, the total distance between two nodes can be 200 meters. You can connect two computers together without the use of a hub by using a crossover cable.

Fiber-optic Ethernet networks run at 10 Mbps and use a medium that contains two strands of 62.5/125 multimode fiber cable. One strand is used to receive signals, and the other is used to transmit them. For 10-Mbps Ethernet, there are two main fiber-optic standards: FOIRL and 10BaseF. 10BaseF defines three fiber-optic configurations: 10BaseFB, 10BaseFP, and 10BaseFL, with 10BaseFL being the most popular.

TABLE 2-7   10-MBPS ETHERNET CABLE SPECIFICATIONS

	DESIGNATION	MAXIMUM SEGMENT LENGTH/METERS	MAXIMUM NODES PER CABLE SEGMENT	CABLE TYPE	CONNECTOR TYPE
Thick Ethernet	10Base5	500 meters	100	RG-8 coaxial	N
Thin Ethernet	10Base2	185 meters	30	RG-58 coaxial	BNC
Twisted Pair	10BaseT	100 meters	2	Category 3 unshielded twisted pair	RJ-45
Fiber Optic	100Base-FL	1,000/2,000	2	62.5/125 multimode fiber optic	ST

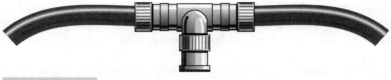

FIGURE 2-17   A thin Ethernet T connector

Now that Fast Ethernet and FDDI are available and both run on fiber-optic cable, it is a waste to underutilize the capacity of the fiber-optic cable by running it at this slower speed.

Fast Ethernet   The Fast Ethernet standard (IEEE802.3u) includes two 100BaseT (UTP) cable specifications: 100BaseTX and 100BaseT4. Both of these cable specifications retain the 100-meter maximum segment length. 100BaseTX is a Category 5 grade cable. Because Category 5 is a higher grade of cable, it provides a better signal transmission capability than does 100BaseT4. Just like 10BaseT, 100BaseTX uses only two pairs of wires in the cable. 100BaseT4 uses the same Category 3 cable as older Ethernet networks, which makes upgrading easier. All four wire pairs are used by 100BaseT4 to transmit and receive.

Gigabit Ethernet   There are two specifications for the Gigabit Ethernet standard: IEEE 802.3z for fiber-optic cable and IEEE 802.3ab for 1000BaseT UTP. The 1000BaseT standard uses Category 5 or Enhanced Category 5 (also known as Category 5E) cable. This standard is designed as an upgrade for existing UTP networks with 100-meter cable segments, and achieves its greater speed by using all four wire pairs and by using a signaling scheme called pulse amplitude modulation-5 (PAM-5). The bandwidth for Category 5 is equal to that of Category 5E (1,000 Mbps) if the installation meets the additional testing parameters published in TIA/EIA TSB-95. The improvement to Category 5E over Category 5 comes primarily in the form of increased resistance to crosstalk.

The Ethernet Frame

The Ethernet protocol encapsulates the data it receives from the network layer protocol in a frame. The frame itself is the sequence of bits that begins and ends every Ethernet packet that is transmitted across the wire. The frame is comprised of a header and a footer. The header and footer are both divided into fields that contain specific information necessary to get each packet to its correct destination. Regular, Fast, and Gigabit Ethernet all use the same frame, shown in Figure 2-18.

The functions of the Ethernet frame fields are as follows:

■ **Preamble (7 bytes)**   The preamble field consists of 7 bytes of alternating 0s and 1s, which the communicating systems use to synchronize their clock signals and then discard. For a DIX Ethernet frame, the preamble is 8 bytes in length.

■ **Start of Frame Delimiter (1 byte)**   The Start of Frame Delimiter (SFD) field contains 6 bits of alternating 0s and 1s, followed by two consecutive 1s, which is a signal to the receiver that the transmission of the actual frame is about to commence and that any data following is part of a data packet

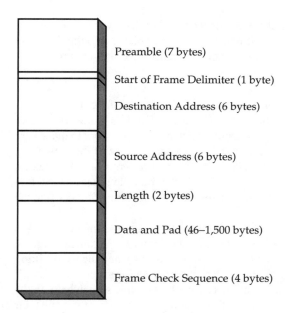

Preamble (7 bytes)

Start of Frame Delimiter (1 byte)

Destination Address (6 bytes)

Source Address (6 bytes)

Length (2 bytes)

Data and Pad (46–1,500 bytes)

Frame Check Sequence (4 bytes)

FIGURE 2-18   The Ethernet frame

that should be placed into the NIC's memory buffer for processing. Unlike IEEE 802.3 frames, the DIX Ethernet frame does not have a separate SFD field. However, the last two bits of the preamble are consecutive 1s, just like the SFD that signals to the receiver that the actual frame is about to commence.

■ **Destination Address (6 bytes)**   The Destination Address field contains the 6-byte hexadecimal address of the NIC on the local network to which the packet is being sent.

■ **Source Address (6 bytes)**   The Source Address field contains the 6-byte hexadecimal address of the sending computer's NIC that generated the packet.

■ **Ethertype/Length (2 bytes)**   In the DIX Ethernet frame, the Ethertype field contains a code identifying the network layer protocol for which the data in the packet is intended. In the IEEE 802.3 frame, the Length field specifies the length of the Data field (excluding the pad, discussed in the next item).

■ **Data and Pad (46 to 1,500 bytes)**   The Data and Pad field contains the data received from the network layer protocol on the transmitting system, which is sent to the same protocol on the destination system. If the data received from the network layer protocol is too short (less than 46 bytes), the Ethernet adapter adds a string of meaningless bits to pad the field out to its minimum length, which is 46 bytes.

■ **Frame Check Sequence (4 bytes)**   The Frame Check Sequence field (FCS) is the frame's footer that carries a 4-byte checksum value that the sending computer creates and places into this field and that the receiving system uses to determine whether the packet was transmitted without error.

CSMA/CD

The Media Access Control (MAC) mechanism called carrier sense multiple access with collision detection (CSMA/CD) is the single most defining element of the Ethernet standard. This is how it works. When a computer on an Ethernet network has data that it needs to transmit, it listens to the network to make sure that it isn't being used by another system. This phase is called the carrier sense phase. If the network is busy, the computer waits for a given period and then checks the status of the network again. If it detects that the network is free, the computer transmits the data packet. This is the multiple access phase. It is called the multiple access phase because all of the devices on the network are contending for access to the same network medium.

Even though the carrier sense phase is in place as a safety feature, it is still possible for a collision to occur on the network. A collision occurs when two or more systems on the network transmit at the same time, resulting in a collision of their signals. It is possible for a collision to occur when the transmitting computer's signal has not yet reached the sensing computer. Because the sensing computer hasn't detected a signal, it commences its transmission. As a result, the two packets collide somewhere on the cable. Both packets are discarded when a collision occurs, which forces both computers to retransmit their packets. Collisions occur normally on an Ethernet network. They are usually not a problem unless computers are unable to detect them or if there are too many collisions occuring.

The collision detection phase is very important because if computers can't tell when collisions occur, corrupt data may be processed as valid. As long as a computer is in the process of transmitting data, it is able to detect a collision on the network. A computer presumes that a collision has occurred on a coaxial network when a voltage spike indicates that a collision has occurred. In half-duplex mode on a fiber-optic or UTP network, a computer presumes that a collision has occurred if the computer detects simultaneous signals on both its transmit and receive wires.

If the packet is too short (less than 64 bytes), or if the network cable is too long, a computer might finish transmitting before the collision occurs. When a collision occurs after the last bit of data has left the transmitting system, it is called a late collision—and this is not a normal Ethernet occurance. When a late collision occurs, it is an indication of a more serious problem, such as a malfunctioning NIC. You must correct this problem as soon as possible.

When a computer does detect a collision, it immediately stops transmitting data and commences sending a jam pattern. This pattern serves as a warning to each computer on the network that a collision has occurred, that they should all discard any partial packets received, and that they should not attempt to transmit any data until the network has cleared. After the jam pattern has been sent, the computer waits for a period of time before it attempts to transmit again. This phase is called the backoff period. Both of the computers involved in the collision use a randomized algorithm called a truncated binary exponential backoff to compute the length of their own backoff periods. This calculation is performed to try to avoid another collision by backing off for different amounts of time.

TOKEN RING BASICS

Token Ring is data link-layer protocol developed by IBM that differs substantially from Ethernet in almost every way. Token ring networks use a different physical layer specification, a different MAC mechanism, and different frame formats. The original token ring standard was privately held by IBM. Later, the protocol was standardized by the IEEE as 802.5. Early token ring networks ran at 4 Mbps, but today virtually all implementations run at 16 Mbps.

Physical Layer Specification

Token ring networks originally used a form of shielded twisted-pair cable called the IBM Type 1 cabling system with proprietary connectors called IBM Data Connectors (IDC). The cables connect the computers to a specialized type of hub called a multistation access unit (MAU). The MAU is the component that implements the logical ring topology on a token ring network, despite it being physically cabled using a star topology.

See the "Ring Topology" section earlier in this chapter for more information.

Today virtually all token ring networks use UTP cables, which IBM refers to as Type 3 cabling. However, the connections to the MAU are the same. Table 2-8 lists some of the cabling guidelines for a token ring network.

Token Passing

The primary difference between a token ring network and an Ethernet network is in its Media Access Control (MAC) mechanism. Token passing is a MAC method that eliminates collisions from the network and supports large amounts of traffic with greater efficiency. Token ring networks use a specialized frame called a token to designate the computer that is permitted to transmit its data. The token is circulated around the network from computer to computer and only the computer in possession of the token is per-

TABLE 2-8	**CABLING GUIDELINES FOR A TOKEN RING NETWORK**	
	TYPE 1 CABLE	**TYPE 3 CABLE**
Maximum Number of Workstations	260	72
Maximum Lobe Cable Length	300 meters	150 meters
Maximum 8-Port MAUs	32	9
Maximum Ring Length @ 4 Mbps	360 meters	150 meters
Maximum Ring Length @ 16 Mbps	160 meters	60 meters

mitted to transmit. Once a computer has completed transmitting its data, it generates a new token and transmits it to the next computer in the ring. After the data circulates throughout the ring to all of the computers on the network, the system that originally generated the data is responsible for removing it. Because there is only one token frame on the network at a time, it is not possible for two computers to transmit data simultaneously. As a result, there are no collisions at all on a token ring network as there are with Ethernet.

Token passing is a highly efficient MAC mechanism that is used by several other protocols including Fiber Distributed Data Interface (FDDI).

Token Ring Frames

Token ring networks use three different types of frames—unlike Ethernet, which has only one. As mentioned in the previous section, the token frame is used solely for Media Access Control and is only 3 bytes long.

The Token Frame   The format of the token frame is shown in Figure 2-19 and the functions of the fields are as follows:

- **Start Delimiter (1 byte)**   The Start Delimiter field is used to indicate the beginning of the frame.

- **Access Control (1 byte)**   The Access Control field contains bits that are used to specify the priority of token ring transmissions.

- **End Delimiter (1 byte)**   The End Delimiter field indicates the conclusion of the frame using the same technique as the Start Delimiter field.

The Data Frame   The token ring data frame is responsible for carrying the actual application data generated by the computers on the network. It is the data frame that is most comparable to the frame used on Ethernet networks. The format of the data frame is shown in a Figure 2-20 and the functions of the fields are as follows:

- **Start Delimiter (1 byte)**   The Start Delimiter field is used to indicate the beginning of the frame.

- **Access Control (1 byte)**   The Access Control field contains bits that are used to specify the priority of token ring transmissions.

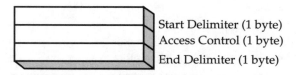

Start Delimiter (1 byte)
Access Control (1 byte)
End Delimiter (1 byte)

FIGURE 2-19   The token frame

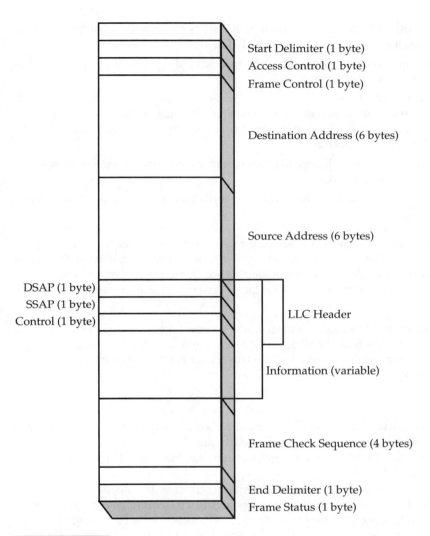

Start Delimiter (1 byte)
Access Control (1 byte)
Frame Control (1 byte)

Destination Address (6 bytes)

Source Address (6 bytes)

DSAP (1 byte)
SSAP (1 byte)
Control (1 byte)

LLC Header

Information (variable)

Frame Check Sequence (4 bytes)

End Delimiter (1 byte)
Frame Status (1 byte)

FIGURE 2-20 The Token Ring data frame

- **Frame Control (1 byte)** The Frame Control field indicates whether the packet contains a data or a command frame.
- **Destination Address (6 bytes)** The Destination Address field specifies the hardware address of the packet's intended recipient, using the standard addresses hard-coded into NICs.

- **Source Address (6 bytes)** The Source Address field identifies the computer that generated the packet using the standard hardware address coded into NICs.

- **Information (variable up to 4500 bytes)** The Information field contains the application data passed down from the network layer protocol.

- **Frame Check Sequence (4 bytes)** The Frame Check Sequence field contains a checksum value generated by the source computer that is compared to a similar computation performed by the recipient for access control purposes. If the value in this field does not match the value generated by the receiving computer, the packet is discarded.

- **End Delimiter (1 byte)** The End Delimiter field indicates the conclusion of the frame using the same technique as the Start Delimiter field.

- **Frame Status (1 byte)** The Frame Status field specifies whether the destination computer has successfully received the frame.

The Command Frame Token command frames use the same format as the data frame, the only differences being in the frame control field value and the information field contents. Command frames do not carry application data and are used to perform control functions only, such as ring maintenance. Command frames are never propagated to other network segments by connection devices such as bridges, switches, or routers.

The Abort Delimiter Frame The abort delimiter frame is only 2 bytes long and consists of the Start Delimiter and End Delimiter fields just like those in the other frame types. Abort delimiter frames are only used in special circumstances to clear the ring of data left over after a problem has occurred such as an incomplete packet transmission.

FDDI BASICS

Fiber Distributed Data Interface (FDDI) was the first commercial data link layer protocol to run at 100 Mbps using fiber-optic cable. Today, FDDI is rarely used because it has been supplanted by the fiber-optic Fast Ethernet and Gigabit Ethernet standards, but in its day FDDI was the primary protocol used for high-speed network backbones.

An FDDI network typically uses 62.5/125 multimode fiber-optic cable in a double-ring topology. Unlike token ring networks, FDDI can use a physical ring topology in which each computer is connected to the next one. To provide fault tolerance on the physical ring, FDDI networks use a double ring topology in which each computer is connected to two separate and independent rings with traffic flowing in opposite directions. If a cable break in the primary ring should occur, traffic is shunted to the other ring so that all the computers on the network remain accessible (a condition called a wrapped ring). Figure 2-21 illustrates the FDDI double ring as well as a wrapped ring.

Computers that are connected to both rings of a double-ring network are called dual attachment stations (DAS). Some FDDI networks also use a hub called a dual attachment concentrator (DAC). The DAC is connected to both rings and creates a logical ring internally, much like a token ring MAU. Computers connected to the DAC are called single attachment stations (SAS).

FDDI Frames

FDDI uses the token passing MAC mechanism just like a token ring network and uses a token frame format virtually identical to that of token ring.

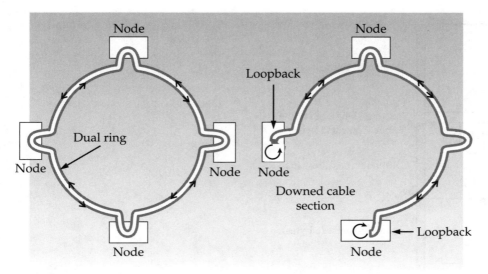

FIGURE 2-21   The FDDI double ring functioning normally on the left, and wrapped on the right

The FDDI data frame, like that of token ring, carries the application data generated by the upper layer protocols. The FDDI data frame is illustrated in Figure 2-22 and the functions of the fields are as follows:

- **Preamble (8 bytes)**   Contains a sequence of bits used to synchronize the clocks of the sending and receiving systems.

- **Starting Delimiter (1 byte)**   The Starting Delimiter field contains a value that indicates the beginning of the frame.

- **Frame Control (1 byte)**   The Frame Control field specifies the type of data carried in the frame. The values for this field can specify that the D field contains station management, Media Access Control, or logical link control data.

- **Destination Address (6 bytes)**   The Destination Address field identifies the computer that will receive the frame using standard hardware addresses coded into NICs.

- **Source Address (6 bytes)**   The Source Address field identifies the computer that generated the frame using standard hardware addresses coded into NICs.

- **Data (variable)**   Contains information generated by a network layer protocol or station management or Media Access Control data, depending on the value of the Frame Control field.

- **Frame Check Sequence (4 bytes)**   The Frame Check Sequence field contains a checksum value used for error detection.

- **Ending Delimiter (4 bits)**   Contains a value indicating the end of the frame.

- **End of Frame Sequence (12 bits)**   Contains Error, Acknowledge, and Copy indicators that are used by intermediate systems to specify the status of the frame.

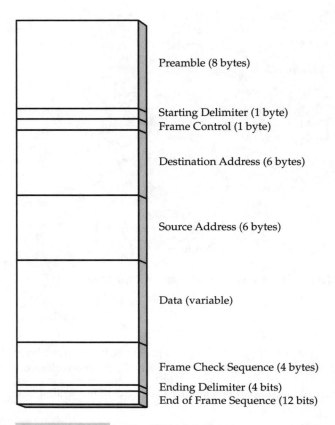

Preamble (8 bytes)

Starting Delimiter (1 byte)
Frame Control (1 byte)

Destination Address (6 bytes)

Source Address (6 bytes)

Data (variable)

Frame Check Sequence (4 bytes)

Ending Delimiter (4 bits)
End of Frame Sequence (12 bits)

FIGURE 2-22   The FDDI data frame

Summary

This chapter covered the basics of network topologies, cabling, and the data link layer protocols. The seven topologies covered were bus, star, star bus, hierarchical star, ring, mesh, and wireless. The cabling covered was coaxial, twisted pair, and fiber optic. We also covered the three elements of data link layer protocols: the format for the frame, the mechanism that regulates access to the shared network, and the network's physical layer guidelines.

Further Study

If you have access to the Internet, take a look at some of these resources:
ANSI Online: **http://www.ansi.org/**
IEEE web site: **http://www.ieee.org/portal/index.jsp**
EIA web site: **http://www.eia.org/**
TIA Online: **http://www.tiaonline.org/**

3

NETWORK PROTOCOLS

When communicating, in both verbal and the written form, it is essential for the communicating parties to understand and adhere to a set of rules. These rules may be as simple as requiring a question mark at the end of a written statement to indicate that a response is required, or they may be a complex and extensive arrangement—as in the case of an entire language such as English or French. Without these rules, it would be difficult—if not impossible—for both parties to interpret each other's meaning.

The same is true in data communication—the communicating devices must agree and adhere to a common set of rules. In other words, they must agree on a common protocol. This protocol, or set of rules, can be as basic as defining when a message starts and when it ends, or it could be a complex set of agreements such as the maximum length of time that is allowed to transpire before a message must be received from either communicating party. Knowing and understanding the rules of a specific protocol is a fundamental requirement in isolating and troubleshooting a problem. Without knowledge of the rules, you would never know when the rule is being broken, and if you do not know when the rule is being broken, it is much more difficult to determine when the communicating devices are functioning properly and how they should be functioning.

In this chapter we will review common networking protocols. First we will examine the Open Systems Interconnection (OSI) model, a reference model developed to describe how data is exchanged between computers across a network. Next, we will explore some of the more common network protocols found in local area networks.

The OSI Reference Model

In1984, the International Organization for Standardization (ISO), a global federation of national standards organizations representing approximately 140 countries, developed a networking reference model called the Open Systems Interconnection, or OSI. The model describes how information from an application in one computer moves through a network medium to an application on another computer. Today, the model is considered the primary architectural model for intercomputer communications and is the framework into which existing standards are slotted.

The purpose of the reference model was to define an architectural framework that defines the logical communication tasks that are required to move information between different computer systems. The basic premise of OSI is to define and group the logical functions of the information flow between systems without attempting to define details of how each function works. To accomplish this, a seven-layer model was developed with each layer representing a group of related logical functions. The internals and details of each layer are left to system developers; instead, the model defines the overall function of each layer and its interface to higher and lower layers.

By standardizing the function of each layer and their interfaces without regard to the details and internals of each layer, OSI facilitates a model that allows interoperability between different manufacturers without the manufacturer having to sacrifice features. The seven layers as defined by the group are

- Layer 7 – Application
- Layer 6 – Presentation
- Layer 5 – Session
- Layer 4 – Transport
- Layer 3 – Network
- Layer 2 – Data Link
- Layer 1 – Physical

Each layer—a logical grouping of tasks—is fairly self-contained so that the tasks defined within a layer can be implemented independently. This allows the development of feature-rich solutions within a layer without affecting the basic functions of other layers.

UNDERSTANDING THE LAYERS

The seven layers of the OSI model can be broken into two categories: upper and lower layers. The upper layers—layers 5–7—address issues that are relevant to applications and are typically implemented in software. The lower layers—layers 1–4—address the transport of the information through the network and may be implemented in hardware, software, and/or firmware.

It is important to note that the model is only a conceptual framework and does not define a method of communication. Communication between computer systems is made possible through protocols that define the rules by which information is exchanged between systems. A protocol implements the functions of one or more layers of the OSI model.

There are many different protocols that are designed to do entirely different tasks. A routing protocol, for instance, operates at layer 3 of the network model and defines the method by which routers decide on the path of a packet as it traverses the network. In contrast, a protocol operating at layer 2—the data link layer—is more concerned with the formatting and addressing—amongst other things—of a packet for a particular transmission medium.

While both protocols are different and behave independently of each other, they must work in harmony to move the packet from one system to another. Since both play an important role in the transport of a packet through the network, it is imperative that the data link layer, for instance, not change the content of the packet it receives from the network layer. Instead, it adds the information it needs to function to the packet. This concept of building upon layers is at the heart of how the OSI model works, but before we explore how the layers work in more detail, we will first take a look at the different layers and what they do.

Layer 1—Physical

Layer 1, the physical layer, defines the electrical characteristics of the network. The physical media—whether it is coax copper, air, or fiber—across which the information flows and the network interface card (NIC) in your PC all operate at this layer. At this level, the information is basically a series of electrical or acoustical impulses that represent the basic ones and zeros of the binary data structure. Regardless of the information, its original structure, or its source, everything boils down to this basic common structure as it wends its way through the network.

A basic principle to remember is that if the physical length of the cable (or wire segment) needs to be extended beyond the defined limits for the particular medium, a *repeater* is required to regenerate the signal. As a result, repeaters as a rule operate at this layer.

Layer 2—Data Link

Layer 2, also called the data link layer, defines the access strategy for sharing the physical medium. It prepares the information, or data, it receives from upper layers for transmission across the specific medium that is installed. At this layer, devices are concerned with two basic pieces of information. The first is the Media Access Control (MAC), which defines the specific properties that are unique to the specific physical media and how it should be shared between multiple devices. The second is the Logical Link Control (LLC) that defines how the link is used, frame synchronization, flow control, and error checking. For this reason, the data link layer is described as consisting of two different sublayers: the MAC and the LLC sublayers.

The LLC is defined in the IEEE 802.2 specification and supports both connectionless and connection-oriented services used by higher-layer protocols. Within the specification, a number of fields in data link layer frames are defined that enable multiple higher-layer protocols to share a single physical data link. The MAC sublayer of the data link layer manages protocol access to the physical network medium. It includes the definition of MAC addresses, which enable multiple devices to uniquely identify one another at the data link layer.

Some functions performed at the data link layer include the following:

- **Physical addressing**   There may be multiple devices on the physical wire segment, as in the case of Ethernet. These devices must be uniquely identifiable through the use of a unique address, called the MAC address. The MAC address is a unique number administered by one of the networking governing bodies—the IEEE—and assigned by the manufacturer.

- **Topology of the local segment**   In addition to the addressing of devices on the local segment, the logical topology of the network is also a factor that must be considered. The topology may be a point-to-point link between devices, or it may be multiple devices sharing a common segment. In the case of the latter, the devices may operate logically as a ring, as a star, or as a bus (as in the case of Ethernet). Additionally, the local segment may be segmented through the use of a bridge. In this case, the bridge keeps a record of the devices that reside on different wiring segments, as shown in Figure 3-1, and directs the data packet to the segment where the target device resides. By only forwarding packets between ports if two devices on separate segments need to communicate, bridges aid in the reduction of unnecessary traffic on segments.

- **Access to the physical medium, flow control, and frame synchronization**   Data packets are encoded and decoded into bits for placement on, and retrieval from, the medium. A packet that is received from the network layer may be further segmented into frames before it is handed to the physical layer.

- **Error detection**   Errors that occur during transmission across the physical medium are detected at this layer. The error detection protects the higher layers from the characteristics of the physical transmission medium. A calculated error control value such as a cyclic redundancy check (CRC) is placed at the tail end of the frame before it is sent to the physical layer. The receiving computer recalculates the CRC and compares it to the one sent with the data. If the two values are equal, it is assumed that the data arrived without errors. Otherwise, a packet may need to be retransmitted by an upper-layer protocol. Although the data link layer implements error detection, it does not necessarily include a function to perform error recovery. This is left for the upper layers to deal with—primarily on the transport layer.

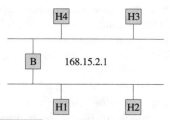

FIGURE 3-1   Bridging between segments

A basic principle to remember is this: multiple wiring segments that share a common network address require a *bridge* or a *layer 2 switch* to connect the segments. Figure 3-2 provides a quick reference on well-known LAN and WAN specifications and how they relate to the physical and data link layers.

Layer 3—Network

The network layer, where the IP protocol resides, is responsible for defining the processes and tasks required to route packets through the networks. As part of this function, layer 3 is concerned with logical addresses of source and target devices and all other devices—routers—that aid in the transport of packets through the network. It is also responsible for determining the path through the network.

If the communicating systems share a common LAN segment, packets may be exchanged directly between them with the help of the data link and physical layers of both the source and target systems. In this instance, the packet is sent from the network layer to the data link and physical layers of the sending system. The data link layer prepares the packets for transmission and places them on to the physical medium. The receiving station receives the bit stream and reassembles it into its original packet structure, which is passed up to the network and upper layers of the receiving device.

If, however, the source and target systems are on different networks, routers are required to move the packets through the network along a path that is already predefined or one that is dynamically discovered. A router is a device that operates at the first three layers of the OSI model, as shown in Figure 3-3. In other words, it has an interface that directly attaches to the physical medium, and it performs layer 2 and layer 3 functions. Routers have the ability to dynamically discover networks through the use of a routing protocol. Alternatively, the path through the network may be predefined through the use of static routes—definitions that indicate the correct outbound interface for each network within the internetwork.

Here's a summary of some of the more basic functions of the network layer:

- Network addressing
- Path determination between source and destination nodes on different networks
- Routing of packets between networks

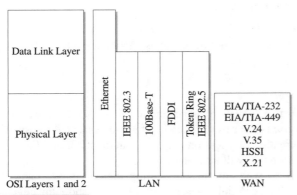

FIGURE 3-2 Common LAN and WAN physical and data link layer specifications

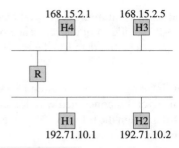

FIGURE 3-3   Routers operate at layers 1–3.

A basic principle to remember is this: where there are multiple networks, a *router* is required to route packets between them.

Layer 4—Transport

Layer 4, or the transport layer, is where TCP resides. The standards describe this layer as responsible for relieving the session layer (layer 5) of the responsibility of ensuring data reliability and integrity. Whereas the network layer is concerned about moving packets from one system to another, the transport layer has a broader objective. It must be concerned with ensuring the delivery and addressing any reported or perceived errors. The following tasks are performed at this layer in order to accomplish these objectives:

- Flow control—used to preserve data integrity.
- Multiplexing of data from upper-layer applications.
- Segmentation of upper-layer datagrams.
- Establishment and teardown of conversations between the communicating endpoints.
- Shielding the complexity of the network from upper layers.
- Ensuring error-free delivery of the data to its destination.
- Ensuring the reliable delivery of the segments, which is not the same as guaranteeing the delivery.
- General connection management and data transfer tasks.

Layer 5—Session

The main function of layer 5, the session layer, is to establish, manage, and terminate sessions between two communicating presentation entities. A *session* is a series of related connection-oriented transmissions between the communicating entities. The creation of a session may entail authentication of a user account and determining the type of communication that will take place.

Consider this: if a user starts buying an item from a web site and begins filling their "shopping cart," it becomes very important that the session remains with the initial web server on which the shopping began. If by chance the user is load balanced across different servers in a server pool, the shopping experience—or the session—may be interrupted. In this instance, it is all right to load balance at the start of a session, but not during the session. For this reason, the device doing the load balancing (which typically operates at the transport layer) must also understand the session layer.

Layer 6—Presentation
The main task of the presentation layer is to define the data formats used to provide a number of services to the application layer. Some of the tasks performed at this layer include protocol conversion, encryption/decryption, and graphics expansion.

Layer 7—Application
Finally, the application layer is the layer that is closest to the end user or end application. The following services are offered at this layer:

- Application services
- Database services
- File services
- Print services
- Message services

To recap, Table 3-1 provides a quick summary of the different OSI layers.

TABLE 3-1   SUMMARY OF OSI LAYERS

LAYER	NAME	DESCRIPTION
1	Physical	Conveys the bit stream through the network at the electrical and mechanical level. It provides the hardware means of sending and receiving data on a carrier.
2	Data link	Provides synchronization for the physical layer and furnishes transmission protocol knowledge and management.
3	Network	Handles the routing and forwarding of the data through the network.
4	Transport	Manages the end-to-end control (for example, determining whether all packets have arrived) and error checking. It ensures complete data transfer.
5	Session	Establishes, coordinates, and terminates conversations, exchanges, and dialogs between the applications at each end. Deals with session and connection coordination.
6	Presentation	Converts incoming and outgoing data from one presentation format to another.
7	Application	Communicating partners are identified, quality of service is identified, user authentication and privacy are considered, and any constraints on data syntax are identified. (This layer is *not* the application itself, although some applications may perform application layer functions.)

HOW THE LAYERS WORK AND INFORMATION FORMATS

As previously discussed, the OSI model is an architectural model describing the way messages or information elements are exchanged between computers. The layered approach of the model is sometimes called a *stack*, and so the model is also often called the *OSI stack*. Conceptually, an element of information flowing from one computer to another flows along a path that begins with the application layer and flows downwards through the stack of layers until it reaches the physical layer. On arrival at the target system, the data must then travel upward through the stack from the physical layer to the application, as shown in Figure 3-4.

Each layer within the OSI model typically communicates with three other layers. (The exceptions are the physical and application layers—they only communicate with two other layers.) These layers are the layers immediately above and below it, and the corresponding layer on the target system—called the *peer layer*.

Two transformations take place to the data as it passes down the stack of the OSI layers in the source system. First, each layer takes the information it receives from the layer above it and breaks it into smaller components. Second, the smaller components each receive additional control information. This additional information is used for the purposes of communicating between the source and peer layers on the target system.

Terminology and Formats

Many terms are used to describe data as it moves from one computer to another. Terms such as "segments," "messages," "packets," "datagrams," "frames," "data units," and "cells" have all been used at one time or another to describe data as it flows from one computer to another. In many cases, they are used interchangeably—a practice that would lead one to believe that they all have the same meaning.

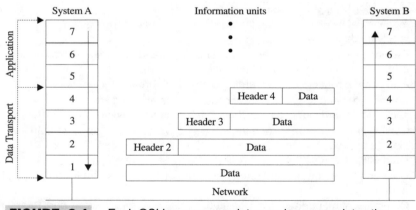

FIGURE 3-4   Each OSI layer encapsulates or de-encapsulates the information it receives.

In reality, the different terminology have specific meanings that are directly related to the structure of the information at any given time in its passage from one computer to another. A *data unit* is a generic term that refers to a variety of information units. However, the other terms all have specific meanings. Common data units are listed here:

- **Service data units (SDUs)**   Information units from upper-layer protocols that define a service request to a lower-layer protocol.
- **Protocol data units (PDUs)**   An OSI term for a packet.
- **Bridge protocol data units (BPDUs)**   A type of data unit that is exchanged between bridges to prevent loops.

A *frame* is a unit of information whose source and destination are the data link layer MAC addresses. It is composed of a header, and possibly a trailer, that contains control information that is specific to that layer. The data portion of the frame actually contains a piece of the original application layer information and other control information that was added by each layer as it passed through the different layers of the stack.

A *cell* is also a term that describes a unit of information that is exchanged between data link layers. However, cells have a fixed size and are used in switched environments, such as Asynchronous Transfer Mode (ATM). A cell is composed of the header and payload. In the case of ATM, the header contains control information intended for the data link layer of the target device and is 5 bytes long. The payload contains upper-layer data that is encapsulated in the cell header and is 48 bytes long.

A *packet* is a unit of information that is exchanged between network layers. The structure at this point is one of a header (and possibly a trailer) that has control information that is specific to the network layer. The data portion consists of control information for the upper layers plus some of the original information. A *datagram* is also a description for units of information that is exchanged between network layers. However, the term usually indicates a *connectionless* network service.

The term *segment* is a reference to units of information whose source and destination is the transport layer. A *message* is a unit of information that is exchanged between any layer above the transport layer—layers 5–7. Figure 3-4 illustrates the concept of how data flows through the stack. Each subsequent layer, depending on the direction of the flow, encapsulates or de-encapsulates the information it receives from adjacent layers. The flow of information between two computers can therefore be summarized as follows:

1. User data is converted to a message.
2. The transport layer converts the message into multiple segments and passes them to the network layer.
3. The network layer takes each segment and breaks it into packets or datagrams, depending on the type of service—connection-oriented or connectionless. The packets and datagrams are handed to the data link layer.
4. The data link layer breaks the packets or datagrams into frames or cells. The frames or cells are streamed on to the physical media.

APPLYING THE MODEL TO THE MICROSOFT WINDOWS ENVIRONMENT

The networking component of the Microsoft Windows operating system maps to the different functions of the OSI layers. In some cases there may not be a perfect one-to-one mapping of a protocol to a specific OSI layer, but even in these cases one can usually find functions within a protocol that perform specific duties that align with the OSI layer model. At the very least, the OSI model is useful for conceptualizing networking components—how the pieces of your system, from the cable through to the Network Neighborhood, fit together to help the computers on your network communicate.

So how does the OSI model relate to Windows NT network communications? We'll once again go through the layers, but this time we'll map the protocols one would likely encounter in NT networking and discuss where those protocols fit in the OSI model and how they cooperate to create a working NT network.

Windows Physical Layer   The components that relate to the physical layer consist of Ethernet, token ring, wireless, and other network interface cards. Of course, the actual physical medium is also included. The physical interface itself is generally mounted within the network interface card itself or through an attachment, as in the case of a PCMCIA Ethernet card. In addition to the card types mentioned, Windows systems also provide the appropriate interface for a dial-up connection. All the physical layer networking hardware components can be viewed on a Windows 2000 system by right-clicking the My Computer icon on your desktop, and then selecting Properties | Hardware | Device Manager (see Figure 3-5).

The physical layer connection within the Windows environment is not limited to network interface cards. Any interface or cable type that facilitates intercomputer communication performs a physical layer

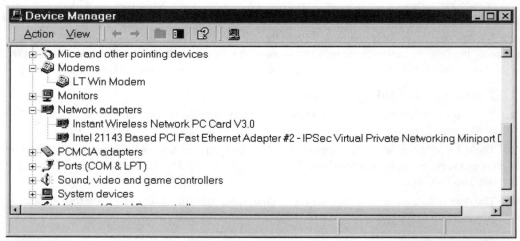

FIGURE 3-5 ╲ Physical layer components can be viewed through the Windows Device Manager.

function. This includes the serial RS232 connector (COM1, COM2, and so forth), the parallel port, and any universal serial bus (USB) ports. In recent years, the USB port has become a popular way to connect broadband networking devices to consumer PCs. When using USB networking, the network interface controller (NIC) is connected to the user's computer using USB.

Windows Data Link Layer   Ethernet is the most common data link layer protocol encountered in the typical Windows LAN environment. The data link layer packages data in frames. Each frame is then given a destination and a source address, which are physical hardware addresses that are burned in to the network card. For this reason, these addresses are sometimes called the burned-in address (BIA)—the proper distinction is the Media Access Control address or the MAC address. These addresses are used to uniquely identify the card from which each frame is being transmitted and the card to which they are being sent. It is important to note that the MAC address is not necessarily the only address of the target computer, as there are some configurations where a single computer may have more than one connection to the same, or a different, LAN.

Ethernet is one of many such data link protocols. Others include Token Ring and Arcnet. If the underlying connection is not a local area network, Windows may use other data link protocols such as Point-to-Point (PPP) or Serial Line Internet Protocol (SLIP), both of which are used across a serial connection.

The PPP and SLIP protocols are outside the scope of this chapter and so we will not examine them in great detail. Both the protocols are used to establish a connection to the Internet that allows Internet programs such as Internet Explorer, Netscape, and other IP applications such as Telnet to operate across a modem connection. The PPP protocol is the newer of the two protocols and is implemented through Dial-Up Networking in the Windows environment. It is a connection-oriented protocol that encapsulates multiple packets of different network protocols so that all the packets can travel across the same link at the same time. PPP contains three parts: one part encapsulates the protocol into generic PPP packets with a header that identifies the network protocol type; a second part creates the connection; and a third part handles any special conditions unique to that protocol, such as resolving IP addresses to hardware addresses.

Some useful links on SLIP and PPP have been provided at the end of the chapter.

Windows Network Layer   One of the principal functions of the network layer is to assign and track logical addresses that identify network nodes within the network. In the Windows environment, the most common network layer protocols are IP and IPX (see the sections, "The Internet Protocol (IP)" and "The IPX/SPX Protocol," later in this chapter). There is typically a one-to-one mapping of a logical network address to a corresponding hardware address. As a result, the network address, or IP address if the protocol is IP, does not necessarily identify a specific computer but a specific hardware interface. A computer may have multiple network interface cards on a single, or a different, LAN, each having its own network and hardware address. It is therefore more appropriate to use the term "network node" to describe the entity that is described by a network address.

In the Windows 2000 environment, selecting the properties of the My Network Places icon and viewing the properties of the Local Area connection accesses the network layer protocols (see Figure 3-6). This is also the place where network addresses are assigned. We will cover network addresses in more detail in the "Network Protocols" section in this chapter. Right-click the My Network Places icon on your desktop and select Properties, then select Local Area Connection and Properties.

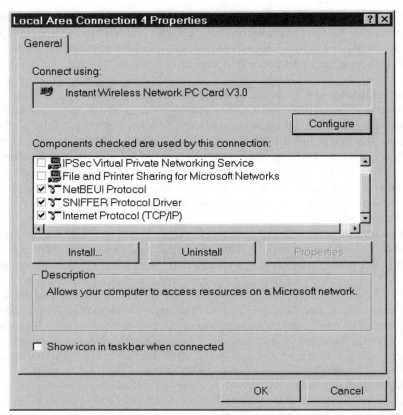

FIGURE 3-6 Network protocols can be viewed by viewing the properties of a local connection.

Behind the scenes, there are many protocols that must operate in harmony to provide a seamless working network. One such protocol is the Address Resolution Protocol (ARP), which we will explore in greater detail in a later section. This protocol is instrumental in logically mapping a network address to a physical hardware address.

Unlike a hardware address that is permanently assigned to a network interface card, the network address is changeable and in some configurations may vary every time the computer reboots. The ARP protocol is used to dynamically assign a correlation between the hardware address and the logical network address.

To view the IP address assigned to the NICs on a Windows 2000 computer, open a command-line window and enter the following:

```
C:\WINNT>ipconfig
Windows 2000 IP Configuration
Ethernet adapter Local Area Connection 4:
        Connection-specific DNS Suffix  . : carty.testdns.com
```

```
IP Address. . . . . . . . . . . . : 192.168.31.101
Subnet Mask . . . . . . . . . . . : 255.255.255.0
Default Gateway . . . . . . . . . : 192.168.31.1
```

The output provides a listing of all the logical network addresses for all active and connected NICs. The output will also show whether or not the physical cable is disconnected from the NIC.

Windows Transport Layer   Network layer protocols such as IP and IPX track layer 3 addresses and decide the most efficient route at any given time. However, these protocols aren't concerned with ensuring that the data is delivered—that job is the responsibility of protocols operating at the transport layer. Ensuring the safe arrival of the packet at its destination is the job of protocols such as TCP for the IP protocol and SPX for IPX. Another IP transport protocol is UDP, which the Windows network uses for program-to-program communication and for applications such as NetBIOS name resolution. Both TCP and UDP rely on IP.

The transport protocols—TCP and UDP—are automatically enabled whenever IP is enabled in the Windows environment. To display the status of all TCP and UDP connections, open a Windows command-line window and enter the following:

```
C:\WINNT>netstat
Active Connections
   Proto  Local Address        Foreign Address        State
   TCP    glen_carty-h1:1060   63.249.162.173:http    ESTABLISHED
   TCP    glen_carty-h1:1061   63.249.162.173:http    ESTABLISHED
   TCP    glen_carty-h1:1062   63.249.162.173:http    ESTABLISHED
   TCP    glen_carty-h1:1069   204.71.191.241:http    ESTABLISHED
```

Windows Session Layer   NetBIOS, short for Network Basic Input/Output, is the standard application programming interface (API) used for services such as locating resources on a Windows network. It is a program that allows applications on different computers to communicate with each other. However, it does not in itself support a routing and transport mechanism and so must rely on another transport protocol such as TCP or UDP. Alternatively, it may use NetBEUI, short for NetBIOS Extended User Interface—a transport protocol developed as an extension to NetBIOS. NetBEUI provides a standard data format for transmission over a wide area network.

A sometimes-confusing element of Windows networking is that NetBIOS is enabled by default whenever TCP/IP is enabled. This is the reason why there is no entry for NetBIOS over TCP/IP (NBT) when installing different networking protocols. In contrast, there is a NetBEUI entry, which actually means NetBIOS over NetBEUI. To load the TCP/IP protocol without the NetBIOS over TCP/IP support, uncheck the Enable Internet Connection Sharing for This Connection option under the sharing tab of the Local Area Connection screen. File and Print Sharing should also be disabled.

Presentation and Application Layers   In the Windows environment, the *redirector* is the application layer function that is responsible for interfacing between application data requests and the OS to determine whether these requests apply to data available locally or to network-accessible resources. It is responsible for directing network requests to networked servers and making sure that local commands go to the local operating system.

The Server Message Block (SMB) is a presentation layer protocol responsible for the enabling of file and printer sharing and the sharing of serial ports over a LAN. It also handles user-based messaging. SMB is a client/server protocol, meaning it uses request/response queries, a request coming from a client and the response coming from the server. SMB is only responsible for the sharing, not the actual transport, so SMB can be used over NetBIOS/NetBEUI or NetBIOS/TCP/IP or IPX/SPX.

Network Protocols

In this section we will examine the common core network protocols that exist in many enterprise networks. For each core network protocol, such as IP or IPX, there are usually many more complementary protocols that span all the different layers of the OSI model. Because the network protocol is the one that is responsible for forwarding packets between two network nodes, and it is the one with the most knowledge of the hosts that are reachable through the local network, it is usually the core protocol around which the other protocols are built. Upper-layer protocols are designed to utilize the services offered by the network protocol, which shields them from the complexity of the underlying network.

This chapter focuses on network protocols, and so we will be examining some of the more common network protocols in some detail. However, a network protocol such as IP is usually dependent on a routing protocol—also a layer 3 protocol—to dynamically route the packet through the network. Although we will be discussing network protocols, we will not delve too deeply into routing protocols, as these will be covered in greater detail in Chapter 14.

Network protocols can operate without the help of a routing protocol. Because they understand the local network, they are efficient for forwarding packets to hosts on the local network. Once these networks are linked, however, they require some help to see beyond the local network boundaries. Routers are layer 3 devices that are used to interconnect different networks. They assist in moving the packet from one network to another. To do this, routers require knowledge of the local networks to which they are attached and the networks that are further downstream. The knowledge of locally attached networks is easily obtained because the routers are directly connected to them. However, things are not so easy when the target host is on another network, several networks away.

In this case, routers need to be told about the networks that are not directly attached but are reachable through another router. This can be accomplished by configuring static routes, which are definitions that define the reachable networks and where to forward packets destined to them. Alternatively, the routers may instead utilize another protocol that will help them learn about these networks.

This is where a routing protocol fits in; these protocols are used to make dynamic decisions about the best way to get a packet from one network to another. They understand the network of networks—the internetwork—and track the areas within the internetwork that are having problems. In this chapter we will make reference to these protocols and provide enough of an explanation to understand how they work in context to the core network protocol. But our main focus will be on the core network protocol.

PROTOCOL BASICS

A protocol is basically a set of rules that have been agreed to beforehand. This is true of all protocols, not just network protocols. The orderly operation of a network is dependent on every participating device obeying and abiding by these sets of rules. To configure, manage, and maintain a network, the network manager must understand how each protocol operates and how they all interact. Without this knowledge, it is nearly impossible to configure and maintain an efficient working network, and even more difficult to perform the task of troubleshooting.

THE INTERNET PROTOCOL SUITE

The TCP/IP protocol, as it is commonly called, is actually two entirely different protocols that operate at layers 3 (IP) and 4 (TCP) of the OSI model. It is generally used to describe a suite of protocols, of which TCP and IP are the two most popular. In this context, a more accurate description is the Internet Protocol suite.

In this section we will examine the IP protocol in detail, as it is the core network protocol around which the other protocols are based and it is the protocol that relates most to the subject of the chapter. We will also take a look at other supporting protocols such as the Address Resolution Protocol (ARP) and Dynamic Host Configuration Protocol (DHCP).

The Internet Protocol (IP)

The IP protocol is based on the concept of hosts and networks. A host is any device in the network that is capable of sending and receiving IP packets across a network. IP hosts, therefore, can be routers, workstations, servers, or any device that has an IP address. A collection of hosts sharing a common address structure is said to be within the same IP network. Typically, these hosts also share a common wire segment such as a common Ethernet segment.

A basic rule in IP networking is that hosts within the same network are able to communicate directly with each other, but if they are in different networks, a router is required to route between the two networks. When viewed in the context of the OSI model, the logic behind this makes sense. A router operates at layer 3, as does the IP protocol. If two hosts reside in two different IP networks, they would have two different network addresses. This is the same as saying they have two different layer 3 addresses. It would require a device operating at the same layer to understand the differences in addressing; such a device is a router.

By understanding this basic rule of IP networking, it quickly becomes obvious why two hosts sharing a common wire but different network addresses will not be able to communicate directly with each other. Even in this configuration, a router would be required for the two hosts to communicate. The fact that they are on the same physical wire does not mean they are able to communicate directly.

Now consider that in some configurations different hosts within the same network may actually reside on different segments. In this case, the two segments must be bridged, which is a layer 2 function. By bridging the two wire segments, the bridge fakes the sending device into believing that the target device is on the same physical wire. The sending device places the frame on to the wire and the bridge forwards it on to the target segment. A logical follow-up question to this process is, "How does the sending device know the physical address of the target if the only reference it knows is its network address?" We will address this in a later section when we discuss the ARP protocol.

Network Addressing

To understand the IP protocol, you must understand the addressing scheme of IP. A solid grounding in IP addressing is the first step in mastering the tasks of configuring, maintaining, managing, and trouble-shooting an IP network. Within a network—whether it is local area network or a network of networks such as the Internet—every host must be given a unique address.

In the same way addresses are used in everyday life to identify specific entities such as a specific building, network protocols identify different nodes within a network. In general, a street address is used to identify a specific building and a ZIP code is used to identify a broad but specific region. An IP address also consists of two components: one to identify the specific host and the other to identify the network in which the hosts reside.

In some cases, names may be assigned to specific addresses—the White House or the Empire State Building, for instance. Names make it easy to identify an address without having to remember the street number and ZIP code. The concept also applies to the IP protocol, and in some cases hosts may be optionally given names. These names negate the need to remember a complex address structure, which makes it a convenient feature. However, from a hardware and software perspective, these names cannot be used to route packets—the actual IP addresses must be used. This raises the question of how these names are mapped to specific addresses. A host file, which is a local file of names that map to specific IP addresses, can be used to correlate names with IP addresses. Windows and other computer systems use this file to resolve names to IP addresses. The following extract is a copy of an actual Windows host file, which is located in the Windows directory. In the extract, the name localhost maps to an IP address of 127.0.0.1, which is a special address called a loopback address for the local machine. The lines preceded by a # are comments only.

```
# Copyright (c) 1994 Microsoft Corp.
# This is a sample HOSTS file used by Microsoft TCP/IP for Chicago
# This file contains the mappings of IP addresses to host names. Each
# entry should be kept on an individual line. The IP address should
# be placed in the first column followed by the corresponding host name.
# The IP address and the host name should be separated by at least one
# space.
#
# Additionally, comments (such as these) may be inserted on individual
# lines or following the machine name denoted by a '#' symbol.
#
# For example:
#      102.54.94.97     rhino.acme.com          # source server
#       38.25.63.10     x.acme.com              # x client host
127.0.0.1        localhost
```

Optionally, the names may be stored on a central server, called a DNS—short for Domain Name Service. If the IP protocol is given a name of a host, it will first attempt to resolve that name by looking at the host file stored locally. If it is not found there, it will look to see if a DNS server address has been configured. If one has been, it will send a request to the DNS server to resolve the name to a real IP address.

IP Address Structure and Address Classes   The IP protocol uses a scheme consisting of 32 bits or 4 bytes expressed as four decimal numbers separated by periods. The addressing scheme is sometime called a dotted decimal address because of the way it is annotated. The four bytes, or decimal numbers, represent a specific host and the network address of that host.

An IP address such as 192.168.14.100 encodes a specific host and network address, but it is not immediately obvious what constitutes the host portion and what constitutes the network. Applying the most basic rule of addressing, one can determine that the network portion is the 192.168.14 and the host portion is 100. So what is this rule?

The rule is that there are three primary classes of IP networks: class A, class B, and class C addresses. A class A network is one where there are a greater number of host addresses compared to network addresses. These addresses logically divide the 32 bits so that the first decimal number represents the network and the remaining numbers represent the host addresses.

A class B network uses the first two decimal positions to denote the network portion of the address and the remaining two for the hosts. The class B network range, therefore, has almost as many networks as there are hosts.

A class C network uses the first three decimal positions to denote the network portion of the address and the fourth decimal position to represent the host address. Using this information, one sees that in the example given of an address of 192.186.14.100, it was determined to be a class C address because the first three octets were said to be the network portion. However, it still does not explain why this address is specifically a class C address. What is it about the address that indicates that the first three octets should be used for the network portion, and not the first one or two octets, which would indicate a class A or class B, respectively? The answer can be found in Table 3-2. It shows the network range for each class.

Using the table, it shows that if the first octet of the IP address falls within the range of 192–223, the address is a class C network, as in our example. Remembering the ranges should be sufficient to recognize the class to which a given network belongs. However, we will delve a bit deeper for the readers that are interested in understanding how these ranges are derived.

The primary classes of network addresses are derived from the first three bits of the 32-bit address. When a router receives a packet, it does not go to a table to decide the class to which an address belongs. Instead, it makes a determination by reading the first three bits—the high order bits—of the address. As shown in Figure 3-7, class A addresses all have the first bit of the first octet set to 0, class B networks have the first bit set to 1 and the second to 0, and, finally, class C networks have both the first and second bits set to 1 and the third bit set to 0.

TABLE 3-2   THE THREE PRIMARY CLASSES OF IP ADDRESSES

CLASS	RANGE OF NETWORK NUMBERS	NUMBER OF BITS	RANGE OF HOST NUMBERS	NUMBER OF BITS
A	0.h.h.h–126.h.h.h	7	n.0.0.1–n.255.255.254	24
B	128.0.h.h–191.255.h.h	14	n.n.0.1–n.n.255.254	16
C	192.0.0.h–223.255.255.h	21	n.n.n.1–n.n.n.254	8

Where h = host
and n = network

	Octet 1	Octet 2	Octet 3	Octet 4
Class A	0 n n n n n n n	h h h h h h h h	h h h h h h h h	h h h h h h h h
Class B	1 0 n n n n n n	n n n n n n n n	h h h h h h h h	h h h h h h h h
Class C	1 1 0 n n n n n	n n n n n n n n	n n n n n n n n	h h h h h h h h

Class A: Start at 0 through 127
Class B: Start at 128 through 191
Class C: Start at 192 through 223

FIGURE 3-7 Primary classes of IP addressing

For the observant reader, the primary classes of networks only address a range of 0–223 in the first octet. The 224–239 range—class D—is reserved for multicast addresses, which are special addresses that are used to address groups of specific hosts. Class E—240–247—is reserved. The remaining addresses through 255 are also reserved, but are typically not grouped into the class E range.

Advanced Concepts in IP Addressing So far we have looked at IP addressing structures that fit within the primary classes. In reality, using addresses that are defined within each class—a concept called classful addressing—can be highly inefficient. The original idea behind classful addressing was to create a structure such that very large networks (of which it was believed there would only be a few) would need an addressing scheme to facilitate thousands of hosts. Large companies such as IBM were assigned a class A network because they fit the profile of a large global network that would need an address space to accommodate the vast number of hosts around the world. The address assigned to IBM is 9.0.0.0.

Companies of intermediate size would be allocated a class B designation, and a small company, which may have a single LAN, a class C designation. That was the logic behind the address structure. What happens, however, when a small company grows to the point where they need more than the one network that is assigned by a class C—as in the example where they are adding two additional LANs? Or, what happens when a class B is assigned to a company, but they really need more than one network address? In these cases, classful addressing is not sufficient to address the requirements.

To overcome the limitations of classful addressing, the concept of subnetting is used. Subnetting is the method by which a classful address can be logically segmented into multiple network addresses by using some of the host bits as bits that indicate a subnetwork. The need for subnetting becomes obvious when one considers how IP addressing works. A network address is required for every wire segment that exists, if the segments are not bridged. If the network assignment were a class B, it would only be of benefit on a single segment. If another wire segment were introduced, another class B address would be required. However, if subnetting is used, a single class B address could be used for both wire segments, as shown in Figure 3-8.

At the core of subnetting is the utilization of subnet masks. A mask is an overlay address structure that is used to indicate which bits of a 32-bit address comprise the network portion of the address. The following table shows the masks for the three classes of addresses already discussed:

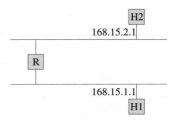

The Class B network 168.15.0.0
is used for both segments
168.15.1.0 is subnet 1
168.15.2.0 is subnet 2

FIGURE 3-8 Subnetting carves multiple
networks out of a classful
network.

ADDRESS CLASS	MASK
A	11111111.00000000.00000000.00000000
B	11111111. 11111111.00000000.00000000
C	11111111. 11111111. 11111111.00000000

Bits that are set to 1 in the mask indicate that the corresponding bits of the IP address are part of the network address. Applying the concept to the class B address of 168.15.1.1, the results would be as follows:

Dotted decimal	168.15.1.100
Binary representation	10101000.00001111.00000001.01100100
Mask	11111111.11111111.00000000.00000000
Mask using dotted decimal	168.15.1.100/16

The mask in this instance indicates that 168.15.0.0 is the network address and the host address is 1.100. The last line of the table shows another way of representing the same information. The number following the dotted decimal address indicates the number of bits used for the mask.

Consider, however, the following mask:

Dotted decimal	168.15.1.100
Binary	10101000.00001111.00000001. 01100100
Mask	11111111.11111111.11111111.00000000
Mask using dotted decimal	168.15.1.100/24

This would indicate that the network address portion of the IP address is 168.15.1.0 and the host address portion is .100. The address is still a class B address, but some of the bits reserved for host addresses are used instead to identify additional subnetworks. In this example, the number of subnets defined by the mask is 254 and the type of subnetting is called fixed-length subnet mask (FLSM).

VLSM   A variable-length subnet mask (VLSM) takes the concept of subnet masking one step further. In the examples given, our implementation of the subnet mask was used in such as way that each additional subnet defined by the mask has an equal number of host addresses. For example, using the class B address we used previously (168.15.0.0), the last two octets are used to represent different host addresses. However, using a 24-bit mask means that the third octet should also be used to denote subnets within the class B network—the host addresses are now represented by the fourth octet only. This means that there can be 254 different subnets (the range spanned by the third octet), each having 254 hosts (the range spanned by the fourth octet).

VLSM is the method by which multiple masks are applied to the same address space to carve out different networks of different sizes. It is a means of right sizing each subnet to fit the specific addressing requirement. VLSM ultimately overcomes the "one size fits all" approach to IP addressing, as is the case in classful addressing (and to some degree, in FLSM).

VLSM provides even greater freedom than fixed-length subnet masking. It is a means by which IP addressing resources can be allocated to subnets according to their individual need rather than some general network-wide rule. Take an Ethernet network, for instance—the greater the number of hosts on an Ethernet network, the more performance degrades. All hosts must vie for access to the physical medium. Because there is no order built into when a host is allowed to transmit, the probability of hosts colliding with each other increases as the number of hosts increases.

The number of host addresses in a class C network is 254. In reality, the performance of an Ethernet network begins to degrade long before the number of hosts that can be accommodated on a single Ethernet segment reaches anywhere near that number. As the number of hosts grows beyond a certain point, it begins to make more sense to create multiple networks, each having a manageable number of hosts. The problem here is that multiple class C addresses would be required for each LAN, with only a subset of the available host addresses being used.

VLSM solves this problem by allowing different masks to be assigned to the single address space, the class C address in this instance. As an example, let's say a network called NETA began life as a single local area network with seven devices attached. The assigned address is a class C address that has the capacity for 254 hosts. Over time the network grows to 72 hosts, but over the same period the performance has also eroded to the point where action has to be taken to address the problem. The network administrator decides to split the network into three different networks that logically group work functions, and link the three networks with a router. The way the network administrator decides to assign the groupings is

LAN 1	Accounting	14 users
LAN 2	Programming	28 users
LAN 3	Sales, Marketing, and Administrative Support	30 users

The network administrator is now faced with a decision; he or she has three networks and one class C address. The choices are to acquire two additional class addresses or to use the existing one more efficiently. The administrator decides on the latter course of action and implements VLSM. Three subnets are created—one that uses a mask that defines 14 hosts, and two others that use a single mask that defines up to 30 hosts per subnet, as shown in the following table:

Original dotted decimal class C address	192.165.11.0	
Binary	11000000.10100101.00001011.00000000	
Natural class C mask	11111111.11111111.11111111.00000000	24-bit mask
First mask allows 15 host bits	11111111.11111111.11111111.11110000	28-bit mask
Second mask allows 31 host bits	11111111.11111111.11111111.11100000	27-bit mask

By using two different masks of 28 and 27 bits, or 255.255.255.240 and 255.255.255.224, the network administrator is able to accomplish the objective. He or she now has the ability to use a single class C address to create three different subnetworks that are more aligned to the company's needs. By using this approach, they gain additional network addresses and conserve on the number of wasted host addresses.

Address Resolution Protocol (ARP)

We have examined the IP protocol and its addressing scheme in which every host is given a unique address that is made up of a host portion and a network portion. The IP packet consists of a source and destination IP address. Routers along the path read the packet to determine the destination address, which they use to make a decision on how best to route the packet.

Regardless of where the destination machine resides, the packet must traverse the LAN to get from the source to the target machine—or a router if the target is on another LAN. The data link layer controls the movement of the packet across the LAN, but at this layer only hardware addresses are understood. Once the packet is handed from layer 3 to layer 2—network layer to data link layer—the data link layer sees the IP address information as data that has no significance to the way in which it operates. How then does the data link layer know the corresponding hardware address of the destination machine? Somehow, the IP address of the target must resolve to a physical hardware address.

The challenge of mapping a logical address to a physical address is known as the address resolution problem. There are two ways in which this has been addressed. Hardware addresses can be manually mapped to a target IP address, or it can be dynamically discovered using the Address Resolution Protocol (ARP).

To manually map an IP address to a hardware address in Windows, go to the command line and type

```
arp -s ip-address hardware-address
```

To display the IP-to-physical address translation tables used by Windows, go to a command line and issue the following command:

```
arp -a
```

ARP—Dynamic Discovery   Manually maintaining a translation table of IP and hardware addresses is not practical in most local area networks. This would require maintaining a table on every host that resides on the LAN, a task that is further complicated when a bridge or a router is in the picture. Furthermore, the changing of NIC cards, the addition of other devices, or the changing of IP addresses would only complicate matters further. It is far more practical to be able to discover these addresses dynamically.

Given the target's IP address, ARP allows a host to find the physical address of a target host on the same physical network. The protocol works by broadcasting a special packet to all hosts on the local network, requesting a response from the owner of a specific IP address. On receiving this packet, the owner of the IP address replies with its physical address. The other hosts ignore the broadcast. On receipt of the reply, the host that originally sent the broadcast uses the physical address embedded in the reply to send packets directly to the target host. Figure 3-9 illustrates the process.

To minimize traffic on the network, ARP maintains a cache of all the recently discovered hosts. By maintaining this cache, the dynamic discovery process is limited to the first time a host wishes to communicate with another. Once the physical address is known, the sending host forwards packets to the target by looking up the physical address in its ARP cache. A computer always checks its ARP cache for a binding of IP and hardware addresses before it embarks on the ARP process.

Once an entry is placed in the ARP cache, it remains there for a limited time. The length of time it stays there is called the age timer, which is refreshed if an ARP packet is received from the network with a matching MAC and IP address. On expiration of the timer, the entry is flushed from the ARP cache. Once the entry ages and is flushed, the process of ARPing for the address through the use of a broadcast packet has to be repeated.

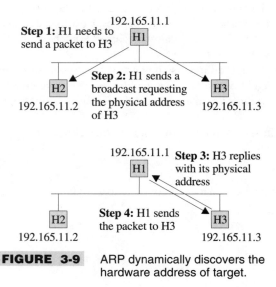

FIGURE 3-9   ARP dynamically discovers the hardware address of target.

Reverse ARP   Reverse ARP (RARP) is just as the name implies—it provides a function that is the reverse of the function provided by ARP. ARP is used to determine the physical address of a known IP address. RARP does the opposite—it is used to find the IP address of a known hardware address.

At first this may seem odd. Why would there ever be a situation where a hardware address is known but the IP address is not? RARP is typically used in diskless workstations. Without a hard disk, the IP address of the machine cannot be stored on the machine. This creates a problem every time the machine reboots. One way of addressing this problem is to code the IP address into the firmware, but this is not practical. Changing the IP address—if it has to move to another network, for instance—would require changing the firmware.

A diskless workstation instead uses RARP to obtain its address from a server. In order to use RARP, a RARP server is required to maintain a mapping of IP and hardware addresses. The process works in the following way:

1. The diskless workstation sends a broadcast—a RARP request—to all hosts on the network.

2. All hosts on the network see the broadcast, but only a machine that is configured to be a RARP server will reply. The server looks up the hardware address to determine that IP address to which it has been mapped. It then replies with the IP address.

3. The workstation receives the reply and stores the IP address in its memory. RARP is not used again until the workstation reboots.

Dynamic Host Configuration (DHCP)

DHCP is also a protocol that is used to dynamically assign an IP address to a workstation. It is the successor to an older protocol called BOOTP that provided the same function. Today, DHCP is very common in many installations of IP networks.

Even the most basic of computers today has some form of storage. In fact, the cost per megabyte of storage is so inexpensive that a typical home computer today has at least several gigabytes of storage. You may be wondering why, then, there is a need for a protocol that assigns IP addresses dynamically when storage is obviously not a problem, as in the case presented with RARP. The answer is convenience.

Today, IP has become pervasive and people have become so mobile that it is inconvenient to use hard-coded addresses. With the growth of laptop computers, a scheme that dynamically assigns an IP address is a lot more appealing than one that requires reconfiguration every time a user has to connect to a new network. Dynamic assignment of IP addresses shields the user from having to know the addressing scheme in use for every network to which they connect. The theme today is "plug and play," and DHCP helps facilitate this theme.

Dynamic assignment of addresses also helps conserve on IP addresses. Hard-coding an address ties up that address even when the machine to which it is assigned is not on the network. With DHCP, the address that is assigned is actually a lease. Once the machine disconnects from the network and the lease expires, the address is released and can be used by another user.

DHCP uses UDP for its transport. It is much more efficient than RARP. With DHCP, a single message can specify multiple items, such as the IP address, the address of the default gateway, or a subnet mask. In fact, a single message can deliver all the configuration information that a computer needs.

DHCP provides complete control over how addresses are assigned. Because the protocol uses the identity of the client to decide how to proceed, the DHCP server can be configured to use different policies of address assignment depending on the identity of the client or the network from which it attaches. DHCP allows three types of address assignments:

- **Dynamic configuration**   Allocates addresses to be leased to a computer for a specific time. The computer uses the assigned address until the lease expires. A common lease time is about three days, after which time the lease expires and a new address is assigned.

- **Manual configuration**   Allows the administrator to configure a specific address for a specific computer.

- **Automatic configuration**   Allocates a permanent address to a computer the first time it connects to the network.

How It Works   A host goes through six states whenever DHCP is used.

- **INITIALIZE**   When the host boots up, it enters the INITIALIZE state. Once the host begins to use DHCP, it becomes a DHCP client by broadcasting a *DHCPDISCOVER* message to determine all the DHCP servers on the network and then transitions to the second state.

- **SELECT**   In this state, the host is receiving *DHCPOFFERs*. DHCP servers that have been configured to respond to the particular client send a *DHCPOFFER*. If there are no servers configured to respond, the client receives no offers; if multiple servers are configured to respond, it receives multiple offers. Each offer contains configuration information. The client must choose one of the offers. Once an offer has been chosen (for example, the first offer received), the client enters into a mode of negotiation—for such things as the length of the lease—with the server from which the offer it accepted was sent. To enter in the negotiation, the client sends a *DHCPREQUEST* and enters into the third state.

- **REQUEST**   In this state, the server acknowledges the request and starts the lease by sending a *DHCPACK*. On receipt of the *DHCPACK*, the client progresses to the fourth state.

- **BOUND**   In this state, the client begins using the assigned address. This is the state during normal operation. The client is allowed to store the address and request it again when it restarts. DHCP allows a client to terminate a lease without waiting for the lease period to expire. To do an early termination of a lease, the client sends a *DHCPRELEASE* message to the server. Once sent, the client can no longer use the address and must return to the first state. There are three timers associated with a lease: renewal, rebinding, and expiration. The default value for the renewal timer is one half the lease time. When this timer expires, the client sends a *DHCPREQUEST* message containing the address currently in use and a request to extend the lease. During the period between when the client sends a request for an extension of the lease and the time when the server responds, the client transitions to the fifth state.

■ **RENEW** During this state the client is waiting on a response from the server on its request for an extension. If the server agrees, it sends a *DHCPACK* and the client returns to the bound state. If not, the server sends a *DHCPNACK*, which causes the client to return immediately to the INITIALIZE state. If, however, the client does not receive a response in a predetermined amount of time—as specified by the rebinding timer, which is about 87.5% of the lease period—the client transitions into the sixth state.

■ **REBIND** The client transitions to this state because it does not receive a response from the DHCP server. In this state, the client assumes the DHCP server is unavailable and begins broadcasting *DHCPREQUESTs* to any DHCP server. Any server that is configured to respond to the client can respond and may approve the extension request, in which case the client returns to the BOUND state, or deny the request, in which case the client goes back to the INITIALIZE state.

If ever the situation arises where the client remains in the REBIND state because there are no available DHCP servers to process the lease extension request, the expiration of the third timer—the lease expiration timer—forces the client back to the INITIALIZE state.

Dynamic Routing Between Networks

We now have an understanding of how a packet from one host gets forwarded to another host on the network. The IP address must first be mapped to a physical hardware address. The data link layer then streams the packets onto the physical medium in the form of frames. The target host receives the frames from the wire, strips off the hardware addresses and data-link-specific control information, then sends the packets to the network layer. The network layer in turn strips the network-layer-specific information and passes it up to the transport layer. The transport layer checks the sequence number of the packet against the number it expects to receive. Depending on the protocol, it may send an acknowledgement. The data is then sent up to upper-layer protocols for them to do their own layer-specific processing.

In the next few paragraphs, we will examine how a packet finds its way through an internetwork and the role dynamic routing protocols play in this process. As previously mentioned, a detailed discussion of routing protocols is outside the scope of this chapter and will be covered in Chapter 14. However, we will explain what they are and what they do in the context of network protocols.

Basic Functions of a Router From the perspective of the sender, the mechanics of sending a packet to a host that is several networks away are the same as if the target host was local to the sender. The only difference in the process is the introduction of a router that is used to receive the packet on one physical network segment and forward it on to another. The sending host must also decide if the target host in on the same network, which is done by comparing the network address of the target host to its own. If the two addresses match, the sender knows the target is local and transmits the packet directly to the target host—a process called direct delivery.

If the two network addresses do not match, the sending host knows that that target is on a different physical network and a router must be used to deliver the packet—a process known as indirect delivery. This also means that the sending host must know the address of a router on the local network to which to send these packets. This router is called the default gateway, which is an address of a router on the local network to which a host sends all packets that it does not have a direct route to. The address of the default gateway may be manually configured on the host. or it may be configured as part of a DHCP request.

A router, by definition, only performs the functions of layers 1–3, and so performs the following basic functions:

1. It receives the frame from a physical network segment.
2. It strips off the data-link-specific information and reads the network layer address of the target machine.
3. It uses the network layer address to decide which output interface it should use to forward the packet on to the target machine.
4. It maps the network address of the next hop, which may be the target host or another router, to a hardware address using either its ARP cache or the ARP process.
5. It assembles the frame for transmission on to the physical medium. The destination hardware address is the next hop address, which may be the actual target machine or another router.
6. It sends the frame out the correct output interface.

Notice that nowhere in the foregoing explanation did we mention any specific protocol. The basic function of a router is the same no matter which protocol suite is in use. As we explore other network protocols, we will make several references to routers. It should be noted that the process for moving a packet through the network and the basic operation of a router are always the same regardless of the specific protocol that is being discussed.

Beyond the Local Network   Routers are used to link different networks. If the target host is beyond the boundary of the local network, a router is required to route between the networks. To do this, routers require knowledge of the local networks to which they are attached and the networks that are further downstream. Knowledge of locally attached networks is easily obtained because the routers are directly connected to them. However, things are not so easy when the target host is on another network, possibly several networks away.

Routers need to be told about the networks that are not directly attached but are reachable through another router. This can be accomplished by configuring static routes or through a dynamic routing protocol. These protocols are used to make real-time decisions about the best way to get a packet from one network to another. They understand the topology of the internetwork and track the regions within the internetwork that are having problems.

Routing protocols see the internetwork as a single entity and are able to make decisions on the best path based on their knowledge of the entire internetwork and what is happening at any given moment in time. The algorithms used by routing protocols to determine the best path between two hosts typically fall into two major categories: distance vector or link state protocols.

Distance vector protocols, such as RIP, base their decision about a best path between two hosts on the distance between them. The distance is measured in the number of hops—routers—between the source and the target. It does not factor in such things as the size of the links to get from source to destination.

Link state protocols, such as OSPF and IS-IS, bases their decision about a best path on several factors, including the size and state of the links the packet must travel on its way between the two hosts. Given two paths, one with three hops each having DS3 links between them, and the other with two hops each having 56KB links, a link state protocol would prefer the three hops, whereas a distance vector protocol would prefer the one with two hops. The logic behind link state protocols is that the faster path is always the best path.

Regardless of the type of routing protocol, they all have the ability to learn different routes through the internetwork. Some routing protocols, such as OSPF, also keep a table of all the routes, but will only select the best route for placement into the router's forwarding table. The forwarding table is the table that the router uses to make its decision on which output interface it should use to forward a packet. The entries in the forwarding table may be taken from a routing table or from the manual assignment of a route through the use of static routes.

THE IPX/SPX PROTOCOL

IPX, short for Internetwork Packet Exchange, is a Novell Netware layer 3 network protocol used to route packets across a network. Developed by Novell in the early 1980s, the protocol is based the XNS protocol developed by Xerox. The IPX protocol had the largest install base of LAN protocols in the late 1980s and early 1990s.

The SPX protocol, which is an abbreviation for Sequenced Packet Exchange, is a connection-oriented protocol that operates at the transport layer of the OSI stack. SPX is the protocol that ensures the reliable delivery of the packet through the network. Like TCP, it is responsible for the retransmission of lost packets and relies on the IPX protocol for the forwarding of packets.

Like IP, IPX operates at layer 3 of the OSI model and requires the use of an addressing scheme that differentiates between nodes from networks. The protocol also requires that every node in the network be given a unique address.

An IPX address is annotated in hexadecimal format and also consists of two parts: a network number and a node number. The network portion of the address is 32 bits long and the node portion, akin to the host portion of an IP address, is 48 bits long. The network administrator defines the network address, but the node address is the MAC address of the network interface card. An example of an IPX network and node address follows:

CA1A20B0.0000.0a5d.ace0

The use of the MAC address as the node address negates the need for an address resolution protocol to bind layer 2 addresses to layer 3 addresses. Using the MAC address allows the sending machine to immediately forward the packet on to the target machine, just by using the node address in the MAC destination field.

IPX networks also uses the concept of an *internal network address*, a term used to describe a logical or virtual network within each server (versions 3.x and 4.x). The internal network is different from the real network, which relates to the actual physical network or cabling system. The internal network number is used to advertise the services of a server.

IPX Encapsulation

Encapsulation describes the way in which upper-layer protocols are packaged into frames by the data link layer for transmission across the wire. In an IPX network, it is possible to define multiple encapsulation types on the same physical network. Encapsulation is an important concept in IPX networks because each encapsulation type is treated as a separate network on the same physical wire segment.

This is an area where a lot of mistakes are made. If multiple encapsulation types are being used on the same physical segment, each encapsulation type must be given its own network address. The problem this creates is that routing between networks requires a router. So, the only way for a client using one type of encapsulation to communicate with a server on the same segment using a different encapsulation is to use a router. The router must have both encapsulation types defined on its interface.

Novell uses four different encapsulation methods for Ethernet:

- **Novell Proprietary**   Also called 802.3 raw or Novell Ethernet_802.3. IPX packets are directly placed within 802.3 frames and do not use 802.2 LLC or SNAP. In Cisco routers this encapsulation type is known as NOVELL-ETHER.

- **Ethernet version II**   Also called Ethernet II, it consists of the standard Ethernet version II header followed by a type field. The type code is 8137. The frame structure is identical to the Novell proprietary except that a type field is used instead of a length field. In Cisco routers, this encapsulation type is known as ARPA.

- **802.3**   Also called Novell_802.2. This is the standard IEEE 802.3 frame format and is the preferred encapsulation for Netware 3.12 and Netware 4.x servers. In Cisco routers, this encapsulation type is known as SAP.

- **SNAP**   Also called Ethernet _SNAP, it extends the 802.2 header by adding a type field. This is generally not used. In Cisco routers, this encapsulation type is known as SNAP.

Service Advertisements

In an IPX network, servers advertise the services they provide. This is the reason why the protocol is sometimes referred to as chatty. The advertisement of services is done though the use of the Service Advertisement Protocol (SAP), an IPX protocol through which network resources such as file servers and print servers advertise their addresses and the services they provide.

The SAP sends its advertisement every 60 seconds and each service advertised is identified through the use of a SAP identifier—a hexadecimal number identifying the service type. Routers in the network build a list of services and their network addresses, which are the internal network addresses or virtual network addresses we discussed previously. The routers then send their SAP table every 60 seconds. It is important to note that IPX servers naturally perform a routing function and so, act as routers.

Clients wishing a particular service make a request for the service and routers respond to the request by supplying the network address of the service. From then on, the client directs its request directly to the address advertising the service. Table 3-3 provides a list of common SAP values.

TABLE 3-3   COMMON SAPS

DECIMAL	HEX	SAP DESCRIPTION
3	0003	Print queue or print group
4	0004	File server (SLIST source)
6	0006	Gateway
7	0007	Print server or silent print server
32	0020	NetBIOS
36	0024	Remote bridge or routing service
39	0027	TCP/IP gateway server
45	002d	Time synchronization server or asynchronous timer
71	0047	Advertising print server
274	0112	Print server (HP)
619	026b	Time synchronization server (Netware 4.x)
632	0278	Directory server (Netware 4.x)
807	0327	Microsoft diagnostics

IPX Routing

The routing of IPX packets on the local LAN is fairly straightforward, because there is no need to go through a process designed to resolve a node address to a MAC. The node address is the MAC address, and so the data link services can proceed with the appropriate encapsulation that is configured and plug the node address into the MAC destination field of the MAC address.

In an internetwork, the IPX also requires a routing protocol. Like IP, it also has a distance vector and a link state routing protocol. The distance vector protocol is RIP, but the logic for calculating the distance is different from the RIP used for IP. The metric used in IPX RIP is ticks, then hops. Ticks are about 1/18 of a second and are a measure of delay. A serial link is six ticks, and Ethernet link is one tick. The path with the lowest number of ticks is used. In the event of a tie, hop count is used as the tiebreaker. IPX RIP advertises the entire routing table every 60 seconds.

The IPX link state protocol is called Novell Link-Services Protocol (NLSP) and was designed to overcome the limitations of IPX RIP and SAP. It is based on the OSI Intermediate System-to-Intermediate System (IS-IS) protocol and was designed to replace RIP and SAP, especially in large internetworks where they are extremely inefficient.

THE APPLETALK PROTOCOL

AppleTalk is a suite of protocols that were developed by Apple computer in the early 1980s. There are two versions of AppleTalk: AppleTalk Phase I and AppleTalk Phase II. The Phase I version was developed for smaller work groups and does not have the capabilities needed for supporting an extended network. The number of hosts in a Phase I network is limited to 135. AppleTalk Phase II increases the number of hosts to 253 on a single segment and supports an extended network.

Like the Internet Protocol suite, the AppleTalk Protocol suite is a suite of protocols that spans most of the seven layers of the OSI model, as shown in Figure 3-10. By applying your knowledge of each layer of the OSI, you can gain an appreciation of the types of functions that would be performed by each of the AppleTalk protocols.

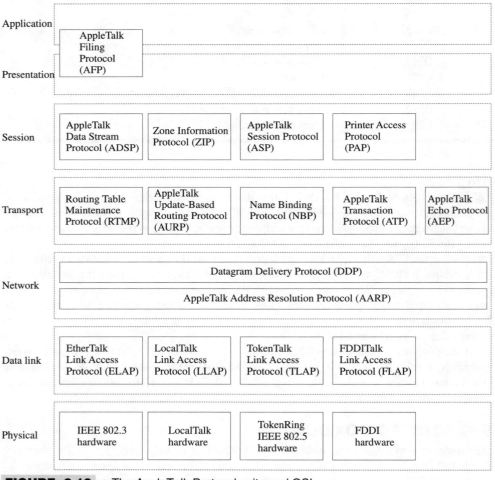

FIGURE 3-10 The AppleTalk Protocol suite and OSI

Sockets, Zones, Nodes, and Networks

An AppleTalk network utilizes a hierarchical structure that consists of sockets, nodes, networks, and zones.

AppleTalk Sockets A socket in effect provides a function similar to a port in TCP parlance. It is a logical connection point between the AppleTalk layer 3 protocol and the upper-layer functions of AppleTalk. The upper-layer functions are called socket clients. A socket client may own one or more sockets, which are used to transfer datagrams. For the most part, sockets are assigned dynamically by a protocol called Datagram Delivery Process (DDP). DDP is a layer 3 network process that operates in much the same way as a routing protocol such as RIP or OSPF. The socket number is an 8-bit number.

AppleTalk Zones AppleTalk zones are logical groupings of nodes or networks. The network administrator configures zones within an AppleTalk network. Networks and nodes do not need to be contiguous to belong to the same zone, as shown in Figure 3-11.

AppleTalk Nodes An AppleTalk node is a device that connects to an AppleTalk network. Within these nodes exist sockets that identify the different software processes that are running. Like IP and IPX, a node belongs to a single network and a single zone. The node address is an 8-bit number.

AppleTalk Networks An AppleTalk network is a local network segment that is running the AppleTalk protocol. An AppleTalk network address is 16 bits long. Unlike an IP network, AppleTalk uses the concept of a nonextended network and an extended network.

A nonextended network is a physical network segment that is assigned a single network number that falls within a range between 1 and 1024. Nodes within a nonextended network must have unique addresses. Also, a nonextended network cannot have more than one zone configured on it.

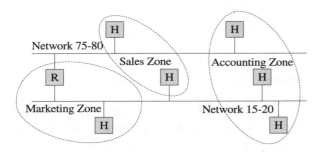

FIGURE 3-11 An AppleTalk network with zones, nodes, and cable ranges

An extended network is one where a physical network segment can be configured with multiple consecutive network numbers. This is a similar concept to that of IPX where a single segment may have different encapsulation types, each having their own network numbers. In the case of AppleTalk, a physical segment that is configured with more than one network number is said to have a cable range configured. Nodes in an extended network must also have unique addresses. The combination of a node address and the network address makes for a unique pairing that identifies a specific node within a specific network.

Multiple zones can be configured on an extended network and a node on any one of the networks configured to the segment may belong to any one zone. Figure 3-11 illustrates the concept of having cable ranges, multiple zones, and node addresses.

Address Assignment   In most installations of AppleTalk, addresses are assigned dynamically when they first attach to the network. An AppleTalk address consists of a 16-bit network address, an 8-bit node address, and an 8-bit socket number.

When an AppleTalk node first starts up, it is given a temporary network address taken from a reserved range of addresses between 65280 and 65534. The node address is randomly chosen. The node then communicates with a router on the network, requesting a valid cable range for the segment on which the node is connecting. The router responds with the valid range, and the node chooses a number from the range. The node then broadcasts a message on the network to see if the randomly chosen node address is taken. If no one responds, the node address is used. If someone responds claiming the address, the process is repeated until a valid node number is found.

Once the network and node address is assigned, normal operation may begin. Like IP, AppleTalk uses a separate protocol to correlate the physical hardware address with a network, node, and socket address. The protocol used for this is the AppleTalk Address Resolution Protocol (AARP). Once the address is found, it is stored in an address mapping table (AMT), which provides a similar function to the ARP cache in the IP protocol suite. Each entry in the AMT is given a timer, which is refreshed if a new packet arrives with a matching binding. The entry is deleted when the timer expires.

Further Study

How to Troubleshoot TCP/IP Connectivity with Windows 2000 or Windows NT:
http://support.microsoft.com/default.aspx?scid=kb;EN-US;q102908
Troubleshooting Novell IPX: **http://www.cisco.com/univercd/cc/td/doc/cisintwk/itg_v1/tr1908.htm**
A User's Guide to TCP Windows: **http://www.ncsa.uiuc.edu/People/vwelch/net_perf/tcp_windows.html**
Campus IPX Internetworking FAQ: **http://www.net.berkeley.edu/dcns/faq/ipxfaq.html**
Cisco - LAN Technologies Technical Tips: **http://www.cisco.com/warp/public/473/**
Cisco – TCP/IP: **http://www.cisco.com/warp/public/535/4.html**
Comparison of Windows NT Network Protocols:
http://support.microsoft.com/default.aspx?scid=kb;EN-US;q128233
DHCP Primer: **http://hotwired.lycos.com/webmonkey/00/39/index3a.html?tw=backend**
Introduction to Internet: **http://www.historyoftheinternet.com/chap4.html**
Introduction to the Internet Protocols:
http://www.cisco.com/univercd/cc/td/doc/cisintwk/ito_doc/introint.htm
Network Calculators: **http://www.telusplanet.net/public/sparkman/netcalc.htm**

SubnetOnline.com Network Resources: **http://www.subnetonline.com/**
TCP/IP and IPX Routing Tutorial: **http://www.sangoma.com/fguide.htm**
USB Networking Drivers: **http://www.mcci.com/mcci-v3/l4_usb_networking_drivers.html**
Using PPP, SLIP, Dial-Up Networking with the World: **http://world.std.com/about/ppp-setup.shtml**

4

NETWORK OPERATING SYSTEMS

CHAPTER AT A GLANCE

As you learned in the first chapter, networks rely on cabling and communication devices to interconnect the hardware of individual PCs and other network devices. Still, hardware alone is not enough to make a network operate. Servers and workstations need an operating system to organize the safe sharing of files and equipment, and all of the information shared across a network must use a protocol (or language) that has been accepted as a standard. This chapter explains the role of a network operating system and studies the major attributes of today's popular NOS types.

Network Operating Systems

Networks are much more than just a series of PCs cobbled together with cabling and communications devices. The whole purpose of networks is to share resources (such as applications, files, messages, printers, scanners, and so on) among those PCs. Sharing requires an operating system (software) that is able to manage the many files and devices that are made available to the network, yet keep those resources secure from intrusion and unauthorized use. This is the role of a *network operating system* (NOS). This part of the chapter introduces the concepts of an NOS and outlines some features that make them different from stand-alone operating systems.

NETWORK SUPPORT

The first thing to understand about an NOS is the way network support is added. Some NOS versions simply add networking features "on top" of the PC's existing operating system, while other NOS versions fully integrate network support into the PC's operating system so a stand-alone OS isn't needed. Novell's NetWare 4.x and 5.x are probably the most familiar and popular examples of an NOS where the client computer's networking support is added on top of its existing computer operating system. This means the desktop computer needs *both* operating systems in order to handle stand-alone and networking functions together. By contrast, most operating systems include networking support natively, such as Windows 2000 Server, Windows 2000 Professional, Windows NT Server, Windows NT Workstation, Windows 98, Windows 95, and MacOS. While these integrated operating systems have some advantages, they do not preclude using other NOS versions. Keep in mind that either approach has its own unique benefits and limitations, and you'll see more about these trade-offs later in the chapter.

MULTITASKING SUPPORT

Networks are busy places, and users often must wait for access (although the wait may only be a few milliseconds) while the server tackles one task at a time. If the server could actually work on more than one task simultaneously, network performance could be substantially improved. A *multitasking* operating system provides the means for a server to process more than one task at a time, and a true multitasking operating system can run as many tasks as there are processors. For example, if a server has four processors, a true multitasking OS can run four tasks simultaneously. More commonly, there are more tasks than processors and the computer must arrange for the available processors to devote a certain amount of time to each task—alternating between tasks until all tasks are completed. With this approach, the computer appears to be working on several tasks at once. There are two primary forms of multitasking:

- **Preemptive**   The operating system can take control of the processor without the task's cooperation. This is often a more versatile approach in a network because the preemptive system can shift CPU activity from a local task to a network task if the situation requires it.

- **Nonpreemptive**   The task itself decides when to give up control of the processor. Programs written for nonpreemptive multitasking systems must include provisions for yielding control of the processor. No other program can run until the nonpreemptive program has given up control of the processor. This is also called *cooperative multitasking*.

Preemptive multitasking is the most common and widely used form of multitasking because of its versatility.

INTEROPERABILITY BASICS

Another NOS issue to consider is *interoperability*—the ability of computer operating systems to function and access resources in different network environments. This is particularly important when setting up a multivendor network environment. For example, a NetWare server can interoperate with other servers such as Windows NT, and users of Apple computers can interoperate with both NetWare and Windows NT servers. Each NOS addresses interoperability in different ways, so you should understand your own network's interoperability requirements when evaluating each operating system. A peer-to-peer network offers relatively poor security (because security is managed on each PC, and the logistics of that management can be daunting) and interoperability because of the limitations inherent in that approach. Security and interoperability are much better on a server-based network.

Server Side or Client Side

You'll also need to determine whether interoperability will be provided as a service on the server-side or as a client-side application on each networked computer. Server-side interoperability is easier to manage because it is centrally located (like other services). By comparison, client-side interoperability requires software installation and configuration at each computer. This can make interoperability much more difficult to manage. In actual practice, it is common to find both methods (a network service on the server and network client applications at each computer) in a single network. For example, Microsoft Windows network interoperability is achieved with a network client application at each personal computer.

You will rarely find only client- or server-side interoperability. Most networks provide interoperability features on *both* the server and client side.

CLIENT AND SERVER SOFTWARE

Normally, a computer's operating system organizes and controls the interaction between the computer hardware and the software (i.e., the applications) that are running. An operating system manages the allocation and use of memory (RAM), processor time, disk access (reading and writing), and peripheral devices (such as video, keyboard, mouse, I/O ports, and so on). In a client/server network environment, this goes a step further, and you'll find that the operating systems used in client and server computers are a bit different. Server network software provides resources to the network clients, and client network software makes those resources available to the client computer. The server and client operating systems are coordinated so that all portions of the network function properly. Network client/server software also offers security by controlling access to data and peripherals.

Client Software

In an individual PC, a user types a command that requires the computer to perform a task. The computer's CPU processes this request. For example, if you want to see a directory listing on one of the local hard disks, the CPU interprets and executes the request and then displays the results in a directory listing in the window. This is a bit different in a network when a user requests a resource that exists on a server in another part of the network. The request has to be forwarded (or redirected) out of the client and onto the network, and from there to the server with the requested resource. This forwarding activity is performed by the *redirector*. A redirector is sometimes referred to as the shell or the requester, depending on the particular networking software. The redirector is a small section of code in the NOS that intercepts requests in the computer and determines if the requests should be handled by the local computer, or be redirected over the network to another computer or server.

Redirection starts in the client computer when a user issues a request for a network resource or service. The user's computer is referred to as a *client* because it is making a request of a server. The request is intercepted by the redirector and forwarded out onto the network. The server processes the connection requested by the client's redirectors and gives them access to the resources they request. The server fulfills the request made by the client. Using redirection, clients don't need to be concerned with the actual location of data or peripherals, or with the complexities of making a connection. To access data on a network computer, a user only needs to type the drive designator assigned to the location of the resource, and the redirector determines the actual routing.

This offers some powerful advantages. Suppose that you need to access a shared directory, and you have permission to access it. With Windows NT, you could use Windows Explorer to connect to the network drive using the Network Neighborhood icon. You can also map to the drive (*drive mapping* is the assignment of a letter or name to a disk drive so that the operating system or network server can locate it). To map to the drive, right-click the directory icon from the Network Neighborhood icon. A dialog box will allow you to assign an available letter of the alphabet as a drive designator (such as G:). Thereafter, you can refer to the shared directory on the remote computer as G: and the redirector will locate it. The redirector also keeps track of which drive designators are associated with which network resources.

Redirectors can send requests to peripherals as well as to shared directories. The request is redirected away from the originating computer and sent over the network to the target. For example, the target may be a print server for the requested printer. With redirection, LPT1 or COM1 can refer to network printers instead of local printers. The redirector will intercept any print job going to LPT1 and forward it out of the client machine to the specified network printer.

Server Software

With networking software for the server, users at client computers can share the server's data and peripherals (including printers, plotters, directories, and so on). Consider a user requesting a directory listing on a shared remote hard disk. The request is forwarded by the redirector onto the network, where it is passed to the file and print server containing the shared directory. The request is granted and the directory listing is provided back to the client.

In simplest terms, server network software allows sharing and security. *Sharing* is a term used to describe resources made publicly available for access by users on the network. Most network operating systems not only allow sharing, but also determine the degree of sharing. Server software can provide different resources to users with different levels of access (that is, users with higher access can use more of the server's resources). Server-side software also coordinates access to resources so that two users do not use the same resource at the same time. As an example, suppose an office manager wants everyone on the network to be familiar with a certain document. The document can be placed on the server to be shared, but access can be controlled so that all users can read it, but only users with a certain level of access will be able to edit it.

Network operating systems also provide security by allowing a network administrator to determine which users (or groups) can access network resources. A network administrator can use the server's network software to create user privileges that define who gets to use the network. The administrator can grant or deny user privileges on the network, and remove users from the list of authorized users. By organizing individuals into groups, the administrator can assign privileges to the group (rather than individually). All group members have the same privileges that have been assigned to the group as a whole. When a new user joins the network, the administrator can simply assign the new user to the appropriate group—with its accompanying rights and privileges.

Finally, some advanced server-side network software includes management tools to help administrators keep track of network behavior. If a problem develops on the network, management tools can detect signs of trouble and present the corresponding data in a chart or other suitable format. With these management tools, the network administrator can take corrective action before the problem halts the network.

NOS INTEROPERABILITY ISSUES

Networks are rarely turnkey systems. Networks typically represent a variety of hardware platforms, a combination of physical topologies, and a collection of server and client software. In most cases, the network's hardware and software have been patched, upgraded, and replaced over a period of years. In order for a network to function properly, it is necessary to find a common language in which all computers can communicate. The server's operating system, the client's operating system, and the redirector must all be compatible. Consequently, it is important for a technician to understand the concepts of interoperability between platforms. For example, interoperability is a major concern when a Windows NT server is supporting a Windows 95 client, a UNIX client, and an AppleTalk client. The differences in hardware, software, and protocols pose potential network problems.

Client/Server Interoperability

There are two approaches that you can take toward interoperability: server-side (or back-end) and client-side (or front-end). The approach that you take will depend on the network products that you're using:

- **Client-side**   In networks that use multiple operating systems, the key to establishing interoperability is the redirector. Just as you can use more than one service provider when connecting to the Internet, your computer can have more than one redirector to communicate over a network with different network servers. Each given redirector handles *only* the packets sent in a language or protocol that it can understand. If you know what your destination is (and which resource you want to access), you can invoke the corresponding redirector, and that redirector will forward your request to the appropriate destination. For example, consider a Windows NT client that needs to access a Novell server. To accomplish this, the network administrator loads the client with a Microsoft redirector (for accessing Novell servers) on top of Windows NT.

- **Server-side**   An alternative method of establishing communication between a client and a server is to install communication services on the server. This is usually the approach used to bring an Apple Macintosh into a Windows NT environment. For example, Microsoft supplies Services for Macintosh software that allows a Windows NT Server–based server to communicate with the Apple client. Once the Windows NT Server has Services for Macintosh installed, Apple users can access resources on the Windows NT Server. The service also converts files between Apple and Windows NT–based computers, so Apple and Windows NT users can utilize their own interfaces to share the same files. With this type of interoperability, an Apple user can follow their own standard procedures and view Macintosh icons (such as the Chooser and Finder) even though that user is accessing resources on a Windows NT server.

Microsoft Interoperability

The Microsoft redirector recognizes Microsoft networks using Windows 2000/NT/95/98. Redirectors are automatically implemented during the operating system installation. A setup utility loads the required drivers, then edits the startup files so the redirector will run when the computer starts. Microsoft redirector software not only makes it possible for clients to access resources, but also provides each Windows NT client with the ability to share its own resources.

Microsoft and Novell products are interoperable, so to connect a Windows NT Workstation client to a Novell NetWare 3.x or 4.x network, use either NWLink and Client Service for NetWare (CSNW) or Novell's NetWare Client for Windows NT. To connect a Windows NT Server system to a NetWare network, use NWLink and Gateway Service for NetWare (GSNW). To connect a Windows 95/98 client to a NetWare network, use IPX/SPX and Microsoft CSNW networks. Microsoft Service for NetWare Directory Services (NDS) is client software for NetWare that incorporates support for Novell Network 4.x and 5.x Directory Services. Microsoft NDS provides users with logon and browsing support for NetWare 3.x and 4.x services.

Novell Interoperability
NetWare character-based clients running MS-DOS can connect to Novell NetWare servers and Windows NT Server–based computers. Windows NT clients running Novell's NetWare requester and the Windows NT redirector can connect to Novell NetWare servers and Windows NT Workstation or Server–based computers. Novell provides requesters (aka Novell redirectors) for client operating systems, including DOS, OS/2, and NetWare Client for Windows NT.

Apple Interoperability
The redirector for AppleShare networking is included with the AppleTalk operating system and provides a file-sharing function. The client software is included with every copy of the Apple operating system. There is also an AppleShare print server (which is a server-based print spooler). AppleShare networking software offers DOS-based clients access to AppleShare file and print servers. With LocalTalk software and a LocalTalk card installed on their personal computers, users can access file server volumes (storage) and printers on an AppleTalk network. The LocalTalk card contains firmware to control the link between the AppleTalk network and the computer. The LocalTalk driver software implements many of the AppleTalk protocols and interacts with the card to send and receive packets.

Using Services for Macintosh, a Windows NT server can be made available to Apple clients. This product makes it possible for DOS and Apple clients to share files and printers. Services for Macintosh includes AppleTalk Protocol versions 2.0 and 2.1, LocalTalk, EtherTalk, TokenTalk, and FDDITalk. In addition, Services for Macintosh supports version 5.2 or later of the LaserWriter printer.

Windows XP

Microsoft has traditionally provided different product families for business and home users. A prime example of this has been Windows Me for home users, and Windows 2000 for network/business applications. Over the last few years, however, Microsoft has been working to merge their personal and business operating systems into a single product family. Initially released in the latter part of 2001, Windows XP is the next version of Microsoft Windows, which brings convergence to Windows 2000 and Windows Millennium. Windows 2000 brings standards-based network security, manageability, and reliability, while Windows 98/Me provides an easy-to-use user interface, excellent hardware compatibility, and innovative support services. Windows XP will be available in two basic versions: XP Home Edition for end users, and XP Professional for business users. This part of the chapter examines the upcoming features common to both versions.

USER INTERFACE
Most Windows users are familiar with navigating the many dialog boxes present in Windows 2000 and 98/Me. The user interface for Windows XP has been redesigned (see Figure 4-1). Common tasks have

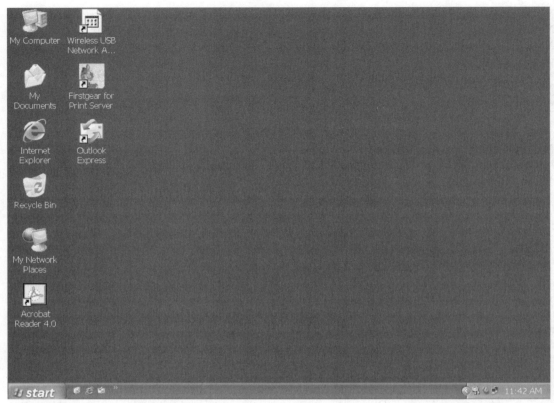

FIGURE 4-1   A typical Windows XP Professional desktop view

been consolidated and simplified, and new visual cues have been added to help you navigate the computer more easily. Windows XP has new visual styles and themes that use sharp 24-bit color icons and unique colors that can be easily related to specific tasks. For example, green represents tasks that enable you to do something or go somewhere (such as the Start menu).

Switching Users
Under current versions of Windows, one user must save their work and log off the computer before a new user can log on. Windows XP employs a fast user switching technique based on terminal services to allow simultaneous user sessions. Users don't need to log off and log on, and each user's data to be entirely separated. For example, one user can log in and balance a checkbook. If they walk away, another user can log in and play a game. The first user's session still runs in the background. In order to run reliable multiuser sessions on a home PC, at least 128MB of RAM is recommended. Fast User Switching is also available on Windows XP Professional if you install it on a stand-alone or workgroup-connected computer. If you join a domain with a computer running Windows XP Professional, you will not be able to use Fast User Switching.

Managing Files
Windows XP uses Webview technology to help you manage files. For example, if you select a file or folder, you see a list of options allowing you to rename, move, copy, e-mail, remove, or publish it to the Web. This is

similar to what you see in Windows 2000 if you right-click on a file or folder, but Windows XP takes this information and brings it into view directly on the desktop. Windows XP also provides a more manageable taskbar, grouping multiple instances of the same application. For example, instead of having nine instances of a Microsoft Word file each arranged horizontally on the taskbar, Windows XP groups them together on one taskbar button. This means you see only one taskbar button that shows the number of files that are open for the application. Clicking the button shows the vertical list of all filenames.

DIGITAL MEDIA

With the explosive growth in digital media for both home and business, Windows XP includes enhanced versions of Windows Media Player and Windows Movie Maker, and improved photo support options.

Media Player 8

Windows Media Player 8 brings together popular digital media activities, including CD and DVD playback, jukebox management and recording, audio CD creation, Internet radio playback, and media transfer to portable devices (such as MP3 players). Windows Media Audio 8 provides nearly three times the music storage of MP3 with faster audio CD burning and intelligent media tracking for more control over digital media. The new My Music folder in Windows XP makes common music tasks easier to perform. In addition, Windows Media Player 8 includes features such as

■ Ability to lock down Windows Media Player features in a managed network
■ Digital broadcast support
■ Accelerated video rendering
■ Video mixing rendering
■ Expanded support for more audio cards and their features

Movie Maker

Windows Movie Maker 1.1 provides basic features for media capture and file creation, simple editing of video and audio, and saving/publishing Windows media files. You can record, edit, organize, and share the home video library from a PC. You could also share the home video with family and friends via e-mail or over the Web. If you want to make a video slide show, you can combine still images and publish into a Windows Media format. Although the utility produces output only in the Windows Media format, it will import all file formats and compression types supported by the DirectShow architecture. If your computer does not include video capture hardware, all other features are available and they allow for the importing and editing of media files that exist on your computer.

Digital Photos

Windows XP expands support for digital devices and provides many options to manipulate images such as publishing pictures to the Web, e-mailing photos (with an option of compressing them for you for smaller file size), displaying pictures in an automatic slideshow, and allowing you to zoom in on images.

HARDWARE COMPATIBILITY

Device and hardware support has been improved for Windows XP. Like Windows 2000, Windows XP simplifies the process of installing, configuring, and managing computer hardware. Windows XP includes Plug-and-Play (PnP) support for hundreds of devices not covered by Windows 2000, and enhanced support for Universal Serial Bus (USB), IEEE 1394, Peripheral Component Interface (PCI), and other bus architectures. Windows XP also supports 200dpi monitors and the new Intel 64-bit Itanium processor.

DVD and CD Support

Advances in storage technology have made it easier and more affordable to work with CDs and DVDs. Windows XP introduces native support for reading and writing to DVD-RAM drives, and can read the Universal Disk Format (UDF) 2.01, the common standard for DVD media, including DVD-ROM discs and DVD videos. By comparison, Windows 2000 can only read UDF 1.02- and 1.5-compatible disks.

Windows XP also allows you to master CDs in the CD-R or CD-RW formats using simple drag-and-drop features and a wizard-based process. When you save or copy a file to CD, the operating system first premasters the complete image on your hard drive, and then streams the data to your CD burner for recording. Premastering effectively minimizes the buffer underruns that generate errors in the recording process and render media useless (an all-too-frequent occurrence when recording "on the fly").

SOFTWARE COMPATIBILITY AND SERVICES

Windows XP will be compatible with almost all of the top 1,000 applications that ran under Windows 9*x*, and almost every application that ran under Windows 2000. The only exceptions are antivirus programs, system utilities, and backup applications—though most manufacturers will have XP updates and patches by the time you install or upgrade to Windows XP. Application improvements in Windows XP help resolve application compatibility problems (such as those that occur when applications incorrectly detect the operating system version or when they reference memory after it has been freed). Fixes are invoked automatically by the operating system to make otherwise incompatible applications function—no user intervention is required. As new applications appear (or new fixes become available), application updates can be downloaded automatically from the Windows Update Web site using the Automatic Updates feature (similar to the feature introduced with Windows Me). There are also numerous file and print service features in Windows XP.

WebDAV

Web Digital Authoring & Versioning (WebDAV) technology in Windows XP enables you to publish documents on Internet servers and update them later. WebDAV is a standard Internet file access protocol that travels via HTTP over the existing Internet infrastructure (firewalls, routers, and so on.). Windows XP includes a WebDAV redirector, which means you can access servers on the Internet just as you would a file share or server share at home or at work. While traditional file-sharing protocols cannot provide you with access to your data in every location, WebDAV uses Internet protocols that allow access to data repositories anywhere on the Internet. WebDAV lets you get to your data from wherever you are while using standard software applications (similar to Novell's iFolder technology for NetWare 6). In general, you can use the WebDAV redirector to publish your own Web data, or to use Internet repositories for storing data and sharing information.

Client-Side Encryption

Windows XP allows you to encrypt the offline files database (also known as the Client-Side Cache, or CSC). Encrypting the offline files database safeguards all locally cached documents from theft, while also providing additional security to your locally cached data. This is an improvement over Windows 2000, where the cached files could not be encrypted. For example, you can use offline files while keeping your sensitive data secure, and network administrators can use this feature to safeguard all local files. CSC is an excellent safeguard if your notebook computer gets stolen with confidential data saved in the offline files cache. Administrative privileges are required to configure how the offline files will be encrypted.

FAT32 for DVD-RAM

You can use a DVD-RAM disk with a FAT32 format and Windows XP will recognize, mount, and format your FAT32 volumes on DVD-RAM disks in superfloppy format (that is, the disk volume has no partition table). You can use a DVD-RAM disk with FAT32 formatting with any common removable media drive (such as magneto-optical and Jaz).

NetCrawler

NetCrawler can find, automatically install, and connect to all of the shared printers that it finds on a home or business network. The NetCrawler enables users who are unfamiliar with networking to have easy, automatically configured access to the computers and devices in a workgroup. It does this by searching the entire network folder and providing links to network resources. For example, if you configure a new computer and you want to print some documents, NetCrawler finds the available printers and displays them for you. Network shares that have not been seen by NetCrawler in 48 hours will be "aged out" of My Network Places by deleting shortcuts to those resources. NetCrawler is on by default when you install Windows XP Home, and on Windows XP Professional when the computer is in workgroup mode (not logged on to a domain). NetCrawler also checks for new resources whenever you log on to a network, and whenever you open or refresh your Printers and My Network Places folders.

Sharing Faxes

Fax sharing lets you send and receive faxes using your fax hardware (such as a fax-capable modem or fax board), or over a computer network offering fax-sharing services. You can send a fax using the Microsoft Outlook messaging and collaboration client (or from any other application that supports printing). The Windows XP fax-sharing feature set provides integration with the contact list in Outlook, the ability to preview a fax before it is sent, and the option to receive an e-mail confirming the fax was received. Administrators can fully control fax capabilities using the Microsoft Management Console (MMC) and the COM API. Fax sharing in Windows XP is fully interoperable with the Back Office Server (BOS)/Small Business Server (SBS) 2000 shared fax service.

NETWORKING AND COMMUNICATIONS

Windows XP simplifies the setup and administration of networks, and provides networks with additional features that expand the capabilities of typical network architectures.

Device Plug-and-Play

Ordinary Plug-and-Play capabilities allow administrators to set up, configure, and add peripherals to a PC. Universal Plug-and-Play extends this simplicity to include the entire network—enabling the discovery and control of devices (including networked devices and services) such as network-attached printers, Internet gateways, and consumer electronics equipment. Universal Plug-and-Play is designed to support zero-configuration, invisible networking, and automatic discovery for a range of device categories from a wide range of vendors. With Universal Plug-and-Play, a device can dynamically join a network, obtain an IP address, convey its capabilities, and learn about the presence and capabilities of other devices—all automatically. Universal Plug-and-Play uses standard TCP/IP and Internet protocols.

Network Connections

First introduced in Windows 98, Internet Connection Sharing (ICS) provides a convenient and economical method for more than one computer to be connected in a home using a single dial-up connection as a gateway (whether for Internet access or to a corporate network). Instead of requiring each device behind the gateway to have a globally unique IP address, it is possible to allocate private addresses to such devices.

In addition, the Home Networking Wizard automates network configuration and Internet Connection Sharing. It uses bridging to allow setup of a LAN without requiring you to know about networking protocols and physical networking requirements. In the past, a typical multisegment IP network required assigning a subnet number to each segment, configuring hosts on each subnet, and configuring packet forwarding between the subnets. Windows XP includes a media-access control (MAC) bridge component that can transparently interconnect network segments using the Spanning Tree Algorithm (STA). The MAC bridge incorporated in Windows XP allows the entire home network to operate as a single IP subnet. A *bridge* is a network device to connect two or more physical networks. It maintains a list of hardware devices on the network and checks the address of each data transmission to see if the recipient is on the network.

REMOTE DESKTOP

With Remote Desktop, you can run applications on a remote computer running Windows XP Professional from any other client running a Microsoft Windows operating system. The applications run on the Windows XP Professional computer and only the keyboard input, mouse input, and display output data are transmitted over the network to the remote location. Remote Desktop lets you access your Windows XP computer from anywhere, over any connection, using any Windows-based client. It gives you secure access to all your applications, files, and network resources—just as if you were in front of your own workstation. Any applications that you leave running at the office are running when you connect remotely. If you're a network administrator, Remote Desktop serves as a rapid response tool. It lets you remotely access a server running Windows 2000 Server or Whistler Server and see messages on the console, administer the computer remotely, or apply headless server control.

SYSTEM RELIABILITY

The reliability of a PC and its resources is critically important for any network installation. Windows XP includes a range of improvements intended to enhance reliability.

Driver Rollback

Driver Rollback helps ensure system stability—much like the Last Known Good Configuration option first available in Windows 2000 Safe Mode and the System Restore. When you update a driver, a copy of the previous driver package is automatically saved in a special subdirectory of the system files. If the new driver does not work properly, you can restore the previous driver. Driver Rollback permits only one level of rollback (only one prior driver version can be saved at a time), and this feature is available for all device classes except printers.

System Restore

System Restore lets you restore your computer to a previous state in the event of a problem without losing personal data files such as documents, drawings, or e-mail. System Restore actively monitors changes to the system and some application files and automatically creates easily identifiable restore points. Windows XP creates restore points each day by default as well as at the time of significant system events such as installing an application or driver. You can also create and name your own restore points at any time. System Restore does not monitor changes to (or recover) personal data files.

System Recovery

The Automated System Recovery (ASR) feature provides the ability to save and restore applications. This feature also provides the Plug-and-Play mechanism required by ASR to back up portions of the registry and restore that information to the registry. This is useful in a variety of disaster recovery scenarios. For example, if a hard disk fails and loses all configuration parameters and information, ASR can be applied to restore the server's data.

Dynamic Update

Reliability is enhanced with dynamic updates that provide application and device compatibility updates, driver updates, and emergency fixes for setup or security issues. Once the need for a Dynamic Update package has been determined, it's provided via the Windows Update Web service. If you choose the Dynamic Update option in Setup, Setup downloads the updates for devices and applications from Microsoft (instead of the original files from the CD). Organizations will also benefit because network administrators can download a complete Dynamic Update package—possibly including an applications compatibility or security fix for their users. Administrators can use the Dynamic Update package to ensure all users who install the operating system get these updated files.

AutoUpdate

This is an option for updating your computer without interrupting your Web experience. You don't have to visit special Web pages, interrupt Web surfing, or remember to periodically check for new updates. These downloads are configured to minimize the impact to network responsiveness, and are automatically resumed if the system is disconnected before an update is fully downloaded. Once the update has been downloaded to the PC, the user can then choose to install it.

Windows Update

Windows Update offers device driver support that supplements the extensive library of drivers available on the installation CD. Windows Update is an online extension of Windows XP, providing a central location for product enhancements, such as service packs, device drivers, and system security updates. For example, if you install a new device, Plug-and-Play will search for a driver locally and online at Windows Update. If your computer is *not* connected to the Internet and no suitable driver is found locally on the system, you will be prompted to go online and search for a driver. If an updated driver is found on Windows Update, the driver's .cab file is downloaded and the Windows Update ActiveX control selects the .INF file for installation.

INTERNET SECURITY

As with any network, security is important to ensure the safety of sensitive files, network resources, and network access. Windows XP provides a suite of enhanced security features that help to protect the network from unauthorized access.

Internet Firewall

Windows XP provides Internet security through a built-in feature called Internet Connection Firewall suitable for home users and small businesses. It protects computers directly connected to the Internet, or connected behind an Internet Connection Sharing host computer that is running the Internet Connection

Firewall. Internet Connection Firewall prevents the scanning of ports and resources (file and printer shares) from external sources. When enabled, the firewall blocks all unsolicited connections originating from the Internet using the logic of a Network Address Translator (NAT) to validate incoming requests for access to a network or the local host. If the network communication did not originate within the protected network, or no port mapping had been created, the incoming data will be dropped. Internet Connection Firewall is available for LAN, PPoE, VPN, or Dial-up connections.

Restriction Policies

Software restriction policies in Windows XP provide a transparent way to isolate and use untrusted, potentially harmful code in a way that protects you against various viruses, Trojans, and worms that are spread through e-mail and the Internet. These policies allow you to choose how you want to manage software on your system. By executing untrusted code and scripts in a segregated area (known informally as the *sandbox*) you get the benefit of untrusted code and scripts that prove to be benign, while the tainted code is prevented from doing any damage. For example, untrusted code would be prevented from sending e-mail, accessing files, or performing other normal computing functions until verified as safe. Software restriction policies protect against infected e-mail attachments. This includes file attachments that are saved to a temporary folder as well as embedded objects and scripts.

Wireless Security

Secure Wireless/Ethernet LAN enhances your ability to develop secure wired and wireless local area networks (LANs). With Secure Wireless/Ethernet LAN, a computer will not usually be able to access the network until the user logs on. However, if a device has "machine authentication" enabled, then that computer can obtain access to the LAN after it has been authenticated and authorized by the IAS/RADIUS server. Secure Wireless/Ethernet LAN in Windows XP implements security for both wired and wireless LANs that are based on IEEE 802.11 specifications. This process is supported by the use of public certificates that are deployed by autoenrollment or smart cards. This enables access control for wired Ethernet and wireless IEEE 802.11 networks in public places such as malls or airports.

Credential Management

The Credential Management feature provides a secure store of user credentials, including passwords and X.509 RSA security certificates. This provides a consistent single sign-on experience for users (including roaming users). If you access an application within a company network, your first attempt requires authentication and you're prompted to supply a credential. After providing this credential, it will be associated with the requesting application. In future access, the saved credential will be reused without having to reenter the credential. It has three components: the Credential Manager, the Credential Collection User Interface, and the Keyring.

Windows 2000

Built on Windows NT technology, the fully integrated Windows 2000 NOS offers built-in Web and application services, Internet-standard security, and good performance. Released in early 2000, it has quickly become a popular operating system for doing business on the Internet (see Figure 4-2). Windows 2000 readily scales from one or two servers with a few dozen clients to hundreds of servers and thousands of clients. It's also regarded as a reliable and robust operating system. Given the recent release of Windows 2000 (and more recently Windows XP Professional), it is the best operating system to take advantage of the latest

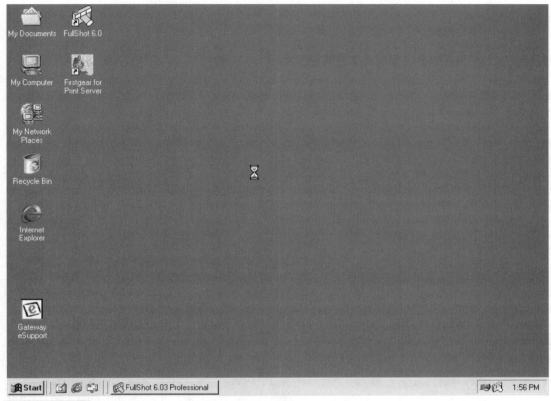

FIGURE 4-2   A typical Windows 2000 Server desktop view

PC hardware (i.e., from small mobile devices to the largest, most powerful servers for e-commerce). Windows 2000 is available in several major variations to best match your particular networking situation:

■ **Windows 2000 Professional**   Supporting up to two CPUs and 4GB of RAM. A reliable operating system for business desktops and notebook computers that is intended for Internet and mobile users. Windows 2000 Professional does not support clustering.

■ **Windows 2000 Server**   Windows 2000 Server is an entry level server software version intended for file, print, intranet, and infrastructure servers. This version will support up to four CPUs and 4GB of RAM and does not support clustering.

■ **Windows 2000 Advanced Server**   Windows 2000 Advanced Server provides improved reliability, availability, and scalability for running e-commerce and line-of-business applications. You'll get support for up to eight CPUs and 8GB of RAM, and clustering support for two-node failover and 32-node network load balancing.

■ **Windows 2000 Datacenter Server**   Windows Datacenter Server is the most powerful server operating system offered by Microsoft. Datacenter Server is intended for enterprises that demand the highest levels of availability and scale. You'll be able to use up to 32 CPUs and 64GB of RAM, along with cascading failover among four clustered nodes and 32-node network load balancing.

You can learn more about Windows 2000 features and support from Microsoft at **www.microsoft.com/windows/default.asp**.

WINDOWS 2000 FEATURES

Windows 2000 Professional is easier to deploy, manage, and support. Centralized management utilities, troubleshooting tools, and support for "self-healing" applications all make it simpler for administrators and users to deploy and manage desktop and laptop computers. In turn, these improvements pay off in reduced costs. It combines the power and security of Windows NT Workstation with the traditional ease of use of Windows 98. It also provides more wizards, a centralized location for common tasks, and menus that adapt to the way you work. When you use Windows 2000 Professional in conjunction with Windows 2000 Server, you can take advantage of IntelliMirror technologies. This technology lets you store your important information and desktop settings on a central computer. IntelliMirror lets you work on any computer attached to your network as if you are at your own desk.

Windows 2000 Professional includes fundamental improvements to reliability (such as modifications to the operating system core to prevent crashes and the ability for the operating system to repair itself) that make it the most reliable desktop operating system Microsoft has ever produced. Windows 2000 also provides comprehensive security features to protect sensitive business data—both locally on your workstation and as it is transmitted over your local area network, phone lines, or the Internet. With its support for Internet-standard security features (such as IP Security, Layer 2 Tunneling Protocol, and Virtual Private Networking), Windows 2000 is considered to be so secure that banks use it.

Windows 2000 Professional includes all the features of Windows NT Workstation, with numerous additions and improvements. The added features are meant to combine the ease of use of Windows 98 with the stability, speed, and security of Windows NT. Many of the improvements are listed here:

■ **64-bit ready**   Microsoft has enabled the Windows 2000 code base to be 64-bit ready and is working toward delivering a full-featured 64-bit OS in the future (this will be fully compatible with existing 32-bit applications). The goal is to take full advantage of Intel's 64-bit "Itanium" processor when it is released.

■ **Active Directory**   This is the integral directory service within Windows 2000. This service improves manageability, enables security, and extends the compatibility between Windows 2000 and other operating systems.

■ **Group Policy**   Group Policy allows an administrator to define and control the state of computers and/or users in an organization. The effect of Group Policy may be adjusted using memberships in security groups.

■ **Hardware Wizard**   This wizard gives you a single, simple interface for dealing with many hardware issues. The options include the ability to add, configure, remove, troubleshoot, and upgrade the peripherals that you use.

■ **Index Server**   This utility runs in the background and creates an index of the contents of the local hard drive or files on a network (if connected). It includes the ability to select what directories and file properties to index. Index Server can operate locally or across a network to improve speed and accuracy, and search results can be ranked according to relevance.

■ **Intellimirror Desktop Management**   This feature allows users to work at any station on a network and maintain their personal desktop settings, application data, and documents. Intellimirror gives administrators the ability to automatically distribute software (including remote OS installation). Administrators can also remotely control desktop configuration and maintenance.

- **Internet Explorer 5.x**   The latest Microsoft browser is fully integrated in the Windows 2000 Professional edition.

- **Network Connections Wizard**   A Network Connections folder in My Computer replaces the Network Settings item in the NT 4.0 Control Panel. Clicking on the Make New Connection icon opens Windows 2000's Network Connection Wizard. The wizard guides you through fewer steps than were required in NT 4.0 to create a new connection. When used with Windows 2000 Server's Active Directory, the OS also adds a series of new management functions designed to simplify running a network.

- **"Open/Save/Save As" dialog boxes**   Windows 2000 provides an Outlook-like directory tree displayed to the left of the Open or Save dialog boxes, allowing for quick and easy navigation to different folders on the hard drive.

- **Personalized Start menu**   Windows 2000 tracks programs and files launched from Start | Programs. After the first six sessions, it alters the Programs menu to show just the most used items. The other entries are collapsed and available by clicking on the double arrows displayed. Windows 2000 continues to monitor file use and make adjustments to the Start menu.

- **Plug-and-Play**   Windows 2000 is compatible with current Plug-and-Play standards, including support for the latest busses (such as USB, IEEE 1394 or "FireWire," and AGP) and other devices, such as DVD players, scanners, and digital cameras.

- **SMP support**   Symmetric multiprocessing allows for multiple processors in the different versions of Windows 2000. The Professional and Standard Server editions support two processors, while the most advanced server edition can support up to eight processors.

- **Windows 2000 Explorer**   The Explorer in Windows 2000 includes all the individual customizable features of Windows 98 Explorer. Added improvements include enabling Thumbnail View on all files instead of on a folder-by-folder basis, customized Windows Explorer toolbars, and Folder Options in Control Panel with a new streamlined Folder Options dialog box.

- **Windows Installer**   This utility allows for easier program installation and reduces problems caused by replacing shared DLL files with different versions during the install process. Windows Installer allows applications to examine existing DLL files in order to keep common files already installed. It also allows for adding program components at a later time and can be used to repair damaged applications. Windows Installer needs cooperative applications, so software publishers must write programs with MSI scripts that take advantage of Installer features.

WINDOWS 2000 INTEROPERABILITY

The Windows 2000 operating system provides or supports a wide range of protocols. Virtually any other platform client can use Windows 2000 Server–based servers, and clients running Windows 2000 Professional can interoperate with server platforms from Novell, IBM, and others. Windows 2000 interoperability includes support for a number of common communications and security protocols, including Transmission Control Protocol/Internet Protocol (TCP/IP), Lightweight Directory Access Protocol (LDAP), Dynamic Host Configuration Protocol (DHCP), the Domain Name Service (DNS) protocol, and the Kerberos version 5 authentication protocol. With this support, Windows 2000 can communicate with operating systems such as Novell NetWare, Macintosh, HP/UX, Solaris, IBM AIX, and Linux; with directory-based services such as Novell NDS, Lotus Notes, Exchange, and LDAP-based directories; and with database platforms, such as those from IBM, Informix, and Oracle.

"Services for UNIX" version 2.0 provides components that can be used to integrate Windows 2000 into existing UNIX environments. This add-on software delivers password synchronization, a Network

Information Service (NIS) server, an NIS-to-Active Directory Migration Wizard, a username mapping service, and Network File System (NFS) server, client, and gateway software. Microsoft Interix 2.2 provides an environment for running UNIX-based applications and scripts on the Windows NT and Windows 2000 operating systems. For IBM support, the Host Integration Server (a successor to SNA Server) lets you integrate the Windows operating system with other non-Windows enterprise systems running on systems such as IBM mainframes, AS/400, and UNIX.

Services for Macintosh is an integrated component of Windows 2000 Server and includes File Server for Macintosh, Print Server for Macintosh, and support for AppleTalk Protocol and AppleTalk Control Protocol (ATCP). Services for Macintosh makes it possible for computers running the Windows and Macintosh operating systems to share files and printers. A computer running Windows 2000 Server with Services for Macintosh installed can function as a file server, remote access server, and print server for Macintosh client computers. In addition, Windows 2000 Server can perform the functions of an AppleTalk router.

Sold as a separate product, Services for NetWare version 5.0 allows Windows 2000 Professional–based clients (and Windows 2000 Server–based servers) to communicate with NetWare-based servers. Services for NetWare includes File and Print Services for NetWare versions 4.0 and 5.0, Directory Service Manager for NetWare, Microsoft Directory Synchronization Services (MSDSS), and File Migration Utility. In addition, Windows 2000 has several built-in technologies that support NetWare. For example, Client Services for NetWare allows Windows 2000 Professional–based clients to connect to resources on NetWare-based servers. Gateway Service for NetWare allows Windows 2000–based servers to communicate with NetWare-based servers.

Windows NT

Unlike the NetWare operating system, Windows NT combines the computer and network operating systems into one integrated platform. Windows NT Server configures a computer to provide server functions and resources across the network, while Windows NT Workstation provides client functions to the network.

 You can learn more about Windows NT features and support from Microsoft at www.microsoft.com/windows/default.asp.

WINDOWS NT VERSIONS AND FEATURES

Windows NT operates on a domain model—a *domain* is a collection of computers that share a common database and security policy, and each domain has a unique name (you'll find that the idea of domains will be very important when actually setting up accounts and groups in Windows networks). Within each domain, one server must be designated as the primary domain controller (PDC). This PDC server maintains the directory services and authenticates any users that log on. Windows NT directory services can be implemented in various ways by using the account and security database. There are several different domain models to choose from. A *single-domain* network maintains the security and accounts database. A *single-master* network may have several domains, but one is designated as the master and maintains the user account information. A *multiple-master* network includes several domains, but the accounts database is maintained on more than one server. This approach is used for very large organizations. A *complete-trust* network uses several domains, but no single domain is designated as a master. All domains work together smoothly.

WINDOWS NT SERVICES

The combination of Windows NT Server and Windows NT Workstation can provide a powerful suite of file, security, printing, and network services to the system.

File Services

There are two approaches for sharing files on a Windows NT network. First, there is simple file sharing, just as there is on a peer-to-peer network. Any workstation or server can publicly share a directory in the network, and set the attributes of that data (i.e., no access, read only, modify, or full access). One difference between Windows NT and other operating systems (like Windows 95/98) is that in order to share a Windows NT resource, you must have administrative privileges. The other method of sharing takes full advantage of Windows NT security features. You can assign directory-level and file-level permissions, so it's possible to restrict access to specified individuals or groups. You will need to use the Windows NT file system (NTFS). During the installation of Windows NT, you can choose between an NTFS or a FAT16 (DOS) file system. You can install both file systems on different hard drives (or on different partitions of a single hard drive), but when the computer is running in DOS mode, the NTFS directories will be unavailable. Any client not using NTFS can share to the network, but is limited to public sharing and cannot take advantage of NTFS security features.

Windows 98 uses the FAT32 file system. Windows NT is not compatible with FAT32, so NT cannot be installed on a FAT32 system, and will not recognize any files on a FAT32 partition.

Security Services

Windows NT provides security for any resource on the network. A Windows NT network domain server maintains all the account records, manages permissions, and stores user rights. To access any resource on the network, a user must have the rights to complete a task and the permission to use that resource.

Printing Services

In a Windows NT network, any client or server can function as a print server. When sharing a printer on the network, it becomes available to anyone on the network (subject to sharing rules established for the network). When installing a printer, designate the printer as a local printer (My Computer) or a network printer. If you choose the network printer, a dialog box will appear listing all of the available network printers—simply select the one you want to use. Remember that you can install more than one printer on the network. If you're installing a local printer, you'll be asked if you want to share the printer with the network for others to use.

Network Services

Windows NT provides several services to help facilitate a smooth-running network. Messenger service monitors the network and receives instant messages for you. Alert service sends notifications that are received by the messenger service. Browser service provides a list of servers available on domains and workgroups. Workstation service runs on a workstation, and is responsible for connections to servers (this is also referred to as the redirector). Server service provides network access to the resources on a computer.

WINDOWS NT INTEROPERABILITY

The NWLink network protocol makes Windows NT compatible with NetWare. The first service is Gateway Services for NetWare (GSNW). All Windows NT clients within a domain must contact a NetWare server through a single source, and GSNW provides the gateway connection between a Windows NT domain and a NetWare server. This works well for slow networks, but can impair performance as the number of requests increases. Client Services for NetWare (CSNW) enables a Windows NT Workstation to access file and print services on a NetWare server—it is included as part of GSNW. File and Print Service for NetWare (FPNW) allows NetWare clients to access Windows NT file and print services (this is not a part of the Windows NT package, and must be purchased separately). The Directory Service Manager for NetWare (DSMN) add-on utility integrates NetWare and Windows NT user and group account information. Finally, the Migration Tool for NetWare is used by administrators converting from NetWare to Windows NT—it sends NetWare account information to a Windows NT domain controller.

Computers running Windows 95 or 98/SE will also work well as clients on Windows NT and NetWare LANs. You'll need to install the respective client software. However, Windows 95/98 users cannot fully benefit from Windows NT security features—those features use the NTFS file format, which is not compatible with Windows 95 or 98.

Novell NetWare

NetWare is one of Novell's most popular network operating systems due to its impressive interoperability. The NetWare operating system employs both network server and network client applications. The client application is designed to run on top of a variety of client operating systems. The server application can be accessed by client computers running under DOS, Windows (3.x, 95, 98/SE, NT, and Windows 2000), OS/2, AppleTalk, or UNIX. Consequently, NetWare is often the preferred operating system in large networks with mixed operating system environments. In small networks, however, NetWare can be difficult and cumbersome for an inexperienced network technician.

You can learn more about NetWare features and support from Novell at **www.novell.com**.

NETWARE VERSIONS AND FEATURES

NetWare version 3.2 is a 32-bit network operating system that supports Windows 3.x/95/98, and NT, along with UNIX, MacOS, and DOS environments. With NetWare 4.11 (also called IntranetWare), Novell introduced its new Novell Directory Services (NDS). NetWare 5.x addresses the integration of LANs, WANs, network applications, intranets, and the Internet into a single global network. NetWare 6 (**http://nw6launch.novell.com/nw6launch/index.jsp**) integrates additional network and Web-related services, supporting up to 32 clustered servers with up to 32 processors.

Novell Directory Services (NDS) provides name services as well as security, routing, messaging, management, Web publishing, and file/print services. Using a directory architecture called X.500, it organizes all network resources (including users, groups, printers, servers, and volumes). NDS also provides a single-point logon for the user, so a user can log on to any server on the network and have access to all their usual user rights and privileges.

NETWARE SERVICES

With NetWare Client installed on a workstation, that client workstation can take full advantage of the file, security, printing, and messaging services provided by a NetWare Server.

File Services

NetWare file services are part of the NDS database. Remember that NDS provides a single-point logon for users, and allows users and administrators alike to view network resources in the same way, but you can also view the entire network in a format that is native to your workstation's operating system. For example, a Windows NT client can map a logical drive to any NetWare file server volume or directory, and the NetWare resources will appear as logical drives on their computer. Such logical drives function just like any other drive in their workstation's computer.

The Internet now connects almost every network in the world to every other network. Yet reaching files on the network from another network remains difficult—sometimes even impossible. New with NetWare 6, Novell's iFolder relieves the restrictions that have traditionally linked users to particular hardware. iFolder also eliminates location as the most important aspect of file access, and provides the tools to synchronize, back up, and access files or applications anywhere and at anytime.

Security Services

NetWare provides extensive security. Logon security provides an authentication of the user's identity based on username, passwords, and time and account restrictions. Trustee rights control which directories and files a user can access (and what they're able to do with them). Directory and file attributes can identify the kinds of actions that can be performed on a file (i.e., read only, write to, copy, share, or delete).

NetWare 6 offers access authentication for every user, but goes far beyond simple directory access. Single sign-on gives a user access to all networked company servers, regardless of type or operating system (with Novell Account Management). Policies controlling groups of users or network resources reduce administration time while allowing great flexibility for users and partners. Novell BorderManager Enterprise Edition is a powerful Internet security management suite that includes firewalls, authentication, virtual private networking tools, and caching services for networks of all sizes. BorderManager integrates tightly with eDirectory, providing the first security management solution to support single sign-on controlled access to company information over any internal or external network. Critical communications within the corporate network or between a company and partners can be guaranteed with the Novell Certificate Server (included in NetWare 6). Novell Certificate Server 2.0 is a scalable, secure public-key cryptography product that creates, issues, and manages certificates. Certificates are digital attachments that verify the identity of the sender of a message. In addition, certificates give receivers a simple way to encode their replies.

Printing Services

Printing services are totally transparent to the client computer's user. Any print request from a client is redirected to the file server, where it is handed off to a print server and, finally, sent to the printer (though the same computer can serve as both file server and printer server). You can share printers that are attached to the server, attached to a workstation, or attached directly to the network by means of the device's own network interface card (NIC). NetWare print services can support up to 256 printers.

Novell provides network printer control by making printers, print queues, and print servers objects inside eDirectory. NetWare 4.x eDirectory made printer administration less time-consuming and more reliable by using the same management tools that are used for every other network resource. Users were able to find and use printers more easily than ever before. Novell Distributed Print Services (NDPS) added even more management and user support. NetWare 6 enhances printer functionality using the "best network print" option as the foundation for Novell Internet Printing. Built upon the IETF-ratified Internet Printing Protocol (RFC-2910-1), Novell Internet Printing introduces printer job control through Web browsers and Web server technology.

Messaging Services

NetWare allows users to send a short message to other users on the network. Messages can be sent to groups as well as to individuals. If all of the intended recipients are in the same group, you'd simply address the message to the group rather than to each individual. Users can also disable or enable the reception for their workstations. When a user disables reception, no broadcast messages will be received by that workstation. Messages can also be handled through the message-handling service (MHS). MHS can be installed on any server and configured to provide a complete messaging system for e-mail distribution. MHS supports most popular e-mail programs.

NETWARE INTEROPERABILITY

Other operating systems provide client software that supports interoperability with NetWare servers. For example, Windows NT provides Gateway Services for NetWare (GSNW). This service allows a server on the Windows NT network to act as a gateway to the NetWare network. Any workstations on the Windows NT network can request resources or services available on the NetWare network, but they must make the request through the Windows NT server. The server will then act as a client on the NetWare network, passing requests between the two networks. With GSNW service, a Windows NT server can obtain access to NetWare file and print services.

Proprietary protocols (such as IPX or DECnet) have given way to standardized protocols like TCP/IP. However, many protocols are still in use, and NetWare 6 supports a variety of different file protocols, all of which are standards in their own markets. File protocols allow different client machines to communicate with the NetWare file system. With NetWare 6, you can now take an iMac out of the box, plug it into your network and immediately begin accessing files off of a NetWare 6 server without installing any additional client software. The same holds true for a Windows client, a UNIX workstation, an FTP client, or a Web browser. The emphasis is to work within an existing infrastructure, capitalizing on the strengths of each platform and clients—not to replace the existing infrastructure.

Linux

In the last part of 1998, a lightweight version of UNIX (called *Linux*) started getting a lot of attention. Since its beginnings in 1991 (and open source release in 1993), Linux has been developed by hundreds of programmers around the world. Its development has been enhanced by one simple fact: the source code for Linux is free, and people are welcome to develop it any way they'd like—the only catch is that any improvements or enhancements made become part of the public domain. Its creator, Linus Torvalds, determines the actual changes to the operating system, and not every change makes it into the "official" version.

As Linux gains popularity from developers, hardware manufacturers, and software makers, Microsoft is becoming increasingly concerned about Linux as a threat to NT or 2000. There is good reason for this—Linux has a dedicated group of developers behind it. Also, the NOS runs on x86 computers, Digital Alphas, and Sun SPARC stations. This means it is actually more flexible than NT (now limited to x86 and Alpha machines). Linux also has relatively light hardware requirements. For example, you can use it to run a Web server from a 486 PC. By comparison, Windows 2000's system requirements are *far* greater.

Today, Linux is the fastest-growing server-side operating system today, and it's making inroads on the desktop. Unlike proprietary operating systems, Linux can be installed and upgraded for free. This makes it extremely attractive to those businesses that don't have a high budget but still want an excellent operating system. But cost is not the main factor. Many companies, large and small, prefer Linux simply because of its reliability—Linux installations have been reported to run for months, even years, without having to be rebooted. And because the source code is open, bugs can be fixed quickly and easily without having to wait for proprietary vendors to issue fixes on their schedule. Businesses also value open source software because it allows groups of companies to collaborate on software problems and issues without being concerned about an antitrust lawsuit. Linux programs can be installed on practically any machine (including older, outdated computers) and offer business owners a degree of flexibility they wouldn't find with other operating systems.

LINUX LIMITATIONS

Still, Linux is not going to conquer the personal computing market any time soon. Users can download the operating system from Red Hat's FTP site (accessible from **www.redhat.com**), order Linux directly on CD, and even buy the OS from their local office/computer superstore. While a growing number of businesses are running Linux servers, limitations in hardware and applications support continue to restrict new Linux installations in favor of high-end business installations such as Windows NT or 2000.

An important issue limiting Linux as a server operating system is the way processing time is divided. Where NT and other major commercial operating systems divide CPU time on a *per-thread* basis for kernel operations, Linux divides time on a *per-process* basis, making the division of CPU resources much less granular. Threads running in user mode (where applications execute) are also scheduled in a way that makes Linux applications less responsive than those designed for NT or 2000. In practice, Linux behaves more like Windows 3.x, using cooperative multitasking to demand that applications release the CPU when they're done. Today's 32-bit versions of Windows use preemptive multitasking that forces applications to give up the CPU at regular intervals. Finally, Linux code is designed to run on only one CPU at a time, so it can't employ multiprocessor hardware. Consequently, it's unable to run some enterprise server applications.

THE FUTURE FOR LINUX

In spite of its limitations, Linux is available from numerous vendors, and is being constantly improved to provide better user functionality, more versatility, and improved performance on a greater number of platforms. Linux versions such as Red Hat 7.2 have found their way onto the servers and desktops of major corporations as well as personal computers. It offers one of the most powerful and reliable systems available. And as an open source system, it can be altered to meet the needs of its users.

Other Operating Systems

While Windows NT/2000 and NetWare are certainly the most popular network operating systems available today, they are hardly the only ones available. UNIX, AppleTalk, and Banyan VINES are other viable products that you may encounter. In addition, Windows 95/98/SE can be configured to serve as a client in other networks. This part of the chapter will briefly introduce these other operating systems.

UNIX

UNIX continues to be a versatile, general-purpose, multitasking, multiuser operating system. The two major variations of UNIX are Linux and Solaris (by Sun Microsystems). Although UNIX was originally designed specifically for large networks, it does have some applications for personal computers (Linux is rapidly gaining popularity on the PC). Generally speaking, a UNIX system consists of one central computer and multiple terminals for individual users. UNIX works well on a stand-alone computer and also performs well in a network environment.

UNIX is very adaptable in a client/server network environment. It can be used as a file server by installing file server software. As a UNIX file server, it can respond to requests from workstations. The file server software becomes just one more application being run by the multitasking computer. A UNIX server can support clients running DOS, OS/2, Windows, or MacOS 7/8 (a file redirector will enable the workstation to store and retrieve UNIX files as if they were in the client's native format).

APPLETALK

Apple network support is fully integrated into the operating system of every computer running the MacOS. The first incarnation (called LocalTalk) was rather slow, but it brought economical networking to computer users. LocalTalk is still part of the Apple OS. AppleTalk directory services are based on *zones*—logical groups of networks and resources. These zones provide a means of grouping network resources into functional units. For example, an AppleTalk phase 1 network consists of no more than one zone, while a phase 2 network can have up to 255 zones. However, these two phases are incompatible, and don't readily support the same network wiring.

The current version of AppleTalk supports high-speed, peer-to-peer networking capabilities among Apple computers, and it also provides interoperability with other computer and network operating systems. However, such interoperability is not part of the Apple operating system. Users of computers other than Apple can connect to resources on an Apple NOS most easily by means of Apple IP (Apple's implementation of the TCP/IP networking protocol). Apple IP allows non-Apple users to access Apple resources such as database files. Computers that are part of the Apple NOS can connect to other networks through services that are supplied by the manufacturers of those other operating systems (running on their network servers). For example, Windows NT Server, Novell NetWare, and Linux all provide Apple interoperability services for their respective platforms. This allows networked Apple users to make use of resources on those network servers.

BANYAN VINES

Another networking system is the Banyan *Virtual Integrated Network Services* (or VINES). Vines is a client/server NOS derived from Xerox Corporation's Xerox Network Systems (XNS) protocols. The current version of Banyan VINES features messaging with Banyan's Intelligent Messaging and BeyondMail software. Network services are created and managed through Banyan's latest version of StreetTalk Explorer. This interface works with Windows user profiles, allowing each user's settings to "follow" them anywhere on the network. VINES also supports TCP/IP server-to-server software, handles up to four processors, and includes client support for Windows NT, Windows 95, and Windows 98 workstations. Banyan Intranet Connect software provides remote client access with a standard Web browser.

POPULAR CLIENTS

As you've seen throughout this chapter, you don't always need a network operating system on a client PC in order to access a network or its resources. In addition to the conventional NOS clients such as Windows 2000 Professional or Windows NT Workstation, other operating systems are also interoperable with many of today's NOS versions—though only in the role of client (workstation). The two most popular "client" operating systems are Windows Me and Windows 98/SE.

Windows Me

Microsoft sought to solidify its hold on the home user PC market with its introduction of Windows Millennium Edition (Me) in September 2000. While benchmarking tests show no real performance advantages with Windows Me over Windows 98/SE, the update package does offer a wide range of enhancements, primarily focused on entertainment, multimedia, and home networking.

Major enhancements over Windows 98/SE include multimedia features such as an automated video editor with high-powered compression and simple import from video cameras, a wizard to automate scanner and still-image camera captures, and a media jukebox/recorder. New system-protection features include a wizard that restores an unstable system to an earlier, functional state, and new easy setup features simplify home networking and broadband access. In addition, support for the Universal Plug-and-Play specification will let Windows communicate with devices such as refrigerators and wearable computers (not that there are immediate applications for such features).

Two important changes are the removal of the standard Windows 9x option to restart or boot to the MS-DOS command prompt (though DOS applications are still usable in DOS windows), and an overhaul of Windows Internet services that improves performance. Windows Me uses the same desktop interface as Windows 2000 Professional, along with the new TCP/IP stack that connects to the Internet, but causes incompatibilities with some widely used Internet software. The help system has vastly improved trouble-shooters and more informative error messages—the whole system is intended to be friendlier to experts and novices alike.

The System Restore feature backs up crucial system files when the computer is idle, making a snapshot of the system state every ten hours of computing time. Additional snapshots can be created at any time by running the System Restore Wizard. If the system stops working, and if you can at least reboot (even if only in Safe mode), you can run the wizard and choose from among the earlier saved system states to restore. The current state of your documents and e-mail won't be overwritten, but the damaged system files will be over-written with working copies. The System Restore component springs into action whenever you delete any potentially important files from the Windows or Program Files folder. For example, if you delete data from the Program Files folder, Windows will work in the background to restore the damage.

The System File Protection feature (based on the similar Windows File Protection in Windows 2000) silently prevents applications from overwriting crucial DLL files with older or nonstandard versions, and should drastically reduce the chance that a newly installed application will stop other programs from working. Users can also switch on the new AutoUpdate feature that downloads newer versions of system files in the background and then prompts you to restore them.

Multimedia   Windows Movie Maker records video from an attached camera or imports existing files, and then splits the video into clips for editing using technology borrowed from high-end video-editing software. Existing videos can be imported from all standard formats (except RealMedia), but can be out-put only in Windows Media Format, not AVI or MPEG.

The Windows Image Acquisition (WIA) feature uses a wizard interface for previewing, creating, and managing images from scanners and digital still cameras. Basic features can be used with any Plug-and-Play scanner, but with a WIA-compatible camera, you can preview and manage pictures without downloading them. More than 60 WIA-enabled camera models (including most released in recent months) are now on the market. The wizard runs automatically when a WIA-enabled camera is plugged into a USB port or a button is pressed on a Plug-and-Play scanner.

The new Windows Media Player 7 works with most standard audio and video formats, with the exception of RealMedia, and includes a Web radio tuner, a jukebox, and a file transfer utility that copies and compresses existing files or streaming media to portable MP3 players and Windows CE devices. The interface is less convoluted than most third-party media players, but Microsoft wastes a lot of screen space in an attempt to make the Media Player look cool, and the program is more crash-prone than anything else in Windows Me.

Networking   A home networking wizard walks you through the process of setting up and customizing file, printer, and Internet sharing on a Windows Me machine connected to any peer-to-peer network. The wizard optionally creates a disk that can be used to install the Windows Me network software on other computers that you want to include on the same network, even if the other computers are running Windows 95 or 98. A new Folder Options applet in the Control Panel provides a direct route to file association and other customization features. To protect against reckless use, crucial system files cannot be viewed in Windows Explorer unless you mark a checkbox in the applet.

If you have ever installed a home network, virtual private network, or broadband software under Windows 95 or 98, you probably bumped into an error message telling you that you could use only six instances of TCP/IP. This meant that Windows 9x could connect to the Internet through no more than six networking components, and that no Internet connections were available for the new software you wanted to install. The new TCP/IP software built into Windows Me removes this limitation, and you can install as many networking features as you want without being forced to remove existing ones.

Internet Explorer 5.5 and Outlook Express 5.5 come with Windows Me, but the only notable enhancement over earlier versions is a new print preview feature in IE. NetMeeting 3.1 is also a part of the package, but its home-networking features are already available in downloadable versions.

Upgrade Recommendations   So, as a technician, should you suggest that your clients upgrade to Windows Me? While Windows Me adds a lot of tools that home users may love, the stability of Windows Me is still being addressed, and benchmark tests suggest that Windows Me is just slightly *slower* than Windows 98/SE. As a rule, wait until Windows Me has undergone some more development (and wait for one or two service packs to become available) before jumping into an upgrade from Windows 98/SE.

Windows 98

With the many new hardware standards and features being developed for the PC, Windows 95 became increasingly hard-pressed to make the fullest use of system resources. Windows 98 builds on Windows 95 by adding a rich suite of refinements and improvements to a full 32-bit OS. New wizards, utilities, and resources work proactively to keep systems running more smoothly. Performance is faster for many common tasks such as application loading, system startup, and shutdown. Full integration with the Internet's World Wide Web aids online work and system versatility. After numerous delays, Windows 98 was finally released in June 1998, and an upgrade containing a year's worth of learning and improvements named "Windows 98 Second Edition" (or "Windows 98 SE") was released in September 1999 (see Figure 4-3). Microsoft has since released the Millennium Edition (called Windows Me), intended to focus on a broad spectrum of home users, but Windows 98/SE continues to be a popular and versatile OS for home and small office users. The most notable features and improvements of Windows 98/SE are outlined here:

- **Backup utility**   A new backup applet supports SCSI tape devices and makes backing up your data easier and more versatile.

- **Broadcast architecture**   With a TV tuner board installed, Windows 98 allows a PC to receive and display television and other data distributed over the broadcast networks, including enhanced television programs (which combine standard television with HTML information related to the programs).

- **Dial-Up Networking improvements**   The dial-up networking included with Windows 98 has been updated to support features like dial-up scripting and support for multilink channel aggregation, which enables users to combine all available dial-up lines to achieve higher transfer speeds.

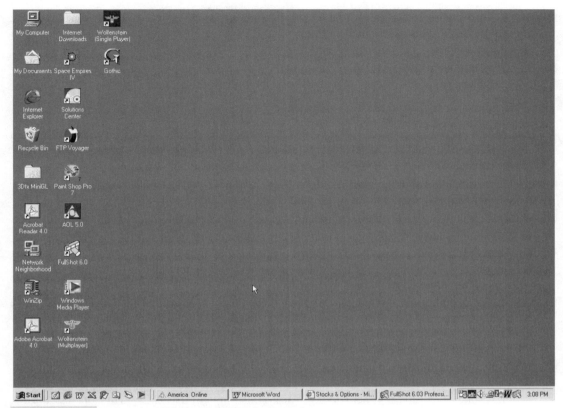

FIGURE 4-3   A typical Windows 98/SE desktop view

- **Disk Defragmenter Optimization Wizard**   This new wizard uses the process of disk defragmentation to increase the speed with which your most frequently used applications run.

- **Display configuration enhancements**   Display setting enhancements provide support for dynamically changing screen resolution and color depth. Adapter refresh rates can also be set with most newer display driver chipsets.

- **Distributed Component Object Model (DCOM)**   Windows 98 (and Windows NT 4.0) provides the infrastructure that allows DCOM applications (the technology formally known as *Network OLE*) to communicate across networks without needing to redevelop applications.

- **Dr. Watson**   Windows 98 includes an enhanced version of the Dr. Watson utility. When a software fault occurs (such as a general protection fault or system hang), Dr. Watson intercepts it and indicates what software failed (and why). Dr. Watson also collects detailed information about the state of your system at the time the fault occurred. A log file is created and can be used by a technician to troubleshoot the problem. Dr. Watson does not run by default; it must be started manually or from a shortcut placed in the Startup folder.

- **Faster shutdown**   The time it takes to shut down the system has been dramatically reduced in Windows 98.

■ **FAT32**   This improved version of the FAT file system allows disks over 2GB to be formatted as a single drive. FAT32 also uses smaller clusters than FAT drives, resulting in a more efficient use of space on large disks.

■ **Infrared Data Association (IrDA) 3.0 support**   Windows 98 supports IrDA for wireless connectivity, which means users can easily connect to peripheral devices or other PCs without using connecting cables. Infrared-equipped laptop or desktop computers have the capability of networking, transferring files, and printing wirelessly with other IrDA-compatible infrared devices.

■ **Intel MMX processor support**   Windows 98 provides support for software that uses the Pentium Multimedia Extensions (MMX and SSE) for fast audio and video support on future generations of the Pentium processor.

■ **Internet connection sharing (for Windows 98/SE)**   This feature enables you to configure your home computer network to share a single connection to the Internet.

■ **Multiple display support**   This feature allows you to use multiple monitors and/or multiple graphics adapters on a single PC.

■ **NetWare Directory Services (NDS) support**   Windows 98 includes Client Services for NetWare that support Novell NDS. This enables Windows 98 users to log on to Novell NetWare 4.x servers running NDS to access files and print resources.

■ **New hardware support**   Windows 98 provides support for an array of innovations that have occurred in computer hardware over the last few years. Some of the major hardware standards supported by Windows 98 include Universal Serial Bus (USB), IEEE 1394, Accelerated Graphics Port (AGP), Advanced Configuration and Power Interface (ACPI), and Digital Video Disc (DVD).

■ **PCMCIA enhancements**   There have been several enhancements to Windows 98 for PCMCIA support, including support for PC Card32 (CardBus) to implement high-bandwidth applications such as video capture and 100 Mbps networking. There is also support for PC Cards that operate at 3.3V, and for multifunction PC Cards (such as LAN and modem, or SCSI and sound) to operate on a single physical PC Card.

■ **PPTP support**   The Point-to-Point Tunneling Protocol provides a way to use public data networks (such as the Internet) to create virtual private networks connecting client PCs with servers. PPTP offers protocol encapsulation to support multiple protocols via TCP/IP connections and data encryption for privacy, making it safer to send information over nonsecure networks.

■ **Power management improvements**   Windows 98 includes support for the Advanced Configuration and Power Interface (ACPI), and support for the Advanced Power Management (APM) 1.2 extensions, including disk spin down, PCMCIA modem power down, and resume on ring.

■ **Remote access server**   Windows 98 includes all the components necessary to enable your desktop to act as a dial-up server. This allows dial-up clients to remotely connect to a Windows 98 machine for local resource access.

■ **System Configuration utility**   This utility allows for the fine-tuning of the Windows 98 startup and shutdown. Individual items in AUTOEXEC.BAT, CONFIG.SYS, SYSTEM.INI, WIN.INI, and the Startup folder can be enabled or disabled to troubleshoot conflicts or problems. It replaces and vastly improves on Windows 95 Sysedit.

■ **System File Checker**   This utility provides an easy way to verify that the Windows 98 system files (*.dll, *.com, *.vxd, *.drv, *.ocx, *.inf, *.hlp, and so on) have not been modified or corrupted. This utility also provides an easy mechanism for restoring the original versions of system files that have changed.

■ **System Information tool**   This utility provides extensive information on the system hardware and software environment. Many of the new troubleshooting, repair, and report utilities are available from the System Information utility through the Tools menu.

■ **System Troubleshooter**   This utility automates the routine troubleshooting steps used by support personnel and users when diagnosing issues with the Windows configuration. The troubleshooters are designed to address specific areas and devices. You can find the troubleshooters listed under the Help utility.

■ **Windows 98 Report tool**   Available under Tools in the System Information utility, this program allows you to submit a problem report to Microsoft. It automatically includes the information about your system that the Microsoft technicians need to have to examine the problem.

■ **Windows Media Player**   Windows 98 supports a new media-streaming architecture called ActiveMovie that delivers high-quality video playback of popular media types, including MPEG audio, WAV audio, MPEG video, AVI video, and Apple QuickTime video. The Media Player supports many popular audio, video, and combined media file formats. Updated Media Players are available for download from Microsoft.

■ **Windows System Update**   This feature helps you ensure that you're using the latest drivers and file systems available. The new Web-based service scans your system to determine what hardware and software you have installed, and then compares that information to a back-end database to determine whether newer drivers or system files are available. If there are newer drivers or system files, the service can automatically install the drivers.

Further Study

AppleShare: **www.apple.com/appleshareip/**
Linux: **www.redhat.com**
Novell NetWare: **www.novell.com**
UNIX: **www.unix.com**
Windows 2000: **www.microsoft.com/windows2000/**
Windows NT: **www.microsoft.com/windows/default.asp**
Windows XP: **www.microsoft.com/windowsxp**

DIRECTORY, NAMING, AND INTERNET SERVICES

There are a number of services at work in modern computer networks. Some are services used to identify computers and other devices, other services help locate objects within the network, and others are used to make the Internet a friendlier place to work and visit. This chapter examines those services—how they work and the most likely sources of trouble.

First, we will examine directory services. These are the tools used to locate any object in a computer network—be it a printer, a document, a user, or a group of users. We'll talk about the basic building blocks upon which directory services are built, then we'll talk about some specific directory services that are offered by Microsoft and Novell.

Next, we'll talk about naming services. These services are used as a means to translate the mystifying Internet Protocol (IP) addresses into something easier to understand by human beings. There are different naming services for different tasks, be it the Domain Name System (DNS), or the Windows Internet Naming Service (WINS). Additionally, for the sake of easy assignment of IP addresses, we'll consider the Dynamic Host Configuration Protocol (DHCP).

Finally, "Internet services" is a broad term used to categorize the various components used on the Internet. Whether it's the protocol used to load web pages, transfer files, or transmit e-mail, there are many different protocols at work behind the scenes.

Directory Services

When you need to find someone, you might pick up the telephone directory and locate their telephone number, or possibly their address. You might also use a church directory or a company's employee roster to track down their phone number, extension, or e-mail address. When you need to find an object on your computer network, the use of a directory service is not too much different. However, in this case, the directory is stored on a network server and its listings contain such information as user groups, printers, folders, and files. Directory services are also used for such tasks as e-mail services, user authentication, and network security. Further, the directory isn't just accessible to the users. Applications can also access these services to help in the performance of their tasks.

Furthermore, the use of directory services allows applications and product upgrades to be automatically sent to each user's computer. Directory services are also used to enable such security features as single sign-on, which allows a user to sign on to the network once and be allowed to access multiple secured locations and applications without having to reenter credentials. This isn't just easier for the user. The administrator saves time and energy because user identification need only be created once and can be centrally managed with the help of the directory service. For example, in a Windows environment, Active Directory allows the management of user credentials across the entire network from a single location. Furthermore, its integration with Microsoft Exchange makes for a seamless work environment both for users and administrators.

Though directory services should appeal to network administrators, they aren't the only ones who receive the benefits. Users also get the privilege of enhanced functionality. For example, users logging on to the network from any computer can get a consistent environment, including desktop options, applications, and data access—whether they sign on at their desk, on the road, or from a branch office.

X.500

X.500 is a standard for directory services by the International Telecommunications Union (ITU). The standard was first developed in 1988, but five years later another version of X.500 was released. Even though the 1993 standard is more recent, most implementations of X.500 still follow the 1988 standard.

To maximize efficiency and availability, X.500 uses a distributed approach to directory services. That is, an organization maintains its information in one or more Directory System Agents (DSAs). A DSA is a database that has two traits:

■ Information is stored in a structure according to the X.500 specification.

■ It has the ability to exchange information with other X.500 DSAs.

DSAs in an X.500 directory service are interconnected based on the tree model we'll explain in more detail later in this chapter. Each DSA holds a piece of the *global directory*, which is the roadmap of sorts to the entire system.

All the information stored within X.500 directory services is stored in *entries*. Entries belong to at least one *object class*. For example, if you wanted to locate Larry Hutchinson in your organization, the entity "LarryHutchinson" might be located as a member of the Production object. The information within each entry is determined by *attributes*. For instance, attributes of the LarryHutchinson entry might include JobTitle, PhoneNumber, EMailAddress, and so forth.

LDAP

X.500 was not a perfect solution, however, to the needs of directory services. Because it was too complex for most directory implementations, the University of Michigan developed a simpler Transmission Control Protocol/Internet Protocol (TCP/IP)-based directory access protocol, known as the Lightweight Directory Access Protocol (LDAP), for use on the Internet.

In most computing environments, employees need to access various services and applications like printers, the e-mail system, and shared files and folders. As such, employees need to be able to access resources located on different platforms (Windows, NetWare, and so forth). In order to locate these resources, a single directory service must be available that can provide authenticated access across the board. This directory service must not only provide usernames and passwords, but it must also store different types of data, like client contact information, application configuration, and personal documents, in a central location. Further, employees must be able to access that database from any workstation on the network, or a remote location if need be.

DIRECTORY TREES

A directory tree is a hierarchical grouping of domains that share a single namespace. Contrary to trees in nature, the top of the tree is called the *root* domain. Sometimes, the root is synonymously referred to as the *parent* domain. As we move down the tree, subdomains (also known as *child* domains) branch out.

The structure of any directory services tree typically is representative of the organization's corporate structure. For example, consider Figure 5-1. In this case, the overall organization is listed at the top, the division is underneath the organization, and so on.

Naturally, the exact structure will differ from company to company, but the basic configuration remains the same. No matter which directory service you use (Active Directory or NDS eDirectory, for example), trees allow the flexibility needed to form an organization's hierarchical structure.

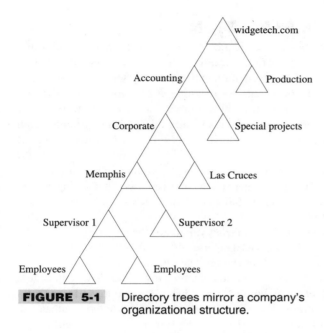

FIGURE 5-1   Directory trees mirror a company's organizational structure.

The directory services love affair with arboreal terminology doesn't end with trees. A collection of trees forms a *forest*. Though the trees each have their own unique namespace, they are joined into a forest through a series of trusts. That is, an administrator of one tree decides that the organization has sufficient enough relationship with another tree that they form a trust, thereby sharing access to each other's resources.

REDUNDANCY

As you can imagine, directory services serve important roles in the organization. As such, if the directory service goes down or fails in any way, then the organization will likely suffer serious repercussions. To avoid problems, it is common for directory service databases to be maintained on several servers. Placing the directory services databases on more than one server is known as *redundancy*. Redundancy is an important concept, because if something happens to one server (or it has to be taken offline for maintenance), another server can take over that server's responsibilities in the organization.

Furthermore, redundancy is an important benefit, especially in large organizations, but multiple servers also provide *load-balancing* features. For example, let's consider an organization with 1,000 client computers. By maintaining three servers on which directory services are deployed, not just one server is responsible for bearing the load alone. Rather, the servers can be set up so that the client load is equally shared across the network.

SYNCHRONIZATION AND REPLICATION

With redundancy comes the need for synchronization and replication. It is because of synchronization and replication that all the servers in an organization can have the same information in their directory services. This is important because without the most up-to-date information in the directory services databases of all an organization's servers, results would be inconsistent. For example, a user could try to locate a resource on one end of the organization (and locate it), while another user who accesses another directory services server that does not have up-to-date information will be unable to find that same resource. Even worse, if a resource is removed or relocated, the lack of current location data will send users to an incorrect location.

In a Windows NT environment, for instance, a hierarchical model was used among servers. That is, there are primary domain controllers (PDCs) and backup domain controllers (BDCs). This is a fine way to control the specifics of your network, and if the PDC were to fail, one of the BDCs would step up to take over its responsibilities. This is illustrated in Figure 5-2.

If a BDC is called upon to take over, it needs to have a current version of the information the PDC used, like a master database of users. When the PDC shares its database with the BDC, it is synchronizing the database. There is a difference between synchronization and replication, however.

Environments using directory services do not use the hierarchical model involving PDCs and BDCs. Rather, they use domain controllers, which are all equal. For instance, when Microsoft moved from Windows NT to Windows 2000 (and now .NET), things beyond the default screen colors and fonts changed. Specifically, Windows 2000 introduced domain controllers (DCs) to the Windows environment.

For the most part, DCs share their tasks equally, as Figure 5-3 shows. Some DCs might take on extra responsibilities (like being a DNS server and so forth), but they all share the basic responsibilities of maintaining a database of the domain-based network's objects. When DCs need to share domain information—because they are all equal—this process is called *replication*. Consider the network shown in Figure 5-4.

In this network, there are half a dozen DCs sharing both LAN and WAN links. At each location, two DCs manage the directory services needs of the LAN. Since there are six DCs, it is necessary to share DC information around the WAN. As such, DC A synchronizes its database with DC B, DC B shares with DC C, and so forth until all the DCs are synchronized.

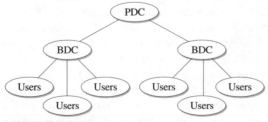

FIGURE 5-2   The PDC/BDC hierarchy

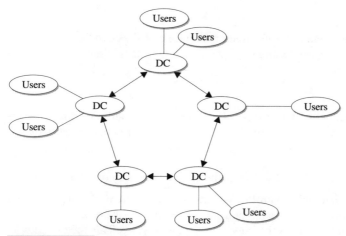

FIGURE 5-3 DCs share the workload, equally.

Synchronization is important so that objects (users, files, devices, and so forth) can be found anywhere within the network. For instance, if a user at location X is attempting to locate a file maintained at location Y, he or she will access the local DC. As such, the DC needs to know where to find the file.

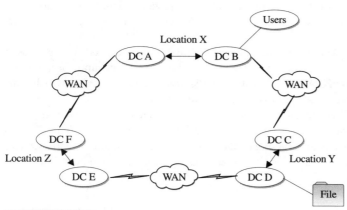

FIGURE 5-4 DC placement and replication need

ACTIVE DIRECTORY

The core feature of Windows 2000's manageability is its directory service called Active Directory (AD). Active Directory, simply put, is a database of your entire network. It maintains lists of data about the different attributes of objects in your system.

Benefits of AD

AD is an exceptional way to manage your network resources. The system takes traditional directory services and allows you to manage them with much more control and flexibility. Other benefits of AD include the following:

- Management is easier because of the centralized nature of the Active Directory database.

- Active Directory uses a series of equal domain controllers—rather than a hierarchical structure. What this means is that if one of the servers containing a domain controller crashes, the other domain controllers will pick up the slack, which minimizes the impact to your enterprise. This feature adds an extra layer of reliability through redundancy.

- Scalability is enhanced, and it allows Active Directory to hold millions of pieces of information without having to modify the administrative model.

- Searchable catalogs let you quickly and easily search through network resources and services.

- Active Directory is extensible. A user or an application can easily add additional data items to the directory.

Structure

The manner in which Active Directory is structured is important. When you read about and deal with X.500-based directory services, you'll encounter a structured, hierarchical way to manage your resources. The language of X.500-based directory services includes organizational units (OU), domains, forests, and trees. These are the building blocks not only of Active Directory, but of other directory services as well.

Figure 5-5 illustrates the structure of Active Directory and other directory services. OUs are groups of people, computers, files, printers, or other resources that need to be combined into one unit. Domains are collections of OUs. Trees are collections of domains. Forests are collections of trees. This network hierarchy allows you much more precise control over your network and its attributes.

Another key component of Active Directory is its *schema*, which is the database's internal structure. The schema defines relationships between classes of objects. For instance, using the example of an address book, there might be a class called Name, having the attribute first and last name, which specifies that objects in the Name class must contain first and last name information. Classes can inherit from other classes, forming a hierarchy of classes.

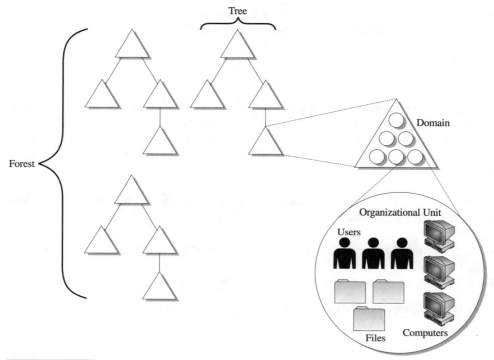

FIGURE 5-5   Active Directory's structure.

SYMPTOMS

When using and installing Active Directory, there are a few common sources of trouble. The following sections illustrate and explain how they can be ameliorated.

SYMPTOM 5-1   **DC fails to promote.**   When upgrading your system to an Active Directory environment, and promoting a PDC or BDC to a DC into an existing domain, you might get a message that the domain isn't a valid Active Directory domain. This is generally a DNS problem. To fix this, make sure that DNS has been correctly installed and that it is functioning properly.

SYMPTOM 5-2   **Installation Wizard hangs.**   If, while installing Active Directory, the process hangs, check to make sure the time on each computer is synchronized. If your servers do not have their clocks synchronized, installation can hang for hours on end. The best thing to do is stop the installation, synchronize your servers, and restart the Active Directory Installation Wizard. This can be accomplished by going to the command line and entering

```
net accounts /synch
```

SYMPTOM 5-3   **Domain user cannot log on.**   If a new user cannot log on to the domain, it's likely a problem with replication latency. That is, the user database has not been replicated to the DC under which he or she will log on. You can either wait for replication to occur, or you can adjust your DC's replication process so there isn't a large lag. This can also happen to users who get their passwords reset.

 Replication settings are a balancing act. You can enable replication to occur very often, but this also comes with lots of network overhead.

If the problem continues, check your event logs to ensure that the DCs are, in fact, replicating successfully.

Other issues to check when a user has a log on problem include the following:

- Is TCP/IP configured properly on the client computer?
- Is a domain controller available?
- Is a global catalog server available?

 The global catalog is a searchable index that allows users to find an object on the network without having to know on which specific domain it is housed.

Monitoring Active Directory

To keep tabs on Active Directory and perform troubleshooting tasks, quite often performance and analysis tools are used. A very powerful tool that has been part of Microsoft Windows servers is Performance Monitor (or System Monitor, as it is called in Windows 2000 and beyond). This tool can be invoked to monitor a plethora of information on your Windows system. To monitor Active Directory, activate Performance Monitor (it can be invoked from the command line by entering **PERFMON.EXE**) and choose NTDS from the list of objects that can be monitored. Table 5-1 lists some third-party tools that can be used to monitor Active Directory.

TABLE 5-1   THIRD-PARTY TOOLS FOR ACTIVE DIRECTORY MONITORING

COMPANY	PRODUCT	WEB SITE
NetPro	DirectoryTroubleshooter	**www.netpro.com**
IBM Tivoli	IBM Tivoli Monitoring	**www.tivoli.com**
NetIQ	NetIQ AppManager	**www.netiq.com**

If you had to restore your system from a backup and used the Restore Wizard, Active Directory can only be restored to its original location. If you specify a different location for the System State files—or if restore is attempted from a remote computer—Active Directory will not restore.

NOVELL DIRECTORY SERVICES (NDS)

Novell's directory services solution is Novell Directory Services (NDS) eDirectory. Novell is especially proud of NDS, because they claim the directory can store a billion pieces of information and perform LDAP searches in less than a second. NDS also provides the foundation for such Novell applications as Certificate Server, digitalme, eGuide, iChain, Net Publisher, and Single Sign-On.

Though designed for NetWare, NDS will work on Windows 2000/NT/XP, Solaris, and Linux operating systems.

Security

Like Microsoft's Active Directory, eDirectory comes complete with a suite of security components to keep out the bad guys:

- **Authentication**   The first layer of security asks users to authenticate themselves when they log on. Authentication support ranges from passwords encrypted over SSL to X.509v3 certificates and smart cards. Additional authentication occurs in the background and is transparent to the user.

- **Novell International Cryptographic Infrastructure (NICI)**   NICI is a cryptographic tool that developers can use to receive the right level of encryption for their application without embedding cryptography in the application.

 The level of encryption is based on the region of the world where the application is being used.

- **Secure Authentication Services (SAS)**   SAS is a modular authentication framework that provides next-generation authentication services. Currently, it provides SSLv3 support.

Management

Novell includes a host of management tools to help you administer the information in NDS. The tools include some that will directly affect your e-business solution (Novell Client), while others will indirectly affect it (NDS Server). Some of the tools included are as follows:

- **NDS Server**   Places replicas of NDS on primary domain controllers (PDCs) and backup domain controllers (BDCs).

- **NetWare Administrator and ConsoleOne**   Helps manage network users and resources.

- **NDS Manager**   Manages partitions, replicas, servers, and the NDS schema.

- **Novell Client**   Gives users access to NDS features.

- **LDAP**   Gives on open infrastructure for applications written on the Internet standard.

- **Bulkload Utility**   Adds millions of objects into the directory at once.

SYMPTOMS

There are a number of places where problems can arise with NDS. Some might seem like insignificant issues (like time synchronization), but some of the biggest problems have their roots in niggling details. The following are some of the more insidious sources of problems with NDS.

SYMPTOM 5-4   **I have problems with NDS server synchronization.**   Ensure that the times on your NDS servers are in synch. Time is important because NDS keeps track of all changes made to the NDS database via timestamps. For example, if your NDS servers are not synchronized and you add an object (a new user, for instance), you might be surprised to find out later that the user is not in the NDS tree. Time synchronization issues can occur for one of several reasons:

- NetWare's time service is not properly configured.

- An equipment failure might prevent servers from talking to each other.

- A server was shut down and the CMOS clock did not match the actual date and time when it was restarted.

- A server was configured with an incorrect time zone.

This is an easy enough problem to fix: simply make sure your servers are in time synchronization with each other.

SYMPTOM 5-5   **Time servers need to be properly configured.**   You should also check your time servers to ensure they've been properly configured. These are the servers that other servers in your organization will contact for time synchronization. NDS uses four types of time servers:

- **Single**   These servers respond to time requests from primary and secondary time servers, but do not change if there is a difference between them.

- **Reference**   These servers respond to time requests from primary and secondary time servers, but will change if there is a difference between them and primary time servers.

- **Primary**   These servers respond to time requests from reference time servers, other primary time servers, and secondary time servers. They can also negotiate minor time changes with other primary time servers.

- **Secondary**   These servers typically receive their time from other time servers.

For more information on selecting the appropriate type of time server and configuration, visit Novell's Support Connection web site at **support.novell.com** and, using the Knowledgebase feature, search for document number 10058645.

SYMPTOM 5-6   **Orphans are causing problems.**   If you change an object in NDS, make sure the change is completely replicated across the network. If a change is made that is not reflected across the entire network, you run the risk of leaving *orphans* behind. Orphans are sub-objects that no longer have a parent object. For instance, if a print server is removed, but the printer is left behind, the printer is an orphan.

To check for orphans, enter the following commands at the server console:

```
SET DSTRACE=+SYNCH
SET DSTRACE=*H
```

If a -637 error appears during the replication process, you might have an orphan (or orphans) in your servers. To clean these out, follow the instructions contained in document 100185121 at **support.novell.com**.

SYMPTOM 5-7   **Servers are not communicating properly.**   If you experience communications disruptions between your servers, you can experience problems with orphans, or your servers can spend hours trying to communicate with each other. You can check for communications problems by entering the following commands at the server console:

```
SET DSTRACE=+SYNCH
SET DSTRACE=*H
```

If you see a -625 error, you should check your communications links. You might have WAN links that are overburdened or bad LAN connections.

SYMPTOM 5-8   **The latest patches and updates have not been installed.**   Novell tries to fix problems through a series of patches and updates. Make sure you are up-to-date on your updating and patching. You can check the list at **support.novell.com/misc/patlst.htm**.

Naming Services

On a network, computers have unique addresses. These addresses allow other devices on the network to know where the computer is located. Additionally, naming services are used to make the process of finding a web site much easier than using the Internet's native IP addressing scheme.

In this section, the issue of naming services is examined in more detail. The most prevalent naming service is the Domain Name System (DNS). This is the naming service used on the Internet, and it is becoming popular on LANs as well. For instance, when you type in **www.whitehouse.gov**, or another address, it is your DNS server that translates that name into an address the computer can recognize. DHCP is a means by which computers logging on to a network are dynamically assigned their own IP address. DHCP is useful because it automates the IP addressing process. Microsoft tried its hand at its own naming system, called WINS. WINS is still a usable naming service that is supported by Windows, but Microsoft has decided to move to DNS rather than WINS. However, since it is still widely used in Windows domains, WINS functionality is explained here.

DOMAIN NAME SYSTEM (DNS)

In order to find a web site on the Internet, you must type a Uniform Resource Locator (URL) into your web browser. A series of unique domain names can be combined with an organization category to form a URL (like **www.whitehouse.gov**, **www.cocacola.com**, or **www.harvard.edu**).

But URLs only exist to make life easier for human beings—they aren't true IP addresses. In order for computers to connect with other computers across the Internet, they rely on 32-bit IP addresses, which act much like telephone numbers. For a URL to be used to connect to a web site, the URL must be converted into the IP address. For instance, if you type the URL **www.cocacola.com** into the web browser, a request is sent to the nearest DNS server, which looks up the URL and converts it to an IP address (in this case, 209.98.82.71).

It's necessary to make this conversion because routers and switches have no idea what a domain name is. In fact, in order to even communicate with your DNS server, an IP address must be entered to make the query. Every address on the Internet is an IP address. Without a DNS server, it would be impossible to use URLs to get where we wanted to go on the Internet.

In Windows 2000, Dynamic DNS (DDNS) was introduced. DDNS enables hosts to update the DNS table with hostnames and addresses as they are added to the network.

Windows Considerations

As we noted earlier, Microsoft's directory service is called Active Directory. DNS plays an important role in the functionality of Active Directory. Before Active Directory is installed, you must have a DNS infrastructure in place or develop a plan to install one. One of the first steps in planning a Windows 2000 or .NET migration is to have a domain name established. This will also be the DNS domain name. When developing an Active Directory network, there are three important roles that DNS plays dealing with naming convention, name resolution, and component locations.

Active Directory needs to use DDNS for setup. Older DNS servers will not work with Active Directory.

Naming Convention   The first role is the naming convention DNS brings to Active Directory. For instance, when developing your Active Directory solution, the root of your domain might be called **widgetech.com**. But this doesn't mean that your DNS domain and your Active Directory domain are one and the same. Remember, Active Directory is a directory service installed on your domain controllers. DNS, on the other hand, is a means of IP address resolution. Internally, your domain might be called **widgetech.com**, but on the Internet you might be found at **www.widgetechinc.com**. Active Directory will contain such entities as printers, users, servers, and so forth. Your DNS domain is hosted by DNS servers that may or may not be collocated with your domain controllers. In fact, they might not even be a flavor of Microsoft Windows.

Your DNS servers contain a database (called a *zone file*) that includes the resource records providing the mappings between hostnames and IP addresses. For instance, a zone file might contain an entry that tells us we can contact the machine domaincontroller5 via the IP address 192.168.1.100.

Name Resolution   Next, DNS is used in Active Directory environments by providing name resolution services. If one machine on your network wants to contact another, it sends out a DNS query to the DNS server to locate the other machine's IP address. In Windows NT 4.0 and earlier, this role was filled by WINS.

Component Location   Finally, DNS helps AD locate specific AD components. For example, since AD is a database containing the components of your network, if you log on to the network and need to find a certain printer, a Global Catalog Server must be located. To handle this type of request, the DNS server uses a resource called a *service record*. Service records are registered by the NetLogon service on a domain controller when it is started.

NSLOOKUP

To help troubleshoot DNS problems you can use the **nslookup** tool. **nslookup** is the name of a program that lets an Internet server administrator or user enter a hostname (for example, **osborne.com** or **whitehouse.gov**) to discover the IP address associated with that domain name. It is also useful for performing a reverse name lookup to find the hostname for an IP address you indicate.

nslookup sends a domain name query packet to a DNS server. The server will depend on the system you're using. Your default DNS server could be one set up on your network, at your service provider, or the root server system for the entire domain name hierarchy. You can also use **nslookup** to switch to a different organization's DNS server.

Using **nslookup**, you can also track down other information associated with the IP address in question, including mail services data. **nslookup** is included with both UNIX-based and Windows operating systems.

The **nslookup** tool can be used to query servers running DNS applications such as Berkeley Internet Name Domain (BIND). To construct a DNS query with **nslookup**, there are three elements that must be present:

- DNS server name or address
- The Internet address that is being queried
- The type of record for which you are searching

nslookup Usage   In a UNIX environment, simply enter **nslookup** at a command prompt. If you're using Windows, enter **nslookup.exe**. Either one of these commands starts the **nslookup** tool.

nslookup is useful when you need to gather different types of information about hosts on the network. For instance, you can get information about mail exchanger records, IP addresses, canonical names, and so forth.

Once you start the **nslookup** application, you'll see the following prompt:

```
>
```

At this prompt, you can enter your DNS query. For example, if you wanted to get the IP address for a specific site, you'd enter the name as such:

```
>osborne.com
```

This will return the IP address's URL:

```
198.45.24.162
```

If you were to enter the IP address, you'd get the canonical name for the entry.

A *canonical name* is the host's name—like **osborne.com**, for instance.

Another very useful feature of **nslookup** is the ability to receive a listing of hosts that serve mail exchange (MX) functions for a given domain.

At the > prompt, entering **?** will generate a list of all the options available with **nslookup**.

If you are looking for a specific type of record (mail exchange, for example), you tell **nslookup** that's the information you want by using the **set type** command.

In Windows environments, **set type** can be replaced with **set q**. In this case, "q" simply means query. The terms "type" and "q" are interchangeable.

For instance, to search for mail exchange information, enter the following:

```
>set type=mx
```

After you've established the type of record for which you're querying, enter the Internet address you are curious about. For example, entering

```
>osborne.com
```

delivers these results:

```
Server:   ra.visi.com
Address:  209.98.98.98
osborne.com     MX preference = 0, mail exchanger = mail.eppg.com
osborne.com     nameserver = NS1.MHEDU.com
osborne.com     nameserver = NS2.MHEDU.com
NS1.MHEDU.com   internet address = 198.45.24.13
NS2.MHEDU.com   internet address = 198.45.24.14
```

From these results, you can see that the machine **mail.eppg.com** is the authorized mail exchange address for all mail coming into **osborne.com**. This result was garnered using the DNS server "ra.visi.com."

If you need or want to check with a DNS server that is the source of authority for another domain, you can establish it as the primary DNS server with the **server** command:

```
> server ns1.mhedu.com
Default Server:  ns1.mhedu.com
Address:  198.45.24.13
```

You can get more detailed information about a mail exchange record by searching for another type of record. In this case, we'll use the **set type** command again, this time to look for host information (HINFO) records:

```
> set type=hinfo
```

This time when we enter **osborne.com**, we get the following detailed information about the host:

```
Server:  ns1.mhedu.com
Address:  198.45.24.13

osborne.com
        primary name server = osborne.com
        responsible mail addr = hostmaster.eppg.com
        serial  = 200204152
        refresh = 3600 (1 hour)
        retry   = 900 (15 mins)
        expire  = 604800 (7 days)
        default TTL = 1800 (30 mins)
```

If you wish to see all the details of a given domain, set the type to "all." This returns all the data for a given domain, as shown in the following example:

```
>set type=all
>osborne.com
Server:  ns1.mhedu.com
Address:  198.45.24.13

Non-authoritative answer:
osborne.com       nameserver = NS1.MHEDU.com
osborne.com       nameserver = NS2.MHEDU.com
osborne.com       MX preference = 0, mail exchanger = mail.eppg.com

osborne.com       nameserver = NS1.MHEDU.com
osborne.com       nameserver = NS2.MHEDU.com
NS1.MHEDU.com     internet address = 198.45.24.13
NS2.MHEDU.com     internet address = 198.45.24.14
mail.eppg.com     internet address = 198.45.24.13
```

An issue that might catch your eye when pouring over **nslookup** information is an entry entitled "non-authoritative answer." For instance, consider the following listings:

```
> whitehouse.gov
Server:  ns1.mhedu.com
Address:  198.45.24.13
```

```
Name:     whitehouse.gov
Address:  198.137.240.92

> whitehouse.gov
Server:   ns1.mhedu.com
Address:  198.45.24.13

Non-authoritative answer:
Name:     whitehouse.gov
Address:  198.137.240.92
```

In each case, we performed a simple **nslookup** on the White House's web site. The first time, we received a very unexciting answer in the form of the White House's IP address. However, when we entered it a second time, before the White House's IP address was returned, we got the qualifier: "non-authoritative answer." Don't be alarmed—this doesn't mean we have shoddy information. The first time we went out for the **nslookup** information, the query results were returned directly to **nslookup** from the White House's DNS server, and they were also cached by our DNS server. The second time we sent an **nslookup** query, the results were delivered from the cache. To indicate that we are getting our results from the cache, **nslookup** adds "non-authoritative answer" before the listing.

nslookup Errors   While using **nslookup**, you might encounter different types of errors:

- **Timed out**   The server did not respond to the **nslookup** request after both a specified amount of time and a number of retries. The timeout period can be adjusted with the **set timeout** subcommand. The number of retries can be adjusted with the **set retry** subcommand.
- **No Response From Server**   No DNS name server is running on the server computer.
- **No Records**   The DNS name server does not have the resource records of the current query type for the computer, even though the name is valid.
- **Nonexistent Domain**   The computer or DNS domain does not exist.
- **Connection Refused**   The connection to the DNS name server could not be made.
- **Network is Unreachable**   The connection to the DNS name server could not be made.
- **Server Failure**   The DNS name server found an inconsistency in its database and could not return an answer.
- **Refused**   The DNS name server refused the **nslookup** request.
- **Format Error**   The request packet sent to the DNS name server was in an incorrect format. This is consistent with an error in **nslookup**.

DYNAMIC HOST CONFIGURATION PROTOCOL (DHCP)

The Dynamic Host Configuration Protocol (DHCP) simplifies the assignment and management of computers connecting to a TCP/IP network. DHCP automatically assigns IP addresses for computers and other devices on the network from a pool of available addresses.

A configured DHCP server provides a database of available IP addresses and can also be set up with configuration options for clients, including the addresses of DNS servers, gateway addresses, and other information. DHCP servers are typically used in large organizations and ISPs because they allow simple assignment and reuse of IP addresses.

When a DHCP client starts, it requests setup information from the DHCP server. This allows the IP address to be automatically assigned, along with subnet masking and other information. The IP address is assigned to each client for a limited amount of time. This is known as a *lease*. Leases can be renewed from time to time, providing an interruption-free session. Leases are renewed about halfway through the lease duration. If the renewal is successful, the IP address remains assigned to the client. If it is unsuccessful, it is returned to the pool for another client to use.

SYMPTOMS

If your DHCP server is having problems, there are a couple scenarios that are common and easily fixed.

SYMPTOM 5-9   **The DHCP server has stopped.**   If your DHCP server stops, first you should check and make sure that the server is authorized to operate on the network. Next, it is easy to overlook a configuration detail, especially if you have just set up or completed administration of the DHCP server. Double-check your settings and make sure you haven't missed a setting.

Examine your system event log and DHCP server audit logs. When a service starts or stops, an explanation is usually present in the log.

SYMPTOM 5-10   **The DHCP server is unable to serve clients.**   If your DHCP server is a multihomed computer and is not providing DHCP service on one or more of its network connections, check your server bindings. Inspect them to see whether they statically or dynamically configure TCP/IP for any installed connections on the server.

"Multihoming" means that the server has more than one network interface card installed and operational on more than one subnetwork.

If your DHCP server's scopes or superscopes have not been configured or activated, ensure that they are properly configured, along with any special options that might be needed on your system. If your scope is in full use and cannot lease addresses to requesting clients, the DHCP server returns a DHCP negative acknowledgement message (DHCPNAK) to the clients. When this occurs, there are four things you can do to stretch your pool of IP addresses:

A scope is a pool of available IP addresses.

- Expand the range of your IP addresses by increasing the end IP address for the current scope.
- Create an additional scope and superscope, then add the existing scope and the new scope to the superscope.
- Deactivate the scope, then activate a new one.
- Reduce the duration of leases.

Your might also find that the range of IP addresses offered by one of your DHCP servers conflicts with the range offered by another DHCP server on your network. To fix this, change the scope address pools for the scopes at each server so you are sure that the pool of IP addresses will not overlap. Further, you can delete client leases and temporarily enable server-side conflict detection to help nail down the problem.

SYMPTOM 5-11   **The DHCP Server has suffered data loss or corruption.**   If the DHCP server is reporting Jet database errors, or you suspect that the database has become corrupted, your DHCP server data recovery options are to restore the database and fix any reported errors. On the DHCP console, you can use the Reconcile feature to verify and reconcile any issues within the database.

DHCP Client Issues

If your DHCP server is working properly, but you're still having problems, the next logical step is to check your DHCP client. There are some common client problems that you should examine.

Reboot   The first place to start is with a simple reboot of the client. Assuming your system has been configured properly to use DHCP, a reboot might be all that's needed to shake the gremlins out of the works. DHCP software still faces some reliability issues that are best resolved by a simple reboot.

Connecting to Another Network   If you are connecting to another network and cannot get access to the DHCP server, again, performing a reboot might be all you need.

Release and Renew   Using the **ipconfig /release**, then the **ipconfig /renew** commands (in a Windows NT/2000/XP environment) or **winipcfg** (in a Windows 9*x* environment) is also a helpful way to shake loose DHCP problems.

Rogue DHCP Servers   Make sure the DHCP server to which your clients are trying to connect is the correct DHCP server. If they are trying to use a so-called *rogue* DHCP server, the server can be dishing out inaccurate information.

WINDOWS INTERNET NAMING SERVICE (WINS)

Windows Internet Naming Service (WINS) is Microsoft's proprietary name resolution service, and isn't primarily used with Windows 2000 or beyond. However, for the sake of backward compatibility, it is still included with Windows releases. Further, since there are many Windows NT environments out there, WINS is still used by many organizations. WINS offers compatibility with services and applications that require NetBIOS-to-IP address resolution.

NetBIOS stands for Network Basic Input/Output System and is a program that allows applications on different computers to communicate within a LAN.

Understanding WINS

WINS contains two high-level components: the WINS server and the WINS client. The WINS client performs two functions: it registers with the WINS server when it first comes up on the network, and it queries the WINS server for IP-to-NetBIOS name resolution. The WINS server receives and processes WINS client registrations and queries, and communicates this information to other WINS servers by sharing its database in a process called *replication*.

A Windows NT network might contain more than one WINS server. In case the primary WINS server is not reachable, clients can attempt to reach the secondary server. WINS servers share their name databases with each other regularly at periods known as the *replication interval*.

Registration, Renewal, and Release

The TCP/IP stack is initialized the first time that the WINS client communicates with the WINS server. The client initiates the request by sending a *Name Registration request* to the WINS server. The WINS server then checks its database to see if the name is already in use. If not, the registration is accepted and written to the database for future lookup requests. Periodically, while connected, the client will query the server to renew its lease—that is, it makes sure it can still use its registration with the WINS server. When a client shuts down, it will contact the server so that the name can be released. The following sections examine the process of registration, renewal, and release in closer detail.

Registration   When the WINS client queries the WINS server, the server will read the request and decide whether to accept or reject the request. Whether the request is rejected is based largely on whether the name is already in use by another network client. If the name is already registered, the server will check the IP address of the requestor. If the name is registered, is still active, and the IP address of the requestor is different, then the WINS server will send a message to the IP addressee for that name. This process starts with a Wait for Acknowledgement (WACK) message, telling the client to wait for the server to finish performing its name query. If the addressee responds, the WINS server tells the first requesting client that the name is already registered and in use. Once the WINS server determines that there is or is not another client with that name, it will send the client either a Positive or Negative Name Registration Response.

Renewal   In order to keep the server's name database from getting clogged with unused names, client names are only granted a finite lifetime. That is, they must periodically be renewed. During the registration process, the client is given a *renewal interval*. When half of the renewal interval has passed, the client must reregister with the server. If the client fails to reregister by the end of the renewal interval, the name is released by the server.

Windows clients renew their leases halfway through the interval. Other clients may have another time at which they perform renewal tasks.

Release   There are two main ways in which a client name is released:

- **Explicit release**   This occurs when the client shuts down normally. It sends out a Name Release Request, telling the WINS server that it will be shutting down and no longer needs the name.
- **Silent release**   This occurs when the client abruptly shuts down. In this case, the Name Release Request is not sent out and when the renewal interval passes, the name is released.

WINS Impact

When implementing WINS on a network, it's a good idea to stick with the default settings unless you have a particularly good reason to change them. Most of the WINS parameters will work fine on their own. Try to set the replication interval between your WINS servers at 15 minutes on a LAN, 60–90 minutes over a domestic WAN connection, and 2–12 hours over an international WAN connection. Depending on the dynamics of your network, you might find that it is more appropriate to adjust these values up or down.

LAN Considerations   When locating a WINS server in your LAN, do yourself a favor—take the time and make the effort to establish primary and secondary WINS servers. That way, if the primary crashes, you won't have to listen to your users griping in unison about the network. Further, it's a good idea to locate your WINS servers in geographically disparate locations, adding physical security to your WINS servers' reliability.

 Geographical disparity need not mean that the servers are located in two different states. They could be in different buildings on the campus, or they could be on different floors of the same building.

WAN Considerations   When WINS are installed on a WAN, it makes sense to install multiple WINS servers. For instance, consider the network shown in Figure 5-6.

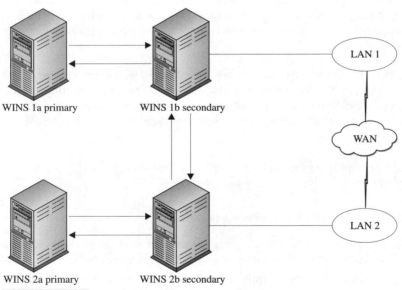

WINS 1a primary   WINS 1b secondary

WINS 2a primary   WINS 2b secondary

FIGURE 5-6   WINS implementation across a WAN

In this case, a primary and a secondary WINS server have been installed on both sides of the WAN. WINS servers 1a and 1b are replication partners, as are WINS servers 2a and 2b. In a large network, it might be necessary to send half of one LAN's traffic to WINS server 1a as their primary, while the other half of the traffic is sent to WINS server 1b. That way, the load is balanced between them. The same thing is occurring on the other side of the WAN, with half the traffic going to 2a and the other half going to 2b. On each side of the WAN, the servers replicate their WINS databases every 15 minutes.

However, in this case the WAN link is heavily utilized and we don't want to clog it even further with unnecessary traffic. Because users on each side of the WAN tend to access resources on their own LAN, we can be fairly secure in the knowledge that WINS converges between sides in less than an hour. To calculate the maximum allowable replication time between 1a and 2a, we add the replication times of each set of WINS servers (in this case, 15 + 15 = 30). This is subtracted from the maximum allowable convergence time of 60 minutes (our convergence goal) to give us the maximum replication time. In this case, we subtract 30 minutes from 60 minutes, giving us a total of 30 minutes maximum for a record to propagate from WINS server 1a to 2a.

Troubleshooting WINS

The following scenarios can help in the troubleshooting of WINS problems. As we noted before, there are two components involved in a WINS system, clients and servers.

Generally speaking, if the server cannot resolve names for clients, it's a good idea to review your WINS configuration and ensure that all the settings have been properly established. The bulk of WINS problems start as failed queries made by the client.

WINS Server Issues   If your WINS server is having problems, the first place to start is by making sure that it is actually up and running. At the Event Viewer or the WINS console, make sure that WINS is started and running. Also, you can use the Services option in the Control Panel to perform this task. If WINS is running, search for the name that was previously requested by the client and check to see if it is in the database.

If a name is not in the WINS database, check to ensure that replication is correctly configured between your WINS servers. Another issue to be cognizant of is whether or not your WINS server is doling out out-of-date information to clients. This can be due to a static mapping blocking the dynamic registration of valid name-to-address mappings. To resolve this, it's best not to use static mappings for clients that dynamically use WINS to update name and address information. If you do encounter out-of-date information, check the name entry on the WINS sever database to see if it was entered statically. If it was entered statically, you can select one of the following options to update it:

■ Enable migrate in Replication Partners Properties.

■ Edit the static mapping to reflect updated information.

■ Delete the static entry.

If there are replication problems between your WINS servers, check the replication partnerships. If your WINS servers use one-way replication partnerships (like push-only or pull-only) the database might not be replicated to all the servers.

If your WINS server experiences problems resolving names sporadically, your WINS server might be registering its names at other WINS servers. This occurs when the WINS server settings configured in the TCP/IP properties of the client point to the IP address of remote WINS servers, rather than a local WINS server. In this case, the correct course of action is to reconfigure the client TCP/IP properties so that WINS points at the local WINS servers.

If your WINS server cannot use push or pull replication with another WINS server, use the Ping tool to ensure that each server is up and running and can be connected to. Also, ensure that each server is properly configured as both a push *and* a pull partner. This setting can be checked in the system Registry under the Push and Pull keys.

The WINS Server Database   If you have established that the WINS service is running on the WINS server, but you still cannot connect using the WINS Manager, the WINS database is either not available or it has become corrupted. Your best course of action is to restore the database from a backup copy. The WINS Manager can be used to restore the WINS database, or you can manually restore the database.

To restore the database manually, the first step is to back up the existing WINS database file. Even though you suspect that it is faulty, this is an easy enough step that can save you headaches later if it turns out that the database was not, in fact, screwy.

Next, in the **\%Systemroot%\System32\Wins** directory, delete these files:

- **J50.log**
- **J50#####.log**
- **Wins.tmp**

Copy an uncorrupted version of **Wins.mdb** to the **\%systemroot\System32\Wins** directory, then restart WINS on your WINS server. The WINS server can be restarted by following these steps:

1. Turn off the server and wait for at least a minute.

2. Turn on the power, restart Windows NT Server, then log on with administrator rights.

3. Open the command prompt and type **NET START WINS**, then press ENTER.

In the event that your WINS server is malfunctioning due to hardware failures, your best course of action is to move WINS to a new server altogether. This involves rebuilding the WINS server. To rebuild a WINS server, follow these steps:

1. If possible, restart your WINS server and make backup copies of all the files in the **\%Systemroot%\System32\Wins** directory. You can use either the Windows GUI or the MS-DOS command prompt, if need be. If neither of these courses of action is an option for you, you will have to use your backup version of the WINS database.

2. Install whichever flavor of Windows you are using, then install TCP/IP (it is part of the installation on Windows 2000 and Windows .NET). Create a new WINS server using the same hard drive location and **\%Systemroot%** directory that was present in your old WINS server.

3. Stop your WINS service on the new server, then use the Registry Editor to restore the WINS keys from the backups.

4. Copy the backups to the **\%Systemroot%\System32\Wins** directory.

5. Restart the computer.

If you need to move the WINS database from one server to another, follow these steps:

1. Stop the WINS service.

2. Copy the files in the **\%Systemroot%\System32\Wins** directory to the new computer. It's best to use the same path that was used on the original computer; however, if that is not possible, then copy **Wins.mdb**, but not any **.chk** or **.log** files.

3. Start WINS on the new server.

WINS Client Issues   If name resolution fails on the client computer, it is likely that the type of name resolution used is inappropriate. You should check which name resolution service is being used on the network: WINS or DNS. Also, check whether the failure is occurring for a NetBIOS or a fully qualified domain name (FQDN).

NetBIOS names are limited to 15 characters or less (DAVESCOMPUTER, for instance) and are used with WINS. An FQDN looks a lot like an Internet address (davescomputer.accounting.widgetech.com, for instance) and is used with DNS. By checking the computer name, you can tell which type of service your network will need.

Next, your client could be using an application or a version of Windows that requires WINS to resolve names. For instance, if a name resolution failed in an attempt to find an Internet web site, the problem is most likely a DNS problem—not a WINS problem. One way to get around this complexity is, if you happen to be in a pure Windows 2000 or .NET environment (meaning all the clients and servers are Windows XP, 2000, or .NET), to use DNS instead of WINS. If any servers are using Windows NT or MS-DOS, a mixed environment would most likely exist.

If yours is a mixed environment, name resolution might fail if a client needs access to a shared resource that is not published via Active Directory. For instance, an application that needs WINS to help with name resolution includes the Map Network Drive, which is in Windows Explorer.

Client configuration is an important place to check in the event of WINS problems. To check your client, you must first establish whether the client is configured to use both TCP/IP and WINS. These settings can be checked manually by examining the client TCP/IP configuration, or dynamically by a DHCP server providing the client with TCP/IP settings. In versions of Windows pre-Windows 2000, clients can use WINS once TCP/IP is installed and configured. In clients using Windows 2000 and later, NetBIOS over TCP/IP (NetBT) can be disabled for each client. When NetBT is disabled, the client cannot use WINS.

You should also use the **ipconfig /all** command to check a client's IP configuration. When the settings are displayed, make sure the following are configured:

- IP address
- Subnet mask
- Default gateway
- Primary and secondary WINS servers

If these settings are not valid, you can either reset these values manually or use the **ipconfig /renew** command to get new configuration details from the DHCP server.

The client might also be experiencing trouble because it does not have connectivity with WINS servers. The first step is to Ping the WINS server by its IP address. If you don't know the IP address of the WINS server, use the **ipconfig /all** command to retrieve the IP address. If the WINS server responds to a Ping, your next step is to use the **nbtstat –RR** command on both the WINS client and the resource server that the client is trying to access. The **nbtstat –RR** command resets the names on both the client and the resource server. In the event the WINS server does not respond to the Ping, you can safely assume that there are network connectivity issues, and a review of your TCP/IP settings and troubleshooting procedures is in order.

Common Internet Services

On the whole, users tend to think of "the Internet" as one gigantic entity. They think e-mail, web pages, and everything else happens because that's what they told Internet Explorer or Outlook to do. In actuality, for all the functions made possible by the Internet, different applications, tools, and protocols are needed.

In this section, the various components used for web page transmission, e-mail, file transfer, Telnet, and Network News are examined.

HYPERTEXT TRANSFER PROTOCOL (HTTP)

The Hypertext Transfer Protocol (HTTP) is the protocol used for exchanging web site components (text, graphics, and other multimedia files) across the World Wide Web. Not only a means to share information across the World Wide Web, HTTP provides a way for pages to contain links to other pages of information. For instance, when you go to **www.whitehouse.gov** and click on a picture of the president, HTTP is the protocol used to deliver another page of information about the president.

Any computer housing a web server is known as an HTTP *daemon*. This is a program that waits for HTTP requests to come in, then handles the task of finding the linked pages. The browser you use to search the Internet is an HTTP client that sends requests to an HTTP server. When you send a request to the server—either by typing in a URL or clicking on a link—the browser forms an HTTP request that is sent to the IP address indicated by the URL. The HTTP daemon at the destination web site receives the request and serves up the requested file.

FILE TRANSFER PROTOCOL (FTP)

File Transfer Protocol (FTP) is an Internet protocol that provides a simple means to exchange files between computers. FTP is similar to HTTP in that it transfers web pages and related files, and is similar to SMTP (which is explained later in this section), which transfers e-mail; however, FTP uses the Internet's TCP/IP protocol suite to transfer files. An FTP server is normally used to transfer files from their origination point to computers around the world.

Users can use FTP either with a simple command-line interface (from an MS-DOS prompt, for instance) or with a program that provides a GUI and a host of added options beyond basic file transfer. Web browsers can also make FTP requests for files. Using FTP, the user (given the appropriate permissions) can also delete, rename, move, and copy files at the server. Accessing an FTP server requires appropriate logon permissions; however, in situations where the public is trying to access the FTP server, logon can be performed anonymously.

NETWORK NEWS TRANSFER PROTOCOL

NNTP (Network News Transfer Protocol) is the principal protocol used by computer clients and servers for managing the discussion postings on Usenet newsgroups. Servers using NNTP manage the worldwide network of Usenet newsgroups. To access the newsgroups stored on these servers, one uses an NNTP client. These are included with most major web browsers, or can be a stand-alone product with additional functionality like Agent or Free Agent. These stand-alone clients are called newsreaders. By default, NNTP uses port 119.

TELNET

Assuming you have the requisite permissions, Telnet can be used to access another individual's computer (called the *host* computer). To be more precise, Telnet is a user command and part of the TCP/IP protocol for accessing remote computers. On the Internet, use of HTTP and FTP allows you to send and receive files for certain remote computers, but you need not actually be logged on to these computers. By using Telnet, when you log on to a host, you will be logged on as a user of that computer. When you log on with Telnet, you do so as a regular user with whatever privileges you have been assigned. For example, Telnet could be used by software developers or anyone who needs to use a certain application or specific data stored on a host computer.

In addition to its use as a tool to access another computer, Telnet is also a very useful troubleshooting tool. Telnet runs on top of TCP/IP, so it establishes a more reliable indication of accessibility than the **Ping** command. Further, Telnet tests higher-level functions of the destination computer. For example, if you're experiencing trouble accessing a multiuser machine, you can Ping it—and you might get a response back. However, the Ping might come back and yet the machine is still inaccessible. This is because the Ping might be responded to by the operating system's kernel. It might accept the TCP connection used by Telnet (also handled by the operating system kernel), but other issues might prevent the login prompt.

Furthermore, Telnet clients allow you to use ports other than the default Telnet port. For instance, you can Telnet to port 25 to ensure that your e-mail server is answering, or port 80 to ensure that your web server is answering.

SIMPLE MAIL TRANSFER PROTOCOL (SMTP)

Simple Mail Transfer Protocol (SMTP) is a TCP/IP protocol used for sending and receiving e-mail. SMTP is normally used in conjunction with one of two other protocols—POP3 or Internet Message Access Protocol (IMAP)—because SMTP has a limited ability to queue messages at the receiving end. When using one of the other protocols, users can save messages in a server mailbox, then download them from the server. In practice, users generally use SMTP when sending e-mail, and POP3 or IMAP to receive messages from their mail server.

To establish this combination of e-mail protocols, most e-mail programs allow you to establish both an SMTP server and a POP server. SMTP generally operates using Transmission Control Protocol (TCP) port 25. In Europe, an alternative to SMTP is called X.400.

SYMPTOMS

When deploying your web solution, you might encounter the following problems.

SYMPTOM 5-12   **There are FTP password errors.**   Because FTP relies on passwords to allow access, you might encounter password errors. The first (and easiest) thing to check is to make sure that the password was entered properly. Make sure the CAPS LOCK key is not on. If this message still appears, make sure you haven't changed your password, or your password hasn't been administratively changed. If you are attempting to log into an anonymous FTP site, it's a good bet that you are not typing the correct information or that anonymous FTP is not—in actuality—being allowed. Contact the site's administrator to find out what's going on.

Passwords are sent in clear (readable) text when using Telnet and FTP, so pick your password carefully.

SYMPTOM 5-13   **There are problems with FTP permissions.**   FTP permissions extend beyond password protection of the site. You might encounter the following error:

```
Server response:filename:Permission denied
```

Even though you had the requisite password to access the site, you might not have the permissions to access a particular file or directory. The similar error message

```
Server file error:filename:Permission denied
```

is generated when you try to do something to a file for which you don't have the appropriate permissions—for instance, if you tried to move, delete, or rename a file. Most FTP sites will allow you to copy a file, but for security (and common sense) reasons, few will allow you to write or alter files. In either of the aforementioned cases, if you are supposed to have access to the file or directory in question, you should contact the FTP site administrator to get the permissions issue straightened out.

SYMPTOM 5-14   **The FTP host is missing.**   When you try to connect to an FTP host, you might get a message that says

```
Error Prompt: Could not find host entry
```

This indicates that the host to which you are trying to connect does not exist. Check to make sure you've entered the hostname correctly. If you have the proper name entered, the next likely explanation is that the site either no longer exists, or has moved.

SYMPTOM 5-15   **The FTP connection is lost.**   After accessing an FTP site, you might receive an error message indicating that the connection was lost. This occurs most often because the FTP program has been sitting idle for too long. You should try to reconnect to the FTP site. Also, it is a good idea to check your FTP program's preferences and change the "on idle, disconnect" (or something like that) setting.

Keep trying to connect. Since you were already able to connect to the FTP server, it is likely that you will be able to reconnect again. Ensure that your computer is not set to disconnect after a period of inactivity and give it another shot.

SYMPTOM 5-16   **The mail delivery system fails.**   In the event that mail delivery fails, sendmail—a prevalent implementation of SMTP—will put the message in a queue and try to deliver it again, later. However, even though a backoff algorithm is used, no mechanism is in place to poll all

Internet hosts for mail. As such, if a host is located behind unreliable connections (like dial-in modems, for instance), SMTP isn't the best choice. A better choice is to configure POP mailboxes and a POP server on the exchange host, then allow all users to be POP-enabled mail clients. Another solution is to organize periodic SMTP mail transfer from the host exchange to another local SMTP exchange host that has been queuing outbound mail.

SYMPTOM 5-17   **There are problems sending and receiving e-mail.**   Generically speaking, one of the first things to check if a user reports problems either sending or receiving e-mail is to ensure that they have the proper incoming and outgoing servers identified in their e-mail program. For instance, incoming mail generally is receivable from a POP3, IMAP, or HTTP server. On the other hand, an SMTP server is used for outgoing mail.

Normally, an organization sets up its e-mail servers with a common naming scheme, save the prefix. For instance, the notional company of Widgetech Inc. would use **pop.widgetech.com** as its incoming message server, but it would use **smtp.widgetech.com** as the outgoing message server. This is a frequently made mistake, but also one that is easy to fix.

SYMPTOM 5-18   **There are problems with port numbers.**   All TCP/IP services (including HTTP, SMTP, Telnet, FTP, and NNTP) access servers using a specific port number. The port number is used to distinguish one TCP/IP service from another. The most commonly used port number for HTTP is port 80, which is the default port number used for web browser access. The default NNTP service port number is 119. If you have problems with port numbers, make sure that your Internet service's port number matches that of the other servers you are connecting to.

SYMPTOM 5-19   **The Telnet system times out.**   If you get a message while using Telnet that says "connection timed out", make sure you are indeed online and connected to the Internet. Try using the destination computer's IP address to connect.

SYMPTOM 5-20   **The Telnet connection fails.**   If, while attempting to connect to another computer using Telnet, you get an error message that the connection has failed, the first thing to check is to ensure you've entered the correct hostname. Make sure that you have entered the name correctly. If it still fails, it is likely that there are problems on the host's end. Try again later.

SYMPTOM 5-21   **I can't connect to a web site.**   This is a very broad problem that can encompass several issues. First, make sure you are connected to the Internet. It's quite possible that you forgot to log on, or sat idle long enough that you were dropped. If you are connected, and you know a web site's IP address, try entering the IP address. If you are able to connect to the web site using an IP address, you know that the problem is with your DNS server.

Further Study

Active Directory: **http://www.microsoft.com/windows2000/technologies/directory/ad/default.asp**
Novell NDS eDirectory: **http://www.novell.com/products/edirectory/**
DHCP: **www.dhcp.org**
WINS:**http://www.microsoft.com/windows2000/techinfo/howitworks/**
communications/nameadrmgmt/wins.asp
DNS: **http://www.ludd.luth.se/~kavli/BIND-FAQ.html**

6

WIRELESS BASICS

In this chapter we will focus our attention on networking without wires. In doing so, we will first obtain an overview of the manner by which different wireless applications operate and how they can be used as a supplement for conventional networking. Once the preceding is accomplished, we will turn our attention to wireless LANs, reviewing the family of IEEE 802.11 standards and basic wireless LAN networking.

Understanding Wireless

Wireless networking actually represents a number of over-the-air technologies—some of which date to the beginning of television broadcasting, while other technologies are based upon recent improvements in chip design. What each wireless technology has in common is the use of predefined frequencies to support their operation. Thus, prior to discussing different wireless applications, we will first focus our attention upon the three related terms of frequency, wavelength, and bandwidth.

FREQUENCY

Frequency is the term used to reference the number of periodic oscillations or waves that occur per unit time. Figure 6-1 illustrates two oscillating sine waves at different frequencies. The top portion of the figure illustrates a sine wave operating at one cycle per second (cps). Note that the term "cycles per second" in general has been replaced by the synonymous term hertz, abbreviated as Hz. The lower portion of Figure 6-1 shows the same sine wave after its oscillating rate is doubled to 2 Hz.

The time required for a signal to be transmitted over a distance of one wavelength is referred to as the "period of the signal." The period represents the duration of a cycle and is also known as the wavelength, which is indicated by the Greek sign lambda (λ). The period or wavelength can be expressed as a function of the frequency. That is, if λ denotes the period of a signal and *f* is its frequency, then

$$\lambda = \frac{1}{f}$$

You can also express the frequency in terms of the period or wavelength of a signal. Doing so gives

$$f = \frac{1}{\lambda}$$

From the preceding, note that the sine wave shown in Figure 6-1 whose signal period is 1s has a frequency of 1/1 or 1 Hz. Similarly, the second sine wave whose period was halved to .5s has a frequency of 1/.5 or 2 Hz. Thus, we can note the relationship between the frequency and the period or wavelength of a signal is an inverse relationship. That is, as the period of a signal decreases, its frequency increases. Similarly, as the wavelength of a signal increases, its frequency decreases.

WAVELENGTH

As previously indicated, the period of an oscillating signal is also known as its *wavelength* (λ). Wavelength in meters can be obtained by dividing the speed of light (approximately 3×10^8 m/s) by the signal's frequency in hertz. That is,

$$\lambda(m) = \frac{3 \times 10^8}{f(Hz)}$$

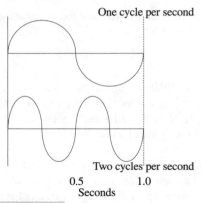

One cycle per second

Two cycles per second

0.5   1.0
Seconds

FIGURE 6-1   Oscillating sine waves at
different frequencies

You can adjust the numerator and denominator of the preceding equation. In doing so, you can adjust the frequency from terms of hertz to kilohertz, megahertz, and gigahertz to determine the wavelength as follows:

$$\lambda(m) = \frac{3 \times 10^8}{f(Hz)} = \frac{3 \times 10^5}{f(KHz)} = \frac{300}{f(MHz)} = \frac{0.3}{f(GHz)}$$

Since the wavelength is expressed in terms of the speed of light divided by the frequency, the frequency also can be defined in terms of the speed of light divided by the wavelength, as shown here:

$$f(Hz) = \frac{3 \times 10^8}{\lambda(m)}$$

Similar to being able to compute the wavelength in terms of varying frequency, you can compute frequency in terms of varying of a wavelength in meters as follows:

$$f(Hz) = \frac{3 \times 10^8}{\lambda(m)}, \ f(KHz) = \frac{3 \times 10^5}{\lambda(m)}$$

$$f(MHz) = \frac{300}{\lambda(m)}, \ f(GHz) = \frac{0.3}{\lambda(m)}$$

For metric computations, you can approximate the wavelength in centimeters as follows:

$$\lambda(cm) = \frac{30}{f(GHz)}$$

For example, assume that a wireless system operates at 5 GHz. Then, its wavelength is approximately 30/5, or 6 cm. For English measurements, you can estimate the wavelength in feet as follows:

$$\lambda(ft) = \frac{1}{f(GHz)}$$

Returning to our previous example, where the frequency is 5 GHz, the wavelength then becomes 1/5 or 0.2 ft. The wavelength of a signal has a significant impact on the length of the antenna required to support a particular wireless application. Most wireless communication antennas are fabricated as a quarter or half wavelength in physical length. This explains why submerged submarines that communicate using very low frequencies unwind a length of wire as an antenna that can be thousands of feet long. In comparison, cellular telephones and wireless LANs that operate in the megahertz and gigahertz portions of the frequency spectrum have a relatively short wavelength. This enables cellular telephones and wireless LAN network adapter cards to be fabricated with relatively short antennas.

BANDWIDTH

Bandwidth represents a measure of the width of a range of frequencies and not the frequencies themselves. For example, if the lowest frequency that can be used in a frequency band is f_1 and the highest is f_2, the bandwidth available is f_2-f_1. While many wireless applications operate at a precise frequency, that frequency is the center frequency around which voice or data is modulated and can change based upon the wireless application. For example, in a cellular telephone environment as a subscriber moves from one cell to another, the frequency used by the cellular telephone can change automatically and transparently to the subscriber. This is because cellular communications support a range of frequencies within each cell that cannot be used in other cells, to avoid interference from communications occurring in adjacent cells. Now that we have an appreciation for frequency, wavelength, and bandwidth, let's turn our attention to obtaining an overview of wireless applications with respect to where they reside in the frequency spectrum.

Applications and Frequency Spectrum

Any discussion of wireless applications requires a brief discussion of national and international organizations responsible for regulating the use of frequency spectrums. Thus, in this section we will briefly examine the role of two U.S. federal government agencies and one international agency.

REGULATORY ORGANIZATIONS

Wireless communications are regulated in most countries by government agencies that are responsible for the use of frequency spectrum. In the United States, the Communications Act of 1934, as revised, resulted in the authority for managing use of the radio-frequency spectrum being partitioned between the U.S. Commerce Department's National Telecommunications and Information Administration (NTIA) and the Federal Communications Commission (FCC). The NTIA administers the frequency spectrum for federal government use. In comparison, the FCC, which is an independent regulatory agency, administers the frequency spectrum for nonfederal government use.

To ensure aircraft can contact ground stations as they pass through different countries and satellites can transmit television signals without encountering or creating interference, the International Telecommunications Union (ITU) functions as a global frequency spectrum usage body. Under the provisions of ITU treaties with most countries, those signatories are obliged to comply with the radio-frequency spectrum allocations specified by the ITU for international use.

Now that we have an appreciation for the fact that the frequencies at which wireless applications operate are regulated, let's turn our attention to examining some common applications and the frequencies allocated for their use.

APPLICATIONS

Table 6-1 lists the frequency bands for 20 common and evolving wireless applications. Of particular concern for this chapter are the cellular, wireless LAN, and fixed wireless frequency bands.

Cellular Bands

Cellular communications in the United States originally occurred in the 806–890-MHz frequency band, which is still used for the initial analog and follow-on time division multiple access (TDMA) cellular systems. More modern cellular telephone systems operate in the 1850–1990-MHz frequency band, which is referred to as the Personal Communications System (PCS) band. Note the PCS band is at a higher frequency than the original cellular telephone band. Because high frequencies attenuate more rapidly than low frequencies, this explains why dual mode cellular telephones that operate in both frequency bands commonly fall back and use an analog frequency. That is, because digital cellular uses higher frequencies than analog, the range of transmission is less. Thus, more cells are required to service a geographic area in the 1850–1990-MHz frequency band than the 806–890-MHz frequency band. While cellular operators provide relatively good digital coverage along interstate highways and within large cities and many suburban areas, when you move into rural areas, communications primarily depend upon the use of older analog base stations. Because it would be very expensive to install a large number of digital base stations to replace analog stations in rural areas, the older analog technology can be expected to continue to be used by dual-band cellular telephones for the foreseeable future.

TABLE 6-1   COMMON AND EVOLVING WIRELESS APPLICATIONS

APPLICATION	FREQUENCY
AM radio	535–1635 KHz
Analog cordless telephone	44–49 MHz
Television	54–88 MHz
FM radio	88–108 MHz
Television	174–216 MHz
Television	470–806 MHz
RF wireless modem	800 MHz
Cellular	806–890 MHz
Digital cordless	900 MHz
ISM band	900–929 MHz
Nationwide paging	929-932 MHz
Satellite telephone uplink	1610–1626.5 MHz
Cellular (PCS)	1850–1990 MHz
ISM band (802.11, 802.11b)	2.4–2.4835 GHz
Satellite telephone downlinks	2.4835–2.5 GHz
Multichannel Multipoint Distribution System	2.5–2.7 GHz
Large disk satellite TV	4–5 GHz
UNII band (802.11a)	5.15–5.35, 5.725–5.825 GHz
Small dish satellite TV	11.7–12.7 GHz
Wireless cable TV/LMDS	28–31 GHz

ISM Bands

Another series of frequency bands that deserves mention are the Industrial, Scientific, and Medical (ISM) bands at 900–929 MHz and 2.4–2.4835 GHz and the Unlicensed National Information Infra-structure (UNII) band at 5.15–5.35 GHz and 5.75–5.825 GHz. These three bands represent unlicensed frequency bands on a near-global basis. Here the term "unlicensed" means that a user of wireless equipment that operates in those bands does not require a license to operate the equipment. However, the equipment must still conform to different national specifications according to the country where it will be used. For example, in the United States the FCC will define the maximum amount of radiated power of the device as well as place constraints on the modulation method used by equipment operating in an unlicensed frequency band.

The first ISM band shown in Table 6-1, from 900–929 MHz, is used by different devices to include many wireless LANs that use proprietary transmission techniques. Because only 29 MHz of bandwidth was available for use, proprietary wireless LANs operating in the 900–929 ISM band tend to be relatively slow, commonly operating at or below 1 Mbps.

The second ISM band shown in Table 6-1 operates in the 2.4–2.4835-GHz frequency band, resulting in 83.5 MHz of bandwidth. This frequency band is used by microwave ovens, certain types of cordless telephones, and (of more interest to readers), two versions of IEEE wireless LANs—technically referred to as 802.11 and 802.11b. The IEEE 802.11 standard for wireless LANs defines a Media Access Control (MAC) method that can be transported by one of three transmission options, each operating at either 1 Mbps or 2 Mbps. The transmission options supported include infrared, frequency hopping spread spectrum (FHSS), and direct sequence spread spectrum (DSSS).

Both FHSS and DSSS represent broadband transmission methods originally developed for military applications as a mechanism to overcome jamming. FHSS results in the use of a pseudorandom sequence of frequencies, with the transmitter hopping from one frequency to another after a short dwell time at a frequency to transmit data. In a wireless LAN environment, each device knows the hopping sequence and the use of a relatively short dwell time ensures that interference occurring at one frequency or even several frequencies has a minimum effect upon overall transmission.

Under DSSS, a spreading code is applied to each data bit such that many bits are transmitted for each data bit. For example, assume the spreading code is 10100. The spreading code is added to each data bit, resulting in five bits being transmitted for each data bit. Thus, if the data bit was a binary 1, this would result in 01011 being transmitted. At the receiver, the same spreading code that was used by the transmitter is used to "despread" or recover the original data bit. That is, if the bit sequence received is 01011 and the spreading code is 10100, adding them results in the sequence 11111. This would indicate that the data bit spread was a binary 1. If an error occurred, the receiver would examine the settings of the five bits and use a majority rules standard to recover the transmitted bit. That is, when a 5-bit spreading code is used, the same value of 3 or more of those despread bits would then represent the despread value. Because DSSS spreads the energy or power of a signal over a large bandwidth, it also represents a mechanism for minimizing interference that can include jamming. The use of infrared results in the transmission of information occurring near visible light. Because this is not considered to represent a radio-frequency signal, there are no regulatory bodies that govern its use. However, due to its limited transmission distance, infrared, while defined under the IEEE 802.11 standard, has yet to be developed by vendors into viable products.

Returning to our discussion of wireless LAN standards, the IEEE 802.11b standard extension defined the use of DSSS at the physical layer to support data rates of 1, 2, 5.5, and 11 Mbps. The third ISM band is referred to as the Unlicensed National Information Infrastructure (UNII) frequency band. This band is currently used by IEEE 802.11a equipment, which defines the use of orthogonal frequency division multiplexing (OFDM) to obtain data transmission rates up to 54 Mbps. Remembering from our physics class that high frequencies attenuate more rapidly than low frequencies, the transmission range of 802.11a-compatible equipment is considerably less than 802.11b products. This means that an organization installing an 802.11a wireless LAN in a building may require significantly more access points than the number of access points required to support a wireless LAN operating in the lower 2.4–2.4835 GHz frequency band.

Fixed Wireless

Two additional frequency bands worth noting on our tour of wireless applications are the 2.5–2.7 GHz band used by Multichannel Multipoint Distribution System (MMDS) applications and the 28–31 GHz frequency band used by Local Multipoint Distribution System (LMDS) applications. Both MMDS and LMDS represent fixed wireless technology developed to provide high-speed broadband communications. MMDS represents a fixed wireless technology that uses the 2.5–2.7 GHz frequency spectrum to provide a data transmission rate up to 10 Mbps. In comparison, LMDS represents a line-of-sight, fixed wireless broadband access technology. The bandwidth allocated to LMDS in the United States is either 150 MHz or 1150 MHz, which is by far the largest allocated to a wireless transmission method.

Under LMDS, it is theoretically possible for a cell to support a data transmission capacity up to 3.5 Gbps. During the late 1990s a considerable investment occurred in MMDS and LMDS technology, with several communications carriers purchasing community television operating licenses from colleges and universities to obtain bandwidth to construct systems. Unfortunately, both technical problems (including echoes from buildings that creates multipath interference) and telecommunications sector financial problems have in effect placed a hold on the potential growth of this technology. Now that we have an appreciation for fixed broadband wireless, we will focus our attention in the remainder of this chapter on wireless LANs, commencing with an overview of the series of IEEE wireless LAN standards.

Wireless LAN Standards

Under the literal IEEE 802.11 umbrella, a number of extensions were added to the basic standard, two of which (802.11b and 802.11a) we briefly mentioned. Table 6-2 provides a summary of the current scope of IEEE standards.

THE BASIC 802.11 STANDARD

As previously mentioned, the 802.11 standard represents the original wireless LAN standard promulgated by the IEEE. This standard specified infrared, FHSS, and DSSS physical layer operations at either 1 Mbps or 2 Mbps. Also included as part of the original IEEE 802.11 standard was a security mechanism in the form of wired equivalent privacy (WEP). WEP was conceived as a mechanism to provide a level of privacy to wireless LAN users equivalent to the level of privacy obtained when transmitting data unencrypted over a wired LAN.

WEP

WEP has several weaknesses that were carried over to the IEEE 802.11b and 802.11a extensions from the basic 802.11 standard. Because security is of prime importance to most organizations, we will focus our attention upon obtaining an appreciation of WEP and its weaknesses prior to discussing other 802.11 standards.

TABLE 6-2   IEEE 802.11 STANDARDS

STANDARD	DESCRIPTION
802.11	Original wireless LAN standard; 1/2 Mbps
802.11b	DSSS extension supporting 1, 2, 5.5, 11 Mbps
802.11a	Operates in 5-GHz band at 6, 9, 12, 18, 24, 36, 48, 54 Mbps
802.11c	Bridging operations
802.11d	Specification for regulatory domains
802.11e	Quality of service (moved to 802.11i in May 2001)
802.11f	Access point interoperability
801.11g	2.4/5-GHz band operations
802.11h	Interference
802.11i	Security features

Wired equivalent privacy represents an encryption method that is applied on a frame-by-frame basis. Under WEP, an initialization vector (IV) that consists of 24 bits is used in conjunction with a secret key configured on each wireless station as a seed to generate a pseudorandom number sequence that is XORed with the plaintext data to create encrypted data. The IV is used to enable each frame to be encrypted independently of preceding and succeeding frames. To enable a receiver to correctly decrypt data, the IV is transmitted in the clear, as illustrated in Figure 6-2. Because each station using WEP is configured with the same secret key, a receiving station concatenates the received IV to its secret key to obtain a seed to generate a pseudorandom number sequence, which is then XORed with the encrypted data to reconstruct plaintext. The integrity check value (ICV) represents a 32-bit cyclic redundancy check (CRC) that permits a receiver to determine if one or more bits are in error in the received frame.

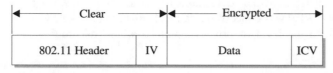

FIGURE 6-2   WEP encryption

Vulnerabilities The pseudorandom generator used by WEP is the RC4 algorithm that is used in many products, ranging from browsers to databases. While RC4 is basically secure in other products, it generates some weak keys that can be used in conjunction with educated guesses about the first byte in the encrypted data to mathematically recover the secret key. Other problems associated with WEP include the fact that, by default, it is disabled, the IV is only 24 bits in length (which means it repeats fairly regularly), and the creation of the ICV represents a linear process. Each of these weaknesses were described over the past few years in various publications that point out that WEP is not secure. Due to the importance of security, we will discuss the insecurity of WEP and current and planned efforts to make it more secure.

Default Setting By default, WEP is disabled on most vendor products. An example of this default setting is shown in Figure 6-3, which illustrates the Encryption tab for the Agere System's Orinoco wireless LAN configuration dialog box for the default profile. Note that the box to the left of the label Enable Data Security is not checked. To enable WEP, a user must first check that box and then enter either alphanumeric or hexadecimal digits for one secret encryption key. The Agere Orinoco configuration dialog box is similar to other products in that it permits up to four encryption keys to be defined; however, only one can be used at a time.

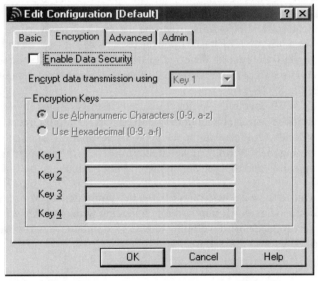

FIGURE 6-3 By default, WEP encryption is disabled on most wireless LAN products.

Because most wireless LAN products disable WEP by default, this fact explains the stories that appeared in the *New York Times*, the *Wall Street Journal*, and other publications during 2001 about the exploits of two men in a van. These two gentlemen were able to travel from parking lot to parking lot in a van in Silicon Valley during 2001 and intercept and understand network transmission. The gentlemen took advantage of the fact that WEP, by default, is disabled. Using a notebook computer and a directional antenna they were able to pick up wireless LAN traffic from over half of the buildings facing various parking lots that they visited.

Other Passive Attacks   Due to the fact that most wireless LAN traffic transports IP packets, it is a relatively easy process to guess the first few bytes transported in each wireless LAN frame. That is, after the beginning of the LAN frame's header, there are certain fields that identify the type of frame being transported. For example, IP is transported in a sub network access protocol (SNAP) frame that is identified by the hex digits AA. Due to the correlation between weak keys generated by the RC4 algorithm used by WEP and the first byte of encrypted data, several researchers discovered methods to recover the secret key used by passively monitoring and collecting between 4,000,000 and 5,000,000 frames of encrypted data. Other researchers claimed to be able to recover the secret key by monitoring between 1,000,000 and 2,000,000 frames, and their work was used by others to place two popular programs on the Internet. Referred to as AirSmart and WEPCrack, both programs permit a third party to passively monitor a wireless LAN and recover the secret key in use. Once the secret key is known, it then becomes relatively easy to use one of several wireless LAN decoding programs that permit a user to enter the secret key in use and decode the data transported in each captured frame.

In addition to publications and programs providing a secret key recovery capability, several papers were written about the weakness of WEP based upon the use of a 24-bit IV. The use of a relatively short IV results in the IV repeating fairly regularly. Referred to as an "IV collision," when this situation occurs the capture of several equal IVs will permit a statistical analysis of encrypted data, which can result in the recovery of the plaintext.

A third weakness of WEP concerns the linear nature of the ICV. This linear relationship enables a "man-in-the-middle" attack in which an unauthorized third party could intercept a frame, flip bits in the encrypted data and ICV fields, and forward the packet to its destination. The receiver would decrypt the packet and after recomputing the ICV find that it matches the ICV in the received field. Thus, it is possible for a third party to change data and that the change would not be detected by the recipient.

Enhancing WEP   Due to the weakness of WEP, the IEEE initiated a task group, Task Group i, under the 802.11 Working Group to develop a standard for enhancing wireless LAN security. This is known as 802.11i. The IEEE also proceeded with developing its 802.1x standard for port-based authentication, both of which will be described later in this section.

Not willing to wait for new standards to plug existing holes in WEP security, several vendors introduced proprietary solutions to overcome WEP vulnerabilities. Most of these proprietary solutions are based on dynamically changing the WEP secret key. Some vendors permit the user to specify the frequency at which the WEP key is changed, while other products do not. However, as long as the frequency of the WEP key change is under every million frames, this should be sufficient to prevent the secret key from being recovered. Now that we have an appreciation for the vulnerability of WEP, let's turn our attention back to the other IEEE extensions to the 802.11 standard.

802.11B

The 802.11b extension to the 802.11 standard is restricted to the use of DSSS at the physical layer. However, the operating rate of equipment was extended from 1 Mbps and 2 Mbps to 5.5 and 11 Mbps. Both the original 802.11 standard and the 802.11b extension operate in the 2.4-GHz frequency band.

802.11A

The 802.11a extension to the 802.11 standard can be considered to represent a high-speed wireless LAN. This extension added data rates of 6, 9, 12, 18, 24, 36, 48, and 54 Mbps; however, only support for 6, 12, and 24 Mbps is mandatory. Unlike the 802.11b extension, equipment that supports the 802.11a extension operates in the 5-GHz frequency band. As we noted earlier in this chapter, because high frequencies attenuate more rapidly than low frequencies, this means the range of 802.11a-compatible equipment is less than wireless LAN products that operate in the 2.4-GHz frequency band.

802.11C

The 802.11c extension to the 802.11 standard defines bridging operations. Because an access point operates as a bridge between a wireless and wired network infrastructure, this extension defines how the access point learns addresses on each infrastructure.

802.11D

The 802.11d extension to the 802.11 standard represents a supplement to the MAC layer to promote worldwide use of 802.11 wireless LANs. The goal of this ongoing effort is to enable access points to operate on acceptable radio channels by adding features to the standard that enable equipment to legally operate in certain countries.

802.11E

The 802.11e extension to the MAC layer represents a developing standard to add a quality of service (QoS) capability to wireless LANs. This QoS capability will enable the transport of voice, data, and video traffic over wireless LANs to be prioritized. In May 2001, this effort was moved to the 802.11i area.

802.11F

The 802.11f extension to the 802.11 standard represents a "recommended practice" being developed to provide multivendor access-point interoperability. This standard will define how access points from multiple vendors can interoperate within a roaming environment and will be available as a flash update for existing equipment by the time you read this book.

802.11G

Because the vast majority of wireless LAN products operate in the 2.4-GHz frequency band, an organization upgrading to a high-speed wireless LAN in the 5-GHz frequency band could not use its investment in access points. The 802.11g standard was developed to provide organizations with both migration options as well as compatibility with older equipment. Equipment supporting the 802.11g standard can operate in the 2.4-GHz band at 11 Mbps or in the 5-GHz band at up to 54 Mbps.

802.11H

In Europe, the 802.11a standard can create interference problems since it shares the 5-GHz band with certain types of radar and satellite communications. The 802.11h specification incorporates transmission power control (TPC) and dynamic frequency selection (DFS) features. TPC enables users close to an access point to reduce their power, while DFS enables devices detecting other signals to switch to an alternative transmission channel.

802.11I

As previously noted, WEP represents a major security weakness of IEEE wireless LANs. The IEEE 802.11i extension represents a set of security features that include the Temporal Key Integrity Protocol (TKIP) and the Advanced Encryption Standard (AES). TKIP represents an interim replacement for WEP that will support legacy client stations and access points through software updates. In comparison, AES will provide a higher level of security, but will more than likely only be available in new hardware. An additional component of the 802.11i extension to the 802.11 standard that warrants discussion is the 802.1x standard. The 802.1x standard defines port-based authentication and provides a method for authenticating clients to access points.

Now that we have an appreciation for the family of IEEE 802.11 wireless standards, let's focus our attention on the structure and operation of 802.11 wireless networks.

Wireless LAN Operations

There are two basic types of wireless LAN devices, referred to as *client stations* and *access points*. Although an access point contains a bridging function to enable frames to flow between a wired and wireless infrastructure, it is also considered to represent a wireless station since it supports radio-frequency communications.

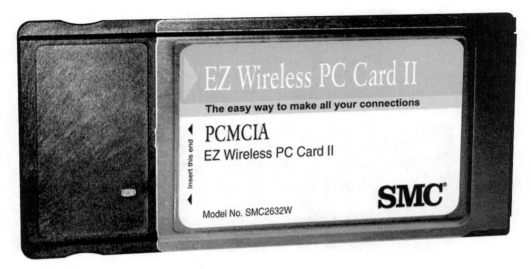

FIGURE 6-4   The SMC PC Card wireless network adapter card (Photograph courtesy of SMC Networks)

OPERATING MODES

IEEE 802.11 wireless LANs operate in one of two modes, referred to as *ad hoc* and *infrastructure*. An ad hoc network represents two or more client stations that communicate directly with one another. In comparison, an infrastructure mode of operation results in all clients communicating with an access point (AP) regardless of the destination of frames. Thus, two clients would communicate with one another through an access point when operating in infrastructure mode.

WIRELESS LAN CLIENT

Figure 6-4 illustrates an example of a wireless LAN adapter card, which with appropriate software turns a laptop or notebook computer into an IEEE 802.11 wireless LAN client. The PC Card shown in Figure 6-4 was manufactured by SMC Networks and includes a built-in antenna encased in plastic on the left portion of the card. That portion of the PC Card will protrude from the PC Card slot when the card is inserted into a laptop or notebook computer.

COMBINED ROUTER/ACCESS POINT

While many vendors manufacture stand-alone access points, some vendors combined the bridging functionality of an access point with basic router and LAN switch features. One such product is the SMC Networks Barricade broadband router that is illustrated in Figure 6-5. This combined wireless access point and router includes three Ethernet 10/100-Mbps LAN switch ports as well as an Ethernet port for connection to a cable or DSL modem. Note the two antennas mounted on the broadband router/access point shown in Figure 6-5. Through the use of two antennas positioned approximately a wavelength apart from

FIGURE 6-5   The SMC Networks Barricade router (Photograph courtesy of SMC Networks)

one another, the device can select the better signal. The use of dual antennas is referred to as *space diversity* and permits better reception of wireless traffic.

THE IBSS AND BSS

When two or more stations communicate directly with one another in an ad hoc mode, the stations form an independent basic service set (IBSS). In an ad hoc mode, stations are limited to communicating with one another as long as they are within transmission range of one another. Figure 6-6 illustrates an example of three client stations in an ad hoc mode forming an independent basic service set. If a client within an ad hoc network requires communications outside of the IBSS, it must change its mode of operation to infrastructure and communicate with an access point.

In an infrastructure mode, each client communicates with an access point (AP). The AP functions as an Ethernet bridge and forwards frames either to another wireless station or onto a wired infrastructure. The access point and clients using the AP form a basic service set. Because the access point in effect functions as a repeater when one station is communicating with another, this permits the range of a BSS to exceed the range of an IBSS. Figure 6-7 illustrates an example of a BSS resulting from a wireless LAN infrastructure type of network.

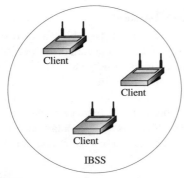

FIGURE 6-6   An example of an ad hoc network
forming an independent basic service
set (IBSS)

THE DISTRIBUTION SYSTEM

In a wireless LAN environment, the coverages of individual basic service sets are linked together through the use of a distribution system (DS). The DS can be formed through the use of a wired LAN interconnecting multiple access points, an intermediate AP functioning as a radio-frequency relay, or another communications system. In fact, under the IEEE 802.11 standard, the formation of the DS is left to the user.

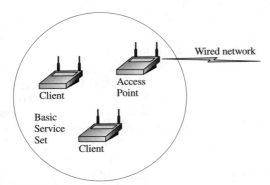

FIGURE 6-7   An example of a basic service set
formed from a wireless infrastructure
network

ASSOCIATION AND AUTHENTICATION

Prior to a station being able to communicate with an access point, it must establish a relationship with the AP. The relationship represents a two-step process that involves three states. In the initial state, a station is not authenticated and not associated with any access point. In a second state, the first step, the station authenticates itself to an access point but remains unassociated. In the third and final state, the second step, the station becomes both authenticated and associated with an access point. Stations transition between these three states by exchanging messages with the access point, in the form of management frames. To appreciate how the authentication and association process occurs, as well as obtain an understanding of another wireless LAN security issue, we will examine how a station discovers and authenticates itself with an access point.

Beacons and the SSID

All access points transmit a beacon management frame at fixed intervals. The beacon frame identifies the access point by incorporating its network name. The network name is technically referred to as a Service Set Identifier (SSID). The SSID is set when the AP is configured, or on some access points, by default, the AP either uses a well-known name such as "wireless" or uses the MAC address burnt into read-only memory (ROM).

A client station will listen for beacon frames as a mechanism to identify access points within range. The client will then select the BSS to join based on the network name configured for its use. Thus, the network name or SSID is viewed by some persons as a network password. Unfortunately, the SSID represents a very poor password for several reasons. First, the SSID within a beacon frame is transmitted in the clear and can be easily discovered by an unauthorized third party. Secondly, you can surf to many Web sites and obtain the manual for different vendor access points, which will indicate the default SSID or network name used by each access point. Third, and perhaps most important for many unauthorized third-party persons who wish to attempt to join an access point, there are two client configuration settings that can usually be used to override the SSID setting used by an AP. The two configuration settings are "any" and a blank. The purpose of using "any" or a blank is to allow a client station to obtain a list of SSIDs or network names from access points within range of the client. The client operator can then select the AP that they wish to communicate with.

Figure 6-8 illustrates the use of the Agere Systems Orinoco Client Manager utility program supporting an Orinoco wireless LAN PC Card accessing an SMC Networks Barricade broadband router/access point. To connect to the SMC Networks access point, this author configured the network name on the Orinoco client to "any". This action enabled a radio connection to the SMC Networks access point that used an SSID in the form of a MAC address. If you carefully examine Figure 6-8, you will note inside the block labeled Status that the access point name is shown as 00-90-4B-08-50-AB. This represents the MAC address of the SMC Networks Barricade router and is the default network name used by that device.

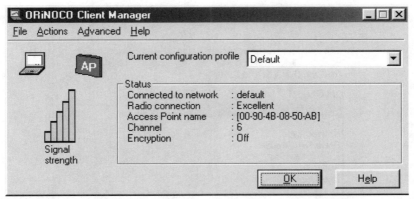

FIGURE 6-8   Using the Orinoco Client Manager to access an SMC Networks access point that uses its MAC address as its network name

Authentication Methods

Once a client station and access point are set to either the same or equivalent network names, both devices will exchange several management frames to mutually authenticate one another. Under the IEEE 802.11 standard, two methods of authentication are supported: *open system* and *shared key*. Open system represents the default authentication method. As its name implies, open system authentication enables anyone that requests authentication to be authenticated. Thus, open system authentication can be viewed as providing a null authentication process.

The second method of authentication is referred to as shared key authentication. This method of authentication is based on the use of the WEP secret key that is configured on the client and access point and is used with the IV to generate a pseudorandom sequence used for encrypting data.

Figure 6-9 illustrates the configuration of an SMC Networks client to use a shared key authentication. When configured in this manner, the station, which becomes the initiator, will transmit an authentication request management frame that indicates that it wishes to use shared key authentication. The recipient of the authentication request, which in this example would be the access point, responds to the client by transmitting an authentication management frame. This frame contains 128 bytes of challenge text generated by the use of the WEP pseudorandom number generator formed from the use of the shared secret key and a randomly selected IV. Upon receipt of the challenge text contained in the management frame, the initiator decrypts the text and uses its shared key and a new randomly selected IV to encrypt it within a new frame. The encrypted management frame is then transmitted to the responder. The responder decrypts the received frame and verifies that the ICV is correct and that the decrypted challenge text matches the 128 bytes transmitted in its original challenge. Assuming the preceding holds true, the authentication process is considered successful. When this situation occurs, the initiator and responder switch roles and the previously described process is repeated to ensure mutual authentication is in effect.

Now that we have an appreciation for client side access to an access point, let's turn our attention to the physical and logical configuration of access points.

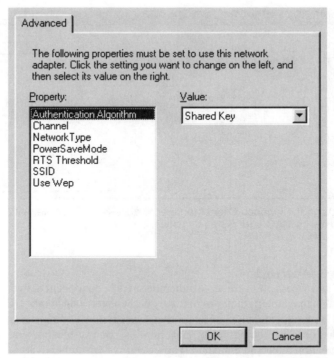

FIGURE 6-9   Using the SMC Networks client configuration dialog box to set authentication to shared key

CONFIGURING AN ACCESS POINT

From a physical perspective, a typical access point is normally cabled to a wired infrastructure to provide a link between wireless and wired stations. The access point functions as a MAC bridge, operating by flooding, forwarding, and filtering frames in a manner similar to an Ethernet wired bridge.

Access points that include a routing capability normally support the Dynamic Host Configuration Protocol (DHCP) and Network Address Translation (NAT). DHCP permits the access point to dynamically assign or lease IP addresses to clients that are authenticated and associated with an access point. Because wireless LAN clients represent stations on a private internal network, it would be a waste of scarce IP addresses to configure each client with a publicly recognizable IP address. Instead, most access points support the use of RFC 1918 addresses. As a refresher, RFC 1918 (titled "Address Allocation for Private Internets") defines three blocks of IP address space for use by private intranets. Those address blocks are

10.0.0.0–10.255.255.255 (10/8 prefix)
172.16.0.0–172.31.255.255 (172.16/12 prefix)
192.168.0.0–192.168.255.255 (192.168/16 prefix)

Note that the first block represents a single class A network number, while the second block represents a set of 16 contiguous class B network numbers. In comparison, the third block represents a set of 256 contiguous class C network numbers.

Duplicate IP addresses would occur if two or more organizations connected private networks using RFC 1918 addresses to the Internet. This would create a routing nightmare and results in the inability to directly use stations configured with RFC 1918 addresses on the Internet. Instead, an intermediate device must be used to perform network address translation. That intermediate device in the world of wireless LAN communications is normally a combined router and access point, such as the SMC Networks Barricade broadband router previously illustrated in Figure 6-5.

Most combined router and access points perform network address translation by translating RFC 1918 addresses assigned to clients via DHCP to a single IP address. To accomplish this while enabling multiple stations to simultaneously access the Internet, the NAT process creates a table of RFC 1918 addresses that are mapped into high port numbers. Sometimes this is also referred to as port address translation (PAT). This action creates a translation table that enables multiple client stations to use one public IP address since one client's RFC 1918 address can be distinguished from another's by the port number used in the mapping process.

Figure 6-10 illustrates the main menu of the Configuration screen of the SMC Networks Barricade wireless broadband router. By examining this screen and a few additional screens associated with this product, we can obtain an appreciation of the settings required to configure access points as well as combined router access points.

In examining the left portion of Figure 6-10, you will note the entry box for a system password. Directly below that box the screen informs the user configuring the device that its default is "admin". SMC Networks, like other vendors, ships its products with default settings that should be changed immediately when the device is placed into a production environment. Otherwise, failing to change the system password can represent a glaring security problem. This problem results from the fact that an access point periodically broadcasts beacon frames that identify the device. With a little bit of effort, such as by searching an online manual or performing a series of Pings, it becomes possible to note the RFC 1918 address used by the private network portion of the router access point. If you examine the address portion of the browser shown in Figure 6-10, you will note that SMC Networks Barricade wireless broadband routers, by default, are configured using the IP RFC 1918 address of 192.168.123.254. Thus, any third party that points their browser to that address would be able to log into the configuration screen if the default system password was not changed.

Once you successfully log into the configuration screen, you obtain a series of configuration options. Figure 6-11 illustrates an example of one of several Barricade wireless broadband router configuration screens as well as the list of options that are available for user selections. Those options available for user selection are shown on the left side of Figure 6-11, with the Primary Setup option shown selected (which results in the display of the window labeled Choose WAN Type). This is shown in the right portion of the referenced illustration. In this configuration screen, you would select one of four options to configure the combined router/access point for connection to a wide area network. Because this author was using a cable modem Internet connection for which his Internet service provider assigns a dynamic IP address, the second option was selected.

In addition to configuring the WAN connection, the SMC Networks series of configuration screens has several security-related configuration tools scattered among different screens. When using this combined router/access point, you can enable WEP using either a 64-bit or 128-bit secret key, and also hide the FTP port if you desire. You can also use an access control configuration screen to filter packets

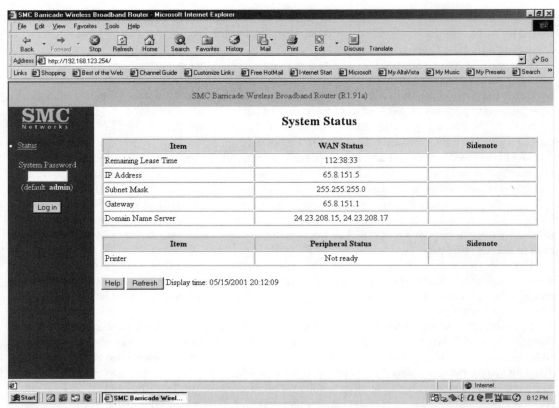

FIGURE 6-10   To log onto the SMC Networks Barricade broadband router, you must enter a system password.

received from the Internet based on several parameters, such as their IP address and port number, in a manner similar to a Cisco router access list. Concerning FTP port hiding, the SMC Networks Barricade wireless broadband router enables a user to configure a different port number than port 21 for FTP access from the Internet. While not truly a security mechanism, it hides an FTP server from casual observance.

Due to the fact that programs such as AirSmart and WEPCrack can discover the secret key by passively recording four to five million frames, several vendors now support dynamic WEP key changes. One example of this capability is obtained from the use of Cisco Aironet wireless access points. You can either accept a default period at which WEP keys are changed or configure Cisco access points to dynamically change the secret key after a predefined period of time.

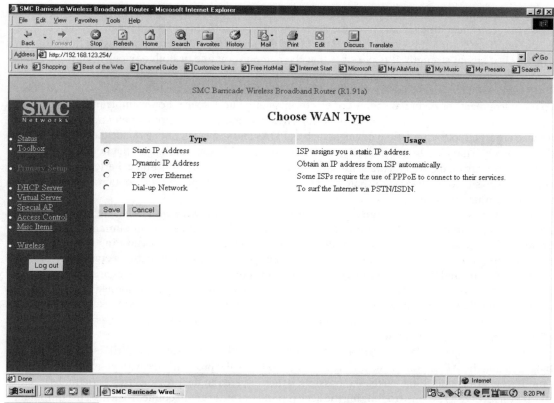

FIGURE 6-11 Selecting the WAN connection for an SMC Networks Barricade broadband router

Troubleshooting

In concluding our discussion of wireless LAN operations, we will turn our attention to a series of techniques you can consider using when your wireless LAN clients appear to receive a signal from an access point but are unable to communicate with one another. If you are using the configuration utility program that is bundled with most client wireless LAN network adapter cards, you will note a signal strength indicator. That indicator may be in the form of a horizontal or vertical bar or series of bars, or may simply indicate a received signal in terms of "excellent," "good," "poor," and "none," or another series of English words. An example of the signal strength in the form of vertical bars was previously illustrated in Figure 6-8.

It is important to note that if you observe a high level of signal strength, this only means that the client station can "hear" the signals from the access point. By itself, this does not mean that the client and access point are compatibly configured. If the client does not display any received signal indication or a low level of signal strength, it is possible that the antennas on one or both devices need to be repositioned.

Check the placement of the AP and the client. If you fail to obtain signal continuity, you should check your environment for potential sources of electromagnetic interference. For example, microwave ovens and newer cordless telephones operate in the 2.4-GHz frequency band. Another potential source of interference are Bluetooth-compatible devices, such as PDAs and some cell phones since they also operate in the frequency band used by the 802.11 standard and the 802.11b extension. Last but not least, make sure that the firmware on the AP and the firmware/software on the client are up-to-date. Periodically check the vendor's web site for updates to the hardware you are using. These updates will contain bug fixes and can also incorporate new features.

Once you determine you have signal continuity between a wireless LAN client and an access point, the next step in troubleshooting is to determine if you have a communications capability between the two devices. To test communications between devices, you can Ping the access point from the client. If you receive a response to the Ping, you have communications continuity between the client station and the access point. In addition, this indicates that both devices are configured correctly in order to receive the response to the Ping. If you do not receive a response to the Ping, it is highly likely that the equipment configurations of the client and access point are not compatible. Thus, you should check the WEP enabled/disabled setting on each device as well as the composition of the secret key on each device.

One quick way to isolate a WEP problem if your Ping fails is to ensure that WEP is disabled on both the client and the AP. If you can now Ping the AP, you know the problem was with your WEP configuration. If you still cannot Ping, check for possible issues covered in the previous two paragraphs.

If you receive a response to Pinging the access point but still cannot connect to a distant computer on the Internet or an organization's wired LAN connected to the AP, the problem more than likely resides in the configuration of the access point's WAN connection. In this situation, you should carefully examine the configuration used for DHCP and NAT to ensure IP addresses are correctly assigned to devices and translated to the correct IP address used for your Internet connection or for the interface to a wired network. By carefully following the previously mentioned steps you should be able to isolate and resolve configuration problems, which contribute to the vast majority of wireless LAN communications problems.

Further Study

Agere Systems Orinoco wireless products: **www.orinocowireless.com/**
Cisco Systems: **www.cisco.com/**
Linksys: **www.linksys.com/**
Netgear wireless products: **www.netgear.com/**
SMC Networks: **www.smc.com**
Institute of Electrical and Electronics Engineers: **www.ieee.org**
Wireless Ethernet Compatibility Alliance: **www.wi-fi.org/**

7

INTRODUCTION TO WAN TECHNOLOGY

The wide area network (WAN) is used to interconnect geographically remote sites. It usually entails the leasing of equipment from a third party, namely a telecommunications service provider or "carrier." The WAN is the single biggest contributor to a corporate network's cost of ownership. Therefore, this is the area where the cost vs. performance trade-off is most pronounced and most critical.

This chapter describes the three fundamental categories of WAN technology: synchronous serial lines, packet-switched technology, and circuit-switched technology. The main technologies that make up these categories will be discussed and analyzed from a design, implementation, and support viewpoint. In this chapter the design issues encountered with the different major WAN technologies will be examined. The driving forces that influence the choice of WAN technology will also be studied.

Wide area network technology is traditionally segregated into three fundamental categories. Synchronous serial or point-to-point leased lines will first be addressed from a network design perspective. The second category to be studied is packet-switched WAN technology. Frame relay, X.25, and ATM can all be loosely described as packet-switched technologies. Frame relay has largely superseded and is replacing X.25, and so the latter technology will not be dealt with in this chapter since it is very unlikely that a new network would be designed around X.25. ATM technically can be described as cell relay, because it switches fixed-length cells rather than variable-length frames. It is nonetheless categorized with frame relay. The motivations for deploying ATM will be addressed, along with the main design issues associated with its implementation. The third category is dial-up WAN or circuit-switched WAN. This will be covered in the form of ISDN. The specific design challenges that relate to the different applications of ISDN will be studied in this chapter.

Synchronous Serial Lines

A serial line can be leased from the telecom service provider to directly connect two sites together. This is illustrated schematically next, where a 256-Kbps leased line connects an office in New York to an office in Chicago.

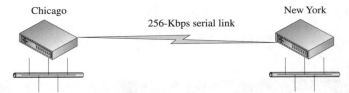

This facilitates communication between the local area networks in each of these offices. For example, clients machines in New York could log on to servers in Chicago by having the appropriate traffic directed over the leased line. Of course, the same could be true of users in Chicago.

In terms of physical connectivity, the leased line connects to the carrier's network via a CSU/DSU (channel subscriber unit/data subscriber unit). This device terminates the leased line on the customer's premises. In the United States, the customer usually purchases the CSU/DSU. However, in other parts of the world it is owned and managed by the carrier. Thus, the demarcation point where the responsibility passes from customer to carrier can vary.

Each end of the link is synchronized from a single clocking source within the public carrier's network. The rate or speed of this clocking is equal to the bandwidth that was purchased. For example a 64-Kbps link is clocked at 64 Kbps. The CSU/DSU acts as the data communications equipment (DCE) and one of its primary functions is to replicate the clocking received from the public network. The CSU/DSU usually connects to a router via a V.35 or X.21 cable. A bridge could also be used to provide an interface between the LAN and the WAN; however, routers have superseded bridges, for reasons discussed in Chapter 14. The router could be connected to the CSU/DSU using an EIA/TIA-232 cable, but this would limit the speed to 115.2 Kbps. The router is the device that is accessing the WAN service, and it is termed the data terminal equipment (DTE).

The serial line speeds have 64 Kbps as their fundamental building block and this has its origins in voice telephony. The audio spectrum for the human voice is 300 Hz to 3.4 kHz. The bandwidth of this spectrum is thus approximately 4 kHz. This is analog voice. When transmitting analog voice over digital circuits, the analog waveform must be sampled and then approximated as a digital bit stream. The Nyquist theorem states that when sampling an analog wave, the digital sampling rate must be at least twice the highest frequency in the waveform. This means that a voice waveform should be sampled at 8 kHz. Each sample is encoded using 8 bits, resulting in an analog voice signal having a corresponding digital bit rate of 64 Kbps.

A single digital channel is therefore 64 Kbps. In the United States, the speed of a single digital channel is often 56 Kbps. This is true when the "robbed bit" signaling technique is employed, which entails the use of one in every eight bits for signaling purposes.

The bandwidth of a serial link can be raised in increments of $n \times 64K$ up to 2 Mbps, which constitutes 30 channels. The backbone speeds of the carrier's network correspond to the Plesiochronous Digital Hierarchy (PDH). Four 2-Mbps circuits are multiplexed into 8 Mbps. The 8-Mbps circuits are multiplexed ($\times 4$) to produce 34-Mbps circuits. Similarly, the next order of circuits are 140 Mbps. The values do not exactly correspond to four times the lower order rate since the actual bit rates are not exactly equal to the rates quoted here. This is due to the fact that some bandwidth must be used for framing, signaling, and management overhead. In the U.S., the PDH hierarchy is slightly different as 56 Kbps is used as the fundamental building block. The following table summarizes the PDH bandwidth values for both the U.S. and Europe, thus representing the two different traditional approaches to digital multiplexing.

EUROPE (BPS)	UNITED STATES (BPS)
64K	56K (DS-0)
2M (E-1)	1.54M (T-1)
8M	
34M (E-3)	45M (T-3)
140M	

A customer can purchase a link at any of these speeds. However, the higher speeds are only likely to be used by customers with very high bandwidth requirements and budgets to match.

The high end of the Plesiochronous Digital Hierarchy (PDH) is giving way to the Synchronous Digital Hierarchy (SDH), or the Synchronous Optical Network (SONET) as it is called in the U.S. This is a high-speed optically based transmission technology intended for the backbone networks of telecommunications service providers. Its basic building block is 155 Mbps, which is termed an STM-1 (Synchronous Transmission Module). An STM-4 corresponds to 622 Mbps. SDH or SONET is a significant advancement on PDH due to increased efficiency in how the multiplexing and demultiplexing is performed, and also its improved manageability.

The higher-order layers of the digital multiplexing hierarchy, however, are not of a direct concern to the small to medium enterprise customer.

Clear channel leased lines are the simplest and most traditional method of interconnecting geographically dispersed sites, but it is also the most expensive method. The main advantage of synchronous leased lines relates to their technological simplicity. This means that less expertise is required to install and troubleshoot the technology, which can ultimately reduce support costs. Point-to-point serial links are also characterized by minimal overhead, thus increasing the effective throughput and eliminating extra contributors to delay and jitter (that is, the variation in delay). Serial links of sufficient bandwidth have the potential to exhibit excellent quality of service (QoS) characteristics. The main contributors to delay and jitter on a serial link are the queuing and packet serialization procedures at the router. Serialization delay can be experienced when a small packet is waiting for a large packet to be sent over the link. This type of delay is more likely on low-speed links. Bandwidth budgets, however, always have a ceiling and there are more cost-effective methods of reducing delay and jitter on serial links. Sophisticated queuing technologies fragment large packets and give higher priority to small packets, thus ensuring a more uniform delay profile on the serial link. This is particularly important for delay-sensitive real-time applications such as packetized voice, video, and multimedia.

The ultimate disadvantage of serial leased lines is cost, so much so that many sections of the industry now regard them as an inefficient use of expensive bandwidth. This has fueled a migration from serial leased line technology to packet-switched technology like frame relay or ATM cell-relay for higher bandwidth requirements.

Synchronous serial links or leased lines are the most traditional of the WAN technologies in wide-spread deployment on modern networks. While it is the simplest type of WAN technology, the following issues should be taken into consideration when deploying serial links on your network:

■ The use of serial leased lines is often the most expensive type of WAN bandwidth. For leased lines to be cost-effective, they should be exhibiting over a minimum of 50-percent bandwidth utilization because the subscriber is being charged for the purchased speed of the link independent of utilization levels. When deciding on an appropriate leased line speed, existing traffic levels should be allowed for with some room being left for growth.

■ Leased lines are less flexible than other WAN technologies in terms of modifying the available bandwidth. Technologies such as frame relay and ATM allow for the purchase of a flexible bandwidth profile that can usually be adjusted with ease. This flexibility is not necessarily true of leased lines. Therefore, a good degree of capacity planning should be done prior to purchasing a serial line.

■ Synchronous serial lines have the advantage of producing less overhead than packet-switched technologies like frame relay or ATM.

The choices of data link layer (layer 2) protocol on serial lines are as follows:

■ **HDLC**   This is a derivative of IBM's SDLC, which was developed to support a single protocol, namely SNA. HDLC was never fully standardized in its support of multiple protocols, and for this reason is a proprietary protocol. Most major networking vendors have their own implementation of HDLC. The upshot of all of this is that HDLC cannot be used on a serial link that connects two routers from different vendors.
The advantages of HDLC are simplicity of operation and configuration. It also entails minimal overhead. These advantages are not to be underestimated, and they mean that HDLC can be an adequate layer 2 serial link protocol in a single router-vendor environment.

■ **Point-to-Point Protocol (PPP)**   PPP is a sophisticated data link layer WAN protocol that can be applied to serial links or ISDN. It will be discussed in more detail in the upcoming section on ISDN. While it is more complex than HDLC, the only major additional features that it provides are that it is a standard (and that could be important) and also the support of CHAP authentication.
Authentication might not be as critical on a serial link as on an open network like ISDN. Nevertheless, it is good practice as part of your security policy.

■ **SLIP**   Don't even think about it! It has been superseded by PPP.

Redundancy on serial links can also be expensive if serial lines are used to back up other serial lines—particularly if it is required that there be no possibility of degraded service in the event of a link failure. Potentially more cost-effective solutions include the following:

■ Purchasing two serial lines that together support the total WAN utilization from a site. These links can then be configured to operate in load-balancing mode. If one link fails, the network may exhibit degraded service due to congestion. This is the classic trade-off of cost vs. performance.

■ Using an alternate technology such as ISDN to restore network connectivity in the event of a serial line failure. ISDN can also be used to back up the serial lines if a certain traffic load is exceeded. This is sometimes termed "bandwidth top-up."

- Implementing compression on serial links. This is often worthwhile—compression algorithms improve throughput across those expensive serial links. The relative improvement in throughput is dependent on the exact type of compression being used and on the protocol to which it is applied. While the advantage of compression is obvious, it does have a couple of potential drawbacks:

  - Compression can be CPU- and memory-intensive for the device that implements it. Compression algorithms use the principle of buffering a certain amount of data and examining it for repeated patterns in order to compress the data. Some compression techniques such as Stacker compression use a very sophisticated algorithm to compress the data. This has the advantage of incurring less memory overhead, as less data has to be buffered. The downside is that because of its complexity, Stacker compression can be very CPU-intensive. Predictor compression is a slightly simpler algorithm that is therefore less processor-intensive. However it must buffer a lot of data before resolving repeated patterns and hence is more memory-intensive than Stacker compression.

  - Compression usually increases latency, which can add up if compression is implemented over multiple serial links between the source and destination. This can also cause a problem for very time-sensitive applications such as SNA or LAT.
    For these reasons, compression should only be used on slower WAN links from 56K up to a maximum of 128K.

There are a number of options to be considered when employing compression. It can be implemented through software running on the router. Alternatively, it can be implemented using hardware that is either integrated or external to the router. The choice here is made against the parameters of cost and performance, which of course vary with the different vendors.

When evaluating compression performance, the different types of compression must be considered against the type of applications and traffic on the network. Most vendors of compression hardware or software support the following types of compression:

- **Full data compression**   This is sometimes called link compression because it compresses all data that crosses the link, both header and payload. Different vendors at either the hardware level or software level support this type of compression. This type of compression is appropriate on point-to-point serial lines. The percentage improvement varies depending of the compression product and the nature of the traffic being compressed.

- **Header compression**   This type of compression is often implemented within the router software and is applicable to traffic that is mainly composed of header—for example, Telnet, LAT, or Xremote sessions. In the case of Telnet, there is a 20-byte TCP header and a 20-byte IP header with just 1 byte of payload. Header compression can be very CPU-intensive since it is more difficult to only compress the header.

- **Payload compression**   This is also CPU-intensive due to the complexity of only compressing the payload. Payload compression can be appropriate for packet-switched media link frame relay or ATM, because the data link header must remain intact when traversing these media. In other words, the DLCI or ATM VPI/VCI cannot be manipulated through compression when crossing a public network. It is also cost-effective due to the more efficient use of bandwidth. For example, multiple small IP packets could be in the same frame relay packet and become the compressed payload. Note that payload compression is not only CPU-intensive, it also increases latency. It should generally not be used if most of the data is traversing a path that consists of more than three router hops. This is, of course, just a rule of thumb, and it is also dependent on how delay-sensitive the traffic is.

PPP AND MULTILINK PPP

The Point-to-Point Protocol is a layer 2 protocol derived from HDLC that can run over any DTE/DCE interface. It supports multiple layer 3 protocols and can support both synchronous and asynchronous transmission. The basic properties of PPP have made it ideally suited for ISDN networks as well as serial links.

PPP has a layer 2 Link Control Protocol (LCP) component, which negotiates link layer establishment, management, and link termination. PPP also supports a family of Network Control Protocols (NCP) that negotiate the support of most of the more common layer 3 desktop protocols, including IP, IPX, DECNET, and AppleTalk.

The main LCP parameters to be negotiated are error detection tests, authentication, compression, and Multilink PPP.

Authentication

The most popular type of authentication used across PPP link is Challenged Handshake Authentication Protocol (CHAP). Other security protocols, such as the more sophisticated TACACS or the simpler Password Authentication Protocol (PAP), are also supported. The advantage that CHAP offers over PAP is that the password is encrypted with CHAP and therefore cannot be detected by a network analyzer. If a password is not encrypted, it is not secure, which makes CHAP the ubiquitous choice of PPP authentication protocol. A further advantage of CHAP is that it is no more difficult to configure or manage than PAP.

Error Detection

Upon link establishment, PPP will send a "magic number" onto the link. This is simply a unique bit stream. If it detects the receipt of this exact bit stream at the same end of the link (that is, back at the point from where it was sent), PPP will conclude that there is a loop on the circuit. This test is often presented as a further example of PPP's sophistication, but it is certainly not the only WAN data link protocol with the capability of loop detection.

Compression

STAC or Predictor compression can be configured for PPP. The throughput improvement can vary depending on the desktop protocol being transported. For example, IP would usually show a slightly higher compression ratio than IPX. When configuring compression, as with authentication, it is important to ensure that the configuration is consistent at both ends of the link. This may sound trite, but these are the simple errors that cause far too many problems in practice.

Multilink PPP

A recent enhancement to PPP is Multilink PPP or MPPP. In the case of traditional PPP over ISDN, there have been problems obtaining an efficient utilization of the two B channels simultaneously. The router can be configured to bring up the second B channel either when an ISDN call is made or when a certain load threshold has been exceeded.

Traffic will normally just propagate across the first channel until the second channel is actually needed to support the throughput. This is often demonstrated by the fact that the second channel sometimes drops on an ISDN call as its idle timer expires, while the first channel remains up.

When the bandwidth requirements increase, the second channel gets utilized. Packets can get randomly sent out on either channel. There is, however, no guarantee that traffic across both channels will take an identical path through the public ISDN network; thus, there is no guarantee that both channels will experience equal delay while getting to the destination. Hence, there is a high probability of packets arriving out of sequence at the destination router. This can cause problems with unreliable protocols or extremely time-sensitive protocols. Even with reliable protocols, a very high number of retransmissions can nullify the effect of using both channels. For example, I have seen instances with TCP-based applications where a high percentage of TCP retransmissions meant that the throughput was not significantly greater with two channels than with one.

The solution to this problem is Multilink PPP. With this enhancement, a sequencing feature has been added that ensures that data is reassembled in the correct order at layer 2, thus eliminating the need for higher-layer retransmissions. MPPP is negotiated during the LCP setup stage and both ends of the link must be configured to support it. The sequencing capability of MPPP allows it to view the two B channels as a logically aggregated link.

Conclusion on PPP

The Point-to-Point Protocol is suitable for serial links that employ different router vendors at each end of the link. For example, your network might standardize on Cisco router, but PPP would have to be used on a serial connection to a business partner that uses Nortel routers on their own network. PPP is a standard, unlike HDLC, and this makes it ideal for mixed-vendor environments.

The loop detection feature and the support of Stacker and Predictor compression are also features of HDLC. The authentication and multilink features are, however, distinct to PPP. Multilink PPP is useful for ISDN, as we shall see later in this chapter. The support of CHAP authentication is another reason why PPP is used for ISDN calls. ISDN is very much a wide open network, and anyone with ISDN in the home is a potential hacker on your corporate network. PPP authentication can also be employed on serial links, but it is less critical.

Packet-Switched Technology

Packet switching is one of the three fundamental categories of WAN technology. The different sites on the enterprise network are interconnected using the public carrier's packet-switched network. Consider two sites shown here:

Traffic going from site A to site B exits the local router at site A and enters the public packet-switched network (which is likely to belong to the telecom carrier). The carrier does not provide a dedicated end-to-end physical connection between the two sites, as would be the case with a direct serial link. Instead, it ensures that its network switches the traffic received from site A so that it ends up exiting the packet-switched network at site B. The traffic is switched on a per-packet basis across a shared public network. Traffic exiting the router shown at site A always terminates at site B so, to some extent, from the customer's perspective it appears like a serial link in terms of traffic flow. However, there are a number of fundamental differences. This type of connection is called a *permanent circuit* since the two endpoints are fixed. But since there is no dedicated physical connection along the entire path, it is termed a *permanent virtual circuit (PVC)*.

The use of PVCs rather than dedicated physical connections is a more cost-effective method for the carrier to provide bandwidth, and this cost saving is passed on to the customer. If you, as a customer, are not using the bandwidth on your PVC, the carrier can give that bandwidth to another customer at that particular instant. The procedure of dynamically allocating bandwidth where it is required is termed *statistical multiplexing* and is performed by the telecom carrier.

While packet-switched technology offers a cost saving over direct serial links, it does not provide the same level of end-to-end bandwidth guarantee since the customer is essentially accessing a shared network. Packet-switched technology does not always provide the same quality of service as serial links. However, given the cost of WAN technology services, this is a trade-off that many customers consider worthwhile.

X.25

X.25 is the oldest type of packet-switching technology and is steadily being replaced by newer technology—in particular, frame relay. This packet-switching technology was designed in an era when WAN links were still relatively unreliable. For this reason, X.25 employs many error-checking features that in most of today's networks only serve to produce unnecessary overhead due to the inherent high reliability of modern WAN circuits. X.25 still warrants some attention, because the robust nature of the protocol has served many clients well and there is a resulting inertia to change. However, because it is a technology whose days are ultimately numbered, it will be treated in less detail than frame relay later in this chapter.

The code example that follows refers to this illustration and shows a simple and typical example of IP over X.25:

The configuration, as it would appear on a Cisco router, is also included for both routers. X.25 is enabled on the router interface using the **encapsulation x25** command. This is the same type of serial interface that could be used to a direct synchronous serial link. Hence, there is no difference in physical presentation. The X.25 network is accessed via a local CSU/DSU. Another point to note is that X.25 is a nonbroadcast medium; therefore, the **broadcast** keyword is required to enable the forwarding of broadcasts such as routing updates.

```
r6#
interface Serial1
ip address 172.16.1.6 255.255.255.0
encapsulation x25
x25 address 20145522
x25 map ip 172.16.1.3 30255533 broadcast
!
```

```
r3#
interface Serial0
 ip address 172.16.1.3 255.255.255.0
 encapsulation x25
 x25 address 30255533
 x25 map ip 172.16.1.6 20145522 broadcast
```

X.25 virtual circuits are identified using X.121 addresses. These addresses are globally significant and are to some extent analogous to telephone numbers. Each device accessing the X.25 network is allocated an X.121 address.

In this example, IP is being run over the X.25 network. This simply means that X.25 virtual circuits are carrying IP network layer traffic. If users on R6's LAN need to access resources on R3's LAN, the R6 router must be programmed to send this traffic to 172.16.1.6, which is the IP address of R3's X.25 interface. However, an additional step is also required. R6 must be "told" what X.121 address corresponds to this IP address since ultimately the traffic must be sent over an X.25 PVC. This is the purpose of the

```
x25 map ip 172.16.1.3 30255533 broadcast
```

statement on R3. The R6 router has a similar mapping statement to resolve R3's IP address to its X.25 address.

Another point to note is that X.25 is a nonbroadcast medium. Therefore, the **broadcast** keyword is required to enable the forwarding of broadcasts such as routing updates.

FRAME RELAY

Frame relay is a packet-switched WAN technology that is still growing in its deployment. There is a trend whereby it is replacing older legacy technologies such as X.25 and point-to-point serial links. The design of the frame relay protocol exploits the improved reliability of modern WAN circuits. The protocol itself employs no error checking, unlike X.25. It delegates error detection and correction procedures to the higher layers of the communications stack. Frame relay does include congestion control in the form of congestion notification messages.

One of the other motivating factors for moving to frame relay is the ability to tailor the purchased bandwidth to the utilization profiles of the applications running on the network. Thus, frame relay provides the potential for a more efficient and cost-effective use of the often expensive WAN bandwidth. Full or partial meshing of the permanent virtual circuits (PVCs) can be employed for network redundancy.

One of reasons frame relay is a popular choice for the core WAN technology is its ability to provide resilience using PVC meshing. It is worthwhile examining the different frame relay topologies in some detail as they apply to any packet-switched technology.

Hub and Spoke

The simplest frame relay topology is the classic hub and spoke (or star) shown here:

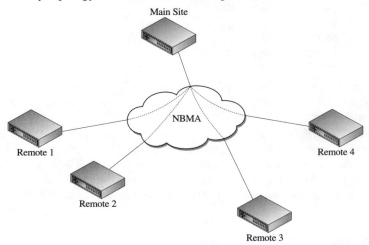

Each remote site has a single PVC to the main site. Any communication between remote sites must take place through the hub site. This is obviously not a resilient design since the failure of any one PVC will cause a loss of WAN connectivity for the remote site that it services.

A second possible issue with the star topology arises if there is a substantial amount of traffic between remote sites. This means that there is a substantial amount of traffic on two PVCs instead of just one, which may not be cost-effective. Also, traffic between remote sites in a star topology always requires at least two router hops, and it is always a design goal to minimize router hops. Therefore, in this instance there may be a case for providing a PVC directly between the sites that exchange a significant amount of data.

Partial Mesh

A partial mesh topology, an example of which is shown next, means that most sites (or indeed all sites) have at least two PVCs connecting to the frame relay network. Therefore, the failure of any one PVC will not cause a loss of WAN connectivity at any site.

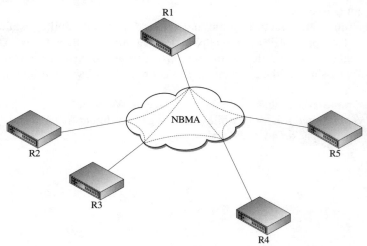

A potential problem with the partial mesh is that there is still a single point of failure at the main site router. This could be overcome by dual-homing the remote sites to different hub site routers, as shown next. This is sometimes called a dual partial mesh. The hub routers could be located at different sites for better redundancy. In this case, the two hub routers would have to be interconnected using two PVCs (for redundancy) or, alternatively, a resilient campus backbone if the two sites are in close geographic proximity. It is not always practical for a company to have two central sites, as there may be only one site that is well suited for housing its main application resources. But even in such a scenario there should be two hub site routers.

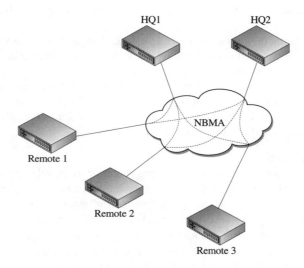

Full Mesh

A fully meshed topology entails directly connecting each site together, as illustrated next. Clearly this results in a fully redundant design, albeit at a cost.

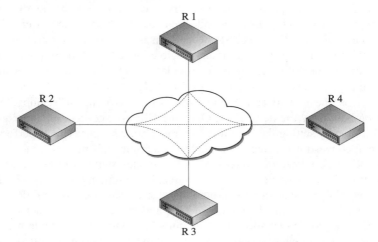

Note that there are four sites fully meshed. A total of six PVCs are required to enable this topology.

More generally, it can be stated that to provide full meshing for n sites, the total number of PVCs required is $n(n-1)/2$. For example, to provide full meshing for 10 sites would require $10 * 9/2 = 45$ PVCs and so on. In terms of resilience in a network of n sites, there are n PVCs from each site and all of these PVCs would have to fail in order to isolate a given site. This sounds impressive, but if one PVC fails due to a local problem it is quite possible that multiple PVCs will fail. This is because absolute resilience is difficult to achieve in the local loop to the frame relay switch. So it would be disappointing to find out that, after spending all this money on resilience, all the PVCs happen to be terminating on the same piece of common equipment in the local central office! Personally, I believe the use of partial meshing with added backup using an alternate technology such as ISDN is a better and more cost-effective solution than the full mesh.

The obvious main limiting factor for full meshing is cost. However, some service providers give competitive rates for PVCs that are used exclusively for backup purposes. So, such a solution should not be discounted on the basis of cost alone without proper cost analysis.

There is, however, another reason why deployments of full-mesh topologies are unusual. Most modern communications infrastructures are not designed to support widespread peer-to-peer communication. The client/server model is far more prevalent, with server resources being centralized at a small number of sites rather than being distributed evenly across the network.

Frame Relay Operation

The frame relay protocol is run between the customer's router or frame relay access device (FRAD) and the local frame relay switch that typically belongs to the service provider. A permanent virtual circuit (PVC) is used for intersite connectivity. The PVC is termed "permanent" since the endpoints are always the same, just like a leased line. The word "virtual" is used since there is no dedicated physical connection along the entire path through the carrier's network. Instead, the carrier programs its switches to ensure that, for example, traffic entering the frame relay network from site A will exit the carrier's network at site B.

Thus, at a very basic level, this may seem similar to the use of a leased line to connect site A to site B. However, there are a number of fundamental and far-reaching differences. Frame relay incurs additional overhead by virtue of the fact that it is a packet-switched technology. The fact that there is no dedicated physical circuit along the entire path enables the carrier to provide a flexible bandwidth offering that may prove cost-effective for the customer. A frame relay service entails the purchasing of a committed information rate (CIR) for each PVC. The CIR is the end-to-end bandwidth that the carrier will guarantee. The customer can also purchase an additional burst rate, and this is the maximum traffic rate that will be supported across the PVC. Obviously, the maximum possible burst rate is the physical speed of the customer's access circuit into the frame relay service provider. However, the carrier does not guarantee that traffic will be transmitted at rates exceeding the CIR. The CIR can be thought of as having a plane ticket, while trying to get across the network at rates above the CIR is like flying on "standby." Whether you get through depends on how busy the network is. Once the CIR is exceeded, all subsequent packets get marked Discard Eligible by setting the DE bit in the frame relay header. This is performed at the local frame relay switch. If congestion is detected at a node in the frame relay network, packets marked DE are the first to be dropped. Upon detecting congestion, a frame relay switch will send a Backward Explicit Congestion Notifier (BECN) message back to the source. If the sending router or FRAD has sufficient intelligence to process this message, it may throttle the sending rate back to the CIR.

A customer can therefore tailor the choice of CIR and maximum burst rate in order to attain a cost-effective bandwidth profile that adequately supports the application's requirements. Applications that use TCP will be more resilient to dropped packets and therefore will incur less of a performance hit than unreliable UDP-based applications. For applications such as voice, an excessive percentage of dropped packets will hinder voice quality. There is an additional problem that may also be perceptible when running voice traffic at rates in excess of the CIR. Apart from dropping DE traffic during times of congestion, the frame relay switch may simply buffer it with a low priority. This means that the traffic may reach the destination, but with a large delay, and exhibit jitter or delay variation, which has a serious effect on the quality of voice or any real-time playback. It should be taken as a general rule to avoid running real-time traffic at rates in excess of the CIR. This is pertinent because frame relay services may entail certain bandwidth guarantees; they do not feature any latency guarantees. This may necessitate using a different PVC for real-time and nonreal-time traffic.

A frame relay network can provide resilience in a cost-effective manner. Backup PVCs can be employed that have a lower CIR than the equivalent primary PVC. Such a backup PVC should ideally reside in a different cable duct than the local frame relay switch, as it is important to ensure that the resilience is not just theoretical.

Frame Relay LMI

Frame relay Local Management Interfaces (LMI) messages are exchanged between the DTE (router) and the DCE (frame relay switch) as a form of protocol keepalive. The DTE sends LMI status inquiry messages to the DCE every 10 seconds by default, and the DCE responds with status replies. It is required by the LMI protocol that the keepalive interval be less on the router than the switch to which it connects. The purpose of the status inquiry and status reply messages is to verify configuration consistency as well as link integrity between the router and the switch, along with the status of configured PVCs. The reporting of PVC status is an extension to the LMI protocol along with other optional extensions such as multicasting, global addressing, and flow control.

A number of LMI parameters such as polling interval and error thresholds are configurable, but it is usually unnecessary to alter these defaults.

Therefore, to summarize the function of the LMI messages exchanged between the router and the local carrier's frame relay switch:

- LMI acts as a keepalive mechanism between the router and switch.
- The LMI messages also contain information on what PVCs terminate on the router, along with the status of these PVCs. For example, are the PVCs active or inactive?

DLCI Mapping

A frame relay PVC is identified locally by a Data Link Connection Identifier (DLCI). This DLCI number is purely of local significance between the router and the local frame relay switch. It is therefore possible for both ends of a PVC to be identified by the same DLCI. The DLCI number is used to locally distinguish between multiple virtual circuits that are on the same physical cable. A site that connects to the frame relay network using just one PVC only requires one DLCI. However, a partially meshed site that has two PVCs must distinguish between them using two different DLCIs. The concept of the DLCI being a locally significant address is different for an X.121 address or an ISDN telephone number, which are both examples of addressing that is globally unique.

So what happens when you run IP over frame relay, as is so typically the case? The router at each of the frame relay PVCs must know what DLCI to use in order to reach the corresponding next-hop IP address. The purpose of the DLCI mapping statement is to map a destination next-hop address for a desktop protocol to a local DLCI. It is important to be clear about what this means, as I have seen the issue of DLCI mapping cause confusion. Remember that the DLCI in the nonextended form is purely of local significance between the DTE and DCE. It distinguishes each of the logical channels on the physical link to the frame relay switch. The frame relay switch then switches each of these channels based on its own configuration for each DLCI. The DLCI mapping statement in effect tells the router, "in order to get to this destination address, use this DLCI." Multiple protocols can have addresses mapped over the same DLCI. In the following example, a Cisco router is configured for frame relay. The IP address of the router's frame relay interface is 192.168.250.2. There are two PVCs terminating on the router, and two DLCIs identify these. The router with an IP address of 192.168.250.1 is connected to on the PVC identified by DLCI 201. DLCI 203 is the PVC connecting to the destination IP address 192.168.250.3. Hence, the local router knows that in order to access 192.168.250.3, the traffic must be sent to the local frame relay switch labeled as DLCI 203 in the frame relay header.

```
interface Serial0
  ip address 192.168.250.2 255.255.255.0
  encapsulation frame-relay IETF
  frame-relay map ip 192.168.250.1 201 broadcast
  frame-relay map ip 192.168.250.3 203 broadcast
```

You will have noticed that the **broadcast** keyword is included at the end of each of the sample mapping statements. Frame relay is a nonbroadcast medium, so this keyword is necessary in order to enable broadcasts to be forwarded across the frame relay network. Without this statement, routing updates, IPX SAPs, and any other broadcast-based traffic will not propagate across frame relay.

Apart from static mapping, the router can discover the destination protocol address that is related to a particular DLCI using Inverse ARP.

ASYNCHRONOUS TRANSFER MODE

ATM is often described as a packet-switched technology since it uses virtual circuits and employs many of the same principles as frame relay. However, technically it is a "cell relay" technology, because ATM access devices fragment the data into fixed-length 53-byte cells in order to minimize delay and jitter.

ATM is a compromise technology designed to combine the consistency in bandwidth and delay that's associated with traditional clear channel time division multiplexing (TDM) technology with the flexibility of packet switching. ATM's higher layers support sophisticated features, such as the dynamic rerouting of switched virtual circuits (SVCs). It is also adaptable to bursty traffic conditions. Small fixed-length 53-byte cells serve to minimize the variation in delay or jitter experienced in the WAN. While ATM employs many similar principles to frame relay, the switching of small fixed-length cells coupled with Quality of Service (QoS) features inherent in the ATM protocol suite make it more suitable for heterogeneous and real-time applications.

Corporate networks that use ATM in the WAN are also likely to have a requirement for high bandwidth. The minimum rate of an ATM PVC is in the T-1/E-1 range, while more typical speeds are of the order to 20 Mbps and beyond. ATM was originally designed to scale though the 155-Mbps bandwidth range and thus go hand in hand with SONET transmission technology.

ATM Resource and QoS Parameters

Frame relay affords the user similar flexibility in bandwidth. With ATM, a sustainable cell rate (SCR) and a peak cell rate (PCR) can be purchased from the service provider. This is very much an equivalent idea to CIR and EIR in frame relay. Thus, as with frame relay, the customer has a certain amount of control over access speeds and can tailor this to application requirements.

ATM incorporates QoS parameters apart from the traffic parameters relating to cell rate. These can be requested at the user network interface and are intended to provide better service for various delay-sensitive and loss-sensitive applications.

Cell Loss Ratio (CLR)   This is the ratio of dropped cells to the total that was throughput across the connection. This ought to be a very small number. The CLR is a parameter that may be set at a particular maximum value for an application that is sensitive to packet loss, such as a UDP-based data application.

Cell Delay Variation (CDV)   The CDV is the average variation in delay across the ATM connection over a specific time interval. A maximum CDV value may be requested from the ATM network for applications that do not tolerate a large variation in delay, such as voice and video.

Cell Transfer Delay (CTD)   The CTD is the total end-to-end latency or delay across the ATM connection. This value may be set for time-sensitive voice or data applications.

ATM also supports a number of fundamentally different classes of service that relate to how bandwidth is allocated on the ATM network.

The ATM forum has specified four service categories:

- **Constant bit rate (CBR)**   This service category ensures a constant bit rate across the ATM PVC. Constant bit rate is a prerequisite for high-quality voice and video transmission. This is the most expensive type of service on a public ATM network because the provider must allocate sufficient bandwidth along the entire path of the PVC in order to meet the specification. The constant bit rate is equivalent to the SCR value purchased from the service provider. If traffic is sent across the PVC at a rate in excess of the SCR, cells may be dropped during times of congestion in the ATM network. The Cell Loss Priority (CLP) bit in the ATM header can determine what traffic is dropped in such instances.

- **Variable bit rate (VBR)**   The bit rate can vary in line with network conditions with this service category. A predefined maximum PCR can be achieved across the PVC when network congestion is completely absent, which, of course, cannot be guaranteed. An average throughput can be negotiated between the ATM access device and the switch for a particular time interval. A guaranteed maximum bit rate can also be negotiated for a short time interval. The VBR class of service is suitable for bursty data applications that are not particularly time-sensitive. VBR has a standard defined for nonreal-time traffic, which is termed VBR-NRT, and this is very typically used for the transport of data traffic. Its real-time equivalent, VBR-RT, is pending ratification.

- **Available bit rate (ABR)**   ABR is a specific type of variable bit rate. A feedback loop is implemented between the ATM switch and router (or whatever ATM adapter is accessing the network). The adapter requests a particular bit rate, but will accept whatever the current network utilization permits. If the bit rate provided by the switch is lower than the requested rate, the switch may increase after a certain time interval when the network is underutilized. Similarly, if the original requested rate is granted by the switch, the switch may subsequently reduce that rate if the network utilization grows. Despite the apparent complexity of ABR, it is less expensive than the CBR or VBR class of service because there is only a limited guaranteed allocation of bandwidth.

- **Unspecified bit rate (UBR)**   There is absolutely no guarantee of bit rate with UBR. All cells sent by the access device may be dropped by the network or may be successfully transported to the destination. The actual throughput achieved depends entirely on network conditions. For this reason UBR is frequently compared to "flying on standby."

The ATM adaptation layer (AAL) prepares cells for transmission over the ATM network. At the sending end, variable-length packets are segmented into fixed-length cells and are reassembled at the receiving end. This particular function of the ATM adaptation layer is called segmentation and reassembly (SAR). Different AAL protocols are defined in order to support optimized transport of traffic types that have different requirements and characteristics.

There are five different AAL protocols that have different characteristics in terms of bit rate profile, connection-oriented/connectionless nature, and timing characteristics. The most commonly used ATM adaptation layer encapsulations are AAL1 and AAL5:

- **AAL1** is connection-oriented and provides constant bit rate. Constant delay is achieved by implementing connection timing end to end between the source and destination. This constant bit rate and delay makes AAL1 ideal for delay-sensitive applications such as voice and video.

- **AAL5** are the most popular ATM adaptation layer protocols used for data transmission. AAL5 is connection-oriented and supplies a variable bit rate.

The type of AAL protocol that is to be used for an ATM PVC is selected and configured on the router and ATM switch. Different AAL protocols can be run on different PVCs. Thus, a particular PVC could be used for voice and video traffic and another PVC could be dedicated to data.

The ability to support different AAL protocols makes ATM a suitable protocol in supporting applications that have different characteristics and networking requirements.

Apart from the inherent delay parameters that can be requested, the ATM transmission profile can also be tailored in other ways to enable the support of traffic types with different transport requirements. Some commentators favor the use of the Cell Loss Priority bit to give a higher priority to delay-sensitive applications such as voice and video. The network will drop traffic with the CLP bit set if the transmission rate is greater than the SCR and congestion is detected. The only advantage to setting it at the ingress to the network is that it affords the customer some control over what cells get set CLP. If, for example, it were decided to mark delay-sensitive UDP-based voice traffic CLP so that it gets dropped rather than delayed, this traffic will always be marked CLP regardless of traffic conditions. Ultimately, it may simply mean that other customers are getting traffic through the carrier's network at your expense.

ATM is typically used for WAN speeds in excess of T-1/E-1 and scales up to the SONET multiples of 155 Mbps. Its niche market is therefore for high-bandwidth requirements and networks that have stringent QoS specifications.

ATM Operation

Despite having many sophisticated features, ATM employs many of the same principles as frame relay. A router that runs ATM exchanges Integrated Local Management Interface (ILMI) messages with the local ATM switch. This acts as a keepalive mechanism between the router and switch. The ILMI messages also allow the router to learn the status of all of its PVCs.

A virtual channel identifier (VCI) and a virtual path identifier (VPI) identify each ATM PVC. A virtual path is simply a group of virtual channels. The VPI/VCI pair, as with a DLCI, is purely of local significance between the router and the ATM switch. The grouping of virtual channels into virtual paths allows ATM switches to switch large groups of virtual channels by making decisions based on the virtual path number. This is a more efficient method of operation at the backbone of a large ATM network.

When deploying IP over ATM, the router at each of the ATM PVC must know what VPI/VCI to use in order to reach the corresponding next-hop IP address at the far end of the PVC. The purpose of the VPI/VC mapping is to map a destination next-hop address for a desktop protocol to a local VPI/VCI. This mapping can be statically configured on the routers, but is more commonly performed using Inverse ARP. Consider, for example, the network displayed next. Router X might resolve that to get to 172.16.1.3, it should use VPI=0 and VCI=19. The packets destined for 172.16.1.3 get segmented into 53-byte cells. The header in each cell contains the VPI/VCI, thus allowing the ATM network to switch each cell to the correct destination.

Circuit-Switched Technology

Circuit switching is a fundamentally different principle than packet switching. With a circuit-switched connection, a dedicated physical circuit is seized end to end for the duration of the switched connection.

PSTN

The oldest example of circuit switching is the public switched telephone network (PSTN). When a call is made, digits are dialed in order to tell the network what destination you want to be switched through to. A dedicated circuit is set up between the calling party and the called party for the duration of the call. This circuit is torn down when the call is terminated. Circuit switching is an effective facilitator of voice communication because it guarantees dedicated end-to-end bandwidth for the call duration. This is a different approach than packet switching, where a shared network is accessed and the amount of available bandwidth may vary during the communication session.

The most basic limitation of the PSTN is bandwidth. The following is a summary of theoretical maximum speeds that can be achieved with the most frequently used modem ITU standard modulation techniques:

MODULATION	SPEED (BPS)
V.32	9600
V.32bis	14.4K
V.34	28.8K
V.34 Annex 1201H	33.6K
V.90	56K

Other limitations of the PSTN include limited intelligence and manageability due to the fact that the local loop between the subscriber and the telecom central office is analog in nature.

ISDN

The Integrated Services Digital Network (ISDN) actually reveals something about itself from its name. It is a fully end-to-end digital network as distinct from the PSTN where, although the switching and transmission technology is 100-percent digital on modern networks, the local loop is still analog. Even on the most modern PSTN implementations, the device signals the digits to the network using analog Dual Tone Multiple Frequency (DTMF) tones. With ISDN, the digits are sent to the local ISDN switch as a digital bit stream.

The term "integrated services" denotes that with sufficient bandwidth allocated, ISDN is capable of supporting heterogeneous services such as data, voice, video, and multimedia.

ISDN is connection-oriented and circuit-switched, similar to the traditional PSTN. The bearer channels (B channels) are each 64 Kbps and therefore optimized for traditional voice traffic. There are two basic ISDN implementations. Basic rate ISDN (BRI) consists of two B channels and a 16-Kbps D-channel for signaling. An ISDN primary rate interface (PRI) consists of 23B+D in the U.S. or 30B+D in Europe. The D-channel is 64 Kbps for primary rate since it has more signaling work to do. Thus, primary rate ISDN offers speeds that may aggregate up to E-1/T-1.

A typical WAN implementation might use BRI at the remote branch offices, with PRI at the central site(s). ISDN is not efficient or cost-effective as a WAN backbone technology in itself. As a general rule of thumb, if the line is up for more than 2–3 hours per day, the costs prove prohibitive and frame relay or a leased line will be more cost-effective. The niche applications of ISDN include periodic connections from remote sites—for example, telecommuters or small branch offices that may only require periodic communication with central site servers. Such ISDN implementations are often referred to as dial-on-demand (DDR). It is very important, however, to correctly configure the routers at the remote sites to ensure that ISDN calls are never needlessly connected for any reason other than the application in question. Application overhead traffic and dynamic routing updates are typical examples of traffic that may result in spurious calls. For this reason, static routing is often employed for ISDN. However, static routes do not scale well on very large networks due to the administrative overhead, thus necessitating careful design and configuration of the dynamic routing protocol.

ISDN also provides a very cost-effective solution for backing up leased line or frame relay connections, because its tariffing is mainly usage-based. Another advantage of ISDN lies in its connection-oriented nature, which ensures that for a single B-channel connection packets can never arrive out of order and should experience a relatively uniform delay pattern. For increased throughput, it may be necessary to combine both B channels to produce 128 Kbps to the same destination. To do this efficiently requires a protocol such as PPP Multilink that has a special sequence field to ensure that packets do not reach the destination out of sequence. Real-time applications cannot tolerate significant variations in delay due to packets taking different paths through the public network, depending on the B channel used. Out-of-sequence packets also cannot be dealt with by unreliable UDP-based applications. Even reliable TCP-based applications may incur an excessive number of retransmissions due to out-of-order packets, thus negating the advantage of using a second channel.

The deployment of ISDN will remain confined to the applications already discussed, primarily due to its strongly usage-based tariff structure.

ISDN Operation

An ISDN basic rate connection normally terminates on an NT-1 device on the customer's premises. The NT-1 performs 2-wire to 4-wire conversion like an analog telephone. It also synchronizes the S-bus and manages contention if there are multiple devices connected to the S-bus. Normally, only a single device connects directly to the NT-1, although the ISDN specification allows for up to eight devices to attach to the S-bus. Obviously, only two of these devices could be active at any one time, because this is the number of available B channels.

A router connected directly to the NT-1, as in the case of a typical scenario, is shown here:

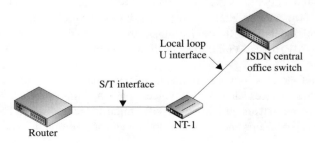

The interface between the ISDN terminal and the NT-1 is termed the S/T interface. This is one of the fundamental reference points used when specifications are drawn up for the different ISDN interfaces. The interface between the NT-1 and the local ISDN central office telecom switch is the U interface. In some parts of the world (most notably in the United States), the ISDN is simply presented as a passive jack on the wall rather than via an NT-1. The customer, in this case, must provide his or her own NT-1. For this reason, many routers are sold with integrated NT-1s. Hence, the ISDN interface on such a router is a U interface rather than an S/T interface.

The ISDN terminal (a router in this example) exchanges layer 2 Q.921 signaling messages periodically with the local ISDN switch. Using these messages, the switch will assign the router a Terminal Endpoint Identifier (TEI) value. The router will not be capable of making an ISDN call until it has been assigned a TEI value.

When the router attempts to make a call, it will send a layer 3 Q.931 signaling message to the local switch. This is a call setup request that includes the destination terminal number that is to be called. ISDN addresses are very similar in nature to PSTN telephone numbers. When the switch receives the Q.931 call setup request, it will switch the call through to the destination in an equivalent manner to a modern digital telephone network.

When running IP over ISDN, the routers must be configured so that they know what ISDN number to call in order to reach the destination IP address at the other end of the network. Consider this illustration:

Router X requires a route in its IP routing table stating that the next-hop address to get to 10.1.1.0/24 is 10.7.7.3. The same router must be configured with a dialer map statement telling it that to get to 10.7.7.3, dial 5551122—which is the ISDN number associated with the HQ router.

Spurious traffic can bring the ISDN line up unintentionally if the network is not configured carefully. Preventing unwanted spurious calls is one of the challenges of implementing ISDN. For example, application layer broadcasts or overhead traffic such as periodic routing updates can bring up the line, resulting in excessive call charges being incurred. Filters can be configured on the routers that prevent unwanted traffic from causing a call to be initiated. Static IP routing is often preferred to a dynamic routing protocol for ISDN for this same reason.

Virtual Private Networks

A virtual private network (VPN) is an encrypted connection between two devices that facilitates secure communication between two trusted networks across an untrusted domain. The connection or VPN tunnel traverses an untrusted network such as the Internet, resulting in the need for encrypting confidential information. A schematic diagram of a simple VPN between two firewall devices is shown here:

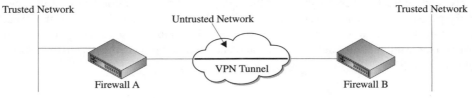

The VPN is a logical point-to-point connection, and the endpoint devices could be of the following combinations:

- Host to host
- Gateway to gateway
- Host to gateway

The hosts in question could be clients or servers and the gateway devices could be routers, firewalls, or intelligent servers.

The VPN is usually considered a security tool, and its use is considered adequate in helping to secure communication between two networks. However, all a VPN does is ensure that a communications link can be established, with the communications link itself being reasonably secure. The endpoints are critical. For example, if the VPN has been established with a business partner, the actual degree of security depends on the security practices at the business partner's site. When using a VPN to connect to another network that does not have the same level of trust as your own network—as is the case with a business partner's network—it is important to ascertain the following information:

- Does your business partner or remote office engage in secure ongoing practices? For example, do they keep updated on new threats and the corresponding patches or solutions?

- Does your business partner have a security policy in place? How well is it being implemented? What aspects of the policy relate to the communication to and from your own network?

IPSEC

IP version 4 was designed for implementation across networks that were presumed secure. Hence, security was not integral to its design. There are, however, a number of security "patch" protocols that can be incorporated with IPv4. One such protocol is IPSec.

With IPv4, IPSec is optional and each end of a connection must ask its peer if the peer supports IPSec or not. With IPv6, IPSec support is mandatory. By mandating IPSec, it can be assumed that your IP communication can be secured whenever you talk to IPv6 devices. The addressing structure of IPv6 uses 128 bits, but there is backward compatibility for IPv4 addresses where the 32 bits are mapped as the least significant bits of the IPv6 address, with the higher-order bits having a constant predefined value.

IP Security protocol, IPSec, is a set of open standards that provides data confidentiality through encryption, information integrity, and authentication between participating peers. IPSec provides these services at layer 3. The Internet Key Exchange (IKE) protocol is used to manage peer negotiation. IKE also generates the encryption and authentication keys that are used by IPSec.

IPSec negotiates secure tunnels between two peers, and in this respect it is similar to the implementation of VPNs. These peers are usually two routers or firewall devices. These endpoint devices must be configured to denote what packets are considered sensitive and should be sent through the secure tunnels. Specifying the encryption and authentication parameters for the tunnel also configures the protection for the tunnels. This protection can be specified through manual configuration or using IKE negotiation between the peers. When so-called "sensitive" data is exchanged between IPSec peers, the IP packets are encapsulated in IPSec packets that contain the security parameters. A schematic representation of an IPSec peer relationship that uses authentication and encryption to protect the data in the IPSec tunnel is shown here:

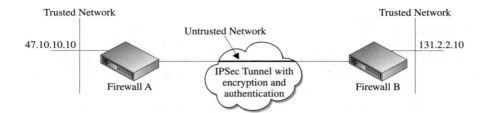

In this example, the IPSec peers are configured to set up a secure tunnel when they receive packets that are exchanged in either direction between 47.10.10.10 and 131.2.2.10. All other traffic passes between the peers without encryption or authentication.

The following is a summary of the security services provided by IPSec:

- **Data authentication**   The data authentication can include two separate concepts.

  - **Data integrity**   The integrity of the data must be verified to confirm that it has not been altered. This is a mandatory element of data authentication.

  - **Origin authentication**   Additional data origin authentication may be performed. This is intended to verify that the data was actually sent by the claimed sender.

- **Data confidentiality**   Encrypting all traffic that passes between the IPSec peers protects data confidentiality. The encryption parameters such as the keys are either statically configured or established via the IKE protocol.

- **Antireplay**   This service enables a receiver to reject old or duplicate packets in order to protect it against replay attacks. The persistent resending of duplicate packets is often characteristic of a denial-of-service attack.

There are a number of issues or restrictions to be considered before implementing IPSec:

- At the time of writing, the IETF has only ratified standards for unicast IPSec traffic. No standards have as yet been developed for multicast or broadcast traffic.

- There are some interoperability issues with Network Address Translation (NAT). Generally, static translations should be used to ensure that there is not a random allocation of external global addresses. Also, the NAT should occur before the IP packet is encapsulated in IPSec. This guarantees that IPSec is used with global addresses.

- A significant overhead and CPU utilization is associated with IPSec. An additional encapsulation step must be done along with authentication and encryption processes. This can increase latency and also place additional processing requirements on the routers at each end of the secure tunnels.

- The act of encapsulating the IP packets in IPSec can potentially cause the packet to exceed the MTU of the transmission medium and hence require fragmentation. The reassembly process incurs additional overhead and further slows down the communication. There is a further issue to be mindful of in relation to fragmentation. Some firewalls may be configured to perform additional checks to detect, and even to drop, fragmented packets because they are often used for denial-of-service attacks. If problems are encountered passing IPSec traffic to a destination firewall, this is an issue that should be checked for.

- IPSec uses IP protocol numbers 50 and 51 and IKE uses protocol 17 with UDP port 500. These protocols and ports must be allowed by firewalls and packet filters along the secured path.

Conclusion

The wide area network is used to interconnect geographically dispersed sites. The different options for the WAN technology are generally divided into three distinct categories: synchronous serial links, packet-switched technology, and circuit-switched technology.

Synchronous serial links represent the simplest type of WAN technology as the sites are interconnected using direct point-to-point links that operate at the speed that was purchased from the telecom service provider. The telecom carrier, through their network, provides a dedicated path at a fixed bandwidth in order to connect the sites. Since this bandwidth is now seized and cannot be given to other customers even if it is not being used, synchronous serial links also represent the most expensive type of WAN solution.

Packet-switched technology uses switched virtual connections to provide intersite connectivity. Traffic is switched by the telecom carrier on a per-packet basis between the source and the destination. Because no dedicated physical paths are provided, different customers can share bandwidth. The method by which the carrier dynamically allocates bandwidth where it is required is termed "statistical multiplexing." This is a more cost-effective WAN solution, but there is a lower guarantee on the end-to-end bandwidth since packet switching involves accessing a highly shared medium. The earliest example of packet-switched technology is X.25, which has been for the most part replaced by frame relay. ATM can be deployed in cases where there is a high-bandwidth requirement.

Circuit-switched technology involves setting up a dedicated physical circuit between a source and a destination site for the duration of a communication session. The oldest example of circuit switching is the PSTN. In this case, a dedicated physical circuit that connects the calling party to the called party is seized across the PSTN for the call duration. The circuit is torn down upon termination of the call. For niche data applications, the ISDN represents an evolution of this principle.

WAN costs usually represent the single highest cost element in owning a network. The choice of WAN technology is therefore a critical network design decision from both a technological and budgetary standpoint. Which technology you choose depends on the bandwidth requirements, traffic profile (for example, is the traffic consistent, periodic, or bursty?), and budgetary constraints. Ultimately, the type of technology deployed and the amount of bandwidth purchased may well come down to a trade-off between cost and performance.

Further Study

Ralph Becker's ISDN Tutorial: **http://www.ralphb.net/ISDN/**
Eicon Networks: **http://www.isdnzone.com/**
Marconi: **http://www.marconi.com/html/education/webbasedwantheory.htm**
ArdRi Communications: **http://site.yahoo.com/cormac-s-long/wantec.html**
RAD Data Communications: **http://www.rad.com/networks/netterms.htm**
TechFest: **http://www.techfest.com/networking/wan.htm**
Stanford Linear Accelerator Center:
http://www.slac.stanford.edu/comp/net/wan-mon/tutorial.html

NETWORK CABLING

Whether working with local or wide area networks, one part of infrastructure will almost always be involved in the maintenance and troubleshooting of the network. That's because, unless the network is a wireless one, some form of cabling will be utilized to physically connect devices together to form a network. The type of cabling used will vary depending on networking application, topology, performance desired, and distance required. With this in mind, there are three basic types of cable used in local and wide area networks, those being coaxial, twisted pair, and optical.

Coaxial Cable

Originally developed during WWII, coaxial cable (sometimes referred to as "coax") can be found in a variety of baseband and broadband applications. Uses for coaxial cable range from local area networking (LAN) to CATV, and even high-speed telephone local loop circuits such as T-3 or DS-3. Some typical coax cable types are listed in Table 8-1.

Physically speaking, coaxial cable consists of a thin, single copper conductor that is encased in a dielectric insulating material, and surrounded by a braided metal that acts as both a shield from interference and an electrical ground. For protection against the environment, the conductor, insulation, and braided metal are fitted with an outer protective jacket. A diagram of coaxial cable can be found in Figure 8-1.

Due to its construction and shielding, coaxial cable is very resilient to various forms of spectral interference, thus it is ideal for use in servicing those distances that unshielded twisted-pair cabling cannot due to excessive signal degradation. For example, Ethernet over RG-58 coaxial cable (10Base2 or thinnet) has a rated maximum distance of 185 meters, and Ethernet over RG-8A/U coax (10Base5 or thicknet) has a maximum distance of 500 meters, whereas the maximum distance of Ethernet over twisted-pair cable (10BaseT) is 100 meters. In addition to a longer transmission distance, coax can be run in spectrally noisy environments, or those with large amounts of electromagnetic interference (EMI) such as in electrical motor rooms and near fluorescent light ballasts.

Unfortunately, also due to its design, transmission rates of 10Base2 Ethernet are limited to 10 Mbps, whereas current maximum speeds of Ethernet over twisted-pair cable reach 1 Gbps (1000BaseT). Keep in mind, however, that higher data rates are possible with coaxial cable, just not when using coax in an Ethernet application.

BASEBAND AND BROADBAND

Over the past few years, the term "broadband" has been used quite freely as more and more homes have become equipped with high-speed always-on forms of Internet connectivity, such as cable modem or DSL access. Traditionally speaking, though, on a universal scale the term "broadband" refers to any transmission medium that exceeds the speed of a regular telephone or plain old telephone service (POTS) line.

TABLE 8-1   COMMON COAXIAL CABLE TYPES AND THEIR ASSOCIATED APPLICATIONS

CABLE TYPE	APPLICATION
RG-58A/U	50-ohm cable primarily used for thinnet (10Base2 Ethernet)
RG-8A/U	50-ohm cable used for thicknet (10Base5 Ethernet)
RG-59/U	75-ohm cable used primarily for CATV
RG-62/U	93-ohm cable used in nearly defunct ARCNET

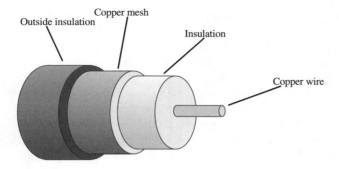

FIGURE 8-1   Coaxial cable diagram

Those media that fall below the 56-Kbps speed limit of a POTS line are typically considered baseband transmission media.

When speaking of coaxial-based data networks, however, these terms take on new meaning. This is due in part to the two means of transmitting data or a signal over coaxial cable. The first means of data transmission involves altering the voltage level of the cable itself in order to signal a 0 or 1 (binary bit). This is done by producing either a −1.5Vdc or a +1.5Vdc voltage level, respectively. Since the entire cable is used as one channel by altering voltage level for signaling, this transmission method is called baseband signaling. As there is only one channel available for the transmission of data in baseband signaling, only one device can transmit at a time, though all devices on the cable network can receive data at all times. As a point of reference, thinnet and thicknet utilize the baseband signaling method for the transmission of data packets across the cabled infrastructure.

The second method of transmission over coaxial cable is considerably more complex than baseband signaling. Since coax has the ability to carry signals at a wide range of frequencies, rather than use the entire cable as a single channel by altering voltage, broadband signaling divides the cable into many channels by transmitting data at a broad range of different frequencies. This creation of channels by altering transmission frequency is known as frequency division multiplexing (FDM). The division of frequency space not only allows multiple devices to transmit at once, but more specifically it allows multiple forms of data or signals to be transmitted (that is, voice, video, and data) simultaneously. Both cable TV (CATV) and cable modem systems utilize broadband signaling for the transmission of video and data to customers.

THINNET AND THICKNET

When Dr. Robert Metcalfe first developed Ethernet in the late 1970s at the Xerox Palo Alto Research Center (PARC), it was designed to run in a bus topology (or a daisy chain of devices) over two different types of coaxial cable, those being RG-58 and RG-8A/U. Ethernet over coaxial cable has been given the names thinnet and thicknet, respectively, due to the diverse thickness of the two cable types they utilize. Each of these cable types has its own set of distinct characteristics, which are shown in Table 8-2, that make each suitable for certain environments.

Thinnet, or 10Base2 Ethernet, is primarily used for the connection of network devices to one another at a speed of 10 Mbps, and over a maximum total distance of 185 meters (from one end of the cable or bus to the other). This maximum distance is due to the attenuation or signal loss over distance of RG-58. As a signal travels down the cable, it will begin to degrade and eventually become so weak that a device further down on the Ethernet bus can no longer receive the signal reliably—or at all. As thinnet is substantially thinner than thicknet, it has a higher attenuation value and is also more susceptible to spectral interference. Note, however, that even though thinnet has a shorter maximum distance than thicknet, it is still preferred for device connection as it is substantially easier to work with given its larger bend radius and simple device connection with BNC T connectors.

As seen in Figure 8-2, a typical thinnet network or bus consists of network hosts or devices connected with RG-58 cable in a linear fashion. Each device is connected to the cabled network with a BNC T connector. The T connector essentially has three BNC connection points—one connects to the device itself and the other two are for the incoming or outgoing RG-58 cable to the next device in the bus. At either end of the cable bus, a terminating resistor must be installed in order to preserve signal level and limit interference and signal distortion.

Thicknet, or 10Base5 Ethernet, on the other hand, is geared more towards long-haul backbone runs between network devices, or for use in spectrally noisy environments. Due to its lower attenuation value of 1.7 db per 100m and considerably thicker insulation, 10Base5 can carry 10 Mbps of data up to 500m before the signal level degrades beyond useful levels. While thicknet can be used to connect network hosts together, it is typically advised against due to the relatively small bend radius (rendering the cable itself hard to work with) and the need for cumbersome vampire taps and drop cables, as opposed to the simpler BNC T connectors.

COAX CONSIDERATIONS

With the advent of twisted-pair and fiber-optic cabling, as well as fairly low-cost Ethernet hubs and switches, coaxial-cable-based networks are being deployed to a lesser degree. So while thinnet and thicknet are no longer in wide use, tools and materials for deploying or maintaining a coaxial-based net-

TABLE 8-2   DIFFERENTIATING CHARACTERISTICS OF THINNET AND THICKNET COAXIAL CABLE

CHARACTERISTIC	THINNET (RG-58)	THICKNET (RG-8A/U)
Conductor diameter	0.94 mm	2.7 mm
Insulation diameter	2.52 mm	6.15 mm
Outer jacket diameter	4.62 mm	10.3 mm
Bend radius	5 cm	25 cm
Attenuation (at 10 MHz)	4.6 dB/100m	1.7 dB/100m

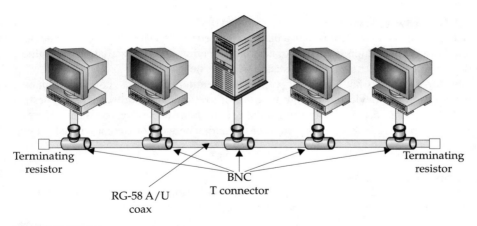

Terminating resistor

Terminating resistor

BNC
T connector

RG-58 A/U
coax

FIGURE 8-2   A typical thinnet network

work are still widely available. However, before considering deploying such a network, there are some points to consider relative to the cost and type of cable used, network topology, installation considerations, and, of course, reliability.

Cost and Cable Type

While at one time coaxial cable was substantially cheaper than twisted-pair cable, the cost difference between the two is now quite marginal. With this in mind, there are a few reasons to consider using coax rather than twisted pair. If the network will be running in EMI-intense environments or over long distances, coax may be a wise decision—providing, of course, the network will not require more than 10 Mbps of bandwidth. Should the bandwidth requirement be higher, multimode fiber-optic cable may be a better choice given its quite long distance limitations and virtual immunity to EMI.

If the bandwidth limitations of coax are acceptable, then the selection of RG-58 over RG-8A/U is largely dependent on two key factors, those being distance and spectral noise. Should the total length of the network not exceed 185 meters, RG-58 is the preferred medium on condition that it provides adequate shielding from any EMI sources.

If, however, the total length requirement exceeds 185 meters but is less than or equal to 500 meters—or greater EMI shielding is required—then RG-8A/U is recommended. While thicknet can be cumbersome to install, it does provide for a neater and more eye-pleasing installation, given the use of drop cables from a backbone hidden in the wall or ceiling.

Lastly, if cable will be installed through an air plenum space, it is required to use plenum-rated cable for the installation. While this cable will be more expensive to purchase, it will cut down considerably on toxic fumes produced by the cable should it catch fire or begin to burn. The increase in cost is related to the difference in jacket materials used—or in most cases, the use of Teflon as opposed to PVC.

Topology and Collision Domains

Thinnet and thicknet are designed to be deployed in a bus (as opposed to a star) topology, thus all devices or hosts are connected in a linear fashion. This type of network sometimes poses installation difficulties, especially if one device is located a considerable distance from the next.

Additionally, this topology does not lend itself well to the creation of multiple collision domains; thus, having too many devices or devices with high network utilization can greatly reduce the performance of the network as collisions occur. If a high number of collisions are occurring, one means of creating another collision domain is to connect two separate coax Ethernet networks together with a bridging or routing device.

Installation Considerations

To ensure a trouble-free network deployment, keep the following installation considerations in mind when planning or reviewing your current coaxial-based network:

- Even though coaxial cable is shielded, it is still a good idea to avoid running cable segments near electrical motors or florescent light ballasts, as this will decrease your chances of interference-related problems.

- Always remember not to exceed the distance limitations of 10Base2 (185 meters) and 10Base5 (500 meters). Aside from actual cable distance, it is good practice to add 6 ft to the total length calculation for each break in the cable (that is, T connector or barrel connector).

- If the network in question requires longer distances than what is permitted, Ethernet repeaters can be deployed up to a maximum of four per network. Should a far-reaching workstation experience problems, try limiting the number of repeaters between the workstation and server to two.

- To ensure proper signal strength throughout the entire network, do not exceed a total of 30 T connectors per network segment. Furthermore, the T connectors should be at least 4 ft apart, and always remember to terminate each end of the network with 50Ω terminating resistors (one of which should be electrically grounded).

- If the installation requires a 10Base5-like installation with the easy to handle cable of 10Base2, consider using a thinnet tap system by manufacturers such as AMP.

Reliability

When used in the proper environment, coaxial-based networks will provide many years of cost-effective trouble-free operation. The relatively simple design of a bus network does have its pitfalls, however—the largest being a single point of failure. This can best be compared to small holiday decorating lights, in that if one part of the bus becomes faulty, the entire network will ultimately fail.

In order to proactively hedge against this occurrence, be sure that all cable connectors are crimped on tightly (not twist-on) and that there is ample contact to the grounding braided metal. Also, remember terminating resistors are required on both ends of the bus, and should be connected tightly as well. Lastly, ensure that all parts of the cabled infrastructure are secured, and not in danger of being stepped on or tripped over.

COAXIAL CABLE TROUBLESHOOTING

While there are typically no active electrical components such as hubs or switches in thinnet and thicknet networks, there are still components that can fail and cause network problems. These components include terminating resistors, BNC T connectors, BNC connectors, network interface cards, or even the cable itself. Fortunately, when working with a coaxial-based network, it can be relatively easy to locate and fix the failed component. Some basic methods employed for this purpose include resistance testing and voltage testing.

Resistance Testing

The object of resistance testing is to locate a broken cable segment or a faulty connector. In order to test the resistance level across the network, it is first necessary to power down all devices on the network. Next, with a standard multimeter or ohmmeter, measure the resistance level at any T connector by applying the meter leads to the copper conductor and coax shielding (outer part of the connector). In a normal 10Base2 or 10Base5 network with all terminating resistors in place, the meter should read approximately 27Ω (±5Ω). Should only one terminating resistor be present, the resistance level will rise to approximately 55Ω (±10Ω), and continue to rise to an infinite amount of resistance should both terminating resistors be removed from the network. These resistance levels would indicate the cable and connectors are good.

With these values in mind, to locate a faulty segment of cable and/or connector, simply remove the terminating resistor from one end of the network and test the resistance level from that end of the cable while using the removed terminating resistor to isolate the network into smaller and smaller segments. For example, by disconnecting one side of a T connector from the network (the side furthest away from the unterminated end) and placing the terminating resistor there, the meter should read a resistance level of 55Ω, indicating that all cable segments and connectors between the multimeter and present location of the terminating resistor are okay. A considerably higher resistance level would indicate a problem exists between those two points, which can be further isolated by moving the terminating resistor to a T connector closer to the multimeter, one cable segment at a time.

Very often a cable segment will appear nonfunctional due to a poorly connected BNC connector and not a failure of the cable itself. If this is the case, cutting the cable ends and installing new crimped BNC connectors may quickly alleviate the problem.

When testing 10Base5 networks, it is necessary to test from vampire taps, as there are typically no T connectors in a 10Base5 network.

Voltage Testing

This method of testing can assist in identifying potential failed media access units (MAUs) in a 10Base5 network. Additionally, it can also identify a ground-loop condition, typically caused by more than one ground in the network. Normal voltage levels of a 10Base5 network should not exceed ±100mV when tested at any vampire tap with a voltmeter. Should the tested voltage level be substantially higher than ±100mV, chances are a short exists in the network.

To locate the short, simply start by disconnecting MAUs one at a time from their associated vampire taps, until the voltage level drops to acceptable levels. If the voltmeter continues to read a value higher than ±100mV after all MAUs are disconnected, check the cable plant for additional grounds, because a ground loop can cause a high-voltage condition as well.

Advanced Testing Tools

While resistance and voltage-level testing can aid in locating common coaxial cable problems, using these methods to locate and rectify the problem in large network environments could take a substantial amount of time. To accelerate the process of locating network malfunctions, there are advanced cable testing devices that can automatically test and identify any present or potential network problem.

These devices are generically referred to as time domain reflectometers (TDRs). Diagnostic tools such as TDRs operate very similar to RADAR or SONAR, in that they work by simply transmitting a signal onto the network cable, and then measuring the time it takes for the device to receive the reflection of that signal. The TDR will then evaluate the strength and distance traveled of the reflected signal to locate and diagnose the network trouble. Some advanced cable testers can also evaluate the network from a data transmission level, and identify performance problems such as high collision rates or corrupt Ethernet frames.

SYMPTOMS

SYMPTOM 8-1   **There is an intermittent loss of connectivity.**   While there can be a multitude of reasons for an intermittent loss of connectivity, the typical malfunctions are all based on physical connection problems. These include faulty or loose BNC or T connectors and failing or loose terminating resistors. Monitoring resistance levels while checking the individual cable connections can sometimes yield the faulty segment or loose connector.

SYMPTOM 8-2   **An entire cable segment has failed.**   Generally speaking, if an entire segment has failed, the problem most likely lies in the cable itself. These problems typically manifest themselves as ground loops or shorts in the cable infrastructure, although the possibility of loose connectors and faulty terminators should not be overlooked.

SYMPTOM 8-3   **You find an unusually high number of collisions.**   Collisions are a normal event in Ethernet networks, especially as the network grows in size and encompasses more hosts or devices. However, an unusually high number of collisions is generally caused by a large number of retransmissions by devices on the network. Retransmissions are typically due to the corruption of frames or packets, which can be due to signal reflections in the cable caused by a lack of terminating resistance. Check to ensure both terminating resistors are connected and are providing ample resistance to the bus. If collisions still persist when resistance values are normal, it may be advisable to create a new Ethernet segment to split up the transmitting devices into smaller collision domains.

SYMPTOM 8-4   **FCS errors occur frequently or intermittently.**   While collisions and fragmented packets are normal in Ethernet operation, an excessive or intermittently occurring number can be an indication of interference. Assuming the measured value of terminating resistance is approximately 27Ω, the cause of interference is most likely an electric motor, copy machine, or florescent light ballast. Check the cable path for any potential sources of EMI, and reroute the cable if possible. Also, it is advisable to ensure all devices on the network are connected to their AC power source with a line noise-filtering device of some type, as these devices can substantially limit possible electrical noise induction.

SYMPTOM 8-5   **There is no (or intermittent) connection after a new workstation is installed.**   A change in the connection status of existing network devices once a new device or workstation is installed would indicate part of the new installation (cable, connectors, NIC, and so forth) is causing a fault in the cable bus. These components should be checked and replaced if necessary. However, should the existing network operate satisfactorily, while the new workstation is experiencing no connectivity, a configuration error may be to blame. Check the NIC on the new workstation, as well as the workstation's configuration. Selecting an incorrect frame type for the network is a common workstation configuration error, and should be verified before replacing the NIC.

Twisted-Pair Cable

While coaxial cable is a great solution for inexpensive installations, small networks, or networks in spectrally noisy environments, twisted-pair cable is far more versatile and scalable, and considerably easier to install and maintain. Twisted-pair cable consists of eight individually insulated copper conductors, arranged into four intertwining color coded sets or pairs. The twisting of each pair in the cable creates a virtual shielding that prevents crosstalk between pairs, and is an effective means of protection against low levels of interference. Additionally, to further prevent noise between pairs, each of the four pairs in the cable are twisted at a different rate of twists per foot. For physical protection from the environment, the four sets of pairs are surrounded by either a PVC or a Teflon (for plenum-rated cable) outer jacket.

Twisted-pair cable is manufactured to different levels of certification, called categories, which are numbered 1–7. Generally speaking, the higher the category, the more twists per foot are in each pair. The increased number of twists allows for higher data rates as less noise is able to penetrate each of the pairs; thus, the faster the network, the higher the category of cable required. Table 8-3 summarizes the common categories of twisted-pair cable available with their typical uses and maximum usable lengths.

 Cable installation accessories such as jacks and patch panels are also manufactured to the same category standards; as such, be sure to install the matching category for the cable in use.

TABLE 8-3   COMMON CATEGORIES OF TWISTED-PAIR CABLE

TWISTED-PAIR CABLE TYPE	TYPICAL USE	MAXIMUM LENGTH
Category 2	Voice	n/a
Category 3	10BaseT Ethernet and Voice	100m (at 16 MHz)
Category 5	100BaseT Ethernet	100m (at 100 MHz)
Category 5e	100BaseT Ethernet 1000BaseT (Minimal Support)	100m (at 100 MHz)
Category 6	1000BaseT Ethernet	100m (at 250 MHz)
Category 7	1000BaseT Ethernet	100m (at 600 MHz)

UNSHIELDED TWISTED PAIR (UTP)

Twisted-pair cable is available in two major varieties, the first being the commonly used unshielded twisted pair or UTP, which is used in 10BaseT, 100BaseT, and even 1000-BaseT networks. It is referred to as "unshielded" because there is no metal shielding around any of the pairs, thus relying on a magnetic field created by the twisting of pairs (which works well in most environments).

When using UTP for Ethernet, each of the eight pairs is crimped into an eight-position (four-pair) modular connector dubbed RJ-45, which is shown in Figure 8-3. This connector resembles the smaller

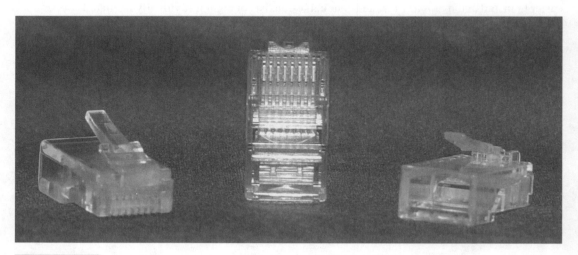

FIGURE 8-3   RJ-45 modular connector for use with twisted-pair cabling

two-pair RJ-11 connector found on most analog phones, and is only available in a crimp-on form, thus special but widely available tools are required to secure the connector to the cable. Each of the conductors must be inserted into the connector on both ends of the cable in a standardized order as specified by Electronic Industry Association/Telecommunications Industry Association's Standard 568B, and as shown in Table 8-4. The connector's pins are numbered from left to right, with the cable end pointing away and the plastic tab facing up. Using the same order on both ends will produce what is termed a "straight-through cable," or one that is used for connecting a host or device to an Ethernet hub or switch. By reversing the order of the transmit and receive pairs, a crossover cable will be rendered that allows two hosts or devices to communicate directly without the need for an Ethernet hub or switch.

One of the many benefits of twisted-pair cabling is its ease of installation and maintenance on a per-node basis; thus, adding or removing a workstation from the network, or a failed cable segment, will not affect other nodes of the network. This is a result of the star topology (as opposed to a bus topology) used in twisted-pair networks, in which each node has its own connection to an aggregating device such as an Ethernet hub or switch.

Twisted-pair cable is generally installed in a patch system fashion; that is, there are very often no direct (or single cable) runs between workstation and hub or switch. Instead, each workstation has a short patch cable that is connected from its NIC to an RJ-45 jack nearby. That jack is hard-wired (either screwed or punched down) with a longer cable run to a central RJ-45 patch panel, which is nothing more than a large number of RJ-45 jacks on a panel. From the patch panel, a short patch cord connects the individual jack to a port on the hub or switch. This system allows for offices to be prewired, and individual runs to be activated on an as-needed basis. It also dramatically improves cable management and troubleshooting.

TABLE 8-4   STANDARD PIN ASSIGNMENTS IN A RJ-45 PLUG, PER TIA/EIA 568B

PIN NUMBER	FUNCTION (WHEN USED STRAIGHT THROUGH)	STRAIGHT-THROUGH CONDUCTOR COLOR	CROSSOVER CONDUCTOR COLOR
1	Transmit data (+)	White-orange	White-green
2	Transmit data (-)	Orange	Green
3	Receive data (+)	White-green	White-orange
4	Unused by 10BaseT	Blue	Blue
5	Unused by 10BaseT	White-blue	White-blue
6	Receive Data (-)	Green	Orange
7	Unused by 10BaseT	White-brown	White-brown
8	Unused by 10BaseT	Brown	Brown

While UTP is fairly resilient to failures, it is not uncommon for self-made cables to fail due to poor connection between the conductors and the RJ-45 plug. To limit this occurrence, as well as save some installation time, it is wise to order premade, machine-crimped patch cables. Many electrical supply companies can manufacture patch cables to any length (and color) required.

Twisted-pair cabling is often offered with two choices of conductor types, those being solid and stranded. Solid conductor twisted pair is typically used for cable runs between patch panels and jacks (within walls), while stranded is generally used in patch cables from jack to NIC as it is a bit more flexible. Either type can be used in each application, providing the connectors and jacks are matched to the type of conductor used. A mismatch will cause shorted or split pairs, and can be detected with a cable scanner.

SHIELDED TWISTED PAIR (STP)

Although UTP is resistant to low levels of external interference, there are some environments that are so spectrally noisy that extra shielding is required for proper operation of the network. In environments such as these, the second major variety of twisted-pair cable, called shielded twisted pair (STP), is quite useful. By incorporating several layers of metallic shielding within the cable, STP is capable of operating in intense interference environments without sacrificing speed or maximum distance.

As STP is almost identical to UTP in construction, color coding, and connectors utilized, it follows the same category manufacturing ratings and can be used in all Ethernet environments without modification. Whereas UTP relies on electromagnetic fields for shielding, STP enhances resilience to interference by first shielding each pair with an aluminum (or equivalent) wrapping, and in some cases following that with a braided metal jacked around all the individually shielded pairs prior to securing the bundle with a PVC or Teflon outer jacket.

Due to extra shielding in STP, it is a bit more difficult to work with than UTP because it is somewhat stiff and does not tend to bend as easily. Also, it is necessary to ensure that both ends of an STP cable are grounded, because improper grounding can lead to inducted noise.

TWISTED-PAIR TROUBLESHOOTING

Unlike coaxial cable, twisted-pair cable is far easier to troubleshoot due in part to its typical star topology. Generally speaking, if an entire network is not functioning properly, chances are a hub or switch is to blame. If a single host is experiencing trouble, the problem is most likely located somewhere between the host itself and its port on the hub or switch, especially if there is difficulty in obtaining a solid link LED on the NIC or hub port. Thankfully, some fairly inexpensive tools (such as basic cable scanners) exist to aid in the troubleshooting of twisted-pair cable problems. Should more advanced testing be desired, there are time domain reflectometer (TDR) type devices for twisted-pair networks that cost between $400 and $10,000, depending on functionality required.

Much like coaxial cable, many twisted-pair problems begin with the connectors and or jacks where UTP runs have been terminated. An easy way to test the cable end to end is with an inexpensive cable scanner. These devices are sold in two-piece sets. One piece is the scanner or continuity tester itself, which will plug into one end of the cable. The other piece is a loopback connector, which looks very much like a mini RJ-45 jack and would be connected to the opposite end of the cable.

Once both ends are connected, a quick test or scan of the cable is performed, and within a few moments the scanner's display will show which conductor or pair is shorted, split, or swapped. Unfortunately, most scanners will not be able to locate the connector that is home to the problem, as such both connectors will need to be removed (cut) and new RJ-45 connectors crimped in place. Should the scanner show no fault, give the cable at either end a little wiggle into the connector, because one of the conductors may not be fully seated against a connector pin. Loose connectors should always be replaced, because even if the cable seems to pass testing, it may fail in the near future.

If after several attempts to crimp new connectors onto the cable the trouble persists, it is possible that stranded conductors are being crimped with solid connectors, or vice versa. Check to ensure that the cable conductor type and connector type match to alleviate this problem.

Time Domain Reflectometers and Advanced Cable Scopes
Even though most UTP and STP cable troubles will exist in the connectors themselves, twisted-pair cable itself can be at fault sometimes—especially if the cable has undergone unusual amounts of physical stress. Furthermore, some cable problems are not always physically obvious, as in the case of near-end crosstalk (NEXT), which essentially is the leakage of signal from one pair to another. It is termed "near-end" because it can occur at an RJ-45 plug at either end of the cable, where pairs are untwisted for crimping.

One popular method of identifying physical cable problems of this nature is by utilizing a TDR for UTP and STP networks. TDRs work by transmitting a signal down the cable, and evaluating the reflected signal in terms of time to return and power level received. By analyzing these factors, a TDR can accurately locate physical problems within the cable. Some advanced cable scanners do incorporate a TDR function to diagnose and locate physical cable issues. One of these devices is the MicroScanner, which is manufactured by Fluke Networks and sells for approximately $400.

Advanced Cable Analyzers
When managing or maintaining a large UTP or STP infrastructure, advanced cable analyzers may assist in keeping the cable plant operating at peak efficiency. Analyzers like the Fluke DSP-4000 series of digital cable analyzers typically combine the features of an advanced cable scanner with digital testing tools. This combination not only allows the analyzer to diagnose and locate physical cable problems, but also detect performance-hindering troubles such as NEXT, inducted interference or noise, and even general Ethernet transmission problems such as high collisions or excessive errors.

Near-end crosstalk is generally caused by untwisted pairs within a cable or on a patch panel. When crimping cable or punching down on a patch panel, it is imperative not to untwist the pairs for more than half an inch. Untwisting more than this length will result in interference between the transmission and receiving signal within a given pair. High levels of NEXT can also be created due to poor-quality cable or patch panels.

Should the analyzer indicate excessive collisions within the network, there is most likely something interfering with the transmission of packets or frames, which can sometimes be attributed to an excessive amount of EMI. If this is the case, ensure that all cable runs are an ample distance from any source of EMI, and relocate any cable runs that may be inducting noise. If the network is still inducting interference, it may be wise to consider upgrading any suspect cable runs to STP cable.

Additionally, a high attenuation level may be to blame for excessive collisions. Ethernet allows for an 11.5-dB signal loss before encountering problems; thus, if a faulty cable is causing additional signal loss, performance-degrading errors such as collisions and frame check sequence (FCS) errors will result.

SYMPTOMS

SYMPTOM 8-6   **The network experiences reduced performance.**   A network-wide reduction in performance can be a result of high collisions, FCS errors, or even high network utilization. It is important to note that high collisions and high network utilization may be the result of too many hosts on a given cable segment. If this is the case, consider moving to a switched rather than a shared Ethernet infrastructure, and if necessary, create multiple collision domains by segmenting either the hub or the switch, or with the creation of VLANs.

FCS errors can also result from interference within the network, such as NEXT or the induction of EMI. Performing a cable test with an advanced cable analyzer should be able to properly diagnose interference-causing problems, though a quick visual inspection of the cable plant for close proximity sources of EMI may be a less costly means of alleviating the problem. Copy machines, light ballasts, and anything with an electrical motor are known sources of EMI. Additionally, all devices on the network, including hubs or switches, should be connected to AC power sources via electrical line-filtering devices, as induction of EMI noise has been observed through AC power lines.

Lastly, always ensure that all cable grades and types are homogeneous throughout the entire network: that is, all cable and terminating devices are of the same category certification, as well as properly matched to either solid or stranded conductors. The maximum distance rating of 100m should also be observed at all times.

SYMPTOM 8-7   **You notice a high number of collisions or fragmented packets.**
Similar to symptom 8-6, a high number of collisions would be indicative of a network congestion problem. If this is the case, try moving to a switched infrastructure, or at the very least move some workstations to another shared Ethernet segment. Additionally, employ a network sniffer or related device to ascertain if a high amount of broadcasts, or broadcast storm, is causing high network utilization, thus leading to

excessive collisions. Alternatively, if the problem includes a high amount of runts or fragments, a transmission problem due to interference could be at fault.

SYMPTOM 8-8   **There is no (or intermittent) connection after a new workstation is installed.**   Connection problems of a newly installed workstation can be attributed to a nonfunctional cable run, a failed NIC, or even a workstation configuration problem. Intermittent problems are generally caused by a loose connection somewhere on the cable run, or a short in the connector due to an improperly seated conductor. Ensure proper connectors are being used with the conductor type in use (solid or stranded), and crimp new connectors to alleviate intermittent shorts or loose conductors within the connectors themselves.

Also ensure that a straight-through patch cable is utilized, rather than a crossover patch cable. Should the workstation or hub indicate a successful link on the cable, check the workstation's configuration for possible errors.

SYMPTOM 8-9   **A workstation fails completely.**   Generally speaking, should a workstation lose its link to the hub or switch after a successful connection was established, a physical cable problem is most likely the culprit. Perform a visual inspection of the cable run, looking for damage or breaks in the cable. Should no obvious signs of wear show, a connector has probably become loose and should be replaced. Lastly, be sure that the hub or switch port has not failed. This can be easily tested by simply moving the failed cable run to a new hub or switch port, and checking for a link LED.

 Electrostatic discharge (ESD) has been known to cause failure in individual switch and NIC ports. Therefore, before working with cable, be sure to ground yourself by touching a bare piece of metal. ESD can even be inducted over a connected cable, thus disabling the connected port.

Optical Cable

Both twisted-pair and coaxial cable provide a cost-effective means of transmitting and receiving data, but both are limited by potential interference as well as short distance limitations. While not the least expensive form of cabling, fiber-optic cable provides everything the aforementioned cabling options do, and then some. Because fiber optics rely on photons for the transmission of data, fiber optics are impervious to EMI and can transmit signals considerably further than even 10Base5 coaxial cable. Much like twisted-pair cable has one pair for transmitting and one for receiving, fiber-optic cabling requires that two separate cables be used for the transmission as well as the reception of photons (though they can be packaged together in one jacket).

Fiber-optic (FO) cable consists of long, thin strands of light-conducting ultrapure silica (or plastic for short-distance needs) called a *core*, which is surrounded by a reflective glass sheath (much like a mirror) called *cladding*. As light photons try to escape the silica core, the cladding reflects them back into the silica. Surrounding the cladding is a plastic buffer, and in some cases an extra strengthening material such as Kevlar. Much like either twisted-pair or coaxial cable, there is an outer PVC or Teflon jacket for exterior protection.

OPTICAL-FIBER TYPES

When either a laser or LED transmits light down fiber-optic cable, the photons are transported down the glass by bouncing off mirrored cladding that surrounds the glass fiber core. As the cladding and core do not absorb any (or very minimal) light, transmitted signals can travel distances up to several thousand kilometers. The maximum speed and distance of transmitted light over fiber-optic cable is a function of how frequently the light is reflected in and out of the core. As such, fiber-optic cable is available in a variety of core diameters—the smaller of which provides for longer and less frequent reflections, thus allowing longer maximum distances. Two major types of fiber-optic cable are single-mode and multimode, each with its own set of attributes and applications.

Multimode Fiber

When speaking of fiber-optic cabling in a LAN or enterprise environment, more often than not multimode fiber is employed. This is due in part to the reduced cost of both short-haul cable and fiber-optic hardware. Multimode fiber is constructed of a relatively large core, typically 50 to 80 micros in diameter; thus, reflections of photons occur more frequently than if the core were smaller or narrower. Rather than use a laser to produce photons, multimode optical hardware uses LEDs that emit infrared light. This difference in transmission hardware results in considerably lower cost.

Two forms of multimode fiber exist, and they are differentiated by the abrupt or gradual change between core and cladding. Step-index multimode cable introduces increased refraction over gradual-index multimode cable, due to its abrupt change between core and cladding. Lower levels of refraction allow for the faster movement of photons. As such, step-index multimode cable is limited to 50 Mbps, while gradual-index multimode cable is limited to 1 Gbps. The latter is used considerably more frequently in LAN and short-haul campus environments.

Still, with gradual-index multimode cable, refraction is still a problem because refraction creates different paths for photons to travel within the cable, a phenomenon known as multimode distortion. As photons move to the outer portion of the cable, they tend to travel faster then photons in the core; thus, some photons may arrive at their destination earlier than other photons. Over short distances (< 2km) this is not a problem, because photons tend to all arrive simultaneously. However, with longer distances this problem can cause the intended signal to become corrupt.

Single-Mode Fiber

While multimode fiber is used for more economic, short-haul applications, single-mode fiber cables (or monomode) are designed for long-haul, high-speed applications such as carrier trunking. The biggest difference between the two is core size, which is a much smaller 7–10 microns in single-mode fiber. As distance limitations are considerably higher with single-mode fiber due to substantially decreased refraction, a laser diode is used for the transmission of high-intensity photons, rather than the weaker LED used in multimode applications.

The smaller silica core and powerful laser diodes increase the cost of single-mode installations to well above the cost of multimode deployments. This increased cost does, however, have advantages, reflected in substantial gains in speed and distance. For example, the ITU has published standard G.652, which supports single-mode cable transmission distances of up to 1000 km at 2.5 Gbps and 3 km at 40 Gbps. While refraction is not a large problem in single-mode cable, another phenomenon known as chromatic dispersion does eventually limit cable distance as well.

Single-mode fiber-optic cable is considerably harder to work with than multimode fiber due to its smaller core diameter. Neither has a very optimal bend radius, thus rendering fiber-optic cable as a whole somewhat hard to utilize.

FIBER CONNECTIONS

Regardless of which type of fiber-optic cable is employed, both utilize a common set of optical connectors for terminating cable into network devices. Typically, receiving devices employ photodiodes for regeneration or translation of light pulses to electrical signals. Common optical connectors include ST and SC connectors, both of which are used in 1000BaseFL applications. Another common connector used in data networking is the MIC connector, commonly found in FDDI environments.

ST Connectors

Straight-tip (ST) connectors are most commonly found in Ethernet environments where media converters are being used between fiber and UTP infrastructure. It resembles a coax-like BNC connector in that it twists on to lock. ST connectors do require the inserted fiber to be polished prior to assembly; as such, it is wise to order premade cables.

SC Connectors

Rather than twist on, straight connection (SC) connectors simply plug into their receptacles. This type of connector is also commonly found in Ethernet environments, especially on gigabit-capable Ethernet switches. As with ST connectors, SC connectors also require fiber to be polished and properly aligned, so ordering premade cables may save time and prevent frustration from faulty self-assembled cables.

MIC Connectors

Medium interface connectors (MICs) are used primarily in FDDI (Fiber Distributed Data Interface) environments. They are similar to SC connectors in that they plug into a receptacle, though they are specially keyed to only allow the transmit connector into the transmit receptacle and so forth.

MT-RJ and VF-45

Two companies have engineered connectors suitable for use in not only a networking environment, but also in a fiber to the desktop environment. Originally developed by Amp, the MT-RJ connector includes both transmit and receive fibers and is designed to be inserted into a receptacle, much like an RJ-45. The 3M VF-45 connector also closely resembles an RJ-45 connector and includes both transmit and receive fibers, but unlike the MT-RJ, it includes a sliding door to prevent dust or debris from entering the connection point.

FIBER-OPTIC ISSUES

While fiber-optic cable does not have many of the limitations of twisted-pair or coaxial cable, it does have a few fairly minor issues to consider. The first and largest issue is flexibility of the cable. As fiber-optic cable is essentially composed of glass or glass-like substances, its bend radius is quite poor. Care must be exercised when working with fiber-optic cabling, and any sharp bends in the cable should be avoided. A good rule of thumb is not to exceed a bend radius that is equal to 20 times the diameter of the cable itself. Additionally, when splicing or adding connectors to fiber-optic cabling, keep an eye out for glass shards that can become lodged in skin quite easily.

While fiber-optic cabling exceeds the distance restrictions of even RG-8A/U coaxial cable, it does have limitations. Current Ethernet standards call for a 550m distance limitation on multimode fiber, and between 2km and 40km (depending on speed) for single-mode fiber.

The last consideration before deploying a fiber-optic infrastructure is cost. While fiber optics do add substantial performance and distance gains, the cost of such an installation is considerably higher than that of a twisted-pair installation. Given the increase in cost, fiber optics should only be employed where and when necessary (that is, for long-distance runs, interswitch trunking, or high-speed connections).

FIBER-OPTIC TROUBLESHOOTING

Similar to twisted-pair cabling, most fiber-optic difficulties will only affect a single node or cable segment. Fortunately, with fiber-optic cabling, there is only one pair of transmit and receive cables to test for problems. Unfortunately, the test equipment for fiber-optic cabling is quite expensive and generally consists of an optical time domain reflectometer (OTDR).

Barring the use of expensive optical meters, there are some methods that can be used as a rapid and considerably cheaper means of identifying problems. First, if a particular cable segment has never been active, it is quite possible that the transmit and receive connectors need to be swapped. These connectors should be installed in a directly opposed order between the two ends of the cable; thus, transmit on one end would be receive on the other.

If possible, perform a visual inspection of the cable run, looking for tight bends—if a proper bend radius is not adhered to, the cable can become damaged. Replace the run if cable damage is suspected or physically observed.

Many fiber-optic devices utilize modular optical transceivers that can be removed or swapped. Should a fiber-optic run test clean but trouble still persists, try swapping the transceiver—it may have failed or become dirty.

Much like coaxial cable, each splice in a fiber run will introduce an increased level of attenuation. As such, too many or poorly executed splices can result in excessive signal loss to the point of corrupted transmissions or complete failure. To avoid excessive attenuation, limit the number of splices in a given fiber run. If attenuation is suspect, an OTDR or light meter may assist in identifying the problem.

Lastly, if a handmade cable is suspect, it may be advisable to swap the cable in its entirety or at least splice on new connectors, because the original splicing may have been faulty.

Never attempt to visually test the transmission ability of a connected fiber-optic cable, because exposure to laser radiation can result in permanent eye damage. Remember that fiber-optic systems typically use infrared wavelengths, which are not in the visible spectrum. If you must visually test an optical cable, use a flashlight.

SYMPTOMS

SYMPTOM 8-10   **There is no connection across the fiber-optic cable segment.**
While a break or faulty splice could be at fault for the connection failure, always ensure that the transmit and receive connectors are not reversed. This is a common problem in fiber-optic installations, and one that is readily corrected. Assuming the swap of connectors does not rectify the problem, check the cable run for excessive bends or breaks. If any physical damage is present it is acceptable to splice over the damaged portion or install a new cable run. It is also essential to check all fiber-optic connectors for improper installation, and correct if necessary.

SYMPTOM 8-11   **There is no (or intermittent) connection.**   An intermittent connection problem is most likely caused by excessive attenuation or a weak signal. Two major causes of either condition include too many splices in the cable run or a poorly constructed or dirty splice/connector. Additionally, a tight bend may also introduce high attenuation into the cable without fully breaking the core.

Check for poorly executed splicing or dust within the connectors, as well as physical damage to the cable. Should no physical damage be present, it is advisable to swap any media transceivers or NICs on the run in case of pending LED or diode failure. If an OTDR or light meter is available, test the cable for signal strength and/or attenuation.

SYMPTOM 8-12   **There is no connection after a new workstation is installed.**   Similar to the prior symptom, a faulty cable run, splice, or connector may be to blame. Use an OTDR or light meter, test the cable run, and replace any component necessary. Should the physical plant test clean, check the transmission equipment at either end for failures and replace as necessary. Lastly, always ensure that the transmit and receive cables are not swapped.

Further Study

3Com: **http://www.3com.com/technology/**
3Com Cable Errors:
http://support.3com.com/infodeli/tools/netmgt/tncsunix/product/091500/c11ploss.htm#14431
Annixter: **http://www.anixter.com/techlib/**
Bell Labs: **http://www.bell-labs.com/technology/lightwave/**
Cisco Systems:
http://www.cisco.com/univercd/cc/td/doc/product/mels/cm1500/manguide/appa.htm
Corning Fiber: **http://www.corningfiber.com**
Evolution of the telephone cable: **http://telecom.copper.org/evolution.html**
Fluke Networks: **http://www.flukenetworks.com**
IEEE: **http://grouper.ieee.org/groups/802/3/**

SERVER MOTHERBOARDS

The *motherboard* (or main board) is at the heart of every server, workstation, or ordinary desktop system that you'll ever work on (see Figure 9-1). Devices on the motherboard provide all of the system resources (i.e., IRQs, DMA channels, and I/O locations) and support the "core processing" devices needed by the system: the CPU, memory, real-time clock, BIOS, and expansion slots. A server's motherboard supports even more resources that are critical to a network: additional CPUs, a video controller, an onboard SCSI host adapter, an onboard IDE controller, and other network-related tools (which you'll see later). This chapter explains the features and layout of a typical server motherboard, highlights the CPUs, memory, and other devices that you'll find there, and explains the essentials of troubleshooting so that you can fix serious server problems as effectively as possible.

Understanding a Server Motherboard

Before you can install, upgrade, or troubleshoot a server's motherboard effectively, it is vital that you know your way around and be able to identify every critical device on sight. While each motherboard is certainly designed a bit differently, the devices are surprisingly simple to sort out. For the purposes of this book, we'll look closely at an Intel L440GX+ server board (see Figure 9-2), and talk a bit about the Intel SKA4 server chassis.

PROCESSOR

You must install at least one processor (i.e., items B and D). A server motherboard will typically support more than one 242-pin cartridge-style processor (i.e., two, four, or eight processors) such as the Pentium II or Pentium III—often Pentium II/III Xeon variations. The L440GX+ processor interface is

FIGURE 9-1   Internal view of the Gateway 7400 server

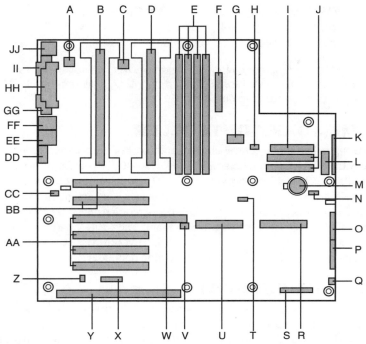

FIGURE 9-2   An Intel L440GX server motherboard (Courtesy of Intel Corporation)

MP (multi- processor) ready and operates at 100 MHz (more recent motherboards will support Socket 370 Pentium III processors at bus speeds of 133 MHz). A local APIC (advanced programmable interrupt controller) is included for interrupt handling in both single- and multiprocessor environments. The cartridge assembly includes the processor core with an integrated 16KB primary (L1) cache and a 512KB secondary (L2) cache. The Pentium II/III L2 cache includes burst pipelined synchronous static RAM (BSRAM), and error-correcting code (ECC) performance operates at half the core clock rate. The processor's numeric coprocessor (the floating-point unit, or FPU) significantly increases the speed of floating-point operations. Cartridge processors are secured by a retention mechanism attached to the server board. The CPU cooling fan for each processor is attached to a local fan power/tachometer connection (items A and C in Figure 9-2, respectively).

MEMORY

Servers require memory—*lots* of memory—in order to store the files and data being demanded by the network. For best performance, you should fill the system with the best-performing memory for your particular motherboard. For the L440GX+, only 100 MHz PC100 ECC (or non-ECC) SDRAM is supported by the server board. Your own motherboard may be quite different, so be sure to double-check the motherboard's specifications. For example, your server may use PC133 SDRAM or PC600/PC800 Rambus DRAM (RDRAM). The L440GX+ partitions memory as four banks of SDRAM DIMMs (item E), each providing 72 bits of noninterleaved memory (i.e., 64-bit main memory plus ECC). You may install 64MB to 2GB of *registered* memory DIMMs, or install 32MB to 1GB of *unbuffered* memory DIMMs. Memory should be added in order from slot 1 to slot 4. The memory controller automatically detects, sizes, and initializes the memory, depending on the type, size, and speed of the installed DIMMs/RIMMs. The controller then reports memory size and allocation to the server using configuration registers.

Never mix registered and unbuffered memory. Non-ECC memory may be installed, but ECC memory is recommended in a server environment for superior data integrity. Mixing non-ECC memory and ECC memory causes all ECC features to be disabled.

HOST BRIDGE/MEMORY CONTROLLER

Server motherboards are designed around a central chipset, and most of the features supported by your motherboard are handled by the chipset. For our example, Intel's L440GX+ board is designed around the Intel 82440GX AGPSet (440GX). The chipset provides 100 MHz processor host bus interface support, DRAM controller, PCI bus interface, AGP interface, and power management functions. The host bus/memory interface in the 440GX is optimized for 100 MHz operation using 100 MHz SDRAM main memory. It also supports a PCI interface that is PCI 2.1 compliant. The 440GX memory controller supports up to 2GB of ECC (or non-ECC) memory using PC100 SDRAM SIMMs. ECC can detect and correct single-bit errors, and detect multiple-bit errors for outstanding data integrity.

PERIPHERAL DEVICE SUPPORT

The server needs a means of communicating with the real world through ports and expansion slots, so you should be familiar with the varied devices and ports incorporated into your motherboard. A super I/O chip controls many of the system's I/O ports. Controllers (such as the National 87309) support two serial ports, one parallel port, the diskette drive, a PS/2-compatible keyboard, and a mouse. The server board provides a connector for each port, as shown in Figure 9-3.

- **Serial ports**   Each serial port (items GG and II in Figure 9-2, or item D in Figure 9-3) can be set to one of four different COM ports, and can be enabled separately. When enabled, each port can be programmed to generate edge- or level-sensitive interrupts. When disabled, serial port interrupts are available for use by other add-in boards.

- **Parallel port**   The super I/O chip provides one IEEE 1284–compatible 25-pin port supporting bidirectional EPP and ECP modes. The parallel port (item HH in Figure 9-2, or item C in Figure 9-3) can be configured with a different port address and interrupt. ECP mode is supported with two possible DMA channels. When disabled, parallel port interrupts are available for use by other add-in boards.

- **USB ports**   USB (universal serial bus) offers a versatile means of connecting various external devices (i.e., scanners or printers) without the need to power down the system and perform intrusive installations. The simple four-wire cables can be attached and removed without interrupting the server's normal operation. Most motherboards (including the L440GX+) provide a dual USB hub (item EE in Figure 9-2, or item H in Figure 9-3).

- **Chassis intrusion**   While most security concerns focus on passwords and authorizations within the network operating system itself, the physical security of the server is often overlooked. A *chassis intrusion* connector (item Z in Figure 9-2) attaches to a physical switch at the chassis cover. If the cover is opened, the server's security system can notify the network administrator (more on server security features later in this chapter).

- **Backup battery**   The information that defines a system's configuration is typically stored in a small area of low-power memory called CMOS RAM. Since that information must be preserved when system

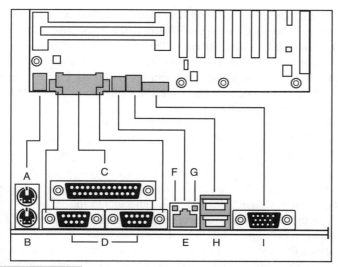

FIGURE 9-3   I/O connections on a server-type motherboard
(Courtesy of Intel Corporation)

power is off, a small battery (item M in Figure 9-2) is used to maintain the CMOS RAM. The battery
must be replaced periodically (see the motherboard's documentation for replacement suggestions).

■ **Expansion slots**   Chances are that you'll need to add one or more expansion devices to the PC.
Video adapters, SCSI adapters, RAID controllers, and network cards are just a few of the devices that
typically find use in a server. In order for an expansion device to work, it must be installed into a suitable expansion slot so that it may communicate with the host system. Your motherboard will generally provide an ISA slot to support legacy devices (item Y in Figure 9-2), and four or more PCI slots.
Modern server motherboards such as the L440GX+ provide four 33 MHz 32-bit PCI slots and two 66
MHz 32-bit PCI slots for even higher performance (items AA and BB in Figure 9-2, respectively). As
a rule, if you install a 33 MHz PCI card into one of the 66 MHz PCI slots, the bus speed for both slots
will be lowered to 33 MHz.

The components on some full-length expansion cards installed in slot 6 may interfere with the DIMM
connector latches. Use caution whenever installing full-length cards.

■ **Video port**   Graphics are certainly not vital elements of the network server, but some motherboards
provide an onboard video controller (item DD in Figure 9-2, or item I in Figure 9-3). The L440GX+
incorporates the Cirrus Logic CL-GD5480 64-bit SVGA controller that is fully VGA compatible. The
standard configuration uses 2MB of 10 ns onboard synchronous graphics memory (SGRAM). The
video controller supports pixel resolutions of up to 1,600 × 1,200 and up to 16.7 million colors. It also
supports refresh rates up to 100Hz for flicker-free displays. You *cannot* add video memory to the
server board, though it can be disabled and replaced with a video adapter card.

■ **SCSI controller**   Many high-end server boards provide an onboard SCSI host adapter for SCSI devices
and RAID support. The L440GX+ motherboard offers an Adaptec AIC-7896 dual-function SCSI controller, providing both UltraWide2 (LVDS) and UltraWide SCSI interfaces as two independent PCI functions
(items U and R in Figure 9-2, respectively). PCI slot 4 is also RAID-upgradable, providing specialized

support for the Adaptec ARO-1130U2 RAIDport controller (item W in Figure 9-2). The SCSI bus is terminated on the server board with active terminators that *cannot* be disabled, so the onboard SCSI controller must always be at one end of the bus. The SCSI device at the end of the cable must also be terminated. LVDS devices generally do not have termination capabilities, but non-LVDS devices (using a traditional single-ended SCSI interface) generally are terminated through a jumper or resistor pack. If the server board includes a SCSI cable, chances are that it has been modified to include active termination. When attaching any SCSI device to the cable, verify that they are *not* terminated—this is usually a configurable option using a jumper or terminator block on the device itself (check the documentation that comes with each SCSI device to locate this option). Termination of the SCSI bus is implemented using the active termination on the server board along with the active termination at the end of the SCSI cable.

- **IDE and floppy controller**   IDE is an inexpensive 40-pin interface designed for 16-bit intelligent disk drives, CD-ROM drives, Iomega Jaz drives, ATAPI IDE tape drives, and other drives with disk controller electronics onboard. The L440GX+ motherboard's PIIX4e chip (also called the PCI/ISA/IDE Accelerator) is a multifunction device on the server board that acts as a PCI-based Fast IDE controller. The PIIX4e controls PIO and DMA/bus-master operations with data transfer rates up to 33 MB/s (Ultra-DMA/33), though other motherboards may support faster Ultra-DMA/66 (66 MB/s) or Ultra-DMA/100 (100 MB/s) data transfers. The IDE controller provides two channels (item J in Figure 9-2), and supports two devices per channel—a maximum of four IDE-type devices. A hard drive activity LED in the server chassis can be attached to the hard drive LED connector (item V in Figure 9-2). Finally, the motherboard incorporates a simple 34-pin floppy drive interface (item I in Figure 9-2).

The maximum IDE cable length is 18 inches. Additional cable length may result in poor data transfer rates or data loss because of electrical signal interference.

- **Network controller (NIC)**   Your server motherboard may incorporate a NIC function that would eliminate the need for a single-channel NIC (item FF in Figure 9-2, or item E in Figure 9-3). The L440GX+ server board includes a 10BaseT/l00BaseTX network interface feature based on the Intel 82559 FastEthernet PCI Bus Controller chip. As a PCI bus-master device, the network controller can burst data at up to 132 MB/s (32 bits at 33 MHz). The network controller contains two receive and transmit FIFO (first in first out) buffers that prevent data overruns or underruns while awaiting access to the PCI bus. The controller has support for both 10 Mbps and 100 Mbps networks, capable of full or half-duplex, with back-to-back transmit at 100 Mbps. It also handles autodetect and autoswitching for 10 or 100 Mbps network speeds. The network status LEDs on the server board indicate transmit/receive activity on the LAN (the green LED: item F in Figure 9-3) and the LAN 10/100 Mbps transfer mode (the orange LED: item G in Figure 9-3).

- **Keyboard and mouse**   The keyboard/mouse controller is PS/2-compatible, and you'll find the keyboard/mouse connectors on the rear I/O panel (item JJ in Figure 9-2, or items B and A in Figure 9-3, respectively). As an added security measure, the server can be configured to lock out keyboard and mouse input after some predefined period of server inactivity. Once the inactivity (lockout) timer has expired, the keyboard and mouse do not respond until the proper server password is entered.

- **Power management (ACPI)**   Virtually all current server motherboards (i.e., the L440GX+) support advanced power management techniques such as the Advanced Configuration and Power Interface (ACPI) defined by the ACPI 1.0 and PC97 (or later) specifications. An ACPI-aware operating system can put the system into a state where the hard drives spin down, the system fans stop, and all processing is halted. However, the power supply will still be on and the processors will still be dissipating some power, so the power supply fan and processor fans will still run. The system will "wake" again when an external event occurs such as a keyboard entry, a mouse movement, or LAN activity sensed through the Wake on LAN connector (item T in Figure 9-2). The L440GX+ supports sleep states s0, s1, s4, and s5 (though the actual states that are available will depend on the version of Windows, UNIX, or Linux being used):

■ **s0**   This is the normal running state of the system.

■ **s1**   This is a processor sleep state where processing slows (throttles back or speed steps) or stops completely.

■ **s4**   This is the hibernate or Save to Disk state. The memory contents and machine state are saved to disk, and the system powers down most devices. Pressing the Power button (or other wakeup event) will restore the system state from the disk and resume normal operation.

■ **s5**   This is a "soft off" condition. Only the RTC (real-time clock) section of the PIIX4 controller and the BMC (Baseboard Management Controller) chips are running in this state. This is very deep power conservation.

■ **Power and cooling**   Power is provided through the 20-pin ATX-style power connector, as well as an optional ATX auxiliary power connector (items F and G in Figure 9-2). The main power connector supplies the various voltages and power signals needed to operate the motherboard and expansion devices. Table 9-1 lists the pinout of an ATX power connector. There are also numerous connections for chassis fans (items H, Q, and CC in Figure 9-2). In most cases, you do not need to use all of the available chassis fan connectors, but a heavily loaded server may easily benefit from the added cooling.

■ **Front panel connector**   You'll need to connect important case controls and indicators to the motherboard, and those connections are made at the front panel connector (item K in Figure 9-2). The L440GX+ provides connections for a power switch, hard drive activity LED, speaker, power LED, reset switch, and sleep (suspend) switch. You can see these connections detailed in Figure 9-4. These connections are often overlooked when replacing or upgrading the motherboard.

TABLE 9-1   ATX 20-PIN POWER CONNECTOR PINOUT

PIN#	DESCRIPTION	PIN#	DESCRIPTION
Pin 1	+3.3Vdc	Pin 11	+3.3Vdc
Pin 2	+3.3Vdc	Pin 12	-12Vdc
Pin 3	Ground	Pin 13	Ground
Pin 4	+5Vdc	Pin 14	PS-ON ("soft" power control signal)
Pin 5	Ground	Pin 15	Ground
Pin 6	+5Vdc	Pin 16	Ground
Pin 7	Ground	Pin 17	Ground
Pin 8	Power Good	Pin 18	-5Vdc
Pin 9	+5Vdc (standby)	Pin 19	+5Vdc
Pin 10	+12Vdc	Pin 20	+5Vdc

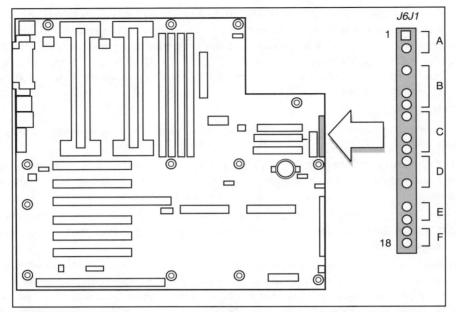

FIGURE 9-4   Close-up of a front panel connector (Courtesy of Intel Corporation)

Server Management and Security Features

Network administrators and technicians will need to access the server for testing and configuration changes. Consequently, you should be familiar with the various management tools supported by the server, and understand the security features that are available. This discussion will cover the features found in the Intel L440GX+ server motherboard.

SERVER MANAGEMENT

Server management is handled through a microcontroller on the motherboard. Intel refers to this as the Baseboard Management Controller (BMC). The BMC is basically an autonomous motherboard subsystem that monitors system events and logs their occurrence in nonvolatile memory called the *System Event Log* (SEL) and the *sensor data record* (SDR). Typical events include overtemperature and overvoltage conditions, fan failure, or chassis intrusion. The BMC provides access to the SEL information so that software running on the server can poll and retrieve the server's current status. A properly powered BMC performs the following functions:

- Monitors the server board's temperature and voltages
- Monitors which processors are present
- Detects and indicates fan failures

■ Manages the SEL and SDR interfaces

■ Monitors the SDR/SEL timestamp clock

■ Monitors the system management watchdog timer

■ Monitors the periodic SMI timer

■ Manages front-panel NMI handling

■ Monitors the event receiver

■ Controls secure mode, including video blanking, floppy write-protect monitoring, and front-panel lock/unlock initiation

■ Manages the sensor event initialization agent

■ Controls "Wake on LAN" support

The BMC and associated circuitry are powered from the ATX +5V standby supply, which remains active even when server power is switched off (the server must still be plugged into ac power). SEL contents can be retrieved after system failure, and used for analysis by field service personnel. Server management software tools (such as Intel Server Control software on the CD included with the L440GX+ server board) can be used to retrieve the SEL. You can generally update the software tools directly from the manufacturer's Web site. For the L440GX+, you'd download the software from **support.intel.com/support/motherboards/server/l440gx**.

Depending on the design of your motherboard, SEL and SDR information may also be available. The L440GX+ makes that data available through Intel's *Intelligent Management Bus* (IMB, shown as item N in Figure 9-2). An emergency server management card such as the Intel LANDesk Server Monitor Module card (SMM) can be inserted into the motherboard (item S in Figure 9-2), obtain the SEL data, and make it remotely accessible using a LAN or telephone line connection. The SMM is available with the LANDesk Server Manager Pro package.

EMERGENCY MANAGEMENT AND EVENT PAGING

Every minute offline can affect the productivity and sales of even a small company, so the purpose of server management tools and data logs is to allow fast, decisive system recovery when trouble strikes. The L440GX+ motherboard includes *Emergency Management Port* (EMP) software that allows remote server management through a modem or direct (serial port-to-serial port) connection. A technician can access and check the server from a remote location (i.e., an offsite support office). The EMP software allows you to connect to a server remotely, power the server on or off, and reset the server. You can also examine the contents of your SEL and SDR in order to check any events that may have precipitated the problem. Obtaining this information from a remote location can allow a technician to select replacement parts and have them on hand before physically reaching the server.

Event paging enables the server to dial out and generate a page when an issue arises. Your server can be configured to automatically dial up a paging service and page you when a platform event occurs (events include out-of-range temperatures, out-of-range voltages, chassis intrusion, fan failure, and so on). This gives technicians and administrators almost immediate warning when server trouble strikes. Since paging is also part of the autonomous BMC, a page can be generated even if the server's processors are down or system software is unavailable. Paging requires an external modem connected to the server's EMP serial connection (typically the COM2 serial port).

SECURITY

Security is a vital concern for network administrators. Unauthorized users must be prevented from accessing the network, and the physical server must be secured to protect the hardware from accidental (or even intentional) damage. The server typically offers both hardware and software security features.

Mechanical Interlocks

If the server supports mechanical interlocks, you can use the chassis intrusion alarm switch. When the server's outer cover is opened, the switch transmits an alarm signal to the server board, where BMC firmware and server management software handle the signal. The server can be programmed to respond to an intrusion by powering down or by locking the keyboard.

Software Locks

The CMOS Setup and the *System Setup Utility* (SSU) provide password security features to prevent unauthorized or accidental access to the system. Once security is enabled, you can only access the system after you enter the correct password(s). For example, software security will

- Enable the keyboard lockout timer—the server requires a password to reactivate the keyboard and mouse after a specified timeout period.
- Set and enable an administrative password.
- Set and enable a user password.
- Set a secure mode to prevent keyboard or mouse input, and prevent use of the front-panel reset and power switches.
- Activate a hot-key combination to start the secure mode.
- Disable writing to the floppy drive when the secure mode is set.
- Disable access to the boot sector of the primary hard disk drive.

Secure Mode

In the secure mode, you can boot the server and the operating system will run, but you must enter the user password to use the keyboard or mouse. You cannot turn off the system power or reset the server from the front-panel switches. The secure mode has no effect on any functions enabled through the *Server Manager Module* (or power control through the real-time clock). Taking the server out of secure mode does *not* change the state of system power. For example, if you press and release the power switch while secure mode is in effect, the system will not be powered off when secure mode is later removed. If the front-panel power switch remains depressed when secure mode is removed, the server *will* be powered off.

Remove a floppy drive and/or CD drive from a production server; this prevents an intruder booting the device by powering down and inserting, say, a UNIX boot floppy—also, most new software is downloaded anyway, so you don't need a floppy/CD. If you must keep these, configure CMOS so that these drives are *not* boot devices.

Installing a Server Motherboard

Whether you're replacing a failed motherboard or upgrading an existing server, chances are that you'll need to install a motherboard at some point. Motherboard installation is a highly intrusive procedure, so great care is required to properly reinstall all of your existing devices. This part of the chapter highlights

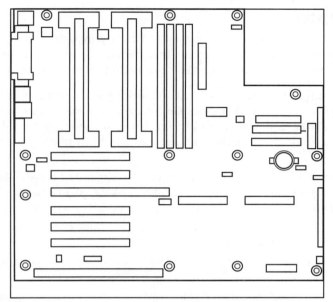

FIGURE 9-5   Mounting locations on a typical ATX server motherboard
(Courtesy of Intel Corporation)

the motherboard installation process, and covers installation of the processor and memory. We'll assume the use of an ATX motherboard such as the Intel L440GX+, as shown in Figure 9-5. Always refer to the documentation accompanying your particular motherboard for specific instructions and cautions.

STANDARD PRECAUTIONS

Before you get started, there are several warnings and cautions that you must understand thoroughly. Take a moment to review this section of the chapter before attempting any work on the network server:

■ *Shut down and unplug the server.* Remember that it's not enough to simply shut down the server through Windows. Standby power is always fed to the system as long as the power supply is connected to ac power. You *must* unplug the ac cord from the wall outlet before opening the chassis or beginning your work. Also, remember to shut off the monitor.

■ *Disconnect peripheral cables.* Power is also present on most peripheral cables attached to the server. Once the system is shut down and the ac power cord is unplugged, be sure to disconnect the network cable, the telephone (modem) cable, and other local peripheral devices (such as a parallel port printer) still under power (or shut those local devices off).

■ *Manage your ESD.* The motherboard—and most other devices in the server—are *extremely* sensitive to damage from accidental electrostatic discharge (ESD). Before opening the server, you must ground yourself using a properly grounded anti-static wrist strap. You should also work on a properly grounded anti-static mat on your work surface. Hold all electronic boards only by their edges. After removing a board from its protective wrapper (or from the server), place the board component side up on a grounded, static-free surface.

REMOVING THE BOARD

Let's start with a review of motherboard removal. This can be particularly important during server upgrades where you'll need to remove the existing motherboard first. Be sure to power down the server and disconnect the ac cord before proceeding. To remove a motherboard, follow these steps:

1. Open the server and remove all peripherals and components blocking access to the server board. In most cases, this will involve the removal of all expansion cards and cables attached to the motherboard, but you may also need to remove one or more drives. It will really depend on the design of your particular chassis (your server chassis manual will probably offer detailed information on this issue).

2. Label and disconnect all internal and external cables connected to expansion boards—labeling will eliminate guesswork when it's time to reconnect things later (taking a digital snapshot of the internal system may help also).

3. Remove all expansion boards. Remember to store the boards on an anti-static mat, or place them in anti-static bags to prevent accidental ESD damage.

4. Label and disconnect all internal and external cables connected to the server board (including the ATX power cable).

5. If you'll be transferring the memory and processor(s) to the new motherboard, remove the memory and processor(s) from the motherboard now. Place these sensitive devices in an appropriate anti-static container until you're ready to reinstall them.

6. Remove the server board retaining screws and set them aside.

7. Remove the server board and place it (component side up) on an anti-static mat, or place it in an anti-static bag to prevent accidental ESD damage.

8. If you're going to be storing the old server board for an extended period of time, remove the backup battery, place the battery into a heavy plastic bag, then tape the bag to the motherboard's anti-static bag.

9. You may also need to remove and save the EMI gasket that covers the I/O connectors on the board (the new motherboard may provide an appropriate new shield).

As with all major computer upgrades, you may want to perform a complete server backup to tape before proceeding. Changes to the drive controller hardware and other main components of the motherboard may sometimes cause unexpected operation of the system—and this may result in accidental data loss.

INSTALLING THE BOARD

Now it's time to install the new motherboard. Use extreme caution when positioning the new board so that standoffs do not scrape the printed circuit runs on the board. At high signal speeds, even minor scratches can impair signal reliability. Serious scratches can even damage the new motherboard. You should generally install the new motherboard first, then install the memory and processor before powering up and configuring the system:

1. You might need to install an EMI gasket on the rear chassis to accommodate the I/O port layout of your new motherboard.

2. Seat the new motherboard in the chassis, and verify that all of the mounting holes align properly. Do *not* proceed with the installation unless all of the mounting points are clear.

3. Insert screws through the mounting holes and into the threaded standoffs. Make sure the board is properly seated, and then tighten all the screws snugly (do not overtighten the screws).

4. Connect the 20-pin ATX power cable to the corresponding power connector on the motherboard.

5. Connect all internal and external cables to the server board, and install a fresh battery to preserve the motherboard's configuration data. When connecting cables, be sure to check the alignment of pin 1 with each cable and header (the red or blue stripe down one side of the cable always represents pin 1).

6. Reinstall all expansion boards and bolt them into place on the chassis.

7. Connect all internal and external cables to the expansion boards.

Double-check that all screws securing the motherboard are snugged into place. Loose screws may work out, drop onto live circuitry or into a fan, and result in serious system problems.

INSTALLING/REPLACING PERIPHERALS

Network servers typically rely on fast processors and a great deal of memory. Once the new motherboard is installed, you'll need to install memory devices and at least one processor before powering up and configuring the server. Be sure to keep the server powered off and unplugged while working inside of it.

Memory

Memory is often installed in the form of DIMMs (dual inline memory modules), and a typical server motherboard will support 1GB or more of synchronous DRAM (SDRAM) memory across up to four DIMM slots (i.e., four 256MB DIMMs), such as in Figure 9-6. Some servers will employ Rambus memory (RDRAM) fitted into RIMM (Rambus inline memory module) slots. This part of the chapter focuses on the more popular DIMM architecture, so RIMM users should refer to the specific instructions and cautions accompanying the motherboard. Since you may need to upgrade memory in an existing configuration, let's look at DIMM removal first:

Memory is extremely sensitive to accidental damage from ESD. Use all anti-static precautions when handling a DIMM.

1. Open the server (if it's not already open) and locate the DIMM slot(s).

2. Gently push the plastic ejector levers out and down to eject the selected DIMM from its slot.

3. Hold the DIMM only by its edges (careful not to touch its components or gold edge connectors) and carefully lift it away from the socket. Store the old DIMM in an anti-static package.

4. Repeat to remove other DIMMs as necessary.

Refer to the motherboard's documentation and select one or more DIMMs to provide an adequate amount of memory for the server. DIMMs must be selected based on capacity (i.e., 128MB), memory type (i.e., SDRAM), speed (i.e., 8 ns cycle time), and error checking (i.e., parity, nonparity, ECC, or non-ECC).

FIGURE 9-6   Servers can easily support 1–2GB of RAM in the form of DIMMs or RIMMs.

DIMMs and sockets may use tin or gold in the connectors, but mixing dissimilar metals (i.e., a DIMM with gold contacts into a DIMM slot with tin contacts) may cause later memory failures—resulting in data corruption. Only install DIMMs with gold-plated edge connectors in gold-plated sockets.

Let's review the process for DIMM installation:

1. Open your server (if it's not already open) and locate the DIMM slot(s).

2. Hold a DIMM only by its edges, and remove it from its anti-static package.

3. Orient the DIMM so that the two notches in the bottom edge of the DIMM align with the keys in the slot.

4. Insert the bottom edge of the DIMM into the slot, and press down firmly on the DIMM until it seats correctly and fully in the slot.

5. Gently push the plastic ejector levers on either end of the slot to the upright (locked) position.

6. Repeat to install other DIMMs as necessary.

Use extreme care when removing or installing a DIMM—too much pressure can damage the slot (and ruin the motherboard). Apply only enough pressure on the plastic ejector levers to release or secure the DIMM. DIMMs are keyed to allow insertion in only one way.

Processor(s)

A server motherboard will normally accommodate two or four (or more) processors. For example, our Gateway 7400 server supports two processors (see Figure 9-7), while the Gateway 8400 version will accommodate up to four processors. You'll need to attach an appropriate heat-sink/fan unit to each processor being installed now, and have a termination card available for other processor slot(s). Refer to the documentation that accompanied the server motherboard and verify the type and speed of compatible processors (i.e., one or two 800 MHz Pentium III processors). If you're adding a second processor, be sure that the new processor matches the existing one (including the processor's manufacturing revision if necessary), or is otherwise suitable for use with the original CPU.

Processors are extremely sensitive to accidental damage from ESD. Use all anti-static precautions when handling a processor.

Let's review correct processor removal first:

1. Open your server (if it's not already open) and locate the processor slot(s).

If the server has been running, any installed processor and heat-sink motherboard will be *hot*. To avoid possible burn injury, allow the system to remain off for at least 15 minutes before servicing the processors.

2. If the selected processor has a heat-sink/fan unit, disconnect the power wire from its connector on the server motherboard:

■ For cartridge-type processors, carefully pull back the tab of the retention mechanism with your left hand until the processor can be rotated out of the slot. With your right hand, grasp the processor on the side closest to the retention mechanism tab you're pulling and rotate the one side of the processor out of the slot. Once that side is free, you can pull the other side out of the slot. This can be a difficult process. Pull the retention mechanism tab just far enough for the retention lock to free the processor.

■ For socket-type processors, locate and disengage the ZIF lever, then raise the lever to the full upright position. You may need to gently rock the processor back and forth to remove it from the socket. Do *not* pry the processor from one side only—this can cause pins to bend and damage the processor.

3. Remove the processor and place it in an anti-static bag or box.

4. Select one or more suitable processors for the motherboard, and verify that their heat-sink/fan units are properly attached.

5. Locate the corresponding CPU slots (or sockets) on the motherboard, and also locate the small fan connectors near each slot (or socket). Virtually all modern server motherboards will autodetect the processor, and configure the bus speed, multiplier, and CPU voltage automatically. This means you rarely need to set jumpers to prepare a motherboard for new CPUs.

You generally must install a termination card into any vacant processor slot to ensure reliable system operation. A termination card contains AGTL+ termination circuitry and clock termination. The server may not boot unless all vacant processor slots contain a termination card.

FIGURE 9-7   The Gateway 7400 supports two Socket 370 processors.

Let's cover the essentials of processor installation now:

1. Open your server (if it's not already open) and locate the processor slot(s):

- If your server has one processor and you're adding a second, you must remove the termination card from the secondary processor slot. Carefully pull back the tab of the retention mechanism until the termination card can be rotated out of the slot. Grasp the card on the side closest to the retention mechanism tab and rotate the one side of the card out of the slot. Once that side is free, you can pull the other side out of the slot.

- If your server has one processor and you're replacing it, leave the termination card in place in the empty secondary slot. Remove the processor you want to replace.

- If your server has two processors and you are replacing one or both, remove the appropriate one(s).

2. Remove the new processor from its anti-static package and orient the processor in its slot (or socket), using special care to align pin 1 properly.

3. For cartridge-type processors, slide the processor into the retention mechanism. Push down firmly, with even pressure on both sides of the top, until the processor is seated. It should click into place.

4. For socket-type processors, seat the processor fully into the socket, then close and lock the ZIF lever.

The grounded retention mechanisms (GRMs) are not compatible with SECC-type processor packaging—the new GRMs only support SECC2-type (i.e., Pentium II/III Xeon) processors. If you plan on using SECC-type (i.e., ordinary Pentium II/III) processors, you must use a universal retention mechanism (URM).

5. Attach the fan power cable to the three-pin connector on the server board.

6. Close the server and secure the outer cover (make sure that any intrusion switch is closed).

7. Connect any remaining external cables and attach the ac power cord.

8. Turn on the monitor and then power up the server. Start the server's setup routine to configure the new server motherboard, memory, and CPU(s).

Configuring the Motherboard

After the motherboard is secured in a server, and the memory and processor(s) have been installed, it's time to configure the motherboard in its new hardware setup. Server configuration usually involves setting the motherboard's jumpers, running the CMOS Setup, and executing other utilities needed to settle the server into its network environment.

SETTING THE JUMPERS

Modern motherboards use relatively few jumpers—the vast majority of the server's configuration is set through the CMOS Setup and other software tools. However, the few jumpers present on your motherboard will affect major security issues (i.e., clearing a password, chassis intrusion, and so on). The documentation accompanying your server motherboard will detail the location and use of each jumper. For the Intel L440GX+ motherboard (see Figure 9-8), you'll need to understand nine critical jumpers:

■ **BIOS Write Enable (BIOS WR EN)** This jumper protects the BIOS boot block. In the set position, the BIOS boot block is protected and cannot be overwritten (aka write protected). In the reset position, the BIOS can be erased and reprogrammed. Note that this protects the motherboard's BIOS only—not the BMC firmware.

■ **Baseboard Management Controller Firmware Upgrade (BMC FRC UP)** This jumper controls the server's boot cycle. In the default state, the server will boot normally. In the program state, the server will attempt to read a floppy disk in order to update the BMC firmware. This jumper must be set in conjunction with the BMC WR EN jumper. Note that this enables the reprogramming of the BMC firmware only—not the motherboard's BIOS.

■ **Baseboard Management Controller Write Enable (BMC WR EN)** This jumper protects the BMC firmware boot block. In the set position, the BMC boot block is protected and cannot be overwritten (it's write protected). In the reset position, the BMC firmware can be erased and reprogrammed. Note that this protects the BMC firmware only—not the motherboard's BIOS.

■ **Clear the CMOS (CMOS CLR)** This jumper protects the contents of the CMOS RAM. In the default protected mode, the CMOS RAM contents are protected (though they can be updated through the CMOS Setup routine). In the erase mode, the CMOS RAM contents are replaced with a set of

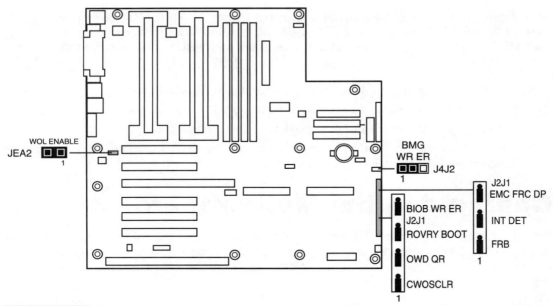

FIGURE 9-8   Jumper locations for a server motherboard (Courtesy of Intel Corporation)

default factory values. This feature is particularly handy for restoring basic functionality to the server after the backup battery is replaced, or when settings are altered incorrectly.

■ **Fault Resilient Booting (FRB)**   This jumper controls the motherboard's fault-resilient booting (FRB) feature. When FRB is enabled, the system will boot from processor 1 if processor 0 (the default processor) does not respond. When FRB is disabled, the system will not boot if processor 0 does not respond.

■ **Intrusion Detection (INT DET)**   When enabled, a switch installed on chassis will send a signal to the server indicating when the outer cover has been removed (this will generate a security warning for the network administrator). If the feature is disabled, the switch is bypassed and no warning will be generated if the cover is removed.

■ **Clear the Password (PSWD CLR)**   In the default protect mode, the system will maintain the current system password (if the password is set). In the erase mode, the system will clear the password. This feature is particularly handy if the system password is forgotten or set improperly.

■ **Recovery Boot (RCVRY BOOT)**   This controls the server's boot cycle. In the default normal mode, the system attempts to boot using the BIOS stored in flash memory. If the jumper is set to the recovery mode, the BIOS attempts a recovery boot, loading BIOS code from a floppy diskette into the flash device. This feature is typically used when the motherboard's BIOS code has been corrupted, or needs to be updated. Note that this feature only controls the motherboard BIOS—not the BMC firmware.

■ **Wake On LAN Enable (WOL EN)**   This jumper enables/disables the motherboard's Wake On LAN (WOL) support. If the motherboard receives adequate standby power (i.e., +5V@0.8A through the standby power line) to support Wake On LAN, you can enable this feature (enabled by default). Otherwise, you must disable this feature.

In virtually all cases, the server should be powered off and unplugged before changing a jumper position. Most jumpers will need to be returned to their original (default) positions after the respective feature has been used (i.e., after the system password has been cleared).

POST

Each time you start (or restart) the server, a power-on self test (POST) program is executed from the motherboard's BIOS. A typical POST checks the server board, the installed processor(s), the installed memory, the keyboard, and most installed peripheral devices. During the memory test, POST displays the amount of memory that it is able to access and test (the length of time needed to test memory depends on the amount of memory installed in the system). If an error is detected in the motherboard, processors, memory, or other installed devices, the POST will generate an error (more about errors in the "General Troubleshooting" section later in this chapter). A normal POST process will proceed similar to the steps shown here:

1. Turn on the video monitor and power up the server. After a moment, the POST will run and the memory count will start.

2. After the memory count, you'll see messages and screen prompts such as

   ```
   Press F2 key if you want to run SETUP

   Keyboard...Detected
   Mouse...Detected
   ```

3. In this example, you'd press F2 to start the system's CMOS Setup routine. Other motherboard and BIOS versions may use different keys, but you'll see the key(s) called out in the message.

4. If you do *not* press the key(s) to start your CMOS Setup, the POST will end and transfer control to the operating system. If you do not have a device (a drive) with an operating system loaded, the above message remains for a few seconds while the boot process continues, and the system beeps once. Then you'll see a message such as

   ```
   Operating system not found
   ```

5. When the operating system is found, the boot process continues. If your motherboard includes an onboard SCSI host adapter, you may see other BIOS messages such as

   ```
   Press <Ctrl><A> to enter SCSI Utility
   ```

6. In this example, you'd press CTRL-A to start the SCSI controller's setup utility. Other motherboard and BIOS versions may use different keys, but you'll see the key(s) called out in the message. Start the SCSI utility if there are SCSI devices installed on the server. When the utility opens, follow the onscreen instructions to configure the onboard SCSI host adapter and devices. If you do not enter the SCSI utility, the boot process continues normally.

7. Press ESC during POST to open a boot menu when POST finishes—from this menu, you can choose the boot device (i.e., the C: drive or D: drive) or enter the CMOS Setup.

8. After the POST cycle is complete, the system beeps once.

9. Now you'll see the operating system logo, and the actual operating system will begin to load.

If the system halts before the POST finishes, the system speaker emits a beep code indicating a fatal system error that requires immediate attention. If the POST has initialized the video system, you may see a message on the video display (and the system may beep twice). Record any beep or text error messages.

CMOS SETUP

The CMOS Setup routine is part of the motherboard BIOS, and the many variables that define the system's configuration are stored in battery-supported CMOS RAM or flash memory. You may elect to enter the CMOS Setup (sometimes referred to as the BIOS Setup or simply Setup) when the server motherboard is upgraded, the backup battery is replaced, or other hardware changes are made to the system that must be identified at the system hardware level. The system's documentation generally lists a selection of common settings. A few reasons to access the CMOS Setup might include

- Identifying the diskette drive
- Selecting a parallel port mode
- Enabling or disabling a serial port
- Setting the time and date
- Configuring an IDE-type hard drive (i.e., cylinders, sectors, heads, and so on)
- Specifying a boot device sequence
- Enabling the SCSI BIOS (and SCSI host controller)
- Setting the processor speed
- Enabling or disabling power conservation modes

If the values stored in CMOS RAM do not agree with the hardware detected by the POST (i.e., after the CMOS RAM is cleared), an error message is generated. In many cases, you can reenter the CMOS Setup to correct the error, or use the Clear CMOS jumper to reset factory default values.

SYSTEM SETUP UTILITY (SSU)

While the motherboard's CMOS Setup routine is vital to the configuration of low-level server hardware, there are several critical issues that are not addressed by Setup. Motherboards (such as the L440GX+) include a System Setup Utility (SSU) on the driver/resource CD. The SSU allows a higher-level configuration of the server. For example, an SSU assigns resources to baseboard devices and add-in cards *prior* to loading the operating system. It allows you to specify boot device order and system security options outside of the CMOS Setup. The SSU permits viewing (and clearing) the system's critical event log, and provides a system-level view of the server's I/O devices. The SSU also allows you to perform basic server troubleshooting when the OS is not operational. Use the SSU when you need to

- Add or remove boards that affect the assignment of resources (i.e., ports, memory, IRQ, or DMA)
- Modify the server's boot device order or security settings
- Change the server configuration settings
- Save the server configuration
- View or clear the System Event Log (SEL)

Legacy and PnP Devices

The SSU is "PCI aware", and it should comply with ISA plug-and-play specifications—the SSU works with any compliant configuration (**.CFG**) files supplied by individual peripheral device manufacturers. As a rule, you do *not* need to run the SSU when adding or removing PnP ISA/PCI devices, but you *must* run the SSU to reconfigure the server when installing or removing a legacy ISA device.

POST checks the system configuration data against the actual hardware configuration. If the two do not agree, POST generates an error message. You must then run the SSU to specify the correct configuration before the server boots. An SSU allows you to specify a system configuration using the information provided by **.CFG** files, configuration registers, flash memory, and any information that you enter manually. The SSU writes this configuration information to flash memory. Changes to the configuration will take effect when you boot the server. The SSU always includes a checksum with the configuration data so the BIOS can detect any potential data corruption before the actual hardware configuration takes place.

Launching the SSU

In most cases, an SSU may be run directly from the motherboard's server resource CD by booting the server system to the CD and selecting Utilities. Running the **SSU.BAT** file provided on the resource CD will start the SSU (if the server boots directly from the SSU media, the **SSU.BAT** file is automatically run). When the SSU starts in the local execution mode (the default mode), the SSU accepts input from the keyboard and/or mouse, and presents a basic graphical user interface (GUI) on the primary monitor.

The SSU runs from writable, nonwritable, removable, and nonremovable media. If the SSU is run from nonwritable media (i.e., a CD-ROM drive), user preference settings cannot be saved.

You could also run the SSU remotely using a remote server fitted with a Server Monitor Module (SMM) card and a local system with remote control software. The SMM (i.e., a LANDesk 2) card provides video memory, keyboard, and mouse redirection support for the remote server and the connection is established through either a modem or an Ethernet link. Since the SSU would be running exclusively on the remote server, any files required for the SSU to run must also be available on the remote server (usually on removable or nonremovable media).

Understanding the Processor

The *processor* (also known as the microprocessor, CPU, or central processing unit) is the single most important component in the PC. This powerful programmable logic device handles all of the program instructions (and much of the data) on the system—including Windows modules, applications, and data files. As a technician, it's important that you understand some of the important issues involved in processor technology and its implications on the desktop or server:

- **System performance**   The processor is probably the most important single factor behind system performance. While other components (i.e., memory, chipset, drive controller, NIC adapter, and so on) also influence overall performance, the processor's capabilities dictate the efficiency with which program instructions are executed.

- **Software support**   The processor can only work with a certain instruction set. For example, Intel and AMD processors typically run "x86" type software such as DOS, Windows, and Linux/UNIX—non-x86 software will not run. Current processors that support instruction extensions (such as MMX, 3DNow, or SME) support software written to take advantage of those special features.

- **Reliability and stability**   The quality and design integrity of the processor determines how reliably your system will run (you may remember the notable bug that occurred with early Pentium processors). Dependability will also vary with the age of the processor and how much energy it consumes.

- **Energy consumption and cooling**   Older processors consumed relatively little power (compared to other system devices), but current Pentium II/III or Xeon processors can consume a great deal of power. Power consumption will have an impact on system cooling and overall system reliability.

- **Motherboard support**   Today's processors require comprehensive support from the motherboard's BIOS and chipset. This means you'll need to select a motherboard that will support your intended processor(s).

KNOWING THE CHIP

It's usually helpful to understand some key physical characteristics of a processor chip. Issues related to the design and manufacture of the physical chip itself will have a direct impact on the chip's size, performance, power consumption, and heat generation. This will consequently have an influence on how the processor is employed in the system.

Versions and Steps

A processor represents a very complex and intricate design. As with any hardware design, there are often bugs that are discovered (i.e., the floating-point bug discovered with early Pentium processors). This means that a given processor may exist in many different design revisions, where newer versions fix the problems encountered with older versions. Intel uses the term "stepping" or "S-step" to indicate a processor's revision, and the S-step is typically marked right on the processor. AMD uses a model number to indicate the processor's revision. For example, a late-model Intel Pentium III processor may use an S-spec of SL3WA. It is not necessary that you be able to interpret the S-spec (or other manufacturer's revision markings) on sight—you can usually find a manufacturer's table that details the processor's characteristics based on its S-spec number.

New features are generally not introduced with higher processor steps—only problems are corrected and performance issues resolved.

As a rule, the processor's revision number will have little (if any) impact on the system's performance, but it might. Problems may be encountered when using particular processor revisions with certain motherboard and BIOS combinations. When you encounter system reliability problems, check with the motherboard maker for possible issues with your processor step. Certain minimum step levels and step matching may also be important when using several processors on the motherboard.

Processor Power and Management

Processors consume a relatively large amount of power. In order to reduce the PC's power demands and improve performance, the traditional +5-volt operating voltages of years past have given way to processors, support chips, and expansion devices that operate at far lower voltages. The first step in this evolution was to reduce the operating voltage level to +3.3 volts. This was apparent in early Pentium processors. Newer processors (such as the Pentium MMX and Pentium II/III) reduce voltage levels even more using a *dual voltage* (or *split rail*) design. A split rail processor uses two different voltages. The external (or I/O voltage) is usually +3.3 volts, and this ensures compatibility with the other chips on the motherboard. The internal (or core voltage) is somewhat lower (usually +2.5 to +2.9 volts, though +1.8- to +2.4-volt operation is appearing in the latest processors). The I/O voltage lets the processor "talk" to the motherboard, while the core voltage allows the processor to run cooler internally.

Traditionally, you'd need to set the correct operating voltage for your particular processor(s) by configuring one or more voltage regulation jumpers on the motherboard. Today, processor voltages are set automatically by voltage selection signals on the processor itself—all you need to do is plug in the processor and boot the computer.

Since the power consumption of a CPU is related to its processing speed and internal activity, Intel eventually developed power management circuitry that enables processors to conserve power (and lengthen battery life in laptop systems). Power management was originally introduced with the Intel 486SL processor (an enhanced version of the 486DX processor), but power management features were soon standardized and incorporated into all Pentium and later processors. These power management features are referred to as "System Management Mode" (or SMM). SMM circuitry is integrated into the physical processor chip, but operates independently to control the processor's power use based on its activity level. SMM allows the system to specify time intervals after which the CPU will be powered down partially or fully (aka throttled back), and also enables the suspend/resume feature that supports today's system *standby* and *hibernate* modes. SMM settings are normally controlled through the CMOS Setup.

Processor Cooling

The millions of transistors operating inside a processor all liberate a small amount of heat each time they switch on or off. When this switching action takes place hundreds of millions of times each second, heat (and its management) becomes a serious concern. Processors have a specified safe temperature range that represents their limits for normal operation. If the processor overheats, serious system problems will usually result. These will usually take the form of system reboots, lockups, or crashes. An overheated processor can also manifest itself through memory errors, application errors, disk problems, or a host of other things. A severely (or repeatedly) overheated processor can also be permanently damaged, though this rarely happens. These problems can be extremely difficult to diagnose because they often appear to implicate other parts of the system. For example, a system crash or lockup is often associated with a software bug or hardware conflict rather than an overheated CPU.

Processors are cooled by active heat sinks—that is, a fast fan mounted to a large metal heat sink with numerous fins. The heat sink pulls heat away from the processor, and the fan in turn cools the heat sink. Air warmed by the heat sink is vented from the case (this is the warm air you feel exhausting from the back of the case). The problem with active heat sinks is that they rely on the fan. If the fan fails, the processor can overheat in a very short time. To protect the processor from an accidental fan failure, many motherboards integrate tachometers that check the fan's rotational speed, and thermostats that measure the processor's case temperature. If the fan stops turning—or the processor's temperature climbs over a preset limit—a warning will indicate the fault and allow you to address the trouble before a crash or other system problem occurs.

Processor Packages

Raw chips (the small "dies") are not used directly—they are far too fragile and sensitive. Instead, the die is placed in a *package* that will protect the die and help it to dissipate heat. The form of that standardized package normally takes the form of a slotted or socketed device. Slot-type processors are normally classified as slot 1, slot 2, or slot A. Socket-type processors are usually denoted as socket 370 or socket A. You can see four slot 1 connectors (marked "H") for the Intel SKA4 quad processor server motherboard in Figure 9-9. Typical processor classifications are highlighted below:

■ **Slot 1**   These single edge contact (SEC) packages are normally associated with Intel Pentium II and Pentium III processors.

■ **Slot 2**   These are slightly larger SEC packages that are intended for Intel Pentium II/III Xeon processors, and are commonly found in server and multiprocessor platforms.

■ **Slot A**   These are SEC packages (almost identical to slot 1) that are found with AMD Athlon processors.

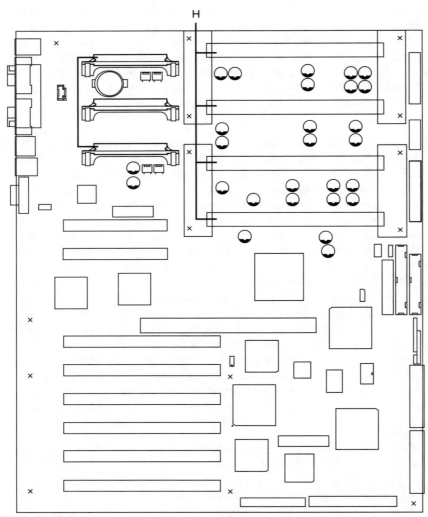

FIGURE 9-9   CPU locations on an Intel SKA4 quad server motherboard (Courtesy of Intel Corporation)

- **Socket 370**   These are 370-pin processor packages that are used with many Intel Celeron processors.

- **Socket A**   These are 460-pin processor packages (sometimes called socket 460) that are used with late model AMD Athlon (Thunderbird), and Duron processors.

- **Socket 423 and 478**   These are PGA packages used to accommodate the current generation of Pentium 4 processors.

MULTIPROCESSING NOTES

Multiprocessing is the technique of running a system with more than one processor. The idea is that you can double system performance using two processors instead of one, quadruple performance with four processors instead of one, and so on. This doesn't always work that well in actual practice, but multiprocessing can result in improved performance under certain conditions. In order to employ multiprocessing effectively, the host computer must have all of the following elements in place:

- **Motherboard support**   You'll need a motherboard capable of handling multiple processors. This means additional sockets or slots for the extra CPUs, and a chipset capable of handling the multiprocessor configuration.

- **Processor support**   You'll need processors that are suitable for use in a multiprocessing system. Not all processors are suitable, and only some versions of the same processor are suitable. Be sure to check the motherboard's documentation for processor recommendations.

- **Operating system support**   You'll also need an operating system that supports multiprocessing, such as Windows NT/2000 or UNIX. Other operating systems, such as Windows 98, do not support multiprocessing.

Multiprocessing is most effective when used with application software designed specifically for it. Multiprocessing is managed by the operating system, which allocates different tasks to be performed by the various processors in the system. Applications designed for multiprocessing use are said to be "threaded"—they are broken into smaller routines that can be run independently. This allows the operating system to let threads run on more than one processor simultaneously, and that is how multiprocessing results in improved performance. If the application isn't designed this way, it can't take advantage of multiple processors (though the operating system can still make use of the additional processors if you use more than one application at a time).

Multiprocessing can be said to be either asymmetric or symmetric. This term indicates how the operating system divides tasks between the processors in the system. *Asymmetric* multiprocessing designates some processors to perform system tasks only, and others to run applications only. This rigid design results in poor performance during times when the computer needs to run more system tasks than user tasks (or vice versa). *Symmetric* multiprocessing (SMP) allows *either* system or user tasks to run on any processor. It's a more flexible approach, and therefore offers better performance. SMP is what most multiprocessing PC motherboards use.

For a processor to support multiprocessing, it must support a multiprocessing protocol that dictates the way that the processors and chipset talk to each other in order to implement SMP. Intel processors typically use an SMP protocol called APIC, and Intel chipsets that support multiprocessing are designed to work with these chips. APIC is a proprietary Intel standard, so even though AMD and Cyrix can make Intel-compatible processors, they cannot make them work in SMP configurations. AMD and Cyrix implement their own SMP standard called OpenPIC.

PROCESSOR MODES

Processors are capable of operating in several different modes. The term "mode" refers to the way(s) in which a processor creates (and supports) an operating environment for itself. The processor mode controls how the processor sees and manages the system memory and the tasks that use it. Three different modes of operation have evolved for the PC: the real mode, the protected mode, and the virtual real mode. You should have a basic understanding of these three modes.

Real Mode

The original IBM PC could only address 1MB of RAM. The decisions made in those early days have carried forward, and in each new processor, the processor had to support a mode that would be compatible with the original Intel 8088 chip—this is called *real mode*. When a processor is running in real mode, it has the advantage of speed, but it otherwise accesses memory with the same restrictions of the original 8088: an addressable RAM limit of 1MB and memory access that doesn't take advantage of the 32-bit processing found in modern CPUs. All processors can support the real mode—in fact, the computer normally starts up in real (DOS) mode. Real mode is used by DOS and standard DOS applications.

Protected Mode

Starting with the IBM AT, a new processor *protected mode* was introduced. This is a much more powerful mode of operation than real mode, and is used in all modern multitasking operating systems. The protected mode has numerous advantages:

- The protected mode offers full access to all of the system's memory (there is no 1MB limit in protected mode).

- The protected mode has the ability to multitask, meaning that the operating system can manage the execution of multiple programs simultaneously.

- The protected mode offers support for virtual memory, which allows the system to use the hard disk to emulate additional system RAM when needed.

- The protected mode also offers faster (32-bit) access to memory, and faster 32-bit drivers to handle I/O transfers.

Each running program has its own assigned memory locations, which are protected from conflicting with other programs. If a program tries to use a memory address that it isn't allowed to, a protection fault is generated. All of the major operating systems today use protected mode, including Windows 9x/ME, Windows NT/2000, OS/2, and Linux. Even DOS (which normally runs in real mode) can access protected mode memory using DPMI (DOS Protected Mode Interface), used by DOS games to break the 640KB DOS conventional memory barrier. The 386 (and later) processors can switch "on the fly" from real to protected mode, and vice versa. Protected mode is also sometimes called 386 enhanced mode, since it became mainstream with that family of processors.

Virtual Real Mode

The third mode of processor operation is actually an enhancement of the protected mode. Protected mode is normally used to run graphical multitasking operating systems such as the various types of Windows. There is sometimes a need to run DOS programs under Windows, but DOS programs need to be run in real mode—not protected mode. *Virtual real mode* was created to solve this problem. It emulates the real mode from within the protected mode and allows DOS programs to run. A protected mode operating system such as Windows can actually create multiple virtual real-mode machines, each of which appears to the software running it as if it were the only software running on the machine. Each virtual machine gets its own 1MB address space, an image of the real hardware BIOS routines, and so on. Virtual real mode is what is used when you use a DOS window or run a DOS game in Windows 95/98. When you start a DOS application, Windows creates a virtual DOS machine for it to run under.

ARCHITECTURAL PERFORMANCE FEATURES

The past several years have seen an explosion of technologies and techniques intended to wring more performance out of a processor. Designers have invested tremendous effort to develop the improvements that we take for granted each time we boot the system. This part of the chapter describes some of the performance-enhancing features found in a modern microprocessor.

Superscalar Architecture

Program instructions are processed through circuits called *execution units*. Superscalar architecture refers to the use of multiple execution units to allow the CPU to process more than one instruction simultaneously. This is a form of multiprocessing within the CPU itself, since multiple processing chores are taking place at the same time. Most modern processors are superscalar at one level or another.

Superpipelining

Instructions are processed in a pipeline, with each step in the pipeline performing a certain amount of work on the instruction. By making the pipeline longer (with more stages), each stage performs less work and the processor can be scaled to a higher clock frequency. This is known as *superpipelining*, and is generally regarded an improvement over regular pipelining.

Speculative Execution and Branch Prediction

Some CPUs have the ability to execute multiple instructions at once. In some cases, not all of the results of the execution will be used because changes in the program flow may mean that the given instruction should never have been executed in the first place. This often occurs in the vicinity of program branches—where a condition is tested, and the program path is altered depending on the results. Branches represent a real problem for pipelining, because you can't always be sure that instructions will go in a linear sequence. A less sophisticated processor may stall the pipeline until the results are known, and this can hurt performance. More advanced processors will *speculatively execute* the next instruction anyway. The hope is that the CPU will be able to use the results if the branch goes the way it thinks it will.

Even more advanced processors combine this with *branch prediction*, where the processor can actually predict (with fairly good accuracy) which way the branch will go based on past history. Branch prediction improves the handling of branches by making use of a special small cache called the *branch target buffer* or *BTB*. Whenever the processor executes a branch, it stores information about it in this area. When the processor next encounters the same branch, it is able to make an informed guess about which way the branch is likely to result. This helps keep the pipeline flowing and improves performance.

Out-of-Order Execution

Processors that use multiple execution units can actually complete the processing of program instructions in the wrong order. For example, instruction 2 can be executed before instruction 1 has finished. This versatility improves performance since it allows execution with less waiting time. The results of the execution are reassembled in the correct order to ensure that the program runs correctly. This is normally done by the *retirement unit* (an instruction handling stage in the processor's circuitry) on translating processors.

Register Renaming and Write Buffers

Register renaming is a technique used to support multiple execution paths without conflicts between different execution units trying to use the same registers. Instead of just one set of registers being used, multiple sets are put into the processor. This allows different execution units to work simultaneously without unnecessary stalls in the pipeline. Write buffers are used to hold the results of instruction execution until they can be written back to registers or memory locations. More write buffers allow more instructions to be executed without stalling the pipelines.

CONTROLLING PROCESSOR HEAT

Heat remains the greatest enemy of the modern processor, so managing that heat is an important priority. Try some of the following suggestions to help you overcome CPU heating issues:

- Use a good-quality heat sink/fan that is more than adequately rated for your particular CPU.

- Use a thin layer of heat-sink compound to improve heat transfer between the CPU case and heat sink (available at Radio Shack; Cat. No. 276-1372).

- For extremely hot CPUs, try a Peltier cooler or similar refrigeration unit.

- Select reliable ball-bearing type fans with extended service lifetimes.

- Fold and tie cables away from areas requiring free air circulation (such as the vicinity of the CPU fan). Keep any obstructions clear.

- Make sure the CPU heat sink/fan is in close thermal contact with the processor surface (using heat-sink compound if needed). It should attach securely to the CPU, or CPU and socket. If not, get a new heat sink/fan.

- Use a CPU cooler with an audio alarm system that will alert you in case of either fan malfunction or excessive CPU temperature.

- If you are overclocking your CPU, compensate for the increased heat generated by using an upsized heat sink/fan or Peltier active cooler.

- Clean fan blades, fan support struts, and power supply louvers of accumulated dirt at least annually. Canned compressed air and vacuum sweeper brushes work well.

- Increase air circulation in and out of your computer case by using an auxiliary fan.

Understanding Bus Architectures

Inside the PC, data is passed from device to device over groups of related signal paths, called a *bus*. CPUs, memory, chipsets, drive interfaces, and expansion cards are just some of the important devices that use buses. There are numerous levels of buses within the PC—a hierarchy where each higher level is further removed from the processor, but each is connected to integrate various parts of the PC. Each higher level is also generally slower than the one below it. The four general bus levels are shown here:

- **Processor bus** This is the fastest, lowest-level bus that the motherboard uses to manage the processor-to-memory interface (e.g., operating at 100 MHz, 133 MHz, 150 MHz, or higher). Some motherboard block diagrams may illustrate this as the "memory bus."

■ **Cache bus**   Many more advanced PCs (such as Pentium Pro, and Pentium II/III systems) employ a dedicated bus for accessing the system cache. This is sometimes called a "backside bus." Some current motherboards and chipsets integrate the cache bus with the standard memory bus.

■ **Local I/O bus**   This is a medium-speed I/O bus used for connecting performance-critical peripheral devices to the system memory, chipset, and processor. For example, video cards, disk controllers, and NIC adapters generally use a bus of this sort. The two most common local I/O buses are the 66 MHz AGP bus and the 33 MHz PCI bus.

■ **Standard I/O bus**   The slowest bus architectures are 8.3 MHz ISA and 10 MHz EISA buses, and these are ideal for interfacing slower peripheral devices (i.e., mice, modems, regular sound cards, or low-speed network cards) to the PC.

Expansion cards use standardized I/O bus slots (i.e., local or standard) that allow you to plug a wide variety of devices (i.e., video cards or NIC adapters) into the system or server. This part of the chapter outlines the concepts of expansion buses, and focuses on the two most popular bus architectures: PCI and AGP.

BUS SIGNALS

Every bus is comprised of two distinct parts: the data bus and the address bus. The *data bus* is the set of signal lines that actually carry the data being transferred between the expansion device and system—the data bus is what most people refer to when talking about a bus. The *address bus* is the set of signal lines that indicate where (in memory) the data is to be transferred to or from. There are also a number of control lines (aka the control bus) that control how the bus functions, and allow devices to signal the system when data is available.

Bus width is another important consideration. Remember that a bus is a channel over which information flows—the wider the bus, the more information that can flow across the channel. The ISA bus used today is 16 bits wide. The other I/O buses (such as PCI and AGP) are 32 bits wide. By comparison, the memory and processor buses on Pentium PCs (and later) are 64 bits wide.

The address bus width can be specified independently of the data bus width. The width of the address bus indicates the number of different memory locations that can be accessed.

BUS SPEED AND BANDWIDTH

The *speed* of the bus indicates how many bits of information can be sent across each wire each second. Most traditional buses transmit one bit of data per data line every clock cycle. However, newer high-performance buses like AGP may actually move two or four bits of data per clock cycle—doubling (even quadrupling) performance. On the other hand, older buses like ISA may take two clock cycles to move one bit—halving the effective performance. By comparison, *bandwidth* (also called throughput) refers to the total amount of data that can theoretically be transferred on the bus in a given unit of time (i.e., MB/s). The *theoretical* bandwidth for most common I/O buses is shown in Table 9-2.

AGP has "x2" and "x4" modes that allow the bus to transfer data at two or four points per clock cycle, resulting in an effective bus speed of 133 or 266 MHz.

TABLE 9-2   BANDWIDTH COMPARISON FOR MAJOR BUSES

BUS	DATA WIDTH	BUS SPEED (MHZ)	MAX. BANDWIDTH (MB/S)
ISA (8-bit)	8	8.3	7.9
ISA (16-bit)	16	8.3	15.9
EISA	32	8.3	31.8
PCI (32-bit)	32	33	127.2
PCI (64-bit)	64	66	508.6
AGP	32	66	254.3
AGP (2X)	32	(66 × 2) 132	508.6
AGP (4X)	32	(66 × 4) 264	1017.2

BUS BRIDGES

When a system has multiple buses, circuitry must be provided on the motherboard to connect the buses and allow devices on one bus to talk to devices on the other. This device is called a *bridge*. The most commonly found bridge is the PCI-ISA bridge—part of the motherboard's chipset. The PCI bus also has a bridge to the processor bus. You can see these devices under System Devices in the Device Manager in Windows (see Figure 9-10).

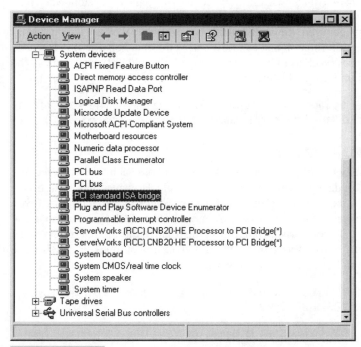

FIGURE 9-10   Checking the PCI-ISA bridge in Windows

BUS MASTERING

One of the problems with traditional PC architectures is that the processor was forced to manage all of the data transfers taking place in the system. As device bandwidth increased, the processor was forced to devote a greater portion of its time to routine data transfer tasks. With the introduction of IBM's PS/2 system (and its MicroChannel bus), it became possible for individual devices to take control of the bus and transfer data themselves. This is called *bus mastering* (or first-party DMA), and devices that can do this are called *bus masters*. Ideally, bus mastering leaves the processor free to do other work simultaneously. The motherboard's chipset arbitrates all requests to assume control of the bus. Most current bus mastering in the PC takes place across devices on the PCI bus.

I/O BUS TYPES

Now that you have a little background in essential I/O bus concepts, it's time to review some specific bus architectures found in PCs and many server-type systems. It's important to remember that you probably won't find all of these buses on any given motherboard, but you may find some of them (i.e., an ISA slot, four or five PCI slots, and an AGP slot). Figure 9-11 illustrates several of these slots.

FIGURE 9-11   The server can easily be expanded by installing devices in one or more bus slots.

ISA (Industry Standard Architecture)

The venerable ISA slot was the first open system bus architecture used for IBM-type personal computers, and any manufacturer was welcome to use the architecture for a small licensing fee. Because there were no restrictions placed on the use of ISA buses (also referred to simply as PC buses), they were duplicated in every IBM-compatible clone that followed—even to this day. Not only did the use of a standardized bus pave the way for thousands of manufacturers to produce compatible PCs and expansion devices, but it also helped to support the use of standardized operating systems and applications software. Both an 8- and 16-bit version of the ISA bus are available, although all motherboards manufactured since the mid-1980s have abandoned the 8-bit XT version in favor of the faster, more flexible 16-bit AT version.

Use of the 8-bit ISA bus started in 1982. The 8-bit ISA bus consists of a single card edge connector with 62 contacts. The bus provides eight data lines and twenty address lines, which allow the board to reside within the XT's 1MB of conventional memory. The bus also supports connections for six interrupts (IRQ2-IRQ7) and three DMA channels (DMA0-DMA2). The XT bus runs at the system speed of 4.77 MHz. Although the bus itself is relatively simple, IBM failed to publish specific timing relationships for data, address, and control signals. This ambiguity left early manufacturers to find the proper timing relationships by trial and error.

The limitations of the 8-bit ISA bus were soon obvious. With a floppy drive and hard drive taking up two of the six available interrupts, COM 3 and COM 4 taking up another two interrupts (IRQ 3 and IRQ 4), and an LPT port taking up IRQ 7, competition for the remaining interrupt was fierce. Of the three DMA channels available, the floppy and hard drives take two, so only one DMA channel remains available. Only 1MB of address space is addressable, and 8 data bits form a serious bottleneck for data transfers. It would have been a simple matter to start from scratch and design an entirely new bus, but that would have rendered the entire installed base of XT systems obsolete.

The next logical step in bus evolution came in 1984/85 with the introduction of the 80286 in IBM's PC/AT. System resources were added to the bus while still allowing XT boards to function in the expanded bus. The result became what we know today as the 16-bit ISA bus. Instead of a different bus connector, the original 62-pin connector was left intact, and an extra 36-pin connector was added. An extra 8 data bits were added to bring the total data bus to 16 bits. Five interrupts and four DMA channels are included. Four more address lines are also provided, in addition to several more control signals. Clock speed is increased on the AT bus to 8.33 MHz. It is important to note that although XT boards should *theoretically* work with an AT bus, not *all* older XT expansion boards will work on the AT bus.

Today, the ISA slot is virtually abandoned in favor of faster and more versatile PCI slots. Many current motherboards include only a single ISA slot for backward compatibility with older expansion devices. Most server-type motherboards have abolished ISA slots entirely.

EISA (Extended ISA)

The EISA bus is a 32-bit bus developed in 1988/89 to address the continuing need for greater speed and performance from expansion peripherals encouraged by the use of 80386 and 80486 CPUs. It also did not make sense to leave the entire 32-bit bus market to IBM's MicroChannel Architecture (MCA) bus. Even though the EISA bus works at 8.33 MHz, the 32-bit data path doubles data throughput between a motherboard and expansion board. Unlike the MCA bus, however, EISA ensures backward compatibility with existing ISA peripherals and PC software. The EISA bus is designed to be fully compatible with ISA boards. The EISA bus switches automatically between 16-bit ISA and 32-bit EISA operation using a second row of card edge connectors and dedicated signal lines. Thus, EISA boards have access to all of the signals available to ISA boards, as well as the second row of EISA signals.

EISA supports arbitration for bus mastering and automatic board configuration, which simplifies the installation of new boards. The EISA bus can access fifteen interrupt levels and seven DMA channels. To maintain backward compatibility with ISA expansion boards, however, there is no direct bus support for video or audio (as there is with the MCA bus). Since the EISA bus clock runs at the same 8.33 MHz rate as ISA, the potential data throughput of an EISA board is roughly twice that of ISA boards. EISA systems are used as network servers, workstations, and high-end PCs of the late 1980s/early 1990s. EISA was typically regarded as the high-end standard of its day for systems such as network servers, and never really filtered down to low-cost consumer systems.

PCI (Peripheral Component Interconnect)

By the late 1980s, the proliferation of 32-bit CPUs and graphics-intensive operating systems made it painfully obvious that the 8.33 MHz ISA bus was becoming obsolete. The PC industry began to develop alternative architectures for improved performance. In mid-1992, Intel Corporation and a comprehensive consortium of manufacturers introduced the PCI bus. Where the older VL bus was designed specifically to enhance PC video systems, the 188-pin PCI bus looked to the future of CPUs (and PCs in general) by providing a bus architecture that also supports peripherals such as hard drive controllers, network adapters, and so on. PCI is a 33 MHz fixed-frequency bus architecture capable of transferring data at 132 MB/sec—a great improvement over the anemic transfer rates of a 16-bit ISA bus. Another key advantage of the PCI bus is that it has automatic configuration capabilities for switchless/jumperless peripherals. Autoconfiguration (the heart of plug-and-play) will take care of all addresses, interrupt requests, and DMA assignments used by a PCI peripheral.

While the 32-bit implementation of PCI is the most common, a 64-bit version of PCI is available. Both 32- and 64-bit cards can be installed in either a 64- or 32-bit slot. When a 64-bit card is installed in a 32-bit slot, the extra pins just overhang without plugging into anything.

The PCI bus supports *linear bursts*, which is a method of transferring data that ensures the bus is continually filled with data. The peripheral devices expect to receive data from the system main memory in a linear address order. This means that large amounts of data are read from or written to a single address, which is then incremented for the next byte in the stream. The linear burst is one of the unique aspects of the PCI bus since it will perform both burst reads and burst writes. In short, it will transfer data on the bus *every* clock cycle. This doubles the PCI throughput compared to buses without linear burst capabilities.

While the 33 MHz implementation of PCI is the most common, a 66 MHz version of PCI is available.

The devices designed to support PCI have low *access latency*, reducing the time required for a peripheral to be granted control of the bus after requesting access. For example, an Ethernet controller card connected to a LAN has large data files from the network coming into its buffer. Waiting for access to the bus, the Ethernet is unable to transfer the data to the CPU quickly enough to avoid a buffer overflow—forcing it to temporarily store the file's contents in extra RAM. Since PCI-compliant devices support faster access times, the Ethernet card can promptly send data to the CPU.

The PCI bus supports bus mastering, which allows one of a number of intelligent peripherals to take control of the bus in order to accelerate a high-throughput, high-priority task. PCI architecture also supports *concurrency*—a technique that ensures the microprocessor operates simultaneously with these masters, instead of waiting for them. As one example, concurrency allows the CPU to perform floating-point calculations on a spreadsheet while an Ethernet card and the LAN have control of the bus. Finally, PCI was developed as a dual-voltage architecture. Normally, the bus is a +5Vdc system like other buses. However, the bus can also operate in a +3.3Vdc (low-voltage) mode.

PCI Interrupts and Bus Mastering   The PCI bus uses its own internal interrupt system for dealing with requests from the cards on the bus. These interrupts are denoted #A, #B, #C, and #D (though they are sometimes numbered #1 through #4) to avoid confusion with the normal numbered system IRQs. These interrupt levels are not generally seen by the user except in the PCI Configuration menu of your CMOS Setup where they can be used to control how PCI cards operate. These PCI interrupts are then mapped to regular interrupts (normally IRQ9 through IRQ12). The PCI slots in most systems can be mapped to four regular IRQs at the most. In systems that have more than four PCI slots (or that have four slots and a USB controller), two or more of the PCI devices share an IRQ.

If you're using Windows 98 or later, you may see additional entries for your PCI devices in the Device Manager—each device may have an additional entry labeled "IRQ Holder for PCI IRQ Steering" (a Windows 2000 display is shown in Figure 9-12). PCI steering is actually a feature that is part of the plug-and-play system, and enables the IRQ used for PCI devices to be controlled by the operating system in order to avoid resource problems. Having an IRQ holder listed in addition to another device in the IRQ list does *not* mean you have a resource conflict.

The PCI bus supports bus mastering, so devices on the PCI bus can take control of the bus and perform data transfers directly without the direct intervention of the system processor. The PCI bus is the first bus to make bus mastering commonplace—probably because for the first time there are operating systems and chipsets that are really capable of taking advantage of it. PCI allows bus mastering of multiple devices on

FIGURE 9-12   IRQ holders for PCI interrupt steering are not always needed if there are no other PCI devices in the server.

the bus simultaneously, with the motherboard's chipset arbitration circuitry working to ensure that no device on the bus (including the processor) locks out any other device. At the same time, it allows any given device to use the full bus throughput if no other device needs to transfer data.

The PCI bus also allows you to set up compatible IDE/ATA hard disk drives to be bus masters. With all of the necessary elements in place, PCI IDE bus mastering can increase performance over the use of traditional PIO (programmed I/O) data transfer modes (which are the default means used by IDE/ATA hard disks to transfer data). When PCI IDE bus mastering is enabled, IDE/ATA devices use DMA modes to transfer data instead of PIO. PCI IDE bus mastering requires all of the following in order to function:

- **Bus-mastering-capable system hardware** This includes the motherboard, chipset, bus, and BIOS. Virtually all current motherboards using a Pentium II/III or AMD Athlon chipset will support bus-mastering IDE.

- **Bus-mastering hard disk** This means that the drive must be capable of at least multiword DMA mode 2 data transfers. Essentially, all Ultra ATA hard disks (i.e., UDMA/33, UDMA/66, and UDMA/100) support bus mastering.

- **32-bit multitasking operating system** This means usually Windows NT/2000, Windows 95/98/ME, or Linux.

- **Bus-mastering drivers** A special driver must be provided to the operating system to enable the system's bus-mastering support.

 It's important to remember that bus mastering will not be a significant performance benefit under DOS and nonmultitasking operating systems (such as Windows 9x/Me).

AGP (Accelerated Graphics Port)

The PC's video system continues to improve in color depth and resolutions. Today's video information generates a tremendous amount of data. Not only does this data require memory, but it also needs a lot of bandwidth to pass that data to the video card. The AGP bus opens a freeway for graphics information that is especially well suited for 3D and visualization applications. For example, the fast floating-point performance of today's CPUs can smooth the drawing of 3D meshes and animation effects, and adds depth to a 3D scene. The next step is to add lifelike realism. To do this, the PC must render a 3D image by adding textures, alpha-blended transparencies, texture mapping, lighting, and other effects. AGP technology accelerates graphics performance by providing a dedicated high-speed bus for the movement of large blocks of 3D texture data between the PC's graphics controller and system memory. In practice, AGP enables a hardware-accelerated graphics controller to execute texture maps directly from system RAM (instead of caching them in the relatively limited local video memory). It also helps speed the flow of decoded video from the CPU to the graphics controller. In addition, off-loading this tremendous data overhead from the PCI bus leaves PCI free to handle drive data transfers and other controllers.

High bandwidth is the key to AGP's power. The 32-bit 66 MHz AGP interface is positioned between the PC's chipset and graphics controller. This architecture significantly increases the bandwidth available to a graphics accelerator. In its basic form, AGP offers a bandwidth of 266 MB/s (twice the bandwidth of PCI). This is referred to as AGP 1X. With advanced data-handling techniques, 2 bytes can be passed on every AGP clock for a bandwidth of 532 MB/s (known as AGP 2X). Further refinements to AGP data handling and the introduction of new chipsets allow 4 bytes to be passed on every AGP clock for a bandwidth of more than 1 GB/s (called AGP 4X). The 32-bit AGP bus gets its roots in the PCI local bus specification, but makes some significant improvements and additions intended to optimize AGP for high-performance

3D graphics. The most notable difference is the clock speed. PCI uses a fixed 33 MHz bus, but AGP ups the clock speed to 66 MHz. There are other major differences, including

- Deeply pipelined memory read and write operations—this hides memory access latency.
- Demultiplexing of address and data on the bus, allowing almost 100-percent bus efficiency.
- New ac timing for the 3.3V electrical specification that provides for one (AGP 1X) or two (AGP 2X) data transfers per 66 MHz clock cycle, allowing for real data throughput in excess of 500 MB/s.
- A new low-voltage electrical specification that allows four (AGP 4X) data transfers per 66 MHz clock cycle, providing real data throughput of over 1 GB/s.
- The bus slot defined for AGP uses a new connector body (for electrical signaling reasons) that is *not* compatible with the PCI connector, so PCI and AGP boards are *not* mechanically interchangeable.

There are a number of different requirements in order to allow a system to take advantage of AGP:

- **AGP video card**   You'll need a suitable video adapter for the AGP slot.
- **Motherboard with AGP chipset**   The motherboard must be fully compliant with AGP, including a chipset, bus slot, and BIOS.
- **Operating system support**   Plan on using Windows 98 or later for full AGP support.
- **AGP driver support**   You'll need drivers to enable the AGP features of the motherboard chipset, as well as video drivers for the AGP card.

I^2O (Intelligent I/O)

Every aspect of computer technology is feeling the demand for more processing power and higher I/O bandwidth. Unfortunately, I/O technology has not kept pace with processor speed, and a bottleneck inevitably occurs—restricting the flow of data. As attempts are made to increase the I/O bandwidth, we increase the number of interrupts sent to the host processor. An interrupt occurs whenever a disk subsystem, a network interface card, or any other real-world I/O device needs attention. In any given operation, an I/O device may interrupt the processor many times. While the processors are startlingly fast at straight computational functions, they were not designed to handle interrupt duties. The answer is to allow the processor to do what it does best—manage the applications, and offload the I/O functions by implementing intelligent I/O processing (known as I^2O).

Intelligent I/O most commonly refers to any server system that uses a processing element as part of the I/O subsystem. The I/O processor performs tasks that would normally be executed by the system processor, reducing the host processor overhead. By giving the processor some relief, overall system response time and I/O throughput are increased. I^2O allows a specialized I/O processor to offload the tasks from the system processor. I^2O allows requests to come in from one PCI device, destined for another PCI device, and the request never has to go through the system processor. The I^2O processor recognizes these requests and handles them locally. It also allows requests to queue up at the I^2O processor while the system processor is working on other important tasks.

Since the initial implementation of intelligent subsystems, vendors have built servers with increasingly high bandwidth I/O. But as demand has increased, software developers have struggled to keep up with the multiple hardware drivers that interface to the various operating systems. The need arose for a hardware standard that would work across diverse operating systems and revisions. In 1996, Intel and other industry leaders formed a special interest group to address the need for a standard interface for intelligent I/O systems. The resulting standard was dubbed I^2O. Peripheral vendors are then spared the task of writing drivers for multiple operating systems. Peripheral vendors only need to write one driver to the I^2O architecture, and the operating system will work with the I^2O subsystem. The I^2O architecture also eases the task of building peripherals by simplifying the demands on the I/O cards—much of the processing that was previously done on the card can now be done by the I^2O processor.

I^2O drivers are divided into two modules: the OS services module (OSM), and the hardware device module (HDM). The OSM interfaces with the operating system, and the HDM interfaces with the hardware device. The two modules exchange information through a two-layer communication system in which a message layer sets up a communication session while a transport layer defines how information will be shared. The modules communicate without knowledge of underlying bus architectures or topologies.

Understanding Server Memory

System memory (called RAM) holds the program code and data that is processed by the server's CPU(s)—and it is this intimate relationship between memory and the CPU that forms the basis of computer performance. Larger and faster CPUs are constantly being introduced, and more complex software is regularly developed to take advantage of that processing power. In turn, the more complex software demands larger amounts of faster memory. Networks and network servers must provide files and applications to a number of simultaneous users (often a *large* number of users), so servers are particularly memory hungry. These demands have resulted in a proliferation of memory types that go far beyond the simple, traditional DRAM. Pipeline-burst cache, fast synchronous DRAM (SDRAM), and other exotic memory types such as Rambus DRAM (RDRAM) now compete for the attention of PC technicians. These new forms of memory also present some new problems. This part of the chapter will provide you an understanding of popular memory types, configurations, installation concerns, and troubleshooting solutions.

MEMORY SPEED

The PC industry is constantly struggling with the balance between price and performance. Higher prices usually bring higher performance, but low cost makes the PC appealing to more people. In terms of memory, cost cutting typically involves using cheaper (slower) memory devices. Unfortunately, when slower memory is used, the CPU must be made to wait until memory can catch up. All memory is rated in terms of speed—specifically, *access time*. Access time is the delay between the time data in memory is successfully addressed, to the point at which the data has been successfully delivered to the data bus. For traditional PC memory, access time is measured in nanoseconds (ns), and current memory offers access times of 50–60 ns—70 ns memory is extremely common in older i486 systems. SDRAM is an exception to this rule, and is typically rated in terms of *cycle time* rather than access time. Cycle time is the minimum amount of time needed between accesses. Cycle time for SDRAM averages around 12 ns (nanoseconds), with 10 ns or 8 ns (and faster) SDRAM devices available.

It is usually possible to use *faster* memory than the manufacturer recommends. The system should continue to operate normally, but there's rarely ever a performance benefit. As you'll see in the following sections, memory and architectures are typically tailored for specific performance. Using memory that is faster should not hurt the memory, or impair system performance, but it costs more and will not produce a noticeable performance improvement—simply because the system is not equipped to employ the faster memory to its best advantage. The only time such a tactic would be advised is when your current system is almost obsolete, and you would want the new memory to be usable on a new, faster motherboard if you choose to upgrade the motherboard later.

Determining Memory Speed

It's often necessary to check memory modules for proper memory speed (aka access time or cycle time for SDRAM) during troubleshooting, or when selecting replacement parts. Unfortunately, it can be very difficult to determine memory speed accurately based on part markings. Speeds are normally marked cryptically by adding a number to the end of the part number. For example, a part number ending in -6 often means 60 ns, a -7 is usually 70 ns, and a -8 can be 80 ns. SDRAM often uses markings such as -12 for 12 ns cycle time, -10 for 10 ns cycle time, or -8 for 8 ns cycle time. Still, the only means of being absolutely certain of the memory speed is to cross-reference the memory part number with a manufacturer's catalog, and read the speed from the catalog's description (i.e., 4Mx32 50 ns EDO).

MEGABYTES AND MEMORY LAYOUT

Now is a good time to explain the idea of bytes and megabytes. Very simply, a *byte* is 8 bits (binary 1s and 0s), and a *megabyte* is one million of those bytes (1,048,576 bytes to be exact, but manufacturers often round down to the nearest million or so). The idea of megabytes (MB) is important when measuring memory in your PC. For example, if a SIMM is laid out as 1M by 8 bits, it has 1MB. If the SIMM is laid out as 4M by 8 bits, it has 4MB. Unfortunately, memory has not been laid out as 8 bits since the days of the IBM XT. More practical memory layouts involve 32-bit memory (for 486 and OverDrive processors), or 64-bit memory (for Pentium II/III/4 processors). When memory is "wider" than 1 byte, it is still measured in MB. For example, a 1M × 32-bit (4 bytes) SIMM would be 4MB (that is, the *capacity* of the device is 4MB), while a 4M × 32-bit SIMM would be 16MB. So when you go shopping for an 8MB 72-pin SIMM, chances are you're getting a 2M × 32-bit memory module.

PRESENCE DETECT

Another feature of modern memory devices is a series of physical signals known as the *presence detect* (or PD) lines. By setting the appropriate conditions of the PD signals, it is possible for a computer to immediately recognize the characteristics of the installed memory devices and configure itself accordingly. Presence detect lines typically specify three operating characteristics of memory: size, device layout, and speed. Many memory devices today use serial EEPROM chips to pass *serial presence detect* (or SPD) data to the motherboard at start time.

MEMORY REFRESH

The electrical signals placed in each RAM storage cell must be replenished (or *refreshed*) periodically every few milliseconds. Without refresh, RAM data will be lost (this is why RAM is referred to as "volatile" memory). In principle, refresh requires that each storage cell be read and rewritten to the memory array. This is typically accomplished by reading and rewriting an entire row of the array at one time. Each row of bits is sequentially read into a sense/refresh amplifier (part of the memory chip), which recharges the appropriate storage capacitors, then rewrites each row bit to the array. In actual operation, a row of bits is automatically refreshed whenever an array row is selected—the entire memory array can be refreshed by reading each row in the array every few milliseconds.

The key to refresh is in the *way* RAM is addressed. Unlike other memory chips that supply all address signals to a chip simultaneously, RAM is addressed in a two-step sequence. The overall address is separated into a row (low) address and a column (high) address. Row address bits are placed on the DRAM address bus first, and the -Row Address Select (-RAS) line is pulsed logic 0 to multiplex the bits into the chip's address decoding circuitry. The low portion of the address activates an entire array row and causes each bit in the row to be sensed and refreshed. Logic 0s remain logic 0s, and logic 1s are recharged to their full value.

Column address bits are then placed on the DRAM address bus, and the -Column Address Select (-CAS) is pulsed to logic 0. The column portion of the address selects the appropriate bits within the chosen row. If a read operation is taking place, the selected bits pass through the data buffer to the data bus. During a write operation, the read/write line must be logic 0, and valid data must be available to the chip before -CAS is strobed. New data bits are then placed in their corresponding locations in the memory array.

Even if the chip is not being accessed for reading or writing, the memory must *still* be refreshed to ensure data integrity. Fortunately, refresh can be accomplished by interrupting the microprocessor to run a refresh routine that simply steps through every row address in sequence (column addresses need not be selected for simple refresh). This "row-only" (or RAS only) refresh technique speeds the refresh process. Although refreshing the RAM every few milliseconds may seem like a constant aggravation, the computer can execute quite a few instructions before being interrupted for refresh. Refresh operations are generally handled by the chipset on your motherboard. Often, memory problems (especially parity errors) that cannot be resolved by replacing a memory module can be traced to a refresh fault on the motherboard.

MEMORY TYPES

In order for a computer to work, the CPU must take program instructions and exchange data directly with memory. As a consequence, memory must keep pace with the CPU (or make the CPU wait for it to catch up). Now that processors are so incredibly fast (and getting faster every few months), traditional memory architectures are being replaced by specialized memory devices that have been tailored to serve specific functions in the PC. As you upgrade and repair various systems, you will undoubtedly encounter some of the latest memory designations explained here (listed alphabetically).

DDR SDRAM

One limitation of SDRAM is that the theoretical limitation of the design is 125 MHz (though technology advances allow up to 133 MHz and 150 MHz operation), but bus speeds will need to increase well beyond that in order for memory bandwidth to keep up with future processors. There are several competing standards on the horizon; however, most of them require special pinouts, smaller bus widths, or other design considerations. In the meantime, *double data rate SDRAM* (DDR SDRAM) allows output operations to occur on both the rising and falling edge of the clock. Currently, only the rising edge signals an event to occur, so the DDR SDRAM design can effectively double the speed of operation up to at least 200 MHz (a prime candidate for AMD Athlon motherboards). There is already one Socket 7 chipset that has support for DDR SDRAM, and more will certainly follow if manufacturers decide to make this memory available.

PC100/PC133 SDRAM

When Intel decided to officially implement a 100 MHz system bus speed, they understood that most of the SDRAM modules available at that time would not operate properly above 83 MHz. In order to support 100 MHz bus speeds, Intel introduced the PC100 specification as a guideline to manufacturers for building modules that would function properly on their 100 MHz chipsets (i.e., the 440BX). With the PC100 specification, Intel laid out a number of guidelines for trace lengths, trace widths and spacing, the number of printed circuit layers, EEPROM programming specs, and so on. PC100 SDRAM on a 100 MHz (or faster) system bus will provide a performance boost for Socket 7 systems of between 10 percent and 15 percent, since the L2 cache is running at system bus speed. Pentium II/III systems will not see as big a boost because the L2 cache is running at half the processor speed (with the exception of the cacheless Celeron chips, of course).

You may encounter even faster types of "certified" RAM, including PC133 (133 MHz) and even PC150 (150 MHz) SDRAM.

RDRAM (Rambus DRAM)

Most of the memory alternatives so far have been variations of the same basic architecture. Rambus, Inc. (joint developers of EDRAM) has created a new memory architecture called the Rambus channel. A CPU or specialized chip is used as the master device, and the RDRAMs are used as slave devices. Sixteen bits of data are then sent back and forth across the Rambus channel at speeds of 600 MHz, 711 MHz, or 800 MHz (dubbed PC800 RDRAM), allowing for theoretical data transfer rates of up to 1.6 GB/s (roughly less than 1 ns of equivalent access time). The problem with RDRAM is that the memory chips generate a great deal of heat (requiring the use of a heat sink or heat spreader) across the Rambus module. While several high-end chipsets now support RDRAM, the overall performance benefits are generally below early Rambus expectations. This means conventional SDRAM DIMMs remain a popular RAM type for servers and other high-end PCs. You can learn much more about Rambus technologies at **www.rambus.com/developer/getting_started.html**.

SDRAM (Synchronous or Synchronized DRAM)

Typical memory can only transfer data during certain portions of a clock cycle. The SDRAM modifies memory operation so that outputs can be valid at *any* point in the clock cycle. By itself this is not really significant, but SDRAM also provides a "pipeline burst" mode that allows a second access to begin before the current access is complete. This "continuous" memory access offers effective access speeds as fast as 8 ns, and can transfer data at up to 100 MB/s. SDRAM is now quite popular on current motherboard designs, and is supported by the Intel VX (and later) chipsets, as well as VIA 580VP, 590VP, and 680VP (and later) chipsets. Like BEDO, SDRAM can transfer data in a 5-1-1-1 pattern, but it can support motherboard speeds up to 100 MHz, which is ideal for the 75 MHz and 82 MHz motherboards, and 100 MHz motherboards that are now so vital for Pentium II/III systems. Current SDRAM types can support 133 MHz and 150 MHz bus speeds. For more information on SDRAM, check out **www.ti.com/sc/docs/memory/brief.htm**.

SRAM (Static Random Access Memory)

The SRAM is also a classical memory design—it is even older than DRAM. SRAM does *not* require regular refresh operations, and can be made to operate at access speeds that are much faster than DRAM. However, SRAM uses six transistors or more to hold a single bit. This reduces the density of SRAM and increases its power demands (which is why SRAM was never adopted for general PC use in the first place). Still, the high speed of SRAM has earned it a place as the PC's L2 (or external) cache. You'll probably encounter three types of SRAM cache schemes: asynchronous, synchronous burst, and pipeline burst:

■ **Asynchronous Static RAM (Async SRAM or ASRAM)**   This is the traditional form of L2 cache introduced with i386 systems. There's really nothing too special about ASRAM except that its contents can be accessed much faster (20 ns, 15 ns, or 12 ns) than DRAM. ASRAM does not have enough performance to be accessed synchronously, and has long since been replaced by better types of cache.

■ **Synchronous burst static RAM (sync SRAM or SBSRAM)**   This is largely regarded as the best type of L2 cache for intermediate-speed motherboards (~60–66 MHz). With access times of 8.5 ns and 12 ns, the SBSRAM can provide synchronous bursts of cache information in 2-1-1-1 cycles (i.e., two clock cycles for the first access, then one cycle per access, in time with the CPU clock). However, as motherboards pass 66 MHz (i.e., 75 MHz and 83 MHz designs), SBSRAM loses its advantage to pipelined burst SRAM.

■ **Pipelined burst static RAM (PB SRAM)**   At 4.5 ns to 8 ns, this is the fastest form of high-performance cache now available for 75 MHz+ motherboards. PBSRAM requires an extra clock cycle for "lead off", but then can sync with the motherboard clock (with timing such as 3-1-1-1) across a wide range of motherboard frequencies.

VRAM (Video Random Access Memory)

DRAM has been the traditional choice for video memory, but the ever-increasing demand for fast video information (i.e., high-resolution SVGA displays) requires a more efficient means of transferring data to and from video memory. Originally developed by Samsung Electronics, video RAM achieves speed improvements by using a dual data bus scheme. Ordinary RAM uses a single data bus—data enters or leaves the RAM through a single set of signals. Video RAM provides an input data bus and an output data bus. This allows data to be read from video RAM at the same time new information is being written to it. You should realize that the advantages of VRAM will only be realized on high-end video systems such as $1024 \times 768 \times 256$ (or higher) where you can get up to 40 percent more performance than a DRAM video adapter. Below that, you will see no perceivable improvement with a VRAM video adapter.

WRAM (Windows RAM)

Samsung Electronics has introduced WRAM as a new video-specific memory device. WRAM uses multiple bit arrays connected with an extensive internal bus and high-speed registers that can transfer data almost continuously. Other specialized registers support attributes such as foreground color, background color, write-block control bits, and true-byte masking. Samsung claims data transfer rates of up to 640 MB/s—about 50 percent faster than VRAM—yet WRAM devices are cheaper than their VRAM counterparts. While WRAM has received some serious consideration in the last few years, it has been largely ignored in favor of SDRAM for video systems.

MEMORY TECHNIQUES

Rather than incur the added expense of specialized memory devices, PC makers often use inexpensive, well-established memory types in unique architectures designed to make the most of low-end memory. There are three popular architectures that you will probably encounter in almost all systems: paged memory, interleaved memory, and memory caching.

Paged Memory

This approach basically divides system RAM into small groups (or pages) from 512 bytes to several KB long. Memory management circuitry on the motherboard allows subsequent memory accesses on the same page to be accomplished with zero wait states. If the subsequent access takes place outside of the current page, one or more wait states may be added while the new page is found. This is identical in principle to fast-page mode DRAM explained earlier. You will find page-mode architectures implemented on high-end i286, PS/2 (model 70 and 80), and many i386 systems.

Interleaved Memory

This technique provides better performance than paged memory. Simply put, interleaved memory combines two banks of memory into one. The first portion is even, while the second portion is odd—so memory contents are alternated between these two areas. This allows a memory access in the second portion to begin before the memory access in the first portion has finished. In effect, interleaving can double memory performance. The problem with interleaving is that you must provide twice the amount of memory as matched pairs. Most PCs that employ interleaving will allow you to add memory one bank at a time, but interleaving will be disabled and system performance will suffer.

Memory Caching

This is perhaps the most recognized form of memory enhancement architecture. *Cache* is a small amount (anywhere from 8KB–2MB) of very fast SRAM that forms an interface between the CPU and ordinary system RAM. The SRAM typically operates on the order of 5 ns–15 ns, which is fast enough to keep pace with a CPU using zero wait states. A *cache controller* chip on the motherboard keeps track of frequently accessed memory locations (as well as predicted memory locations) and copies those contents into cache. When a CPU reads from memory, it checks the cache first. If the needed contents are present in cache (called a cache hit), the data is read at zero wait states. If the needed contents are not present in the cache (known as a cache miss), the data must be read directly from DRAM at a penalty of one or more wait states. A small quantity of very fast cache (called tag RAM) acts as an index, recording the various locations of data stored in cache. A well-designed caching system can achieve a hit ratio of 95 percent or more—in other words, memory can run *without* wait states 95 percent of the time.

There are two levels of cache in the contemporary PC. CPUs from the i486 onward have a small *internal cache*—known as L1 cache or processor cache—while *external cache* (SRAM installed as DIPs or COAST modules on the motherboard) is referred to as L2 cache. The i386 CPUs have no internal cache (though IBM's 386SLC offers 8KB of L1 cache). Most i486 CPUs provide an 8KB internal cache. Early Pentium processors are fitted with two 8KB internal caches: one for data and one for instructions. Today's Pentium II/III Slot 1 CPU incorporates 256KB–512KB of L2 cache into the processor cartridge itself. Xeon processors intended for server use may support up to 2MB of L2 cache.

RAID cache is another powerful application of cache that works by allowing the RAID controller card to write data to cache memory (RAM) on the RAID controller itself (rather than directly to the drives). A server can access the RAID controller's cache memory (called the array accelerator) more than 100 times faster than accessing a disk. Once data is cached in the array accelerator, the RAID controller will write the data to the disk array at a later time when the controller would otherwise be idle. The use of RAID caching also increases server performance during disk reads by anticipating read requests. This anticipated data is read into the array accelerator and is ready before you access it. When the RAID controller receives a read request for the cached data, it can immediately transfer that data into system memory (RAM) at PCI bus speeds.

CPU and drive data caching is often implemented as write back and write through. In *write back* cache (also called copy back cache), any new data that is written to the cache (such as the CPU's L1 cache) is *not* immediately written to memory (or disk). The data is written later, usually when a lull in the processing allows time to write the data. This behavior gives write back caching a performance edge because you're not forced to wait for the system to save the cache data immediately—it's written in the background as processing time allows. The problem with write back cache is that it can cause system problems if the system crashes before the cache is saved. *Write through* caching saves data in the cache immediately, so the cache and memory (or disk) contents always match. This method is a bit slower, but is more reliable (especially in mission-critical systems).

Shadow Memory

ROM devices (whether the BIOS ROM on your motherboard, or a ROM chip on an expansion board) are frustratingly slow, with access times often exceeding several hundred nanoseconds. ROM access then requires a large number of wait states, which slow down the system's performance. This problem is compounded because the routines stored in BIOS (especially the video BIOS ROM on the video board) are some of the most frequently accessed memory in your computer.

Beginning with the i386-class computers, some designs employed a memory technique called *shadowing*. ROM contents are loaded into an area of fast RAM during system initialization, then the computer maps the fast RAM into memory locations used by the ROM devices. Whenever ROM routines must be accessed during runtime, information is taken from the shadowed ROM instead of the actual ROM IC. The ROM performance can be improved by at least 300 percent.

Shadow memory is also useful for ROM devices that do not use the full available data bus width. For example, a 16-bit computer system may hold an expansion board containing an 8-bit ROM IC. The system would have to access the ROM not once but *twice* to extract a single 16-bit word. If the computer is a 32-bit machine, that 8-bit ROM would have to be addressed four times to make a complete 32-bit word. You may imagine the hideous system delays that can be encountered. Loading the ROM to shadow memory in advance virtually eliminates such delays. Shadowing can usually be turned on or off through the system's CMOS Setup routines.

MEMORY MODULES

Memory has always pushed the envelope of integrated circuit design. This trend has given us tremendous amounts of memory in very small chips, but it also has kept memory relatively expensive. Traditional PCs often included a small amount of RAM on the motherboard, and provided slots for additional RAM modules. Today, virtually every motherboard relies on standardized memory modules for all system memory. You'll find three essential types of memory modules—SIMMs, DIMMs, and RIMMs—as detailed here.

SIMMs and DIMMs

By the time 386 systems took hold in the PC industry, proprietary memory modules had been largely abandoned in favor of the standard 30-pin memory module. A SIMM (single inline memory module) is light, small, and contains a relatively large block of memory, but perhaps the greatest advantage of a SIMM is *standardization*—using a standard pin layout, a SIMM from one PC could be physically installed into almost any other PC. The 30-pin SIMM provides 8 data bits, and generally holds up to 4MB of RAM. The 30-pin SIMM proved its worth in 386 and early 486 systems, but fell short when providing more memory to later-model PCs. The slightly larger 72-pin SIMM replaced the 30-pin SIMM version by providing 32 data bits, and may hold up to 32MB (or more).

You'll also find such structures referred to as DIMMs (or dual inline memory modules). DIMMs appear virtually identical to SIMMs (see Figure 9-13), but they are physically *larger*. And where each electrical contact on the SIMM is tied together between the front and back, the DIMM keeps front and back contacts separate—effectively doubling the number of contacts available on the device. For example, if you look at a 72-pin SIMM, you will see 72 electrical contacts on both sides of the device (144 contacts total), but these are tied together, so there are only 72 signals (even with 144 contacts). On the other hand, a DIMM keeps the front and back contacts electrically *separate* (and usually adds some additional pins to keep SIMMs and DIMMs from accidentally being mixed). Today, virtually all DIMM versions provide 168 pins (84 pins on each side). DIMMs first appeared in high-end 64-bit data bus PCs (such as Pentium, PentiumPro, and PowerPC RISC workstations). As PCs have continued to advance, DIMMs have completely replaced SIMMs as the preferred memory expansion device, and the typical DIMM today can provide 128MB or 256MB of very fast memory (such as PC133 SDRAM). As a result, a server can be populated with 512MB of RAM or more with just a *few* memory modules.

Finally, you may see SIMMs and DIMMs referred to as "composite" or "noncomposite" modules. These terms are used infrequently to describe the technology level of the memory module. For example, a *composite* module uses older, lower-density memory, so more chips are required to achieve the required storage capacity. Conversely, a *noncomposite* module uses newer memory technology, so fewer chips are needed to reach the same storage capacity. In other words, if you encounter a high-density SIMM with only a few memory chips on it, chances are that the SIMM is noncomposite.

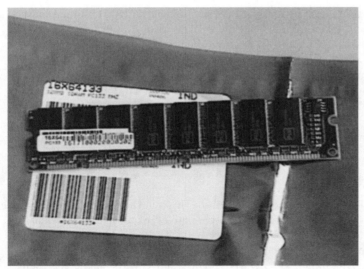

FIGURE 9-13   A basic DIMM used in many PCs, servers, and workstations

RIMMs

RDRAM is used on RIMMs (Rambus inline memory modules). RIMMs appear almost identical to DIMMs, but are slightly bigger (with several keys between the metal contact fingers). Early RIMM implementations used 168 pins, but the 600 MHz, 711 MHz, and 800 MHz (PC800) RIMMs available today use 184 pins. Figure 9-14 shows a typical RIMM and also illustrates the heat sink (or *heat spreader*) used to manage the elevated operating temperatures encountered with RDRAM chips. Table 9-3 outlines the general information contained on a typical RIMM.

UNBUFFERED, BUFFERED, AND REGISTERED

Memory modules may be unbuffered, buffered, or registered. This distinction is defined by the way in which electrical signals are handled by the memory module, and your choice of module will affect the maximum amount of RAM that can be installed on the server motherboard. An *unbuffered* memory module contains only memory devices, and the raw data is not boosted by buffers on the module itself.

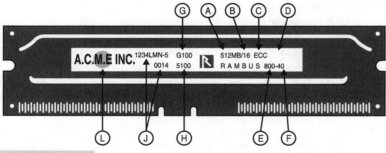

FIGURE 9-14   A basic RIMM (Courtesy of Rambus)

TABLE 9-3   READING A TYPICAL RIMM

ITEM	DESIGNATION	DESCRIPTION	TYPICAL VALUES
A	Memory Capacity	The 8-bit or 9-bit RDRAM storage capacity in the RIMM module	(i.e., 512MB, 256MB, 128MB, 64MB)
B	RDRAM Devices	The number of RDRAM devices (chips) on the RIMM module	(i.e., 16, 8, 4, 2)
C	ECC Support	Indicates whether the RIMM module supports ECC	(Blank is 8-bit non-ECC, ECC is 9-bit)
D	Reserved	Reserved for future use	
E	Memory Speed	Data transfer speed for RDRAM RIMM module	(i.e., 800, 711, or 600 MHz)
F	t_{RAC}	Row Access Time (optional)	(i.e., -40, -45, -50, or -53 ns)
G	Gerber Version	PCB Gerber file revision used on RIMM module (optional)	Rev 1.00 = G100
H	SPD Version	SPD code version (optional)	Rev 1.00 = S100
J	Vendor	Vendor-specific part number, date code, or manufacturer codes	
K	Vendor	Vendor-specific barcode information (optional)	
L	Vendor	Vendor logo area or country of origin	

Unbuffered modules are fast because there is no buffering circuitry to slow the signals, and their slightly lower cost makes them ideal for use in everyday PCs. Unfortunately, unbuffered electrical signals are prone to attenuation, so only a few unbuffered modules (usually one or two) can be used at a time.

By adding *buffers* or *registers* to the memory module, the electrical signals entering and leaving the memory module are strengthened. This slows the module's performance by a few nanoseconds, but allows the use of additional memory modules—thus the motherboard can support much *more* memory (this is particularly important for memory-hungry systems such as network servers). For EDO and FPM memory modules, the process of redriving memory signals is called *buffering*. For SDRAM memory modules, the process of redriving memory signals is called *registering*. Registering is similar to buffering, but registering clocks data into and out of the module using the system's clock. The motherboard's memory controller chip determines the type of memory modules required, so you cannot use unbuffered and buffered (or registered) modules together on the same system (they're also keyed differently so that you cannot use them on an incompatible motherboard).

PARITY AND ECC

As you might imagine, it is *vital* that data and program instructions remain error free. Even one incorrect bit due to electrical noise or a component failure can crash the PC, corrupt drive information, cause video problems, or result in a myriad of other faults. PC designers approached the issue of memory integrity by employing a technique known as *parity* (the same technique used to check serial data integrity). More recently, PCs (especially mission-critical PCs such as servers) employ a more robust and versatile error scheme called error correction code (ECC).

The Parity Principle

The basic idea behind parity is simple: each byte written to memory is checked, and a ninth bit is added to the byte as a checking (or parity) bit. When a memory address is later read by the CPU, memory-checking circuitry on the motherboard will calculate the *expected* parity bit, and compare it to the bit actually *read* from memory. In this fashion, the PC can continuously diagnose system memory by checking the integrity of its data. If the read parity bit *matches* the expected parity bit, the data (and indirectly the RAM) is assumed to be valid, and the CPU can go on its way. If the read and expected parity bits *do not* match, the system registers an error and halts. Every byte is given a parity bit, so for a 32-bit PC, there will be 4 parity bits for every address. For a 64-bit PC, there are 8 parity bits, and so on.

While parity has proven to be a simple and cost-effective means of continuously checking memory, there are two significant limitations. First, though parity can detect an error, it cannot correct the error because there is no way to tell *which* bit has gone bad. This is why a system simply halts when a parity error is detected. Second, parity is unable to detect multibit errors. For example, if a 1 accidentally becomes a 0 and a 0 accidentally becomes a 1 within the same byte, parity conditions will still be satisfied. Fortunately, the probability of a multibit error in the same byte is extremely remote. You are not required to employ parity checking, and nonparity RAM is quite common in desktop systems. However, the critical nature of servers demands that some form of error checking be implemented to prevent the server from suffering major (and costly) data errors.

ECC and EOS

In the world of personal computing, parity is an ancient technique. Frankly, it could easily be replaced by more sophisticated techniques such as error correction code (ECC) or ECC on SIMM (EOS). ECC (which is a popular technique used on today's high-end PCs and file servers) uses a mathematical process in conjunction with the motherboard's memory controller, and appends a number of ECC bits to the data bits. When data is read back from memory, the ECC memory controller checks the ECC data read back as well. ECC has two important advantages over parity. It can actually *correct* single-bit errors on the fly without the user ever knowing there's been a problem. In addition, ECC can successfully detect 2-bit, 3-bit, and 4-bit errors, which makes it an incredibly powerful error-detection tool. If a rare multibit error is detected, ECC is unable to correct it, but it will be reported and the system will halt.

It takes 7 or 8 bits at each address to successfully implement ECC. For a 32-bit system, you'll need to use x39 or x40 SIMMs (i.e., 8Mx39 or 8Mx40). These are relatively new designations, so you should at least recognize them as ECC SIMMs if you encounter them. As an alternative, some 64-bit systems use two 36-bit SIMMs for a total of 72 bits—64 bits for data and 8 bits (which would otherwise be for parity) for ECC information.

EOS is a relatively new (and rather expensive) technology that places ECC functions on the memory module itself, but provides ECC results as parity—so while the memory module runs ECC, the motherboard continues to see parity. This is an interesting experiment, but it is unlikely that EOS will gain significant market share. Systems that use parity can be fitted with parity memory much more cheaply than EOS memory.

General Troubleshooting

While most server motherboards should provide years of reliable operation, there are certainly many problems that can arise with the motherboard and peripheral devices. Servers present a special challenge for technicians, because server problems affect the entire network, and a down server can cost a busy company thousands of dollars in lost sales and productivity for every hour that it's offline. As a technician, it's vital that you recognize server problems and be equipped to correct them promptly.

RESETTING THE SYSTEM

Some server problems may be caused by external factors such as power glitches or software bugs, and may easily be corrected by just resetting the server. There are three ways to reset a server: a warm reboot, a hard reset, or a cold start:

■ A warm reboot will clear system memory and reload the operating system. Press CTRL-ALT-DEL to invoke a warm reboot.

■ A hard reset will clear system memory, restart the POST, and reload the operating system. This may be necessary if the system crash disables the keyboard (rendering CTRL-ALT-DEL ineffective). Press the Reset button to use a hard reset.

■ A cold start will clear system memory, restart the POST, reload the operating system, and halt power to all peripherals. This may be necessary after making hardware upgrades or corrections. Press the Power button.

INITIAL SYSTEM STARTUP PROBLEMS

A server must boot, pass the POST, and load the operating system properly before it can service the network. If the server fails to boot properly, the network will remain offline until you can identify and correct the problem. Fortunately, initial system startup problems are usually caused by incorrect device installation (or configuration). The following checklist will help you isolate potential problems:

■ See that the system power cords are properly connected to the system.

■ Press the system Power button on the front panel and verify that the power LED is on. Cooling fans should also be running properly.

■ Check to see that all internal and external cables are correctly connected and secured.

■ Check to see that the processors are fully seated in their slots on the baseboard. CPU slots without a processor should have a terminator card.

■ Verify that all PCI boards are fully seated in their expansion slots and secured to the chassis.

■ Verify that all switch and jumper settings on the motherboard are correct.

■ Verify that all the jumper and switch settings on expansion boards and peripheral devices are correct.

■ Check that all DIMMs are installed correctly and securely. The DIMMs should be the correct type and speed and error-correction scheme for the motherboard. On some server motherboards, the system will not start unless all DIMM slots are filled.

■ Check that all peripheral devices are installed correctly.

■ If the system has a hard disk drive, verify that it is properly partitioned, formatted, and configured in the CMOS Setup.

■ Verify that all device drivers are properly installed. You may need to load updated versions of critical device drivers for best operation (i.e., SCSI host adapter drivers or NIC drivers).

■ Verify that all configuration settings made with the SSU are correct.

■ Check that the operating system has properly loaded.

SOFTWARE ISSUES

In addition to hardware issues, software problems (namely software bugs and incompatibilities) can also interfere with normal server operations. Problems that occur when you run new application software are usually related to the software:

- Verify that the PC meets the minimum hardware requirements for all installed software.
- Verify that you're using an authorized copy of the software (rather than a modified or OEM version).
- Verify that your original installation media is good (try a known-good installation CD).
- Verify that the CD is not damaged or scratched.
- Verify that the software is installed correctly (recheck the installation).
- Check that the correct device drivers are installed.
- Check that the software is correctly configured for your particular system.
- Check the software user manual and see that you're using the software correctly.

WHEN PROBLEMS OCCUR

Even when the system hardware and software are proven out, problems can occur after the server has been in operation for a period of time. Issues that occur *after* the system hardware and software have been running correctly often indicate hardware failure (i.e., a drive or controller failure). System upgrades and alterations may also cause hardware problems. In most situations, server hardware problems are not difficult to identify and correct, but the following checklist may help isolate the more obvious trouble:

- If you're running software from a diskette, try a new copy of the software on a fresh diskette, or clean the floppy drive and try the diskette again.
- If you're running software from a CD-ROM, try a different CD to see if the problem occurs on all discs, try the CD in another drive, clean the suspect disc or drive, or replace the suspect CD-ROM drive.
- If you're running software from a hard drive, try running it from a diskette or CD. If the software runs correctly, there may be a problem with the copy on your hard drive. Reinstall the software on the hard disk and try running it again. Make sure all necessary files are installed.
- If the system problems are intermittent, there may be a loose cable or expansion card, a marginal power supply, or other component failure(s) in the system. Run diagnostics or look for specific error messages to help isolate the exact problem.
- Keyboard and mouse input problems are usually caused by accumulations of dirt or debris, and can almost always be corrected by cleaning the keyboard or mouse.
- If you suspect that a transient voltage spike, power outage, or brownout might have occurred, reload the software (or reboot the system) and try running the system again. Symptoms of voltage spikes include a flickering video display, unexpected system reboots, and the system failing to respond to user commands.

 If you're getting random errors in your data, the files may be corrupted by voltage spikes on the ac power line. You may want to install a new surge suppressor between the power outlet and the system power cords.

UNDERSTANDING SEL MESSAGES

The System Event Log (SEL) viewer is the user interface that allows users or technicians to access the SEL. This interface can be accessed both from the Emergency Management Port (EMP) and the System Setup Utility (SSU). The viewer extracts information from the SEL and presents it to the user in either a "hex" or "verbose" format. Users can also save the current SEL data to a file (for later analysis) or clear the current SEL records at the server. This part of the chapter highlights the typical codes found in the SEL for server motherboards such as the L440GX+. An administrator or technician can use this SEL information to monitor the server for warnings (i.e., the chassis door has been opened), or potentially critical problems (i.e., a processor has failed or a temperature threshold has been exceeded). For current server systems, events can be generated from the Baseboard Management Controller (BMC), Hot Swap Controller (HSC), and BIOS.

Sensor Events

Sensors are commonly used to detect real-world conditions in and around the server (such as voltage levels, temperature levels, fan operation, and chassis intrusion). When an event is detected by a sensor, it is logged in the SEL. For example, if the server backplane temperature exceeded a preset limit, a temperature sensor would log the event as "01 01" (if the "hex" view is used). Table 9-4 lists the sensor types and numbers that are typically available on a server.

TABLE 9-4   TYPICAL SEL SENSOR EVENTS

SENSOR TYPE		SENSOR NUMBER	SENSOR NAME	GENERATOR ID
Verbose	/Hex			
Temperature	01h			
		01h	Backplane Temperature	HSC
		17h	Primary Processor Temp	BMC
		18h	Secondary Processor Temp	BMC
		19h	Baseboard Temperature 1	BMC
		1Ah	Baseboard Temperature 2	BMC
Voltage	02h			
		01h	Baseboard 5V	BMC
		02h	Baseboard 3.3V	BMC
		03h	Primary Processor	BMC
		04h	Secondary Processor	BMC
		05h	Processor 2.5V	BMC
		06h	5V Standby	BMC
		07h	SCSI-W LVDS Term1	BMC
		08h	SCSI-W LVDS Term2	BMC
		09h	3V Standby (Wake on LAN)	BMC
		0Ah	Baseboard -12V	BMC
		0Bh	Baseboard SCSI-W SGL Term	BMC
		0Ch	Processor 1.5V	BMC
		0Dh	Baseboard -5V	BMC

TABLE 9-4   TYPICAL SEL SENSOR EVENTS (CONTINUED)

SENSOR TYPE		SENSOR NUMBER	SENSOR NAME	GENERATOR ID
		0Eh	Baseboard +12V	BMC
Fan	04h			
		0Ch	Backplane Fan 1	HSC
		0Dh	Backplane Fan 2	HSC
		0Fh	Baseboard Fan 0	BMC
		10h	Baseboard Fan 1	BMC
		11h	Processor Fan 0	BMC
		12h	Processor Fan 1	BMC
		1Fh	Digital Fan 1	BMC
		20h	Digital Fan 2	BMC
		21h	Digital Fan 3	BMC
		22h	Digital Fan 4	BMC
Physical security	05h			
		26h	Chassis Intrusion	BMC
Secure mode	06h			
		27h	EMP Password	BMC
		28h	Secure Mode Sensor	BMC
Processor	07h			
		1Bh	Primary Processor Status	BMC
		1Ch	Secondary Processor Status	BMC
Memory	0Ch			
		EFh	Memory Trouble	BMC
Drive slot (bay)	0Dh			
		02h	Drive Slot 0 Status	HSC
		03h	Drive Slot 1 Status	HSC
		04h	Drive Slot 2 Status	HSC
		05h	Drive Slot 3 Status	HSC
		06h	Drive Slot 4 Status	HSC
		07h	Drive Slot 0 Presence	HSC
		08h	Drive Slot 1 Presence	HSC
		09h	Drive Slot 2 Presence	HSC
		0Ah	Drive Slot 3 Presence	HSC
		0Bh	Drive Slot 4 Presence	HSC
POST error	0Fh			
		25h	System Error (see POST table)	
Watchdog	11h			
		1Dh	BMC Watchdog	BMC
System event	12h			
		EFh	System Error	
Critical interrupt	13h			
		1Eh	Front Panel NMI	BMC

BIOS Events

The system BIOS is responsible for monitoring and logging several different system events, memory errors, and critical interrupts. The BIOS sends an event request message to BMC in order to log the event. Some errors (such as a processor failure) are logged during the early POST. When an event is detected by the BIOS, it is logged in the SEL. For example, if a system boot event occurs, the BIOS would log the event as "12 EF E7 01" (if the hex view is used). Table 9-5 lists the BIOS events that are typically available on a server.

POST Events

Serious errors in critical devices (such as a processor failure) are logged during the early POST. When an event is detected by the BIOS early in the POST, it is logged in the SEL. For example, if a fixed disk failure occurs, the BIOS would log the event as "0F – 00 02" (if the hex view is used). The advantage of POST-related errors in the SEL is that you can see many POST errors without the need for a POST reader card. Table 9-6 lists the POST events that are typically logged by the BIOS.

POST CODES AND MESSAGES

When serious system problems arise, the motherboard probably will not boot completely—this may make it impossible to load the operating system or run diagnostic software. Fortunately, the BIOS places two-digit hexadecimal codes (called POST codes) on I/O port 80h during the boot process. If you install an ISA POST reader card, you can see these codes as they flash by. If the system halts or freezes on a particular code, you can cross-reference the code with the POST status and determine the last step to be successfully completed. Table 9-7 lists a typical set of POST codes for a current server-type BIOS. If the system boots to a point that initializes the video system, errors may be displayed as four-digit codes as shown in Table 9-8. You'll need the documentation that accompanies your particular server motherboard in order to decode the exact meaning of each code.

TABLE 9-5   TYPICAL SEL BIOS EVENTS

SENSOR TYPE	SENSOR NUMBER	EVENT DESCRIPTION (HEX)	EVENT TYPE
12	EF	---	---
		E7 01	System boot event
		E7 00	System reconfiguration
0C	EF	---	---
		E7 40 [DIMM#]	Single-bit memory error
		E7 41 [DIMM#]	Multibit memory error
		E7 02	Memory parity error
13	28	---	---
		E7 00	Front-panel NMI
13	EF	---	---
		E7 01	Bus timeout
		E7 02	I/O check
		E7 03	Software NMI
		E7 04	PCI PERR

TABLE 9-6   TYPICAL POST EVENTS

EVENT TYPE	EXPLANATION
00 02	Failure fixed disk
00 81	Processor 0 failed BIST
01 04	Invalid system configuration data—run configuration utility
01 06	Device configuration changed
01 81	Processor 1 failed BIST
02 06	Configuration error—device disabled
03 04	Resource conflict
04 04	Resource conflict
04 05	Resource conflict
04 81	Processor 0 internal error (IERR) failure
05 04	Expansion ROM not initialized
05 05	Expansion ROM not initialized
05 81	Processor 1 internal error (IERR) failure
06 04	Warning: IRQ not configured
06 05	Warning: IRQ not configured
06 81	Processor 0 thermal trip failure
07 81	Processor 1 thermal trip failure
08 81	Watchdog timer failed on last boot
0A 81	Processor 1 failed initialization on last boot
0B 81	Processor 0 failed initialization on last boot
0C 81	Processor 0 disabled, system in "uniprocessor" mode
0D 81	Processor 1 disabled, system in "uniprocessor" mode
0E 81	Processor 0 failed FRB level 3 timer
0F 81	Processor 1 failed FRB level 3 timer
10 02	Stuck key
10 81	Server Management Interface (SMI) failed to function
11 02	Keyboard error
12 02	Keyboard controller (KBC) failed
13 02	Keyboard locked—unlock key switch
20 02	Monitor type does not match CMOS—run Setup
20 81	IOP subsystem is not functional
30 02	System RAM failed at offset <xxxxx>
31 02	Shadow RAM failed at offset<xxxxx>
32 02	Extended RAM failed at offset <xxxxx>
50 02	System battery is dead—replace and run Setup
50 81	NVRAM cleared by jumper
51 02	System CMOS checksum bad—default configuration used
51 81	NVRAM checksum error—NVRAM cleared
52 81	NVRAM data invalid—NVRAM cleared
60 02	System timer error

TABLE 9-6   TYPICAL POST EVENTS *(CONTINUED)*

EVENT TYPE	EXPLANATION
62 01	BIOS unable to apply BIOS update to processor 1
63 01	BIOS unable to apply BIOS update to processor 2
64 01	BIOS does not support current stepping for processor 1
65 01	BIOS does not support current stepping for processor 2
70 02	Real-time clock (RTC) error
97 02	ECC memory error in base (extended) memory test in bank <xx>
B2 02	Incorrect drive A: type—run SETUP
B3 02	Incorrect drive B: type—run SETUP
D0 02	System cache error—cache disabled
F5 02	DMA test failed
F6 02	Software NMI failed

TABLE 9-7   TYPICAL POST CODES

CODE	BEEPS	ERROR
02h		Verify real mode
04h		Get processor type
06h		Initialize system hardware
08h		Initialize chipset registers with initial POST values
09h		Set in POST flag
0Ah		Initialize processor registers
0Bh		Enable processor cache
0Ch		Initialize caches to initial POST values
0Eh		Initialize I/O
0Fh		Initialize the local bus IDE
10h		Initialize power management
11h		Load alternate registers with initial POST values
12h		Restore processor control word during warm boot
14h		Initialize keyboard controller
16h	1-2-2-3	BIOS ROM checksum
18h		8254 timer initialization
1Ah		8237 DMA controller initialization
1Ch		Reset Programmable Interrupt Controller 0
20h	1-3-1-1	Test DRAM refresh
22h	1-3-1-3	Test 8742 Keyboard Controller
24h		Set ES segment register to 4GB
28h	1-3-3-1	Autosize DRAM
2Ah		Clear 512K base RAM
2Ch	1-3-4-1	RAM failure on address line <xxxx>

TABLE 9-7 TYPICAL POST CODES *(CONTINUED)*

CODE	BEEPS	ERROR
2Eh	1-3-4-3	RAM failure on data bits <xxxx> of low byte of memory bus
30h	1-4-1-1	RAM failure on data bits <xxxx> of high byte of memory bus
32h		Test processor bus-clock frequency
34h		Test CMOS
35h		RAM initialize alternate chipset registers
36h		Warm start shut down
37h		Reinitialize the motherboard chipset
38h		Shadow system BIOS ROM
39h		Reinitialize the motherboard cache
3Ah		Autosize cache
3Ch		Configure advanced chipset registers
3Dh		Load alternate registers with CMOS values
40h		Set new initial processor speed
42h		Initialize interrupt vectors
44h		Initialize BIOS interrupts
46h	2-1-2-3	Check ROM copyright notice
47h		Initialize manager for PCI option ROMs
48h		Check video configuration against CMOS
49h		Initialize PCI bus and devices
4Ah		Initialize all video adapters in system
4Bh		Display QuietBoot screen
4Ch		Shadow video BIOS ROM
4Eh		Display copyright notice
50h		Display processor type and speed
51h		Initialize EISA board
52h		Test keyboard
54h		Set key click if enabled
56h		Enable keyboard
58h	2-2-3-1	Test for unexpected interrupts
5Ah		Display prompt: "Press F2 to enter Setup"
5Ch		Test RAM between 512 and 640K
60h		Test extended memory
62h		Test extended memory address lines
64h		Jump to UserPatch1
66h		Configure advanced cache registers
68h		Enable external and processor caches
6Ah		Display external cache size
6Ch		Display shadow message
6Eh		Display nondisposable segments
70h		Display error message(s)
72h		Check for configuration errors

TABLE 9-7   TYPICAL POST CODES (CONTINUED)

CODE	BEEPS	ERROR
74h		Test real-time clock
76h		Check for keyboard errors
7Ah		Test for key lock on
7Ch		Set up hardware interrupt vectors
7Eh		Test coprocessor if present
80h		Detect and install external RS232 ports
82h		Detect and install external parallel ports
85h		Initialize PC-compatible PnP ISA devices
86h		Reinitialize on board I/O ports
88h		Initialize BIOS Data Area (BDA)
8Ah		Initialize Extended BIOS Data Area (EBDA)
8Ch		Initialize floppy controller
90h		Initialize hard disk controller
91h		Initialize local bus hard disk controller
92h		Jump to UserPatch2
93h		Build MPTABLE for multiprocessor boards
94h		Disable A20 address line
95h		Install CD-ROM for boot
96h		Clear huge ES segment register
98h	1-2	Search for option ROMs. Two short beeps on checksum failure
9Ah		Shadow option ROMs
9Ch		Set up power management
9Eh		Enable hardware interrupts
A0h		Set time of day
A2h		Check key clock
A4h		Initialize typematic rate
A8h		Erase F2 prompt
Aah		Scan for F2 key stroke
Ach		Enter SETUP
Aeh		Clear in-POST flag
B0h		Check for errors
B2h		POST done—prepare to boot operating system
B4h		One short beep before boot0
B5h		Display MultiBoot menu
B6h		Check password (optional)
B8h		Clear global descriptor table
BCh		Clear parity checkers
Beh		Clear screen (optional)
BFh		Check virus and backup reminders
C0h		Try to boot with INT 19
D0h		Interrupt handler error

TABLE 9-7   TYPICAL POST CODES *(CONTINUED)*

CODE	BEEPS	ERROR
D4h		Pending interrupt error
D6h		Initialize option ROM error
D8h		Shutdown error
Dah		Extended block move
DCh		Shutdown 10 error
FFh		POST finished

TABLE 9-8   TYPICAL POST ERROR MESSAGES

CODE	ERROR
0162	BIOS unable to apply BIOS update to processor 1
0163	BIOS unable to apply BIOS update to processor 2
0164	BIOS does not support current stepping for processor 1
0165	BIOS does not support current stepping for processor 2
0200	Failure: fixed disk
0210	Stuck key
0211	Keyboard error
0212	Keyboard Controller (KBC) failed
0213	Keyboard locked—unlock the key switch
0220	Monitor type does not match CMOS—run SETUP
0230	System RAM failed at offset <xxxxx>
0231	Shadow RAM failed at offset <xxxxx>
0232	Extended RAM failed at offset <xxxxx>
0250	System batter is dead—replace battery and run SETUP
0251	System CMOS checksum bad (default configuration used)—replace CMOS RAM chip
0260	System timer error
0270	Real-time clock (RTC) error
0297	ECC memory error in base (or extended) memory test in bank <xx>
02B2	Incorrect drive A: type—run SETUP
02B3	Incorrect drive B: type—run SETUP
02D0	System cache error—cache disabled
02F5	DMA test failed
02F6	Software NMI failed
0401	Invalid system configuration data—run the configuration utility
0403	Resource conflict
0404	Resource conflict
0405	Expansion ROM not initialized
0406	Warning: IRQ not configured

TABLE 9-8   TYPICAL POST ERROR MESSAGES *(CONTINUED)*

CODE	ERROR
0504	Resource conflict
0505	Expansion ROM not initialized
0506	Warning: IRQ not configured
0601	Device configuration changed
0602	Configuration error—device disabled
8100	Processor 1 failed BIST
8101	Processor 2 failed BIST
8104	Processor 1 Internal Error (IERR) failure
8105	Processor 2 Internal Error (IERR) failure
8106	Processor 1 thermal trip failure
8107	Processor 2 thermal trip failure
8108	Watchdog timer failed on last boot
810A	Processor 2 failed initialization on last boot
810B	Processor 1 failed initialization on last boot
810C	Processor 1 disabled, system in uniprocessor mode
810D	Processor 2 disabled, system in uniprocessor mode
810E	Processor 1 failed FRB level 3 timer
810F	Processor 2 failed FRB level 3 timer
8110	Server Management Interface (SMI) failed to function
8120	IOP subsystem is not functional
8150	NVRAM cleared by jumper
8151	NVRAM checksum error—NVRAM cleared
8152	NVRAM data invalid—NVRAM cleared

THE SERVICE PARTITION

The *service partition* is a special hard disk partition—it is established when you initially set up the server system and it contains utilities, diagnostics, and other software required for remote management. The service partition is not marked as an active partition, and the server will only boot from it by special request. It is not normally visible to a user because it has a special nonstandard partition type that does not appear as an accessible file system. However, low-level disk utilities can "see" the partition entry as an unknown type. As a rule, you should install the service partition before installing an OS. Here's a quick way to install a service partition:

1. Boot to the server's software CD.

2. When the Server Board CD-ROM menu appears, select the Utilities menu and press ENTER.

3. Select Run Service Partition Administrator and press ENTER.

4. Choose "Create service partition".

5. Follow the instructions to select the hard drive for service partition installation.

6. Reboot to the server's software CD.

7. When the Server Board CD-ROM menu appears, select the Utilities menu and press ENTER.

8. Select Run Service Partition Administrator and press ENTER.

9. Choose "Format service partition and install software".

10. Follow the instructions to format the service partition and install the partition software.

Not all systems use a service partition. The documentation that accompanies your server should indicate if a service partition is employed.

REPAIRING DIMM/RIMM SOCKETS

If there is one weak link in the architecture of a DIMM or RIMM, it is the socket that connects it to the motherboard. Ideally, the memory module should sit comfortably in the socket, then gently snap back—held in place by two clips on either side of the socket. In actual practice, you really have to push that module to get it into place. Taking it out again is just as tricky. As a result, it is not uncommon for a socket to break and render your extra memory unusable.

The best (aka, "textbook") solution is to remove the damaged socket and install a new one. Clearly there are some problems with this tactic. First, removing the old socket will require you to remove the motherboard, desolder the broken socket, and then solder in a new socket (which you can buy from a full-feature electronics store such as DigiKey). In the hands of a skilled technician with the right tools, this is not so hard. But the printed circuit runs of a computer motherboard are *extremely* delicate, and the slightest amount of excess heat can easily destroy the sensitive, multilayer connections—ruining the motherboard entirely.

Fortunately, there are some tricks that might help you. If either of the module clips has been bent or broken, you can usually make use of a medium-weight rubber band that is about 1-in shorter than the socket. Wrap the rubber band around the module and socket, and the rubber band should do a fair job holding the memory module in place. If any part of the socket should crack or break, it can be repaired (or at least reinforced) with a good-quality epoxy. If you choose to use epoxy, be sure to work in a ventilated area, and allow plenty of time for the epoxy to dry. This does not fix the problem, but it does contain the damage, and may allow the motherboard to serve a long and reliable working life.

CONTACT CORROSION

Corrosion can occur on SIMM/DIMM/RIMM contacts if the module's contact metal is not the same as the socket's contact metal. This will eventually cause contact (and memory) problems. As a rule, check that the metal on the socket contact is the same as the memory module contacts (usually tin or gold). You may be able get around the problem in the short term by cleaning corrosion off the contacts manually using a cotton swab and good electronics-grade contact cleaner. In the meantime, if you discover that your memory and connectors have dissimilar metals, you may be able to get the memory seller to exchange your memory modules.

PARITY ERRORS

Parity errors constitute many of the memory faults that you will see as a technician. As you saw earlier in this chapter, parity is an important part of a computer's self-checking capability. Errors in memory will cause the system to halt, rather than continue blindly along with a potentially catastrophic error. But it is not just faulty memory that causes parity errors. Parity can also be influenced by your system's configuration. Here are the major causes of parity problems:

- One or more memory bits are intermittent or have failed entirely.
- Poor connections between the SIMM/DIMM/RIMM and socket.
- Too few wait states entered in BIOS (memory is too slow for the CPU).
- An intermittent failure or other fault has occurred in the power supply.
- A bug, computer virus, or other rogue software is operating.
- A fault has occurred in the memory controller IC or BIOS.

When you're faced with a parity error after a memory upgrade, you should suspect a problem with wait states or memory type settings in the CMOS Setup routine, so check them first. If the wait states or other memory settings are correct, systematically remove each memory module, clean the contacts, and reseat each module carefully. If the errors continue, try removing one bank of memory modules at a time (chances are that the memory is bad). You may have to relocate memory so that bank 0 remains filled. When the error disappears, the memory you removed is likely to be defective.

When parity errors occur spontaneously (with no apparent cause), you should clean and reinstall each memory module first to eliminate the possibility of bad contacts. Next, check the power supply outputs—low or electrically noisy outputs may allow random bit errors. You may have to upgrade the supply if it is overloaded. Try booting the system clean from a write-protected floppy disk to eliminate the possibility of buggy software or computer viruses. If the problem persists, suspect a memory defect in the memory module.

SYMPTOMS

Even though the general troubleshooting guidelines presented in this chapter will help you isolate many potential problems with a server, there may be times when specific troubles strike your network. Use the following symptoms to help you identify specific corrective actions.

SYMPTOM 9-1   One CPU is always shown "busy" on a multiprocessor computer.
When you view CPU usage using the Windows 2000 Task Manager, one processor may appear to be busy (between 50 percent and 70 percent use), even when the computer is idle. This trouble can occur if your computer uses an ASUS P2B-D, P2B-DS, XG-DLS, P2L97-D, or P2L97-DS motherboard, *and* you choose to install the Advanced Configuration and Power Interface (ACPI) Hardware Abstraction Layer (HAL) during or after Windows 2000 Setup. If you're actually using an ASUS motherboard, contact ASUS to obtain a BIOS update for the motherboard (to enable ACPI support). For additional information, check the ASUS Web site at **www.asus.com/Products/Techref/Acpi/win2000.html**. You can also work around this problem:

1. Start Windows 2000 Setup again.
2. Press the F5 key when you see the following prompt:
   ```
   Press F6 if you need to install a 3rd party SCSI or RAID driver.
   ```
3. When you are prompted for the type of computer you are using, choose MPS Multiprocessor PC, and then continue Setup normally.

SYMPTOM 9-2   **The server power LED does not light.**   In virtually all cases, this is a power issue. Check to see that the ac cord is attached securely (and verify that there is ac available at the wall or UPS output). If the server's power supply has a "master power" switch, see that the switch is in the ON position. Check the system fans. If the fans are turning, there is a more serious problem with the server motherboard (or other device in the system). If ac is available, the supply is switched on, and the fans are *not* turning, the supply is probably defective and should be replaced.

If the power LED is out but the system seems to be operating normally, check to see that the LED is securely connected to its proper place on the motherboard.

SYMPTOM 9-3   **The system is not producing any beep at start time.**   Normally, the successful completion of the POST sequence will result in a single beep through the server's speaker. If there is no beep, and the system seems to be operating properly, chances are that the speaker is defective or not connected securely to its place on the motherboard. Check the speaker's connection and replace the speaker if necessary. If there is no beep, and the system is not responding, there may be a serious problem with system power (the power supply). There may also be trouble with the motherboard or primary processor (the system is not completing the POST).

SYMPTOM 9-4   **The system produces a beep error code.**   The BIOS keeps track of the system's current test state during the POST by outputting a two-digit hexadecimal code to I/O port 80h. If a POST reader board is installed, it displays the two-digit code on a pair of seven-segment LEDs. When the POST encounters a problem, the system will usually beep to warn you of the trouble, and you can use a POST reader card to indicate the last successful POST step to be completed. By comparing the last POST step with a list of codes for your particular BIOS version (check your system documentation), you can determine the point at which the POST failed, and make an informed decision regarding the probable failure. In many cases, serious failures detected through the POST can be corrected by replacing the motherboard.

SYMPTOM 9-5   **The system produces a POST error message.**   If the system is able to initialize the video system, any subsequent errors can be presented in the form of a numerical code on the monitor. By comparing the POST error code with a list of codes for your particular BIOS version, you can determine the point at which the POST failed, and make an informed decision regarding the probable failure. In many cases, serious failures reported with a POST error message can be corrected by replacing the motherboard or a peripheral device.

SYMPTOM 9-6   **You have trouble mixing processors on the server motherboard.** In most cases, servers require that you use processors of the same engineering step—it's not impossible to "mix" processors, but it's not possible to verify the reliability of every processor combination. Follow the guidelines below to prevent matching issues:

- Pentium II, Pentium III, and Pentium 4 processors should *never* be mixed on the same system.
- Processor core and bus speeds should *never* be mixed on the same system (i.e., one 900 MHz processor and one 1.2GHz processor generally won't work).
- ECC and non-ECC memory devices should *never* be mixed on the same system.
- Processor L2 cache sizes should *never* be mixed on the same system.
- As a rule, mixing processor steps *should* function correctly, but the core step should not vary by more than one step for both processors in the server. The primary processor should be plus or minus one step from the secondary processor.

SYMPTOM 9-7 **SPD data is overwritten.** Some combinations of server hardware may corrupt the DIMM EEPROM SPD (*serial presence detect*) data. Certain bits of the 256-byte SPD data area are overwritten. The data corruption only occurs in the SPD data area—not to main memory. The SPD data of the EEPROM is read only during system boot. If a DIMM's SPD data is corrupted, the bank of memory that contains the DIMM will be disabled, and this will result in a failure:

■ If only *one* bank of memory is installed, the system will not boot (all memory in the system has been disabled).

■ If *more* than one bank is installed, memory will be reduced by the number of banks disabled (up to and including all memory).

It seems that the memory module board itself has a problem caused by improperly terminated outputs on the circuit that controls memory bank selection. The potential for overwriting EEPROM SPD data only appears to exist on "unlocked" (write-enabled) DIMM EEPROMs since data can be written to the unprotected 256-byte SPD data area. "Locked" EEPROM SPD memory does not suffer this problem since it is write-protected. When this situation occurs, try using different memory modules, or check with the motherboard manufacturer for available BIOS upgrades.

SYMPTOM 9-8 **You notice false voltage events entered in the SEL.** Some server motherboards may indicate voltage threshold events being recorded in the *System Event Log* (or SEL). These events may be reported for the +12V, +5V, and +1.5V supply rails (and for multiple components). It is possible that you're seeing false signals, and these can be ignored. However, you may wish to replace the power supply, use a UPS, and see if the problem goes away.

SYMPTOM 9-9 **The server's PCI configuration space is not updated properly.** Some server systems may hang or malfunction after adding certain PCI add-in cards with an Intel i960 I/O microprocessor. This problem has been observed with some server motherboards and the AMI MR493 RAID card (but other hardware combinations may also suffer this problem). You also may not be able to install Windows 2000 after configuring the system with "PCI Hot Plug" (PHP) enabled. This can hang Windows 2000.

This problem has been identified as a system BIOS PCI resource allocation issue. This problem is caused by a BIOS routine that creates a 1MB memory aperture on the primary side of the PCI-PCI bridge. However, the PCI-PCI bridge cannot properly close the memory aperture. You may need to change the hardware configuration (usually the suspect PCI devices) to devices that do not suffer this trouble, or check for an available BIOS upgrade that will correct the issue (or upgrade the motherboard outright).

SYMPTOM 9-10 **Your server encounters a power-on failure in the standby mode.** This may occur on some server motherboards using certain power supplies. In the standby mode (ac is applied to the system prior to powering the system on), the Power OK signal was not in compliance with the ATX Specification—which requires the Power OK signal to be held at a low level (i.e., less than +0.4 volts). On the failing power supplies, the Power OK signal was observed to be between +0.6 volts and +2.0 volts. The inconsistency of the Power OK signal prevented the motherboard from powering up. Replace the power supply with a model that has been tested/recommended for use with the system, or check with the motherboard manufacturer to see if a validation procedure is available for other supplies.

SYMPTOM 9-11 **Server diagnostics may lock up while running RTC accuracy tests.** While running the RTC accuracy test on your server board, the test hangs (requiring a system reboot). In most cases, the RTC test module was found to have a problem. Under some circumstances, this generates unexpected interrupts that the motherboard's BIOS was not designed to support. Check for a patched or updated RTC accuracy test that corrects this condition. There are no other suitable workarounds other than to avoid using the RTC accuracy test.

SYMPTOM 9-12   **The server will not power on, but ac is available.**   Start with the obvious issues and verify that the server's ac cord is securely plugged into the power supply and wall. If the supply is attached to a UPS or power strip, see that the source is switched on. Some ATX power supplies have a "master" power switch on the back of the power supply next to the fan. If your supply is configured that way, verify that the supply is switched on. Also verify that the front-panel power switch cable is properly connected to the front-panel header pins on the motherboard.

For an SSI-compliant power supply, make sure the proper power supply connector is attached to the auxiliary signal connector. "SSI" power supplies require a +3-volt sense signal to properly power auxiliary devices. If an SSI connector is available with your power supply, make sure that it is firmly seated in the Auxiliary Signal connector.

Remove all expansion cards and see if the server boots using just the onboard components. If so, replace the expansion cards one at a time and see if you can pinpoint the suspect device(s). Remove the processor (and any processor "terminator cards") and reseat them carefully. Remove and reseat all memory modules (try using memory modules from a known working server system). Also check to see that you have enough memory modules (some servers require a set of four memory modules).

SYMPTOM 9-13   **The system boots up after installing a PCI adapter.**   Server management features require full-time "standby" power—this means that power is still provided to parts of the system, even if the user has turned the system off using the front-panel power switch. There are also signals in the PCI connectors that tell the system to boot (normally used by server management adapters or NICs/modems with "Wake on LAN/Wake on Ring" capability). Plugging in the adapter with ac power still applied through the power cord can cause false signals to be transmitted causing the system to boot. Be sure to disconnect the ac power cord before installing the PCI device.

SYMPTOM 9-14   **The system boots automatically after powering up a power strip.** You probably powered down the system incorrectly. Some server systems normally save the "last known power state" since the last ac power connection. If you remove ac power *before* powering down the system with the front-panel power switch, your system will automatically attempt to return to the "on" state that it was in once you restore ac power. Allow your system to fully power up and then power down the system using the front-panel power switch.

SYMPTOM 9-15   **The server takes too long to boot.**   This is a common problem with various possible causes, but you need to understand the boot process. The boot process normally involves several distinct phases:

- ■ **BIOS power-on self test (POST)**   This includes the memory count, the keyboard/mouse check, and IDE drive check.

- ■ **Option-ROM loading**   Each device may load a portion of its operating code (or "option ROM") into memory. You may see messages identifying add-in devices such as a SCSI controller BIOS.

- ■ **Operating system boot**   After initialization, the operating system takes control of the server and performs whatever checks/setups are necessary for operation. For example, you'll see a Windows "splash screen."

Large memory configurations can slow boot time. Large memory installations can take one or two minutes to check. Extended memory tests can be disabled in CMOS Setup to speed up the boot process (especially when performing service that requires multiple reboots). However, this memory test should be enabled for normal system operation. Multiple SCSI adapters can also load slow boot times. SCSI adapters take time to load their "option ROMs" and execute the code that scans for drives. Detection and ROM loading takes additional time.

SYMPTOM 9-16   The server won't boot with a single processor installed.   Make sure that the processor is the correct speed for the system bus. Chances are that the server board only supports processors of a certain bus speed. For example, the Intel 5KA4 server board only supports Pentium III processors for the 100 MHz system bus. Verify that the processor is in the primary processor slot.

Check that the secondary processor slot contains a terminator card. The Pentium III processor architecture requires nonpopulated processor slots to be terminated. Without proper termination, the signals may cause errors. Some server boards will not boot up if they don't detect a "terminator card." Verify that the processor and terminator card are firmly seated. The retention mechanisms are designed to hold the processor and terminator card firmly in place, so ensure that the processor and termination card have "snapped" into the retention mechanism.

SYMPTOM 9-17   Your cartridge-style processor isn't supported with "grounded retention mechanisms" (GRMs).   Some server boards use grounded retention mechanisms to seat the Pentium III processor. New GRMs will only support processors manufactured with SECC2 packaging. Older Pentium II/III processors that use SECC processor packaging will not fit into the new GRMs. You can continue to use universal retention mechanisms (URMs) to support processors in the SECC package. Install URMs, or exchange the processor types.

SYMPTOM 9-18   You may damage processors when removing them from "grounded retention mechanisms."   Care must be taken when removing Pentium III processors from the "grounded retention mechanisms" (GRMs) used on some server boards. With the tight grip provided by a GRM, it is possible to damage the GRM, the server board, the processor slot, and even the processor if a careful processor extraction procedure is not followed. It is easiest to remove the processor with the server board mounted in a chassis—this will provide support and help prevent bending of the server board. Place the system on its side, remove the side cover, and then carefully disengage the processor from the GRM.

SYMPTOM 9-19   Fast Pentium III processors are not supported on your motherboard. For example, this is a known issue with server motherboards such as the L440GX+ using Pentium III/600E and faster processors. You'll probably find that faster Pentium III processors will physically fit onto the older server boards, but they will produce an unstable server platform, and may cause damage to either the server board or the processor. In most cases, the problem occurs because the offending server board doesn't include the correct voltage regulation module (VRM) needed for faster processors. You may be able to replace the VRM(s) to accommodate later processors, or upgrade the motherboard to a version that is compatible with the processors that you require.

SYMPTOM 9-20   A server motherboard may lock up when expansion cards are added to PCI slot 5 or 6.   There is no issue when expansion cards are only installed in PCI slots 1 through 4. You may encounter a system lockup on some servers by installing PCI cards requiring a high I/O bandwidth (such as a SCSI RAID controller) into PCI slot 5 or 6. The fault may occur after POST while booting the operating system, or while performing data transactions on the secondary PCI bus using a "system stress" program. In most cases, you'll find that the server utilizes a PCI "riser card" in PCI slot 5. This problem may also occur when PCI expansion cards are plugged into riser cards. The issue is not OS dependent, nor is it related to any specific add-in card. You'll usually find that the problem is in the motherboard itself, and *not* in the OS or expansion card(s). The trouble is frequently caused by manufacturing issues that adversely affect the operation of bus interface circuits. Check for a BIOS upgrade that can compensate for this type of problem. Otherwise, you should upgrade the server motherboard.

SYMPTOM 9-21   **BMC features are compromised when the BMC firmware is updated.**
You may notice that the BMC no longer functions after performing a flash update of the *Baseboard Management Controller* (BMC) firmware on your server motherboard. With the loss of your BMC, all server management functions are disabled. For example, you'll lose the ability to power down the system from the front panel, the system will no longer log system events in the System Event Log (SEL), and server management software will not be able to communicate to the onboard sensors. This occurs because the method used to update the firmware is damaging the information retention properties of the flash chip. This causes corruption to the BMC firmware, resulting in the eventual loss of BMC functionality—a BMC failure may occur immediately after updating the firmware, or it may occur at some time after the update. Before flashing the BMC firmware, check to see that you're using the latest flash loader utility from the manufacturer. Otherwise, you'll need to replace the motherboard.

SYMPTOM 9-22   **A server with redundant power supplies will not boot with your server motherboard installed.**   When using a server chassis with redundant power supplies and a server board (i.e., the Intel L440GX+), the system will not boot. Chances are that the server motherboard cannot be used with the redundant power supply feature of your particular server chassis. A later-version motherboard may correct the problem, or the redundant supply may need to be disabled.

Further Study

Gateway: **www.gateway.com**
Intel: **developer.intel.com/design/servers/**
Compaq: **www.compaq.com**
Hewlett-Packard: **www.hp.com**
Dell: **www.dell.com**

10

NETWORK ADAPTERS AND LAN TROUBLESHOOTING

Networks allow computers to share files, printers, applications, Internet access, and other resources. However, computers must be connected in order to operate on the network. Computers are interfaced to network media using a *network interface card* (NIC), as shown in Figure 10-1. Servers typically use one or more multiport NICs, and workstation/desktop systems need only a single-port NIC. If you spend any time working with networks, chances are that you'll need to upgrade or replace network cards. This chapter

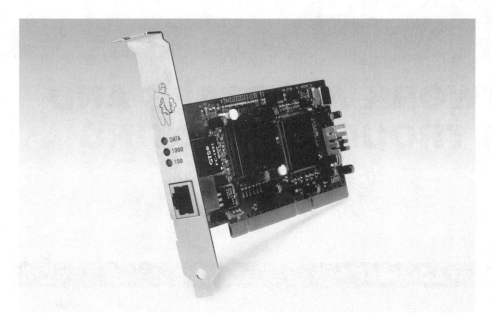

FIGURE 10-1   The Netgear GA622T Gigabit Ethernet NIC (Courtesy of Netgear)

explains the characteristics of a typical NIC, reviews an installation process, and outlines a series of handy troubleshooting guidelines.

NIC Basics

Simply stated, a network interface card (or NIC) is an expansion board device that fits into a computer and provides that computer with a connection to a network. You may use a different type of NIC depending on whether you're working with a workstation/desktop or server system—there is a difference. A desktop NIC is installed in a desktop PC or workstation and only supports a single user (i.e., a single-port NIC). A server NIC is used in a server system intended to connect many users, and this supports important business and mission-critical network situations. Consequently, a server NIC is usually (but not always) a multiport NIC, and it must provide greater functionality (such as increased reliability and throughput), reduced CPU overhead, and better overall communications performance. If a server NIC is inadequate for the network (or fails), it can affect the productivity and profitability of an entire workgroup, department, or company. Just consider the difference in features shown in Table 10-1.

While a server may often use multiple NICs (or a multiport NIC), it can certainly work with a regular single-port NIC—but traffic congestion may occur on a busy network.

Network cards act as the physical interface between the computer (server or workstation) and the network cable. A NIC converts the parallel data of the PC's internal bus into serial signals for transfer over coaxial, twisted-pair, or fiber-optic cables (and back again). Before you can install and configure a NIC, you'll need to understand the ideas of network addressing and system resource assignments (i.e., inter-

TABLE 10-1 NIC COMPARISON

FEATURE	SERVER NIC	DESKTOP NIC
Single-port NIC	X	X
Multiple ports per NIC	X	
Multiple NICs per system	X	
Port aggregation/load balancing	X	
32-bit PCI bus attachment	X	X
64-bit PCI bus attachment	X	
Automatic detection of port failures	X	
Automatic failover to standby port	X	

rupts, I/O, and memory). You'll also need to understand the factors that influence NIC performance on the network. In general, a NIC performs four essential tasks:

■ It prepares the parallel data from the host computer's (server or workstation) bus into serial data suitable for the network cable.

■ It transmits that serial data to another computer on the network.

■ It controls the flow of data between a computer and the network cabling.

■ It receives incoming serial data from the network cable and translates it into parallel data that can be passed to the computer's bus and processed by the system's CPU.

 In strict networking circles, a NIC implements the logical link control and Media Access Control functions in the data link layer of an OSI model.

NIC NETWORK ADDRESSING

The NIC also has to advertise its own location (or address) to the rest of the network in order to distinguish it from all the other NICs on the network. The Institute of Electrical and Electronics Engineers (IEEE) has assigned blocks of addresses to each NIC manufacturer, and each manufacturer hardwires these addresses onto their cards—this essentially "burns" the address into the card. Each NIC (and therefore each computer) has a unique address on a network. A computer with more than one NIC will have an address for each NIC. The physical (or MAC) address is typically a 6-byte hexadecimal number (such as 00:04:5A:D1:9D:25). The NIC also performs several other functions as it takes data from the computer and prepares it for the network cable:

■ The computer and NIC must communicate in order to move data from the computer to the card. If your NIC card can utilize direct memory access (or DMA) data transfers, the computer will assign some of its memory space to the NIC.

■ The NIC then signals the computer and requests the computer's data.

■ The computer's bus then moves the data from system memory (RAM) to the NIC.

Because data can often move faster on the PC bus or the network cable than the NIC can handle, the data is sent to an onboard buffer (a reserved portion of RAM on the NIC). The data is held in that buffer temporarily during both the transmission and reception of network data.

NEGOTIATING DATA

Before the sending NIC actually sends data over the network, it carries on a complex electronic dialog with the receiving NIC (called "negotiation") so that both cards agree on the following:

- The maximum size of the data blocks to be sent
- The amount of data to be sent before confirmation of receipt is issued
- The time intervals between sending data chunks
- The amount of time to wait before confirmation is sent
- How much data each card can hold before its buffer overflows
- The speed of data transmission (such as 10/100/1,000 Mbps)

For example, if a newer, faster, more sophisticated NIC needs to communicate with an older, slower NIC, both devices need to negotiate a common transmission speed and other parameters that each can accommodate. Many newer NICs incorporate circuitry that allows the faster card to adjust to the rate of the slower card. Each NIC signals to the other, indicating its own parameters and accepting or adjusting to the other card's parameters until a "lowest common denominator" is found. After all of the communication details have been worked out, the two cards begin to exchange data.

PORT FAILOVER

Failover is a method of redundancy that provides protection from system failures on servers running mission-critical applications. During a port failure, failover keeps the connection to the server established by moving all traffic on the affected segment to a standby NIC (or NIC port). When a failure is detected on the primary port, that port is disabled and a secondary port takes over to carry the load, and keeps the network running without interruption. Failover operation occurs when there is a network (i.e., Ethernet) link loss, a watchdog timer expires, an abnormal hardware interrupt occurs, or abnormal send/receive counts occur on the segment (such as too many collisions or errors).

PORT AGGREGATION

Port aggregation is a software-supported NIC feature that provides network path redundancy and increased bandwidth for network (i.e., Fast Ethernet) servers running mission-critical applications. Port aggregation works by load balancing the data throughput over multiple ports. With port aggregation, you can create a virtual port by grouping multiple ports together. This grouping distributes the network load by sharing the resources of all ports in a group. In the port aggregation group, one port becomes the primary port and its Media Access Control (MAC) address is given to the protocol. The entire group behaves as a single interface, allowing the software to manage the combined resources of the group efficiently. In the event of a port failure, the remaining ports carry the load and keep the network running and uninterrupted.

Not all NICs and network operating systems support port aggregation. For example, Adaptec Duralink64 port aggregation software is compatible with Adaptec ANA-69011/TX and ANA-62011/TX single-port NICs, ANA-62022 dual-port NICs, and ANA-62044 quad-port NICs. Duralink64 port aggregation software supports Windows NT 4.0 and 3.51, as well as Novell NetWare 4.x– and 5.0–based servers (Windows 95/98/SE doesn't support port aggregation). A server with Duralink64 port aggregation can use up to 12 Adaptec PCI Fast Ethernet ports in one aggregated group (at 1.2 Gbps per group). If any of the supporting members of a specific aggregated group should fail, that member is excluded from the group, and the remaining ports balance the existing load. The combination of failover and port aggregation technologies can help you to create a network that is both fast and fault tolerant.

FEC (FAST ETHERCHANNEL)

Fast EtherChannel (FEC) is a technology developed by Cisco Systems (based on standard Fast Ethernet) to provide the additional bandwidth that network backbones need today. FEC combines two or four Fast Ethernet links to a single logical connection capable of carrying 800 Mbps of aggregate full-duplex data throughput. In addition to scalable bandwidth, the technology also provides fault tolerance and resiliency—protecting the network from outages due to failed links. Fast EtherChannel allows grouping of ports or NICs, enabling full utilization of available bandwidth (up to 800 Mbps). Up to four single-port NICs, two two-port NICs, or one four-port NIC can be grouped. This technology also provides load balancing and management of each link by distributing traffic across multiple links in the channel. As an example, Adaptec Duralink64 v4.2 software and all of the Adaptec DuraLAN NICs support Fast EtherChannel technology, allowing redundancy and high-speed aggregation between switches and servers.

Fast EtherChannel is available on select Cisco Catalyst switches and Cisco routers. For additional information on Cisco's Fast EtherChannel technology, visit the Cisco Systems Web site: **http://www.cisco.com/warp/public/729/fec**.

FULL DUPLEX

Full-duplex support allows a NIC to send and receive data at the same time—effectively doubling your available network bandwidth. To implement full-duplex operation on your network, you'll need both a NIC and a switch (or router or any suitable interconnection device) that supports full duplex. Full duplex can also be enabled point-to-point with a crossover cable instead of a switch.

BNC connections do not support full-duplex operation.

MICROSOFT CLUSTERING

Microsoft Clustering is Microsoft's implementation of server clustering technology. The term "clustering" refers to a group of independent systems that work together as a single system. Fault tolerance is built into the clustering technology. Should a system within the cluster fail, the cluster software will disperse the work from the failed system to the remaining systems in the cluster. Clustering is not intended to replace current implementations of fault-tolerant systems—although it does provide an excellent enhancement.

JUMBO FRAME SUPPORT

Normally, jumbo frames are treated as an error, but some advanced NICs (such as the SMC EtherPower II Gigabit Ethernet card) can be configured to use jumbo frames. This effectively increases the maximum Ethernet frame size from 1,514 bytes up to 9,014 bytes. Using jumbo frames greatly reduces the packet processing overhead for the host CPU, and can boost throughput by up to 300 percent for bulk data transfers. However, to use jumbo frames, both communicating computers *must* have network cards that support this feature. Network devices connecting the two computers (such as hubs, switches, and routers) must also support jumbo frames—otherwise, communication problems will certainly occur.

VIRTUAL LAN SUPPORT

Some advanced NICs (such as the SMC EtherPower II 1000 network card) support the IEEE 802.1Q virtual LAN (VLAN) standard, and can be configured to participate in a network with other devices that use VLANs. An IEEE 802.1Q VLAN is a group of ports that can be located anywhere in the network but communicate as though they belong to the same physical segment. VLANs help to simplify network management by allowing you to move devices to a new VLAN without having to change (rewire) any physical connections. VLANs can be easily organized to reflect departmental groups (such as Marketing or R&D) or usage groups (such as e-mail or video conferencing).

VLANs provide greater network efficiency by reducing broadcast traffic, but also allow you to make network changes without having to update IP addresses or IP subnets. VLANs inherently provide a high level of network security, since traffic must pass through a router or a switch to reach a different VLAN. VLANs are usually configured within IEEE 802.1Q VLAN-enabled switches in the network, and computers are assigned to a VLAN ID based on the switch port number. However, current NICs overcome this limitation by allowing up to 16 VLAN IDs to be configured directly within the network card. Using this feature, a network server can share its resources with up to 16 VLANs when connected to a switch port configured with overlapping VLANs, significantly reducing the latency between clients and the server.

The VLAN IDs configured within the card must match those in the IEEE 802.1Q-compliant switches throughout the network.

Current VLAN-enabled NICs also support the IEEE 802.1p "Quality of Service" standard. Each VLAN is assigned a priority level in the VLAN ID table. By defining priority levels in the network card, it allows the card to work with other network devices to deliver higher-priority packets first. Remember that the IEEE 802.1p standard must also be supported by the other devices in the network.

You can learn more about the specifics of IEEE standards at **standards.ieee.org**.

NIC Configuration Issues

Since a NIC is an internal device, it must be configured to use the computer's hardware resources (typically interrupts, I/O addresses, memory range, and transceiver type). With the standardized use of Plug-and-Play (PnP) BIOS and operating systems, many network cards can automatically configure themselves to the computer's available resources. However, older cards (or cards used with older computer platforms) may need to be configured manually using jumpers or DIP switches. There are several types of resource assignments that you should be familiar with.

RESOURCE ASSIGNMENTS

Interrupt request lines (or IRQs) are hardware signal lines over which devices such as I/O ports, keyboards, disk drive controllers, and NICs can demand the attention of the computer's CPU. Interrupt lines are accessible from the bus, and each IRQ is assigned different levels of priority so that the CPU can determine the relative importance of incoming service requests. Lower IRQ levels represent a *higher* priority. For example, the system processor will service IRQ3 before IRQ12—even if the signals are asserted together. Given the importance of NIC performance, you should try to use the *lowest* available IRQ for your NIC. In most cases, IRQ3 or IRQ5 can be used for the NIC. IRQ5 is typically the recommended setting (if it is available), and it is the default setting for most systems.

Although an interrupt can get the processor's attention, there must still be a means of passing commands and data between the NIC and host PC. By assigning a base *I/O port*, the NIC establishes a channel for communication with the system.

Direct memory access (or DMA) is a technique that allows data to be moved from place to place inside the computer (i.e., between system RAM and the NIC buffer) without the direct control of your computer's

CPU. Otherwise, the CPU would need to manage every data transfer (known as "programmed I/O" or PIO). Not all network cards support DMA data transfers, but those that do—especially newer NICs—will usually provide better performance.

It is important that each device in the computer use a different IRQ, I/O, DMA, and memory resource assignment. If more than one device uses the same resource, a hardware conflict will result, and that can cause the NIC (or other system devices) to behave unexpectedly.

Many NICs utilize a certain amount of memory (RAM) space that serves as a buffer—a temporary storage area that can handle incoming and outgoing *data frames* (a packet of information transmitted as a unit on the network). By setting a *base RAM address* (sometimes called a RAM start address), you can control the memory range occupied by the NIC. Often, the base RAM address for a NIC is D0000h, though there is typically a selection of possible addresses that can be selected (i.e., D8000h).

The same situation is true for ROM address space. Most NICs incorporate their onboard instructions (or firmware) on a BIOS ROM chip located on the network card itself. Remember that the motherboard has a BIOS, and other devices in the system often use a BIOS (i.e., video BIOS or SCSI controller BIOS). This means you must set the *base ROM address* (or ROM start address) so that the NIC will occupy a ROM memory range not used by other devices in the system. Often, the base ROM address for a NIC is D0000h, though there is typically a selection of possible addresses that can be selected (i.e., D8000h).

A NIC that does not use system RAM will not have a setting for the base memory address. However, some NICs offer a setting that allows you to specify memory blocks to be set aside for storing data frames. For example, some cards let you specify either 16KB or 32KB of memory. Configuring more memory provides better network performance, but leaves less memory available for other uses.

SELECTING A TRANSCEIVER

Finally, some network cards come with one external and one onboard *transceiver* (the circuit that drives the network cable). When you connect a cable directly to the NIC, you're using the card's *internal* transceiver. When you must connect a transceiver module to the NIC first (then connect the cable to the module), you're using an *external* transceiver. If your NIC offers this selection, you would have to decide which transceiver to use, and then make the appropriate choice on your card using a jumper or DIP switch (though some NIC models may autoselect the transceiver).

TYPICAL NIC SETTINGS

Now that you've reviewed the elements involved in NIC configuration, you can see the default settings for typical NIC shown below. Keep in mind that these are usually default settings and can be adjusted manually (through the use of jumpers and DIP switches) or automatically (through the use of PnP).

- **Interrupt**   IRQ5 (with a second choice of IRQ2)
- **DMA**   DMA1 or DMA3 (when using 16-bit network adapters, try DMA5)
- **I/O port**   300h usually will work fine
- **Base address**   D0000h or above
- **ROM address**   D0000h or above

Remember that the card's real-mode (DOS) drivers *must* match the card's physical configuration. Network operating systems create these drivers in different ways. For example, 3Com (and many other manufacturers) adjusts the software driver in the **CONFIG.SYS** using some optional command-line switches. By comparison, Novell creates the driver with either SHGEN (NetWare 2.1x) or GENSH (NetWare 2.0a). In either case, your driver parameters must match the card.

NIC BUS SLOTS AND CABLES

To ensure the compatibility between a computer and the network, the NIC must interface with the host computer's data bus architecture (i.e., an ISA or PCI bus) and have the right type of cable connector for network cabling. For example, a NIC that would work in an Apple computer communicating in a bus network will not work in an IBM computer using a token ring environment. You should understand the different data bus architectures and network cabling/connector variations that are available.

Data Bus Architectures

On the personal computer platform, there are four types of computer bus architectures: ISA, EISA, MicroChannel, and PCI. Each type of bus is physically different from the others, but it is essential that the NIC and the bus match. You must select a NIC to match the bus slot(s) available in your PC.

Industry Standard Architecture (ISA)   The venerable *Industry Standard Architecture* is the first open system bus architecture used for IBM-type personal computers—any manufacturer was welcome to use the architecture for a small licensing fee. Since there were no restrictions placed on the use of ISA buses (also referred to simply as "PC buses"), they were duplicated in every IBM-compatible clone that followed. Not only did the use of a standardized bus pave the way for thousands of manufacturers to produce compatible PCs and expansion devices, but it also helped to support the use of standardized operating systems and applications software. Both 8-bit and 16-bit versions of the ISA bus are available, although all motherboards manufactured since the mid-1980s have abandoned the 8-bit XT version in favor of the faster, more flexible 16-bit AT version.

Extended Industry Standard Architecture (EISA)   The *Extended ISA* bus is a 32-bit bus developed in 1988/89 to address the continuing need for greater speed and performance from expansion peripherals caused by the use of 80386 and 80486 CPUs. It also did not make sense to leave the entire 32-bit bus market to IBM's MicroChannel Architecture (MCA) bus. Even though the bus works at 8.33 MHz, the 32-bit data path doubles data throughput between a motherboard and expansion board. Unlike the MCA bus, however, EISA ensures backward compatibility with existing ISA peripherals and PC software. The EISA bus is designed to be fully compatible with ISA boards, and can switch automatically between 16-bit ISA and 32-bit EISA operation using a second row of card edge connectors. Thus, EISA boards have access to all of the signals available to ISA boards, as well as the second row of EISA signals.

MicroChannel Architecture (MCA)   With the introduction and widespread use of 32-bit microprocessors such as the Intel 80386 and 80486, the 16-bit ISA bus faced a serious data throughput bottleneck. Passing a 32-bit word across the expansion bus in two 16-bit halves presented a serious waste of valuable processing time. Not only was data and CPU speed an issue, but video and audio systems in PCs had also been improving—and demanding an increasing share of bus bandwidth. By early 1987, IBM concluded that it was time to lay the ISA bus to rest and unleash an entirely new bus structure that it dubbed the *MicroChannel Architecture*. IBM incorporated the MCA bus into their PS/2 series of personal computers, and also in their System/6000 workstations. Not only can an MCA bus work as a 16-bit or 32-bit bus, but it was also the first PC bus design to support basic bus mastering for improved device performance.

Peripheral Component Interconnect (PCI)   By the late 1980s, the proliferation of 32-bit (Pentium) CPUs and graphics-intensive operating systems made it painfully obvious that the 8.33-MHz ISA bus was no longer satisfactory. The PC industry began to develop alternative architectures for improved performance. In mid-1992, Intel Corporation and a comprehensive consortium of manufacturers introduced the powerful 33-MHz *Peripheral Component Interconnect* (PCI) bus. Where the older video local (or VL) bus was designed specifically to enhance PC video systems, the 188-pin PCI bus looked to the future of CPUs (and PCs in general) by providing a bus architecture that also supports peripherals such as hard drive controllers, network adapters, and so on.

Beyond speed, another key advantage of the PCI bus is that it has automatic configuration capabilities for switchless/jumperless peripherals. Such *autoconfiguration* (the heart of Plug-and-Play) will take care of all addresses, interrupt requests, and DMA assignments used by a PCI peripheral. The PCI bus supports bus mastering, which allows one of a number of intelligent peripherals to take control of the bus in order to accelerate a high-throughput, high-priority task. PCI architecture also supports *concurrency*, a technique that ensures the microprocessor operates simultaneously with these masters, instead of waiting for them.

The ISA, EISA, and MCA bus architectures are now considered obsolete. In virtually all cases, you will be installing and servicing NICs in PCI slots. The only time that you will deal with older bus types (generally ISA) is when you're using an outdated PC or legacy NIC in your network.

Cabling and Connectors

To select the appropriate NIC for your network, you must also determine the type of network cabling and cable connectors to be used. Remember that each type of network cable has different physical characteristics that the NIC must accommodate. Each card is built to accept at least one type of cable—the most common cable types are *coaxial* (usually thinnet), twisted pair, and fiber optic. Some NICs have more than one network cable connector. For example, it is not uncommon for a NIC to have a thinnet, thicknet, and twisted-pair connector. If a card has more than one network connector and does not have built-in interface detection, you should make a selection manually by setting jumpers on the card itself (or by using a software-selectable option).

Use particular caution when working with thicknet connections. A thicknet network connection uses a 15-pin *attachment unit interface* (AUI) cable to connect the 15-pin (DB-15) connector on the back of the NIC to an external transceiver. The external transceiver uses a "vampire tap" to connect to the thicknet cable. Do not confuse a 15-pin joystick port with an AUI external transceiver port. They may look alike, but some joystick pins carry +5 volts dc, which can be harmful to network hardware as well as to the computer.

There are other potential connection problems to be aware of. Do not to confuse 25-pin SCSI ports with parallel printer ports. Some older SCSI devices communicated through the same kind of DB-25 connector as these parallel ports, but neither device will function when plugged into the wrong connector. Finally, an unshielded twisted-pair connection uses an RJ-45 connector. The RJ-45 connector is similar to a RJ-11 telephone connector, but the RJ-45 is larger in size and has eight conductors—an RJ-11 only has four conductors.

NICS AND NETWORK PERFORMANCE

Since the NIC has a direct relationship to data transmission across a network, your choice of NIC will have a profound impact on the performance of that network. If the NIC is slow (such as 10 Mbps), data will not pass to and from the network as quickly—on a bus network where no one can use the network until the cable is clear, a slow NIC can increase wait times for all users. After identifying the physical requirements of a NIC (i.e., the bus type, the type of network connector, and the type of network in which the NIC will operate), it's necessary to consider several other factors that will affect the capabilities of the card. While all NICs conform to certain minimum standards and specifications, some cards feature the following enhancements that greatly improve server, client, and overall network performance:

- Select a NIC that supports *direct memory access* (DMA). DMA allows a computer to move data directly from the NIC's buffer to the computer's memory (RAM) without the direct intervention of the system processor. This frees the CPU for other tasks and improves relative computer performance.

- Select a NIC that supports *shared adapter memory*. The NIC supplies a buffer (RAM) that it shares with the computer, and the computer identifies this buffer RAM as if it were actually part of the computer's system RAM.

- As an alternative to shared adapter memory, you can try a NIC with *shared system memory*. With this technique, the NIC's onboard controller selects a section of the system's memory (RAM), and uses it to process data.

- If you're using a NIC intended for a PCI slot, select a *bus mastering* NIC. With bus mastering, the NIC takes temporary control of the computer's PCI bus, bypasses the computer's CPU, and moves data directly to the computer's system memory. This speeds up computer operations by freeing the system processor to deal with other tasks, and that can improve network performance.

- Employ *RAM buffers* wherever possible. Network traffic often travels too fast for most NICs to handle, so RAM chips on the NIC serve as a buffer. When the card receives more data than it can process immediately, the RAM buffer holds some of the data until the NIC can process it. This speeds up the card's apparent performance to the network and helps keep the card from becoming a bottleneck.

- Employ *NIC processors* wherever possible. With an onboard processor (also referred to as a microcontroller), the NIC has much lower reliance on the system processor for handling data. This offloads more tasks from the system processor and can improve network performance.

As a rule, you should select the best possible NIC for your server since a server generally handles the majority of network traffic. High-performance NICs (such as 1,000-Mbps Ethernet NICs) are frequently employed in servers. By comparison, workstation/desktop network users can often work adequately with less expensive single-port NICs (such as 10/100-Mbps Ethernet NICs). Older NICs will work when their activities are limited to low-traffic applications (such as word processing). Keep in mind that bus networks can be impaired by a single slow NIC. There are also specialized NIC types that you should be familiar with.

Wireless NICs

There are some installations that simply cannot be physically cabled. When these cases occur, you'll need an alternative to cabled computer networking. Wireless NICs (like the Linksys WPC11 in Figure 10-2) are available that support the major network operating systems and often come with many features, including an indoor omnidirectional antenna and antenna cable, network software to interface the NIC with a particular network, and diagnostic software for troubleshooting. In fact, wireless NICs can be used to create an all-wireless LAN, or to add wireless stations to a cabled LAN. Typically, wireless NICs are

FIGURE 10-2   The Linksys WPC11 wireless NIC (Courtesy of Linksys)

used to communicate with a component called a wireless concentrator that acts as a transceiver to send and receive wireless signals.

Fiber-Optic NICs
Data transmission speeds are constantly increasing to accommodate bandwidth-intensive applications and multimedia data streams so common on today's networks. Rather than the use of copper coaxial or twisted-pair cabling, fiber-optic network cards allow direct connections to high-speed fiber-optic networks using thin fiber-optic cables. Fiber-optic cards (such as the SMC EtherPower II 1000 network card) have recently become quite cost effective compared to conventional copper NICs. You can often tell a fiber-optic installation by the "S" designator (such as 1000BaseSX), where a "T" designator usually denotes a twisted-pair copper installation (such as 1000BaseTX).

Remote-Boot PROMs
In some environments, network security is such an important consideration that individual workstations do not have floppy disk drives. Users cannot copy information to floppy or hard disks, so they cannot take any data from the work site. However, since computers normally start from either a floppy or a hard disk, there has to be another source for the software that initially starts (or boots) the computer and connects it to a network. In these cases, the NIC can be equipped with a special chip called a remote-boot PROM (a programmable read-only memory) that contains the code needed to start a computer and connect the user to the network. This allows diskless workstations to join the network when they start. You can see a boot PROM socket in Figure 10-3.

FIGURE 10-3   An SMC EtherPower II 10/100 Ethernet NIC (Courtesy of SMC)

Installing NIC Hardware

The first step is to install the network card itself. For this discussion, we'll consider a recent PCI-based card such as an Adaptec NIC. This installation process is virtually identical to the installation of any other PnP PCI expansion device. There are three basic steps involved in NIC installation: installing the card, connecting the network cable, and configuring the card. Experienced readers can skip this section, but many technicians may find this part of the chapter to be helpful. The minimum system requirements for using an Adaptec NIC and for running its diagnostics utility are as follows:

- **Single-port PCI NIC**   Available bus-mastering PCI slot—most recent PCI system BIOS recommended (multiport NICs require a PCI 2.1–compliant bus)
- **Quad or dual NICs**   System BIOS supporting PCI-to-PCI bridge chip with Windows NT
- **Diagnostic software**   Requires MS-DOS 3.3 or later
- **CPU**   Intel x86 (IBM PC compatible) platform with single or multiprocessor
- **RAM**   16MB RAM or more
- **Software**   Windows NT 3.51 or 4.0 workstation or server, Windows 95/98/2000 (or NetWare 4.x or 5.0) or later

STARTING THE INSTALLATION

Turn off the power to your PC and disconnect the power cord from the wall outlet. During the installation, you may ground yourself by touching any unpainted surface of the PC case. Then, follow these steps:

1. Remove the outer cover from your computer according to the manufacturer's instructions.

2. Carefully remove the NIC from its anti-static container. Verify the model by looking at the model name on the NIC itself (keep the anti-static container for future use).

3. Check the NIC for any visible signs of damage that may have occurred during shipping or handling. If you find a problem, immediately notify your network supplier and the shipping service that delivered your NIC—you'll need to arrange for a replacement NIC.

4. Once the PC is opened, locate an unused expansion slot (a PCI slot in this case). Remove the bracket screw and remove the expansion slot bracket that covers the card slot's opening.

PCI slots and NICs come in two varieties: 3.3 volt, and the more common 5 volt. PCI NICs generally support 5-volt slots. Some models also support 3.3-volt slots. To improve performance with multiport NICs, install these NICs in higher-priority slots such as PCI bus slot 0.

5. Insert the NIC into the PCI expansion slot, pressing down firmly and evenly until the bus contacts are seated in the slot.

6. Secure the NIC in the expansion slot with the bracket screw you removed earlier.

7. Replace the computer's outer cover on the computer.

8. Reconnect any other devices and cables that you might have removed during the installation. Do not reapply power to the computer yet.

ATTACH THE CABLES

For a thinnet cable, connect the T connector to the card's BNC connector. Align the T connector's slots with the pegs on the card's BNC connector. Push the T connector in and twist it clockwise until it stops (you'll feel a slight click as the barrel rotates far enough). Attach the cable from the network to one side of the T, and place a terminator on the other side (or the cable to the next workstation).

For a twisted-pair cable, make sure that the RJ-45 connector on your cable is wired appropriately for standard 10Base-T adapter (you'd be surprised at how often these connectors are wired wrong). Align the RJ-45 plug on the end of the twisted-pair cable with the notch on the adapter's connector, and insert the cable into the card's RJ-45 socket. See that the other end of the cable is attached to the network.

For thicknet cable (when a 15-pin attachment unit interface, or AUI, is needed), locate the card's AUI connector and move the slide latch to the open position. Connect the AUI cable or transceiver to the AUI connector on the NIC. Move the slide latch to the closed position to lock the cable into place. Connect the other end of the AUI cable to the external transceiver.

The card's selection of cabling should normally be automatic. When the appropriate driver is installed for a particular operating system, the driver automatically selects the media type based on the type of cable connection. If you change the cable type later, you must reinstall the driver for it to automatically detect the cable type. If the driver *cannot* detect which cable is connected (or whether a cable is connected), the Auto Select Media Type function defaults to the type of connector stored in the card's firmware. For example, the default is AUI for a 3Com 3C900-COMBO NIC. You can change this default by selecting another media type from the list of options.

If you install a quad- or dual-port NIC and a port does not have a cable attached, you may receive a startup error message on your server. This is normal and does not affect performance.

CONFIGURING THE NIC

Since most NICs are now PnP compliant, your computer's BIOS *may* determine the available NIC resources and configure the PCI NIC automatically. However, depending on your particular system, you may need to configure the card yourself (or verify that the settings are correct). To do this, enter your computer's CMOS Setup and select Advanced Settings from the Main menu. Make sure the following settings are enabled (your BIOS may not match the following options exactly, so refer to your system manual for specific CMOS Setup options):

- **PCI Slot Enabled**   Enable all of the PCI slots in your system.
- **Bus Mastering**   Enable PCI bus mastering for the slot(s) being used by the NICs.
- **PCI INTA**   Assign an ISA interrupt (10, 11, 12, etc.) to PCI interrupt vector A.
- **PCI INT Vector**   Assign PCI interrupt vector A to the PCI slot(s) used by the NIC.
- **PCI Bus Latency**   Set to a value between 40 and 80.
- **Triggering**   Set the slot to level triggering rather than edge triggering.

Quad and dual NICs typically employ the motherboard's PCI-to-PCI bridge chip. If your system's BIOS does not support the PCI-to-PCI bridge chip, such NICs will not be configured properly. Contact your computer manufacturer to obtain a new BIOS version that supports the PCI-to-PCI bridge chip.

Installing the NIC Drivers

After installing the NIC itself, you must install the appropriate NIC driver. Depending on your particular NIC device and your network operating system, you may install one of three drivers: a standard driver, a failover driver, or a port aggregation driver. Please note that you may install one type only. As an example, the Adaptec Duralink64 diskettes provide the following drivers:

- The *standard* driver (i.e., a DuraLAN Standard Driver) uses each port independently.

Not all versions of Windows support the NIC's failover or port aggregation drivers. For example, Windows 9x and Novell Client32 do not support Adaptec's Duralink64 failover. Install the standard driver for these operating systems.

- The *failover* driver (i.e., a Duralink64 Failover Driver) groups two NIC ports as a set—one as the primary port and the other as the backup port. The ports may be connected to a hub or switch.
- The *port aggregation* or *Fast EtherChannel* driver (i.e., a Duralink64 Port Aggregation Driver) groups up to 12 ports together, and must be used with a switch. In addition, Fast EtherChannel (FEC) can be arranged in groups of two or four, though this type of setup requires a switch that supports Fast EtherChannel.

REMOVING OLD DRIVERS

If you're replacing or upgrading a NIC device (or upgrading the drivers), it is often necessary to remove the older NIC drivers *first*—this ensures that there is no software conflict between the older and newer software. This part of the chapter shows you how to remove the older drivers for an Adaptec DuraLAN NIC—your own NIC may indicate different entries, but the overall process should be quite similar. For example, if you're using Windows NT as your network operating system, follow the steps below as guideline for removing old NIC drivers:

1. Double-click My Computer on your desktop.
2. Double-click Control Panel.
3. Double-click the Network icon.
4. In the Network window, click the Adapters tab.
5. In the Network Adapters list, click the NIC you want to remove (i.e., Adaptec DuraLAN NIC) and then click Remove.
6. When asked if you wish to continue, click Yes.
7. Repeat the previous two steps until all of the related drivers (i.e., Adaptec DuraLAN) are removed.
8. When you're done, click OK.
9. Click Close to close the Network window.
10. Click Yes to restart your computer.

 When you restart Windows NT, a message may indicate that at least one service failed to start. This message will not appear after you add the new driver, so simply click OK.

INSTALLING NEW DRIVER(S)

Once you've cleared old drivers from the system, you can install the current NIC drivers for your particular network operating system. Before proceeding, it's usually a good idea to check for driver updates and patches at the NIC manufacturer's Web site. This section of the chapter illustrates the installation process for Adaptec DuraLAN drivers under Windows NT/2000 and NetWare.

Windows NT 4.0

If you are installing Windows NT at this time, start with step 6 when prompted for the DuraLAN NIC. To install the DuraLAN driver on a Windows NT 4.0 platform, follow these steps:

1. Start the system to Windows NT.
2. From the Start menu, point to Settings and then click Control Panel.
3. In the Control Panel, double-click the Network icon.
4. In the Network window, click the Adapters tab.
5. In the Adapters tab, click Add.
6. In the Select Network Adapter window, click Have Disk.
7. At the Insert Disk window, insert the driver diskette (i.e., Duralink64 for Windows NT diskette) and then click OK.

8. In the Select OEM Option window, click the NIC model that's installed (i.e., DuraLAN NIC) and then click OK.

9. In the installation window that appears (i.e., Adaptec DuraLAN NIC Driver Installation window), select the desired driver and then click OK.

10. Continue on to install the standard driver, the failover driver, or the port aggregation driver.

Windows 2000
Use the following procedure to install the driver and diagnostics on a computer that is running Windows 2000:

1. Reboot the computer and then start Windows 2000.

2. Log on to a suitable Windows 2000 administrator account. The Windows 2000 Found New Hardware Wizard detects the new NIC(s) and begins the driver installation.

3. Insert the NIC driver CD (i.e., a 3Com EtherLink Server CD) in the CD-ROM drive.

4. Select NIC Software from the Main menu.

5. Click NIC Drivers and Diagnostics from the list that appears.

6. Follow the wizard's prompts.

7. Choose Typical or Custom installation. The Please Wait screen appears. After the installation is completed, an Update dialog box appears.

8. Click OK, and a Setup Complete screen appears.

9. Click Finish to complete the installation.

10. Click Exit. You may need to reboot the system so that your new drivers take effect.

Novell NetWare
With NetWare installed and the NetWare file server up and running, complete the following steps to install and configure the drivers. Your first task is to load the driver CD (i.e., a 3Com EtherLink Server CD) in the server's CD-ROM drive.

1. Under NetWare 4.2, insert the CD in the CD-ROM drive and enter the following commands:

```
load cdrom
cd mount ecd210p980x
```

2. Under NetWare 5.x, insert the CD in the CD-ROM drive and enter this command:

```
load cdrom
```

3. Wait for a message that states the CD is mounted successfully, and then proceed to copy the driver as shown in the example below (be sure to check the documentation with your own NIC for specific instructions).

4. Using NetWare 4.2, use the command **load install**. Under NetWare 5.x, use the command **load nwconfig**.

5. In the Configuration Options screen, select Driver.

6. In the Driver Options screen, select Configure.

7. If the Additional Driver Actions screen appears, choose Select (a screen appears listing all previously saved NIC drivers in the system). A new NIC that has not been previously installed will not appear in the list.

8. Press Insert. A system message appears for you to select a disk drive.

9. Press F3.

10. Enter a path to the volume that contains the driver—for example, **ecd210p980x:/nwserver**. The Select a Driver to Install screen appears with your driver name (i.e., 3Com EtherLink Server NIC) highlighted.

11. Press ENTER to select the driver.

12. Select Yes when prompted to confirm the name of the driver to copy. The installation program copies the driver to the appropriate server subdirectory. The Configuration screen appears.

13. At this point, you can specify a slot number for the NIC and load the driver. You need not specify the slot number if you are installing only one NIC.

14. In the Configuration screen, select Slot Number.

15. Enter the slot number of the NIC that you want to install (i.e., 10001).

16. Select Save to set your parameters and load the driver. The installation program loads the configured driver, then writes the appropriate **load** and **bind** commands to the **AUTOEXEC.NCF** file. The system assigns a network number.

17. Enter a network number (or press ENTER to select the system-assigned number). If no errors are encountered, the installation program asks whether you want to select an additional network driver.

18. Select Yes to set up another NIC.

19. Repeat the process for all NICs to be set up. After all NICs are set up, press ESC several times to return to the Installation Options screen. At this point, you can configure groups.

20. From the Configuration Options screen, select NCF files options (this lets you create or edit server startup files).

21. Select Edit **AUTOEXEC.NCF** file.

22. Make the following changes to the **AUTOEXEC.NCF** file:

   - Add a command to load the SE and LBRSL drivers before any commands to load LAN drivers—for example, **load se load lbrsl**.

   - Add or verify the **load** commands for the LAN drivers for all slot-frame instances.

   - For each load-balancing/RSL group, load the same protocols and frame types on the primary and all secondary NICs.

   - On the primary NIC only, bind a protocol to each slot-frame instance.

   - Remove any protocol **bind** commands from each secondary NIC.

   - For each group, add an **lbrsl group** command to group the primary and secondary NICs together. There can be only one **lbrsl group** command per group, and it must list the primary and all secondary NICs. Place this command after the LAN driver.

23. Save the **AUTOEXEC.NCF** file and return to the system prompt.

VERIFY THE WINDOWS DRIVER(S)

After drivers are installed, you should verify that the Windows driver is installed properly. Use the following steps for Windows 2000:

1. Right-click My Computer, choose Properties, and then select the Hardware tab.

2. Click the Device Manager button.

3. In the Device Manager screen, expand the Network Adapters entry. Your NIC should appear under Network Adapters (see Figure 10-4). Close the window. If the NIC does not appear, it has not been installed properly. If a yellow exclamation mark appears beside your NIC entry, the drivers may be incorrect. Remove the NIC driver and reinstall it (check for driver updates if possible).

4. If the Device Manager window lists both old and new NICs, you should remove the old NIC entry from the Device Manager and reboot so that any traces of the old NIC are removed.

VERIFY THE NETWARE DRIVER(S)

To verify that the driver has been properly loaded on the NetWare server, perform the following procedure:

1. At the system prompt, type **load monitor**. The NetWare Monitor screen appears.

2. From the Available Options menu, select LAN/WAN Drivers. The Available LAN Driver menu appears. If the driver has been properly loaded, the driver and frame types associated with the driver appear on this menu.

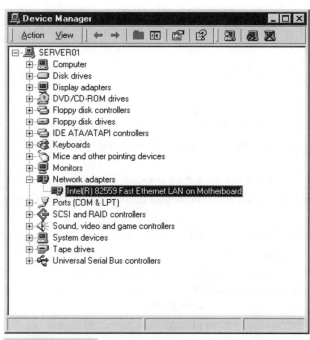

FIGURE 10-4   Checking for your NIC under Windows 2000

3. Select a driver to view its related statistics (a functioning driver displays packets being sent and received).

4. To verify that the server is communicating over the network, perform the last two steps.

5. Set up a NetWare client on a LAN supported by the server to be tested.

6. Log in or map to the server. If you cannot log in or map to the server, the link is not functional. If the link is functional, the following message appears on the server console:

```
Link integrity test for primary slot #XXXXX passed
```

CONFIGURING THE STANDARD DRIVER(S)

If you select the standard NIC driver, you'll need to configure that driver now. The actual setup will depend on whether you use Windows NT, Windows 2000, or Novell NetWare. The following section shows you a configuration example using Windows NT:

1. In the New Hardware Found window, each NIC port is assigned to autodetect and use a default connection type that will always detect the port connection and negotiate a compatible speed and transmission mode.

If you're required to insert the Windows NT CD, you must reinstall the latest version of the Windows NT Service Pack and then restart the system.

2. In the New Hardware Found window, make sure that all the NIC ports appear.

3. In the New NIC Port(s) Available window, click the appropriate port.

4. In the Connection Types list, click the connection type for your network, or use Autodetect Default Connection.

5. Click Apply.

6. Repeat the first four steps for each existing port.

7. When you're done, click OK.

8. When you're done, click Close in the Network window.

9. Restart the system.

SETTING UP THE FAILOVER SYSTEM

If you have multiple ports or adapters on your server, you can employ advanced techniques such as adapter teaming (aggregation), load balancing, and so on. You can see an example in the NIC setup of Figure 10-5. As an example, if you're using Windows NT 4.0, you can elect to use the failover driver on a server. This will allow you to incorporate a certain amount of redundancy in the network. This example looks at the setup of a failover driver.

Configuring the Ports

You'll need to set up the ports on your NIC. Use the following steps as a guideline for configuring the NIC:

1. In the New Hardware Found window, each NIC port is assigned to autodetect and use a default connection type that will always detect the port connection and negotiate a compatible speed and transmission mode.

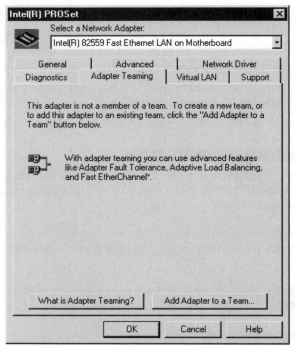

FIGURE 10-5   Configuring a server's NIC features under
Windows 2000

2. In the New Hardware Found window, make sure all of the NIC ports appear.

3. In the New NIC Ports Available box, click the appropriate port.

4. In the Connection Types list, click the connection type for your network, or use Autodetect Default Connection.

5. Click Apply.

6. Repeat the first four steps for each existing port.

7. When you're done, click OK.

Selecting a Failover Pair

You can create failover pairs in Windows NT 4.0 through the Configuration tab. A failover pair consists of two ports: the primary port and the backup port. Follow these steps:

1. From the Available Ports box, click a port to be designated as a primary port.

2. Click Add. The port is added under Primary Port in the Failover Pair list.

3. To assign a backup to the primary port, click the appropriate port from the Available Ports box and then click Add. The port is added in the Backup Port field.

4. Click Apply.

5. Repeat the first four steps to create another failover pair.

To remove a failover pair, click the port from the Primary Ports list and then click Remove. Both ports will return to the Available Ports box. Click Apply.

6. When you're done, click OK and you'll return to the Adapters tab.

7. If SNMP is not set up, you'll receive an error message. Click OK.

8. Enter the protocol information (consult your Windows NT 4.0 documentation for help configuring the protocol, if necessary).

9. When you're done, remove the driver disk from the floppy drive and restart the system.

 If you're required to insert the Windows NT CD, you must reinstall the latest version of Windows NT Service Pack and then restart the system.

Monitoring Failover Pairs

You can use the tools under Windows NT or the failover software to monitor the status of failover pairs in several ways:

■ **SNMP Manager**   When a failover occurs, SNMP traps are sent to network management stations and error logs are updated through the operating system event log. For example, in order to manage SNMP agents, compile the following MIB file on the SNMP management station: **a:\snmpmibs\ duralink.mib**.

■ **Event Viewer dialog box**   The local Event Viewer dialog box will log port failures in Windows NT.

■ **Manufacturer's failover software**   The manufacturer may provide software (such as Adaptec's Duralink64 failover software) that monitors the traffic and health of your failover pairs.

SETTING UP THE PORT AGGREGATION SYSTEM

If you're using Windows NT 4.0 or 2000, you may be able to employ the port aggregation drivers for your NIC. This will share the data transmission load between your NIC ports and increase your effective data bandwidth.

 The guidelines in this section generally assume that you're using Windows NT. If you're using Windows 2000 or some other network operating system, check the NIC user guide for specific installation instructions.

Configuring the Ports

You'll need to configure the NIC ports for failover operation. Use the steps below as a guideline for failover configuration for Windows NT:

1. In the New Hardware Found window, each NIC port is assigned to autodetect and use a default connection type that will always detect the port connection and negotiate a compatible speed and transmission mode.

2. In the New Hardware Found window, check to make sure that all the NIC ports appear.

3. In the New NIC Ports Available box, click the appropriate port.

4. In the Connection Types list, click the connection type for your network or use Autodetect Default Connection.

5. Click Apply.

6. Repeat the previous five steps for each existing port.

7. When you're done, click OK.

8. Now create your port aggregation groups as shown in the next section.

Creating Aggregation Groups

Now you must assign NIC ports to your port aggregation group—effectively creating a virtual NIC port. As an example, use the following steps to configure your port aggregation system for Windows NT:

1. In the Group(s) field, click Create New Group and then type the new group name. The group name may be up to 20 characters. If you skip this step, the system assigns a default group name (i.e., GroupX).

2. In the Link Aggregation Type field, click the appropriate link type.

3. In the Available Ports box, click an available port to add it to the group and then click Add.

Repeat step 3 for each additional port you wish to aggregate. Remember that you must assign the same connection type to each port in the same group. To remove a port from the group, follow these steps:

1. Click the appropriate port from the Group Ports box and then click Remove.

2. When you're finished configuring the group, click Apply.

3. To create another group, repeat the previous five steps.

4. If you want to rename a group, select the default group name in the Group(s) list box, type the new name, and then click Apply.

5. When you're finished configuring all the groups, click OK.

6. If SNMP is not set up on the computer, you will receive an error message, but just click OK.

7. In the Network window, click Close.

8. Now assign the TCP/IP address for the aggregated group.

Creating FEC Groups

Cisco's Fast EtherChannel option allows you to fully aggregate two or four ports over transmit and receive under all protocols. The ports that are configured as the Fast EtherChannel group must be physically connected to the Fast EtherChannel ports on a Cisco switch (see your Cisco switch documentation to configure the ports in Fast EtherChannel mode). If you select Fast EtherChannel on the server, the connection type for each port is automatically configured to 100-Mbps TX/Full Duplex. You must also configure the ports on the Cisco switch (used by the Fast EtherChannel group) to either Auto Negotiation or 100-Mbps/Full Duplex mode under Windows NT, as shown in the following example:

1. In the Group(s) field, click Create New Group and then type the new group name. The group name may be up to 20 characters. If you skip this step, the system assigns a default group name (i.e., GroupX).

2. In the Link Aggregation Type field, click the appropriate link type.

3. In the Available Ports box, click an available port to add it to the group, then click Add.

Repeat step 3 for each additional port. Remember that you must assign the same connection type to each port in the same group. To remove a port from the group, follow these steps:

1. Click the appropriate port from the Group Ports box and then click Remove.
2. When you're finished configuring the group, click Apply.
3. To create another group, repeat the previous five steps.
4. If you want to rename a group, select the default group name in the Group(s) list box, type the new name, and then click Apply.
5. When you're finished configuring all groups, click OK.
6. If SNMP is not set up, you'll receive an error message, but simply click OK.
7. In the Network window, click Close.
8. Now assign the TCP/IP address for the aggregated FEC group.

Assigning a TCP/IP Address

Once you've configured port aggregation, Windows NT prompts you to configure the protocol. IP addresses for groups and stand-alone ports are assigned in the IP Address tab. Ports assigned to a group use the same IP address, so it must be entered only once. Follow these steps to assign a TCP/IP address:

1. In the IP Address tab, click the NIC port (i.e., DuraLAN NIC) from the Adapter list.
2. In the IP Address field, type the IP address.
3. In the Subnet Mask field, type the subnet mask number (and Gateway address if necessary), and then click Apply.
4. Repeat the previous steps for any other port or group.
5. Click OK when you're finished configuring all groups.
6. Restart your computer to complete the changes—click Yes at the message prompt to restart your computer. You may now check system status or modify your groups, if needed.

Adjusting Port Aggregation Groups

After the port aggregation driver is installed and the groups are configured, you may modify the group or port configurations. The following procedures show you how to rename groups, as well as add or remove ports from existing groups under Windows NT. To rename a group, follow these steps:

1. In the NIC's port aggregation windows (i.e., a Duralink64 Port Aggregation window), go to the Configuration tab.
2. From the Group(s) field, select the appropriate group and then type the new name.
3. Click Apply to save your changes.

To add or remove a port, follow these steps:

1. In the NIC's port aggregation windows (i.e., a Duralink64 Port Aggregation window), go to the Configuration tab.

2. In the Group(s) field, click Create New Group and then type the new group name (or select the appropriate group you want to modify):

   ■ To add ports to the group, click the appropriate port from the Available Adaptec Ports box and then click Add.

   ■ To remove ports from the group, click the appropriate port from the Group Ports box, and then click Remove.

3. Repeat the previous step for each appropriate port.

4. Click Apply to save your changes.

5. When you're finished, click OK.

6. If SNMP is not set up on the computer, you will receive an error message, but just click OK.

7. When adding or deleting a group or port, you'll receive another error message, but click OK again.

8. In the Network window, click Close.

If you add or remove a port to or from a group, any existing group or port IP address is removed automatically. Keep track of any IP addresses you plan to use again.

Checking System Status

You can review group and independent port status using the following steps:

1. From the Start menu, point to Settings and then click Control Panel.

2. In the Control Panel, double-click Network.

3. In the Network window, click the Adapters tab.

4. In the Adapters tab, select the NIC (i.e., Adaptec DuraLAN NIC). The NIC's Port Aggregation window appears.

5. Click Properties.

6. Click the Status tab to view the group and independent port information.

7. When you're satisfied with the information, click OK to exit.

Basic NIC Troubleshooting

Although the vast majority of NIC devices should install and operate without errors, there are certainly many situations when a server or workstation system may encounter problems. Trouble can surface in the hardware setup, network cabling, driver installation, or the system configuration. As a technician, you should be able to quickly identify and correct NIC problems. This part of the chapter outlines some of the more common symptoms and solutions for a typical NIC, and explains some common diagnostic commands for an Adaptec DuraLAN NIC.

USING PERFORMANCE MONITOR

Windows NT/2000 provides you with a Performance utility that you can use to view system traffic for selected groups and stand-alone ports (as well as many other parameters). In this window, each line represents the performance of the group or port listed at the bottom of the screen. When a group or port's activity drops, its line drops. Use the following instructions to select the ports and groups you wish to view under Windows 2000:

1. From the Start menu, highlight Programs, point to Administrative Tools, and then click Performance. The Performance dialog box appears, as in Figure 10-6.

2. In the Performance dialog box, click the Add button to enter the Add Counter window.

3. From the Performance list box, select Network Interface.

4. In the Counters box, click the desired elements that you want to monitor (such as Bytes Total/sec), and then click the appropriate instance(s) (such as your NIC). Click Add to start recording.

5. To distinguish elements in the Performance dialog box, click the Properties button (see Figure 10-7) and adjust the chart's appearance.

6. Repeat steps 4 and 5 for each desired port or group (or other element) to be monitored.

7. When you wish to exit, click the Close button.

GENERAL TROUBLESHOOTING TIPS

Before you jump right into a series of specific symptoms, you should always start a troubleshooting effort by reviewing the basic installation and setup of a NIC. If your NIC is not functioning properly, verify that

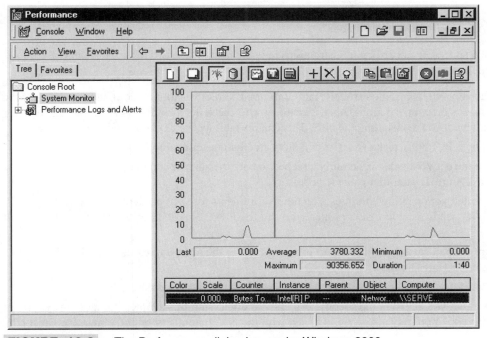

FIGURE 10-6 The Performance dialog box under Windows 2000

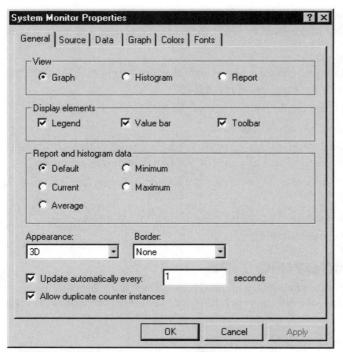

FIGURE 10-7   Adjust the chart's appearance through its
Properties dialog box

it was installed and set up according to instructions in its manual. These tips offer some general trouble-shooting guidelines:

- Verify that your NIC is installed properly and configured correctly in the host computer according to the manufacturer's recommendations. Also, take the time to check the manufacturer's knowledge base for the OS in which you're installing the NIC. This can reveal important OS compatibility problems.

- When using a PCI NIC, make sure the PCI slots are bus-master enabled.

- Make sure the network cable is securely attached to both the adapter and the rest of the network (i.e., the network hub). Try another cable if necessary.

- Make sure that your cabling complies with the requirements for your particular NIC (for example, a Gigabit NIC needs a cable that complies with the IEEE 802.3z 1000BaseSX standard for Gigabit Ethernet).

- Make sure the hub, switch, or router port is configured for the same duplex mode as the adapter (i.e., Full Duplex or Half Duplex).

- Verify that the NIC driver (i.e., Adaptec DuraLAN driver) is installed correctly.

- Make sure that you're using the specific drivers that come with this adapter (rather than generic or default drivers). You may also wish to check with the NIC manufacturer and obtain the latest NIC drivers.

■ If there are other network cards in the computer, they may be causing conflict. Remove all other cards from the computer (if possible) and test the NIC separately.

■ Verify that you are using the latest BIOS for your computer.

■ Verify that your cable, terminators, and connectors are functioning properly, or install the NIC in a different PCI bus slot.

■ If you're replacing an existing adapter under NetWare, make sure the **link** statements in your NET.CFG are correct for the new adapter. For example, the **link** statement for a NetWare client should be **link driver e100bodi**.

■ Under NetWare, verify that the Frame type in your **NET.CFG** file matches your server.

■ If setting up a server under NetWare, check your **load** and **bind** statements.

■ Under Windows NT, make sure the driver is loaded and the protocols are bound. See the Network Bindings dialog box in Windows NT to make sure. If the problem persists, try the following:

   1. Replace the NIC with the same type of NIC that is known to work. If the new NIC functions properly, the problem is related to the original NIC (which is probably defective and should be replaced).

   2. Install the NIC in another functioning computer and run the tests again. If the NIC works in another machine, the problem is related to one of three areas: the original computer is faulty, there is a hardware conflict in the original computer, or there are problems with the cables or connectors in the original computer.

PCI Compatibility
Early PCI BIOS versions do not properly support the PCI specification, and may stop responding when a network card driver tries to load. If this occurs, make sure your BIOS correctly supports the PCI Local Bus Specification (v2.0 or later), or upgrade your computer BIOS to the latest version. Some PCI-based computers are not self-configuring, and require you to perform some or all of the following functions by motherboard jumper changes or adjustments to the CMOS Setup program:

■ Verify that the PCI slot is enabled as a bus-master slot (not a slave PCI slot). Most network cards must be installed in a PCI bus-master slot. In some computers, the PCI slot must be configured to enable bus mastering. Refer to your PC's manual and check the CMOS Setup program to be sure the PCI slot is an enabled bus-master slot.

■ In some cases, your PC's motherboard will require bus-master drivers before bus-mastering operation is supported. Be sure that this software is installed, and update the software if necessary.

■ In some computers, you may be required to disable Plug-and-Play (PnP) in the CMOS Setup program if resources are not properly assigned between the network card and other installed cards. This may require you to configure expansion devices manually.

■ Some computers may require you to reserve interrupts and memory addresses for installed ISA (legacy) cards to prevent PCI cards from using the same settings. Refer to your PC's manual and check the CMOS Setup program configuration options for ISA cards.

■ Make sure the NIC's PCI slot is configured to support INTA.

■ Be sure that INTA for the slot is assigned to a free interrupt (IRQ) number.

■ Check the CMOS Setup program parameters for the PCI slot where the network card is installed. Be sure the slot is configured for level-triggered interrupts instead of edge-triggered interrupts. An example of typical PCI parameters follows:

■ PCI Slot #: (slot number where the network card is installed)

■ Master: Enabled

■ Slave: Enabled

■ Latency Timer: 40 (range is 20 to 255)

■ Interrupt Type: Level-Triggered

■ Interrupt Number: (Choose any number supplied by the CMOS Setup that does not conflict with another installed card)

USE NIC DIAGNOSTICS

Network failures can cost a busy company a tremendous amount of money, so it's worthwhile for NIC makers to provide built-in diagnostic tools in order to speed the troubleshooting process. Diagnostics will let you test the basic functions of the network card, and check its ability to communicate over the network with another card, so any troubleshooting should use the card's diagnostic feature. There are generally two types of tests: local and remote.

Local Tests

Local tests can be used to test the basic functions of the network card. Select the Run Loopback Tests and Run Internal Tests to put the NIC through its paces. For example, the selected tests will show Ready as the status in the test list box. Then click on the Run Local Tests button to start the tests. The progress of each test is shown by the Test Progress status bar. When the tests are complete, click on the View Test Results button to display the test results. As a rule, loopback or internal test failures generally mean that the NIC has failed (or has been installed improperly).

Remote Tests

Remote tests (also called *send and receive* tests) verify that the network cable is connected correctly, so that the network card can transmit and receive data. The test requires two computers with compatible network cards installed. One computer is configured in Send mode to generate and send test messages. The other computer is configured in Receive mode to receive the test messages and transmit them back to the sender. For example, to run the test, simply click the Send button on one computer and click the Receive button on the other. You can view the test results by clicking on the View Test Results button. If local tests pass but remote tests fail, you can be certain that the trouble is with the cabling, connections, or internetworking devices (i.e., hubs, routers, or switches) between the stations. It is also possible that one of the two stations is not configured properly (such as using the wrong protocol).

NIC Diagnostic Software

Many NIC devices are supplied with a versatile real-mode (DOS) diagnostic software that can be used to check a NIC's performance. This part of the chapter reviews the diagnostics included with an Adaptec DuraLAN NIC. While diagnostics included with your own NIC may be quite different, this section may help to familiarize you with some of the more common diagnostic commands.

Launching the Diagnostic Utility   Make sure **HIMEM.SYS** and **EMM386.EXE** are currently in the **CONFIG.SYS** file and that a **files=30** entry is present. If they are not, add the following lines to the top of the **CONFIG.SYS** file and follow these steps:

```
device=c:\dos\himem.sys
device=c:\dos\emm386.exe /noems
files=30
```

Use the correct path to the DOS programs if it is not found in **c:\dos**.

1. Create a directory for the diagnostics on your hard drive.

2. Copy all files from the original diagnostic directory to the new diagnostic directory on the hard drive.

3. At the DOS prompt, type **go_diags** and then press ENTER.

The easiest way of testing a DuraLAN NIC is running the self-test feature.

Understanding Typical Commands   Once your diagnostic is running, you can use the commands in Table 10-2 to test your Adaptec DuraLAN NIC. Remember that the diagnostics included with your NIC may be different, but this list of commands may serve as a handy example and guide.

This test requires a hub, switch, or loop-back cable. Also, autonegotiate defaults to 10 Mbps if the cable is not connected.

TABLE 10-2   TYPICAL NIC* DIAGNOSTIC COMMANDS

COMMAND	PURPOSE	VALUES	MEANING
Address_filter	This tests Ethernet packet-filtering capabilities.		
Autonegotiate \<speed\>	This tests the speed at which the card negotiates. This test has five options:	0	Tests for full autonegotiation (highest speed)
		10	Forces test at 10-Mbps half duplex
		20	Forces test at 10-Mbps full duplex
		100	Forces test at 100-Mbps half duplex
		200	Forces test at 100-Mbps full duplex
Checksum	This tests the ability to calculate a TCP/IP checksum.		
Display	This displays the values of all chip registers on the NIC.		

TABLE 10-2   TYPICAL NIC* DIAGNOSTIC COMMANDS *(CONTINUED)*

COMMAND	PURPOSE	VALUES	MEANING
Echoer #/sender #	This test is useful for testing the network and verifying that data is being passed between the echoer and the sender.		
Eeprom	This tests the contents of the NIC's serial eeprom and displays it on screen.		
Exit	This exits the diagnostics utility.		
External_10	This test requires a loopback cable. It tests the loopback from the cable at 10 Mbps.		
External_100	This test requires a loopback cable. It tests the loopback from the cable at 100 Mbps.		
hbi_dma	This checks DMA transfers to and from the board.		
hbi_slave	This tests slave accesses, checks the serial eeprom, and checks register accesses to the chip.		
Internal_10_mac	This tests internal loopback at 10 Mbps within the chip.		
Internal_10_phy	This tests loopback from the physical device at 10 Mbps.		
Internal_100_mac	This tests internal loopback at 100 Mbps within the chip.		
Internal_100_phy	This tests loopback from the physical device at 100 Mbps.		
Io	This forces the slave access set to I/O mode.		
Loop	This command performs multiple tests consecutively.		
Mac	This tests registers and various functions of the Ethernet controller.		
Mem (default)	This forces the slave access set to Memory mode.		
Mod (mac offset data)	This feature allows the modification of the Ethernet controller registers.		
Pause	This tests the flow controller features of the chip.		
Port X	This specifies the port you want to test.		
Power-management	This tests the power-down features of the Ethernet controller.		

TABLE 10-2   TYPICAL NIC* DIAGNOSTIC COMMANDS (CONTINUED)

COMMAND	PURPOSE	VALUES	MEANING
Selftest	This verifies a variety of card functions. You should run this test first to isolate common NIC errors.		
Statistics	This verifies the statistics-gathering features of the chip.		
Timer	This tests the interrupt delay time feature of the Ethernet controller.		

*These commands are for an Adaptec DuraLAN NIC, but commands for your own NIC may be similar.

CREATING A BOOT/LOGON DISKETTE

When trouble arises with a NIC or its access to the network, you may need a boot/logon disk to boot the system to the real mode (DOS) and access the network. The following procedure illustrates a typical process for creating a Windows NT 4.0 boot/logon diskette for an Intel PRO/100+ LAN adapter card (your own NIC will probably require slightly different files, but the overall process should be quite similar for Windows NT 4.0). To perform this task, you'll require the latest driver disk for the network adapter you're using and a Windows NT 4.0 server with client directories (or the Windows NT 4.0 installation CD).

1. Create a DOS boot disk on a machine running MS-DOS 6.2x or newer.

2. Place the diskette in the disk drive on the Windows NT 4.0 server.

3. Select Start | Programs | Administrative Tools (Common) | Network Client Administrator.

4. Be sure the Make Network Installation Startup Disk option is selected and click Continue.

5. If you're using the defaults, Use Existing Shared Directory should be selected. Click OK.

6. Select the Network Client v3.0 for MS-DOS and Windows in the Network Client window.

7. From the list of adapters under Network Adapter Card, select your NIC (i.e., Intel EtherExpress 16 or 16TP) and then click OK.

8. Type in the name of the computer that you will be booting. Type in the username that you will log on as. Type in the domain. Choose the appropriate network protocol. Click OK.

9. Be sure the diskette is in the disk drive and Click OK again. Click OK after the disk is created and exit from Network Client Administrator. Click OK if there's a final message about memory management.

10. After the disk is created, you'll need to edit three text files on the disk. Use any text editor to edit **A:\AUTOEXEC.BAT**. Delete the last two lines that read

```
echo Running Setup...
z:\msclient\netsetup\setup.exe /$
```

and save the file.

11. Now edit **A:\NET\SYSTEM.INI**. Go to the section labeled [network drivers]. You'll see this line:

```
netcard=exp16.dos
```

12. Change the name of the driver after the equal sign to the name of the **.DOS** (NDIS) file on the driver disk for your NIC. For example, if you're using an Intel PRO/100+ adapter, the line will read

```
netcard=e100b.dos
Save the file.
```

13. Edit **A:\NET\PROTOCOL.INI**. Go to the section labeled [ms$ee16]. You'll see this line:

```
drivername=EXP16$
```

14. Change the name of the driver after the equal sign to the name of the **.DOS** (NDIS) file. For example, if you're using an Intel PRO/100+ adapter, the line will read

```
drivername=e100b$
```

15. Save the file.

16. Copy the NDIS driver (usually a **.DOS** file) from the NIC's driver disk to the **A:\NET** directory on the boot disk.

17. You should be able to boot to this disk and it will log you on to the Windows NT 4.0 server.

SYMPTOMS

If you're still faced with problems after reviewing the general guidelines and issues above, you can refer to a whole series of solutions for specific NIC-related symptoms. This part of the chapter outlines many of the most common symptoms that you will encounter.

SYMPTOM 10-1   **The NIC is conflicting with an installed PCI SCSI adapter.**   Chances are that there is an IRQ conflict (or other resource conflict) between the two devices. Configure the NIC and SCSI adapters to use different interrupts via the BIOS (the CMOS Setup), the System Configuration Utility (SCU), or the EISA Configuration Utility (ECU) provided by the system vendor. If the SCSI adapter is not PnP-compliant, you may consider upgrading the SCSI adapter to a PnP (PCI bus) version that the host system can configure and manage automatically.

SYMPTOM 10-2   **The NIC passes its diagnostic test, but the network connection fails.** In other words, the NIC has passed its local diagnostics but failed its remote diagnostics. This is frequently a problem with the network connections or configuration. Start by checking the network cable and verify that the network cable is securely attached (and terminated if necessary). Under NetWare, make sure to specify the correct frame type in your **NET.CFG** file. Finally, check your duplex modes and see that the duplex mode setting (i.e., half vs. full duplex) on the NIC matches the setting on the hub, switch, or router.

SYMPTOM 10-3   **The computer hangs when the drivers are loaded.**   In most cases, this type of problem suggests that the NIC is not configured properly for the host computer—usually because the PCI bus settings have not been adjusted correctly through the CMOS Setup. You may find that the PCI interrupt settings are wrong. Even if the settings are acceptable for the NIC, try another suitable PCI interrupt assignment. If you're using a system that loads EMM386, verify that it's version 4.49 or later (the version that ships with MS-DOS 6.22 or later).

SYMPTOM 10-4   **The NIC driver fails to load, or fails to recognize your NIC.**   This is normally a system configuration problem—typically related to the PCI bus setup. Recheck the card's installation first. Check the BIOS settings against the BIOS setup recommendations for your NIC (using the

CMOS Setup), and see that all recommended BIOS settings have been configured appropriately. Sometimes the PCI bus-master feature is disabled by default. If so, reenable the bus mastering on the system.

SYMPTOM 10-5   When installing the NIC drivers, the Setup routine reports the adapter is "Not enabled by BIOS".   The driver installation software cannot find the NIC. In virtually all cases, the system BIOS has not been configured properly (using the CMOS Setup) to accommodate the PCI NIC. Check the BIOS tips in the installation section above, or check the NIC user manual for specific BIOS setting recommendations.

SYMPTOM 10-6   You encounter persistent problems with an adapter card set to IRQ 15. This problem occurs in Novell NetWare, and is almost always a hardware resource issue (usually due to conflicting IRQs). Either disable IRQ 15 or change your NIC to utilize another interrupt.

SYMPTOM 10-7   The system hangs at boot up.   This is frequently an issue that occurs after the NIC's installation. First make sure that the NIC is seated properly in the PCI slot (also double-check the system's internal cabling). You may also need a BIOS update, so check your system vendor for the latest BIOS. If the problem persists, there may be a hardware conflict between the NIC and another device in the PC. Check the Device Manager and reconfigure any conflicting devices.

SYMPTOM 10-8   The NIC's LED does not light when running autonegotiation in the card's diagnostic utility.   In most cases, you've forgotten to attach a proper loopback cable before testing the NIC. Use an appropriate loopback cable from the card maker (or make your own loopback cable according to the NIC user manual).

SYMPTOM 10-9   The network card's "Link" (LNK) LED doesn't light.   The NIC is not providing a connection to the network. There can be numerous reasons behind this problem, but the most common solutions are outlined here:

■ Check your drivers and see that you've loaded the latest network drivers for the NIC.

■ Check all network connections at the adapter and the hub.

■ Try another port on the hub (the hub port may be defective).

■ Verify that the "duplex mode" setting on the adapter (i.e., half duplex or full duplex) matches the setting on the hub.

■ Make sure you have the correct type of cable between the adapter and the hub—some hubs require a crossover cable, while others require a straight-through cable.

SYMPTOM 10-10   The network card's "Activity" (ACT) LED doesn't light.   First, the network may simply be idle—that is, no traffic is passing. Try accessing a server and see if the ACT LED lights. If the NIC does not respond, see that you've loaded the latest network drivers. If the problem persists, the NIC is not transmitting or receiving data. This almost always means that the NIC (or that NIC port) is defective, so try another NIC (or NIC port).

SYMPTOM 10-11   The NIC stopped working when another NIC was added to the computer.   In virtually all cases, this is a hardware conflict issue between the two NICs. Check the resources allocated to each NIC and see that none of the cards are using overlapping resources (IRQ, DMA, I/O, RAM, or ROM assignments). Try reseating the NICs. Check the BIOS, OS, and NICs to see that all support "interrupt sharing" (for PCI cards). If either the BIOS, OS, or NIC does *not* support "interrupt sharing," you may need to update that element of the system to fully support additional NICs. For example, you may be using an older system whose motherboard BIOS does not fully support PCI and PnP implementations, or you may be using an older ("legacy") NIC or the OS/2 operating system that doesn't support PCI interrupt sharing. Aside from hardware issues, check the network cable(s) and verify that each NIC port has a valid network cable connection.

SYMPTOM 10-12 **A BNC connection is not detected under Windows 2000.** You find that when you're using the NIC in "autodetect" mode, a BNC connection is *not* detected. Network adapters normally have BNC, AUI, or twisted-pair connectors, and the software drivers for most adapters can automatically detect which connector type is being used. In some cases, however, the drivers only detect twisted-pair-type connections, and may be unable to detect BNC or coaxial-cable-type connections. This problem can occur if Windows 2000 does not correctly detect that the BNC connector type is being used. To work around this problem, configure the adapter to specifically use BNC instead of using the automatic detection feature (this setting is usually found in the properties for the network adapter in Device Manager).

SYMPTOM 10-13 **The NIC was working, then stopped working without apparent cause.** When a NIC stops working, you should always try to run the card's diagnostic first. If diagnostics *cannot* access or locate the NIC, try reseating the card first—then try a different slot if necessary. Also, the NIC driver file(s) may be corrupt or deleted. Delete and then reinstall the latest NIC drivers. If diagnostics *can* access the card and report that the card itself is defective, you should replace the NIC with a comparable model. If the NIC responds and checks OK, there may be some other hardware or software problem with the host system that needs to be isolated. Check all of the other devices in the system, and verify that no new software was added to the system prior to the problem (also check the network for viruses).

SYMPTOM 10-14 **You encounter trouble using a Xircom CE3 NIC under Windows 2000.** When you use an early version of the Xircom CE3 NIC, you may experience numerous symptoms. Network connectivity may be lost during a large file transfer (connectivity can be established again by removing and reinserting the NIC). Alternatively, if the NIC is inserted without a cable attached, CPU usage jumps to maximum—causing the computer to crash. In other cases, the network appears to be connected even without a cable attached. This is strictly a hardware problem, and it occurs if you're using a Xircom CE3 NIC revision 0340C (or earlier). Check the firmware version of the NIC (on most Xircom cards, you can view the firmware revision by looking at the serial number sticker on the card). If you find an older card, you'll need to contact Xircom to obtain updated firmware for the NIC, or replace the NIC outright.

SYMPTOM 10-15 **You see a message such as "Adapter configuration not saved. View configuration to determine current settings".** This problem almost always indicates that the NIC detected a problem during software configuration and did *not* save any changes. View the current software configuration and check that any configuration changes were *not* discarded. Use the adapter configuration utility on the NIC's driver diskette to change the adapter's configuration settings again. Alternatively, install the adapter in another computer and run the software configuration utility on that system.

SYMPTOM 10-16 **The communication between your NIC and echo server has failed.** The adapter (i.e., an EtherLink 16) cannot exchange (transmit and receive) packets with a known functioning echo server. Chances are that the echo server is not running properly. Make sure that the echo server computer set up on the network is functioning properly and not reporting any errors. Check the cable connections on the adapter and on the network echo server adapter.

SYMPTOM 10-17   **You see an error indicating that the "Address PROM" has failed.**
This is a serious fault with the NIC—it cannot read information stored on the card's address PROM, and the card's internal diagnostics failed. There is a fault with the PROM chip or with the adapter's ability to access the PROM. The PROM chip may be loose. Remove the NIC from the computer and make sure the address PROM is properly installed on the board, then reinstall the NIC in the computer. If the problem persists, the NIC may have failed. Try another NIC.

SYMPTOM 10-18   **You see an error indicating that the "interrupt test failed".**   T h e network card's interrupt level is inappropriately configured for the computer (i.e., edge-triggered rather than level-triggered), or the adapter is not properly installed. Reconfigure the card's interrupt level to a different setting using the configuration utility on the driver diskette. If changing the interrupt level is ineffective, remove and reinstall the NIC in the computer—or try another card outright.

SYMPTOM 10-19   **You see an error such as "network coprocessor chip test failed".**
The network card's network coprocessor chip failed diagnostic testing. There is either a fault with the network coprocessor chip or with the card's ability to access the chip. Double-check the card's installation and verify that the card is installed and configured properly. If the problem persists, the chip (and card) is probably defective and should be replaced.

SYMPTOM 10-20   **You see an error indicating that the "RAM test" has failed.**   T h e network card's onboard RAM (the "buffer") failed during diagnostic testing. The *RAM base address* setting for the NIC may conflict with other devices. Also, there may be a fault with the RAM (or with the card's ability to access the RAM). Check the card's configuration and see that the card is configured properly—select an appropriate RAM base address and try the card again. If the card is configured properly, remove and reinstall the card. Otherwise, replace the defective NIC.

SYMPTOM 10-21   **You see an error such as "simple transmit test failed".**   The NIC cannot transmit small data packets to the transceiver, and failed diagnostic testing. In virtually all cases, there is a fault with the network connection. Make sure the adapter is connected to a network (or to a loopback plug). Remember that if you're using a loopback plug, the adapter's "Transceiver Type" software option must be set to ONBOARD. Use the configuration utility on the driver diskette to verify or change the settings for this option (if necessary).

SYMPTOM 10-22   **You see an error such as "unable to locate an echo server".**   The adapter card cannot locate an echo server on the network. Make sure that another functioning computer is set up on the network as an echo server, and is *not* transmitting error messages. In most cases, the network cabling is at fault, so check the cable connections on the NIC *and* on the echo server's adapter. If the problem persists, the echo server may be defective—try the workstation with another server.

SYMPTOM 10-23   **You see an error such as "your system has RAM caching in high memory—you must disable caching at RAM base address 64KB".**   This is almost always due to a RAM conflict. If your system has RAM access caching in high memory, the caching is probably conflicting with the adapter's configured RAM size setting. Be sure that a RAM size of 64KB is used with a *RAM base address* of F00000h or higher (i.e., F20000h, F40000h, F60000h, F80000h) only. Either disable RAM caching on the system or set the noncached address region.

SYMPTOM 10-24   **You see an error such as "RAM size is too large for the RAM base address 0d8000. Set RAM size to either 16KB or 32KB".**   The *RAM base address* is too large. At the 0D8000h RAM base address, you may be forced to use a smaller buffer size such as 16KB or 32KB only. If the RAM size is set larger (i.e., 48KB or 64KB), the setting automatically changes to the 32KB RAM size—which is the largest RAM buffer size setting for the base address setting of 0D8000h. Either accept the RAM size selected automatically (i.e., 32KB) or select a lower RAM base address so that you may increase the RAM size to a level greater than 32KB.

SYMPTOM 10-25   **You see an error such as "RAM base address F00000 or higher must use RAM size 64KB".**   If the RAM base address is set to 0F00000 or higher (i.e., F20000h, F40000h, F60000h, or F80000h), the RAM buffer size must be set to 64KB only. If the RAM base address is set to F00000h or lower, the RAM size setting can be in the 16KB to 64KB range. These error messages are generated by the system if the RAM base address and RAM size settings are *not* compatible with each other. Either disable RAM caching on the system or adjust the noncached address region.

SYMPTOM 10-26   **You see an error such as "All DMA channels failed—unable to locate another channel".**   The adapter's DMA channels (i.e., channels 1, 2, and 3) failed diagnostic test. Make sure that the NIC is installed and configured properly. Make sure that the proper value for the DMA channel is used in the diagnostic test program. Otherwise, the NIC may be defective and should be replaced.

SYMPTOM 10-27   **You see an error such as "ASIC test failed".**   The adapter's custom chip—the application-specific integrated circuit (ASIC)—failed its diagnostic tests. The ASIC (or the circuitry used to access the chip) may not be functioning. Make sure that the adapter is installed properly, and that the ASIC is fully seated in its socket. Otherwise, the NIC may be defective and should be replaced.

SYMPTOM 10-28   **You see an error such as "DMA channel <x> failed—try DMA channel <y>".**   This is almost always a system configuration issue. The adapter's DMA channel <x> failed during diagnostic tests, but DMA channel <y> was usable. DMA channel <x> (the current setting) may be in use by another installed board or other device in the system. Try changing the board's DMA channel to <y>.

SYMPTOM 10-29   **You find that workstations cannot connect to the NetWare server.**
Make sure the workstation and server are using the same frame type. Add the following two lines to the NetWare Server **STARTUP.NCF** file:

```
set minimum packet receive buffers=512
set maximum packet receive buffers=1024
```

For Failover and Port Aggregation NetWare servers, verify that **IPX RETRY COUNT=255** is on each workstation.

SYMPTOM 10-30 **You encounter error messages during NetWare driver installation.**
Chances are that you require a NetWare update. Install NetWare Service Pack 6 (IWSP6) or later, select
the ODI 3.31 specification, and then install the NIC driver. Check with Novell for updates
(**www.novell.com**).

SYMPTOM 10-31 **Your NetWare server returns the error "Router configuration error
detected".** This error message is almost always caused by inconsistency in the network numbering
scheme. Each segment of an IPX network must have a *unique* IPX external network number assigned for
each frame type. That network number must be constant for all devices (servers, routers, and so on)
attached to that segment, and using that frame type. Remember that a *segment* can be defined as any
shared network communication medium such as a contiguous coaxial cable run, a hub (or multiple hubs),
or either of the preceding joined by a repeater or layer 2 switch.

This error most commonly occurs when IPX is bound to two different NICs with the same frame type
on the same segment, but with different IPX external network numbers assigned to each. IPX external network numbers are assigned when you bind IPX to a logical board, and must be *unique* for each segment
(rather than an IPX internal network number, which is assigned on server startup and must be unique for
each server). For example, suppose you're using two Intel EtherExpress PRO/10+ PCI adapters on a
twisted-pair network in your NetWare server, and the following is your **AUTOEXEC.NCF** file:

```
LOAD E100B SLOT=13 FRAME=ETHERNET_802.2 NAME=CARD1
LOAD E100B SLOT=14 FRAME=ETHERNET_802.2 NAME=CARD2
BIND IPX TO CARD1 NET=1
BIND IPX TO CARD2 NET=2
```

As long as each of the two cards is connected to a separate hub, this would work without error. However, if you connected the two hubs together with a twisted-pair cable (joining them into a single "segment"), the computer will respond with the above error message. Look for loops in your network
connections that might join different segments together. Check the configuration of all devices (servers,
routers, network printers, and so on) connected to the suspected segment—making sure that the net number is consistent for that frame type. If no discrepancies are found, check for a malfunctioning or improperly configured router.

SYMPTOM 10-32 **The NetWare server reports "Insufficient receive buffers. Set
maximum packet receive buffer size to 1536 in STARTUP.NCF".** This is a known problem with Intel NICs using EtherExpress LAN drivers, and is usually related to an incorrect command line
in **STARTUP.NCF**. Check the file for a command line such as

```
SET MAXIMUM PHYSICAL RECEIVE PACKET SIZE=2048
```

This parameter determines how much memory your server allocates to each packet buffer, but it has no
effect on the size of the actual packets.

SYMPTOM 10-33 **The NetWare server reports "Loader cannot find public symbol:
<symbol name>".** If this error appears while loading the LAN driver for your NIC, it usually indi-
cates that an older network support NLM is in use (especially the files **MSM.NLM**, **NBI.NLM**, and

ETHERTSM.NLM for Ethernet adapters, or **TOKENTSM.NLM** for token ring adapters). Update your NetWare server to the latest network support. It is also important to apply the latest patches or service packs to your server.

SYMPTOM 10-34   **The NetWare server reports "NetWare does not support protected mode BIOS accesses. PCI drivers may fail without a loader patch".**   This error may appear when loading a 3.3x ODI LAN driver. It's caused by the latest patch(s) being applied improperly—or due to out-of-date NLMs. Make sure that your NetWare server has the latest 3.3x version NLMs and the latest patches. If the latest patches have already been applied, make sure the loader patch was properly applied using the LSWAP utility according to Novell's instructions.

Further Study

Adaptec: **www.adaptec.com**
D-Link: **www.dlink.com**
Linksys: **www.linksys.com**
Netgear: **www.netgear.com**
SMC: **www.smc.com**

RAID ADAPTERS AND TROUBLESHOOTING

Networks are intended to handle huge amounts of valuable data, but networks are hardly infallible. Hardware failures and software incompatibilities can easily interrupt network operations. Such interruptions can compromise data transfers and secure transactions, and cause countless other faults that will interfere with your day-to-day business. Networks try to overcome potential problems *before* they occur using techniques of fault tolerance. One of the most common fault-tolerance techniques available to network planners is RAID—a *redundant array of independent disks*. RAID allows you to use multiple physical drives to create a variety of logical volumes that can mirror drives or share data across several physical drives to boost performance. This chapter reviews the essential concepts of RAID systems, outlines RAID installation and configuration, and presents common troubleshooting issues.

 Keep in mind that RAID can be implemented with IDE or SCSI drives, depending on which type of RAID controller is selected. Small business servers often save money using IDE RAID, but large high-end servers will normally implement SCSI RAID.

RAID Primer

In simplest terms, a *disk array* is formed from a group of two or more physical disk drives that appear to the system as a *single* drive. The advantage of an array is to provide better performance and data *fault tolerance*. Better performance is accomplished by sharing the data transfer workload in parallel among multiple physical drives. Fault tolerance is achieved through data redundant operation, where if one (or more) drives should fail (or suffer a sector failure), a mirrored copy of the data can be found on another drive(s). For optimal results, select identical drives for installation in disk arrays. The drives' *matched performance* allows the array to function better as a single drive. The individual disk drives in an array are called *members*. Each member of a specific disk array is coded in its *reserved sector* with configuration information that identifies the drive as a member of the given array.

LOGICAL DRIVES

A *logical drive* is storage space that is distributed across multiple physical drives in an array (except for online spares). Distributing the storage space in this way provides some significant advantages. For example, data can be accessed on all the physical drives at once, resulting in much higher performance data storage and retrieval. Fault-tolerant RAID levels may be used to protect your data against hardware failures. Finally, an array can consist of several logical drives, each spanning multiple physical drives in the array (for maximum space efficiency, all physical drives in each array should also be the same size).

DISK ARRAY ADAPTER (DAA)

This is the generic term used for the RAID controller—the device that supports your striped or mirrored disks (which are generally termed the *disk array*). Most RAID controllers are implemented using the SCSI interface such as the Adaptec SCSI RAID 3410S (Figure 11-1), but Promise Technologies offers the FastTrack100, which supports RAID functions for UDMA/66 or UDMA/100 hard drives. The controller will virtually always incorporate a BIOS that fully supports the drive operations (i.e., SCSI or UDMA/100), and provide a setup feature (similar to the CMOS Setup) that will allow you to configure the RAID controller's many features.

Adapter Types

There are typically two approaches to implementing a RAID controller: host-based or SCSI-to-SCSI. Both approaches will provide acceptable levels of service, but there are some tradeoffs that you should be aware of.

Host-Based   A host-based RAID device puts all of the RAID "intelligence" on an adapter card that is installed in a network server. Since this dedicates RAID services to a hardware device, host-based RAID also provides the *best* performance. For our Gateway 7400 server, the AMI MegaRAID Express Plus is

FIGURE 11-1   The Adaptec SCSI RAID 3410S RAID controller (Courtesy of Adaptec)

part of the file server, so it can transmit data directly across the computer's PCI bus at data transfer speeds up to 132 MBps. However, as a hardware device, host-based solutions must provide suitable OS-specific drivers. The available sequential data transfer rate is determined by the following factors:

- The sustained data transfer rate on the motherboard PCI bus
- The sustained data transfer rate on the i96ORP PCI-to-PCI bridge
- The sustained data transfer rate of the SCSI controller
- The sustained data transfer rate of the SCSI devices
- The number of SCSI channels
- The number of SCSI disk drives

SCSI-to-SCSI   A SCSI-to-SCSI RAID controller puts the RAID "intelligence" inside the RAID chassis, and uses a plain SCSI host adapter installed in the network server. This means the data transfer rate is limited to the bandwidth of the SCSI channel. For example, a SCSI-to-SCSI RAID system that has two wide SCSI channels that operate at speeds up to 80 MBps must squeeze the data into a single wide SCSI (40 MBps) channel back to the host computer. However, a SCSI-to-SCSI RAID implementation allows the hard drive subsystem to use only a single SCSI ID, which allows you to connect multiple drive subsystems to a single SCSI controller.

Software-Based   A third—rarely used—RAID implementation is based on software. Rather than hardware, the disk array is managed by software running on the server. This is the least desirable form of RAID control because of the added processing load on the system CPU and the need for OS-specific control software. Also, a system crash may interfere with RAID operation, and this may result in data corruption. As a rule, avoid the use of software-based RAID systems if possible.

RESERVED SECTOR

Vital information is saved in a special location on each disk member, called the *reserved sector*. This area contains array configuration data about the drive and other members in the disk array. If reserved data on any member of the array becomes corrupted or lost, the redundant configuration data on the other members can be used for automatic rebuilds. As a rule, disk array members do not have specific drive positions. This allows drives to be placed on different RAID controller connectors or cards within the system without reconfiguring or rebuilding the array.

DISK STRIPING

Disk striping writes data across multiple disk drives instead of just one disk drive. Disk striping involves partitioning each drive storage space into stripes that can vary in size from 2KB to 128KB. These stripes are interleaved in a repeated sequential manner. The combined storage space is composed of stripes from each drive. For example, in a four-disk system using only disk striping (as in RAID level 0), segment 1 is written to disk 1, segment 2 is written to disk 2, segment 3 is written to disk 3, and so on. Disk striping enhances storage performance because multiple drives are accessed simultaneously. However, disk striping does *not* provide data redundancy.

The *stripe size* is the length of the interleaved data segments that the RAID controller writes across multiple drives. RAID controllers such as the AMI MegaRAID Express Plus supports stripe sizes of 2KB, 4KB, 8KB, 16KB, 32KB, 64KB, or 128KB. *Stripe width* is the number of disks involved in an array where striping is implemented. For example, a four-disk array with disk striping has a stripe width of four.

DISK SPANNING

Disk spanning allows multiple disk drives to function like one big drive. Spanning overcomes lack of disk space and simplifies storage management by combining existing resources (or adding relatively inexpensive resources). For example, four 400MB disk drives can be combined to appear to the operating system as one single 1,600MB drive. Spanning alone does *not* provide reliability or performance enhancements—it simply offers increased storage capacity. Spanning is sometimes termed JBOD (or *just a bunch of disks*). Spanned logical drives must have the same stripe size and must be contiguous. However, here are some examples of how spanning is implemented in typical RAID setups:

■ Configure a RAID 10 array by spanning two contiguous RAID 1 logical drives. The RAID 1 logical drives must have the same stripe size.

■ Configure RAID 30 by spanning two contiguous RAID 3 logical drives. The RAID 3 logical drives must have the same stripe size.

■ Configure RAID 50 by spanning two contiguous RAID 5 logical drives. The RAID 5 logical drives must have the same stripe size.

Spanning two contiguous RAID 0 logical drives does not produce a new RAID level or add fault tolerance. It does increase the size of the logical volume and improves performance by doubling the number of spindles.

DISK MIRRORING

With *mirroring* (used in RAID 1), data written to one disk drive is simultaneously written to another disk drive. If one disk drive fails, the contents of the other disk drive can be used to run the system (and reconstruct the failed drive). The primary advantage of disk mirroring is that it provides 100-percent data redundancy. Since the contents of the disk drive are completely written to a second drive, it does not matter if one of the drives fails. Both drives contain the same data at all times, and either drive can act as the operational drive. Disk mirroring provides 100-percent redundancy, but is expensive because each drive in the system must be duplicated. For example, to mirror a 10GB drive, you'd need a second 10GB drive.

PARITY

Parity is a type of redundancy that generates a set of "redundancy data" from two or more parent data sets. The redundancy data can then be used to reconstruct one of the parent data sets, if necessary. Parity data does *not* fully duplicate the parent data sets (such as mirroring would). In RAID, this method is applied to entire drives (or stripes across all disk drives in an array). The types of parity are

■ **Dedicated parity**   The parity of the data on two or more disk drives is stored on an additional disk.

■ **Distributed parity**   The parity data is distributed across all drives in the system.

Parity provides redundancy for one drive failure *without* duplicating the contents of entire disk drives, but parity generation can slow the write process (reducing array performance). For example, if a single disk drive fails, it can be rebuilt from the parity and the data on the remaining drives. RAID 3 combines dedicated parity with disk striping—the parity disk in RAID 3 is the last logical drive in a RAID set. RAID level 5 combines distributed parity with disk striping.

HOT SPARES

A *hot spare* is an extra (unused) disk drive that is part of the disk subsystem. It is usually in "standby mode"—ready for service if a drive fails. Hot spares permit you to replace and rebuild failed drives without a system shutdown or user intervention. Many RAID controllers (such as the AMI MegaRAID Express Plus) provide automatic and transparent rebuilds using hot spare drives, providing a high degree of fault tolerance and zero downtime. The RAID Management software allows you to specify physical drives as hot spares. When a hot spare is needed, the RAID controller assigns the hot spare that has a capacity closest to (and at least as great as) that of the failed drive to take its place. However, hot spares are only employed in arrays with redundancy (such as RAID 1, 3, 5, 10, 30, and 50). As a rule, a hot spare connected to a specific RAID controller can only be used to rebuild a drive that is connected to that same controller.

DISK REBUILD

The RAID controller can *rebuild* a disk drive by re-creating the data that had been stored on the drive before the drive failed. *Standby rebuild* (warm spare) is employed in a mirrored (RAID 1) system. If a disk drive fails, an identical drive is immediately available. The primary data source disk drive is the original disk drive. A hot spare can be used to rebuild disk drives in RAID 1, 3, 5, 10, 30, or 50 systems. If a hot spare is not available, the failed disk drive must be replaced with a new disk drive so that the data on the failed drive can be rebuilt. If a hot spare is available, the rebuild starts automatically when a drive fails. The RAID controller automatically restarts the system and the rebuild if the system goes down during a rebuild.

 Rebuilding can only be performed in arrays with data redundancy such as RAID 1, 3, 5, 10, 30, and 50.

The RAID controller automatically and transparently rebuilds failed drives with user-definable rebuild rates. The *rebuild rate* is the fraction of a system's processing power (CPU cycles) dedicated to rebuilding failed drives. A rebuild rate of 100 percent means the system is totally dedicated to rebuilding the failed drive. Many RAID controllers offer rebuild rates between 0 and 100 percent. At 0 percent, the rebuild is only done if the system is not doing anything else (idle). At 100 percent, the rebuild has a higher priority than any other system activity.

RAID LEVELS

Techniques such as striping, mirroring, and spanning all work to improve data throughput, increase storage capacity, or achieve data redundancy—in most cases, these techniques are combined to offer even more features. You learned a bit about these technologies earlier in this chapter, and now it's time to look at RAID levels in more detail. Table 11-1 compares the major RAID levels.

Remember that all disk members in a formed disk array are generally recognized as a single logical drive volume to the host system—though the array can be broken up into more than one logical drive.

RAID 0 (Striping Only)

RAID 0 provides disk striping across all drives (between 1 to 32 drives) in the RAID subsystem. RAID 0 offers the best performance of any RAID level, but does *not* provide any data redundancy—a failure in any striped drive will corrupt the entire disk array. RAID 0 breaks up data into smaller blocks and then writes a block to each drive in the array. The size of each block is determined by the *stripe size* parameter (set during the creation of the RAID set). RAID 0 offers high bandwidth. By breaking up a large file into smaller blocks, the RAID controller can use several drives to read or write the file faster. RAID 0 involves no parity calculations to complicate the write operation. This makes RAID 0 ideal for applications that require high bandwidth, but do not require fault tolerance.

RAID 1 (Mirroring Only)

This approach writes duplicate data onto a pair of drives, while reads are performed in parallel (improving read performance). RAID 1 is fault tolerant because data is duplicated, and each drive of a mirrored pair is installed on separate connectors. The RAID controller performs reads using data-handling techniques that distribute the workload in a more efficient manner than using a single drive. When a read request is made, the controller selects the drive positioned closest to the requested data, then looks to the *idle* drive to perform the next read access.

If one of the mirrored drives suffers a mechanical failure (i.e., a spindle failure) or does not respond, the remaining drive will continue to function (this is the *fault tolerance*). If one drive has a physical sector error, the mirrored drive will also continue to function. On the next reboot, the RAID software utility will display an error in the array and recommend to replace the failed drive. Users may choose to continue using their PC; however, it's often best to replace the failed drive as soon as possible. RAID 1 normally supports 2, 4, 6, or 8 drives.

Due to redundancy, the drive capacity of the array is half the total drive capacity. For example, two 1GB drives that have a combined capacity of 2GB would have 1GB of usable storage. With drives of different capacities, there may be unused capacity on the larger drive. To improve performance in configurations with more than two drives, the data is striped across the drives (this is also referred to as RAID 1+0 or RAID 10).

If two drives being mirrored to each other fail, the volume is failed and data loss may occur.

RAID 0+1 (Striping/Mirror)

This is a combination of the array types detailed earlier. It can increase performance by reading and writing data in parallel while protecting data with duplication. A minimum of four drives need to be installed.

TABLE 11-1 COMPARISON OF RAID LEVELS

LEVEL	DESCRIPTION AND USE	PROS	CONS	MAX DRIVES	FAULT TOLERANT
0	Data divided in blocks and distributed sequentially (pure striping). Use for noncritical data that requires high performance.	High data throughput for large files	No fault tolerance. All data lost if any drive fails.	1 to 32	No
1	Data duplicated on another disk (mirroring). Use for read-intensive fault-tolerant systems.	100% data redundancy	Doubles disk space. Reduced performance during rebuilds.	2, 4, 6, or 8	Yes
3	Disk striping with a dedicated parity drive. Use for noninteractive apps that process large files sequentially.	Achieves data redundancy at low cost	Not as good as RAID 1	3 to 8	Yes
5	Disk striping and parity data across all drives. Use for high read volume but low write volume, such as transaction processing.	Achieves data redundancy at low cost	Not as good as RAID 1	3 to 8	Yes
10	Data striping and mirrored drives.	High data transfers, complete redundancy	More complicated	4, 6, or 8	Yes
30	Disk striping with a dedicated parity drive.	High data transfers, redundancy	More complicated	6 to 32	Yes
50	Disk striping and parity data across all drives.	High data transfers, redundancy	More complicated	6 to 32	Yes

With a four-drive disk array, two pairs of drives are striped, and each pair mirrors the data on the other pair of striped drives. The data capacity is similar to a standard mirroring array with half of the total capacity dedicated for redundancy.

RAID 1+0 or "10" (Striping/Mirror)

This is an alternative combination of mirroring (RAID 1) and striping (RAID 0). As with RAID 0+1, it can increase performance by reading and writing data in parallel while protecting data with duplication. A minimum of four drives need to be installed. However, with a four-drive disk array, only one pair of drives is striped, and one pair mirrors the data on the other pair of striped drives. This provides RAID 1–type fault tolerance, and high I/O rates are provided by striping those RAID 1 elements. This type of configuration is most frequently seen in database servers where high performance and fault tolerance are vital. RAID 0+1 should *not* be confused with RAID 1+0.

RAID 2 (Striping with ECC)

When a block of data is written, the data is broken up and distributed (interleaved) across all of the data drives (see "RAID 0 (Striping Only)" earlier) along with error-checking data. Error checking and correction (ECC) require a larger amount of disk space than parity checking, but ECC data provides better data protection than parity.

RAID 3 (Striping with Parity)

RAID 3 provides disk striping and complete data redundancy through a dedicated parity drive. The stripe size must be 64KB if RAID 3 is used. RAID 3 handles data at the block level (not the byte level as in RAID 5) so it is ideal for networks that often handle very large files, such as graphic images. However, the additional I/O required for parity may produce a data bottleneck during random I/O operations. RAID 3 breaks up data into smaller blocks, calculates parity on the blocks, and then writes the blocks to all but one drive in the array. The parity data created during the write is then written to the last drive in the array (aka dedicated parity). The size of each block is determined by the *stripe size* parameter that is set during the creation of the RAID set.

If a single drive fails, a RAID 3 array continues to operate in "degraded mode." If the failed drive is a data drive, writes will continue as normal, except no data is written to the failed drive. Reads reconstruct the data on the failed drive by performing a check on the remaining data in the stripe and the parity for that stripe. If the failed drive is a parity drive, writes will occur as normal, except no parity is written. Reads retrieve data from the disks. RAID 3 supports from three to eight disks.

In actual practice, you may find that RAID 5 is preferable to RAID 3 even for applications characterized by sequential reads and writes, because most RAID controllers have very robust caching algorithms. The benefits of RAID 3 disappear if there are many small I/O operations scattered randomly and widely across the disks in the logical drive. The RAID 3 fixed parity disk becomes a bottleneck in such applications. For example, the host attempts to make two small writes and the writes are widely scattered, involving two different stripes and different disk drives. Ideally, both writes should take place at the same time. But this is not possible in RAID 3, since the writes must take turns accessing the fixed parity drive. For this reason, RAID 5 is the clear choice in this type of situation.

RAID 3+0 or "30"

RAID 30 is a combination of RAID 0 and RAID 3, which provides high data transfer speeds and high data reliability. RAID 30 is best implemented on two RAID 3 disk arrays with data striped across both disk arrays. RAID 30 breaks up data into smaller blocks, and then stripes the blocks of data to each RAID 3 set. RAID 3 breaks up data into smaller blocks, calculates parity on the blocks, and then writes the blocks to all but one drive in the array. The parity data created during the check is then written to the last drive in each RAID 3 array. The size of each block is determined by the *stripe size* parameter that is set during the creation of the RAID set.

Use RAID 30 for sequentially written and read data, prepress, and video-on-demand that requires a higher degree of fault tolerance and medium to large capacity. It provides data reliability and high data transfer rates, and RAID 30 can sustain one to four drive failures while maintaining data integrity (if each failed disk is in a different RAID 3 array). Unfortunately, RAID 30 is expensive to implement because it requires 2–4 times as many drives as RAID 3, and can support 6–32 drives.

RAID 4 (Data Guarding)
Data guarding (also called RAID 4) assures data reliability while using only a small percentage of the logi-cal drive storage capacity. A single designated drive contains *parity* data. If a drive fails, the controller uses the data on the parity drive—and the data on the remaining drives—to reconstruct data from the failed drive. This allows the system to continue operating with slightly reduced performance until you replace the failed drive. Data guarding requires a minimum of *three* drives (two *data* drives and one *parity* drive) in an array, and allows the maximum number of drives allowed by the server. For example, in an array containing three physical drives, data guarding uses only 33 percent of the total logical drive storage capacity for fault tolerance. By comparison, an 18-drive configuration (17 data drives and one parity drive) uses only 6 percent.

Given the reliability of a particular generation of hard drive technology, the probability of an array experiencing a drive failure increases with the number of drives in an array.

RAID 5 (Striping with Parity)
RAID 5 includes disk striping at the byte level along with parity, and the parity information is written to sev-eral drives (aka distributed parity, sometimes called *distributed data guarding*). RAID 5 is best suited for networks that perform a lot of small I/O transactions simultaneously. RAID 5 addresses the bottleneck issue for random I/O operations. Since each drive contains both data *and* parity, numerous writes can take place concurrently. In addition, robust caching algorithms and hardware-based exclusive-or assist make RAID 5 performance exceptional in many different environments. RAID 5 normally uses three to eight drives.

Since RAID 5 provides high data throughput (especially for large files), use RAID 5 for transaction processing applications because each drive can read and write independently. If a drive fails, the RAID controller uses the parity drive to re-create all missing information. RAID 5 is also a good implementation for office automation and online customer service that requires fault tolerance—or any application that has high read request rates but low write request rates. However, disk drive performance will be reduced if a drive is being rebuilt. Environments with few processes do not perform as well because the RAID over-head is not offset by the performance gains in handling simultaneous processes.

RAID 5+0 or "50"
RAID 50 provides the features of both RAID 0 and RAID 5. RAID 50 includes both parity and disk strip-ing across multiple drives. RAID 50 is best implemented on two RAID 5 disk arrays with data striped across both disk arrays. RAID 50 breaks up data into smaller blocks, and then stripes the blocks of data to each RAID 5 set. RAID 5 breaks up data into smaller blocks, calculates parity on the blocks, and then writes the blocks of data and parity to each drive in the array. The size of each block is determined by the *stripe size* parameter, which is set during the creation of the RAID set.

RAID 50 works best when used with data that requires high reliability, high request rates, and high data transfer, and medium to large capacity. RAID 50 can sustain one to four drive failures while main-taining data integrity (if each failed disk is in a different RAID 5 array). However, RAID 50 can be very expensive to use because it requires 2–4 times the number of drives for a RAID 5 implementation.

THE ARRAY ACCELERATOR
Even in today's world of fast-transfer, high-RPM hard drives, accessing a drive and moving data can take milliseconds. That's a long time for current PCs, and even longer for busy networks. Several RAID control-lers (such as the Compaq SmartArray 4250ES) incorporate an *array accelerator* feature that can cache the write and read operations of a RAID array. Caching improves the "apparent" performance of the read and write commands, and relieves the system hesitation that often occurs while waiting for drive access to finish.

A RAID array accelerator works by allowing the RAID controller to write data to cache memory (RAM) on the RAID controller itself (rather than directly to the drives). A server can access the RAID controller's cache memory more than 100 times faster than accessing a disk. Once data is cached in the array accelerator, the RAID controller will write the data to the disk array at a later time when the controller would otherwise be idle. The RAID controller also uses an array accelerator to increase performance during disk reads by anticipating read requests. This anticipated data is read into the array accelerator and is ready before you access it. When the RAID controller receives a read request for the cached data, it can immediately transfer that data into system memory (RAM) at PCI bus speeds.

Since the array accelerator uses RAM as the cache, the RAM contents must be protected in the event of an accidental power loss. Battery backup and ECC memory are used to ensure cache reliability. This offers some interesting benefits to server technicians. The ECC technique is actually capable of correcting single-bit errors, so lost bits can be restored in real time without interrupting system operation. Rechargeable backup batteries can preserve data in the array accelerator for several days. When power is restored to the system, an initialization process writes the preserved data to the disk drives. The batteries are typically recharged with a "trickle charge" applied while system power is present. If cached write data was stored in the array accelerator and power loss occurs, you must reinstate power to the accelerator before the batteries discharge; otherwise, the data will be lost. Since the array accelerator module is often removable, the accelerator card can be moved from one compatible RAID controller to another—a handy tip if the RAID controller fails before the cached accelerator data could be written to disk.

When installing a RAID controller with a battery-supported array accelerator, chances are that the batteries will be discharged when the card is first installed. It can take up to 36 hours for the system to fully charge the batteries and enable array accelerator support. If the battery charge is low, the RAID controller will report an error at boot time, and the array accelerator will be disabled until the batteries are charged.

CHANGING THE ARRAY STORAGE CAPACITY

You can normally adjust capacity by expanding or extending a given array. These are subtle differences that you should understand. *Capacity expansion* means increasing the size of an array by adding physical drives and creating additional logical drives. By comparison, *capacity extension* means increasing the size of an array by adding physical drives and "growing" your existing logical drive(s) without adding more logical drives. In either case, more hard drives must be added to the server. Capacity can be adjusted through the RAID controller's configuration utility. The RAID controller will redistribute data in the original logical drive to a logical drive that spans *all* of the physical drives in the array (including the added drives). The room left over is then used to increase the size of a logical drive (extending) or to create additional logical drives that also span the physical drives (expanding). The resized (extended) logical drive is within the larger drive array. When logical drives are added (expanded), the logical drives are then included in the larger drive array. Altering the capacity of an existing logical drive can be done offline by backing up all data, reconfiguring the array, and then restoring the data. To alter capacity online (with the server running), your operating system *must* support a logical drive increasing in size.

The RAID controller's configuration utility will typically allow you to increase the size of existing logical drives under any operating system. However, only Windows NT 4.0 and OS/2 allow you to resize a partition inside the extended (bigger) logical drive using third-party tools like Partition Magic 3.0 or later (**www.powerquest.com**).

Example

Let's consider an offline example. Suppose that you have a total of 14 drives in your current drive array, and you want to expand this to 18 drives. Simply install four matching drives in some available empty drive bays. Start the RAID controller's configuration utility. While the utility runs, the RAID controller redistributes the data to an equal portion of all the drives, using the same fault-tolerance method (RAID level) as the original configuration. The first logical drive remains first, but it now spans 18 drives instead of 14. The configuration utility also detects the unused space on each drive (because each drive now contains 14/18ths of the data that it did before capacity was increased) and helps you configure the extra capacity into a second logical drive if you wish. This new logical drive will have its own fault tolerance distributed over the extra space of all the drives. When this process is finished, both logical drives (one containing the original data and the new empty one) will be configured into a single array with more total capacity than the original one.

When resizing your drive array, there are several important issues to keep in mind. First, it is not necessary for all logical drives in an array to be the same size—or even have the same fault-tolerant configuration (RAID level). Each logical drive is treated as a separate entity (no matter how many physical drives it crosses), and each may be configured to best suit your needs. Also remember that all *physical drives* in an array should be the same size (capacity). Since each drive contains an equal portion of one or more logical drives, the portion sizes can only total the size of the smallest drive. Although you can certainly install larger drives, the extra drive space cannot be used. Finally, when you expand an array that initially has two or more logical drives, the redistribution of data takes place one logical drive at a time. When the capacity increase has finished, any newly created logical drive will become available. Under Windows NT and NetWare, the new logical drive can then be appended to your existing logical volume.

In certain cases, the RAID controller and its configuration utility may support making storage capacity changes online *without* downing the server or storage system. These features are available if you're using either Windows NT or NetWare operating system (NetWare 3.11 not supported) along with hot-pluggable drives. Hot-pluggable drives are required for online storage changes because conventional (non-hot-pluggable) drives require that the server be powered down to add or remove the drive(s). To use hot-pluggable drives, your server (i.e., a Compaq ProLiant or Gateway 7400 server) must support hot-pluggable drives.

Using Larger Hard Drives

Additional storage space in a fault-tolerant configuration may be obtained with the same number of physical drives by systematically replacing your existing drives with higher-capacity drives. By replacing the drives one at a time, the data on the new drive is re-created from redundant information on the remaining drives. After each new drive has been rebuilt, the next drive can be replaced. When all drives have been replaced and rebuilt, the additional capacity on each drive can be utilized by increasing an existing logical drive (extension) or adding a new logical drive (expansion). The RAID controller's configuration utility automatically recognizes the unused space and guides you through the procedures to use it.

CONTROLLER FAULT MANAGEMENT FEATURES

Depending on your particular RAID level, your server can realize faster data access and fault tolerance (often both). The problem is that failures are usually assumed to occur with the hard drives—the RAID controller itself is often overlooked as a source of system problems. Today, RAID controllers offer the intelligence and features that can help identify and correct problems in the drive array, as well as the controller itself. This part of the chapter highlights some of the fault management features found in a typical SCSI RAID controller and supported by network operating systems.

Redundant Controllers

Controllers are often the weak link in a RAID setup. However, advanced servers support a *redundant controller* arrangement. One controller is used as the primary controller, while the second controller operates in an active standby mode. If the primary controller fails, the active standby controller immediately assumes control of the disk array with no data loss or interruption in server operation. For example, Compaq SmartArray 4250ES SCSI RAID controllers have this capability when used on servers with 64-bit PCI and extended SCSI connectors. The SCSI buses are routed to both extended SCSI connectors so that either controller can read or write to the disk array. Another SCSI channel is routed between the two connectors, and this provides an intercontroller link for the two controllers to monitor each other's status and maintain cache integrity between them. Both controllers send status information to each other. In the unlikely event of one controller failing, the operating system is notified by the other controller. If the primary controller fails to respond, the secondary controller will take over operation of the drive array. If the secondary controller fails to respond, the primary controller would simply notify the operating system that redundancy is no longer available.

Autoreliability Monitoring

Automatic reliability monitoring (ARM) is a background process that scans for bad sectors on hard drives within fault-tolerant logical drives. ARM also verifies the consistency of parity data in drives with data guarding or distributed data guarding. This routine process assures that you can recover all data successfully if a drive failure occurs in the future. ARM operates only when you select RAID 1, RAID 4, or RAID 5.

Dynamic Sector Repairing

It's not uncommon for age and use to affect the integrity of drive sectors. A RAID controller that supports on-demand *dynamic sector repairing* (DSR) can automatically remap any sectors with media faults that are detected either during normal operation or during autoreliability monitoring.

Drive Parameter Tracking

Drive parameter tracking (also known as *drive performance tracking*) is a feature that monitors numerous drive parameters and functional tests. For RAID controllers such as the Compaq Smart Array 4250ES, this includes monitoring parameters such as "read/write/seek errors," "spin-up time," "cable problems," and functional tests such as "track-to-track seek time," "one-third stroke seek time," and "full stroke seek time." Drive parameter tracking allows the RAID controller to detect drive problems and predict drive failures before they actually occur.

Interim Data Recovery

If a drive fails in RAID 1(or higher) fault-tolerant configuration, the system continues to operate in an *interim data recovery* mode. For example, if you selected RAID 5 for a logical drive using four physical drives, and one of the drives fails, the system continues to process I/O requests, but at a reduced performance level. Replace the failed drive as soon as possible to restore performance and full fault tolerance for that logical drive.

Automatic Data Recovery

After you replace a failed drive, *automatic data recovery* reconstructs any lost data and places it on the replacement drive. This feature allows the rapid recovery of operating performance without interrupting normal system operations. In general, the time required for a rebuild is approximately 15 minutes per gigabyte (GB). However, the actual rebuild time depends on the rebuild priority set for the amount of I/O activity occurring during the rebuild operation, the disk drive speed, and the number of drives in the array

(RAID 4 and RAID 5). For example, in RAID 4 and RAID 5 configurations, the rebuild time varies from 10 minutes/GB for three drives to 20 minutes/GB for 18 drives (using 9GB SCSI Ultra Wide hard drives).

You must specify RAID 5, RAID 4, or RAID 1 through the RAID controller's configuration utility in order to make the recovery features available.

Hot-Pluggable Drives

You can install or remove hot-pluggable drives without turning off the system power. This greatly speeds service time because the system does not need to be shut down, opened, serviced, then brought back online. This feature operates independently of the network operating system and requires a RAID controller used with a server chassis that supports "hot-pluggable" drives.

Never turn off the hot-pluggable server when removing or installing the pluggable replacement drives. If you turn off the storage subsystem while server power is on, the RAID controller marks all the drives as "failed", and that could result in permanent data loss when the storage system is turned back on.

Controller Duplexing

Some operating systems support *controller duplexing*, a fault-tolerance feature that requires two RAID controllers. Using duplexing, the two controllers each have their own drives that contain identical data. In the unlikely event of a RAID controller failure, the remaining drives and RAID controller service all requests.

Since both RAID controllers would be connected to the same SCSI buses, controller duplexing is an operating system feature that is not supported by all RAID controllers. For example, the Compaq SmartArray 4250ES does not support controller duplexing.

Software-Based Drive Mirroring

Some operating systems support software-based *drive mirroring* as a fault-tolerance feature. Software drive mirroring resembles hardware-based drive mirroring (RAID 1), except that the operating system mirrors logical drives *instead* of physical drives. The problem with software-based drive mirroring is that the operating system believes each logical drive is a separate physical drive. If you mirror logical drives in the same array and a physical drive fails, both logical drives in the mirrored pair will fail, and you will not be able to retrieve your data. If you choose software-based drive mirroring, create at least two arrays with RAID 0 to achieve maximum storage capacity. When configuring your drive mirroring through the operating system, mirror logical drives residing in *different* arrays.

Installing and Configuring a RAID Controller

Before you can use a RAID controller, you'll need to install it in the server. This part of the chapter outlines the general process for installing and configuring a typical SCSI RAID controller card in a server both with and without PCI hot-plug support. If you're installing a second RAID controller (i.e., an AMI MegRAID Express Plus or Compaq SmartArray 4250ES) to provide array controller redundancy, make sure that both of the controllers have been upgraded to the latest firmware version, and see that the system BIOS has been upgraded to the latest version. Also see that the firmware version is the same on both controllers. Start with the following preinstallation steps.

If your RAID controller uses 64-bit PCI slots with extended SCSI connectors, be sure to install the controllers *only* into those slots. Installing the controller in slots without these connectors will cause the system to malfunction.

1. Always start by backing up data from any hard drive(s) that will be moved to the new controller.
2. Upgrade the existing array controller firmware and system BIOS.
3. Remove the server access panels for the PCI and SCSI bus connectors (i.e., the 64-bit PCI bus with extended SCSI connectors).
4. Install additional internal drive cages in the server, if necessary.
5. Attach the preinstalled SCSI RAID controller 68-pin Wide SCSI ribbon cables to the appropriate internal drive cage(s).
6. Connect the ports to the drives (i.e., SCSI port 1 to drive cage 1, port 2 to drive cage 2, and so on).
7. Install drives in the drive cages.

If your server supports hot-plug operation, you do not have to power off the server to install the RAID controller:

1. Unlock and open the server's hot-plug access panel(s).
2. Use the PCI Hot Plug button (or software application) to turn off power to the desired slot. A green LED will flash during the power-down transition and will turn off when power-down is complete.
3. Press the top of the appropriate expansion slot release lever and open the lever toward the rear of the expansion slot. Be sure to use the correct expansion slot.
4. Position the RAID controller board into the appropriate expansion slot alignment guides.
5. Insert the RAID controller until it's resting on the top of the slot connector.
6. Secure the controller board by pushing the ejector levers down.
7. Close the expansion slot release lever from the rear of the unit to secure the board. Make sure the lever latches into the closed position.
8. Activate power to the slot through the PCI hot-plug application (or by pressing the PCI Hot Plug button associated with the corresponding PCI slot).
9. Review the LEDs for slot status—a green LED flashes during the power-up transition, and will turn on when the power-up is complete.
10. Close and lock the server hot-plug access panels.
11. Run the server's configuration utility and the RAID controller's configuration utility as required to set up the RAID card.

Make sure that the appropriate hot-plug drivers are installed for your operating system. If they are *not* installed, the system will halt when a controller is removed or inserted.

If your server does *not* support hot-plug operation, you *will* have to power off the server (and allow internal devices to cool) before installing the RAID controller:

1. Back up all data from any hard drives that will be moved to the new controller.
2. Power down the server and disconnect the power cord(s).

3. Remove the server access panels for the PCI and SCSI bus connectors (i.e., the 64-bit PCI bus with extended SCSI connectors).

4. Position the RAID controller board into the appropriate expansion slot alignment guides.

5. Insert the controller board until it's resting on the top of the slot connector.

6. Secure the board by pushing the ejector levers downward.

7. Close the expansion slot release lever from the rear of the unit to secure the board. Make sure the lever latches into the closed position.

8. Close and lock the server access panels.

9. Power up the server.

10. Run the server's configuration utility and the RAID controller's configuration utility as required to set up the RAID card.

CONFIGURING THE SERVER

After the RAID controller is installed in the server, you'll need to access the server's system configuration utility. The system configuration utility allows the configuration of hardware installed in (or connected to) the server. This utility detects each hardware device and configures the server to work with it. You can use the utility to

■ Automatically configure PCI boards

■ Provide device switch and jumper settings

■ Resolve resource conflicts in areas such as memory, port addresses, and interrupts (IRQs)

■ Manage the installation of memory, processor upgrades, and mass storage devices (such as hard drives, tape drives, and diskette drives)

■ Set and store power-on features like date and time

■ Store configuration information in nonvolatile memory

■ Assist in the installation of the network operating system

■ Assist in running server diagnostic tools

For servers such as the Compaq ProLinea line, the system configuration utility can be run directly from the driver/software CD supplied with the server or Compaq devices (i.e., the Smart Array 4250ES). You may already have a version of this utility in the system partition of the boot disk, but it is often best to use the very latest version of the utility. If your server does not have a bootable CD-ROM drive, create diskettes of the system configuration utility from the support CD.

The following instructions outline the general steps involved with a Compaq ProLinea server system, so check the documentation with your own server for specific instructions.

Starting the Utility

In order to configure the server to accept the new RAID controller, you'll need to start the server's SSU or suitable setup software for your particular RAID controller. The following steps outline a typical process:

1. Place the bootable support CD in the server's CD-ROM drive, or place utility diskette 1 in the server's floppy drive.

2. Reboot the server. During the boot, several messages appear. At least one message will indicate that a new device (i.e., the RAID controller) was detected in an option slot.

3. Press the required key(s) to continue booting, and start the system configuration utility.

4. If you're given a choice of *autoconfiguration*, choose Yes—the server then loads configuration files for all detected devices.

5. In the Configuration Complete screen, choose Review or Modify Hardware Settings.

6. In the Steps In Configuring Your Computer screen, select View or Edit Details.

7. Scroll down to the option slot where your new RAID controller is installed and edit the configuration as outlined here.

Configuring Controller Order

Select the order in which you want the new RAID controller to be recognized. All hard disk controllers (including the integrated SCSI controller on the system board, if present) must be assigned a unique order number from first to fifteenth. The first controller is the primary disk controller that contains the boot disk. The first disk drive on this controller is the one the server will boot from. Subsequent controllers are assigned numbers from second to fifteenth.

When installing a new RAID controller, you must determine if the boot disk is to be handled by a new controller, by another SMART controller, or by the integrated SCSI controller on the motherboard. If the new RAID controller will be the primary controller, choose "first". If you want the order of the integrated SCSI controller to be something other than second, scroll down and set the controller order manually. When installing a new RAID controller in a system with an existing array controller, you can either place the new controller at the end of the controller order or reorder the controllers. Reordering changes the current drive letter assignments for *all* drives on the system. To avoid changing the drive letter assignments, place the new controller at the *end* of the controller order.

If there are already other RAID controllers in the system, do not create a primary partition on any of the disks added with your new RAID controller.

Saving and Exiting

Once you've configured the server to accept the new RAID controller, you'll need to save your changes and exit the setup as outlined here:

1. Review and edit the controller characteristics of all other array controllers in the View or Edit Details screen.

2. Exit the screen when finished editing.

3. Select Save and Exit at the Steps in Configuring Your Computer screen.

4. Choose Save the Configuration and restart the computer at the Save and Exit screen.

5. Press ENTER at the Reboot screen.

6. Remove the CD or utility diskette and verify that the server boots normally without POST errors—this should complete the configuration at the server level.

CONFIGURING THE RAID CONTROLLER

Once you've configured the new RAID controller in the server's system configuration utility, you'll need to run the RAID controller's configuration utility in order to set up the controller card itself. The configuration utility allows a wide range of disk array management controls, such as adding more disk drives, selecting RAID levels, creating new arrays, expanding and extending capacity, changing stripe sizes, and the ability to modify other key RAID features.

Depending on the network operating system in use, you may need to take the network offline before using the configuration utility. For example, the configuration utility with the Compaq SmartArray 4250ES is an online utility in servers running Windows NT and late versions of Novell NetWare, but it is an offline utility for the other operating systems.

Starting the Configuration Utility Online

If you're using a network operating system that supports the RAID controller's configuration utility online (i.e., Windows NT), you can install and run the utility while the network is running. When you install the Software Support Diskette for Windows NT (NT SSD), the diskette prompts you to insert the configuration utility diskette to install the utility. A program icon is created automatically. Simply select the icon to run the configuration utility. To run the configuration utility from the RAID controller's support CD, insert the CD in the CD-ROM drive and power up the server. When you see the menu, select the Configuration Utility option. After completing the configuration, remove the CD and restart the server.

Using Configuration Wizards

If your RAID controller offers Configuration Wizards, you can check and optimize your drive array almost automatically. When you start the RAID controller's configuration utility, the software checks the configuration of the controller and its drive array(s). If the arrays are unconfigured or the configuration is less than optimal, the Configuration Wizard tool can often guide you through the configuration process. This provides a particularly handy tool when setting up new RAID installations. A RAID controller with a Configuration Wizard (such as the SmartArray 4250ES) recognizes the following conditions:

- **Unconfigured controller**   When the configuration utility detects an unconfigured controller, the Configuration Wizard leads you through the controller configuration process.

- **Unused physical drives**   When the configuration utility detects unused physical drives, the Configuration Wizard provides an easy way to add them to an array. For example, the capacity expansion capability of the SmartArray 4250ES allows the configuration utility to add new physical drives to an existing array without destroying data on the existing logical drives.

- **Unused space on an array**   If the configuration utility detects unused capacity in an array, the Configuration Wizard leads you through the process of configuring the space into one or more logical drives.

MANUAL CONFIGURATION

Rather than using the Configuration Wizards to enable your drive array, you can use the RAID controller's configuration utility to manually configure the controller and your drive array. The following procedures outline the techniques used with a SmartArray 4250ES RAID controller to create a new array, expand an array, extend a logical drive, alter the stripe size, and alter the RAID level.

Creating a New Array

To create a new drive array, you'll need to choose a RAID controller to manage the array, group selected drives (of the same size) into the array, then create logical drives from the physical array. Suppose that you have four 4.3GB drives and two 9.1GB drives connected to your SCSI RAID controller. You'd probably create two arrays. Array A would consist of three 4.3GB drives (with the fourth 4.3GB drive used as a spare), and array B would be the two 9.1GB drives. The fault-tolerance method for all logical drives in array A might be RAID 5 (distributed data guarding), and the fault-tolerance method for all logical drives in array B may be RAID 1 (drive mirroring). Let's review the steps to set up this type of example manually:

1. Start the RAID controller's configuration utility. In the Main Configuration screen, select the Controller Selection box.

2. Select one of the listed controllers. If there is only one RAID controller in the server, only one controller should be listed.

3. Click the Controller Settings button, and the Controller Setting screen appears (see Figure 11-2).

4. Select the correct operating system.

5. Click the Create Array button, and the Create Drive Array screen appears (see Figure 11-3).

6. Select the three drives you want to make up array A from the drives listed (for example, SCSI IDs 0, 1, and 2). Remember to always group physical drives of the *same* size—if you mix drive sizes, the capacity of the larger drives is wasted.

7. Click the Assign Drive(s) to Array button.

8. Select the last 4.3GB drive (ID 3) and click the Assign Spare to Array button. Remember that the same spare drive may be assigned to multiple arrays, but spare drives should have the same (or greater) capacity as the drives in the array.

9. Click the Done button to return to the Main Configuration screen.

10. Select the controller again, then click the Create Array button to create array B.

11. Assign both 9.1GB drives to the array and click the Done button.

12. Select array A (or the Unused Space icon under array A) in the Logical Configuration View.

13. Click the Create Logical Drive button. A Create Logical Drive dialog box appears (see Figure 11-4).

14. Select your RAID level. For our example, click the Distributed Data Guarding (RAID 5) option button.

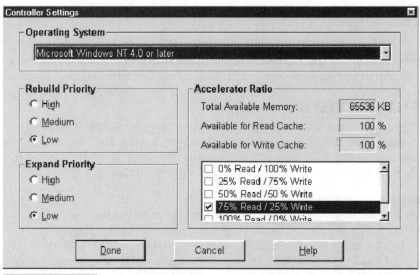

FIGURE 11-2   A basic RAID Controller Settings dialog box

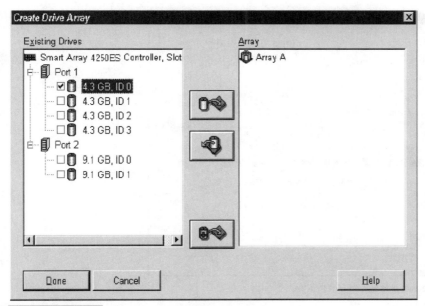

FIGURE 11-3   Creating a RAID drive array

15. Click the Array Accelerator Enable button (if your controller provides array acceleration).

16. Select your stripe size. Stripe size can be left at the default for the selected RAID level, or set to another value.

17. Size your logical drive. The Logical Drive Size area includes a graphical representation of the storage capacity available. To create a single logical drive across this array, accept the default values.

18. Click the Done button.

19. Click array B (or the Unused Space icon under array B) in the Logical Configuration View.

20. Repeat the steps above to create a single logical drive on array B, this time selecting RAID 1 fault tolerance.

21. This should complete the basic configuration of your drive array(s).

Expanding Capacity

Capacity expansion involves adding storage capacity (drives) to an array that has already been configured. If an existing array is nearly full of data, you can expand the capacity *without* disturbing the existing data. When you run the RAID controller's configuration utility, the program checks the drive hardware and configuration. If the configuration utility discovers a physical drive that is not being used, the Configuration Wizard leads you through the steps for adding the drive, or you can expand the capacity manually:

1. Install the new physical drive(s). Always group physical drives of the same size—if you mix drive sizes, the capacity of the larger drives is wasted.

2. Assign the new physical drive(s) to an existing array. An existing logical drive(s) will automatically expand across the physical drives (including the newly added ones).

3. Create a new logical drive to use the extra space on the expanded array.

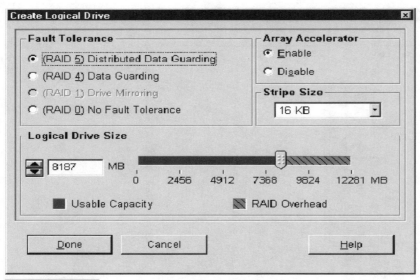

FIGURE 11-4   Creating a logical RAID drive

Consider a configuration similar to the previous example: three 4.3GB drives in array A (no spare), and two 9.1GB drives in array B. If a fourth 4.3GB drive is added later, you can expand array A to include the fourth drive:

1. Select array A and click the Expand button.

2. Select the unassigned 4.3GB drive, then click Assign Drive(s) to Array.

3. Click the Next button at the bottom of the screen.

4. Click the Create Logical Drive button (see Figure 11-5).

5. Set the fault tolerance, enable the array accelerator, set the stripe size, and set the size for logical drive 2.

6. Click the Done button.

7. Back at the main screen, select Controller and Save Configuration from the menu bar. This saves the new settings for logical drive 2 and starts the capacity expansion process.

In the event of power loss, capacity expansion information is temporarily stored in the array accelerator's memory. To prevent the loss of data in the expanding logical drive, do not interchange RAID controllers or array accelerator boards during a capacity expansion process.

Extending Capacity

Logical drive extension allows you to increase the size of existing logical drives without disturbing the data on those logical drives. Keep in mind that logical drive extension is *not* supported by all operating systems. If an existing logical drive is full of data, you can extend the logical drive when there is free space

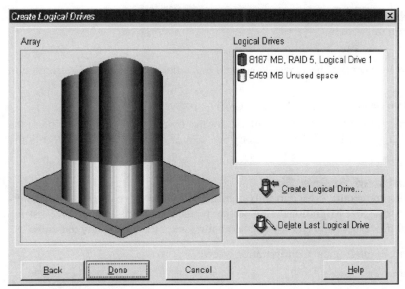

FIGURE 11-5   Expanding the capacity of a RAID array without disturbing data

in the array. If there is no free space available, you can add drives to the array and proceed to extend the logical drive:

1. Click on the logical drive that you want to extend.
2. Click the Drive menu.
3. Select Extend Logical Drive.
4. The Extend Logical Drive screen displays the current capacity and RAID overhead of the selected logical drive (see Figure 11-6).

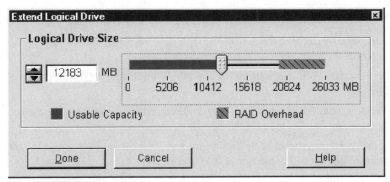

FIGURE 11-6   Extending capacity of a logical drive when physical space is available

5. Click the slider control to change (increase) the size of the logical drive. You cannot reduce the size of the logical drive from this screen.

6. Click Done.

7. Save the logical drive by opening the Controller menu and selecting the Save Configuration option.

8. The logical drive will be restructured so that its data will be preserved.

9. Make the extended space of the logical drive available for use by creating a new partition in the extended space of the logical drive, or by increasing the size of an existing partition(s) in the extended logical drive.

Changing RAID Level and Stripe Size

Use the RAID Level dialog box to reconfigure a currently configured logical drive to a new fault-tolerance (RAID) level, or use the Stripe Size Migration dialog box to change an existing logical drive's stripe size to a new stripe size. Both processes can be accomplished online without causing any data loss:

1. Select a logical drive from the Logical Configuration View.

2. Select the Drive menu.

3. Click the Migrate RAID/Stripe Size option button.

4. Select a new RAID level (i.e., click the RAID 5 Distributed Data Guarding button).

5. The stripe size can be left at the default for the selected RAID level, or set to another value. For example, you can set the stripe size to 16KB.

6. Click Done.

EXCHANGING AN ARRAY ACCELERATOR MODULE

Many high-end RAID controllers incorporate a large cache module called an array accelerator (i.e., the Smart Array 4250ES has a removable 64MB array accelerator, and the AMI MegaRAID Express Plus can support up to 128MB of onboard RAM). An array accelerator holds data between the system and disk array so that power failures and disk faults will not corrupt that data. An array accelerator is normally implemented as a removable daughter board so that it can be easily replaced if necessary—in fact, given the fault-tolerant nature of most RAID controllers, the array accelerator module *must* be attached before the controller can be used. An array accelerator has several unique features:

■ It accelerates data storage by temporarily caching the data at high internal bus rates, while transferring the data to the drives at their slower write speeds.

■ It uses its own batteries to keep the data valid without board power—even if the array accelerator is removed from RAID controller.

■ The memory supports error checking and correcting (ECC), so data reliability is improved with error detection and correction.

■ In a single RAID controller configuration, the module can be moved to another compatible RAID controller to complete the data transfer should the original RAID controller fail.

■ In a redundant RAID controller configuration, it is typically not necessary to move the array accelerator in the event of a single controller failure—the posted write data is automatically synchronized between the two RAID controllers.

Removing the Accelerator

Because an array accelerator is normally implemented as a daughter card, it is secured to the RAID controller with a variety of screws. These steps describe the removal of an accelerator from a SmartArray 4250ES RAID controller, which is a good overall example:

1. Use a Torx T-10 screwdriver to remove the two screws from the top of the array accelerator board.
2. Turn the RAID controller board over and remove the five screws that secure the stiffener bracket to the RAID controller.
3. Remove the stiffener bracket.
4. Remove the remaining screw from the accelerator board bracket.
5. Remove the accelerator board bracket.
6. Turn the board over and twist the latch 90 degrees to release the array accelerator module from the RAID controller.
7. Lift the array accelerator board gently (near the top of the board) to separate it from the signal connectors on the RAID controller.
8. To install the array accelerator board on the RAID controller, just reverse these removal steps.

Installing Operating System Drivers

Once the physical RAID controller is installed and configured, you'll need to install the drivers for the particular operating system. This part of the chapter covers the installation guidelines for controllers (such as the Compaq SmartArray 4250ES) under Windows 2000/NT, Novell NetWare, and Linux. Before installing the operating system drivers, you should update your server BIOS (if necessary) and configure your drive array(s) with the RAID controller's configuration utility.

These procedures are intended to serve as examples. Always refer to the documentation that accompanies your particular RAID controller for detailed installation instructions.

WINDOWS 2000

Most current RAID devices include driver support for Windows 2000 (i.e., Windows 2000 Server). For example, the AMI MegaRAID device drivers for Windows 2000 are provided as a miniport driver. Perform the following procedure to add the AMI MegaRAID Windows 2000 drivers and utilities to an existing system running Windows 2000:

1. After installing the physical RAID controller, boot the system to Windows 2000. The Found New Hardware Wizard appears.
2. Click Cancel on all the new devices (do not allow the wizard to identify the controller device automatically).
3. Click Start | Settings | Control Panel.
4. Double-click the Add/Remove Hardware icon. The Add/Remove Hardware Wizard appears. Click Next.

5. The Choose a Hardware Task screen appears. Select Add/Troubleshoot a device, and then click Next.

6. The Choose a Hardware Device screen displays. Select the PCI device listed in the device list with the exclamation mark (!)—it should be the first device listed. Click on Next.

7. After you complete the Add/Remove Hardware Wizard, click Finish.

8. Click on Next to start the Welcome to the Upgrade Device Driver Wizard dialog box, then click Next.

9. The Install Hardware Device Drivers screen displays. Be sure to list all available drivers.

10. Insert the CD that contains the RAID driver.

11. The Hardware Type screen displays. Select SCSI and RAID controller from the list, then click Next.

12. The Select a Device Driver screen displays. The screen prompts you for the driver that you want to install for this device. Select the manufacturer and model of your hardware device, then click Next.

13. A list of all controllers of that device class will appear. Select the model of your controller and press ENTER.

14. The Start Device Driver Installation screen displays. Click Next to begin driver installation for the selected hardware device.

15. After you have added the driver for all the SCSI controllers, click Finish to close the wizard. This should complete the driver installation.

WINDOWS NT 4.0

To install a RAID controller's Windows NT driver on your server, you will need the controller's driver/support CD, blank diskettes, and access to a server or workstation with a bootable CD-ROM drive (in most cases, this may be the system where you install the RAID controller). To access the driver on your support CD, you'll first need to create the Windows NT SSD diskettes. These diskettes will contain the latest operating system software, drivers, and support documentation for the controller. To create the diskettes, follow these steps:

1. Boot the server from the controller CD.

2. From the System Utilities screen, select Create Support Software.

3. From the Diskette Builder screen, select Create Support Server Diskettes from CD.

4. Scroll down the list and select Support Software for Windows NT.

5. Follow the instructions on the screen to create the Windows NT SSD diskettes.

Installing RAID Controller with Windows NT

You can install the RAID controller's driver during the initial installation of Windows NT 4.0 using the files on the Windows NT SSD diskettes:

1. Begin the Windows NT 4.0 installation process.

2. Setup automatically detects mass storage devices. Press S when prompted to specify additional mass storage devices.

3. From the list, highlight Other (Requires Disk Provided by Manufacturer) and press ENTER.

4. Insert Windows NT 4.0 SSD diskette #1 and press ENTER.

5. Select the RAID controller (i.e., Compaq Integrated Smart Array 42XX Controllers for Windows NT 4.0) from the list of displayed controllers and press ENTER.

6. Press ENTER again and continue installation of Windows NT 4.0.

7. Reinsert the Windows NT 4.0 SSD diskette when prompted—Setup copies the drivers to your system.

Updating RAID Controller's Driver

Updating a RAID controller's driver is normally a two-step process: remove the old driver, then reinstall the new driver. With the Windows NT SSD Setup program, you can skip the remove/add steps and update the driver by following these steps:

1. Start Windows NT and log in to an account with administrative privileges.

2. Insert the Windows NT SSD diskette (diskette #1) into the floppy drive.

3. Start Setup by typing **a:\setup** (where **a:** is the letter of the diskette drive).

4. Select Custom Setup.

5. Select your RAID controller (i.e., Compaq Integrated Smart Array 42XX Controller), then click Update.

6. The Setup program updates the driver on your system from the Windows NT SSD diskettes.

7. Select Close and exit the Setup program.

8. Remove the Windows NT SSD diskette, shut down Windows NT, and reboot the system to load the new driver.

Installing RAID Controller after Windows NT

If you must install the RAID controller *after* Windows NT is installed, you can use the Setup utility located on the Windows NT SSD diskettes. Setup identifies hardware components that are physically installed in the system, and recommends the device drivers that you should install or update:

1. Start Windows NT on the system where you're installing the drivers, and log on to an account with administrative privileges.

2. Insert the Windows NT SSD diskette #1 into the floppy drive.

3. From the Program Manager, select File and then select Run.

4. Type in **a:\setup** and press ENTER.

5. Select Custom.

6. Select the RAID controller (i.e., Compaq Integrated Smart Array 42XX Controllers). If you have previously installed this driver on your system, Setup indicates if the driver can be updated. If it can, click Update. If you have not installed the driver, click Install and insert the correct diskettes as prompted during the installation.

7. You can install other components through Setup, or click Close if you're done. Setup prompts you to reboot the system to enable the newly installed/updated driver.

Removing the Driver

It might be necessary to remove the RAID controller's driver prior to upgrading the controller or resolving device conflicts. Device drivers can only be done through the Control Panel as shown for Windows NT here:

Do *not* remove this driver if the system is booting from a device attached to the RAID controller. You'll get a dialog box reporting that the selected controller is used as a boot device—removing it may cause the system *not* to boot.

1. Start Windows NT and log in to an account with administrative privileges.
2. From the Control Panel, launch the SCSI Adapter utility.
3. Select the Drivers tab.
4. Select the controller (i.e., Compaq Integrated Smart Array 42XX Controllers), then click Remove.
5. After the driver has been removed, click OK. You must reboot the system for the removal to take effect.

Installing Redundancy Software

If your operating system supports redundancy software, you can install the software following the steps as shown for Windows NT here:

1. Start Windows NT on the system where you're installing the redundancy software, and log on to an account with administrative privileges.
2. Insert the Windows NT SSD diskette (usually diskette #7) into the floppy drive.
3. From the Program Manager, select File, and then select Run.
4. Type **a:\setup** and press ENTER.
5. Select the RAID controller's redundancy software component. If you've previously installed this software on your system, Setup indicates whether it can be updated. If so, click Update. If you have not installed the software, click Install.
6. You can install other components through Setup, or click Close if you're done. Setup will prompt you to reboot the system and load the newly installed software.

Removing Redundancy Software

If you have installed a RAID controller's redundancy software on the server, you may remove the software using these steps:

1. Start Windows NT on the system where you've installed the redundancy software, and log on to an account with administrative privileges.
2. Insert the Windows NT SSD diskette #1 into the floppy drive.
3. Open the Program Manager, select File and then select Run.
4. Type **a:\setup** and press ENTER.
5. Select the RAID controller's redundancy software component and click Remove.
6. You can install or remove other components through Setup, or click Close if you're done. Setup will prompt you to reboot the system and load the newly installed software.

NOVELL NETWARE 5.0

To install a RAID controller's NetWare driver on your server, you will need the controller's driver/support CD, blank diskettes, and access to a server or workstation with a bootable CD-ROM drive (in most cases, this may be the system where you install the RAID controller). To access the driver on your support CD, you'll first need to create the Novell Support Software Diskettes (SSD) diskettes. These diskettes will contain the latest operating system software, drivers, and support documentation for the controller. To create the diskettes, follow these steps:

Before installing the device drivers, install and load the latest Support Pack or operating system patch. Novell's Support Packs and patch kits are available for download directly from Novell.

1. Boot the server from the controller CD.
2. From the System Utilities screen, select Create Support Software.
3. From the Diskette Builder screen, select Create Support Server Diskettes from CD.
4. Scroll down the list and select Support Software for Novell NetWare.
5. Follow the instructions on the screen to create the Novell SSD diskettes.

Installing the Driver

The support CD automatically detects the newly installed controller, then copies the necessary drivers and updates the server **STARTUP.NCF** file. The process for installing or upgrading device drivers is relatively simple under NetWare. To install the driver for your RAID controller on a NetWare v3.20, v4.2, or v5.0 server, copy the required files from the Novell SSD (usually diskette #3) to the server startup directory (and to the **SYS:SYSTEM** directory if desired). After the driver installation is complete, refer to your NetWare installation documentation for information about installing and mounting volumes associated with your new disk subsystem.

NetWare and Drive Mirroring

NetWare recognizes each logical drive in an array as a separate physical drive. If you mirror logical drives on the same array and a physical drive fails, both logical drives in the mirrored pair will fail—and your data will be lost. To avoid this, you must mirror logical drives on separate arrays. Use the RAID controller's configuration utility for NetWare (i.e., **CPQONLIN.NLM**) on Novell SSD disk #1 to view the logical configuration for the controller. Record the logical drives (and the arrays on which they reside). When configuring NetWare for drive mirroring, select equally sized logical drives on *different* arrays.

Do *not* use NetWare drive mirroring if you do not have at least two arrays.

Handling Drive Failures Under NetWare

While drive failures are certainly not common, it is vital for you to protect your critical data. The best way to recover from a failed drive is to configure your drive system with some form of fault tolerance. With fault-tolerance techniques, the controller can also perform a background surface analysis on the hard drives to check for bad sectors (and to remap data to a new location on the media). This feature enhances the reliability and availability of your data. In all cases, you should employ sound backup procedures to protect your data in the event of a catastrophic failure. Use this general protocol if you discover a failed drive:

1. Identify and document the physical drive that has failed—note the drive type and capacity.

2. Note which partition and volume (if any) have failed. Such information is provided in the error message on the server console. It is also recorded in the server error log file, which can be viewed using the SYSCON utility or NWADMIN utility.

3. Make sure that you have a recent backup. If the drive is part of a fault-tolerant mirrored volume, or a hardware fault-tolerant volume, you can probably restore the lost data without using the backup, but a backup is still an important part of data protection.

4. Locate a replacement drive of the same type and capacity.

Use the following instructions for replacing a drive for your server configuration. Keep in mind that NetWare does not mirror information on DOS partitions—only hardware fault tolerance supports mirrored DOS partitions. If you have a mirrored drive containing a DOS partition, you'll need to restore the DOS partition information from another backup source. If the failed drive contains a DOS partition, NetWare cannot access information on that partition. For example, files on the DOS partition include **STARTUP.NCF** and Novell disk drivers. To prevent NetWare from attempting to read from or write to the failed device, execute the following command from the console:

```
REMOVE DOS
```

If your server is *not* configured for hardware fault tolerance and the failed drive contained the DOS partition used to boot your server, you will *not* be able to restart the server once it has been powered off. Schedule maintenance time as soon as possible and follow these steps:

1. Power down your server.

2. Replace the failed physical drive.

3. Reboot the system with the server's configuration utility diskette.

4. Select the option to Install a System Partition on your DOS boot device.

5. Exit the server's configuration utility.

6. Locate a DOS bootable diskette that contains the DOS FDISK and FORMAT programs.

7. Use the FDISK program to create a primary DOS partition on the replaced drive—your DOS partition should be at least 60MB.

8. Set the active partition to the DOS partition you just created.

9. Use the FORMAT command to format the DOS partition to include the necessary files to make the partition bootable (for example, FORMAT C: /S).

10. If you have a backup of your DOS partition, use it to create the previous image. Otherwise, use your NetWare server diskettes and copy the following files to a NetWare directory on your DOS partition:

```
SERVER.EXE
INSTALL.NLM
VREPAIR.NLM
MONITOR.NLM
CLIB.NLM
STREAMS.NLM
```

11. Copy the required disk drivers, LAN drivers, and utility **.NLM** files that should reside on the DOS partition from the Novell SSD.

12. Copy any other necessary information to the DOS partition, then reboot your system. You can now start your NetWare server (you may need to create your **STARTUP.NCF** file).

If you have chosen "no fault tolerance" for the drives connected to your RAID controller, but have configured NetWare mirroring or NetWare controller duplexing, perform the following steps to recover the data after a drive failure:

1. Identify the failed physical drive that caused the NetWare device to be deactivated. Record the device number and device name of the failed logical drive, such as

   ```
   NWPA: [V503-A2-D1:0] Compaq SMART-2 Slot 8 Disk 2 NFT
   ```

2. The failure messages are recorded on the server console and also in the server error log file, which may be viewed using the SYSCON utility or the NWADMIN utility. You will use this information later to create a valid partition.

3. Load **INSTALL.NLM** and select the Disk Options Mirroring menu. Select the mirrored logical partition that was affected by the drive failure. Record the device number and partition number of the operational logical drive in this mirrored group. This information will be used later to remirror the repaired logical drive.

4. Delete the unavailable (possibly out of sync) device from the Mirror Partition group—this device is unavailable due to the drive failure.

5. Record the drive bay location of the failed physical drive—the new physical drive must be inserted in this drive bay.

6. If the failed drive is hot-pluggable, you do not need to power down the server. Otherwise, schedule server downtime, take the server offline, and power off the unit.

7. Insert the replacement physical drive in the drive bay where the failed drive was located. The physical drive *must* be of the same capacity as the failed drive. Be sure that all cable connections are secure.

8. Activate the replaced device. Use the **MONITOR.NLM** Disk Information option to select the device. Some versions of NetWare will cause a "device activate" to occur automatically when this option is chosen. Other versions of NetWare require manual activation of the device by changing the operating status to "active." If reactivation of the failed logical drive is *successful*, the driver sends a console alert.

9. Use the **INSTALL.NLM** option Change Hot Fix (that is, look at the information provided about the mirrored drive, not the failed drive) to determine the number of *Hot Fix Redirection* blocks set up for this partition.

10. Use the **INSTALL.NLM** utility to delete and create the partition on the repaired logical drive.

Although the logical drive may have a valid partition table, the data on this logical drive is *not* valid. Some data may appear valid because the failed physical drive was only a portion of the arrayed logical drive. However, there is a "hole" in the logical drive's data at this point. Delete any old or invalid data, then create a new partition on the logical drive.

11. From the **INSTALL.NLM** Disk Options menu, select the Modify Disk Partitions and Hot Fix options.

12. In the **INSTALL.NLM** Available Disk Drives menu, select the previously failed logical drive, which has now been repaired (the device information was recorded in step 1).

13. Select the Delete Partition option. **INSTALL.NLM** may display several error messages. Since you will delete this partition, do *not* update any Volume Definition Table information. Continue until the partition has been deleted.

14. If **INSTALL.NLM** reports that it cannot delete the partition because another process has it locked, unload any NLMs that have the partition locked. After you create the partition and volume information, reload those NLMs.

15. Create the partition on the same logical drive.

16. Return to the Disk Options Mirroring menu and select the previously mirrored NetWare 386 partition number (which you recorded in step 2).

17. Press INSERT for a list of partitions available to remirror. Select the partition associated with the repaired device (listed in step 1). This causes NetWare to resynchronize the mirrored partitions. A console message indicates successful completion of the resynchronization step.

If you configured no fault tolerance at all in your server, you must recover the data from a backup media using the following steps:

1. Identify the failed physical drive that caused the NetWare device to be deactivated. Record the device number and device name of the failed logical drive, such as

```
NWPA: [V503-A2-D1:0] Compaq SMART-2 Slot 8 Disk 2 NFT
```

The failure messages are recorded on the server console and also in the server error log file, which may be viewed using the SYSCON utility or the NWADMIN utility. You will use this information later to create a valid partition.

2. Remove the failed drive.

3. Insert the replacement physical drive in the same drive bay where the failed drive was located. The physical drive must be of the same capacity as the failed drive.

4. Activate the replaced device. Use the **MONITOR.NLM** Disk Information option to select the device. Some versions of NetWare will cause a "device activate" to occur automatically when this option is chosen. Other versions of NetWare require manual activation of the device by changing the operating status to "active." If reactivation of the failed logical drive is successful, the driver sends a console alert.

5. It may be possible to use the **INSTALL.NLM** option Change Hot Fix to determine the number of Hot Fix Redirection blocks set up for this partition.

Although the logical drive may have a valid partition table, the data on this logical drive is *not* valid. Some data may appear valid because the failed physical drive was only a portion of the arrayed logical drive. However, there is a "hole" in the logical drive's data at this point. Delete any old or invalid data, and then create a new partition on the logical drive.

6. Return to the **INSTALL.NLM** Disk Options menu and select the Modify Disk Partitions and Hot Fix options. The driver should reactivate the failed logical drive. The driver sends a console alert if reactivation of the failed logical drive is successful.

7. In the **INSTALL.NLM** Available Disk Drives menu, select the previously failed logical drive, which has now been repaired (the device information was recorded in step 1).

8. Select the Delete Partition option. **INSTALL.NLM** may display several error messages. Delete the volume associated with this partition. Since you will delete this partition, do *not* update any Volume Definition Table information. Continue until the partition has been deleted.

9. If **INSTALL.NLM** reports that it cannot delete the partition because another process has it locked, unload any NLMs that may have the partition locked. After you create the partition and volume information, reload these NLMs.

10. Create the partition on the same logical drive.

11. Create and mount the volume.

12. Locate the recent backup media and restore the data to this server volume.

LINUX

With the growth in popularity of Linux operating systems, you may need to install or update the RAID drivers on a Linux server. Use the following procedure to install AMI MegaRAID controller drivers along with Red Hat Linux 6.2:

1. Boot to CD-ROM with Disk 1.

2. Type **expert** at the boot prompt on the Welcome screen, then press ENTER.

3. Copy the driver image for Linux from the RAID driver CD to diskette, then insert the diskette with driver image.

4. Select English as the default language and click OK.

5. Select US as the type of system keyboard and click OK.

6. Select Local CD-ROM as the type of media that contains the packages to be installed, then click OK.

7. Select Add Device to add SCSI devices and click OK.

8. Select SCSI, then click OK.

9. Scroll down to select AMI MegaRAID Adapter Driver. This will locate and load the driver for your SCSI device. Click OK.

10. The Mouse Configuration screen appears. Select the type of system mouse that you use and click OK.

11. The GUI Welcome screen appears. Click Next.

12. The Install Options screen appears. Select Custom and click Next.

13. Initialize drives. At the Partitions screen, select Add to make partitions.

14. Type a forward slash (/) for the mount point.

15. Tab down to Size (MB), type the size of the array that you want to use, and then press ENTER. Make sure that you enter a number larger than 1,515MB or it will not allow you to install. Notice that the highlighted Partition Type is Linux Native. This means that you are choosing the hard disk space.

16. The Partitions screen appears. Select Add to make another partition.

17. Select Linux Swap as the Partition Type.

18. Tab down to Size (MB). Type **125** and click OK.

19. Click OK at the next screen.

20. The LILO Configuration screen appears. Deselect "Create boot disk" and click on OK. This is a user preference option—it is not necessary to make a boot disk for the installation to continue.

21. The Time Zone Select screen appears. Select the time zone that your system is in and click OK.

22. The Account Configuration screen displays. Select and type a root password, then confirm. Click on Next. Be sure to remember the password so you can log in after installation is completed.

23. The Authentication Configuration screen appears. Click Next.

24. The Select Package Group screen appears. Scroll down and select Everything, then click Next.

25. The X-Configuration screen appears. Select the appropriate monitor and video card, then click Next.

26. Click Next to begin installation of Linux 6.2.

27. Click Exit to complete installation.

28. The system will now reboot.

Altering the Controller Setup

Once a RAID controller is installed and operational, you may need to adjust the setup and make changes to the controller's installation. Before attempting to make any changes to an existing RAID setup, you should carefully review the precautions and requirements for your particular RAID controller and server chassis. Here are some points to check before proceeding:

■ Each RAID channel may support a large number of drives (i.e., up to 14 drives), but the controller will be limited by the number of physical drives supported by your server.

■ Check for acceptable drive combinations. Some RAID controllers allow the use of Wide Ultra2 SCSI, Wide Ultra SCSI-3, or a mixture of the two in servers and storage systems supporting hot-pluggable drives. However, that may not be true for all controller/server combinations.

■ Drives may not require termination. For example, Compaq servers and internal cabling provide the required termination of the SCSI bus.

■ Check the acceptable drive sizes. Your RAID controller may be limited in the sizes and interfaces that can be supported.

■ Drives should be of the same capacity to provide the greatest storage space efficiency when grouped in the same drive array.

■ Check for "reserved IDs." For example, external (or non-hot-pluggable) drives that are attached to some RAID controllers (i.e., a Compaq SmartArray 4250ES) must not be installed as SCSI ID6—SCSI IDs 6 and 7 are reserved for redundant controller operation.

TWEAKING THE FAULT TOLERANCE

You may find it necessary to alter the *fault tolerance* (RAID level) used in an array. This may be necessary when drives are added or removed from the server, or when the network's needs change. For example, early implementations of a network may emphasize data storage performance over fault tolerance, but the need to protect valuable data may require you to update the RAID fault-tolerance selection. Here are the general steps:

1. *Pick the new RAID level.* The first task is to decide which level you'll need to use (see the "RAID Levels" section earlier in the chapter).

2. *Back up the disk array.* A RAID level can typically be migrated without data loss using the RAID controller's configuration utility. If this is not possible (the configuration utility should inform you when this is not possible), you'll need to back up your data first and then change the RAID level.

3. *Configure the array.* Run the RAID controller's configuration utility in order to reconfigure your drive array with the new fault-tolerance method. If an error message states that the number of sectors needs to be increased, you must delete the old volume and reconfigure it as a new volume with the different fault-tolerance method you've selected.

4. *Restore the data.* Copy your protected data back into the same logical drives (if necessary). Your system automatically redistributes the data according to the new fault-tolerance scheme.

TWEAKING THE STRIPE SIZE

You may find it necessary to alter the *stripe size* used in an array. This may be necessary when drives are added or removed from the server, or when the network's needs change. The typical guidelines are listed here:

1. *Pick the new stripe size.* Select the desired stripe size for your array and RAID level (see the "Disk Striping" section earlier in this chapter).

2. *Back up the disk array.* Stripe size can typically be migrated without data loss using the RAID controller's configuration utility. If this is not possible (the configuration utility should inform you when this is not possible), you'll need to back up your data first and then change the stripe size.

3. *Configure the stripe size.* Run the RAID controller's configuration utility in order to reconfigure your drive array with the new stripe size. If an error message states that the number of sectors needs to be increased, you must delete the old volume and reconfigure it as a new volume with the different stripe size that you've selected.

4. *Restore the data.* Copy your protected data back into the same logical drives (if necessary). Your system automatically redistributes the data according to the striping scheme.

MOVING DRIVES WITHIN AN ARRAY

It is possible to move drives (use alternate ID assignments) on any given RAID controller. This allows drives to be easily replaced and reallocated at any point after an array is established. To move drives, the server power must be off (including all system components), the move must not result in more than 32 logical drives (volumes) connected to a single controller, and the array should be in its original configuration with no active spare drives. It is also helpful to be using the latest RAID controller firmware. When the required conditions are met, follow these steps:

 Anytime you move drives or change a RAID configuration, you should perform a complete backup of all data.

1. Power off the system.

2. Move your drives as required.

3. Restore system power.

4. Run the RAID controller's configuration utility to view and verify the new drive configuration.

An error message (i.e., a 1724 POST message) should indicate that drive positions were changed, and the configuration was updated. If a "not configured" error appears (i.e., a 1785 POST message), turn the system off immediately to avoid data loss and return the drives to their original positions.

MOVING ARRAYS BETWEEN CONTROLLERS

It is possible to move entire disk arrays from one controller to another, or consolidate arrays existing on multiple controllers to a single controller. To move arrays, the server power must be off (including all system components), the move must not result in more than 32 logical drives (volumes) connected to a single controller, and the array should be in its original configuration with no active spare drives. It is also helpful to be using the latest RAID controller firmware. In addition, *all* of the drives in an array must be moved at the same time, but the positions of drives on the destination controller should not be changed at that time. When the required conditions are met, follow these steps:

1. Power off the system.
2. Move your array as required (include all drives in the array).
3. Restore system power.
4. Run the RAID controller's configuration utility to view and verify the new drive configuration.

An error message (i.e., a 1724 POST message) should indicate that logical drives were added to the configuration, and the configuration was updated. If a "not configured" error appears (i.e., a 1785 POST message), turn the system off immediately to avoid data loss and return the drives to their original positions. If you move arrays from a multichannel controller to a single-channel controller, you may get an error message indicating a configuration error. If you get such an error message, follow these steps:

1. Return to the previous multichannel controller configuration.
2. Back up *all* data on the array.
3. Move the drives to the single-channel controller.
4. Run the RAID controller's configuration utility on the single-channel controller to configure the array.
5. Restore data to the array.
6. Run the RAID controller's configuration utility to view and verify the new drive configuration or assign spare drives if necessary.

If any drives are missing or have failed, *all* data on the moved array(s) could be lost. Anytime you move arrays or change a RAID configuration, you should perform a complete backup of all data.

Consider a system with two SCSI RAID controllers (each with a different array). Suppose controller 1 has an array of four drives (IDs 0, 1, 2, and 3), and controller 2 has an array of two drives (IDs 0 and 1). If you move the array from controller 2 to controller 1, controller 1 will now have an A array of four drives (IDs 0, 1, 2, and 3) and a B array of two drives (reassigned to IDs 4 and 5). Controller 2 would then have *no* arrays.

A spare drive can be added as part of an array during this procedure, but it will not be restored as a spare until you run the RAID controller's configuration utility.

RESTORING AN ARRAY

In addition to moving an array, you can also restore an array to its original controller. This may be necessary if you encounter server problems with an array or controller, or if the network's needs change. The actual physical process of restoring an array is straightforward (see the "Moving Arrays Between Controllers" section above), but the logical sequence of events required to restore an array to its original controller (or to a new controller in the event of RAID controller failure) is a bit more convoluted. To restore an array, the server power must be off (including all system components), the move must not result in more than 32 logical drives (volumes) connected to a single controller, and the array should be in its original configuration with no active spare drives. It is also helpful to be using the latest RAID controller firmware. When the required conditions are met, follow these steps:

These steps are intended to provide general guidelines only. Always refer to your specific server platform and RAID controller documentation for specific instructions. Any deviation from the manufacturer's instructions can result in the loss of all data across all moved arrays.

1. Power off the system.

2. Move your array back to the original controller (include all drives in the array), but retain its drive position from the consolidated configuration.

3. Restore system power.

4. Each of the controllers will indicate a "missing drives" error (i.e., a 1789 POST message). Press the appropriate key (i.e., F2) to fail the missing drives.

5. Run the RAID controller's configuration utility to remove the appropriate failed arrays.

6. Reboot the server.

Consider a SCSI RAID controller with an A array of four disks (IDs 0, 1, 2, and 3) and a B array of two disks (IDs 4 and 5). Moving the B array back to controller 2 creates an interim four-array state—array B on controller 1 and array A on controller 2 appear to the server as failed. You'll need to run the RAID controller's configuration utility to remove the failed arrays and restore the original two-array configuration.

RAID CONTROLLER UPGRADE/REPLACEMENT GUIDELINES

As you work with networks and network servers, you will probably be required to replace the RAID controller as part of an upgrade or system repair. While the precise upgrade process will vary between controllers, this part of the chapter outlines some general hardware and software guidelines for a typical SCSI RAID controller (i.e., the SmartArray 4250ES) that may help to ease your upgrade problems. Always back up your disk array(s) before starting the upgrade. Be sure to verify the backups *before* proceeding with the following steps. The general steps are listed here:

If you're upgrading to a newer controller from an older controller, do *not* expect the older drivers to support the newer controller properly. You must load the new drivers for the new controller *before* replacing the existing controller.

1. Run the server's "system configuration" utility and document the *boot controller order*—this information will help to ensure that the server will boot correctly after your upgrade.

2. Verify that your server is using the latest BIOS version, and upgrade the BIOS if necessary.

   Skip to the instructions for your network operating system here and see that the drivers are loaded properly. Return to the following steps when you're done:

3. Verify that the server is off.

4. Replace the previous controller with the new controller card.

5. With the controller's driver CD in the drive, power on the server and run the server's system configuration utility.

6. Verify that the Boot Controller Order is exactly the same as the information you recorded above. The old controller should now appear as the new controller.

7. Save any changes made by the server's system configuration utility.

8. Reboot the server and remove the driver CD. This should complete the physical upgrade.

9. See that all drives are identified as they were previously by the operating system, and verify that everything is operating as before.

10. If you have no other older array controllers in the system, remove the old controller driver—you'll usually see error messages that will prompt the driver removal.

Windows NT 4.0

If you're using Windows NT as your operating system, follow these steps:

1. Run the Windows NT Disk Administrator and write signatures to the drives. This will ensure drive letters do not move during the upgrade. After the upgrade is complete, run Disk Administrator again and verify that all drives are associated with the proper data.

2. Insert the new controller's driver CD and install the latest controller applets for Windows NT. Do *not* reboot the system (especially if you're prompted to do so).

3. Open Control Panel | SCSI Adapters | Have Disk to manually install the new drivers from the controller's CD. Browse to the **.INF** file for your specific controller. After selecting the correct controller (or controller family), click OK.

4. Browse the CD to the same folder, select Open, and click OK. This will install your new drivers.

5. Shut down the server.

6. Return to the general instructions listed above.

NetWare 4.2 and 5

If you're using NetWare as your operating system, follow these steps:

1. Enable your CD-ROM. If the CD-ROM drivers are not already loaded, type **load cdrom** and press ENTER at the system console. After the CD-ROM driver has loaded, type **cd mount all** (NetWare 4.x only) and press ENTER at the system console. For NetWare 5, the CD will be automatically mounted after a few seconds.

2. From the system console, type **volumes** and press ENTER. Make a note of the current controller's volume name (i.e., CPQSMST430).

3. Access the available driver files. For example, from the system console, type **load cpqsmst430:cpqsupsw\nssd\install\cpqnssu** and press ENTER. Replace the CPQSMST430 reference with the volume name of your new controller's CD, if necessary.

4. Expand the list of available files for your controller and select the correct file(s) according to the controller's instructions.

5. Highlight the Install Selected Files option and press ENTER. The driver files will be copied to **SYS:SYSTEM** and **C:\NWSERVER**. After the files have finished copying, press ENTER to continue.

6. At the selection screen, highlight Return To Main Menu and press ENTER.

7. At the main menu, highlight Exit and press ENTER. Highlight YES and press ENTER when prompted.

8. At the system console, type **down** and press ENTER. Type **exit** and press ENTER to return to the DOS prompt if necessary.

9. Leave the driver CD in the CD-ROM drive.

10. Shut down the server.

11. Return to the general instructions listed above.

UnixWare 7.x

If you're using UNIX as your operating system, follow these steps:

1. Check with SCO for any required system patches, and install any necessary patches.

2. Make a set of EFS diskettes from the driver CD by booting the CD and selecting Create Support Software. Select SCO UnixWare EFS and follow the instructions.

3. Upgrade the IDA driver from the HBA diskette by typing **pkgadd -d diskette1 ida**. This step should properly update the driver for the new controller, but installing the remainder of the EFS 7.26 is usually recommended.

4. Relink the kernel and shut down the server.

5. Return to the general instructions listed above.

CONTROLLER FIRMWARE UPGRADE GUIDELINES

From time to time, servers and option devices—such as your RAID controller—may need to receive firmware updates. Updates effectively correct firmware bugs, fix hardware or operating system incompatibilities, and add features as they become available. Firmware is typically stored on a *flash BIOS* chip (as with most current PC motherboards), and can be reprogrammed easily using a flash loader utility. For example, the Compaq line of servers and controllers use a utility called ROMPaq. Since reprogramming can be accomplished using software tools and files, updates can be downloaded free from the Internet and installed without actually having to open the server or remove expansion devices. Compaq ProLiant servers use two ROMPaq utilities:

Before you install the new RAID controller into your server, you update the system BIOS.

■ **System ROMPaq**   This updates the system BIOS in all Compaq servers supporting flash ROM. You might use the System ROMPaq utility when installing a new RAID controller in a Compaq server in order to verify that the server can use all the capabilities offered by the controller.

■ **Options ROMPaq**   This updates the onboard ROM on all Compaq option devices that support flash programming. You might use the Options ROMPaq utility when new versions of a Compaq RAID controller's firmware or SCSI drive firmware become available in order to use additional capabilities.

If you have two RAID controllers (a primary controller and a secondary controller) in your server, make sure both controllers are running the same firmware version. The redundant controller feature will work only if both controllers are running the same firmware version.

Creating ROMPaq Diskettes

In virtually all cases, flashing is accomplished from one or more diskettes that can be created as needed. Let's examine the typical process used to create and use ROMPaq diskettes for Compaq ProLiant servers and option devices. To create the ROMPaq utility diskette(s), you will need the installation/driver CD accompanying the RAID controller (i.e., the Compaq SmartArray 4250ES CD), and one blank diskette (for System ROMPaq) or up to five blank diskettes (for Options ROMPaq), depending on your server. You will also need access to the server or a workstation with a bootable CD-ROM drive. This can be the system in which you are installing a new RAID controller. Use these steps to create ROMPaq diskettes:

Keep in mind that this discussion is strictly an example. Always refer to the documentation accompanying your server and optional devices for specific flash upgrade instructions.

1. Boot the server from the Compaq CD.

2. From the Compaq System Utilities screen, select Create Support Software.

3. At the Diskette Builder screen, scroll down the list and select either System ROMPaq or Options ROMPaq.

4. Follow the instructions on the screen to finish creating the ROMPaq diskette(s).

Using System ROMPaq Diskettes

System ROMPaq updates the BIOS in Compaq servers (such as the ProLinea line). When you plan to install a new device with enhanced capabilities (i.e., a Compaq Smart Array 4250ES), your server may need updated firmware to take advantage of these capabilities. Since it is difficult to determine when the firmware needs to be updated, run the latest System ROMPaq on all servers when installing a new device. To run a System ROMPaq diskette, follow these steps:

1. Place the System ROMPaq diskette in the server's diskette drive.

2. Boot the server by turning on the power.

3. Press ENTER at the Welcome screen.

4. In the Select A Device screen, select your server from the list of the programmable devices (the server may be the only item in the list) and press ENTER.

5. In the Select An Image screen, you will see information regarding your devices to reprogram, the current ROM version, and the latest ROM version. Press ENTER.

6. Review the information on the Caution screen, then press ENTER to reprogram the system ROM. You can also press ESC to discontinue reprogramming and return to the Select An Image screen.

7. The message "Reprogramming Firmware" indicates that the system ROM is being reprogrammed. *Do not interrupt the reprogramming process, or the BIOS may be corrupted.* You'll be notified when reprogramming is complete.

8. When ROMPaq finishes reprogramming the system ROM, press ESC to exit the System ROMPaq utility.

9. Remove the System ROMPaq diskette and reboot the server by cycling the power (initiate a cold boot of the server).

10. If you have not installed your new option devices (i.e., the SmartArray 4250ES), you may do so now.

Using Options ROMPaq Diskettes

The Options ROMPaq updates the firmware in Compaq option devices (such as the Compaq Smart Array 4250ES). Since it is difficult to determine when the firmware needs to be updated, run the latest Options ROMPaq on all devices whenever updates are released. To run the Options ROMPaq diskette(s), follow these steps:

1. Place the Options ROMPaq diskette 1 in the server's diskette drive.

2. Boot the server by turning on the power.

3. Press ENTER at the Welcome screen.

4. In the Select A Device screen, select your desired device from the list of the programmable devices (such as ALL COMPAQ Smart Array 4250ES Array Controller(s)) and press ENTER.

5. If the firmware version in the selected device is the same or newer than that on the Options ROMPaq diskette, you will get the message "The ROM image files found for the device selected are not newer than the current ROM image." Press ENTER to skip the next three steps.

6. If the firmware version in the selected device is older than that on the Options ROMPaq diskette, you will see the Select An Image screen listing the device to reprogram, the current ROM version, and the new ROM version. Press ENTER.

7. Review the information on the Caution screen, then press ENTER to reprogram the system ROM. You can also press ESC to discontinue reprogramming and return to the Select An Image screen.

8. The message "Reprogramming Firmware" indicates that the option ROM is being reprogrammed. *Do not interrupt the reprogramming process, or the firmware may be corrupted.* You'll be notified when reprogramming is complete.

9. When ROMPaq finishes reprogramming the system ROM, press ESC to exit the Options ROMPaq utility.

10. Remove the Options ROMPaq diskette and reboot the server by cycling the power (initiate a cold boot of the server).

RAID Troubleshooting

RAID controllers and servers are generally regarded as some of the most reliable PC hardware available today, and the fault-tolerance features of most modern RAID controllers allow defective hard drives to be replaced without losing any data (often without even taking the server offline). However, disk arrays and controllers are not problem-free, and the steps taken immediately after a fault can have a profound impact on the integrity of your valuable data. This part of the chapter shows you how to recognize and deal with drive failures, then highlights the numerous problems that can occur with the RAID controller itself. The first step in recovering from a drive problem is to identify a drive problem in the first place. In most installations, a drive failure can be detected in several ways:

- The operating system (or network console) indicates a logical drive failure.

- An LED illuminates on failed drives in a hot-pluggable drive tray.

- An LED illuminates on the front of a server (such as a Compaq ProLiant server) if failed drives are inside (though other problems such as fan failure or overtemperature conditions will also cause this LED to illuminate).

- The server's power-on self test (POST) message lists failed drives whenever the system is restarted.

- The RAID controller's diagnostic (i.e., an array diagnostics utility, or ADU) lists all failed drives.

Problems such as reduced system performance or general disk errors reported by the operating system do not necessarily indicate that a drive has or has not been failed. If drive failures or repeated errors are suspected, run the array diagnostics.

HANDLING DRIVE FAULTS

The server informs you that a drive has failed. Depending on your level of fault tolerance, the network may (or may not) still be functioning. Still, you will have to take immediate corrective action to repair the fault and prevent further data loss. If your RAID controller is configured to support hardware fault tolerance, use these general steps to correct the trouble:

1. *Find the faulty drive.* While the operating system will typically report the logical drive failure, you will still need to determine which *physical* drive failed. With hot-pluggable drives in a server (such as a Compaq ProLiant system) or storage system, faults are indicated by an LED (i.e., an amber "Drive Failure LED" on each drive tray).

2. *Evaluate a server shutdown.* If the server containing the failed drive does not support hot-pluggable drives, perform a normal system shutdown of the server. If hot-pluggable drives are supported, you may not need to shut down the server.

3. *Replace the faulty drive.* Remove the failed drive and replace it with a drive that is of the same capacity. For hot-pluggable drives, the LEDs on the drive each light once in an alternating pattern to indicate that the connection was successful (after you secure the drive in the bay). The online LED blinks (if the server is so equipped) indicating that the controller recognized the drive replacement and began the recovery process.

4. *Restart the server.* Power up the server (if necessary).

5. *Allow the recovery to finish.* The RAID controller's firmware reconstructs the information on the new drive based on information from the remaining physical drives in the logical drive array. While reconstructing the data on hot-pluggable drives, the Online LED blinks. When drive rebuild is complete, the Online LED is illuminated.

In the event of a drive failure, the condition of the corresponding logical drive varies depending upon the fault-tolerance level used. Since a single array of physical drives can contain multiple logical drives with different fault-tolerance methods, the condition of each logical drive on the same array is not necessarily the same. If more drives are failed at any one time than the fault-tolerance level allows, fault tolerance is considered to be compromised and the condition of that logical drive can be referred to as "failed." If a logical volume is failed, all requests from the operating system to access that logical drive will be rejected with "unrecoverable" data errors. The system will respond to faults based on the RAID level that you have selected as shown here:

- **RAID 0 (Striping)**   Under RAID level 0, there is no fault tolerance, and your disk array cannot sustain any drive failures. If any physical drive in the array is failed, the condition of *all* non–fault-tolerant logical drives in the same array will also be failed. This is because data is striped across all drives in the array.

- **RAID 1 (Mirroring)**   This type of fault tolerance replaces the failed drive with the mirrored copy. Mirroring can sustain multiple drive failures (as long as failed drives are not mirrored to one another), so a RAID 1 drive will only be failed if the two failed drives are mirrored to one another. RAID 1 will attempt to rebuild data if a failed drive has been replaced, or if a spare drive kicks in to take the place of the defective drive.

- **Spare drives**   In the event of a drive failure, the spare drive acts as an immediate replacement for the failed drive (if a spare drive is assigned and available). Data is reconstructed automatically from the remaining drive(s) in the volume, and written to the spare drive using the automatic data recovery process. Once the spare drive is completely built, the logical drive again runs at full fault tolerance, and is able to sustain another subsequent drive failure. However, if another drive fails before the spare drive is completely built, the spare drive cannot prevent failure of the entire logical drive. Also note that it is possible for noncorrectable disk errors to prevent completion of the automatic data recovery process.

Drive Replacement Notes

As a rule, failed drives in hot-pluggable trays can be removed and replaced while host system and storage system power are both *on* (hot-pluggable drives can also be replaced when the power is *off*). However, *never* turn off an external storage system while the host system (server) power is on. This results in the failure of all drives in the storage system, which would likely compromise your fault tolerance. When a hot-pluggable drive is inserted, all disk activity on the controller is temporarily paused while the drive is spinning up (usually 20 seconds or so). If the drive is inserted into a fault-tolerant configuration while system power is on, the recovery of data on the replacement drive begins automatically (normally indicated by a blinking LED). Non-hot-pluggable drives should be replaced only while the system power is off.

Be sure to check the SCSI ID jumpers on all non-hot-pluggable drives to make sure that the correct drive is being replaced. Also verify that the SCSI ID jumpers are set to the same SCSI ID on the replacement drive. The SCSI ID jumpers may be located at different places on different drive models, but it is necessary that the SCSI ID on the replacement drive *always* be set to the same value as the original failed drive to prevent SCSI ID conflicts that could compromise the fault tolerance.

The capacity of replacement drives must be at least as large as the capacity of the other drives in the array—drives of insufficient capacity will be failed immediately by the controller without starting the automatic data recovery process.

Always replace a failed drive with a new or known-good replacement drive. In some cases, a drive that previously had been marked as failed by the controller may appear to be operational after the system is power-cycled, or after removal and reinsertion of a hot-pluggable drive. This practice is highly discouraged because the use of such marginal drives may eventually result in data loss.

ADR Notes

If a drive in a fault-tolerant configuration is replaced while the system power is *off*, the RAID controller displays a power-on self test (POST) message during the subsequent system startup. This indicates that the replacement drive has been detected, and that automatic data recovery (ADR) may need to be started. If ADR is not enabled, the logical drive remains in a "ready-to-recover" condition, and the same query appears at the next system restart.

Replacement drives are not considered to be online until ADR is complete. Any drives that are not yet online are treated as if they are failed when trying to determine whether fault tolerance will be compromised. For example, in a RAID 5 logical drive with no spare and one drive rebuilding, another drive failure at this time would result in a failure condition for the entire logical drive.

In general, the time required for a data rebuild is approximately 15 minutes per gigabyte (GB) of data. The actual rebuild time depends upon the rebuild priority set for the amount of I/O activity occurring during the rebuild operation, the disk drive speed, and the number of drives in the array (RAID 4 and RAID 5). In RAID 4 and RAID 5 configurations, the rebuild time varies from 10 minutes/GB for three drives to 20 minutes/GB for 14 drives (using 9GB Wide Ultra SCSI hard drives).

ADR Failures   If the online LED of the replacement drive stops blinking during ADR (and all other drives in the array are still online), the automatic data recovery process may have abnormally terminated due to a noncorrectable read error from another physical drive during the recovery process. Background autoreliability monitoring usually helps prevent this problem, but it cannot do anything about certain issues such as SCSI bus signal integrity problems. Reboot the system—a POST message should confirm the diagnosis. Retry ADR. If the trouble persists, a backup of all data on the system, surface analysis, and restore are recommended.

If the online LED of the replacement drive stops blinking during ADR and the replacement drive is failed (a failure LED lights or other LEDs go out), the replacement drive is producing unrecoverable disk errors. In this case, the replacement drive should be removed and replaced once again.

Handling Compromised Fault Tolerance

If fault tolerance is ever compromised due to failure of multiple drives, the condition of the logical drive will be failed and unrecoverable errors will be returned to the host system, and data loss will occur in most cases. Inserting replacement drives at this time will not improve the condition of the logical drive. If this occurs, try turning the entire system off and on. In some cases, an intermittent drive will appear to work again (perhaps long enough to make copies of important files) after cycling power.

Fault tolerance may be compromised due to nondrive problems such as a faulty cable, faulty storage system power supply, or a user accidentally turning off an external storage system while the host system power was on. In such cases, the physical drives do not need to be replaced, but data loss can occur (especially if the system was busy at the time the problem occurred). In cases of legitimate drive failures, replace any drives that have failed (once copies of important data have been made). After these (multiple) drives are replaced, the fault tolerance may again be compromised, power may need to be cycled, and you may need to re-create your partitions and restore all data from a backup.

Given the risk that fault tolerance may be compromised at some point in the future, always make regular backups of all logical drives.

REMOVING A RESERVED SECTOR

When any array is created using a RAID controller, a *reserved sector* is placed on each drive that belongs to the newly created array. This reserved sector allows the RAID controller to identify which drives belong to which array. The reserved sector also contains file allocation information that is needed for reading and writing to any array. The reserved sector can become corrupt or bad from time to time, causing any number of issues to arise, such as

■ An inability to partition or format a drive successfully.

■ The volume name is unreadable when attempting to remove a partition with FDISK—making it impossible to complete the removal.

■ Problems with reading/writing to the drives or array (such as fatal errors or data corruption).

■ The array constantly goes into Critical or Offline mode during a reboot.

■ Problems with rebuilding mirrored (RAID 1) and mirrored/striped (RAID 0+1) drives.

Removing the reserved sector will remedy most issues related directly to a "Bad Reserve Sector" error. The following steps outline the process for an IDE RAID controller such as a FastTrak 66/100:

Always perform a complete backup of the array before attempting to remove the reserved sector on a drive. When removing the reserved sector on drives that belong to any mirror, you should remove the sector from the mirrored drive first—remove the sector on the master drive only as a last resort. Finally, removing the sector from any striped drive will cause a nonfunctional array.

1. When the controller's BIOS banner comes up, press the required key combination to enter the controller's Setup utility (i.e., CTRL-F).

2. Select View Drive Assignments and highlight the suspect drive.

3. Opt to delete the reserved sector. A message will appear indicating that the reserved sector on the disk will be wiped. Press Y to confirm the deletion.

4. Repeat this for each member of the particular array that is having a problem.

5. When finished, reboot the system.

Now re-create the drive array, then partition and format it. You should be using FDISK and FORMAT to set up the array. Reload your data from a current backup.

HANDLING ERRORS

The firmware incorporated into most RAID controllers will execute an onboard POST process when the server initializes. If an error is encountered with the controller, the system will generate a corresponding POST code on the display, and you can use the code to quickly cross-reference the error. Table 11-2 lists the error codes for a typical RAID controller, and offers suggestions for corrective actions.

Always refer to the documentation for your specific RAID controller for detailed error code meanings and suggested solutions.

TABLE 11-2   INDEX OF TYPICAL RAID CONTROLLER POST CODES

MESSAGE	DESCRIPTION
1702. SCSI Cable Error Detected. System Halted.	This message indicates a termination or cabling problem with the server system board's integrated SCSI controller. Check the SCSI system termination, and replace the SCSI signal cable(s) if necessary.
1720. Slot "x" Drive Array—SMART Hard Drive Detects Imminent Failure SCSI: Port "y": SCSI ID "x".	The indicated drive has reported a SMART predictive-failure condition—the drive may fail at some time in the future. If this drive is part of a non-fault-tolerant configuration, back up all data before replacing the drive as soon as possible, and restore all data afterwards. If this drive is part of a fault-tolerant configuration, do not replace this drive unless all other drives in the array are online.
1722. Slot "x" Drive Array—Redundant Controller Pair Not Operating Redundantly.	This is usually due to incompatible RAID controller models, or the intercontroller communication has failed. In either case, the RAID controllers are not operating properly. In a redundant configuration, both controllers must be the *same* models. If they are, one of the controllers (or the motherboard) is defective and must be replaced, or the controllers are using dissimilar firmware versions that may need to be upgraded. Finally, the controller array accelerator cards may use different amounts of RAM. See that both controllers have the same accelerator installed when operating in Redundant mode.
1723. Slot "x" Drive Array—SCSI Connection Problem.	To improve signal integrity, internal SCSI connector should be removed if external drives are attached to the same SCSI port. Try detaching the internal SCSI port interface board from the RAID controller. Try replacing the dual-connector internal SCSI interface board with a single-connector internal SCSI interface board. Try moving the internal SCSI interface board to port 2 (with system power off). Try moving the external SCSI cable to port 2 (with power off).
1724. Slot "x" Drive Array—Physical Drive Position Changes(s) Detected.	This message indicates that the logical drive configuration has been updated automatically following physical drive position changes. You may have reinstalled one or more drives in the wrong locations, or assigned SCSI IDs improperly.
1726. Slot "x" Drive Array—Array Accelerator Memory Size Change Detected.	This message indicates that the array accelerator configuration has been updated automatically due to replacement of an array accelerator (or controller) with one having a different memory size. You may need to reconfigure the RAID controller with a suitable accelerator—especially when using matched RAID controllers.
1727. Slot "x" Drive Array—New Logical Drive(s) Attachment Detected.	If there are more than 32 logical drives, this message will be followed by "Auto-configuration failed: Too many logical drives." This message indicates that the controller has detected an additional array of drives that was attached when the power was off. The logical drive configuration information has been updated to add the new logical drives, but the maximum number of logical drives supported is 32—additional logical drives will not be added to the configuration.

TABLE 11-2	**INDEX OF TYPICAL RAID CONTROLLER POST CODES** *(CONTINUED)*
MESSAGE	**DESCRIPTION**
1729. Slot 1 Drive Array—Disk Consistency Initialization in Progress.	RAID 4 or 5 performance may be lower until autoreliability monitoring (ARM) has completed automatic background parity consistency initialization. This message is normal following the initial configuration of RAID 4 or RAID 5 logical drives. This POST error message will disappear (and performance of the controller will improve) after the parity data has been initialized by ARM.
1762. Redundant Controller Operation Is not Supported in this Firmware Version.	When you attempt to use two RAID controllers in the same system, both must have the same firmware version. Please remove the redundant RAID controller or upgrade the controller's firmware. The controller will remain disabled until this problem is resolved.
1763. The Array Accelerator Card Is Detached—Please Reattach.	The controller's daughter card is disconnected or defective. Reconnect or replace the accelerator. The RAID controller will remain disabled until this problem is resolved.
1764. Slot "x" Drive Array—Capacity Expansion Process Is Temporarily Disabled.	You cannot expand the disk array capacity. In most cases, the array accelerator has been disconnected or has failed. Check the accelerator installation, or replace the accelerator board. In other cases, the accelerator's backup battery has not fully charged, so the accelerator will be unavailable until the unit fully charges. Also, the expansion process may be interrupted until automatic data recovery (ADR) is completed. If the array accelerator has been removed, you must reinstall it for capacity expansion to continue.
1766. Slot "x" Drive Array Requires System ROM Upgrade.	Download and upgrade the server's BIOS to the latest version.
1768. Slot "x" Drive Array—Resuming Logical Drive Expansion Process.	This message appears whenever a controller reset or power cycle occurs while array expansion is in progress.
1769. Slot "x" Drive Array—Drive(s) Disabled Due to Failure During Expansion.	Data has been lost while expanding the array, so the drives have been temporarily disabled. The expansion process has been aborted due to unrecoverable drive errors or array accelerator errors. The array accelerator has failed or has been removed, and expansion progress data may have been lost. Acknowledge the data loss and reenable the logical drives, then restore data from a backup. If the array accelerator has failed, replace the accelerator board after the expansion process has terminated. Note: *Never* turn off the system and replace the array accelerator board while capacity expansion is in progress.
1774. Slot "x" Drive Array—Obsolete Data Found in Array Accelerator.	The data found in the accelerator was older than data found on the drives—obsolete data has been discarded. This occurs if drives have been disconnected, used on another controller, and then reconnected. You may need to clear the array accelerator, or reload data from backups.
1775. Slot "x" Drive Array—Storage System Not Responding.	Check the storage system's power switch and cables. Turn the system power off while checking the power and cable connections, then turn the system power back on. Remember that external drives must all be powered up before (or at the same time as) the main system.

TABLE 11-2 INDEX OF TYPICAL RAID CONTROLLER POST CODES *(CONTINUED)*

MESSAGE	DESCRIPTION
1776. Slot "x" Drive Array—SCSI Bus Termination Error.	Internal and external drives cannot be attached to the same SCSI port simultaneously. The internal and external connectors of the specified SCSI port(s) are both attached to drives. However, the SCSI bus is not properly terminated when internal and external drives are attached concurrently to the same SCSI bus. The indicated SCSI bus is disabled until this problem is resolved. Turn off the server's power and check the cabling and termination at the specified SCSI port.
1777. Slot "x" Drive Array—Server Storage Enclosure Problem Detected.	A serious fault has occurred with the server chassis management, and you may see additional error messages, such as *Cooling Fan Malfunction Detected *Overheated Condition Detected *Side-Panel Must Be Closed to Prevent Overheating *Redundant Power Supply Malfunction Detected *Wide SCSI Transfer Failed SCSI Port "y": Interrupt Signal Inoperative Check the cooling fan's operation by placing your hand over the fan. Check the internal plenum cooling fan in tower servers or storage systems. If the fan is not operating, check for obstructions and check all internal connectors. Replace the server unit's side panel if removed. Suspect a power issue. If the server storage system's power LED is amber instead of green, this indicates a redundant power supply failure. Check SCSI cables. If the message indicates a SCSI cable problem, refer to the cabling information that accompanied your server. If the routing is correct, replace cables on the specified port until the POST message is eliminated.
1778. Slot "x" Drive Array Resuming Automatic Data Recovery Process.	No action is required on your part. This message appears when the RAID controller resets (or power cycles) while automatic data recovery (ADR) is in progress.
1779. Slot "x" Drive Array—Replacement Drive(s) Detected or Previously Failed Drive(s) Now Appear to Be Operational: Port "y": SCSI ID "x".	This message appears once immediately following drive replacement, and before data is restored from backup. Restore data from backup once the replacement drive x has been installed. If this message appears and drive x (identified by its SCSI ID) has *not* been replaced, this indicates an intermittent drive failure. Check your drive power and signal cabling.
1783. Slot "x" Drive Array Controller Failure.	If this message appears immediately following a ROM installation, the ROM is defective or not installed properly. Check to see if the array accelerator board is attached properly, and check that the RAID controller is firmly inserted in its slot. Try upgrading the system ROMs. Otherwise, replace the RAID controller outright.
1784. Slot "x" Drive Array Drive Failure: SCSI Port "y" SCSI ID "x".	The indicated SCSI drive(s) should be replaced. Check for loose power and signal cables first. Replace defective drive x and/or cable(s).

TABLE 11-2   INDEX OF TYPICAL RAID CONTROLLER POST CODES *(CONTINUED)*

MESSAGE	DESCRIPTION
1785. Slot 1 Drive Array Not Configured.	There are numerous possible issues that can cause this error, so check each issue carefully before taking corrective action: *Run the RAID controller's array configuration utility to configure the controller properly. *No drives detected. Turn off the system and check all SCSI cable connections to make sure drives are attached properly. *Array accelerator memory size increased. Run the server's configuration utility. *External cable(s) attached to wrong SCSI port connector(s). Turn the system power off and swap the SCSI port connectors to prevent data loss. *Drive positions cannot be changed during capacity expansion. Turn the system power off and move the drives to their original positions (run the drive array's advanced diagnostics if previous positions are unknown). *Drive positions appear to have changed. To avoid data loss, turn system power off and reattach the drives to the original controller. *Configuration information indicates drive positions beyond the capability of this controller. This may be due to drive movement from a controller that supports more drives than the current controller. *Configuration information indicates that drives were configured on a controller with a newer firmware version. To avoid data loss, reattach drives to the original controller or upgrade controller firmware to the version on the original controller.
1786. Slot "x" Drive Array Recovery Needed: SCSI Port "y": SCSI ID "x". or Slot "x" Drive Array Recovery Needed. Automatic Data Recovery Previously Aborted: SCSI Port "y": SCSI ID "x".	The indicated SCSI drive(s) need automatic data recovery (ADR). You may continue with the recovery of data to the drive, or continue without data recovery. The indicated SCSI drive(s) need ADR. You can normally choose to retry ADR or start without ADR. This message normally appears when a drive was replaced in a fault-tolerant configuration with system power off. In this case, you can elect to start the ADR process. The "previously aborted" version of the 1786 POST message will appear if the previous rebuild attempt was aborted for any reason (run the array diagnostics utility for more information). If the replacement drive was failed, try using another replacement drive. If the rebuild was aborted due to a read error from another physical drive in the array, you'll need to back up all readable data on the array, run a diagnostic surface analysis, and then restore your data.
1787. Slot "x" Drive Array Operating in Interim Recovery Mode: SCSI Port "y": SCSI ID "x".	The indicated SCSI drive(s) should be replaced. Following a system restart, this message reminds you that drive x is defective, and fault tolerance is being used. Drive x needs replacement as soon as possible—a loose or defective cable may also cause this error.

TABLE 11-2 INDEX OF TYPICAL RAID CONTROLLER POST CODES *(CONTINUED)*

MESSAGE	DESCRIPTION
1788. Slot "x" Drive Array Reports Incorrect Drive Replacement: SCSI Port "y": SCSI ID "x".	The indicated SCSI drive(s) should have been replaced, or the drives were installed in the wrong place, so they have been disabled. Reinstall the drives correctly. You can elect to continue (the drive array will remain disabled) or elect to reset the configuration (all data will be lost). Run the array diagnostic for more information. Error 1788 might also be displayed due to a bad power cable connection at the drive or a defective SCSI cable. If this message was due to a faulty power connection, repair the connection and continue. If this message was not due to a bad power cable and the drive was not replaced, this could indicate a defective SCSI cable.
1789. Slot "x" Drive Array Physical Drive(s) Not Responding: SCSI Port (y): SCSI ID (x).	This message indicates that previously operating drives are missing (or inoperative) following a cold or warm reset. Check your cables or replace the indicated drive(s). You can elect to continue and the drive array will remain disabled, or elect to fail the drives that are not responding—interim recovery mode will be enabled if the array is configured for fault tolerance. Turn off the system and check your cable connections. If the cables are connected, replace the drive.
1792. Slot "x" Valid Data Found in Array Accelerator.	Data is automatically written to the drive array. Power was interrupted while the system was in use, or the system was restarted while data was in the array accelerator memory. Power was then restored within an acceptable period, and data in the accelerator was flushed to the drive array safely.
1793. Slot "x" Drive Array—Array Accelerator Battery Depleted.	Data in array accelerator has been lost (error message 1794 also appears). While the system was in use, power was interrupted while data was in the array accelerator memory. Power was *not* restored within four days, and data in the array accelerator was lost. Check all array files for potential data corruption.
1794. Slot "x" Drive Array—Array Accelerator Battery Charge Low.	The array accelerator is temporarily disabled. The battery charge is below 90 percent, and posted writes are disabled. When the batteries are fully charged, the array accelerator will automatically be reenabled, and this POST message will be discontinued. Replace the array accelerator or the RAID controller if those backup batteries do not recharge within 36 (power-on) hours.
1795. Slot "x" Drive Array—Array Accelerator Configuration Error.	The data stored in the array accelerator does not correspond to this drive array, and the array accelerator is temporarily disabled. Match the array accelerator to the correct drive array, or run the RAID controller's configuration utility to clear data in the array accelerator.
1796. Slot "x" Drive Array—Array Accelerator Is not responding.	The array accelerator is temporarily disabled, and is not responding. Replace the array accelerator or the RAID controller.
1797. Slot "x" Drive Array—Array Accelerator Read Error Occurred.	Data in the array accelerator has been lost, and the accelerator is disabled. Replace the array accelerator or the RAID controller to correct the error, and then restore your data from backup.

TABLE 11-2 INDEX OF TYPICAL RAID CONTROLLER POST CODES *(CONTINUED)*	
MESSAGE	**DESCRIPTION**
1798. Slot "x" Drive Array—Array Accelerator Write Error Occurred.	The array accelerator is disabled due to a write error. Replace the array accelerator or the RAID controller to correct the error.
1799. Slot "x" Drive Array—Drive(s) Disabled Due to Array Accelerator Data Loss.	Data stored in the array accelerator has been lost, so the drives have been temporarily disabled. Elect to continue with your logical drives disabled, or elect to accept data loss and reenable logical drives. Restore any lost data from your backup.

SYMPTOMS

In addition to the general RAID troubleshooting guidelines presented above, you may encounter specific problems. This part of the chapter highlights many of the common symptoms that occur with RAID installations.

SYMPTOM 11-1   **The system hangs when scanning for SCSI RAID devices.**   In most cases, this indicates a problem with SCSI termination (which is required at both ends of the SCSI bus). The SCSI bus must be properly terminated at both ends so that commands and data can be transmitted between devices on the bus. Recheck the termination on your SCSI bus and see that only the ends of the chain are terminated (i.e., the RAID controller card and the last SCSI drive). Also, recheck all cabling to verify that cables are connected securely, and try a new high-quality SCSI cable. In addition, each SCSI device must have a unique SCSI ID. Devices that are "missing" may be incorrectly sharing IDs with other devices. Check each drive and see that they are all assigned a unique ID (usually starting with ID0).

SYMPTOM 11-2   **The system fails to boot after installing the RAID controller.**   There are numerous possible problems that can prevent the system from starting, but this is almost always due to an error or oversight during controller installation:

■ *Check the basics.* Always start by checking system power, then see that all cables (especially SCSI drive cables) and other devices in the server are securely installed.

■ *Verify the installation.* Remove and recheck the controller and see that it has been configured, installed, and connected according to the manufacturer's instructions. You may need to configure the server and run configuration software in order to fully configure the controller in the server.

■ *Try a minimal system.* Remove all components except minimal memory and a processor (and processor termination card in multiprocessor systems) and reboot. Check individual components (especially processors and memory) in a known-good system (if possible).

■ *Check the processors.* See that all processors have been properly installed. If only one processor is in use on a multiprocessor motherboard, see that the processor "termination card" is fully seated.

■ *Check the memory.* See that all DIMMs are securely installed, and that they are fully compatible with the motherboard. For example, you can check for memory that has been tested on the Intel L440GX+ memory module at **support.intel.com/support/motherboards/server/L440GX/compat.htm**.

■ *Check the "array accelerator" memory.* See that the proper RAM has been installed in your RAID cache (aka "array accelerator") module. For example, the Mylex AcceleRAID 250 controller uses EDO cache memory.

SYMPTOM 11-3   **The system cannot spin all RAID drives at once.**   Hard drives consume a lot of power, and a large RAID system can easily overload a power supply if many drives try to spin simultaneously (especially at power-up). If your RAID drives are not spinning properly—and possibly causing boot problems—check the RAID controller's setup and configure the RAID system to spin fewer drives, or spin drives only when needed. In some cases, you may need to install a second power supply to accommodate the needs of many RAID drives (the server chassis and RAID system must accommodate such an arrangement).

SYMPTOM 11-4   **When a RAID controller is installed, you encounter an error such as "BIOS Not Installed".**   Always start by checking your attached hard drives—this error will appear normally if there are no drives attached (or are configured improperly). In most cases, the problem is related to an incompatibility with the host system. In order for a current PCI RAID controller to function, the host system must support version 2.1 (or later) PCI bus slots with bus-mastering capability, and a current BIOS that supports bus mastering. Check the specifications for the host system or motherboard and verify the compatibility of the system. If the hardware meets all requirements, check to see if a motherboard BIOS upgrade is available from the system maker.

SYMPTOM 11-5   **You have trouble working with an IDE RAID controller.**   You may encounter this type of trouble with IDE controllers such as the FastTrak100. In most cases, the problem is an old firmware version. The FastTrak 100 is known to have this trouble when using driver version 1.20 or earlier. You should upgrade to the latest BIOS and driver versions. For the FastTrak 100, you'd upgrade to the 1.30 driver and BIOS version 1.20 (or higher) at **www.promise.com**.

SYMPTOM 11-6   **An array created by the RAID Configuration Utility uses too many drives.**   The RAID Configuration Utility is designed to create your first RAID volume. It automatically creates an array using up to eight available disks, and places a volume on the array. If you would like a certain number of disks to be excluded from the first array, then mark the disk(s) as *spare* in the RAID Configuration Utility (or disable the disks in the system by disconnecting them from the SCSI controller and power supply). Once you have created a volume on the remaining disks using RAID Configuration Utility, you may bring additional disks online and configure them with the RAID controller's management software.

SYMPTOM 11-7   **The RAID SCSI boot device cannot be found.**   This is normally an issue with the server's setup. Enter the system CMOS Setup utility and configure the server so that the RAID volume is selected as the primary boot device (or first in the boot device list). If the RAID controller card is physically moved from one PCI slot to another and the boot device is a RAID volume controlled by the RAID card, some systems will automatically reconfigure some system BIOS settings (such as the boot device order). This issue is related to how the system BIOS operates and may not occur with all systems.

SYMPTOM 11-8   **You cannot boot from an IDE-type RAID controller.**   Even when the RAID controller is installed and recognized properly, you may not be able to boot from the controller due to incorrect boot order, an undefined array, an improperly selected array, or an incorrect CMOS Setup entry. Always make sure that you have an array defined. If the array is defined, there is an option in the controller's BIOS to make the array bootable. Make sure the array that you are using is set as the "boot array." For controllers such as the FastTrak 100, this is denoted with an asterisk next to the array number in the FastBuild utility. If your array does not have an asterisk next to it, highlight the array and press the SPACEBAR to make that array the boot array. If your array is already set as a bootable array, you will need to check the CMOS Setup of your host computer and ensure that your "Disk Drive Sequence" assigns the "System BIOS Boot Devices" first and the "FastTrak RAID Controller" second. Also verify that the boot sequence includes drive C:.

SYMPTOM 11-9   **You find that a particular hard drive constantly forces an array to be rebuilt or remain offline.**   This is almost always a cabling problem or a drive fault. For example, the SCSI cable may be bad. Swap the cable and the suspect drive to another channel (i.e., move the cable and hard drive from channel 2 to channel 3). If the move corrects the problem, the first channel could be bad—replace the RAID controller. Otherwise, the cable may be bad—replace the cable. If the problem persists, try replacing the hard drive outright.

SYMPTOM 11-10   **You cannot locate all of the drives connected to the RAID controller.** In most cases, this indicates a problem with SCSI termination (which is required at both ends of the SCSI bus). The SCSI bus must be properly terminated at both ends so that commands and data can be transmitted to and from all devices on the bus. Recheck the termination on your SCSI bus and see that only the ends of the chain are terminated (i.e., the RAID controller card and the last SCSI drive). Also, recheck all cabling to verify that cables are connected securely.

Each SCSI device must have a unique SCSI ID. Devices that are "missing" may be incorrectly sharing IDs with other devices. Check each drive and see that they are all assigned a unique ID (usually starting with ID0). Finally, verify that only acceptable drives are connected to the RAID controller's SCSI bus. For example, CD-ROM or tape drives are often valid SCSI devices, but are prohibited from a SCSI RAID bus because of their slow data transfer times—at best, you may see poor RAID system performance. Make sure that only high-performance hard drives are on the RAID SCSI bus. If the RAID controller offers a separate SCSI bus for other devices, you may connect CD-ROM, tape, or other drives there.

SYMPTOM 11-11   **You find that UDMA drives appear to fall off the array at random.** You generally notice this behavior with the fastest Ultra-DMA/66 or Ultra-DMA/100 drives. In most cases, the RAID controller is not fully compliant with UDMA 66/100 standards, and cannot reliably support the drives at their top data transfer speeds. You may need to upgrade the RAID controller (or its BIOS version) to improve UDMA support. As a workaround, you can disable the UDMA 66/100 mode in your array drive(s)—this can usually be accomplished using a utility from the drive manufacturer.

SYMPTOM 11-12   **A drive in the array seems to fail frequently.**   In most cases, you may see this as a logical failure requiring you to rebuild the drive (typically resulting in poor storage system performance during rebuild processes). Recheck the drive and see that it's cabled securely, and try installing a new high-quality cable. If the problem continues, replace the drive outright. Be sure to match the new drive to the other drives in the array.

SYMPTOM 11-13   **The video card is not working properly even though it is sharing resources with the RAID controller.**   This is usually due to a resource conflict. Virtually all RAID controllers are fully PnP compliant, so the resources assigned to various devices are determined by the PnP BIOS on the motherboard. Most controllers will support PCI IRQ sharing, but this will not work unless *all* the concerned devices support IRQ sharing. If your motherboard allows you to control the assignment of these resources, you may be able to remedy the problem by manually adjusting the resource assignments. You can also try resetting/clearing the "PnP Configuration" entry in the CMOS Setup. If the setting is disabled, set it to "enabled," then save your changes and reboot the system. Otherwise, switch the PCI slot that the controller card is in—reinstall the controller in a lower-priority slot.

SYMPTOM 11-14   **The server will not boot from the support CD.**   After installing the RAID controller, you find that the server will not start from the motherboard's software CD. Try the following:

■ *Check the boot order.* The BIOS boot priority order may be set incorrectly. Start the server's CMOS Setup routine (the server's "configuration utility") and set the boot order so that the CD-ROM drive appears first in the order. Save your changes and reboot the server.

■ *Check the controller's configuration.* For most RAID controllers, the onboard BIOS must be enabled, and its "CD-ROM boot" feature must be enabled. You may need to access the controller's setup routine (i.e., ALT-M during boot) and see that these items are configured correctly.

SYMPTOM 11-15   **The RAID controller reports a disk array at a much smaller capacity.** For example, the Promise SuperTrak Pro's SuperBuild BIOS utility is known to report the capacity of Maxtor 40GB drives to be only between 5GB and 7GB in size. In virtually every case, this type of reporting problem is due to a fault in the RAID controller's firmware and utility software. Contact the controller maker for updated firmware and software. For the SuperTrack Pro, the problem is with BIOS version 1.0 build 4 and the Promise RAID ISM version b146. This problem has been resolved by updating the Promise RAID ISM version to b156, and updating the firmware from **support.promise.com/Support/Default.htm**.

SYMPTOM 11-16   **You experience lower than expected data transfer rates with the RAID controller.**   In virtually all cases, poor data transfer performance is caused by PCI bus latency between the RAID controller and another high-bandwidth device (such as a video capture card). For example, you may notice dropped frames when capturing video on a RAID system. If you can identify the device that is demanding the additional bandwidth, you can disable or adjust the device's performance in order to free additional bandwidth on the PCI bus for the RAID controller—or remove the contending device entirely. Otherwise, you may need to adjust the RAID controller's PCI utilization (if possible), which will almost always impair the disk array's overall performance.

SYMPTOM 11-17   **You encounter problems when the system attempts to use a "hot spare" or "hot swap" drive.**   In many cases, you may experience problems such as the rebuild process freezing, or the disk array management utility (such as FastCheck for the Promise FastTrak 66/100) cannot recognize failed or newly installed drives. Try the following:

■ *Check the firmware.* Make sure that you're using the very latest firmware version for your RAID controller.

■ *Check the drivers and software.* Make sure that you've installed the very latest drivers and utility software for your RAID controller on your particular operating system. Update the drivers and software if necessary.

■ *Eliminate background software.* Reduce of the number of additional programs running in the background that might interfere with the RAID disk checking utility.

■ *Check the drive.* Verify that the suspect drive is *good* by testing it on another controller and/or computer.

■ *Remove the reserved sector.* You may need to remove the "reserved sector" from your suspect hard drive, and allow the system to redetect and reinstall the drive. Remember that removing the "reserved" sector of an array disk will destroy all data on that disk, so perform a complete system backup first.

SYMPTOM 11-18   **You have trouble partitioning and formatting a disk array when a SCSI controller is also present in the system.**   You may see indications of "bad capacity", bad reserved sectors, or other boot or operating system issues. If you have a SCSI drive controller in the system, the computer will attempt to boot from whichever controller is "seen" first. For one controller to be identified before another, you must get its BIOS to load *first*. Manipulating the BIOS address that the card is set to use will normally do this. For fully PnP controllers (such as the FastTrak 100), however, only the PnP BIOS on the motherboard can control which resources a card uses. The PCI slot with the *highest* priority (normally PCI slot 1) will be assigned to the *lowest* BIOS address—and load first—so you may need to shuffle expansion cards so that the RAID controller is located in the higher-priority slot. Some CMOS Setup utilities support "Scan Order Toggles" that dictate how the PCI slots and onboard devices are scanned for bootable devices. In other cases, you may be able to clear the trouble by changing the "boot order" in the system's CMOS Setup so that "SCSI" is *after* C: or your RAID disk array.

SYMPTOM 11-19   **You encounter data corruption or disk lockups during array access.** You may also notice this when partitioning or formatting the array. There are several possible issues that you should be aware of:

■ *Check your cables.* The drive signal cables may be faulty or attached improperly. Recheck the connections and replace the signal cables if necessary.

■ *Check the CMOS Setup.* Recheck the CMOS Setup and verify that the motherboard clock and PCI bus clocks are running within acceptable levels. For example, overclocking a motherboard can result in higher PCI bus rates, and this may result in data errors at the RAID controller. Try restoring "BIOS Defaults" in the CMOS Setup.

■ *Check the RAID memory.* The memory (aka "array accelerator") on the RAID controller may be faulty. Verify that the memory on the RAID controller is appropriate and installed properly. Replace the memory module on the RAID controller. Try memory from another recommended manufacturer.

■ *Install the chipset drivers.* Most modern motherboards require drivers in order to manage advanced features such as bus mastering or AGP support. Be sure that you install the latest version of your motherboard drivers (i.e., the VIA "4-in-1" drivers for VIA based motherboards).

SYMPTOM 11-20   **You receive errors when copying files to a server experiencing disk stress.**   This is known to occur under Windows 2000 and Windows NT when you perform a large amount of network file transfers to a server, and is usually designated as "Error 3013", such as

```
Error 3013, The redirector has timed out to <servername>
```

These redirector timeouts may cause write operations to a server to be unsuccessful. While there are many causes of redirector timeout errors, this error typically occurs because of a cache manager problem when you write large files to disk on a computer that has a large amount of memory. The available bandwidth to the disk is less than what is required by the writer to finish its task in one cycle, so the writer may end up holding file resources for very long periods of time. The write operation takes too long to finish the operation, and the client redirector finally times out. This problem is mostly encountered when you use Windows NT 4.0 clients to connect to a server running Windows 2000, and the server is using RAID that slows down disk throughput—such as RAID 5 (striping with parity). To resolve this problem, obtain the latest service pack for Windows 2000 and/or Windows NT.

SYMPTOM 11-21   **You encounter an error such as "Scanning PCI bus mechanism #2".** This type of error often occurs when booting with a Windows 98 CD boot disk (i.e., preparing for a clean install of Windows NT 4.0 or Windows 2000). This is almost always a resource assignment error, and this problem occurs when certain resources are assigned to the RAID controller by the system BIOS. You should check with the RAID controller manufacturer and see if there are any suggested resource assignments or workarounds available. For example, this is a known issue with the Promise SuperTrak Pro, and a workaround is listed at **support.promise.com/techsupport/trouble/scanning_pci_bus_using_Mechanism_2.htm**.

SYMPTOM 11-22   **The OS won't load after installing a RAID adapter.**   This is almost always a server hardware configuration issue (not an OS driver problem). Check the system's CMOS Setup for PCI interrupt assignments and verify that a unique interrupt is assigned for RAID controller—the controller should not be sharing IRQs with other devices. You may also try moving the RAID controller to a higher-priority PCI slot. In some cases, you may need to initialize and configure the drive array before installing the operating system.

SYMPTOM 11-23   **You receive an FTDISK internal error when starting Windows NT/2000.**   If your primary operating system drive fails (or goes offline) while in a RAID 1 "mirrored" configuration, Windows NT/2000 continues to run from the mirrored drive, and flags the registry on the current drive to reflect the "broken mirror" condition. When you try to restart Windows NT/2000, you'll see an error such as

```
STOP: 0x00000058 FTDISK_INTERNAL_ERROR
```

Windows NT/2000 uses this protection scheme because processing continued on the mirrored drive while the primary drive was offline—any data saved to the mirrored drive would be lost if you were to boot from the primary drive again. Use the following steps to prevent data loss:

1. Use a Windows Fault Tolerance boot diskette to boot from the mirrored (secondary) system drive.

2. Run Disk Administrator. You'll see that the primary operating system disk partition is red (indicating that the mirror is "broken"). The primary drive will show the drive letter C:—it must be changed to a new drive letter by "breaking the mirror." Highlight the partition, select Fault Tolerance, and choose Break Mirror. On the Partition menu, click Commit Changes Now.

3. Once the mirror is successfully "broken" and you have two separate partitions, complete a tape backup of the mirrored drive that you're running from—this is the most current data you have, and contains all the information saved since the primary operating system drive failed.

4. Mark as active the primary partition on the secondary drive (a reboot may be required).

5. Delete the primary drive partition so you can remirror the current operating system back to the primary drive. Select the primary drive partition and click Delete on the Partition menu. On the Partition menu, click Commit Changes Now.

 If the entire C: drive was mirrored (and does not have another primary partition to mark "active"), Disk Administrator may not allow you to delete the active partition. Moving the drive to a secondary nonbootable drive position (i.e., SCSI ID 1 or higher, or slave IDE drive) should allow you to delete the primary partition. Alternatively, you can use Norton Utilities Disk Editor (**DISKEDIT.EXE**) to remove the boot flag from the partition table manually.

6. Remirror the drives. Highlight the current operating system drive partition and, while holding down the CTRL key, highlight the free space created in step 5 above. Click Establish Mirror on the Fault Tolerance menu. On the Partition menu, click Commit Changes Now.

7. Verify that the mirror is established by exiting and restarting Disk Administrator to check on the status of the mirror.

8. Once this mirror is successfully established, you have the most current data on the primary disk—unfortunately, you cannot reboot from the primary disk now because it is only a mirror. Rebreak the mirror again as shown in step 2 above.

9. Once the mirror is broken again, mark the partition "active" if it is the primary boot partition.

10. Perform a normal shutdown, and reboot from your primary operating system drive. Once Windows is running, delete the partition and reestablish the mirror to restore your fault-tolerant RAID 1 configuration.

SYMPTOM 11-24 **You have trouble with the "Standby" mode when using certain RAID controllers.** Some RAID controllers (such as the Mylex DAC960) do not properly recover when the Windows 2000 host computer returns from its "Standby" mode. This is due to issues with the particular RAID controller, which is not fully ACPI compliant. To correct this problem, update the RAID controller's BIOS (and possibly its drivers), replace the RAID controller with an ACPI-compliant model, or disable the host computer's "Standby" mode.

Further Study

Adaptec: **www.adaptec.com**
Compaq: **www.compaq.com**
Gateway: **www.gateway.com**
Intel: **www.intel.com**
Promise: **www.promise.com**
Tekram: **www.tekram.com**

12

SCSI ADAPTERS AND TROUBLESHOOTING

Network servers and high-performance workstations depend on a fast, reliable storage subsystem that can handle a large mix of diverse drives without the need for multiple controllers. The *small-computer system interface* (or SCSI) was introduced around 1986, and has emerged as the premier interface for servers and other demanding PC storage applications. A system fitted with a single typical SCSI adapter can support up to seven unique SCSI devices simultaneously—all daisy-chained to a single cable. A modern server with a current SCSI host adapter (such as the Adaptec 39160 host adapter in Figure 12-1) can handle up to 30 SCSI devices on two independent controller channels capable of 160 Mbps data transfers. This chapter provides an overview of SCSI technology and hardware, covers typical hardware and software installation, and outlines the solutions for many common SCSI problems.

FIGURE 12-1   An Adaptec 39160 dual-channel Ultra160 SCSI adapter
(Courtesy of Adaptec)

Understanding SCSI Concepts

Ideally, peripheral devices should be *independent* of the microprocessor's operation. The computer should only have to send commands and data to the peripheral, and wait for the peripheral to respond (printers work this way). The parallel and serial ports are actually *device-level* interfaces. The computer is unconcerned with what device is attached to the port. In other words, you can take a printer built 12 years ago and connect it to a new AMD Athlon-based system, and the printer will work just fine because only data and commands are being sent across the interface. Very simply put, this is the concept behind SCSI. Computers and peripherals can be designed, developed, and integrated without worrying about hardware compatibility—such compatibility is established entirely by the SCSI interface.

From a practical standpoint, SCSI is a *bus* and a *command set*. The bus is an organization of physical wires and terminations where each wire has its own name and purpose. The command set is a limited set of instructions that allow the computer and peripherals to communicate over that physical bus. The SCSI bus is used in systems that want to achieve device independence. For example, all hard disk drives look alike to the SCSI interface (except for their total capacity), all optical drives look alike, all printers look alike, and so on. For any particular type of SCSI device, you should be able to replace an existing device with another device without any system modifications, and new SCSI devices can often be added to the bus with little more than a driver upgrade. Since the intelligence of SCSI resides in the peripheral device itself and not in the computer, the computer is capable of employing a small set of standard commands to accomplish data transfer back and forth to the peripheral.

SCSI VARIATIONS

At this point, let's take a look at the evolution of the SCSI interface, and examine the ways in which it has evolved and proliferated. SCSI began life in 1979 when Shugart Associates (PC old-timers might remember them as one of the first PC hard drive makers) released their Shugart Associates Systems Interface (or SASI) standard. The X3T9.2 committee was formed by ANSI in 1982 to develop the SASI standard (later renamed SCSI because ANSI won't name a standard after a product). SCSI drives and interfaces that were developed under the evolving X3T9.2 SCSI standard were known as SCSI-1, though the actual SCSI-1 standard (ANSI X3.131-1986) didn't become official until 1986. SCSI-1 provided a system-level 8-bit bus (referred to as "narrow") that could operate up to eight devices and transfer data at up to 5 MB/s. However, the delay in standardization led to a lot of configuration and compatibility problems with SCSI-1 setups. Table 12-1 compares the specifications of each SCSI standard.

Although SCSI-1 was supposed to support all SCSI devices, manufacturers took liberties with the evolving standard. This frequently led to installation and compatibility problems between SCSI-1 devices that should theoretically have worked together perfectly. Today, all obsolete SCSI-1 adapters should be upgraded to SCSI-3 installations.

Earlier in 1986 (even before the SCSI-1 standard was ratified), work started on the SCSI-2 standard that was intended to overcome many of the speed and compatibility problems encountered with SCSI-1. By 1994, ANSI blessed the SCSI-2 standard (X3.131-1994). SCSI-2 was designed to be backward compatible with SCSI-1, but SCSI-2 also provided for several variations. *Fast SCSI-2* (Fast SCSI) doubles the SCSI bus clock speed and allows 10-MB/s data transfers across the 8-bit SCSI data bus. *Wide SCSI-2* (Wide SCSI) also doubles the original data transfer rate to 10 MB/s by using a 16-bit data bus instead of the original 8-bit data bus (the SCSI clock is left unchanged). To support the larger data bus, Wide SCSI uses a 68-pin cable instead of the traditional 50-pin cable. Wide SCSI can also support up to 16 SCSI devices. Designers then combined the attributes of fast and wide operation to create Fast Wide SCSI-2 (Fast Wide SCSI), which supports 20MB/s data transfers across a 16-bit data bus. Whenever you see ref erences to Fast SCSI, Wide SCSI, or Fast Wide SCSI, you're *always* dealing with a SCSI-2 implementation.

But SCSI advancement hasn't stopped there. ANSI began development of the SCSI-3 standard in 1993 (even before SCSI-2 was adopted). SCSI-3 is intended to be backward compatible with SCSI-2 and SCSI-1

TABLE 12-1   COMPARISON OF COMMON SCSI FEATURES

TERMS	NAME	MHZ	BUS WIDTH	MB/S	MB/S
SCSI-1	SCSI-1	5	8	5	40
Fast SCSI	SCSI-2	10	8	10	80
Fast-Wide SCSI	SCSI-2/ SCSI-3	10	16	20	160
Ultra SCSI	SCSI-3	20	8	20	160
Ultra-Wide SCSI	SCSI-3	20	16	40	320
Ultra2 SCSI	SCSI-4	40	8	40	320
Ultra2-Wide SCSI	SCSI-4	40	16	80	640
Ultra3 SCSI	Ultra 160	40*2[1]	8	80	640
Ultra3-Wide SCSI	Ultra 160	40*2[1]	16	160	1,280
Ultra4 SCSI	Ultra 320	Undefined			
Ultra4-Wide SCSI	Ultra 320	Undefined			

1. Ultra3 features the same base frequency as Ultra2 (40MHz), but transmits 2 bytes per data clock, thus doubling the total throughput.

devices, and there are many SCSI devices and controllers that are making use of the advances offered by SCSI-3 development. These typical SCSI-3 devices are generally known as Fast-20 SCSI (or Ultra SCSI-3, also termed Ultra-SCSI). Ultra-SCSI uses a 20-MHz SCSI bus clock with an 8-bit data bus to achieve 20-MB/s data transfers. By using a 16-bit data bus, SCSI-3 offers Wide Fast-20 SCSI (or Ultra Wide SCSI-3, also termed Ultra Wide SCSI), which handles 40-MB/s data transfers. SCSI development continued with the SCSI-4 implementations. The SCSI-4 standard covers Fast-40 SCSI (called Ultra2 SCSI-4 and Ultra2 SCSI) using a 40-MHz bus clock to provide 40-MB/s data transfers with an 8-bit data bus. The 16-bit data bus version is known as Wide Fast-40 SCSI (called Ultra2 Wide SCSI-4, or Ultra2 Wide SCSI), which is supposed to support 80-MB/s data transfers. Whenever you see references to Ultra2 or Fast-40, you're almost certain to be faced with a SCSI-4 setup.

But SCSI advances have not stopped there. The Ultra3 SCSI standard (known as Ultra160) employs a 40-MHz bus clock that is "double transitioned." This allows twice the effective data transfer on the same 40-MHz clock, yielding data transfers up to 80 MB/s. The Ultra3 Wide SCSI standard offers 16 data bits rather than 8. On the same double-transitioned 40-MHz clock, Ultra3 Wide SCSI can achieve data transfers up to 160 MB/s. While Ultra360 (Ultra4) SCSI standards have not yet been fully defined, you can be sure that even faster SCSI implementations are on the horizon. Also keep in mind that SCSI has traditionally been a *parallel* bus—that is, 8 or 16 bits of data are transferred at a time across parallel data lines. SCSI-3 is proposing three new *serial* connection schemes. You'll see these noted as Serial Storage Architecture (SSA), Fibre Channel, and IEEE 1394 (called Fire Wire). These serial schemes will offer faster data transfers than their parallel bus cousins, but are *not* backward compatible with SCSI-2 or SCSI-1.

SINGLE-ENDED AND DIFFERENTIAL

The signal wiring used in a SCSI bus has a definite impact on bus performance. There are two generally used wiring techniques for SCSI: single-ended and differential. Both wiring schemes have advantages and disadvantages.

The *single-ended* (SE) wiring technique is just as the name implies—a single wire carries the particular signal from initiator to target. Each signal requires only one wire. Terminating resistors at each end of the cable help to maintain acceptable signal levels. A common ground (return) provides the reference for all single-ended signals. Unfortunately, single-ended circuitry is not very noise resistant, so single-ended cabling is generally limited to about 6 meters at data transfer speeds of 5 MHz or less. At higher data transfer speeds, cable length can be as short as 1.5 meters. In spite of the disadvantages, single-ended operation is simple and popular because of its simplicity.

The *differential* (DIF) wiring approach uses *two* wires for each signal (instead of one wire referenced to a common ground). A differential signal offers excellent noise resistance because it does not rely on a common ground. This allows much longer cables (up to 25 meters) and higher-speed operation (10 MHz). An array of pull-up resistors at each end of the cable help to ensure signal integrity. The problem with differential wiring is that it is more complicated than single-ended interfaces. *Low-voltage differential* (or LVD) SCSI is an emerging standard defined in the SPI-2 document of SCSI-3 that runs on 3.3Vdc rather than 5Vdc. The goal of LVD is to allow higher data rates while combining the benefits of single-ended and differential SCSI bus schemes. LVD is less sensitive to electromagnetic noise and allows high data rates at greater cable lengths than a single-ended bus. LVD is the interface specified for use with Ultra-2 SCSI and Ultra160/m specifications. While LVD is not directly compatible with single-ended wiring, the devices will use multimode driver circuits that automatically detect the type of bus used and switch to the appropriate mode of operation. This will allow you to use an LVD/SE device on a single-ended bus without having to set any switches or jumpers. Therefore, LVD has been introduced gradually without the loss of the current investment in single-ended devices. Still, the advantages of LVD are lost when an LVD/SE device is used in a single-ended bus—as soon as one single-ended device is connected to a LVD/SE bus, the whole bus switches to single-ended mode (with all its limitations).

BUS LENGTH

As you're already aware, SCSI devices are daisy-chained together with a 50-pin or 68-pin cable. The total length of this cable makes up the overall SCSI bus. When there are only *internal* SCSI devices, the bus length is measured from the SCSI host adapter to the last internal SCSI device on the chain (the terminated device). When there are only *external* SCSI devices, the bus length is measured from the SCSI host adapter to the last external SCSI device on the chain (it should also be terminated). When there are *both* internal and external SCSI devices, the bus length is measured from the last external device to the last internal device. There are finite limits on the length of your SCSI bus. As SCSI implementations have become faster over the years, that effective bus length has shortened. Table 12-2 illustrates the maximum SCSI bus lengths for single-ended, differential, and low-voltage differential (LVD) signaling approaches.

TERMINATORS

When high-frequency signals are transmitted over adjacent wires, signals tend to degrade and interfere with one another over the length of the cable. This is a very normal and relatively well-understood electrical phenomenon (you saw this as *attenuation* in Chapter 8). In the PC, SCSI signal integrity is enhanced by using powered resistors at each end of the data cable to "pull up" active signals. Built-in pull-up resistors at drives and controller cards already terminate most high-frequency signal cables in the PC. The small resistor array is known as a *terminator*. Since there is a distinct limit to the number of devices that can be added to a floppy drive or IDE cable, designers have never made a big deal about termination—they just added the resistors and that was it. With SCSI, however, up to eight devices can be added to the bus cable. The SCSI cable also must be terminated, but the location of terminating resistors depends on which devices are added to the bus, and *where* they are placed. As a result, termination is a much more

---

TABLE 12-2   COMPARISON OF SCSI BUS LENGTHS

TERMS	SINGLE-ENDED	DIFFERENTIAL	LVD
SCSI-1	6m	25m	$12m^2$
Fast SCSI	3m	25m	$12m^2$
Fast Wide SCSI	3m	25m	$12m^2$
Ultra SCSI	1.5m–3m	Up to 25m	Up to 12m
Wide Ultra SCSI	Up to 3m	Up to 25m	Up to 12m
Ultra2 SCSI	[1]	25m	12m
Wide Ultra2 SCSI	[1]	25m	12m
Ultra3 SCSI	[1]	25m	12m
Wide Ultra3 SCSI	[1]	25m	12m

1. Single-ended and high-powered differential are not defined at Ultra2 and Ultra3 speeds.
2. Only if all devices on the bus support LVD.

vital element of SCSI setup and troubleshooting. Poor or incorrect termination can cause intermittent signal problems. Here are some general guidelines for termination:

■ The last devices in a SCSI chain (cable) must be terminated. For an internal installation, the SCSI host adapter and last (endmost) internal device must be terminated, and other devices must be unterminated. For an external installation, the SCSI host adapter and last (endmost) external device must be terminated. In an internal/external installation, the SCSI host adapter is normally unterminated, and the endmost internal and external SCSI devices are terminated.

■ Internal Ultra160 and Ultra2 SCSI devices (such as drives) come from the factory with termination *disabled* and cannot be changed. The built-in terminator at the end of the 68-pin internal LVD SCSI cable provides proper termination for these internal devices.

■ Termination on Wide SCSI, Narrow SCSI, and Ultra SCSI devices usually is controlled by manually setting a jumper or a switch on the device, or by physically removing or installing one or more resistor modules on the device—this is the "traditional" means of selecting terminators.

■ Termination on most external SCSI devices is controlled by installing or removing a SCSI terminator block on the last device's passthrough port. However, termination on some external SCSI devices is enabled or disabled by setting a switch on the back of the SCSI device.

■ By default, termination on the Adaptec SCSI host adapter card is set to Automatic (the preferred method). This means the card will be terminated or unterminated as it deems necessary. Most SCSI host adapter manufacturers recommend that you do not change this default setting.

Termination is typically either active or passive. Basically, *passive* termination is simply plugging a resistor pack into a SCSI device. Passive resistors are powered by the TERMPWR line. Passive termination is simple and effective over short distances (up to about 1 meter) and usually works just fine for the cable lengths inside a PC, but can be a drawback over longer distances. *Active* terminators provide their own regulated power sources, which make them most effective for longer cables (such as those found in external SCSI devices like page scanners) or Wide SCSI systems. Most SCSI-2 implementations (and later) use active terminators. A variation on active termination is *forced perfect termination* (or FPT). FPT includes diode clamps that prevent signal overshoot and undershoot. This makes FPT effective for long SCSI cable lengths.

SCSI IDS AND LUNS

A typical SCSI bus will support up to eight devices, called *logical units*, and these devices are each identified using an ID. This means each device on the bus must have its own unique ID number (0–7). If two devices use the same ID, there will be a conflict. IDs are typically set on the SCSI adapter and each SCSI device using jumpers or DIP switches (see Figure 12-2). Typically, the SCSI adapter is set for ID7, the primary SCSI hard drive is set to ID0, and a second SCSI hard drive is ID1. Other devices can usually be placed anywhere from ID2–ID6. Wide (16-bit) SCSI bus implementations can support up to 16 devices with IDs from 0 to 15. The Adaptec 39160 provides two 16-bit channels, so can support up to 30 SCSI devices—two 16-bit channels offer 32 IDs, minus one ID for the controller of each channel, leaving 30 available IDs. Here are some general guidelines for SCSI IDs:

■ For internal SCSI devices, the SCSI ID is usually set by configuring a jumper on the device.

■ For external SCSI devices, the SCSI ID is usually set with a switch on the back of the device.

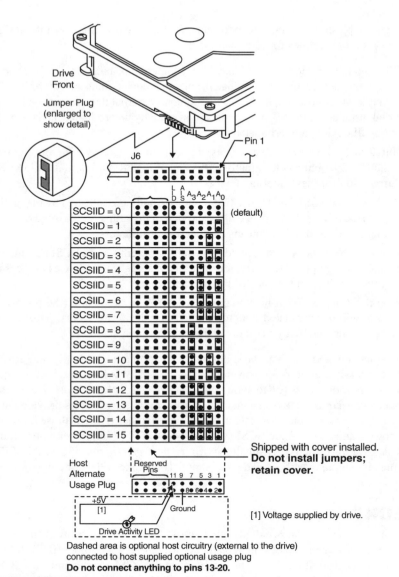

FIGURE 12-2   Setting a SCSI ID jumper (Courtesy of Seagate)

■ SCSI ID numbers do not need to be sequential, as long as the SCSI host adapter and each device use a *different* number.

■ SCSI ID 7 has the *highest* priority on the SCSI bus. The priority of the remaining IDs (in descending order) is 6 to 0, then 15 to 8.

■ On most SCSI bus systems, the host adapter is set to ID7 for highest priority. On multiple SCSI bus adapters such as the Adaptec 39160, both SCSI bus channels are preset to SCSI ID7 and should not be changed.

- Most internal SCSI hard disk drives come from the factory preset to SCSI ID0.

- If you have 8-bit (Narrow) SCSI devices, they must use SCSI IDs 0, 1, 2, 3, 4, 5, or 6. SCSI ID0 is recommended for the first SCSI hard drive.

- If you're booting a computer from a SCSI hard drive, the SCSI host adapter's internal setup must usually list the same ID as the bootable drive. For example, when booting from an Adaptec 39160 controller, the *Boot SCSI ID* setting in the SCSISelect utility must correspond to the SCSI ID of the device you're booting from. By default, the *Boot SCSI ID* is set to 0 for the first SCSI hard drive. You generally need not change this setting.

Logical unit numbers (LUNs) are similar to SCSI IDs because both identify SCSI devices. However, LUNs indicate devices within devices—divisions within IDs. Every SCSI ID from 0–7 can have up to eight LUNs (64 LUNs in SCSI-3), or eight subdevices for every given device ID. Suppose you needed to use more than eight devices on a SCSI bus. You could cause your device to respond to a SCSI ID, and have each device using the ID respond to a different LUN. For example, if you had three hard drives E:, F:, and G:, you could have all three drives use ID2, but E: could be assigned LUN0, F: could be assigned LUN1, and G: could be assigned LUN2. This is often the case with SCSI RAID systems where there are far more drives than available SCSI IDs. Unfortunately, a SCSI user cannot arbitrarily decide to use LUN assignments—the hardware must be designed for that purpose. Also, LUNs are seldom used, and many SCSI adapters don't check for them. This shortcut speeds bus scanning a bit. If you have a device that uses LUNs (such as a CD jukebox), you may need to enable LUN support in the host adapter's BIOS or device driver. Windows 2000 lets you see the SCSI ID and LUN assignments of installed SCSI devices (such as in Figure 12-3).

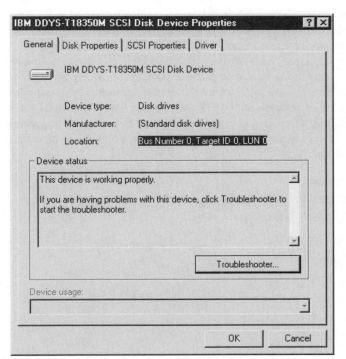

FIGURE 12-3   Using the Windows 2000 Device Manager to check the ID and LUN assignments of SCSI drives

SCSI BUS OPERATION

Now that you have learned about SCSI bus concepts and structure, you can see how the interface behaves during normal operation. Since bus wires are common to every device attached to the bus, a device must obtain permission from all other devices before it can take control of the bus. This attempt to access the bus is called the *arbitration phase*. Once a device (such as the SCSI controller) has won the bus arbitration, it must then make contact with the device to be communicated with. This device selection is known as the *selection phase*. When this contact is established, data transfer can take place. This part of the chapter will detail negotiation and information transfer over the SCSI bus.

Negotiation

Devices must *negotiate* to access and use a SCSI bus. Negotiation begins when the bus is free and Busy (BSY) and Select (SEL) lines are idle. A device begins arbitration by activating the BSY line and its own data ID line (data bit D0–D7, depending on the device). If more than one device tries to control the bus simultaneously, the device with the *higher* ID line wins. The winning device (an initiator) attempts to acquire a target device by asserting the SEL line and the data ID line (data bit D0–D7) of the desired device. The BSY line is then released by the initiator, and the desired target device asserts the BSY line to confirm it has been selected. The initiator then releases the SEL and data bus lines. Information transfer can now take place.

Information

The selected target controls the data being transferred and the direction of transfer. Information transfer lasts until the target device releases the BSY line, thus returning the bus to the idle state. If a piece of information will take a long time to prepare for, the target can end the connection by issuing a *disconnect* message. It will try to reestablish the connection later with a new arbitration and selection procedure.

During information transfer, the initiator tells its target how to act on a command, and establishes the mode of data transfer during the *message-out phase*. A specific SCSI command follows the message during the *command phase*. After a command is sent, data transfer takes place during the *data-in* and/or *data-out* phases. The target relinquishes control to the initiator during the command phase. For example, the command itself may ask that more information be transferred. The target then tells the initiator whether the command was successfully completed or not by returning status information during a *status phase*. Finally, the command is finished when the target sends a progress report to the initiator during the *message-in* phase. Consider this simple SCSI communication example:

1. **Bus free phase**   System is idle.
2. **Arbitration phase**   A device takes control of the bus.
3. **Select phase**   The desired device is selected.
4. **Message-out phase**   Target sets up data transfer.
5. **Command phase**   Send command.
6. **Data-in phase**   Exchange data.
7. **Status phase**   Indicate the results of the exchange.
8. **Message-in phase**   Indicate exchange is complete.
9. **Bus free phase**   System is idle.

Installing a SCSI System

Today, virtually all SCSI host adapters are Plug-and-Play (PnP) devices that are designed for automatic detection and resource assignment in a motherboard's PCI slot. Still, most SCSI host adapter problems *start* when the card is first installed in the system—usually due to inadequate or incorrect installation of the hardware and software. This part of the chapter offers an overview of the SCSI adapter installation process and SCSI BIOS setup so that you can check your own installation for missing steps.

If your server motherboard incorporates a SCSI host adapter, you can generally skip the installation steps and focus on the SCSI setup and configuration issues.

INTERNAL HARDWARE INSTALLATION

Implementing SCSI on your server or workstation requires that you install a SCSI host adapter (called a "controller") and at least one SCSI device. The steps below outline the installation of a typical SCSI host adapter:

1. Shut down your system, then turn off and unplug the computer.

2. Unbolt the outer case, then remove the housing and set it (and the screws) aside in a safe place.

3. If you're replacing an existing SCSI host adapter with a newer, faster model, you'll need to remove the old SCSI adapter first. Disconnect the internal and external SCSI cable(s) from the SCSI adapter. Unbolt the old SCSI card bracket from the chassis and remove the old SCSI adapter from its expansion slot. Be sure to set the old SCSI adapter aside on a static-safe surface, or in an anti-static bag.

4. Locate a slot for the new SCSI host adapter card. Most current SCSI host adapter devices will require a 32-bit PCI slot, though some older SCSI cards will use an ISA slot. Some new high-end SCSI cards may require a 64-bit PCI slot (usually found on server motherboards). Find an available bus-mastering PCI slot that's appropriate for your SCSI adapter card. Remove the cover for the slot you intend to use (if it's not already removed), and save the screw for the mounting bracket.

5. Insert the SCSI host adapter card. Push the card in firmly and evenly until it's fully seated in the slot. Do *not* use excessive force—you can break the card, and perhaps even damage the motherboard. Replace the screw to secure the bracket of your SCSI card to the computer's chassis.

6. If you're connecting any internal SCSI devices, plug the 50-pin or 68-pin SCSI connector on the end of the internal SCSI ribbon cable into the SCSI card's header. Make sure to align pin 1 on both connectors.

7. Connect your computer's drive activity LED cable to the appropriate connector on the SCSI card (if desired). This is designed to operate the front panel LED found on most PC cabinets to indicate activity on the SCSI bus.

8. Make any external SCSI bus connections that may be required (for example, from your SCSI scanner or external SCSI drives).

The SCSI bus requires proper termination, and no duplicate SCSI IDs. Before you attempt to reboot the computer, verify the SCSI IDs for each SCSI device, and double-check the SCSI termination at the end(s) of your SCSI chain.

If your server's motherboard provides an onboard SCSI host adapter, remember that the onboard adapter may be terminated by default. If you cannot disable the onboard adapter's termination, you may be limited to using only internal or external SCSI devices, but not both. See your motherboard's documentation for specific limitations.

SCSI Connection Notes

Although the SCSI interface is designed to accommodate a wide range of devices, their installation often presents some wrinkles you need to be aware of. As a rule, there are three things you need to check before connecting a SCSI device to the host adapter: check the SCSI IDs, check the termination, and connect power cables. Below are some guidelines for setting SCSI IDs and termination on your various devices.

Since setup procedures can vary from device to device, always refer to each device's documentation for specific instructions.

Check the SCSI IDs   The SCSI host adapter and each SCSI device must have a unique ID. For example, each of the Adaptec 39160 SCSI card's channels is set to ID7, and each device you connect to a given channel must have a SCSI ID number ranging from 0 to 15. No two devices on the same SCSI channel can have the same SCSI ID. If you boot from a SCSI hard drive, make sure the drive ID is set to 0. (Most SCSI hard drives are preset to SCSI ID 0 at the factory.) The SCSI IDs for internal devices are usually set with jumpers, and the SCSI IDs for external devices are usually set with a switch on the back of the device.

Terminate the Cable   To ensure reliable communication on the SCSI bus, the device at the end of each cable (or the end of the cable itself) must have a *terminator* installed (or must have its internal termination enabled). Terminators must be removed (or termination must be disabled) on devices between the ends of each cable. When connecting Ultra160 or Ultra2 SCSI devices, the SCSI bus must be terminated either on the end of the cable (with a permanent terminator) or with a separate terminating connector. Ultra SCSI and earlier single-ended devices can terminate the bus directly from the device. If you use an Ultra SCSI terminator on an LVD Ultra160 and Ultra2 SCSI bus, you will force the bus to single-ended mode, limiting the speed and cable distance. For this reason be sure that you have the necessary Ultra160 or Ultra2 cable or terminator before installing Ultra160 SCSI devices.

Connecting Internal Ultra160 and Ultra2 Devices   A special 68-pin internal LVD (low-voltage differential) cable is needed to connect internal Ultra160 or Ultra2 SCSI devices. If your cables are not marked, you can identify most LVD cables as having twisted pairs of the flat ribbon cable between the device connectors. Some cables are laminated so that they lay flat. Internal LVD cables usually have a terminator built into the end of the cable. SCSI host adapters such as the Adaptec 39160 have two separate Ultra160 SCSI channels, and each channel has an internal LVD/SE connector where you can connect internal SCSI devices. Follow these steps to connect your internal Ultra160 and Ultra2 devices:

1. Locate a 68-pin internal LVD SCSI cable (which may have either twisted wires or flat wires). As a rule, keep your Ultra160 and Ultra2 SCSI devices on a separate SCSI channel from your older Ultra SCSI devices. This allows the newer Ultra160 and Ultra2 SCSI devices to transfer data at their maximum speed.

2. Connect the nonterminated end of the cable(s) to the internal LVD/SE connector(s) at the SCSI adapter.

3. Plug the internal Ultra160 and Ultra2 SCSI devices to the other cable connectors, starting with the connector at the terminated end of the cable.

4. Connect a power cable from your computer's internal power supply to each internal SCSI device.

Internal Ultra 160 and Ultra2 SCSI devices come from the factory with termination disabled and cannot be changed. Proper termination is provided by the terminator at the end of the LVD SCSI cable.

Connecting Wide SCSI Devices   You can connect Wide SCSI devices to the internal LVD/SE connectors. However, it is usually recommended that you connect them to the SCSI channel A LVD/SE connector, and that you connect all newer Ultra160 and Ultra2 devices to the SCSI channel B connector. Follow these steps to connect Wide SCSI devices:

1. Locate a 68-pin internal Wide SCSI cable.

2. Connect one end of the cable to the Channel A internal 68-pin connector on the SCSI host adapter.

3. Connect the other end of the cable to a *terminated* Ultra/Fast Wide SCSI device.

4. If you have other Ultra/Fast Wide SCSI devices, attach them to the connectors between the two ends of the cable. Be sure these other devices are *unterminated*.

5. Connect a power cable from your computer's internal power supply to each internal device.

Connecting Internal Ultra/Fast Narrow SCSI Devices   If you have internal Ultra/Fast Narrow SCSI devices with standard 50-pin connectors, you can connect them to the 50-pin internal SE Narrow SCSI connector. Follow these steps to connect the devices:

1. Locate a 50-pin internal Ultra Narrow SCSI cable.

2. Connect one end of the cable to the 50-pin internal SE Narrow SCSI connector on the SCSI host adapter.

3. Connect the other end of the cable to a terminated Ultra/Fast Narrow SCSI device.

4. If you have other Ultra/Fast Narrow SCSI devices, attach them to the connectors between the two ends of the cable. Be sure these other devices are *unterminated*.

5. Connect a power cable from your computer's internal power supply to each internal device.

Connecting External SCSI Devices   You can connect external Ultra160 and Ultra2 SCSI devices to the 68-pin external LVD/SE SCSI connectors. Each external device will require a 68-pin VHDCI external LVD SCSI cable. Follow these steps to connect your external SCSI devices:

1. Connect one end of an external SCSI cable to one of the external Ultra160 connectors on the SCSI host adapter (such as the Adaptec 39160 SCSI card). Connect *only* Ultra160 and Ultra2 SCSI devices to the external SCSI connectors in order to achieve the maximum data transfer rate. Also, do not combine older SCSI devices with the newer Ultra160 and Ultra2 SCSI devices on the same SCSI channel of the host adapter card.

2. Connect the other end of the cable to a SCSI connector on the back of an external device. If you are installing only one external device, terminate the device and skip to step 4.

3. Connect the other external SCSI devices by linking each device to the previous one (in a "daisy chain fashion). Terminate only the device at the end of the chain.

4. Connect power cables to all external device(s) and to the computer.

SCSI Drive Notes

While connecting and terminating SCSI drives is a relatively straightforward process, there are certain nuances to keep in mind as you configure each device. The following tips should help you to make the most of your new and existing SCSI drives:

- If you connect a SCSI hard drive to a new SCSI host adapter that was previously connected to a different SCSI card, you must repartition and reformat the drive before you can use it. Back up the data on the drive before you move it! In some cases, you may need to low-level format the SCSI drive using a utility integrated into the SCSI host adapter's firmware.

- Every SCSI hard drive must be physically low-level formatted, partitioned, and logically formatted before it can be used to store data. Most SCSI drives are preformatted at the factory. If your SCSI hard disk drive has not been preformatted (and if your computer is running under DOS or Windows), you can format the disk with the DOS FDISK and FORMAT commands.

- When using a dual-channel SCSI host adapter, connect your LVD (Ultra160 and Ultra2) SCSI devices to SCSI Channel B and your non-LVD SCSI devices (if any) to SCSI Channel A. This allows the LVD SCSI devices to run at their maximum performance levels of 160 MB/s or 80 MB/s, respectively. Or, you can connect LVD SCSI devices to both SCSI channels. If you combine LVD and non-LVD SCSI devices on the same SCSI channel, the data transfer rate of the LVD SCSI devices will drop down to non-LVD SCSI performance levels of up to 40 MB/s.

- Internal Ultra2 and Ultra160 SCSI devices come from the factory with termination *disabled* and cannot be changed. Proper termination is provided by the terminator at the end of the internal LVD SCSI cable.

Combining SCSI and Non-SCSI Devices

You can install the SCSI host adapter in a computer that already has a non-SCSI controller (such as an EIDE or Ultra-DMA controller). However, you cannot mix devices on the same interface—SCSI devices must be connected to the SCSI host adapter, EIDE/UDMA devices must be connected to their controller, and so on. When you install the SCSI host adapter and SCSI disk drives in a computer that boots from a non-SCSI disk drive, the computer will continue to boot from the non-SCSI disk drive unless you change the computer's CMOS configuration. You do not need to change the configuration if you just want to use the SCSI drives for additional file storage space. If your computer's motherboard BIOS supports the BIOS Boot Specification (or BBS) feature, you can select a different boot device without much difficulty. Table 12-3 outlines what to do in order to use different kinds of disk drives in the same computer.

SOFTWARE INSTALLATION

Now that the physical hardware for your new SCSI host adapter card has been installed, it's time to install the SCSI adapter drivers and application software that you'll need to identify the device under the operating system. The following steps illustrate a typical procedure for Windows 2000, NT, 98, and NetWare, but check the adapter's recommendations for other operating systems (such as UnixWare or Linux installations). Leave the computer's housing off for now, but reconnect the ac cord to the computer and prepare to start the system again.

Always refer to the **README** file on the SCSI adapter card's driver disc to obtain the very latest feature descriptions and software installation guidelines for your particular card.

TABLE 12-3 BOOT POLICIES FOR SCSI-EQUIPPED SYSTEMS

DOES COMPUTER BIOS SUPPORT BBS?	WANT COMPUTER TO BOOT FROM SCSI DRIVE?	THEN DO THIS:
No	No	No action required. SCSI drives and non-SCSI drives can be used together.
No	Yes	Run CMOS Setup program. Change primary Hard Disk setting to None or Not Installed (see computer documentation). You will not be able to use the non-SCSI drive(s) at all when you boot from the SCSI drive.
Yes	No	No action required. SCSI drives and non-SCSI drives can be used together.
Yes	Yes	Run CMOS Setup program and select SCSI drive as boot device. SCSI drives and non-SCSI drives can be used together.

Installing Windows 2000 Drivers

Virtually all current SCSI host adapters are Plug-and-Play devices that are automatically detected by Windows 2000. If you're adding or upgrading SCSI support to a server or workstation, perform the following steps to add the Windows 2000 driver to a previously installed Windows 2000 system:

1. Install the SCSI host adapter card.

2. Power up the computer. Windows 2000 detects the SCSI host adapter and starts the Found New Hardware Wizard. Click Next.

3. Select "Display a list of the known drivers for this device so that I can choose a specific driver" and then click Next.

4. Select "SCSI and RAID controllers" in the Hardware Types list, then click Next.

5. Click Have Disk. The Install From Disk dialog box opens.

6. Insert the diskette that contains the SCSI host adapter's driver into an appropriate drive, then type the location of the Windows 2000 driver (i.e., **a:/w2k**) and click OK.

7. Select the appropriate driver for the device (i.e., QLogic QLA1280, 64-bit PCI DUAL LVD SCSI HBA), then click Next. Windows 2000 indicates that the wizard is ready to install the device. Now click Next.

8. If the Digital Signature Not Found dialog box appears, click Yes, then click Finish.

9. Finally, click Yes to restart the system.

Updating Windows 2000 Drivers   From time to time, it may be necessary to update a SCSI driver in order to fix bugs or improve device performance. Follow these steps if you're updating the driver for an existing SCSI host adapter:

1. Click Start, then select Programs | Administrative Tools | Computer Management.

2. Double-click System Tools, and then double-click Device Manager.

3. Double-click "SCSI and RAID controllers".

4. Double-click the appropriate SCSI host adapter (i.e., QLogic QLA1280, 64-bit PCI DUAL LVD SCSI HBA), and then select the Driver tab (see Figure 12-4).

5. Click Update Driver. The Upgrade Device Driver Wizard dialog box appears. Click Next.

6. Select "Display a list of the known device drivers for this device so that I can choose a specific driver", then click Next.

7. Click Have Disk. The Install From Disk dialog box appears.

8. Insert the diskette that contains the QLogic driver into an appropriate drive, type the location of the Windows 2000 driver (i.e., **a:\w2k**), and click OK.

9. Select the appropriate SCSI adapter (i.e., QLogic QLA1280, 64-bit PCI DUAL LVD SCSI HBA), and then click Next. Windows 2000 indicates that the wizard is ready to install the device. Now Click Next.

10. If the Digital Signature Not Found dialog box appears, click Yes.

11. Click Finish, and then click Yes to restart the system.

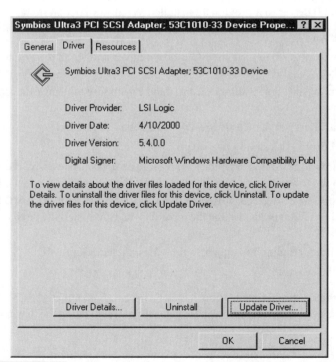

FIGURE 12-4   Windows 2000 SCSI drivers can be updated through the Drivers tab in the device's Properties dialog box.

Installing Windows NT Drivers

The procedures for installing Windows NT drivers are a bit different than under Windows 2000, but the basic ideas are still the same. Perform the following steps to add the Windows NT driver to a previously installed Windows NT 4.0 system:

1. Select My Computer from the desktop, select Control Panel, and then select SCSI Adapters.
2. Select the Drivers tab and click Add.
3. Insert the diskette that contains the SCSI host adapter NT driver into an appropriate drive and click Have Disk.
4. Type the path to the Windows NT driver on the diskette (i.e., **a:\nt**) and click OK.
5. Select the proper driver (i.e., QLogic QLA1280, 64-bit PCI DUAL SCSI LVD HBA) and click OK.
6. Remove the diskette and click Yes to restart the system.

Updating Windows NT Drivers   From time to time, it may be necessary to update a SCSI driver in order to fix bugs or improve device performance. Perform the following steps if a Windows NT driver is already installed and you want to install an updated version of the SCSI driver:

1. Open a DOS command prompt window.
2. Change the current directory to the Windows NT driver directory (i.e., **cd \winnt\system32\ drivers**).
3. Make a backup copy of the old driver. You can copy the file into the same directory with a **.SAV** extension, indicating that it is the saved file (i.e., **copy ql1280.sys ql1280.sav**).
4. Insert the diskette that contains the new SCSI host adapter driver into an appropriate drive.
5. Copy the new driver over the old driver (i.e., **copy a:\nt\ql1280.sys**).
6. Reboot your system to load the driver.

Installing NetWare Drivers

NetWare will require some real-mode tactics in order to define the proper SCSI host adapter driver. Follow these steps to install the SCSI drivers on an existing NetWare 4.x/5.x system:

1. Start NetWare and load the NetWare Install program from the NetWare server prompt (:). For example, if you're using NetWare 4.11 or 4.2, type **load install**. If you are using NetWare 5.X, type **load nwconfig**.
2. Select "Driver options" from the main menu.
3. Select "Configure disk and storage device drivers".
4. Select "Select an additional driver".
5. Press INSERT to install an unlisted driver.
6. Insert the diskette that contains the SCSI host adapter driver into an appropriate drive.
7. Press ENTER to select the proper **.HAM** driver.
8. Select Yes to copy the driver from the diskette to the server directory.
9. If you have a CD-ROM attached to the SCSI card, you must also load **CDROM.NLM**, which is provided with NetWare to mount CD-ROM volumes on the server (i.e., **load cdrom.nlm**).

10. If you're attaching multiple LUN devices (such as tape changers), add the /LUN switch to the LOAD line (i.e., **load ql1280.ham slot=xx /lun**).

11. If ASPI support is required for the SCSI devices, you must load the **NWASPI.CDM** module, which is provided by NetWare (i.e., **load nwaspi.cdm**).

Installing Windows 98 Drivers

While Windows 98/Me isn't a viable choice for server applications, it remains a popular alternative for workstations, and readily supports SCSI host adapters. Perform the following steps to install the SCSI host adapter driver on a system with the Windows 98 operating system already installed:

1. Install the new SCSI host adapter.

2. Reboot your system. The New Hardware Found window pops up after detecting the PCI SCSI host adapter card.

3. Insert the diskette that contains the SCSI driver into an appropriate drive, then click Next.

4. Select "Display a list of all the drivers in a specific location, so you can select the driver you want", then click Next.

5. If prompted to select a device type, select SCSI Controllers and then click Next.

6. Click Have Disk and type **a:\win9x** with the path to the new driver, then click OK.

7. Make sure the new SCSI adapter (i.e., QLogic QLA1280 LVD PCI Dual SCSI Adapter) is selected, and then click Next.

8. Click Next again, then click Finish when the wizard finds the updated driver.

9. When prompted, remove the diskette from the disk drive and reboot your system.

CONFIGURING THE SCSI BIOS

Whether added as an expansion device or integrated into your server's motherboard, the vast majority of SCSI host adapters will employ BIOS (or *firmware*) to configure the adapter's various operations. In most cases, the default settings of your SCSI BIOS are adequate, and you should not need to change the default configuration of the host adapter. However, you may decide to alter these default values if there is a conflict between device settings, if you need to optimize the system's performance, or if you need special SCSI features (such as low-level formatting a SCSI hard drive). This part of the chapter outlines the default settings of a common Adaptec SCSI host adapter, and explains many of the SCSI BIOS settings that you may encounter. Typical default settings are listed in Table 12-4.

Using the SCSI BIOS

The SCSI host adapter's firmware can be accessed in the moments following the POST—just after the PC lets you enter the CMOS Setup. As the initialization process continues, you'll see a message such as

```
Press <Ctrl><A> for SCSISelect Utility
```

Press the specified keys to start the SCSI Setup utility (i.e., SCSISelect). If there is more than one available channel, you can specify the channel (such as channel A or channel B) to work on. The setup menu appears, so use the arrow keys to navigate through the various options, and press ENTER to make selections. When you're done reviewing or changing SCSI options, press ESC until you're prompted to exit and save changes. Select Yes and the PC will reboot.

TABLE 12-4 COMMON SCSI BIOS SETTINGS USED TO CONFIGURE A SCSI HOST ADAPTER

SCSI SELECT OPTIONS	AVAILABLE SETTINGS	DEFAULT SETTING
SCSI Bus Interface Definitions		
Host Adapter SCSI ID	0–15	7
SCSI Parity Checking	Enabled, Disabled	Enabled
Host Adapter SCSI Termination:	Ch. A: Automatic, Low On/High On, Low Off/High Off, Low Off/High On	Automatic
	Ch. B: Automatic, Enabled, Disabled	Automatic
Boot Device Options:		
Boot Channel	A First, B First	A First
Boot SCSI ID	0–15	0
Boot LUN Number	0–7	0
SCSI Device Configuration:		
Sync Transfer Rate (MB/s)	160, 80.0, 53.4, 40.0, 32.0, 26.8, 20.0, 16.0, 13.4, 10.0, ASYN	160
Initiate Wide Negotiation	Yes, No	Yes (Enabled)
Enable Disconnection	Yes, No	Yes (Enabled)
Send Start Unit Command	Yes, No	Yes (Enabled)
Enable Write Back Cache	Yes, No, N/C (No Change)	N/C (No Change)
BIOS Multiple LUN Support	Yes, No	No (Disabled)
Include in BIOS Scan	Yes, No	Yes (Enabled)
Advanced Configuration Options:		
Reset SCSI Bus at IC Initialization	Enabled, Disabled	Enabled
Display <CTRL> <A> Messages during BIOS Initialization	Enabled, Disabled	Enabled
Extended BIOS Translation for DOS Drives > 1 GB	Enabled, Disabled	Enabled
Verbose/Silent Mode	Verbose, Silent	Verbose
Host Adapter BIOS	Enabled, Disabled: Scan Bus, Disabled: Not Scan	Enabled
Domain Validation	Enabled, Disabled	Enabled
Support Removable Disks Under BIOS as Fixed Disks	Disabled, Boot Only, All Disks	Disabled
BIOS Support for Bootable CD-ROM	Enabled, Disabled	Enabled
BIOS Support for Int 13 Extensions	Enabled, Disabled	Enabled

The instructions and options shown here are provided as an example, and may vary greatly between SCSI adapters. Instructions for navigating the menus, and specific options available to your particular SCSI host adapter, can be found in the adapter's user manual.

SCSI BIOS Settings   Once the SCSI BIOS Setup utility is running, you'll be able to adjust a large number of settings and operating parameters such as the ones listed below (default settings are listed in parentheses):

- **Host Adapter SCSI ID (7)**   This sets the SCSI ID for the SCSI card. Most SCSI cards (such as the Adaptec 39160) are set at 7, which gives them the highest priority on the SCSI bus. As a rule, you should not change this setting.

- **SCSI Parity Checking (Enabled)**   When set to Enabled, this feature verifies the accuracy of data transfers on the SCSI bus. Leave this setting enabled unless any SCSI device connected to the SCSI host adapter does *not* support SCSI parity.

- **Host Adapter SCSI Termination (Automatic)**   This determines the termination setting for the SCSI card. The default setting is Automatic, which allows the SCSI card to adjust the termination as needed. As a rule, you should not change this setting.

- **Boot Channel (A First)**   This specifies which of the two SCSI channels the boot device is connected to (if the computer boots from a SCSI device). If you change this setting, the change automatically applies to both SCSI channels. This type of option will not be available on SCSI host adapters with only one channel.

- **Boot SCSI ID (0)**   This specifies the SCSI ID of your boot device, which is ID 0 by default. As a rule, you should not change the default setting. If you change this setting, the change automatically applies to both SCSI channels.

- **Boot LUN Number (0)**   This specifies which LUN (Logical Unit Number) to boot from on your boot device. This setting is not valid unless the *Multiple LUN Support* feature is enabled. If you alter this setting, the change automatically applies to both SCSI channels.

- **Sync Transfer Rate (160)**   This determines the maximum synchronous data transfer rate that the SCSI card supports. As a rule, you should leave the maximum (default) value of 160 MB/s.

- **Initiate Wide Negotiation (Yes)**   When set to Yes, the SCSI card attempts 16-bit data transfer (wide negotiation). When set to No, the SCSI card uses 8-bit data transfer unless the SCSI device specifically requests wide negotiation. Set Initiate Wide Negotiation to No if you're using an 8-bit SCSI device that hangs or exhibits other performance problems with 16-bit data transfer rate enabled.

- **Enable Disconnection (Yes)**   When set to Yes, this allows the SCSI device to disconnect from the SCSI bus. Leave the setting at Yes if two or more SCSI devices are connected to the SCSI card. If only one SCSI device is connected, change the setting to No for slightly better performance.

- **Send Start Unit Command (Yes)**   When set to Yes, this sends the Start Unit Command to the SCSI device at bootup. (The following three options have no effect if the SCSI Card BIOS is disabled—the SCSI Card BIOS is normally enabled by default.)

- **Enable Write Back Cache (N/C)**   This option can be used to enable or disable the write-back cache on SCSI disk drives connected to the host adapter. Leave this option set to its default setting (N/C), which usually allows for optimum drive performance.

- **BIOS Multiple LUN Support (No)**   Leave this setting on No if the device does not have multiple Logical Unit Numbers (LUNs). When set to Yes, the SCSI BIOS provides boot support for a SCSI device with multiple LUNs (i.e., a CD "jukebox" in which multiple CDs can be accessed simultaneously).

- **Include in BIOS Scan (Yes)**   When set to Yes, the SCSI BIOS includes the device as part of its BIOS scan at bootup.
- **Reset SCSI Bus at Initialization (Enabled)**   When set to Enabled, the SCSI card generates a SCSI bus reset during its power-on initialization and after a hard reset.
- **Display Messages during BIOS Initialization (Enabled)**   When set to Enabled, the SCSI BIOS displays the logon message (i.e., "Press <CTRL> <A> for SCSISelect Utility") during system bootup. If this setting is disabled, you can still invoke the SCSI BIOS utility by pressing the required keys after the SCSI BIOS banner appears. If you change this setting, the change automatically applies to both SCSI channels.
- **Extended BIOS Translation for DOS Drives > 1GB (Enabled)**   When enabled, this provides an extended translation scheme for SCSI hard disks with capacities greater than 1GB. This setting is necessary only for DOS 5.0 and later, and is not required for other operating systems like NetWare or Linux/UNIX.

Changing the translation scheme destroys all data on the drive. Be sure to back up your disk drives before changing the translation scheme.

- **Verbose/Silent Mode (Verbose)**   When set to Verbose, the SCSI card BIOS displays the host adapter model on the screen during system buildup. When set to Silent, the message will not be displayed during bootup. If you change this setting, the change automatically applies to both SCSI channels.
- **Host Adapter BIOS (Enabled)**   This feature enables or disables the SCSI card BIOS. If you change this setting, the change automatically applies to both SCSI channels. Leave this setting enabled to let the SCSI BIOS scan and initialize all SCSI devices. Set to Disabled: Not Scan if the devices on the SCSI bus (i.e., CD-ROM drives) are controlled by software drivers and do not need the BIOS, and you do not want the BIOS to scan the SCSI bus. Set to Disabled: Scan Bus if you do not need the BIOS, but you want it to scan the SCSI devices on the bus and you need to spin up the device. (The following four options have no effect if the SCSI BIOS is disabled.)
- **Domain Validation (Enabled)**   This determines the optimum transfer rate for each device on the SCSI bus and sets transfer rates accordingly. This also displays the resulting data transfer rate. If you change this setting, the change automatically applies to both SCSI channels.
- **Support Removable Disks Under BIOS as Fixed Disks (Disabled)**   This determines which removable-media drives are supported by the SCSI card BIOS. When disabled, no removable-media drives are treated as hard drives. Software drivers are required because the drives are not controlled by the BIOS. In Boot Only mode, only the removable-media drive designated as the boot device is treated as a hard disk drive. In All Disks mode, all removable-media drives supported by the BIOS are treated as hard disk drives.
- **BIOS Support for Bootable CD-ROM (Enabled)**   When set to enabled, the SCSI BIOS allows the computer to boot from a CD-ROM drive.
- **BIOS Support for Int 13 Extensions (Enabled)**   When set to enabled, the SCSI card BIOS supports Int 13h extensions. The setting can be either enabled or disabled (if your system is not Plug-and-Play).

SCSI Troubleshooting

As far as the *bus* is concerned, there is very little that can go wrong—wires and connectors do not fail spontaneously. However, it never hurts to examine the wiring, connectors, and terminator network(s) to ensure that the physical connections are intact (especially after installing or configuring new devices). The most likely areas of trouble are in the installation, setup, and operation of the devices residing on the bus.

ISOLATING TROUBLE SPOTS

Assuming that your SCSI devices have been installed correctly, problem scenarios can occur during normal operation. The first indication of a problem usually comes in the form of an error message from your operating system or application program. For example, your SCSI hard drive may not be responding, or the host PC may not be able to identify the SCSI host controller board, and so on.

The advantage to SCSI architecture is that it is reasonably easy to determine problem locations using intuitive deduction. Consider a typical SCSI system with one initiator (a host controller) and one target (such as a hard drive). If the hard drive fails to function, the trouble is either in the host controller or the drive itself. When you see drive access being attempted, but an error is generated, the trouble is probably in the drive. If no drive access is attempted before an error is generated, the error is likely in the host controller. As another example, consider a setup with one initiator and two or more targets (i.e., a hard drive and CD-ROM). If *both* the hard drive *and* CD-ROM become inoperative, the problem is likely in the host controller card since the host adapter controls both targets. If only *one* of the devices becomes inoperative (and the other device works just fine), the trouble is likely in the particular device itself.

GENERAL TROUBLESHOOTING TIPS

No matter how many precautions you take, you cannot always prevent problems from striking during SCSI installations or replacements. Fortunately, if you are installing devices one by one, you'll have far fewer problem areas to check. Your first diagnostic for a SCSI installation should be the host adapter's SCSI BIOS initialization message. If you see no initialization message when the system powers up, the problem is likely with the host adapter itself. Either it is not installed properly, its BIOS is disabled, or the adapter is defective. Make sure that the adapter is set to the desired ID (usually ID 7). Try a new or alternate SCSI adapter. If the adapter provides its initialization message as expected, the problem is probably related to driver installation. Check the installation and any command-line switches for each device driver. When installing a SCSI hard drive instead of IDE hard drives, you must ensure that any previous hard drive references are "mapped out" of the CMOS setup by entering "none" or "not installed". If preexisting drive references are not removed, the system will try to boot from IDE drives that aren't there.

Be aware that faulty SCSI ID settings can result in system problems such as "ghost" disks—disks that the system says are there but that cannot be read from or written to. Some peripherals may also not work properly with the ID that has been assigned. If you have problems interacting with an installed device, try the device with a different ID, and make sure that there are no two devices using the *same* ID. Don't be surprised to find that certain types of cables don't work properly with SCSI installations. Make sure that everything is terminated correctly. Also be sure that any external SCSI devices are powered up (if possible) before the PC is initialized. If problems persist, try different cables. A quick-reference checklist is shown here:

- Check the power to all SCSI devices (make sure that the power supply has enough capacity to handle all of your attached SCSI devices).

- Check the 50- or 68-pin signal cable to all SCSI devices. It should be a good-quality cable that is attached securely to each device.

- Check the orientation of each connector on the SCSI cable. Pin 1 must always be in the proper orientation.

- Check the SCSI ID of each device. Duplicate IDs are *not* allowed unless you're using LUN designations—this can occur when using a large number of SCSI devices such a RAID system.

- Check that both ends of the SCSI cable are properly terminated, and that the terminators are active.

- Check the SCSI controller's configuration (IRQ, I/O, BIOS addresses, and so on). Verify that the SCSI controller is not conflicting with other devices in the system.

- Check SCSI host adapter BIOS. If you're not booting from SCSI hard drives, you can often leave the SCSI BIOS disabled. This will also simplify the device configuration. You may be able to upgrade the host adapter's BIOS to resolve performance problems or compatibility issues.

- Check the CMOS Setup for drive configurations. When SCSI drives are in the system and IDE/EIDE drives are not, be sure that the drive entries under CMOS are set for "none" or "not installed".

- Check the PCI bus configuration in the CMOS Setup. See that the PCI slot containing the SCSI host adapter is active, and is using a unique IRQ (usually named IRQ A). PCI bus mastering should also be enabled.

- Check for the real-mode drivers under DOS or network OS versions like NetWare. If you're working under DOS, see that any needed drivers for the host adapter and non-HDD devices are installed in the CONFIG.SYS and AUTOEXEC.BAT files.

- Check for the protected-mode drivers under Windows 98/Me/NT/2000. If you're working under Windows, see that any needed Protected mode drivers for the host adapter and SCSI devices are installed. The SCSI host adapter should be properly identified in the SCSI Adapters Wizard.

- Try remarking-out Real mode drivers if problems occur only under Windows 98/Me/NT/2000. Real-mode SCSI drivers can sometimes interfere with Protected mode SCSI drivers. If the SCSI system works fine in DOS, but not in Windows, try temporarily disabling the DOS drivers in your startup files.

SCSI SYMPTOMS

Even the best-planned SCSI setups go wrong from time to time, and SCSI systems already in the field will not run forever. Sooner or later, you will have to deal with a SCSI problem. This part of the chapter is intended to show you a variety of symptoms and solutions for many of the problems that you will likely encounter.

SYMPTOM 12-1   **You see an error such as "Device connected, but not ready".** This error indicates that the host computer received no answer when it requested data from an installed SCSI device (i.e., a hard drive). Run the SCSI BIOS Setup utility and set the Send Start Unit Command to Yes for the particular SCSI device ID (for example, the first SCSI HDD is usually ID 0). Also verify that the suspect device is set to spin up when the power is switched on. The spin-up option is typically set by a jumper on the device itself, so you may need to refer to the device's documentation for specific jumper assignments.

SYMPTOM 12-2   **You see an error such as "Start unit request failed".**   The SCSI BIOS was unable to initiate a Send Start Unit Command to one of the installed SCSI devices. First, verify that the device is connected and powered properly. Next, run the SCSI BIOS Setup and disable the Send Start

Unit Command for that particular device. If the problem persists, the SCSI device itself may be defective and require replacement.

SYMPTOM 12-3   **You see an error such as "Timeout failure during...".**   An unexpected timeout occurred while attempting to communicate with a SCSI device. First, verify that the SCSI bus is properly terminated, and ensure that all power and signal cables are properly connected. Next, isolate potentially defective SCSI devices—try disconnecting the SCSI device cables from the SCSI card and then starting the computer. If the computer successfully restarts, the disconnected SCSI device may be defective.

SYMPTOM 12-4   **You see an error such as "Too many devices terminated on the SE connectors".**   The SCSI BIOS has detected more than two terminated devices on the SE (single-ended) cable segment. Verify the termination on the 68-pin or 50-pin internal SE connectors, and terminate only the last SCSI device at the end of each cable. Remove or disable the terminators on the SCSI devices between the ends of the cables. If no SCSI devices are connected to either of the connectors, set the SCSI BIOS termination option for the SE connector to Automatic or Enable.

SYMPTOM 12-5   **You see an error such as "Insufficient termination detected on SE connectors".**   The SCSI BIOS has detected only one terminated device (or no terminated devices) on the SE (single-ended) cable segment. Verify the termination on the 68-pin or 50-pin internal SE connectors. Terminate only the last SCSI device at the end of each cable. Remove or disable the terminators on the SCSI devices between the ends of the cables. If no SCSI devices are connected to either of the connectors, set the SCSI BIOS termination option for the SE connector to Automatic or Enable.

SYMPTOM 12-6   **You see an error such as "Too many devices terminated on LVD/SE connectors".**   The SCSI card BIOS has detected more than two terminated devices on the LVD/SE SCSI cable segment. Verify the termination on the internal and/or external 68-pin LVD/SE connectors. Terminate only the last SCSI device at the end of each cable. Remove or disable the terminators on the SCSI devices between the ends of the cables. If no SCSI devices are connected to either of the connectors, set the SCSI BIOS termination option for the LVD/SE connector to Automatic or Enable.

SYMPTOM 12-7   **You see en error such as "Insufficient termination detected on LVD/SE connectors".**   The SCSI card BIOS has detected only one terminated device (or no terminated devices) on the LVD/SE segment. Verify the termination on the internal and/or external 68-pin connectors. Terminate only the last SCSI device at the end of each cable. Remove or disable the terminators on the SCSI devices between the ends of the cables. If no SCSI devices are connected to either of the connectors, set the SCSI BIOS termination option for the LVD/SE connector to Automatic or Enable.

SYMPTOM 12-8   **After initial SCSI installation, the system will not boot from the floppy drive.**   You may or may not see an error code corresponding to this problem. Suspect the SCSI host adapter first. There may be an internal fault with the adapter that is interfering with system operation. Check that all of the adapter's settings are correct and that all jumpers are intact. If the adapter is equipped with any diagnostic LEDs, check for any problem indications. When adapter problems are indicated, replace the adapter board. If a SCSI hard drive has been installed and the drive light is always on, the SCSI signal cable has probably been reversed between the drive and adapter. Make sure to install the drive cable properly.

Check for the SCSI BIOS message generated when the system starts. If the message does not appear, check for the presence of a ROM address conflict between the SCSI adapter and ROMs on other expansion boards. Try a new address setting for the SCSI adapter. If there is a BIOS wait state jumper on the adapter, try changing its setting. If you see an error message indicating that the SCSI host adapter was not found at a particular address, check the I/O setting for the adapter.

Some more recent SCSI host adapters incorporate a floppy controller. This can cause a conflict with an existing floppy controller. If you choose to continue using the existing floppy controller, be sure to disable the host adapter's floppy controller. If you'd prefer to use the host adapter's floppy controller, remember to disable the preexisting floppy controller port.

SYMPTOM 12-9   **The system will not boot from the SCSI hard drive.**   Start by checking the system's CMOS Setup. When SCSI drives are installed in a PC, the corresponding hard drive reference in the CMOS Setup must be changed to "none" or "not installed" (this assumes that you will *not* be using IDE/EIDE hard drives in the system). If previous hard drive references have not been "mapped out," do so now, save the CMOS Setup, and reboot the PC. If the problem persists, check that the SCSI boot drive is set to ID 0. You will need to refer to the user manual for your particular drive to find how the ID is set.

Next, check the SCSI parity to be sure that it is selected consistently among all SCSI devices. Remember that *all* SCSI devices must have SCSI parity enabled or disabled—if even one device in the SCSI chain does not support parity, it must be disabled on *all* devices. Check the SCSI cabling to be sure that all cables are installed and terminated properly. Finally, be sure that the hard drive has been partitioned and formatted properly. If not, boot from a floppy disk and prepare the hard drive as required using FDISK and FORMAT.

SYMPTOM 12-10   **The SCSI drive fails to respond with an alternate HDD as the boot drive.**   Technically, you should be able to use a SCSI drive as a nonboot drive (i.e., drive D:) while using an IDE/EIDE drive as the boot device. If the SCSI drive fails to respond in this kind of arrangement, check the CMOS setting to be sure that drive 1 (the SCSI drive) is "mapped out" (or set to "none" or "not installed"). Save the CMOS Setup and reboot the PC. If the problem persists, check that the SCSI drive is set to SCSI ID 1 (the nonboot ID). Next, make sure that the SCSI parity is enabled or disabled consistently throughout the SCSI installation. If the SCSI parity is enabled for some devices and disabled for others, the SCSI system may function erratically. Finally, check that the SCSI cabling is installed and terminated properly. Faulty cables or termination can easily interrupt a SCSI system. If the problem persists, try another hard drive.

Later SCSI host adapters use BIOS that allows SCSI drives to boot even *with* IDE/EIDE drives in the system. In such a configuration, the "Boot Order" entry in CMOS Setup will determine whether A:, C:, or SCSI will be the boot device.

SYMPTOM 12-11   **The SCSI drive fails to respond with another SCSI drive as the boot drive.**   This typically occurs in a dual-drive system using two SCSI drives. Check the CMOS Setup and make sure that both drive entries in the setup are set to "none" or "not installed". Save the CMOS Setup. The boot drive should be set to SCSI ID 0, while the supplemental drive should be set to SCSI ID 1 (you will probably have to refer to the manual for the drives to determine how to select a SCSI ID). The hard drives should have a DOS partition and format. If not, create the partitions (FDISK) and format the drives (FORMAT) as required. Check to be sure that SCSI parity is enabled or disabled consistently throughout the SCSI system. If some devices use parity and other devices do not, the SCSI system may not function properly. Make sure that all SCSI cables are installed and terminated properly. If the problem persists, try systematically exchanging each hard drive.

SYMPTOM 12-12   **The system works erratically. The PC hangs or the SCSI adapter cannot find the drive(s).**   Such intermittent operation can be the result of several different SCSI factors. Before taking any action, be sure that the application software you were running when the fault occurred did not cause the problem. Unstable or buggy software can seriously interfere with system operation. Try different applications and see if the system still hangs up (you might also try any DOS diagnostic utilities that accompanied the host adapter). Check each SCSI device and make sure that parity is enabled or disabled consistently through out the SCSI system. If parity is enabled in some devices and disabled in others, erratic operation can result. Make sure that no two SCSI devices are using the same ID. Cabling problems are another common source of erratic behavior. Make sure that all SCSI cables are attached correctly and completely. Also, check that the cabling is properly terminated.

Next, suspect that there may be a resource conflict between the SCSI host adapter and another board in the system. Check each expansion board in the system to be sure that nothing is using the same IRQ, DMA, or I/O address as the host adapter (or check the Device Manager under Windows). If you find a conflict, you should alter the most recently installed adapter board. If problems persist, try a new drive adapter board.

SYMPTOM 12-13   **You see a 096xxxx error code.**   This is a diagnostic error code that indicates a problem in a 32-bit SCSI host adapter board. Check the board to be sure that it is installed correctly and completely. The board should not be shorted against any other board or cable. Try disabling one SCSI device at a time. If normal operation returns, the last device to be removed is responsible for the problem (you may need to disable drivers and reconfigure termination when isolating problems in this fashion). If the problem persists, remove and reinstall all SCSI devices from scratch, or try a new SCSI adapter board.

SYMPTOM 12-14   **You see a 112xxxx error code.**   This diagnostic error code indicates a problem in a 16-bit SCSI adapter board. Check the board to be sure that it is installed correctly and completely. The board should not be shorted against any other board or cable. Try disabling one SCSI device at a time. If normal operation returns, the last device to be removed is responsible for the problem (you may need to disable drivers and reconfigure termination when isolating problems in this fashion). Try a new SCSI host adapter board.

SYMPTOM 12-15   **You see a 113xxxx error code.**   This diagnostic code indicates a problem in a system (motherboard) SCSI adapter configuration. If there is a SCSI BIOS ROM installed on the motherboard, be sure that it is up-to-date and installed correctly and completely. If problems persist, try replacing the motherboard's SCSI controller chip (if possible), or replace the system board outright. It may be possible to circumvent a damaged motherboard SCSI controller by disabling the motherboard's controller, then installing a SCSI host adapter card.

SYMPTOM 12-16   **You see a 210xxxx error code.**   There is a fault in a SCSI hard disk. Check that the power and signal cables to the disk are connected properly. Make sure the SCSI cable is correctly terminated. Try repartitioning and reformatting the SCSI hard disk. Finally, try a new SCSI hard disk.

SYMPTOM 12-17   **A SCSI device refuses to function with the SCSI adapter even though both the adapter and device check properly.**   This is often a classic case of basic incompatibility between the device and host adapter. Even though SCSI-2 and later standards help to streamline compatibility between devices and controllers, there are still situations when the two just don't work together. Check the literature included with the finicky device and see if there are any notices of compatibility problems with the controller (perhaps the particular controller brand) you are using. If there are warnings, there may also be alternative jumper or DIP switch settings to compensate for the problem and allow you to use the device after all. A call to technical support at the device's manufacturer may help shed light on any recently discovered bugs or fixes (for example, an updated SCSI BIOS, SCSI device driver, or host adapter driver). If problems remain, try using a similar device from a different manufacturer (such as try a Connor tape drive instead of a Mountain tape drive).

SYMPTOM 12-18   **You see a "No SCSI Controller Present" error message.**   Immediately suspect that the controller is defective or installed improperly. Check the host adapter installation (including IRQ, DMA, and I/O settings), and see that the proper suite of device drivers has been installed correctly. If the system still refuses to recognize the controller, try installing it in a different PC. If the controller also fails in a different PC, the controller is probably bad and should be replaced. However, if the controller *works* in a different PC, your original PC may not support all the functions under the interrupt 15h call required to configure SCSI adapters (such as an AMI SCSI host adapter). Consider upgrading the PC BIOS ROM to a new version—especially if the PC BIOS is older. There may also be an upgraded SCSI BIOS or host adapter driver to compensate for this problem.

SYMPTOM 12-19   **The PCI SCSI host adapter is not recognized, and the SCSI BIOS banner is not displayed.**   This often occurs when installing new PCI SCSI host adapters. The host computer must be PCI REV. 2.1 compliant (or later) and the motherboard BIOS must support PCI-to-PCI Bridges (PPB) and bus mastering. This is typically a problem (or limitation) with some older PCI motherboard chipsets, and you'll probably find that the PCI SCSI adapter board works just fine on newer systems. If the system doesn't support PPB, it may not be possible to use the PCI SCSI adapter. You can try an ISA SCSI adapter instead, or upgrade the motherboard to one with a more recent chipset.

If the system hardware does offer PPB support and the problem persists, the motherboard BIOS may still not support PPB features as required by the PCI 2.1 (or later) standard. In this case, try a motherboard BIOS upgrade if one is available. If the problem continues, either the board is not in a bus-mastering slot, or the PCI slot is not enabled for bus mastering. Configure the PCI slot for bus mastering through CMOS Setup, or through a jumper on the motherboard (check your system's documentation to see exactly how).

SYMPTOM 12-20   **During bootup, you see a "Host Adapter Configuration Error" message.**   In virtually all cases, there is a problem with the PCI slot configuration for the SCSI host adapter. Try enabling an IRQ or assigning a higher-priority IRQ for the SCSI adapter's PCI slot (usually accomplished through the CMOS Setup). Alternatively, you can try moving the PCI card to a higher-priority slot. Make sure that any IRQ being assigned to the SCSI adapter PCI slot is not conflicting with other devices in the system.

SYMPTOM 12-21   **You see an error message such as "No SCSI Functions in Use".** Even when a SCSI adapter and devices are installed and configured properly, there are several possible causes for this kind of an error. First, make sure that there are no hard disk drivers installed when there are no physical SCSI hard disks in the system. Also make sure that there are no hard disk drivers installed (i.e., in **CONFIG.SYS**) when the SCSI host adapter BIOS is enabled. HDD drivers aren't needed then, but you could leave the drivers in place and disable the SCSI BIOS. Finally, this error can occur if the HDD was formatted on another SCSI controller that does not support ASPI, or uses a specialized format. For example, Western Digital controllers only work with Western Digital HDDs. In this case, you should try a more generic controller.

SYMPTOM 12-22 **You see an error message such as "No Boot Record Found".** This is generally a simple problem that can be traced to several possible issues. First, chances are that the drive has never been partitioned (FDISK) or formatted as a bootable drive (FORMAT). Repartition and reformat the hard drive. If you partitioned and formatted the drive with a third-party utility (such as TFORMAT), be sure to answer "Y" if asked to make the disk bootable. A third possibility can occur if the disk was formatted on another manufacturer's controller. If this is the case, there may be little alternative but to repartition and reformat the drive again on your current controller.

SYMPTOM 12-23 **You see an error such as "Device fails to respond. Driver load aborted".** In most cases, the problem is something simple such as the SCSI device not being turned on or cabled correctly. Verify that the SCSI devices are on and connected correctly. In other cases, the SCSI device is on, but fails the INQUIRY command—this happens when the SCSI device is defective, or not supported by the host adapter. The device may need default jumper settings changed (for example, the drive should spin up and become ready on its own). You may find that the SCSI device is sharing the same SCSI ID with another device. Check all SCSI devices to verify that each device has separate SCSI ID. You may have the wrong device driver loaded for your particular device type. Check **CONFIG.SYS** to make sure the correct driver is loaded for the drive type (for example, **TSCSI.SYS** for a hard disk, not a CD-ROM).

SYMPTOM 12-24 **You see an error such as "Unknown SCSI Device" or "Waiting for SCSI Device".** The SCSI hard disk has failed to boot as the primary drive—check that the primary hard disk is set at SCSI ID 0. Make sure that the drive is partitioned and formatted as the primary drive. If necessary, boot from a floppy with just the ASPI manager loaded in **CONFIG.SYS** and no other drivers, *then* format drive. It may also be that the SCSI cable termination is not correct (or TERMPWR is not provided by the HARD DISK for the host adapter). Verify the cable terminations and TERMPWR signal.

SYMPTOM 12-25 **You see an error such as "CMD Failure XX".** This typically occurs during the FORMAT process—the "XX" is a vendor-specific code (and you'll need to contact the vendor to determine what the error means). The most *common* problem is trying to partition a drive that is *not* low-level formatted. If this is the case, run the low-level format utility that accompanied the SCSI drive or built into the SCSI host adapter, then try partitioning again. If you're suffering a different error, you may need to take other action depending on the nature of the error.

SYMPTOM 12-26 **After the SCSI adapter BIOS header appears, you see a message like "Checking for SCSI target 0 LUN 0".** The system pauses about 30 seconds, then reports "BIOS not installed, no INT 13h device found". The system then boots normally. In most cases, the BIOS is trying to find a hard drive at SCSI ID 0 or 1, but there is no hard drive available. If you do not have a SCSI hard drive attached to the host adapter, it is recommended that the SCSI BIOS be disabled.

SYMPTOM 12-27 **The system hangs up when the SCSI BIOS header appears.** This is usually caused by a terminator problem. Make sure that the SCSI devices at the end of the SCSI chain (either internally or externally) are terminated. Check all device IDs to make sure that they are unique, and also check for system resource conflicts (such as BIOS address, I/O address, and interrupts). You may also need to disable the Shadow RAM feature in the CMOS Setup.

SYMPTOM 12-28 **The SCSI BIOS header is displayed during system startup, then you get the message "Host Adapter Diagnostic Error".**   The card either has a port address conflict with another card, or the card has been changed to port address 140h and the BIOS is enabled. Some SCSI host adapters are able to use the BIOS under port address 140h, so check for I/O conflicts. You may need to reconfigure the SCSI host adapter.

SYMPTOM 12-29 **Adaptec EasySCSI software causes an invalid page fault error under Windows 9x/Me.**   When you reinstall the Adaptec EZ-SCSI version 4.0x software, you may receive the following error message:

```
ADPST32 caused an invalid page fault in module MSCUISTF.dll at 015f:007d1bf7.
```

After you receive this error message, the computer may hang up. This problem can be caused when an Adaptec 3940UW Dual Channel SCSI adapter is installed on your computer, when you previously set the Write and Read Cache settings to Enable in SCSI Explorer (included with EZ-SCSI 4.0x), or when you uninstalled the EZ-SCSI software and then restarted the computer before attempting to reinstall the EZ-SCSI software. You should restore the firmware defaults for the SCSI BIOS:

1. Reboot the computer. When you see the SCSI BIOS banner, press CTRL-A to start the SCSI BIOS Setup program.
2. In the SCSI BIOS Setup program, press the F6 (or other appropriate) key to restore the factory default settings. You must do this for both channels if you're using a dual-channel SCSI host adapter.
3. Turn your computer off and back on.
4. Uninstall and then reinstall the EZ-SCSI software.

SYMPTOM 12-30 **You encounter problems with a BusLogic PCI SCSI controller.**   If your computer includes a PCI BusLogic SCSI controller, the Windows Device Manager displays an exclamation point in a yellow circle next to the PCI BusLogic SCSI controller, or the system performance is not a good as you expect with the PCI BusLogic SCSI controller. This fault can occur if the BusLogic card is not configured as a "true" PCI device.

To configure the BusLogic card as a "true" PCI device, remove the jumpers in the bottom-right corner of the card. If you remove the jumpers, the card can be enumerated. If you leave the jumpers on the card, the card is detected as a "legacy" device and is *not* enumerated by the PnP system. Also, if you leave the jumpers on, the I/O range is set to a standard address (such as 330h, 334h, 130h, or 134h) instead of a high PCI address. As a rule, if the version number in the top-right corner of the BusLogic card is -01-4.23K or later, the card is supported in true PCI mode and you should remove the jumpers. If the version is earlier than -01-4.23K, leave the jumpers on the card.

SYMPTOM 12-31 **You encounter problems with an Adaptec SCSI controller and CD-RW drive.**   Your computer may hang up when you start your Windows 98 computer, or your computer may run slowly when you try to access drives in your computer. This problem can occur if you're using an Adaptec AHA-2940U2W SCSI host adapter with a SCSI CD-RW drive. The AIC78U2.MPD driver file included with the Adaptec AHA-2940U2W SCSI adapter is *not* completely compatible with Windows 98. To correct this problem, download the **7800W9X.EXE** file from Adaptec's Web site. This self-extracting file contains updated drivers for the Adaptec AHA-2940U2W SCSI adapter.

SYMPTOM 12-32 **Windows 98 cannot locate the SCSI CD-ROM after upgrading.**
When Windows 98 Setup restarts your computer for the first time, Setup may be unable to access your SCSI CD-ROM drive, and you may receive error messages stating that files cannot be found (the filenames vary depending on your computer's hardware). Once Setup is completed and you attempt to start Windows 98, your computer may hang up, and only a blinking cursor may be displayed on a black screen. In virtually every case, this problem will occur if the **HIDE120.COM** file (a file related to an LS120 drive) is being loaded from the **AUTOEXEC.BAT** file. Open your **AUTOEXEC.BAT** file and disable (that is, REM-out) the HIDE120 command line, such as

```
REM d:\lsl120\hide120.com
```

Further Study

Adaptec: **www.adaptec.com**
Ancot: **www.ancot.com**
Maxtor: **www.maxtor.com**
Qlogic: **www.qlogic.com**
Quantum: **www.quantum.com/src/**
SCSI guide: **www.delec.com/guide/scsi/**
SCSI Trade Association: **www.scsita.org**
Seagate: **www.seagate.com**
Symbios articles: **www.lsilogic.com**
Symbios specs: **www.symbios.com/x3t10**
Western Digital: **www.wdc.com**

13

REPEATERS, HUBS, AND SWITCHES

With rare exception, as a network grows there are certain pieces of network hardware that will find their way into the LAN or WAN that is being maintained. Some hardware such as repeaters, hubs, and switches simply allow one workstation to communicate with another on the same local network, while other network hardware such as bridges, routers, and gateways allow two workstations in geographically diverse areas or diverse network topologies to communicate. These devices vary in intelligence and complexity based primarily on the layer of the OSI model at which they operate. In this chapter the former group of network hardware will be addressed, because all will typically reside within a local area network environment.

Repeaters

As with any electrical signal, data transmissions have a tendency to slowly degrade over distance traveled. This degradation of signal is a condition known as *attenuation*, and often limits the diameter of a given data network to at most a few hundred meters. For example, in 10Base2 or thinnet networks, the entire bus (or total length of all cable segments) cannot exceed 185 meters. To overcome this distance limitation and allow thinnet networks to reach total distances of up to 925 meters, repeaters were created for Ethernet data transmission.

 Repeaters are not limited to just wired electrical networks, as they can also be found in optical and wireless varieties.

A repeater is a fairly simple device that operates at the physical layer (or layer 1 in the OSI model), and acts as a signal amplifier to the medium to which it is attached. Essentially, a signal enters the repeater on one of its ports, which is then amplified and retimed, then retransmitted in its amplified form out all other ports. Basic repeaters have only two ports, while more advanced or multiport repeaters may have more.

In the case of thinnet, up to five total segments can be created with up to four repeaters, but only three of the segments can be host to workstations. The other two segments are used strictly for extending the distance of the network, and no workstations should be located on these segments. This limitation of repeaters in Ethernet networks is known as the 5-4-3 rule, which exists due to propagation delays that result when a network becomes too lengthy. Essentially, as a network grows, the time for a signal to travel from one end of the network to the other increases, thus workstation X at one end of the network may have trouble accurately detecting when workstation Y at the other end of the network is transmitting—causing a high rate of collisions. Should network issues arise when using repeaters in a thinnet network, it may be wise to move the server or servers in a given network towards the middle of all segments. Although not required, this ensures that any given workstation would not need to cross more than two repeaters to communicate with the server, and may clear minor network difficulties.

Because repeaters operate at the physical layer, they can clean noise from and amplify a received signal, but they cannot correct a corrupted signal. Thus, as the adage goes, garbage in equals garbage out. Additionally, repeaters have no means of detecting where data should be sent; thus, networks cannot be segmented into multiple collision domains with devices of this nature. This simplicity does have its benefits, however, in that a repeater can typically be placed into a network with minimal (if any) configuration required. As its name implies, simply supply power and cable—and the repeater will repeat anything it receives.

Hubs and MAUs

As networks migrated from coaxial to twisted-pair infrastructure, a new device was required to input the signal received from one workstation on a twisted-pair network and repeat it to another. A problem existed in that most twisted-pair networks contain more than two workstations in a given network segment; thus, a single twisted-pair crossover cable between two devices would not suffice. To satisfy this new requirement, a multiport repeater for twisted-pair cable was created. For Ethernet networks, this device was designated a hub, and a similar device for token ring networks is called a media access unit or MAU.

HUBS

Similar to a repeater, the hub operates at the physical layer (or layer 1 in the OSI model), and simply listens for transmissions on any one of its RJ-45 ports. When a transmission or signal is received, the hub amplifies and retimes the signal, then retransmits it to every other port that a workstation or server is connected to. As the hub is an amplification device, each workstation connected to it can be a maximum distance of 100m from the hub itself.

Classes of Hubs

When deciding on which hub to install, it is important to realize that not all hubs are created equal. In fact, there are three very distinct classifications of hubs, each building on the functionality of the class before it. These three major classes of hubs are passive, active, and intelligent, all of which are generally available with anywhere between 4 and 48 or more RJ-45 Ethernet ports.

- **Passive**   As the name somewhat denotes, this class of hub simply accepts a signal from one port and retransmits it without any form of amplification to all other nodes. As a result, this hub should only be used in very small environments where workstations are fairly close together, as the total length of *all* cable used cannot exceed 100m. This class also happens to be the least expensive class of hub available.

- **Active**   Addressing the need for larger networks, the active hub provides amplification and retiming to a signal prior to retransmission. This increase in functionality allows for each workstation or server to be a maximum of 100m from the connected hub, without any risk of excessive signal degradation due to attenuation. As an added benefit, fewer collisions should occur in active hub networks, as hosts do not have to retransmit packets that have minor transmission errors due to timing.

- **Intelligent**   Intelligent hubs are essentially active hubs with some remotely accessible management functionality added. This is clearly the most expensive class of hub, but does provide statistical reporting on utilization and errors within the network, as well as a means of remotely enabling or disabling an individual port on the hub for security or troubleshooting purposes. Statistical information is generally available though a variety of means, including serial console, command line (Telnet) or web-based GUI via the network, or through a network management protocol known as SNMP.

It should also be noted that hubs are available in a variety of supported Ethernet standards, including but not limited to 10BaseT and 100BaseT. Some hubs may only support one or the other, while more advanced hubs can support both through a method known as auto-negotiation. It is important to ensure that workstation NICs and connected hubs support the same Ethernet standard—for example, a 10BaseT NIC will not function when connected to a 100BaseT or Fast Ethernet hub. Additionally, when referring to Fast Ethernet, the IEEE 802.3u specification classifies hubs or repeaters into two groups, those being class I and class II. The difference between the two classes is based around the number of hubs or repeaters that can be between any two given hosts on a network. For example, class I devices allow for only one hub or repeater between any two given hosts, while class II devices allow for no more than two hubs or repeaters between any two given hosts. This limitation is due to the delay that each of the aforementioned devices introduces into a Fast Ethernet network.

Installing Hubs

Aside from intelligent hubs, most hubs can be placed into a network without any prior configuration. Because they are similar to repeaters (in that hubs merely repeat a signal and are not concerned with the sender or intended receiver of a particular packet), very often no further configuration is necessary. Intelligent hubs, however, may require configuration to allow access to their management functions.

Physically speaking, to connect a hub, simply apply power to the device and connect the RJ-45 cables from any required workstation to the hub. A successful connection between hub and workstation would be indicated by a solid link LED on both hub and workstation NIC. In addition, some hubs will also indicate the port speed if more than one speed is supported (that is, 10 Mbps or 100 Mbps).

Should a hub not have an ample number of ports, two or more 10BaseT hubs may be chained together to grow a network. Unless otherwise specified by the hub manufacturer, only two 100BaseT class II hubs may be chained together over a maximum distance of 5 meters between hubs. This chaining or cascading of hubs is typically performed through an uplink port, which is an RJ-45 receptacle specially designated for connection between hubs. Some hubs allow the uplink port to share the same capabilities as a normal workstation port, which is indicated through a user-selectable switch to determine the operating mode of the port. Additionally, more advanced or stackable hubs may have a coaxial 10Base2 BNC port for trunking, or even a proprietary uplink port and cable for a high-performance interconnection between hubs.

If a hub does not have an uplink port, a normal workstation port can be used, providing a twisted-pair crossover cable is used to connect the two hubs.

Hub Management Notes

Since hubs are fairly simplistic devices, there is not a whole lot to manage on a device of this nature. Those that are manageable, however, do provide for the reporting of utilization and error statistics, as well as port-by-port administration. Aside from this advanced reporting functionality, almost all hubs have very basic means of reporting activity through front-panel diagnostic LEDs. With this in mind, most hubs have the following indicators:

■ **Power**   Typically indicated by a solid green LED, indicating the hub is powered on and operating properly.

■ **Activity**   This indicator will vary from hub to hub; some will have a single activity light indicating there is transmission activity through the entire attached network. Other hubs may have an activity light per port indicating transmission activity on a per-port basis.

■ **Link**   Most hubs will have a link LED per port, indicating a successful connection has been made between the hub and connected device. Some hub link LEDs also double as activity indicators.

■ **10/100**   Those hubs that support multiple speeds may have a per-port LED to indicate at which speed the port is operating.

■ **Collisions**   The only LED on a hub that should call attention to the device is the collision indicator. While it is normal for this indicator to blink occasionally, excessive actuation would indicate a transmission or performance problem on the network.

For intelligent hubs with management functionality, statistical and error information is most often accessed in one of the following ways:

■ **Direct console access**   This requires a terminal or computer to be connected to the hub's serial connector—typically via a null-modem serial cable, though some devices may require a straight-through or proprietary serial cable. Once connected, using any terminal emulation program such as HyperTerm will provide access to a command-line-based management system. While console settings vary from vendor to vendor, generally a setting of 8 bits, no parity, and one stop bit (or 8-N-1), and a port speed of 9,600 bps with VT100 terminal emulation selected should provide smooth connectivity to the device. Commands do vary from vendor to vendor, so be sure to check the manual that came with the hub, though typing **?** once logged into the hub is a good place to start.

■ **Remote command-line access via Telnet**   In order to access a network-based command line via Telnet, it is necessary to first configure the hub with at least an IP address and subnet mask. This can generally be accomplished by first connecting to the hub via its serial console. Once an IP address has been configured, simply Telneting to the configured IP address should provide access to the hub's command line.

■ **Web-based GUI access**   Should a graphical management interface be desired, some devices provide such an interface via a small web server embedded into the device itself. To access this management interface, the device must first be configured with at least an IP address and subnet mask, generally set through direct console access. Once configured, access to the graphical interface is typically performed through a standard web browser such as Microsoft Internet Explorer or Netscape Navigator. Some devices only support a proprietary graphical application, which should be shipped with the device on a disk or CD-ROM.

When configuring a hub or any device for management, be sure to change and save the default administration password. Additionally, if configuring the device for access via a network, it is wise to configure an IP address and subnet mask, but not a gateway address. This will inhibit anyone on the outside from directly accessing the hub's management functionality. Always be sure the configured IP address is available and not in use by any other device.

Hub Troubleshooting

The greatest benefit of the star topology formed by the use of hubs and twisted-pair cabling is almost certainly the ease in troubleshooting it provides. Unlike the linear bus that is used in 10Base2 and 10Base5 networks, a failed cable segment will affect only one node—as opposed to all nodes on the bus in a 10Base2 network. Additionally, being that all nodes are aggregated at one point (hub) in a star topology, it provides a central location from which to test.

When troubleshooting a connectivity problem, the first step is to check the diagnostic indicators on the hub and workstation NIC in question. The absence of a link LED in either location would most likely be indicative of a physical connectivity problem. However, make sure that the port is enabled on both the host and hub (if manageable). Should link be present on one side of the connection and not the other, it may be a physical connectivity problem as well, or it is possible that either device is not set at the proper speed (that is, 10 or 100 Mbps). While a mismatch in transmission speed should not allow for a proper link to be established, some older devices may not act as expected in this scenario. Should a physical problem be suspected, check the cable run for physical damage and loose connectors. If possible, use a cable tester or scanner to verify the cable is in working order. Remember to always observe the 100m distance limitation of twisted-pair cabling.

The link LED should not be considered an absolute certainty in cable diagnostics, however, because it is possible that either the hub port or NIC has failed. To test this, simply move the cable segment to a new (and known working) hub port and check for a link LED. If there is still an absence of link, try swapping patch cables at either end, and check the cable run with a tester. Finally, swap the workstation NIC if there is still difficulty in obtaining link. For further twisted-pair cable troubleshooting, refer to Chapter 8.

 Always ensure that the NIC and hub support the same speed Ethernet, as a 10BaseT NIC will not work with a 100BaseT- or Fast Ethernet-only hub, and vice versa.

Other hub status and diagnostic indicators are useful in troubleshooting as well. For instance, if users are reporting slow network performance, check the collision indicator on the hub for excessive actuation. While this LED should indicate occasional collisions, a high number of collisions is not normal and is due to either a transmission difficulty with one or more nodes or network utilization that is too high, and thus the network should be segmented to allow for additional collision domains.

If a transmission error is suspected, it may be possible to visually ascertain which node or nodes are causing the problem by looking for synchronous actuation between the collision LED and an individual port's activity LED. Additionally, disconnecting ports one by one until the collision LED resumes a normal indication rate can also aid in locating the node in trouble. Lastly, if a manageable hub is in use, the hub's command line or graphical interface may be able show per-port statistics such as collisions or transmission errors on a per-port basis. Once the troubled node has been identified, be sure to check the cable segment for both physical and EMI interference problems with a cable scanner, if possible.

Occasionally, a manageable hub may seemingly disappear from the network, in that it no longer responds to either Telnet or web-based management requests. This has been known to occur when the device supports a protocol known as BOOTP or DHCP. Essentially, when a BOOTP-enabled device first boots it will send a broadcast request to any and all BOOTP or DHCP servers, requesting an IP address and associated information. If such a server exists on the local network, the hub will be given a new IP address, which is most likely not the address to which it was originally configured. To ascertain if this potential problem exists, connect to the hub's console port and check to ensure that BOOTP configuration is disabled. Be sure to give the device a new IP address and save the configuration before exiting the console.

MAUS

Similar to hubs in an Ethernet environment, media access units (MAUs) physically connect workstations in a star topology with twisted-pair cabling. Rather than use Ethernet as the network medium, though, an IBM-developed technology called token ring is used instead. While both technologies physically form a star topology, the similarities end there as token ring MAUs actually create an internal bus, thus making a logical ring of all workstations in the network. Also, unlike Ethernet, there is no contention for transmission on a token ring network, as a transmission control device known as the token is used to allow all workstations to transmit within a given time period. There is a disadvantage to token ring networks, however, in that until recently they were limited to speeds of either 4 Mbps or 16 Mbps. While faster speed token ring networks are now available, Fast Ethernet and Gigabit Ethernet technologies have become quite popular in terms of LAN connectivity.

On a basic level, token ring works by putting all workstations on a ring constructed by the MAU. Then, each host waits for the token to come so they can transmit. While a workstation has the token, it is free to transmit and can do so without any risk of collisions. Once it is done transmitting, the token is released and passed to the next workstation in the ring. Without the token, a workstation is not permitted to transmit.

The ring itself is constructed by electrical relays within the MAU, which essentially connect one port's transmitting pair with the next port's receiving pair. This continues from port to port until all ports collectively produce the ring. If a particular port is not in use, that port is put in a bypass mode; thus, the ring is passed to the next active port.

When a new workstation is attached to the network, the MAU's port starts in a bypass mode that essentially provides a loopback to the connected workstation. In order to be inserted into the ring, the workstation places a low level of voltage on its transmitting pair, thus indicating it is ready to participate in the ring. The MAU detects this voltage and the workstation's receiving pair is connected to another port's transmitting pair, while the new workstation's transmitting pair is connected to a different port's receiving pair. This method of bringing a workstation into the ring is called *insertion*. Should voltage ever drop from a particular port, the MAU will consider that node to be down and will remove it from the ring by putting the port into bypass mode.

Classes of MAUs

Again similar to their Ethernet cousin, MAUs are available in three major classes: passive, active, and controlled. Passive MAUs are nothing more than a box of electrical relays designed to produce an internal ring with connected workstations. They do not incorporate any type of signal amplification; thus, distances for a passive MAU-based token ring network are somewhat limited.

Active MAUs, on the other hand, include signal amplifiers, and they are able to extend the size of a token ring network to far beyond the reaches of a passive MAU-based network. They are typically available with port configurations from 8 up to 16 or more, but are not available in a manageable or intelligent variety.

Instead of a manageable MAU, token ring networks can contain controlled access units (CAUs). Aside from the availability of management functionality, CAUs differ from MAUs in that they do not allow for workstations to directly connect to them. In order to connect a workstation to a CAU, an additional module called a lobe attachment is required.

MAU Troubleshooting

Token ring networks have a series of fault recovery algorithms built into the workstation NICs; thus, many errors that occur on a network of this type will go undetected. However, as with any wired infrastructure, cable faults can occur and hardware can fail. Because of this, troubleshooting physical issues in a token ring environment is very similar to that in an Ethernet environment. In fact, many MAUs do have diagnostic LEDs in much the same way Ethernet hubs do.

In token ring networks, connectivity problems are mostly the cause of a cable fault or failed hardware. As such, anytime a workstation is experiencing difficulty attaching to the ring, its cable should always be tested first. Should the cable test good, try moving it to a new MAU port. Lastly, the workstation's NIC may be the culprit, and should be swapped out to test this possibility. Thankfully, some token ring cards do ship with diagnostic software, which may be able to identify or provide information on an error condition that is causing the connectivity problem.

Switches

Many times in this book the phrase "collision domains" has been mentioned, but until this point a device that could support creating these separate virtual or physical network segments has not been discussed. Switches have the ability to create separate collision domains either physically or virtually, because they operate at the data link layer (or layer 2 in the OSI model), and higher in cases of a multilayer switch.

When operating at layer 2, a device has the ability to make intelligent decisions on how to handle a given packet of data based on the source and destination MAC address. A Media Access Control (MAC) address is essentially a unique identifier that is hard-coded into every network device at the time of production.

In this chapter, Ethernet switches—which switch frames of data between ports—will be discussed. Other network switches do exist—for example, frame relay switches are used largely by telecommunications carriers, as are Asynchronous Transfer Mode (ATM) switches. ATM switches are also found in large enterprise networks, but differ greatly from Ethernet switches in that they switch in cells and not frames. ATM switches also cost considerably more than Ethernet switches, but have some large performance advantages to go with the increased price tag.

While on the surface an Ethernet switch may look similar to a hub, switches do not just receive a signal on one port and repeat it to all other ports. Instead, a switch will receive a packet of data on one port and actually read the header information in the packet. By reading the header information, the switch can deduce where the packet originated from and where it is supposed to go. As a result, the switch will transmit the frame out (and only out) the destination port that connects to the intended recipient. The exception to this process occurs when a workstation sends a broadcast packet, which (since the data is intended for all workstations) the switch will retransmit across all ports.

Forwarding frames only to the port that connects to the intended recipient has many advantages, the greatest being performance, because many nodes on the network can transmit at once without risk of collision. Another advantage of a switched architecture is enhanced security. In shared or hub-based environments, all traffic is repeated to all ports; thus, any workstation could eavesdrop or "sniff" another workstation's network communications. In switched environments, however, because traffic is forwarded only to its intended recipient, no other workstations can sniff out data that is not intended for it. Many other advantages exist, too, including full-duplex operation, the creation of virtual LANs or VLANs, and enhanced network manageability.

Switches are not designed merely to connect workstations together; they also excel at aggregating multiple hubs together. This saves bandwidth and increases performance, because the switch will only send packets to the connected hub that hosts the recipient workstation of the packet.

FULL-DUPLEX OPERATION

Another large performance gain in the use of switches comes from the ability of a workstation to transmit and receive at the same time, or operate in full-duplex mode. This differs from the typical half-duplex environment in which a workstation can only transmit when it is not receiving data, or vice versa.

To understand how this is accomplished, first understand that the switch port and the host that is connected to it establish a private point-to-point Ethernet circuit (as opposed to shared among multiple switch ports). This allows both the switch and host to transmit and receive concurrently because there is no contention for transmission ability or bandwidth. The switch will transmit packets it receives for a given destination immediately unless data is already being transmitted out the destination port. In this case, the switch will buffer the frame and transmit it when the port is again available. This eliminates collisions and retransmissions resulting from collisions.

A huge performance gain results from not only the elimination of collisions and retransmissions, but also from the workstation or server NIC no longer having to divide its time of transmitting and receiving. The result is a performance gain of almost 100 percent or double over a shared half-duplex environment.

SWITCH TECHNIQUES

Ethernet switches use two main techniques for the switching of data between network ports. Each method has its own advantages over the other, and the choice of which technique to purchase depends heavily on the environment in which it will be operating. Regardless of which method is chosen, all switches make use of a port forwarding database or FDB, which allows wire-speed switching to occur because the device can store a table of hosts and their respective ports for later reference.

In the first method of switching, data arrives at the switch and is immediately acted upon by the switch—often before the transmission is complete. The switch ascertains which port to forward the frames of data to and begins the bridging process. This fast-acting method is called cut-through switching, as the switch forwards the data as soon as it can figure out where to send it (rather than buffering it), and bases this information on the first frame received. Because the data is forwarded before the source has completed transmitting all frames, the switch does not have a chance to accomplish any form of error correction on the data. While this method is the faster of the two in many circumstances, it can become considerably slower if data is corrupt, or if the switch has to buffer frames due to a slower or busy receiving switch port.

The second method of switching is termed *store and forward*, and as the name implies, data that arrives at the switch is first stored in buffers until the switch has received a complete frame. As the data is being stored, the switch analyzes it for destination information. Once a complete frame is stored, the switch performs a CRC error check on the frame prior to forwarding it to the recipient's switch port. Should the recipient port be busy, the switch will keep the frame stored until it can successfully forward it. This is often the preferred method, because in many cases a switch will temporarily have to buffer outgoing data due to a slow or busy recipient, and with store-and-forward switches an additional error check is performed—while with cut-through switches, there is no error check. As a point of reference, the average latency or delay introduced into a transmission by a cut-through switch is 45.6 microseconds. This is less than 6 microseconds faster than a store-and-forward switch, which introduces a 51.5 microsecond delay into the transmission. This marginal difference between switches typically makes store and forward the method of choice.

USING A SWITCH

When deploying a switch, it is suggested to first plan where the switch will be placed in the network. For example, while a switch can be connected directly to each and every workstation, this is an expensive proposition when such high performance is not required. Rather, it may be wise to connect servers to the switch, and workstations to small departmental hubs that are then aggregated by the switch.

As seen in Figure 13-1, this architecture provides direct high-speed full-duplex connectivity to the servers, while allowing for a few sets of workstation groups or workgroups, each in their own collision domain, to access the servers with a reduced chance of collisions occurring. This keeps network performance and deployment costs at optimal levels.

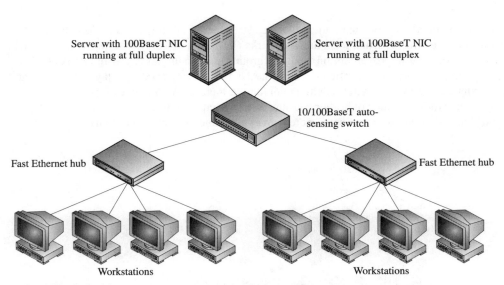

FIGURE 13-1   In this example, switches are used to aggregate two hub-attached workgroups, while providing full-duplex 100BaseT to the servers.

In a deployment of this nature, much like a hub, the switch does not require that any special configuration be performed. Once inserted into the network, the switch will learn the port locations of all workstations and servers automatically, and save that information in its port-forwarding database. Should switch management access be desired, an IP address and subnet mask would have to be configured on the switch, and can be accomplished via the switch's serial console port.

Bridging Groups

Basic layer 2 switches typically support a means of segmenting or dividing the switch ports into smaller logical groupings called *bridging groups*. This feature is useful when a physical division or separation of two or more networks is desired. For example, lets assume that the finance department occupies switch ports 1–7, the marketing department occupies ports 8–15, and the sales department occupies ports 16–23.

Assuming each department has its own server, the switch can be configured into three separate bridging groups that would ensure that each department can only access resources designated for them. Additionally, segmenting a switch also cuts down on broadcasts within a given network segment because there are fewer workstations in the group, which (much like a reduction in collisions) increases the performance of a network.

VLANs

As switches have matured, so, too, have their feature sets. One of the biggest additions to Ethernet switches is the ability to create virtual local area networks (VLANs), not only within a switch but also between switches. As a big improvement on bridging group functionality, VLANs have many advantages, including the ability to move traffic between VLANs (when supported by a layer 3 switch) and physically moving users between switches while maintaining their VLAN membership.

Referring back to the discussion of bridging groups, and as seen in Figure 13-2, we have three departments, all of which have their own set of network resources available to them. A problem exists, however,

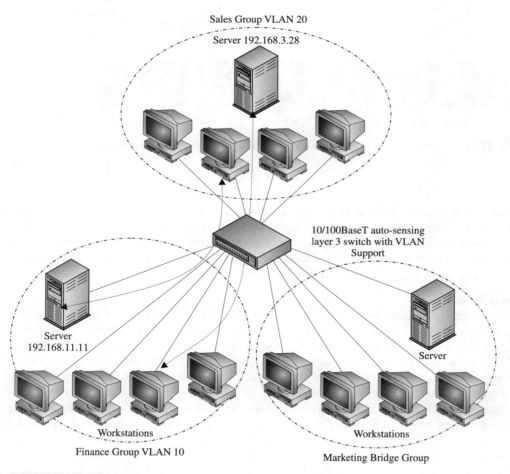

FIGURE 13-2   The difference between bridge groups and VLANs for the separation of broadcast domains

in that if a user in the finance department does need to gain access to a server in the sales department, he or she physically cannot. By placing each of these groups into their own VLANs, we now have a variety of options available to handle this dilemma. Note that a layer 3 switch can route between VLANs, but not bridging groups. Additionally, most switches do not support both VLANs and bridge groups.

One option is to allow routing between VLANs. This functionality is supported by an external router, which will be covered in Chapter 14, or a layer 3 switch, which can operate at both the data link and network layers. In this instance, a user in the sales VLAN (called VLAN 20) will simply access the server in the finance VLAN (called VLAN 10) by the server's IP address. The switch will recognize the IP address as belonging to VLAN 10 and virtually route data between VLANs as needed. Once again, this allows for the creation of smaller broadcast domains, which can enhance the performance of the network as a whole.

The last example of VLAN advantages is shown in Figure 13-3, which shows four switches connected via fiber-optic trunks. As illustrated in this figure, there are three different VLANs, all of which

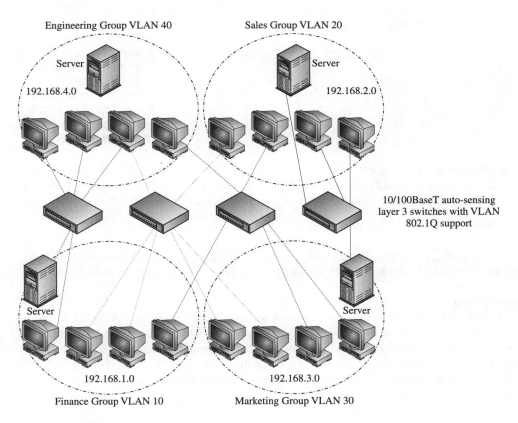

FIGURE 13-3   802.1Q VLAN tagging between switches

reside across all switches. By utilizing a trunking protocol known as 802.1Q, every switch in the trunk group is able to tag each frame of data with a VLAN identifier. As a result, when data moves from switch to switch, the receiving switch will examine the frame's 802.1Q tag for a VLAN ID, and based on that information forward the frame to the proper VLAN and/or broadcast group. This functionality can allow users in a given VLAN to move from switch to switch without losing connectivity to their own workgroup's VLAN, which in turn can ease some fairly large management difficulties from moves, adds, and changes.

The 802.1Q tag is actually 4 bytes of data that are added to the traditional Ethernet 802.3 frame format, and specify not only VLAN membership information but also 802.1p frame priority information. The 4-byte tag is broken down into four separate fields, which are as follows:

LABEL	FIELD NAME	SIZE	DESCRIPTION
TCI	Tag Control Info	2 bytes	If set to a value of 8100, it indicates that the frame uses 802.1Q and 802.1p tags.
P	Priority	3 bits	Indicates the 802.1p priority level of 0–7.
C	Canonical Indicator	1 bit	Specifies if the MAC addresses are in canonical format. Ethernet frames typically have this value set to 0.
VLAN	VLAN ID	12 bits	Specifies which VLAN the frame belongs to.

The configuration of VLANs in a switch is not a complex process and can typically be done with just a few commands. For example, to add ports 1, 2, 3, 5, 7, 23, and 24 to VLAN 10 (which was already created) on an Extreme Summit Ethernet switch, the following command could be used:

```
Switch-1: configure vlan 10 add ports 1,2,3,5,7,23,24
```

Should the switch be running at layer 3 as well, a configured VLAN might require its own IP address for the virtual routing interface in that VLAN. Without it, routing between VLANs may not be possible.

Port Mirroring

When complex network issues arise, sometimes the only means of locating a problem is by actually examining the data being sent over the network with a network analyzer or sniffer. Now, this might sound easy if the network is composed of all Ethernet hubs—thus all ports receive any and all data being transmitted. Considering, however, that a switch is designed to specifically shield ports from receiving traffic that is not intended for them, how does one examine all data being sent on the network?

Thankfully, many switch vendors have considered this issue and have devised a solution called *port mirroring*. With this feature, a switch can be configured to literally mirror traffic from any individual or group of ports on the switch to any other port that is configured as the mirror port. Additionally, switches can even be configured to mirror one or more VLANs to a single port for testing purposes.

For example, to enable mirroring on an Extreme Summit Ethernet switch from VLAN 1 to port 48, the following commands would be used:

```
Switch-1: enable mirroring to port 48
Switch-1: configure mirroring add VLAN 1
```

Often when mirroring is enabled on a given port, that port may not be usable for normal network transmissions.

SWITCH MANAGEMENT NOTES

Because switches are fairly complex devices that can read and analyze data being transmitted, they provide quite a wealth of information in terms of statistical data as well as per-port utilization and error counters. Additionally, the switch should be able to provide the MAC address and, in the case of a layer 3 switch, the IP address of workstations located on each port. This information can be quite valuable when trying to locate a bandwidth hog or workstations generating errors on the network.

As with even the most basic hubs, nearly all switches also have front-panel diagnostic LEDs, as such the layout of these indicators very often mimics that of an intelligent hub.

Switch management interfaces can provide great information in terms of network utilization, error rates, and other real-time statistical information. While this information is accessible via either the command line or even a web-based GUI interface, it may also be helpful to access this information via the Simple Network Management Protocol (SNMP). This allows for the aggregation and proactive monitoring of a group of network devices from a central monitoring application. Some devices even support configuration changes via an SNMP software console, which may assist in reducing administration time if multiple switches are being employed.

When using SNMP, it is recommended for security purposes to change the default public and private SNMP community strings. Additionally, if supported by the device, a suggested practice is to limit which hosts have access via SNMP or Telnet on a per-IP-address basis.

SWITCH TROUBLESHOOTING

As switches are very similar to hubs, troubleshooting procedures are nearly identical with only a few switch-specific additions. Refer to the earlier section on hub troubleshooting for basic star topology troubleshooting guidelines.

General Troubleshooting

In addition to general hub troubleshooting, remember that switches (as well as intelligent hubs) have the added benefit of monitoring transmissions and errors on a per-port basis. As such, be sure to reference the switch's management interface to locate those workstations that may be experiencing trouble in transmitting or receiving data. A high number of errors may signify a physical cable problem, but be sure to look for an incrementing count because the present number may have accumulated over a long duration.

Always make use of the port forwarding database (FDB) whenever possible. For example, if two computers have somehow been configured with identical IP addresses, generally Windows will advise of such and also reference the offending workstation's MAC address. With this information, the MAC address can be looked up in the FDB to determine its location or at least physical port number, which can be temporarily disabled to allow one of the two workstations to communicate properly.

Should a workstation be moved between ports, it might be necessary to clear the port forwarding database (or even ARP cache on layer 3 switches), because some switches may not age out the entry for the original connected port. Keep in mind that this action may slow switch performance down temporarily while the FDB is rebuilt. As a preliminary and less intrusive method, first try to Ping the host's gateway from the host itself once it is powered up and connected to the network.

Another common problem among switches is the lack of compatibility in the auto-negotiation function many switches employ. Whenever using an auto-negotiating switch and NIC card, it is wise to manually configure both devices for whichever port speed and duplex mode is desired. Very often an undesired duplex mode (generally half duplex) is auto selected—or in some cases the mode intermittently changes between the two devices, causing intermittent connectivity issues. This most often occurs when one of the devices is set to full duplex, while the other is set to auto-negotiate. Generally speaking, both NIC speed and duplex can be configured on the workstation through the adapter's properties or driver settings. Be sure to see both hub and NIC card documentation for the specific means of adjusting these values.

Always ensure that the NIC and switch support the same speed Ethernet, as a 10BaseT NIC will not work with a 100BaseT- or Fast Ethernet-only switch, and vice versa.

VLAN Troubleshooting

With the added benefit of VLANs comes potential trouble and confusion with VLANs. It is not uncommon for a user to seemingly not have network access when they are configured for one VLAN but actually reside in another. This can be rectified rather easily with the MAC address of the workstation in question. With the address in hand, look up its entry in the FDB and find its corresponding port number. Next, verify what VLAN that port resides in and if it is incorrect, simply modify that port's VLAN membership configuration such that it will reside in the proper VLAN.

Another common VLAN problem is trouble with inter-VLAN routing. An easy means of testing where routing may be broken is with the **traceroute** or **tracert** command-line utility often found in most operating systems and network devices. To use this utility, simply type **traceroute** (or the equivalent) followed by a destination IP address that is believed to be reachable through routing. The Traceroute utility will then list all devices or hops that are taken to get to the destination. When routing fails, hops will be listed with "* * *" indicating a timeout. The routing issue is most likely located between the hop that times out and the previous reachable hop.

If the previous hop is the switch (assuming a layer 3 switch), be sure to check the switch for a default route and any other route that may be needed. Remember that in order to route between VLANs, all switches require an IP address in each subnet that VLANs will be routed between.

SYMPTOMS

While many connectivity issues can be isolated to physical cabling problems, often a simple configuration error can cause many problems as well. Some typical host and network configuration errors are described next.

SYMPTOM 13-1   **There is no connection between segments linked by a switch.**
Assuming both segments have obtained a good link to the switch, the problem most likely is a switch configuration issue. Because switches can be divided into bridge groups or VLANs, it is entirely possible that the two segments in question are in two different groups or VLANs. To verify this, check the switch configuration for each of the connected ports, and make changes as needed.

SYMPTOM 13-2   **You're faced with persistent broadcast storms.**   One of the unfortunate side effects of using Microsoft Windows is the increasingly large broadcast storms that are created as more and more nodes are brought onto a LAN segment. One method of reducing broadcasts is to create several smaller broadcast domains. This can be done quite easily with switch VLANs, and should allow for a reduction in broadcast storms while permitting all nodes to communicate with each other.

SYMPTOM 13-3   **There is consistently low data throughput at the switch.**   A common reason for low data throughput is often a mismatch in duplex settings. For example, if a server's switch port is hard-coded to 100-Mbps full duplex and the server itself is configured to auto-negotiate, the server will "negotiate" the connection to 100-Mbps half duplex. To rectify this, manually set any suspected switch ports to 100 Mbps and full-duplex operation if possible. Also, be sure to check the switch's management interface for an excessive number of port errors on any port, as this will help identify other ports with possible duplex or connectivity issues.

SYMPTOM 13-4   **You cannot access the switch using Telnet, SNMP, or web browser software.**   Before any switch will be accessible via the network, be sure to configure at least an IP address and subnet mask. Assuming this is already configured, ensure that the workstation from which the switch is being accessed is in the same local subnet as the switch. If it is not, the switch will need to be configured with a gateway address so that it can communicate outside of its local subnet. Lastly, the switch may have been configured to only accept network management connections from certain IP addresses. Connect to the switch via its console port to verify your source IP address is listed.

If none of the above pertain, it is possible that a BOOTP or DHCP server has dynamically reconfigured the switch. To check this, connect to the console port of the switch and verify its IP address information. If the address has changed, check to see that BOOTP and DHCP have been disabled, and if not disable them now. Always remember to save the configuration before exiting the configuration interface.

SYMPTOM 13-5   **You cannot access the switch through its serial port connection.**
Some network devices require null-modem cables to connect to their console ports, others require regular serial cables, and yet others require proprietary cables to connect successfully. Check the switch manual to ensure that you are using the right cable and proper terminal emulation settings. If trouble is still experienced, try using a different cable because the current cable may have failed. It is rare for a console port to fail, but it is possible. Lastly, the device may have frozen its management interface, and a reset may restore normal operation.

Further Study

Cisco – Ethernet Technology:
http://www.cisco.com/univercd/cc/td/doc/cisintwk/ito_doc/ethernet.htm
Cisco – Troubleshooting Ethernet:
http://www.cisco.com/univercd/cc/td/doc/cisintwk/itg_v1/tr1904.htm
Charles Spurgeon's Ethernet Web Site:
http://www.ethermanage.com/ethernet/ethernet.html
Extreme Networks Technology Guide:
http://www.extremenetworks.com/technology/technology.asp
IEEE: **http://grouper.ieee.org/groups/802/3/**
Lantronix Networking: **http://www.lantronix.com/learning/index.html**
TechFest: **http://www.techfest.com/networking/**

14

BRIDGES, ROUTERS, AND GATEWAYS

As data networks begin to move from the local area to metro and wide area, network devices must become more and more intelligent in how they transmit data between networks. This increased intelligence is required, because whether the environment requires additional collision domains for growth or the transmission of data between two or more geographically disperse networks, simply repeating all traffic from one network to another (much like a hub or repeater) will not suffice—bandwidth constraints alone will begin to cause problems.

In order to efficiently transport data in these increasingly complex environments, network devices need to operate at not only the physical layer but also the data link, network, and in some cases even higher layers. Devices that operate in these layers include bridges, routers, and gateways, and are more often than not used in wide area networking applications. This chapter will explore these devices from both a functional and a troubleshooting perspective in both a local and a wide area networking capacity.

Bridges

The first device in this group is the bridge, which operates at layer 2 or the data link layer of the OSI model. Bridges are devices with two or more ports that are used as intelligent repeaters in that they are designed to connect two or more networks together in one common broadcast domain. Depending on the type of bridge employed, this connectivity can take place in a local area or wide area environment.

The delineation between a repeater and a bridge comes from an increased level of intelligence in transmission of data between the two networks. While a repeater simply retransmits all data it receives on one port to all other ports, a bridge will read the data frames it receives and determine based upon the destination address whether or not to forward the frame to one or more of its bridge ports. The forwarding decision is made by comparing the data frame's destination to a table of connected hosts on all bridge ports. Should the bridge match the frame's destination to one of its connect bridge ports, it will accept the frame and retransmit it only on the bridge port that the intended recipient is reachable through. This conserves bandwidth and general network utilization of all connected networks. If the destination is not found in the table, it will transmit the frame out all bridge ports.

> While the operation of a bridge may sound somewhat similar to the functionality of a switch, remember that a layer 2 switch is simply a multiport bridge.

Adding bridging functionality to a network brings many benefits and abilities to an environment. Some of these useful abilities include

- The isolation of general network problems between two LAN segments
- The general filtering of frames between two LAN segments for traffic and network utilization purposes (that is, separating local area networks into smaller collision domains)
- Extending a LAN to great distances within the local area (that is, within a building) by bridging two or more segments together with copper- or fiber-connected bridges, all while isolating individual collision domains and maintaining the broadcast domain
- Connecting two geographically dispersed networks together over a dedicated leased data line, while maintaining the broadcast domain

BRIDGING PROCESSES

A closer look at the operation of a bridge shows four major processes that contribute as a whole to the functionality of the device. The first process is termed *learning* or *listening* and describes the routine of simply listening to network traffic. Essentially, during this process the bridge watches network traffic on all interfaces, and creates a table of which hosts reside on what ports. To ensure that information contained in the table remains current, the bridge will expire or remove entries once a specified period of time elapses with no traffic seen to or from a particular host. The information collected and maintained in the table is used by a second process, called *forwarding*.

As noted earlier, when a bridge receives a frame on one of its interfaces, the bridge compares the destination address of the frame to the forwarding table built with the learning process. Assuming a match for the destination is found, the bridge forwards the packet to the appropriate interface. Should no match be found, the bridge uses a third process called *flooding*, in which the bridge sends the frame to all ports and waits to receive a reply from the frame's destination.

The last process, called *filtering*, allows for the minimization of unnecessary traffic within or between network segments. For example, on a basic level a bridge employs filtering to ensure that communications between any two given hosts on the same segment are not forwarded or flooded to other bridge ports. In an advanced implementation, filtering can be used to limit communications between hosts on different network segments as well.

SPANNING TREE ALGORITHM

While bridges work quite well when installed as the sole bridge in a given network, problems in the form of bridging loops can arise when two or more bridges are implemented in the same network. This occurs when a host on one network transmits data to a host on another network, which are connected by two or more bridges. As each bridge receives the frames of data, the devices look up the location of the recipient and forward the frames accordingly. Unfortunately, because each bridge received and forwarded the frames to the recipient's network, there is now a duplication of each frame. Additionally, through the process of learning or listening, each bridge now believes that both hosts are on the same network segment; thus, through filtering, they will no longer attempt to forward frames between these two hosts, and as a result the hosts can no longer communicate.

To address this potential issue, and make use of the redundancy gained with multiple bridges in a given environment, bridges support a feature called spanning tree for the management of paths to a given network segment. The spanning tree algorithm (STA) was originally developed by Digital Equipment Corporation, and was later revised by the IEEE 802 committee when it was published in their 802.1d specification.

STA works by first determining which bridge in a given environment is the root bridge, by choosing the bridge with the lowest bridge identifier or MAC address. STA then computes the best bridge path from any given bridge to the root bridge, based on configuration messages that have been received from all bridges in the network. Once all paths are computed, the bridge that has the best path from a given segment to the root bridge becomes the designated bridge for that segment. Any bridge that is not deemed as being part of the best path (or is a duplicate path to a given network) is put into a standby or blocking mode. When in blocking mode, a bridge port does not listen, forward, or flood frames; thus, if STA is running, there should be no bridge loops because duplicate bridge ports on any given segment have effectively been disabled.

When employing STA, all bridges in a given network exchange configuration messages, or bridge protocol data units (BPDUs), to ascertain which bridges have access to what network segments. These messages are exchanged every few seconds to ensure the known network topology stays up-to-date. Additionally, should any one bridge fail to send BPDUs to the other bridges, the device is then presumed to be no longer a valid path to any network segments and is removed from the known topology. Anytime a change in the topology of a network is detected (that is, bridge no longer sends BPDUs), each bridge reruns the STA once again to ascertain which ports to use to reach what networks.

BRIDGE TYPES

As the individual applications in which a bridge can be deployed vary considerably, there are three major types of bridges, including local, remote link, and translation—each with their own specialized functionality for an environment. As bridges listen to all traffic on a network (promiscuous mode), they can repeat data to all connected network segments, though very often they employ MAC layer filtering (source and/or destination address based) to only retransmit data that needs to be sent to another network. The extent of filtering employed is sometimes a function of the environment in which the bridge is operating, as well as the bandwidth available between the two or more bridged networks.

Local Bridge

This type of bridge generally contains two or more homogeneous LAN ports (that is, all Ethernet ports, all token ring ports, and so forth) for the purpose of connecting two or more similar local area network segments together within a given area such as a building. The first typical use for a local bridge addresses the need to separate one large LAN segment into two or more smaller segments for the purpose of creating additional collision domains, thereby increasing network performance. In this application, one dual or multiport bridge is used between hubs, MAUs, or 10Base2/10Base5 network segments and only retransmits traffic between the various segments when needed, thus limiting collisions and allowing each segment to communicate efficiently with lower contention for the network. This type of bridge most closely resembles the functionality of a layer 2 switch; as such, both devices should be considered for an application of this nature.

Remote Bridge

When two or more geographically dispersed local area networks need to be connected, the use of a remote bridge is generally a good solution. This type of bridge will typically combine a LAN port with a WAN port for the purpose of connecting both a LAN and wide area link (that is, T-1) to the bridge. Additionally, remote bridges perform address-based filtering on data to be passed to other remote networks, thus allowing the efficient utilization of bandwidth available over the wide area, which is typically far less than that available in the local area.

As an example of a remote bridge application, as seen in Figure 14-1, there are two local area Ethernet networks: one in New York and the other in Denver. In order to connect the two into one bridge group, two remote bridges must be deployed—or one for each LAN location. In either location, the LAN bridge port will connect to the local network, and the WAN bridge port will connect to a T-1 leased

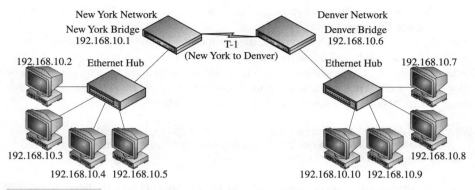

FIGURE 14-1 Two geographically diverse networks being connected with Ethernet bridges

line, which runs between the two bridges. As a data frame destined for a Denver workstation originates on the New York network, the bridge will see the frame and compare it to the stored host address table. Because the destination address of the frame resides on the Denver network, the bridge will transmit the frame over the T-1 to the remote bridge, where it will be retransmitted onto the Denver LAN. Unless configured otherwise (or a router is installed), broadcast frames will also be sent across the T-1 for retransmission on the remote network.

Translation Bridge

Because the situation may arise when two different network types (that is, Ethernet and token ring) must be connected, a translation bridge is designed to connect two different types of LANs together. This function is performed by converting the data for the destination network type, in terms of differences in frame layout and speed between the two connected networks. Certain types of wireless bridges may fall into the translation bridge category, because they must handle the differences in frame layout and speed between some wireless technologies and the connected LAN. It is important to note that some routers can be configured to perform the functions of a translation bridge; thus, both devices should be considered for such an application.

BRIDGE MANAGEMENT NOTES

Much like a switch, bridges are for the most part "plug and play" and do not require a tremendous amount of configuration or management. In actuality, once a bridge is installed and powered, it will begin its own process of learning the networks attached to it. As a frame appears on the network for an unknown destination address, the bridge will attempt to locate the destination host by transmitting the frame on all ports or segments except for the port where the frame originated. Should a host respond to the bridge's frame, an entry is made into the bridge port forwarding database, and all future frames destined for that address will automatically be forwarded to the appropriate port.

Given this automatic process of network discovery, many times the default configuration of a local bridge will suffice; however, should broadcast or forwarding limitations be required, changes to the configuration will be needed. Filtering configurations of this type will be based on MAC address (source or destination) filtering and have the ability of statically (rather than dynamically or transparently) forwarding or even dropping frames based on the source or destination MAC address.

While a local bridge may not need to be configured to operate properly, it is important to at least change the default login information for the device. This will prevent operational and security-related problems from manifesting in the future.

While the transparent bridging functions of a remote link bridge can successfully build a port forwarding database without any manual configuration changes, very often the WAN ports on remote link bridges will require configuration prior to operation. This is due to the various port configurations that can be used in the wide area. Additionally, in the case of T-1 WAN links, some bridges will be equipped with V.35 serial ports (rather than internal CSUs), thus requiring external CSUs with each device requiring its own configuration. A similar configuration effort may be required in wireless bridges, because for security purposes it is highly advisable to not operate under the default settings.

Because bridges will retransmit all broadcasts (or frames intended for all hosts) to every connected segment by default, it is important to keep an eye on the level of broadcasts throughout the network. An excessive number of broadcasts or broadcast storms can significantly impede the performance of a network. Should this start to occur, either employ some form of limitation on the amount of broadcasts a bridge port will process or consider the use of routers instead of bridges, because routers create separate broadcast domains that will not repeat broadcasts from one segment to another.

To aid in managing bridged segments, most bridges do have a fairly complete command-line or web-based graphical interface that can provide real-time statistics on frames and broadcasts transmitted to each segment. Additionally, it is through this interface that filters can be configured to limit what frames can traverse between the various connected network segments. Access to this interface is typically made through a direct serial-console connection (similar to that of a switch), through a connected network via Telnet/SSH, or through a web-based GUI. Some advanced bridges may also support SNMP (Simple Network Management Protocol) for the advanced monitoring and reporting of usage and error statistics to a central SNMP management console.

Particularly in the more advanced bridges, it is always advisable to stay up-to-date with bridge firmware revisions. Various changes in firmware may handle certain tasks more efficiently or securely, and staying current with the latest tested version may limit future problems. Remember to save a copy of the operating configuration to another location because, should the bridge fail, it will substantially decrease the time to install and configure a new device. This operation can be performed with file transfer protocols such as the Trivial File Transfer Protocol (TFTP) or the File Transfer Protocol (FTP).

Particularly useful in larger environments, it is wise to have supporting services such as a TFTP server (for configuration downloads), an NTP server for a centralized clock, and a SYSLOG server for centralized logging of device errors. These services will aid in diagnosing network problems and help identify potential issues.

BRIDGE TROUBLESHOOTING

Bridge problems will typically reside within one of the connected networks, though on occasion a configuration error may be at fault. The determination of where the trouble lies is best performed by eliminating bridge-related trouble first (as it will be easier to diagnose). One of the biggest problem-causing configuration errors is incorrect port speed or duplex setting, on not only the bridge but also whatever device it is connected to. Ensure that both sides of the connecting link between the bridge and network are set for the appropriate port settings. Also, be sure to consult the bridge utilization and error statistics, and note any elevated values. It is not uncommon for high network utilization to cause high buffer utilization in a bridge, particularly when a high number of broadcasts are present within a network. Should this be the case, try to identify the cause of the broadcast storm with a sniffer or protocol analyzer.

If a remote link bridge is in use, be sure to check for any errors, as well as the average and peak utilization of the connecting WAN link. Unfortunately, because most WAN link bandwidth rates are a fraction of bandwidth that is typically available in a LAN, it is entirely possible that the current WAN link may be too small for the current environment or saturated. If this is the case, consider moving to a larger form of WAN connectivity, or look for means of reducing internetwork traffic. A common way of reducing internetwork traffic is by creating local servers for each of the remote offices; in this fashion, the local workstations need not cross the bandwidth-limited WAN link for the majority of their work.

If performing remote server backup through a remote link bridge, be sure to schedule the backup operation at night when network utilization is lowest. In addition, it is good practice to perform incremental (as opposed to full) backups to limit the data crossing the bandwidth-limited WAN link.

Generally Poor Network Throughput

As mentioned earlier, many performance-related problems are most likely caused by one of the connecting networks. To this end, we cannot stress enough the importance of a good protocol analyzer or network sniffer. Software packages like SnifferPro are a cost-effective means of providing an insider's view to the current state of the network, because they allow the analysis of not only an entire network's traffic, but also individual communications between two or more devices. They also excel at identifying many common and not so common performance-hindering problems, and can very often locate the hardware or MAC address of the offending device. Always remember, a high incidence of collisions or other errors on the network will cause performance to degrade heavily, and reporting of such errors can typically be found in a switch or bridge on the network.

Missing or Dropped Frames

As a general rule of thumb, frames do not just jump off the network and vanish into thin air; however, frames can be incorrectly forwarded, filtered, or just dropped from the interface due to high utilization. If it appears that frames are not arriving at their destination, first check the bridge for high utilization because this may cause packets to be dropped due to full buffers. Assuming utilization is normal, verify any custom filters that have been put in place and ensure that the suspected frames are not being incorrectly filtered by the bridge. Also, be sure that no incorrect static forwarding entries have been entered into the bridge, causing it to potentially misforward a frame to an incorrect network segment. If all else fails, check the current dynamic or learned forwarding database for any incorrect entries, particularly verifying the source and destination addresses to ensure they are listed on their respective bridge port. If no problem is found there, a clearing of the forwarding database may resolve the issue.

Bridging Loops Due to Redundant Bridges

In an environment where there is more than one bridge in a given network for redundancy, it is imperative to have the spanning tree algorithm (STA) configured on both bridges. Without spanning tree, bridging loops will occur, causing erroneous network traffic and dropped frames. With STA one bridge effectively blocks its redundant port until it is needed for bridging, thus limiting bridging loops.

Trouble with Connecting Different Network Types

Network problems originating on either network type can severely impede the performance of a multinetwork bridge; therefore, unless both networks are in pristine operating order, problems will most likely exist. If troubles do exist, first check both network segments for trouble—in addition to the error and utilization statistics on the bridge that may help to isolate the problem to one of the two networks. If problems still persist, it may be wise to consider using a router for this function as they are known to be more reliable for applications of this nature.

Routers and Gateways

So far in Chapters 13 and 14, we have discussed those network devices that operate at the first and second layers of the OSI model. These devices perform well for the tasks of repeating, bridging, and switching within a network, but they do not address the need for transporting data between two or more networks.

Filling this void is a device that operates at the network (or third) layer of the OSI model and has the ability to route data between two or more like or unlike networks, based on source, destination, or both. In the early days of the Internet, this device was called a gateway, because initially it connected mainframe computers together over a wide area. Later, however, these devices connected LANs together and now, true to its chief function, this device is known as a router.

ROUTER BASICS

On a basic scale, a router is a network device that has two or more interfaces, which are typically connected to local area networks or WAN links (that is, ISDN, DSL, T-1, T-3, and so forth), and simply routes data from one network to another. It varies from a bridge in that the data is being transported at the network layer; thus, routers are able to transport data across completely separate networks, which may or may not be of a similar link layer type (that is, Ethernet, token ring, FDDI, ATM, frame relay). Additionally, network broadcasts do not normally cross between routed networks, though some routers do support a broadcast relay or proxy function for protocols like BOOTP and DHCP. An overview of the routing process looks something like the following:

1. Once a frame of data has been received, strip off frame information and analyze the datagram for errors. Correct any errors if possible and forward the datagram up the stack.

2. The network layer locates the destination address in the header, and identifies the network portion of the address for lookup in the routing table.

3. Look up the destination network in the routing table, attempting to match the most specific route available (for example, using the route for 192.168.4.0 instead of 192.168.0.0). If a route cannot be found, reply to the source address with an ICMP "Network Unreachable" message.

4. Modify the datagram's TTL or Time-To-Live field as needed. This field is instrumental in detecting routing loops. Should the TTL counter reach a value of zero, the datagram will be dropped and an ICMP "TTL Expired" message transmitted.

5. Prepare to forward the datagram on to its next hop as indicated by the routing table. Verify the MTU or maximum transmit unit of the next hop network (for example, the MTU of Ethernet is 1,514 bytes per frame), and fragment the datagram if necessary to accommodate the network's MTU.

6. Send the ready to transmit packet of data to the necessary output interface queue, and forward the packet on to its next hop. If the queue is full or the route has become invalid, drop the packet and notify the source if possible.

Since routers transport data at the network layer, a network layer protocol must be employed to package data into a routable form. Examples of major routable network layer protocols include Internet Protocol (IP) and Internetwork Packet Exchange (IPX), though the former is considerably more prevalent in today's networks and is used as the sole network layer protocol on the Internet.

The Internet Protocol (IP) addresses hosts with a 32-bit or 4-octet address, by which a router can identify the source and destination of a particular packet. As such, each host has its own unique IP address that would look something like "192.168.4.28." Hosts are separated into logical networks with a network mask, which tells both host and router what network they reside in. Essentially, the network mask (or netmask) provides a delineation as to which part of the IP address identifies the network and which part identifies the host. For example, an IP address of 192.168.6.7 with a netmask of 255.255.255.0 translates to be host 7 in the 192.168.6 network, while an IP address of 10.20.4.13 with a netmask of 255.255.0.0 translates to host 4.13 in network 10.20. This means of addressing is very similar to that of our telephone network, in that the area code and prefix identify a central office (or in our terms, a network) and the last four digits identify the actual phone line (or in our terms, host) within the central office.

In order for routers to move traffic between two different networks, not only must the router be directly connected to each of the networks, but also it must have an IP address in each of the logical networks between which it will route traffic. For example, in Figure 14-2, we have two networks addressed 192.168.11.0 and 192.168.4.0, each with a netmask of 255.255.255.0. These networks are connected to a router with addresses of 192.168.11.1 and 192.168.4.1, respectively, and each host within the network has an appropriate IP address, netmask, and gateway configured (the local router). Initially, host 192.168.11.46 transmits a packet of data to 192.168.11.18. Because both reside in the same IP network, the data moves between the two workstations and never passes through the router or gateway. Next, host 192.168.11.46 transmits a packet of data to 192.168.4.13, which is located in another IP network. In this case, the packet is first sent from the workstation to its configured gateway or router of 192.168.11.1. The router examines the header of the packet and reads the destination IP address. The address is then compared to the router's route table for a matching route. In this case, the destination network is directly connected, so the router knows how to reach the 192.168.4.0 network and releases the packet to its directly connected interface in the 192.168.4.0 network. Finally, the packet arrives at its destination address of 192.168.4.13.

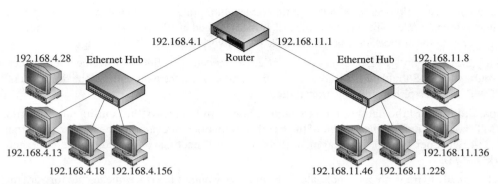

FIGURE 14-2   Two networks within different IP subnets, connected with a
single router

Hosts and network devices that reside within the same IP network still use MAC addressing at the link layer, and construct their own IP-to-MAC address table by utilizing the Address Resolution Protocol (ARP). To see a given host's ARP table, the command **arp –a** can be used on a Windows-based system, or **show ip arp** on a Cisco router.

Now that we have examined the process of routing from one directly connected network to another, the question becomes, "If a router can only route between two directly connected networks, how does one route to **www.yahoo.com**?" While it is true that individual routers can only route between directly connected networks, it is also true that routers can work together, thus providing paths for one another to get from point A to point B. This process is also known as taking "hops" through networks.

FINDING PATHS

In order for one router to route traffic through a multitude of other routers, it must know by which path to send the packet—otherwise referred to as the packet's next hop. This information of paths is shared among routers, and is exchanged by employing one or more routing protocols such as RIP, OSPF, or BGP.

Generally speaking, there are three types of routes—those being connected, static, and dynamic. Connected routes have been demonstrated earlier in this chapter, and are created when a router has physical direct connectivity to a given network. Static routes are a bit different in that they must be manually entered and simply state the next hop for a given destination network. Routes, in general, also specify a route cost or metric that is used by the router to determine when to use one route over another. As a general rule of thumb, the lower the route cost or metric, the more preferable the route.

An excellent example of a static route is the all-important default route. A default route tells the router where to forward data if no route for the destination network can be found in the forwarding table. In a Cisco router's configuration file, a default route would look something like

```
ip route (Destination Network) (Destination Netmask) Next-hop Metric
```

or

```
ip route 0.0.0.0 0.0.0.0 192.168.100.1 0
```

The destination network of 0.0.0.0 and netmask of 0.0.0.0 specify any network; thus, if the router cannot find a more specific match in its forwarding table, it will follow this route and send data for this route to a next hop of 192.168.100.1. Many dedicated Internet connections work in this fashion, where the customer's router has one default route that sends all data to the connected provider. From there, the ISP network will route data as needed to its intended recipient.

> Default routes can be distributed through dynamic routing protocols as well, but it is highly advisable to specify a static default route with a high metric or cost as a worst-case route, should dynamic routing fail.

The last type of route, dynamic, is actually a route that can be learned from one of many different dynamic routing protocols. They are termed "dynamic" because the routes can dynamically change as the path to a given network changes. A router must only be configured to listen or participate in a given dynamic routing protocol, and told which routers it is to listen to for routes—otherwise known as the router's neighbors.

Dynamic routing protocols are broken into two major groups based on where within a network the protocol is utilized; thus, the groups are coined as "interior" and "exterior" routing protocols. Interior routing protocols can best be described as the means of exchanging routing information within a given set of internal networks or an autonomous system (AS). An autonomous system is nothing more than a grouping of networks within an organization or managed by a central organization. Typically, an ISP operates its own AS, which all its customers will fall under. An AS generally has more than one method of accessing or connecting to other external networks; thus, many organizations with a single means of connectivity do not have their own AS.

The most common interior routing protocols include the Routing Information Protocol (RIP) and the Open Shortest Path First Protocol (OSPF). While RIP is still in use in many networks, OSPF has become quite common in larger network environments because it handles routing updates in a considerably more efficient fashion.

The largest difference between RIP and OSPF, however, is the method in which each protocol determines which route is best to a given destination. For example, RIP utilizes the distance-vectoring method of routing, in which it bases its routing decisions on the distance or number of hops and vector (or direction) that a packet must travel to reach its destination. Once RIP has collected the distance and vector information for a given network, The Bellman-Ford algorithm analyzes the collection of information and determines which path is best.

OSPF differs from RIP in that it employs the link state method of routing that collects routing information on a network-wide topographical level. This information is then analyzed by the Dijkstra algorithm to calculate the current forwarding table. OSPF is superior to RIP in many respects, but this is especially apparent in large network environments where the fast and efficient route updates of OSPF contribute greatly to the stability of networks during changes in routing. In OSPF, whenever a router needs to update its available routes to other routers, it issues a link-state advertisement (LSA) flood to all adjacent or neighboring routers. This LSA is then analyzed and integrated into the forwarding table of the neighboring routers, which then issue their respective LSA floods to other neighboring routers, and so on. This process only occurs when there is a change in a given router's forwarding table due to a changed route or link state—as opposed to RIP, which sends routing updates regardless of changes in routes.

Another key feature of OSPF, which keeps route convergence time to a minimum as well as keeping LSA floods from becoming intrusive, is the use of areas within the routing hierarchy. Essentially, a large network can be broken up into several smaller OSPF routing areas, each with their own link state database and LSA floods when routing updates are needed. To integrate a series of OSPF areas, there is a concept of a backbone area or area 0, into which all other OSPF areas populate link state information for the aggregation of routes between areas.

Generally speaking, the OSPF routing protocol works in the following manner:

1. OSPF is configured on each router in a given area. During configuration, the router is given a unique router ID by setting it manually or automatically, using the highest interface IP address as the ID.

2. OSPF now attempts to create adjacencies (or communication channels for routing information) between it and its neighboring routers. OSPF neighbors can be located across point-to-point links (T-1, T-3, and so forth), across broadcast links (Ethernet networks), or even across NBMA (nonbroadcast multiple access) links such as ATM or frame relay.

   A. To limit the number of adjacencies required within a given network, OSPF classifies routers into types. For example, in certain OSPF network deployments, a designated router (DR) is elected to be the master route server; thus, all routers in that OSPF network will send their LSAs to the master, rather than to every router within the network. If OSPF areas are being utilized, each area will have one or more area border routers (ABRs) that relay routing information between their own areas and the backbone area.

3. Actual OSPF communications consists of these three major processes:

   A. Initially, a router running OSPF will issue a "hello" in an attempt to discover and initiate communications with a neighboring OSPF router. "Hello" is also used to elect the DR within a given network.

   B. Once an adjacency is established, the router then uses the "exchange" process to share information about its own links with various other neighbors. Additionally through this process, the router receives information from its neighbors about other links. All exchanged data is stored in a link state database, which is synchronized between all routers within a given OSPF network through the exchange and flooding processes.

   C. Once the exchange process is complete, OSPF routers will use the flooding process to update its neighbors about any changes in a given link's status. This is done by issuing or flooding LSAs to all active OSPF interfaces on a given router. LSAs are analyzed by receiving routers and added to the link state database, if required.

4. The link state database does not actually provide the route or forwarding table; instead, the Dijkstra algorithm is run against the link state database to analyze and produce the shortest path to a given network, which is then added to the router's forwarding table.

While interior routing protocols provide dynamic routing within an AS, exterior routing protocols provide routing between autonomous systems. One of the most commonly used exterior routing protocols is the Border Gateway Protocol(BGP). This protocol is typically run on one or more border routers, which provide a gateway from one AS or grouping of networks to another AS.

An excellent example of BGP utilization is by ISPs. These ISPs use BGP to exchange routing information between one another. While it is rare for an ISP to provide routing to a customer with BGP, it is sometimes necessary if the customer is multihomed or connected to more than one ISP. BGP is designed to provide routing between large networks; thus, it is able to handle the over 100,000 routes that each ISP border router uses to efficiently forward data throughout the Internet. The following is an example of an ISP's routing table, which lists destination networks followed by their current best next hop:

```
Gateway of last resort is 10.0.1.1 to network 0.0.0.0
B    208.221.13.0/24 [20/0] via 10.26.199.239, 1w4d
B    206.51.253.0/24 [20/0] via 10.26.199.239, 1w4d
B    205.204.1.0/24 [20/0] via 10.26.199.239, 1w4d
B    204.255.51.0/24 [20/0] via 10.26.1.236, 3d11h
B    200.68.140.0/24 [20/0] via 10.26.199.239, 1w4d
B    199.221.26.0/24 [20/0] via 10.26.29.249, 1w0d
B    199.0.199.0/24 [20/0] via 10.26.196.111, 1w4d
B    192.68.132.0/24 [20/0] via 10.26.17.244, 11:23:10
     170.170.0.0/16 is variably subnetted, 3 subnets, 3 masks
B        170.170.0.0/19 [20/0] via 10.26.199.239, 1w4d
B        170.170.224.0/20 [20/0] via 10.26.199.239, 1w4d
B        170.170.254.0/24 [20/0] via 10.26.33.249, 1w4d
B    216.239.54.0/24 [20/0] via 10.26.17.244, 4d14h
```

Discussing OSPF, BGP, or any other routing protocol can occupy an entire book; thus, if more information is desired on any of the routing protocols, it is advisable to consult one of the technical resources at the end of this chapter for an in-depth explanation on the inner workings of routing protocols.

INSTALLING AND CONFIGURING ROUTERS

Routers, physically speaking, are fairly easy to install, because in a corporate environment most routers will not exceed three or four network interfaces. To illustrate the installation and configuration process, we will be installing a router into the environment pictured in Figure 14-3.

The sample environment consists of two local networks named network A and B, each with their own IP subnet. Additionally, there is one wide area T-1 connection to an ISP. The local networks are addressed as 192.168.4.0 and 192.168.11.0, respectively, and the router will have interfaces at 192.168.4.1 and 192.168.11.1 for the local networks, and 10.3.28.86 for the T-1 interface. Because Cisco routers are quite common in environments of this type, we will be using a Cisco 3640 router in this example. Given the information above, this router will be equipped with three interfaces, those being two Fast Ethernet interfaces and one serial (T-1) interface with an integrated CSU.

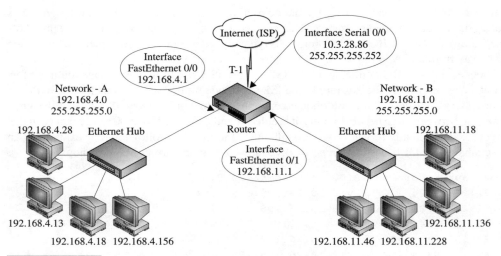

FIGURE 14-3   Sample network that is the basis for our router configuration

To install the router, start by connecting the power cable to the device. Next, connect the router to each of the respective local networks by using Ethernet patch cables. The Fast Ethernet ports on the router should be labeled as Fast Eth 0 and Fast Eth 1. For this example, be sure to connect network A to Fast Eth 0 and network B to Fast Eth 1. Lastly, connect the T-1 with a T-1 patch cable to the RJ-45 port marked Serial 0.

Some installations may require the use of crossover patch cables as opposed to straight-through. For this reason, always have a few of each on hand, and if there is difficulty in obtaining link, try using a different cable type. Also, be careful not to connect an Ethernet network to a serial port and vice versa, as the receptacles on the router are identical.

As a point of reference, Cisco IOS recognizes network interfaces with the convention of *Interface_Type Slot_Number/Port Number*. As such, if all interfaces to be configured in this example reside in slot 0, the configuration will reference the Fast Ethernet Ports as FastEthernet 0/0 and FastEthernet 0/1. Additionally, the T-1 interface will be referenced as Serial 0/0.

Prior to powering on the router for the first time, it is good practice to first connect to the console of the device. This will enable you to view the router's startup diagnostics and boot cycle, which can call attention to a potential hardware problem. To connect to the console, first locate the blue or black console cable that shipped with the router. Most of the more recent Cisco models have an RJ-45 serial console port labeled as "Console" or "CON". Once located, connect the RJ-45 end of the cable to the router's console port, and the DB9 serial end (a serial port adapter may be required) to a VT100 terminal or workstation with terminal emulation software. Once connected to the workstation or terminal, configure the terminal or software with communication settings of 9600 baud, 8 Data Bits, No Parity, and 1 Stop Bit. When ready, power-on the router and the following should appear:

```
System Bootstrap, Version 12.0(3)T, RELEASE SOFTWARE (fc1)
Copyright (c) 1999 by cisco Systems, Inc.
```

The router will now run through its diagnostics and begin to load the internetwork operating system (IOS). Additionally, the router will identify what interfaces and storage systems it is able to recognize by displaying something similar to the following:

```
cisco 3640 (R4700) processor (revision 0x00) with 44032K/5120K bytes
of memory.
Processor board ID 28351804
R4700 CPU at 100Mhz, Implementation 33, Rev 1.0
Bridging software.
X.25 software, Version 3.0.0.
2 FastEthernet/IEEE 802.3 interface(s)
1 Serial network interface(s)
DRAM configuration is 64 bits wide with parity disabled.
125K bytes of non-volatile configuration memory.
8192K bytes of processor board System flash (Read/Write)
16384K bytes of processor board PCMCIA Slot0 flash (Read/Write)
```

Once the router has finished its boot process, the message "Router con0 is now available, Press RETURN to get started" will be displayed. To begin configuration, simply press ENTER on the terminal keyboard. The router may now recognize that it has been booted for the first time, and ask if you wish to run a configuration script. For the purposes of this example, answer no and the routers prompt of "Router>" will appear.

Before configuration is possible, the console session must be put into enable mode or given a privilege level of 15. This is performed by entering **enable** at the current command prompt. Under typical circumstances, a password is required to enter enable mode, but because no password has been set as of yet, the router will respond with a new prompt of "Router#" indicating that enable mode has been reached.

Before continuing with configuration, it is highly advisable to first set the system clock, because diagnosing problems with incorrectly dated log entries can be quite tedious. To set the router's clock, simply use the command **clock set *HH:MM:SS MONTH DAY YEAR*** or, as an example, **clock set 09:00:00 June 07 2002**. The router will not confirm the entry—it will just return a command prompt if the setting was successful.

When the router first booted, it created a very basic configuration that is currently running the router. To view the current running configuration, simply type **show running-config**, or **show run** for short. The currently running configuration will then be displayed one screen at a time on the terminal.

To begin configuring the router for our example, the router first needs to be put into configuration mode. This is done by typing **configure terminal** or **config t**, which should be followed by a new prompt of "Router(conf)#" indicating configuration mode.

Be *very* careful when in configuration mode, because any and all changes are immediate and can have adverse effects on your network if you are not careful in entering the proper configuration commands.

As a general rule of thumb, to get a list of what commands are available at any given prompt, simply type **?** and a list of available commands with descriptions will be displayed. To list the possible completions for a given command, simple type the command followed by a **?**. This command completion functionality is available in all modes (including configuration mode) and is quite helpful in learning what functions can be configured on a given router. For the most part, configuration commands can be negated or reversed by placing a "no" in front of the command. For example, if when configuring an interface the administrator enters the command **shut**, the interface will be put into an administratively down status. To reverse or reenable the interface, the configuration command **no shut** can be used to remove that command from the configuration.

The following commands will be used in this configuration. Keep in mind this is a basic configuration, and other commands may be required to reach the desired operational functionality.

- **hostname** This command configures the router's hostname. Once configured, it will replace the "Router>" prompt with the entered text.

- **aaa new-model** This tells the router that we will be configuring the account, authentication, and authorization features using the new command set, thus disabling the old commands.

- **aaa authentication** Enables per-user authentication on the router.

- **username USER PASSWORD** Adds a user and their respective password to the local user database.

- **enable secret** Sets the enable mode password using a higher encryption algorithm than the old **enable password** command.

- **clock timezone** Sets the time zone for the routers locale.

- **ip subnet-zero** Enables subnet-zero subnet types.

- **ip domain-name** Sets the domain name for the router.

- **ip name-server** Instructs the router to use the specified name server for DNS resolution.

- **interface Serial | FastEthernetX/X** Prepares the router to accept configuration commands for the specified interface.

- **ip address ADDRESS NETMASK** Configures the IP address and netmask for the currently configured interface.

- **speed 100** Sets the Ethernet port speed to 100 Mbps.

- **full-duplex** Forces the Ethernet port to full-duplex mode, which should limit problems caused by auto-negotiation.

- **ip classes** Tells the router to allow classes subnets for routing purposes.

- **ip route NETWORK NETMASK INTERFACE or NEXT-HOP METRIC** Configures a route for the specified network. In our example, we will only be configuring a default route, so the router will forward any nonlocal traffic to the ISP connected to the Serial0/0 interface. Additionally, a next-hop IP address could be used in place of the "Serial0/0" interface statement.

- **line con | aux | vty** Prepares the router to accept configuration commands for the specified terminal device.

With these commands in mind and the router in configuration mode, enter the following commands to configure the router for our example:

```
hostname ExampleRouter

aaa new-model
aaa authentication login default local enable
username jdoe password hound
enable secret AgoodPassword

clock timezone EST -5
ip subnet-zero
ip domain-name sampledomain.com
ip name-server 10.99.99.28

interface Serial0/0
 ip address 10.3.28.86 255.255.255.252
 encapsulation ppp
 no fair-queue
 service-module t1 timeslots 1-24

interface FastEthernet0/0
 ip address 192.168.4.1 255.255.255.0
 speed 100
 full-duplex

interface FastEthernet0/1
 ip address 192.168.11.1 255.255.255.0
 speed 100
 full-duplex

ip classless
ip route 0.0.0.0 0.0.0.0 Serial0/0 0
no ip http server


line con 0
 password consolepasswordhere
 transport input none
line aux 0
 password auxpasswordhere
line vty 0 4
 password telnetpasswordhere

end
```

Be sure to modify any usernames and passwords as needed. Once these are set, you will need to use the configured credentials to access the router!

Assuming the configuration was entered properly, the router's command prompt should return, only it should now appear as "ExampleRouter#". To verify the interface configuration, type **show ip interfaces brief** and a table of the three configured interfaces should appear and will look similar to this:

```
Interface           IP-Address      OK? Method Status     Protocol
FastEthernet0/0     192.168.4.1     YES manual up         up
Serial0/0           10.3.28.86      YES manual up         up
FastEthernet0/1     192.168.11.1    YES manual up         up
```

After verifying the interface configuration, be sure to save the current running configuration, by issuing the command **copy running-config startup-config**, or **copy ru st** when abbreviated. Additionally the older **write memory** command may be used, though that command has become obsolete and will probably be removed from the Cisco IOS in the near future. Without issuing the **copy** command, the configuration would be lost if the router was ever rebooted. Upon saving the configuration, exit the console session by using the **logout** command. The router should now be ready for use.

MANAGEMENT NOTES

Routers are extremely intelligent devices, and thankfully have fairly straightforward management interfaces to access and manage the intelligence and versatility of the device. As alluded to earlier in the chapter, there are a few different methods of accessing a router's management functionality. Some access methods include direct console access, Telnet access, SNMP, and in some cases a web-based GUI via HTTP.

The console access method is supported in nearly every router, and is typically provided through an RJ-45 or DB-9 serial port. Some routers require special or proprietary console cables that ship with the device, so be sure to keep the cable in a safe place when not in use. In most cases, a terminal emulation program with settings of 8-N-1 will provide sufficient access to the text-based command-line interface. While various vendors use different commands in their management interface, most will have some form of a command completion function, thus always start by typing **?** or **help**, because it may provide suitable assistance in producing the necessary commands or configuration options.

Many routers also support accessing their command-line interface via the network-based Telnet. This is generally accessed on a router by using a Telnet client to connect to one of the router's interface IP addresses. In the case of Cisco routers, these connections are referred to as VTY sessions, and are configured in the "Line VTY" section of the configuration. While this method does typically offer near-identical access to that of a console connection, always be sure to not modify a setting that may hamper your access or disconnect the current Telnet session from the router. This is especially true if the administrator is located some distance away from the device.

Many administrators make use of the Cisco **reload in XX** command to issue scheduled reboots when doing major configuration changes that may impede access accidentally. Once a reload has been configured, if not cancelled, the router will reload the previously saved configuration and should once again be accessible. This, of course, assumes the administrator did not save the newly edited configuration. Note, however, that once the router has begun a reload, no traffic will be forwarded until the reload has completed.

Some routers also support a web based GUI to access the management functionality of the device. While GUIs are very good at simplifying a device's management interface, many advanced routers require some configuration functions to be performed through a command-line interface (CLI). If a GUI is in use, however, be sure to take appropriate steps to secure the interface with IP access lists or some other form of access control.

To maintain a proactive approach to router management, many organizations make use of an SNMP solution. SNMP allows a management console (such as HP OpenView or, on a smaller scale, SNMP-C) to poll network devices for key statistics such as a given interface's throughput or error count. SNMP also allows for the unsolicited transmission of "traps" or alarms from a device, should an error condition occur such as a power supply failure or high-temperature alarm. Additionally, freeware programs such as MRTG can poll a router via SNMP to collect information such as bandwidth utilization, and produce some fairly meaningful graphs to assist in trending just about any value desired.

When using SNMP, it is highly advisable to change the public and private community strings to a noncommon value. Additionally, if the router supports some form of IP address filtering for SNMP access, we suggest that you enable that function in an effort to increase the security of the device.

If there will be more than one router in the network, management can be simplified somewhat by incorporating a SYSLOG server into the environment. SYSLOG allows for a central logging facility that all network devices can send log events to. This can aid greatly in diagnosing network troubles, because all log information can be found in one place. Also, note that some network devices dump their log files when rebooted; thus, if a router reboots suddenly, there may not be much in the way of evidence as to why the reboot occurred.

Many vendors produce new firmware releases on a fairly regular schedule. It is highly recommended to stay up-to-date with firmware releases. In many instances, aside from adding new functionality or modifying existing functionality, these releases also patch newly discovered security holes or vulnerabilities. This is not to say that every new release should be applied to the router; instead, as new firmware versions are released, first read their release notes and ascertain if the new release is needed for a specific reason. If possible test the new firmware release on a nonproduction device prior to uploading it onto a production router.

On a security note, many routers support some type of packet filtering based on any combination of source, destination, and port number. In Cisco IOS, this functionality is referred to as access lists, which are set up while in configuration mode. This feature can be particularly useful in protecting the network should a firewall not be in place. Additionally, it can be used to block specific hosts or networks from accessing the internal network, again based on destination IP address or port number. For more information on this functionality, consult the respective router's manual or contact the vendor.

As a word of caution, be careful not to block administrative or legitimate user access to the router when working with access lists. If in doubt about the configuration, it is best to verify the command context first or at the very least schedule a reload in case access to the router is lost.

One of the most useful routing functions is called Network Address Translation (NAT). NAT allows for a local network to be addressed with private or reserved IP address space. When a host or device with a private IP address attempts to send data through the router, the router will intercept the packet and almost seamlessly map the private IP address of the sender to a public and routable IP address before the packet leaves the network. When the destination host sends data back, the router will remember (through a translation and session table) what host on the internal network requested incoming data from the outside and route it accordingly.

This function works particularly well with most applications, but in some cases where the external sender changes the source or destination port numbers that were previously in use, the router will have a hard time determining what host to pass the data to on the private network. In instances of this nature, a one-to-one NAT mapping is required; thus, data arriving at the router for IP address X will always be mapped to internal or private IP address Y.

It is important to note that there are some applications that will not work with any form of NAT whatsoever.

Commands of Note

While commands can vary from router to router, there are a few basic commands to keep in mind when administering a device of this nature. The commands noted here are from the Cisco IOS, but many other vendors do have equivalent commands.

■ **show ip arp** The command will retrieve the routers current Address Resolution Protocol (ARP) table. The ARP table provides a mapping of IP address to host MAC address. This can be useful in locating a duplicate IP address problem.

■ **show ip route** This command will list the current IP route or forwarding table. In many smaller environments, there will only be a default route (0.0.0.0, 0.0.0.0) and routes to any other directly connected interface. In larger environments, however, the table may be substantially larger. To retrieve or check the current route for a specific destination, the command **show ip route DESTINATION_IP** can be used, rather than sifting through an entire route table.

■ **show ip interface brief** Mentioned earlier in this chapter, this command will provide a summary of all configured interfaces within the router. The summary includes information such as the interface IP address and its current status. Also, **show ip interface INTERFACE** can be used to get detailed information (such as utilization, errors, or dropped packets) on a given router interface.

■ **show interface INTERFACE** Similar to the previous command, this command will provide detailed information of an interface, but at a hardware level rather than the IP or protocol level.

■ **show process cpu | memory** When the router appears to be sluggish in operation, this command can help to isolate the cause. Depending on which option is used, the command will either give you current and historical information on CPU load and various processes running on the CPU, or information on memory utilization in terms of individual process utilization.

■ **copy running-config tftp** It is always good practice to have an offline copy of the router configuration. This command allows for the transfer of the running configuration to an external server such as a TFTP server (or FTP if the router is properly configured). Additionally, the configuration can be copied back to a new router if needed by using the same command with different options.

TROUBLESHOOTING ROUTERS AND GATEWAYS

Because routers operate at layer 3, most troubles will exist at the network layer or in a logical as opposed to physical manner. With this in mind, many problems can be isolated with the use of a few commands, and even if the problem is related to a physical failure of some type, chances are it can be clearly identified in short order.

The most common complaint an administrator will hear is generally due to a loss of connectivity. In cases like this, it is best to first perform a Traceroute or Ping from the host experiencing the loss of connectivity. The Traceroute will send a series of ICMP packets toward the destination specified, and should report on the reply time of each hop the packet must take to reach the destination. Once this test is complete, one of four things will be evident:

- Connectivity to the destination is fine, in which case the problem most likely lies at the application layer of the troubled host. Windows-based PCs are notorious for this, and typically a reboot can rectify the problem. It is sometimes advisable to perform a Traceroute from the outside in, utilizing sites like **http://www.traceroute.org** if the destination is reachable from the Internet.

- The Traceroute is able to reach the destination, but is reporting a high round-trip time or excessive latency at or after hop X. This information will point to a network problem occurring somewhere between the last good traced hop and the hop reporting high latency, or in a worst-case scenario a complete timeout. If the troubled hop is outside the local network and past the router, there is not much that can be done. If the hop is within the upstream ISP's network, notify them of the problem. Should the troubled hop be within the local network, check for a physical problem between the troubled hop and the previous good hop. If one of the hops in question is within the router, log on to the router and check any of the interfaces involved for high utilization, high error rates, or dropped packets. Any of these values would be indicative of either a physical problem (such as local network trouble or a failing T-1) or high utilization. If the WAN link is at fault, be sure to report it to the provider immediately, and be sure to get a trouble ticket number to track.

- After hop X, the Traceroute appears to "bounce" between two of the same hops continuously. This situation is indicative of a routing loop, and the bouncing routers should be checked to verify that two conflicting routes do not exist. The ISP may need to be involved in this effort if the loop is between the local WAN interface and the remote WAN interface, or if the loop is occurring within the network or the Internet. Lastly, verify that the router's forwarding table has a valid route for the destination in question.

- The Traceroute does not show any hops that are reachable, or are timing out at hop 1. This would indicate a physical failure within the local network, or possibly a configuration error on the troubled host. If all hosts are experiencing the same loss of connectivity, it is possible that the router or router interface has failed. Ensure that the local gateway on the workstation in question is correctly set to the Ethernet interface of the router. Lastly, it is possible that an access control list (ACL) on the first hop router is preventing the transmission of Traceroute messages or data in general; thus, the router should be checked for such an ACL.

Should the router be performing in a slow or latent fashion as indicated by high latency Pings, check the router's interface statistics for high utilization. If this is occurring, the router will attempt to buffer outbound packets until the buffers are full, at which point the router will simply drop the packets. Additionally, check the CPU and memory utilization of the router, as there may be a process that is draining the router's resources. Load issues of this nature are sometimes due to denial-of-service (DoS) attacks, and should be brought to the attention of the upstream ISP if suspected. Lastly, never discount the router's log files, as they will undoubtedly provide some insight as to what problems or issues the router is encountering.

If connectivity seems somewhat sporadic but no physical problems are evident, be sure to check the maximum transmit unit (MTU) and maximum receive unit (MRU) configured values for each interface (if possible). If these values are misconfigured, sporadic performance problems will result due to high packet fragmentation rates.

If there are sporadic problems with certain applications, an access list may be blocking certain ports with which the application communicates. Verify that any configured access lists are not blocking required TCP or UDP ports. Additionally, if employing Network Address Translation (NAT), realize that not all network applications work well with NAT; thus, a one-to-one mapping may be needed for a particular application to work.

SYMPTOMS

Bridges and routers are fairly complex devices, which in turn can make troubleshooting problems quite difficult at times. Thankfully, as both devices operate in a logical and procedural fashion, a network diagram and good understanding of the device configuration can assist greatly in rectifying the problem. To aid in the troubleshooting process, the following are some typical symptoms that may be present in a network, as well as their respective courses of action.

SYMPTOM 14-1   **You cannot access the cable/DSL router.**   If a Ping to the router's local interface fails, check to ensure that all physical cabling on both ends is in working order. Additionally, verify that the configuration of both devices is correct in terms of IP address and subnet mask. Lastly, log on to the router with a console cable, if necessary, and try clearing the device's ARP cache after verifying all other network settings.

SYMPTOM 14-2   **If equipped, the router's diagnostic LEDs don't follow the correct bootup sequence.**   This may indicate a current or potential problem with the device. Consult the router's manual for LED boot sequence codes, and check the router's console upon bootup for any suspect messages.

SYMPTOM 14-3   **The router's link or Activity LEDs do not light.**   There is most likely a physical cable problem between the router and the connected device. Check the cable and replace if necessary. Also, be sure to use the proper type of cable in terms of straight-through rather than crossover, or vice versa. From a configuration standpoint, ensure that the router's interfaces have not been administratively shut down. Also, if either device's interfaces have been set to auto-negotiate, it may be prudent to manually set both settings on either device.

SYMPTOM 14-4 **Your broadband router stops working or locks up.** Broadband routers are subject to DoS attacks, and due to their always-on nature they seem to get their share. This can sometimes occur when a large amount of traffic is targeted at a particular administrative port on the device. Often, the simplest method to rectify this problem is a quick device reboot. If the device continues to lock up, check its logs for any indication of a resource issue or high error counts on a given interface. Additionally, check with the device's manufacturer, because there may be a new version of firmware recently released that addresses the problem.

SYMPTOM 14-5 **You cannot connect to other computers through the router.**
Check your workstation settings, in particular verifying the IP subnet mask as well as any static routes that have been defined in the workstation itself. Should the target computers be on a different IP subnet, ensure that your default gateway is set properly on the workstation, and that the router has a valid route for the destination computer. Additionally, check to ensure the destination computer has a valid IP configuration.

SYMPTOM 14-6 **You cannot browse the Internet through the router.** Check the router's management interface for error statistics of the WAN link. If the link is an SDSL or cable link, try rebooting the router to force a retrain to the network. Should IP-addressed Pings pass through the router, but no named URLs can pass, check to ensure that there is a valid DNS server or servers configured on the workstation in question.

SYMPTOM 14-7 **Your web page hangs and downloads are corrupt.** This condition may indicate a duplex issue between your workstation and the hub/switch, or between the hub/switch and the router. Additionally, check the router's interface statistics for any high error rates that may exist within the local network or on the WAN links connected to the router.

SYMPTOM 14-8 **You cannot get an IP address through the cable modem or DSL router.** Some broadband modems "lock onto" the MAC address of a connected device; thus, if you recently swapped two devices between the modem, you may not be able to obtain an IP address via DHCP. Try to clear the router's MAC or ARP table by powering it off for a few short moments. Additionally, verify that no personal firewalls are running, because these are known to cause some problems with DHCP address assignments on occasion.

If the problem is with a DSL router, ensure that the router is configured to serve IP addresses via DHCP, and that there are enough available IP addresses in the address pool to serve all hosts on the LAN.

SYMPTOM 14-9 **The e-mail program doesn't receive e-mail through the router.**
Should your e-mail client be experiencing trouble receiving mail, verify that port 110 (for POP3 communications) is not being blocked. If using another mail protocol, ensure that it is not being blocked either. Also, some mail servers will not accept mail from or deliver mail to hosts at IP addresses that do

not have proper reverse DNS entries. This can be checked at a site such as **http://www.samspade.org**, by performing a name lookup on your current IP address. Contact your ISP if a proper reverse DNS entry is not present.

SYMPTOM 14-10   **You cannot get the router to work with NetMeeting.**   If the router is configured with NAT or ACLs, you may want to consider running NetMeeting with a host that has static mappings defined and is clear of any ACL that would restrict the operation of NetMeeting. This application uses a variety of ports for its various subapplications, all of which should be checked to ensure that no ACL inhibits the function of these ports.

SYMPTOM 14-11   **You cannot get the router to connect to your ISP.**   Ensure that all interface settings are correct. If using a T-1 for connectivity, check that all line settings such as framing type and timing are set properly. Verify that the router is showing the interface and protocol status as Up, and if not, attempt to verify with the ISP all configuration settings. Lastly, have them perform a remote loopback test to your router, if possible, to verify the operational status of the T-1—and if necessary, involve the carrier to test the circuit from a pure transport perspective (that is, testing to the smart jack, if available).

SYMPTOM 14-12   **Trying to access the router through the web page fails.**   Verify the operating port for the router's web server. If the port has changed, you will need to specify it in the URL as **http://1.2.3.4:8000** (or whatever port number is now in use). If bad authentication credentials were used, you may need to shut down all open web browsers prior to attempting to access the device again.

Further Study

Bridge Functions Consortium at UNH IOL: **http://www.iol.unh.edu/consortiums**
Cisco "Bridging and Switching Basics":
http://www.cisco.com/univercd/cc/td/doc/cisintwk/ito_doc/bridging.htm
Cisco "OSPF": **http://www.cisco.com/univercd/cc/td/doc/cisintwk/ito_doc/ospf.htm**
Cisco "Troubleshooting transparent bridging environments":
http://www.cisco.com/univercd/cc/td/doc/cisintwk/itg_v1/tr1920.htm
Cisco routing: **http://www.cisco.com/warp/public/732/Tech/routing.shtml**
IEEE: **http://grouper.ieee.org/groups/802/3/**
Juniper Networks: **http://www.juniper.net/techcenter**
TCP/IP and IPX Routing Tutorial: **http://www.sangoma.com/fguide.htm**

15

FIREWALLS AND PROXY SERVERS

Two of the most popular and important tools used to secure networks are firewalls and proxy servers. The basic function of a firewall is to screen network traffic for the purpose of preventing unauthorized access to or from a computer network. Proxy servers are used to complete requests on behalf of internal users when communicating with untrusted (that is, external) entities. Proxy services can be provided directly by the firewall or on a separate host working in conjunction with a firewall.

Understanding a Firewall

Firewalls take on many different shapes and sizes, and sometimes the firewall is actually a collection of several different computers. For the purposes of this chapter, a *firewall* is the computer or computers that stand between trusted networks (such as *internal* networks) and untrusted networks (such as the Internet), inspecting all traffic passing between them. To be effective, firewalls must have the following attributes:

■ All communications pass through the firewall.

■ The firewall permits only traffic that is authorized.

■ The firewall can withstand attacks upon itself.

The effectiveness of the firewall is greatly reduced if an alternate network routing path is available—unauthorized traffic can simply be sent around the firewall (it's like guarding the front door but leaving the back door open). Additionally, if the firewall cannot be relied upon to differentiate between authorized and unauthorized traffic, or it is configured to permit dangerous or unneeded communications, its usefulness is also diminished. Finally, because the firewall is relied upon to stop attacks and nothing is deployed to protect the firewall itself against them, it must be capable of withstanding attacks directly upon itself.

A firewall can be a router, a personal computer, a host, or a collection of hosts set up specifically to shield a private network from protocols and services that can be abused from hosts outside the trusted network. A firewall system is usually located at a network perimeter directly between the network and any external connections. However, if additional security needs are warranted, additional firewall systems can and should be located inside the network perimeter to provide more specific protection to a smaller collection of hosts.

The way a firewall provides protection depends on the firewall itself and the policies/rules that are configured on it. The four main categories of firewall technologies available today include

■ Packet filters

■ Application gateways

■ Circuit-level gateways

■ Stateful packet-inspection engines

FIREWALLS AND TCP/IP

Before we can fully understand the differences and functions provided by firewalls, it is necessary to have a solid understanding of the Transmission Control Protocol/Internet Protocol (TCP/IP). While networking was discussed previously in this book, we will take a moment to point out some attributes of TCP/IP that are integral to firewall operation. The fundamental purpose of TCP/IP is to provide computers with a method of transmitting data from one computer to another over a network. The purpose of a firewall is to control the passage of TCP/IP traffic between hosts and networks.

In actuality, TCP/IP is a suite of protocols and applications that perform discrete functions corresponding to specific layers of the Open Systems Interconnect (OSI) model. Data transmission using

TCP/IP is accomplished by independently transmitting blocks of data across a network in the form of *packets*. Each layer of the TCP/IP model adds a header to the packet. Depending on the firewall technology in use, the firewall will use the information contained in these headers to make access control decisions.

A Discussion on Ports

To enable effective communications, most well-known services are run on universally known "ports." Almost all firewalls base some or all of their access control decisions on the port information contained within packet headers.

Without using universally known ports, providers of services would need to inform their users of the proper ports to use. For example, port 80 is well known as the port for HTTP, and almost all web servers on the Internet are configured to service HTTP requests on port 80. Connecting on any other port would result in an error. If an administrator chose to have the web server service requests on port 81, he or she would have to inform all users to connect on port 81 (usually done in a browser by specifying the port at the end of the URL, http://www.somewebserver.com:81). Port 80 (or port 81 in our alternative example) is considered the TCP destination port, and this information is contained within the TCP packet header.

From a security perspective, security is not increased by running your web server on a nonstandard port. Attempts at "security through obscurity" almost always fail. Be aware that hackers spend a lot of time performing *port scans*. Port scanning is the process of systematically attaching to each port on a system and determining the response or lack of response. Thus, your web server on port 37244 will soon be discovered!!

In addition to destination ports, TCP (and UDP) packets also contain a source port. The source port is the port that the user TCP/IP stack uses to communicate with a server's destination port. It also becomes the server's destination port for packets from the server to the user. The source port is normally assigned semirandomly by the TCP (or UDP) process on the source host and is typically some number above 1023

Outgoing HTTP Request TCP Packet Headers:
TCP Source Port: 1085 TCP Destination Port 80

Returning HTTP Answer TCP Packet Headers:
TCP Source Port: 80 TCP Destination Port 1085

Internet user wishes
to open a Web page

Web Server listening on
Port 80 for HTTP requests

FIGURE 15-1   TCP port numbers in an HTTP request

but below 65535, although this is not a requirement. Figure 15-1 shows how port numbers are used within TCP/IP packets.

The list of TCP port numbers and the applications they are associated with is available in RFC 1700, "Assigned Numbers." For a full listing of TCP & UDP assigned port numbers reference: http://www.iana.org/assignments/port-numbers. Table 15-1 is a small list of the most popular services and their assigned ports.

PACKET-FILTERING FIREWALLS

Packet-filtering firewalls provide network security by filtering network communications based on the information contained within the TCP/IP headers of each packet. The firewall examines the header of each packet and uses the information contained within to make a decision on whether to accept and route the packet along to its destination or deny the packet by dropping the packet silently or rejecting it (that is, dropping it and notifying the sender that the packet was dropped).

Packet filters make their decisions based on the following header information:

- The source IP address
- The destination IP address
- The network protocol in use (TCP, UDP, or ICMP)
- The TCP or UDP source port
- The TCP or UDP destination port
- If the protocol is ICMP, the ICMP message type

TABLE 15-1   BRIEF LISTING OF POPULAR TCP AND UDP PROTOCOL PORT NUMBERS

SERVICE	PROTOCOL	PORT
FTP	TCP	21
FTP-data		20
Secure Shell Protocol (SSH)	TCP	22
Telnet	TCP	23
Simple Mail Transfer Protocol	TCP	25
DNS (Zone Transfers)	TCP	53
DNS (Queries)	UDP	53
HTTP	TCP	80
NetBIOS	TCP	137–139
	UDP	
Pop-3	TCP	110
IMAP	TCP	143
SNMP	UDP	161
SNMP Traps	UDP	162
HTTPS	TCP	443
X Windows	TCP	6000

In addition to this information, a good packet filter can also make a decision using information not directly contained within the packet header—such as which interface the packet is received upon.

Essentially, a packet filter has a dirty interface, a set of filters, and a clean interface. The dirty side is exposed to the untrusted network and is where traffic enters. As packets enter the dirty interface, they are processed according to the set of filters being used by the firewall (commonly called *rules*). Based on these filters, the packets will either be accepted and sent out the clean interface to their destination, silently dropped, or rejected. The next section contains an example of a packet filter.

Packet Filtering Example

Our example network will have one web server and one mail server that will be accessible from the Internet. In addition, administration of these servers will be permitted via the SSH protocol from the Internet; however, use of this protocol will be restricted to the source network of 128.5.6.0/24. Figure 15-2 shows a diagram of this configuration. Enabling inbound communications via a packet filter would result in the rules shown in Table 15-2.

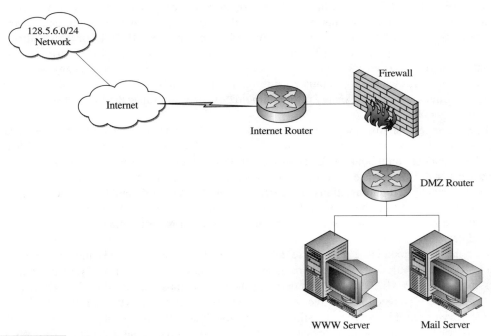

FIGURE 15-2   Example diagram

TABLE 15-2   EXAMPLE INBOUND PACKET-FILTER RULE SET

RULE	PROTOCOL	SOURCE ADDRESS	DESTINATION ADDRESS	SOURCE PORT	DESTINATION PORT	ACTION
1	TCP	128.5.6.0/24	129.1.5.155 128.1.5.154	>1023	22	Permit
2	TCP	Any	129.1.5.154	>1023	80	Permit
3	TCP	Any	129.1.5.155	>1023	25	Permit
4	Any	Any	Any	Any	Any	Deny

Translating the rules in Table 15-2, rule 1 permits hosts in the 128.5.6.0/24 (that is 128.5.6.0–128.5.6.255) network to send packets to the web or mail servers with a source port above 1023 and a destination port 22. Remember, a packet filter doesn't actually understand SSH, only the attributes of its TCP/IP headers. If the packet attributes do not completely match rule 1, they are then compared to the next rule. Rule 2 permits any network to send packets to the web server with a destination port of 80 (the well-known port for HTTP) and a source port above 1023. If the packet attributes do not match, they are compared to rule 3. If the packet is still not accepted, it is processed according to the "catchall" rule that has been configured to drop any traffic that wasn't permitted by any of the previous rules. Remember, firewalls should only permit traffic that is authorized and therefore, in accordance with best practices, the last rule of any rule set should be to drop all traffic that wasn't expressly permitted by an earlier rule.

There are several significant things to note about the rule set depicted in Table 15-2. First, rules are processed from top to bottom, and once a match occurs no further processing is performed. Second, it should be considered an inbound rule set only—not only because it's enforced on packets entering the external (that is, dirty) interface of the firewall, but because TCP communications are really two-way conversations. For actual communications to occur, a compatible set of outbound filters is required to permit return traffic back through the firewall. If all traffic is permitted outbound, this is not necessary. Most organizations, however, wish to screen outbound traffic to prevent information from leaking to the untrusted network.

To define an outbound rule set, reverse the source and destination addresses and ports. For example, return traffic for our rule 2 above would have a source address:port of 129.1.5.154:80 and a destination address:port of any: > 1023. Rather than defining such a rule, most packet filters have functionality to allow "established" connections to traverse an interface. The filter does this by examining the TCP packet header to see whether it is part of an existing conversation. It does this by looking to see whether the TCP header SYN bit has been cleared. Note that the filter does not track the actual connections, but relies on the state of this bit. As an improvement over filtering on "established" connections, stateful packet filters were developed. These are discussed in more depth later in this chapter.

Note that although there are various strategies for implementing packet filters, the following two prevail as security practitioner favorites:

■ Build rules from most specific to most general. This is done so that a general rule does not "step on" a more specific but conflicting rule that falls within the scope of the general rule.

■ Rules should be ordered such that the ones used most often are at the top of the list. This is done for performance reasons: A screening device can stop processing a list when a complete match is found.

Advantages and Disadvantages of Packet Filtering

From the preceding conversation, it is evident that defining specific and accurate packet-filtering rules can become very complex. While considering the deployment of a packet filter, you should assess the advantages and disadvantages. Some advantages of packet filters include

■ **Performance**   Filtering can be performed at near line speeds with today's processors.

■ **Cost-effective**   Packet filters are relatively inexpensive or free. Most routers have packet-filtering capabilities integrated with their operating systems.

■ **Good method to perform traffic management**   Simple packet filters can be used to drop obviously unwanted traffic at network perimeters and between different internal subnets.

■ **Transparency**   User behavior is not altered by the implementation of a packet filter.

Some major disadvantages of packet filters include the following:

■ Direct connections are permitted between untrusted and trusted hosts.

■ Packet filters do not scale well. As rule sets get large, it becomes difficult to prevent enabling "unintended" communications. In addition, due to the dynamic nature of some protocols, it may be necessary to open large ranges of ports to permit their proper function. The worst example of this is FTP. FTP requires an inbound connection from the server to the client, so packet filters would require large ranges of open ports to permit these transfers.

■ Packet filters can be vulnerable to spoofing attacks. These types of attacks usually entail faking information contained within the TCP/IP headers. Popular attacks include spoofing source addresses and making packets appear to be part of already established communications.

APPLICATION GATEWAYS

The term *application gateway* has come to mean a number of different things. It has become synonymous with terms such as *bastion host*, *proxy gateway*, and *proxy server*. As mentioned earlier, proxy services can be run directly on the firewall or on a separate server running in conjunction with a firewall.

An application gateway makes access decisions based on information contained within a packet at all seven layers of the OSI model. Because of this, application gateways are often thought of as being "application aware."

The application gateway provides a higher level of security than that of a packet filter, but does so at the loss of transparency to the services that are being proxied. The application gateway often acts as the intermediary for applications such as e-mail, FTP, Telnet, HTTP, and so on. Specifically, the application gateway acts as a server to the client and as a client to the true server—actually completing requests on behalf of the users it's protecting.

Being application aware permits the firewall to perform additional verification of communications over that of a basic packet filter. An application gateway can verify that the application data is in an acceptable format. It can even handle extra authentication and increased logging of information; it can also perform conversion functions on data, if necessary and capable. For example, an application gateway can be configured to restrict FTP connections to only *get* commands, and to deny *put* commands. This is useful if you want to allow users to download files but provide an additional layer of protection against those users from putting files on the FTP server. The next subsection examines the process used by an application gateway for proxying internal user Telnet requests.

Application Gateway Example

Our sample company decides to host a Telnet server so that remote administrators can perform certain functions on a particular host. They advertise the Telnet gateway, and not the actual hostname of the server, in order to mask its true identity from untrusted networks. The process that occurs for connecting to the specific host happens like this.

1. A user Telnets to the application gateway over port 23. The screening device checks the source IP address against a list of permitted sources. If connections are allowed from the source IP address, the connection proceeds to the next step. If not, the connection is dropped.

2. The user is prompted for authentication. Optionally, as part of the authentication, the user is required to specify the ultimate host he or she wishes to use.

3. If authenticated, the user is given a prompt or a menu of systems that he or she is allowed to connect to. These IP addresses are not directly accessible from the Internet—they only accept connections from the gateway.

4. The user selects the system to connect to. This selection initiates a *new* TCP connection to the destination host, from the application gateway.

5. The user is prompted for additional authentication information, if applicable.

 The proxy daemon is a hardened application, which makes it more difficult to compromise and provides a single location to update in the event a new vulnerability is discovered.

Disadvantages of Application Gateways

The security provided from application gateways comes at a price. The following is a list of common disadvantages when implementing application gateways:

- **Slower performance**   Each user request is in reality two separate connections, one between the user and gateway and one between the gateway and the true destination host. This requires double the connections and processing than that of a packet filter. In addition, the additional application layer inspections that are performed also require more and longer processing times. Today's high-bandwidth streaming applications, such as videoconferencing, may not be able to tolerate the latency of a proxy server.

- **Lack of transparency**   Most proxy servers require modification to clients and/or user behavior. At times, client software may not be able to use a proxy server for its connections. In addition, proxy servers rely on the ability to insert the proxy between the end user and the true server.

- **Need for proxies for each application**   Although proxy servers for popular services are widely available, proxies for newer or less frequently used services are harder to find. Most application gateways offer a default "plug" proxy to get traffic through the gateway. However, this plug isn't application aware and reduces the gateway to an expensive packet filter.

- **Limits to application awareness**   The gateway must be able to differentiate between safe functions of an application and dangerous functions. If the proxy cannot make such differentiations or the proxy cannot strip out the unwanted without impacting desired operations, usefulness is reduced.

CIRCUIT-LEVEL GATEWAYS

Circuit-level gateways are similar to application gateways, but are not application aware. A circuit-level gateway operates by relaying TCP connections from the trusted network to the untrusted network. However, a direct connection between the client and server never occurs. Because the circuit-level gateway cannot understand the application protocol, it must have the connection information supplied to it by clients that understand and are programmed to use them. In general terms, application gateways use modified procedures while circuit-level gateways use modified clients.

The main advantage of a circuit-level gateway is that it provides services for many different protocols and can be adapted to serve an even greater variety of communications. However, protocols that require some application-level awareness (such as FTP, which communicates port data dynamically) are more suited for application gateways than circuit-level gateways. A SOCKS proxy is a typical implementation of a circuit-level gateway.

 A discussion on SOCKS is beyond the scope of this chapter. For a full discussion on SOCKS, please see RFC 1928.

Circuit-Level Gateway Example

Our sample company decides to permit its internal users to browse the Internet. However, they are worried about allowing direct connections between their users and untrusted web servers on the Internet. To reduce this risk, they decide to implement a circuit-level gateway to control such traffic. The process that occurs for a user retrieving a web page would occur as follows (as noted earlier, specific configuration or special software is required when circuit-level gateways are used): This communication is illustrated in Figure 15-3.

1. When retrieving web pages, the end user's system actually only knows about the session between itself and the gateway. A user opens a browser and attempts a connection to the destination URL. The browser is specifically configured to use the proxy server and makes the request directly to the web server.

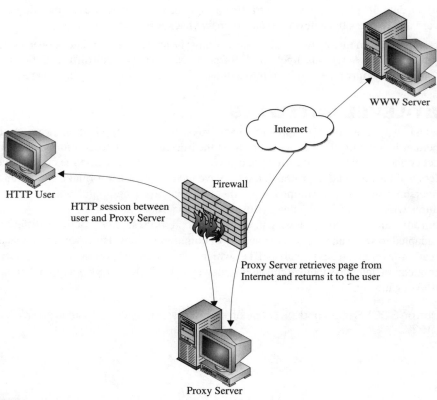

FIGURE 15-3   User retrieving a web page via a proxy server

2. The proxy server receives the user request and checks its configuration to see if the communication is permitted, requires authentication, or is denied. If authentication is required, the authentication process is initiated. If denied, the gateway will often redirect the response to a "denied" page, informing the user that the communication is denied.

3. Once authentication is successful, the gateway performs any additional tasks such as comparing the URL to a list of explicitly permitted or denied URLs.

4. The gateway sends an independent request to the web server to retrieve the information.

5. Once retrieved, the information is provided back to the requesting client.

A major performance benefit of HTTP proxies is the ability to cache the results of user requests. Instead of re-retrieving web sites each time a new user requests it, an HTTP proxy can cache the initial retrieval and then serve future requests from this cache. This cuts down on bandwidth usage and speeds performance as requests can be served to the user locally instead of needing to be retrieved from the Internet.

Disadvantages of Circuit-Level Gateways

There are several other disadvantages to using a circuit-level gateway as the sole means of protecting a network. The following is a list of some common disadvantages:

- **Require clients that can specifically use them**   Some client applications cannot be modified to support a circuit-level gateway, thus limiting their ability to access external resources. In other cases, considerable expense is involved in deploying an application that supports this functionality, which may limit the number of applications or the scope of deployment of applications that can access external resources.

- **Are not capable of application layer inspection**   This allows applications to utilize TCP ports that were opened for other, legitimate applications. Several peer-to-peer applications can be configured to run on arbitrary ports, such as TCP 80 and TCP 443 (commonly opened for web browsing). This opens the possibility for misuse and exposes potential vulnerabilities inherent in these applications.

STATEFUL PACKET INSPECTION FIREWALLS

A stateful packet inspection (SPI) firewall permits and denies packets based on a set of rules very similar to packet-filtering rules. However, when a firewall is "state" aware, it makes access decisions not only on IP addresses and ports but also on the SYN, ACK, sequence numbers, and other data contained in the TCP header. Whereas packet filters can pass or deny individual packets, and require permissive rules to permit two-way TCP communications, stateful packet inspection (SPI) firewalls track the state of each session and can dynamically open and close ports as specific sessions require.

SPI firewalls were developed to combine the speed and flexibility of packet filters with the application-level security of application proxies. This has resulted in a compromise between the two firewall types: an SPI firewall is not as fast as a packet-filtering firewall and does not have the same degree of application awareness as an application protocol. This compromise, however, has proven to be very effective in providing strong network perimeter policy enforcement.

When a packet arrives on an interface, several things happen within the inspection engine:

1. When a packet is received on an interface it is first inspected to determine whether it is part of an existing, established communication flow. A packet-filtering firewall can only search for signs that a packet is part of an existing TCP conversation by looking at the state of the SYN bit (either set or cleared). An SPI firewall will compare the characteristics of the packet with a connection table of existing valid connections to see whether there is a match. This is accomplished by maintaining a connection table on the firewall that consists of, at a minimum, source and destination IP addresses and transport layer source and destination ports. Virtually any information contained within the packet header can be tracked, including TCP sequence numbers, which assist the firewall in correctly recognizing the packet as part of an existing conversation.

2. Depending on the protocol, the packet may be inspected further. There are a number of well-known and commonly exploited vulnerabilities in several high-use protocols, including FTP and SMTP. Firewall vendors have implemented functionality to improve a firewall's ability to protect hosts from malicious activity. If the firewall includes functionality for the packet's protocol, it will read into the data portion of the packet. It will then make forwarding decisions based on the contents of the data.

3. If the packet does not have a corresponding entry in the connection table, the firewall will inspect the packet against its configured rule set. The rule set for most SPI firewalls is similar to a packet-filtering firewall's rule set: source IP address and port, destination IP address and port, and protocol. The packet-filtering rule set can then be optionally extended to include the examination of the data, as indicated earlier.

4. If the packet is permitted based on source, destination, protocol, and packet content, the firewall will forward the packet toward its final destination and build or update a connection entry in its connection table for the conversation. It will use this connection entry as the method for validating the return packet in lieu of requiring a specific rule defined.

5. The firewall will typically use timers and identification of a TCP packet with the FIN or RST bit set as a way of determining when to remove the connection entry from the connection table.

Advantages and Disadvantages of Stateful Inspection

The processes just described have two primary advantages over packet-filtering technologies. The connection table greatly reduces the chance that a packet will be spoofed to appear as if it were part of an existing connection. Because packet-filtering firewalls do not maintain a record of the pending communications, they must rely on the format of the packet—specifically, the status of the SYN bit in a TCP packet—to determine whether the packet is part of a previously approved conversation. This opens the possibility of packet spoofing of TCP packets and does not provide any method of determining the status of UDP or ICMP packets. By maintaining a connection table, the firewall has much more information to use when determining whether to permit a packet to pass.

A second advantage to SPI firewalls over packet-filtering firewalls is their ability to look into the data of certain packet types. This has become a very valuable feature due to a number of well-known and well-publicized vulnerabilities in common protocols. An example of this in the FTP protocol is an examination of commands to determine whether a command is being transmitted in the correct direction. Given the TCP port information, the firewall is able to determine which side of the conversation is the client and which is the server. The firewall then can look for commands from both sides to ensure that the server does not send the client incorrect commands, and vice versa.

The main disadvantage of an SPI firewall is that it permits direct connections between untrusted and trusted hosts. Thus, reliance must be placed on the host process instead of the hardened proxy service.

Network Security Basics

Now, having defined the specific firewall technologies available today, we may ask why a firewall is necessary. Why not just configure individual systems to withstand attack? The simplest answer is that the firewall is dedicated to only one thing—deciding between authorized and unauthorized communications. This prevents having to make compromises between security, usability, and functionality.

Without a firewall, systems are left to their own security devices and configurations. These systems may be running services that increase functionality or ease administration but are not overly secure, are not trustworthy, or should only be accessible from specific locations. Firewalls are used to implement this level of access control.

If an environment lacks a firewall, security relies entirely on the hosts themselves. Security will only be as strong as the weakest host. The larger the network, the more complex it becomes to maintain all hosts at equally high levels of security. As oversights occur (such as only applying a critical security patch to 14 of the 15 web servers), break-ins occur because of simple errors in configuration and inadequate security patching.

The firewall is the single point of contact with untrusted networks. Therefore, instead of ensuring multiple machines are as secure as possible, administrators can focus on the firewall. This isn't to say that the systems available through the firewall shouldn't be made as secure as possible; it just provides a layer of protection against a mistake.

Firewalls are excellent auditors. Because all traffic passes through them, the information contained in their logs can be used to reconstruct events in case of a security breach.

In general, firewalls mitigate the risk that systems will be used for unauthorized or unintended purposes (for example, getting hacked). What exactly are the risks to these systems that firewalls are protecting against? Corporate systems and data have three primary attributes that are protected by a firewall:

■ **Risk to confidentiality**   The risk that an unauthorized party will access sensitive data or that data is prematurely disclosed. A business could easily lose millions of dollars from simply having their business plan, company trade secrets, or financial information exposed.

■ **Risk to data integrity**   The risk of unauthorized modification to data, such as financial information, product specifications, or prices of items on a web site. This applies to general confidentiality, integrity, and availability issues. In the context of firewalls, this involves just malicious users and/or data manipulation.

■ **Risk to availability**   System availability ensures systems are appropriately resilient and available to users on a timely basis (that is, when users require them). Unavailable systems cost corporations real dollars in lost revenue and employee productivity as well as in intangible ways through lost consumer confidence and negative publicity.

COMMON TYPES OF ATTACKS

The preceding section discussed why individuals and corporations implement firewalls. Now the question is, exactly how do attackers gain unauthorized access to systems? Motivations for such attacks are numerous and often range from "to see if it could be done," to using the compromised systems to attack other systems, to performing corporate espionage—and even for malicious reasons such as disrupting and/or damaging systems.

There are literally dozens of different ways an intruder can gain access to a system. A brief list of the most common attacks is provided here:

■ **Social engineering**   An attacker tricks an administrator or other authorized user of a system into sharing his or her login credentials or details of the system's operation.

■ **Software bugs**   An attacker exploits a programming flaw and forces an application or service to run unauthorized or unintended commands. Such attacks are even more dangerous when the program runs with additional or administrative privileges. Such flaws are commonly referred to as *buffer overflow attacks* or *format string vulnerabilities*.

For excellent reading on the buffer overflow and format string attacks, refer to the following sites:
http://www.insecure.org/stf/smashstack.txt
http://www.insecure.org/stf/mudge_buffer_overflow_tutorial.html
http://julianor.tripod.com/teso-fs1-1.pdf

■ **Viruses and/or Trojan code**   An attacker tricks a legitimate user into executing a program. The most common avenue for such an attack is to disguise the program in an innocent-looking e-mail or within a virus. Once executed, the program can do a number of things, including installing backdoor programs, stealing files and/or credentials, or even deleting files.

■ **Poor system configuration**   An attacker is able to exploit system configuration errors in available services and/or accounts. Common mistakes include not changing passwords on default accounts (both at the system and application levels) as well as not restricting access to application administration programs or failing to disable extraneous and unused services.

In addition to attempting to gain unauthorized access to systems, malicious individuals may attempt to simply disrupt systems. For critical and highly visible applications, the cost to the business could be just as severe. These attacks are referred to as denial of service (DoS) attacks. A DoS attack is an incident in which a user, network, or organization is deprived of a resource or service they would normally have. The loss of service is usually associated with the inability of an individual network service, such as e-mail or web, to be available or the temporary loss of all network connectivity and services.

GOOD SECURITY PRACTICES

Although a complete discussion on best practices regarding firewall configuration and management is beyond the scope of this chapter (many volumes are available on this topic), it is still useful to introduce a number of important concepts that can and will improve the overall security of a firewall. These concepts apply to both the firewall and the systems protected by that firewall. Also note that the following concepts and practices are not mutually exclusive, and when properly implemented together, they can achieve higher levels of security.

Help Your Systems Help Themselves

Except in some very rare situations, systems and applications are not installed in their most secure configurations. In addition, services extraneous to the desired functionality of your system or application are most likely installed and activated by default. It is good practice to enable only the bare minimum services and accounts necessary for the proper operation of a system. Countless intrusions occur because an unused service or account superfluous to the operation of a system was compromised. The practice of disabling unnecessary services and reconfiguring other services for greater security is often referred to as *host hardening*. Here is a small checklist to follow when hardening hosts:

1. Disable any and all unneeded or unnecessary services.

2. Remove unneeded accounts and groups. Change the passwords to and/or disable default application and system accounts. Disable accounts that do not require interactive logins.

3. Reconfigure remaining services for increased security.

4. Secure any and all administrative functions.

5. Use strong passwords. Strong passwords are passwords that are greater than seven characters and are a mixture of uppercase and lowercase letters, numbers, and other alphanumeric characters.

 The SANS institute (www.sans.org) publishes a number of "best practice" guides for securing operating systems.

Patch! Patch! Patch!

Consistently applying the torrent of patches released today is a daunting and often overlooked process. New vulnerabilities are being discovered constantly. A system that was secure one minute could turn completely vulnerable the next. To stay on top of your systems, subscribe to multiple bug-notification mailing lists as well as vendor mailing lists for installed software. Popular vulnerability notification services are maintained by the following organizations:

- Internet Security Systems maintains its xforce database and mailing list at http://www.iss.net/xforce.
- SecurityFocus maintains a copy of the Bugtraq archive and mailing list at http://www.securityfocus.com.
- The Computer Incident Emergency Response Team (CERT) can be found at http://www.cert.org.
- The Common Vulnerabilities and Exposures (CVE) database is available at http://www.cve.mitre.org.

 After applying patches, ensure that system security was not weakened. As an example, Sun is notorious for having their Solaris cluster patches reenable services.

Appliance Versus Operating System

Historically, firewalls have run on top of general-purpose operating systems such as Windows NT or Unix. They function by modifying the system kernel and TCP/IP stack to monitor traffic. These firewalls can be at the mercy of problems present in the operating systems they run on top of. To achieve a high level of security, it is necessary to harden, patch, and maintain the operating system (as described in the previous section). This can be a time-consuming and difficult task, especially if there is a lack of expertise or time to adequately secure and maintain a fully functional operating system. As an alternative, a number of firewall vendors distribute their firewalls as appliances.

Appliances integrate the operating system and the firewall software to create a fully hardened, dedicated firewall device. The integration process removes any and all functionality not required to screen and firewall packets. In addition, a fully functional administrative interface is provided to further simplify configuration and maintenance of the firewall. Firewall appliances do not require a significant amount of host hardening when being deployed (usually changing default passwords is all that is required). Administrators can focus on developing rule sets instead of reconfiguring and patching a general-purpose operating system. Appliances significantly reduce operating and maintenance costs over operating system–based firewalls. Popular appliance firewalls include the Cisco PIX, Netscreen, SonicWall, and Check Point FireWall-1 on the Nokia IPSO platform.

Layer Defenses

Although the firewall itself is an excellent security tool, it should not be completely relied upon. As stated before, firewalls cannot protect against what is authorized. What happens if an intruder bypasses the firewall? Consider the scenario in which an intruder is able to use HTTP to exploit your web server, gaining shell access to that system. The firewall will permit this traffic because HTTP is permitted to the web server, and the attacker can use this as a conduit to attack other servers and systems on the network without the protection of the firewall. If these systems are not configured in a secure manner, it won't be long until the entire infrastructure is compromised.

When designing systems, it is good practice to implement redundant controls to limit or prevent system damage in the event a control fails. (It's like having a steering wheel lock for your car, even though there is a lock on the door.) Layered controls would include the following:

- Hardening your internal hosts to withstand attacks in case the firewall fails or is bypassed.

- Running services in restricted environments (for example, via the UNIX **chroot** command) and with minimal privileges such that the compromising of the service does not immediately compromise the entire system.

- Implementing multiple firewalls from different vendors or implementing packet filters on network routers. This reduces exposure to a specific flaw in the firewall itself.

- Implementing human controls such as education, log monitoring, and alerting.

- Putting in place systems to automatically detect and alert administrators to unauthorized or malicious activity. These systems are referred to as intrusion detection systems (IDS).

Create a Security Policy

The corporate information security policy is the foundation that establishes information as an asset that must be protected. It defines the corporation's sensitivity to risk and the consequences for a breach of security. The security policy also defines how data should be protected; the firewall is an implementation of this policy.

For smaller organizations that do not have a large database of formalized policies, it is incredibly useful to document the purposes of the network and use the firewall to restrict usage accordingly.

Policy empowers administrators to deny the many requests for new firewall access that are always submitted. Without clearly defining what should and should not be permitted through the firewall, over time the firewall's effectiveness is reduced as more and more services are permitted.

Monitor and Log

Any system can be penetrated given sufficient time and money. But penetration attempts will leave evidence, entries in logs, and so on. If people are watching systems diligently, the likelihood of detecting an attack increases dramatically. Therefore, it is extremely important that system activity be monitored. Applications should record system events that are both successful and unsuccessful. Verbose logging and timely reviews of those logs can alert administrators to suspicious activity before a serious security breach occurs.

The evidence from probes and attempted attacks may be strewn across logs from many different servers. And piecing together these bits of information may be critical to detecting some attacks. If the timestamps for these log entries vary greatly across the servers, correlating the events becomes even more difficult. It is considered best practice to implement the Network Time Protocol to ensure that system clocks across servers are synchronized.

Audit and Test

One of the most important things that can be done after configuring your firewall is to ensure that the level of security you planned to achieve is in fact what was achieved and to verify that nothing was overlooked. A number of freeware and commercial tools are available that can be used to test the security of the firewall and the systems behind it. One of the best freeware tools is Nessus, available at www.nessus.org.

Intrusion Detection and Incident Response

Intrusion detection is the process of monitoring network and system activity for the purposes of detecting and alerting appropriate personnel to the presence of unauthorized activity. Incident response is the process by which organizations respond to problems and outages, including detected intrusions. A full discussion of intrusion detection and incident response is beyond the scope of this chapter, but it is important to introduce the topic here.

Intrusion detection systems (IDS) differ from firewalls in that they do not actively interact with network traffic (though some have the ability to take specific actions based on configured alarms). An IDS will passively monitor resources for signs of malicious activity and alert appropriate personnel as alarms are triggered. There are two main types of IDS available today—network-based and host-based. A network-based IDS will monitor networks for malicious packets while host-based systems monitor individual hosts for unauthorized activity.

Before deploying a commercial or open-source-based IDS system, it is extremely important for an organization to have an incident response plan implemented for dealing with suspected attacks on their infrastructure. Having well thought out and predefined responses to suspected intrusions could prevent panic and costly mistakes. In addition, creating and reviewing response procedures will identify weaknesses and failures in the organization's ability to detect, respond, and recover before it's too late. The ultimate goal of any incident response plan is to resume normal operations as quickly and smoothly as possible.

The first obstacle to effective incident response is detecting the actual intrusion. The biggest failure when deploying an IDS is mistuning the alarms. If the system generates too many false positives, people will stop responding to the alarms (remember the old adage about the boy who cried wolf!). On the flip side, if the system alarms aren't triggered during a legitimate attack, the system is also useless. It takes many long hours and expertise to strike the appropriate balance.

However, before deploying an IDS, be sure to leverage any and all capabilities of the existing infrastructure. Firewalls and servers are capable of producing logs full of important information about the traffic flowing through them. Almost all attacks will leave evidence of preliminary probing and hacking attempts in those logs long before they become successful. Administrators should configure their systems for appropriate logging and review those logs on a regular basis.

Once a potential security breach is detected, the next step of a good incident response plan is notification. Depending on the size of the organization, an entire incident response team may be trained and maintained. A clear and simple mechanism should be available to notify appropriate staff of a suspected incident. A quick response may mean the difference between a minor incident and a major security breach.

Once the proper personnel have been notified, an evaluation should be performed. The immediate purpose of the evaluation will be to assess the state of affairs and identify appropriate actions to contain and prevent further damage to systems. The immediate questions to answer are

- Has the attacker successfully penetrated your systems?
- Is the attack still actively in progress?

If the attack is not currently active or not obviously successful, the response team may have more time to respond. If the attack appears successful or is still in progress, the team will want to take decisive action quickly.

The actual actions taken will be influenced by the ultimate goals of an organization. Should an organization wish to prosecute an intruder, response plans should be careful to include methods to preserve and collect evidence. There are a number of legal requirements that must be satisfied to have system evidence admissible in court. If an organization is not interested in prosecution, but only in recovery, immediately shutting down affected systems/network connections may be the most appropriate response.

Be careful not to make the intrusion worse by logging right in and issuing commands, especially as an administrator. Intruders may be waiting for such a thing to complete their attack!

Ultimately, the emergency team should dictate the initial response. If the team feels that the security breach may not be limited to a single host, shutting down all external connections may be the appropriate response. However, it may not be possible to detach production systems (that is, cause more damage by being out than by allowing attack to continue). Imagine if Yahoo! or eBay shut down every time an attack was detected. Proper planning and understanding the infrastructure are integral to defining an appropriate response. For example, it is probably not advisable to shut off network connectivity if downtime costs the corporation $100,000 per hour when the estimated damages from the breach are only $10,000.

After the initial attack has been contained, the response team should move into recovery mode. This may entail moving processing to backup machines, ensuring the security hole is adequately closed, restoring systems from trusted backups, patching systems, notifying appropriate personnel, and so forth.

The best avenue of recovery after an intrusion is to rebuild affected systems from scratch or restore from a trusted backup tape (one created before the intrusion occurred—not necessarily the backup from last night). Intruders can and will install programs and back doors (commonly called root kits) to ensure and maintain their access. For example, they may replace the Telnet daemon with a version that allows connections without a password. In addition, they may Trojan common binaries such as *who* and *ps* to not report their presence while on the system!

The last and most important step is review. There are multiple reasons for performing a review. These include the following:

- Perform a damage assessment. If the attack was not successful, significant work may not be required. However, even if the attack was unsuccessful, the organization may wish to increase their monitoring—especially if the intruder was aggressive and persistent.
- Identifying how the intrusion occurred.
- Ensuring appropriate steps were taken to close the security hole.
- Reviewing procedures to identify how the hole may have come into existence (that is, failure to apply a patch, misconfiguration of a service, unauthorized change to a configuration, and so forth).
- Should legal proceeding be under consideration, adequately collect, label, and store any and all evidence.
- Finally, a review of how the organization detected and responded to the emergency should be performed. By reviewing the response, an organization can refine and improve the process.

Firewall Troubleshooting

Whenever network connectivity issues arise, the firewall is almost always blamed. To follow are a number of suggestions and tips to help administrators troubleshoot connectivity problems and actually determine if the problem is in fact the firewall.

As mentioned previously, proper logging is integral for detecting potential security breaches. However, they are just as valuable for troubleshooting network connectivity problems. If a user cannot connect to a specific site with a service, the first place to check is the firewall logs for evidence that the firewall is denying the connection.

It is also useful to ask a number of questions, such as, "Was this something that was previously working and has now stopped?" If it was previously working, administrators should begin to determine what has changed in the environment. Common culprits when things "mysteriously" stop working are network and host routing changes as well as DNS outages.

When all else fails, network sniffers are invaluable tools to an administrator. Use a sniffer to track packets through a network to pinpoint the exact location at which a connectivity problem is occurring. Are the host's packets reaching the firewall? Can you still see them on the remote site of the firewall? If packets aren't making it through the firewall, check your rule-sets.

SYMPTOMS

Here is a common list of network "symptoms" and helpful hints towards resolving them.

SYMPTOM 15-1   **A LAN workstation can't access the Internet.**   This is almost always due to a misconfiguration of the local workstation's TCP/IP properties. Check to ensure that the workstation's subnet mask and default gateway are properly set. Try and Ping their default gateway. Also, check if other workstations on the subnet can access the Internet. If the problem is not limited to the one workstation, begin by checking the network gateways for proper route entries and check to then ensure such access is permitted by the firewall rule set.

SYMPTOM 15-2   **The DMZ server is unreachable from the Internet.**   This can be a number of problems. Check to ensure that TCP/IP and routing has been properly configured between all hosts and routers. If NAT is in use, make sure appropriate translation entries have been made and ARP tables have correct entries. And, as always, ensure that the firewall rule set permits such communications.

SYMPTOM 15-3   **You have problems with sending e-mail to the ISP's mail server from your LAN.**   First, ensure that the ISP does not have any filters preventing your use of the mail server. Next, make sure the firewall permits outbound SMTP traffic on port 25. Note that mail retrieval occurs on a different set of ports (IMAP is 143 and POP3 is 110). Also, if you are sending mail via a domain name, make sure DNS is working properly. Can you send mail by IP address? If you can connect using the IP address and not the domain name, the problem is most likely DNS related.

SYMPTOM 15-4   **The firewall's log reports "Disk Full".**   This is obviously a disk space issue. After freeing up appropriate disk space, look into compressing and archiving log files automatically. A best practice is to log to a remote host so that a full disk won't cause an outage.

SYMPTOM 15-5   **The administrator password has been changed or lost.**   Unfortunately, password recovery procedures are different from vendor to vendor. Consult your vendor to see if password recovery is possible. However, it is a good idea to have backups of all configuration files in case the machine should ever need to be rebuilt. It would also be a good idea to investigate how the password got changed, as this could be a symptom of a network intrusion.

SYMPTOM 15-6   **You notice that "auth" connections are blocked.**   If connectivity for a specific service is not working, check the firewall rule set to see if the traffic is permitted. If it is not, update the rule set appropriately.

SYMPTOM 15-7 **A specific subnet can't access the Internet across the firewall.**
The first place to check is the network and firewall routing tables. If routing appears to be correct and other networks can access the Internet, check your rule set to ensure that the subnet is permitted access to the Internet.

Further Study

Firewalls: The Complete Reference, Strassberg, Gondek, Rollie, et al., Osborne McGraw-Hill, 2002
Check Point: **http://www.checkpoint.com**
Cisco: **http://www.cisco.com/go/pix**
NetScreen: **http://www.netscreen.com**
SonicWALL: **http://www.sonicwall.com**
Netfilter: **http://www.iptables.org/**
Squid Web Proxy Cache: **http://www.squid-cache.org**
SecurityFocus: **http://www.securityfocus.com**
NTSecurity.com: **http://www.ntsecurity.com**
Carnegie Mellon University CERT Coordination Center: **http://www.cert.org**
Internet Security Systems: **http://www.iss.net**
Snort – Open Source Network Intrusion Detection System: **http://www.snort.org**
Network Working Group Site Security Handbook: **http://www.ietf.org/rfc/rfc2196.txt**
Network Working Group Network Ingress Filtering: **http://www.ietf.org/rfc/rfc2827.txt**

16

PRINT SERVERS

Printers present some unusual challenges for network administrators. Individual printers are often underutilized, and a large number of printers creates a maintenance nightmare for technicians as they struggle to support a diverse array of printer models. By putting printers on the network, administrators are able to achieve much higher utilization from fewer printers—often centralizing the printing activities of a workgroup or department. With fewer printers to contend with, a support staff can stock a smaller assortment of supplies, and focus on just a limited number of driver updates and printer upgrades. Printers are shared through a device called a *print server*. While traditional print servers required the services of a networked PC (where the printer was attached to the printer's LPT port), a growing number of networks are using dedicated print servers such as the Netgear PS110 print server (see Figure 16-1). This chapter

FIGURE 16-1   The Netgear PS110 print server allows up to two parallel port printers to exist on an Ethernet network. (Courtesy of Netgear)

covers the installation, setup, testing, and troubleshooting of print server devices across several popular operating systems.

Network Printing Options

A traditional print server required a basic PC with a printer attached—nothing fancy, just enough to hold an operating system, printer drivers, and spool files. Old 486 PCs (even later model 386s) were frequently pressed into service as print servers. The PC was then attached to the network, and printing requests were made to the PC, which in turn passed the print jobs to its attached parallel port printer. The problem with this configuration is that the PC is often tied up with print jobs, and cannot handle other tasks.

Today, PC-based print servers are giving way to dedicated print servers (such as in Figure 16-1). Dedicated print servers connect directly to the network. They are cheaper than a PC, and can attach anywhere from two to five printers at the same location (centralizing the department's print services). The dedicated print server is typically managed from another PC on the network using a suite of software that can access the device's settings and control its configuration. More powerful print servers can support a variety of network protocols such as IPX/SPX (NetWare), TCP/IP (Windows or UNIX **lpr/lpd**), NetBEUI (Windows), and AppleTalk.

A third network printing option is to select "network-ready" printers with their own NIC—these can connect directly to the network at a switch or hub just like any workstation. While network-ready printers are often more expensive than parallel port or USB printers, they can be located almost anywhere on the network (they are also usually designed for higher monthly utilization). Network-ready printers can often be managed through Web-based software (for example, simply access the selected printer's IP address in the Web browser such as **http://10.0.0.12**).

DEDICATED PRINT SERVERS

Dedicated print servers are available with a range of features and capabilities to suit your particular needs, but look for the following features when making a selection:

- **Network support** The print server should be compatible with your network architecture (i.e., 100BaseT).

- **Protocol support** The print server should match your network protocol (i.e., TCP/IP).

- **Ports** The print server can provide a single printer port to as many as five ports (perhaps more). Select a server that is appropriate for your printing needs. Choose bidirectional printer ports for higher speed and better compatibility with IEEE 1284 printers.

For example, the Linksys EtherFast 10/100 three-port print server offers bidirectional printing ports that can simultaneously handle multiple print jobs. It is also compatible with half- and full-duplex network implementations. A 256KB buffer helps offload printing traffic, and its 512KB firmware chip can be flashed with firmware upgrades. Hewlett-Packard's JetDirect is another very popular print server.

Interpreting the LEDs

Print servers often provide a suite of LEDs that can help you determine the activity and status of the unit on the network. The actual LEDs will vary depending on your print server model, but the most common indicators are shown here:

- **Power** The Power LED lights up green when the print server is powered on.

- **Link** The Link LED lights up green when a successful connection is made between the print server and your network through the print server's Uplink Port.

- **Status** The Status LED lights up green when the print server runs a self-diagnostic test while booting up. It turns off when the diagnosis is successfully completed. If this LED stays on, troubleshooting or replacement may be required.

- **Error** The Error LED lights up red if there's a problem with the print server, or it is writing information to the print server. When assigning an IP address, this LED will also light up for a few seconds.

- **LPTx** There may be an activity LED for each printer port.

If your dedicated print server incorporates switch ports, there may be additional LEDs such as

- **Link/Act** This LED lights up a solid green when the print server is successfully connected to a device through that port. If this LED is flickering green, the print server is actively sending or receiving data through that port.

- **Full/Col** This LED lights up solid green when a successful full-duplex connection is made through that port. When this Full/Col LED is off, the data is transmitting in half-duplex mode. If the green LED flickers, that connection is experiencing collisions (infrequent collisions are normal). If the switch seems to experience excessive collisions, verify that your network cabling is securely crimped and installed correctly. If this LED flickers too often, troubleshooting or network load balancing may be required.

- **100** The 100 LED lights up orange when a successful 100-Mbps connection is made through that port. When the 100 LED is off, the data transfer rate is 10 Mbps.

Configuration Settings

Your print server may include several DIP switches to set basic configuration options. While the location and number of switches can vary among print server models, there are several popular options:

- **Autonegotiation** This switch controls the Autonegotiation mode, which enables the print server to automatically detect the speed (10 Mbps or 100 Mbps), polarity, and duplex of your network cabling. If the switch is in the off position, the unit will not automatically detect speeds.

- **Speed** This switch controls the print server's speed (i.e., 10 Mbps/100 Mbps). For example, set the switch off for 100-Mbps data transfer, or set the switch on for 10-Mbps data transfer.

- **Duplex** This switch controls the duplex mode of data transfer. When this switch is set on, data transfer runs in half-duplex mode. When this switch is set off, data transfer runs in full-duplex mode.

General Hardware Installation

Most dedicated print server devices are not terribly difficult to install, but it does require a little bit of preparation. The device uses an ac adapter, and can support several printers, so you will need adequate ac outlets for the server and printer(s). Before you start the installation, you'll need to locate the server's *default name* and *node address*. This information is usually printed on a sticker located on the back or bottom of the unit. Locate that sticker now, because it may be hard to find once the print server is fully installed. Write down the unit's default name (such as SC483081). You'll need to know this when installing the drivers. Also, record the print server's node address (such as 00C002123456), which is the physical address of the unit (i.e., the MAC address).

The guidelines provided here are presented as a general reference only. Always refer to the manufacturer's directions for specific instructions and cautions.

Most print servers do not have an on/off power switch—whenever its ac power adapter is plugged into a power supply, the print server is powered on. Fortunately, the print server can be powered on before, during, or after your network power. Simply plug the power adapter into the print server's power port (on the back of the unit), then plug the power adapter into the wall. The print server's Power LED should light up green. Finally, connect your print server with a Cat 5 UTP cable from the RJ-45 port to a standard port on your switch or hub.

Power down your printers and connect them to a corresponding parallel port on the print server. If you're using IEEE 1284 printers, be sure to use good-quality shielded parallel port cables intended for high-speed bidirectional communication. You can power on the printers after they're connected. You can now install the software drivers and/or administrative software for your print server. In virtually all cases, this software only needs to be installed once on the administrator's PC.

Configuring and Using Print Servers

As a network device, a print server device is accessible to all of your network stations once it's installed and printers are connected. In some cases, print server drivers may need to be installed on each workstation that must access the print server, but most print server devices are fully functional network devices that require no drivers (see the instructions that accompany your print server for more specifics). However, virtually all print servers will utilize some form of management software (such as *PS Admin* for a D-Link print server and *Bi-Admin* for a Linksys print server) that allows an administrator to access and alter the print server's configuration.

INSTALLING ADMINISTRATION SOFTWARE

The administrator should install management software on their workstation. If you find that the management platform does not support the system requirements, it may be possible to use Telnet access instead. For example, D-Link's PS Admin uses the IPX protocol for communicating with the print server, so you need to have the IPX network protocol and the Novell NetWare client services enabled. The following steps outline the installation of typical administration software:

1. Insert the software installation disk 1 into your system's 3.5" floppy drive (**A:** or **B:**).

2. If you are using Windows 3.1x or Windows NT 3.51, choose Run from the Program Manager's File menu. Under Windows 9x/Windows NT 4.x (or later) operating systems, choose Run from the Start menu on the taskbar. When the dialog box appears, type the pathname of the Setup program on the floppy drive (such as **a:\setup**) and click OK.

3. The Setup program will begin by copying some files and ask for your confirmation. Click the Next button to continue.

4. The Setup program will then ask you to select a directory on your hard disk where you want it to install the administration program. If you want a destination directory path other than the default, click the Browse button to select it. Click the Next button to continue the installation.

5. The Setup program will copy program files to the directory you selected, and create a corresponding program group. Press the Finish button to complete the installation.

6. Once the installation is complete, you can begin using the software.

INITIAL SETUP

Before you're able to print over the network using your print server, you may need to perform some basic setup tasks. When trouble arises with a print server, it's often helpful to check these basic setup options. Typical options require you to

■ Select a name for your print server.

■ Set a password to protect your print server's settings from unauthorized modifications.

■ Choose names for the print server's individual printer ports, and select appropriate port settings.

■ Test the operation of the print server, and verify that the print server is connected properly.

■ Once you have finished with these tasks, you can proceed to set up network printing for Novell NetWare, Microsoft Networks, AppleTalk networks, and UNIX TCP/IP systems.

Select a Name

Each network print server has a *server name*. When the print server is shipped from the factory, it has a default name such as SC483081, where the digits often represent the last six digits of the Ethernet address (normally found on the print server's underside sticker). You can stay with the default name or choose any name you like for your print servers, provided that

■ The server name is less than 15 characters long.

■ The server does not have the same name as any file server on your network.

■ The server does not have the same name as any print servers configured for your network.

■ The server does not have the same name as any client or server.

Uppercase and lowercase letters are not distinguished in print server names.

Most manufacturers recommend that you limit your print server name to 15 characters—including the letters A through Z, the digits 0 through 9, and the hyphen ("-") character. Names that violate this recommendation may not be usable with some networks. A typical print server's name can be changed using the steps outlined here:

1. Select the print server in the PS Admin main window's server name display (or extended server display).

2. Choose Server Device from the Configuration menu, or press the Configure Server button in the toolbar. (If you have already assigned a password to the server, you will have to enter it at this point.) PS Admin will display the Configuration – Server Device window.

3. In the Server Name field, enter the name you have chosen for the server and press OK.

4. Choose Save Configuration from the Configuration menu, or press the Save Configuration button on the toolbar. This will store the new settings into the print server and restart it. Your print server will now be accessible under the new name.

Select a Password

Unless you set a password, anyone on your network will be able to change your print server's settings. If your local network is connected to the Internet, it may be possible to change your print server's configuration from anywhere in the world using the Telnet interface. To protect your print server's integrity, you should set a password for your print server, and record it in a safe place. To set the print server's password, follow these steps:

1. Select the print server in the administration software's server name display (or extended server display).

2. Choose Server Device from the Configuration menu, or press the Configure Server button in the toolbar. (If you have already assigned a password to the server, you will have to enter it at this point.) The software will display the Configuration – Server Device window.

3. In the Password field, enter the password you have chosen for the server and press OK.

4. The software will ask you to confirm your new password. Enter the password a second time and press OK.

5. Choose Save Configuration from the Configuration menu, or press the Save Configuration button on the toolbar. This will store the new settings into the print server and restart it.

Do not forget or lose your print server password. If you forget it, you will have to contact your D-Link service representative to change the password.

Adjust Port Settings

The individual printer ports on the print server can also be adjusted for optimum performance. For example, you can usually adjust the following characteristics of each port:

■ The name of the port

■ A comment describing the port

■ Parallel port speed

■ Parallel port support for HP's PJL (Printer Job Language) protocol

■ Serial port speed (baud rate)

■ Number of serial port data bits

■ Number of serial port stop bits

■ Serial port parity (even or odd)

■ Serial port software flow control (XON/XOFF)

■ Serial port hardware flow control (DTR/RTS)

There are typical steps to set the parameters for a printer port:

1. Select the print server in the administration software's server name display (or extended server display).

2. Choose Server Device from the Configuration menu, or press the Configure Server button in the toolbar. (If you have assigned a password to the server, you will have to enter it at this point.) The software will display the Configuration – Server Device window.

3. Press the button corresponding to the port you wish to change. You can change the following parameters for a parallel port:

■ **Port Name**   This is the name by which the port is known on network systems. The port name should be at most 32 characters long, and may consist of letters, numbers, and hyphens. Spaces are not allowed. If the port will be used for LAN Manager clients, the port name cannot exceed eight characters.

■ **Description**   A comment describing the port.

■ **Speed**   Determines whether the print server can send data to the printer at high speed. Most newer printers can accept high-speed data transmission. If your printer loses characters, you may need to choose the low-speed mode.

■ **PJL Printer**   This determines whether or not the printer accepts Hewlett Packard's PJL printer job control language commands. PJL allows users to get feedback on the printer's status. If the printer connected to the port supports PJL, set this field to Yes.

You can change the following parameters for a serial port:

■ **Port Name**   This is the name by which the port is known on network systems. The port name should be at most 32 characters long, and may consist of letters, numbers, and hyphens. Spaces are not allowed. If the port will be used for LAN Manager clients, the port name cannot exceed eight characters.

■ **Description**   A comment describing the port.

■ **Baud Rate**   This sets the serial communications bit rate (in bits per second). Most printers default to 9,600 bps—rates from 300 bps to 115,200 bps are often available.

■ **Data Bits**   This sets the number of bits transmitted (per byte) on the serial port. Most modern printers use 8-bit data.

■ **Stop Bits**   This sets the number of stop bits transmitted (per byte) on the serial port. Most modern printers use serial protocol with one stop bit.

■ **Parity**   This sets the type of parity check bit sent with each byte on the serial port. Most modern printers use a nonparity serial protocol.

■ **Software Flow Control**   This determines whether or not the print server should respond to software flow control requests from the printer. When software flow control is used, the printer will send an XOFF character (CTRL-S) to the print server when its buffer is getting full, and an XON character (XON) when the buffer is no longer full.

■ **Hardware Flow Control**   This determines whether or not the print server should respond to hardware flow control requests from the printer. When hardware flow control is used, the printer will use the DTR, RTS (or both control lines) to control the print server's transmission of data in order to prevent the printer's buffers from getting full.

4. Once you've made the necessary changes, click OK to exit the Port Settings dialog box.

5. Click OK to exit the Server Device dialog window.

6. Choose Save Configuration from the Configuration menu, or press the Save Configuration button on the toolbar. This will store the new settings into the print server and restart it.

Test the Print Server

Once you have set all of the necessary parameters, and have finished connecting your printer(s) to the print server, you should test each of the printer ports using the Print Test function. Follow these steps for each port you wish to test:

1. Select the print server in the software's server name display (or extended server display).

2. Choose Print Test in the Tools menu. The software will prompt you for the port you wish to test.

3. Choose a port and click OK. The print server should print out a test page.

4. Repeat this procedure for each printer port with an attached printer.

Printing Under Novell NetWare

Many current network print server devices support both the Bindery server database used with NetWare 3.x networks, and the NetWare Directory Services (NDS) network-wide database used with NetWare 4.x/5.x networks. This part of the chapter explains how to use the network print server in an NDS environment.

NETWARE DIRECTORY SERVICES (NDS)

NetWare version 3.x stores information about users, file server volumes, print servers, print queues, and other objects in a database called the *Bindery*. NetWare server administration programs (such as SYSCON, PCONSOLE, and so on) modify entries in the Bindery to manage the operation of the file server. The main disadvantage of the Bindery database is that it is limited to a single server. Networks with a large number of servers can become difficult to manage, because each server has to be configured separately. In large enterprises, this can result in disorganization as each department tries to administer its own NetWare servers—each in a different way. It can become troublesome (even impossible) to coordinate the administration of file servers across the entire enterprise.

For this reason, NetWare version 4.x introduced NetWare Directory Services (NDS), which allows administration on a global (as well as local) scale. NDS organizes objects not by file server, but by administrative domain. The Network Directory Services database stores "objects" in a tree structure. Branches in the tree represent different regional offices, divisions, departments, or other ways of dividing administrative responsibility. Objects, such as users, servers, server volumes, print servers, print queues, and so on, can be placed anywhere within the tree structure. The whole tree structure is shared by all servers using the same tree. Changing a setting in the tree affects all servers, making it less critical to manage servers individually. For compatibility with existing NetWare 3.x clients and servers, NetWare 4.x/5.x provides Bindery emulation, which exposes objects in the server's context as Bindery objects.

NETWARE 5.X CONFIGURATION

To enable your print server device as a NetWare NDS print server, you'll first need to create several NDS objects. You can do this using the DOS-based PCONSOLE or NWADMIN programs, or the Windows-based NWADMN32 NetWare 5.x Administrator program. NWADMN32 is used in this example, but consult your NetWare documentation for information about using PCONSOLE or NWADMIN to perform the setup. First, determine a unique name and permanent name for each print server on the network, then follow these steps to configure your print server in Pserver mode for NetWare 5.x NDS printing:

 Remember that you may also need to install manufacturer's configuration software for the print server.

1. Use a Windows 9x (running Client32) and execute the NWADMN32 program from the system volume (for example, **F:\public\win32**) on the file server.

2. Log into your NDS network as Admin (or as a user with Administrator access privileges). Make a note of the NDS tree and NDS context name that appear on the screen—this information is used later to configure the print server.

3. Access the file server's Quick Setup option.

4. Select a context where you want to add the new print server object, printer object, and print queue object.

5. Select Tools from the NWADMN32's menu bar.

6. Select Print Services Quick Setup (Non-NDPS).

7. Type your print server name in the Print Server Name field (manufacturers often recommend that you use the default name).

8. Type the printer name you want in the Name field (within the "Printer" section of the Quick Setup Window).

9. Select Parallel in the Type field.

10. Select Text in the Banner field.

11. Type the Queue name you want in the Name field (within the Print Queue section of the Quick Setup Window).

12. Select the NetWare File server volume in the Volume field.

13. Now save your changes and launch the print server's Administration utility. For a Netgear print server, you would select Netgear Print Server Administration from the FirstGear for Print Server icon on your desktop.

14. Select Print Server from the Active Print Server list.

15. Select NetWare Pserver.

16. Select the Advanced icon.

17. Select NetWare Pserver.

18. Click on Print Server Mode.

19. Select the NDS Tree Name.

20. Enter the Context Name.

21. Click on Save to Device.

For more information about configuring print servers, printers, and print queues, consult your NetWare documentation.

REMOTE PRINTER CONFIGURATION

Your network print server may also be configured as NetWare 4.x/5.x remote printer. This allows slightly easier administration, but may increase printing delays. Use the following guidelines to set up a printer port as a remote printer port:

1. Make sure you are logged on to your NetWare server as Admin, or that you have permissions equivalent to Admin.

2. Make sure that the NetWare protocol is enabled in the server. This setting is found in the Configuration - Server Device window, accessible by selecting the print server and choosing Server Device from the Configuration window.

3. Make sure you have a NetWare print server created and running on your NetWare file server. Consult your NetWare documentation for instruction on how to do this.

4. Choose NetWare Protocol from the Configuration menu in your print server's administration software (or click the Configure NetWare button in the toolbar). Click on the Remote Printer tab.

5. Click on the port number button corresponding to the port you will be using for remote printer service.

6. Click on the NDS Remote Printer selection. The print server's administration software will display the tree structure of the NetWare NDS contexts accessible from your network.

7. Enter the name of the context you'll be using, and enter the name of the print server in that context.

8. Determine what printer numbers are available on the given print server, and enter an unused printer number in the Printer Number field. Printer numbers can range from 0 to 15.

9. Click OK, then choose Save Configuration from the Configuration menu (or press the Save Configuration toolbar button) to change the settings in the print server. The print server will restart itself and begin serving as a remote printer for the specified print server.

PRINTING FROM CLIENTS

Once your print server device is set up for printing from the file server, your network's client workstations can each connect to the file server's print queue. The actual process will depend on the each client's operating system.

Windows 9x Clients

Unless you're using the 32-bit NetWare requester from Novell, Windows 9x does not directly support NDS access. You can access NetWare 4.x printer queues using Bindery Emulation.

Windows NT 4.0 Clients

A workstation running Windows NT 4.0 (or later) can print to a NetWare print queue using steps similar to those shown here:

1. Open the Start menu, choose the Settings submenu, and then select the Printers item. Windows will display the Printers folder.

2. Double-click on the Add Printer icon in the Printers folder. Windows will start the Add Printer Wizard.

3. Choose the Network Printer selection and click the Next button to continue.

4. Locate the print queue you wish to attach to in the browser, and click OK. NetWare NDS contexts may be found beneath the NetWare or Compatible Network item.

5. Windows will display a message—press OK to continue.

6. The Add Printer Wizard will ask you to choose the appropriate printer driver, and may ask you to insert your Windows NT installation media to locate driver files.

7. When installation is complete, the Add Printer Wizard will display another message. Click Finish to complete printer installation.

Printing Under Microsoft Networks

Microsoft Networking services prior to Windows 2000 are based on the NetBEUI protocol, which provides network users with peer-to-peer network services. In addition to accessing files and printers on a central server, any workstation can share its file directories and printer ports, making them accessible to other workstations. Most network print servers are also capable of making attached printers accessible to Microsoft Networking workstations running network operating systems such as Windows 9x/NT/2000, LAN Manager, and IBM LAN Server. Also, to improve printing efficiency, Microsoft Networking services clients can choose to print to a print queue stored on a Windows NT server—which can then forward the print jobs to the print server device. This part of the chapter examines common techniques for configuring and using a print server device with Windows operating systems.

WINDOWS CONFIGURATION

Little additional setup is necessary for the print server to be usable from Microsoft Networking clients. First, the NetBEUI check box in the Configuration – Server Device window needs to be checked. Select the print server and choose Server Device from the Configuration menu to display this window. You should also set the workgroup name and maximum allowed connections. These settings are accessible from the Configuration—NetBEUI dialog window, which you can display by choosing NetBEUI Protocol from the Configuration menu.

Each Microsoft Networking workstation or server has a workgroup name. The workgroup name determines what servers and resources will show up by default in lists of accessible resources. You should assign to the print server the same workgroup name as the users who will be accessing it most often. Network path names for printers on Microsoft Networking systems are of the form

```
\\computer name\printer name
```

When a print server device is used with Microsoft Networking, the Server Name (set from the Configuration – Server Device window) is used for the computer name in the path, and the Port Name (set from the Configuration – Parallel Port or Configuration – Serial Port window) is used for the printer name. For example, the printer connected to the port named DJ-660C on server PS-142634 would typically be referred to by the path

```
\\PS-142634\DJ-660C
```

UTILIZING THE WINDOWS NT PRINT QUEUE

Although it is possible for client workstations to connect directly to a network print server device, the print server's memory is limited, and a client may have to wait for large print jobs to complete (instead of letting the print server queue the entire job). To reduce wait times for clients, you may wish to store the print queue on a Windows server. Use the following steps to do this under Windows NT:

1. Make the networked printer usable from the NT server machine using the Add Printer Wizard as described earlier.

2. In the Printers window, right-click on the networked printer and choose the Sharing item.

3. Enable sharing, and set the Sharing Name of the printer.

4. Optionally, select the operating system version(s) you'll be providing the printer driver on the server. You will need to have operating system distribution disks for these operating system versions.

5. Click OK. The printer will now be accessible to other network users by way of the Windows NT server machine—taking advantage of additional memory on the server.

PRINTING FROM CLIENTS

Once your print server device is set up for printing on a Microsoft network, your network's client workstations can each connect to the file server's print queue. The actual process will depend on each client's operating system.

Windows 9x Clients

Use the following steps as a guideline to allow your Windows 9x (or later) workstation to print over the Microsoft network directly through your network print server device:

1. Open the Start menu, choose the Settings submenu, and then select the Printers item. Windows will display the Printers folder.

2. Double-click on the Add Printer icon in the Printers folder. Windows will start the Add Printer Wizard. Press the Next button to continue to the next screen.

3. Choose the Network Printer selection and click the Next button to continue.

4. Enter the network path for your network print server device, specifying which port you want to connect to. For instance, to use the printer connected to the port named PS-142634-P2 on the print server named PS-142634, enter (see Figure 16-2)

```
\\PS-142634\PS-142634-P2
```

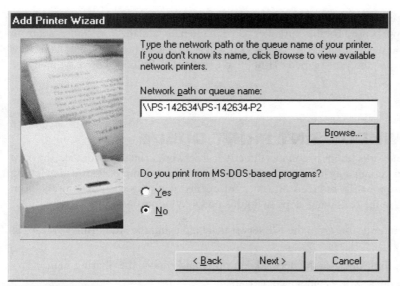

FIGURE 16-2 The Add Printer Wizard allows you to enter a path to a printer that includes the print server.

As an alternative to entering the network path, you can also use the Browse button to locate the print server and printer. Press the Next button to continue.

5. At this point Windows will ask you to choose the correct printer driver for the printer. Choose your printer's make and model from the list, or use the driver disk included with the printer. When you have chosen the correct printer, click Next to continue.

6. Windows will ask for a name for the printer. Enter a name (or accept the default). Then press Finish to complete the installation.

Windows NT 4.0 Clients

A workstation running Windows NT 4.0 (or later) can print over a Microsoft network directly to the print server device using steps such as the ones shown here:

1. Open the Start menu, choose the Settings submenu, and then select the Printers item. Windows will display the Printers folder.

2. Double-click on the Add Printer icon in the Printers folder. Windows will start the Add Printer Wizard.

3. Choose the Network Printer selection and click the Next button to continue.

4. Enter the network path for your network print server device, specifying which port you want to connect to. For instance, to use the printer connected to the port named PS-142634-P2 on the print server named PS-142634, enter

   ```
   \\PS-142634\PS-142634-P2
   ```

   As an alternative to entering the network path, you can also browse the network to locate the print server and port. Press the Next button to continue.

5. Windows will display a message. Press OK to continue.

6. At this point Windows will ask you to choose the correct printer driver for the printer. Choose your printer's make and model from the list, or use the driver disk included with the printer. When you have chosen the correct printer, click OK to continue.

7. If you already have a default printer, Windows will ask if you wish to use the newly installed printer as the new default.

8. When installation is complete, Windows will display another message. Press the Finish button to complete installation.

Printing Under UNIX TCP/IP

Some network print server devices (such as D-Link print servers) can provide print services to systems using the **lpr/lpd** network printing protocol. Most UNIX systems are capable of supporting **lpd**. This part of the chapter explains how to use the print server's administration software to configure the print server for TCP/IP printing, and how to configure your UNIX workstations to print to the print server. For TCP/IP networks *without* a Windows-based workstation available, you can generally use the print server's Telnet interface to configure the print server.

CONFIGURING TCP/IP SETTINGS

To use a typical print server device in the UNIX environment, you'll need to configure the network print server to allow TCP/IP-based printing, as well as SNMP and Telnet-based management. The steps below outline one possible set of procedures:

1. Start the print server's administration software and make sure the TCP/IP protocol is enabled. The TCP/IP check box in the Configuration – Server Device window needs to be checked. Select the print server and choose Server Device from the Configuration menu to display this window.

2. Choose TCP/IP Protocol from the Configuration menu.

3. Configure the print server's IP address, local network subnet mask, and default gateway.

4. Press OK, then choose Save Configuration from the Configuration menu (or press the Save Configuration toolbar button) to change the settings in the print server. The print server will restart itself and will be available for **lpd**-protocol printing, as well as management using the Telnet protocol and SNMP-based centralized network management.

UNDERSTANDING SNMP MANAGEMENT

Simple Network Management Protocol (SNMP) has become a standard protocol for managing large networks using central management consoles. Some network print servers (such as D-Link servers) support the SNMP *Management Information Base* (known as MIB-II), which collects basic statistics on the print server's basic TCP/IP and Ethernet networking operations. SNMP (version 1) implements a rudimentary form of security by requiring that each request include a *community name*. A community name is an arbitrary string of characters used as a "password" to control access to the hub. If the hub receives a request with a community name it doesn't recognize, it will trigger an authentication trap. Network print servers such as the D-Link allow up to three different community names to be defined, and the access rights for each community can be separately set to either *read only or read/write*. You will need to coordinate these names with the community name settings you use in your network management system. To set community names for your print server, start the print server's administration software and review these general steps:

1. Choose TCP/IP Protocol from the Configuration menu.
2. Press the SNMP button to open the SNMP Configuration window.
3. As necessary, add community names and set the access level for each.
4. Press OK to exit the SNMP Configuration window.

The print server also sends out SNMP *traps* to network management stations whenever certain exceptional events occur—such as when the print server is powered on, or when an SNMP request is made using an unknown community name. The print server allows traps to be routed to up to three different network management hosts. To enable traps for your print server, start the print server's administration software and follow this guide:

1. Choose TCP/IP Protocol from the Configuration menu.
2. Press the Trap button to open the Trap Configuration window.
3. Check the SNMP Trap box to enable the sending of SNMP traps.
4. Set IP addresses and community names for each trap recipient.
5. Click OK to exit the Trap Configuration dialog box when you're done.

TEXT PRINTING UNDER UNIX

Text files on UNIX systems contain lines that end with "newline" characters, as opposed to DOS and Windows operating systems that end with a carriage return followed by a linefeed. Most printers require a carriage return/linefeed pair at the end of each line, making it necessary for some translation to be done before UNIX text files can be printed on most printers. For this purpose, you can define two "printers" for the same printer port: one that prints to the port itself, and one that prints to the port name with _TEXT added to the name. Files printed to the second port will be translated so that the printer has the carriage return/linefeed pairs that it needs. For example, you could define a printer hp5l that prints to port PS-142634-P1, and a printer hp5lt that prints to port PS-142634-P1_TEXT. You graphics files could then be printed to the hp5l printer, and "raw" text files could be printed to the hp5lt printer.

PRINTING UNDER BSD UNIX

For UNIX versions derived from or related to BSD releases (such as SunOS 4.x, Linux, BSD/OS, FreeBSD, or NetBSD), you can use the following procedure to enable users to print to a printer connected to your network print server device:

1. Log in as the **superuser** (root).
2. Add an entry for the print server in the host's **/etc/hosts** file, giving a hostname for the print server's IP address. A line in **/etc/hosts** contains an IP address and one or more aliases for the host. For example: **202.39.74.40 ps-142634 ps-142634.dlink.com.tw**. If you use DNS (the Domain Naming Services protocol), you can add an address record entry to your DNS database for the print server.
3. Create a spool directory for the printer. On SunOS systems, create the directory as a subdirectory of **/var/spool**, with the same name as the printer. On Linux systems, create the directory as a

subdirectory of **/usr/spool/lp**. On BSD/OS, FreeBSD, or NetBSD systems, create the directory as a subdirectory of **/var/spool**.

4. Change the owner and permissions of the directory so that it is owned and writable by group daemon, using the following commands:

```
chown bin.daemon /var/spool/hp51
chmod 775 /var/spool/hp51
```

5. Add an entry for the printer to **/etc/printcap**, similar to the following:

```
hp51:\
:lp=:sd=/var/spool/hp51:mx#0:\
:rm=ps-142634:rp=PS-142634-P1:
```

6. The directory path in the sd spool directory entry should match the directory name you created above. If your entry requires more than one line, you can escape the newline with a backslash. The meaning of each of the entries is described here:

- **lp=**   The lp entry is used to specify a local printer device. Since the printer is a remote printer, this entry should be blank.
- **sd=dir**   The location of the printer's local spool directory.
- **mx#blocks**   The limit for print job files in the local spool directory; 0 means no limit.
- **rm=address**   The host where the remote printer is located—in this case the D-Link print server.
- **rp=printer**   The name of the printer on the remote host. For the D-Link print server, the port name (case-sensitive) should be used.

7. Issue the command to start a spool daemon for the printer (the printer will then be available for use):

```
lpc start hp51
```

8. Optionally, add another printcap entry (and issue another **lpc start** command) for a second printer, using the port_TEXT port. This second printer name can be used for printing text files. Entries in **/etc/printcap** begin with a name for the printer or a list of names, separated by "|" (a vertical bar).

PRINTING UNDER WINDOWS NT

Windows NT versions 3.51 (and later) support printing using the lpd protocol. To print to a network print server (such as a D-Link device) from a Windows NT 4.0 workstation or server, follow these guidelines:

1. Make sure that you have installed the TCP/IP protocol and the Microsoft TCP/IP Printing service. You can install these from the Network control panel if necessary.

2. Open the Start menu, choose the Settings submenu, and then select the Printers item. Windows will display the Printers folder.

3. Double-click on the Add Printer icon in the Printers folder. Windows will start the Add Printer Wizard.

4. Choose the My Computer selection and click the Next button to continue.

5. Click the Add Port button to add the lpd print server to the list of ports.

6. Choose the LPR Port type and click New Port.

7. Enter the IP address of your network print server, and the port name of the printer you wish to use.

8. Click OK to return to the Printer Ports window, and then click Close to return to the Add Printer Wizard.

9. Click Next to continue installing the printer, following the on-screen instructions. The Add Printer Wizard will ask you to select the proper driver for the printer, and will ask you to give a name to the printer. When you are done installing the printer, you will be able to use any of the usual printing commands to print to your printer.

Telnet Administration Basics

Most print server devices come bundled with management software (such as Bi-Admin for Linksys or PS Admin for D-Link). This management software is more than adequate for checking device status and making adjustments to the print server's configuration. However, there may be times when the management software simply isn't available, or your administration platform does not meet the requirements for the management applet. When this occurs, you may be able to access and control the print server device through Telnet. This part of the chapter provides examples of manual configuration procedures using common network tools.

SETTING AN IP ADDRESS

The administration software (such as PS Admin) program allows you to set your print server's IP address (and other TCP/IP parameters). If you don't have a Windows-based workstation and you need to set the print server's address, you can use a BOOTP (Boot Protocol) server, or the manual method described as follows. If you want to use BOOTP, your local Ethernet network needs to have a BOOTP server. The BOOTP server table needs to have an entry listing the print server's Ethernet (MAC) address, the IP address you want to assign to the print server, the network's mask, and the default gateway (router) address. If you aren't using BOOTP, you can manually set the IP address using the following method as an example:

Consult your BOOTP server documentation for information about how to add an entry to the server table.

1. Note your print server's Ethernet (MAC) address. The Ethernet address is a 12-digit hex number printed on a sticker at the bottom of your print server.

2. Use a host on the same local Ethernet network as the print server. Change your host's ARP (Address Resolution Protocol) table to add a mapping from the IP address you want to assign to the print server's Ethernet address. For many TCP/IP systems, this is done with a command of the form:

```
arp ip-address ethernet-address
```

3. For example, to assign the address 202.39.74.40 to the print server with MAC address 00 80 C8 14 26 34, use this command:

```
arp 202.39.74.40 0080C8142634
```

4. On a UNIX-based system, you will need to have superuser (root) permission to execute the **arp** command. From the host with the modified ARP table, send an ICMP echo request to the print server using the **ping** command:

```
ping 202.39.74.40
```

```
**************************************
* Welcome to Print Server          *
* Telnet Console                    *
**************************************
Server Name   : PS-132544
Server Model  : DP-3xx
F/W Version   : 1.02
MAC Address   : 00 80 C8 14 26 34
Up Time       : 5 days, 06:14:38
Please Enter Password:
```

FIGURE 16-3   Some print servers provide a Telnet interface for administration.
The initial login reports details of the print server's operation.

5. When the print server receives an ICMP request at its own Ethernet address, but with a different IP address than the one it was expecting, it changes its IP address setting.

6. The print server will now respond to the new IP address. At this point you can use the Telnet interface (as described next) to change the host's other settings.

USING TELNET

You can access your print server's Telnet interface using an ordinary Telnet client program. On many systems, the command to invoke the Telnet client is

```
telnet ip-address
```

where ip-address is the IP address you have assigned to the print server. When you first Telnet to the print server, it displays its login message as in Figure 16-3 above.

At this point, you can enter the password assigned to your print server. If you have not yet assigned a password, just press ENTER. The print server will then display the Telnet interface main menu as in Figure 16-4.

```
[Main Menu]
1 - Server Configuration
2 - Port Configuration
3 - TCP/IP Configuration
4 - AppleTalk Configuration
5 - Display Information
6 - Tools
7 - Save Configuration
0 - Quit
Enter Selection:
```

FIGURE 16-4   The Telnet main menu lets you configure the
major aspects of a print server's operation.

```
[TCP/IP Configuration]
1 - IP Address <168.8.100.52>
2 - Subnet Mask <255.255.0.0>
3 - Default Gateway <168.8.100.254>
4 - SNMP Community
5 - SNMP Traps
0 - Return to Main Menu
Enter Selection:
```

FIGURE 16-5   The TCP/IP menu allows you to manage
the print server's network behavior.

CHANGING TCP/IP SETTINGS

Once you have set the print server's IP address for the first time, you may wish to change the address or other TCP/IP configuration information such as the local network mask, the default gateway, the accepted SNMP community names, or the list of SNMP trap recipients. From the main menu, choose TCP/IP Configuration. The print server will display the TCP/IP Configuration menu (such as Figure 16-5 above).

To change the IP address, local subnet mask, or default gateway, select the corresponding menu item. The print server will prompt you for a new value for the setting. Enter the new value and press ENTER. To change the SNMP community names, choose the appropriate menu item. The print server will display the SNMP Community menu (as shown in Figure 16-6).

For each of the three community name "slots" that the print server supports, you can set the community name and the level of access (such as read-only or read/write) given to each request. SNMP-compatible *Network Management System* (NMS) stations can use the community names you've set to access management information and statistics collected by the print server. To change an entry, select the corresponding menu item. When the print server prompts you for the new value, enter the value and press ENTER. When you're done changing community name settings, choose 0 to return to the TCP/IP Configuration menu. To modify the SNMP trap settings, choose the appropriate menu item from the TCP/IP Configuration menu. The print server will display the SNMP Trap menu (as in Figure 16-7).

By default, SNMP traps are disabled. Select the Traps item to enable or disable the sending of traps. Once traps are enabled, you can assign up to three different hosts as designated trap recipients. With each trap recipient IP address, there is also an associated SNMP community name that will be included in the IP request. To change an IP address or community name, select the appropriate menu item and enter the

```
[SNMP Community]
1 - Community 1 Name <public>
2 - Community 1 Access <Read Only>
3 - Community 2 Name <>
4 - Community 2 Access <Read Only>
5 - Community 3 Name <>
6 - Community 3 Access <Read Only>
0 - Return to TCP/IP Menu
Enter Selection:
```

FIGURE 16-6   The SNMP Community menu lets you tweak the SNMP
management parameters for the print server.

```
[SNMP Traps]
1 - Traps <Disable>
2 - Target 1 IP Address <0.0.0.0>
3 - Target 1 Community Name <>
4 - Target 2 IP Address <0.0.0.0>
5 - Target 2 Community Name <>
6 - Target 3 IP Address <0.0.0.0>
7 - Target 3 Community Name <>
0 - Return to TCP/IP Menu
Enter Selection:
```

FIGURE 16-7   SNMP Traps allow you to change the way
SNMP interacts with your print server.

desired value. When you're done changing TCP/IP settings, choose 0 to return to the main menu. Finally, choose the Save Configuration option and confirm the save. The Telnet connection will drop, and the print server will reset itself so that the new TCP/IP settings take effect.

CHANGING PRINT SERVER SETTINGS

From the Server Configuration menu, you can change the server name, as well as the Location and Contact fields (used for identifying the location of the print server and the person responsible for maintaining it). To change print server settings, choose Server Configuration from the main menu—the print server will display the Server Configuration menu (as in Figure 16-8).

To change the server name, location, or administrative contact, choose the appropriate menu item. The print server will prompt you for the new value. When you're done changing the server settings, choose 0 to return to the main menu. Choose the Save Configuration option and confirm the save. The Telnet connection will drop, and the print server will reset itself so that the new server configuration will take effect.

CHANGING THE PRINT SERVER PASSWORD

A print server password is used to protect the print server's configuration from unauthorized changes—either through the administration software or through the Telnet interface. To change the print server's password, choose the Server Configuration option from the main menu. The print server will display the Server Configuration menu (shown in Figure 16-8).

Choose the Change Password menu item. The print server will prompt for the old password (if there is no password, just press ENTER). The print server will prompt you to enter the new password (password

```
[Server Configuration]
1 - Server Name <PS-142634>
2 - Location <Massachusetts Office>
3 - Admin Contact <Joseph>
4 - Change Password
0 - Return to Main Menu
Enter Selection:
```

FIGURE 16-8   You can manage key settings on the print
server using the Server Configuration menu.

characters will be displayed as asterisks "*"), then you'll be prompted a second time. Enter the same password as before to confirm that you've typed it correctly. Choose 0 to return to the Main Menu and save the configuration. The Telnet connection will drop, and the print server will reset itself to let the new password setting take effect.

CHANGING PORT SETTINGS

Each port on the print server has several settings that you may need to adjust in order to suit your configuration and the physical printer you have attached to the port. To change one or more port settings, choose Port Settings from the main menu. The print server will display the Port Menu. Select the port you wish to configure. The print server will display a menu appropriate to the port's type (serial and parallel ports will have different menus).

To change any of the displayed settings, choose the appropriate menu item. The print server will prompt for the new value. When you're done changing settings for the port, choose 0 to return to the port menu. When you're done changing port settings, choose 0 to return to the main menu. Choose the Save Configuration menu item and confirm the save. The Telnet connection will drop, and the print server will reset itself to let the new port settings take effect.

DISPLAYING INFORMATION

The print server Telnet interface provides two menu selections for displaying information about the print server and about the printers connected to it. From the main menu, you can select the Display Information selection to display the Display Information menu. The Display Configuration selection displays several pages of information about the print server's hardware and internal software, as well as its configuration settings. Information about the port settings is also included. The Display Port Status selection displays statistics and information about the jobs printed on each of the print server's ports (such as in Figure 16-9).

```
Port Number         1              2              3
=========================================================
[Total Status]
Jobs                45             1              0
Sizes (KB)          23179          0              0
Timeouts            0              0              0
---------------------------------------------------------
[Current Job]
Printer Status      On Line        Off Line       On Line
Index               0              1              0
Protocol NETWARE
Name 00C60001
Spooling Bytes      0              172032         0
Printing Bytes      0              153600         0
=========================================================
1 - Refresh Port Status
0 - Return to Display Information Menu
Enter Selection:
```

FIGURE 16-9   The Telnet interface also supplies a detailed report of the print server's various ports.

RESETTING THE PRINT SERVER

There are times when it may be necessary to restart the print server—this will reset its internal statistics counters and clear other status information. The Telnet interface provides two different types of reset; an ordinary reset and a factory reset. An *ordinary reset* has the same effect as powering off the print server and powering it back on again. Statistics counters will be cleared, but all of the print server's configuration settings will be retained. A *factory reset* not only restarts the print server, but changes all of its configuration settings back to their original values (as the print server was shipped from the factory).

Do not perform a factory reset unless you are absolutely sure this is what you want. All settings (including the print server's TCP/IP network address) will be erased and replaced with their original values.

To reset the print server, choose Tools from the Main Menu. Choose the Reset or Factory Reset option, depending on the type of reset you wish to perform. The print server will ask for confirmation. Confirm the reset and press ENTER. The Telnet connection will drop, and the print server will reset itself. If you selected Factory Reset, all of the print server's default configuration values will be restored.

Troubleshooting Print Servers

Current print servers are usually reliable devices that can be installed and maintained with a minimum of fuss. Still, there are times when troubles arise with the device itself, the attached printers, or the server's configuration in the network. When problems strike your print server, you can take steps to quickly evaluate and correct the trouble.

DIAGNOSTIC TESTING

Most print servers perform a self test when power is first applied. The results are presented on the print server's LEDs. A normal (no fault) result is signaled by three flashes of the LPT indicator and the start of normal print server operation. If any error condition is found during the component test series, the test will halt with the LPT LED continuously signaling the particular error. Table 16-1 illustrates the error codes for a D-Link print server, but check your documentation for codes specific to your particular model.

FIRMWARE UPGRADES

The print server's internal software is stored in flash memory, which allows you to upgrade it to an updated version without shipping the print server back to the manufacturer. Check the manufacturer's Web site for new firmware downloads when they become available. Print server firmware updates are often contained in two related files: a larger one with a **.bin** extension, and a smaller one with a **.dwl** extension—both of these files are necessary for the flash update to be completed successfully. Once you've obtained the updated firmware, it's time to perform the update. One possible example is shown here:

1. Make sure you have backup copies of the previous version of the firmware image files before overwriting them with the new ones.

2. Start the print server's administration software (or Telnet interface). Choose Reload Firmware from the Tools menu. The print server will ask for the filename of the updated **.bin** image file.

3. Type in the pathname of the **.bin** file, or click the Browse button to locate the file using a standard dialog box.

TABLE 16-1	LED DIAGNOSTICS FOR A TYPICAL D-LINK PRINT SERVER
LPT FLASH PATTERN	**ERROR TYPE**
Steady long flashes	Firmware Reload Required
Continuous on	DRAM Error
One long, two short flashes	Timer INT Error
One long, three short flashes	Flash Protected
One long, four short flashes	Flash ID Error
One long, five short flashes	Flash Erase / Program Error
One long, six short flashes	LAN Controller Error
One long, seven short flashes	LAN Memory Error
One long, eight short flashes	Parallel Controller Error
One long, nine short flashes	LPT Error
Steady short flashes	EERPROM Error
One long, eleven short flashes	LAN I/O Base Error

4. Click OK. The administrative software will usually display an informational warning message.

5. Click OK. The flash update will begin, and the print server's administrative software will display the progress of the update.

6. When the update is complete, the software will display an informational message, and you may need to cycle the power to your print server.

When flashing the firmware, be very careful not to interrupt the transfer by powering down the print server or disconnecting it from the network. The print server should be able to recover from an interrupted transfer in most cases. In some situations, however, it may be necessary to return your print server for servicing in order to recover from an interrupted flash cycle.

SYMPTOMS

In addition to LED self-test results, there are numerous symptoms that can help pinpoint specific problem areas with your print server.

SYMPTOM 16-1 **There are no LEDs illuminated on the print server.** This can almost always be traced to a power problem—either the ac adapter has been disconnected or it has failed. In either case, check power to the print server. Replace the ac power adapter or try another print server.

SYMPTOM 16-2 **The print server's status LED is continuously lit.** The print server has crashed. In most cases, a "cold reboot" of the print server will clear the problem. Unplug and reconnect power at the print server. If the problem persists, replace the print server.

SYMPTOM 16-3 **The print server's status LED and power LED are continuously lit.** The print server has crashed. You can often clear this type of problem by resetting the print server with the Reset button, or unplug and reconnect power at the print server.

SYMPTOM 16-4   **When using DHCP, the print server gets an IP address conflict involving the print server.**   This is a common addressing problem that can occur with dynamically addressed network devices. If the print server is left on when the DHCP server is turned off, the print server will retain its IP address without informing the DHCP server. Reset the print server so that it will obtain a new IP address. This problem also arises if you assigned a static IP address within the range used by the DHCP server. If so, use another address *not* within the range used by the DHCP server.

SYMPTOM 16-5   **You have problems using WPCONFIG to configure the print server in Windows 9x.**   This is a software compatibility problem. Be sure that the administration software that you're using is compatible with your operating system. WPCONFIG is designed for Windows 3.1 only. For Windows 9x or NT, use a more appropriate utility such as Bi-Admin, PS Admin, or other administration software.

SYMPTOM 16-6   **The LED on the side of the three-port print server is not lighting up.** This is a cabling problem. Check your cabling and make sure that the Link LED on your hub or switch is lit. Change the DIP switch settings on the print server, if necessary, to adjust the print server's configuration.

SYMPTOM 16-7   **When using 10BaseT cabling, the print server unit does not work.** Check that the Link LED on your switch or hub for the print server port is lit. If it's off, there is a problem in the network cable. If using 10BaseT or 100BaseTX, check the LED next to the connector. It should be on if the network connection is OK. If the LED is out, try reconnecting the cable, or try a different cable. You may also try attaching the print server to a different port on the hub or switch. Also, check and modify the DIP switch settings on the print server if necessary, and remember to reset the print server each time you change any of the DIP switches.

SYMPTOM 16-8   **A printer connected to the print server cannot print (or prints garbage).**   This kind of problem is often traced to the printer itself. Verify that the printer is on and working properly (reboot the printer and try a self test). If the self test fails, the printer itself is defective and should be replaced. If the self test works properly, check the cabling between the printer and print server—it should be a good-quality cable (preferably a shielded IEEE 1284 cable) attached securely at both ends. Also verify that the total cable distance between the print server and the printer does not exceed 10 feet (try a shorter cable). Finally, verify that the printer driver operating the printer (as well as the printer selected in the particular application) is the latest available version.

SYMPTOM 16-9   **You cannot alter the print server's configuration.**   For example, the Configuration button on the Printer Status screen in Linksys Bi-Admin software is grayed out—even though the printer is bidirectional. This is usually caused by printer activity. You cannot alter a print server's configuration until the printer has finished its print job and is idle. Make sure that any pending print jobs are completed before attempting to configure the print server.

SYMPTOM 16-10   **The print server prints garbage under NetWare.**   First, print out a diagnostic file using PSCONFIG or the print server's administration utility (i.e., the Linksys Bi-Admin program). For example, run PSCONFIG and select your print server from the list, then select Print Diagnostic Report. Select each port in turn and print a diagnostic report. Check to see if the diagnostic report printed. If the diagnostic report prints properly, the problem may be caused by incorrect system configuration. If the diagnostic report printout is not correct, check your printer. If you do not find faults while inspecting your printer, the print server may require replacement.

Next, print a test text file and a test graphic file. If the text file prints correctly but the graphic file prints garbage, then specify the /NT (no tabs) option for **nprint** or **capture** commands and print again. If both tests print incorrectly, temporarily disable the print server handling the print queue and try the following steps. For NetWare 2.x and 3.x:

1. Run PCONSOLE.
2. Select Print Queue Information and select the print queue that the print server handles, then select Current Queue Status.
3. Set the "Servers can service entries in queue" option to NO.
4. Press ESC and select Print Queue ID. Record the queue ID.
5. Send your test files to the print queue using normal print commands.

For NetWare 4.x and 5.x Bindery & NDS modes:

1. Run PCONSOLE.
2. Select Print Queues, select the print queue that your print server handles, and then select Status.
3. Set the "Allow service by current print servers" option to NO.
4. Press ESC and select Information, and record the queue ID.
5. Send your test files to the print queue using normal print commands.

Remember to reset these changes later once the problem is corrected.

If the problem persists, reroute network printing to local printing. Disconnect the printer attached to your print server and connect it to LPT1 of your PC. Change to the drive and then the directory on the file server that contains the print queue. The directory will have the name of the queue ID (such as **\queues\Q_ID** for NDS mode, or **system\Q_ID** for Bindery mode). The test files you printed earlier should be in the queue directory. Print these files to the local printer using the COPY command with the **/b** option, such as

```
copy /b test.txt LPT1
```

Compare the printouts from the PC-driven and the print-server-driven exercises. If the printouts are the same, then the problem is *not* the print server. The problem might be that an incorrect printer driver was chosen, or the timeout setting in the **capture** command is too short. If the printouts are *not* the same, there may be a problem with the print server device. Try replacing the print server.

SYMPTOM 16-11   **The print server does not appear in the Active Device List of NetWare's PSCONFIG program.**   This type of problem can sometimes be caused by a problem in the arrangement of your physical network. Make sure that the print server is on the same network segment as your PC. If the print server is on a different network segment, you may need to access it from another administrative PC on that network segment (i.e., another PC running the print server's administration software, such as Bi-Admin or PS Admin).

In some cases, you may need to load a compatible protocol on the PC. For example, you may need to load NetBEUI on your PC so that the print server's administration software can connect with NetBEUI. Check the documentation for your print server to verify that your administrative PC meets all of the system requirements for the print server's software. Once you can get the print server to connect, verify that the NetWare protocol is enabled on the PC. Finally, the Ethernet frame type of your PC may be different than the frame type used with your print server—enable all Ethernet frame types and try the print server again.

SYMPTOM 16-12   **The print server is configured for NetWare, but cannot log in to a file server.**   This is almost always a problem in the print server's configuration. Start by checking the device configuration through PSCONFIG or the print server's administration software (such as Bi-Admin or PS Admin). If the device is configured as a NetWare print server, the information will look similar to Figure 16-10.

Make sure that the Master File Server name is assigned correctly, then check the current status of Your_File_Server, such as

- **Connected**   No action is required—the device is responding normally.
- **No file server**   Assign a master file server using PSCONFIG or the print server's administration software.
- **Connecting to server**   Wait and check if the file server exists.
- **Password mismatch**   Clear the NetWare password with PCONSOLE, or set the correct password for the print server using PSCONFIG or administration software.
- **Print server not defined**   Install the print server again.

Check NetWare to see if the login status of the print server to the file servers is ready. If it is not, check the error message and perform the required corrective action(s). Next, check the NetWare file server's name for character length. It should not be over 15 characters long (using letters, numbers, and a hyphen). If the name is incorrect, set a more appropriate name for the file server. Finally, if the file server is not in the status list and the print server has logged into the master file server, it means that the file server has not been serviced by the print server. Check to see if the file server is in the list of File Server To Be Serviced items under PCONSOLE. If not, insert the file server name to the list.

```
Server Name                : SC110049
NetWare Information         :
Master File Server         : ICE
Print Server Mode Status    :
Your_File_Server           : Current Status
Remote Printer Mode Status : N/A
```

FIGURE 16-10   Checking the print server's configuration can usually reveal obvious setup problems.

SYMPTOM 16-13 **The print server is configured as a NetWare Remote Printer, but can't log in to the NetWare print server.** Start by checking the print server's configuration and gathering its configuration data as described in the previous symptom. Now check the Remote Printer Mode Status field(s). For each logical printer, there will be a status entry. The status will be one of the following:

- **Connected** No action is required—the device is responding normally.
- **Unable to find server** Load the NetWare print server software.
- **Connecting to server** Wait and check if the NetWare print server is loaded.
- **Printer not defined** Install the print server as a remote printer of a NetWare print server.

Check NetWare to see if the print server device is ready. If it is not, check the error message and perform the required corrective action(s). Finally, check the NetWare file server's name for character length. It should not be over 15 characters long (using letters, numbers, and a hyphen). If the name is incorrect, set a more appropriate name for the file server.

SYMPTOM 16-14 **The print server cannot print the jobs sent to the NetWare print queue.** Start with the printer attached to the print server, and see that the printer is powered and online. Also check to verify that the print server device is logged into the NetWare file server, and see that the NetWare printer number is correct, such as

- 0 = parallel port 1 of the PrintServer
- 1 = parallel port 2 of the PrintServer
- 2 = parallel port 3 of the PrintServer

Check the current status of the print queue. Run PCONSOLE and select Print Queue Information. Then select the queue and select Current Queue Status. See if there are three YESes. If not, set the three entries to YES and try the print job again.

Next, check to see if the print server device is acting as a static queue server to the print queue. Run PCONSOLE and select Print Server Information. Select Print Server Configuration and select Queues Serviced by Printer. Then select your desired printer and check if the queue is on the list. If not, insert the queue into the list by pressing the INSERT key and select the queue. Then reset the print server to service the new queue. Finally, the total number of queues to be serviced may be over the limit (such as 56). If so, reduce the number of queues to an appropriate level and try the print job again.

SYMPTOM 16-15 **You used the NetWare capture command to print a job, but the job was separated into two parts.** The timeout setting in the **capture** command may be too short. Increase the timeout value of the **capture** command by using the option **/TI=n** of the **capture** command to increase the timeout value, where **n** is the value of timeout.

SYMPTOM 16-16 **PSCONFIG or the administration software shows "No Response".** There are several possible issues that can cause this problem. Excessive network traffic is one example—if the network is busy, wait a bit and try the print job again later. It is also possible that the print server device is powered down or disconnected. Check the print server's power and network cable. Finally, the node address of the print server may be the same as the node address of another device on the network. You may need to change the node address of the print server (or the conflicting device).

SYMPTOM 16-17   **The QUICKSET command times out when checking if the device had logged in to the file server.**   This often means that the print server device did not log in to the master file server. This is usually because the Ethernet frame types do not match. Try to determine the frame type of the print server using PSCONFIG or the device's administration software (such as Bi-Admin). Set the print server's frame type to match the frame type that the master file server uses (and disable all other frame types).

SYMPTOM 16-18   **You cannot receive Notify messages in a NetWare 4.x environment.**   This is frequently a configuration problem. Make sure that you are a Notify member of the print server. Also run NetAdmin and set the name of the default server to receive notification.

SYMPTOM 16-19   **You can't see the printer status, or server status indicates that it's "down".**   For example, you cannot use PCONSOLE or the print server's software (such as Bi-Admin) to see printer status. In addition, the current server status in Print Server Information is showing Down in a NetWare 4.x environment. It may be that you created the print server object in a NetWare 3.x environment and used PCONSOLE in NetWare 4.x to view the status. Ensure that the print server is ON, and delete the *print server* object of the print server device. If necessary, install the print server device again in your NetWare 4.x NDS environment.

SYMPTOM 16-20   **The "String Before Job" and/or "String After Job" settings in the Logical Printers don't work properly.**   Check the length of the control strings (no string can exceed 15 characters). Also check that the control strings are in hexadecimal.

SYMPTOM 16-21   **You have trouble servicing additional NetWare bindery file servers.**   If your print server device is configured as a NetWare Print Server and you want it to service more than one bindery file server, try the following steps:

1. Log in (with supervisory rights) to the other file servers that you want the print server device to handle.
2. Create queues and a print server name for your print server on each file server you want to handle.
3. Log in (with supervisory rights) to the master file server of your print server.
4. Run PCONSOLE.
5. Select Print Server Information, then select your print server device in the print server list.
6. Select Printer Server Configuration, then select File Server To Be Serviced.
7. Insert the file server name(s) of the other file server(s) to be handled by your print server device.
8. Reset the print server.

SYMPTOM 16-22   **You have trouble attaching to more than one NetWare Print Server.**   In NetWare Remote Printer mode, if you want each port of the print server to attach to a different NetWare print server, use PCONSOLE to create and assign the required printers and queues. Now run PSCONFIG and select Set to NetWare Remote Printer Mode. Enter the correct NetWare print server name(s) in the print server name field(s), and then select Execute Setup.

SYMPTOM 16-23   **Windows applications do not print correctly.**   For example, when printing from some Windows applications (such as PowerPoint), printing takes a long time and the printout is incorrect. The problem is usually due to the printer being configured to start printing *after* the first page is spooled. Use the following steps to change spool settings:

1. Open the Control Panel, then double-click the Printers folder.

2. Right-click your printer and select Properties, then select Details.

3. Click the Spool Settings button.

4. Choose "Start printing after last page is spooled" and click OK. Now try printing again.

SYMPTOM 16-24   **While adding a Windows 9x printer, you received a "Printer could not be found" message.**   When configured as a local printer, some printer drivers will poll the printer to see if it is connected. Since the printer is networked, the printer cannot be detected (and an error is generated). To fix this, try the following steps to reinstall the network printer:

1. When the Add Printer Wizard asks "How is the printer attached to your computer", select Network Printer.

2. When prompted for Network Path or Queue Name, enter a dummy value such as **\\SCnum\P1** (or **P2** or **P3** for LPT2 or LPT3, respectively) and select Next.

3. The Printer Wizard will display a message stating the network printer is offline—continue to install the printer as normal.

4. When finished, open the Control Panel and double-click the Printers folder to select your printer—the printer icon will be grayed out (indicating the printer is not ready).

5. Right-click the printer and select Properties, then select the Details tab. In the "Print to the following port" box, select Print Server.

6. Click Apply, then OK, then close the Properties dialog box.

7. Select the printer, then go to the File menu and see that the Work Offline option is OFF.

8. If the printer is connected and powered properly, the printer icon should no longer be grayed out, and you should be able to print.

SYMPTOM 16-25   **You connect and configure a WPS (Windows Printing System) printer, but can't get the print job to run.**   WPS printer drivers poll the printer before sending print data. Since the printer is networked, the printer is not found and no data is sent. The solution is to add your printer as a network printer as described in the previous symptom above. The following is a list of a few common WPS printers to be aware of:

- Canon LBP-430W
- Epson ActionLaser 1300/W, Epson EPL-5500/W
- HP LaserJet 5L, Lexmark WinWriter Series
- NEC SuperScript series, Olivetti PG304
- Samsung MyLaser Series
- HP DeskJet CX and CS Series

SYMPTOM 16-26   **Text prints just fine under Windows, but graphics contain a lot of garbage.**   This is often a driver problem. Obtain and install the latest driver for your printer from the manufacturer. Also try changing the spool settings such as in this example:

1. Click Start | Settings | Printers.

2. Right-click on the selected printer and choose Properties.

3. For Windows 9x users, click the Details tab, then click on Spool Setting and change the setting to Spool Data Format (RAW). For Windows NT users: Open the Properties window for your printer and click on General. Click on Print Processor and choose RAW or EMF. Click the Always Spool RAW Data Type.

4. Click OK, then OK again.

SYMPTOM 16-27 **You receive an "SPX Connect Error".** For example, when trying to configure or change the TCP/IP settings on the print server device, you get an "SPX Connect Error". This is often a protocol problem that occurs when the utilities used by your print server require the IPS/SPX protocol to be installed. If so, you may need to install IPX/SPX before using the print server. Also, check your cabling and make sure there is a Link LED on the hub and print server. If necessary, you can reset or restore the print server's factory defaults using the print server's administration software (such as Bi-Admin) or the Telnet interface.

SYMPTOM 16-28 **Some DOS programs don't work in a Windows 9x peer-to-peer environment.** Some DOS applications require an LPT port to print. If so, you can enable the NetBEUI protocol and capture a port for DOS support. You must have NetBEUI installed for your network. Follow the instructions below as an example:

1. Run the print server's administration software (such as Bi-Admin), select the Configuration Menu option, then choose NetBEUI.

2. At the Domain prompt, enter your network workgroup name.

3. Click on Save to Device.

4. Open your Network Neighborhood. You should see the print server device on your network. If not, press F5 a few times to refresh the window.

5. Double-click on the print server device (such as "SCE15223" or "SCC15232").

6. You should see the port in the form of "Pn" (such as P1, where *n* is the port number on the print server).

7. Right-click on the port you want to capture (such as P1) and select Capture Printer Port.

8. A window will appear asking for a device. Select the port you want to use (such as LPT1 or LPT2).

9. Put a check on the "Reconnect at logon" option so that you can connect to the print server when you reboot your computer.

10. To set up the printer, click on Start | Settings | Printers.

11. Right-click on the printer you want to set up, and select Properties.

12. Click the Details tab.

13. Change the "Print to the LPT port" number you selected in step 8.

14. Click Apply, then OK to finish.

15. Reboot your PC.

Consult your operating system documentation for more information on NetBEUI.

Further Study

D-Link: **www.dlink.com**
Hewlett Packard: **www.pandi.hp.com/seg/ps_ns.html**
Intel: **support.intel.com/support/network/index.htm**
Linksys: **www.linksys.com**

17

POWER SUPPORT

Network implementations of all shapes and sizes depend on an adequate supply of commercial power (or "ac" for *alternating current*). A network administrator is tasked with managing that power in order to ensure that the network utilizes power in a responsible fashion, and that operation continues uninterrupted in the face of storms, accidents, and other factors often beyond control. This chapter presents a discussion of power management techniques, and covers the use of backup power devices.

Network Power Management

While networks are getting bigger and more sophisticated, the increasing expense of electricity (coupled with today's growing emphasis on power conservation) makes *power management* a priority for network administrators who must frequently juggle performance and accessibility against limited utility budgets. By designing PCs that use less power, and employ comprehensive power-down techniques during periods of nonuse, a computer can actually be left on all the time, yet use only about 5W of power in its "deepest" power-saving state (less than most nightlights). This also reduces electric bills and lowers the cost of running a network. This part of the chapter explains the power conservation technologies commonly employed in modern computers, and offers some techniques for minimizing power use on idle devices.

POWER MANAGEMENT AND WINDOWS 2000

There are several important elements required to support power management: the BIOS, chipset, devices, and operating system. The operating system provides the controls and dialog boxes needed for selecting your power management strategy, and it runs the various drivers needed to control each piece of "power managed" hardware. While Windows 98 and Windows Me are largely considered to be the premier "end user" operating systems for power management, Windows 2000 also offers a robust suite of power management features. You can configure just about any "power managed" part of the PC through the Windows Power Options Properties dialog box. The dialog box for Windows 2000 is shown in Figure 17-1.

Power management under Windows begins by selecting a "power scheme"—this basic categorization uses a collection of predefined settings that control the power-down timing of your hardware devices. However, you can also tailor the settings of a given scheme to suit your particular tastes. There are three classic power-saving modes that you should be familiar with:

- **Basic conservation**   You can turn off your monitor (or LCD backlight) and hard drive(s) automatically after a given period of inactivity (conserving a great deal of power while the rest of the system may be running normally).

- **Standby**   You can put the computer into a "standby" mode when it's idle. While in "standby" mode, your monitor and hard drive(s) turn off, and some computer devices are powered down. When you want to use the computer again, it comes out of "standby" mode quickly, and your desktop (along with your important work) is restored exactly as you left it. Standby is particularly handy for saving battery power in laptop computers.

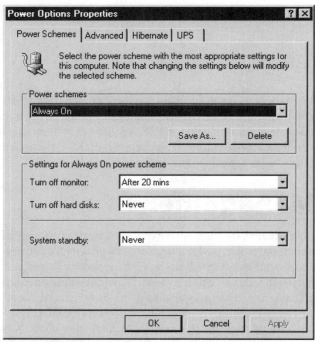

FIGURE 17-1   The Power Options Properties dialog box under Windows 2000

■ **Hibernation**   You can put your computer into "hibernation" mode after longer periods of inactivity (i.e., you leave your office for the day). Power management's "hibernate" feature turns off your monitor and hard drive(s) first (i.e., it enters the "standby" mode first). If idle time continues, the system will save everything in memory on disk, then turn off your computer. When you restart your computer, your computer's last state is restored to memory from the disk, and your desktop is restored exactly as you left it.

The following sections outline a number of techniques that you can use to control power management under Windows 2000.

Selecting a Power Scheme

To enable the system's "standby" mode and take advantage of your computer's power management features, you first need to select a "power scheme." Click Start, highlight Settings, click Control Panel, then double-click the Power Options icon. The Power Options Properties dialog box will appear (see Figure 17-1). Click the "Power schemes" drop-down menu and select from the available choices that loosely define how the PC is used:

■ Always on
■ Home/Office Desk
■ Portable/Laptop
■ Presentation
■ Minimum Power Management
■ Maximum Battery

When you select a scheme, you'll notice that the settings for that power scheme ("System standby", "Turn off monitor", and "Turn off hard disks") will be updated to their default values. If you wish to tweak the default timer values (i.e., you want to add more time before the system drops into "standby" mode), you can simply click on the respective timer and select the desired time value from the drop down list. Using these timer entries, you can configure the monitor, hard drive, and "standby" delays according to your own personal preferences. Be sure to Apply your changes before clicking OK.

If you're using a laptop computer, you can specify a different "standby" delay for battery power, and a different setting for ac power.

Saving/Deleting a Power Scheme

If you've made changes to your power scheme's timer value(s), you can save all of those settings as a unique power scheme. Once you have your timer settings the way you want them, simply click Save As, then enter the name for your new scheme—the new scheme is added to the "Power schemes" drop-down list. If you no longer wish to save a particular power scheme on your system, simply select the scheme from the "Power schemes" drop-down list and click Delete.

Manually Invoking the "Standby" Mode

The easiest way to place your PC in the "standby" mode is to use the Shut Down Windows dialog box (see Figure 17-2). You can also configure the system to let you use the "standby" mode whenever you press the Power button on your system (or whenever you close the lid on your laptop). Click Start, highlight Settings, click Control Panel, then double-click the Power Options icon. The Power Options Properties dialog box

FIGURE 17-2 Using the Standby feature of the Windows 2000
Shut Down dialog box

will appear. Click the Advanced tab (see Figure 17-3). Locate the entry "When I press the power button on my computer", then click Standby. If you're using a laptop, locate the entry "When I close the lid of my portable computer", then click Standby. Click Apply (or OK), then turn off the power or close the laptop's lid.

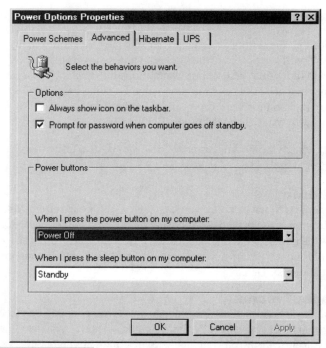

FIGURE 17-3 The Advanced Power Options Properties
dialog box under Windows 2000

It's a good idea to save your work *before* putting a computer into "standby" mode. While the computer is in "standby," information in RAM is *not* saved to your hard drive—if there's an interruption in power, the information in memory can easily be lost.

Manually Invoking the "Hibernation" Mode

When you put your computer in "hibernation," *everything* in the computer's memory is saved on your hard disk. When you turn the computer back on, all programs and documents that were open when you put the PC into "hibernation" are restored on the desktop. Click Start, highlight Settings, click Control Panel, then double-click the Power Options icon. The Power Options Properties dialog box will appear. Click the Hibernate tab and select the "Enable hibernate support" check box (see Figure 17-4). Click the Advanced tab and locate the entry "When I press the power button on my computer", then click Hibernate. If you're using a laptop, locate the entry "When I close the lid of my portable computer", then click Standby. Click Apply (or OK), then turn off the power or close the laptop's lid.

If the Hibernate tab is not displayed, your computer does not support this feature with its current set of hardware and software.

Passwords in "Standby" or "Hibernation"

In order to prevent anyone from moving a mouse or pressing a key to bring your system out of "standby" or "hibernation", you can use passwords to protect your system on waking. Click Start, highlight Settings, click Control Panel, then double-click the Power Options icon. The Power Options Properties dialog box will appear. Click the Advanced tab, and then click "Prompt for password when computer goes off

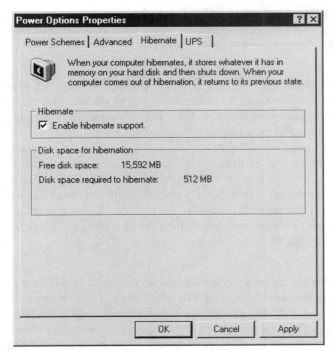

FIGURE 17-4   Enabling the Hibernate power-saving
mode under Windows 2000

standby". You use your Windows password for both standby and hibernation. Remember that you are not required to use a password, but it does afford a certain amount of security since your system will be running while you're away from it.

ADVANCED CONFIGURATION AND POWER INTERFACE (ACPI)

The *Advanced Configuration and Power Interface* (or ACPI) is an open industry specification that defines a flexible and extensible hardware interface for the system board. Software designers use this specification to integrate power management features throughout a computer system, including hardware, the operating system, and application software. This integration enables Windows 2000 to determine which applications are active and handle all of the power management resources for computer subsystems and peripherals. For example, an ACPI system can turn off (or "throttle back") a wide range of devices such as CD-ROMs, DVD-ROMs, modems, network devices, and so on. ACPI also allows the system to "wake" and perform predetermined tasks based upon real-world events. For example, an ACPI system may "wake" when the modem receives a call, connect and exchange data, then return to a "standby" or "hibernate" state after the call is completed. Current PCs use ACPI 2.0 introduced in July of 2000.

ACPI design is essential to take full advantage of power management and Plug-and-Play in Windows 2000. If you are not sure if your computer is ACPI compliant, check your manufacturer's documentation.

In addition to enabling OS-controlled power management, ACPI provides a generic system event mechanism for Plug-and-Play, and an OS-independent interface for device configuration control. This means your ACPI system can actually manage device configuration as well as power. In effect, ACPI is a "marriage" of PnP and APM that offers much more precise and versatile control over a system's devices.

ACPI BIOS

A computer's BIOS is a set of software through which the operating system (or Setup) communicates with system hardware devices. The ACPI is the current standard for power management implemented in the BIOS. Windows 2000 supports not only ACPI-compliant BIOS versions, but also some BIOS versions based on older *Advanced Power Management* (APM) and Plug-and-Play designs.

Some ACPI-based BIOS versions are not compliant with the standard. The more recent the version of an ACPI BIOS, the more likely that it is compliant. An ACPI-based BIOS that is not compliant with the ACPI standard might not support workable communication between the operating system (or Setup) and your hardware. If workable communication is not supported, Setup stops and displays instructions for contacting your hardware manufacturer and taking other steps to solve the problem. This is one reason why it's helpful to document the system's BIOS version before installing (or upgrading to) Windows 2000. A BIOS that is not ACPI compliant can usually be upgraded.

ACPI and PnP

To take full advantage of Plug-and-Play, you must use an ACPI-based computer, running in ACPI mode (configured through the CMOS Setup), and all hardware devices must be fully PnP compliant. Remember that the operating system (not the hardware) configures and monitors the computer under ACPI. The Windows 2000 operating system determines which programs are active and manages all of the power requirements for your computer subsystems and peripherals. ACPI lets the operating system direct power to devices as they need it, preventing unnecessary power demands on your system.

Because Windows 2000 controls your computer's resources and configuration, you can install PnP hardware devices without restarting. Windows 2000 automatically identifies the new hardware and installs the drivers it may need. If you are using any other type of computer, you may need to perform some manual setup and restart your computer when installing new hardware devices.

TROUBLESHOOTING POWER MANAGEMENT

Power management offers some compelling advantages for the PC where systems can be extremely responsive, yet use very little power in the idle state. Ideally, the BIOS, chipset, devices, and operating system must work together seamlessly in order to avoid system crashes and data corruption. Unfortunately, this doesn't always happen (especially with older systems). BIOS incompatibilities, buggy drivers, and noncompliant hardware devices are just some of the issues that can result in power management problems. This part of the chapter explores a range of power management symptoms and solutions.

ACPI SYMPTOMS

The Advanced Configuration and Power Interface (ACPI) is now the standard power management technology employed by current PCs such as network servers and late-model workstations. While ACPI offers more comprehensive and versatile control over the many devices in a system, there is also far more latitude for problems to occur. The symptoms below offer a cross-section of common ACPI issues that you should be familiar with.

SYMPTOM 17-1   **You receive an error after disabling ACPI support.**   If the ACPI option is enabled in your computer's BIOS when you initially install Windows 2000, and you later disable the ACPI option in your computer's BIOS, you receive the following error message on a blue screen when you start Windows 2000:

```
0x00000079 (0x00000004, 0x0000AC31, 0x00000000, 0x00000000)
```

This error occurs because Windows 2000 uses a separate hardware abstraction layer (HAL) for ACPI support. If you want to disable ACPI support *after* Windows 2000 is installed, you must reinstall Windows 2000 with APCI *disabled* in the computer's BIOS. Since numerous changes are made to the Registry and system files, an upgrade installation does not work.

SYMPTOM 17-2   **The system cannot go into standby mode.**   Hibernation is a special form of sleep in which the entire system context is paged to a reserved area on the hard disk, and is restored when a wakeup event occurs. Not all ACPI computers support Hibernate mode. On ACPI computers that support hibernation, the ACPI driver checks each device to determine the lowest sleep state supported by that device. The ACPI driver then determines each device's lowest sleep state that responds to a wake event. If a wake level is unsupported by a device, the ACPI driver expects the device to send an "undefined" response for that state. When you attempt to put your Windows 2000 computer into Hibernate or Standby mode, you may receive the following error message:

```
The system cannot go to standby mode because the driver <drive>\<device
driver name> failed the request to standby.
```

Unless *every* device supports hibernation, the computer cannot go into Hibernate mode. As a rule, device drivers that are poorly written or devices that do not properly respond to ACPI queries may still attempt to hibernate. When a device does not respond to an ACPI mode transition request, the error message occurs.

This problem can occur if the driver for the device is not ACPI compliant. If a device is not ACPI compliant, contact your hardware manufacturer to inquire about the availability of a fix or upgrade for this issue. The problem can also appear if the device driver does not support a sleep level sufficient for hibernation—this can be caused by a number of factors, including out-of-date device drivers or the presence of Windows NT 4.0 device drivers in Windows 2000. Verify that you are using the latest device driver written for Windows 2000, and verify the device supports hibernation properly.

SYMPTOM 17-3 **You cannot opt to turn off the monitor through Power Options.** When you check the Windows 2000 Power Options dialog box, the Turn Off Monitor option may be missing. This issue can occur if your video adapter and your video adapter driver do not support ACPI power management. The video adapter driver must be ACPI compliant and properly map the control methods that are read by the **ACPI.SYS** file to construct the options that are displayed in the Power Options dialog box. For example, this problem can occur if you're using an out-of-date video adapter driver, or if the ACPI Control Method description block was improperly implemented.

To work around this issue, contact the manufacturer of your video adapter to inquire about the availability of a Windows 2000-specific video adapter driver (preferably, a driver that supports all of the features of ACPI power management).

SYMPTOM 17-4 **Windows 2000 sleep timer settings are ignored.** When you specify sleep timer settings in the Power Options dialog box, the settings may take effect. However, you may be unable to resume from Suspend mode without cycling computer power off and back on, and you may receive "divide by 0" error messages. ACPI-compliant computers require a separate real-time clock that is used to regulate power management events. This timer (a hardware device on the motherboard) determines when parts of the computer should be suspended and resumed. If the BIOS is not written properly, the operating system may ignore the clock and the problem may occur. This problem is commonly caused by a problem with a computer's ACPI BIOS. To correct this problem, contact the computer manufacturer to inquire about the availability of an updated BIOS for your computer.

SYMPTOM 17-5 **OpenGL screensavers prevent power management standby modes.** When you configure your Windows 2000 computer to use an OpenGL screensaver and the System Standby feature in *Advanced Power Management* (APM), your computer may not enter the Standby mode. This problem can occur if the OpenGL screensaver starts before the time you configured for the Standby mode to start has elapsed. This happens because ACPI puts the computer in the Standby mode only *after* the CPU has been idle for the specified period of time. When an OpenGL screensaver starts, the CPU is no longer idle and the ACPI timer for the Standby mode is reset. You can work around the problem by disabling OpenGL screensavers.

SYMPTOM 17-6 **You cannot disable IRQ steering on an ACPI computer.** You do not have the option to disable IRQ steering in Device Manager on a Windows 2000-based computer with ACPI support installed. In Windows 2000 on non-ACPI-compliant computers, the ability to disable IRQ steering may help resolve problems with loading certain devices. The majority of cases that require this option involve legacy Windows NT 4.0 drivers installed in Windows 2000. These issues should be resolved as manufacturers release fully Windows 2000–compliant ACPI BIOS versions. This is almost always a BIOS issue, so contact your motherboard or PC manufacturer for an updated ACPI-compliant BIOS.

 Fully compliant ACPI computers with ACPI support installed in Windows 2000 do not require this option because of the nature of the ACPI specification.

SYMPTOM 17-7   **Windows 2000 loses its date and time on every boot.**   After you install Windows 2000 and reboot, you may receive a message stating that the system's date and time are invalid. For example, the date may be set for January 1, 1601 (or another invalid date), and the clock may be counting the time from 12:00 A.M. If you reset the date and time correctly and boot to another operating system (such as Windows NT or Windows 9x), the date and time remain accurate after rebooting. However, the problem returns whenever you boot into Windows 2000. This problem can occur if the computer's BIOS is not 100-percent ACPI compliant—Windows 2000 is the only operating system that relies on the ACPI BIOS entries to be valid. Contact the computer manufacturer to inquire about a flash BIOS update that resolves this issue. If available, apply the update according to the manufacturer's instructions.

To work around this problem, reinstall Windows 2000 without ACPI support. Press the F7 key during the first phase of Setup (at the "Setup is inspecting your computer's hardware configuration" screen). This forces Setup to install a non-ACPI hardware abstraction layer (HAL).

SYMPTOM 17-8   **You receive a STOP 0x9F error in Windows 2000.**   You may receive a "STOP 0x0000009F DRIVER_POWER_STATE_FAILURE" error message in Windows 2000. This error occurs when drivers do not handle power state transition requests properly. The error message most often occurs during one of the following actions:

■ Shutting down
■ Suspending or resuming from Standby mode
■ Suspending or resuming from Hibernate mode

To prevent the error message from occurring, update or remove the offending driver. This problem is not limited to device drivers—it can also occur with file system filter drivers (for example, drivers installed by an anti-virus, remote control, or backup program). To isolate the driver that is causing the problem, use the following steps:

1. Check to be sure your computer and all devices are on the hardware compatibility list (HCL) and have WHQL signed and certified drivers. You can use **SIGVERIF.EXE** to check for unsigned drivers.
2. Check for driver updates that may be available for your hardware.
3. Update software that uses filter drivers (i.e., anti-virus software).
4. Uninstall any noncritical devices and software to help isolate the device/software that may be causing the problem.
5. Install Windows 2000 in a new folder. Add drivers and restart as you proceed to isolate the driver that is causing the problem.

SYMPTOM 17-9   **You have trouble saving data on a Windows 2000 system on battery.**   Unsaved application data may be lost if your computer completely loses power, or if you leave your computer unattended/idle for a long period of time. You can lose unsaved data if a power or system failure causes the computer to shut down while programs with unsaved data are running. This can also happen if computers in standby mode, while running on battery power for an extended period of time, eventually lose power and shut down. Finally, this can happen if Windows 2000 doesn't support "wake on low battery" or wake events from battery devices. Use the following recommendations to avoid losing unsaved application data when the computer experiences power failure, system failure, or enters a power-saving mode:

■ Save data often.
■ Save data before leaving the computer unattended.

- Save data before entering Standby or Sleep modes.
- Save data before leaving a power management-enabled computer unattended.
- Configure the computer power management settings to enter Hibernate mode.
- Set the first system idle timeout event to Hibernate.
- Configure the system battery alarms to enter Hibernate mode (when applicable).

SYMPTOM 17-10   **Power features are not available under standard VGA.**   The Hibernate and Standby features are not available when you use the Windows 2000 Power Options tool in Control Panel or when you shut down the computer. This problem occurs if the computer is using a VGA video driver. The VGA driver supplies basic video functionality only. The VGA driver does not supply power management functionality—those features are specific to individual video cards. To make the Hibernate and Standby options available, install the correct video driver for your system.

SYMPTOM 17-11   **The PC may hang when using SYSPREP.**   After you run SYSPREP under Windows 2000 to build a master copy of a hard disk, the computer may crash with a blank desktop on an ACPI-enabled computer. To resolve this problem, obtain the latest service pack for Windows 2000. The English version of this fix should have the following file attributes or later:

```
04/07/2000  04:47p  5.0.2195.2020  45,840  Sysprep.exe
```

SYMPTOM 17-12   **The PC hangs when running in ACPI mode.**   When your Windows 2000–based computer running in ACPI mode uses the ACPI Power Management Timer (PMTimer) as a high-resolution counter, you may experience any of the following symptoms:

- You may experience problems or poor performance when playing back audio or video streams.
- Your computer may display an error message on a blue screen and crash.

This issue occurs if your computer has a chipset that causes the PMTimer to make time appear to run backwards. The following chipsets are known to cause these issues on Windows 2000–based computers:

- VIA
- SIS
- ALI
- RCC

To resolve this issue, obtain and install Windows 2000 Service Pack 1 or later.

SYMPTOM 17-13   **Windows 2000 uses IRQ6 even if floppy controllers are absent.** Windows 2000 may claim IRQ6 settings that are usually reserved for floppy disk controllers. This happens even if the floppy disk controller is unavailable in the BIOS, or the floppy disk drive has been physically removed. If you disable the floppy disk controller in Device Manager, and then click the Resources tab in System properties, you may receive the following message:

```
The Device is not using any resources because it is not currently enabled
```

If you use the Computer Management tool in Control Panel, click System Information, click Hardware Resources, and then click IRQs to view the resources—the IRQ6 setting is not reported as being used. However, if you attempt to configure another ISA device to use IRQ6, you receive a message that states that the resource is already in use. This issue occurs because non-ACPI-based systems that use a PnP BIOS always report a device node for the floppy disk controller on x86-based systems. For ACPI-based systems, **ACPI.SYS** enumerates floppy disk controllers from BIOS tables that are exported to the operating system (only devices that are present are reported in this file).

To resolve this issue, update your system BIOS to an ACPI-compliant BIOS version. If you're already using an ACPI-based BIOS, modify the system BIOS so that it does not report a floppy disk controller when the controller is unavailable (disable the floppy controller through the CMOS Setup). Contact your system manufacturer for a BIOS update. If the BIOS is an ACPI-based BIOS, remove the PNP0700 device node from the ACPI tables, and a floppy disk should *not* be reported.

SYMPTOM 17-14   **An NMI is not recognized on an ACPI multiprocessor system.**
A nonmaskable interrupt (or NMI) may not be recognized on your Windows 2000 ACPI system with multiple processors. This problem can occur if the processors are not installed contiguously (sequentially) in the CPU slots for the multiprocessor system. This is a problem with Windows 2000. As a workaround, you can try rearranging the processors into contiguous sockets. A supported fix is now available from Microsoft, but it is only intended to correct the problem described in this article and should be applied only to systems experiencing this specific problem. The English version of this fix should have the following file attributes or later:

```
2/19/2001   05:12p   5.0.2195.3273   81,760   Halaacpi.dll
2/19/2001   05:12p   5.0.2195.3273   82,656   Halmacpi.dll
```

SYMPTOM 17-15   **You receive a STOP 0xA error in Windows 2000 with ACPI.**   The error may occur after a period of time when you're using an ACPI driver under Windows 2000 SP1. For example, if you install a thermal monitor driver for your motherboard, but the thermal monitor system device is not fully ACPI compliant, you may receive a STOP 0x0000000A error message. This problem occurs because the ACPI embedded controller driver (**ACPIEC.SYS**) can call the device driver multiple times. These calls can generate a STOP error message if the device itself is not fully ACPI compliant. This is a problem with Windows 2000. To correct the problem, download and install the latest service pack for Windows 2000.

SYMPTOM 17-16   **A PC with an OSB4 chipset may crash.**   On a computer with a Reliance Computer Corp./ServerWorks OSB4 chipset running Windows 2000 (SP1 or SP2) in ACPI mode, the following symptoms might occur when you are using the ACPI Power Management Timer (PMTimer) as a high-resolution counter:

■ You may experience problems or poor performance when playing back audio or video streams.

■ Your computer may display an error message on a blue screen and crash.

The problem can occur in this chipset when the chipset causes the PMTimer to make time appear to run backwards. To determine whether your computer uses the chipset, follow these steps:

1. Click Start, highlight Settings, and then click Control Panel.

2. Double-click the System icon.

3. On the Hardware tab, click Device Manager.

4. Double-click the System Devices branch to expand the branch.

5. Locate the PCI-to-ISA Bridge device. This device should contain a description that identifies the chipset.

You can correct this issue by editing the Registry:

Editing the registry incorrectly can cause serious problems that may require you to reinstall your operating system. You should back up the registry before you edit it. If you are running Windows NT or Windows 2000, you should also update your Emergency Repair Disk (ERD).

1. Make sure that you're running Windows 2000 SP1 or later (you may wish to update Windows 2000 before proceeding).

2. Start Registry Editor (**REGEDT32.EXE**).

3. Locate and click the following registry key:

   `HKEY_LOCAL_MACHINE\SYSTEM\CurrentControlSet\Control\HAL`

4. On the Edit menu, click Add Value and then add the following value:

   ```
   Value name: 11660200
   Data type: REG_DWORD
   Data: 00000001
   ```

5. Quit Registry Editor, and then restart the computer.

UPS Implementation

Networks rely on the constant operation of servers, workstations, and other devices. In many cases, equipment is running continuously. Operation depends on an adequate supply of commercial power (the ac from a wall outlet). Unfortunately, power distribution is not perfect, and interruptions such as brownouts, blackouts, surges, and spikes do occur. Power interruptions can cause erratic server operation or reboots. In more extreme cases, power problems can corrupt data, and even damage your network equipment. The *uninterruptible power supply* (or UPS) is a device used to provide power when such interruptions occur (see Figure 17-5). The UPS is inserted inline between an ac outlet and the computer equipment that you need to protect. When a power problem occurs, the UPS switches over to a battery-based power source that will keep the equipment running—at least long enough to save data and initiate an orderly shutdown. In most cases, a UPS also contains protective circuitry that will prevent sudden voltage surges or spikes from passing into the computer equipment.

UNDERSTANDING THE UPS

There are basically two types of UPS designs: online and offline. An *online* UPS is a system where the *inverter* (the circuit that changes dc power to ac power) is constantly operating and powering the computer equipment. In effect, the PC is constantly running from battery power even though ac is readily available and keeping the UPS batteries charged. The ac from the wall is translated into dc, which charges the batteries, and then that dc battery voltage is inverted back into ac to run the computer equipment. This is often referred to as a "double conversion" UPS, and both voltage and frequency can be highly regulated. A second type of online UPS became popular by 1990. This is referred to as a "single-conversion," "delta conversion," or

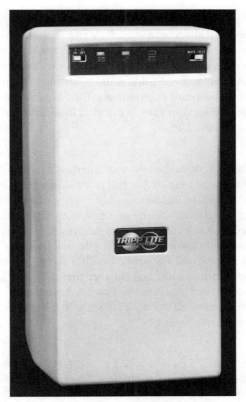

FIGURE 17-5   A Tripp Lite BCPro 600 UPS (Courtesy of Tripp Lite)

"parallel online" UPS. In this design, only a portion of the output power of the UPS has been processed by the ac-to-dc-to-ac process.

By comparison, an *offline* UPS only runs (provides battery power) when ac is lost. These are traditionally referred to as a "battery backup system" or "standby UPS." When ac fails, the UPS inverter kicks in and runs the PC equipment entirely from battery power. This type of UPS is a bit simpler to design and maintain, but it's hard on the batteries because they are often heavily discharged to support the attached PC load. In normal applications, a standby UPS is used to protect less critical loads for short periods of time (i.e., a workstation).

Line interactive UPS systems are a dramatic improvement over standby systems because they are able to correct modest undervoltage (*brownout*) or overvoltage (*surge*) conditions without depleting the batteries. By using a boost function to raise utility voltage up, or a buck function to reduce incoming voltage, the line interactive UPS postpones using battery power until the voltage is substantially out of range. A line interactive UPS typically includes a display showing the percent of load, percent of battery capacity remaining, and other status information. They are excellent choices for almost any critical load.

UPS systems are almost always battery based. However, some advanced UPS systems may use gasoline-powered generators to supplement battery power and provide greatly extended running time.

Transfer Time

Most offline UPS systems do not respond instantaneously. It takes a finite amount of time to recognize a loss of ac power, start the inverter, and make that standby power available to the PC equipment. This response time is known as *transfer time*, and UPS transfer times can vary dramatically depending on the quality of the UPS model. It's not uncommon to see transfer times anywhere from 3 ms to 13 ms. The general cutoff for PC equipment is 7 ms—this means PC equipment (or other critical load devices) may crash or reboot spontaneously if ac fails for longer than 7 ms. If a critical load demands a very fast transfer time (i.e., approaching 0 ms), consider an online UPS.

Communication

Power loss is generally considered to be a critical failure, and batteries cannot provide power to PC equipment indefinitely. This means that even the best UPS is still just a safety net that provides a few crucial minutes of additional running time so that files can be saved and systems shut down in an orderly fashion. Unfortunately, there is no guarantee that a technician or administrator will be available to handle the system shutdown when a power loss occurs. Most current UPS systems include a built-in controller that monitors power levels and communicates with the attached PC equipment (usually through a serial cable). When power fails and the system is running on UPS power, the UPS can signal the PC to start a shutdown process automatically. This requires a serial connection between the UPS and PC, as well as appropriate client software to monitor the UPS condition. You may even be able to send an alert to the network administrator (via e-mail or pager). If power is restored while the UPS is active, the UPS will notify users that the power has returned and abort the shutdown process.

Running Time

As you might expect, the batteries in a UPS cannot power a load forever. This means a UPS can only power certain pieces of equipment for a limited amount of time. The exact amount of time depends on the *load* (the amount of equipment) that you've attached to the UPS and the size (capacity) of the UPS itself. For a UPS of any given capacity, a *higher* load will result in *shorter* running time. Lightening the load (or using a larger-capacity UPS) will increase the running time. The real trick is to determine your running time by checking the load that you're planning to attach.

All UPS systems are rated in terms of volt-amperes (or VA), which is a more technical indication of power (usually measured in watts, or W). The power requirements of your equipment should be less than or equal to the VA capacity of the UPS. For example, an IBM OfficePro 700 UPS provides 700VA capacity. A VA capacity will generally operate a load at that level for about 8–10 minutes. That means the 700VA UPS should power 700VA worth of PC equipment for about 10 minutes. If you're using half the load (350VA), the UPS should operate for twice as long (i.e., 16–20 minutes). If you're using a quarter of the load (175VA), the UPS should operate for four times as long (i.e., 35–40 minutes), and so on. In practice, the actual amount of running time will be a bit longer if the load is measurably lower than the UPS capacity (i.e., the UPS is overrated for the load).

The real trick is to calculate the load that you're attaching. All PC equipment makers list a load rating for their devices. This rating is usually listed on the nameplate or label near the line cord on the rear of the device. The rating may be in VA, in watts (W), or in amps (A). Ideally, all loads should be denoted in VA so that the loads can simply be added together. If a load is in watts, convert to VA by multiplying $W \times 1.4$. If a load is in amps, convert to VA by multiplying $A \times 120$ (for a 120V device) or $A \times 230$ (for a 230V device). Suppose you want to use a UPS to run a monitor, PC, and tape drive. A typical example may be

Computer VA	=	120V × 2A	=	240VA
Monitor VA	=	100W × 1.4	=	140VA
Tape drive VA	=	120V × 1A	=	120VA
Total			=	**00VA**

In this example, a 500VA UPS will run this load for about 8–10 minutes, or a 1,000VA UPS will run this equipment for about 20 minutes. Table 17-1 compares basic load and runtimes for several common UPS capacities.

Do not connect laser printers to a UPS! The power requirements of a typical laser printer are much larger than the requirements of other computer peripherals, and may trip the UPS system's protective circuit breaker. Plug laser printers into a good-quality surge suppressor. Print jobs can always be requeued when the power is restored.

UPS Selection Criteria

The following questions will help the network administrator determine which UPS system best fits the needs of the network:

- Will the UPS meet the basic power requirements of this network?
- How many components can the UPS support (number of outlets)?
- Does the UPS communicate with the server to notify it when a power failure has occurred and the server is running on batteries?

TABLE 17-1 A TYPICAL COMPARISON OF UPS RUNTIME VS. LOAD

LOAD	250VA	400VA	450VA	600VA	900VA	1,250VA
50VA	37 min	100 min	120 min	145 min	220 min	270 min
75VA	29 min	72 min	88 min	105 min	155 min	210 min
100VA	23 min	47 min	65 min	79 min	110 min	160 min
150VA	14 min	30 min	41 min	54 min	83 min	115 min
200VA	8 min	19 min	32 min	41 min	65 min	92 min
250VA	5 min	13 min	24 min	31 min	47 min	75 min
300VA	--	9 min	18 min	22 min	40 min	64 min
350VA	--	7 min	14 min	17 min	35 min	54 min
400VA	--	5 min	11 min	13 min	29 min	46 min
450VA	--	--	8 min	10 min	24 min	40 min
500VA	--	--	--	7 min	20 min	34 min
550VA	--	--	--	6 min	17 min	29 min
600VA	--	--	--	5 min	15 min	25 min
700VA	--	--	--	--	13 min	22 min
800VA	--	--	--	--	11 min	17 min
900VA	--	--	--	--	10 min	13 min
1,000VA	--	--	--	--	--	10 min
1,250VA	--	--	--	--	--	9 min

■ Does the UPS include surge protection to guard against power spikes and surges?

■ What is the life span of the UPS battery?

■ How long can a UPS be inactive before its batteries starts to degrade?

■ Will the UPS warn the administrator and users that it is running out of power?

INSTALLING A UPS

Installing a UPS is certainly not a difficult or time-consuming process, but there are some common steps that can help you streamline the installation. Your UPS manual should provide detailed instructions, but the general guidelines are shown here:

1. *Connect the battery connector.* In many cases, a UPS is shipped with the actual battery pack disconnected (often done for safety during shipping). Connect the battery pack before proceeding.

2. *Connect the equipment and power to the UPS.* Connect equipment to the UPS outlets. Plug the UPS into a two-pole, three-wire grounding receptacle only. Avoid using extension cords and adapter plugs.

3. *Turn on and check the UPS.* Make sure the battery is connected before turning on the UPS. Press the power button on the front panel to power up your UPS—this will power up connected equipment (connected equipment should be switched ON). The UPS charges its battery pack when it is connected to utility power. The batteries charge fully during the first few hours of normal operation. You probably won't get full run time during this initial charge period. The unit performs a self-test automatically when turned on and every two weeks thereafter (by default). Check the site wiring fault indicator located on the UPS. It lights up if the UPS is plugged into an improperly wired ac power outlet. Wiring faults include missing ground, hot-neutral polarity reversal, and overloaded neutral circuit. If a fault is indicated, contact a qualified electrician to fix the trouble.

4. *Install optional software and accessories.* You can connect the serial cable between the UPS and PC (if so equipped), along with power utilities needed for proper PC management in the event of a power fault.

Always refer to your manual for specific installation instructions and cautions.

Understanding the LEDs

Most UPS systems provide an array of LEDs used to indicate power status, remaining charge, critical errors, and so on (see Figure 17-6). Any UPS installation should include an understanding of the available LEDs.

Not all UPS units will offer the same suite of indicators. Be sure to check the documentation for your own UPS for specific details.

Load   The five-LED display on the left of the front panel shows the percentage of available power used by the connected equipment (the *load*). For example, if three LEDs are lit, the connected load is drawing between 50 percent and 67 percent of the UPS capacity. If all five LEDs are lit, the connected load is drawing between 85 percent and 100 percent of capacity. Thoroughly test your entire system to make sure that the UPS will not become overloaded. The UPS maintains battery charge when it is plugged in (and utility voltage is present).

Self-Test   The UPS performs a self-test automatically when powered on (and every two weeks thereafter)—you can change the default interval. Automatic self-test eases maintenance requirements by elim-

FIGURE 17-6   UPS units like the APC Smart UPS use LEDs to report line voltage, remaining charge, alert conditions, and so on.

inating the need for periodic manual self-tests. During the self-test, the UPS briefly operates the connected equipment on-battery. If the UPS passes the self-test, it returns to online operation. If the UPS fails the self-test, the UPS lights the Replace Battery LED and immediately returns to online operation. The connected equipment is not affected by a failed test. Recharge the battery for 24 hours and perform another self-test. If it fails, the battery must be replaced.

Utility Power   During normal operation, the UPS monitors the utility power and delivers power to the connected equipment. If your system is experiencing excessive periods of high or low voltage, have a certified electrician check your installation for electrical problems. If the problem continues, you may need to use an alternate source of commercial power.

Online   The online indicator illuminates when the UPS is supplying utility power to the connected equipment. If the indicator is not lit, the UPS is supplying battery power and the UPS sounds an alarm—four beeps every 30 seconds.

Utility Voltage (120/230Vac)   The UPS has a diagnostic feature that displays the utility voltage. Plug the UPS into the normal utility power. Press and hold the button to view the utility voltage bar graph display. After a few seconds the five-LED display on the right of the front panel shows the utility input voltage. Refer to the figure at left for the voltage reading (values are not listed on the UPS). The UPS starts a self-test as part of this procedure. The self-test does not affect the voltage display. The display indicates the voltage is between the displayed value on the list and the next higher value. For example, with three LEDs lit, the input voltage is between 114 and 124Vac. If no LEDs are lit and the UPS is plugged into a working ac power outlet, the line voltage is extremely low. If all five LEDs are lit, the line voltage is extremely high and should be checked by an electrician.

AVR Trim/Boost   The AVR Trim LED indicates that the UPS is compensating for a *high* utility voltage. The AVR Boost LED indicates that the UPS is compensating for a *low* utility voltage.

On Battery   If the utility power fails, the UPS can provide power to the connected equipment from its internal battery for a finite period. The UPS sounds an alarm (four beeps every 30 seconds) while operating on battery power. The alarm stops when the UPS returns to online operation. When the On Battery power indicator is lit, the UPS is supplying battery power to the connected equipment.

Battery Charge   The five-LED display on the right of the front panel shows the present charge of the UPS battery as a percentage of the battery capacity. When all five LEDs are lit, the battery is fully charged. The LEDs extinguish (from top to bottom) as the battery capacity diminishes. As a low battery warning, any illuminated LEDs flash and the UPS beeps. The low battery warning default setting can be changed from the rear panel (or through the optional power software).

Overload   The UPS emits a sustained alarm tone and the LED illuminates when an overload condition occurs (that is, when the connected equipment exceeds the specified "maximum load"). The alarm remains on until the overload is removed. The UPS continues to supply power as long as it is online and the breaker does not trip, but the UPS will not provide power from batteries in the event of a utility voltage interruption. Disconnect nonessential equipment from the UPS to eliminate the overload. If a continuous overload occurs while the UPS is on battery, the unit turns off output in order to protect the UPS from possible damage.

Replace Battery   Failure of a battery self-test causes the UPS to emit short beeps for one minute and the Replace Battery LED lights. LED flashes indicate the battery is disconnected. The UPS repeats the alarm every five hours. Perform the self-test procedure after the battery has charged for 24 hours to confirm the replace battery condition. The alarm stops if the battery passes the self-test. Otherwise, replace the battery pack.

Testing the UPS
After the UPS has had several hours to charge its batteries, turn on the UPS system's power control and switch on your computer equipment. The UPS indicator should be illuminated and your equipment should operate normally. To test the operation of a UPS, simply unplug its input cord (or press and hold the Test/Alarm Disable switch on units so equipped) to simulate a utility blackout. The UPS will immediately transfer your equipment to power from the UPS internal battery. During this time, the UPS will emit a beep once every few seconds to remind you that your equipment is operating from a source of power that is limited in duration. Restore power to the UPS by plugging in the line cord (or releasing the Test control switch). Observe that your equipment operates normally during the transfer from and to ac power. Repeat this test four or five times to ensure proper operation.

If the total power requirement of your attached equipment is much greater than the capacity of the UPS, the rear circuit breaker on the UPS may trip—this is an overload situation. Once the circuit breaker trips, the UPS will attempt to operate the load using its internal batteries, but this may result in an unexpectedly short runtime. If the overload is severe, the UPS will immediately shut down and cease to power the load. In this case, the UPS will emit a loud tone to alert you of the overload. If this occurs during your test, turn off the UPS and disconnect any nonessential equipment from the UPS. The circuit breaker may be reset when the overload is removed.

UPS Support and Windows 2000

UPS systems are particularly important in server environments where the sudden loss of power can result in interrupted network traffic and unexpected data loss. A UPS is normally a key part of network availability, and some UPS systems (such as an APC Back-UPS Office UPS) can communicate with the server through a serial cable (see Figure 17-7) and corresponding UPS management software (i.e., APC's PowerChute for Windows 2000). This connection allows automated, orderly shutdown of the server when power is lost. Some configurations also allow a number of intelligent features such as the following:

- Perform scheduled or unscheduled UPS self-tests
- Schedule system shutdowns or reboots
- Data logging
- Alert e-mail and paging support (for administrators or technicians)

Once the UPS is properly installed, you'll need to attach the serial port on the UPS to an available serial port on the server using the cable supplied with the UPS. You'll then need to configure management options under Windows 2000 through the Power Options icon. Open the Control Panel and double-click the Power Options icon. Look for two tabs: Hibernate and UPS.

Most UPS systems will support operating systems other than Windows, including Linux, NetWare, Solaris, OS/2, and more. If you're using an OS other than Windows 2000, refer to the installation instructions (or OS manufacturer's documentation) for specific software installation and setup guidelines.

FIGURE 17-7   A UPS with a serial interface can automatically test or shut down a server or PC when power fails.

Hibernate   The Hibernate tab (see Figure 17-4) is optional—it's not available on all PCs. If your server contains the proper hardware for hibernation (saving the system's state to disk rather than shutting down power completely) and a minimum of 128MB, you can select "Enable hibernate support" and click Apply. This will enable the UPS to hibernate your server in the event of an extended power failure.

UPS   The UPS tab (see Figure 17-8) provides the main options needed to configure the UPS for your server. Click Select, choose the manufacturer (i.e., American Power Conversion), select the model (i.e., Smart-UPS), and choose the COM port attached to the UPS (i.e., COM1). Click Finish to complete the configuration and return to the UPS tab. If you've enabled hibernation support, click Configure, select Hibernate (rather than Shutdown) for the "Next, instruct the computer to" setting. Now click Finish, and click Apply so that any changes can take effect.

UPS MAINTENANCE ISSUES

Fluctuations and interruptions in commercial power distribution can interfere with computer operation and result in sporadic crashes or reboots. While such problems may have little consequence for individual PCs, the effects on network servers can be horrendous. Uninterruptible power supply (UPS) systems are designed to keep a server running in the event of a power problem. Rather than running a server directly from an ac wall outlet, the UPS is plugged in to the ac outlet, and the server (and other peripheral equipment) is powered from the UPS. If ac power is interrupted briefly, the UPS keeps power levels steady and prevents server crashes. If ac power fails completely, the UPS continues to provide power for several minutes. Today's UPS systems also communicate with the server, so the system administrator can be informed when power events occur, and an orderly system shutdown can be invoked.

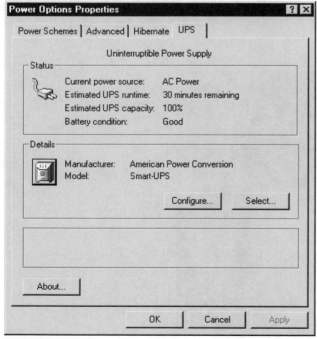

FIGURE 17-8   The UPS tab lets you configure the server to work with your UPS.

While most UPS systems use batteries as the source of backup power, some more sophisticated systems supplement the battery power with a gasoline generator that can keep a server running for hours.

UPS Battery Testing

Batteries are electrochemical devices. This means a battery will eventually wear out after an ample number of charge and discharge cycles, and you'll need to replace them. As a rule of thumb, you can expect to change your batteries every 3–5 years under normal use. Other circumstances such as bad commercial power sources, elevated temperatures where the batteries are stored, and improper maintenance procedures can all reduce the working life of a battery. You should suspect battery problems when they cannot hold a charge (i.e., you experience short runtimes and "low battery" alarms even after ample charging time). The UPS internal diagnostics will typically report battery problems as they develop. For example, a battery service indicator may appear on the UPS, or UPS software on the server may report battery trouble. In many cases, you can test batteries yourself using steps similar to those shown below (for +12Vdc batteries):

- Make sure that your BPS or UPS is connected correctly, and has at least 50 percent of its total load devices plugged in (desktop unit, monitor, scanner, and so on).
- Turn the system and attached peripherals on, and allow the PC to boot normally.
- Simulate a power outage by disconnecting the BPS or UPS line cord.
- Use a standard digital voltmeter and measure each individual battery voltage.
- Each +12Vdc battery should read between +11.5Vdc and +12.5Vdc. Any battery measuring outside of that range should be considered defective and should be replaced.
- All batteries should measure about the same. Any battery that differs more than 0.4 volts from the rest of the batteries should be considered bad and replaced.
- Wait about five minutes and repeat the test (looking for one weak battery to discharge faster than the others). If any battery appears to be discharging faster than the others, it should be considered bad and replaced.

UPS Battery Replacement

If you find that battery replacement is required, you can use the following guidelines to replace the UPS batteries. Remember that you *must* replace batteries with the exact same make and model as the original batteries, or use a suitable substitute recommended by the UPS manufacturer. If you must substitute batteries, it may be necessary to replace all of the batteries in that UPS (even if only one is weak). Be sure to consult with the UPS manufacturer for their recommendations. As a rule, UPS systems allow for "cold" (UPS off) and "warm" (UPS on) battery substitution.

Preparing for Cold Substitution   The safest way to replace UPS batteries is through *cold* substitution—powering down the UPS and all load devices, then replacing the batteries. Use the following steps for cold battery replacement:

1. Shut down all load devices (the server, monitor, printer, etc.).
2. Take the UPS out of its Operate mode (i.e., press the Standby button on the UPS). The ON LED goes out, and power to the load receptacles stops.
3. Disconnect the UPS from utility (ac) power.
4. Wait at least 60 seconds for the UPS internal circuitry to discharge.

Preparing for Warm Substitution   In general, UPS batteries may be replaced without powering off the UPS (hot-swapped) if the UPS is not currently charging the batteries and the UPS is not supplying battery power to load devices—that is, normal ac power is available. In order to determine if warm substitution is safe, be sure to check the UPS indicators to verify that the batteries are fully charged and that it is supplying utility power rather than battery power.

Older batteries may register as fully charged but still be incapable of providing adequate backup for load devices. This means the battery charge LEDs may indicate the batteries are fully charged, while the UPS diagnostics have determined that the batteries need to be replaced.

Removing the Battery Pack   Now use the following steps as a general guideline to remove the old battery pack from the UPS (your own UPS may be different, so check with the manufacturer for their recommendations):

1. Open the UPS cabinet to access the battery pack. The exact procedure may vary between UPS models, so be sure to review the procedures for your own UPS system. In many cases, you must remove several screws holding a faceplate, then detach the faceplate to reveal the LED display cable.

2. Disconnect the LED display cable from the faceplate, then set the faceplate aside—take care to avoid damaging the printed circuit board behind the LED display.

3. Remove the screws that are retaining the battery pack.

4. Slide the battery pack partially out of the UPS chassis to access the battery terminals.

5. Disconnect the negative (black) battery pack terminal connections.

6. Disconnect the positive (red) battery pack terminal connections.

7. Slide the battery pack out in order to access the battery cable-retaining bracket. Remove the screw and battery cable retainer bracket.

8. Carefully slide the battery pack out until the plastic handle(s) is accessible.

9. Remove the battery pack and set it aside for proper disposal.

Remember that UPS battery packs are generally quite heavy, and can often exceed 60 lbs. Get some help when transporting the battery pack, and be sure that there is a safe location to set the pack once it's removed.

Installing the New Battery Pack   With the old battery pack removed, use the steps below as a guideline to install the new batteries in a UPS (your own UPS may be different, so check with the manufacturer for their recommendations):

1. Slide the new battery pack into the chassis—leave room to replace the battery cable retainer bracket.

2. When installing the bracket, position the cables to lie flat and to run under the plastic handling strap(s).

3. Reconnect the positive (red) battery pack terminal connections.

4. Reconnect the negative (black) battery pack terminal connections.

5. Reinstall the screw(s) holding the battery pack to the UPS chassis.

6. Reinstall the display faceplate, if necessary. Attach the LED display cable to the LED display.

7. Replace the screw(s) holding the faceplate to the chassis.

Testing the Battery Pack   After the new battery pack is installed, run a UPS self-test or diagnostic (i.e., press the Test/Alarm Reset button). Refer to the documentation that accompanied your specific UPS for self-test or diagnostic instructions. Remember that most UPS systems will not invoke a self-test until the new batteries are 90-percent charged or more, so you may need to wait a little while until the new battery pack is charged. If there are problems with the new installation, one or more battery warning displays (i.e., a battery service indicator) will light. You may need to go back and check your terminal connections.

Disposing of Old Batteries   Due to the dangerous and caustic chemicals used in batteries, it is virtually impossible to discard used batteries. When you replace UPS batteries, most vendors will also provide instructions and suitable packaging for you to ship the batteries to an appropriate disposal facility. If the vendor does not provide adequate disposal options, check your local yellow pages for a recycling center that meets all local environmental protection standards.

Prolong Shutdown Time

During a Windows NT/2000 system shutdown (i.e., power fails and a UPS switches to battery), each running process in the system is given 20 seconds to perform cleanup work by default. If a process does not respond within this timeout period, the system opens the Wait, End Task, Cancel dialog box, which asks the user to either wait for another 20 seconds, terminate the process, or cancel the shutdown. When applications need more time to close properly, you may need to increase the system shutdown time. The default timeout value, 20 seconds, is stored in the HKEY_CURRENT_USER\Control Panel\Desktop registry key under the WaitToKillAppTimeout value (the value of this timeout period for Windows NT 4.0 has been inadvertently moved to HKEY_USER\.DEFAULT\Control Panel\Desktop). This value is expressed in milliseconds. You can use **REGEDIT.EXE** to modify this value in the Registry, and restart for the change to take effect.

 Modifying the Registry incorrectly can cause serious, system-wide problems that may require you to reinstall Windows to correct. Always make a backup copy of the system Registry before proceeding.

In general, you should avoid increasing the shutdown time unless it's absolutely necessary. For example, if your computer loses power, it is possible that your UPS cannot provide backup power for the computer long enough to allow all the processes, as well as the operating system, to shut down properly.

Dealing with Common "Alarm" Conditions

Many of the current-generation UPS systems incorporate a certain amount of "intelligence" which oversees features such as battery charging and self-diagnostics. When important conditions are not met, or errors are detected, the BPS/UPS will produce an "alarm." While the actual means used to present the alarm (i.e., beeps, seven-segment codes, or alphanumeric LCD readouts) can vary quite a bit, you should understand the essential alarm meanings, and know how to respond quickly:

- **Batteries Disconnected**   The UPS batteries are not properly connected. Verify the connection of all batteries in the UPS. The UPS will *not* protect your system until this fault is corrected.

- **Batteries Undercharged**   The PC is receiving power, but the batteries have an insufficient charge and will not protect your system for long. See that the batteries are allowed ample time to charge. If this is a persistent problem, you may wish to inspect each of the batteries.

- **Check Battery**   The UPS has detected a possible problem with its batteries. Verify that all of your batteries are properly connected in the UPS. You should test and replace any defective batteries as necessary.

- **Check Fan**   The cooling fan inside the UPS is not functioning properly. The fan may need to be replaced, or the UPS may require factory service or replacement.

■ **Check Fuse Board**   The UPS has detected a possible problem with an internal fuse board. It may be possible to check/replace the fuse board, but this usually means that the BPS/UPS has failed, and is in need of factory service or replacement.

■ **Check Inverter**   The UPS has detected a possible problem with its inverter circuit (the circuit which actually turns battery dc back into ac for the computer). This usually means that the BPS/UPS has failed, and is in need of factory service or replacement.

■ **Check MOVs**   The UPS has detected a problem with a MOV (Metal Oxide Varistor) inside the unit. This usually means that the BPS/UPS has failed, and is in need of factory service or replacement.

■ **Check Power Supply**   The unit has detected a possible problem with the unit's internal power supply (which powers the UPS microprocessor controls). This usually means that the UPS has failed, and is in need of factory service or replacement.

■ **Circuit Breaker Warning/Shutdown**   There is high-output current being provided by the UPS. This usually occurs because excessive PC equipment is overloading the UPS. Shut down all of the PC equipment and reset the UPS. Then disconnect the extra PC equipment that is overloading the UPS.

■ **High ac Out/Shutdown**   The UPS is generating an unusually high ac output voltage, and will shut down to prevent damaging the PC equipment. This usually means that the UPS has failed, and is in need of factory service or replacement.

■ **High Ambient Temperature**   The temperature inside the UPS is too high. Make sure that the UPS is placed in a room where the temperature is within the system's recommended range (high-temperature industrial environments are typically bad). Also see that there is nothing blocking the cooling vents in the UPS.

■ **High Battery**   The battery voltage in the UPS is high. There may be a problem with the battery charger settings, the charging circuit itself, or one or more batteries. This usually means that the UPS has failed, and is in need of factory service or replacement.

■ **Low ac Out/Shutdown**   The UPS is generating an unusually low ac output voltage, and will shut down to prevent damaging the PC equipment. This usually means that the UPS has failed, and is in need of factory service or replacement.

■ **Low Battery**   Battery voltage is too low for the UPS to operate on battery power, and the unit will subsequently shut down. In most cases, you should see a low runtime error first. If the batteries are too low even while the UPS is operating from ac, there may be a problem with the charging circuit or batteries in the unit.

■ **Low Runtime**   The PC is running on battery power, and the amount of battery time remaining is low (usually two minutes or less). Do an orderly shutdown of your PC equipment immediately. In most cases, you do not need to shut off the UPS (when ac power returns, the UPS can automatically restart and begin to recharge its batteries).

■ **Memory Error**   On startup, the UPS unit has failed its automatic memory validity test (usually in "intelligent" microprocessor-based UPS units). This usually means that the UPS has failed, and is in need of factory service or replacement.

■ **Output Short Circuit**   Similar to "Overload" below. This is usually signaled by a continuous error tone, and typically indicates an overload condition when the UPS unit it turned on. Check the wiring and verify that you're not loading down the UPS with excessive equipment.

■ **Overload** The PC equipment is drawing more power than the UPS is designed to provide. This can seriously reduce battery runtime. You'll need to shut down extra PC equipment (i.e., scanners, printers, and so on) until the error stops.

■ **Replace Batteries** This error is typically generated as one or more beep patterns from the UPS, and suggests that one or more batteries in the unit will not hold a proper charge. You should check each battery in the UPS, and replace any questionable batteries at your earliest convenience.

■ **UPS Fault** This indicates that a serious error has occurred in the UPS. The UPS will probably not protect your system during this error condition until the fault is cleared or the UPS is replaced.

UPS SYMPTOMS

Most UPS systems will provide a lifetime of reliable service for your system, but there are numerous problems that can interfere with normal UPS operation. This part of the chapter outlines a selection of common symptoms that you may encounter when dealing with UPS problems.

SYMPTOM 17-17 **The UPS will not turn on.** There are a variety of simple problems that may be responsible for this kind of symptom, so use a systematic approach to identify the issue:

■ *The unit is not on.* Press the On button once to power the UPS and the connected equipment.

■ *Check the source power.* The UPS may not be connected to an ac commercial power source. Check that the power cable from the UPS to the utility power supply is securely connected at both ends.

■ *Check the circuit breaker.* Chances are that the UPS input circuit breaker tripped. Reduce the load on the UPS by unplugging equipment and resetting the circuit breaker (on the back of UPS) by pressing the plunger in.

■ *Very low (or no) utility voltage.* Check the ac power supply to the UPS by plugging in a table lamp. If the light is very dim, have the utility voltage checked.

■ *Battery is not connected properly.* Check that the battery connectors are fully engaged.

SYMPTOM 17-18 **The UPS will not turn off.** In virtually all cases, this is an internal problem with the UPS itself that will require repair or replacement. Do not attempt to use the UPS—unplug the UPS and have it serviced immediately.

SYMPTOM 17-19 **UPS is on battery, but normal ac exists.** When ac is present at the wall outlet, but the UPS is running from battery power, check the ac input circuit breaker. A surge or excessive load may have tripped the breaker—cutting off ac to the UPS. If the breaker trips repeatedly, reduce the load on the UPS by unplugging equipment and resetting the circuit breaker (on the back of UPS). Another common problem is distorted (i.e., high or low) ac line voltage, which can often happen when problems strike commercial power distribution centers. A common example is a brownout condition in the summer when the power grid is loaded by air conditioning systems (inexpensive fuel-powered generators can also distort the voltage). Move the UPS to an outlet on a different circuit. Test the input voltage with the utility voltage display. If the voltage level is acceptable to the connected equipment, reduce the UPS sensitivity.

SYMPTOM 17-20 **The UPS does not provide the expected backup time.** In virtually all cases, this is a battery issue. The UPS battery pack may be weak due to a recent outage (it has not yet fully recharged), or the battery pack is near the end of its service life. Charge the battery pack. Batteries require recharging after extended outages. They wear faster when put into service often or when operated at elevated temperatures. If the battery is near the end of its service life, consider replacing the battery (even if the *replace battery* LED is not yet lit).

SYMPTOM 17-21   **All UPS indicators are lit, and the unit beeps constantly.**   In some cases, the UPS is overloaded. Check the UPS load display, unplug unnecessary equipment (such as printers), and reset the UPS if necessary. If the trouble persists, chances are that there is a serious internal fault with the UPS itself. Do not attempt to use the UPS—turn the UPS off and have it serviced immediately.

SYMPTOM 17-22   **UPS panel indicators are flashing sequentially.**   This is usually not an error condition. Instead, the UPS has been shut down remotely through software (or an optional accessory card). The UPS will restart automatically when utility power returns.

SYMPTOM 17-23   **All indicators are off, but the UPS is plugged in.**   The UPS is shut down because the battery has discharged from an extended outage. There is little to be done in a case like this except to restore normal ac. The UPS will return to normal operation when the power is restored and the battery has regained a sufficient charge.

SYMPTOM 17-24   **The Replace Battery LED is lit.**   The battery pack is discharged or failing. Allow the battery to recharge for at least four hours, and then perform a UPS self-test. If the problem persists after recharging, replace the battery pack. In a few cases, you may find that the battery pack is not connected properly—check that the battery connectors are fully engaged.

SYMPTOM 17-25   **The UPS indicates a site wiring fault.**   In most cases, the UPS has detected improper wiring at the ac receptacle. For example, the ac receptacle is ungrounded (or there's no ground wire in UPS power cord). You may also find that the line and neutral wires have been reversed in the ac receptacle (or in the UPS power cord). In either case, contact a qualified electrician to correct the condition.

SYMPTOM 17-26   **A "high voltage" warning LED appears on the UPS.**   This usually means that the ac voltage is too high (outside of the UPS operating range). When this occurs, the UPS typically switches to battery power in order to protect the computer equipment. If this happens repeatedly, contact a qualified electrician to check and correct any ac voltage level problems. Once the ac level returns to normal, you may need to reset the alarm condition.

SYMPTOM 17-27   **A "low voltage" warning LED appears on the UPS.**   This usually means that the ac voltage is too low (outside of the UPS operating range). When this occurs, the UPS typically switches to battery power in order to protect the computer equipment. If this happens repeatedly, contact a qualified electrician to check and correct any ac voltage level problems. Once the ac level returns to normal, you may need to reset the alarm condition.

SYMPTOM 17-28   **The UPS frequently switches between utility and battery power.** In most cases, the UPS is performing normally by protecting the computer equipment from high/low ac voltage levels. First, check the ac level to see that it is in an acceptable range for the UPS. If not, contact a qualified electrician (or your utility company) to correct the problem. If ac is acceptable but the UPS still switches frequently, you may need to adjust the UPS switching sensitivity (to make the unit less sensitive to ac changes). If the problem persists, there may be trouble with the UPS itself.

SYMPTOM 17-29   **A "load" warning LED appears on the UPS.**   In addition to an LED indicator, you may also find that the output circuit breaker trips. This usually means that there is excessive load (too many devices) on the UPS. Make sure that the total load (in volt-amperes or VA) does not exceed the UPS capacity. If so, disconnect unnecessary devices or upgrade the UPS to a larger model. If the load is within acceptable limits, the UPS itself may be damaged.

SYMPTOM 17-30   **The UPS tab is not available in the Power Options dialog box.** When trying to configure the UPS, you may notice that the UPS tab isn't available in the Windows 2000 Power Options dialog box. In virtually all cases, the UPS has not properly identified itself to the server. UPS support has been integrated into Windows 2000, and most UPS devices have either a serial or Universal Serial Bus (USB) connection to a computer.

A UPS that is connected using a USB cable is represented as a battery in Windows 2000, and is configured using the Alarms and Power Meter tabs in the Power Options dialog box. On laptops and desktops with a USB-connected UPS, there is no UPS tab in Power Options. In this case, the UPS presents itself as a *human input device* (HID)–compliant device, and Windows 2000 automatically installs the necessary drivers. Make sure that the proper USB support is installed in the PC, and recheck the USB cable between the UPS and the system.

A UPS that is connected using a serial cable is configured using the UPS tab in the Power Options tool. Windows 2000 may or may not recognize a serial PnP UPS. By default, Windows 2000 contains serial support for the following American Power Conversion UPS devices:

- Back-UPS
- Back-UPS Pro
- Basic Port on Communications Accessory
- Basic signaling to any APC UPS
- Matrix-UPS
- PowerStack
- Smart Signaling to any APC UPS
- Smart-UPS
- Symmetra Power Array

You can also click Generic in the Manufacturer box, and then click Custom in the Model box to manually configure the UPS signal polarity. Check your UPS documentation for information about how to configure the UPS service for your UPS. It is important to remember that UPS devices offering a serial connection may use a variety of proprietary cables (with different cables providing different levels of functionality). If you have problems configuring your UPS, it may help to contact the UPS manufacturer for information about your specific UPS cable requirements.

SYMPTOM 17-31   **The UPS enters Battery mode during Windows 2000 installation.** When you install Windows 2000 on a computer that has a UPS attached, the computer may unexpectedly go into "battery" mode. This problem occurs during Setup when the serial enumeration driver (**SERUNUM.SYS**) attempts to detect what exists on the serial ports. The UPS is started when the driver engages the serial port. Unfortunately, this is a known problem with Windows 2000. To work around this problem, disconnect the serial cable from the UPS during Windows 2000 Setup—the problem does not occur after Setup is finished.

SYMPTOM 17-32   **The UPS enters battery calibration mode during Windows 2000 installation.**   When you install Windows 2000, certain UPS systems that are in *Smart Signaling* mode may go into a Battery Calibration mode. This behavior may cause the battery to unexpectedly drain over time. This problem can occur when Window 2000 tries to detect a serial mouse during Setup. When this occurs, Windows sends an ASCII character "D" to the serial port, which causes some UPS units to enter Battery Calibration mode. This problem has been fixed in Windows 2000 Service Pack 2 and later. The English version of this fix should have the following file attributes (or later):

```
06/21/2000  09:40p  229,264  Setupldr.bin
```

To work around this problem, disconnect the UPS before you run Setup from a CD-ROM installation. If you are deploying Windows using an unattended installation, replace the **SEUPLDR.BIN** file in the I386 folder with the **SETUPLDR.BIN** file provided in this fix.

SYMPTOM 17-33   **A simple signaling UPS doesn't power off after a system shutdown.** If you have a "simple signaling" UPS attached to a Windows 2000 computer, you may find that the UPS does *not* power off after a system shutdown—thus the UPS continues to use battery power. This behavior doesn't occur with the same UPS under Windows NT 4.0. This problem is caused by a change in Windows 2000. In Windows NT 4.0, processes can run with limited resources after the shutdown. This allows the Windows NT 4.0 UPS service driver to signal the UPS to turn off over the serial port. In Windows 2000, all processes are automatically terminated by the operating system during shutdown. This prevents the UPS service driver from signaling the UPS to power down after shutdown. There is no workaround for this issue, but some UPSs allow you to set an internal timer that turns off the UPS automatically when it is running on battery power and there is no load. Check your documentation to see if such a feature is available in your UPS.

SYMPTOM 17-34   **The UPS can't access its COM port.**   This is known to occur under Windows 2000 (SP1 and SP2). When you try to choose a manufacturer for a UPS using the UPS tab in the Power Options dialog box, you may receive the following error message:

```
The UPS service could not access the specified Comm Port.
```

This problem can occur if your computer only has one COM port that is not configured as COM1. The default value for the COM port when installing a UPS is COM1, so this setting is automatically written to the Registry when you click the UPS tab. Until the actual COM port is selected, the registry setting remains at COM1. To work around this problem, manually select the COM port:

1. Click Start, highlight Settings, click Control Panel, and then double-click Power Options.
2. Click the UPS tab, and then click Select.
3. In the On Port box, click your COM port. Note that you may only have one choice.
4. Click Finish, and then click OK.

SYMPTOM 17-35   **Windows shuts down immediately during a power failure.**   Y o u find that Windows NT/2000 shuts down immediately when power fails—even though a working UPS is attached. This is normally caused by a UPS that doesn't have the ability to send a low battery signal to the computer. If a UPS cannot send a signal to the computer to inform it of a low battery condition, Windows NT/2000 instead relies on information provided by the user to determine the length of time that the system can be run on battery power. When the battery power reaches two minutes of life remaining, Windows begins a shutdown of the system.

When you boot Windows NT/2000, it starts under the assumption that the battery is completely drained. This is a safety feature that assumes a computer has just been turned on, and that the UPS battery is not charged yet. Windows NT/2000 then computes the amount of life it expects the battery to have based on the "Expected battery life" and "Battery recharge time per minute of run time" settings in the UPS Service setup screen. For example, if the battery recharge time is set to 100 minutes, the system must run 100 minutes for Windows to believe that the battery has a one-minute charge. It must run 200 minutes for Windows NT to calculate a two-minute charge, and so on.

Since Windows NT/2000 will begin a shutdown immediately if the power fails when the battery life is calculated to be two minutes or less, Windows may shut down immediately if the power fails and the calculated battery life is two minutes or less. Thus, Windows may shut down sooner than expected after a power failure if the computer was rebooted recently—even though the UPS may be fully charged. This action is by design because Windows NT/2000 assumes worst-case conditions for unattended UPS monitoring.

SYMPTOM 17-36   **There is trouble with the UPS serial connection.**   You may note that the UPS tab in your Windows 2000 Power Options dialog box reports that UPS communication has been lost. Before you attempt to reconfigure the UPS, check that you're using the cable that accompanied the UPS (rather than a standard serial cable). Also check the UPS tab and verify that the correct UPS make and model were selected. Next, open the Device Manager and expand the COM Ports listing. Double-click the COM port used for UPS communication. In the Port Properties dialog box, verify that the required port settings are configured (check the UPS manual for specific settings). As a rule, the following settings are adequate:

- **Data Rate (bps):** 2,400
- **Data:** 8-bit
- **Parity:** none
- **Stop:** 1
- **Flow Control:** none

Further Study

TrippLite: **www.tripplite.com**
APC: **www.apcc.com**
Best Power: **www.bestpower.com**
Microsoft: **www.microsoft.com**

NETWORK STORAGE

Today's networks handle far more than the text, spreadsheets, and other common data types that we traditionally associate with networking—modern bandwidth-hungry networks exchange high-end graphics, voice, and even real-time video data. Such demands stretch the network's connectivity, but also place a tremendous strain on network storage capacity. Administrators are realizing that a few drives tucked into a server are no longer enough to support the network's storage needs. A new generation of *network attached storage* (NAS or "storage appliance") devices is emerging to provide convenient, high-capacity storage solutions. The NAS is basically a dedicated file server that simply attaches to the existing network through a hub or switch. These storage appliances allow administrators to add storage quickly, and distribute storage to different areas of the network (reducing the traffic congestion that often occurs at a file server). This chapter details several common types of storage appliances, and outlines the concepts of a storage area network (or SAN).

Fixed Disk Servers

The most common type of NAS unit is the fixed disk (hard drive-based) file server such as the Maxtor NAS 3000 in Figure 18-1. These are dedicated file servers which include an array of drives (which can be configured in a variety of RAID levels), a network interface, and all of the necessary processing components

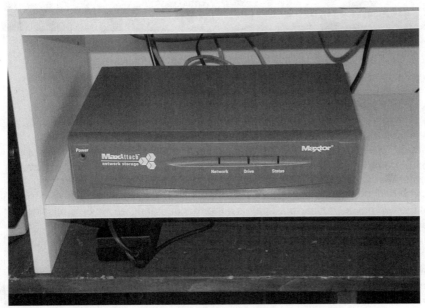

FIGURE 18-1   Maxtor's NAS3000 provides up to 40GB of storage with a simple Ethernet connection.

and software needed to run the unit. In most cases, using a NAS server involves just attaching it to the network and running software to initialize and configure the unit's storage characteristics. Once online, the NAS can usually be managed through a Web browser.

UNDERSTANDING INDICATORS

Dedicated storage appliances (such as the NAS 3000) rely on a series of indicators to report the unit's status and any problems that might be occurring. Before installing the unit, take some time to familiarize yourself with the indicators available on your unit. Typical indicators include the following:

- **Power LED**   When the power LED indicates that the unit is powered on. If the light is blinking, the unit is either starting up or shutting down.
- **Network LED**   The Network LED can be green or orange. For example, green represents a 10-Mbps connection, and orange represents a 100-Mbps connection to the network. When the light is solid, a network connection is established. When the light is blinking, there is network traffic (similar to a Link/Activity LED found in many switches and routers).
- **Drive LED**   The drive LED represents drive activity. When it is solid, there is extensive drive activity. Otherwise, the LED will blink to indicate varying levels of activity.
- **Status LED**   When the status LED is lit, the NAS is generating an alert (usually available on the NAS unit's home page). The light may be on steadily, or blink to indicate a specific error. Table 18-1 lists some common alerts for the Maxtor NAS—other NAS units may use different indicators. NAS units like the Maxtor NAS3000 generate LED blink codes to indicate the device's status and errors.

TABLE 18-1	COMMON ALERTS FOR THE MAXTOR NAS
STATE	**DESCRIPTION/SOLUTION**
Steadily on	A serious fault has occurred in the NAS unit, which should be replaced.
2 blinks	A server on the network has the same name as the NAS. The name assigned to the NAS must be unique, so assign a new network name.
3 blinks	An operating system update was not successful. The NAS reverts to using the previous version and reports the "Operating System Update Failed" alert.
4 blinks	A device on the network has the same IP address as the NAS. The IP address assigned to NAS must be unique. Assign a static IP address to the NAS.
5 blinks	The temperature of the NAS's internal CPU is too high. When the warning occurs, the temperature is still 10 percent below the threshold temperature at which the unit will be shut down automatically. Power off the NAS and check ventilation.
6 blinks	One of the two drives in a mirrored pair is either encountering errors or is missing.
7 blinks	Both drives in a mirrored pair are encountering errors.
8 blinks	The NAS is recording a high number of drive errors, and reports the "High Number of Drive Errors" alert.
10 blinks	One of the disks is full, and this produces the "Disk Volume Full" alert.
12 blinks	The temperature/voltage sensor has failed, and the NAS should be replaced.

BASIC INSTALLATION

Since NAS units are basically dedicated computers, installation generally consists of attaching the unit to an available port on the network, then installing a software utility on the administrator's console. However, the NAS can still be accessed and managed from any station using a Web browser interface. The following steps outline a typical installation:

1. To connect the NAS unit to the network, insert a Category 6 cable into the network connection on the back of NAS (see Figure 18-2), then insert the other end into a 10/100BaseT Ethernet connection on your network hub or switch. Connect the NAS unit to power using an ac cord or adapter.

2. Power on NAS by pressing the On/Off button in the back of the unit. On the front panel of the box, the power light will flash for several minutes during the power-up cycle. When the power light stops flashing and the network light is on, your NAS is ready to configure.

3. Insert the NAS unit's software CD into the Administrator's PC that is logged into the network (though any workstation will usually suffice). The software will launch automatically and begin the installation process. Simply follow the on-screen prompts to install the NAS software.

4. When the installation is complete, you will be given the option to launch. Click Finish to launch the software. A window will appear and the software will search the network for attached NAS units. This process may take a few minutes, depending on your network configuration.

5. When the search is complete, a window will display the NAS unit(s) on your network. Double-click the desired unit to display the status, unit name, IP address workgroup name, and other information of each NAS unit (see Figure 18-3). This information confirms the operation of your NAS, and you can proceed to configure the unit.

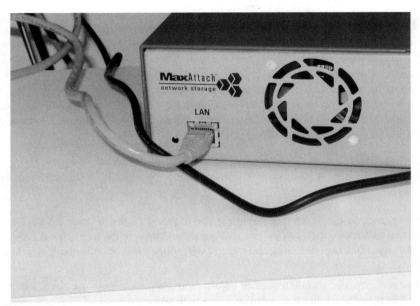

FIGURE 18-2 The NAS3000 connects to an Ethernet network with a single RJ-45 cable.

 Remember to add the NAS to your network documentation along with details like the IP address, MAC address, and unit name.

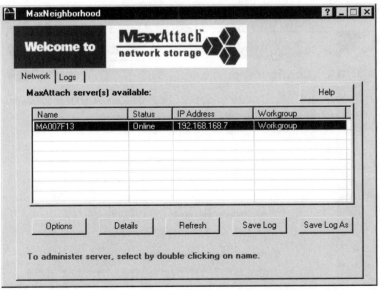

FIGURE 18-3 After connecting the NAS unit, installation software will automatically detect any NAS attached to the network, and provide details of the device.

CONFIGURING THE NAS

Once the NAS unit is attached and operational, you'll need to configure the unit and perform some administrative tasks. The first time that you configure the NAS, you'll need to launch the configuration process from the unit's software. For example, to launch the Maxtor NAS 3000 Configuration Wizard, highlight and double-click the name of your unit in the software window (such as MA007F13). The Configuration Wizard will appear in your Web browser window (see Figure 18-4). It will walk you through setting the clock, assigning an administrator password, and assigning a unit and workgroup name. Click Next to start the configuration, then enter the following parameters:

Remember that these discussions are presented as an example only—your particular NAS may offer more and different options. Always refer to documentation for specific setup and management instructions.

■ **Clock**   When setting the clock, simply complete the required fields. If you and the unit are not located in the same time zone, you can enter *either* your local time or the unit's local time. To apply daylight savings time, click the check box and the unit will adjust the clock automatically. When completed, click Next.

■ **Password**   For security, you should assign an administrator's password to the NAS. Enter and confirm the password, then record the password in a secure location.

■ **Name and Workgroup**   Now enter a unit name and workgroup identification for the NAS. Enter a name for your unit so users can find it in the Network Neighborhood or Windows Explorer. When creating a unit name (use up to 15 characters), be sure it is unique—it should *not* have the same name as

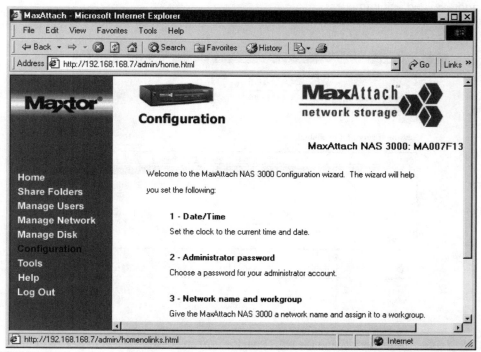

FIGURE 18-4   The NAS Configuration Wizard allows you to set up the NAS unit for operation.

any other device on your network. If you haven't changed your PC or laptop's workgroup name, the default name will be "Workgroup". Click Next.

In most cases, this will complete the initial configuration, and you simply need to reboot the NAS so that your changes will take effect. When the reboot is done, you'll be asked to enter your password. Type it and press the ENTER key or click OK. Your NAS unit is now ready for use. If your NAS resides on a different subnet than the workstation you're using to configure the unit, you may need to assign a temporary IP address to the NAS. This means that your unit is acting as a DHCP server. Assign an IP address and subnet mask. After you assign an IP address, click Next, and then click Reboot. Once the NAS reboots, you'll be asked to enter your password. Type it and press the ENTER key or click OK. You now need to change the range of IP addresses that your NAS unit can assign. To do this, click on the Manage Networks menu, and then click on the DHCP server tab. Modify the range according to your new address and click Apply.

Even though an NAS may support DHCP, you're not obligated to use it. Since the NAS is acting as a file server, you may prefer to use a static IP address for the unit(s) to ensure that their IP address doesn't change.

NAS MANAGEMENT NOTES

After the NAS unit has been initially configured, you can create users and groups, build shares/folders, and apply security—or select NT Passthrough if you are using a primary domain controller. You can access the administrator program either through a Web browser or NAS software utility. For a Web browser, simply type the unit's IP address in the browser's Address line (i.e., **192.168.1.106**) and enter the correct password. The NAS home page will appear (see Figure 18-5), providing important network, disk, and alert information about the NAS.

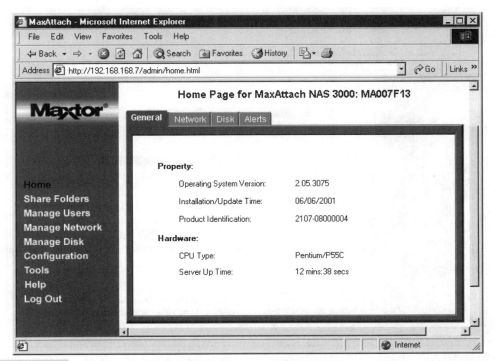

FIGURE 18-5   The NAS unit can be managed completely through a browser-based interface.

Share Folders

Click the Share Folders menu to manage shares on the NAS. There is already a default public share available (called \Public) unless you've changed the factory default drive configuration. At this point, any user connected to the unit through your network has access to this share. To create a new share, click on Share Folders in the left navigation bar. A screen will appear with default folders (as in Figure 18-6). If you've created any private folders, they will also appear. Choose your folder, and then click the New Folder button. Enter a name for your new folder. Click OK. Click on your new folder. It is currently not shared. To grant access, click on either the SMB or NFS box. Verify the share name, and click Apply. You now have a new share for the network.

NAS units such as the Maxtor NAS 3000 allow you to define the access rights and security for the shares that you create. For example, select a share and click on the User Access tab. By default, all new shares are given Read/Write status to the group AnyOne. To restrict access, this must be changed to None or Read Only. Click one or the other and click Apply. To grant rights to a user or group, highlight the user or group and select the access rights. Then, click Apply.

Manage Users

You can also control the various users and groups that access your NAS. To create users and groups, click Manage Users on the left navigation bar (see Figure 18-7). Click the Add New User button. Enter the user's login name and password for the Windows 9x/NT/2000 system. Enter the password again to confirm it, and click OK. You can now create a private/home folder for this user. To do this, click the check box that says Private folder and click Apply (to create additional users, just click Add New User and repeat the process).

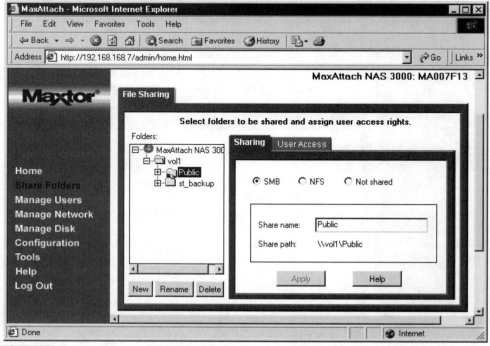

FIGURE 18-6   The Share Folders menu lets you manage shares on the NAS.

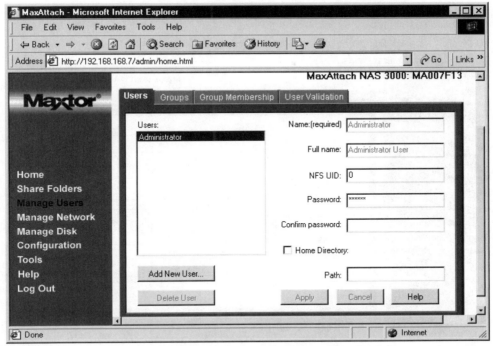

FIGURE 18-7   The Manage Users menu lets you control the users and groups that use the NAS unit.

You can also create a group. A group is a collection of users with the same access rights to folders. Group assignments are particularly handy when you wish to assign the same resources and rights to a large number of users. To create a group, click on the Groups tab at the top. Click the Add New Group button. Enter a group name and click OK. Click on the Group Membership tab at the top. Select the user or users you wish to add to a group(s). Select the group, click Add, and then click Apply. Finally, you can select a method for checking passwords using the User Validation tab.

Manage Network

If you need to adjust the way your NAS behaves on the network, select the Manage Network entry on your menu (see Figure 18-8). From here, you can tweak the unit's IP address, identification (i.e., name or workgroup settings), WINS setup, and DHCP server settings (if you need the NAS to provide DHCP services). When the NAS is being serviced by another DHCP server, and is receiving its IP address and subnet automatically, select the Network tab and click "Obtain an IP address from a DHCP server". The Identification tab lets you set different device and workgroup names for the NAS. If you're using WINS, the WINS tab allows you to enable WINS and enter the WINS server IP address. When there is no other DHCP server supporting the NAS, you can select the DHCP Server tab and configure the IP address range managed by the NAS.

Manage Disk

NAS units such as the Maxtor NAS 3000 typically provide more than one disk for storage. If your NAS offers several disks, you can manage the way that those disks are used. By default, the NAS will usually span multiple disks to create a single large volume. For example, an NAS with two 60GB drives can span

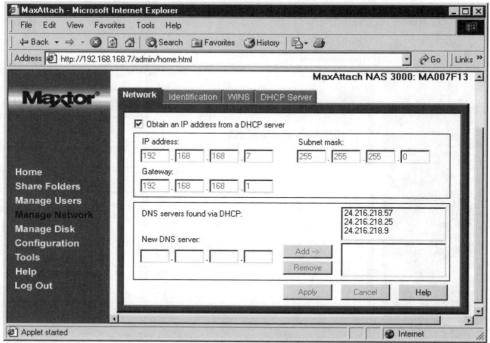

FIGURE 18-8   The Manage Network menu lets you adjust the way your NAS unit behaves on
the network.

to create a single logical volume up to 120GB. Alternately, you may use the Manage Disk menu (see
Figure 18-9) to select other available disk configurations such as the following:

- Two individual disks (no RAID)
- One active/one backup disk (basic mirroring)

Of course, a more sophisticated NAS with multiple disks (i.e., four disks, six disks, eight disks, or
more) may support additional configuration schemes. If you do alter the disk configuration, you'll also
need to apply the change(s), and usually reformat the affected disk(s).

NAS TROUBLESHOOTING

NAS units are intended to provide easy installation, good performance, and long-term reliability on your
network—but this doesn't mean that they're problem-free. As an administrator or technician, you should
understand the important issues needed to support typical NAS devices, and familiarize yourself with the
most common symptoms.

DHCP Services

If your NAS unit supplies DHCP services, you'll need to understand a few special rules when planning an
NAS installation. If you're installing your unit into a network that already provides DHCP services (usually on a network with a server or other device with built-in DHCP services), your unit will automatically
obtain an IP address for the NAS unit—you don't need to take any further action.

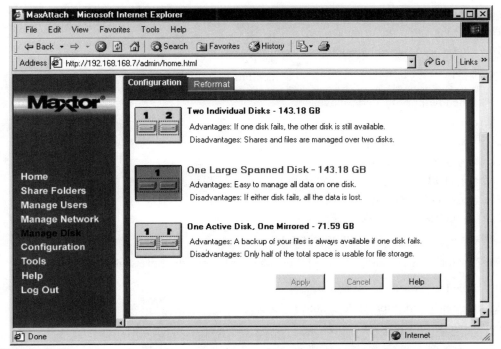

FIGURE 18-9   The Manage Disk menu lets you configure NAS units with more than one
internal drive.

If you installed your unit into an environment *without* a DHCP server, then your NAS unit will
become a DHCP server with a default static address (i.e., **192.168.42.252**) and default subnet (i.e.,
255.255.255.0). Your own NAS unit may offer different default settings, but this is a good example. In
order to configure your NAS unit, you'll need access to a computer with an address within this IP
range—you may need to change the IP address for your computer temporarily. Otherwise, the NAS configuration software will return an error when you try to select the NAS unit.

If you later move the NAS unit into a DHCP environment (for example, you install the NAS in a different subnet on your network), you must ensure that DHCP services are reselected. To do this, open NAS
in your Web browser, select the Manage Network menu, and check the "Obtain IP Address Automatically" box. Failing to reconfigure the relocated NAS may cause interruptions in your network.

Using Alerts

When trouble strikes, most NAS units will generate a suite of error or diagnostic messages that are stored
in a log file. If a user reports trouble accessing a NAS, the administrator or technician should check this log
first. Corrective action(s) can then be based upon any errors or alert messages generated. The Maxtor
NAS generates the following low-priority alert messages:

- There is a server name conflict.
- The OS has been updated successfully.
- Volume 1 or 2 is 2% full.
- Volume 1 or 2 is 90% full.

- The CPU temperature is too high.
- The CPU voltage is out of range.
- There have been five failed attempts on admin password.

The Maxtor NAS generates the following medium-priority alert messages:

- All of the low-priority alerts above.
- There is a file system consistency check (fsck).
- Disk space is exceeded by a user.
- There is a duplicate IP address.
- There is a CPU temp/voltage sensor failure.
- There is an OS update in progress.
- The OS update failed or was successful.
- There is a SMART (disk diagnostic) error.

The Maxtor NAS also produces the following high-priority alert messages:

- All of the low-priority alerts above.
- All of the medium-priority alerts above.
- The network collision rate is high.

Clearing Alerts   The NAS alert log should be checked routinely as a matter of standard operating procedure. This allows the administrator to detect and correct any problems before they become critical. The typical steps needed to check and clear alerts are outlined here:

1. Click Home.
2. If the Alerts tab is not displayed, click Alerts.
3. Review the alerts listed in the Alert box.
4. To see a description of an alert, select the alert and click Help.
5. To clear the alerts, click Clear Alerts.

E-Mail Alerts   Rather than checking the NAS log manually, many administrators prefer to receive alerts via e-mail. If your NAS supports e-mail alerts (and your network uses an SMTP mail server), you can use steps such as the following to request alert notification by e-mail:

1. Click Tools.
2. If the E-mail tab page is not displayed, click E-mail.
3. Type in the address for your SMTP server.
4. Type in the e-mail address to which you want the messages sent (for example, John.Smith@yourcompany.com).
5. Select the priority level of alerts you want sent (you may wish to start with *all* alerts).
6. To be sure the e-mail information you typed is correct, click Test.

7. Clicking Test prompts the NAS to send a test message to the e-mail address at the mail server you identified previously. If the message arrives, you know the information is correct.

8. When the information is correct, click Apply.

Operating System Management

An NAS is basically a dedicated file server computer that includes the manufacturer's own operating system version. From time to time, manufacturers will release a new operating system to fix bugs, improve compatibility, and enhance performance. You can typically update the OS directly from the manufacturer's Web site. Before considering an OS update, check the unit's general operating status for current information about file server software and hardware. For example:

1. Access the NAS management software using a Web browser.

2. Click Home.

3. If the General tab page is not displayed, click General.

4. Review the information on the page. General operating information often includes the following details:

   ■ **Operating system version** Version of the operating system currently in use.

   ■ **Installation/update time** Date on which the operating system was installed (or last updated).

   ■ **Product identification** An internal number identifying NAS.

   ■ **CPU type** Model and clock speed of the file server's CPU.

   ■ **Server up time** Length of time the NAS has run since it was last restarted.

Updating the OS You'll normally receive a notification from the manufacturer when a new OS version becomes available (along with a URL and filename required for download). OS updates are usually quite safe, but be sure you're using a computer with a Web browser that can connect to the Internet. Also, since the file server restarts at the end of the update process, do not update the operating system while people are using the file server. To update an OS, follow these steps:

1. Access the NAS management software using a Web browser.

2. Click Home.

3. If the General tab page is not displayed, click General.

4. Write down the number that identifies the current version of the operating system.

5. Click Tools.

6. If the Update tab page is not displayed, click Update.

7. Click Update.

8. When the browser opens, follow the instructions for downloading the new operating system. Remember that the NAS will be inaccessible by network users during the update process.

9. When NAS restarts, click Home.

10. If the General tab page is not displayed, click General.

11. Verify that the server is running the new version of the operating system.

Operating system upgrades will normally fail for the following reasons:

- The network connection was lost during upgrade.
- The upgrade file was corrupted in transfer.
- The NAS power went out.
- The system is already running the most current version.
- There isn't enough space on the hard drive to download or apply the upgrade.

Managing LMHOST

If you wish to use server names (rather than IP addresses) to administer your NAS, you may need to modify or create an LMHOSTS file. Try the following steps to manage an LMHOSTS file:

1. If you have an existing LMHOSTS file (for example **LMHOSTS.SAM**), open it with Notepad. If you don't have an existing LMHOSTS file, just open an empty Notepad file. If you edit the file, open it and save a copy for backup (as another filename such as **LMHOSTS.OLD**). If there's a problem or error in the edited LMHOSTS file, you can restore the backup.

2. Create an entry by typing your IP address, followed by five spaces, and then your chosen server name. Your server name can only be 15 characters. It should look something like this:

   ```
   192.168.42.252 server_name
   ```

3. Save the file as its original name if you are modifying an existing LMHOST file. If you're creating a new file, save it as LMHOST in your Windows 9x subdirectory (or in your **WINNT** subdirectory).

4. Reboot your computer. Your LMHOST file and server name will now become active.

Passthrough Mode

Some NAS devices provide a *passthrough mode* that takes user and group information from a *Primary Domain Controller* (PDC) server. This means that you do not have to create users or groups on the NAS system, nor do you have to manage the users or groups separately. You simply manage access rights on local NAS shares and folders. The following steps give an example of the way to enable the passthrough mode:

1. Select the Manage Users tab, click on User Validation, and then click the Passthrough button.
2. Enter your NetBIOS server name.
3. Enter the IP address of the PDC server and click Apply.
4. Answer Yes in the warning window, and your previous configuration and user rights will be deleted. Another warning window will appear reminding you to reboot your system. Click OK to reboot—this will activate the passthrough mode.
5. Select to the Tools menu and click the Shutdown tab.
6. Choose the number of minutes to shutdown (choose zero minutes for an immediate response) and click Restart. Your system should now be in passthrough mode.

Select the Manage Users tab—your system should show users and groups assigned according to your NT PDC Server. If you don't see your lists of users and groups, any user should access a share or folder on the NAS unit. This should initiate the database download. After you do this, select Refresh in your browser window, and your groups should appear. You must log out of your PC or laptop for any changes to take place (there is no need to log out of the NAS). Reboot the workstation to log out.

The NT PDC does not grant access rights to the NAS share; it only validates the Users Passwords and Group Membership—rights to shares must be granted on NAS.

NAS Backup/Restore

Even though an NAS can be configured for RAID operations, protecting important data still requires a complete backup. That backup can then be restored if necessary. This section outlines the general process used to back up and restore files from a typical NAS. For example, to backup existing NAS data, follow these steps:

1. Use a client station to log in to the NAS as an Administrator.

2. Click the Tools option from the Main Menu, and the Tools applet will appear.

3. Click on the Backup tab, and then click on the Backup Now button. The backup will be saved as **config.dat** that is stored in the **\\vol1\st_backup** folder. After completion, a backup window will appear indicating that the NAS configuration settings were successfully backed up. Click on the OK button to continue.

4. Click on the Share Folders option from the Main Menu, and the Share Folders applet will appear.

5. Click on the Shares Tab, highlight the **\st_backup** folder, and select the Shared radio button. The **\st_backup** folder name will appear in the field provided. Click on the Apply button to save the changes.

6. Click on the User Access tab, highlight the User Administrator, and click on the Read/Write radio button. Click on the Apply button to save the changes.

7. Copy the **\\vol1\st_backup** folder to either another network share or to a local hard drive.

8. Back up existing data on the NAS using a standard backup application (i.e., Veritas Backup Exec, Computer Associates ArcServe, Native NT Backup, and so on). If you do not have such an application, you may copy the data to another source (such as a networked share or local disk drive).

9. Shut down the NAS unit.

You can also restore data to an NAS using steps such as those shown here:

1. Connect the replacement NAS unit to its power and network cables, then apply power to the NAS unit.

2. Execute the NAS software from a system that has the software installed, and enter all requested information. Make sure to give the replacement unit the same password, network name, and IP address.

3. Login to the NAS as Administrator, then click on Manage Disks from the Main Menu.

4. Configure the NAS unit to the same disk configuration (i.e., mirrored, JBOD, or spanned) as the original unit. Restart the NAS unit when disk configuration is complete.

5. Restore the file and directory structure from the backup application (or from your copy of the data). Restart the NAS unit when restoration is complete.

6. Log in to the NAS as Administrator once again.

7. Click the Tools option from the Main Menu, and the Tools applet will appear.

8. Click the Restore tab and select the **config.dat** file that was previously copied to a network share (or to a local hard drive). Once selected, click on the Restore Now button.

9. Restart the NAS unit after the **config.dat** file has been restored.

10. At this point, the file and directory structure should be the same as the original unit. Users and groups that share permissions should also be the same as they were on the original NAS unit. Confirm access by having multiple users log in and access shares.

SYMPTOMS

Although most NAS units are designed to provide "plug and play" storage solutions for your network, there are some common problems that can occur. Most trouble can be corrected through visual checks and configuration changes, but this part of the issue outlines a series of specific problems that demand detailed corrective actions to resolve.

SYMPTOM 18-1   **You cannot administer the NAS unit.**   Always check power and connections first. Make sure that the NAS is connected to a power source and the power light is on. Plug in the unit and power it on if necessary. If the unit is powered on, check that the Network light is on. If not, check your network cable connection. Use the cable that came with the unit. Insert the cable into the connection labeled LAN on the back of NAS. Insert the other end into a suitable network connection (i.e., 10/100BaseT Ethernet) on your network hub or switch. Try a different port on the hub or switch, or try a different network cable. If you're using a hub or switch with an "uplink" port, avoid using the "uplink" port unless you have the Uplink button in the proper position. Do not connect the cable directly to your PC or laptop unless you have a specialized crossover cable for your NAS (which must be purchased separately). If the problem persists, reboot the NAS and see if the trouble clears. Otherwise, the NAS unit may be experiencing problems and require replacement.

SYMPTOM 18-2   **You cannot find the NAS in your network.**   For example, you cannot locate the unit in your Network Neighborhood (Windows 9x) or My Network Places (Windows 2000). Start by reviewing the suggestions of Symptom 18-1. If the NAS is not on, is connected improperly, or the corresponding hub or switch port is defective, the NAS will not be able to communicate on the network (and it will not be seen by the network). Verify that your NAS unit is in the same workgroup as the PC or laptop you're currently using. To do this, go to Network Neighborhood or My Network Places and double-click on Entire Network. Look for your NAS workgroup name (i.e. "Workgroup"). If the NAS workgroup name is there, double-click on your unit's name, and it should appear. You can see the NAS unit MA007F13 along with the server SERVER01 in Figure 18-10.

If your NAS unit is still not there under Windows 9x, click Start | Find | Computer. Type in your NAS unit's name (i.e., MA007F13) and click Find Now. Your computer will search for your unit name, and if located, it will be displayed. Double-click on the name and your share(s) will appear. Under Windows 2000, you can search once you've selected Entire Network from the My Network Places dialog box. If the problem persists, reboot the NAS and see if the trouble clears. Otherwise, the NAS unit may be experiencing problems and require replacement.

SYMPTOM 18-3   **Your administration program does not display properly.**   First, make sure that you can indeed manage the NAS using a Web browser. If not, you may need to install a NAS-specific management utility on your administrator's console before you're able to access the NAS. If you can manage the NAS using a Web browser, be sure that you're using an adequate version of the browser (such as IE 4.01 or later). If you're using the correct Web browser, be sure that the browser is configured to show Java applets and accept cookies. Otherwise, the administrator's program may not appear properly (if at all).

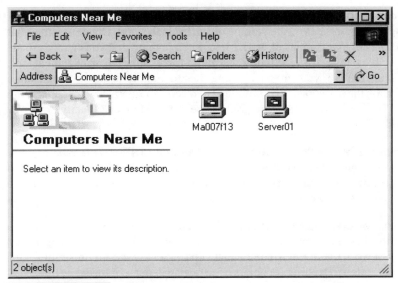

FIGURE 18-10   It's easy to see the NAS unit in your network, and browse it as you would any other storage unit.

SYMPTOM 18-4   **The administrator's password is lost.**   Reset the NAS unit. Some NAS units can be reset by pressing a Reset button while power is applied. Other NAS units may require you to power off the unit first, then use a ballpoint pen to depress the Reset button on the back of the NAS before restoring power. Continue to hold the Reset button for 3–5 seconds. Resetting the file server will preserve the data volumes and security database, but all server configuration settings will be cleared. The file server will assume it is a brand new system when it restarts. It will go through the first time Configuration Wizard as if it were going through initial setup. This includes reassigning the IP address. It will reset WINS setting (to none). If you've backed up your configuration settings, you can restore those settings now according to the manufacturer's instructions.

SYMPTOM 18-5   **An error reports that your "Disk mirror is in a degraded state".** When your NAS is configured to provide disk mirroring, this error means that one of the two drives in a mirrored pair is encountering errors (or is missing entirely). The other drive is still running, and supporting your data. If you know that one of the drives is physically missing (for example, it was removed so you could replace it), you can simply ignore this alert—it will disappear once the missing drive is replaced. However, if both drives are present, you may have a serious hardware problem. Power off the NAS and restart it. If the problem is not resolved, a disk may have failed, or there is some other problem with the NAS that will require replacement from the manufacturer.

SYMPTOM 18-6   **An error reports that the "Disk mirror is in a failure state".**   This is a serious fault that indicates *both* drives of your mirrored pair are encountering errors. This type of error usually means that any data on the NAS has been compromised (and is likely to be inaccessible). Power off the NAS and restart it. If the problem is not resolved, you may need to replace the affected drives, or replace the NAS outright. In either case, you may need to restore the contents of your mirrored disk array from a recent backup.

SYMPTOM 18-7   **An error reports that the "Disk volume is full".**   This is a straightforward error—there is no more space to store files on the volume identified in the alert. Delete any files that are no longer used (such as old files or extra copies of work files). Keep in mind that you cannot use the administration software to delete files. Instead, use Windows Explorer (or another file management tool) to delete unneeded files. As an alternative, you can move some files to another location (such as to a backup tape or another file server on the network). If you continue to receive the alert, consider upgrading your existing NAS to include a second drive, consider upgrading the NAS to higher-capacity drives, or add another NAS to the network.

SYMPTOM 18-8   **An error reports a "High number of drive errors".**   This type of error indicates that there are serious problems with one or more of the NAS unit's hard drives. You can try to clear the problems by powering off the NAS and then restarting it. If you continue to receive the error, the NAS may require repair or exchange from the manufacturer.

SYMPTOM 18-9   **An error reports "Low disk space".**   This error usually means that less than 10 percent of the space on the disk is available to store files. Delete any files that are no longer used (such as old files or extra copies of work files). Keep in mind that you cannot use the administration software to delete files. Instead, use Windows Explorer (or another file management tool) to delete unneeded files. As an alternative, you can move some files to another location (such as to a backup tape or another file server on the network). If you continue to receive the alert, consider upgrading your existing NAS to include a second drive, consider upgrading the NAS to higher-capacity drives, or add another NAS to the network.

SYMPTOM 18-10   **An error reports "The user at <IP address> has issued 5 incorrect passwords".**   One of the users on your network (the IP address in the message identifies the computer that the person is using) has tried to log in as the administrator at least five times, but the person is using the wrong password for the "Administrator" username. This is a serious security breach (hacking) that should be dealt with immediately—there are likely to be other violations of use being attempted by the offending user.

SYMPTOM 18-11   **You're not receiving e-mail alerts from the NAS.**   You configure the NAS to send you alerts by e-mail, but even though alerts are being generated, you're not receiving them. This type of problem can almost always be traced to NAS configuration errors. First, confirm that the mail server you identified is an SMTP server. For example, to find out what server you identified, click Tools and display the E-mail tab page. Verify that the mail server is directly connected to your network. If the mail server is only available after you dial in to the network (or through another indirect connection), you will not be able to receive alerts.

Try sending a test message to confirm that the e-mail information you entered is correct. To send a test message, click Tools, display the E-mail tab page, and click Test. Also make sure that you have requested Low, Medium, or High priority alerts—if you selected None, no alerts will be sent. Finally, if the mail server receives its IP address from a DHCP server, confirm that it also receives a hostname. This provides the server with a valid DNS domain name.

SYMPTOM 18-12   **A user can see the NAS, but cannot save files in a particular folder.**   In most cases, you can trace this to a share problem. Verify that the folder, which the user is trying to access, is a share folder (share folders are marked with a hand). Also, make sure the person has Read/Write access to the folder (and to the parent folders). For example, to check user access, click Share

Folder, display the User Access tab page, and select the share folder from the folder tree. Determine what access rights are assigned to the user (and any groups to which the user belongs). Make any necessary corrections to the user's rights.

SYMPTOM 18-13 **You cannot update the NAS with a new operating system.** Normally, an OS update can be downloaded and installed directly from the manufacturer's Web site. When you see a message such as

```
Unit has not been updated successfully with a new operating system
```

it means that the operating system has not been downloaded and updated. The NAS will typically revert to using the operating system it was using before you tried to download a newer version. You can continue to use the current version, or try the download again (be sure you're trying to download the correct OS file). If you continue having trouble, check the current OS version and contact the NAS manufacturer for additional assistance—you may need to download an alternate file, or return the unit to the manufacturer for service. See the section above on "Operating System Management."

CD Servers

Busy networks frequently need to share CDs. This is normally accomplished using a CD jukebox. But CD servers (such as the Linksys 20GB GigaCD Server in Figure 18-11) have emerged as a valuable alternative—allowing users to upload frequently used CDs, graphic storage CDs, standard audio CDs, games, or any other high-demand CD and avoid having to locate it or swap it out with other users. A CD server

FIGURE 18-11 The Linksys GigaCD server allows you to store CD images for access by the entire network.

allows your CD-ROM data to become simultaneously available to multiple network users (accessible from the Network Neighborhood). If you don't have a CD-ROM drive installed on your network PC, just access the CD server and use the CD data there. For example, a CD server lets you

- Share access to CD-ROM titles through the network.
- Run CD-ROM applications without a CD-ROM drive on your workstation.
- Store up to 30 full-length (650MB) CD-ROMs.
- Use all audio CD formats.
- Utilize remote device monitoring and shutdown features.
- Update firmware from any PCs on the network.
- Act as a DHCP server or client.

As with fixed disk file servers like Maxtor's NAS, CD file servers are remarkably self-contained dedicated network appliances designed to integrate into your existing network with a minimum of installation and configuration hassles. All you need is to insert a CD and copy it to the internal disk drive—that image is then made available to your network.

UNDERSTANDING INDICATORS

Dedicated storage appliances (such as the Linksys GigaCD Server) rely on a series of indicators to report the unit's status and any problems that might be occurring. Before installing the unit, take some time to familiarize yourself with the indicators available on your unit. Typical indicators may include the following:

- **Ready**   This green LED will blink during startup and shutdown, and turn off once completed. During a software upgrade, both the Ready and Error LEDs will blink.
- **Error**   This amber LED will blink during startup. However, if it remains on, there is a hardware error. During a software upgrade, both the Ready and Error LEDs will blink.
- **LAN**   When a network connection is established, this green LED will illuminate. While data is being sent or received over your network, this green LED will flash.
- **Disk**   This green LED will flash whenever the unit's internal hard drive is accessed.
- **Disk Full**   This green LED will normally be off. It will begin to blink to indicate that the hard drive is 98 percent full, and remain on to indicate that the hard drive is completely full.
- **Copy Error**   This amber LED will normally be off. Should an error occur during the image copying procedure, this LED will remain on until the CD is ejected.

Buzzer Indications

Dedicated storage devices such as the GigaCD Server often use a buzzer to report key events or device errors that require attention. Buzzers may provide error or informational messages such as the following:

- **One beep**   The Reset IP/Password Button or Power Switch has been pressed.
- **Two beeps**   This is usually repeated every five seconds for one minute. The server is a DHCP client, but no DHCP server responded to the DHCP client request.
- **Three beeps**   This is usually repeated every 15 seconds for three minutes. The server's hard disk is more than 98 percent full.

■ **Five beeps**   This is usually repeated every 15 seconds for three minutes. The server is overheating. Some servers will automatically shut down (i.e., three minutes after the first beep).

BASIC INSTALLATION

Since CD server units are basically dedicated computers, installation generally consists of attaching the unit to an available port on the network, then installing a software utility on the administrator's console. However, the CD server can still be accessed and managed from any station using a Web browser interface. The following steps outline a typical installation (your own CD server may be different):

1. Connect a network cable from the RJ-45 port in the back of the server to your hub or switch to which the server will be connected. The server will autosense a 10BaseT or 100BaseTX connection at full or half duplex.

2. Connect ac power and power on the CD server.

3. Check the startup process. During startup, the unit's LEDs (i.e., Ready, Error, Disk Full, and Copy Error LEDs) will blink or stay on for a few seconds. If the Error LED remains lit, there is a hardware problem. Otherwise, the hardware installation process is basically complete.

4. Now it's time to install the required software on your administrator's PC. Insert the Setup CD-ROM into the CD drive on your PC. The Setup program should start automatically (if it doesn't, select **setup.exe** on your CD drive).

5. Select the "Administrator Installation" option and follow the prompts to install the CD server's manager utility, then start the utility once installation is complete.

6. Once the main menu appears (see Figure 18-12), select the CD server to be configured. If prompted for a password, click OK (there is no password by default). Select the Setup icon and start Quick Setup. The typical Quick Setup options are shown in Table 18-2. Once you save your Quick Setup entries, the CD server should be operational.

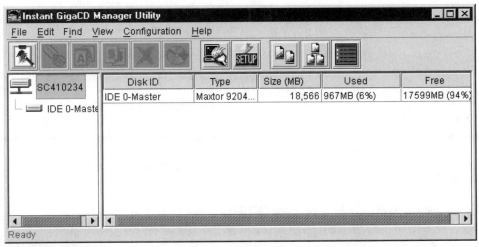

FIGURE 18-12   The CD Manager lists any CD server(s) available on the network.

TABLE 18-2   TYPICAL QUICK SETUP OPTIONS FOR THE LINKSYS GIGACD SERVER

SETTING	EXPLANATION
Server Properties:	
Server Name	This will show the default name, which you can change however you wish.
Comment	Any optional comments can be placed here.
Date/Time	Adjust the system's time setting here.
Time Zone	Adjust the time zone for your location here.
TCP/IP Properties:	
Obtain IP Address Automatically	You can enable this setting if there is a DHCP or Bootp server connected to your LAN used to obtain the CD server's IP address. Since this is a server, it is best to use a fixed IP address.
Fixed IP Address	You can enter your fixed IP address here.
IP Address	Quick Setup will suggest unused values from within the address range used on this segment of the LAN. If the suggested value is currently being utilized by a device that has been turned Off, change the address to one that is not being used.
Network Mask	This should use the same values as the other PCs on your LAN. The default value for the CD server is **255.255.255.0**.
Gateway	This should also use the same values as the other PCs on your LAN.
Enable DHCP Server	If selected, the CD server will provide IP addresses and related data to PCs on the network. PCs can only request such data if they are set up as DHCP clients.
Start IP Address	This is the first value for the IP addresses allocated by the DHCP server.
Finish IP Address	This is the final value for the IP addresses allocated by the DHCP server. The range between the Start IP Address and Finish IP Address should be large enough to hold all of the DHCP clients.
Microsoft Networking Properties:	
Workgroup Name	This name should correspond with the name used by the PCs on your LAN.
Code Page	You will want to select the appropriate region within which you are running the CD server.

 Remember to add the NAS to your network documentation along with details like the IP address, MAC address, and unit name.

CD SERVER MANAGEMENT NOTES

After the CD server has been initially configured, you can use the server's management utility to select and manage the unit. As an example, the Linksys GigaCD Server provides management software that lets you set passwords, handle system settings, make network setup changes, and use built-in utilities. This part of the chapter walks you through an example of CD server management options and their meanings.

CD server administration usually starts by launching the management software from the administrator's PC (or accessing the CD server using a Web browser if your unit supports it). Management software will automatically scan the network for CD servers, and then the main screen will appear (as in Figure 18-12). You will see a display of the CD servers currently connected to your network. Click to highlight the server that you wish to access (you'll be prompted for a password if one has been set). Once the CD server is selected, any "cabinets" within will be listed and available CD images will be listed within a selected cabinet.

If your CD server allows you to set a password (most do), it's a good policy to set the password during the unit's initial configuration. This protects the unit from unauthorized configuration changes. Be sure to record the password in a safe place.

System Configuration

System configuration options typically cover the major operating parameters of the device. General settings let you set the name that the CD server will use in your network. You can also set the date and time. Copy settings let you set the default location of saved CD images in your network. E-mail options enable e-mail messages to you or another administrator in the event of a CD server problem (if your CD server supports this feature). Finally, shutdown options let you specify the times and dates when the CD server will shut down (or respond to shutdown events).

General   General settings are usually entered during the server's initial configuration, but your selections can be changed here (see Figure 18-13). This can be particularly handy when moving the CD server to a new location or network, or when adjusting daylight savings time.

- **Server Name**   You can change the name of the CD server on your network. However, if you change the server's name, remember that any shortcuts to locations on the server will no longer work. Remember that punctuation and special characters (i.e., %#@) cannot be included in the server's name.

- **Comment**   This handy field allows you to enter a comment for the CD server. A comment may come in handy—such as denoting the server's physical location or administrator's contact information.

- **Current Date/Current Time**   The server's internal calendar will be set according to the information in these fields.

- **Time Zone**   Find and select your correct time zone in this field.

Copy   Copy options let you set the default destination for CD images copied from the server (see Figure 18-14). This is particularly important information because it affects where CD information is stored.

- **Select Disk**   Select the internal hard drive that you'll use as the default destination for CD image files.

- **Cabinet Name**   Enter the name of the "cabinet" (or folder) you wish to use as the default destination for CD images—if no such cabinet exists, it will be created.

- **Image Name**   Enter a name to be used as a default image name—this will be used only in the event that the Volume Name on the CD is blank.

- **Copy image in compressed mode**   Check this box to save CD images in a compressed format. However, if the CD image is compressed, file sharing is *not* possible because the compressed image file cannot be read by other PCs.

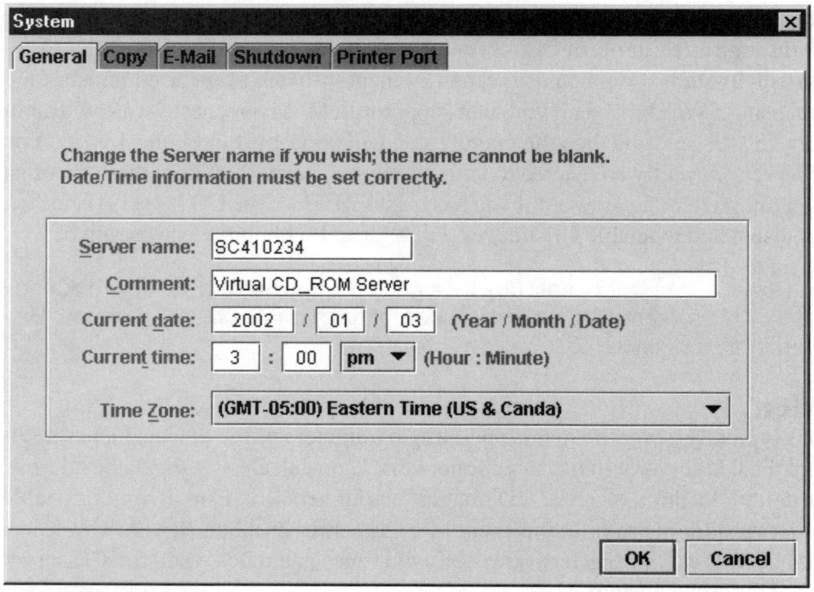

FIGURE 18-13   General settings can be used to make basic configuration changes to the CD server.

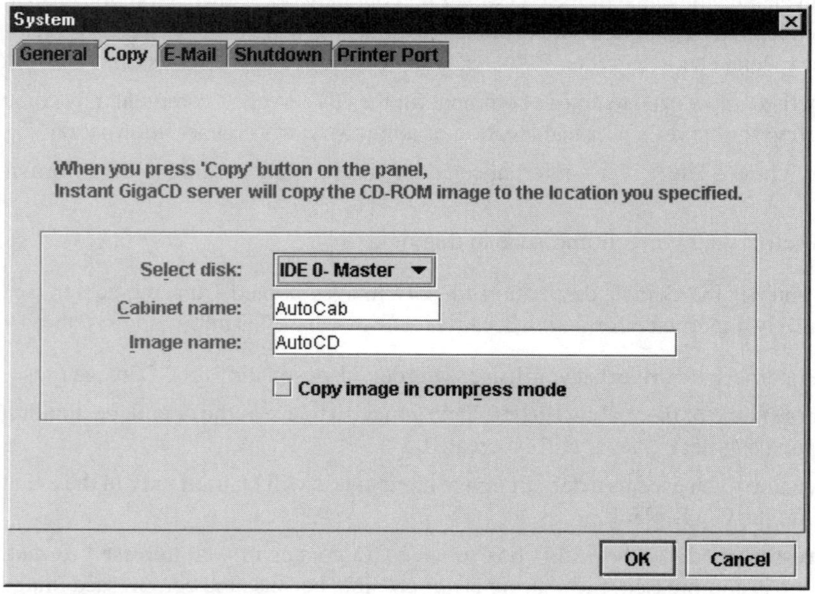

FIGURE 18-14   Copy options allow you to set a destination for CD image files.

E-Mail   Some CD servers can send an e-mail message or alert to an administrator or authorized technician. This can be a very important feature in busy networks where problems must be identified and corrected as soon as possible. To use e-mail messages, you must enable e-mail support, enter the destination e-mail address for any such messages, and denote a subject line (i.e., "CD Server Problem") for e-mail messages.

If you enable e-mail messages, be sure to test the messaging system so you know that e-mail is being sent as expected.

Shutdown   Some CD servers provide a mechanism to shut down the unit, or schedule routine shutdowns for maintenance and service. Using the Shutdown dialog box, you can shut down or reboot the server on-demand or set a shutdown schedule. After a shutdown, you must manually switch the server back on. Typical options include

- **Reboot**   Select this option to restart the server on demand.
- **Shutdown now**   Select this option to shut down the server immediately. After shutting down, the server will not restart.
- **Shutdown in xxx minutes**   This option will start a delayed shutdown with a maximum delay of 999 minutes.
- **Start**   This button will begin the selected action.
- **Weekdays/Saturday/Sunday**   Select the appropriate check box to schedule a shutdown, then enter the time when you'd like the shutdown to occur.
- **Save**   This button will save the scheduled data.

Network Configuration

Network configuration options typically cover the issues related to network operations. The TCP/IP tab lets you adjust IP address and related data (including the DHCP server function). The DNS tab lets you configure DNS entries. Finally, a Networking tab organizes information needed to identify the unit (such as Workgroup Name and Code Page).

TCP/IP   You can use the TCP/IP dialog box (such as in Figure 18-15) to alter DHCP and IP address settings for the CD server. Ordinarily, these parameters are established when the device is first configured, but you can change them as needed.

- **DHCP Client**   A DHCP (Dynamic Host Configuration Protocol) server provides an IP address to PCs and other devices on the network. This should be selected if you have a DHCP server on your network.
- **Fixed IP Address**   If your network does not have a DHCP server, select this option and enter the appropriate IP data.
- **IP Address**   The selected IP address must be unused and compatible with the other devices on your network. This usually means that the first three fields should be the same as your PC and the last field should be an unused number between one and 254.
- **Network Mask**   This should be the same network mask used by the other devices on your network.
- **Gateway (Router)**   If your network has a router or other gateway, enter its IP address here.
- **Enable DHCP Server**   When this option is enabled, the server will provide IP addresses and related data to other, networked PCs upon request. To use this feature, the PCs in your network must be

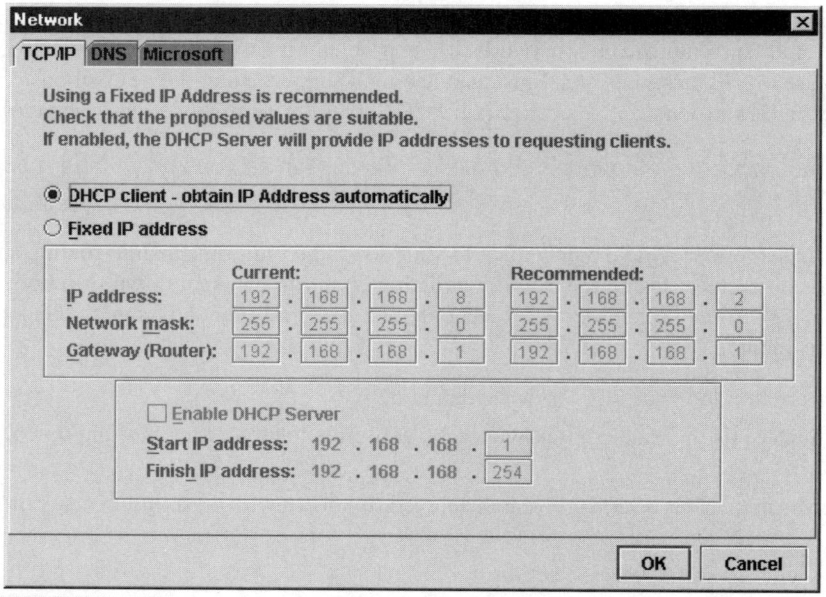

FIGURE 18-15   The TCP/IP tab lets you configure the CD server for other network segments, or even find an IP address automatically.

configured as DHCP clients. If enabled, you should enter at least one DNS (Domain Name Server) value on the DNS tab. Never enable this if you already have a DHCP server in your network.

■ **Start IP Address**   Enter the first number in the range of IP addresses in your network to be allocated by the DHCP Server. This number must be between one and 254.

■ **Finish IP Address**   Enter the last number in the range of IP addresses in your network to be allocated by the DHCP Server. The range should be large enough to cover all the possible DHCP clients.

DNS   The DNS tab allows you to enter up to three DNS IP addresses so that the CD server can find the DNS server on your network. IP address entry one is for the first DNS server, but the second and third IP addresses are optional. You will need to enter this IP information (for the first IP address at least) if you're using the CD server as a DHCP server. If you're using the CD server as a DHCP client (there's another network device acting as the DHCP server), you may leave these IP address entries blank.

Networking   The Networking tab is used to enter information necessary to identify the device on a Microsoft-compatible network. For example, the unit's workgroup name should match the name of your network's workgroup (though users in other workgroups will still be able to use the CD server). A code page entry lets you select the geographic region where you're running the server. This tab may also let you enable the WINS client and enter the WINS server IP address (if your network is using WINS).

IMAGE MANAGEMENT

The entire purpose of a CD server is to create "disc images" from CDs to an internal hard drive, then allow PCs on the network to share those CD images—effectively replacing a CD jukebox. Ultimately, you'll need to create CD images, manage those images, and allow other PCs on the network to use those images.

To accomplish this, you'll need to use the CD server's management utility, and install client software on PCs that access the CD server.

Cabinets

CD images can be organized and stored in folders on the CD server (sometimes called *cabinets*). However, cabinets cannot be nested—that is, one cabinet cannot be placed inside another. For example, to create a new cabinet, start the server's management software. Once the software is running, select File | New | Cabinet from the menu, and enter the new cabinet's name (see Figure 18-16). You can modify the new cabinet's description by selecting the Properties icon and entering the new description. You can also cut, copy, paste, and delete cabinets (or CD images) to organize your data, but you cannot copy a CD image from one server to another.

Creating an Image

To create an image file for a CD, place the new CD in the server and close the unit. If the server's management software isn't running already, start it now. You can click an icon to start the build process, or use the menu such as File | New | CD. A new CD image dialog box will appear, such as in Figure 18-17, and you'll need to enter some information about the new image:

- **Use Compression** If this is selected, the CD image file is stored in compressed form, and will occupy less space on the hard disk. However, selecting Use Compression prevents file sharing.

- **File Sharing** If this option is selected, users within your network will be able to access the CD images on the server.

- **Name** Enter the name for this CD image here.

- **Description** Enter a description of the CD image's contents here.

- **CD-Key** This is the serial number or other identifier from the original CD, which some programs will require to access the CD image.

- **Cabinet** Select the cabinet on the server where the image is to be stored.

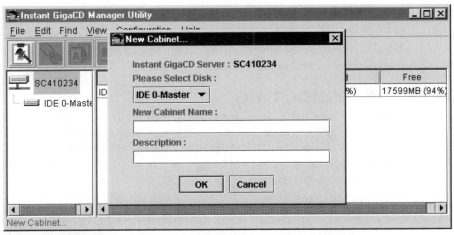

FIGURE 18-16   Create a new cabinet to hold CD image files.

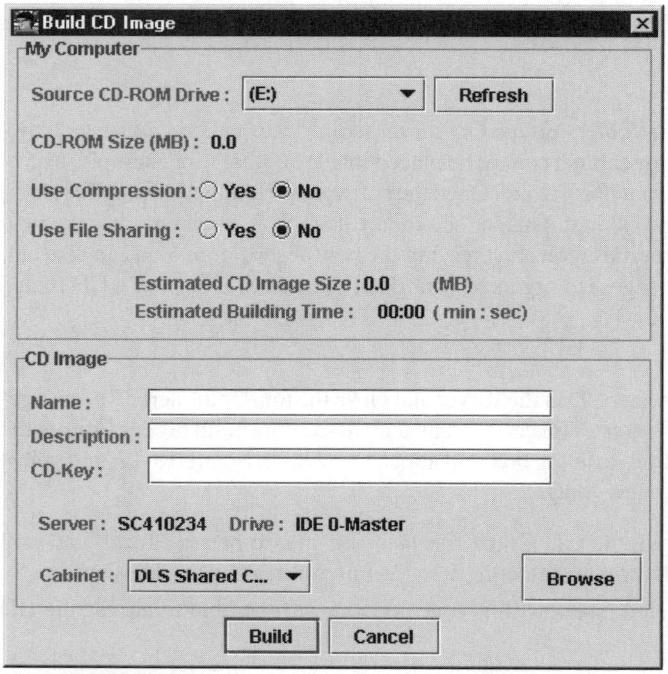

FIGURE 18-17   Set up your CD image file using the
Build CD Image dialog box.

After completing the new CD image dialog box, click Build to start creating the CD image. Building a CD image requires processing on the CD server, and may slow access for other users—it is best to build new images when the server is being lightly used. You can suspend the build process by using the Pause/Resume button, or press Cancel to stop the build process completely.

Using an Image
You'll need to install client software on each workstation that accesses the CD server. This will install the CD server's driver on each PC, and install a selector program to enable access to CD image files. Use the selector program on each workstation to locate the server (see Figure 18-18), and the CD images are then available to that PC as if a real CD were located in the local CD-ROM drive.

CD SERVER TROUBLESHOOTING
CD servers are intended to provide easy installation, good performance, and long-term reliability on your network (mainly because many CD image files can be stored and accessed without the need for a large, cumbersome CD jukebox)—but this doesn't mean that they're problem-free. As an administrator or technician, you should understand the important issues needed to support typical CD server devices, and familiarize yourself with the most common symptoms.

Disk Diagnostics
Devices like the Linksys GigaCD Server incorporate an internal hard drive to store CD image files. Over time, these hard drives may experience bad sectors or other disk errors that will compromise the CD

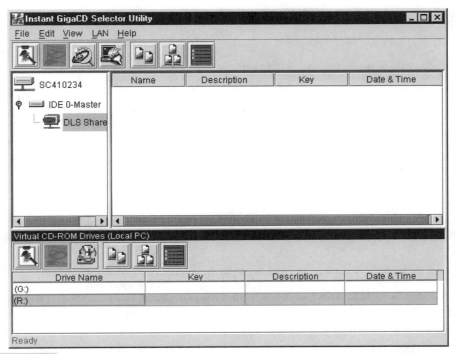

FIGURE 18-18   The CD server's "selector" utility lets you access CD image files.

images, or make the images inaccessible. A technician or administrator should check the disk status periodically to verify that the CD server is running properly. If your CD server provides disk diagnostics (see Figure 18-19), you can check your disk and take corrective action if necessary.

Activity Log

Most CD server devices will maintain an activity log that can help in management and troubleshooting tasks. Some servers write their activity log to an external text file, but others will record an internal log accessible from the device's utility menu. When trouble is reported with server access or performance, always check the log before taking corrective action.

Firmware Upgrades

If your CD server provides a firmware upgrade utility, you may use this feature to upgrade the device's firmware. In most cases, you'll need to download the updated firmware file from the manufacturer first. Open the upgrade utility and enter the full path of the upgrade file (i.e., **c:\program files\Virtual CD-Rom Utility\manager\DS36799.rpm**), then start the update process. Remember that the server will be unavailable during the upgrade process, and all connections are lost (including the one used to start the upgrade). The upgrade procedure may take up to ten minutes. Once the upgrade is completed, reboot the CD server (if it does not do so automatically) and reestablish the connection to your network, and clients may once again access the CD images.

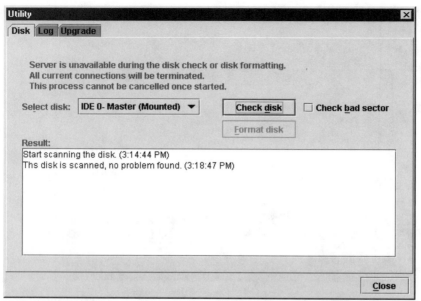

FIGURE 18-19   Utilities allow you to check the disk(s) and report any problems.

SYMPTOMS

Although most CD server units are designed to provide "plug and play" storage solutions for your network, there are some common problems that can occur. Most trouble can be corrected through visual checks and configuration changes, but this part of the issue outlines a series of specific problems that demand detailed corrective actions to resolve.

SYMPTOM 18-14   **You cannot connect to the CD server to configure it.**   Always check power and connections first. Make sure that the NAS is connected to a power source and the power light is on. Plug in the unit and power it on if necessary. If the unit is powered on, check that the LAN light is on. If not, check your network cable connection. Use the cable that came with the unit. Insert the cable into the connection labeled "LAN" on the back of the CD server. Insert the other end into a suitable network connection (i.e., 10/100BaseT Ethernet) on your network hub or switch—they should be on the same network segment. Try a different port on the hub or switch, or try a different network cable. If you're using a hub or switch with an uplink port, avoid using the uplink port unless you have the Uplink button in the proper position.

IP addresses may be another issue. Make sure that your suspect workstation is using an IP address within the range compatible with the CD server. For example, a range of **192.168.0.3** to **192.168.0.254** would be compatible with a CD server's default IP address of **192.168.0.2**. If the problem persists, reboot the CD server and see if the trouble clears. Otherwise, the unit may be experiencing problems and require replacement.

SYMPTOM 18-15   **Your workstation cannot find the CD server when browsing the network.**   This can usually be traced to a TCP/IP problem on the workstation. First verify that the TCP/IP protocol is installed on the workstation—if not, add the protocol. Also verify that the TCP/IP protocol is bound to your network card (NIC). Select your network card, click Properties, and then click the Bindings tab. If TCP/IP is not checked, select it now. The TCP/IP and network card must also be bound to the Client for Microsoft Networks service. Select the TCP/IP entry for your network card, click Properties, and then click the Bindings tab. If Client for Microsoft Networks is not checked, select it now.

There may also be a problem with IP addressing. If you don't have a router, check that your IP address is compatible with the CD server's IP address. It needs to be from the same address range (i.e., **192.168.0.3** to **192.168.0.254**) and use the same subnet mask (i.e., **255.255.255.0**). If you do have a router, check that your gateway IP address is set correctly.

SYMPTOM 18-16 **You cannot change the CD server's drive letter under Windows 2000.** A Windows 2000 system only allows one CD drive be assigned on installation—the drive letter cannot be changed (the next drive letter will always be used). After the first installation and reboot, you can use the CD server's Setup feature to create new virtual CD-ROM drives and set their drive letters as desired. When you do this, you need to reboot. After rebooting, Windows 2000 will prompt you to reboot a second time. There is no need for a second reboot—you can cancel this prompt.

SYMPTOM 18-17 **An error reports "Low disk space".** CD image files are stored on the server's hard drive. This error usually means that less than 10 percent of the space on the disk is available to store image files. Delete any image files that are no longer used (such as old clipart or archival images) using the CD server's management software. If you continue to receive the alert, consider upgrading your existing CD server to include a second drive, consider upgrading the CD server to higher-capacity drives, or add another CD server to the network.

SYMPTOM 18-18 **You're not receiving e-mail alerts from the CD server.** You configure the CD server to send you alerts by e-mail, but even though alerts are being generated, you're not receiving them. This type of problem can almost always be traced to CD server configuration errors. First, confirm that you've enabled e-mail alerts, and entered the proper e-mail address to receive them. Try sending a test message to confirm that the e-mail information you entered is correct. Also make sure that you have elected to receive all alerts and messages—if you elected no alerts, no alerts will be sent.

SAN Basics

Most small to mid-sized networks employ traditional server-based storage principles. That is, storage takes place on servers, local PCs, or in "storage appliances" (such as the Maxtor NAS 3000 or Linksys GigaCD Server you've seen earlier in this chapter). While this approach is simple to understand and easy to implement, the sheer amount of data traveling over the network media (cable) can result in storage performance bottlenecks—a problem that worsens quickly as networks become larger. Some networks have enhanced storage performance with load-balancing and aggregation techniques. For example, a server may employ several NIC ports rather than just one, so the server (and its available storage) can be accessed using more than one "connection." In addition, the server can remain accessible if one or more connection should fail. This idea is taken a step further with "server clustering," where multiple servers can be aggregated together to provide a service (i.e., file serving).

Still, large networks face three perplexing storage problems: application-shared databases, busy applications, and high-availability demands. An *application-shared database* supports multiple types of applications from common information. When shared databases are used in applications that are distributed across multiple servers, the database itself must also be distributed, which can cause database synchronization problems. *Busy applications* may cause a similar problem. Most businesses have a few core applications that most users must access. Often the activity on these critical applications is high enough to load a single server excessively, but dividing the application across multiple servers produces the "shared database" problem. *High-availability* issues are another important concern. A single server may be able to carry the entire load storage, but it can't provide insurance against hardware/software problems. If a parallel server is used to back up the primary server, databases must be synchronized between the two, and we're back to shared database problems.

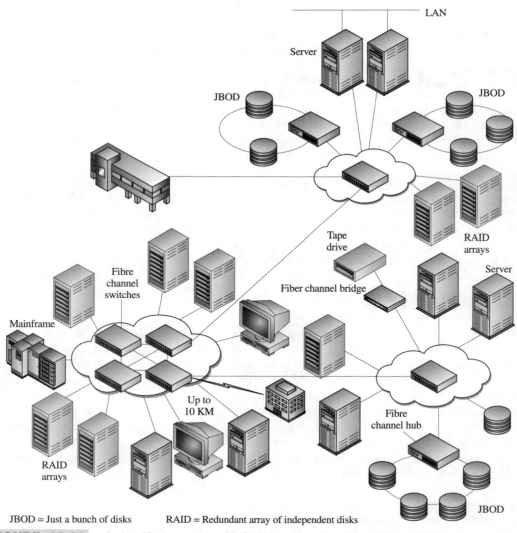

JBOD = Just a bunch of disks   RAID = Redundant array of independent disks

FIGURE 18-20   A simplified example of a SAN in action (courtesy of NetworkMagazine.com)

UNDERSTANDING THE SAN

Network developers have resolved these issues using a *storage area network* (or SAN). Simply stated, a SAN is a separate network for servers and storage devices existing alongside your LAN, and connected with dedicated high-speed switches dubbed *storage servers* (see Figure 18-20). Data can even be moved between SAN devices without having to be processed through a host server. SANs provide a versatile "any-to-any" mechanism for multiple servers to access multiple disk resources—a kind of disk-sharing technology that takes place behind the server. On the SAN side, each server is connected to a switching infrastructure (typically Fibre Channel or Gigabit Ethernet connections) that provides access to individual storage arrays set up as nodes on the SAN.

A typical SAN will generally comprise servers attached through a SAN interface adapter card that emulates a standard disk interface (such as SCSI) to the server. In addition, a SAN will include storage devices (tapes and disk arrays), and bridges and multiplexers, all connected to Fibre Channel (or high-speed Ethernet) switches. As with LANs or WANs, the switches furnish the backbone for all connected devices, with one or more switches acting as a Fibre Channel switching fabric. SAN switch fabrics allow attachments of thousands of nodes supporting vast amounts of storage.

FC-based SANs also can incorporate a Fibre Channel Arbitrated Loop (FC-AL), a type of shared-media network. The FC-AL architecture allows for up to 126 devices per loop (either attached directly to Fibre Channel switches, or to hubs that in turn connect to switches). Further, Fibre Channel SANs help take the load off servers, which have historically been given the added burden of transferring data to storage devices and to the LAN. Now, servers can offload data transfer to the SAN itself, and quickly return to their original processing role. With a SAN, a server simply monitors the storage process rather than directly controlling it.

When planning Ethernet as the SAN connection architecture, don't share devices or Ethernet trunks between the SAN and LAN/WAN. Storage network traffic levels are very high and can severely impair network performance for other applications. Contention between SAN and LAN/WAN traffic creates timing problems between the two that are nearly impossible to reproduce—and correct.

FIBRE CHANNEL CONSIDERATIONS

Fibre Channel SANs can be designed as both *shared-media* and *switched-access* networks (sometimes a mix of the two). In shared-media SANs, all devices share the same gigabit loop. Unfortunately, throughput goes down as more devices are added. While this might be acceptable for very small environments, a backbone based on Fibre Channel switches will increase a SAN's aggregate throughput. One or more switches can be used to create the Fibre Channel switching fabric. Accessing the services available from the switching fabric is possible only if the network interface card of each storage device can connect to the fabric as well as to the operating system and the applications. Basically, the NIC becomes a part of the storage network by logging into the fabric. This function is simply called fabric login, and it's important to use NICs that support fabric login in building a SAN.

Another key issue for devices attached to the SAN is the ability to discover all the devices in the switching fabric. Fibre Channel defines a discovery mechanism (called *simple name service* or SNS) that learns the address, type, and symbolic name of each device in the switching fabric. SNS information resides in Fibre Channel switches, and NICs and storage controllers request SNS data from the switches. Network managers opting for Fibre Channel should look for Fibre Channel NICs and storage controllers that support SNS.

For error recovery and fault isolation, Fibre Channel has an optional feature called *registered state change notification* (RSCN). This issues updates to devices on configuration changes. RSCN is frequently used when RAID arrays, non-RAID disks, tape devices, and hosts are directly attached to a switching fabric rather than to shared-access loops (since faulty nodes won't affect any other fabric-attached devices). Switched networks also recover from faults a lot faster than shared-media nets because problem devices or links can be isolated.

SAN MANAGEMENT

In terms of SAN management, network administrators should be able to use all the tools and systems they use for LANs and WANs. That means you should look for SAN devices that can be managed via SNMP or through the Web. Devices also should support Telnet (for remote diagnostics or servicing). All of these management tools should furnish detailed information on device status, performance levels, configuration and topology changes, and historical data. Key status and performance information would include throughput and latency details. Some SAN devices may even deliver tuning and optimization tools.

In FC-AL networks, the FC hub furnishes management information on all devices within the loop, but the hub can't report on devices outside the loop. Of course, when loops are attached to a switching fabric, remote management and diagnostics are possible for all devices.

Further Study

Chi Storage Solutions: **www.chicorporation.com**
Fibre Channel Association: **www.fibrechannel.com**
Linksys: **www.linksys.com**
Maxtor: **www.maxtor.com**
Storage Networking Industry Association (SNIA): **www.snia.org**

19

NETWORK VIRUS PROTECTION

While most of the software products in the marketplace today are useful, constructive, and beneficial, there is also other software that serves a darker purpose—the *computer virus*. Such rogue software is designed to enter a network without the user's knowledge, often hiding in normal programs or even e-mail. Viruses also execute their functions without prompting users for permission, they do not warn of potential dangers to the system, and they do not produce error messages when problems are encountered. Essentially, a computer "virus" is a fragment of executable code that runs secretly and is capable of cloning itself in other programs.

Technically, there is nothing in this definition to indicate that a virus is necessarily *destructive*—that's a twist added by the virus programmers themselves. But legitimate software does not *need* to run secretly, hide itself in other programs, or duplicate itself without a user's knowledge or permission. So the very nature of a computer virus makes it an ideal vehicle for spreading computer chaos. In today's networked world, where all manner of LANs depend on Internet access, computer viruses are more pervasive and dangerous than ever. This chapter is intended to explain the nature and operations of computer viruses, show you how they spread and manifest themselves, and explain some procedures you can take to protect your network users from their effects.

Virus Basics

We use the term *virus* to describe virtually any type of destructive software. Although this is a good, general term, it is also a misnomer—a virus is actually only one of many destructive software types. There are many types of recognized rogue software, and most are considered every bit as hazardous as a virus. Each type of software has a different mode of operation. As a technician, you should understand how these classic software types operate.

Today, you may see the term *malware* used more frequently to describe destructive software.

SOFTWARE BUGS

A *software bug* is basically an error in program coding or logic that results in faulty or unexpected operation. Bugs are rarely intentional, but the vast majority of *serious* system-crippling bugs are caught during the developer's alpha and beta testing processes. In order for serious bugs to get through into a finished product (the kind of bugs that can cause serious memory errors or hard drive file loss), the developer would have to do little (if any) testing on various PC platforms. Serious bugs are certainly not intended as malicious, but they suggest a dangerous lack of concern on the part of the software developer. There are two clues that suggest the presence of software bugs: first, it is only a single program (usually the one you just installed or started using) that causes the problem, and the problem will not be detected by any anti-virus tool (the application will be reported as clean). Software containing serious or persistent bugs is often referred to as "bug ware". Fortunately, bugs are usually corrected by software patches or updates from the manufacturer.

TROJAN HORSES

The *Trojan horse* is largely considered the grandparent of today's virulent software. It is a destructive computer program concealed in the guise of a useful, run-of-the-mill program such as word processor or graphics program. Well-developed user shells or seemingly normal operations trick the user into believing that the program is harmless—until the virulent code is triggered—then the program's *true* nature is revealed. The Trojan horse tactic is the most popular means of introducing viruses by distributing seemingly harmless software that actually contains virulent code. Fortunately, most virulent code can be detected by scanning new software before it is executed for the first time. To prevent the spread of Trojan horses, be suspicious of unwanted or unsolicited software arriving through the mail, or as e-mail attachments. Also beware of software that sounds *too good* to be true (i.e., a TSR that will increase Windows performance by 100 times, get SVGA graphics on an EGA video adapter, use AOL for free, and so on).

SOFTWARE BOMBS

The *software bomb* is just what the name implies—when the infected program is launched, the virulent "bomb" code executes almost immediately and does its damage. Software bombs typically contain no bells or whistles—unlike a virus, they also make little effort to cloak themselves, and almost no effort to replicate. As a consequence, the software bomb is quick and easy to develop. Its somewhat clumsy nature also makes it fairly easy to spot with anti-virus tools.

LOGIC BOMBS

Where the software bomb is used for immediate and indiscriminate destruction, a *logic bomb* is set to go off when a particular logical condition is met. For example, the logic bomb may "detonate" (erase files, calculate subsequent payroll records incorrectly, reformat the disk, or so on) if payroll records indicate that the bomb's author is fired or laid off, or their payroll statements do not appear for over four weeks. A logic bomb can be triggered by virtually any system condition. However, the "bomb" approach is also fairly easy to spot with anti-virus techniques.

TIME BOMBS

Instead of triggering a bomb immediately or through system status conditions, a *time bomb* uses time or repetition conditionals. For example, a time bomb can be set to "detonate" after some number of program runs, on a particular day (i.e., April 1st or Friday 13th), or at a certain time (i.e., midnight). Time bombs are often used as a means of "making a statement" about a particular date and time. This kind of bomb architecture is relatively easy to spot with anti-virus tools. You can research current activation dates at **www.mcafee.com/anti-virus/**. The advantage of a virus calendar is that you can quickly reference potential virus problems, then search for more detailed information from a virus library such as **vil.mcafee.com**.

REPLICATORS

The purpose of a *replicator* (also called a *rabbit*) is to drain system resources. It accomplishes this function by cloning copies of itself. Each clone copy is launched by the parent that created it. Before long, the multitude of copies on disk and in memory soak up so many resources that the system can no longer function. In effect, the system is crippled until the copies are removed and the replicating virus is eliminated. This type of behavior is particularly effective at shutting down large, multiuser systems or networks. Since the virulent code is self-replicating, it is easy to spot with anti-virus tools.

WORMS

The *worm* was one of the first rogue software types known to attack computer networks. The worm travels from computer to computer—usually without doing any real damage. Worms typically replicate in order to continue traveling through the network, and attempt to delete all traces of their presence. A worm is another typical network presence used to seek out and selectively alter or destroy a limited number of files or programs. For example, a worm can be used to enter a network and alter or erase passwords. Since worms can be tailored for specific jobs, they are often difficult to spot unless the worm is known.

VIRUSES

The most recognized and dynamic type of rogue software is the *virus*. A virus modifies other programs to include executable virulent code—in some cases, the virulent code mutates and changes as it is copied. Expertly engineered viruses do not change the infected file date, time stamps, file size, its attributes, or its checksums. As a result, viruses can be extremely difficult to detect and even harder to erase. The task becomes even more difficult as viruses become increasingly powerful and sophisticated. With today's "high overhead" operating systems such as Windows 9x/Me/XP and network operating systems like Windows NT/2000, viruses can usually hide and replicate quite easily in any of the numerous **.DLL** files, **.VXD** files, or other modules normally in operation. Given their predilection toward stealth and replication, viruses tend to linger in systems to spread themselves between hard drives and floppy disks, and network connections where they disrupt data, cause system errors, and generally degrade system performance. Eventually, most viruses will self-destruct, typically taking the hard drive files with them.

Virus Types

As you might have suspected, all virulent code is not created equal. Viruses are as varied as legitimate application software, and each technique provides the virus author with an array of advantages and disadvantages. Some viral techniques are preferred because they are more difficult to detect and remove, but require extra resources to develop. Other viral techniques are easier to develop, but lack the stealth and sophistication that more powerful viruses demand. Still other viral techniques stand a better chance of infecting multiple systems.

Boot-Sector Viruses   Early PCs loaded their operating systems from floppy disks. Virus authors quickly discovered that they could substitute their own program for the executable code present on the boot sector of every floppy disk formatted with DOS—whether or not it included system files. Unsuspecting users thus loaded the virus into memory every time they started their computers with an infected disk. Once in memory, a virus can copy itself to boot sectors on other floppy or hard disks. For example, those who unintentionally loaded "Brain" from an infected floppy found themselves reading an "advertisement" for a computer consulting company in Pakistan. With that advertisement, Brain pioneered another characteristic feature of modern viruses—the *payload*. The payload is the prank or malicious behavior that (if triggered) causes effects that range from annoying messages to data destruction. It's the virus characteristic that draws the most attention. Many virus authors now write their viruses specifically to deliver their payloads to as many computers as possible.

For a time, sophisticated descendants of this first boot-sector virus represented the most serious virus threat to computer users. Variants of boot-sector viruses also infect the master boot record (MBR), which stores partition information. Nearly every step in the boot process (from reading the MBR to loading the operating system) is vulnerable to viral sabotage. Some of the most tenacious and destructive viruses still include the ability to infect your computer's boot sector or MBR. Loading a boot-sector virus at boot time can give a virus a chance to do its work before your anti-virus software has a chance to run. Some anti-virus tools anticipate this possibility by allowing you to create an "emergency disk" that you can use to boot your computer and remove infections.

File Infection Viruses   At about the same time as the authors of the Brain virus found vulnerabilities in the DOS boot sector, other virus writers found out how to use existing software to help replicate their creations. An early example of this type of virus showed up in computers at Lehigh University in Pennsylvania. The virus infects part of the DOS command interpreter (**COMMAND.COM**), which it uses to load itself into memory—once there, it spreads to other uninfected **COMMAND.COM** files each time a user enters any standard DOS command that involves disk access. Early iterations of this virus limited its spread to floppy disks that contained a full operating system.

Later viruses quickly overcame this limitation—sometimes with fairly clever programming. For example, virus writers might have their virus add its code to the beginning of an executable file. When users start a program, the virus code executes immediately, then transfers control back to the legitimate software (which runs as though nothing unusual has happened). Once it activates, the virus "hooks" or "traps" requests that legitimate software makes to the operating system and substitutes its own responses. Particularly clever viruses can even subvert attempts to clear them from memory by trapping the CTRL-ALT-DEL keyboard sequence for a warm reboot, then faking a restart. Sometimes the only outward indication that anything on your system is amiss (before any payload "detonates") might be a small change in the file size of infected legitimate software.

Stealth, Mutating, Encrypted, and Polymorphic Viruses   As unobtrusive as they might appear, changes in file size and other scant evidence of a virus infection usually gives most anti-virus software enough of a clue to locate and remove the offending code. One of the virus writer's principal challenges is to find ways to hide their handiwork. The earliest disguises used a mixture of innovative programming and obvious giveaways. For instance, the Brain virus redirected requests to see a disk's boot sector away from the actual location of the infected sector to the new location of the boot files, which the virus had moved. This "stealth" capability enabled this and other viruses to hide from conventional search techniques.

Because viruses needed to avoid continuously reinfecting host systems (doing so would quickly balloon an infected file's size to easily detectable proportions, or would consume enough system resources to point to an obvious culprit), virus authors also needed to tell them to leave certain files alone. They addressed this problem by having the virus write a code "signature" that would flag infected files with the software equivalent of a "do not disturb" sign. Although that kept the virus from giving itself away immediately, it opened the way for anti-virus software to use the code "signatures" themselves to find the virus.

In response, virus writers found ways to conceal the code signatures. Some viruses would "mutate" or write different code signatures with each new infection. Others encrypted most of the code signature or the virus itself—leaving only a couple of bytes to use as a key for decryption. The most sophisticated new viruses employ stealth, mutation, and encryption to appear in an almost undetectable variety of new forms. Finding these "polymorphic" viruses requires software engineers to develop very elaborate programming techniques for anti-virus software.

Macro Viruses   By 1995 or so, the virus war had come to something of a standstill. New viruses appeared continuously (prompted in part by the availability of ready-made virus "kits" that enabled even some nonprogrammers to whip up a new virus in no time). Most existing anti-virus software could easily be updated to detect and dispose of the new virus variants, which consisted primarily of minor tweaks to well-known templates.

But 1995 marked the emergence of the "concept" virus, which added a new and surprising twist to virus history. Before "concept" viruses, most virus researchers thought of data files (the text, spreadsheet, or drawing documents created by the software you use) as *immune* to infection. Viruses, after all, *are* programs, and as such needed to be run the same way executable software did in order to do their damage. On the other hand, data files are simply stored information that you entered when you worked with your software.

That distinction melted away when Microsoft began adding "macro" capabilities to Word and Excel—the flagship applications in its Office suite. Using a stripped-down version of its Visual BASIC language, users could create document templates that would automatically format and add other features to documents created with Word and Excel. Virus writers seized the opportunity that this presented to conceal and spread viruses in documents that you, the user, created yourself. The exploding popularity of the Internet and of e-mail software that allows users to attach files to messages ensured that macro viruses would spread very quickly and very widely. By the late 1990s, macro viruses had become the most potent virus threat ever.

Java and ActiveX   Programs based on Java and ActiveX come in a variety of forms. Some are special-purpose miniature applications (or "applets") written in Java—a relatively new programming language first developed by Sun Microsystems. Others are developed using ActiveX—a Microsoft technology that programmers can use for similar purposes.

Both Java and ActiveX make extensive use of prewritten software modules (or "objects") that programmers can write themselves, or take from existing sources and fashion into the plug-ins, applets, device drivers, and other software needed to power the Web. Java objects are called "classes," while

ActiveX objects are called "controls." The principle difference between them lies in how they run on the host system. Java applets run in a Java "virtual machine" designed especially to interpret Java programming and translate it into action on the host machine, while ActiveX controls run as native Windows programs that link and pass data between existing Windows software.

The overwhelming majority of these objects are useful (even necessary) parts of any interactive Web site. But despite the best efforts of Sun and Microsoft engineers to design security measures into them, determined programmers can use Java and ActiveX tools to plant harmful objects on Web sites, where they can lurk until visitors unwittingly allow them access to vulnerable computer systems. Unlike viruses, harmful Java and ActiveX objects usually don't seek self-replication as their primary goal—the Web provides them with plenty of opportunities to spread to target computer systems, while their small size and innocuous nature makes it easy for them to evade detection. In fact, unless you specifically tell your browser software to block them, Java and ActiveX objects automatically download to your system whenever you visit a Web site that employs them.

Instead, harmful objects exist to deliver their equivalent of a virus payload. For example, programmers have written objects that can read data from your hard disk and send it back to the Web site you visited. These objects can "hijack" your e-mail account and send out offensive messages in your name, or they can watch data that passes between your computer and other computers.

Practical Anti-Virus Components

Today, anti-virus software is far more than just a simple command-line-driven utility. Modern anti-virus software (especially network anti-virus software) is actually a combination of powerful interrelated tools that each serve a specific purpose on your system. This part of the chapter examines the components of a current anti-virus software package such as Norton AntiVirus Corporate Edition.

This discussion is for example purposes only. Your own anti-virus software may use more or fewer components, but the basic suite of features will probably be quite similar.

- Symantec System Center (console applet and Alert Management System), which you use to centrally manage Symantec products and alerting functions.
- Norton AntiVirus Corporate Edition management snap-in, which extends the Symantec System Center console so you can manage Norton AntiVirus Corporate Edition on servers and clients.
- Norton AntiVirus Corporate Edition (and includes support for Windows NT/2000 Servers, NetWare Servers, Windows NT/2000 clients, Windows 9x/Me/XP clients, and Windows 3.x/DOS clients).
- LiveUpdate Administration Utility, which you can use to download updates to your intranet FTP server or other internal server. Servers and clients then retrieve updates from the designated server.
- Central Quarantine, which you can use to centrally manage infected files detected on servers and clients.
- Norton AntiVirus Corporate Edition includes a Microsoft Management Console snap-in. Use this snap-in to manage Norton AntiVirus Corporate Edition from the Symantec System Center console.
- Importer tool, which you can use to import computers located in non-WINS environments.
- Roaming Client Support, which you can use to ensure that Norton AntiVirus Corporate Edition clients (including mobile clients) are assigned to the best servers based on speed and proximity.
- ACL Fix Tool, which limits Registry writes on a Windows NT platform to administrators.

SCANNING

Of course, the best anti-virus software available won't do any good unless it's configured to seek out viruses and actively protect your network. Modern anti-virus tools allow you to perform several types of scanning for both routine and on-demand situations. For example, the Symantec System Center console (managing Norton AntiVirus) lets you configure the following scans for servers and clients:

- **Virus sweeps** This lets you inspect all drives on all servers and clients belonging to the selected "object"—normally a group of systems on the network that you've defined. Virus sweeps provide immediate results from a scan on large areas of the network (or the entire network).

- **Manual (on-demand) scans** Use this feature to inspect selected folders and drives on selected computers. Manual scans provide immediate results from a scan on a small area of the network or a local hard drive, and are particularly useful for testing suspect PCs without bogging down large areas of the network.

- **Scheduled scans** This feature lets you inspect selected folders and drives on selected computers at a predetermined time or regular schedule (i.e., daily or weekly). Scheduled scans are ideal for large areas of the network because you can run the scans during off-hours when network traffic is low.

- **Realtime scans** These scans inspect files as they are read from or written to a server or client computer in real time. Norton AntiVirus also lets you configure native e-mail scanning for 32-bit client computers.

You can also set up manual, scheduled, and real-time scans for folders and files on the Norton AntiVirus Corporate Edition client, and select two additional types of scans:

- **Custom scans** Run a scan manually at a later time.
- **Startup scans** Run a scan automatically when the client computer starts.

Virus Sweeps

From the anti-virus management software (i.e., Symantec System Center console), you can launch an immediate scan of both servers and clients with a single button. You can perform a *virus sweep* by selecting the entire system (aka, System Hierarchy), one or more server groups, or one or more servers in the Symantec System Center console tree. After starting a virus sweep on the System Hierarchy, you'll know within minutes that your entire network is virus-free (you do not have to send messages that ask users to scan their computers to ensure that the network is clean). The virus sweep ensures that there are no viruses on servers or workstations.

 You cannot interrupt or stop a virus sweep of the network after it has started. You must let it finish.

Manual Scans

A *manual scan* quickly lets you investigate a targeted area of your network. Unlike the virus sweep—which scans *all* files on all drives—you can configure a manual scan to narrow the scope of your scans. From the anti-virus management software (i.e., Symantec System Center console), you can launch an immediate scan of one or more Norton AntiVirus Corporate Edition servers in the same server group, or one or more clients managed by the same Norton AntiVirus server.

Scheduled Scans

From the anti-virus management software (i.e., Symantec System Center console), you can set up a scan to run at a specific time of day using daily, weekly, or monthly intervals. Scheduled scans must be created separately for servers and clients. For example, schedule server scans by selecting server groups or a server in the Symantec System Center console tree, or schedule client scans by selecting a server or a client in the Symantec System Center Console tree. One handy suggestion is to time your scheduled scans to closely follow your schedule for updating virus definitions files so that any newly introduced viruses are handled efficiently.

Real-Time Scans

From the anti-virus management software (i.e., Symantec System Center console), you can set up file system real-time protection on both Norton AntiVirus Corporate Edition servers and Norton AntiVirus clients. You can set up mail data real-time protection for supported e-mail applications installed on the Norton AntiVirus client. You configure server and client real-time protection separately. After you configure real-time protection, you only need to change it if your network environment or security policy changes.

UNDERSTANDING SERVER SCANS

Regular server scans are particularly important because infections can quickly spread to clients and cripple a busy network. You can scan or configure one or more Norton AntiVirus Corporate Edition servers. The number of servers that you scan or configure depends on the object that you select:

- **All servers in the network**   For example, if you select the entire network (i.e., the System Hierarchy object) in the Symantec System Center console tree, you can run a virus sweep to scan all Norton AntiVirus Corporate Edition servers in the network. A virus sweep scans not only the Norton AntiVirus server, but any Norton AntiVirus clients managed by the server.

- **All servers in selected server groups**   If you select the System Hierarchy object in the Symantec System Center console tree, then select multiple server groups in the right pane, you can either run a virus sweep or configure a scheduled scan. A virus sweep scans all the Norton AntiVirus Corporate Edition servers and their clients in the selected server groups, while a scheduled scan scans only the servers.

- **All servers in a server group**   If you select a server group object, you can run a virus sweep or configure a scheduled scan for all servers in the server group.

- **Some servers in a server group**   If you select the server group object, then select multiple servers in the available list, you can perform either a virus sweep or manual scan on all selected servers (though you cannot select multiple servers to configure scheduled scans).

- **A single server**   If you select a single server object, you can run a virus sweep to scan the server and all of its clients, scan just the server by performing a manual scan, or configure a scan of the server or its clients using a scheduled scan.

UNDERSTANDING CLIENT SCANS

Use the anti-virus management software (i.e., Symantec System Center) to scan or configure one or more Norton AntiVirus Corporate Edition client computers. The level of configuration depends on the object that is selected:

- **All clients in the network**   If you select the entire network (i.e., the System Hierarchy object in the Symantec System Center console tree), you can run a virus sweep to scan all 32-bit and 16-bit Norton AntiVirus Corporate Edition clients in the network. A virus sweep also scans all the Norton AntiVirus servers that manage the clients.

■ **All clients in selected server groups**   If you select the System Hierarchy object in the Symantec System Center console tree, then select multiple server groups in the right pane, you can run a virus sweep. The virus sweep scans all Norton AntiVirus Corporate Edition servers and their 32-bit and 16-bit clients in the selected server groups.

■ **All clients in a single server group**   If you select the server group object, you can run a virus sweep to scan all 32-bit and 16-bit clients in a single server group.

■ **All clients connected to a single server**   If you select a server object, you can run a virus sweep or configure a scheduled scan. The virus sweep scans all 32-bit and 16-bit clients that are managed by the server. The scheduled scan scans only the 32-bit clients that are managed by the server.

■ **Selected 32-bit clients on the same server**   If you select a server in the console tree, then select multiple 32-bit client computers in the right pane, you can perform a manual scan.

■ **A single 32-bit client**   If you select a 32-bit client object, you can perform a manual scan or set up a scheduled scan for only that computer.

■ **16-bit clients**   You cannot individually configure or scan 16-bit client computers. However, 16-bit computers are included in virus sweeps, and you can set real-time protection options for 16-bit clients at the server or server group level.

UNDERSTANDING "FALSE DETECTIONS"

A "false detection" (also called a "false positive") occurs when your anti-virus software sends a virus alert message (or makes a log file entry) that identifies a virus where none actually exists. You're more likely to see false detections if you have anti-virus software from more than one vendor installed on your computer, because some anti-virus software stores the code signatures it uses for detection unprotected in memory. The *safest* course to take when you see an alert message or log entry is to treat it as a genuine virus threat, and to take the appropriate steps to remove the virus from your system. But if you believe that the anti-virus software has generated a false detection (i.e., it flags a file as "infected" when you have used it safely for years), check for one or more of the following situations before you contact the anti-virus software maker:

■ *You have more than one anti-virus program running.* If so, one of the scanners might detect unprotected code signatures that another program uses and report *them* as viruses. To avoid this problem, configure your network to run only one anti-virus program—this may include uninstalling unneeded anti-virus software from servers and clients.

■ *You have a BIOS chip with anti-virus features.* Many current BIOS versions provide anti-virus features (intended to prevent boot sector infection) that can trigger false detections when anti-virus software runs. If a particular client or server reports virus issues, you can try disabling the anti-virus protection in system's BIOS through the CMOS Setup.

■ *You have older PCs on the network.* Some older PCs (from manufacturers like HP) modify the boot sectors on their hard disks each time they start up. Anti-virus software might detect these modifications as viruses—when in fact they are not. To solve the problem, upgrade the offending PC(s), or use the command-line version of your anti-virus software to add validation information to the startup files themselves. This method does not save information about the boot sector or the master boot record.

■ *You have copy-protected software.* Depending on the type of copy protection used, your anti-virus software might detect a virus in the boot sector or the master boot record on some floppy disks or other media. Check with the author of the suspect software and see if there is a patch or update (or other installation option) that will correct this problem.

If none of these conditions are true, you should contact the anti-virus software maker and inform them of the false detection so that they can investigate the matter and make suitable corrections in subsequent patches and data updates.

Anti-Virus Installation

With the exception of a few powerful firewall products that incorporate virus checking "into the box" (like SonicWall's SOHO2 product), anti-virus products are implemented as software (such as Symantec's Norton Internet Security in Figure 19-1) that must be installed on individual PCs. For network users, anti-virus tools must be installed on *both* servers and client PCs. Once the anti-virus software is in place, it must be routinely updated to include the very virus definitions and other protective techniques. This part of the chapter outlines the basic installation of both end-user and network-based anti-virus tools.

INDIVIDUAL PC INSTALLATION

Installing anti-virus software on individual PCs is typically an automatic process—driven by an installation wizard launched by an autorun file when you insert the CD in your drive. Installation is then simply a matter of following the wizard, which will perform an initial scan of the system, copy files to your PC, make the necessary system changes, then reboot the system so that the anti-virus software will be running in the background. If you have a peer-to-peer network established, each peer will need a copy of the anti-virus software.

FIGURE 19-1   Norton Internet Security is a premier anti-virus/firewall tool for PCs and workstations. (Courtesy of Symantec)

With a peer-to-peer network, you will still need a multiuser license to install the anti-virus software on more than one PC. Larger server-based networks will use a corporate (enterprise) edition of the anti-virus tool—including a site license.

NETWORK INSTALLATION

When you're administering a network with one or more servers and numerous client systems, implementing anti-virus software becomes a bit more complicated. You'll certainly need to install anti-virus utilities on your server(s) and clients, but the order in which you install the products can be important. For example, Symantec recommends the following order for their corporate edition of Norton AntiVirus:

1. Install Symantec System Center before you install the Norton AntiVirus Corporate Edition management snap-in.

2. Install the Norton AntiVirus Corporate Edition management snap-in before you attempt to manage Norton AntiVirus Corporate Edition from the Symantec System Center console.

3. Roll out Norton AntiVirus Corporate Edition to servers before you roll out Norton AntiVirus Corporate Edition to clients. If you install to clients first, they will not be able to connect to a Norton AntiVirus Corporate Edition server and will run in "unmanaged" mode.

4. Install other products and utilities in the order that works best for you.

Lab Testing on Servers

One of the risks with important network software is unexpected interruptions (i.e., network crashes) due to unforeseen problems with the new software. For example, if the new anti-virus software isn't compatible with other software on the server or client(s), you may suffer performance problems, crashes, and other problems. Before you perform a full-scale installation, it's a good policy to install the anti-virus software in a remote (noncritical) lab environment for a learning and evaluation period. This lets you examine the software closely, familiarize yourself with its options, and address any compatibility or performance issues before full enterprise deployment.

For best testing results, install the anti-virus software on at least two servers, mixing Windows NT/2000 and NetWare if needed. The communication protocols in your test environment should match those in your actual network environment. Also, include routers in your test environment (particularly for mixed protocol environments). Perform a complete install to each server, including any important management utilities. After installing the software to your test servers, take the following steps:

1. Configure virus scanning options for maximum protection (i.e., scan all files, all drives, and so on).

2. Test maintenance features like virus definition file downloads and server-to-server updates.

3. Create a virus test file (not a real virus) to see how the virus-catching mechanisms work without introducing a real virus on your computer.

4. Let scheduled scans and other automated functions run for several days.

5. Verify that management software (such as Symantec's Alert Management System) can view servers on both sides of your routers (if necessary).

6. Verify that log files and reports accurately reflect the expected data.

Virus Test Files   It's important to test the anti-virus software to see how it behaves, but it's dangerous to try a real virus. However, you can create a text file that will be detected as a virus, which you can use to verify detection of viruses, logging, and alert functioning. Copy the following line into a separate text file, saving it as **TestVirus.com**. This file is *not* a virus, but will be detected as the EICAR Test String.70 virus (you may need to disable real-time file protection temporarily before saving the file).

```
X5O!P%@AP[4\PZX54(P^)7CC)7}$EICAR-STANDARD-ANTIVIRUS-TEST-FILE!$H+H*
```

 Do not include spaces above, below, in front of, or behind this string. Spaces might prevent the string from being detected.

Lab Testing on Clients

As with servers, client systems and software should also be tested before implementing new anti-virus software. Test client programs in a noncritical environment to locate any potential compatibility or performance problems that might interfere with productivity. Perform tests in an environment with a hardware and software setup that closely matches the actual network environment. Here are some guidelines when testing:

■ Install the anti-virus software to all operating systems that you expect to use.

■ Install the anti-virus software to connected and stand-alone clients, if necessary.

■ Match all IP/IPX protocol combinations that exist in your environment.

■ Match client-to-server OS combinations (for example, allowing Windows NT workstation to log on to NetWare servers, and so on).

■ Hardware setups should reflect minimum and maximum configurations.

After installing the new anti-virus software to your test clients, take the following steps:

1. Configure the anti-virus software options for maximum protection (i.e., scan all files, all drives, and so on).

2. Test virus definitions file downloads.

3. Use a virus test file (that you created above) to trigger the alerting system.

4. Let scheduled scans and other automated functions run for several days.

5. Verify that management software can view clients on both sides of routers.

6. Verify that connected clients appear in the management software under the correct parent server.

7. Lock some client scanning parameters using management software and verify that clients cannot change these settings.

8. Launch a virus sweep and verify that the client scans take place.

9. Verify that log files and reports reflect the expected data.

Phased Installations

After lab testing is complete, you may need to test and roll out new anti-virus tools in phases (or stages) to guarantee that there are no interruptions in actual network operation. A phased installation method is common for larger organizations. This involves first installing the anti-virus software to a test server, then systematically expanding to additional groups of servers in stages over a period of time so that any potential issues within your environment are discovered prior to a full-scale deployment on the network. The actual process is largely up to you. For example, you may start installing managed clients after you install the anti-virus software to one or more servers, or install all servers first and then all clients. As other examples, a staged installation may include installing to Windows NT/2000 servers, then NetWare servers, or just to Windows clients. You can then include other operating systems to work out any issues on a per-platform basis. The main idea is to move in small, carefully planned steps rather than risk serious network problems by moving ahead all at once.

Typical Server Installation

Now it's time to examine the installation process for a typical enterprise-type anti-virus software package. For this example, we'll look at Symantec's Norton AntiVirus Corporate Edition server program and Alert Management System utility software. Always be sure to check the specific procedures recommended for your own particular software. As a rule, always install support or management tools along with the anti-virus software. For example, when installing Norton AntiVirus Corporate Edition to Windows NT/2000 servers or workstations (or NetWare servers), you can also install the Alert Management System program that runs on every primary server. While AMS is only required on the primary server to configure and view alerts, install AMS on computers where you install Norton AntiVirus for the server. This lets you make any of these computers a primary server. If a secondary server needs to be made primary, AMS events will not be lost.

 If you're working with other operating systems such as Linux/UNIX or MacOS, you should refer to the manufacturer's installation instructions that accompany the particular anti-virus version.

Windows NT/2000 Servers   Here are the typical steps to install Norton AntiVirus Corporate Edition on Windows NT/2000 servers:

1. Start the installation wizard. Click Install Norton AntiVirus To Servers, then ensure that Install Norton AntiVirus Server is selected. Alternatively, if you installed the Symantec System Center add-ons first, click AV Server Rollout from the Symantec System Center Tools menu.

2. Click Next. Read the license and warranty, click I agree, and then click Next.

3. Ensure that the Server Program and Alert Management System (AMS) options are checked, and then click Next. Only the primary server uses the AMS files. If you select the AMS option, the service is installed on each server where you install the Norton AntiVirus server program. This lets you change primary servers without reinstalling AMS on the new primary server. If you do not plan to change your primary server, uninstall the AMS files from nonprimary servers.

4. Double-click Microsoft Windows Network.

5. Select a server on which to install, then click Add.

6. Repeat this step until you've included all of the required servers.

7. If you created a text file containing IP addresses to import computers located in non-WINS environments, continue to step 8. If you did not create a text file containing IP addresses to import computers located in non-WINS environments, continue with step 12.

8. Click Import to import the list of servers. The Import feature is designed for use with Windows NT-bases systems only. It is not intended for use with NetWare.

9. Locate and double-click the text file that contains the computer names. A summary list of computers to be added to the Available Computers list appears. During the authentication process, you may need to provide a username and password for computers that require authentication.

10. Click OK.

11. During the authentication process, setup checks for different error conditions. You are prompted to view this information interactively on an individual computer basis or to write the information to a log file for later viewing. If you create a log file, it is located at a specific location (such as **c:\Winnt\Navcesrv.txt**).

12. Click Yes to write to a log file, No to display the interactive information.

13. Click Next.

14. Accept the default anti-virus install path or change it as necessary (select a computer and click Change Destination), then click Next.

15. Type a name for a new server group, then click Next. You'll be prompted to confirm the creation of the new server group. Alternatively, select an existing server group to join, then click Next and type the server group password when prompted.

16. Click Automatic or Manual startup. If you click Automatic, the Norton AntiVirus services (and AMS services if you installed them) will start automatically if you need to restart the server. If you click Manual, you will have to start these services manually when you restart the server.

17. Click Next. The Using the Symantec System Center Program screen appears.

18. Click Next. The Setup Summary screen appears indicating the default password used to unlock the server group (for our example, the default is symantec).

19. Click Finish. The Setup Progress screen shows the status of server installations.

20. When Norton AntiVirus is installed to all of the servers you specified, check to see if any errors were reported. For example, select a server and click View Errors for more information.

21. Click Close when completed. This should complete the server installation.

NetWare Servers   When installing Norton AntiVirus to NetWare Directory Services (NDS), it is recommended that the computer performing the installation use the Novell Client for NetWare. If you encounter problems installing to NDS with the Microsoft Client for NetWare, install the Novell Client for NetWare and try the installation again. Here are the typical steps to install Norton AntiVirus Corporate Edition on Novell NetWare servers:

1. Log on to all NetWare servers where you want to install Norton AntiVirus Corporate Edition.

2. Start the installation wizard. Click Install Norton AntiVirus To Servers. Alternatively, from the Symantec System Center console, click Tools | AV Server Rollout (available only if you installed the Symantec System Center add-ons).

3. Ensure that Install Norton AntiVirus To Servers is selected, then click Next.

4. Read the license and warranty, click I agree, then click Next.

5. Ensure that Server Program is checked, and then click Next.

6. If you're using the Novell Client for NetWare, double-click NetWare Services. If you are using the Microsoft Client for NetWare, double-click NetWare Or Compatible Network.

7. Select the client that you're using:

   ■ **Novell Client for NetWare**   To install to a Bindery server, double-click NetWare Servers and select a server (indicated by a server icon).

   ■ **Novell Client for NetWare**   To install to NDS, double-click Novell Directory Services, then select the SYS volume object where you want to install Norton AntiVirus.

■ **Microsoft Client for NetWare**   To install to a bindery server, select a server (indicated by a server icon).

■ **Microsoft Client for NetWare**   To install to NDS, select the SYS volume object where you want to install Norton AntiVirus.

8. Click Add. If you're installing to NDS, you are prompted to enter a container, username, and password. If you enter an incorrect username or password at this stage, installation will continue normally. However, when you attempt to start Norton AntiVirus on the NetWare server, you will receive an authentication error and will be prompted for the correct username and password.

9. Repeat steps 7 and 8 until volumes for all servers you are installing to are added.

10. Click Next.

11. Accept the default Norton AntiVirus Corporate Edition install path or change it as necessary, then click Next.

12. Type a name for a new server group, then click Next, then click Yes to confirm. Alternatively, select an existing server group to join, then click Next and provide the server group password when prompted.

13. Click Automatic Startup or Manual Startup, then click Next. If you click Automatic Startup, **vpstart.nlm** starts automatically each time the server starts (you must complete the installation before this takes effect). If you click Manual Startup, run **vpstart.nlm** each time you start the server.

14. Click Next until you reach the final dialog box, then click Close.

15. After the install is complete, run **vpstart.nlm** on each NetWare server to which you installed. You can do this at the server console (or you can use RConsole if you have rights). The first time that you load **vpstart.nlm** after installation, you must use the **/Install** switch—for example, **load Sys:Nav\Vpstart.nlm /Install**. This should complete the server installation.

Remember that these procedures are presented as an example only. Always follow the specific installation instructions provided with your anti-virus server software.

Typical Client Installation

Once you've installed anti-virus software on the server(s), you'll also need to install client versions of the software on each workstation. Popular anti-virus products allow you to install client software from a client disk image on the server, or install locally using the installation CD on each client individually. For this example, we'll look at installing Norton AntiVirus (but always be sure to check the specific procedures recommended for your own particular software).

Installing a Disk Image   When you install Norton AntiVirus Corporate Edition to servers, the Setup program creates a client disk image (or installation folder) on each protected server. Client users can then run the Norton AntiVirus setup program directly from the servers they connect to. The anti-virus client will install in Managed mode and display in the management software (i.e., Symantec System Center) when its associated server is selected in the console tree. When the client runs in managed mode, you can configure automatic definition file updates for the client and administer them from the management software.

On Windows NT/2000 servers, for example, the default shared folder is **\\Server\Vphome\Clt-inst**, and every user has read permissions. On NetWare servers, the default shared directory is **\\Server\Sys\Nav\Clt-inst**. Setup also creates a group called **nortonantivirususer**. If you add users to this group, they'll have the rights they need to run the client installation program from the client disk image on the server. Alternatively, if you make the installation CD available on a shared network drive, users will need to map that drive on their workstations to ensure successful installation of all components. To install the client disk image from a server, follow these steps:

1. Verify that users have rights to the client disk image on the server.

2. Give the user the path and (if necessary) drive mapping to the client disk image. For NetWare servers, the default path is **\\Server\Sys\Nav\Clt-inst**. For Windows NT servers, the default share path is **\\Server\Vphome\Clt-inst**.

3. Make sure the user knows which platform to install. For Norton AntiVirus, these installation folders and Setup programs are available under the **Clt-inst** folder on each server:

   ```
   Clt-inst\Win32\Setup.exe
   Clt-inst\Win16\Setup.exe
   Clt-inst\Dos\Install.bat
   ```

Remote Installations   You can remotely install the Norton AntiVirus client onto any Windows NT/2000 or NetWare computer connected to the network, and you can install to multiple clients at the same time without having to physically go to each workstation. An advantage to remote installation is that users do *not* need to log on to their computers as administrators prior to the installation (if you have administrator rights to the domain that the client computers belong to). To install Norton AntiVirus, follow these steps:

1. Start the anti-virus setup program and click Install Norton AntiVirus To NT Clients. The Welcome screen appears.

2. Click Next and double-click Microsoft Windows NT Network.

3. Select a computer and server running Norton AntiVirus, then click Add.

4. Repeat this until all the clients that you want to manage are added.

5. If you created a text file containing IP addresses to import computers located in non-WINS environments, continue to step 6. If you did not create a text file containing IP addresses to import computers located in non-WINS environments, continue with step 10.

 The Import feature is designed for use with Windows NT/2000/XP only. It is not intended for use with NetWare.

6. Click Import to import the list of computers.

7. Locate and double-click the text file that contains computer names. A summary list of computers to be added to the Available Computers list appears. During the authentication process, you may need to provide a username and password for computers that require authentication.

8. Click OK.

9. During the authentication process, Setup checks for different error conditions. You are prompted to view this information on an individual computer basis, or to write the information to a log file for later viewing. If you create a log file, it is located on the **C:** drive (such as **c:\Winnt\Navcecln.txt**).

10. Click Yes to write to a log file, No to display the interactive information.

11. Click Finish.

Virus Signatures

Anti-virus tools operate by comparing file contents to a list of known virus "signatures"—traces that indicate the presence of a virus. Today, there can be well over 50,000 virus signatures in a signature file, and new signatures are being identified every day. This means you'll need to update your virus signature file on a very regular basis in order to maintain optimum protection for your network. In most cases, you can download new virus signature files directly from the anti-virus maker's Web site (often automatically), then "push" the new virus signature files to the clients on your network. This process greatly simplifies the task of virus management by allowing an administrator to update protection across the entire network without having to download or transfer the signature updates on each PC individually.

Removing Infections

Although far from harmless, most viruses that infect your network will not destroy data, play pranks, or render your computer unusable. Even the comparatively rare viruses that do carry a destructive payload usually produce their nasty effects in response to a trigger event. In most cases (unless you actually see evidence of a payload that has activated), you will have time to deal with the infection properly. The very presence of these small snippets of unwanted computer code can, however, interfere with a computer's normal operation, consume system resources, and have other undesirable effects, so you should take them seriously and be sure to remove them when you encounter them.

Another issue to keep in mind is that odd computer behavior, unexplained system crashes, or other unpredictable events might have causes other than virus infections. If you believe you have a virus on your computer because of such occurrences, scanning for viruses might not produce the results you expect, but it will help eliminate one potential cause of your computer problems.

When you install anti-virus software, its setup routine starts the anti-virus application to examine your computer's memory and your hard disk boot sectors in order to verify that it can safely copy its files to your hard disk without risking their infection. If the application does not detect any infections, continue with the installation and then scan your system thoroughly as soon as you restart your computer—file-infector viruses that don't load into your computer's memory or hide in your hard disk boot blocks might still be lurking somewhere on your system.

INFECTIONS UPON INSTALLATION

If the anti-virus application detects a virus during its setup process, you'll need to remove it from your system before you install the program. The following steps provide an example of virus removal during the initial anti-virus installation process:

1. Quit Setup immediately, then shut down your computer. Be sure to turn the power to your system off completely. Do not use CTRL-ALT-DEL or reset your computer to restart your system—some viruses can remain intact during this type of "warm" reboot.

2. If you created an anti-virus emergency startup disk during installation, write-protect the disk and insert it into your floppy drive. Some anti-virus installation CDs provide you with a bootable CD version of the emergency disk. If you did not create an emergency disk (and your computer is configured to start with a bootable CD), insert the Installation CD in your CD-ROM drive before proceeding to the next step.

3. Wait at least 15 seconds, then start your computer again.

4. As your computer restarts, the emergency disk runs a batch file that leads you through an emergency scan operation. The batch file first asks you whether you cycled the power on your computer. Type **Y** to continue.

5. Read the notice shown on your screen, then press any key to continue.

6. The emergency disk will load the files it needs into memory.

7. The command-line scanner that comes with the emergency disk (i.e., **BOOTSCAN.EXE**) will make four scanning passes to examine your hard disk boot sectors, your Master Boot record (MBR), your system directories, program files, and other likely points of infection on all of your local computers' hard disks.

The emergency disk will not detect macro viruses, script viruses, or Trojan horse programs, but it will detect common file-infecting and boot-sector viruses.

8. If **BOOTSCAN.EXE** finds a virus, it will try to clean the infected file. If it fails, it will deny access to the file and continue the scan operation. After it finishes all of its scanning passes, it shows a summary report of the actions it took for each hard disk on the display. If the scanner detects a virus, it beeps and reports the name and location of the virus on the screen.

9. When the scanner finishes examining your hard disk, remove the emergency disk from your floppy drive (or CD-ROM), then shut your computer off again.

10. When **BOOTSCAN.EXE** finishes examining your system, you can either try reinstalling the anti-virus software again or try to clean any remaining viruses and continue.

INFECTIONS AFTER INSTALLATION

When your anti-virus software detects a virus, an alert message displays onscreen to notify you. The best course of action is to attempt to clean the infected file. Cleaning removes the virus from your server, client, or wireless device and attempts to repair the infected file. You can typically deal with a virus in one of four ways:

■ *Attempt a repair.* You may be offered the option to repair a file—this attempts to delete the infection but save the file and continue using it. This process is not always perfect, and many users prefer the added safety of deleting the infected file.

■ *Quarantine the file.* Select Quarantine to isolate the infected file. Once you have quarantined the infected file, use Instant Updater to download the most current anti-virus signature files. Then you can make another attempt to clean the infected file.

■ *Delete the file.* When you click Delete, both the virus and the infected file are removed from your computer. Choose Delete only if a backup copy of the file is available to you.

■ *Stop the operation.* If all else fails, select Stop to stop scanning and use the emergency disk method of repair described above.

Troubleshooting Anti-Virus Tools

The key to dealing with computer viruses is the proper use of anti-virus tools. A quick walk through almost any software store will show you just how many anti-virus products are available. Being able to use those products properly and successfully is not always a simple task. This part of the chapter offers some guidelines to help you handle problems with the tools themselves.

INSTALLATION ISSUES

Most anti-virus installations (even enterprise installations) can be accomplished smoothly, but there are instances where trouble occurs. A failed installation can cause software problems that are difficult to isolate. The major causes of installation failure include hard drive errors, temporary (**.TMP**) files that conflict with the installation, and attempting to install the anti-virus software while other software is running. Try the following procedure to minimize common installation errors.

Drive Cleanup

Disk problems can easily interfere with the installation of new software. If it's been a while since using routine diagnostic tools, run Disk Cleanup and Disk Defragmenter to clear space and reorganize files on your hard drive:

1. Click Start, highlight Programs, select Accessories, choose System Tools, and then click Disk Cleanup.

2. Select your disk. Windows 2000 will calculate the space that can be freed (see Figure 19-2).

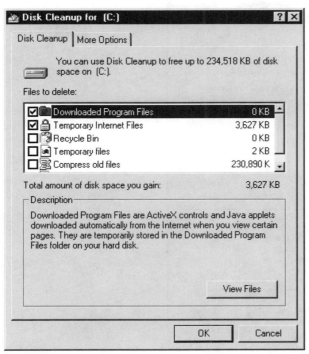

FIGURE 19-2 Disk Cleanup for Windows 2000 lets you recover space on your hard drive(s).

3. Select the component(s) to be cleaned using their check boxes.

4. Windows will proceed to erase the selected files. Depending on the size of your hard drive, this cleanup may take several minutes to finish.

5. The Disk Cleanup dialog box will automatically close when finished.

6. Click Start, highlight Programs, select Accessories, choose System Tools, and then click Disk Defragmenter.

7. Click the Analyze button. After a few moments, a detailed report of the drive will appear (see Figure 19-3) including a recommendation of whether to defragment the drive. Close the report when you're done.

8. Once the report closes, you'll see a graphical representation of the disk appear (see Figure 19-4).

9. Click the Defragment button, if necessary, and allow the disk to reorganize. Depending on the speed of your computer and the size of your drive, this may take several minutes to complete.

10. Close Disk Defragmenter when it has finished defragmenting your disk.

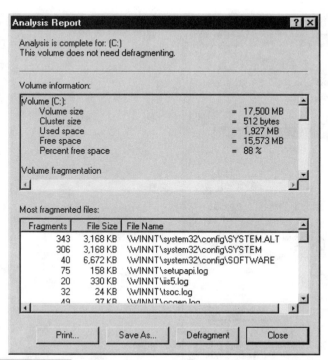

FIGURE 19-3   Windows 2000 will generate a detailed report of disk use and fragmentation.

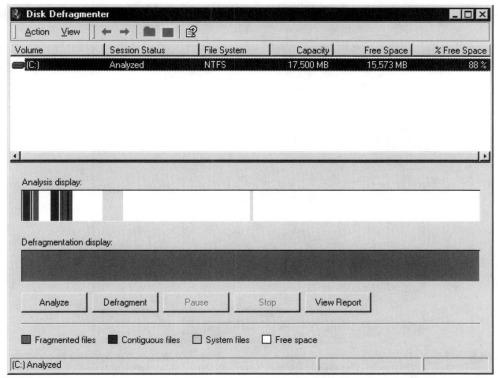

FIGURE 19-4 You can see a graphical representation of disk fragmentation under Windows 2000.

Close Other Software

Some software running in the background on your server or client may interfere with the anti-virus installer. Disable all unnecessary software on the system before attempting to install the software again:

1. Press CTRL-ALT-DEL. The Windows Security dialog box appears. Click the Task Manager button (see Figure 19-5).

2. Click End Task for every unneeded item on the list.

3. Repeat steps 2 and 3 until you've closed everything that you don't need.

4. When you've closed unneeded applications, close the Task Manager and try installing the anti-virus software again.

PREVENTING MACRO VIRUSES

Macro viruses can be detected by most of the current anti-virus tools now available (and you should regularly scan documents for macro viruses), but you may be able to reduce the risk of macro virus effects with the following tips:

■ Mark the **NORMAL.DOT** template file as "read-only". This generally protects the **NORMAL.DOT** file from infection.

FIGURE 19-5 The Windows 2000 Task Manager allows you to close processes in order to isolate applications that may interfere with anti-virus installation or operation.

■ Use Word 7.0a or later from Microsoft. These versions present an Alert box when the file you are going to open contains macros or customization information. You also have the opportunity to disable unknown macros before they operate.

Removing a Macro Virus

Chances are that you're receiving virus alerts for macro viruses in one or more Microsoft Word or Excel documents. If you've tried to repair the documents with your anti-virus software but the software has been unsuccessful, you may be able to remove the macro virus manually. The steps below will only remove the virus from existing documents, and should be considered an emergency repair. If the virus that's creating the infected macros is still on your system or network, the infection will reoccur the next time the infected document is opened. As a rule, you should avoid the use of macros (if possible) in applications such as Word, Excel, or PowerPoint, and never allow macro auto-open/execution. Please follow these steps to manually remove the macro virus from a document and recover its text:

 Before proceeding, make a backup of the suspect documents to clearly labeled media such as a floppy disk.

1. Click Start, highlight Find, and click Files or Folders. The Find dialog box appears.

2. Type **NORMAL.DOT** and click Find Now.

3. Once the file is found, right-click the filename and click Rename on the shortcut menu.

4. Rename the file to **NORMAL.OLD** and press ENTER.

5. Close the Find dialog box.

6. Start Word—this will re-create the **NORMAL.DOT** template.

7. Choose the File menu and click Open.

8. Navigate to the folder containing the infected file and select it.

9. Press and hold the SHIFT key and click Open. Continue to hold the SHIFT key until the affected file is open in Word (holding the SHIFT key while opening a file keeps any macros from running).

10. Choose the Tools menu, point to Macro, and then click Macros.

11. In the Macros In list box, select "All active templates and documents".

12. Select the suspect macro and click Delete. Click Yes to confirm.

13. Repeat the previous step for *all* suspect macros.

14. Click Close.

15. Choose the Edit menu and click Select All.

16. Press SHIFT-LEFT ARROW to deselect the last paragraph mark in the document.

17. Choose the Edit menu and click Copy.

18. Choose the File menu and click New. Select the desired template and click OK.

19. Choose the Edit menu and click Paste.

20. Repeat steps 10–14 to verify that the viral macros have not replicated again.

21. Save the document.

22. Repeat these steps for any document you think may contain a macro virus.

SYMPTOMS

Once you've installed your anti-virus software and it's operational, it should run on servers and clients without difficulty. However, there are situations when anti-virus problems occur. This part of the chapter examines several of the most common symptoms and solutions.

SYMPTOM 19-1   **You cannot run more than one anti-virus product at a time.**   This is not an uncommon problem, and occurs most frequently when memory-resident virus protectors conflict with file-based anti-virus tools. When you run more than one anti-virus program, there is always the risk of strange results and false alarms. For example, some anti-virus programs store their "virus signature strings" unprotected in memory. Running incompatible or conflicting anti-virus tools may detect other signature strings or memory-resident activity as a virus. Run only one anti-virus program at a time.

SYMPTOM 19-2   **Your anti-virus tool does not function, or causes other drivers to malfunction.**   Some "terminate-and-stay-resident" (TSR) software may conflict with some anti-virus programs, especially memory-resident anti-virus programs. When problems occur, try booting the system from a clean bootable disk so that there are no other drivers or TSRs in the system aside from the anti-virus tool.

SYMPTOM 19-3   **You notice that your anti-virus tool is slowing disk access dramatically, or it locks up under Windows.**   Normally, many anti-virus tools (especially memory-resident tools) will slow disk access a bit. When there is a tremendous reduction in disk performance, or the tool freezes during operation, it may be that the disk cache being used conflicts with the anti-virus product. Try increasing the number of buffers in the **CONFIG.SYS** file. If problems continue, try disabling the disk caching software while running the anti-virus product. In other cases, a patch or update from the anti-virus manufacturer may help correct the problem.

SYMPTOM 19-4   **The anti-virus tool is reporting false alarms.**   It is not uncommon for anti-virus products to report false alarms. This happens most often due to conflicts with other memory-resident software running in the system. Try running the software from a clean boot disk. The nature of anti-viral detection techniques also plays a role in reporting false errors. For example, file comparison is a typical technique, but files can be changed for many reasons other than a virus, so false alarms are a strong possibility. Other techniques also have flaws that may result in false alarms. You should try updating the virus signature database from your anti-virus software provider.

SYMPTOM 19-5   **You are unable to remove the memory-resident anti-virus tool.** There is probably another TSR or background application running in the system that is conflicting with the anti-virus tool. You may have to reboot the system in order to clear the anti-virus tool. In the future, try loading the anti-virus tool last—after all other drivers and TSRs or background applications are loaded.

SYMPTOM 19-6   **The virus scanner is only scanning files very slowly.**   This is usually an issue with certain older virus scanning software. Ideally, you should be able to correct this problem by upgrading to the latest patch or version of your virus scanner. If you cannot patch or update the program, try scanning only the "Program files" and not "All files" or "Compressed files".

SYMPTOM 19-7   **The virus scanner seems to conflict with the boot sector when it scans.**   If the virus scanner is conflicting with your boot sector (either upon installation or after installing), try choosing the "Custom" setup feature and disable the initial system scan during installation. Then edit the scanner's configuration to skip the boot scan. As an example, for McAfee's VirusScan product, edit your **DEFAULT.VSC** file and under the [Scan Options] section, change bSkipBootScan=0 to bSkipBootScan=1. This will skip the boot-sector scan when you run VirusScan. This will mean that the boot sector will not be scanned for viruses.

SYMPTOM 19-8   **You encounter NDS errors installing to a NetWare 4.x server.**   F o r example, if you install an anti-virus product like Norton AntiVirus Corporate Edition to a NetWare 4.x server with an outdated version of the **clib.nlm** file, you will see these error messages:

```
Error importing NWDSCreateContextHandle
Error (0xa0000014)(-1610612716) initializing DS in DS Preliminaries Error
Error: 0xa0000014(-1610612716) in line 255: [DSPROFILE] Error
Error: Not authenticated with Novell Directory Services in line 278:
[DSOBJECTS]
```

Use the latest Novell **clib.nlm** file. This file is contained in the latest version of the NetWare update patch (LIBUPF or newer), which you can download from the Novell Support Web site at **support.novell.com**. Install this patch on your NetWare 4.x server, and then reinstall the anti-virus software to resolve this problem.

SYMPTOM 19-9   **You encounter a "third-party rollout" error.**   For anti-virus products like Norton AntiVirus Corporate Edition, the error is designated 0x20000046E. This normally occurs if you roll out the anti-virus software with an installation method not provided for in the product—the error normally occurs when attempting manual or scheduled scans. You may need to let the anti-virus product interact with the desktop (i.e., check the Norton AntiVirus Service and ensure that the check box to interact with Desktop is checked), or uninstall the anti-virus software completely, then reinstall it according to the manufacturer's instructions.

SYMPTOM 19-10   **You encounter an error such as "Unable to load <filename>".**   For example, you may see an error such as "Unable to load listview.ocx" after installing Norton AntiVirus. This means that one or more files were not registered during installation. For the Norton AntiVirus error, the unregistered files may include **clntcon.ocx**, **srvcon.ocx**, or **ldvpocx.ocx**. This situation might occur if the installation was not complete when you exited the Setup program, or if an important **.DLL** file (i.e., **transman.dll**) is missing from the directory where you installed the anti-virus software. The best solution is usually to uninstall the anti-virus software, then reinstall the product from scratch.

SYMPTOM 19-11   **You encounter startup issues after installing anti-virus software.** For example, your Windows client systems may display a yellow exclamation mark on the anti-virus icon in the system tray. The exclamation point appears after you restart, and real-time protection is not enabled. On Windows computers, you may see an error message such as

```
RTVSCN95 caused a General Protection Fault in module krnl386.exe
```

These problems are usually caused by a timing conflict between the anti-virus software (i.e., Norton AntiVirus Corporate Edition) and another program or service loading at startup. To resolve the issue on Windows NT/2000 computers, change the load order of the Norton AntiVirus Corporate Edition Client service by creating a dependency on another service.

For instructions on creating a dependency, please see the Microsoft Knowledge Base Article Q193888.

SYMPTOM 19-12   **You encounter shutdown issues after installing anti-virus software.** For example, when you attempt to shut down or restart the computer where you've installed your anti-virus software, it may stop responding, or you may see the following error message:

```
The application cannot respond to the End Task request.
```

Some anti-virus tools (i.e., Norton AntiVirus Corporate Edition) scan the **A:** drive during restart or shutdown to prevent your computer from becoming infected by a boot-sector virus. On some computers, the shutdown floppy disk drive scan causes timing problems during shutdown. To correct the problem, you'll need to edit the Registry. Start by backing up the Registry:

Back up the system registry before making any changes. Incorrect changes to the registry can result in permanent data loss or corrupted files. Modify only the keys specified.

1. Click Start.
2. Click Run. The Run dialog box appears.
3. Type **Regedit** and click OK. The Registry Editor opens.
4. On the Registry menu, click Export Registry File.

5. Verify the following items in the Export Registry File dialog box:
   - **Save in:** Desktop
   - **File name:** Registry Backup
   - **Save as type:** Registration Files
   - **Export range:** All
6. Click Save.
7. Exit the Registry Editor and verify that the file Registry **Backup.reg** is on the Desktop.

Now adjust the registry to shut down the floppy scan:

1. Click Start.
2. Click Run. The Run dialog box appears.
3. Type **Regedit** and click OK. The Registry Editor opens.
4. Navigate to the following subkey:

   HKEY_LOCAL_MACHINE\Software\Intel\LanDesk\VirusProtect6\CurrentVersion
5. In the right pane, right-click and click New | DWORD Value.
6. Name the value **Skipshutdownfloppycheck**.
7. Right-click the new Skipshutdownfloppycheck and click Modify.
8. In the Value Data text box, type **1**.
9. Repeat steps 4–7 to create a new value named **Skipshutdownscan** with a value of **1**.
10. To reenable the shutdown floppy disk drive scan, set the Skipshutdownfloppycheck and Skipshutdownscan values to 0.
11. On the Registry menu, click Exit to save the changes.

SYMPTOM 19-13   **A 16-bit client appears twice in your management software after an update.**   When you update the 16-bit client for your anti-virus software, you initially see two copies of the same client computer displayed in the anti-virus management software (i.e., Symantec System Center). This is because the old client still exists in the anti-virus server's client list. When the server refreshes its client list, it clears the old copy of the 16-bit anti-virus client. Afterwards, only the updated 16-bit client appears in management software.

SYMPTOM 19-14   **You have difficulty loading the anti-virus software for NetWare.** For example, you may receive the following error message when loading Norton AntiVirus Corporate Edition for NetWare:

RTVSCAN could not load NDS function.

This type of error usually occurs because of software incompatibility. For Norton AntiVirus, you may be using an outdated **dsapi.nlm** file. Update your **dsapi.nlm** file by downloading the latest version from Novell at **www.novell.com**, and reinstall the anti-virus software (i.e., Norton AntiVirus Corporate Edition).

You may want to use Config Reader to identify any outdated NLMs. Config Reader can take input from a **CONFIG.TXT** file and present it in a way that provides you with more options than viewing it through a text editor. Config Reader is available from the Novell Web site.

Further Study

Command Worldwide: **www.commandcom.com**
EICAR: **www.eicar.org**
IBM: **www.research.ibm.com/antivirus/**
McAfee: **www.mcafee.com** or **www.networkassociates.com**
NCSA (TrueSecure): **www.trusecure.com**
Dr. Solomon: **www.drsolomon.com**
Symantec: **www.symantec.com/avcenter/**

NETWORK BACKUP AND RESTORATION

When trouble strikes, it usually strikes without warning, and important network data is usually caught in the crossfire. While it's easy for a technician to replace failed components or rewire damaged cabling, lost data is virtually impossible to re-create—it must be replaced. More than one company has lost income (and even gone out of business) after losing important data. Data-crushing disasters can be caused by a wide range of natural or man-made events, including the following:

- Component failure (i.e., NIC adapter failure)
- Computer viruses (introduced by file transfers or infected applications)
- Data deletion and corruption (i.e., sabotage by a disgruntled employee)
- Fires caused by arson or electrical mishaps
- Natural disasters (i.e., lightning, floods, tornadoes, or earthquakes)
- Power supply failure and power surges
- Theft and vandalism

Consequently, the techniques of making, verifying, and restoring backups are essential parts of network maintenance. The simplest, most inexpensive way to avoid such a disastrous loss of data is to implement a schedule of periodic backups (preferably using storage facilities off-site). Tape backups (see Figure 20-1) provide a simple and economical way to ensure that important network data remains safe and usable. A reli-

FIGURE 20-1 The Seagate 240 DAT autoloader tape drive (Courtesy of Seagate)

able backup strategy minimizes the risk of losing data by maintaining a *current* backup—copies of existing files—so that operating systems, applications, and data files can be recovered if the original data is lost or damaged. This chapter explores the concepts and practices of tape backups, and covers a series of common troubleshooting issues.

Tape Basics

So when should backups be performed? It's not a simple answer because each network situation is different. When selecting a backup schedule, follow a simple rule: *If you cannot get along without it, back it up*. Critical data should be backed up daily, weekly, or monthly—it really depends on how critical the data is and how frequently it is updated. It is best to schedule backup operations during periods of low system use (i.e., during late evening or weekend hours). Users should be notified when the backup will be performed so that they will not be using the server during the backup period.

Whether you back up entire disks, selected directories, or individual files will depend on how fast you will need to be operational after losing important data. Complete backups make restoring disk configurations much easier because all files are restored at once, but they can require multiple tapes (especially if there are large amounts of data). Backing up individual files and directories generally goes faster and requires fewer tapes, but could require you to manually restore disk configurations. Ideally, a tape drive should have more than enough capacity to back up a network's largest server. It should also provide error detection and correction during backup and restore operations.

BACKUP TECHNIQUES

There is no single way to back up a server. You can choose from several common backup practices, and most administrators will use a combination of techniques:

- **Full backup** A full backup is used to save and mark selected files regardless of whether or not they have changed since the last backup. This provides the most complete and convenient data protection, but it takes the longest to implement.

- **Copy** A copy backs up all selected files without marking them as being backed up.

- **Incremental backup**   This process saves and marks selected files only if they have changed since the last time they were backed up.

- **Daily copy**   This is a variation of copy that saves only those files that have been modified that day, without marking them as being backed up.

- **Differential backup**   This saves selected files only if they have changed since the last time they were backed up, without marking them as being backed up.

For example, you may choose to start a backup cycle on Monday with a full backup, then perform an incremental backup each day through the rest of the week to preserve the files that have changed, then repeat the cycle again on the following Monday. Of course, the actual frequency of your backups will depend on your particular network needs. Most backup strategies will involve numerous tapes rotated on a regular basis.

Backups are useless if they cannot be restored, and any experienced technician will tell you to test (aka verify) a backup. Network administrators will periodically perform disaster recovery drills by making a backup, deleting files, restoring the data, and attempting to use that data. In many cases, these drills are handled by less senior technicians (under the supervision of the administrator) to reinforce the necessary recovery steps. These drills are used to verify that the necessary files are indeed backed up, and that a reliable recovery procedure is in place.

Regardless of what backup plan you adopt, don't skimp on tape quality. Tapes cannot be reused indefinitely, so selecting a quality, name-brand product that is recommended for your particular tape drive will help you to achieve the most uses and longest data retention.

Incremental vs. Differential

A full backup takes the most time to make and restore, but it can restore your system to the way it was when the backup was made (you don't need to mess with hardware setup or individual applications). *Incremental* and *differential* backups will save only the files that have changed since the last backup process. However, incremental backups will mark files that have changed, but differential backups will not. This means that differential backups will grow larger as time goes on because they constantly include all files that have changed since the full backup. Incremental and differential backups involve fewer files, and are usually faster to make and restore, but don't involve the entire system.

In actual practice, you'd usually start with a full backup of the system, then periodically make incremental backups as the system and its data changes. You'd restore the full backup first, then systematically add each incremental backup until the system "catches up" to its latest state. However, restoring a lot of incremental backups can take a great deal of time. If you prefer differential backups, you'd restore the full backup, then restore the latest differential backup—since the last differential backup will include all files changed since the full backup, it may be a more efficient than incremental backups when relatively few files are involved.

Let's try an example. Suppose you make a full backup of your system, then spend the next week working on FILE A. If you perform an *incremental* backup, only FILE A would be saved. If you then work on FILE B and perform another incremental backup, only file B would be saved. If you need to restore the system, you'd restore the full backup first, then restore the incremental backup with FILE A, then restore the full backup with FILE B, and so on. If you work on FILE A and perform a *differential* backup, FILE A would also be saved, but when you finish FILE B and perform another differential backup, both FILE A and FILE B would be saved. When you restore the system, you'd use the full backup and the *last* differential backup because that would have *all* the files that have changed since the last full backup. In short, differential backups can save you time during restoration.

BACKUP LOGS

Backup procedures should also be logged (either as a separate record or as part of your server maintenance log). A complete backup record can be critical for proper data recovery later, and should include the following information:

■ Date of the backup

■ Tape set number (or other identifier)

■ Type of backup performed (i.e., full, incremental, and so on)

■ Which computer/server was backed up

■ Which drives/files were backed up

■ Who performed the backup

■ The physical location of the backup tapes (if the tapes are stored off-site)

TAPE ROTATION TACTICS

Tape cartridges are certainly the most common medium for network backup systems. Although the number of backups you perform per week or per month will depend entirely on the amount of activity on your system or network, backup integrity is limited by the tapes themselves. By using more than one tape as part of your backup regimen, you will not find yourself writing over a current backup (potentially disastrous if the backup process is interrupted). Tape rotation is a common tactic that helps to ensure that data is protected and integral at all times.

 There are many practical tape rotation procedures. This section outlines only a few common tactics.

Two Tapes

This is generally considered to be the most rudimentary strategy—ideal for individual or infrequent PC users. There are usually two variations with a two-tape strategy. The most common implementation is simply to make full backups (alternating the tapes each time). For example, tape A is reformatted and used for a backup on March 1, tape B is reformatted and used in April 1, then tape A is reformatted and reused for a complete backup on May 1, and so on. This approach guarantees that you are never overwriting a current backup. An alternative strategy is to create a total backup on tape A, then make modified backups on tape B as needed.

Three Tapes

The three-tape cycle is frequently used for small offices or home offices where there are a limited number of files changing from day to day. The process is easy to understand if you look at it over a one-week period. On Monday, make a complete backup on tape A. Tuesday through Friday, make modified (aka incremental) backups on tape B. The next week, make a total backup on tape C, and store tape A in a secure location off-site. Erase or reformat tape B, then use it for modified backups throughout the week. On Monday of the subsequent week, store tape C off-site, and return tape A to be erased or reformatted for a new complete backup. Thus, tapes A and C are alternated each week for complete system backups, while tape B remains on-site for daily modified backups.

If you are not using the system enough to justify daily maintenance, try a weekly approach. Use tape A for a total backup on the first of the month, then use tape B for modified backups once a week during the month (or whenever important new files must be protected). The first of the next month, perform a total backup on tape C and store tape A in a secure location off-site. Erase tape B and reuse it for modified backups throughout the month. On the first of the third month, move tape C off-site, erase tape A, and perform a complete backup, then erase tape B and use it for modified backups. This way, tapes A and C are alternated the first of every month rather than the first of every week.

Six Tapes

The six-tape rotation is intended for businesses and busy offices where important files are changed and updated daily. Start the week by erasing or reformatting tapes A and F, then creating total backups on both tapes. Store tape F in a secure location off-site. Use tapes B, C, D, and E to perform modified (incremental) backups on Tuesday through Friday. On the subsequent Monday, tapes A and F would be erased and backed up once again. Each day through the week, the tape designated for that particular day would be erased and saved with a modified backup.

Ten Tapes

When you need to maintain weekly and monthly off-site archives of ongoing work, you can use a ten-tape rotation cycle (which is really just an adjustment to the six-tape cycle). By adding four more tapes to the six-tape cycle, you can create a total backup the first of every week, then store those weekly backups off-site. For example, on the first Monday of the month, a total backup is made on tapes A and F (just as in the six-tape rotation) and tape F is stored off-site. On Tuesday through Friday, tapes B, C, D, and E hold modified backups of each day. Tape F becomes the archive of week 1. The next week, total backups are made on tapes A and G, while tapes B, C, D, and E provide modified backups. Tape G would be the archive for week 2. The third week, tapes A and H would be the total backups, and tape H would archive the third week. Tapes A and I would hold total backups on the forth week, so tape I would archive the fourth week. Finally, tape J would be used as a total backup on the last day of the month. While this process is overkill for many businesses, it may come in handy for businesses that require long-term archives of their work (i.e., government contractors).

Tape Drive Installation

Drive installation is generally a straightforward proposition that typically includes simply mounting the drive, cabling to an available SCSI (sometimes IDE) adapter, then providing power. Once the drive is installed, it performs a self-test on power up; then, you'll need to install the appropriate drivers and backup software. This part of the chapter reviews the essentials of hardware and software installation.

HARDWARE INSTALLATION

Hardware installation basically involves mounting and cabling the tape drive properly. Here are the general installation steps for an internal drive model:

 These steps are intended to provide general guidelines. Always follow the manufacturer's instructions when configuring and installing a tape drive.

1. Unpack the tape drive and configure it for use on your server. This includes configuring the drive's SCSI ID, SCSI parity (even or odd), and parity checking (enabled or disabled). Be sure that the SCSI ID does not conflict with other SCSI devices on the system. If you're installing an ATAPI IDE tape drive, you'll need to configure the drive as a master or slave IDE device.

2. Power down and unplug the server where you'll install the tape drive (make sure that any users are adequately alerted and given an opportunity to log off before proceeding). Also disconnect the server from the rest of the network.

3. Open the server and uncover a drive bay to receive the new drive. Slide the drive into place and secure the drive with four mounting screws—fewer screws may allow the drive to vibrate excessively.

4. Connect the SCSI (or IDE) signal cable to the drive. If the SCSI drive is the last device in the SCSI chain, be sure to terminate the SCSI cable properly.

5. Now connect an available drive power cable and see that it's inserted completely.

6. Route the cables properly and see that they're out of the way of fans or other devices. Do not replace the outer covers or reconnect the server back onto the network until you've proven the installation.

Power On Testing

Once the drive is installed, you may power up the server and check the drive's operation. Verify that the power LED is on, and check for any POST indications from the drive. Table 20-1 lists the indicators for a typical tape drive. For example, the DLT2000 follows a well-defined sequence of events starting with right-side indicators:

1. Indicators on right side of the front panel turn on sequentially (from top to bottom).

2. All indicators remain on for approximately 3 seconds.

3. The "Tape in Use" indicator blinks and turns off.

Several possible situations may occur:

■ If no tape cartridge is loaded, the Operate Handle indicator turns on and a beeper sounds.

■ If a tape cartridge is loaded, the Tape in Use indicator remains blinking and stops when the drive is ready.

■ If the handle is open, the Operate Handle indicator blinks, telling you to close the handle. The Tape in Use indicator blinks, the Operate Handle indicator blinks again, and a beeper sounds.

If the drive's indicators respond as expected, chances are that the drive has been installed properly and is operating correctly. You can proceed to install drivers and check the drive. If the drive does not power on properly, you must recheck the installation, and replace the suspect drive if necessary.

SOFTWARE INSTALLATION

After the tape drive is installed and operating properly, it's time to install the software needed for proper drive operation. Device drivers must be installed first so that Windows NT/2000 (or other operating systems) can access the drive; then, you'll need to install a suitable backup utility to organize files, scheduling, media spanning (multiple tapes), and other features. Let's start with driver installation.

Loading Device Drivers

As with most devices on the PC, drivers are critical so that an operating system can access various pieces of hardware. The device drivers supplied on the drive's CD are required if you intend to use native operating

TABLE 20-1   OVERVIEW OF LED ASSIGNMENTS FOR A DLT2000 TAPE DRIVE

INDICATOR	COLOR	STATE	OPERATING CONDITION
Write Protected	Orange	On	Tape is write-protected.
		Off	Tape is write-enabled.
Tape in Use	Yellow	Blinking	Tape is moving.
		On	Tape is loaded and ready for use.
Use Cleaning Tape	Yellow	On	Drive head needs cleaning, or the tape is bad. Cleaning tape attempted to clean the drive head, but the tape expired so cleaning was not done. Problem data cartridge; try another cartridge.
		Off	Cleaning is complete, or cleaning is unnecessary.
Operate Handle	Green	On	Okay to operate the cartridge/insert release handle.
		Off	Do not operate the cartridge insert/release handle.
All right-side indicators	Blinking	---	A drive error has occurred.
2.6	Yellow	On	Indicates the tape is recorded in 2.6 format.
		Blinking	Indicates the tape is recorded in another density.
6.0	Yellow	On	Indicates the tape is recorded in 6.0 format.
		Blinking	Indicates the tape is recorded in another density.
10.0	Yellow	On (default)	Indicates the tape is recorded in 10.0 format.
		Off	Indicates the tape is recorded in another density.
Compress	Yellow	On	Compression mode enabled.
		Off	Compression mode disabled.
Density Override	Yellow	On	You have selected a density from the front panel.
		Off (default)	Density to be selected by the host (automatic).
		Blinking	You are in density selection mode.

system backup applications, though many commercial backup applications provide all necessary device driver support. Here are the steps to install typical drivers under Windows NT:

1. Insert the drive's CD into drive x (where "x" is the CD-ROM drive letter).

2. Click the Start button, point to Settings, and click on Control Panel.

3. Double-click the Tape Devices icon. If there are no tape device drivers installed, the Install Driver menu will appear when you click Tape Devices in the Control Panel. Alternatively, if there is already a tape driver installed, you will see the Tape Devices menu. From there, click on the Drivers tab, then Add to get to the Install Driver menu.

4. From the Install Driver menu, click Have Disk and the Install from Disk window should display.

5. Under the Copy Manufactures' Files From area, select the CD-ROM drive letter.

6. Click on Browse and the Locate File window will appear.

7. Click the **nt_driver** folder and check that OEMSETUP is displayed.

8. Click Open.

9. The Install from Disk window should be displayed. Copy manufacture's files from **x:\nt_driver** (where "x" is the CD-ROM drive designator).

10. Click OK.

11. The Install Driver window will appear. Click OK.

12. Click OK when the New SCSI Tape Device Window is displayed.

13. The Windows NT Setup window will appear.

14. Enter **x:\nt_driver** (where "x" is the CD-ROM designator).

15. Click Continue and the driver will be loaded.

16. The Tape Devices Window will be displayed. Click OK.

17. Remove the CD from the CD-ROM drive and restart the system.

18. Once the system is restarted, click the Start button, point to Settings, and click on Control Panel.

19. Double-click the Tape Devices icon to see if the driver has been loaded.

20. If the driver is not loaded, make sure the tape drive is properly connected to the system and repeat process from step 1 if necessary.

Here are the typical installation steps under Windows 2000:

1. Start up the system and bring up Windows.

2. Right-click on the My Computer icon and select Manage. This will bring up the Computer Management applet.

3. In the Computer Management applet window (see Figure 20-2), highlight Device Manager. A list of device subsystems is displayed in the right view.

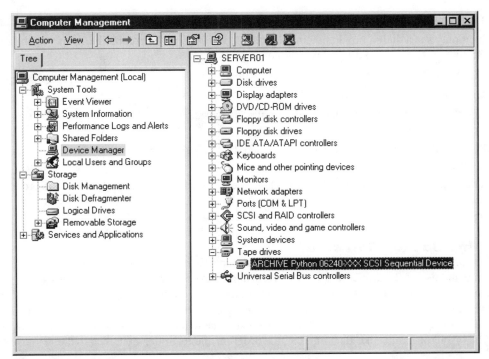

FIGURE 20-2   Use the Windows 2000 Device Manager to identify the installed tape drive on your PC or server.

4. The target tape drive may be found in either the Tape Drives or Other Devices section. Expand the section where the target drive is located. Right-click the target drive and select Properties.

5. If Windows 2000 does not see the drive in the Tape Drives or Other Devices sections, you'll need to troubleshoot the drive. Do not continue installation until this is resolved.

6. In the Properties window, verify that the SCSI ID matches that of the tape drive you are installing.

7. Select the Driver tab and then select Update Driver. This will start the Upgrade Device Driver Wizard.

8. In the device dialog, select Next.

9. Select the "Display a list of the know drivers for this device so that I can choose a specific driver" radio button.

10. Select Next.

11. If the drive is unknown to the system, the next view is Hardware Type. Otherwise, the Select a Device Driver view is displayed.

12. For Hardware Type view, select either Other Devices or Tape Drives. Then select Have Disk on the next view.

13. For Select a Device Driver view, select Have Disk.

14. Insert the CD into the CD-ROM drive, and make sure the path is **x:\2000_driver** (where "x" is the CD-ROM drive designator).

15. Click OK.

16. Highlight the listed driver for the tape drive and then click Next.

17. You may see a dialog box indicating that the driver may not be compatible with your hardware. Select Yes to continue driver installation.

18. The Start Device Driver Installation view is displayed.

19. Click Next to install the driver.

20. Should the wizard indicate that the driver already exists on the system and prompt you for a selection, select New.

21. The Windows 2000 Setup window is displayed. Verify the correct path to the driver, then select Continue.

22. The next view is Completing the Upgrade Driver Wizard. Click Finish. You may be prompted to reboot your system.

23. The tape driver is installed.

Installing Backup Software

With your drivers installed, it's time to install the backup software. This part of the chapter looks at the installation and use of BackupExec software. To install BackupExec directly from your CD-ROM, just insert the CD into your CD-ROM drive. The Auto-run routine starts, so just follow the instructions on your screen to install the program. Most types of backup devices are automatically detected and configured the first time you run BackupExec. Your backup device will be listed in the Where to Back Up box. When you install programs like BackupExec, the program and its folder are added to the Windows Start menu (if you have the Backup Exec icon added to your desktop during installation, you may double-click this icon to open the program). To start the software manually, follow these steps:

1. Click the Start button on the Windows taskbar.
2. Select Programs, BackupExec and point to the BackupExec folder.
3. Click BackupExec.
4. BackupExec opens (and appears on the taskbar).
5. The BackupExec Startup window appears.

Automatic Data Protection   Automatic Data Protection (ADP) ensures that your data is backed up on a regular basis. When you first start the backup application, you are prompted with the option of initiating Automatic Data Protection. Any backup job created with Automatic Data Protection can later be edited with BackupExec. If you configure your Advanced Power Management settings to turn off the hard disks after a set period of time, BackupExec will not be able to restart your computer in order to run a scheduled backup job. Follow these steps to use ADP:

1. Select a day of the week for the backup job to run, or select Day or Weekday.
2. If you choose a day of the week, the New and Changed Files option is displayed. If you choose Day or Weekday, the New and Changed Files option is not displayed, and All Selected Files backups are automatically performed.
3. Click OK.

One-Button Backup   The one-button backup feature launches a backup of all local hard disks—including the System State. To use the one-button backup feature:

1. Double-click the One-Button Backup icon on the Desktop. Or, click the Start menu, select Programs | Backup Exec, and then click One-Button Backup.
2. The One-Button Backup dialog box appears (see Figure 20-3).
3. Select a device in the drop-down list box (your tape drive).
4. Click Start.

 If your backup job exceeds the space available on a single tape, BackupExec will prompt you to insert another blank tape when the current one has been filled.

5. The backup will run as either a full or differential backup (with default settings) depending on the following criteria.
6. An All Selected Files backup is performed if ten differential backups have been performed since the last All Selected Files backup (regardless of dates), or if more than seven days have passed since the last backup.
7. A differential backup is performed if no more than seven days have passed since the last All Selected Files backup.

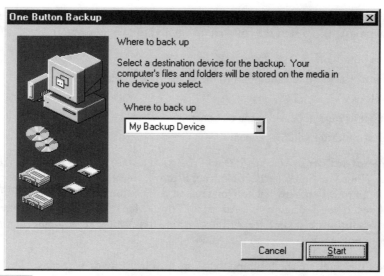

FIGURE 20-3 One-button backup simplifies the backup process for busy administrators.

One-Button Restore The One-Button Restore button launches a series of dialog boxes that help you perform a system restore in just a few steps. To run a one-button restore, follow these steps:

1. Click the Start menu, select Programs, BackupExec, and then click One-Button Restore.

2. The One-Button Restore dialog box appears.

3. Select a device in the drop-down list box.

4. Click Next to continue.

5. Check the drives, folders, and files you want to restore.

6. Click Start to begin restoring your files.

 If your backup job exceeds the space available on a single tape, BackupExec will prompt you to insert another blank tape when the current one has been filled.

Performing a Backup

BackupExec uses backup jobs to save and reuse file and option selections. You create a backup job by selecting desired drives and files for backup, choosing program settings and options, and saving your selections with a new job name. A backup job includes all selections made at the time it is saved:

■ Drives, folders, and files to back up

■ Backup type

■ Backup device

■ Options selected or default selections

Backup jobs can be opened, saved, and deleted using the Job menu. In the Backup window, you can open a backup job with the Backup Job list. To change a backup job, simply make new file or option selections. When you run a backup, your changes are automatically saved. To save your changes under a different name, choose Save As from the Job menu and enter a new name (or type the new name in the Job Name field). If you attempt to save a new job using an existing name, the program asks you to overwrite the existing job. If you choose Overwrite, the new job replaces the existing job.

Backup Wizard   You can use the Backup Wizard to create new backup jobs or you can modify and rename existing job files. By saving your backup jobs, you can run them again without making your selections again. The Backup Job box lists your saved backup jobs. Type a new name in the box to save the job under a different name. Let's take a look at a typical backup with the Backup Wizard:

1. Click Backup Wizard in the Startup window, then click OK. Alternatively, click the Backup Wizard icon on the toolbar. The What to Back Up window of the Backup Wizard appears (see Figure 20-4).

2. Select the drives and files you want to back up. To back up all files, folders, and drives on your computer, click Back Up My Computer. Click Next to continue. The Backup Type Wizard window appears. Alternatively, to back up only some of the files, folders, or drives on your computer, click "Back up selected files, folders and drives". The Backup Wizard Selection dialog appears.

3. Select the specific drives, folders, and files you want to back up. Click Next to continue. Select a backup type.

4. Click All Selected Files to back up all selected files, then click Next. Alternatively, click New and Changed Files Only to back up only files that are new or have changed since the last All Selected Files backup and click Next.

5. Select a destination for the backup from the Where To Back Up list.

6. Click Next to continue. The How to Back Up Wizard window appears (see Figure 20-5).

7. Select your backup options for this screen. Click Next to continue. The When to Back Up Wizard appears.

8. Click Now to begin this backup immediately, or click Later to schedule this backup for a later time. To back up later, specify the frequency, then set the time, date, and/or days of the week to run this backup job.

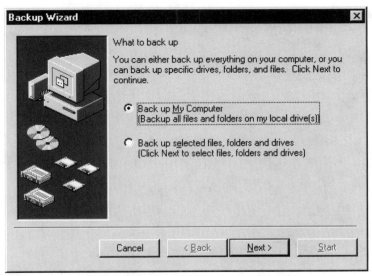

FIGURE 20-4   Starting the Backup Wizard and selecting complete or partial backups

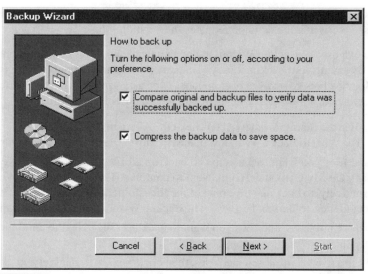

FIGURE 20-5 Making compare and compress selections in the Backup Wizard

9. Click Next to continue. The Name the Backup Job window appears (see Figure 20-6).

10. Type a name for this backup job. Review the backup job's summary. To change an option, use the Back and Next buttons. Click Start to begin this backup job. The Backup Progress window appears. Or, Click OK to run your job as scheduled.

 If your backup job exceeds the space available on a single tape cartridge, BackupExec will prompt you to insert another blank tape when the current one has been filled.

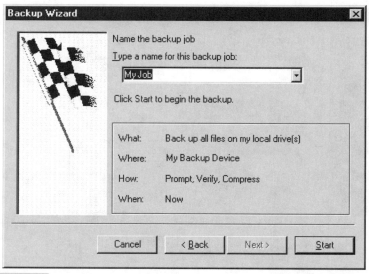

FIGURE 20-6 Naming and starting the backup using the Backup Wizard

Performing a Compare

Compare is a separate function of your backup software designed to provide maximum data integrity. After you create a backup set, you use the BackupExec Compare window to verify that the information contained on the backup tape is identical to the data on the hard disk (and that the data is readable and can be restored later). You should perform compares after your first few backups, and after changing your system's configuration—this will confirm BackupExec is running properly on your computer. Performing a compare at any time in the future lets you see how the files in the backup set differ from the files currently on the hard disk. Selecting the Compare tab (see Figure 20-7) gives you quick access to the compare options. It consists of three main sections:

- **Compare from**   The Compare from drop-down box lists all available backup devices to compare from. To change the drive you want to compare from, select another drive in the drop-down list box.

- **What to compare**   This area lets you select specific files to compare by folders, media, or device.

- **Where to compare**   You'll usually want to compare files to the same drive and directory as the one from which they were backed up. If their location has changed, however, the "Where to compare" box lets you specify where the original files are now located.

After making your selections, simply click Start to start comparing your files. When the compare process is complete, the OK and Report buttons become available. Click Report for a summary of your compare operation, or click OK to continue.

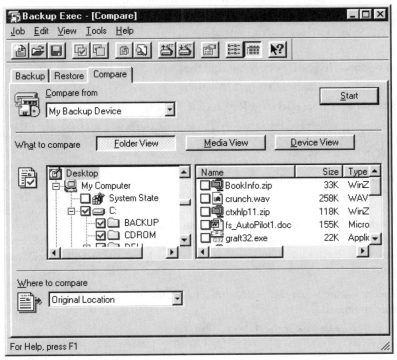

FIGURE 20-7   Performing a compare will verify the current backup and improve reliability for future restore operations.

Performing a Restore

The BackupExec Restore feature reads selected backup sets and restores those files to a specified location (usually their original location). You can restore one file, several selected files, or all files from a backup set. You can also select individual versions of a file, specify the destination for the restored files, and set options. Let's take a look at disaster recovery, and the Restore Wizard.

Disaster Recovery   This first procedure gives you a method to quickly and easily restore all your files in the event of a hard disk failure (this procedure can also be used to transfer all your files to a new computer). Before you can restore your files after a hard disk failure, you must prepare your hard disk (i.e., Fdisk and Format), and reinstall Windows, then follow these steps for Windows 2000:

1. With the hard drive working and Windows 2000 reinstalled, install and configure BackupExec (or your own backup software).

2. Collect the tapes containing your most recent All Selected Files (full) and your New and Changed Files (incremental) backups. The exact backup sets you'll need to restore depend on your backup strategy. If you performed

- **All Selected Files only**   Restore only your most recent backup set.

- **All Selected Files and Differential New and Changed Files**   Restore your All Selected Files backup first, and then restore the most recent differential backup set.

- **All Selected Files and Incremental New and Changed Files**   Restore your All Selected Files backup first, and then restore each of the incremental backup sets in order, starting with the oldest.

3. Restore the All Selected Files backup set. Make the following option selections on the Restore window:

- **What to restore**   Click Device view, and then select each local drive.

- **Where to restore**   Choose Original Locations.

- **How to restore**   Choose Always Replace.

Restoring the system state may cause serious problems if your hardware configuration has changed since you last backed up the system state.

4. If your system's hardware configuration and system settings have *not* changed since the last backup of the System State, place a check mark beside the System State icon in the Restore Window selection pane. All of the files consisting of the System State will be restored along with all selected local drives. However, if your system's hardware configuration *has* changed (i.e., you've added a new drive or changed the IRQ settings on a card), make sure the Restore System State check box is *not* selected. Only files selected from your local drives will be restored.

5. Click Start.

6. When the restore is complete, you're prompted to reboot your computer. Click Yes to reboot the system as recommended.

7. Now restore any New and Changed Files backup sets.

Restoring Bindery Files   You can also restore Bindery files. If you backed up files on your SYS volume or Novell Server and checked the Back up NetWare Bindery option, you can restore your bindery files using steps similar to these:

1. Click the Restore tab. The Restore window appears.

2. In the selection panes, select any file(s) on the SYS volume.

3. When prompted whether or not to restore the bindery, click Yes.

Restore Wizard   Of course, the easiest way to restore lost or corrupted files is to use the BackupExec Restore Wizard, which simply guides you through the steps and options required to create your restore job. To create your restore job using the Restore Wizard, follow these steps:

1. Click Restore Wizard in the Startup window and click OK, or click the Restore Wizard button on the toolbar, or select Restore Wizard from the Tools menu. The Restore From window appears (see Figure 20-8).

2. Choose the backup device to restore from, then click Next. The View files to restore window appears.

3. You may select your files from the catalog stored on your hard disk or from the media in your drive. Click Next to continue. The Restore selection pane window appears (see Figure 20-9).

4. Click the check boxes next to the items you want to restore. Click Next to continue. The Where to Restore window appears.

5. Choose a destination for your restored files. If you choose to restore to another location, type a path into the text box or click Browse. Files are restored in their original folder structure unless you check "Restore all files to a single folder". Click Next to continue. The How to Restore window appears (see Figure 20-10).

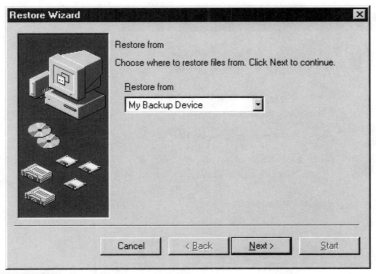

FIGURE 20-8   The Restore Wizard lets you choose where to restore files from.

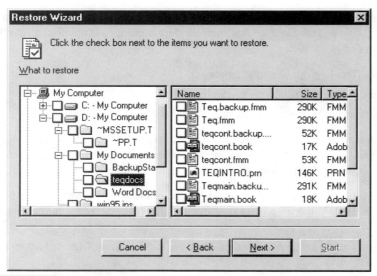

FIGURE 20-9   Check the boxes next to the item(s) that you want to restore.

6. Select an option and click Start.

7. The Media Required box appears. Follow the instructions on the screen, then click OK. The Restore Progress window appears.

 If your backup job spanned more than one tape, insert the first tape of the backup set. BackupExec will then prompt you to insert each additional tape as needed.

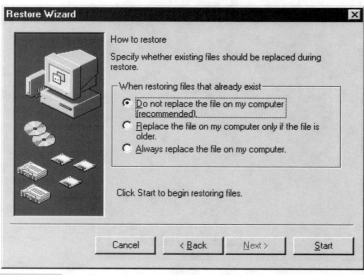

FIGURE 20-10   Select how files are to be restored using the Restore Wizard.

Checking the Installation

After you install your new tape drive and software like Seagate BackupExec, you should make sure that your computer and backup software can recognize your new drive before you try to back up your data. Launch Seagate BackupExec. Look down the list of target drives in the "Where to back up" menu box. If your tape drive is listed in this drop-down list, Seagate BackupExec has recognized your new drive. This means that your tape drive and software are ready to back up data. If your drive is not listed in the drop-down list, the software cannot find the drive.

Tape Drive Troubleshooting

Tapes and tape drives are designed to be rugged and provide a long reliable service life when properly cared for. However, tape systems are notoriously proprietary. Drive mechanisms, device drivers, backup software, and tape media must all be compatible. This means proper installation is critical, routine maintenance is vital, and you'll need to recognize drive problems quickly. This part of the chapter examines common tape and drive issues, and offers solutions for the most common problems.

COMMON BACKUP PROBLEMS

While backups are usually considered to be a cost-effective form of data archiving and a reliable means of data protection, backups are hardly perfect. There is a wide range of issues that can adversely affect your backup efforts (or those of your customer). Here are some common pitfalls to look out for when planning and executing backups:

■ *Backups are performed irregularly or inconsistently.* This is probably the single most troublesome problem when implementing a backup strategy. In order to be effective, backups must be performed *regularly*. All too often, users make some initial backups on schedule, but fail to follow through with subsequent backups. Before long, the backups that *were* made fall so far out-of-date that they become useless. When trouble occurs, the investment in equipment and media just does not pay off. Administrators must make it a point to implement regular backups and follow through with them consistently.

■ *Backups are poorly labeled and stored.* This problem is typical of large tape rotations. Often, tapes and other backup media are left strewn around an office or department with little or no indication of what is on them. Effective backup strategies demand that each tape be marked and identified clearly so that no one will accidentally discard or overwrite it. Groups of tapes should always be kept together in a secured drawer or on a shelf, the same way you would organize volumes of books. It's hard enough to keep regular backups without having to search for the tapes and guess which ones to use. Make it a point to keep tapes (and all magnetic media) away from telephones, monitors, power supplies, excessive heat, extreme cold, and all forms of moisture.

■ *Inadequate disaster preparation.* Here's another real impediment to successful backups. Too often, businesses invest serious money in backup equipment—only to leave the tapes sitting on top of the backed-up system. If you rely on backups to store your vital files, those tapes should be stored in a location that is reasonably safe from disasters (i.e., fire, flood, theft, or sabotage). Often, a fireproof safe or file cabinet will perform quite well. The same concern is true for off-site storage.

■ *Inadequate testing and maintenance.* Some businesses are so preoccupied with *performing* a backup that they do not check to confirm that the backup is any good. When trouble strikes, they are horrified to find that the backup lacks vital files, is unreadable, or does not restore properly—leaving the backup virtually useless. After a backup is made, it should be tested using a "compare" or "verify" function of the backup software to check the tape contents against the disk files. Although this takes a bit longer, it need not be done each time a backup is made. When errors are indicated, it usually means that the drive is failing or has not been routinely cleaned as required. Try cleaning the backup drive as recommended by the manufacturer and perform the backup again. Every so often, it may be worth testing your backup capability with a backup drill.

■ *Inadequate attention to the media.* Like diskettes, tapes are magnetic media. Unfortunately, magnetic media does not last forever. One of the big problems with frequent backups is that users mistake backup or compare errors as a problem with the drive or backup software, where it is actually the *tape* that has worn out. As a general rule, plan on replacing your tapes at least once a year. If you are performing frequent backups, plan on replacing your tapes even more frequently. Tape life is also dependent on tape quality. High-quality tapes last longer than low-quality tapes. It is often more prudent to spend a bit more for a reliable, good-quality tape than save a little money on a low-cost tape—only to find that the tape wears out much sooner, or loses data when it's needed.

DRIVE AND TAPE MAINTENANCE

Tape drives require periodic maintenance for proper operation. In general, there are two types of maintenance that you will need to handle: drive cleaning and tape maintenance. While these hardly sound like exciting procedures, they can have profound effects on your drive's overall performance, and the reliability of your backups.

 These are only general guidelines. Refer to the user's manual for your particular drive for specific cleaning recommendations, and cautions listed by the manufacturer. Every drive has slightly different cleaning and preventive maintenance procedures. Some drives may also require periodic lubrication.

Drive Cleaning

As with floppy disk drives, tape drives bring magnetic media directly into contact with magnetic R/W heads. Over time and with use, magnetic oxides from the tape rub off onto the head surface. Oxides (combined with dust particles and smoke contamination) accumulate and act as a wedge that forces the tape away from the head surface. Even if you never have cause to actually disassemble your tape drive, you should make it a point to perform routine cleaning. Regular cleaning improves the working life of your recording media and can significantly reduce the occurrence of data errors—especially during file restores where problems can keep you shut down.

The objective of drive cleaning is remarkably simple: remove any buildup of foreign material that may have accumulated on the R/W head. The most common cleaning method employs a pre-packaged cleaning cartridge. The cartridge contains a length of slightly abrasive cleaning material. When cleaning tape is run through the drive, any foreign matter on the head is rubbed away. The cleaning tape can often be used for several cleanings before being discarded. Some cleaning tapes can be run dry, while others may have to be dampened with an alcohol-based cleaning solution. The advantage to a cleaning cartridge is *simplicity*—the procedure is quick, and you never have to disassemble the drive. Since QIC and Travan-type tape moves much more slowly across a R/W head than floppy media does, you need not worry about damaging the R/W head due to friction. DAT and 8mm (helical) heads *do* move across the tape quickly, so you must be cautious about cleaning times. You will likely have better results over the long term using dry cleaning cartridges that are impregnated with a lubricating agent to reduce friction.

Cleaning cartridges are typically not rewindable—once they have been run through the drive, they are simply discarded. However, many tape drives do not detect the "end" of a cleaning tape. Be sure to inspect the cleaning cartridge regularly, and discard it after it is exhausted.

Autoloader Cleaning   The *autoloader* is a feature that loads and unloads helical scan DAT tapes (in much the same way that VCRs use automatic loaders and unloaders). In some DAT drives, the loader mechanism retrieves cartridges from a magazine, inserts them in the DAT drive inside the autoloader, and returns them to the magazine when the cartridges are unloaded and ejected by the internal drive. Autoloader mechanisms and guide paths should also be cleaned (and lubricated if necessary) on a regular basis—often once a month, or when an autoloader front panel error is displayed.

Tape Maintenance

Tape cartridges are one of the more rugged items in the PC world—tape is contained in a hard plastic shell, and the R/W head aperture is usually guarded by a metal or plastic shroud. However, tapes are certainly not indestructible. They must be handled with care to ensure the integrity of their data. The following guidelines will help you get the most from your tapes:

■ *Avoid fingerprints on the tape.* Do not open the tape access door of the cartridges or touch the tape itself. Fingerprints can prevent the drive from reading the tape and result in errors.

■ *Set the write protect switch.* Be sure to set the write-protect switch after backing up your data—this will reduce the possibility of accidentally overwriting critical data if you forget to label the tape.

■ *Careful of magnetic fields.* Tapes are sensitive to magnetic fields from monitors, electromechanical telephone ringers, fans, and so on. Keep the tape away from sources of magnetic fields.

■ *Careful of toner.* The toner used by laser printers and photocopiers is a microfine dust that may filter out of the device in small quantities. Keep your tapes away from printers and copiers to avoid accidental contamination by toner dust.

■ *Careful of the tape environment.* Keep the tape out of direct sunlight, keep the tape dry, and keep the tape safe from temperature extremes (sudden hot-to-cold or cold-to-hot transitions). Before using a tape, allow it to slowly assume the current room temperature.

■ *Retension your tapes regularly.* Before using a tape that has been idle for a month or more, use your backup software to retension the tape first. This removes any "tight spots" that often develop on the tape.

You've probably noticed that if you play a videotape often, the picture and sound quality on the tape will begin to degrade. This is a natural effect of wear as the media passes repeatedly over the R/W heads. Tapes do not last forever, and after a period of use, they should be destroyed before their reliability deteriorates to a point where your data is not safe. Tape life is generally rated in terms of *passes*. But passes are difficult to track because a single backup or restore operation may involve many passes. Tape life also depends on how the tape is used. For example, a nightly backup to an 8mm tape may use only the first half or the tape, but leave the last half of the tape almost unused. As a rule, follow the "20-use" rule: If a tape is used daily, replace the tape every month. If a tape is used weekly, replace the tape every 6 months. If a tape is only used monthly, replace it every 18–24 months.

Regardless of how you schedule tape replacement, you should replace a tape immediately if it has been physically damaged, if it has become wet, frozen, or overheated, or if your backup application reports repeated media errors.

Errors Due to Cleaning Neglect

Tape drives are some of the most susceptible to the buildup of contaminants. If a tape drive is not kept clean, increased dropouts will occur where the drive cannot read or write to the tape (you may lose as much as 20 percent of backup capacity and performance if the recommended head cleaning schedule is not followed). High-end tape drives typically monitor the total number of dropouts. When the number reaches a predetermined threshold (defined in the drive's firmware), an LED on the drive will slowly flash, indicating the tape drive needs cleaning. These are some of the errors that can result from failure to observe routine tape drive maintenance and cleaning:

- **Dropouts**   A *dropout* is caused by weak signal strength from dirty read/write heads, and can result in reduced tape capacity and backup performance.

- **Media errors**   The backup tapes can be jammed, torn, or otherwise damaged by a dirty read/write head. This may require you to replace the effected tape cartridge.

- **Read or write errors**   Data may not be recorded on the tape during backup because of a dirty read/write head. Even if the data is on the backup tape, retrieval may not be possible if the dirty head cannot read the data.

- **Format failures**   During backup, data is laid on the tape in a certain format for easy retrieval. A dirty write head can cause format failures, which means that data can be lost or impossible to retrieve.

- **Bad blocks**   The tape may not accept backup data because of media damage. Also, the read/write head may be unable to retrieve data from bad blocks caused by tape failures.

Media Problems and DAT Drives

DAT drives are particularly sensitive to contaminants and media problems. If the DAT media is marginal or defective, it will cause the drive to report an error that is either displayed on the drive's indicator(s) or passed to the backup software. There are several characteristics of a DAT tape cartridge that can cause DAT drives to fail:

- **Head clogs**   These are the most common media problem, caused by loose media particles deposited on the read/write heads. These deposits prevent the drive from reading or writing to the tape. Head clogs are reported in several ways (depending on the firmware version in use). When a head clog occurs, clean the drive at least four times to ensure the heads are clean. Tape media problems can also result in head clogs. Keep track of when tapes fail and when they are successful for the first three uses—if a tape fails two out of three times, the tape is failing and must be replaced.

- **High-torque cartridges**   These may be wound incorrectly during manufacturing (the tape rubs against the top and/or bottom of the inside of the tape cartridge shell). This creates enough resistance to prevent the DAT drive from moving the tape consistently. For example, autoloaders will display the message "BAD TPE #", where # is the slot number of the tape (so you can find it in the autoloader magazine). High-torque tapes *must* be replaced.

- **BOT/EOT prism problems**   These are caused by bad cartridges. They are not common, but when they happen, they will intermittently prevent the drive from sensing the end or beginning of tape. This causes the motors that move the tape to stop suddenly, resulting in an error message. The cartridge must be replaced.

- **Physical tape damage**   This may be caused by the drive, or may occur during tape manufacturing. This problem always occurs on the exact same location on tape. This problem can only be verified by testing with a special debug tool that can eject the tape without rewinding so the damage is visible, and requires that the tape be captured. It is generally recommended that tapes reporting these errors be replaced.

■ **Tape hub alignment**   These problems typically cause noise during high-speed tape motion such as a "rewind." When this occurs, it is recommended to replace the tape.

Recommended Cleaning Guide for DAT Drives   To optimize the performance and reliability of DAT drives, follow these recommendations for cleaning:

■ When using new tape media for backups, DAT drives need to be cleaned after each 8 hours of read/write operation until the entire data cartridge has been used five times.

■ When using data cartridges that have already been used five times or more, clean DAT drives after each 25 hours of read/write operation.

■ Clean DAT drives before performing a complete server (or major system) backup.

■ Clean only once for routine cleaning, to minimize head wear. Occasionally a single cleaning cycle will not fully clean read/write heads on a DAT drive. If the backup software reports errors, clean the drive again to eliminate the possibility that dirty heads are causing the error.

■ Clean the drive four times after a failure to ensure the heads are cleaned. A single cleaning cycle may not remove a head clog adequately.

■ When using an autoloader, keep a cleaning cartridge in the last slot. Refer to your software user manual for instructions on how to schedule and perform automatic cleaning operations using the backup software.

■ DAT cleaning cartridges typically last 30 cleaning cycles (passes). Remember to replace the cleaning cartridge after it has been exhausted.

SYMPTOMS

While guidelines can help to correct many simple issues and oversights, there are times when you'll require more specific information. The following situations outline frequent drive and software problems, and offer corrective actions to help remedy the trouble.

SYMPTOM 20-1   **The tape drive does not work at all.**   Begin your repair by checking for obvious setup and configuration errors. First, make sure that power is available to the drive (a power indicator will usually be lit on the drive). An internal tape drive is usually powered from the host computer, so be sure that the internal four-pin power connector is correctly attached. External drives are almost always powered from a separate ac adapter or power supply, but a few proprietary drives can be powered through their interface cables. Check the output of any external ac adapter or power supply. If the ac adapter output is low or nonexistent, replace the ac adapter.

Check that the interface cable between drive and tape controller card is connected properly. Also, check that your backup software is running and properly configured to your particular drive. If you are troubleshooting a new, unproved installation, inspect the tape controller board address, interrupt, and DMA settings as necessary—configuration conflicts can lock up a software package or render a drive inoperative. Check the tape itself to be sure it is inserted properly and completely.

Check the drive for indicator patterns (i.e., blink codes) that may suggest a drive problem. If the error indicates a fault in the drive, the drive mechanism must be replaced. If the drive is simply not communicating with the system, check the drive's installation, controller, driver, and backup software.

SYMPTOM 20-2   **The tape doesn't read or write, but the tape and head seem to move properly.**   You will probably find read/write errors indicated by your backup software. Start your repair by inspecting the tape cartridge itself. The cartridge should be inserted completely and properly into the drive, and sit firmly over the reel. If the current tape is inserted properly, try loading from another tape. Old tapes may have degraded to a point where data can no longer be read or written reliably. If an alternate tape works properly, discard and replace the old tape. If problems persist, try cleaning the tape drive's R/W heads. Excessive buildups of dust or residual oxides can easily interfere with normal tape recording/playback operations. If you still encounter R/W trouble, the R/W heads or their associated circuitry has probably failed. Try replacing the tape drive.

SYMPTOM 20-3   **The drive writes to write-protected tapes.**   When a tape is write-protected, the drive should not be able to write to that protected tape. Your first step should be to remove and inspect the tape itself. Check to make sure that the write-protect lever is in the "protect" position. If the protect lever is not in the right place, the tape is vulnerable to writing. If the tape protect lever is set properly, replace the entire drive.

SYMPTOM 20-4   **The backup software indicates "Too many bad sectors" on the tape.** You may also see an error such as "Error correction failed". This type of error generally indicates that more than 5 percent of the sectors on a tape are unreadable. In many cases, this is due to dirty R/W heads. Try cleaning the R/W head assembly. If problems continue, try a new tape cartridge. If problems persist, check the drive's power and signal cables and make sure that they are installed properly and completely.

SYMPTOM 20-5   **The tape backup software produces a "Tape drive error XX" error.** The "xx" fault type will depend on the particular drive and tape backup software you are using, so refer to the user manual for exact code meanings. The following code examples are for Colorado tape backup software:

- **0Ah** (Broken or dirty tape)   Clean the R/W heads carefully, and replace the tape (if broken).
- **0Bh** (Gain error)   Reformat the tape before attempting a backup.
- **1Ah** (Power-on reset occurred)   Check the drive's power and signal connections and try again.
- **1Bh** (Software reset occurred)   Shut down any application that might be conflicting with the tape backup software.
- **04h** (Drive motor jammed)   Remove the tape and make sure that there is nothing (including the tape) blocking the motor(s). Insert a new tape and try the system again.

SYMPTOM 20-6   **The tape drive works in DOS, but refuses to work in Windows 9x or later.**   First make sure that the backup software you're using under Windows 9x is able to detect the tape drive. If the backup software is working properly, chances are that one or more Windows 9x drivers are interfering with the tape drive. Try starting Windows 9x in the Safe mode and try your tape access again. If the tape drive is accessible now, you're going to have to check for driver or software conflicts. This often happens with parallel port tape backups when Windows 9x drivers block parallel port access using third-party printer drivers loaded by **SYSTEM.INI**. You should check the [386Enh] section of **SYSTEM.INI** and use semicolons to "remark out" any offending "device=" lines.

SYMPTOM 20-7   **The backup software generates an overlay error such as "Could not open file: QBACKUP.OVL".**   Failures to open overlay files are often due to insufficient buffers. For example, you should usually have a BUFFERS=30 or higher entry in your **CONFIG.SYS** file. Otherwise, the backup utility may not function properly. If you do edit changes to your **CONFIG.SYS** file, remember to save your changes before rebooting the computer.

Always make it a point to have backup copies of your **CONFIG.SYS** and **AUTOEXEC.BAT** files available before making changes to them. That way, you can easily restore original startup files without having to reedit the files.

SYMPTOM 20-8   **You encounter "media errors", "bad block errors", "system errors", or "lock-ups".**   These types of problems are known to occur with Travan tapes, and there are several possible problems to consider. First, try removing and reinserting the Travan data cartridge. In many cases this allows the drive mechanism to clear any errors. If problems continue, try reinitializing the data cartridge (typically handled through backup software such as "Tools" and "Initialize"). Note that reinitializing the cartridge will render all data on it unusable. Finally, try disabling data compression—especially if you notice a high frequency of "shoe shining," which often results in error messages.

All TR-4 data cartridges are preformatted, and these TR-4 tapes cannot be reformatted unless your tape drive mechanism is designed to format TR-4 tapes. As a consequence, do *not* "bulk erase" a TR-4 cartridge using an electromagnet or similar device.

SYMPTOM 20-9   **During initialization under DOS or Windows, the SCSI tape driver (i.e., BPASPI.SYS) reports the error "An ASPI drive was not found".**   In many cases the driver's test for enhanced parallel ports is causing the problem, so try disabling the EPP test by adding a command-line switch to the ASPI tape driver—for example,

```
device=\bpaspi\bpaspi.sys NOEPP
```

Note that your particular drive mechanism and driver may use different command-line switches. Once you make the changes to **CONFIG.SYS**, save your changes, then turn off the tape drive and computer before rebooting the system.

SYMPTOM 20-10   **When using a Colorado Trakker tape drive, you cannot get the drive to save or restore files reliably.**   You will probably see error messages like: "Unable to transfer data properly. Retry the operation", "Tape header contains unexpected or invalid values", "Microsoft Backup encountered an error reading this tape. This error may be caused by an unformatted or incorrectly formatted tape. Reformat the tape, and then try again." In virtually all cases, the drive (or backup software) does not function with EPP or ECP type parallel ports. You should enter the CMOS Setup and change the parallel port mode to "Compatibility mode."

You may not receive any error messages when you back up files, but you may then be unable to compare or restore the files. If you *can* restore the files, the data that is restored to your hard disk may be damaged.

SYMPTOM 20-11   **It takes much longer than you expect to perform a backup.**   This poor backup performance may also be accompanied by poor hard disk performance while you perform other tasks in Windows or later. There are a number of problems that can cause this poor performance. First, there may be a lack of available RAM—you may have too many programs open at the same time, or not have enough physical RAM installed in the computer. Try closing all programs before starting the backup process. If performance does not improve, remove all programs from the Startup folder, and from the load= and run= lines in **WIN.INI**, then restart Windows. If performance is still poor, you may need to add more physical RAM to your computer to improve performance.

One or more of your hard disks may be running in the Compatibility mode. If the Performance tab in System properties shows that one or more of the hard disks in your computer is using the MS-DOS Compatibility mode, resolving this problem should improve performance in Backup. You may need a new protected-mode driver for the hard drive. Even if your hard disks are not using MS-DOS Compatibility mode, the speed of your backup may be affected by the overall performance of your hard disks. For example, if you are using an IDE hard disk, the performance of the hard disk may be affected by another device that is connected to the same IDE controller channel (such as CD-ROM drives). Try moving the slower device to a separate IDE controller, or to the second IDE channel on an EIDE dual-port controller.

If you're using disk compression on a computer with an older CPU, hard disk performance may not be as good as if you were not using disk compression. If you are using third-party disk compression software that uses a real-mode driver to access your compressed drives, you may be able to improve performance by replacing the real-mode driver with a protected-mode driver (contact the maker of your compression software).

Check the file fragmentation on your hard drive. Badly fragmented hard disks can affect the performance of backup software, as well as the performance of other tasks in Windows. Run DEFRAG to defragment your hard disks. Finally, backup software can often detect and avoid unusable sectors on a tape, but the process that it uses to do so can be time-consuming. If you suspect that performance problems are caused by unusable sectors on a tape, try using a new tape, or a tape that you know does not contain unusable sectors.

SYMPTOM 20-12   **You experience excessive "shoe shining" during backups.** In normal tape drive operations, the tape drive writes data to a single track from one end of the tape to another: It then writes data in a parallel data track back to the beginning of the tape, and so on, until the tape is full. *Shoe shining* refers to frequent back-and-forth tape motion. If you have the backup window open, minimize it. With the window open, the system has to continually update the screen, and this takes resources away from the software sending data to the tape drive. If the PC offers a "turbo mode", try disabling the turbo mode (especially when using parallel port tape drives).

Further Study

Computer Peripherals: **www.cpuinc.com**
Exabyte: **www.exabyte.com**
Seagate: **www.seagate.com**
Tandberg Data: **www.tandberg.com**
Overland Data: **www.ovrland.com**
Hewlett-Packard: **www.hp.com/tape/colorado/index.html**
AIT Technology: **www.aittape.com**
DLT Standards: **www.dlttape.com**
LTO Standards: **www.lto-technology.com**

21

IMPLEMENTING A BASIC NETWORK

Networks don't simply appear. They are crafted into being with a carefully conceived plan that is based on a solid understanding of the hardware and software elements involved. Implementing a successful network requires an ample amount of planning and selection. If you're working with an existing network, it's imperative that you have access to all of the documents, maps, layouts, and other administrative information available. With this information as your guide, you can select new hardware, software, and cabling that will be compatible with the current network design. Starting a new network from scratch is actually a more difficult endeavor. You'll need to evaluate the needs of your organization and its workers, select the hardware and software to fit the needs (and budget), plan and implement the installation, then establish security with accounts and shares. The bottom line is that good planning and a methodical approach are essential to upgrading an existing network or implementing a new network. In this chapter, you'll learn some elements and see some examples of network planning, then cover basic concepts of setup and problem solving.

Planning a Basic Network

Whether you're updating an existing network or planning a new network, the first step in implementing the work is *planning*. This may sound painfully obvious, but you'd be amazed at the amount of labor spent correcting oversights and fixing compatibility issues. Proper planning and review will eliminate a *lot* of potential problems (and needless expense) when you're actually doing the work. The planning process can usually be divided into five main areas: setting network objectives, evaluating current resources, developing a plan, reviewing the plan, and implementing the plan. Ideally, your implemented plan will meet (or exceed) the objectives set out at the beginning of the project.

DEFINE THE OBJECTIVES

Surprisingly, setting clear objectives is often the most difficult and frustrating part of the process. The idea here is to identify what needs to be done, and what the work will accomplish. While this may not be so critical if you simply need to add a workstation or upgrade a NIC, it is absolutely essential when building or expanding a network—setting objectives will lay the foundation of the entire project. For example, a typical planning process may require you to answer the following questions:

- How many users must be networked together?
- How many existing computers must be connected?
- How many existing devices (e.g., printers) must be connected?
- How many new computers (if any) must be added?
- How many new devices (e.g., printers) must be added?
- Is there a need for future expandability? If so, how many users or devices?
- Are any unusual resources required (e.g., Internet connectivity for a particular user or group)?
- Who is responsible for network maintenance and administration?

Of course, there are countless variations to these questions, and each situation may require more or less information. Ultimately, the goal here is for you to get a clear picture of just what needs to be done, and what your customer expects when the network is completed. By clearly defining your objectives, you can be sure to meet the needs of your customer. The problem with setting objectives is that your customer (perhaps an outside company, or maybe a department head in your own company) may not have a clear knowledge of just what's needed. You may simply be told, "I want everyone in the company (or department) to be on a network." Remember that your customer will probably not know as much about networking as you do, and you may need to ferret out the specific details in order to present a specific plan.

EVALUATE CURRENT RESOURCES

Once you've got a clear picture of just what's required of the network, the next step is to evaluate the current hardware and software resources available to work with. Remember that many users in the company or department may already have a computer available to them. In some cases, those computers may even have network cards or network-related software installed, or be part of some preexisting network infrastructure. Before you recommend the purchase of new equipment, it's important to determine what is already in service. For example, suppose that you're faced with a variety of individual PCs running Windows 9x. Chances are that you'll need to replace or upgrade at least some of the oldest systems, add network cards to the remaining systems, and update the system designated as the server with Windows NT/2000 or NetWare. You will need to take account of hardware, software, connectivity, and network resources.

Checking Hardware

If you've ever had to check the minimum system requirements on that new game or PC productivity package, you already know that software makes certain demands on PC hardware. The PC must meet or exceed those minimum levels in order to support the software properly. This is even more important in a network environment. By evaluating the hardware that is available now, you can make informed decisions about which systems must be replaced, upgraded, or added. Knowing the specifications of each system now will prevent serious performance or compatibility problems later. Identifying specific key devices will also make it easier for you to track down updated drivers, if necessary. For each computer, you will need to gather information such as

- PC make and model (e.g., Gateway Performa 1100).
- Processor manufacturer and speed (e.g., Intel Pentium III 1.1GHz).
- Amount of memory (RAM) installed (e.g., 256MB).
- The manufacturer and size of each hard drive (e.g., C: Maxtor 30GB HDD).
- Details of any other installed drives (e.g., CD-ROM, floppy drive, or Iomega drives).
- Monitor characteristics (e.g., Gateway Vivitron21 21 in).
- Video card characteristics (e.g., Voodoo3 3Dfx 16MB).
- NIC card characteristics (if installed).
- Denote any installed peripherals (e.g., printers or scanners) and see that you have the original installation diskettes or CDs for each.
- Note the system bus (e.g., EISA, ISA, or PCI) and check to see how many slots are free. This will be important if you need to add a network card or upgrade a drive controller.

Checking Software

While you're checking each system's hardware, take some time to survey the software being used on that system. This information can be important because it may affect hardware compatibility. For example, if you updated all the computers to Windows 2000 during network implementation, you might find that some of the existing programs (perhaps used on a daily basis) no longer run. This is particularly tricky when the company or department uses custom-designed or proprietary programs such as accounting databases that have been written especially for the company. Few proprietary programs will run properly on a network (if at all). In other cases license agreements may not allow network use. You might need to contact the software manufacturer for information about running proprietary programs on the network. Gather the following information for the operating system and each software program:

- Program name.
- Program version number.
- See that you have the original installation diskettes or CDs for each program.
- Check the licensing information for each program (an upgrade may be required to allow use on the network).

It's amazing how software compatibility issues will surface when you actually sit down and see what everyone is using. For example, the accounting department might be using WordPerfect, while the sales department may be using Microsoft Office. You may need to upgrade certain applications in order to standardize on one suite of software for the entire network. This in turn may demand additional training for users that are not familiar with the chosen software.

Checking Connectivity

Today, most networks include some form of telecommunications connectivity in order to use Internet connections or some form of remote access server (RAS—a host on a LAN that includes modems and enables users to connect to the network over telephone lines). Take note of the phone line(s) wired into each office or user location. For example, if a company or department has an electronic telephone system, telephone outlets might be located in every office, but chances are they're not capable of a modem connection. A separate telephone outlet might be required for voice and data communication. Similarly, a digital telephone service (a PBX) may not support standard modems at all. In short, see what's available for telephone connections just in case you need them.

Check Network Resources

A final area to evaluate is the presence of *existing* network resources (if any). Check for patch panels, RJ-45 or BNC wall outlets, previously installed network cable plants, or any existing infrastructure that you may be able to use. If the company or department had already been wired for Category 5 UTP in every office—perhaps when the building was constructed—this may *greatly* simplify the physical implementation (and reduce the costs) of your network's wiring. Rather than wiring a building from scratch, it may simply be a matter of adding or modifying the cabling in order to support your users. In many cases, you should have a set of building plans available so that you can trace existing wiring and plan new wiring as necessary.

Now is also a good time to consider the physical plant where the network will be installed. Based on the size of the facility, the number of users, and the environment (e.g., office or manufacturing), you can give some thought to how a network will be wired, and what kind of media (e.g., coax or twisted pair) is best suited for your particular situation.

PLAN THE WORK

The next step is to actually plan the work that will be needed to implement your network. Ultimately, a plan will start with the resources that are currently available and detail the work needed to reach the network objectives. Such a plan may include upgrading or replacing existing systems, adding systems for other users, outfitting those systems for network operation, installing the wiring, installing the software, and configuring the network as needed. This planning process usually includes timeframe and budget considerations. In most cases, a plan must be presented to (and approved by) your customer before the actual work can begin.

Stick with the Budget

The greatest technical design in the world is useless if it will cost too much money to implement. If the money for a project is not in the budget, no amount of creativity will make the design work. Before you become involved in a project, find out about the budget—know the monetary parameters for the design and stay within them. If you think the budget for the project is unrealistic, say so up front. You may be able to modify the budget (or the project) to be more appropriate.

You may find that you can offer nearly the same amount of functionality within a design by substituting less-expensive components for more costly ones. However, do not use substandard products—you'll only end up spending the money you saved initially on increased repairs and support costs. If you scale back your design to the point that you can no longer offer the same level of functionality that was initially envisioned, and the project will still go over budget, you'll need to inform management that you'll have to sacrifice low-priority features. It's better to provide a stable set of core functionality and cut out less important features than to skimp on the entire project.

Network Types

If you're developing or updating a network, you must decide whether the network will be peer-to-peer or server-based. This is an important decision because it will affect number of users, expandability, security, budget, traffic, and administrative management involved. You will often be working with a server-based network by default. However, you should still understand the considerations involved in selecting a network type.

Peer-to-Peer   Small businesses or groups with just a few users benefit quite well from a peer-to-peer network approach. All users on the network are equal, and each will have equal access to all other computers on the network—provided that other PC users have shared resources with the network. There is no centralized administration or management support for a peer-to-peer network. Responsibility for running the network is distributed to everyone, and individual users determine which information or resources on their computers will be shared. This is often a plus in small businesses that cannot afford a full-time network administrator.

However, there are some disadvantages to a peer-to-peer network. All PCs and resources must be running. For example, if a user with a laser printer turns their PC off, no one else will be able to share the laser printer. As another example, if one computer freezes or reboots while another tries to access resources, that computer will be effectively disconnected. Performance is also limited. If a user is accessing resources on your computer, that user will also be using processor time on your computer. This means your PC's performance will be impacted whenever someone else is accessing your system. Peer-to-peer networks are generally not feasible with more than ten users.

Server-Based   On a server-based network, resources are usually centralized to a few key computers, but many clients can access those resources. For example, one server manages all the printers, another server manages all the files, and so on. Since servers are rarely turned off (ideally never), resources will always be available to the network. Since other clients access servers rather than other users' systems, only server performance is affected by network traffic (workstation performance is unaffected). Server-based networks are also *scalable*—servers can be upgraded (and more servers added) to compensate for increased network traffic.

The centralized nature of server-based networks makes them more secure than peer-to-peer networks. With a peer-to-peer network, all resources are shared equally across the network. For example, if Accounting shares a directory that contains salary files, everyone else on the network can also access these files. This is clearly not secure. By comparison, server-based networks use accounts and permissions, so particular users (and groups of users) may access certain files or directories without making the data available to everyone on the network.

Hybrids   It is certainly possible to combine peer-to-peer and server-based approaches. Many small companies looking to expand at some point in the future may elect to install a peer-to-peer network in order to service a few users, but also install a dedicated computer as a file server/print server. With this approach, access to the file/print server requires an account and permissions, while access to other computers on the network is shared equally. As the network and its traffic grow, users may be shifted off the peer-to-peer network into more traditional server-based architectures (e.g., bus, star, or ring), and placed alongside new users.

Topology and Architecture

With an understanding of the network type, you can work to choose an appropriate network topology: bus, ring, or star (these topologies are detailed in Chapter 2). The bus topology is often referred to as a "linear bus" because the computers are connected from one to another. It consists of a single cable called a *trunk* (also called a *backbone* or *segment*) that connects all of the computers in the network in a single line. This is the simplest and most common method of networking a relatively small number of Ethernet computers. Since data is sent to the entire network in the form of an electronic signal, it travels from one end of the cable to the other. If the signal is allowed to continue uninterrupted, it will keep bouncing back and forth along the cable and prevent other computers from sending signals. Therefore, the signal must be stopped after it has had a chance to reach the proper destination address. To stop the signal from bouncing, a component called a *terminator* is placed at each end of the cable to absorb free signals. Absorbing the signal clears the cable so that other computers can send data.

In the star topology, cable segments from each computer are connected to a centralized component called a *hub* (a *switch* can also be used when connecting groups of computers). Hubs (or switches) can be grouped together to support a large number of PCs. Figure 21-1 shows a simple network with two workstations and a server connected to a hub using the star topology. Signals are transmitted from the sending computer through the hub to all computers on the network. This topology originated in the early days of computing when computers were connected to a centralized mainframe computer. The star topology offers the advantage of centralized resources and management, and is commonly employed for 10/100/1000 Ethernet networks (Chapter 2 covers the ideas of Ethernet). However, since each computer is connected to a central point, this topology requires a great deal of cable in a large network installation. Also, if the central point fails (e.g., the hub), the entire network goes down (you can learn more about hubs, switches, and other interconnection devices in Chapters 13 and 14).

The ring topology (almost always used for token ring networks) connects computers on a single circle of cable. Unlike the bus topology, there are no terminated ends. The signals travel around the loop in one direction and pass through each computer, which can act as a repeater to boost the signal and send it on to the next computer. The failure of one computer can have an impact on the entire network. In actual practice, a ring topology resembles a star, where all PCs are wired to a central point called a Multipoint Access Unit (MAU). The "loop" is formed by circuitry within the MAU, and MAUs can be grouped together to

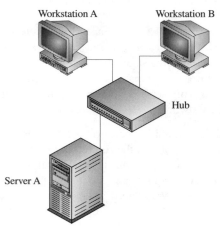

FIGURE 21-1 A simple network with two PCs and a server

support a large number of users. Networks based on the ring topology offer superior self-diagnostic capabilities (Chapter 2 outlines token ring architecture).

Wireless Options

While the vast majority of networks rely on some form of physical cabling for data transport, there are times when cabling is not a suitable solution. Often, the building's design doesn't easily accommodate the installation of new cabling. In other cases, the user may require a degree of mobility that cannot be achieved with cabling. Wireless access techniques can be employed to ease tricky cabling issues and provide mobility for the user (wireless concepts are detailed in Chapter 6).

Wireless installations are implemented with a *wireless access point* (or WAP—do not confuse this with the wireless application protocol used with wireless devices), which serves as a radio transceiver and provides a physical connection to the cabled network. One or more workstations with a wireless NIC can then exchange data with the WAP—accessing the rest of the network (as in Figure 21-2). Where additional range is needed (such as for added mobility), several WAPs can be installed at various locations around the network, and users can roam between adjacent access points.

Common Considerations

It's important for you to understand is that there is no one "right" way to design a network—there are as many design preferences as there are designers. However, some guidelines can help you get your fledgling network on the right track. The following guide will help you determine whether a peer-to-peer or server-based environment is most appropriate for your site, help you form a general picture of the role that servers should play in your network, and help you choose an appropriate topology. Simply check the appropriate answer to each question and add up the results—the answer with the most checks is usually the best decision:

■ Roughly how many users will the network serve (or will be expected to server in the near future)?

0–10	Select a peer-to-peer scheme
11+	Select a server-based scheme

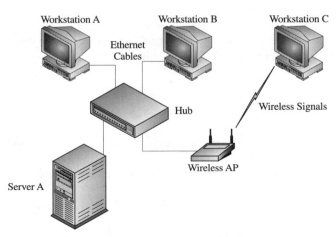

FIGURE 21-2   A basic network with wireless support added

■ Will data and resources on your network need to be restricted or regulated through a common security scheme?

No	Select a peer-to-peer scheme
Yes	Select a server-based scheme

■ How will computers on the network be utilized?

Client/Server	Select a peer-to-peer scheme
Client	Select a server-based scheme
Server	Select a server-based scheme

■ Will network users be able to handle their own administration and management tasks?

No	Select a server-based scheme
Yes	Select a peer-to-peer scheme

■ Will network users be allowed to share their own resources and set other network policies for their own computer?

No	Select a server-based scheme
Yes	Select a peer-to-peer scheme

■ Will your network have one central administrator who sets network policies and privileges?

No	Select a peer-to-peer scheme
Yes	Select a server-based scheme

■ Will your network use centralized servers?

No	Select a peer-to-peer scheme
Yes	Select a server-based scheme

If you opt for a server-based network, the following questions can help you to predict and resolve capacity and location issues that often arise in a server-based environment:

■ Identify the tasks that your server(s) must support:

Communication	Backup/redundancy	Application
Database	E-mail	Fax
Print	User directories	General data storage

■ Are some of the servers designated for special tasks (such as a Web or FTP server)?

Yes
No

■ Approximately how many servers does your network have now (or is expected to have in total)?

0–5
6–10
11–50
51–100
100+

■ Will the network servers be centrally located or spread out in different locations?

Centrally located
Spread out (why?)

■ Will some (or all) of the network servers be placed in a secure location?

Yes
No (why?)

Now it's time to select the network topology. If you're not clear on the choice of one topology over another, the following questions can help you to choose an appropriate topology for your network:

■ Roughly how many users will the network serve (or be expected to serve in the near future)?

| 0–10 | Select a bus topology (though any topology will suffice) |
| 11+ | Select a star or ring topology |

■ Is real-time performance a consideration in choosing the network topology?

| No | Any topology will be suitable |
| Yes | Ring stations have predictable timing, so select ring topology |

■ Is automated troubleshooting important?

| No | Any topology will be suitable |
| Yes | Ring topology detects inserted/removed stations, so select ring topology (if compatible with other decisions here) |

■ Is ease of troubleshooting important?

| No | Any topology will be suitable |
| Yes | Star topology allows for easy connection and cross wiring of stations |

■ Does the current physical layout of the computers and office spaces naturally lend itself to a particular topology?

| No |
| Yes (what topology?) |

■ Is ease of reconfiguration important?

No	Any topology will be suitable
Yes	Star topology allows for easy connection and cross wiring of stations

■ Can the existing wiring in the building be used for your new network?

No	
Yes (what topology?)	

Of course, these questions offer only one generic guideline, and you may include any other important considerations in this decision-making process.

Selecting Media

Now that you've established a physical and logical layout, it's time to select wiring (media) for the network. This is an important decision because the labor required to wire a building is generally quite high—a cost that is exacerbated if inadequate or inappropriate wiring has to be replaced. Not only must the media be appropriate for your network type, it must also be appropriate for the particular requirements of the location. For example, if several workstations are located in a manufacturing environment where lots of electrical noise is generated, fiber-optic cable might be required because it is unaffected by electrical signals. By comparison, ordinary twisted-pair (or shielded twisted pair) cable will usually be appropriate in an office (cabling is detailed in Chapter 8).

The other aspect of network media involves future expandability of the network. Using the minimum cable for your traffic today may save money, but if users and traffic increase, your wiring may become totally inadequate in the future and require a time-consuming and expensive rewiring process. As an example, you might decide to install Category 3 UTP cable on a small network. This would certainly support a few workstations, but limit the network speed to 10 Mbps. A few years down the road, that network may have many more workstations, and a 10-Mbps network would become painfully slow. If you look ahead and install Category 5 UTP (or better) now, you could upgrade the network to 100 Mbps (even faster) at any time in the future without having to rewire the building—and enjoy that capability for just a few cents more per foot. Also, there are a growing number of wireless NIC and access point solutions for situations when it's physically difficult to install permanent wiring between a PC and a hub or switch.

Research suggests that over 80 percent of all new network installations are using UTP cable in an Ethernet star topology. Since most cable installation costs are due to labor, there is often little cost difference between using Category 3 UTP cable and Category 5 UTP cable (or even higher grades such as Category 6 or 7). Most new installations use Category 5 or higher because it supports transmission speeds of up to 100/1000 Mbps. For example, Category 6 allows you to install a 100-Mbps network solution now, and upgrade it to a 1,000-Mbps solution later. However, UTP cable might not be suitable for all networking situations. If you're not clear on the choice of network media, the following series of questions can help you to identify media that is most appropriate for your situation:

■ Is ease of troubleshooting and inexpensive cable maintenance/upgrades important?

No	Any cable type will be suitable
Yes	UTP cable is readily available and inexpensive (STP cable can also be used)

■ Are most of your computers located within 100 meters (328 feet) of your wiring closet or patch panel?

No	Coaxial or fiber-optic cable is better for longer runs
Yes	UTP cable is well suited for short runs

■ Is ease of reconfiguration important?

No	Any cable type will be suitable
Yes	UTP cable uses RJ-45 connectors, which can be relocated as needed

■ Does your network have any existing STP cabling?

No	Any existing cable type will be suitable
Yes	STP cable should be used if it's already in use in the network, or if electrical noise issues require its use

■ Does the topology or NIC you want to use require the use of STP cable?

No	The choice of STP (vs. UTP) would then depend on other factors
Yes	STP cable should be used if the station's NIC requires it

■ Do you need cable that is more resistant than UTP to EMI or RFI

No	UTP cable would be suitable (depending on other factors)
Yes	STP, coaxial, or fiber-optic cable would be superior choices for EMI/RFI

■ Do you need network cabling that is *completely* immune to EMI or RFI?

No	Any existing cable type will be suitable
Yes	Fiber-optic cable is the only choice for total immunity from EMI/RFI

■ Do you have existing coaxial cabling in your network?

No	Any existing cable type will be suitable
Yes	Coaxial cable should be used if there is coax already in the network

■ Do you have any equipment that currently needs token ring NICs (such as an IBM mainframe) or otherwise uses token ring?

No	Any existing cable type will be suitable
Yes	Ring architecture should be considered to support existing infrastructure

■ Is the network very small (10 or fewer computers)?

No	Any existing cable type will be suitable
Yes	Coaxial cable (bus) or UTP cable (star) would be suitable choices

■ Do you need network cabling that is relatively secure from most eavesdropping or intelligence-gathering equipment?

No	Any existing cable type will be suitable
Yes	Fiber-optic cable is extremely secure

■ Do you need network transmission speeds that are higher than those supported by copper media?

No	Any existing cable type will be suitable
Yes	Fiber-optic cable supports very fast transmission speeds

■ Do users on the network need to physically move their computers in the course of their workday?

No	Any existing cable type will be suitable
Yes	Wireless network components allow free movement (within a range)

■ Are there physical limitations that make it very difficult (or impossible) to cable computers to the network?

No	Any existing cable type will be suitable
Yes	Wireless network components can eliminate cabling headaches

Logical and Physical Mapping

At this point, you can start to lay out the actual network on paper. This normally involves creating both a physical and logical layout of the proposed network, which includes all of the users and peripheral devices. The physical layout is typically a *map* that illustrates the building layout, the location of each piece of hardware, and a general wiring plan between the server, each PC, and a peripheral device(s)—such as the basic network in Figure 21-3. If there's a preexisting network infrastructure in place, it should also be included in your layout. You should also create a *logical* layout of the network topology (e.g., bus or star), which also includes the server(s), each PC, and all peripheral devices. Not only will this documentation help when the network is implemented, it will also be a tremendous asset for troubleshooting and network expansion. This documentation will also help other technicians to learn about the network.

Recognize Potential Bottlenecks

If the existing network has been properly designed to support its current applications, be careful to anticipate what new requirements your design will place on the network. For example, if a router or other device is already operating at near 100-percent utilization, you may need to include an upgrade to those devices within your design. For server-based applications, you may need to plan for a RAM upgrade, or you may need to add a second or third CPU.

Don't make the mistake of underestimating the impact your design will have on the network. If you need to perform a comprehensive analysis to determine the current operational environment of the production network, do the analysis before you begin your design. Before the analysis begins, you should have already identified the areas within the network that your design will have the most impact on. For example, if you plan to add a new server-based application to an existing server, you'll know that the application will place requirements on the CPU, on memory, and on the disk channel on the server. Network traffic associated with application usage will also increase. Focus on these areas during your initial analysis to determine what stresses the devices involved are experiencing.

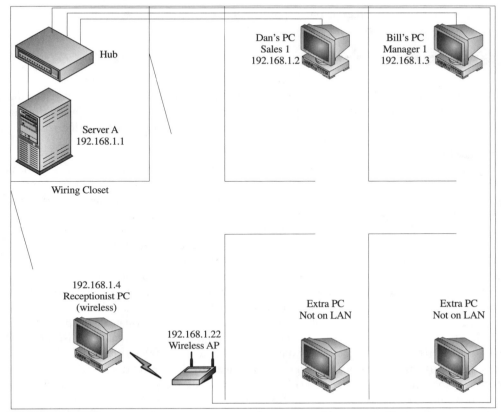

FIGURE 21-3   A physical map will help you to identify the location and address of all
network devices.

One way to predict how your design will impact the network is to closely analyze how your design
operates once it is implemented in the pilot project. Utilize tools like Performance Monitor and network
protocol analyzers to get a clear view of your design's performance requirements.

Even if you don't have the budget to upgrade the components that will be operating beyond operational efficiency, identify those impacted areas in your design (some parts of your network may fall
outside your department's responsibility).

REVIEW THE PLAN

Once you have completed your plan, it's time to sit down and present that plan to your customer. This type
of meeting is often informal, but it is *always* important. Reviewing the plan lets your customers ask questions, and ensures that they are getting the network that they need. Weaknesses or oversights in your plan
will usually surface during a review, and any last-minute ideas or requirements can be addressed *before*
money is actually spent. It may be necessary for you to go back and tweak some decisions in order to
address all of the network issues and budget constraints, then review the plan once again. It's not uncommon to have several reviews before a final network plan is approved (even more if the network is

particularly large or complex). After the customer approves your plan (and no other issues are raised), it's time to implement the network plan.

IMPLEMENT THE PLAN

The next step is to implement the network according to the plan that you've prepared. If you've done an adequate job of planning, you should know exactly what hardware and software to order, and understand the wiring that must be installed to support each device. Typical implementation usually involves installing the wiring, locating each device, connecting the devices, installing the software, and configuring the network.

Wiring Installation

At this point, you (or a professional installation team) will need to run the physical wiring. It's an ideal time to start with the wiring while other equipment is on order. In virtually all cases, this will involve running wiring through walls, ceilings, and floors. For the sake of an example, let's look at the installation of a basic Category 5 Ethernet cabling system. The simplest way to lay out a network in a small-office environment is to use a physical star topology. The center of any star will be a *patch panel*. A patch panel is a box with an array of RJ-45 female connectors that have terminals for connecting the wires.

A typical patch panel may have 12 or more RJ-45 connectors and each connector has eight connection points—one pin for each of the eight twisted-pair wires. In most cases, connections are color-coded for easy installation. The idea is to mount the patch panel(s) in a central location—often in a designated wiring closet or near the hub (usually next to the server)—so that you can easily make connections to the network. You'll need to install a Category 5 outlet near the hub and on the other end of each cable so that you can patch a PC's NIC to the cable. By configuring your wiring scheme in this fashion, it's a simple matter to disconnect or reconnect workstations (at a nearby wall jack), or quickly reconfigure PCs at the patch panel.

For example, suppose that a PC stopped working. You can easily disconnect the PC at one wall jack and connect it to another unused jack to see if the PC is still working. If it is, you know that the problem is in the wiring, patch panel, or hub/switch. As another example, suppose that the hub/switch port fails. You can easily use a patch panel to "patch" the PC over into another working hub/switch port. This can all be accomplished without disturbing the permanent wiring in walls, ceilings, and floors.

Remember that any cables run above the ceiling or below the floor must meet local construction and fire codes. Use plenum-grade cable where it is required.

Device Installation

When wiring is completed and each device is located, it's time to connect the devices. Connections are straightforward, and are made by attaching a relatively short patch cable between the NIC port and the RJ-45 outlet in the wall or floor. If you're using a hub, you will also need a short patch cable to connect the patch panel to a corresponding outlet on the hub. In other words, to connect a PC to the network, you need to patch a hub port to an RJ-45 outlet on the wall. That outlet is cabled to another RJ-45 outlet located near the respective PC. Another patch cable will connect that RJ-45 outlet on the wall to the PC's NIC. This completes the path from the PC to the hub. A separate connection then connects the hub to the server (hopefully located nearby).

Software Issues

After the hardware is installed, you should turn your attention to software issues. This usually involves the installation of server-side and client-side applications, drivers, redirectors, and so on. The network must then be configured with permissions and shares (aka security) so that users can access the server, exchange messages, and so on.

PRACTICAL EXAMPLES

Now that you've seen some of the guidelines and issues involved in network planning, it's time to see some examples in action. As you've seen, there is no one single "right" way to design or implement a network, but these examples apply the major ideas that have been outlined thus far, and tie together many of the things you've seen in earlier chapters.

Example: Connecting a New PC

When you designed the network for that manufacturing company, you took into account the possibility that it would eventually be necessary to add additional computers. The business manager has acquired an additional computer and brought it to you unannounced. He expects you to have it connected to the network as soon as possible so that a new employee can begin working in two days. The computer does not have a network interface card installed. You'll need to take the steps necessary to install a NIC and connect the new PC to the existing network (Chapter 10 details NIC installation and troubleshooting).

First, set up the new computer and verify that it's in good working order. If the operating system allows it, check for available interrupts in case this information is needed when you configure the NIC. Make a note of the installed RAM and disk capacity (these might be inadequate for network use or for resource-intensive applications). Now close any applications and shut down the PC. Disconnect all cables and open the system. Examine the main board for available bus slots. If a PCI slot is available, it should be your preferred choice. If not, an older ISA slot might be available.

Obtain a NIC for the correct bus slot, network architecture (e.g., Ethernet or token ring), and cable connector type (e.g., BNC or UTP) for the company's existing network. Remember that if the existing network has 100-MHz UTP cabling or faster, the card needs to be capable of operating at that speed. Drivers for the OS normally accompany a NIC (usually on floppy or CD). If the new computer does not have a CD-ROM drive installed, you might have to copy the drivers onto floppy disks using a computer that has a CD-ROM installed.

Install the NIC in the appropriate bus slot and reconnect the computer cables. Start the computer and install the latest drivers after the computer has recognized the NIC. Before you can communicate with the network, you'll have to install the appropriate communication protocols (such as IPX/SPX or TCP/IP). This software can normally be installed through the OS. Once the NIC is installed and recognized, and any necessary communication protocols have been installed and bound to the NIC, you may connect the network cable to the connection jack on the NIC. Finally, test the completed installation by checking for network resources in whichever way is appropriate for the network. For example, you can confirm the presence of the new PC by looking for its name under My Network Places.

Example: A Peer-to-Peer Solution

Here's a more complicated problem that requires a bit of creativity. A small company in Vermont designs and manufactures kits for building log houses. The owner of the company wants to connect the office by means of a network that is capable of supporting as many as 10 computers and users. The company employs two salespeople, an office manager, a drafter, a graphic designer, the mill foreman, and a number of employees who do not use computers.

The owner's computer is running Windows 98 with a standard suite of office application software and a popular project management software application. The office manager, whose Windows 98 machine runs the same kind of office application suite as the owner, prints to a letter-size laser printer that is connected directly to the computer. The company also employs a CAD operator who makes fabrication drawings for the employees in the mill. His computer operating system is Windows NT, and his primary application is a vector CAD program that plots to a roll-feed device that is cabled directly to that computer's printer port.

The two salespeople have portable computers that run Windows 98, and their major applications are included in the same office suite. The computer graphic artist, who creates catalog art and presentation material, uses an Apple G3 computer running high-end graphics software as well as the same office suite as the owner and office manager. Her computer prints to a high-resolution color PostScript printer through its standard port. Ultimately, the owner wants everyone on this network to be able to exchange files and use both printers. The owner has made it clear that they do *not* want a network that requires high administrative overhead.

One Solution   There are many possible solutions, but here is one set of suggestions. First, since the owner is unwilling to consider a network that requires significant administrative overhead, a peer-to-peer network seems appropriate. This is acceptable because there are relatively few users on the network. A server-based approach would also work technically, but would impose network administration that the owner doesn't want. By enabling the peer-to-peer networking that resides in the company's existing computers (that is, enabling file and print sharing) and by connecting the computers with 100-Mbps UTP Ethernet cabling and TCP/IP, an adequate degree of interoperability is achieved.

File and print sharing also let users share the laser and color postscript printer connected to their current machines. However, you may suggest moving the printers to an Ethernet print server device (Chapter 16 covers print servers in detail), which allows the two printers to be centrally located and self-standing so that the office manager and graphic artist don't need to leave their PCs running all the time. The print server simply connects to an Ethernet hub or switch port.

Talking to the Apple PC adds a little wrinkle, but enabling Apple services on the Windows NT computer creates a path between the graphic designer (who uses the Apple OS) and the others (who use two of the Windows network operating systems).

Example: Connecting Buildings

Here's a third example that explores long-distance considerations within and between buildings. A small marketing firm leases two groups of offices in Building B and Building H of a suburban office park. The business staff (including the human resources and accounting departments) has 12 people, and is located in two offices in Building B. The creative staff (including copy writing, graphics, and production departments) includes 22 employees and is housed in Building H. Building B and Building H are about 600 meters (about 1,970 feet) apart.

The business staff in Building B is networked with a five-year-old coaxial bus that ties their PC-compatible computers together in a peer-to-peer workgroup. The creative staff in Building H has a conglomeration of computers (including Apple Macintoshes and PC-compatibles) that are not networked. The owners of the company would like to network all the computers for the creative staff and connect the creative staff network to the business staff network. They would also like to standardize the type of network used in both buildings to keep troubleshooting issues to a minimum. What network type should be used? What architecture should be used within buildings? What architecture should be used between buildings?

Keep in mind that there is no single "right" answer to this problem because there are many variables to consider. It is entirely possible that you will find another solution that works better than the one we suggest.

Selecting a Network Type   A server-based network is suggested because the total number of workstations (34) exceeds the recommended limit of 10 for a peer-to-peer network. Also, because this company uses a variety of computers (PCs and Macintoshes), it will be easier to implement the server-based network. By getting all the computers standardized and networked, this company is moving toward a more centralized administration. Installing the server-based network now will put them well on their way to a more centralized system and open future expansion. A peer-to-peer network would certainly limit future expansion. Since the company needs a server-based operating system that serves both Macintoshes and PCs, you could choose Microsoft Windows NT/2000 Server, although there are several other server-based operating systems, such as NetWare, that could complete the same functions.

Architecture Within Buildings   Within the offices, Ethernet 100BaseT is the suggested solution because it is supported on all platforms and is easy to troubleshoot and install. Token ring and ArcNet solutions would also work, but LocalTalk would not meet the requirements because it is slow, and it is difficult to find LocalTalk cards for personal computers.

Architecture Between Buildings   A fiber-optic Ethernet solution (called 100BaseF) is suggested between the two buildings, for two reasons. First, fiber-optic cable offers the distance capabilities necessary to cover 600 meters (2,000 feet). Second, a repeater can be used to connect the fiber-optic cable from one building to the 100BaseT cable in the other.

Adding Internet Access

Today, networks rarely exist by themselves. Local area networks are often combined to form wide area networks (WANs), or connected to that ultimate WAN—the Internet. Internet access is a powerful feature for a LAN, and network users can exchange e-mail and access the Web as part of their daily routine. In this part of the chapter, you'll learn about the options available for LAN Internet access, and see some examples of access with a basic network.

WAN ACCESS

LANs have physical and distance limitations. Since LANs are not adequate for all business communication, they must be able to connect between LANs and other types of environments to ensure access to full communication services. Using components such as routers, along with communications service providers, a LAN can be expanded from an operation that serves a local area to encompass a wide area network that can support data communications statewide, countrywide, or even worldwide. To the user, the WAN appears to function like a local area network—when properly implemented, it appears indistinguishable from a LAN. To create a WAN, LANs are linked with mediums that include

- Packet-switching networks
- Fiber-optic cable
- Microwave transmitters
- Satellite links
- Cable television coaxial systems

These WAN links are usually leased from service providers. Communication between LANs will involve one of the following transmission technologies:

- Analog
- Digital
- Packet switching

Analog Connections

The same *public switched telephone network* (PSTN) that your telephone uses is available to computers. The PSTN offers voice-grade dial-up telephone lines, and can be thought of as one large WAN link. Since the PSTN was designed primarily for voice-grade communication, data communication can be very slow, and the connection quality is inconsistent. Any single communication session will be only as good as the circuits linked for that particular session. However, DSL technology is becoming available for "always on" high-speed connections using the existing telephone system.

Digital Connections

In some cases, analog lines provide sufficient connectivity. However, when an organization generates so much WAN traffic that the transmission time makes an analog connection inefficient and expensive, it might be time to consider alternatives. For example, organizations requiring faster data transmission can turn to *digital data service* (or DDS) lines. DDS provides point-to-point synchronous communication at 2.4, 4.8, 9.6, or 56 Kbps. Point-to-point digital circuits are dedicated circuits that are provided by several telecommunications carriers. The carrier guarantees full-duplex bandwidth by setting up a permanent link from each endpoint to the LAN. The primary advantage of digital lines is that they provide transmission that is nearly 99-percent error free. Digital lines are available in several forms, including DDS, T1 (1.544 Mbps), Fractional T1 (64-Kbps increments of the T1 bandwidth), T3 (45 Mbps), T4, and switched 56. Because DDS uses digital communication, it does not require modems. Instead, DDS sends data from a bridge or router through a device called a *Channel Service Unit/Data Service Unit* (CSU/DSU).

This is also a fair analogy of high-speed cable service. A NIC (using TCP/IP protocols) in the PC exchanges data with the cable provider's CSU/DSU (called a "cable modem," which is technically incorrect), which is attached to the cable network. The connection is always on, and provides higher bandwidth than is possible with ordinary dial-up services. For example, a computer user can easily establish high-speed Internet service from their local cable service using a cable CSU/DSU (such as in Figure 21-4). The PC uses an Ethernet NIC to communicate with the cable modem, which is then wired into the cable network.

Multiplexing   T1 uses *multiplexing* (or *muxing*) to allow more than one signal to share the same physical signal line(s). Several signals from different sources are collected into a device called a *multiplexer* and fed into one cable for transmission. At the receiving end, the data is demultiplexed back into its original form. This approach emerged when telephone cables (which carried only one conversation per cable) became overcrowded. The solution to the problem, called a T-Carrier network, allowed the telephone system to carry many calls over one cable.

Packet Switching

Networks that send packets from many different users along many different possible paths are called "packet-switching networks" because of the way they package and route data. Packet technology is fast, convenient, and reliable, so it is used to transmit data over extensive areas such as across cities, states, or

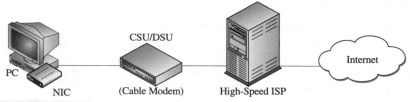

FIGURE 21-4   Adding high-speed Internet access for an individual PC

countries. The original data package is broken into packets, and each packet is tagged with a destination address and other information. This makes it possible to send each packet separately over the network. Packets are then relayed through stations in a computer network along the best route currently available between the source and the destination.

Each packet is switched separately. This means two packets from the same original data package can follow completely different paths to reach the same destination. The paths selected for individual packets are based on the best route open at any given instant. Even when each packet travels along a different path and the packets composing a message arrive at different times or out of sequence, the receiving computer is still able to reassemble the original message. Switches direct the packets over the possible connections and pathways, and exchanges in the network read each packet and forward them along the best route available at that moment. Packet size is kept small, so retransmitting a small packet is easier than retransmitting a large packet (small packets tie up switches for only short periods of time).

Virtual Circuits   Many packet-switching networks use *virtual circuits* employing a series of logical connections between the sending computer and the receiving computer. The circuit is bandwidth provided on demand—not an actual cable or permanent physical link between two stations. The connection is made after both computers exchange information and agree on communication parameters that establish and maintain the connection. These parameters include the maximum message size and the path the data will take. Virtual circuits can last either as long as the conversation lasts (temporary) or as long as the two communicating computers are up and running (permanent).

ROUTERS

Creating a WAN is basically a matter of joining two or more LANs together. In an environment with several network segments using differing protocols and architectures, you need a device that not only knows the address of each segment, but can also determine the best path for sending data and filtering broadcast traffic to the local segment. Such a device is called a *router* (Chapter 14 covers routers in detail).

Routers work at the network layer of the OSI reference model. This means they can switch and route packets across multiple networks. They do this by exchanging protocol-specific information between separate networks. Routers read complex network addressing information in the packet, and use this information to improve packet deliveries. Routers are used in complex networks because they provide better traffic management. Routers can share status and routing information with one another and use this information to bypass slow or malfunctioning connections.

Routers do not talk to remote computers. Instead, they understand only the network numbers that allow them to communicate with other routers and local NIC addresses. Routing is handled through the use of *routing tables* that include

- All known network addresses
- Instructions for connection to other networks
- The possible paths between routers
- The efficiency of sending data over those paths

Thus, a router uses its routing table to select the best route for the data based on efficiency and available paths. When routers receive packets destined for a remote network, they send them to the router that manages the destination network. This is an advantage because it means routers can segment large networks into smaller ones, act as safety barriers between segments, and prevent broadcast storms (broadcasts are not forwarded).

Internet Routers

While individual PC users can enjoy high-speed Internet access with a DSL or cable provider, obtaining high-speed service for multiple users can quickly become an expensive proposition. Small networks can use an *Internet router* (as in Figure 21-5) to interface the LAN to a cable or DSL modem—effectively sharing a single high-speed Internet service among multiple Ethernet LAN users. The router uses one IP address, so it appears as one device to the DSL or cable provider, yet the router can support up to 253 users on the LAN. Some Internet routers also include features like a four-port or eight-port switch (so PCs can be connected directly to the router rather than a separate hub or switch), a firewall, a DHCP server, and so on.

Figure 21-6 adds a typical Internet sharing scheme to our basic network. In this case, a one-port Internet router is used (because all existing workstations are connected to a switch), so the router's LAN port is simply connected to an available port on the switch. The router's WAN port is then connected to the cable/DSL modem—which in turn is attached to the telephone or coaxial cable medium. With the router properly installed and configured, each workstation in the network will now have Internet access. As workstations are added to the network, they will each have Internet access.

Of course, there are practical limits to this scheme. Each user accessing the Internet will demand a certain part of the cable/DSL modem's available bandwidth, so more simultaneous users will mean slower Internet performance. For example, if a single user can download a file from the Internet at 50 Kbps, two users may only be able to download at 25 Kbps, four users may only be able to download at 12.5 Kbps, and so on. If you require additional bandwidth, you may need to upgrade to even faster communication channels such as T1 service, and employ high-end routers such as Cisco and Bay Systems devices.

PRACTICAL EXAMPLES

Now that you've seen some of the guidelines and issues involved in connecting networks, it's time to review several examples. As you've seen, there is no one single "right" way to design or implement WAN access, but these examples apply the major ideas that have been outlined thus far, and tie together many of the things you've seen in earlier chapters.

FIGURE 21-5   The Linksys BEFSR81 Internet router with eight-port switch

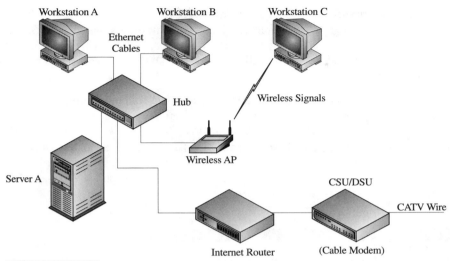

FIGURE 21-6   Adding high-speed Internet access to our basic network

Example: SOHO Internet Access

A small design firm in Massachusetts already has numerous PCs and servers networked together allowing designers and sales staff to share information and documents. However, only one of the workstations has Internet access through a dial-up modem. The managing partners feel that Internet access would help the firm by allowing users to access e-mail and search the Web for new vendors and materials as needed. However, they don't want to install multiple modems and tie up multiple phone lines with dial-up access—but they also cannot afford (and don't need) high speeds such as T1.

High-speed cable Internet service is available from the local cable provider. By installing a cable modem, connecting the cable modem to an Internet router, then attaching the Internet router to an open port on the network switch, all workstations on the network can access the Internet through a single account (which may also provide an e-mail address for each user).

Example: Connecting Two Networks

A magazine publisher based in Seattle has branch offices in Florida and New York. Each office is internally and separately networked. The networks were implemented five years ago, and each has a coaxial linear-bus topology supporting Ethernet 10-Mbps traffic. The branch offices stay in touch with each other by telephone and Federal Express. Recently, the company has begun to develop projects that involve team members from more than one office. Each office has resources that the other two do not, and current projects require all of these resources. The internal networks have had frequent cable problems, and each time they have a problem, the entire office network goes down until the problem is resolved (due to the bus topology).

Management would like a network design that offers easier troubleshooting, less downtime, and provides WAN communication between the three sites. They would like the WAN connection to be able to support about 256 Kbps of data and several analog telephone conversations between sites (the long-distance bills have been unacceptably high). The combination of long-distance and Federal Express charges should be eliminated by the WAN. Management would like the WAN to be able to continue operating even if one of the WAN links should fail.

Site Upgrades   The networks on each site will require some upgrades in order to ease troubleshooting and reduce downtime. For example each site should consider switching from a bus to a 100BaseT Ethernet star topology, connecting each station to a hub or switch. In addition, each PC will need a 10/100 Ethernet card to support 100-Mbps data transfers, and a cable upgrade to 100-Mbps Category 5 (or better) to replace the coaxial bus cable now in use.

WAN Links   The separate branch offices need to maintain voice and data communications with each other, so consider a T1 (or a less-expensive fractional T1) link because they can carry voice and data simultaneously. Frame relay service may be another viable option to consider. These services are available through national carriers (such as AT&T, MCI, Sprint, and others). E1 service is available outside of the U.S., and provides roughly the same level of service. Each site will need a multiplexer to mix voice and data signals, and place them on the same WAN link, as well as a router to connect each LAN to the multiple WAN paths between offices.

Configuring Network Access

With the physical server-based network implemented as planned, it's time to configure access for each of the network's users. In a client/server network, resource sharing is managed through the use of accounts. By creating accounts (and organizing individual accounts into groups), a network administrator has the tools necessary to provide a higher level of security. Each workstation must have client software installed and be configured as a network client. You will have to establish the computer's network identity, enable sharing, and set access privileges for the resources the computer will share. The actual procedure for installing and configuring client software depends on the operating system you are using (and the operating system of the network on which you intend to share resources). This part of the chapter will illustrate user and group accounts, highlight the appropriate types of accounts for a given network environment, and outline the process for creating user and group accounts.

UNDERSTANDING ACCOUNTS

Simply stated, an *account* provides users with access to files, directories, and devices (such as printers). In a client/server network, accounts are created and managed by the network administrator. An account is composed of a username and logon information established for each user. Logon information can include which computer(s) the user can work at, the days and times during which access is allowed, user passwords, and more. Account information is entered by the administrator and usually stored on the server through the network operating system. A network checks the username and other parameters to verify the account when the user attempts to log on.

User Accounts
The first step in enabling a new user is to create an account for that user. An administrator can use a network utility to enter and edit account information for a user. The new user account requires a complete set of information that defines a user to the network security system. This includes a username and password, rights for accessing the system and its resources, and the group(s)—if any—to which the account belongs. Administrators can also configure a number of parameters for a user. Logon times can be entered to restrict access to certain hours of the day. A home directory can be assigned to give a user an area to store private files. And an expiration date can be included to limit a temporary user's access to the network (e.g., a temporary employee).

You should also be familiar with administrator and guest accounts. When a network operating system is first installed, the setup program automatically creates an account with complete network authority. In a Microsoft networking environment, this account is called *administrator*. In the Novell environment, this is the *supervisor* account. Under Linux, it is known as *root*. After logging on as administrator, that user has full control over all network functions. For example, an administrator can start the network, set the initial security parameters, and create other user accounts. By comparison, a guest account is usually a basic default account intended for individuals who do not have a valid user account but need temporary access to some low level of the network.

Group Accounts

Once a user account is created, that account generally has no rights—this is a common default used for security purposes. User accounts are assigned particular rights through *group memberships*. All user accounts within a particular group will have certain access rights and activities (according to the assigned group). By assigning permissions and rights to a group, an administrator can treat the group as a single account. Groups are commonly used to grant access to resources—the permissions granted to a group are automatically granted to all of its members. Groups also assign rights to perform system tasks (such as to back up and restore files or change the system time). Grouping users together can also simplify communications by reducing the number of individual messages that need to be sent (messages can be sent to the group instead). For example, if an administrator wanted a certain user to have administrative capabilities on the network, the administrator might make that user a member of the Administrators group.

Do not underestimate the power of group accounts. Client/server networks can support hundreds (even thousands) of accounts. There will be occasions when an administrator needs to send messages to large numbers of users notifying them about an event or network policy, or identify every account that has a particular access. If 100 users need a change in their access, the administrator would need to change 100 individual accounts. Clearly, working with individual accounts is a time-consuming and error-prone approach. On the other hand, if those 100 accounts were placed in one group, the administrator would simply send one message to the group account (and each member of the group would automatically get the message). Permissions could be set or changed for the group, and all members of the group would automatically receive the same permissions.

Account Passwords

In most situations, each username is coupled with a *password*. Passwords help to protect network security by ensuring that each username is authenticated by a secret word—usually consisting of letters, numbers, and other characters—known only to the user (and encrypted on the network). Initially, the password is assigned by the network administrator, but can often be changed later by the user (an administrator can require users to do this automatically by setting a password change time interval for the user). Keep in mind that passwords are not necessarily *required* by a network operating system. In some low-security network environments, it is possible to configure an account so that it no longer needs a password. When selecting a password, avoid obvious choices such as birth dates, social security numbers, or the names of spouses, children, pets, and so on. Never write down the password—memorize it instead. If the password has an expiration date, the system will typically warn you when you're 30 days or so from expiration so you can change the password before it expires and locks the user out of the network.

Removing Accounts

When an account is no longer needed, it can generally be disabled or deleted. This will prevent the user from accessing the network. Disabling an account is a handy measure when an account must be stopped temporarily. It will still remain on the network, and can be reactivated later if necessary. For example, if an employee will be on vacation or a leave of absence, their account can be disabled until they return. An account can also be deleted, which will erase the user's information from the network. An account can be deleted when a user leaves the company or moves to another part of the company where no network access is required.

MANAGING ACCOUNTS UNDER WINDOWS 2000

Now that you've covered some account basics, let's look at an example of account and group creation under Windows 2000. The Microsoft Windows 2000 Server network utility for managing accounts and groups is called Computer Management, which you access by clicking Start | Programs | Administrative Tools | Computer Management. The Computer Management dialog box will open, and you can expand the Local Users and Groups entry as in Figure 21-7.

Highlight the Users entry, and a listing of users will appear in the right pane. To add a new user, simply right-click on Users and select New User. This opens the New User dialog box in Figure 21-8, and you can enter the User Name, Full Name, Password, and other account parameters (you could also disable an existing account). When you've created the new user, click Create, and the new user will be added to the list of users in the Computer Management dialog box. Similarly, you can check or adjust other users by double-clicking the desired user from the right pane of the Computer Management dialog box, or right-clicking the user and selecting Properties.

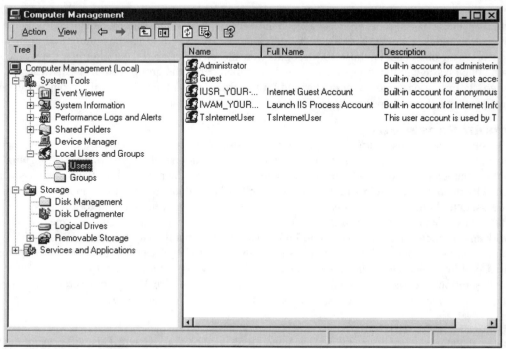

FIGURE 21-7   The Computer Management dialog lets you access users and groups under Windows 2000.

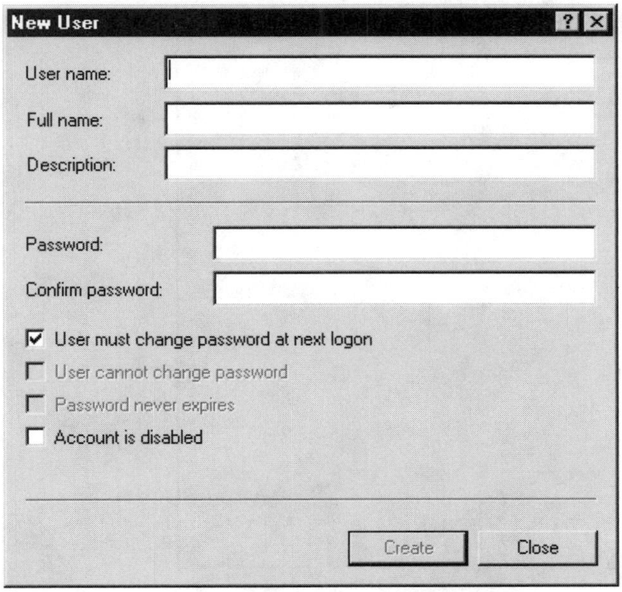

FIGURE 21-8   The New User dialog box lets you define a new network user under Windows 2000.

Managing Groups

Managing groups under Windows 2000 is just about as easy. With the Computer Management dialog box open, highlight the Groups entry and a list of available groups will appear in the right pane. A typical list of groups may include

- Administrators
- Backup Operators
- Guests
- Power Users
- Replicator
- Users
- DHCP Administrators
- DHCP Users

To add a new group, simply right-click the Groups entry and select New Group. The New Group dialog box will appear as in Figure 21-9, and allow you to define the group name, a description, and add or remove members. Click Create to form the new group, and it will be added to the list under Computer Management. You may add members to a group by double-clicking the desired user, clicking the Member Of tab, and then adding the user to the desired group. Alternatively, you can right-click the group and select Properties. When the group opens, you see a list of members. Click Add and choose the member(s) that you'd add to the group, then click Apply and OK to save your changes.

FIGURE 21-9   The New Group dialog box lets you establish new network groups under Windows 2000.

MANAGING ACCOUNTS UNDER WINDOWS NT

Under NT, network management tools can be accessed by clicking Start | Programs | Administrative Tools (Common). The Microsoft Windows NT Server network utility for creating accounts is called the *User Manager*. After you start the User Manager tool, select the User menu and then select the New User option. A window appears for entering the new user information such as username, full name, account description, and password.

Windows NT Server also offers an "account-copying" feature that allows an administrator to create a template that has characteristics and parameters common among multiple users. To create a new account with template characteristics, highlight the template account, select User | Copy (F8), then enter the new username and other identifying information.

Profiles are often used to configure and maintain a user's logon environment (including network connections and the appearance of the desktop). This is an extremely handy feature because it allows a user to see their own familiar desktop even though they may be logging on from other computers on the network. Profile settings include printer connections, regional settings, sound settings, mouse settings, display settings, and other user-definable settings. Profile parameters can also include special logon conditions and information about where the user can store personal files. Profiles can be accessed from the User Manager.

Windows NT Server disables guest accounts by default after installation. The network administrator must manually reenable the guest accounts if they will be used.

An administrator can also disable and delete users. Windows NT Server uses the User Properties window in User Manager to disable users. Simply double-click the name of the account, select the Account

Disabled check box, and then click OK. The account is now disabled. To delete an account, open the User Manager, select the account to be deleted, and then press the DEL key and click OK. Another dialog box will ask for confirmation of the user account deletion. Click Yes to delete the account (click No to cancel the deletion). Remember that deleting an account permanently removes the account (and the permissions and rights associated with it). Re-creating the user account with the same name will not automatically restore the user's rights or permissions—those will have to be generated from scratch.

Managing Groups

Windows NT uses four types of group accounts: local, global, system, and built-in. *Local groups* are implemented in each local computer's account database, and contain user accounts and other global groups that have access to a resource on a local computer. Local groups cannot contain other local groups. *Global groups* are used across an entire domain. They are created on a primary domain controller (PDC) in the domain where the user accounts reside, and can contain only user accounts from that domain. Global groups cannot contain local groups or other global groups. *System groups* automatically organize users for system use. Administrators do not assign users to system groups. Instead, users are members by default, or become members during network activity. *Built-in groups* are a feature offered by many network vendors, and are included with the network operating system. Administrators can save time and trouble assigning users to built-in groups rather than creating unique groups to do the same basic jobs.

Windows NT provides numerous built-in groups. The administrator group contains local and domain administrators. This group can create, delete, and manage user accounts, global groups, and local groups. They can also share directories and printers, grant resource permissions and rights, and install operating system files and programs. User and guest groups contain users that are able to perform tasks for which they have been given rights. They can also access assigned resources. User groups can be modified by administrators and account operators. Members of the server operator group can share resources, lock a server, format the server's disks, log on at servers, back up and restore servers, and shut down servers. Server operator groups can be modified by administrators only. The printer operator group can share and manage printers. This group can also log on locally at servers and shut servers down. Backup operator members can log on locally, back up and restore servers, and shut down servers. Account operator members can create, delete, and modify users, global groups, and local groups, but cannot modify administrator or server operator groups.

You can also use the User Manager to create and assign groups under Windows NT. Access the User Manager by clicking Start | Programs | Administrative Tools (Common). After you start the User Manager tool, select the User menu and then select the New Local Group option. This presents you with a dialog box for entering the information to create a new local group. The Group Name field identifies the local group. A group name cannot be identical to any other group or username of the domain or computer being administered. The Description field contains text describing the group (or the users in the group). The Members field shows the usernames of each group member. Keep in mind that a newly created group account will have no members until an administrator assigns one or more existing users to the group. This is accomplished from the New Local Group dialog box by clicking Add and selecting the user account to be added.

Further Study

3Com: **www.3com.com**
CNET: **www.cnet.com**
IT Toolbox: **www.ittoolbox.com**
Network Magazine: **www.networkmagazine.com**
ZDNet: **www.zdnet.com**

NETWORK MAINTENANCE AND UPGRADES

Networks are used to connect busy people and share resources. When network devices fail, everyone using that network comes to a halt. Regardless of your network's size, PC problems typically result in lost productivity—and often lost data. In order to minimize the impact of network problems, servers and workstations must be maintained in a prompt and professional manner. The idea of maintenance is not new, but its many roles often vary from company to company (and even between networks in the same company) depending on the size and traffic being supported. For our purposes, maintenance involves all types of upgrades and routine replacement tasks such as BIOS upgrades, CPU and memory upgrades, drive replacement and retirement, and all types of network expansions (i.e., adding a workstation). This chapter is intended to familiarize you with the essential requirements for these general maintenance tasks.

Server Maintenance Guidelines

Server maintenance is often more of an art than a science—there is no one way to do it right. Still, a good technician should understand the server, be familiar with its components, and have the tools available to boot and restore the server when trouble strikes. The following guidelines may help you to prepare for server maintenance tasks a bit more clearly.

KNOW THE SERVER

A network server is essentially a powerful PC with server software. As with any PC, you should know the various components that your server can accept, as well as the parts currently installed. For example, if the server can accept two Pentium III CPUs up to 1.4 GHz, but only one Pentium III 1-GHz CPU is installed, you should know this. Such knowledge will make it easier to identify and gather up replacement parts quickly and effectively—especially if the server is at a remote site. Write this information in your notebook or maintenance log where it is easily accessible. As a minimum, record the following:

- CPU speed (installed and maximum)
- Number of CPUs installed/supported
- CPU step (version designation)
- Amount of RAM (installed and maximum)
- Configuration of installed RAM (i.e., PC133 SDRAM 256MB DIMMs)
- BIOS manufacturer and version number
- Manufacturer and size(s) of your system drive(s)
- RAID controller make and model (and its firmware version number)
- SCSI controller make and model (and its firmware version number)
- NIC adapter make and model (and its firmware version number)

If the server was purchased "off the shelf", you should also record the system's make and model, as well as its service tag/serial number, along with the manufacturer's technical support telephone number—this will make it easier to find support information later.

KNOW THE SOFTWARE

Network hardware is useless without the network operating system and applications. You should make it a point to identify the critical software installed on your server. This can be particularly important when planning the installation of service packs or maintenance patches, and can help you prevent software compatibility problems. As a minimum, record the following:

- System operating system version (with any service packs, patches, or updates installed)
- Network operating system version (with any service packs, patches, or updates installed)
- Driver versions for the RAID and NIC adapters
- Any system diagnostics, virus checkers, or other tools needed for network support

It's usually a good idea to have all of the installation CDs or diskettes for this software at your disposal. Be sure to have a current boot diskette that can start the server in the event of an unrecoverable drive failure.

CHECK AND TUNE DRIVES REGULARLY

Hard drives are generally quite reliable, but they are certainly not infallible. Common disk problems include lost clusters and cross-linked files. File fragmentation is also an issue. Part of your routine maintenance policy should be to run ScanDisk and Disk Defragmenter (or other suitable disk tools) to check for file problems, surface defects, and efficient file organization. You may elect to wait for such procedures until hours of low network use (such as evenings or weekends), or until other routine procedures are required such as drive installations.

BACKUP RELIABLY

Select a backup system based on your needs and the sensitivity of your data. Busy corporate networks or sales entry systems may require daily backups (perhaps several times per day). The main issue to consider is that after you develop a backup plan, you must implement that plan consistently. Be sure to *verify* your backup. A poor or incomplete backup is worse than no backup at all—there's nothing worse than trying to restore a damaged or incomplete backup. Backups should ideally be stored off-site in a protected location, but you should periodically plan on practicing a restoration procedure to keep your skills sharp. Remember that time is money, so the ability to recover from a disaster is one of the most valuable maintenance skills available.

CHECK FOR VIRUSES

Networks are ideal for transferring viruses, especially if your network allows access to the Internet. Your network software should certainly include a comprehensive network virus checker, and that virus checker should be updated regularly to include the latest signature files and patches. Be sure to scan all files when the virus checker is first installed, then scan files that change (or new files) on the network. Users should be briefed on proper safety procedures regarding file downloads and even e-mail.

MAINTAIN THE ENVIRONMENT

Servers are normally stored in closets or rooms where they are protected from casual access. However, servers can dissipate a great deal of heat from the multiple CPUs and drives in the system. Be sure that your server location provides adequate cooling and power. Excessive dust and heat can be detrimental to system cooling. When extensive network equipment is involved, dust filters and air conditioning equipment may be needed to maintain suitable levels of temperature and humidity.

KEEP YOUR MAINTENANCE LOGS

Each time that work is performed on a server, that service should be entered into a permanent written log. It is very important for maintenance logs to be kept up-to-date as service and upgrades are performed. Careful records help to keep system maintenance current, prevent duplicated effort, and serve as a guide to future upgrades. It also makes technicians accountable for their work. Maintenance logs should be kept with the server and other network equipment.

Network Upgrades

Networks are surprisingly dynamic systems—they're constantly growing, changing, and improving as users and resources are brought to bear. The need for upgrades is often unclear, but changes in performance and user feedback will help to indicate when upgrades warrant consideration. For example, an eventual decline in network data transfer performance may indicate that an upgrade is needed. This means a large portion of your maintenance efforts will focus on network upgrades and enhancements. In most cases, upgrades are intended to improve the network's performance (i.e., increase throughput), increase storage or add fault tolerance, and add support for more users. This part of the chapter will examine BIOS, processor, memory, NIC, and storage upgrades.

NETWORK ARCHITECTURE AND MEDIA

Two important considerations in the design and implementation of a network are the architecture and the media. The *architecture* is the network's structure or topology (i.e., ring or bus). The *media* is the cabling that connects network devices (i.e., copper or fiber). There may be situations when it's necessary to make upgrades to the network architecture or media. While such upgrade processes are beyond the scope of this book, you should consider these upgrades when fundamental network performance upgrades are needed. Consider the following examples:

■ If a network has been designed using a bus topology (and its users are complaining of frequent network crashes or downtime due to cabling issues), it might be necessary to upgrade to a star or ring topology.

■ If the size and number of networked buildings are expanding, upgrading to fiber-optic media for the network backbone could be a worthwhile investment. Fiber-optic media can also be used for cable runs between remote buildings.

■ If the network was configured with copper-based media (and devices have been added that create large amounts of electrical interference), it might be necessary to upgrade using fiber-optic media.

■ If online conferencing or advanced Web-based applications at the desktop are being introduced, the network could also benefit from an upgrade to fiber-optic cable.

■ Network users that require mobility or relocate their workstations frequently may benefit from wireless connections.

There are other factors to consider before making an architecture or media upgrade decision (such as cost). Although the price of fiber-optic media is dropping, the installation of fiber-optic cable requires a trained technician—an added expense. Remember that the network interface cards, hubs, and other network hardware will need to be upgraded at the same time, so there may be additional upgrade procedures that need to be conducted at the same time.

HARDWARE COMPATIBILITY

One of the most important issues of network upgrades is hardware compatibility, especially when working with business-oriented operating systems such as Windows NT or 2000. Since networking is so hardware-dependent, verifying the correct choice of hardware is an important step in network planning. Otherwise, hardware purchases may not function as expected (if at all). This part of the chapter explains the importance of compatibility checking prior to implementing an upgrade, and offers some suggestions for resolving compatibility issues.

Identifying Problems

In today's computer industry, hardware and software incompatibilities are simply a fact of life. Hundreds of manufacturers develop hardware and software. Even with well-established standards and protocols, each developer has a unique perspective on the best way to accomplish the same task, and each will provide a unique solution. This is a mixed blessing—competition between developers keeps prices low and selection high, but not all products work together. Consequently, evaluating and selecting suitable products is a major part of planning for network implementation.

If you have the luxury of designing a network from the ground up, you can generally just choose your product vendors and place the burden of compatibility on them. The best way to avoid problems is to research your key items *before* you make purchases. You might consider giving your vendors a list of the hardware and software you plan to use and ask them to certify that those items are compatible with that vendor's products. For example, if you are considering the purchase of two devices, ask both vendors if their product is compatible with the other. Compare the responses you get, because they may help you to find an incompatibility you would otherwise fail to detect.

In most cases, you'll need to create a network out of an existing collection of hardware, and the likelihood of problems developing from incompatible hardware is very high. The most common incompatibilities occur between existing hardware and new software, or new hardware and existing software. Changing or upgrading a computer or network operating system can lead to major compatibility problems. For example, Windows 98/SE provides excellent support for USB ports, but Windows NT does not. If you need to use Windows NT in order to create a network, and you're relying on that USB printer for the network, you may find that the Windows NT upgrade has effectively disabled your printer.

Checking Documentation and Requirements

The manuals that accompany a product can yield valuable information about compatibility issues. This is especially true for product Web sites where manufacturers can quickly post known issues (and any workarounds that have been discovered). Online product FAQs can often address a wide range of common questions and problems.

You must also verify that your system meets the minimum (preferably the recommended) system requirements for any hardware or software that you plan to install. Issues of processor speed, memory (RAM), and available disk space are particularly important. For example, Table 22-1 lists some minimum requirements for several common network operating systems.

Checking the HCL

Operating systems and network operating systems are extensively tested with a vast array of hardware devices. If you're planning a hardware upgrade, or need to verify that an NOS upgrade will continue to support your existing hardware, you can check the Hardware Compatibility List (HCL) for your NOS. For example, Microsoft maintains a comprehensive HCL for Windows 2000 at **http://www.microsoft.com/ WINDOWS2000/upgrade/compat/default.asp**. If your hardware is not listed in the HCL, it may still work with third-party or manufacturer-specific drivers, but at least this might alert you to the possibility of trouble.

When you install a new computer or network operating system, the installation routine will usually attempt to detect the hardware in the system during the installation process, then load the appropriate drivers

TABLE 22-1	COMMON NOS SYSTEM REQUIREMENTS			
	NETWARE 5	**WINDOWS NT SERVER 4.0**	**WINDOWS 98**	**RED HAT LINUX 7.2**
Processor	Pentium processor	486 33 MHz or higher	486 66 MHz or higher	Pentium 200 MHz
Memory	64MB	16MB	16MB	64MB
Disk Space	200MB	125MB	225MB	650MB
Disk	CD-ROM	CD-ROM	3.5" high density	CD-ROM
Monitor	VGA	VGA	VGA	VGA
NIC	Yes	Yes	Yes	NIC

for each device. Check the list of detected hardware and ensure that it matches what is already in the machine. For example, if you're installing Novell's IntranetWare, the install utility will automatically scan your computer for devices such as hard drives, CD-ROM drives, and NICs. Detection should also occur when a new device is added to an existing network operating system. If the devices are recognized, the appropriate drivers will be loaded for the recognized devices. If a device is not detected, check to see if a manufacturer-specific driver or other supporting software is available. Otherwise, you may not be able to use the device.

BIOS UPGRADES

BIOS is *firmware*—software that has been permanently recorded onto one or more memory chips and is used to operate the PC. When bugs are corrected, compatibility issues are resolved, and performance is tweaked in the BIOS code, it may be necessary for you to update the BIOS in your own server to the latest version available. Traditionally, updating the BIOS required you to physically replace the chip(s) or even update the entire motherboard. Today, virtually all PCs use flash BIOS, which allows the BIOS to be reprogrammed on the chip right in the system. This means you can download the updated BIOS file and flash loader utility from the motherboard maker's Web site and install it yourself.

Checking Your BIOS Version

Before you attempt a BIOS upgrade, it's important to determine the current version of your BIOS. Once you know the version that's on your system, you can ensure that you're installing a later/better version. BIOS is identified in the moments following the initial power up, but before the operating system starts to load—usually while the memory count is taking place. Keep in mind that the BIOS ID string only appears for several seconds, so you may need to reboot the system more than once in order to get the entire code. Although the BIOS ID may appear as a jumble of codes, you should pay particular attention to the BIOS maker and its release date. For example:

```
Sample BIOS 4.65 12/25/2000
```

When selecting a BIOS upgrade, be sure that the BIOS is correct for your exact server. If you install the wrong BIOS version, your system may fail to run properly (if it starts at all).

Preparing the Upgrade Process

BIOS upgrades require a little bit of preparation. You'll need to download the appropriate flash file to a bootable floppy diskette, then decompress the flash file into its constituent files (usually a flash loader utility, a new BIOS data file, and a **readme** file). These steps cover a basic example:

Please review the specific instructions distributed with the flash loader upgrade utility before attempting a BIOS upgrade.

1. Make a clean bootable diskette using either DOS or Windows 98/SE.
2. The BIOS upgrade file is usually a compressed self-extracting archive that contains the files you need to upgrade the BIOS. Copy the BIOS upgrade file to a temporary directory on your hard disk.
3. From the C: prompt, change to the temporary directory.
4. To extract the upgrade file, type the name of the BIOS upgrade file—for example,

```
10006BC1.EXE
```

5. Press ENTER and the file will decompress. The extracted file will include files such as

```
LICENSE.TXT
README.TXT
BIOS.EXE
```

6. Read the **LICENSE.TXT** file, which contains the instructions for the BIOS upgrade on your specific system.

7. Insert the bootable floppy disk into drive A:.

8. Extract the flash loader (i.e., **BIOS.EXE**) file to the floppy disk, change to the temporary directory containing the flash loader file, and type

```
BIOS A:
```

9. Press ENTER.

10. The bootable diskette now holds the BIOS upgrade and recovery files.

Completing the Upgrade Process

Once you've prepared your diskette for the BIOS upgrade, use the steps below as a guideline for the new BIOS installation:

1. Boot the computer with the floppy disk in drive A:. The "BIOS upgrade utility" screen appears.

2. Select Update Flash Memory From a File.

3. Select Update System BIOS and press ENTER.

4. Use the arrow keys to select the correct **.BIO** file and press ENTER.

5. When the utility asks for confirmation that you want to flash the new BIOS into memory, select Continue with Programming and press ENTER.

6. When the utility displays the message Upgrade is Complete, remove the floppy disk and press ENTER.

7. As the computer boots again, check the BIOS identifier (the BIOS version number) to verify that the upgrade was successful.

8. To enter the CMOS Setup program, observe the BIOS banner such as

```
Press <F2> Key if you want to run SETUP
```

9. For proper operation, load the CMOS Setup program defaults and press ENTER to accept the defaults.

10. Reset any critical entries in the CMOS Setup.

11. Accept and save the settings, then turn off the computer and reboot.

 Remember that most computers protect the BIOS with one or more jumpers (i.e., the BIOS Write Enable jumper). You should configure the server to accept the new BIOS file before booting the system.

Using BIOS Recovery

In most cases, the BIOS upgrade should proceed without interruption. However, using an incorrect BIOS version or suffering a power interruption can result in serious BIOS corruption, rendering the server unbootable. Fortunately, many of today's motherboards offer "boot block" features that protect essential

BIOS operations. Even when the BIOS is corrupted, this minimum piece of protected BIOS code (the boot block) will read a floppy disk and allow the system to reinstall the original (or correct) BIOS. The following steps explain a typical procedure to recover the BIOS if an upgrade should fail:

Given the small amount of code available in the boot block area, there is no video support—you will not see anything on the screen during the recovery procedure. You can monitor the procedure by listening to the speaker and looking at the floppy drive LED.

1. Turn off all peripheral devices connected to the computer, then turn off the computer.

2. Remove the computer cover and locate the BIOS recovery jumper.

3. Set the recovery jumper to the reprogram position.

4. Insert the bootable BIOS upgrade floppy disk into floppy drive A:.

5. Turn on the computer and allow it to boot—the recovery process will take a few minutes.

6. Listen to the speaker.

7. Two beeps (and the end of activity) in drive A: indicate a successful BIOS recovery, but a series of continuous beeps indicates a failed BIOS recovery (if recovery fails, return to step 1 and try recovery again).

8. If recovery is successful, turn off the computer and reset the recovery jumper to the protect position.

9. Replace the computer cover and restart the system to the CMOS Setup. Select the default values and reenter any critical settings.

10. Reboot the system normally.

NIC UPGRADES

As users come onto the network and traffic levels increase, you may need to improve the data transfer capacity (throughput) of your network. This means you'll need to replace your NIC adapter. The upgrade process is virtually identical to the installation of any other PnP PCI expansion device, and follows four basic steps: remove the existing card, install the new card, connect the network cable, and configure the new card.

Removing the Old Drivers

If you're replacing or upgrading a NIC device (or upgrading the drivers), it is often necessary to remove the older NIC drivers first. This ensures that there is no software conflict between the older and newer software. This example shows you how to remove the Windows NT drivers for an Adaptec DuraLAN NIC:

1. Double-click My Computer on your desktop.

2. Double-click Control Panel.

3. Double-click the Network icon.

4. In the Network window, click the Adapters tab.

5. In the Network Adapters list, click the NIC you want to remove (i.e., Adaptec DuraLAN NIC), and then click Remove.

6. When asked if you want to continue, click Yes.

7. Repeat the previous two steps until all of the related drivers (i.e., Adaptec DuraLAN) drivers are removed.

8. When you're finished, click OK.

9. Click Close to close the Network window.

10. Click Yes to restart your computer.

When you restart Windows NT, a message might indicate that at least one service failed to start. This message should not appear after you add the new driver, so simply click OK.

Removing the Existing Card

After the old drivers are removed, it's time to uninstall the old NIC. Follow these steps to remove your old NIC adapter:

1. Turn off the power to your PC and disconnect the power cord from the wall outlet. During the removal, you should ground yourself by touching any unpainted surface of the PC case.

2. Remove the outer cover from your computer according to the manufacturer's instructions.

3. Disconnect the network cabling from your existing NIC.

4. Remove the screw holding the NIC in place, then gently remove the card from its slot.

Before shutting down the PC to remove the NIC, it might be necessary to remove the NIC driver(s) and supporting software.

Installing the New Card

With the old NIC out of the system, go ahead and install the new NIC using the following steps:

1. You should ground yourself by touching any unpainted surface (the chassis) of the PC case.

2. Carefully remove the new NIC from its antistatic container. Verify the model by looking at the model name on the NIC itself (you may place the old NIC in the antistatic container).

3. Check the NIC for any visible signs of damage that may have occurred during shipping or handling. If you find a problem, immediately notify your network supplier and the shipping service that delivered your NIC—you'll need to arrange for a replacement NIC.

4. Because the PC is already opened, locate an unused expansion slot (a PCI slot in this case). Remove the bracket screw and remove the expansion slot bracket that covers the card slot's opening.

PCI slots and NICs come in two varieties: 3.3 volt, and the more common 5 volt. PCI NICs generally support 5-volt slots. Some models also support 3.3-volt slots. To improve performance with multiport NICs, install these NICs in PCI bus slot 0.

5. Insert the NIC into the PCI expansion slot—press down firmly and evenly until the bus contacts are seated in the slot.

6. Secure the NIC in the expansion slot with the bracket screw you removed earlier.

7. Replace the computer's outer cover on the computer.

8. Reconnect any other devices that you might have removed during the installation.

Reconnecting and Reconfiguring

Carefully reconnect the network cabling to the new NIC adapter (after the NIC drivers are installed, the card's selection of cabling should normally be automatic). Depending on your particular system, you may need to configure the card through the server's CMOS Setup. You may also need to adjust the card's configuration through its own onboard setup.

Installing the New Drivers

After installing, connecting, and configuring the new NIC hardware, you must install the appropriate NIC driver for your particular network operating system. Before proceeding, it's usually a good idea to check for driver updates and patches with the NIC manufacturer. This section of the chapter illustrates the typical installation process for an Adaptec DuraLAN NIC under Windows NT:

1. Start the system to Windows NT.

2. From the Start menu, point to Settings and then click Control Panel.

3. In the Control Panel, double-click the Network icon.

4. In the Network window, click the Adapters tab.

5. In the Adapters tab, click Add.

6. In the Select Network Adapter window, click Have Disk.

7. At the Insert Disk window, insert the driver diskette (i.e., Duralink64 for Windows NT diskette), and then click OK.

8. In the Select OEM Option window, click the NIC model that's installed (i.e., DuraLAN NIC), and then click OK.

9. In the installation window that appears (i.e., Adaptec DuraLAN NIC Driver Installation window), select the desired driver and click OK.

10. Continue on to install the standard driver, the failover driver, or the port aggregation driver.

Verifying the Driver(s)

After the drivers are installed, you can use the steps below to verify that the standard driver is installed properly under Windows NT:

1. From the Start menu, point to Settings | Control Panel.

2. In the Control Panel, double-click the System icon.

3. In the Device Manager tab, look under Network Adapters.

4. Your NIC should appear under Network Adapters. Click OK. If the NIC does not appear, it has not been installed properly.

5. If a yellow exclamation mark appears beside your NIC entry, the drivers may be incorrect. Remove the NIC driver and reinstall it (check for driver updates if possible).

6. If the Network window lists both old and new NICs, you should remove the old NIC entry from the Device Manager.

STORAGE UPGRADES

Networks rely on a great deal of storage for the many files and applications that are needed. This means you'll be adding and replacing drives to accommodate the server's storage needs. Servers typically use removable media and hot-pluggable drives (as in Figure 22-1) to provide storage. Removable media drives include floppy, tape, and CD type drives. Hot-pluggable drives include all types of SCSI hard drives—usually configured for RAID applications.

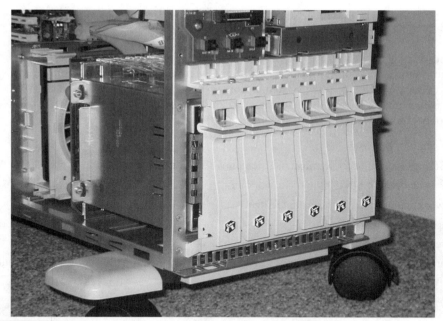

FIGURE 22-1   The Gateway 7400 server uses hot-pluggable drives for storage.

Removable Media Drives

Removable media drives can typically be removed from a rack-mounted server using the these steps:

1. Extend the server out from the rack to the locked position and remove cover plate.
2. Remove the Y brace and card bracket brace.
3. Slide the base frame back to access cables in the drive cage.
4. Lift the protective cover and disconnect power and signal cables to the drive.
5. Remove the media trim piece retaining screws (two of them) from the front bezel.
6. Remove the storage device retaining screws (two of them) and slide the drive out.

Simply reverse these steps to install the drive. It's important to remember that not all drives are supported in every bay. For example, a 1.44MB 3.5-in floppy drive may only work in bays 5 and 6, while a CD-ROM drive may only work in drive bay 5, and a TurboDAT drive may only work in bay 7. You should research the server's documentation to be certain that you know which drives are compatible in each of the server's drive bays.

Hot-Pluggable Drives

Hot-pluggable drives can be removed and replaced while the server power is still applied. In most cases, it is not necessary to set the SCSI ID jumpers on a replacement hot-pluggable hard drive—the SCSI ID is set automatically by the motherboard and the hot-pluggable tray when the drive is installed. When a drive (configured for fault tolerance) is replaced, the replacement drive will automatically begin being restored after the installation is replaced. While a drive is being restored, the online LED will flash green. The LED will continue to flash until the drive is completely restored. The following guidelines must be followed when replacing hot-pluggable hard drives:

- *Never remove more than one drive at a time.* When a drive is replaced, the controller uses data from the other drives in the array to reconstruct data on the replacement drive. If more than one drive is removed, a complete data set is not available to reconstruct data on the replacement drive(s).

- *Never remove a working drive when another drive has failed.* Drives that have been failed by the controller are indicated by an amber drive failure LED on the drive tray. Permanent data loss will occur if a working drive is removed when replacing a failed drive.

- *Never remove a drive while another drive is being rebuilt.* A drive's online LED will flash green whenever it is being rebuilt. A replaced drive is restored from data stored on the other drives.

- *Never turn off a drive (storage) system while the controlling server is powered on.* This would cause the server's SMART controller to mark all the drives as failed—this could result in permanent data loss.

- *If an online spare drive is installed, wait for it to finish rebuilding before replacing the failed drive.* When a drive fails, the online spare will become active and begin being rebuilt as a replacement drive. Once the online spare has finished being rebuilt, the failed drive should be replaced with a new replacement drive. Do not replace the failed drive with the online spare.

- *A POST error message (i.e., code 1786) will occur during server power up if a drive has been replaced while the system is off.* When this occurs, you'll be prompted to continue booting and rebuild the replaced drive, or continue booting and not rebuild (this will result in data loss).

It's a relatively simple matter to replace a hot-pluggable hard drive. In most cases, drives are accessed from the front of the rack and do not require that the server be extended from the rack. To remove the drive, press the releases on the ejector levers and swing the levers out (see Figure 22-2). This will pull the drives out of the backplane connector. Slide the hot-pluggable hard drive out of the chassis. To replace the drive, slide the hot-pluggable hard drive all the way into the drive cage. Mate the drive with the backplane

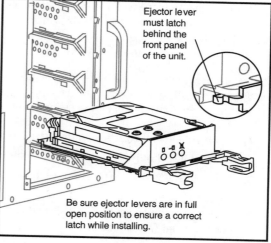

Ejector lever must latch behind the front panel of the unit.

Be sure ejector levers are in full open position to ensure a correct latch while installing.

FIGURE 22-2 Installing a hot-pluggable hard drive (Courtesy of Compaq)

connector and swing the ejector levers back into place. When routing cables, always make sure that the cables are not in a position where they will be pinched or crimped.

In many cases, SCSI hard drives on the same SCSI bus must be internal (within the server) or in an external storage system, but not both. A configuration with both internal and external SCSI hard drives requires more than one single-channel SCSI controller. A multichannel controller (such as the Compaq SMART SCSI Array Controller) supports both internal and external SCSI hard drives on separate SCSI buses.

MEMORY UPGRADES

Server memory is often installed in the form of DIMMs (dual inline memory modules), and a typical server motherboard will support 768MB to 1GB (or more) of fast Synchronous DRAM (SDRAM) memory across up to four DIMM slots (i.e., four 256MB DIMMs). Some servers will employ Rambus memory (RDRAM) fitted into RIMM (Rambus Inline Memory Module) slots. As server complexity and traffic increase, more memory may be necessary to handle the larger number of open files. Because you might need to upgrade memory in an existing configuration, let's look at DIMM removal first:

All forms of memory are extremely sensitive to accidental damage from ESD. Use all antistatic precautions when handling a DIMM or RIMM.

1. Open the server (if it's not already open) and locate the DIMM slot(s).

2. Gently push the plastic ejector levers out and down to eject the selected DIMM from its slot.

3. Hold the DIMM only by its edges (careful not to touch its components or gold edge connectors) and carefully lift it away from the socket. Store the old DIMM in an anti-static package.

4. Repeat to remove other DIMMs as necessary.

Use extreme care when removing or installing a DIMM or RIMM—too much pressure can damage the slot (and ruin the motherboard). Apply only enough pressure on the plastic ejector levers to release or secure the module. Modules are keyed to allow insertion in only one way.

Refer to the motherboard's documentation and select one or more DIMMs to provide an adequate amount of memory for the server. DIMMs must be selected based on capacity (i.e., 128MB), memory type (i.e., SDRAM), speed (i.e., 8-ns cycle time), and error checking (i.e., parity, non-parity, ECC, or non-ECC). Let's review the process for DIMM installation:

DIMMs and sockets may use tin or gold in the connectors, but mixing dissimilar metals (i.e., a DIMM with gold contacts into a DIMM slot with tin contacts) may cause later memory failures—resulting in data corruption. Only install DIMMs with gold-plated edge connectors in gold-plated sockets.

1. Open your server (if it's not already open) and locate the DIMM slot(s).

2. Hold a DIMM only by its edges, and remove it from its anti-static package.

3. Orient the DIMM so that the two notches in the bottom edge of the DIMM align with the keys in the slot.

4. Insert the bottom edge of the DIMM into the slot, and press down firmly on the DIMM until it seats correctly and fully in the slot.

5. Gently push the plastic ejector levers on either end of the slot to the upright (locked) position.

6. Repeat to install other DIMMs as necessary.

CPU UPGRADES

A server motherboard will normally accommodate two or four (or more) processors. While one processor should work fine for most end users, network servers can employ additional processors to manage more users and open files. You'll need to attach an appropriate heat sink/fan unit to each processor being installed now, and have a termination card available for other unused processor slot(s). Refer to the documentation that accompanied the server motherboard and verify the type and speed of compatible processors (i.e., one or two 1-GHz Pentium III processors). If you're adding a second processor, be sure that the new processor(s) match the existing one (including the processor's manufacturing revision if necessary), or is otherwise suitable for use with the original CPU.

All processors are extremely sensitive to accidental damage from ESD. Use all anti-static precautions when handling a processor.

Select one or more suitable processors for the motherboard, and verify that their heat sink/fan units are properly attached. Locate the corresponding CPU slots (or sockets) on the motherboard, and also locate the small fan connectors near each slot (or socket). Virtually all modern server motherboards will auto-detect the processor and configure the bus speed, multiplier, and CPU voltage automatically. This means you rarely need to set jumpers to prepare a motherboard for new CPUs. Let's cover the essentials of processor installation now:

If the server has been running, any installed processor and heat sink will be hot. To avoid possible burn injury, allow the system to remain off for at least 15 minutes before servicing the processors.

1. Open your server (if it's not already open) and locate the processor slot(s).

2. If your server has one processor and you're adding another, you must remove the termination card from the next processor(s) slot. Carefully pull back the tab of the retention mechanism until the termination card can be rotated out of the slot. Grasp the card on the side closest to the retention mechanism tab and rotate the one side of the card out of the slot. Once that side is free, you can pull the other side out of the slot.

You generally must install a termination card into any vacant processor slot to ensure reliable system operation. A termination card contains AGTL+ termination circuitry and clock termination. The server may not boot unless all vacant processor slots contain a termination card.

3. If your server has one processor and you're replacing it, leave the termination card in place in the empty secondary slot. Remove the processor you want to replace.

4. If your server has two processors and you're replacing one or both, remove the appropriate one(s).

5. Remove the new processor from its anti-static package and orient the processor in its slot (or socket) using special care to align pin 1 properly. For cartridge-type processors, slide the processor into the retention mechanism. Push down firmly, with even pressure on both sides of the top, until the processor is seated. It should click into place.

6. For socket-type processors, seat the processor fully into the socket, then close and lock the ZIF lever.

The grounded retention mechanisms (GRM) are not compatible with SECC type processor packaging—the new GRMs only support SECC2 type (i.e., Pentium II/III Xeon) processors. If you plan on using SECC type (i.e., ordinary Pentium II/III) processors, you must use a universal retention mechanism (URM).

7. Attach the fan power cable to the three-pin connector on the server board.

8. Close the server and secure the outer cover (make sure that any intrusion switch is closed).

9. Connect any remaining external cables and attach the ac power cord.

10. Turn on the monitor and then power up the server. Start the server's CMOS Setup routine to configure the new server motherboard, memory, and CPU(s).

Processor Card Notes

In some cases, rack-mounted servers (especially older servers such as the Compaq ProLiant 4500) might include the processor(s) on a removable card as shown in Figure 22-3. Such a processor card typically includes the BIOS and many of the core processing elements normally found on an ordinary motherboard. This approach allows designers to simplify the rack's main board, and install the processor card as an expansion card, which can easily be replaced for repairs or upgrades. Today, the high-frequency signaling used with modern processors does not lend itself well to processor card technology, so processors are included on the motherboard (much the same way that CPUs are installed on desktop PCs).

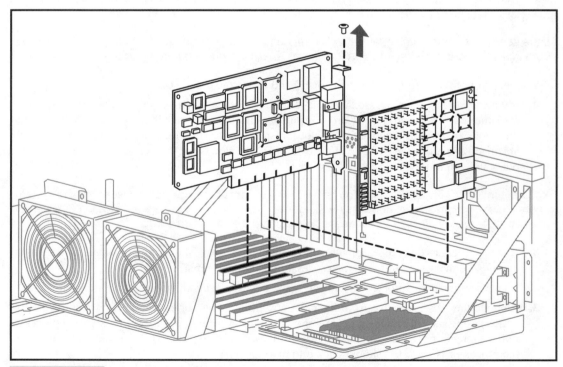

FIGURE 22-3   Removing processor and option card(s) from a rack-mounted server (Courtesy of Compaq)

Processor Matching Notes

Even processors with identical speed and voltage ratings may be slightly different internally. Such changes occur when bugs are fixed and performance enhancements are made to the processor's design. In many cases, the processors used in a typical network server should be matched. So, not only should the processors use the same speed and voltage, they should all be of the *same* engineering revision level. For example, Intel processors use "S-spec" numbers to represent the revision level. Matching is not required on every server motherboard (the newest server motherboards are more tolerant of CPU mismatches), but matching is generally regarded as the best default configuration policy. If matching is required for your server, but you cannot match new processors (i.e., because the engineering level of the existing processors is too old and stock is no longer available), you may need to install an entirely new suite of processors that are matched.

Conflict Detection and Resolution

Every device installed in the server (i.e., a NIC or video card) uses system resources in order to obtain the system's attention and communicate data with memory or the CPU. All PCs (including servers) offer only a limited amount of resources, and no two devices can use the same resources; otherwise, a *hardware conflict* will result. Low-level software (such as a device driver) that uses system resources can also conflict with each other during normal operation. This part of the chapter explains the concept of system resources, then shows you how to detect and correct conflicts that can arise in both hardware and software.

UNDERSTANDING SYSTEM RESOURCES

The key to mastering and eliminating conflicts is to understand the importance of each system resource that is available to you. PCs and servers provide three typical types of resources: interrupts (or IRQs), DMA channels, and I/O areas. Many controllers and network devices also utilize BIOS, which requires memory space. Do *not* underestimate the importance of these resource areas—conflicts can occur anywhere, and carry dire consequences for a system.

Interrupts

An *interrupt* is probably the most well known and understood type of resource. Interrupts are used to demand attention from the CPU. This allows a device or subsystem to work in the background until a particular event occurs that requires system processing. Such an event may include receiving a character at the serial port, striking a key on the keyboard, or any number of other real-world situations. An interrupt is invoked by asserting a logic level on one of the physical interrupt request (IRQ) lines accessible through any of the motherboard's expansion bus slots. AT-compatible computers provide 16 IRQ lines (noted IRQ 0 through IRQ 15), as outlined in Table 22-2. Keep in mind that Table 22-2 covers common *hardware interrupts* only. There are also a proliferation of processor and software-generated interrupts.

After an interrupt is triggered, an interrupt handling routine saves the current CPU register states to a small area of memory (called the *stack*), then directs the CPU to the *interrupt vector table*. The interrupt vector table is a list of program locations that correspond to each interrupt. When an interrupt occurs, the CPU will jump to the interrupt handler routine at the location specified in the interrupt vector table and execute the routine. In most cases, the interrupt handler is a device driver associated with the board generating the interrupt. For example, an IRQ from a network card will likely call a network device driver to operate the card. For a hard disk controller, an IRQ calls the BIOS ROM code that operates the drive. When the handling routine is finished, the CPU's original register contents are popped from the stack, and the CPU picks up from where it left off without interruption.

TABLE 22-2   A LISTING OF TYPICAL INTERRUPT ASSIGNMENTS

IRQ	FUNCTION
0	System timer chip
1	Keyboard controller chip
2	Second IRQ controller chip
3	Serial port 2 (COM2: 2F8h-2FFh and COM4: 2E8h-2EFh)
4	Serial port 1 (COM1: 3F8h-3FFh and COM3: 3E8h-3EFh)
5	Parallel port 2 (LPT2: 378h or 278h)
6	Floppy disk controller
7	Parallel port 1 (LPT1: 3BCh [mono] or 378h [color])
8	Real-time clock (RTC)
9	Unused (*redirected to IRQ 2*)
10	USB (on systems so equipped—can be disabled)
11	Windows sound system (on systems so equipped—can be disabled)
12	Motherboard mouse port (PS/2 port)
13	Math coprocessor
14	Primary AT/IDE hard disk controller
15	Secondary AT/IDE hard disk controller (on systems so equipped—can be disabled)

As a technician, it is not vital that you understand precisely how interrupts are initialized and enabled, but you should know the basic terminology. The term "assigned" simply means that a device is set to produce a particular IRQ signal. For example, a typical IDE hard drive controller board is assigned to IRQ 14 (primary controller) and IRQ 15 (secondary controller). Assignments are usually made with one or more jumpers or DIP switches, or are configured automatically through the use of Plug-and-Play (PnP). Next, interrupts can be selectively enabled or disabled under software control. An "enabled" interrupt is an interrupt where the PIC has been programmed to pass on an IRQ to the CPU. Just because an interrupt is enabled does not mean that there are any devices assigned to it. Finally, an "active" interrupt is a line where real IRQs are being generated. Note that active does not mean assigned or enabled.

DMA Channels

The CPU is very adept at moving data. It can transfer data between memory locations, I/O locations, or from memory to I/O and back with equal ease. However, PC designers realized that transferring large amounts of data (one word at a time) through the CPU is a hideous waste of CPU time. After all, the CPU really isn't *processing* anything during a data move—it's just shuttling data from one place to another. If there were a way to off-load such redundant tasks from the CPU, data could be moved faster than would be possible with CPU intervention. Direct memory access (DMA) is a technique designed to move large amounts of data from memory to an I/O location, or vice versa, without the direct intervention of the CPU. In theory, the DMA controller chip acts as a stand-alone data processor, leaving the CPU free to handle other tasks.

A DMA transfer starts with a DMA request (DRQ) signal generated by the requesting device (such as the floppy disk controller board). If the channel has been previously enabled through software drivers or BIOS routines, the request will reach the corresponding DMA controller chip on the motherboard. The DMA controller will then send a Hold request to the CPU, which responds with a Hold Acknowledge (HLDA) signal. When the DMA controller receives the HLDA signal, it instructs the bus controller to effectively disconnect the CPU from the expansion bus and allow the DMA controller chip to take control of the bus itself. The DMA controller sends a DMA Acknowledge (DACK) signal to the requesting device, and the transfer process may begin. After the transfer is done, the DMA controller will reconnect the CPU and drop its HOLD request—the CPU then continues with whatever it was doing without interruption. Table 22-3 illustrates common DMA channel assignments.

As with interrupts, a DMA channel is selected by setting a physical jumper or DIP switch on the particular expansion board (or through Plug-and-Play). When the board is installed in an expansion slot, the channel setting establishes a connection between the board and DMA controller chip. Often, accompanying software drivers must use a command-line switch that points to the corresponding hardware DMA assignment. Also, DMA channels cannot be shared between two or more devices. If more than one device attempts to use the same DMA channel at the same time, a conflict will result.

I/O Space

All computers provide space for I/O (input/output) ports. An I/O port acts very much like a memory address, but it's not for storage. Instead, an I/O port provides the means for a PC to communicate directly with a device—allowing the PC to efficiently pass commands and data between the system and various expansion devices. Each device must be assigned to a unique address (or address range). Table 22-4 lists some typical I/O port assignments.

I/O assignments are generally made manually by setting jumpers or DIP switches on the expansion device itself (or automatically through the use of Plug-and-Play). As with other system resources, it is vitally important that no two devices use the same I/O port(s) at the same time. If one or more I/O addresses overlap, a hardware conflict will result. When a conflict occurs, commands meant for one device may be erroneously interpreted by another. Keep in mind that while many expansion devices can be set at a variety of addresses, some devices cannot.

Memory Assignments

Memory is another vital resource for the PC. While early devices relied on the assignment of IRQ, DMA channels, and I/O ports, most current devices (i.e., SCSI controllers, network cards, video boards, modems, and so on) are demanding memory space for the support of each device's onboard BIOS ROM (their firmware). No two ROMs can overlap in their addresses; otherwise, a conflict will occur. Table 22-5 lists a memory map for a modern PC.

TABLE 22-3	A LISTING OF TYPICAL DMA ASSIGNMENTS	
DMA	**TRADITIONAL FUNCTION**	**CURRENT FUNCTION(S)**
0	Dynamic RAM refresh	Audio system
1	Unused	Audio system or parallel port
2	Floppy disk controller	Floppy disk controller
3	Unused	ECP parallel port or audio system
4	Reserved (used internally)	Reserved (used internally)
5	Unused	Unused
6	Unused	Unused
7	Unused	Unused

TABLE 22-4 TYPICAL I/O ASSIGNMENTS

ADDRESS RANGE	TYPICAL ASSIGNMENT
0000h–000Fh	PIIX4-DMA 1
0020h–0021h	PIIX4-interrupt controller 1
002Eh–002Fh	Super I/O controller configuration registers
0040h–0043h	PIIX4-counter/timer 1
0048h–004Bh	PIIX4-counter/timer 2
0060h	Keyboard controller byte—reset IRQ
0061h	PIIX4—NMI, speaker control
0064h	Keyboard controller, CMD/STAT byte
0070h	(Bit 7) PIIX4—enable NMI
0070h	(Bits 6–0) PIIX4—real-time clock, address
0071h	PIIX4—real-time clock, data
0078h	Reserved—board configuration
0079h	Reserved—board configuration
0081h–008Fh	PIIX4—DMA page registers
00A0h–00A1h	PIIX4—interrupt controller 2
00B2h–00B3h	APM control
00C0h–00DEh	PIIX4—DMA 2
00F0h	Reset numeric error
0170h–0177h	Secondary IDE controller
01F0h–01F7h	Primary IDE controller channel
0200h–0207h	Audio/game port
0220h–022Fh	Audio (Sound Blaster compatible)
0240h–024Fh	Audio (Sound Blaster compatible)
0278h–027Fh	LPT2
0290h–0297h	Management extension hardware
02E8h–02EFh	COM4/video (8514A)
02F8h–02FFh	COM2
0300h–0301h	MPU-401 (MIDI)
0330h–0331h	MPU-401 (MIDI)
0332h–0333h	MPU-401 (MIDI)
0334h–0335h	MPU-401 (MIDI)
0376h	Secondary IDE channel command port
0377h	Secondary floppy channel command port
0378h–037Fh	LPT1
0388h–038Dh	AdLib (FM synthesizer)
03B4h–03B5h	Video (VGA)
03BAh	Video (VGA)
03BCh–03BFh	LPT3
03C0h–03CAh	Video (VGA)
03CCh	Video (VGA)

TABLE 22-4 TYPICAL I/O ASSIGNMENTS *(CONTINUED)*

ADDRESS RANGE	TYPICAL ASSIGNMENT
03CEh–03CFh	Video (VGA)
03D4h–03D5h	Video (VGA)
03DAh	Video (VGA)
03E8h–03EFh	COM3
03F0h–03F5h	Primary floppy channel
03F6h	Primary IDE channel command port
03F7h	Primary floppy channel command port
03F8h–03FFh	COM1
04D0h–04D1h	Edge/level triggered PIC
0530h–0537h	Windows Sound System
0604h–060Bh	Windows Sound System
LPT n + 400h	ECP port, LPT n base address + 400h
0CF8h–0CFBh	PCI configuration address register
0CF9h	Turbo and reset control register
0CFCh–0CFF	PCI configuration data register
0E80h–0E87h	Windows Sound System
0F40h–0F47h	Windows Sound System
0F86h–0F87h	Yamaha OPL3-SA configuration
FF00h–FF07h	IDE bus master register
FFA0h–FFA7	Primary bus master IDE registers
FFA8h–FFAFh	Secondary bus master IDE registers

TABLE 22-5 A TYPICAL PC MEMORY MAP

ADDRESS RANGE (DECIMAL)	ADDRESS RANGE (HEX)	SIZE	DESCRIPTION
1024K–262144K	100000–10000000	255MB	Extended Memory
960K–1024K	F0000–FFFFF	64KB	BIOS
944K–960K	EC000–EFFFF	16KB	Boot block (available as UMB)
936K–944K	EA000–EBFFF	8KB	ESCD (PnP/DMI configuration)
932K–936K	E9000–E9FFF	4KB	Reserved for BIOS
928K–932K	E8000–E8FFF	4KB	OEM logo or scan user flash
896K–928K	E0000–E7FFF	32KB	POST BIOS (available as UMB)
800K–896K	C8000–DFFFF	96KB	Available high DOS memory
640K–800K	A0000–C7FFF	160KB	Video memory and BIOS
639K–640K	9FC00–9FFFF	1KB	Extended BIOS data
512K–639K	80000–9FBFF	127KB	Extended conventional memory
0K–512K	00000–7FFFF	512KB	Conventional memory

RECOGNIZING AND DEALING WITH CONFLICTS

Fortunately, conflicts are almost *always* the result of a PC upgrade gone awry. Thus, a technician can be alerted to the possibility of a system conflict by applying the Last Upgrade rule. The rule consists of three parts:

■ A piece of *hardware* and/or *software* has been added to the system very recently.

■ The trouble occurred *after* a piece of hardware and/or software was added to the system.

■ The system was working fine *before* the hardware and/or software was added.

If all three of these common-sense factors are true, chances are very good that you are faced with a hardware or software conflict (rather than a defective device). Unlike most other types of PC problems, which tend to be specific to the faulty subassembly, conflicts usually manifest themselves as much more general and perplexing problems. The following symptoms are typical of serious hardware or software conflicts:

■ The system locks up during the POST or operating system initialization.

■ The system locks up during a particular application.

■ The system locks up when a particular device (i.e., a TWAIN scanner) is used.

■ The system locks up randomly or without warning regardless of the application.

■ The system might not crash, but the device that was added may not function (even though it seems properly configured). Devices that were in the system previously may still work correctly.

■ The system may not crash, but a device or application that was working previously no longer seems to function. The newly added device (and accompanying software) may or may not work properly.

The severity and frequency of a fault (as well as the point at which the fault occurs) depend on such factors as the particular *devices* that are conflicting, the *resources* that are conflicting among the devices (i.e., IRQs, DMAs, or I/O addresses), and the *function* being performed by the PC when the conflict manifests itself. Since every PC is equipped and configured a bit differently, it is virtually impossible to predict a conflict's symptoms more precisely.

Confirming and Resolving Conflicts

Recognizing the possibility of a conflict is one thing, but proving and correcting it is another issue entirely. However, there are some very effective tactics at your disposal. The first rule of conflict resolution is *last in first out* (LIFO). The LIFO principle basically says that *the fastest means of overcoming a conflict problem is to remove the hardware or software that resulted in the conflict*. In other words, if you install board X and board Y ceases to function, board X is probably conflicting with the system, so removing board X should restore board Y to normal operation. The same concept holds true for software. If you add a new application to your system, then find that an existing application fails to work properly, the new application is likely at fault. Unfortunately, removing the offending element is not enough. You still have to install the new device or software in such a way that it will no longer conflict in the system.

Dealing with Software Conflicts

Device drivers present a potential conflict problem. Some server hardware upgrades require the addition of one or more real-mode (aka DOS) device drivers. Such drivers are called from the **CONFIG.SYS** file during system initialization (or loaded with Windows), and use a series of command-line parameters to specify the system resources that are being used. This is often necessary to ensure that the driver operates its associated hardware properly, and is very common with NetWare-based servers. If the command-line options used for the device driver do not match the hardware settings (or overlap the settings of another device driver), system problems can result. If you suspect that a device driver is causing the problem, find its reference in the **CONFIG.SYS** file and disable it by placing the command REM in front of its command line, such as

```
REM DEVICE = C:\DRIVERS\NEWDRIVE.SYS /A360 /I:5
```

The REM command turns the line into a "REMark", which can easily be removed later if you choose to restore the line. Remember that disabling the device driver in this fashion will prevent the associated hardware from working, but if the problem clears, you can work with the driver settings until the problem is resolved. Remember to reboot the computer so that your changes will take effect. Finally, consider the possibility that the offending software is buggy or defective. Try contacting the software manufacturer. There may be a fix or undocumented feature that you are unaware of. There may also be a patch or update that will solve the problem.

Dealing with Hardware Conflicts and Error Codes

Consider an example. A PC user recently added a CD-ROM and adapter board to their system. The installation went flawlessly using the defaults—a 10-minute job. Several days later, when attempting to backup the system, the user noticed that the parallel port tape backup did not respond (although the printer that had been connected to the parallel port was working fine). The user tried booting the system from a clean bootable floppy disk (no **CONFIG.SYS** or **AUTOEXEC.BAT** files to eliminate the device drivers), but the problem remained. After a bit of consideration, the user powered down the system, removed the CD-ROM adapter board, and booted the system from a clean bootable floppy disk. Sure enough, the parallel port tape backup started working again.

Stories such as this remind technicians that hardware conflicts are not always the monstrous, system-smashing mistakes that they are made out to be. In many cases, conflicts have subtle, noncatastrophic consequences. Since the CD-ROM was the last device to be added, it was the first to be removed. It took about five minutes to realize and remove the problem. However, *removing* the problem is only part of conflict troubleshooting—reinstalling the device without a conflict is the real challenge.

Fortunately, Windows provides a Device Manager that tracks the devices in your system and identifies the resources and drivers assigned to each device. As an example, under Windows 2000, when you open the Device Manager, double-click the Computer entry at the top of the device list. The Device Manager dialog box will open. Select View, choose Resources by type, and expand the resource list you'd like to see (see Figure 22-4) and you can check the assignments for IRQs, DMA, I/O, or Memory. By reviewing these entries, you can quickly determine which resources are assigned and which are free.

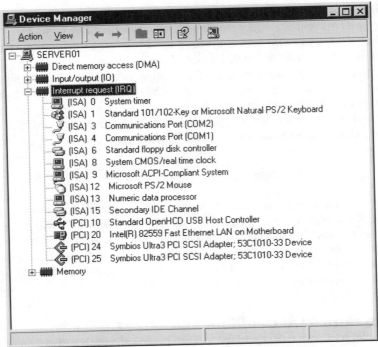

FIGURE 22-4 Determining resource assignments under Windows 2000

The Windows 95/98/2000 Device Manager is a very powerful resource that's designed to help you inspect the configuration and settings of almost every device in your system. When a problem occurs, the Device Manager can often identify the problem and provide valuable clues that will help you resolve the trouble. Before we start working through the conflict resolution process, let's take some time to study the typical Device Manager errors. Check your Device Manager for error codes under Windows 2000:

1. Right-click My Computer.

2. Click Properties.

3. Select the Hardware tab and click the Device Manager button.

4. Double-click a device type (i.e., Network adapters) to see the devices in that category.

5. Double-click a device to view its Properties dialog box (see Figure 22-5).

6. If an error code has been generated, the code appears in the Device status box on the General tab. If there is a problem with the device, click the Troubleshooter button.

Interpreting Device Manager Codes

After you've opened the Device Manager under Windows 98/ME, you can use the Device Manager to examine the status of each device. If there is a problem with a device, it is listed in the device list under the Computer entry. The problem device has a symbol indicating the specific nature of the problem:

- A black exclamation mark ("!") on a yellow field indicates the device is experiencing a problem (though it may still be functioning). A problem code explaining the problem is displayed for the device.
- A red "X" indicates a disabled device. A disabled device is a device that is physically present in the system and consuming resources, but it does not have a protected-mode driver loaded.
- When viewing device resources in Computer properties, a blue "i" on a white field (over a device resource) indicates that the Use Automatic Settings feature is not selected for the device, and that the resource was manually selected. It does not indicate a problem or disabled state.
- A green question mark ("?") in Device Manager means that only a compatible driver for the given device is installed—there's a possibility that all of the device's functionality may not be available.

Select a specific device in Device Manager and click Properties—you'll see a Property dialog box. When you click the Resource tab (see Figure 22-6), the Resource settings window in the middle of the dialog box indicates which resource type(s) are used for that device. The box at the bottom of the dialog box contains a Conflicting device list, and this list indicates a conflict with an error code. Observe the "Use automatic settings" check box. If Windows successfully detects a device, its check box is selected and the device should function correctly. However, if the resource settings are based on "Basic Configuration x" (where x is a number from 0 to 9), it may be necessary to change the configuration by selecting a different basic configuration from the list. If the particular configuration you want for the device is not listed as a

FIGURE 22-5   A typical device Properties dialog box under Windows 2000

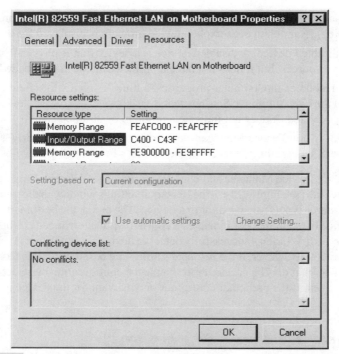

FIGURE 22-6   Adjusting resource assignments (if necessary) under Windows 2000

basic configuration, you may need to click the Change Setting button to manually adjust the resource values. For example, to edit an I/O range setting, follow these steps:

1. Highlight the Input/Output Range to be changed and uncheck the "Use automatic settings" box.

2. Click the Change Setting button.

3. Select the appropriate I/O range for the device.

   Remember to save your changes and reboot the system (if necessary). If the device uses jumpers or DIP switches, you must configure the device manually rather than through the Properties dialog boxes.

Further Study

APC: **www.apcc.com**
Dell: **support.dell.com**
Gateway: **www.gateway.com**
Intel: **www.intel.com**
Kingston: **www.kingston.com**
Microsoft: **support.microsoft.com**

WEB SERVER BASICS

The Internet explosion of the last few years has been largely driven by availability of the World Wide Web (or simply the Web). The Web can trace its roots back to 1989 when the European Center for Nuclear Research (CERN) in Geneva started a project to publish and link research information on the Internet. Since then, Web technologies have become a cornerstone of personal and professional publishing—there is scarcely a company in existence today that doesn't support a Web presence, and even individuals routinely update their family Web sites with photos and video clips. Today, there are hundreds of thousands of Web servers in operation across the Internet, serving many millions of Web pages to eager shoppers, readers, researchers, students, and so on. Your corporate network probably contains one or more Web servers. In this chapter, we'll look at the functions of a typical Web server based on Microsoft's Internet Information Server (IIS) 5.0 for Windows 2000, and examine some of the common problems associated with operating a Web server on the Internet today.

Web Server Software Basics

Web servers rely on server software to accept browser requests and retrieve files (typically Web pages), then execute any associated CGI scripts and serve them back to the client. The first Web software used a command-line interface. However, as the technology developed, graphics were incorporated. In early 1993, the Mosaic browser (a fully graphical browser) was developed at the National Center for Supercomputing Applications (NCSA), under the leadership of Marc Andreessen. He later went on to play a role at Netscape and develop the Netscape Navigator browser—ushering in the age of modern Windows Web browsers that we enjoy today. Today, Web pages are created using the Hypertext Markup Language (HTML) and travel across the Internet using the Hypertext Transfer Protocol (HTTP). The Web server runs continuously and works through a port (usually port 80) on the server machine. Browsers send requests to these ports. Some server software on the market also provides other network service functionality such as FTP or multimedia services.

Just as browser software has evolved rapidly over the last few years, server software has also grown considerably. New functionality has been added to provide support for new kinds of information (particularly with multimedia) and new management tools have been developed. Some server software is even available on the Internet at no cost. There are several popular types of server software available today:

- **Apache**   A freely distributed Web server available at **www.apache.org**. It is estimated that about 50 percent of Web servers are running Apache. The Apache Web server has been ported to many different computer system platforms such as Windows NT/2000, UNIX/Linux, and Novell NetWare.

- **Microsoft IIS**   The Microsoft Internet Information Server (IIS) Web server software comes free with its Windows NT and 2000 operating systems. The Windows NT Option Pack (available for download) contains components to upgrade it to IIS version 4.0, though IIS version 5.0 is available free with Windows 2000. Microsoft also has a Personal Web server for its Window 9x operating system family, downloadable from **www.microsoft.com**.

- **iPlanet Web Server**   Formerly Netscape's enterprise version of its Web server as the result of their alliance with Sun, and now supported by iPlanet. You can find information about iPlanet servers at **http://www.iplanet.com/products/iplanet_web_enterprise/home_web_server.html**.

- **Jigsaw Web Server**   This is a Java-based Web server created and maintained by the World Wide Web Consortium. The Jigsaw Web server is freely available from **http://www.w3.org/Jigsaw/**.

ADVANTAGES OF THE WEB

The Web's popularity stems from its great versatility. Posting text and graphics is a traditional application, but those are only a few basic capabilities of the Web. The advances in Web languages and increases in communication speeds have resulted in an explosion of creativity that continues to this day. Modern Web sites enable virtual meetings (aka, Web conferencing), remote device access and management, remote database access, streaming media (i.e., radio and television), download libraries, help desk automation, and countless other creative applications. Here are just a few general uses for the Web.

Distribute and Gather Information

Web content can be a big paper saver. Rather than creating memos informing people of a change in company policy or inviting them to the company holiday party, you can create a Web page with the information. This not only saves you the trouble of distributing the memos, but also allows you access to design elements not always possible in e-mail—without requiring people to have access to the application in which the original document was created (such as Adobe Acrobat). Posting the documents to the Web site also prevents people from tampering with the original document.

Another advantage to publishing documents on the Web is that you can confirm that people have read them. You're not limited to just posting the information and hoping it got to the people who needed to see it. Just create a section where people can click on a button saying, "Yes, I've read and understood this" to send a confirmation e-mail to the business manager (or whomever else needs to know). You could do something similar to have people RSVP for the office conference, creating a form in which people can indicate whether they'll be attending, how many guests they'll be bringing, and any other relevant information.

Communicate and Collaborate

Chat sessions can be a means of getting people together for meetings when physical meetings are difficult or impossible. A chat application is one way of doing this, but a Web-based chat is another—and one that can be used by anyone with a browser (not just people with a chat application installed). Video conferencing can also be supported via a Web interface. Web meeting services (such as WebEx at **www.webex.com**) let Web users view presentations, and share applications and desktops for a true collaborative experience. With Web-based scheduling applications, the Web can also be used in group scheduling for those times when virtual meetings won't do the trick. For example, Lotus Organizer has a Web plug-in so that people can plan their schedules on their personal computers or PDAs, and then upload the information to a Web-based calendar so that coworkers know where everyone is.

As another example, a corporate Web can help workers find each other in the first place. Many big companies are a maze of cubicles or offices, and in a large company not everyone can know each other by sight. One solution to this problem is to prepare an online map of the corporate offices that shows the location of each person's office. Let users plug in a name, and the map highlights the location of that person's office *and* pulls up a picture of the person whose name you entered.

Improve Support

A Web-based user help desk can streamline the support process. First, many user requests are predictable—they want access to a particular folder, can't reach their e-mail, can't find a file, and so on. You can create a form listing common problems, inviting users to pick their problem from a list. If their problem isn't listed, they can explain it in a text box on the Web page. The Web page can also link to FAQs, file patches and updates, and other support resources that are frequently needed.

Writing down the problem or choosing from a set of options encourages users to think about what's wrong and describe it more fully than they might over the telephone or in person. You often have to go through the initial process of isolating the problem, getting from "WordPerfect isn't working" to "WordPerfect is shutting down after a message comes up saying that the computer is low on resources". Isolating the problem can take several minutes, or even longer. It's simpler, and less frustrating for everyone, to allow the user to write down the problem or choose his or her problem from a list. This won't completely eliminate the need to isolate some problems, but it should help. Telephone follow-up is always an option if more information is needed.

Finally, submitting problems by Web-based e-mail reduces both the time it takes to report the problem and the time required for the support person to listen to it. Additionally, e-mail is usually available—the person reporting the problem doesn't have to wait for a free line to the support center to open up.

Database Access

An increasingly popular use for a corporate intranet Web is to provide a front end to a database for salespeople or managers. It's a great improvement over printing out standard reports every month. A canned report may not answer a specific set of questions that a salesperson or manager has. Moreover, the distribution problem surfaces again—generating and distributing those reports to everyone in a widely distributed company can take a great deal of labor.

At some corporations, users can send database server queries via e-mail without having to know Structured Query Language (SQL) syntax. The users phrase the questions using standard language that will trigger a previously prepared query. More advanced users familiar with SQL syntax can e-mail queries using SQL and thus get custom reports. Additionally, when people need to edit the database or create reports, a properly designed Web application lets users do it without having to understand how to use a database front end (such as Access). The interface on the front end can be designed to translate the user-phrased queries into the SQL that databases use.

Distribute Files

It's entirely possible that you may want people to have access to certain files, but not to the directories in which those files are stored. Perhaps the directories are across a slow WAN connection, or other files are stored in the directories that you don't necessarily want everyone to know exist. In such a case, you can set up an FTP site to function as a central repository for files coming in and going out. Users can upload and download files from a "public" directory. The degree of security depends on how you configure it (whether access is dependent on a password, restricted to certain users, or open to anyone who logs in). For example, if you have computer-savvy users on your network, you can store software upgrades in a central location. Users can run the Setup files from the FTP site, saving themselves the trouble of looking for their own disks or getting the support person to upgrade their applications.

Publish Research

One more use for the Web is to share research between departments of a large organization. For example, several agencies within the U.S. Department of the Army share a corporate intranet. On this intranet is a Web-based database called IntelLink that publishes the data collected by analytical departments. Users of IntelLink (including policymakers, soldiers, management, and anyone else with access) can refer to a database of country reports, pictures, maps, and military hardware. Without this Web-based application, these people would have to call the analysts to prepare reports for them. Analysts will still make custom reports and briefings, but often-requested information doesn't require any more work on the analysts' part.

MARKUP LANGUAGES

If you've ever worked with the Web, you know that there's a lot more to a Web page than just the text and graphics that you see. You can't just drop text onto a Web page and have it look right—it must be coded so that a browser can present the page as it was intended. We often refer to this as Web "programming," but it's more accurate to say that the page is "marked up" for a browser. A *markup language* is basically a series of codes that are inserted into the body of a document. These codes define how the text, graphics, and other visual items should look when printed or displayed (or to define its logical structure such as paragraphs and bullets). Without such a markup language, the data to be displayed would be raw text with no character or paragraph formatting.

A markup language defines document appearance with codes (called *tags*) that take the form of <tag>…</tag>. The first tag indicates the point where the formatting should *begin* and the second tag (with the slash) indicates where the coding should *end*. If you forget the second tag, the coding for the first tag is applied until the end of the document. For example, if you wanted to bold a sentence using a basic markup language, the syntax would appear as

```
<strong>
This is the bold sentence.
</strong>
```

When you view this text in a browser, the sentence will be bolded. The markup language can be applied to raw text using a text editor (such as Notepad) or with a graphical tool (such as FrontPage) that adds the code when you visually arrange the text as you want it to appear. Graphical tools are easier to work with when you're learning, but they're not always as precise and efficient as text-based editing. There are several types of markup languages that you should be familiar with.

This is certainly not intended to be a detailed discussion on Web design or markup languages, but you can see the importance of each language.

Hypertext Markup Language (HTML)

The Hypertext Markup Language (or HTML) is the basis of Web page coding, and the backbone of most Web pages. HTML allows you to publish text and figures, display the contents of spreadsheets, or even create database reports to be read online. It's good for organizing and formatting any kind of static information. HTML codes let you

- Set text sizes and fonts
- Apply bold, italic, or underlined formatting to text
- Define links to other pages (called "hyperlinks")
- Insert images (such as **.JPG** or **.GIF** files)
- Create a title for the page
- Create tables
- Insert metadata for use by search engines

Metadata is hidden data that does not appear on the Web page, but may be picked up by a search engine to direct people to a site.

There are three types of HTML tags: tags that format text or individual characters, tags that format paragraphs or other chunks of text, and tags that are invisible but provide other functionality (such as metadata for searches). You can see an example of HTML source code in Figure 23-1. While more recent markup languages are often used to supplement HTML, it has the advantage of virtually universal support. Just about any browser (certainly any modern and graphics-capable browser) supports the current version of HTML, and this may not be true of other languages like Dynamic HTML (DHTML), XML, or Java and ActiveX. If you need your Web sites to be accessible to a variety of browser types, HTML is the way to go.

Dynamic HTML (DHTML)

Dynamic HTML (or DHTML) makes HTML a bit more flexible. Rather than presenting a static Web page to the world, you can use DHTML and make a page customizable by the person using it, *without* corrupting the original document source. For example, a page prepared with DHTML can include elements that a user can drag around on the page to rearrange its contents. When the page is refreshed, however, the changes are lost and the page is restored to its original appearance. DHTML has support for the following features not included in HTML:

- Dynamic styles
- Precise positioning
- Data binding
- Dynamic content

FIGURE 23-1   You can tell a browser to display the HTML source code that makes up a Web page.

Dynamic styles are based on the principles of *cascading style sheets* (CSS), applying style sheets to a page instead of formatting the various sections by hand. If you use a modern word processor, you're probably familiar with style sheets that automatically format text blocks a certain way (depending on the style you assign to them). This formatting can include text color, font, positioning, visibility, and just about anything else to do with how text can be presented. CSS (and by extension DHTML) is the same kind of thing, only applied to Web pages instead of word processors. DHTML's dynamic styles have capabilities not included in word processors. For example, you could mark up text to make links automatically change color when you position your mouse over them, or show text when you move your cursor over a certain blank space. The only catch to these styles is that they require you to put most documents in style sheets—a time-consuming task for those new to style sheets or who are having to convert documents. When properly implemented, style sheets also allow the Web publisher to easily change the appearance of a page or set of pages. Dynamic content allows the Web user to change the appearance of a page by running a script in order to

■ Insert or hide elements of a page

■ Modify text

■ Change the page layout

■ Draw data from back-end sources and display it based on a user request

Unlike HTML, which can only change page contents *before* the page is downloaded to the user's browser, DHTML can accept changes at any time. When used with scripts that allow users to define the elements they want to see, dynamic content can provide a high degree of interactivity.

Another feature of DHTML is its ability to define exactly where on a page an element will appear, using "x" (horizontal), "y" (vertical), and even "z" (object placement in 3D allows you to make objects overlap) coordinates to define object placement. Precise positioning makes wrapping text around images possible and repositions objects according to the size of the browse window. HTML without CSS does not support exact placement. Instead, the positioning of elements depends on the browser.

To give users access to back-end information (such as that stored in a database) normal HTML pages must contact the server holding the original data and ask for permission to let users manipulate data. DHTML allows the data to be bound to a particular page, permitting users to work with the bound data without disturbing the source data, or even touching the server storing the original data. Instead, the data source is part of the page and can be sorted and filtered like a database. Not only does this reduce load on the servers, but it also allows users to view and manipulate data without giving them access to the source.

Extensible Markup Language (XML)

The Extensible Markup Language (or XML) is a relatively new Web coding language that supports HTML, making Web pages a little more flexible. When you're formatting a page with HTML, you can change the appearance of text with the tags for boldface, italic, paragraph break here, and so forth. These tags don't really tell you anything about the text's content, but only format its appearance. XML is not limited to tags that say what text is supposed to look like. Instead, you can use it to tag the text with what it is (names, addresses, product names, and so on).

This kind of metadata can make it easier for search engines to find predefined elements. If you searched your corporate Web site (created with HTML) for "name," looking for all the names mentioned, the search would return all the instances of the word "name", but not names. If the site were coded with XML, however, the search would return any text tagged as a *name*. Also, tagging parts of text is useful if you want to apply a rule (such as color or language) only to parts of a Web document. Suppose that the online document is a short story in Spanish with translation in English. Rather than having to switch from Spanish to English support in the document, you could define all the parts of the story with a <story> </story> tag and apply the Spanish rule to those parts only, with the translations remaining in English. Essentially, if your Web page design would be made easier by making certain parts of its text isolated elements, you could benefit from using XML.

APPLICATION AND SCRIPTING LANGUAGES

Up to now, markup languages are used to make a Web page look a certain way, and present data within the page. However, the pages themselves don't "do" anything except display information. Developers have integrated application and scripting languages into Web design, allowing Web pages to acquire information and interact with users in useful ways. On the client side, this could take the form of *ActiveX* controls or *Java* applets. Client-side Web applications and executables are downloaded from the Web server to the client, and are executed on the client using the client machine's resources. Client-side applications may include such features as chat programs or other applications likely to be used more than once while a page is still open.

On the server side, such miniprograms might use a *Common Gateway Interface* (or CGI) front end to a program stored on the server, or a script embedded in the page itself with Microsoft's *Active Server Pages* (ASP). Server-side Web applications execute on the server, using a server operating environment and resources. Server-side applications are more likely to be one-time applications (such as search engines).

The advantage to server-side applications is their compatibility—the browser doesn't have to support the client-side application language. The approaches to storing and loading these programs may differ. For example, CGI servers access an application stored on the server, where Active Server Pages store the script to be executed in the HTML page itself.

Java and ActiveX

Java is a cross-platform language developed by Sun Microsystems. The concept behind Java is interoperability—*Java applets* (miniature applications) are able to run on any platform (including DOS, Windows, UNIX, NT, and so on). When a Java applet runs, it first creates an execution environment (called a *sandbox*) for itself, and then runs in the context of this sandbox. In theory, the sandbox lets an applet execute on any platform because the sandbox creates the operating environment that the applet needs. It also keeps the applet from doing anything to the native operating environment.

Java applets that you might already have encountered include Netscape Communicator's Netcaster as well as the trip planners used on some travel Web sites. Netcaster is the front end to Netscape pull technology (that is, pulling content from Web sites without requiring that you actually visit the sites). The trip planners take the preferences you enter and search a database of airline flights that correspond to your needs and then return the possible matches.

ActiveX is similar to Java in that it's a way of attaching miniapplications to Web pages, but it's not identical. Rather than being a platform-independent programming language, ActiveX is a set of controls that can make applications written in a variety of languages (such as C++, Delphi, J++, and Visual Basic) accessible via the browser. ActiveX controls do *not* run in a sandbox—they run like any other application in the user operating environment.

CGI and ASP

The Common Gateway Interface (CGI) is a standardized way of passing information from a Web user's input to a back-end application or script, and then passing back information to the client's browser. For example, when you fill out an online registration form and click the Submit button, the information that you supplied may be passed via a CGI to a database. Once the information has been processed, you get a "Thank you!" message back, via the CGI. CGI's biggest advantage is consistency—it doesn't matter what platform the server is running on—the data can be passed from the user to the application, regardless. This isn't very different from what you'd get using a scripting language. It just works differently. A script is attached to a specific Web page, but an application accessible through CGI is not linked to a specific page (rather to a specific gateway), so any Web page can associate itself with that gateway.

Active Server Pages (ASPs) are an alternate means of getting Web pages to do a job. Some Web pages have scripts embedded in them that can be run when conditions require it (for example, when a user clicks a search engine's Find button, or fills out a form and clicks OK). You can create an ASP file by including in an HTML document a script written in VBScript or another supported scripting language, and then renaming the document with the **.ASP** suffix. When the user loads that page and fulfills the conditions, the script will run.

PUBLISHING CONTENT

Creating Web content is just the beginning—you still need to make Web content available on a server (that is, "publish" the Web content). Almost every operating system has the ability to add an HTTP server, and thus the ability to create an intranet or Internet site. There are various options for publishing HTML documents both inside (intranet) and outside (Internet) your network. When you publish HTML documents, all you're basically doing is placing a copy of the HTML documents on a server. Your visitors (using a browser) tell the server what to get, and the server responds by displaying the requested pages. In general, you can publish your HTML documents in three ways:

- Through your ISP or Web hosting service to the Internet
- Through a corporate IS department to an intranet or Internet
- Through your own server to an intranet

Virtual Domains

In the old days of the Internet, a URL would include the name of your ISP's server. For example, if you're a business called *SuperWidgets* and you're doing business with an ISP called **myweb.com**, your home page's URL might look like this:

```
http://www.myweb.com/~superwidgets/home.htm
```

This would be the URL that someone would need to enter into a browser in order to find your home page (and some budget ISPs still work this way for individuals). While this is technically fine, it's not intuitive, and few people would know to look for your site on another server. Fortunately, you're not limited to using the server name as the hostname portion of your URL. Instead, you can use a *virtual domain*. This gives you a hostname of your own, but your files still reside on the ISP's server(s). By creating a virtual domain such as **superwidgets.com**, customers can easily try an intuitive URL like

```
http://www.superwidgets.com
```

Today, virtual domains are a very popular way for small companies and organizations to have their Web content hosted by an ISP, but give the appearance of their own servers (and make it easier for customers to find them). But having a virtual domain goes beyond a matter of vanity or identity. There are very real advantages. For example, a virtual domain gives you consistency—you can keep the same domain (and URL) even if you move or change ISPs. Without a virtual domain, moving ISPs (or establishing your own Web server) would change your address and make it more difficult for customers to find you.

The easiest way to get a virtual domain is to ask your ISP to set it up for you. You usually pay between $20 to $100 for setup, plus a $50 fee for registering your domain name with InterNIC (**www.internic.net**, the main domain name registration service) for two years. If you do a little homework with your ISP, you can set up a virtual domain yourself and save a few dollars. Follow this process to check a domain name:

1. Go to **www.networksolutions.com**.
2. In the box that says "Enter a domain name", enter the domain you wish to register. For example, you might enter **breakfastbuffetatnight.com** or **eatmoreofjoesgreatburgers.com**. If you're lucky, you will see a list of possible names, including the one you entered—this means that your domain name is available.
3. Register the name yourself or ask your ISP to do it for you. Most ISPs will register domain names free if they'll be hosting them, or they charge a reasonable fee (usually $100 or less) for the service, plus hosting charges. If you really want to do it yourself, all the information and instructions you'll need are available at the Network Solutions site.

Of course, once the Web server is running, you'll need to support each virtual domain. One way is to assign an IP address to each domain and assign all of those IP addresses to the same host running the Web service—when you connect to port 80, the IP address is used to direct you to the correct page. Another way is to use a single IP address and the server software gets the right page based upon the name in the URL. This is really the heart of what the Web server administrator needs to know and needs to troubleshoot.

ISPs and Web Hosting

One of the most common places to publish HTML documents is on Web space provided by an Internet service provider (ISP). ISPs usually provide a slew of Internet-related services (including Web space) and help with your Web development needs. ISPs often provide a range of services, and you'll need to do some research to find out what each offers, as well as startup fees and monthly costs. In general, though, most ISPs offer either individual or business accounts.

Another option is to use a Web-hosting service. These services do not provide dial-up Internet access, but simply provide a location from which you can serve your Web content. Generally, you use Web-hosting services in conjunction with an ISP (combining the best Web-hosting deal with reliable dial-up access). Although it's possible that a single company could meet all your needs, shopping for these services separately can be useful.

Chances are that you're setting up your own Web server(s), but working with an ISP is a fine option for new businesses that wish to pass the server cost and support to a third party.

Individual Accounts   Individual users and small businesses can benefit from the low costs and ready availability of individual accounts. Generally, ISPs provide individual subscribers with access to the Internet, one or more e-mail accounts, and a relatively small amount of space on a Web server (5–50MB). Many ISPs also provide other services (such as forwarding the results of a form via e-mail). Exactly which services you'll need depends on what you want to do with your HTML pages. For example, if you plan to create and publish simple HTML documents, you may only need a bit of Web space. On the other hand, if you plan to create an enormous Web site, or one loaded with multimedia and downloadable files, you may need additional Web space. If you plan to include forms or use server-specific capabilities, you may need some server access or specific programs available on the server. First figure out what you want to do, and then find an ISP that can meet your needs. There are also other factors to consider:

- *Know the server and platform.* Once you identify the server and the platform, you can tell which scripts are available. For example, if an Apache server is running on a Sun SPARCstation (a likely ISP scenario), you can reasonably request that your server administrator install specific Perl scripts. However, if you're on an intranet with a Windows NT–based Netscape server and you discover enhancement to the WebStar server on a Macintosh, the two are incompatible.

- *Know the security.* For example, when testing pages on the server, you don't want the whole world to see them. Setting password-restricted access to the whole site helps with this. Additionally, if you have some pages that you want to make available to only a few people (or to everyone except a few people), you need to be able to set passwords (ideally with little hassle and wasted time). If you need security, be sure to know the capabilities—and limitations—of each service.

- *Know the scripts.* If you can install and run your own scripts, you'll have a lot more flexibility and capability than you might otherwise. If you're limited to what your ISP has already installed for your use, you are likely to have access to certain limited special capabilities (such as chat rooms), but not the flexibility to go with what you really want.

- *Know the reporting and logging features.* If you're selling services, promoting your company, or doing anything else that involves a significant number of people seeing your message, you'll need to see that accesses are logged, and you'll need to learn how to access those logs. If your ISP doesn't provide access and activity logs, you may need to select a different service.

■ *Know the service and support.* Web content needs to be available constantly, so your ISP must provide a high level of reliability. Know how to contact your ISP's support services when trouble strikes. You should also know how to make backups, and restore those backups if necessary.

Business Accounts   If you are running (or considering) a business with an Internet presence, consider establishing a business account with an ISP. Business accounts are generally more expensive than individual accounts, but almost always include more Web space (i.e., 100–500MB), better access to server-side programs (such as CGI scripts for complex forms), and more comprehensive services that sometimes include Web page design. In addition, some business accounts may include guaranteed uptime, regular backups, and more attention to business needs.

Corporate Servers
Another place to publish Web documents is on a corporate Web server—typically at your place of employment. If you work for a large company or an educational institution, or if you work with an organization or group that handles system administration tasks, you'll probably have little to do when it comes to accessing a Web server. All the necessary pieces (such as access, administration, and security) are likely to be in place, and you'll simply step in and start using the server.

The level of access and control that you actually have will vary from company to company. In the ideal situation, someone else takes care of running the server, but gives you great flexibility in using the server. You'd ideally get help setting up and running server-side programs, and can essentially do anything you need to in order to provide information. At the other extreme, you must adhere to a rigid process in submitting information to the intranet. You'd submit HTML documents, and then have little control over where they're placed or how they're linked. Chances are that your company will be somewhere in the middle, with an established procedure for accessing the corporate intranet, but a substantial amount of freedom to do what you need to do. If the process of providing content is tightly controlled, you may want to see about running your own server.

Your Own Servers
Finally, you might choose to publish your Web documents on your own server. If you have the technical savvy and existing infrastructure, running your own server affords you the most flexibility and best range of resources for Web development. One good reason to run your own server is that it's a more authentic environment for developing and testing pages—you can run pages "live" without releasing them to the rest of the company (or the Internet). For example, if you have server-sensitive URLs in links, they'll work properly if you're loading the files from a server, but not if you're loading the same file locally.

If you have a relatively new desktop machine, you can certainly use it as a Web server. For example, an older Pentium or Pentium II computer with 32–64MB of RAM (or more) can run an adequate Windows NT/2000 server for testing purposes (that is, the PC is being used for testing purposes, and is not intended to service heavy traffic). It can also run a Linux Web server if you'd prefer. To run a public server, whether at home or at work, you'll need a dedicated network connection—anything from a full-time ISDN line to a direct cable/DSL connection will work (at least for testing purposes).

IIS 5.0 for Windows 2000 Server

Now that you've seen a bit on Web basics, it's time to examine the features, installation, and use of a real Web server. While there are several servers available, we'll use *Internet Information Services* (IIS) 5.0 included with Windows 2000—this is the Windows 2000 Web service that lets you publish information on your intranet or on the Internet. Internet Information Services 5.0 has many new features to help Web administrators to create scalable, flexible Web applications.

INSTALLING IIS

Internet Information Services is available on a Windows 2000 Server by default, though you will need to install and run it. You can remove IIS or select additional components by using the Add/Remove Programs application in Control Panel. Follow these steps to install IIS, add components, or remove components under Windows 2000:

1. Click Start, highlight Settings, click Control Panel, and launch the Add/Remove Programs Wizard.

2. Select Configure Windows, click the Components button, and then follow the on-screen instructions to install, remove, or add components to IIS (see Figure 23-2).

 If you upgraded to Windows 2000, IIS 5.0 will be installed by default only if IIS was installed on your previous version of Windows.

One note about uninstalling IIS—it won't always uninstall completely (especially if there is user information on the server). The following directories containing user content will remain on your system after you completely uninstall IIS:

- **\Inetpub**
- **\%systemroot%\Help\iisHelp**
- **\%systemroot%\system32\inetsrv**

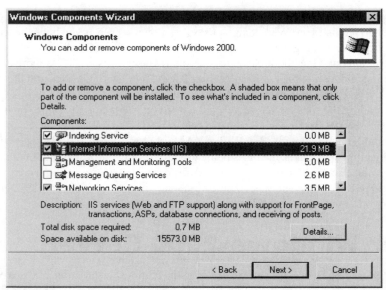

FIGURE 23-2   Use the Windows 2000 Components Wizard to install, remove, or alter the installation of IIS.

QUICK SITE SETUP WITH IIS

IIS creates a default Web site and FTP site when you install Windows 2000 Server. Once IIS is installed, you can use the general procedures below to publish information to the default site(s). Use the following steps to publish content on your Web site:

1. Use an authoring tool (such as Microsoft FrontPage) to create a home page for your Web site.
2. Name your home page file **default.htm**, **default.html**, or **default.asp**.
3. Copy your home page into the default Web publishing directory for IIS. The default Web publishing directory is also called the *home directory*, and the location provided by Setup is **\Inetpub\Wwwroot**.
4. If your network has a name resolution system (typically DNS), visitors can simply type your computer name (such as **author1.example.net**) in the address bar of their browsers to reach your site. If your network does not have a name resolution system, visitors must type the numerical IP address of your computer.

It is also a simple matter to publish content on your FTP site:

1. Copy or move your files into the default FTP publishing directory. The default directory provided by Setup is **\Inetpub\Ftproot**.
2. If your network has a name resolution system (typically DNS), visitors can type **ftp://** followed by your computer name in the address bar of their browsers to reach your site. If not, visitors must type **ftp://** and the numerical IP address of your computer.

Adding Sites

Your Web server can normally support a number of sites, and you can add new sites to a computer by launching the site wizard. You can easily add a new site to your Web server using the following steps:

1. Select the computer (or a site) in the Internet Information Services snap-in, and click the Action button.
2. Click New, and then Web Site (or FTP Site) to launch the site wizard (see Figure 23-3).
3. Follow the on-screen directions to assign identification information to your new site. You must provide the port address and the home directory path. If you're adding additional sites to a single IP address by using host headers, you must assign a host header name.

All Unassigned refers to IP addresses that are assigned to a computer, but not assigned to a specific site. The default Web site uses all of the IP addresses that are not assigned to other sites. Only one site can be set to use unassigned IP addresses.

BASIC SITE ADMINISTRATION

Once the Web site is established, you will need to administer IIS by using the Internet Information Services snap-in. The IIS snap-in is hosted in the Microsoft Management Console (MMC). This is a powerful site administration tool that provides access to all of your server settings. Use the IIS snap-in to manage a complex site on your corporate intranet or publish information on the Internet.

The Internet Information Services snap-in is an administration tool for IIS 5.0 that has been integrated with other administrative functions of Windows 2000. In previous releases, this tool was called the Internet Service Manager.

FIGURE 23-3   The Web Site Creation Wizard lets you establish a new Web
site on your server.

Site Management

Whether your site is on an intranet or the Internet, the principles of providing content are the same. You
place your Web files in directories on your server so that users can establish an HTTP connection and view
your files with a Web browser. But beyond simply storing files on your server, you must manage how your
site is deployed—and more importantly, how your site evolves. Today, an engaging Web site is seldom a
static collection of pages. Most successful Web administrators are kept busy accommodating ever-changing
Web content. In this part of the chapter, you'll learn the basics of managing a Web site's infrastructure.

Starting and Stopping   By default, sites start automatically when your computer restarts. Stopping
a site stops Internet services and unloads Internet services from your computer's memory. Pausing a site
prevents Internet services from accepting new connections but does not affect requests that are already
being processed. Starting a site will restart or resume Internet services. To start, stop, or pause a site, select
the site you want to manage using the Internet Information Services snap-in, then simply click the Start,
Stop, or Pause button on the toolbar.

If a site stops unexpectedly, the Internet Information Services snap-in may not correctly indicate the
state of the server. Before restarting, click Stop, and then click Start to restart the site.

In IIS 5.0, you can stop and restart all of your Internet services from within the IIS snap-in. This makes
it unnecessary to restart your computer when applications misbehave or become unavailable. To restart
IIS, highlight the computer icon in the Internet Information Services snap-in and click the Action button,
then select Restart IIS. From the drop-down menu (see Figure 23-4), select Restart Internet Services, Stop
Internet Services, Start Internet Services, or restart the computers, as appropriate.

Restarting IIS will stop all **drwtsn32.exe**, **mtx.exe**, and **dllhost.exe** processes in order to restart
Internet services.

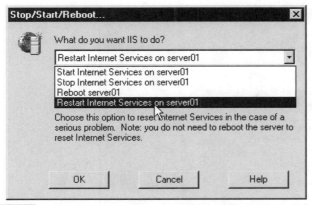

FIGURE 23-4   Use IIS to stop, start, or restart Web services.

Directories   You should set up your Web site(s) by indicating which directories contain the documents that you want to publish. The Web server cannot publish documents that are not within these specified directories. So, the first step in deploying a Web site should be to determine how you want your files organized. You then use the Internet Information Services snap-in to identify which directories are part of the site. You can get started right away without having to create a special directory structure. If all of your files are all located on the same hard drive (of the server running IIS), you can publish your documents immediately by copying your Web files into the default home directory **C:\InetPub\Wwwroot** (for an FTP site, copy your files into **C:\InetPub\Ftproot**).

Each Web or FTP site must have one home directory. The *home directory* is the central location for your published pages. It contains a home page or index file that welcomes customers and contains links to other pages in your site. The home directory is mapped to your site's domain name or to your server name. For example, if your site's Internet domain name is **www.dlspubs.com** and your home directory is **C:\Website\Dlspubs**, browsers use the URL **http://www.dlspubs.com** to access files in your home directory. On an intranet, if your server name is **acct_server**, then browsers use the URL **http://acct_server** to access files in your home directory. To change the home directory, select a Web or FTP site in the Internet Information Services snap-in and open its property page. Now click the Home Directory tab (see Figure 23-5) and then specify where your home directory is located. You can select

- A directory located on a hard disk on your computer
- A shared directory located on another computer
- A redirection to a URL (browsers requesting this URL are forwarded to a new URL), though you cannot redirect an FTP directory

In the text box, specify the path name, share name, or URL of your directory. If you select a directory on a network share, you may need to enter a username and password to access the resource. If you use an account that has administration permissions on the server, clients can gain access to server operations—this seriously compromises the security of your network.

Virtual Directories   To publish from any directory (not contained within your home directory), you would create a virtual directory. A *virtual directory* is a directory that is not contained in the home directory but appears to client browsers as though it were. A virtual directory has an *alias* (a name that Web

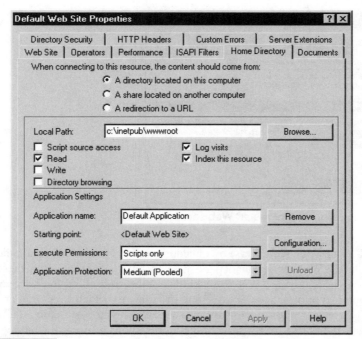

FIGURE 23-5   Use the Home Directory tab to specify a new home directory for your Web site.

browsers use to access that directory). Since an alias is usually shorter than the path name of the directory, it is more convenient for users to type. An alias is also more secure—users do not know where your files are physically located on the server, and cannot use that information to modify your files. Aliases make it easier for you to move directories in your site. Rather than changing the URL for the directory, you'd change the mapping between the alias and the physical location of the directory.

For a simple Web site, you may not need to add virtual directories. You can simply place all of the files in your site's home directory. If you have a complex site, or want to specify different URLs for different parts of your site, you can add virtual directories as needed.

To create a virtual directory, use the Internet Information Services snap-in to select the Web site or FTP site where you want to add a directory. Click the Action button, then highlight New and select Virtual Directory. Use the New Virtual Directory Wizard to complete this task. To delete a virtual directory, select the virtual directory you want to delete in the Internet Information Services snap-in. Click the Action button and select Delete. Deleting a virtual directory does *not* delete the corresponding physical directory or files.

If you are using NTFS, you can also create a virtual directory by right-clicking a directory in Windows Explorer, clicking Sharing, and then selecting the Web Sharing property page.

Site Naming and Header Names   Each Web site (aka virtual server) has a descriptive name and can support one or more host header names. *Host header names* make it possible to host multiple domain names on one computer. Not all browsers support the use of host header names. Internet Explorer 3.0, Netscape Navigator 2.0, and later versions of both browsers support the use of host header names—earlier versions of the two browsers do not. For example, if a visitor attempts to contact your site with an older browser that does not support host headers, the visitor is directed to the default Web site assigned to that IP address (if a default site is enabled), which may not necessarily be the site requested. Also, if a request from any browser is received for a site that is currently stopped, the visitor receives the default Web site instead. For this reason, carefully consider what the default Web site displays. Typically, ISPs display their own home page as the default, and not one of their customers' Web sites. This prevents requests for a stopped site from reaching the wrong site. Additionally, the default site can include a script that supports the use of host header names for older browsers.

To name a Web site, select the Web site using the Internet Information Services snap-in and open its property page. On the Web Site tab, type a descriptive name for the site in the Description box. To assign a host header name, you'll first need to add the new site name mapping for your static IP address to your name resolution system (typically DNS). Select the Web site using the Internet Information Services snap-in and open its property page. On the Web Site tab, click the Advanced button. On the Advanced Multiple Web Site Configuration property dialog box (see Figure 23-6), click the Add button to assign a host header name, IP address, and port for a Web site.

Redirects   When a browser requests a page on your Web site, the Web server locates the page identified by the URL and returns it to the browser. When you move a page on your Web site, you can't always

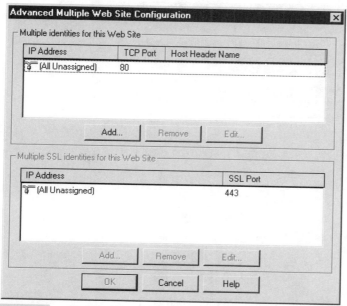

FIGURE 23-6   You can assign names and other configuration information to your Web site.

correct *all* of the links that refer to the old URL of the page. To ensure that browsers can find the page at the new URL, instruct the Web server to give the browser the new URL. The browser uses the new URL to request the page again. This process is called *redirecting* a browser request (or *redirecting* to another URL). Redirecting a request for a page is similar to using a forwarding address with a postal service. Redirecting a URL is useful when you're updating a Web site and need to make a portion of the site temporarily unavailable, or when you've changed the name of a virtual directory and want links in the original directory to access files in the new virtual directory.

To redirect requests to another directory or Web site, select the Web site or directory in the Internet Information Services snap-in and open its property page. Click the Home Directory, Virtual Directory, or Directory tab, then select "A redirection to a URL" (see Figure 23-7). In the Redirect To box, type the URL of the destination directory or Web site. For example, to redirect all requests for files in the **/Catalog** directory to the **/NewCatalog** directory, type **/NewCatalog**.

To redirect all requests to a single file, select the Web site or directory in the Internet Information Services snap-in and open its property page. Click the Home Directory, Virtual Directory, or Directory tab and select A Redirection to a URL. Type the URL of the destination file in the Redirect To box. Select The Exact URL Entered Above option to prevent the Web server from appending the original filename to the destination URL. You can use wildcards and redirect variables in the destination URL to precisely control how the original URL is translated into the destination URL.

Finally, you can redirect all requests for files in a particular directory to a specific program. Generally, you also want to pass any parameters from the original URL to the program, which you can do by using redirect variables. To redirect requests to a program, select the Web site or directory in the Internet Information

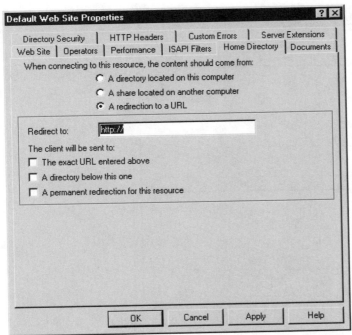

FIGURE 23-7   Using the Home Directory tab to apply redirection to a Web site

Services snap-in, and then open its property page. Click the Home Directory, Virtual Directory, or Directory tab, and select A Redirection to a URL. In the Redirect To box, type the URL of the program (including any redirect variables needed to pass parameters to the program). For example, to redirect all requests for scripts in a Scripts directory to a logging program that records the requested URL and any parameters passed with the URL, type

```
/Scripts/Logger.exe?URL=$V+PARAMS=$P
```

where *$V* and *$P* are redirect variables. Also, select The Exact URL Entered Above to prevent the Web server from appending the original filename to the destination URL.

Content Expiration   If you have time-sensitive information on your Web site, you can configure settings that will ensure that obsolete information isn't published. You can configure your Web site content to automatically expire at any point in time by using the HTTP Headers property page. When content expiration is enabled, the Web browser compares the current date to the expiration date to determine whether to display a cached page or request an updated page from the server. To set the expiration of Web site content, select the Web site, virtual directory, directory, or file (that you want to set content expiration for) using the Internet Information Services snap-in. Right-click the Web site, virtual directory, directory, or file and select Properties. Select the HTTP Headers property sheet (see Figure 23-8), and check the Enable Content Expiration check box. Select the "Expire immediately", "Expire after", or "Expire on" radio button and enter the appropriate expiration information in the corresponding box.

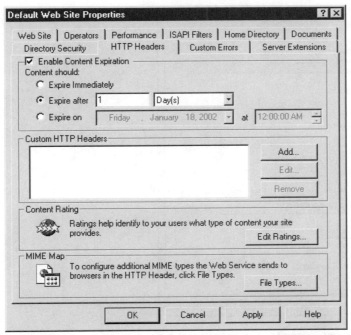

FIGURE 23-8   Use content expiration to eliminate dated material from your Web site.

Content Ratings   You can configure your IIS 5.0 Web server's content rating features to embed descriptive labels in your Web page's HTTP headers. Some Web browsers (such as Internet Explorer 3.0 or later) can detect these content labels and help users to identify potentially objectionable Web content. Your Web server's default *Platform for Internet Content Selection* (PICS) based rating system uses a system developed by the Recreational Software Advisory Council (RSAC), which rates content according to levels of violence, nudity, sex, and offensive language. Before setting your Web content ratings, you should fill out an RSAC questionnaire to obtain the recommended content ratings for your particular Web content. To set content ratings, follow these steps:

1. Select a Web site, directory, or file using the Internet Information Services snap-in and open its property page.

2. Click the HTTP Headers tab, and then click Edit Ratings under Content Ratings.

3. In the Ratings property page, select the "Enable Ratings for this resource" check box (see Figure 23-9).

4. In the Category box, click a ratings category. Use the rating slider to set the level of potentially objectionable material for the category. Each setting displays a description of the rating level.

5. Under "Email name of person rating this content", type the e-mail name of person who rated the content, and then select the Expire On list and choose a ratings expiration date from the calendar.

6. Click OK.

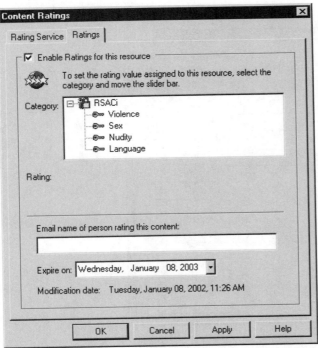

FIGURE 23-9   Apply content ratings to identify sites that may be potentially objectionable.

Protecting the IIS Configuration   You can back up your current IIS configuration so that it is easy to return to a previous state in case of a setup or configuration error. These procedures illustrate the steps needed to create and restore an IIS backup (though restoring a configuration may depend on whether you removed and reinstalled IIS). Follow these steps to back up your IIS configuration:

1. Highlight the Computer icon under the Internet Information Services snap-in.
2. Click the Action button and select Backup/Restore Configuration.
3. Click the Create Backup button, choose a name for your backup file, and click OK (by default, the backup file will be stored in the **\Winnt\system32\inetsrv\MetaBack** directory).
4. Click Close.

This backup method will provide a way to restore only your IIS settings, not your content files. It will still be necessary to maintain a full backup of your Web content.

To restore your IIS configuration, follow these steps:

1. Highlight the Computer icon under the Internet Information Services snap-in.
2. Click the Action button and select Backup/Restore Configuration.
3. Select a backup file and click the Restore button. When asked whether to restore your configuration settings, click Yes.

Security is an important issue of any Web server. Be sure to familiarize yourself with any potential security risks and features available in your Web server product.

Assigning Operators   Unless you plan to manage the Web server all by yourself, you'll need to assign one or more operators. Web site Operators are Windows user (or group) accounts that have limited administration privileges on a Web site, so you can allow others to perform day-to-day tasks (such as updating new content), but maintain overall administrative rights for yourself. The following steps show how to add a Web site operator:

1. Select the Web site in the Internet Information Services snap-in and open its property page.
2. Select the Operators tab, then click the Add button. This opens the Add Users and Groups window.
3. Either select a user or group from the Names list or select another name list from the List Names From box.
4. Select a member from a group of users by clicking the Members button and selecting the member from the window, or search for a user or group on a network by clicking the Search button.

To remove an operator later, return to the Operators tab, highlight the user or groups, and then click the Remove button.

Managing IIS Applications

It is possible to execute applications through your Web site using the Web server (such as IIS). An IIS *application* is any file that is executed within a defined set of directories in your Web site. When you create an application, you use the Internet Information Services snap-in to designate the application's *starting point directory* (also called an *application root*) in your Web site. Every file and directory under the starting point directory in your Web site is considered part of the application (until another starting point directory is found). Internet Information Services supports ASP, ISAPI, CGI, IDC, and SSI applications. Applications are powerful tools because they can share information among the files in the application. For example, ASP applications share context flow, session state, and variable settings across the pages of the application.

Application protection refers to the way in which applications are run, and IIS 5.0 offers three levels of application protection. In IIS 4.0, applications could be set to run either in the same process as Web services (**inetinfo.exe**) or in a process separate from Web services (**dllhost.exe**). In IIS 5.0, applications can be run in a pooled process (another instance of **dllhost.exe**). These different options provide varying levels of protection for situations where a misbehaving application could fail and cause the process in which it is running to stop responding. By default, Web services will run in its own process, and other applications will be run in a single, pooled process. You can then set high-priority applications to run as isolated processes. For performance reasons, you should not run more than ten isolated applications.

Finally, there is a trade-off between performance and the level of application protection. Applications run in the Web services process result in higher performance, but with a greater risk that a misbehaving application can make Web services unavailable. The recommended configuration is to run **inetinfo.exe** (Web services) in its own process, run mission-critical applications in their own processes, and run remaining applications in a shared, pooled process.

Creating Applications   To create an application, you first designate a directory as the starting point (application root) for the application. You can then set properties for the application. Each application can have a user-friendly name—this name appears in the Internet Information Services snap-in and gives you a way to distinguish applications (the application name is not used anywhere else). To create an application, follow these steps:

1. Select the directory that is the application starting point using the Internet Information Services snap-in. You can designate the home directory of a Web site as an application starting point.

2. Open the directory's property page and then click the Home Directory, Virtual Directory, or Directory tab.

3. Click the Create button (see Figure 23-10). If there is a Remove button instead of a Create button, an application has already been created.

4. In the Application name text box, type a name for your application.

You must also set permissions for an application:

- Set permissions to None to prevent any programs or scripts from running.

- Set Scripts only to enable applications mapped to a script engine to run in this directory without having Execute permission set. Use Script permission for directories that contain ASP scripts, Internet Database Connector (IDC) scripts, or other scripts. Script permission is safer than Execute permission because you can limit the applications that can be run in the directory.

- Set Scripts and Executables to allow any application to run in this directory, including applications mapped to script engines and Windows binaries (such as **.dll** and **.exe** files).

You can also remove a directory from the application boundaries. Requests to files in that directory and its subdirectories will no longer start the application. Removing a directory from an application boundary does *not* delete the directory from either your Web site or from your server's hard drive. To remove a directory from the application, repeat the process above, but click the Remove button (instead of Create). To stop an application and unload it from memory, click the Unload button. If the Unload button is dimmed, you are not in the application's starting point directory.

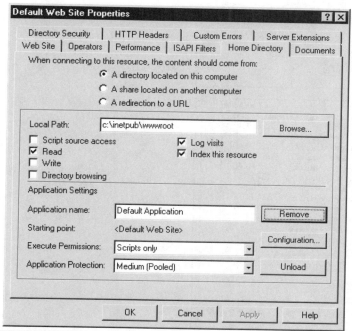

FIGURE   23-10   You can remove and create applications for your Web site.

 Select the Run in Separate Memory Space (Isolated Process) check box to run the application in a process separate from the Web server process. This protects other applications (including the Web server itself) from crashing if the application fails.

Mapping Applications   Internet Information Services lets you develop Web applications in a number of programming and scripting languages. IIS uses the filename extension of a requested resource on your Web site to determine which ISAPI or CGI program to run to process a request. For example, a request for a file ending with an **.asp** extension causes the Web server to call the ASP program (**asp.dll**) to process the request. The association of a filename extension with an ISAPI or CGI program is called *application mapping*. IIS is preconfigured to support common application mappings. You can add or remove mappings for all applications on a Web site or for individual applications. To map an extension to an application, follow these steps:

1.   Select the Web site or the starting point directory of an application in the Internet Information Services snap-in.

2.   Open the directory's property page, and then click the Home Directory, Virtual Directory, or Directory tab.

3.   Click the Configuration button, and then click the App Mappings tab (see Figure 23-11).

4.   Click Add, and in the Executable box, type the path to the ISAPI or CGI program that will process the file. You must specify a program in a local directory on the Web server.

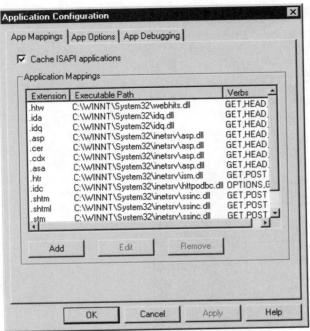

FIGURE 23-11 You may configure the application mappings for your Web site.

5. In the Extension box, type the filename extension you want to be associated with the ISAPI or CGI program. When the Web server receives a URL identifying a file with this extension, it calls the associated program to process the request.

6. To allow the processing for files of this type in a directory with Script permission, select the Script Engine check box. When a directory has Script permission set (instead of Execute permission), only files associated with applications that are designated script engines can be processed in the directory.

To remove an application mapping, open the App Mappings property page, select the filename extension, and then click the Remove button. Requests for files with this filename extension will no longer be processed in this Web site or directory.

Configuring ASP Applications Properties can be set for each ASP application that you have installed on your Web server. For example, you can turn on the use of session state in the application or set the default scripting language. Remember that application properties apply to all ASP pages in the application unless you directly override the property on an individual page. To configure an ASP application, follow these steps:

1. Select the Web site or the starting point directory of an application using the Internet Information Services snap-in.

2. Open the directory's property page and then click the Home Directory, Virtual Directory, or Directory tab.

3. Click the Configuration button and then click the App Options tab.

4. Set the properties for the application.

You can use Microsoft Script Debugger to look for errors in your ASP scripts. To use the debugger on your Web server, you must first configure the server for debugging as described here:

For information on using the debugger to examine your scripts, see the Microsoft Scripting Technologies Home Page at **msdn.microsoft.com/isapi/redir.dll?prd=scripting&ar=home&pver=4.0.**

1. Select the Web site or the starting point directory of an application in the Internet Information Services snap-in.

2. Open the directory's property sheets and then click the Home Directory, Virtual Directory, or Directory tab.

3. Click Configuration, then click the App Debugging tab.

4. To enable debugging, select Enable ASP Server-Side Script Debugging. The debugger will start when an error is generated from a script, or when ASP encounters a breakpoint in a script.

Configuring CGI Applications Internet Information Services supports CGI applications. *CGI programs* are executed when the Web server receives a URL that contains the CGI program name and any parameters required by the program. If your CGI program is compiled into an executable file (**.exe**), you must give the directory that contains the program Execute permission so that users can run the program. If your CGI program is written as a script (for example, a Perl script), you can give the directory either Execute permission or Script permission. To use Script permission, the script interpreter must be marked as a script engine. To install and configure CGI applications, do the following:

For general information on programming CGI applications, see the MSDN Online Library at **msdn.microsoft.com/isapi/redir.dll?prd=msdn&ar=library&pver=6.0**.

■ Set up a directory for your CGI programs. For extra security, you should separate your CGI programs from your content files. You do not need to name the directory Cgi-bin, although you can do so if you want.

■ If your CGI programs are scripts, obtain and install the appropriate script interpreter. For example, to run Perl scripts, you must obtain a Perl interpreter. Windows operating systems do not provide versions of Perl, SED, or AWK, but interpreters can be obtained from third-party developers.

■ If your CGI programs are **.exe** files, give the directory Execute permissions. If your CGI programs are scripts, you can give the directory either Execute or Script permission.

■ If you choose Script permission, you must mark the script interpreter as a script engine in the property sheets for the directory. Only interpreters that are marked as script engines are allowed to execute in the directory. Executable files (**.dll** and **.exe** files) cannot be directly executed—a browser request cannot launch an executable file *on the Web server* by including the program name in the URL. Using Script permission with the Script Engine option allows you to safely put content files (such as **.htm** or **.gif** files) in the same directory as your CGI scripts. Content files will be displayed in the browser and scripts will be executed, but no one can run an unauthorized program—nor will script commands be displayed in the browser.

If you give Read permissions to directories that contain executable files, visitors to your site can download and run your executable files. For security purposes, it is best to always keep executable files in a separate directory that does not have Read permissions set.

- For CGI scripts, create an application mapping between the filename extension of your script and the script interpreter.

- IIS maps filename extensions to an interpreter. For example, if you are using Perl scripts stored in files with a **.pl** extension, map the **.pl** extension to the program that runs Perl scripts. Map **.bat** and **.cmd** files to the command interpreter (**Cmd.exe**).

- If you are using NTFS access permissions, be sure that all users who need to run the program have Execute permissions for the directory. If your Web site accepts anonymous users, be sure the anonymous user (the IUSR_*computername* account) has Execute permissions.

- If your script accesses a script mapped to **cmd.exe** running on a remote server, the default working directory is set to **%SYSTEM32%** on the local computer. The default value of **%SYSTEM32%** is **\Winnt\System32** (on Windows 2000) and **\Win95\System** (Windows 95 or later).

For faster execution, consider developing an ISAPI extension instead. For ease of development, consider developing an ASP application. ASP is particularly attractive for new programmers or scripters because it handles many of the chores traditionally associated with writing CGI applications, such as parsing HTTP headers.

Using ISAPI Filters   Like ISAPI extensions, ISAPI filters are programs that respond when the Web server receives an HTTP request. They are different from applications since they are driven by Web server events rather than by a client request. You can associate an ISAPI filter with a particular Web server event—the filter is then notified every time its associated event occurs. For example, a filter could be notified when a Read or Write event occurs and then encrypt the raw data to be returned to the client. You can install ISAPI filters for all sites on a server (global filters), and you can install filters for individual Web sites. If you install both global filters and site filters, the two filter lists are merged for the site.

When several filters have registered for the same event, they are called sequentially. Filters with a higher priority are run before filters with a lower priority. If several filters have the same priority, global filters set in the master properties are run before filters set at the site level. Filters with the same priority at the same inheritance level are run according to the order in which they were loaded. You can change the filter load order on the property sheets for the Web server or Web site. To add a filter to a Web server or Web site, do the following:

1. Select the Web server or Web site using the Internet Information Services snap-in, and open its property page.
2. Click the ISAPI Filters tab (see Figure 23-12).
3. Click the Add button.
4. Type the name of the filter in the Filter Name box and either type or browse for the DLL file in the Executable box.
5. Click OK.

If you have added or changed a global filter, you must stop and restart the Web server to load the new filters into memory. A filter added at the Web site level is automatically loaded when you add it.

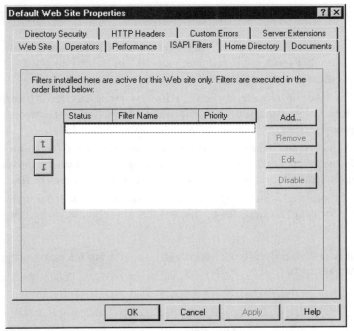

FIGURE 23-12   Configuring ISAPI filters for your Web site

SITE SECURITY BASICS

Whether you're responsible for single Web servers or an entire network, security is an ever-growing concern. Proper security safeguards on your Web server can reduce or eliminate important security threats from malicious individuals, as well as from well-intentioned users who might accidentally gain access to restricted information or inadvertently alter important files. Internet Information Services 5.0 provides five main security elements that you should be familiar with: authentication, access control, encryption, auditing, and certificates. This part of the chapter shows you how to configure both your Web server and Windows to properly secure your Web site and to carry out other essential security functions.

Security Standards

IIS 5.0 incorporates a range of security features, and many of the security features in IIS implement Internet community standards. These standards help to facilitate uniformity and cross-platform utilization of applications and information. There are six major security features that you should be familiar with in IIS:

■ **Fortezza**   The U.S. government security standard commonly called Fortezza (**developer. netscape.com/tech/security/formsign/fortezza.html**) is supported in IIS 5.0. This standard satisfies the Defense Message System security architecture with a cryptographic mechanism that provides message confidentiality, integrity, authentication, nonrepudiation, and access control to messages, components, and systems. These features are implemented both with server and browser software and with PCMCIA card hardware. Fortezza is a widely used mechanism within the U.S. government.

■ **Secure Sockets Layer (SSL 3.0)**   The Secure Sockets Layer (**home.netscape.com/eng/ ssl3/index.html**) is a public key-based security protocol implemented by the Secure Channel

(Schannel) security provider. SSL security protocols are used widely by Internet browsers and servers for authentication, message integrity, and confidentiality.

- **Basic authentication**   Basic authentication (**www.w3.org/Protocols/HTTP/1.0/spec.html**) is a part of the HTTP 1.0 specification that sends password over networks in Base64 encoded format. Most browsers support this specification.

- **Digest authentication**   The use of Digest authentication (**www.ics.uci.edu/pub/ietf/ http/rfc2069.txt**) is a new feature of IIS 5.0 that sends authentication information over networks as a *hash* and is compatible with proxy servers.

- **PKCS #7**   The Public Key Cryptography Standard #7 (**www.rsasecurity.com** and search for a list of documents) describes the format of encrypted data such as digital signatures or digital envelopes that securely contain information. Both of these are involved in the certificate features of IIS.

- **PKCS #10**   The Public Key Cryptography Standard #10 (**www.rsasecurity.com** and search for a list of documents) describes the format of requests for certificates that are submitted to certification authorities.

For additional information about Windows and network security issues, visit the Microsoft security Web site at **www.microsoft.com/security**.

Security Practices

Before configuring your Web server security, determine the level of security that you will require to protect your Web and FTP sites. For example, if you intend to create a Web site that allows special users to access private information (such as financial or medical records), you will require a robust security configuration. This configuration should be able to reliably authenticate designated users and restrict access to only those users. Much of your Web server's security relies on your Windows security configuration. If you do not properly configure your Windows security features, you cannot secure your Web server. Be sure to implement the following:

- Configure the Windows Administrator account.
- Create and manage user accounts.
- Create and manage groups.
- Define Windows security policies.

As part of your security configuration, you should also convert your hard disk partition(s) to an NTFS partition. NTFS hard disk partitions offer precise file and directory access control, and save information more efficiently than File Allocation Table (FAT) partitions. You can use the Windows Convert utility to convert a hard disk partition to NTFS. Next, determine which files and directories will be publicly available to users visiting your Web and FTP sites. Keep public and restricted content in separate directories. Here is a listing of potential security concerns, and recommendations for improving security:

- *Use NTFS.* The NTFS system is more secure than the FAT system.
- *Check NTFS permissions on network drives.* By default, Windows creates new shared resources and assigns Full Control permissions to the Everyone group.
- *Review directory permissions.* By default, Windows creates new folders and assigns Full Control permissions to the Everyone group. This may not be desirable in your particular situation.

■ *Set access control for the IUSR_computername account.* This will help limit the access that anonymous users have to your Web server.

■ *Keep executable files in a separate directory.* This makes it easier to assign access permissions and auditing.

■ *Review user accounts often.* Check for new accounts that were not created by a valid administrator. Review the rights given to the IUSR_*computername* account. All users gaining anonymous access to your site have the rights assigned to this account. You can also use auditing to monitor when and by whom security policies are changed.

■ *Choose difficult passwords.* Passwords are more difficult to guess if they consist of a combination of lowercase and uppercase letters, numbers, and special characters.

■ *Maintain strict account policies.* Keep track of what types of access are given to important user accounts and groups. This includes knowing who has the ability to change security policies.

■ *Limit the members of the Administrators group.* This group typically has full access to the computer, so limiting the individuals with full access will help to improve security.

■ *Assign a password to the Administrator account.* By default, the password used for the Administrator's account is blank. To improve security, set a difficult password for this account.

■ *Run minimal services.* Run only the services that are absolutely necessary for your particular situation. Each additional service that you run presents an entry point for malicious attacks.

■ *Do not use PDC as a Web server.* The primary domain controller (PDC) is constantly processing authentication requests. Running a Web service on the PDC will decrease performance. It could also expose your PDC to attacks that could render your entire network nonsecure.

■ *Enable auditing.* Auditing is a very valuable tool for tracking access to secure or critical files. Auditing can also be used for tracking server events, such as a change in your security policy. Audit logs can be archived for later use.

■ *Use encryption with remote administration.* Remote administration usually involves the exchange of sensitive information (such as the password for the Administrator's account). To protect this information over open networks, use Secured Sockets Layer (SSL) encryption.

■ *Use a low-level account to browse the Internet.* Using the Administrator, Power User, or other highly privileged account to browse the Internet can potentially open entry points on your computer for attacks. Also, never browse the Internet from the primary domain controller (PDC).

■ *Back up vital files and the registry often.* No security effort can guarantee data safety, so always implement a consistent regimen of backups and disaster planning for your Web server (and entire network).

■ *Run virus checks regularly.* Any computer on an open network is susceptible to computer viruses. Regular checkups can help avoid unnecessary data loss.

■ *Unbind unnecessary services from your network adapter cards.* This simplifies the platform's configuration, and reduces possible areas of attack. However, this could have undesirable effects on other users of your system.

■ *Use the most secure form of authentication possible.* Use the most secure authentication that your clients support. For example, integrated Windows authentication and Digest authentication are more secure than Basic authentication. Client certificates can also be used for highly secure authentication.

- *Use the most restrictive permission possible.* For example, if your Web site is used only for viewing information, assign only Read permissions. If a directory or site contains ASP applications, assign Scripts Only permissions instead of Scripts and Executables permissions.

- *One-to-one mapping versus many-to-one mapping.* You can use either or both of these methods to map client certificates to Windows user accounts. One-to-one mapping offers a higher level of certainty, but requires a copy of the client certificate to be stored on the server. Many-to-one mapping is easier to implement and does not require a copy of the certificate to be stored on the server.

- *Synchronize Web and NTFS permissions.* If Web permissions and NTFS permissions are not synchronized, the more restrictive of the two is used. Synchronization can be done manually, or by using the IIS Permissions Wizard.

- *Careful with Write and Scripts and Executable permissions.* Use this combination with extreme caution. It can allow someone to upload potentially dangerous executable files to your server and run them.

- *Lock the desktop.* When you're not at the computer, lock the desktop by pressing the CTRL-ALT-DELETE keys and selecting Lock Workstation.

- *Use a password-protected screen saver.* The time delay before invoking the screen saver should be short so that no one can use the computer after you leave. The screen saver should be blank (animated screen savers can decrease server performance).

- *Physically lock up the computer.* Keep the computer locked in a secure room in order to reduce the chance of access by malicious individuals.

- *Use different Administrator accounts.* Each individual who has administrative privileges should be given a distinct user account and password. This will make it easier to track any changes that are made.

- *Use nondisclosure agreements.* The accountability of administrators can be enforced by using nondisclosure agreements (i.e., to keep usernames and passwords confidential).

- *Periodically reassign accounts.* To reduce the risk of user account information being compromised, periodically assign new user accounts to personnel with Administrator or other high-level privileges.

- *Quickly disable or delete unused accounts.* This will reduce the risk of a disgruntled former employee or vendor gaining access to your network.

- *Delete sample files in default locations.* This prevents intruders from perusing common default files that you may not want visitors to see.

- *Put IIS on a different logical drive.* Access to the drive with IIS still prevents intruders from accessing drives with other OS and critical administrative information.

Authentication   Security starts with *authentication*—proving the identity of a user. Five methods of authentication are supported in IIS 5.0 so that you can confirm the identity of anyone requesting access to your Web sites:

- **Anonymous authentication** allows anyone access without asking for a username or password.

- **Basic authentication** will prompt the user for a username and password, which are sent *unencrypted* over the network.

- **Digest authentication** is a new feature that operates much like Basic authentication except that the passwords are sent as a *hash* value. A hash value is a number derived from a text message, such as a password, from which it is not feasible to decipher the original text. Digest authentication is available only on domains with a Windows 2000 domain controller.

■ **Integrated Windows authentication** uses hashing technology to identify your user without actually sending the password over the network.

■ **Certificates** are digital credentials that can be used for establishing a Secure Sockets Layer (SSL) connection. They can also be used for authentication.

You can use these methods to grant access to public areas of your site, while preventing unauthorized access to your private files and directories.

Access Control   NTFS access permissions are the foundation of your Web server's security, allowing you to define the level of file and directory access granted to Windows users and groups. For example, if a business decided to publish its catalog on your Web server, you would need to create a Windows user account for that business and then configure permissions for the specific Web site, directory, or file. The permissions would enable only the server administrator and the owner of the business to update the Web site's contents. Public users would be allowed to view the Web site, but cannot alter its contents.

WebDAV (supported in IIS 5.0) is an extension of the HTTP 1.1 protocol that facilitates file and directory manipulation over an HTTP connection. Properties can be added to and read from files and directories through the use of WebDAV *verbs* (or commands). Files and directories can also be remotely created, deleted, moved, or copied. Additional access control can be configured through both Web server permissions and NTFS.

Certificates   Certificates are digital identification documents that allow both servers and clients to authenticate each other. They are required for the server and client's browser to set up an SSL connection over which encrypted information can be sent. The certificate-based SSL features in IIS 5.0 consist of a server certificate, a client certificate, and various digital keys. You can create these certificates with Microsoft Certificate Services or obtain them from a mutually trusted, third-party organization called a certification authority (CA).

Server certificates provide a way for users to confirm your Web site's identity. A server certificate contains detailed identification information, such as the name of the organization affiliated with the server content, the name of the organization that issued the certificate, and a *public key* used in establishing an encrypted connection. This information helps to assure users of the authenticity of Web server content and the integrity of the secure HTTP connection. With SSL, your Web server also has the option of authenticating users by checking the contents of their *client certificates*. A typical client certificate contains detailed identification information about a user and the organization that issued the certificate and a *public key*. You can use client certificate authentication, along with SSL encryption, to implement a highly secure method for verifying the identity of your users.

Encryption   You can allow users to exchange private information with your server (such as credit card numbers or phone numbers) in a secure way by using *encryption*. Encryption "scrambles" the information before it is sent, and decryption "unscrambles" that information after it is received. The foundation for this encryption in IIS is the SSL 3.0 protocol, which provides a secure means of establishing an encrypted communication link with users. SSL confirms the authenticity of your Web site and, optionally, the identity of users accessing restricted Web sites.

Certificates include *keys* used in establishing an SSL secure connection. A *key* is a unique value used to authenticate the server and the client in establishing an SSL connection. A *public key* and a *private key* form a *key pair*. Your Web server utilizes the key pair to negotiate a secure connection with the user's Web browser to determine the level of encryption required for securing communications. For this type of connection, both your Web server and the user's browser must be equipped with compatible encryption and decryption capabilities. During the exchange an encryption (or *session*) key is created. This secret session key is sent by the client to the server using a public key scheme (such as RSA).

Both your server and the Web browser use the session key to encrypt and decrypt transmitted information. The session key's degree of encryption (or *strength*) is measured in bits. The greater the number of bits in the session key, the greater the level of encryption and security. Although these greater encryption key strengths offer greater security, they also require more server resources to implement. Your Web server's session key is usually 40-bits long, but can be 128-bits long depending upon the level of security required. To enable encryption, follow these steps:

1. Select a Web site, directory, or file using the Internet Information Services snap-in, and open its property page.

2. If you have not previously created a server key pair and certificate request, select the Directory Security or File Security tab, then under Secure Communications click Server Certificate (see Figure 23-13). The Web Server Certificate Wizard will guide you through the procedures. If you have previously created a server key pair and certificate request, select the Directory Security or File Security tab, then under Secure Communications click Edit.

3. In the Secure Communications dialog box, select the "Require secure channel (SSL)" check box.

4. Instruct users to establish a secure HTTPS connection with your Web content (that is, the URL for the restricted Web site should start with **https://** rather than **http://**).

 Encrypted transmissions can significantly reduce transmission rates and server performance, so consider using SSL encryption only for sensitive information such as financial transactions.

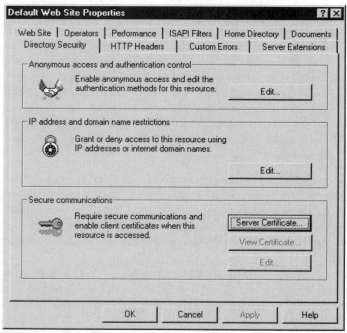

FIGURE 23-13   Configuring a server certificate for your Web server

You can also configure your Web server to require a 128-bit minimum session-key strength (rather than the default 40-bit key strength) for all SSL secure communication sessions. If you set a minimum 128-bit key strength, users attempting to establish a secure communications channel with your server must use a browser capable of communicating with a 128-bit session key. To set encryption strength, do the following:

1. Select a Web site, directory, or file using the Internet Information Services snap-in, and open its property page.

2. If you have not previously created a server key pair and certificate request, select the Directory Security or File Security tab. Under Secure Communications, click Server Certificate. The new Web Server Certificate Wizard will guide you through the procedure. If you have previously created a server key pair and certificate request, select the Directory Security or File Security tab. Under Secure Communications, click Edit.

3. In the Secure Communications dialog box, select the "Require secure channel (SSL)" check box.

4. Select the "Require 128-bit Encryption" check box if this level of encryption is required.

5. Click OK.

Server-Gated Cryptography (SGC) is an extension of SSL that allows financial institutions with export versions of IIS to use strong (128-bit) encryption. Although SGC capabilities are built into IIS 5.0, a special SGC certificate is required to use SGC.

Auditing   Finally, administrators can use security-auditing techniques to monitor a broad range of user and Web server security activity. It is recommended that you routinely audit your server configuration to detect areas where resources may be susceptible to unauthorized access and tampering. You can use integrated Windows utilities or the logging features built into IIS 5.0, or use Active Server Pages (ASP) applications to create your own auditing logs.

SITE ACTIVITY LOGGING

You can configure your Web or FTP sites to record log entries about user and server activity. IIS log data can help you regulate access to content, determine content popularity, evaluate security requirements, and troubleshoot potential Web site or FTP site problems. This part of the chapter explains the principles and procedures needed to manage logging on your Web site. Remember that logging IIS site activity should *not* be confused with the event logging carried out by Windows 2000 and viewed using the Event Viewer—the logging in IIS is more extensive.

Log File Types

Web or FTP site logging is carried out by modules that operate independently of other activities on the server. You can choose the format of your logs for each individual Web or FTP site. If logging is enabled for a site, you can disable or enable it for individual directories on that site. The logs created by IIS can be read in a text editor, but the files are usually loaded into a report-generating utility. ODBC logging is logged to a database and the database can be used to generate reports.

The times listed in log files reflect the times the server uses to process requests and responses— these do not reflect network travel time to the client, or client processing time.

W3C Extended Log Format   W3C extended log file format is a customizable ASCII format with a variety of different fields. You can include fields important to you, while limiting log file size by omitting unwanted fields. Fields are separated by spaces. Time is recorded as UTC (Greenwich Mean Time). The following example shows lines from a W3C file using the Time, Client IP Address, Method, URI Stem, HTTP Status, and HTTP Version fields:

```
#Software: Microsoft Internet Information Services 5.0
#Version: 1.0
#Date: 2002-05-02 17:42:15
#Fields: time c-ip cs-method cs-uri-stem sc-status cs-version
17:42:15 172.16.255.255 GET /default.htm 200 HTTP/1.0
```

The preceding entry indicates that on May 2, 1998 at 5:42 P.M. (UTC), a user with HTTP version 1.0 and the IP address of **172.16.255.255** issued an HTTP GET command for the file **default.htm**. The request was returned without error. The #Date: field indicates when the first log entry was made, which is when the log was created. The #Version: field indicates that the W3C logging format was used. To customize W3C Extended logging, follow these steps:

1. Select a Web or FTP site and open its property page.
2. Enable logging (if it is disabled) and select the W3C Extended log file format.
3. Click Properties.
4. On the Extended Properties property sheet, select the fields you want to log. By default, Time, Client IP Address, Method, URI Stem, and HTTP Status are enabled.
5. Click Apply.

For more information on the W3C Extended format specification, see the W3C site at **www.w3.org**.

Microsoft IIS Log Format   The Microsoft IIS log format is a fixed (noncustomizable) ASCII format that records more items than the NCSA Common format. The Microsoft IIS format includes basic items such as the user's IP address, username, request date and time, HTTP status code, and number of bytes received. In addition, it includes detailed items such as the elapsed time, the number of bytes sent, the action (for example, a download carried out by a GET command), and the target file. Commas separate the items, so the format is easier to read than the other ASCII formats, which use spaces for separators. The time is recorded as local time. When you open a Microsoft IIS format file in a text editor, the entries are similar to the example here:

```
192.168.114.201, -, 03/20/2001, 7:55:20, W3SVC2, SALES1, 192.168.114.201,
172.21.13.45, 4502, 163, 3223, 200, GET, DeptLogo.gif
172.16.255.255, anonymous, 03/20/98, 23:58:11, MSFTPSVC, SALES1,
192.168.114.201, 60, 275, 0, 0, 0, PASS, intro.htm
```

In the example, the first entry indicates that an anonymous user (actually the Web guest user IUSER_computername) with the IP address of **192.168.114.201** issued an HTTP GET command for the image file **DeptLogo.gif** at 7:55 A.M. on March 20, 2001, from a server named SALES1 at IP address **172.21.13.45**. The 163-byte HTTP request had an elapsed processing time of 4,502 milliseconds (4.5 seconds) to complete, and returned, without error (200 reply code), 3,223 bytes of data to the anonymous user. In the log file, all fields are terminated with a comma. A hyphen (-) acts as a placeholder if there is no valid value for a certain field.

NCSA Common Log File Format   The NCSA Common log format is a fixed (noncustomizable) ASCII format available for Web sites (but not for FTP sites). It records basic information about user requests, such as remote hostname, username, date, time, request type, HTTP status code, and the number of bytes received by the server. Items are separated by spaces, and time is recorded as local time. When you open an NCSA Common format file in a text editor, the entries are similar to the following example:

```
172.21.13.45 — REDMOND\fred [08/Apr/2002:17:39:04 -0800] "GET
/scripts/iisadmin/ism.dll?http/serv HTTP/1.0" 200 3401
```

The entry indicates that a user named Fred in the REDMOND domain, with the IP address of **172.21.13.45**, issued an HTTP GET command (that is, downloaded a file) at 5:39 P.M. on April 8, 2002. The request returned 3,401 bytes of data (without error) to the user named Fred.

ODBC Logging   The ODBC logging format is a record of a fixed set of data fields in an ODBC-compliant database (such as Microsoft Access or Microsoft SQL Server). Some of the items logged are the user's IP address, username, request date and time, HTTP status code, bytes received, bytes sent, action carried out (for example, a download carried out by a GET command), and the target (for example, the file that was downloaded). The time is recorded as local time. With this type of log, you must specify the database to be logged to, and set up the database to receive the data.

Process Accounting   Process accounting is a new feature in IIS. It can be enabled on a per-site basis, and adds fields to the W3C Extended log file to record information about how Web sites use CPU resources on the server. This information is used to determine if sites are using an unusually high amount of CPU resources, or to detect malfunctioning scripts or CGI processes. Process accounting does not provide details on CPU usage of individual applications, and logs information only about out-of-process applications. It is available only for Web sites (not FTP sites) and is recorded only when the W3C Extended log file format is selected. Generally, the information gained from process accounting can be used to determine if *process throttling* should be enabled on a Web site. Process throttling limits the amount of processor time a Web site can use. To enable process accounting to track processor use, do the following:

1. Select a Web site and open its property page.
2. On the Web Site tab, click the Properties button.
3. Select the Process Accounting check box on the Extended Properties page (see Figure 23-14).
4. Click OK.

Log Management
You can enable logging for individual Web and FTP sites and choose the desired log format. When logging is enabled, it is enabled for all the site's directories, but you can disable it for specific directories. To enable logging on a Web or FTP site, follow these steps:

1. Select a Web or FTP site, and open its property page.
2. On the Web Site or FTP Site property page, select the Enable Logging check box.
3. Select a format in the "Active log format" list (see Figure 23-15). By default, the Enable Logging check box is selected and the format is W3C Extended Log File Format, with the following fields enabled: Time, Client IP Address, Method, URI Stem, and HTTP Status.
4. Click Apply.
5. Click OK.

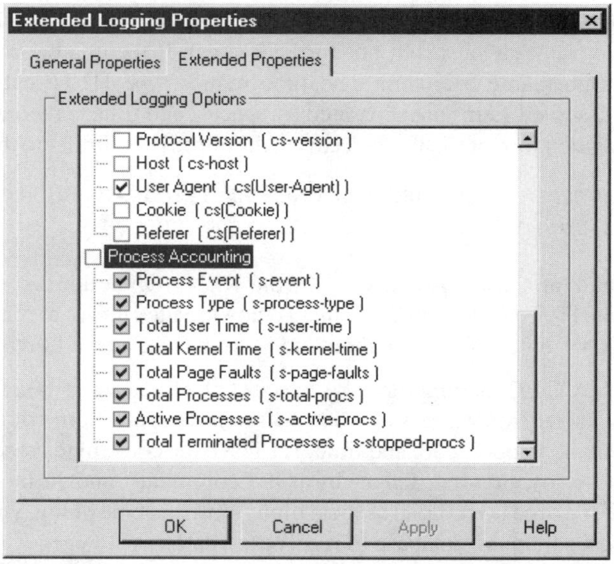

FIGURE   23-14   Enabling process accounting for your Web site

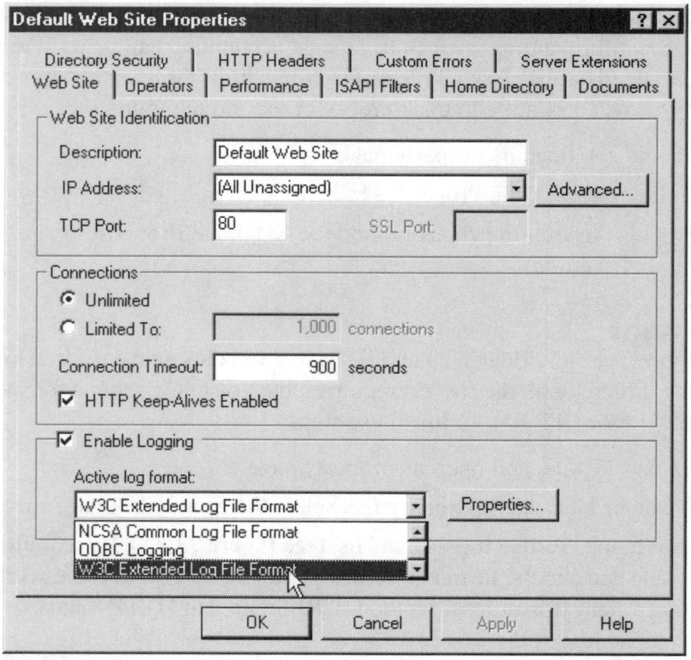

FIGURE   23-15   Selecting a log file format for your site logging

If you select ODBC logging, click Properties and then type the Data Source Name and the name of the table within the database in the boxes. If a username and password are required to access the database, type these also and click OK.

To disable or enable logging for a specific directory on a site, do the following:

1. Select the directory and open its property page.

2. On the Home Directory or Directory tab, find the Log visits check box. By default, the check box is selected.

3. To disable logging for that directory, clear the check box. To enable logging again, select the check box. These settings do not affect process accounting.

Saving Log Files

You can specify the directory where log files are saved, and specify when new log files are started. This is how to set options for saving log files:

1. Select a Web or FTP site and open its property page.

2. Click Properties on the Web Site or FTP Site tab.

3. On the General Properties tab, select the option to use when starting a new log file. The options are

- ■ **Hourly**   Log files are created hourly, starting with the first entry that occurs for each hour. This feature is typically used for high-volume Web sites.

- ■ **Daily**   Log files are created daily, starting with the first entry that occurs after midnight.

- ■ **Weekly**   Log files are created weekly, starting with the first entry that occurs after midnight Saturday.

- ■ **Monthly**   Log files are created monthly, starting with the first entry that occurs after midnight of the last day of the month.

- ■ **Unlimited file size**   Data is always appended to the same log file. You can access this log file only after stopping the site.

- ■ **When file size reaches**   A new log file is created when the current log file reaches a given size (specify the size you want).

4. Under Log file, type the directory where log files should be saved. The directory must be a local drive and the path cannot be relative. You cannot use mapped drives or UNC paths such as **\\server1\share1** when you specify the log file directory.

5. Click Apply.

PERFORMANCE TUNING

Hardware needs vary depending on the service provided. For example, the FTP service uses less memory than the Web service. In addition, Active Server Pages (ASP) applications, Common Gateway Interface (CGI) scripts, database queries, and video files are more processor-intensive than static HTML pages. Consequently, you must ensure that server performance is optimal in order to provide a satisfactory experience for users. Performance also changes over time as traffic and site content change. To efficiently tune performance, the server administrator must plan a monitoring strategy using a variety of tools. This part of the chapter examines the concepts and tactics of site performance tuning.

Tuning Basics

Performance testing and tuning is an ongoing process. To work effectively, you must carefully plan an evaluation strategy for your Web server. The first step is to measure the current level of performance. Since performance of the server can vary greatly over time, be sure to monitor long enough to capture a true picture of server activity. You must also examine all parts of the system for potential bottlenecks. Bottlenecks can be caused by inadequate or improperly configured hardware, or by software settings in either IIS or Windows 2000. A good monitoring plan checks on performance in all areas.

Once you know how your server is performing, you consider changes aimed at improving performance. Any changes should be made one at a time, or it becomes impossible to assess the impact of individual changes. After a change is made, continue monitoring to see if the change had the desired effect (or if it had undesirable side effects). Since changes to one resource can cause bottlenecks to appear in other areas, it is important to check on the performance of *all* resources after you make a change. Once you have assessed the impact of a change, you can determine whether further changes are necessary.

Monitoring Tools

Monitoring the server is a crucial part of server administration. By using suitable monitoring tools, you can detect server problems, evaluate the result of changes to your Web site content, and plan upgrades to make your sites more accessible to users. The best choice of monitoring tool (and method) depends on the information you need. For example, if you're trying to measure the overall load on your Web server, you could use System Monitor to render a weeklong plot—showing information such as the number of computer connections and file transfers. As another example, if you notice a slowdown in your server's performance, you can check for errors in Event Viewer (the tool for viewing logs generated by Windows 2000). You can also monitor your server by examining logs generated by IIS (see the discussion on Site Activity Logging earlier). Windows 2000 provides a variety of tools for monitoring.

System Monitor   System Monitor is a powerful tool that you can use to monitor your server's activity and summarize its performance at selected intervals (both short and long term). With this tool, you can display performance data in real-time charts or reports, collect data in files, and generate alerts that warn you when critical events occur. System Monitor examines the output of *counters* that monitor the activity of specific *objects* (specific services or mechanisms controlling server resources). For example, if you view the object called Web Service, you can see counters that monitor bytes received per second or connection attempts per second.

Windows 2000 includes a number of counters, and you can supplement these with counters for disk usage and TCP activity by using utilities available in the Windows 2000 Resource Kits. In addition, IIS installs special counters, including Web service counters, FTP service counters, counters for Active Server Pages applications, and global counters for Internet Information Services. The Web, FTP, and Active Server Pages counters monitor connection activity, while the Internet Information Services Global counters monitor things such as bandwidth usage and caching activity for all IIS services.

Event Viewer   Windows 2000 includes an event-logging service, which records events such as errors or the successful starting of a service. These event logs are viewed by using Event Viewer. You can use Event Viewer to monitor System, Security, and Application event logs. With this information, you can better understand the sequence and types of events that led up to a particular performance problem.

Task Manager   Task Manager can be used to view ongoing tasks and threads. It can also be used to change the assigned priority of processes. However, once the process has completed, the new priority setting is lost. CPU and memory usage can be seen in real time, but information is not saved over time.

Network Monitor   The Network Monitor utility captures information on traffic to and from a computer, and gives detailed information about the frames being sent and received. This tool can help you analyze complex patterns of network traffic. Using Network Monitor, you can view the header information included in HTTP and FTP requests to your server. Generally, you need to design a *capture filter*, which functions like a database query and singles out a subset of the frames being transmitted. You can also use a *capture trigger* that responds to events on your network by initiating an action (such as starting an executable file).

Disk Optimization

Hard disk bottlenecks are most often seen on sites with very large file sets that are accessed randomly. How often IIS needs to access the hard disk is directly related to the amount of RAM and the number and size of requested files. If the amount of RAM is small and a large number of different files are being requested (or the size of the requested files is large), IIS is unable to maintain copies of the files in RAM for faster access. In this case, IIS must access the files from the hard disk (using a swap file). The access speed and size of the hard disk determine how quickly IIS can locate a requested file.

To monitor your disk drives, use System Monitor to log the percentage of CPU utilized, network card saturation, and the % Disk Time counter of the Physical Disk object (see Figure 23-16). If the % Disk Time counter is high (but the CPU and network card are not saturated), the disk drive is creating a bottleneck.

To improve disk access, use RAID configured with striped disk sets. If your server is used heavily for database work, you may need a large amount of RAM (1GB or more) so you can minimize drive access delays, or a RAID controller with a large RAM cache. You should also maintain redundancy so that you're not forced to restore from backup copies when a single drive ceases to function. Many newer controllers permit hot swapping, so that when a drive fails, it can be replaced without forcing server downtime. Still, it's a good policy to maintain proper backups, and to keep one backup copy off-site.

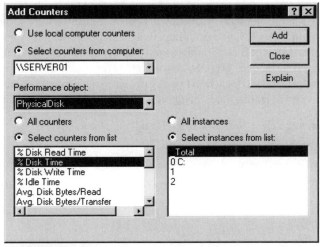

FIGURE 23-16   Adding counters to the System Monitor

Memory Optimizations

As any good PC technician knows, RAM is the memory space used by programs when they are running. Typically, when you start an application, the computer copies the necessary application files from the hard disk to RAM, and the application runs from RAM. RAM has much faster access time than the hard disk, so the less the computer accesses the hard disk, the faster applications can run. When IIS is running, it is using some portion of RAM, depending on a number of other factors, including

- The amount of RAM used for cache
- The size of swap file
- The amount of free disk space
- The number of services running
- The type of processor(s)
- The number and size of content files (such as HTML files)
- The number of connections that are currently open
- Other active applications that require RAM

Cache RAM   When a request for a static file is received by IIS, a file handle is cached in RAM by IIS and Windows 2000 caches the file. As subsequent requests are received for the same file, IIS uses the copy cached in RAM (rather than going back to the hard disk to retrieve the file again). This reduces the time IIS takes to fulfill a request, and makes access faster for visitors. However, the amount of time a file is kept in cache is dependent on a number of other things. As different files are requested from IIS, older cached files are purged to make room for the new files. This means that if you have a large number of files available through IIS, and you only have a small amount of RAM, access may be slowed because IIS must retrieve many files from the hard disk. If you're using other applications on the same computer that also use RAM, cached copies of files are pushed out of RAM to make room for the new files. IIS may be unable to maintain cached files in RAM. Again, the result is slower IIS access as files are brought from the hard disk.

Since large files take up more space in RAM than small files, requests for large files (such as audio or video files) may cause a high turnover in cached files when the amount of available RAM is small. If your documents are large, if you're publishing a large number of documents, or if you're running other RAM-intensive applications on the computer hosting IIS, you can improve system performance by adding RAM. However, if you have a very small number of files to publish (and the files are relatively small), adding RAM does *not* improve Web server performance. You can also affect performance by adjusting the amount of memory that Windows 2000 allocates for file cache. If you're primarily using your server as a Web server, configure it as an application server (rather than the default setting of file server):

1. On the desktop, open My Computer, and select Network and Dial-up Connections.
2. Right-click Local Area Connection and open its property sheet.
3. Select File and Printer Sharing for Microsoft networks and select Properties.
4. On the Server Optimization property sheet, select "Maximize data throughput for network applications" (see Figure 23-17).

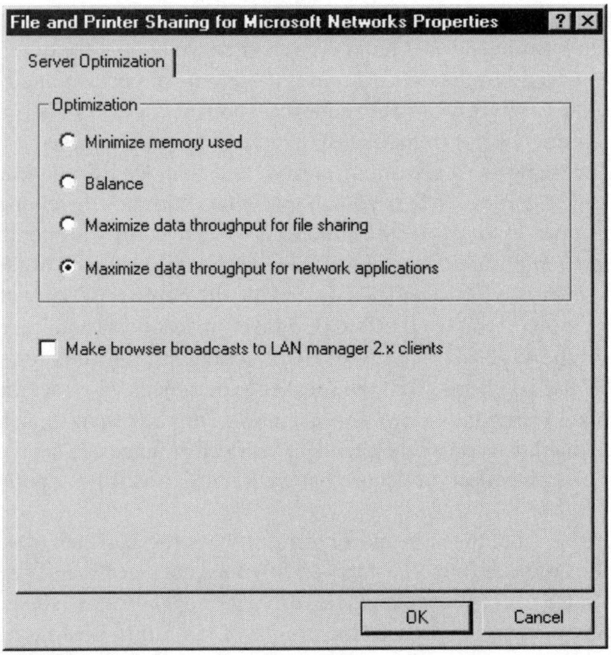

FIGURE 23-17   Optimizing the server for network applications

You can use System Monitor to evaluate the performance of your server's cache. When selecting the performance object, choose Internet Information Services Global and then use the following counters to view cache activity:

- Cache Flushes
- Cache Hits
- Cache Hits %
- Cache Misses
- Cached File Handles
- Directory Listings
- Objects

The value of Cache Hits % should be as *high* as possible. A low value (particularly if it is accompanied by a high value of the % Disk Time counter of the Disk object) indicates that your server is not able to get enough of its files from cache. This is caused either by many different files being requested or your cache is too small and needs to be enlarged.

Memory Versus Response   To increase request response speed, you typically must dedicate memory or processor resources to individual connections—reducing resources available for other applications during times when requests are not being received. Maximizing memory performance for all applications running on your server may mean slightly slower request responses for users visiting your site (because memory and processor resources are not immediately available for the requests).

As a rule, set the estimated number of requests in a 24-hour period, and then let IIS automatically adjust to balance memory use against response time. When you change this estimate, IIS changes the number of sockets dedicated to listening for new requests. If the number is set just slightly higher than the actual number of connections, connection attempts are made faster. If the number is set much higher than the actual number of connection attempts, memory is wasted. To determine the number of daily connections to your server, use System Monitor to log the value of the Total Connection Requests counter and the Current Connections counter (both within the Web Service object). Collect data in log files for several days (if possible) to get a realistic record of the conditions that your server experiences. Now set the number of daily connections from your estimate. Using the Internet Information Services snap-in, select the Web site and click the Properties button to display its property page. On the Performance tab, set the value slightly larger than the estimated number of connections you anticipate receiving in a 24-hour period (see Figure 23-18).

In IIS 5.0, sites with different IP addresses (but the same port number) share the same set of sockets. So creating multiple sites with different IP addresses (but all using port 80) does not significantly increase the nonpaged memory consumption of IIS. IIS uses these sockets flexibly among all of these sites, reducing its resource consumption. This "socket pooling" increases the ability of IIS 5.0 to host many more

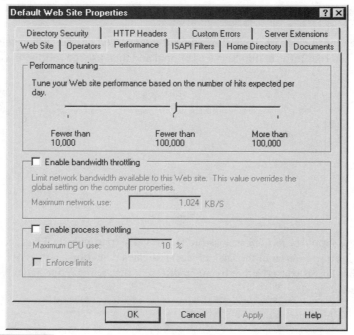

FIGURE 23-18   Configuring Web server performance based on the estimated number of connections

sites on the same hardware than was possible in IIS 4.0. However, socket pooling causes IIS to listen on all IP addresses, which may present a possible security risk for secure domains with multiple networks. Also, bandwidth throttling and performance adjustments will apply to *all* Web sites configured for the same port number. If you use bandwidth throttling (or do other performance tuning) on a per-site basis, you must disable socket pooling for the sites you want to throttle.

Processor Optimizations

As Web servers have matured, performance has become increasingly important. Today, with the growth of Web applications for database publishing, content indexing, and collaboration, maximizing hardware and software performance has become a priority. This part of the chapter focuses on processor aspects of performance, and makes recommendations for upgrades based on performance monitoring tests.

CPU Bottlenecks   The CPU does the actual processing of instructions received by the computer. Information moves between the various components of the computer (such as the CPU, hard disk, and RAM) depending on the clock speed of the CPU and the size of the data bus the CPU uses to move the information. Clock speeds are usually expressed as megahertz (MHz) or gigahertz (GHz). A typical data bus can carry 16, 32, or 64 bits of data on each clock tick. You can use System Monitor to measure processor performance. Processor bottlenecks are characterized by very high CPU % Utilization numbers while the network adapter card remains well below capacity. If CPU % Utilization is high, you can

- Upgrade the CPU.
- Add additional CPUs to the same computer.
- Replicate the site on another computer and distribute traffic across both computers.
- Move processor-intensive applications such as database applications to another computer.

Processor Throttling   You can limit the percentage of time that a CPU spends processing out-of-process WAM, ISAPI, and CGI applications for individual Web sites by enabling *process throttling*. Limiting access to the CPU is useful if you host multiple sites on one computer, and you're concerned about out-of-process applications on one site using all of the CPU capacity (preventing other sites from using the processor). If a restricted site's application(s) uses more than the assigned percentage of processor time during a specified time interval, the event is logged based on the amount of overrun of the assigned percentage. For example,

- **Level 1**   An event is written to the Windows 2000 Event Log when the total processor use exceeds a limit over the specified time period.
- **Level 2**   If the processor use exceeds 150 percent of a preset limit, an event is written to the Event Log, and all the out-of-process applications on that Web site have their CPU priority set to Idle.
- **Level 3**   If the processor use exceeds 200 percent of a preset limit, an event is written to the Event Log, and all the out-of-process applications on that Web site are stopped.

Once a site has reached a Level 2 or Level 3, the event remains in effect until the next time interval. For example, if a site's out-of-process applications are restricted to 10 percent of the CPU processing time (during a 24-hour interval), the site's applications should be using the CPU for only 2.4 hours out of 24. If the site uses the CPU longer than 2.4 hours, but less than 3.6 hours, the only consequence is that an event is written to the Event Log. Once the site uses the CPU for more than 3.6 hours, all out-of-process applications on the site are set to Idle. If the server is not very busy and the applications continue to use processor time, eventually reaching 4.8 hours of use during the 24-hour interval, the out-of-process applications are stopped on the Web site. To throttle processor use by a Web site, follow these steps:

1. Select the Web site where you want to restrict processor use through the Internet Information Services snap-in.

2. Open the Web site's property page, and then click the Performance tab.

3. Select "Enable process throttling" (see Figure 23-18 earlier) and enter the percentage of the CPU time that you want this site to be limited to.

4. Select "Enforce limits" if you want to enable the Level 2 and Level 3 consequences of processor time overrun.

If you enable process throttling, you should probably *lower* the CGI timeout interval. By default, the interval is set to 5 minutes. If the CGI applications fails, the thread is not released until the timeout value is reached. The time between failure and when the thread is finally released is counted as time that the application is using the processor. The CGI timeout in IIS 5.0 is the total amount of time a CGI application is given to complete (not the time until I/O must occur).

Bandwidth Throttling

Every connection provides a given amount of bandwidth. By throttling the connection bandwidth used by IIS, you can maintain available bandwidth for other applications (such as e-mail or news servers). If you're running more than one Web site on IIS, you can also throttle bandwidth on each of the Web sites individually—throttling bandwidth on individual sites assures that bandwidth is available for all the sites sharing the network card. Remember that bandwidth throttling limits only the bandwidth used by static HTML files.

Keep in mind that while the total number of connection attempts in a day may give you an idea of the overall activity on your site, you'll also need to consider changes in the connection rate (connections per second) to see if you're having congestion problems at peak times. If you're regularly using more than 50 percent of your total connection bandwidth, you may need to consider upgrading your connection. If you're just setting up a Web site and have no available data to analyze, but do plan to run multiple services (such as a Web server, mail server, and news server), you may want to start by restricting your Web server to 50 percent of the available bandwidth. Once you've been in operation for a short time, you can analyze site performance and adjust bandwidth accordingly.

To manage bandwidth throttling, first determine how much bandwidth your server is using. Use System Monitor to examine the Bytes Total/sec or Current Bandwidth counter in the Network Interface object. If you'd rather compare incoming and outgoing traffic, you can examine both Bytes Sent/sec and Bytes Received/sec. Compare the values with the total bandwidth of your network connection. With a normal load, your server should not use more than 50 percent of its total available bandwidth. The remaining bandwidth is used during peak periods. To throttle the bandwidth used by IIS, do the following:

1. Select the computer running IIS using the Internet Information Services snap-in.

2. On the Internet Information Services property page, select the Enable Bandwidth Throttling check box.

3. In the Maximum Network Use box, type the maximum number of kilobytes per second (Kbps) you want to be used by IIS.

To throttle the bandwidth used by an individual Web site, do this:

1. Select the desired Web site using the Internet Information Services snap-in, and click the Properties button to display its property page.
2. On the Performance tab, select enable bandwidth throttling (see Figure 23-18 earlier).
3. In the Maximum Network Use box, type the maximum number of kilobytes per second you want to be used by the site.

LAN Connection Capacity   In addition to the hardware inside a server, the type of network connection can directly affect server performance. If your network connection cannot handle the amount of data being sent across it, the performance of your server is drastically reduced. The bandwidth available to IIS is also affected by other applications running on the computer that require network bandwidth (such as e-mail). On a fairly busy site, IIS can completely saturate a 10-Mbps Ethernet card. To prevent the server from being restricted by limited network capacity, use either several 10-Mbps Ethernet cards or install a 100-Mbps Ethernet NIC.

To check for network saturation, use System Monitor to check for CPU % Utilization on both the client and the server. If neither the client nor the server is restricted by the CPU capacity, something else is causing the problem. You can also use Network Monitor for Windows 2000 to check the network utilization. If the network is close to 100-percent utilized (for either the client or the server), the network is likely to be the bottleneck. Remember that different brands of network cards perform differently. The performance of a network card is affected by the drivers and driver settings used when configuring the network card. Also check with the maker of your network card to see if updated drivers are available.

Internet Connection Capacity   Internet bandwidth determines how fast data arrives at your computer, and also how many requests can be serviced simultaneously. If you don't have sufficient bandwidth for the number of requests coming to your site, delays or failures can occur. Your computer connects to the Internet through a network adapter card or other network device (such as a modem or ISDN card). The amount of bandwidth available is a function of the type of connection you select.

In addition to the number of simultaneous users you anticipate supporting, you should also consider the speed at which your files (Web pages) are sent to users. File transfer speed is a function of connection speed and file size. A general guideline is that it should take less than five seconds to send a page (this does not include external graphics, audio, or video). External files typically load after the text loads. A general rule for external files is that they should load in less than 30 seconds. Once you've determined the amount of bandwidth needed for your Web or FTP server, consider whether you will be offering other services that require bandwidth. These services can include e-mail, news, or audio or video streaming.

Typically, your Internet connection comes to a router, and a network adapter card connects your computer to the router. You need a high-performance network card to prevent a bottleneck between your Internet connection and your computer. For example, if your connection to the Internet is a T1 line with 1.54-Mbps bandwidth, having your servers on an Ethernet LAN with a 10-Mbps bandwidth should be more than sufficient. However, if you have a T3 connection to the Internet, you might consider using a Fiber Distributed Data Interface (FDDI) LAN for your servers because the T3 bandwidth of 45 Mbps is much greater than the Ethernet bandwidth of 10 Mbps, or even 100 Mbps.

Page Compression   Page performance can also be improved using compression. HTTP compression provides faster transmission time between compression-enabled browsers and IIS. Compressed files download faster, and are particularly beneficial to the performance of any browser that uses a network connection with restricted bandwidth (such as a modem). You can compress static files alone, or both static files and applications. If your network bandwidth is restricted, you may consider HTTP compression (at least for static files). However, if processor use is already extremely high, the additional processor overhead needed for compression (especially compressing dynamic content) may actually impair server performance.

When IIS receives a request, it checks to see if the browser is compression-enabled. IIS then checks the filename extension to see if the requested file is static or dynamic. If the file is static, IIS checks to see if the file has previously been requested (and is already available in compressed format in the temporary compression directory). If the file is not already in compressed format, IIS sends the uncompressed file to the browser, and then adds a compressed copy of the file to the temporary compression directory. If the file is stored in a compressed format, IIS sends the compressed file to the browser. No files are compressed until they have been requested once by a browser. If the file contains dynamic content, IIS compresses the file as it is generated and sends the compressed file to the browser—no copy of the file is stored.

You can easily test the effectiveness of HTTP compression. Before enabling compression, use System Monitor to log the % Processor Time counter of the Processor object over several days to establish a baseline. This counter has a Total instance and a separate instance for each processor in the system. If your server has more than one processor, you should probably watch the individual processors as well as the total to discover any imbalance in the workload. Now, enable HTTP compression:

1. Select the computer icon in the Internet Information Services snap-in, and click the Properties button to display its property page.

2. Select WWW Service under Master Properties.

3. Click the Edit button.

4. On the Service tab, select "Compress static files" (see Figure 23-19) to compress only static files for transmission to compression-enabled clients.

5. To compress application files, select both "Compress static files" and "Compress application files".

6. Type the path to a local directory in the Temporary folder box, or use the Browse button to locate a directory where compressed files will be kept. The directory must be on a local drive and it must be on an NTFS partition. The directory should not be shared and cannot be a compressed directory.

7. Set the maximum size to allow for the folder to Unlimited, or limit the size by typing a number in the Limited to text box.

After enabling compression, continue to log the value of these counters for an extended period (preferably for several days) so you have a good basis for comparison. Compare the values without and with compression. If you see signs of bottlenecks during the test, you should promptly stop—a significant drop in performance indicates that server performance with compression enabled has decreased (compared to performance without compression enabled).

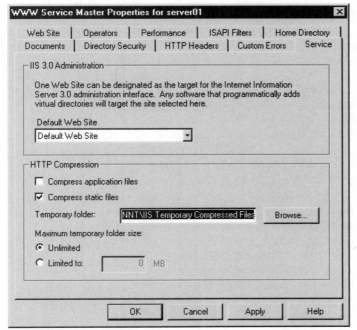

FIGURE 23-19   Configuring HTTP compression to speed the download of Web pages

Limiting Connections   Limiting connections is another way to conserve bandwidth for other uses (such as e-mail or news servers, or for another Web site running on the same Web server). All connection attempts beyond the connection limit are rejected. To test connection limits, use System Monitor to log the Current Connections, Maximum Connections, and Total Connection Attempts counters in at least the Web Service and FTP Service objects. Continue logging (for several days or a week) until you establish the normal range. If you want to limit the number of connections:

1. Select the desired Web site using the Internet Information Services snap-in, and click the Properties button to display its property page.
2. On the Web Site tab, select the "Limited to" option.
3. Type the maximum number of simultaneous connections you want to allow in the Maximum Connections box (see Figure 23-20). The Unlimited option permits as many simultaneous connections as your bandwidth and processor can support.
4. Type the connection timeout value in seconds in the Connection Timeout box.

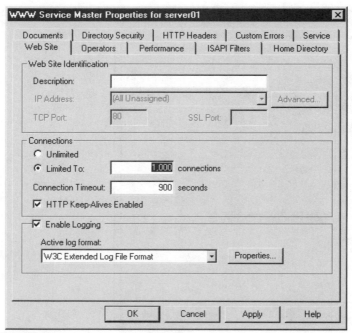

FIGURE 23-20 Throttle bandwidth by manually limiting active connections to the Web server.

Further Study

Apache: **www.apache.org**
FrontPage: **www.microsoft.com/isapi/redir.dll?prd=frontpage express&ar=home**
ICANN: **www.icann.org**
IIS: **www.microsoft.com/isapi/redir.dll?prd=ieak&ar=isn**
Learn ASP: **http://www.learnasp.com/aspng/index.aspx**
Microsoft Universal Data Access Web: **www.microsoft.com/isapi/redir.dll?prd=mdac**
Microsoft: **www.microsoft.com**
SANS Institute: **www.sans.org**
Windows Update: **windowsupdate.microsoft.com/isapi/redir.dll?prd=windowsupdate**
World Wide Web Consortium: **www.w3.org**

WINDOWS 2000 ADMINISTRATION AND SECURITY

Windows 2000 is a versatile OS platform for all sizes of network installations, and Windows versions such as NT/2000 are widely regarded as the most popular network OS available (Windows XP is also appearing on some platforms). It offers a suite of powerful features right out of the box, including IIS (Web and FTP services), Telnet server, clustering, DNS and DHCP support, and more. Also, its well-known graphic interface makes Windows 2000 comfortable for administrators and users of varied experience levels. However, the many features provided by Windows 2000 present a steep learning curve that makes it difficult to master. This chapter provides administrators with an overview of Windows 2000 features, installation, and basic testing, and then covers the basics of user administration and security.

For detailed information on Windows 2000 and administration, you can refer to the Windows 2000 Resource Kit, or any number of comprehensive books on the subject.

Installation Basics

Unless Windows 2000 is preinstalled on your server, you'll need to go through the installation process. The actual installation is very automated, but you will need to make some important choices along the way. There are numerous ways to install Windows 2000 Server, but you only have two real choices to begin the installation—boot from the Windows 2000 Server CD or prepare boot diskettes. Most servers less than five years old are able to boot from their CD-ROM drives (and this is certainly the best way to approach the installation). However, if you find that you need to prepare boot diskettes (i.e., the intended server PC doesn't have a CD-ROM), you can do so by running the **makeboot.exe** program found in the **\Bootdisk** folder of the Windows 2000 Server CD. The installation overview in this chapter assumes that you're booting from the Windows 2000 Server CD.

RUNNING SETUP

If you've installed any version of Windows in the past, you already know that you need to run the Setup routine. Windows 2000 installation is no different. When you boot from the Windows 2000 Server CD, you'll first see a real-mode (aka DOS) display that takes you through the early installation choices. Press ENTER to confirm that you wish to install Windows 2000 Server (or press F3 to exit Setup). Next, choose to install Windows 2000 Server, or to repair an existing Windows 2000 Server installation. You press ENTER to install Windows 2000 Server. Now you're faced with the lengthy Windows 2000 Server license agreement. Read and understand the agreement, and press F8 to agree and proceed.

Managing Partitions

The installation process begins, and you'll see a listing of all available disk partitions where you can install Windows 2000 Server. You can use the arrow keys and press ENTER to select an existing disk partition, or press C on the keyboard to create a new disk partition (you usually must do this with a new server installation). Alternately, press D on the keyboard to delete an existing partition (you usually do this when removing all traces of a previous operating system before creating the installation partition you need). When you opt to create a partition, you're prompted for the size of the partition you wish to create. By default, the maximum size partition will be offered. To accept this choice, simply press ENTER and the new partition will be created. You then see the screen listing all partitions, including the new partition you just created—shown as New (Unformatted). Choose this new partition and press ENTER to proceed.

After selecting the new partition, you must choose a disk format—either FAT or NTFS. For most servers, you use only NTFS partitions, so choose NTFS and press ENTER to continue. Setup then formats the partition for you. When formatting is completed, Setup automatically copies the files needed to continue the Windows 2000 Server installation to the new partition. In many cases, administrators select at least two partitions—one for the OS, and one for the applications. Once the files are copied, the system is automatically restarted, and the GUI portion of the installation routine starts automatically.

Device Identification

The GUI-based Setup program walks you through various installation choices you must make during the setup process, and sets a basic configuration for the server. First, the GUI Setup program attempts to detect and configure all of the devices installed in the computer—this process takes five to ten minutes (depending on the number of devices installed in the server). After the hardware devices are installed and configured, choose the location and keyboard settings for your system. These choices default to English (United States) and U.S. Keyboard Layout (if you're using a copy of Windows 2000 Server purchased for the U.S.), so you can usually just click Next to continue.

Licensing

Now it's time to enter your name and organization name. Most companies prefer that you not personalize the operating system for a particular individual. Instead, use a name like "Sales Department" and then enter your company's name in the field provided. Click Next to continue. You're prompted to choose how the server will manage its Client Access Licenses (CALs). Windows 2000 Server supports Per Server and

Per Seat licensing. *Per Server licensing* means the CALs are assigned to the server, and the server will only allow as many connections from computers as there are installed CALs on that server. *Per Seat licensing* means you have chosen to purchase a CAL for each of your client computers, and this gives them the right to access as many Windows 2000 servers as they wish (and the servers don't limit the number of connections). Microsoft recommends that you use Per Server licensing when running a single server and Per Seat licensing when running multiple servers. If you're unsure of which mode to use, choose Per Server because you can change to Per Seat mode once at no cost. Choose the appropriate option button. If you chose Per Server licensing, select the number of licenses you own. Click Next to continue.

Next, enter the name of the server where you're installing Windows 2000 Server, along with the initial Administrator password. These are very important selections. The computer name you choose will be the name of the server, and the name seen by users when they browse the servers on the network. If possible, choose a name that you won't need to change later. The administrator's password is key to doing anything critical with the server, so select a strong password that is not easy to guess. As a rule, choose an administrator's password with eight or more characters that has both letters and numbers. Also, make sure it's also a password you'll remember. After completing the fields, click Next to continue.

Optional Components

Next, you'll see a dialog box that lists all the different components you can optionally install with Windows 2000 Server. For this chapter, only the essential choices for a file and print server will be selected. However, the following list outlines your choices (though you can choose to add these components later):

- **Certificate Services** Certificate Services are needed to enable public-key applications (such as when you're setting up a secure Web server). You do not need to install this option unless you have an application that requires these services.

- **Cluster Services** Windows 2000 Cluster Services enable two or more servers to share a common workload and to provide failover support in the event that one of the servers experiences a hardware failure. For example, cluster services allow multiple file and print servers to appear as one server to the network. You do not need to install this option unless you are building a server cluster to provide high availability.

- **Internet Information Server (IIS)** IIS allows a Windows 2000 Server to operate as a Web and FTP server. Choosing this option installs IIS along with a number of support features. You do not need to install IIS for an everyday file and print server.

- **Management and Monitoring Tools** This option installs supplemental server management tools. The Connection Manager helps you manage RAS and dial-up connections. The Directory Service Migration Tool helps you migrate from NetWare Directory Services (NDS) to Windows 2000 Active Directory. Network Monitor Tools perform rudimentary network packet analysis and decoding. Simple Network Management Protocol (SNMP) allows Windows 2000 Server to report management information to an SNMP management computer on the network. For a basic file and print server, you may choose to install the Network Monitor Tools portion of this option, which you can select by clicking the Details button and then choosing just that option.

- **Message Queuing Services** These services queue network messages used with certain client/server applications. You do not need to install this option unless it's required by a specific application.

- **Microsoft Script Debugger** This option adds tools that enable you to check and debug scripts written in VBScript and JScript. You may occasionally need to access the Internet through a Web browser on the server (for example, to download driver updates), or you may develop server-based scripts written in VBScript or JScript, so you should choose to install this option.

- **Networking Services**   This installation choice includes a wide variety of network services that you may choose to install on your server. Several of these options are ideal for a file and print server. Consider installing Dynamic Host Configuration Protocol (DHCP). This allows the server to manage a range of IP addresses, and assign addresses automatically to client computers. Also consider installing Windows Internet Name Service (WINS) to provide name resolution and browsing support to client computers that are running pre-Windows 2000 operating systems using TCP/IP (such as Windows NT and Windows 9x). However, neither of these options is required for a basic file and print server.

- **Other Network File and Print Services**   This option lets you install the additional support required to share the server's files and printers with Macintosh computers and UNIX-based computers. You don't need this option if all of your client computers are running some version of Windows.

- **Remote Installation Services (RIS)**   RIS lets you remotely install Windows 2000 Professional onto network computers that support a feature called *Remote Boot*. This is handy if you're adding a lot of workstations, and don't want to tote the Windows 2000 Professional CD from PC to PC. You'll need a dedicated partition on the server to host the Windows 2000 Professional disk images, but you don't need this option for a basic file and print server.

- **Remote Storage**   This feature lets you configure a Windows 2000 Server disk to automatically move infrequently used files to an available tape drive or writable CD (a CD-R or CD-RW drive). The operating system can automatically recall these files if they're needed. This feature isn't needed for most servers because there is ample disk space.

- **Terminal Services and Terminal Services Licensing**   Windows Terminal Services work similar to mainframes, where all the work is performed on the mainframe and the client acts only as a terminal to the mainframe. These two options let a Windows 2000 Server host multiple Windows sessions for remote computers. The applications execute on the server, and the client computer handles only the display and keyboard/mouse input for the application. You do not need these options for file and print servers.

Final Selections

After selecting the desired options, click Next to continue. You'll be prompted for information about a modem attached to the server (if one exists). You can provide your area code, any number you need to dial to get an outside line, and whether the phone line supports tone dialing or pulse dialing. Complete the requested fields and click Next to continue. You're then prompted to enter the correct date and time, as well as the time zone where the server resides. Update these fields, if necessary, and click Next to continue. Select your network settings. You can choose *Typical* settings or *Custom* settings. For a small network, you can usually choose Typical settings. Custom settings enable you to define details (such as what networking components will be installed and how each is configured).

Domain or Workgroup

Next, you're prompted to set up the Windows 2000 Server as a member of a workgroup or a domain. A *domain* is a sophisticated administrative grouping of computers on a Windows 2000 network that allows the network's resources to be administered from a single point and where strong security can be implemented. Domains enable you to manage many Windows 2000 or Windows NT servers more easily. By comparison, a *workgroup* is a simple collection of computers on a network, and is only suited to peer-to-peer networks. Windows 2000 Servers can be configured in one of three modes to support either domains or workgroups. *Domain controllers* hold the domain's Active Directory information and authenticate users and access to resources. Most Windows 2000 networks will consist of at least one domain, and will need at least one domain controller. *Member servers* are part of a domain, but do not hold a copy of the Active Directory information. *Stand-alone servers* do not participate in a domain, but instead participate in a workgroup.

Remember that you cannot join the new server to a domain unless the domain already exists and a domain controller is available to validate the new server into the domain. For a new server (even one that will be a domain controller), choose workgroup and click Next to proceed. The setup program then completes its portion of the installation of Windows 2000 Server using the information you provided.

CONFIGURING THE SERVER

Once Windows 2000 has been installed, the system reboots, and you'll need to configure the server. At the Windows 2000 Server login prompt, press CTRL-ALT-DEL and log into the server—you log in as Administrator, using the password you defined as part of the setup process. After logging in, the Windows 2000 Server desktop appears, along with the Windows 2000 Configuration Wizard (see Figure 24-1), which walks you through the remaining steps needed to make the server operational. If you're setting up a single server for a small network, you can choose "This is the only server in my network" as shown in the figure. For more sophisticated Windows 2000 installations, choose "One or more servers are already running in my network", though this requires more detailed setup knowledge. You'll see a confirmation screen confirming that you want to set up the server with services like Active Directory, DHCP, and DNS (standard for a single server in a network). Click Next to proceed, or learn more about these services by clicking the links shown in the Server Configuration Wizard.

Now you're prompted for the name of the domain you'll create. Remember that the domain name cannot have spaces, and you should choose a simple name—many companies choose the name of their

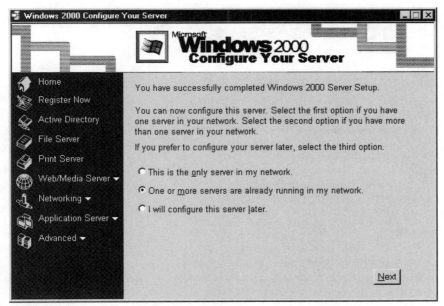

FIGURE 24-1   After installing Windows 2000 Server, the Configuration Wizard walks you through the remainder of the server's setup.

company, or some abbreviation thereof, for their domain name. You must also enter any Internet domain name that exists for your network. The Internet domain name is one owned or controlled by your company. For example, if you work for a company called Widget Corporation, you can call your Windows 2000 domain *widget*, and your Internet domain would probably be **widget.com**. If you don't have an Internet domain name registered, enter **local** in the field instead. For example, the Windows 2000 domain name will be **admintration.dls** and the Internet domain name will be **admintration.dls.com**. Enter your information and click Next to continue.

After a pause, you'll see that the choices you've made will be installed, and the server will be restarted. Click Next a second time to proceed (you may be prompted for a Windows 2000 Server CD-ROM during this process). After the system installs the necessary components and restarts, you need to finish up some final steps in the Server Configuration Wizard before you're done:

1. Right-click My Network Places and select Properties.

2. Right-click Local Area Connection and choose Properties. This opens the Local Area Connection Properties dialog box (see Figure 24-2).

3. Choose the Internet Protocol (TCP/IP) entry and click the Properties button.

4. On the General tab, click the "Use the following IP address" radio button and enter the IP number for this server to use as its IP address. If you don't have an existing range of numbers (and your network isn't directly connected to the Internet), use **192.168.1.1** as the IP address.

5. Enter the correct subnet mask. If your network hasn't used subnet masks before, choose **255.255.255.0**.

6. In the Preferred DNS Server field, repeat the IP address you assigned to the server (e.g., **192.168.1.1**). Click OK to close the various Properties dialog boxes.

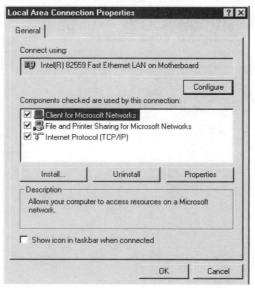

FIGURE 24-2   The Local Area Connection Properties dialog box allows you to configure the server's communication on the network.

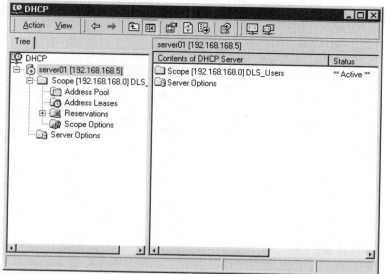

FIGURE 24-3 Use the DHCP Manager to let the server fulfill DHCP requests to clients.

7. Now authorize the DHCP services. Click Start | Programs | Administrative Tools | DHCP. You should see the DHCP Manager (see Figure 24-3).

8. Expand the tree in the left pane, then right-click your new server. Choose All Tasks and click Authorize. This lets the server fulfill DHCP requests and assign IP addresses to client computers on the network.

9. Shut down and restart the server for your changes to take effect. This should complete the basic installation and configuration of a Windows 2000 server.

CONFIGURING A CLIENT

Once Windows 2000 Server is installed and the server is running, you may still want to perform some basic testing to ensure that the server is accessible to client systems elsewhere on the network. This means you'll need to create a user account, create a shared resource on the server for the client computer to access, configure a client to connect to the server, then log into the server with the client computer and verify that the shared resource is accessible. Experienced administrators may skip this step, but it's a handy exercise if you need practice with accounts and shares.

Create a Test Account

While you can try logging into the server as an administrator, it's usually better to create a generic user account that you can use for testing purposes:

1. Click Start | Programs | Administrative Tools | Active Directory Users and Computers. This opens the Windows management console with your server's Active Directory Users and Computers settings (see Figure 24-4).

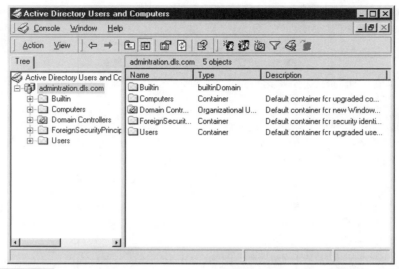

FIGURE 24-4   Use Active Directory to manage your server's users and groups.

2. Right-click the server (i.e., **admintration.dls.com**) in the left-hand pane, select New, and then choose User. The Create New Object (User) dialog box appears (see Figure 24-5). Enter the first and last name for the test user account. The remaining fields are generated automatically based on the server's configuration, although you can change fields if required. In the figure, the user *stephen_bigelow* will log into Active Directory using the user account **stephen_bigelow@admintration.dls.com**. Click Next to continue.

3. Now, enter a password for the account you just created (for a quick test, simply use the password *password*). Click Next to continue, and then click Finish to complete the new user account.

Create a Shared Resource

Once you have a valid user account, there must be something on the server for that user to access. Windows 2000 Server shares folders through a mechanism called a *share*. A share is a browsable resource that remote users can access (provided they have the appropriate privileges). Let's create a folder on the server that a user can access from the network. First, create a normal folder on one of the server's disk drives. Right-click the folder and choose Sharing from the menu. The Sharing tab of the folder's Properties dialog box appears (see Figure 24-6). Click the "Share this folder" radio button and check the share name. The share name is automatically assigned based on the folder's name, but you may change it if you wish. Click OK to share the folder.

Configure a Client

Pick a Windows PC on the network and configure it to access the new server. If the PC has been working on the network already, chances are that many of the following steps have already been completed, but it's a good exercise to check each setting and enter the new server's domain name before proceeding. Follow these steps to configure your client:

1. Open the Control Panel and double-click the Network icon.

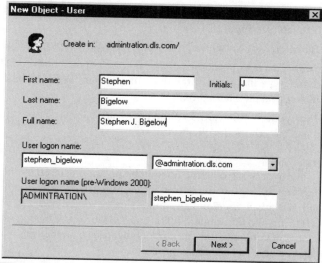

FIGURE 24-5 Create a temporary user account so that you can test the connection to your new server.

2. Click Add, choose Client in the Select Network Component Type dialog box, and then click Add.

3. Choose Microsoft from the list of Manufacturers, and then choose Client for Microsoft Networks in the Network Clients area. Click OK to continue.

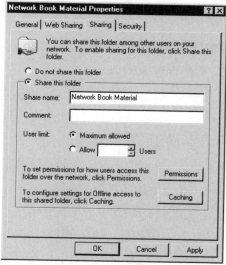

FIGURE 24-6 Use the Sharing tab to share a resource that you've created on the server.

4. The Network Properties dialog box will appear with both the Client for Microsoft Networks and the TCP/IP protocol installed (see Figure 24-7).

5. Highlight the "Client for Microsoft Networks" entry and click the Properties button.

6. In the Client for Microsoft Networks Properties dialog box, select the checkbox "Log onto Windows NT domain" and then type the name of the domain. For our example, the domain name is *admintration*. Click OK to close the dialog box.

7. You may be prompted for your Windows CD (if the necessary files are not available on the PC already), and will then need to reboot the client PC.

Test the Connection

With everything configured, you can now log onto the domain being administered by the new Windows 2000 Server and browse the files you placed into the shared folder. When the client computer restarts, use the test user account name (such as *stephen_bigelow*), the domain name (*admintration*), and the password you selected (such as *password*) to log into the domain. If you enter the information correctly, you will log into the domain. If any problems occur—such as an unrecognized user name, password, or domain name—you will see an error and be able to correct the problem.

Open the Network Neighborhood on the client's desktop. The new server should appear in the list. Opening the server shows you any shares that you have access to. You will see netlogin and sysvol, as well as the folder you created and shared (see Figure 24-8). You should be able to open the test folder and see any files you placed there. You should be able to manipulate those files, delete them, rename them, open them, and so on (just as if you were working with the files on a local hard drive).

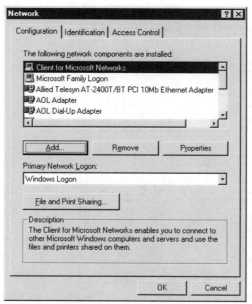

FIGURE 24-7   Be sure to configure the client PC for proper communication over the network.

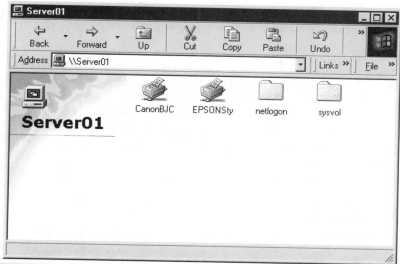

FIGURE 24-8   Check Network Neighborhood to see your available shares after logging onto the server.

Basic Administration

Now that you've successfully installed, configured, and tested Windows 2000 Server on your new server platform, it's time to focus on the more involved tasks of server administration. Proper administration helps to ensure that your servers remain productive and secure, so you must develop and enforce security policies that are appropriate for your network environment. For example, forcing the use of frequently changing 20-character passwords will virtually guarantee that users must write the passwords down somewhere—ultimately compromising the strong security that you're trying to employ. Strong security measures also mean that users will have trouble logging onto the network, and require additional support from the administrator. This part of the chapter covers basic administrative duties like adding new users, deleting old users, assigning permissions to users, and so on.

USER ACCOUNTS

In order to access a Windows 2000 server, every network user (even the administrator) must have a user account on the server or in the domain (a collection of security information shared among Windows 2000 servers). The user account defines the user's name (the name by which the user is known to the system) and the user's password, along with an assortment of other information specific to each user. Windows 2000 Server allows you to create, maintain, and delete user accounts with a minimum of fuss.

Understanding SIDs

Every user account created for a Windows 2000 Server domain is assigned a special number called a Security ID (or SID), and the user is really known to the server using this number. The SID is made up of a unique number assigned to the domain and then a sequential number assigned to each created account. SIDs are completely unique, so no two users will ever have the same SID—even if they have the same user name or password. If you have a user called "bill", then you delete that account and create another account called "bill" later, both accounts will have different SIDs, so no user's account will accidentally receive permissions originally assigned to another user of the same name.

New User Accounts

To manage user accounts, you must use the Active Directory Users and Computers management console available in Start | Programs | Administrative Tools. Once the console starts (see Figure 24-5), open the tree for the domain you're administering and then click the Users folder in the left pane. A list of existing users will appear in the right pane. To add a new user, right-click the Users folder, choose New from the menu, and select User. The Create New Object (User) dialog box appears (see Figure 24-5). Enter the First name, Last name, and User logon name fields (you can adjust other fields if necessary). Click the Next button to create the new user's password profile (see Figure 24-9). Enter the initial password to be used by the new account, confirm the password, and select any applicable options:

■ *User must change password at next login.* Selecting this checkbox forces users to choose their own password when they first log into the system.

■ *User cannot change password.* This option is sometimes used for accounts where the password should change without the administrator's input (i.e., on more secure networks). However, this checkbox is usually *not* selected.

■ *Password never expires.* This option allows the password to remain valid for as long as the user chooses to use it. Selecting this option is generally considered to be a poor security practice, so this checkbox is usually *not* selected.

■ *Account disabled.* Selecting this option causes the new account to be disabled, though it can easily be enabled again when needed. This is handy when creating a new account, but the new user isn't ready to start using the network yet.

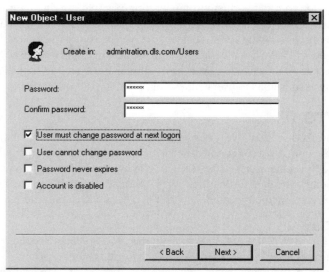

FIGURE 24-9   Be sure to set a suitable password when creating a new user account.

After entering the password and selecting the desired options, click Next to continue. You will then see a confirmation screen, so click Next again to create the account (or click Back to make any needed changes to the new account).

Naming Schemes   Most small organizations generally assign logon names that include the user's first or last name. However, you can have several common names in an organization of any size, so rather than reworking your logon naming scheme when you run into problems, select a good naming scheme up front and make sure other administrators use it. When naming accounts, you should use a consistent procedure that allows your user base to grow, limits the possibility of name conflicts, and ensures that your accounts have secure names that aren't easily exploited. Here are some guidelines that may help to ease naming issues:

- *User's first name and last initial.* Take the user's first name and combine it with the first letter of the last name to create the logon name. For Stephen Bigelow, use *stephenb* or *steveb*, though this naming scheme isn't practical for large organizations.

- *User's first initial and last name.* Take the user's first initial and combine it with the last name to create the logon name. For Stephen Bigelow, you would use *sbigelow*. This naming scheme isn't practical for large organizations.

- *User's first initial, middle initial, and last name.* You combine the user's first initial, middle initial, and last name to create the logon name. For Stephen J. Bigelow, you would use *sjbigelow*.

- *User's first initial, middle initial, and first five characters of the last name.* You combine the user's first initial, middle initial, and the first five characters of the last name to create the logon name. For Stephen J. Bigelow, you would use *sjbigel*.

- *User's first name and last name.* You combine the user's first and last name, and use an underscore character (_), period (.), or hyphen (-) to separate the two. For Stephen Bigelow, you could use *stephen_bigelow*, *stephen.bigelow*, or *stephen-bigelow*.

Secure Passwords   Passwords are case-sensitive strings that can contain up to 104 characters with Active Directory directory service (and up to 14 characters with Windows NT Security Manager). Valid characters for passwords include letters, numbers, and symbols. When you set a password for an account, Windows 2000 stores the password in an encrypted format in the account database. But simply having a password isn't enough—the key to preventing unauthorized access to network resources is to use *secure* passwords. The difference between an average password and a secure password is that secure passwords are difficult to guess and crack. Make passwords difficult to crack by using combinations of all the available character types (including lowercase letters, uppercase letters, numbers, and symbols). For example, instead of using *crazydays* for a password you would use *crAZy2Days&*, *Cr**y!dayS*, or even *c*AZY%d*ys*.

Changing User Accounts

Creating a new account is a relatively quick and simple procedure, and there are few options to contend with. However, there are many other options available to document the user and set a variety of security options, and this means you'll need to update the account. To update an existing user account, open the list of users in your management console, right-click the particular user that you need to update, and then choose Properties from the menu. The user's Properties dialog box opens (see Figure 24-10).

The General and Address tabs let you enter additional information about the user (such as their title, mailing address, telephone number, e-mail account, and so on). Active Directory integrates with new

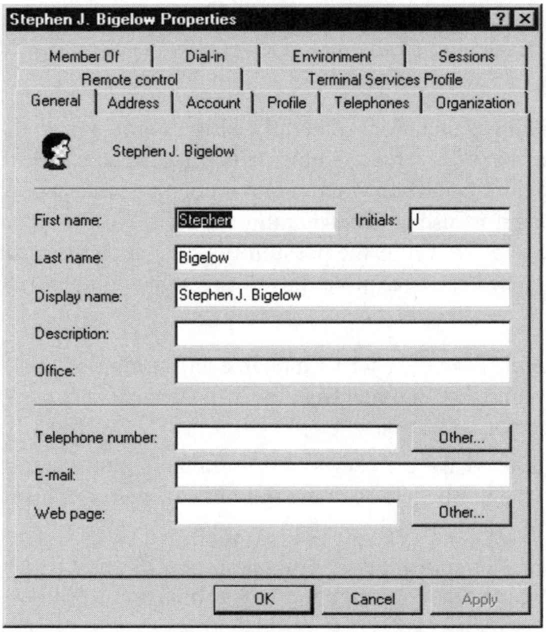

FIGURE 24-10   You can manage all of the details of a user account through the user's Properties dialog box.

versions of Exchange Server, so this information may be important for your network. You can set some4 important user account options using the Account tab (see Figure 24-11). This lets you change the User logon name, the server domain, the User logon name (pre-Windows 2000, which can be used to log into the domain from a Windows NT computer or using an application that doesn't support Active Directory logins).

By default, users are permitted to log on to the network at any time, any day of the week, and this policy is usually fine for small networks. However, you can use the Logon Hours button to restrict the days and times that a user can log on to the network. Restricting logon days/times is more important in larger networks where additional security is warranted. When setting these restrictions, be sure to leave a bit of additional time before and after work hours as a cushion. By default, users can log on to any workstation in the domain and the domain authenticates them. In some cases, stricter security may require that you limit which computer(s) a user account can log on to. Use the Logon To button to restrict the user's logon destinations.

The Logon To feature only works if NetBIOS or NetBEUI protocols are being used—this feature will not work with TCP/IP-only networks.

The Account options portion of the Account tab lets you to select additional account options using checkboxes. The two most important additional options are "Account is disabled" and "Account is trusted for delegation". When the account is disabled, the user cannot use their account, but the account remains set up in Active Directory. You need to deny access to the network temporarily (i.e., while the user is on vacation), but reenable it again in the future without deleting it. When trusted for delegation, you can

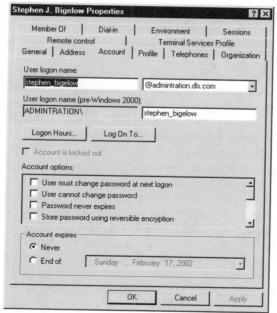

FIGURE 24-11 Enforce security in the user's account through the Account tab.

designate the user account to administer some part of the domain (Windows 2000 Server lets you to grant administrative rights to portions of the Active Directory tree without having to give administrative rights to the entire domain). The last option on the Account tab to be familiar with is the Account expires (expiration date) feature. By default, the expiration is set to Never. However, you may define an expiration date, and the account is automatically disabled (not deleted) when the expiration date is reached. This is particularly handy when setting up a temporary account for a user (like a temporary employee).

Removing User Accounts

As users change departments or leave the company, their accounts will need to be removed. This helps with the administrative "housekeeping" of the network, and helps to ensure security by preventing unauthorized (perhaps disgruntled) former employees from accessing the network. To delete a user account, open the Users folder in the management console, right-click the user, then select Delete from the menu. To delete multiple accounts, select all of the accounts to be deleted, then right-click on them and select Delete.

 If you'd rather disable an account than delete it, simply right-click the user(s) and select Disable Account.

USER GROUPS

While user accounts provide very precise control over a user's activities on a network, managing users alone would quickly become an administrative nightmare. For example, suppose that your sales department has access to 30 folders on the server. If you were only able to manage individual accounts, you'd need to look up those 30 folders each time a new salesperson was hired so that you'd know what permissions to assign. As another example, when a user changes departments and access to different folders is required, you'd need to research the new permissions required for that user—you can see how this would easily overwhelm a busy administrator.

To simplify the drudgery of network privileges, network operating systems support the idea of *groups* (sometimes called *security groups*). The idea is to create a group, assign appropriate permissions to that group, and then assign users to their particular group. When you assign permission to a folder on the server, you give network permission to the group, and all users that are assigned to the group automatically inherit those permissions. A group scheme makes the ordeal of managing network permissions much easier. This way, you'd assign access to those 20 sales-related folders to the Sales group. When you create an account for the new salesperson, you'd simply add them to the Sales group—automatically giving them access to the necessary folders. If that salesperson later moves over to a service position, you can just reassign that user to the Service group, thus changing all necessary permissions.

Group assignments also support *group hierarchies*, where groups can be members of other groups. For example, suppose that you had a group for Sales, and a broader group for Administration (which accesses other folders). You'd first create a Sales group, then create the Administration group, and the Sales group would be made a member of the Administration group. This approach allows for a logical assignment of resources. If a resource is just for a specific department, assign the resource to that departmental group. If a resource is for a higher group, you assign that resource to the higher group, and all the individual departmental groups below will inherit permission to access that resource. If a resource were for everyone (i.e., a folder with HR guidelines or benefits handbooks), you would assign that resource to the master, top-level group.

Creating a Group

To create and manage groups, you must use the Active Directory Users and Computers management console available in Start | Programs | Administrative Tools. Once the console starts (see Figure 24-4,), open the tree for the domain you're administering (such as **admintration.dls.com**). Groups appear in the Built-in and Users folders. The Built-in groups are fixed and cannot be deleted, and they can't be made members of other groups. Built-in groups have certain important permissions already assigned to them, and other groups you create can be assigned membership to the Built-in groups. If you want to disable a particular Built-in group, you just remove all of its member groups. In most cases, you'll work with groups listed in the Users folder. You can distinguish user groups from user accounts by the "two-person" icon and the Type designation. To add a new group, right-click the Users folder, choose New from the menu, and select Group. The Create New Object (Group) dialog box appears (see Figure 24-12).

Enter the name of the new group in the "Name of new group" field. You'll see that new name echoed in the "Group name (pre-Windows 2000)" field. This field lets you to use a different group name for Windows NT computers (which should be avoided wherever possible). Select the appropriate options in the lower half of the dialog box. "Group scope" indicates how widely the group is used throughout a domain. A *Universal* group exists throughout an organization—even when the network includes many individual domains. Universal groups can also contain members from any domain in an organization's network. A *Global* group can only contain members from the domain where they exist, but global groups can be assigned permissions to any domain within the network (even across multiple domains). *Domain local* groups only exist within a single domain, and can only contain members from that domain.

Finally, select between a Security group or a Distribution group. *Distribution* groups have only one function—to create e-mail distribution lists. You use distribution groups with e-mail applications (such as Microsoft Exchange) to send e-mail to the members of the group. As with a security group, you can add a

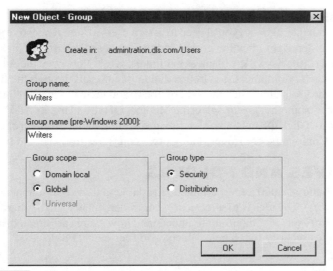

FIGURE 24-12   Create new groups to organize users and assign access to resources.

contact to a distribution group so that the contact receives e-mail sent to the group. Distribution groups play no role in security (you do not assign permissions to distribution groups), and you cannot use them to filter Group Policy settings. By comparison, *security* groups are an essential component of the relationship between users and security. Security groups manage user and computer access to shared resources, and filter Group Policy settings. You collect users, computers, and other groups into a security group and then assign appropriate permissions to specific resources (such as file shares and printers) to the security group. This simplifies administration by letting you assign permissions once to the group instead of multiple times to each individual user. When you add a user to an existing group, the user automatically gains the rights and permissions already assigned to that group.

Small Organizations   Some small organizations will choose to use security groups with *universal* scope to manage all their group needs. For organizations that expect to grow, use universal groups initially and then convert to the Global/Local pattern recommended for medium to large organizations. Alternatively, some growing small organizations will choose to implement the Global/Local pattern from the start. Since groups with universal scope (and their members) are listed in the global catalog database, a large number of universal groups—especially where membership changes frequently—can cause a lot of replication traffic. If this is the situation, use the guidelines for medium to large organizations.

Medium/Large Organizations   Medium to large organizations use Account (global) groups and Resource (local) groups to achieve flexibility, scalability, and ease of administration when managing security groups. Put users into security groups with global scope. A *global* group can usually be thought of as an Accounts group (a group that contains user accounts). Alternatively, put resources into security groups with *domain local* (or machine local) scope. A local group can usually be thought of as a Resource group (a group where you assign permissions to access a resource). You can also put a global group into any domain local (or machine local) group in the forest (this is especially efficient when more than one domain is involved) or assign permissions for accessing resources to the domain local (or machine local) groups that contain them.

Assigning Group Members

New groups are created without members, so you'll need to assign users to their respective groups. Locate the new group in the Users folder, right-click the group, and then choose Properties. Click the Members tab for a list of current members (the list will be blank as in Figure 24-13). Now click the Add button—this opens the Select Users, Contacts, Computers, or Groups dialog box. Scroll through the list, select each member you want to add to the group, and click the Add button to add them to the list of members. If you want the group to be a member of another group, select the Member Of tab and use its Add button (just like adding members to the group). Click OK when you've finished adding members, then click OK to close the Select Users, Contacts, Computers, or Groups dialog box. Your new group should be populated.

MANAGING DRIVES AND FOLDERS

Drives and folders under Windows 2000 Server are made available to users over the network as shared resources (simply called *shares*). The idea is to select a drive or folder, enable it to be shared, and then set permissions for the share. However, it's important to understand how shares are created, and know how Windows 2000 Server handles security for shares, folders, and files on NTFS drives.

Creating Shares

To create a new share, use either My Computer or Windows Explorer on the server. Right-click the folder or drive you want to share and choose Sharing from the menu. You will see the Properties dialog box with the Sharing tab selected (see Figure 24-6). Click the "Share this folder" radio button and assign a Share name (along with a descriptive Comment that users will be able to see). Now select a limit to how many

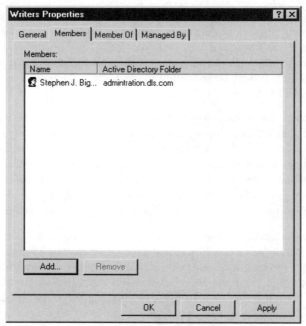

FIGURE 24-13   Populate the group by adding members (even other groups).

users can access the share simultaneously. Generally, you may leave the User limit set to "Maximum allowed".

Now you should set permissions for the share. Click the Permissions button to open the Permissions dialog box (see Figure 24-14). The default settings for a share are the Everyone group with the fullest possible access to the share. This is usually adequate. If you need to restrict access to the share in some fashion, the Permissions dialog box lets you fine-tune the access. Click Add to see the Select Users, Contacts, Computers, or Groups dialog box, then choose the users and groups that need permissions to the share. Once a user or group is added, you can use the checkboxes in the Permissions window to set the exact permissions you want: Full Control, Change, or Read. Click Apply and OK to save your permissions, then click Apply and OK again to save the changes to your new share.

Once a share is created, users can browse it through either Network Neighborhood under Windows 9x\NT or My Network Places under Windows 2000. Double-clicking the share will open it (depending on the permissions). You could also make a share hidden, but still available for users who know the share name. Just create the share normally, but append the '$' symbol to the end of its name. For example, *myfiles$* is a share name that is not seen when browsing available network shares.

Drive Mapping

You may need to simulate a connected hard disk on your computer with a share from the network. For example, many applications that store files on the network require the network folders to be accessible as a normal drive letter. The process of simulating a disk drive with a network share is called *mapping*, where you create a map (a link) between the drive letter you want to use and the actual network share (such as a folder) that's assigned to that drive letter. To map a drive, open Network Neighborhood on the client PC and locate the share you want to map. Right-click the share and select Map Network Drive. The name of the domain and share will appear for you (such as **\\author1\my doc c**). Just select a drive letter for the

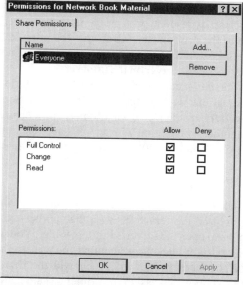

FIGURE 24-14   Set permissions on your share(s) to secure the information on your server.

mapping and click OK. From then on, the share will appear as that drive letter on your client computer, and can be seen as a drive in My Computer.

MANAGING PRINTERS

Printers can be expensive to buy and supply, and they're rarely used at their maximum throughput (pages per month). This means a lot of printer capacity is wasted. In addition, administrators are often tasked with supporting different printer makes and models for a variety of users. It's possible to share printers across a network, and allow many network users to employ the same printer. With a shared printer, a print job is redirected to a print queue on the network (rather than the local printer port). The job will remain in the print queue (usually a temporary file on the print server) until the print server can send the job to the printer. Printer queues can hold a large number of jobs from any network users. Once the job is completely sent to the printer, the print server removes the job from the queue.

Print serving can be accomplished in many different ways. If the printer being used is connected to a server or workstation on the network, *that* server or workstation handles the print server tasks. If the printer is directly connected to the network (i.e., the printer has its own network port), the printer usually has a built-in print server as part of its network hardware. This built-in print server has the intelligence to log in to the network and service a particular printer queue.

For networks larger than 20 users, you're better off buying printers with network interfaces and built-in print servers, or using dedicated print server devices that interface the printer to the network.

Print jobs start with the printing application (such as Corel on a workstation). The application sends its printer output to the local operating system (maybe Windows 2000 Professional). The local operating system uses the printer driver requested by the application to construct the actual print job for the printer. The local operating system then uses the installed network client software to send the formatted print job to the print queue—where the job sits until the printer is available. The print server takes the print job from the queue and sends it to the actual printer.

Remember that driver discrepancies may result in print problems with the shared printer. The network workstation that sends the print job to the print queue will format the print data using a printer driver intended for the workstation's operating system. When the job reaches the PC acting as the print server, the job will be sent to the local printer using the driver on the print server. This means a job formatted for an HP LaserJet 6 on a Windows 98 workstation may not print properly when the job is served by a LaserJet 6 driver under Windows 2000 Server (if that's where the shared printer is). Some items may print perfectly, but you may find that some exotic or specialized print jobs may show errors in the final output. The fix is often to try the print job from another workstation with an OS that matches the OS used by the print server (i.e., if the print server PC is using Windows 2000 Server, try printing from a Windows 2000 Professional workstation).

Sharing a Printer

Let's share a printer attached to our Windows 2000 server. The printer is a conventional parallel port printer already attached and configured on the server PC with the appropriate Windows 2000 drivers installed. Click Start | Settings | Printers to open the server's Printers folder. You will see all of the printers currently installed in the Printers folder. Right-click the printer that you want to share, and choose Sharing from the menu. The Properties dialog box for the printer will appear with the Sharing tab selected (see Figure 24-15). Click the "Shared as" radio button and assign the printer a share name for use by client computers (such as CanonBJC). You can click the OK button and allow the default permissions for a shared printer (the Everyone group can print to it).

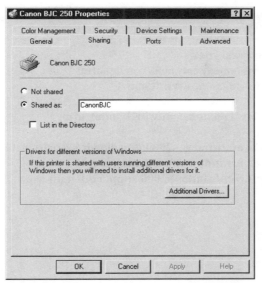

FIGURE 24-15   Share printers with the users on your network.

 If this is a new printer that's not yet been installed, open the Printers folder and use the Add Printers Wizard to configure the printer on the server before trying to make the printer available on the network.

For high-throughput printing requirements, you may use the printer pooling feature. This lets you set up a number of identical printers—all connected to a single printer queue—which appear as one printer on the network. Users print to "one" printer, and the first available physical printer services the job. With printer pooling, you can have a whole set of printers appear as one printer to network users, and dramatically increase the amount of print requests you can handle. However, pooled printers must be identical because they will all use the same print driver. To activate printer pooling, select the shared printer's Ports tab, click the "Enable printer pooling" checkbox, and then select the additional port(s) that also has the same type of printer installed.

To set the permissions for a shared printer, use the Security tab of the printer's properties dialog box, and note the default group assignments. Three main permissions are assigned to each group: Print, Manage Printers, and Manage Documents. The Everyone group has permission to Print, but not to manage documents in the queue. However, a special group called Creator Owner has permission to manage documents. This means the user who sent the print job automatically has permission to modify or delete their own print job (but not others waiting in the queue).

Further Study

Computer Security Institute: **www.gocsi.com**
Hardening Windows 2000: **www.systemexperts.com/win2k.shtml**
International Computer Security Association: **www.icsa.net**
Microsoft: **www.microsoft.com**
NSA Security Guidelines: **nsa1.www.conxion.com/win2k/index.html**
SANS: **www.sans.org**
Security Updates: **www.microsoft.com/windows2000/downloads/security/default.asp**
Windows 2000: **www.microsoft.com/windows2000/default.asp**
Windows Support: **www.microsoft.com/windows2000/support/default.asp**

LINUX ADMINISTRATION AND SECURITY

The Linux operating system has come a long way in the last few years. Once largely regarded as a limited niche OS, Linux has matured into a serious platform for client and server systems. Versions of Linux (such as Red Hat) also provide a suite of powerful server-related features right out of the box, including a news server, Web server, FTP server, file server, DNS server, SQL database server, and more. Installation and maintenance are also much easier than in years past—mainly due to vast improvements in the Setup routine and use of a comfortable graphic interface. This chapter provides administrators with an overview of Red Hat Linux 7.2 features, installation, and basic testing, then covers the basics of user administration and security.

 For detailed information on Red Hat Linux and administration, you can refer to the Red Hat site at **www.redhat.com**.

Installation Basics

Unless Linux is preinstalled on your server, you'll need to go through the installation process. The actual installation of Red Hat 7.2 is very automated, but you will need to make some important choices along the way. There are numerous ways to install Red Hat Linux, but you only have two real choices to begin the installation—boot directly from Linux installation CD 1, or prepare boot diskettes. Most servers less than five years old are able to boot from their CD-ROM drives (and this is certainly the best way to approach the installation). However, if you find that you need to prepare boot diskettes (i.e., the intended server PC doesn't have a CD-ROM), you can do so by running the **rawrite.exe** program found in the **\dosutils** directory of the Linux CD on a Windows-based PC. You will be prompted for the source file (**\images\boot.img** on the Linux CD) and destination floppy diskette. The installation overview in this chapter assumes that you're booting from the Linux installation CDs.

CHECK THE HARDWARE

While Linux has made great strides in hardware compatibility, it still lacks the broad scope of device compatibility enjoyed with operating systems like Windows XP/2000. As a result, you should take the time to inventory the server's hardware prior to installation. First, verify that the server meets the minimum hardware requirements (such as memory and available disk space) for your version of Linux. Also verify that any particular hardware devices (including the video adapter, sound device, NIC, SCSI host adapter, and so on) are present on the *hardware compatibility list* (HCL) for your Linux version. For example, the Red Hat HCL can be found at **www.redhat.com/hardware**, and Caldera's HCL is at **www.caldera.com/products/openlinux/hardware.html**.

RUNNING SETUP

When you're ready to start the installation, put the first Linux installation CD in the CD-ROM drive and reboot the PC. As the PC restarts, it will automatically read the CD and launch the installation routine. You'll see a text display that lets you choose between text or graphic installations, along with several other choices. Simply press ENTER to use the graphics-based installation routine and the Linux GUI will load.

If the PC doesn't boot from the CD-ROM, you may need to change the PC's boot order in the CMOS Setup so that the system first checks the CD-ROM drive for bootable media before the hard or floppy drives.

Basic Choices

Now it's time to make some basic choices about your system and geographic location in order for Linux to prepare the installation. Fortunately, the Linux GUI installer provides you with a comfortable "point and click" interface, along with context-sensitive help, so you can make informed decisions as the installation progresses.

Language   Select the language you would prefer to use for the installation and as the system default. Selecting a language will also help target your time zone configuration later in the installation (the installation program will try to define the appropriate time zone based on what you specify here). Once you select the appropriate language, click Next to continue.

Keyboard   Choose the keyboard model that best fits your system. If you cannot find an exact match, choose the best generic match for your keyboard type (such as Generic 101-key PC). Now choose the correct layout type for your keyboard (such as U.S. English). Creating special characters with multiple keystrokes (such as Ñ, Ô, and Ç) is done using *dead keys* (also known as *compose key sequences*). Dead keys are enabled by default—if you don't want to use them, select "Disable dead keys." To test your keyboard, use the blank text field at the bottom of the screen to enter text. Click Next to continue.

Mouse   Choose the correct mouse type and interface (i.e., serial or PS/2) for your system. If you cannot find an exact match, select one of the generic entries, based on the number of buttons and interface.

If you have a PS/2 or a bus mouse, you do not need to pick a port and device. If you have a serial mouse, choose the correct port and device that your serial mouse is on. The "Emulate 3 Buttons" checkbox allows you to use a two-button mouse as if it had three buttons. In general, the X-Window system is easier to use with a three-button mouse—you can emulate a third (middle) button by pressing both mouse buttons simultaneously.

Install Type   After a brief splash screen, it's time to select your install type. Red Hat Linux supports several classes of installation. A *workstation* installation is usually best if you're new to Linux. A workstation installation will create a system for your home or desktop use. A graphical, Windows-like environment will be installed. A *server* installation is most appropriate for you if you would like your system to function as a Linux-based server, and you don't want to customize your system configuration. A *laptop* installation simplifies Red Hat Linux installation on laptops. As with a workstation installation, it will make sure you have the appropriate packages needed, and offer you an automated installation environment. *Custom* installation allows you the greatest flexibility during your installation. You can choose your boot loader, the packages you want, and so on. Custom installations are most appropriate for users already familiar with Red Hat Linux installations and needing complete flexibility. If you already have a version of Red Hat Linux (3.0.3 or greater) running on your system, and you need the latest packages and kernel version, then an *upgrade* installation is most appropriate.

Managing Linux Partitions

At this point in the installation, you'll need to create partitions for Linux—this is a bit different than Windows-type partitioning. Under Linux, each partition is *mounted* at boot time. Mounting makes the contents of that partition available as if it were just another directory on the system. For example, the root directory (/) is on the first (root) partition. A subdirectory called **/usr** exists on the root directory, and additional partitions can be mounted under the **/usr** directory. Since all the mounted partitions appear as a unified directory tree (rather than separate drives), the installation software does not differentiate between one partition and another. The only concern is which directory each file goes into. The installation process automatically distributes its files across all the mounted partitions (so long as the mounted partitions represent different parts of the directory tree where files are usually placed). The most significant grouping of Linux files happens in the **/usr** directory, where all of the actual programs reside. A typical Linux tree structure is shown in Figure 25-1.

Let's look at each of these major partitions:

- **/usr**   This is where all the program files will reside (similar to the Program Files folder under Windows).

- **/home**   This is where every user's home directory will be (assuming this server will house them). This is useful for keeping users from consuming an entire disk and leaving other critical components (such as log files) without space.

- **/etc**   This partition contains many of the Linux configuration files and directories. If you're looking for files that affect the setup of a Linux platform, this is the place to check.

- **/var**   This is the final destination for log files. Since log files can be affected by outside users (such as individuals visiting a Web site), relegating logs to a separate partition can prevent a Denial of Service (DoS) attack by generating so many log entries the entire disk fills.

- **/tmp**   Temporary files are located here. Since any user can write to this directory (similar to the **C:\TEMP** directory under Windows), you need to make sure that users don't fill the entire disk by keeping it on a separate partition.

```
/     (root)
/usr
      /usr/share
      /usr/include
      /usr/lib
      /usr/bin
      /usr/doc
/home
/etc
/tmp
/var
/boot
```

FIGURE 25-1   The Linux tree structure is composed of mounted partitions that appear as directories under the system's root.

■ **Swap**   This is where the virtual memory file is stored. While Linux (and other UNIX versions) can use a normal disk file for virtual memory—the way Windows does—having the swap file on its own partition improves performance.

Linux provides some options for automatic partitioning, and allows you to have some control concerning what data is removed (if any) from your system. You have three options:

■ *Remove all Linux partitions on this system.* Select this option to remove only Linux partitions (partitions created from a previous Linux installation). This will not remove other partitions you may have on your hard drive(s).

■ *Remove all partitions on this system.* Select this option to remove all partitions on your hard drive(s), including partitions created by other operating systems such as Windows 9x/NT/2000.

■ *Keep all partitions and use existing free space.* Select this option to retain your current data and partitions—assuming that you have enough free space available on your hard drive(s) for the Linux installation.

Using your mouse, choose the hard drive(s) where you want Red Hat Linux to be installed. If you have two or more hard drives, you can choose which hard drive(s) should contain this installation. Unselected hard drives (and any data on them) will not be touched. To review and make any necessary changes to the partitions created by automatic partitioning, select the Review option. After selecting Review and clicking Next to move forward, you will see the partitions created for you in Disk Druid. You will also be able to make modifications to these partitions if they do not meet your needs. Click Next to proceed once you have made your selections.

Boot Loader

In order to boot your Red Hat Linux system without a boot disk, you usually need to install a boot loader. You can choose to install either GRUB (selected by default) or LILO (LInux LOader). GRUB is a software boot loader that can be used to start Red Hat Linux, as well as other operating systems such as Windows 9x. If you choose *not* to install a boot loader, make sure that you create a boot disk at the end of installation, or have another way to boot Linux (such as a third-party boot loader). Once you have chosen to install a boot loader (GRUB or LILO), you must determine where it will be installed. You may install your boot loader in one of two places:

- **The master boot record (MBR)**   The MBR is a special area on your hard drive that is automatically loaded by your computer's BIOS, and is the earliest point at which the boot loader can take control of the boot process. This is the recommended place to install a boot loader, unless the MBR already starts another operating system loader (such as System Commander or OS/2's Boot Manager). If you install a boot loader in the MBR, GRUB (or LILO) will present a boot prompt when your machine starts. You can then boot Red Hat Linux or any other operating system that you have configured the boot loader to launch.

- **The first sector of your root partition**   This is recommended if you're already using another boot loader on your system (such as System Commander). In this case, your other boot loader will take control first. You can then configure that boot loader to start GRUB (or LILO), which will then boot Linux.

Select where you want GRUB (or LILO) to be installed on your system. If your system will use only Red Hat Linux, you should choose the MBR. For systems with Windows 9x, you should also install the boot loader to the MBR so that it can boot both operating systems. Every bootable partition is listed—including partitions used by other operating systems. The partition holding your Linux root file system will have a "Boot label" of **linux**. Other partitions may also have boot labels. If you would like to add boot labels for other partitions (or change an existing boot label), click once on the partition to select it, then change the boot label. Finally, you should create a GRUB password to protect your system. This will prevent users from passing options to the kernel, which can compromise your system security. Enter and confirm the password, then continue.

Network and Firewall Configuration
Next, you'll need to configure the network card in your PC. If you have multiple NIC devices, you'll see a tab for each device. You may switch between devices (for example, between **eth0** and **eth1**), and the information you provide on each tab will be specific to that particular device. Indicate if you would like to configure your IP address using DHCP (Dynamic Host Configuration Protocol). If you select "Activate on boot", your network interface will be started each time the system boots. Next, enter the IP Address, Netmask, Network, and Broadcast addresses where applicable. If you have a fully qualified domain name for the network device, enter it in the Hostname field. Finally, enter the Gateway and Primary DNS addresses (and the Secondary DNS and Ternary DNS addresses if applicable). Click Next to continue.

Red Hat Linux integrates firewall protection for enhanced system security. Choose the appropriate security level for your system: High, Medium, or No firewall. If you choose High security, your system will not accept connections (other than the default settings) that are not explicitly defined by you. By default, only DNS and DHCP connections are allowed. If you're connecting your system to the Internet, but do not plan to run a server, this is the safest choice. If additional services are needed, you can choose Customize to allow specific services through the firewall.

If you choose Medium security, your firewall will not allow remote machines to have access to certain resources on your system. If you want to allow resources such as RealAudio, while still blocking access to normal system services, choose medium and select Customize to allow specific services through the firewall. The No firewall option provides complete access to your system, and does no security checking. This should only be selected if you're running on a trusted network (not the Internet) or plan to do more firewall configuration later. Choose Customize to add trusted devices or allow additional incoming services.

Language and Time Zone

Red Hat Linux can install and support multiple languages for use on your system. You must select a language to use as the default language (the default language will be used on your Linux system once installation is complete). If you choose to install other languages, you can change your default language after the installation. In most cases, you're only going to use one language on your system, so selecting that one language will save significant disk space. To use more than one language on your system, check the specific languages to be installed (or select all available languages).

You can set your time zone by selecting your computer's physical location, or by specifying your time zone's offset from coordinated universal time (UTC). Notice the Location and UTC Offset tabs at the top of the screen. The first tab allows you to configure your time zone by your location. You can specify different areas to view on the map, or click on a specific city—a red X will appear indicating your selection. You can also scroll through a list and choose a time zone. The second tab allows you to specify a UTC offset. There is a list of offsets to choose from, as well as an option to set daylight saving time. Please check the "System clock uses UTC" box if you know that your system is set to UTC.

Account Configuration

Next, the Account Configuration screen allows you to set your root password. Additionally, you can set up user accounts to log in with once the installation is complete. These are particularly important steps in the Linux setup process, and you should put a bit of thought into secure passwords.

Root Password   Your root account is similar to the administrator account used on Windows NT/2000 machines. The root account is used to install packages, upgrade RPMs, and perform most system maintenance functions (such as managing user accounts). Logging in as root gives you complete control over your Linux system, so password selection should be a serious issue. As a rule, use the root account *only* for system administration, and create a nonroot account for your general use (covered in the next section). By working through an ordinary account for everyday use, then switching to the root account for important management tasks, you'll minimize the chances of a typo or an incorrect command impairing your system.

The installation program will prompt you to set a root password for your system (you *must* enter a root password, or the installation program will not let you proceed). The root password must be at least six characters long, and you must enter the password twice for confirmation. Remember that the password is case sensitive. If you write down your password, keep it in a secure place. However, it is recommended that you do not document any password you create.

A root password is the administrative password for your Linux system. You should only log in as root when needed for system maintenance. Changes made as root can have implications for your entire system.

User Account   This is also a good point for you to create at least one user account for yourself so that you'll be able to immediately log on to the Linux system once the installation is finished. This lets you easily log into your computer without having to switch to the root first in order to create your user account. Enter a brief account name, then enter and confirm a password for that user account. Enter the full name of the account user and press Add. Your account information will be added to the account list, and the user account fields will be cleared so that you can add another user (if you'd like to set up several accounts in advance). You can also Edit or Delete the user accounts you have created.

Package Selection

Linux operating systems (such as Red Hat) include a large number of optional features (called *packages*) that can be installed. Packages include the preferred desktop, Web and FTP servers, news servers, SQL servers, and so on. At this point, you'll need to select the additional package(s) to be installed. If you have plenty of space available on the system (about 1.7GB), you can certainly opt to install additional packages now, but running unnecessary packages may have an adverse effect on the server's performance—not to mention security implications. You can select components (which group packages together according to function such as C Development, Networked Workstation, or Web Server), individual packages, or a combination of the two. To select a component, click on the checkbox beside it. Select each component you wish to install. This is the easiest way to proceed.

If you want more control over the files placed on your Linux system, you may select packages individually. Check the "Select Individual Packages" box at the bottom of the screen. After selecting the components you wish to install, you may then select or deselect individual packages. You can choose to view the individual packages in tree view or flat view. *Tree view* allows you to see the packages grouped by application type, while *flat view* lets you to see all of the packages in an alphabetical listing on the right of the screen. For example, tree view shows you a listing of package groups. When you expand this list and pick one group, the list of packages in that group appears in the panel on the right. To select an individual package, double-click the checkbox beside the package name. A checkmark in the box means that a package has been selected, and package information will appear at the bottom of the screen.

Unresolved Dependencies Many software packages depend on other software packages that must be installed on your system. For example, many of the graphical Red Hat system administration tools require the **python** and **pythonlib** packages. To make sure your system has all the packages it needs in order to be fully functional, Red Hat Linux checks these *package dependencies* each time you install or remove software packages. If any package requires another package that you have not selected, the program presents a list of these unresolved dependencies, and gives you the opportunity to resolve them.

The Unresolved Dependencies screen appears *only* if you're missing packages that are needed by the packages you have selected. At the bottom of the screen (under the list of missing packages), an "Install packages to satisfy dependencies" checkbox is selected by default. If you leave this checked, the installation program will resolve package dependencies automatically by adding all required packages to the list of selected packages.

Video Configuration

X-Windows is the foundation for the Linux GUI. It is X-Windows that actually talks to the system's video hardware, and passes that information to the Gnome or KDE front end. The last bit of information needed by Linux prior to installation is the proper identification of your system's video adapter. The X Configuration screen will present a list of video cards for you to choose from. In most cases, Linux setup will identify your video system properly, but you should always double-check the selected video adapter against your hardware inventory. If your video card does not appear on the list, X may not support it. However, if you have technical knowledge about your card, you may choose the Unlisted Card option and attempt to configure it by matching your card's video chipset with one of the available X servers.

Next, enter the amount of video memory installed on your video card (such as 16MB or 32MB). It will not damage your video card by choosing more memory than is available, but the X server may not start correctly if you do. If you decide that the values you have selected are incorrect, you can click the "Restore original values" button to return to the suggested settings. You can also select "Skip X Configuration" if you would rather configure X after the installation (or not at all).

The X-Window configuration tool will present a list of monitors for you to choose from. You can either use the monitor that is auto-detected for you or choose another monitor from the list. If your monitor doesn't appear on the list, select the most appropriate generic model available. If you select a generic monitor, setup will suggest horizontal and vertical sync ranges (these values are generally found in the documentation that accompanies your monitor). Suggested horizontal and vertical resolution ranges are also displayed on this screen. If you decide that the values you have selected are incorrect, you can click the "Restore original values" button to return to the suggested settings. Click Next when you've finished configuring your monitor.

Start the Installation

You should now see a final screen preparing you for the installation of Red Hat Linux. To cancel this installation process, press your computer's Reset button or use the CTRL-ALT-DEL keys to restart your machine. Otherwise, simply start the installation and allow it to proceed. Eventually, you'll need to insert the second Linux installation CD. Make it a point to create a boot diskette when you're prompted to do so. After the installation is complete, you'll be prompted to reboot the system. Remove any diskette in the diskette drive or CD in the CD-ROM drive. If you did not install a boot loader, you will need to use your boot disk now. After your computer's normal power-up sequence has completed, you should see the graphical boot loader prompt, which will allow you to boot the system and begin using your Linux platform.

For your reference, a complete log of your installation can be found in **/tmp/install.log** once you reboot your system.

CONFIGURING THE SERVER

The default settings for your Linux installation are not necessarily the correct settings for your network. Once Linux is successfully installed and the system has restarted, take a moment to review the Linux network settings, and make any needed changes to the configuration. Fortunately, the KDE and Gnome desktops under Red Hat Linux 7.2 offer a GUI dialog box that makes it easy to check and adjust network settings. Follow the steps below when you're using the KDE desktop:

1. Click the "K" logo in the lower-left corner of the desktop. This opens a list of application groups.
2. Select System | Network Configuration.
3. Enter the root password (you need this to adjust network settings), then click OK.
4. The Network Configuration dialog box opens (see Figure 25-2).

Hardware

The Hardware tab appears by default and lists the physical description of your NIC. Use the Hardware tab to Add, Edit, or Delete any physical Ethernet, modem, ISDN, and token ring hardware configurations in the Linux server. For example, you can select a NIC and use Edit to configure the type of adapter (manufacturer and model) and kernel device name for an Ethernet device. The type of adapter you select determines which kernel module (driver) is loaded for the network interface card. After selecting the adapter, select the kernel device name for the network interface card (such as **/dev/eth0** or **/dev/eth1**). You can also configure the device's system resource settings such as IRQ or DMA.

Devices

The Devices tab (see Figure 25-3) allows you to Add, Edit, or Delete logical network devices related to your physical network hardware. For example, once you've installed or replaced a NIC and identified it

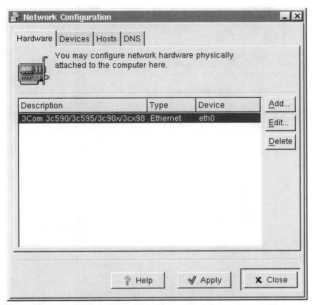

FIGURE 25-2   The Linux Network Configuration dialog box lets you configure the physical and logical aspects of the PC's network connection.

properly in the Hardware tab, use the Device tab to configure its network attributes. Highlight the desired device and click Edit. A Device dialog box will open—for example, an Ethernet device will be shown in an Ethernet Device dialog box where you can adjust General, Protocol, and Hardware Device settings. The General tab gives the device a nickname, lets you activate the device when the computer boots, and allows users to enable and disable the device. The Protocols tab lets you edit the TCP/IP settings such as the IP address (including DHCP), hostname, and static network routes. Use the Hardware Device tab to configure a device alias. A *device alias* allows you to set up multiple virtual devices for one physical device.

Hosts

The Hosts tab (see Figure 25-4) allows you to Add, Edit, or Delete static IP address mappings, which are stored in the **/etc/hosts** file. This file contains IP addresses and the hostnames to which the IP addresses should be resolved. When your system tries to resolve a hostname to an IP address (or determine the hostname for an IP address), it refers to the **/etc/hosts** file before using the name servers (if you're using the default Red Hat Linux configuration). If the IP address is listed in the **/etc/hosts** file, the name servers are not used. To add an entry to the **/etc/hosts** file, click Add in the Hosts tab, provide the requested information, and click OK. Click Apply to write the entry to the file.

DNS

If your Linux system is part of a network, it's a good idea to employ a DNS server. Name servers are used to look up other hosts on the network, so the DNS tab allows you to configure the system's hostname, domain, name servers, and search domain. The DNS tab (see Figure 25-5) lets you configure the system's hostname and domain, and specify up to three DNS server addresses. You can also use this dialog box to

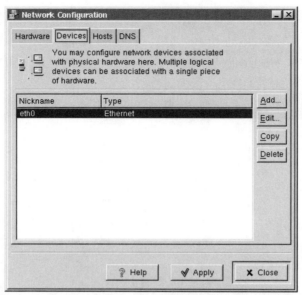

FIGURE 25-3   The Devices tab lets you configure the logical elements of NIC identification.

Edit or Delete domain names in the DNS search path, and change the search order of domain names. Keep in mind that the name server entries do not configure the system to be a name server.

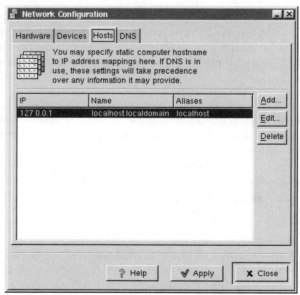

FIGURE 25-4   The Hosts tab lets you configure static IP mapping on the Linux system.

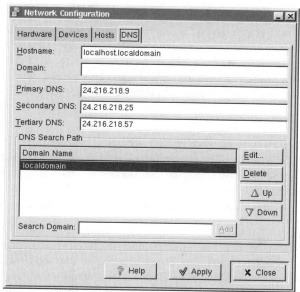

FIGURE 25-5 The DNS tab lets you identify domain name servers for your Linux system.

 When updating the Linux system configuration, remember to apply and save any changes. You typically do not need to reboot the Linux system for your changes to take effect.

CHECK THE CONNECTION

Once the Linux system is configured and receiving its IP address from your network's DHCP server, check that the new system appears when other workstations browse the network. For example, the Linux system should appear in Network Neighborhood or My Network Places under Windows 9x/2000. You'll see it as an icon with its workgroup name (i.e., a default workgroup of Mygroup, and a default name of Localhost). Remember that even though the new Linux system may appear in your LAN, you still need to establish shares on it before other users can share files and other resources like printers. You may need to configure Samba on the Linux system so that Windows users can access Linux shares.

Basic Administration

Now that you've successfully installed, configured, and tested Red Hat Linux on your new server platform, it's time to focus on the more involved tasks of server administration. Proper administration helps to ensure that your servers remain productive and secure, so you must develop and enforce security policies that are appropriate for your network environment. Under Linux, *users* can either be people (accounts tied to a physical user) or logical users (accounts that exist for applications so that they can perform specific tasks). Both types of users have a user ID (or UID, which is usually unique) and group ID (or GID). By comparison, *groups* represent logical organization on the system—groups tie users together and give them permissions to read, write, or execute a given file. Any file created is assigned a user and group when it is made. It is also assigned separate read, write, and execute permissions for the file's owner, the group assigned to the file, and any other users on that host. The administrator (root) can then change the user and group of a particular file (as well as the permissions on that file). This part of the chapter covers basic administrative duties like adding new users, deleting old users, changing passwords, and so on.

USER ACCOUNTS

An administrator must be concerned with the state of user accounts. In order to access a Linux system, every network user (even the administrator—or *root*) must have a user account on the server. The user account defines the user's name (the name by which the user is known to the system) and the user's password, along with an assortment of other information specific to each user. A Linux server provides graphical tools that allow you to create, maintain, and delete user accounts with a minimum of fuss.

New User Accounts

You'll need to create new accounts whenever a new user is added to the network (or needs to use a particular system). Accounts are handled through the Linux User Manager. To start the User Manager, click the "K" logo in the lower-left corner of the desktop, select Red Hat | System | User Manager. The User Manager dialog box will open (see Figure 25-6). User Manager allows you to view, modify, add, and delete local users and groups. Click the Users tab to view a list of all local users on the system, or click the Groups tab for a list of all local groups on the system. If you need to find a specific user or group, type the first few letters of the name in the Filter by field, then press ENTER or click the "Apply filter" button. The filtered list will be displayed. Table 25-1 shows the listing of standard users (people and processes) installed with Linux.

To add a new user, click the New User button at the top of the User Manager. A Create New User dialog box will appear (see Figure 25-7). Type the username and full name for the new user in the appropriate fields. Type the user's password in the Password and Confirm Password fields (the password must be at least six characters or longer—preferably with a combination of letters, numbers, and special characters). Now select a login shell. If you're not sure which shell to select, simply accept the default value of **/bin/bash**. The default home directory is **/home/<username>**, though you can certainly change the home directory that is created for the user (or you may choose not to create the home directory by deselecting "Create home directory").

Red Hat Linux also employs a *user private group* (or UPG) scheme. The UPG scheme does not add or change the way UNIX handles groups—it simply offers a new convention. By default, a unique group with the user's name is created whenever you create a new user. If you don't want to create this group, deselect "Create new group for this user." Click OK to create the user. To add the user to more user groups, click on the User tab, select the user, and click Properties. In the User Properties window, select the Groups tab. Select the groups that you want the user to be a member of (more on group assignments later in the chapter).

Shadow Passwords

If you are in a multiuser environment (and not using a networked authentication scheme such as Kerberos), you should consider using shadow utilities—also known as *shadow passwords*—for the enhanced protection offered for your system's authentication files. In fact, Linux password files are readable by default, so professional administrators often require the use of shadow passwords to decrease password vulnerability. During the installation of Red Hat Linux, shadow password protection for your

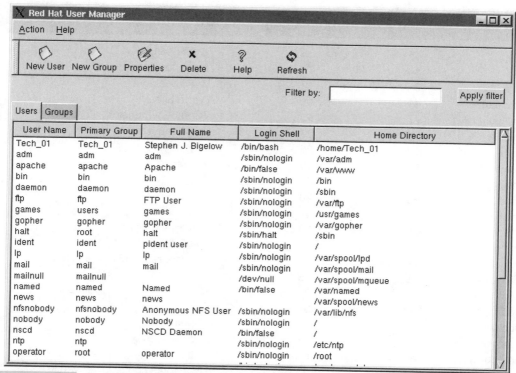

FIGURE 25-6   The User Manager dialog box allows you to administer users and groups.

TABLE 25-1	LISTING OF STANDARD USERS UNDER RED HAT LINUX 7.2

USER	UID	GID	HOME DIRECTORY	SHELL
Adm	3	4	/var/adm	
Amanda	33	6	/var/lib/amanda/	
Apache	48	48	/var/www	
Bin	1	1	/bin	
Daemon	2	2	/sbin	
Ftp	14	50	/var/ftp	
Games	12	100	/usr/games	
Gdm	42	42	/var/gdm	
Gopher	13	30	/usr/lib/gopher-data	
Halt	7	0	/sbin	/sbin/halt
Ident	98	98	/	/sbin/nologin
Junkbust	73	73	/etc/junkbuster	

TABLE 25-1   LISTING OF STANDARD USERS UNDER RED HAT LINUX 7.2 (*CONTINUED*)

Ldap	55	55	/var/lib/ldap	
Lp	4	7	/var/spool/lpd	
Mail	8	12	/var/spool/mail	
Mailman	41	41	/var/mailman	
Mailnull	47	47	/var/spool/mqueue	
Mysql	27	27	/var/lib/mysql	
Named	25	25	/var/named	
News	9	13	/var/spool/news	
Nobody	99	99	/	
Nscd	28	28	/	
Operator	11	0	/root	
Piranha	60	60	/etc/sysconfig/ha	
Postgres	26	26	/var/lib/pgsql	
Pvm	24	24	/usr/share/pvm3	/bin/bash
Radvd	75	75	/	
Root	0	0	/root	/bin/bash
Rpc	32	32	/	
Rpcuser	29	29	/var/lib/nfs	
Rpm	37	37	/var/lib/rpm	
Shutdown	6	0	/sbin	/sbin/shutdown
Squid	23	23	/var/spool/squid	/dev/null
Sync	5	0	/sbin	/bin/sync
Uucp	10	14	/var/spool/uucp	
Wnn	49	49	/var/lib/wnn	
Xfs	43	43	/etc/X11/fs	

system is enabled by default along with MD5 passwords (an alternative method of encrypting passwords for storage on your system). Shadow passwords offer several distinct advantages over Linux/UNIX password storage methods, and include features such as

- Improved system security placing the encrypted passwords (normally found in **/etc/passwd**) into **/etc/shadow**, which is readable only by root.
- Information concerning password aging (how long since a password was last changed).
- Control over how long a password can remain before the user is required to change it.
- The ability to use the **/etc/login.defs** file to enforce a security policy, especially concerning password aging.

Changing User Accounts

It will be necessary for you to update various user accounts as network needs change over time. Open the User Manager dialog box, select the Users tab, select the user from the User list, and click the Properties button (or

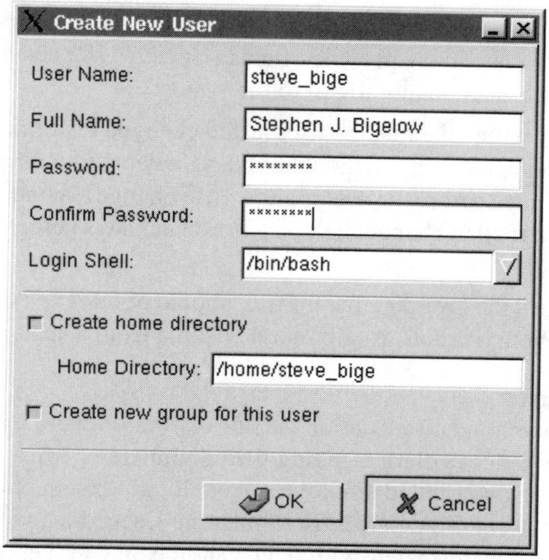

FIGURE 25-7   Enter details for new user accounts in the Create New User dialog box.

choose Action | Properties from the menu). The User Properties dialog box will appear (see Figure 25-8), and is divided into four tabs:

■   **User Data**   This tab contains the user's basic information that was configured when you initially added the user. Use this tab to change the user's full name, password, home directory, or login shell.

FIGURE 25-8   Modify user data, account and password info, and group assignments through the User Properties dialog box.

- **Account Info**   This tab lets you select "Enable account expiration" so that the account expires on a certain date (enter the expiration date in the provided fields). Select "User account is locked" to lock out the user's account so that the user cannot log in to the system.

- **Password Info**   This tab shows the date that the user lasted changed his or her password. To force the user to change their password after a certain number of days, select "Enable password expiration". You can also set the number of days before the user is allowed to change his or her password, the number of days before the user is warned to change their password, and days before the account becomes inactive.

- **Groups**   This tab lets you select the group(s) that the user should be assigned to. You may assign the user to several or all groups, though this is usually not advisable from a security standpoint.

Removing User Accounts

When users leave the organization or move to a location outside of your domain, it is usually good policy to delete the unused account. This reduces clutter (giving the administrator fewer accounts to manage) and enhances security by preventing disgruntled employees from logging on later or passing their logon information to other unauthorized users. To delete a user, open the User Manager, select the Users tab, select the user to be removed, then click the Delete button. Depending on your version of Linux, you may be asked what you want to do with the user's data (such as archive the data, delete it, or leave it in place). If you suspect that you'll need to access the user's work files, leave the data in place. If the user might come back, archive the data (or simply lock out the account instead). Otherwise, just delete the data and reclaim the disk space.

USER GROUPS

Linux works a bit differently from operating systems like Windows. Where Windows makes a distinct separation between users and groups, Linux tends to blur that line a bit—mainly because user accounts are often coupled with a corresponding group automatically. For example, creating a user called **pwruser1** will also create a **pwruser1** group for that user by default (unless you deselect "Create new group for this user" when establishing the account). With a group generated for every user automatically, it's possible for the list of groups to grow unwieldy in a very short time.

Creating a Group

Still, Linux allows unique groups to be created and managed through the User Manager dialog box (as in Figure 25-6, earlier). Click the Groups tab to see a current listing of groups. As with users, there is a set of standard groups that are implemented during a Linux installation. Table 25-2 shows the standard groups as shown in the **/etc/group** file. To add a new group, click the New Group button. A Create New Group dialog box will appear where you'll be prompted to enter a group name. Type the name of the new group and click OK—the new group name will appear in the list.

To view the properties of an existing group, select the group from the Group list and click the Properties button (or choose Action | Properties from the menu). A Group Properties dialog box will appear. The Group Data tab simply lists the name of the group (which you can change if necessary). The Group Users tab (see Figure 25-9) displays which users are members of the group. Select additional users to add them to the group, and deselect users to remove from the group. Click OK or Apply to modify the users in your selected group, and check the Group list to see that the desired users have been added to your group. Finally, you can delete a group that's no longer needed. With the Groups tab open in your User Manager, simply select the group to be removed, and click the Delete button.

TABLE 25-2 LISTING OF STANDARD GROUPS UNDER RED HAT LINUX 7.2

GROUP	GID	MEMBERS
Adm	4	root, adm, daemon
apache	48	apache
bin	1	root, bin, daemon
daemon	2	root, bin, daemon
dip	40	
disk	6	root
floppy	19	
ftp	50	
games	20	
gdm	42	gdm
gopher	30	
ident	98	ident
junkbust	73	junkbust
kmem	9	
ldap	55	ldap
lp	7	daemon, lp
mail	12	mail
mailman	41	mailman
mailnull	47	mailnull
man	15	
mem	8	
mysql	27	mysql
named	25	named
news	13	news
nobody	99	
nscd	28	nscd
piranha	60	piranha
popusers	45	
postgres	26	postgres
pppusers	44	
pvm	24	pvm
root	0	root
rpc	32	rpc
rpcusers	29	
rpm	37	rpm
slipusers	46	
slocate	21	
squid	23	squid
sys	3	root, bin, adm
tty	5	

TABLE 25-2   LISTING OF STANDARD GROUPS UNDER RED HAT LINUX 7.2 (*CONTINUED*)

GROUP	GID	MEMBERS
users	100	
utmp	22	
uucp	14	uucp
wheel	10	root
wnn	49	wnn
xfs	43	xfs

LINUX SHARES

Once a Linux server is running on your network, you'll generally want to configure other network PCs to access files and printers across the network connection. With Linux, you'll need to employ the Samba utility (using the SMB protocol) to share files and printers across a network connection. Samba is particularly useful if you have a network with both Windows and Linux machines. Samba will allow files and printers to be shared by all the systems in your network, though the process is a bit more involved than creating shares in a Windows system. For example, if you have a user account named **Tech_01** in the default folder of **/home/Tech_01**, you can select this "folder" as a share in the **smb.conf** file.

Linux "shares" can be confusing—especially if you're used to the ease of Windows file and folder sharing. Linux does not provide "shares" the way that Windows does. This discussion is only a brief overview of Linux shares. Linux documentation includes far more information regarding the use of Samba to connect Linux machines to a Windows network. For more information on Samba, check **www.redhat.com/support/resources/print_file/samba.html**. Samba is not required for pure Linux-to-Linux file sharing.

Updating SMB.CONF

Samba uses **/etc/samba/smb.conf** as its configuration file. If you change this configuration file, the changes will not take effect until you restart the Samba daemon with the command **service smb restart**. The default configuration file (**smb.conf**) in Red Hat Linux 7.2 allows users to view their Linux home directories as a Samba share on the Windows machine after they log in using the same username and password. It also shares any printers configured for the Red Hat Linux system as Samba shared printers, so you can attach a printer to your Red Hat Linux system and print to it from the Windows machines on your network. To specify the Windows workgroup and description string, edit the following lines in your **smb.conf** file:

```
workgroup = WORKGROUPNAME
server string = BRIEF COMMENT ABOUT SERVER
```

Replace **workgroupname** with the name of the Windows workgroup to which this Linux machine should belong. The **brief comment about server** is an optional entry, and will be the Windows comment about the Samba system. To create a Samba share directory on your Linux system, edit the Shares section to your **smb.conf** file such as in Figure 25-10. This allows the **Tech_01** share in the **/home/Tech_01** path to be publicly available to the network.

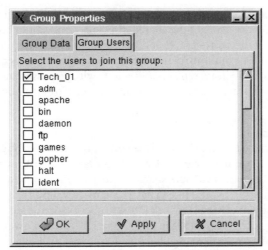

FIGURE 25-9   Assign users to one or more groups using the Group Properties dialog box.

Linux Connections

To connect to a Samba share from a Linux system, from a shell prompt, type the following command:

```
smbclient //hostname/sharename -U username
```

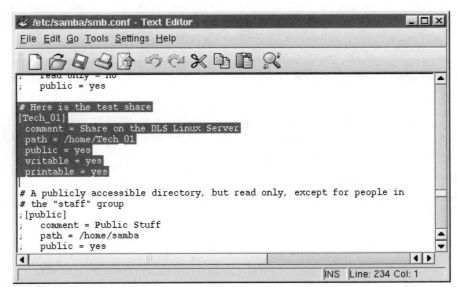

FIGURE 25-10   A sample of the updated **smb.conf** file creating a Linux share through Samba

You will need to replace *hostname* with the hostname or IP address of the Samba server you want to connect to, replace *sharename* with the name of the shared directory you want to browse, and exchange *username* with the Samba username for the system. Enter the correct password (or press ENTER if no password is required for the user). If you see the **smb:\>** prompt, you have logged in successfully. If you wish to browse the contents of your home directory, replace *sharename* with your username. If the **-U** switch is not used, the username of the current user is passed to the Samba server. To exit **smbclient**, type **exit** at the **smb:\>** prompt.

Windows 9x Connections

Once you've established a share on the Linux PC, edited the **smb.conf** file properly, and restarted the **smb** service, you should see the Linux server in the Network Neighborhood of your Windows 9x clients. Simply browse to the Linux server to open the available share(s). Keep in mind that you may need to enter a password before accessing the share(s). If you'd like to have a share show up as a drive letter (such as **e:**, **f:**, and so on), right-click on it and select Map Network Drive to choose a drive letter. You can also specify whether you want to reconnect each time you log in to Windows. If you don't want to browse Network Neighborhood each time you need to access a share (and you don't want to assign a drive letter), you can also drag an icon of a share onto your desktop.

Windows NT/2000 Passwords

Although Windows NT/2000 machines should easily browse Linux shares through My Network Places, differences in the password scheme between Linux and Windows NT/2000 raise a compatibility issue for technicians. The Microsoft SMB protocol originally used plain text passwords, but Windows 2000 and Windows NT 4.0 (with Service Pack 3 or higher) require encrypted Samba passwords. To use Samba between a Red Hat Linux system and a system with Windows NT/2000, you can either edit your Windows Registry to use plain text passwords, or configure Samba on your Linux system to use encrypted passwords. If you choose to modify your Registry, you must do so for all your Windows NT/2000 machines—a tricky and time-consuming proposition. To configure Samba on your Red Hat Linux system to use encrypted passwords, follow these steps from the command prompt:

1. Create a separate password file for Samba. For example, type the following command to create one based on your existing **/etc/passwd** file:

```
cat /etc/passwd | mksmbpasswd.sh > /etc/samba/smbpasswd
```

2. The **mksmbpasswd.sh** script is installed in your **/usr/bin** directory with the Samba package. Now use the following command to change permissions on the Samba password file so that only the root has read and write permissions:

```
chmod 600 /etc/samba/smbpasswd
```

3. The script does not copy user passwords to the new file. To set each Samba user's password, use the following command (and replace *username* with each user's username):

```
smbpasswd username
```

4. A Samba user account will not be active until a Samba password is set for it. The next step is to enable encrypted passwords in the Samba configuration file. In the file **smb.conf**, uncomment the following lines:

```
encrypt password = yes
smb passwd file = /etc/samba/smbpasswd
```

5. To have the changes take effect, restart Samba by typing the following command at a shell prompt:

```
service smb restart
```

 These types of procedures require you to have a knowledge of the Linux command-line interface. Refer to Linux documentation for specific command descriptions and details.

Further Study

Caldera Linux: **www.caldera.com**
Kerberos: **web.mit.edu/kerberos/www**
Linux: **www.linux.org**
NSA: **www.nsa.gov**
RedHat Linux: **www.redhat.com**
Samba Tips: **www.redhat.com/support/resources/tips/Samba-Tips/Samba-Tips.html**
SANS: **www.sans.org**
SuSe Linux: **www.suse.com/index_us.html**

26

LOGON TROUBLESHOOTING

A particularly frustrating experience for users is when they have trouble just trying to log on to the computer network. The problem here could be something as basic as a user not having permission to use the color printer, or something more insidious—like not being able to log on whatsoever.

But login problems aren't just time-consuming irritations to the user. A study conducted by the Network Applications Consortium estimated that 70 percent of an administrator's time is spent resetting lost or forgotten passwords.

This chapter examines the issues surrounding logon in Windows, NetWare, and UNIX/Linux environments. In addition to basic logon issues, this chapter also covers user rights and permissions management, and how they can be administered.

Windows Logon

The various flavors of Windows offer different means of logon and user rights, account management, and permissions. In addition, scripts can be used to establish specific work environments for users and groups of users.

This section takes a closer look at what's involved for logon in a Windows environment, and how the logon process can be managed. Additionally, the issue of user rights and permissions management is explored to shed light on this subject.

THE NETLOGON SERVICE

In Windows, the NetLogon service is used by clients to establish a connection with NT, 2000, and .NET Servers. This service is necessary for you to log onto a domain. The logon process is explained in terms of action on the Windows client and the Windows server machines.

Clients

On Windows client machines, user login requests are processed by the Local Security Authority (LSA), and if there is no match to an entry in the local user account database, the LSA passes the request to the NetLogon service—which forwards the request to a domain controller. The NetLogon service on NT Servers passes these requests to the secure domain directory database or passes requests through to a controller in another domain if the resources requested are located in that domain.

The NetLogon service requires the Workstation and Server services. When connecting NT Workstation clients that have been configured in stand-alone or workgroup mode, be certain these services have been set for automatic startup. This can be verified and set in the Services window of the Control Panel. It also requires the Access this Computer from Network right, which is set in the User Manager. Note that the default settings for this right include permission for everyone to have access to the computer. This means that any domain user can sit at the client and log into the domain.

Before the NetLogon service can perform these operations, it must first locate the relevant machine (or machines in the case of NT Server NetLogon service). This process is called *discovery* and it begins as soon as the service is started on bootup. A client NetLogon service will try to "discover" the NetLogon service of the NT Server. If the received username and password information are in the security database, the machines establish a *secure communications channel*. If the discovery fails, the NetLogon service on the client will use cached information for the user, created from the last login. This means that the user will be logged into the client and will have the local privileges that existed at the time of the last login.

If discovery is successful, but no user account is found on the server, there are two possibilities:

- If Guest accounts are enabled and no Guest password is set, the user will be logged on as a Guest; otherwise, the login fails.

- In Windows NT, if the client is attempting to log in to a backup domain controller (BDC), the BDC NetLogon service will pass authentication through to the PDC if that machine is available. This can occur in cases where a user password has been changed at the PDC, but that change has not yet been replicated to the BDC (see more on this in the next section). In this case, the PDC would allow the login.

Clients *not* running a Windows client or server have their access to network resources authenticated by the NetLogon service on the appropriate domain controllers. However, users on these clients have no restrictions on their access to local resources.

Domain Controllers

The NetLogon service on domain controllers responds to domain client authentication requests and also establishes secure communication channels with all domain controllers with which it has trust relationships. On startup, the domain NetLogon service will attempt discovery with all trusted domains. If necessary, each domain is polled three times within 5 seconds of bootup. If the discovery fails in this period, the domain controller will repeat the attempt any time that a request for authentication is received from a client that requires access to resources outside the domain. If no requests are received, the controller will attempt discovery every 15 minutes.

In NT Server, this service receives requests for authentication from clients and passes requests through to trusted servers in other domains when necessary. This includes both logon authentication and requests to access resources (files or printers). If a logged-on user seeks to map a network drive outside the domain, the PDC NetLogon service will pass the request to the PDC or DC (if using Active Directory) of a trusted domain. If the username and password match the security database in that domain, the request will be honored. If there is a failure, the server will prompt the user to enter a username and password, thus allowing access if the user has two accounts in different domains, or knows the username and password of a valid account in that domain.

The NetLogon service is also responsible for synchronizing the security database between the domain controllers. Changes to user or group accounts (passwords, group membership, or user or group rights, for instance) are stored in a change log (kept both in memory and on disk \%*Systemroot*%**Netlogon.chg**). The default size of the change log is 64K, and once full, new changes bump the oldest changes out of the log file.

Windows 2000 and Kerberos

Windows 2000 adds an additional layer of security when a user logs on. When a user attempts to log on to a Windows 2000 workstation, the Kerberos security protocol is invoked. As such, logon involves the following steps (as illustrated in Figure 26-1):

1. *The user requests admission to the ticket-granting service for the domain.* To accomplish this, an authentication service (AS) exchange occurs between the Kerberos Security Support Provider (SSP) on the client and the Kerberos Key Distribution Center (KDC) on the domain controller. If the process is successful, the user will receive a ticket-granting ticket (TGT) that can be used for future logons.

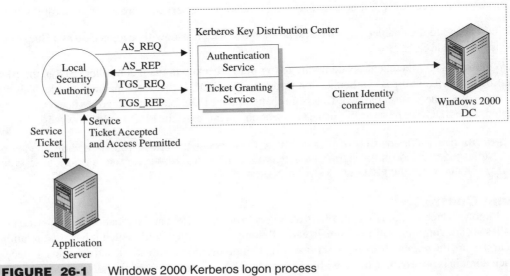

FIGURE 26-1 Windows 2000 Kerberos logon process

2. *The user requests a ticket for the computer.* A ticket granting service (TGS) exchange occurs between the Kerberos SSP on the client and the KDC for the user's account domain. The result is a ticket the user can present when requesting permission to access the network.

3. *The user requests permission to local system services on the computer.* In the final step, the Kerberos SSP presents a session ticket to the client computer's Local Security Authority (LSA). If the computer and the user are on different domains, an additional step is necessary. Before requesting a ticket for the computer, the Kerberos SSP must first ask the user's domain account KDC for a TGT good for admission to the KDC in the computer's account domain. Next, it presents the TGT to the KDC for a session ticket for the computer.

ACCOUNT POLICY ISSUES

In Windows NT, administrators use the System Policy Editor tool to manage user and computer configurations stored in the NT registry database. Using System Policy Editor, you create system policies to control user work environment and actions and to enforce configuration settings for all computers running NT.

Windows 2000/XP/.NET uses the Group Policy MMC snap-in tool, which offers enhancements over the System Policy Editor and provides refined capabilities for specifying user and computer configurations for users and user groups. Group policies define components of the user's environment that system administrators need to manage, such as policy settings for security options, software deployment, and scripts.

Group Policy Snap-In Extensions

The Group Policy snap-in includes several snap-in extensions. A snap-in extension can expand both User and Computer Configuration nodes in either the Windows Settings node or the Software Settings node. Snap-ins typically extend both of these nodes, but usually with different options. The following list describes the snap-in extensions included with Windows 2000:

- **Administrative Templates**   Includes registry-based policy settings, which are used to control the registry settings that manage the appearance and functionality of the desktop. It also manages disk quotas and remote installation features.
- **Security Settings**   This extension establishes security configurations for computers within a Group Policy object. You can establish local computer, domain, and network security settings.
- **Software Installation**   Used to manage software distribution within your organization.
- **Scripts**   Used to automate computer startup and shutdown, and user logon and logoff.

Make Your Own Group Policy Snap-Ins

You can build your own custom Group Policy that includes selections from the Group Policy snap-in extensions. For example, you could create a snap-in that just uses the Software Installation snap-in. This feature allows you to establish modular settings to create a customized console. Next, you must determine which users and groups you will allow access to the Group Policy object and the associated Active Directory location.

To start Group Policy as a stand-alone snap-in, follow these steps:

1. Click Start, click Run, type **MMC**, and then press ENTER.

2. In the MMC window on the Console menu, select Add/Remove Snap-in.

3. On the Standalone tab, click Add.

4. In the Add Snap-in dialog box, click Group Policy and then select Add.

5. In the Select Group Policy object (GPO) dialog box, click Browse to find the GPO you want to manage.

6. Click Extensions, and select the extension snap-ins you want to use.

7. Click Finish.

8. Click OK. The Group Policy snap-in opens with focus on the GPO you specified.

9. After you specify the policies you want to use, click Save As on the Console menu to save your settings (make sure you save your file with a **.msc** file extension).

To set access permissions, use the Security tab on the Properties page of the selected GPO. These permissions allow or deny access to the GPO by specified groups.

USER RIGHTS

When a user is added to a Windows environment, various rights can be immediately assigned to him or her. This streamlines the process of establishing new user accounts because a number of rights and privileges can be established and waiting for the user when they log on.

Creating Users

To create a new user account in Windows 2000, open Computer Management from Administrative Tools in the Start menu. In the console tree, in Local Users and Groups, click Users. Next, click Action, and then click New User.

Creating a new user account in Windows NT is similar, but you use the User Manager instead of the Computer Management tool.

Next, fill out the information in the dialog box shown in Figure 26-2 (this is used in Windows 2000 and XP, but the information sought is similar in a Windows NT environment).

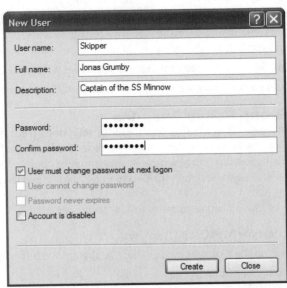

FIGURE 26-2 The New User dialog box asks for the user's screen name, real name, and password options.

Select or clear the check boxes for the following:

- User must change password at next logon
- User cannot change password
- Password never expires
- Account is disabled

To add another user, click Create and repeat the aforementioned process. Otherwise, to finish, click Create and then click Close.

> A username cannot be identical to any other user or group name on the computer being administered. It can contain up to 20 characters (uppercase or lowercase), except the following:
> " / \ [ ] ; : | = , + * ? < >
> Also, a username cannot consist solely of periods or spaces.

In NT, the User Manager also houses three policy editors. They are found under the menu item Policies and are called Account, User Rights, and Audit. These policy editors are also found in the Windows 2000 Security Policy tool. They are used to provide a homogenous environment for the users as well as to set some security measures against weak passwords, unauthorized logon attempts, and rights granted unknowingly to users.

The Account policy editor (here using a Windows XP interface) illustrated in Figure 26-3 allows you full control over users' password properties and account lockout for all users in the domain. It is possible to set password criteria based on length, and you may force users to change their password after a given time. It can even disallow reusing passwords for a given amount of history. Account lockout is mostly used to disable an account if there has been a series of incorrect login attempts. This essentially is a security measure to prevent unauthorized users from trying repeatedly to guess a password. The settings you choose for both the password criteria and account lockout will depend on how much security you want to impose on the users.

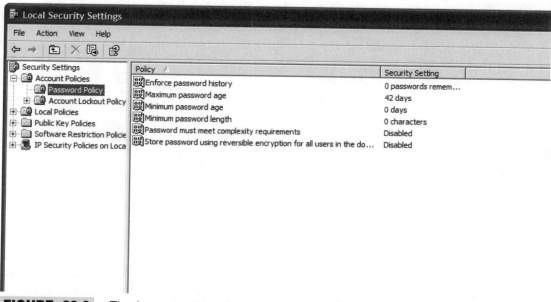

FIGURE 26-3 The Account policy editor sets logon policies for all users.

The User Rights assignment policy editor controls more precisely which rights a user or group may possess. In Windows NT, if you select Show Advanced User Rights, you will get a list of over 20 rights—ranging from simple rights, such as the ability to change the time, to more obscure rights like the ability to create a token object. For example, in Figure 26-4 (shown on a Windows XP computer) the right to log on locally to the machine is granted to the Administrators, Backup Operators, Guests, Power, and Users. You can easily add or remove groups or users, although you should be aware of the ramifications of doing so—many rights may not seem crucial to the functioning of an account, but prove to be after you remove it. Be cautious adding or removing rights, because the result may not always be what you intended!

Because the job of the Audit policy is to set which *system* events are to be saved in the security log, this tool seems out of place in the User Manager. The security log can be viewed using the Event Viewer in Administrative Tools. Figure 26-5 shows the GUI for selecting which events to audit. Figure 26-5 uses Windows XP, but the tool looks similar in other flavors of Windows. Here, failed logon attempts, successful access of directory services, and all privilege uses are audited. This information may prove quite useful in troubleshooting a system problem or sniffing out a potential intruder.

USER PROFILES

Many logon issues can be eliminated by using user profiles. These settings are created for every user who logs onto a computer for the first time. User profiles control more detailed information about the user's

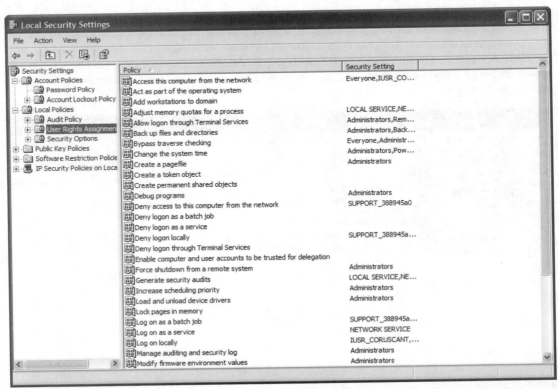

FIGURE 26-4 User Rights Assignment Policy editor assigns specific rights to users or groups.

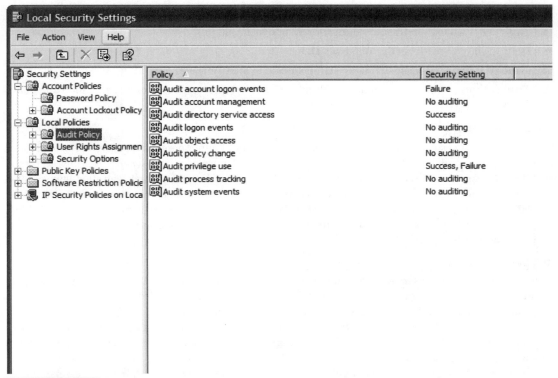

FIGURE 26-5   The Audit policy editor configures which events will be logged.

environment compared to system policies. They allow users to customize their desktops so that whatever changes they have made will be present next time they log on. If a user has a roaming profile, these settings will "follow" them to every computer on the network they log onto, providing a consistent user environment. If the administrator decides that users should have the same desktop environment each time they log on, mandatory profiles can be used.

Settings

User profiles are contained in a tree structure of folders in the **\%Systemroot%\Profiles\username** directory and also in a data file called **NTUSER.DAT**. The profile tree structure contains information about shortcuts, printers, recently accessed files, and other application-specific data. The **NTUSER.DAT** file contains cached information from the Windows NT registry **HKEY_CURRENT_USER**. This registry tree contains information about installed software, environmental settings, and general user-specific information.

User profiles can contain settings for the following:

- **Display**   Background, screen saver, and color scheme
- **Menu**   Start menu items and desktop icons
- **Mouse**   Settings for the mouse
- **Connections**   Network and printer connections

- **Window**   Layout maintains window sizes and positions
- **Explorer**   All user-definable settings for Windows Explorer
- **Help**   All bookmarks in the Windows Help system
- **Control Panel**   All user-definable settings made in the Control Panel
- **Applications**   All changes made to Windows user-specific applications such as the Calculator, Clock, Paint, HyperTerminal, and so forth

Local Profiles

There are three types of profiles offering you the flexibility to either control the users' environment or allow them to control their own desktop settings. Local profiles are generated when a user logs on for the first time. They are given a copy of the profile called Default User. From there, they can alter their settings, and expect them to be saved when they log off. Next time they log on, their own customized profile will be loaded. Local profiles can only be used for that system. If a user has accounts on more than one machine, each machine will have a separate user profile for that user. Changing a setting on one will have no effect on the other profiles.

Roaming Profiles

Roaming profiles allow users to create and maintain a single profile that is used throughout the domain. No matter where the user logs on, they will get the same desktop settings and their changes will be saved and reapplied next time they log on, regardless of which machine it is.

In a Windows 2000 environment (if you're using Active Directory), user profiles follow the user around the network. Under Windows NT, and in non-Active Directory environments, for users to have a roaming profile you must set up a path to their profile under User Manager for Domains under the Profile button. If you have many users, you might have an entry like *\\servername\profile path*%**username**%. This allows you to copy this user many times without having to change the name of the profile path, because you use the environmental variable %**username**%. Next, you need to go to the User Profiles tab in the Systems Properties window, found in the Control Panel. Here you can change the type of the profile from Local to Roaming if a path has been set up in User Manager for the user.

It is important to note that if you need to copy a profile from one user to another, you need to use the Copy To button. Simply copying the **NTUSER.DAT** file and the profile tree structure using File Manager or Explorer will not create the appropriate registry entries. Windows NT will not be aware of or know how to load the profile.

Mandatory Profiles

Mandatory profiles are a kind of roaming profile that can't be updated by users. Administrators and technical support staff would certainly appreciate it if everyone had the same desktop settings. This consistency would help support staff troubleshoot problems and talk users through problem resolution. Coupled with editing system policies, you can exert a great deal of control over the user's environment using a mandatory profile.

To change a normal roaming profile to a mandatory profile, copy a profile to another account, modify it to fit your needs, and simply change the name of **NTUSER.DAT** to **NTUSER.MAN**. Now when this user (or users if multiple users are going to use the same profile) logs on, your settings will be enforced and any changes they are permitted to make during that session will not be saved to the profile. For future modifications, you can make changes offline on a copy of the profile and then copy it over the working version of the profile.

LOGON SCRIPTS

Although user profiles can control most aspects of the user's environment, there are times when you still need to run a program or a batch file when the user logs on. To do this, you enter the path and name of the script in User Properties, Profile button in the User Manager for Domains or the Local Users and Groups MMC snap-in in Windows 2000. Since user profiles can specify which network connections to make, you no longer need to include those in the script. However, other operating systems' clients that don't have user profiles can take advantage of logon scripts. Another situation in which you'd employ a logon script is for running a certain application. For example, you might want all users to run a virus scan program at login.

Historically, people have placed script commands in a batch file to run at logon. You could, for example, have all users mount a shared drive on a server by including

```
net use s: \\servername\sharename
```

Troubleshooting Scripts

In Windows environments, logon scripts can be used to define the environment in which the user is logging on. Establishing a logon script is a three-step process, which will vary depending on which version of Windows you are using. In Windows NT, the steps are as follows:

1. Open User Manager for Domains.
2. Double-click on the user from the generated list, then choose Profile.
3. Enter the filename of the logon script in the Logon Script Name text box.

In Windows 2000 and .NET, the process is similar, but uses the Microsoft Management Console (MMC):

1. Open the Local Users and Groups snap-in to the MMC.
2. Double-click on the user from the generated list, then choose Profile.
3. Enter the filename of the logon script in the Logon Script Name text box.

When entering the filename, it's important to be mindful of the file extension of your logon script. In a Windows environment, use **.bat** as the extension. If you use **.exe**, Windows perceives this as an executable file and launches the filename application. If there is no application, the logon script simply won't run. The following scenarios illustrate potential problems and their solutions when developing scripts for Windows logons.

Executable Launches Without a Command in the Logon Script   If a user complains about an unwanted application launching every time they log on, the first place to check is the logon script itself. If you don't see anything in the logon script that would be launching the application, the **autoexec.bat** file is the next stop. Run down the file, line by line, and ascertain whether or not the application is being started because of an entry in the **autoexec.bat** file. It's very likely that the command won't be present in either the logon script or the **autoexec.bat** file.

The next place to check is the system registry. Using the **regedit.exe** tool, open the system registry and navigate to HKEY_CURRENT_USER\Software\Microsoft\Windows\CurrentVersion. This is the registry key containing the configuration items that start whenever Windows starts.

The registry is not something to be trifled with. If you aren't 100 percent sure what you're doing, stay out of the registry. A simple typo in the registry can cause any number of horrible things to happen to your computer!

Examine the data in the entries named in "run." If there are any entries that indicate a program that will be run, open the data item and delete the entry.

Don't Reinvent the Wheel   You can save yourself some headaches when assigning logon scripts to users by having standard scripts on hand. When a new user comes on board, you simply give them the same script that other members of his or her group have. This streamlines the scripting process. First, you need not rewrite the script. Secondly, this method ensures that everyone in the group has the same properties identified in their script. Finally, it's a good way to avoid trouble. Because you know the script already works for others in the group, there's no worry that a typo will cause the script to malfunction.

In a Windows environment, you can use Group Policy to determine which network permissions your users will be able to access. However, there are any number of reasons why you might want to use a script. First, maybe you don't want to manage user permissions. Also, you might have to connect to a resource that is not manageable by Group Policy (like a setting associated with another operating system, and so forth).

We'll create a brief script to demonstrate what goes into the file. In this case, the script gives the user access to the active files on the organization's production server. The script is

```
net use z:\\production\current
```

In this example, there are three components to the script:

- The drive letter (in this case, z:)
- The name of the computer to which we want to grant access (in this case, the production server)
- The name of the share containing the desired files (in this case, current)

Next, name the script (ensuring to add **.bat**) to the end. This file might be called **production.bat**. Next, you indicate the path to the logon script, as mentioned earlier in this section.

Time Management   When you look at the details of a file or folder, you'll see a variety of information, including who created the file, when it was created, when it was last accessed, and so forth. Since timestamps are so important, it's a good idea to use logon scripts to ensure that your client machines are in synchronization with your servers.

A simple script to accommodate time synchronization is

```
net time \\server /set /yes
```

The components of this script are as follows:

- **net time** is the command.
- **\\server** is the name of the server with which you want your client to synchronize time.
- **/set** tells your client to set its time with the server's value.
- **/yes** confirms that you wish to change the client's time and data to the value of the server.

Script Creation Tools   When creating scripts, it's important to use a text editor. Without pure, clean ASCII text, the script can be misread, causing errors and any number of problems. At first blush, you might be thinking that you don't want to use a word processor like Word to create your scripts. You're correct. However, if the next idea for script creation is Windows Notepad, try again.

Even though Notepad has the veneer of a plain text editor, it can still dirty things up by using Unicode characters. These characters have the detrimental effect of interfering with a script. Your best bet is to use the editor that runs in MS-DOS.

Although Microsoft has been threatening to do away with the DOS prompt for the last umpteen versions of Windows, it persists in the latest versions of Windows. To start the MS-DOS editor, open a command line and enter

```
edit filename.bat
```

This starts up the MS-DOS editor and saves the file without any extraneous code.

SYMPTOMS

You've probably read and scoffed at some of those "real-life help desk call" e-mails that circulate about. Generally, they're full of the stupid things people do that common sense could have solved—for instance, the woman who wanted to know how to get the pop can holder to come out (turns out it was the CD-ROM drive), or the guy who couldn't get a CD-ROM to fit into the A: drive, so he used a scissors to trim down the CD-ROM so it would fit. "But the darn thing *still* doesn't work…"

As funny as those things are, the fact is we all get a brain cramp now and again. While we might not be so dense as to chop up a CD-ROM, we do occasionally forget and leave the CAPS LOCK on, or maybe the keyboard cable has come unplugged from the computer. These are all easily overlooked places to first check for problems.

A more insidious problem stems from all the policies that Windows allows you to keep in place. Although Microsoft should be commended for trying to include as many options as possible with their password policies, the more they include, the more cautious an administrator must be when trying to set up and manage passwords.

SYMPTOM 26-1   **I'm having problems with password policies.**   The best way to avoid problems with passwords is to plan out password policies that ensure the security you want, without becoming a convoluted mess. Password policies are stored—in Windows 2000 or .NET—in the Security Policy tool. On Windows NT, they are located in the Account Policy dialog box. Policies can be managed either by the individual user or by user groups.

Microsoft allows the following settings to be managed for user passwords:

- **Maximum Password Age**   From 1–999 days, or Password Never Expires
- **Minimum Password Age**   From 1–999 days, or Allow Changes Immediately
- **Minimum Password Length**   From 1–14 characters, or Permit Blank Password
- **Password Uniqueness**   Allows you to determine how many times a new password must be created before a previously used password can be reused. You can set this number from 1–24 for new passwords. In Windows 2000, this is listed under Enforce Password History.
- **Account Lockout**   From never through 999. This tells the computer how many times a user can goof up the password before Windows will no longer even let them try to enter a password. Within this

policy, you must also specify the Reset Counter (from 1–99999), which is the number of minutes that can elapse between any two failed logon attempts. Lockout Duration tells the computer to lock out that user forever (requiring the administrator to unlock it) or enter a specific duration (from 1–99999 minutes) until the account is unlocked.

■ **User Must Logon in Order to Change Password**   This policy establishes whether the user is able to change his or her expired password, or if the administrator must do it. If the policy is not selected, the user is able to change the expired password without having to bother the administrator.

On the surface, these policies seem like they should work and play well with each other. However, there are combinations of these policies that—like mixing an acid and a base—are just asking for trouble. For instance,

■ If, within the Minimum Password Age policy, you enable the Allow Changes Immediately option and establish a Password Uniqueness policy, you'll have trouble. Rather, *do not* establish a Password Uniqueness policy and instead make sure the Do Not Keep Password History radio button is selected.

■ If you elect to use Password Uniqueness, make sure you enter a minimum number of days in the Minimum Password age policy.

■ Policies permitting blank passwords and minimum password length do not mix. If you use one policy, don't use the other.

■ When configuring a lockout duration, the amount of time specified in the Lockout Duration must be equal to or greater than the amount in the Reset Counter After value. If it isn't, the configuration won't work.

SYMPTOM 26-2   **A user has forgotten his or her password.**   Try not to be too hard on a user who forgets his or her password. It happens. At least it's better that they come to you for help than posting the password on the side of their monitor with a sticky note. If you're using Windows XP as client workstations, the problem can be resolved without your ever having to get involved. Windows XP Professional allows the use of a password recovery disk, which enables the user to save face when a password is forgotten and fix the problem themselves.

However, if your system does not support password recovery disks, you'll have to reset the user's password. You can also elect to force the user to enter a new password at the next logon. This option is found in the User Properties dialog box.

SYMPTOM 26-3   **Unlocking the locked-out user.**   As mentioned earlier in this section, a user can be locked out for any number of reasons: his or her password could have expired, the maximum number of logon attempts could have been reached, and so forth. To un-lockout a user, you have a couple different methods at your disposal.

To unlock a workstation, open User Manager for Domains (NT) or the Local Users and Groups MMC-snap in (2000 and .NET) and double-click on the selected user. The Account Locked Out field is selected and only needs to be deselected. If the lockout is going to expire after a predetermined amount of time, the user can either wait for the duration to expire (however, they must be cognizant of this duration and willing to wait it out) or come to you, with hat in hands, seeking that the workstation be unlocked.

SYMPTOM 26-4   **Give the user a heads up.**   When you set a minimum and maximum value for password changes, Windows automatically tells the user that they must change their password within 14 days. Two weeks is the default value, but you can change this value to any number you like. For instance, if you've established that passwords must be changed weekly, a 14-day heads up won't really work. On the other hand, maybe you've decided that users need 30 days to really get into the groove of password management.

No matter what your need, you can change this setting by editing the registry. Follow these steps:

1. Open **regedit.exe** and navigate to the HKEY_LOCAL_MACHINE\SOFTWARE\ Microsoft\WindowsNT\CurrentVersion\Winlogon key.

2. Create a REG_DWORD item named PasswordExpiryWarning.

3. Enter data establishing the number of days before the password expiration that you want a warning to be given to the user.

SYMPTOM 26-5   **The user cannot log on to a domain because there is a time difference.**   When you add your computer to a Windows 2000 domain, then attempt to log on to the domain, you might get a message saying that you cannot log on due to a time difference between the client and the server.

This is because the Kerberos authentication protocol inspects the timestamp of the authentication request that the client sends. This timestamp is compared to the current time of the domain controller. If there is a significant difference between the times (the default setting is 5 minutes), authentication fails.

To fix this problem, make sure that the client and the server have the same time. Furthermore, make sure that the correct time zone is entered on each computer, because Kerberos converts all times to Greenwich mean time for its comparison.

SYMPTOM 26-6   **Domain does not recognize a client computer after it has been renamed.**   If you rename a client computer, often the logon domain won't recognize the new name. To avoid this problem, when renaming a Windows client, follow these steps:

1. Create a new computer account under the new computer name.

2. Leave the domain by joining a workgroup.

3. Restart the client when Windows prompts you.

4. Rejoin the domain by using the new computer name.

5. Restart the client when Windows prompts you.

Linux/UNIX Logon

Even though Windows is the big dog on the client OS block, Linux/UNIX computers are still prevalent in many work settings. Quite often, a Linux/UNIX server will feed various clients, running all sorts of operating systems.

This section examines various client components of a Linux/UNIX environment. Not only are issues of logon examined, but so are client connections using the Network Information Service (NIS) and connecting Linux/UNIX with other types of clients, using such intermediary tools as SAMBA.

NETWORK INFORMATION SERVICE

Depending on your organization's need and mission, computer networks can be complex environments with different services offered in different locations. As such, users and network administrators might need to log on to a different computer to access a particular resource. As users access other workstations, they still come to expect a familiar desktop and computing environment. However, anticipating user logon needs and implementing them here and there on a network is a nightmare.

The Network File System (NFS) provides a server environment that allows for the roaming user settings we explained earlier. Within NFS is the Network Information Service (NIS). NIS supports distributed databases for maintaining certain administrative files for an entire network, including password information, group information, and host addresses.

NIS was developed by Sun Microsystems in the 1980s, and for a long time was known as *Yellow Pages* (or *YP*). As time went by, Yellow Pages evolved into a management system known as NIS+. Even though NIS and NIS+ are used on the major variants of UNIX, and run in basically the same way, NIS+ provides enhanced security over NIS.

NIS/NIS+ runs in a client/server model. An NIS client runs processes that request data from the NIS servers. Applications using NIS/NIS+ don't need to know the location of the computer housing the information that they need. It's NIS/NIS+'s job to locate the information on an NIS server, and give it to the application in the format it requests.

There are two types of NIS/NIS+ servers, as shown in Figure 26-6:

- **Domain masters**   These servers store all the database source files for an entire domain.
- **Slaves**   Since NIS/NIS+ services are so important, they need to be accessible even if the NIS/NIS+ server is down. As such, a domain master periodically sends a copy of all its source files to a slave, which is a backup server.

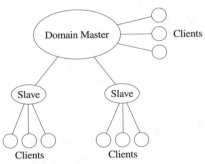

FIGURE 26-6   Deployment of NIS/NIS+ servers

NIS/NIS+ provides a screening mechanism to authenticate users requesting a shared resource. For example, if you want to use a file housed on another computer on the network, NIS/NIS+ determines whether you are allowed to use the resource before NFS mounts it. Further, if you want to perform remote procedure calls (RPCs), NIS/NIS+ ensures that you have access to the command as well as the resource on the networked computer.

Don't misunderstand—NIS/NIS+ does not perform authentication. It simply returns database entries. For instance, if a password database is accessed, NIS/NIS+ locates the desired information—the application must determine whether or not the user has the requisite permissions to access it.

NIS+ is used by a daemon called **rpc.nisd**. This daemon starts the NIS+ service in one of two ways:

- NIS+ can run with all its service features.
- NIS+ can be run in *NIS compatibility mode* by using the –YB option. This allows computers that are on a network to use resources as if they were using the older NIS.

Troubleshooting NIS

Even though NIS/NIS+ provides an additional layer of functionality in UNIX environments, you can bet that it also adds its own problems. The following are some problems that can occur with NIS and NIS+.

SYMPTOM 26-7 **The user cannot log in or use rlogin to another domain.** If a user is unable to use **rlogin** to access another domain, the problem can be attributed to many issues, including

- **Forgotten password** If the user forgot his or her password, run **nispasswd** for that user on another computer.
- **Mistyped password** A painfully common problem—make sure CAPS LOCK is not on and the users are aware of case-sensitivity in passwords.
- **Expiration** Have the user's password privileges expired?
- **Inactivity** The user has exceeded the inactivity maximum for his or her account.

rlogin will be explained in more detail later in this section.

SYMPTOM 26-8 **The user's new password does not work.** If a user has recently changed the password and is unable to log in, or can log in on some computers but not others, there are two likely problems:

- It might take a while for the new password to propagate through the network. Try the old password.
- The password was changed on a computer that was not running NIS+.

SYMPTOM 26-9 **The user is unable to log in to a remote domain.** If a user uses the **rlogin** command on a computer and is greeted with a "permission denied" message, make sure the user has local credentials on that machine. Run **nismatch** *username.domainname.cred.org dir* in the other domain to see if the user has the requisite local credentials.

To assign the user the appropriate credentials, do the following:

■ On the remote domain, use the **nisaddcred** command to create a local credential for the user on that domain.

■ Edit the **/etc/security/login.cfg**, **etc/security/user** and **/usr/lib/security/methods.cfg** files (or create them if they do not exist) and ensure they contain the following lines:

```
NISPLUS
    program=/usr/lib/security/NISPLUS
```

SYMPTOM 26-10   **The user is unable to change his or her password.**   If the user is unable to change his or her password, the most likely causes are mistyping or forgetting the old password. Other causes include

■ The password Min value has been set greater than the password Max value.

■ The password is locked or has expired.

SYMPTOM 26-11   **The user doesn't have the requisite permissions.**   The most prevalent permission problem is also the easiest to resolve. Simply put, the user doesn't *have* permission to access a network resource. Use the **niscat –o** command on the object the user is trying to access; this will show the user's permissions. Either the owner of the object or the system administrator can make the requisite changes.

SYMPTOM 26-12   **The user does not have the appropriate credentials.**   If the user doesn't have the correct credentials, many operations will fail. Use the **nismatch** command on the home domain's cred table to ensure the right credentials are present.

SYMPTOM 26-13   **The user and computer share the same name.**   A user and computer cannot share the same name. If a user is given the same name as a computer (or a computer given the same name as a user), the first object cannot perform operations requiring secure permissions because the second object's key has overwritten the first object's key in the cred table. Furthermore, the second object now has the permissions that were originally granted to the first object. Some of the symptoms of this problem include

■ The user or computer experiences "permission denied" error messages.

■ The user or the root for the computer cannot run **keylogin**.

■ The error message "Security exception on LOCAL system. UNABLE TO MAKE REQUEST" appears.

The best course of action in this case is to change the computer's name and then delete the computer's entry from the cred table. Next, use **nisclient** to reinitialize the machine as an NIS+ client. You might have to replace the user's credentials in the cred table.

SAMBA

In today's networking environments, it's rare to see a wholly homogenous environment. That is, most of the company might be using Windows clients, but there are going to be UNIX and Linux servers or clients sprinkled here and there. In order for all these computers to work and play well together, there needs to be a way for one vendor's clients to access another vendor's servers.

At the end of this chapter is a link to the SAMBA web site where you can get your own copy of SAMBA.

One very popular method of providing Windows clients with access to UNIX drives is the SAMBA server package. This is freeware that runs on UNIX servers and provides a Windows client access to UNIX mounts. Before you turn away from the concept of using a noncommercial product in your organization, you need to know that SAMBA has been in existence for a considerable period and has been widely used in both academic environments (where it was developed) and in several large corporate sites. SAMBA is a robust, well-tested, and well-documented software package that is worth considering if your goal is to allow clients on a Windows network to read and save files that exist on UNIX systems.

SAMBA is based on the Server Message Block (SMB) protocol that Windows uses for sharing files. SAMBA works by the creation of UNIX support for the SMB protocol. The SAMBA daemon responds to SMB requests from Windows network clients and becomes a server to respond to those requests.

Since SAMBA is a process that is installed entirely on UNIX systems, a UNIX system administrator will need to install the SAMBA server. The Windows systems administrator has almost nothing to do when connecting network clients to a SAMBA server. If you are aware of the many various versions of UNIX that may be in use, rest easy because SAMBA is compatible with all major versions of UNIX (such as products from Apollo, HP, DEC, NeXT, SCO, Sun, and SGI, among others). This section will include a brief description of the requirements for having SAMBA working with Windows.

NT Network Client Requirements

While there are no SAMBA client files that must be installed in Windows 9x, 2000, XP, or NT machines, these computers must have appropriate network protocols and services running to be able to connect to the UNIX machines that they will gain access to. These required elements are the TCP/IP protocol and DNS services.

If DNS is unavailable, the UNIX machine DNS names and IP numbers can be placed in the HOSTS file located in the **%Systemroot%\System32\drivers\etc** directory.

UNIX Configuration

The SAMBA server configuration is set in the **smb.conf** file. This text file has a section structure that would feel familiar to anyone who has edited a Windows **SYSTEM.INI** file. There are separate sections for each share that will be created that permit setting valid users, read-write privileges, and public access. The following is an example of an **smb.conf** file:

```
[global]
workgroup = ACCOUNTING
```

```
server string = Accounting Department's Samba Server
encrypt passwords = True
security = user
smb passwd file = /etc/smbpasswd
log file = /var/log/samba/log.%m
socket options = IPTOS_LOWDELAY TCP_NODELAY
domain master = Yes
local master = Yes
preferred master = Yes
os level = 65
dns proxy = No
name resolve order = lmhosts host bcast
bind interfaces only = True
interfaces = eth0 192.168.1.1
hosts deny = ALL
hosts allow = 192.168.1.4 127.0.0.1
debug level = 1
create mask = 0644
directory mask = 0755
level2 oplocks = True
read raw = no
write cache size = 262144

[homes]
comment = Home Directories
browseable = no
read only = no
invalid users = root bin daemon nobody named sys tty disk mem kmem users

[tmp]
comment = Temporary File Space
path = /tmp
read only = No
valid users = admin
invalid users = root bin daemon nobody named sys tty disk mem kmem users
```

There are also two sections that are very important for use in the enterprise environment with large numbers of clients. The **[homes]** section will automatically permit users that already have accounts on the UNIX system to connect to their home directories without having to create individual shares for every account. The **[global]** section sets several comprehensive properties of the server. Of greatest importance are the security options that determine the method of authenticating users. There are three security modes that can be specified in the **[global]** section under the **security=** entries:

■ **Security=share** The *valid users* entry in each share section can specify specific users and their privileges within that share. This is a relatively insecure method and is limited to users who already have UNIX accounts, so it is a poor method for general access for Windows network users within the enterprise.

■ **Security=user** In this mode, all authentication occurs via the UNIX user accounts. In those cases where all Windows network clients also have accounts on the UNIX system, this is a secure and efficient system. For those enterprises that already have UNIX accounts for every user of the network, this is a viable option.

■ **Security=server** This mode is the clear choice when all users do not have or should not have UNIX accounts. In this mode, user access is authenticated through a server other than the UNIX SAMBA server—for example, a Windows 2000 DC. This could allow a single Windows machine to grant access to both Windows 2000 and SAMBA resources using a single database of usernames and passwords. It also has the great advantage of not requiring users to change their passwords on two different systems. When this entry is made in the **[global]** section, the name of the server that will perform the authentication must be added in the **password server=** entry.

This name will be the NetBIOS name of the server. For that machine to be found, it will have to be added to the **/etc/hosts** file on the UNIX system.

A drawback to SAMBA is that it is only useful if your clients use SMB protocols. This will include Windows 9*x*, 2000, XP and NT, but not NetWare or Macintosh clients.

LINUX/UNIX LOGON PROBLEMS

Because UNIX is a multiuser system, passwords are required to give access to your files. If you enter the wrong password, you can expect to see the following:

```
login: wildbill
Password:
Login Incorrect
login:
```

The **Password:** prompt will appear, even if you enter an incorrect or nonexistent login name. This is by design, rather than a flaw—it prevents someone from guessing login names and getting the **Password:** prompt if they happen to guess right.

The administrator can set a maximum number of times that a login and password can be incorrectly entered before the LAN or dial-in connection is terminated. Further, the system administrator can be notified if a failed attempt to log on has been made. Additionally, unless the user logs on within a predetermined amount of time (for instance, a minute) the connection will be terminated.

If you have problems logging in, the first place to check is to ensure that the CAPS LOCK key has not been pressed. Since UNIX/Linux logons are case sensitive, the CAPS LOCK key will cause incorrect login and password information to be sent to the server.

There are four ways that you can access a multiuser UNIX system. Depending on which way you connect, you might face different logon issues.

Direct Connect

The first way to connect is via a direct connection. In this scenario, workstations and PCs are connected to the UNIX system. This type of configuration is most often seen with dedicated systems, small offices, or labs. Once the PC is booted and the terminal emulator invoked, the CARRIAGE RETURN or ENTER key is hit and the UNIX System prompt appears:

```
login:
```

Dial-In Access

Another way to access a UNIX system is remotely via a dial-in connection. The terminal emulator is used to dial the UNIX system access number. Once the familiar modem high tone is heard, some characters appear on the screen. If these characters do not appear, press the ENTER key.

Next, you should see the UNIX system login prompt. You might see some strange characters (for instance, "]]]{{kDFwr|>>f:"). This might mean that the system is capable of connecting at different rates of speed and the wrong speed has been selected for your dial-in connection. To ameliorate this problem, hit the RETURN or BREAK key. Each time you press RETURN or BREAK, the system tries to send to your terminal using a different connection rate. Ultimately, the correct speed will be found, and you'll see the familiar

```
login:
```

If you still see garbage on your screen, you should check your parity settings and try again.

LAN

A LAN is the most prevalent way users connect to a UNIX server. The settings used will depend on your LAN environment. A number of LAN environments exist, including LAN Manager and NetWare. Each LAN environment includes a set of software that is used in conjunction with a network interface card (NIC), enabling you to connect your client to the server.

Clients and servers might be running Windows, UNIX, or a combination of both (as we've already explored). Most often, the TCP/IP protocol is used to connect these clients and servers; however, such protocols as IPX and SPX are also widely used in LANs. For example, a group of Windows PC clients could be connected to a server running UnixWare 7, Solaris, or Linux.

When accessing a UNIX system on a LAN, first you must configure your PC to be able to recognize the system to which you wish to connect. This ensures the proper protocols are in place.

Internet

The fourth way to connect to a UNIX system is via an IP network, like the Internet or an intranet. In this scenario, you use the **telnet** command to access any computer on the network allowing such connections. The computer you access could be a UNIX computer or a computer using another operating system. This computer could be located two cubicles away from you or on the other side of the country.

Remote Login

The UNIX environment incorporates Berkeley remote commands. These are commonly known as the *r* commands*, because they all start with "r". These commands are used for various functions on remote machines linked to your computer via TCP/IP. The command we're most interested in here is the **rlogin** command, which is used to log in to a remote host.

You might find the need to log in to a remote UNIX computer on a TCP/IP network for a number of reasons. By using the **rlogin** command, you log into a remote computer as if you were using it as a local computer. The command is used as such:

```
$ rlogin computername
```

The **rlogin** command supplies the remote machine with your user ID and tells it what kind of terminal you are using by sending the value of the *TERM* variable. You can also log on to a remote terminal using a different user ID and password. This is achieved by using the **–l** option in conjunction with the **rlogin** command. For example, to log in to the computer gilligan with the user ID skipper, you'd enter the following command:

```
$ rlogin -l skipper gilligan
```

This type of login is different from Telnet, because Telnet allows you to remotely access computers using different operating systems. Telnet does not pass information about your environment to the remote computer, whereas **rlogin** does.

When using **rlogin**, there are times when you can log onto a remote machine without having to enter your password. Other times, you will be required to supply a password. Still other times, you will not be able to log in at all, because there is no entry of you in the computer's password database.

If you have an entry in the password database and your computer is listed in the remote machine's **/etc/hosts.equiv** file, you are allowed to log in because the remote machine trusts your local machine.

You can also log in without having to supply a password if the name of your local machine is not in the **/etc/hosts.equiv** file, but there is a line in the **.rhosts** file in the home directory of the login on the remote machine that contains your local computer's name (if the login name is the same as yours, or if both the local computer name and your login ID are listed).

If you do have an entry in the password database of the remote computer, but your computer's name is not listed in the **/etc/hosts.equiv** file and there is no appropriate line in the **.rhosts** file in the home directory of the login on the remote machine, the remote computer will prompt you for a password. However, your permissions are restricted even though you supplied the appropriate login and password, and you'll not be able to run remote processes.

If you use **rlogin** to attempt to log on to a computer that your computer is not aware of, your computer will search its database, then send back a message that the remote computer could not be found, as shown below:

```
$ rlogin gilligan
gilligan: unknown host
```

NetWare Logon

The last section of this chapter examines NetWare logon issues and environments. First is a discussion of Novell Directory Services and the single sign-on tool that makes signing on to multiple resources much smoother. Next is a discussion of logging on to NetWare and troubleshooting logon problems.

NOVELL DIRECTORY SERVICES

Chapter 5 explained Novell Directory Services (NDS) in greater detail than we cover here. However, what's important to know is that NDS allows network objects (printers, users, files, and so forth) to be located anywhere on the network. This allows users and applications to find resources much more easily.

When logging on to NDS, the user sees everything in a tree structure. That is, smaller objects are placed beneath their larger objects. For instance, a given computer will have users and hard drives listed beneath it. Beneath the hard drives will be lists of files, as exemplified in Figure 26-7.

Novell set out to simplify logon procedures with the Novell Single Sign-on (NSSO) Bundle and NDS Authentication Services (NDS-AS) 3.0. Both products are used with NDS eDirectory.

The NSSO Bundle combines two single sign-on products:

- Novell Single Sign-on 2.0
- v-GO for Novell Single Sign-on

The NSSO Bundle can be used to access most Windows, web, and host-based applications. To bolster NSSO, NDS-AS extends user authentication across multiple platforms and legacy applications whether or not they use the NSSO Bundle. NSSO Bundle and NDS-AS can be used for single sign-on across a number of platforms, including

- Windows 2000 and NT
- OS/390
- Solaris
- HP-UX
- AIX

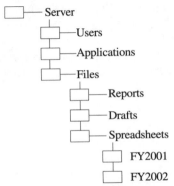

FIGURE 26-7   NDS users see network resources as a tree.

- Linux
- Radius
- Internet Information Server (IIS)

The NSSO Bundle captures logons at the source, using the user's workstation or remote PC, and then stores the passwords as encrypted files in SecretStore, a protected location within NDS.

When a user comes to a password-protected application or web site, the appropriate name and password combination is retrieved from SecretStore and entered without the user having to bother himself or herself with it.

Additionally, the NSSO Bundle accommodates all password management tasks, including logon, password selection, change, and reset. Additionally, administrators need not manage multiple passwords for each user. From a central console, the administrator can manage a host of user settings. Users benefit from the NSSO Bundle because they won't have multiple passwords to keep track of, and they are less likely to compromise network security by writing down the passwords and losing the list.

Logon information is encrypted by Novell International Cryptographic Infrastructure (NICI). Additionally, if a user steps away from his or her computer, the NDS Screen Saver requires the user to log back on to the computer.

NDS-AS bolsters NDS security with such features as:

- Intruder detection
- Password rules
- User disablement to other platforms

NDS-AS is a server-based application that protects the network by denying hackers the ability to access passwords through workstations or remote consoles.

LOGGING ON

When logging on to a single NetWare server, the process is quite straightforward. One simply enters his or her username and password into the dialog box, then clicks the Login button. NetWare also offers two other ways to log on to its servers, including logging on to multiple servers and logging on from the command line.

Multiple Servers

To log into multiple servers in the NetWare Access Manager, open the Server menu and select Login (Multiple Servers). The NetWare Login Manager window shows a list of NetWare servers you can log on to. Follow these steps to log on:

1. The check box by Reuse Login Name and Password is enabled by default. This configuration allows one login and password combination to log into multiple servers. If you have different login and password combinations on each server, clear this check box.

2. You can log into multiple servers in one of two ways:

   - If you want to log into selected servers, select the servers from the list and click Login.
   - If you want to log into all the displayed servers, click on Login (All Servers).

3. Depending on whether you will reuse the same login and password combination for all servers, you must do one of the following:

   ■ If Reuse Login Name and Password is enabled, enter your NetWare login password and click Login.

   ■ If Reuse Login Name and Password is disabled, you are prompted to enter a separate login and password for each server.

4. The Message window will display the logins that were successful and the ones that failed.

5. Click OK.

6. In the NetWare Login Manager window, pull down the Server menu and select Exit.

Command-Line Logon

Alternately, you can use the command line from your UNIX or Linux client to log in to a NetWare server. The command is **nwlogin** and uses the following syntax:

```
nwlogin [-p] server_name [/user_name]
```

A username can be used if it is specified in the **nwlogin** command. If no username is specified, **nwlogin** uses the client's login name. **nwlogin** prompts for your NetWare password, then uses it to log in to the NetWare server you specified. After the login and password have been verified, you are logged on to the NetWare server. If the login is successful, no results are displayed.

Some **nwlogin** options are

■ **-p**   Cancels the prompt, and uses the next line from standard input as the NetWare password.

■ *server_name*   The name of the file server you want to log on to.

■ *user_name*   The user's NetWare login name. If this value is not specified, your current client login name is used.

NETWARE LOGON PROBLEMS

A mixed environment exists when clients use one type of operating system (Windows, for instance) to access resources stored on a server using a different type of operating system (NetWare, for instance). Immediately, the opportunity for logon problems should be apparent. It's one thing when programmers and developers try to hammer out the problems of connecting computers using the same operating system, but it's another thing entirely when two different operating systems have to come together.

The following are some common problems that can occur in a mixed NetWare/Windows environment.

SYMPTOM 26-14   **I'm having problems with logon scripts.**   If you are connecting to a NetWare server, or are running NetWare Client Services, it's likely that you will use a NetWare login script, as this is the only way to establish environment and user settings. Some common scripting errors include

■ **Mapping error when establishing a duplicate drive**   If you encounter an error telling you that a drive mapping was attempted on a non-NetWare network drive, it's likely the drive mapping you've established in your script is attempting to map an already mapped drive.

■ **ENDIF command fails** If your script runs under Client Services for NetWare (CSNW) or Gateway Services for Netware (GSNW) and the script contains an **ENDIF** command, a message will appear telling you that the line could not be interpreted. This is because **ENDIF** can only be used in a script on a NetWare client. With CSNW and GSNW, use **END** rather than **ENDIF**.

SYMPTOM 26-15 **I'm having problems in my mixed environment.** There are other problems that can arise when working in a mixed environment, including the following:

■ **A new script doesn't work** If you've just written a script, it's likely that the script hasn't propagated to the domain controllers yet. You could wait until your NT domain replicates or the 2000/.NET domain synchronizes. However, if you need to speed things up, you can force synchronization by going to the command prompt and entering

```
net accounts /sync
```

■ **Check permissions** If your logon script is stored on a server using the NTFS file system, read permissions must be given to the user the script belongs to. You'll know this is a place to check, because if there are no read rights assigned, no error message will appear when the script fails.

SYMPTOM 26-16 **I'm having trouble with the Net Use command.** The **Net Use** command can be a source of friction between Windows and NetWare operating systems. It's not uncommon to see an error message telling the user that the network password is incorrect. This error is not due to the password's veracity. However, it is a problem with NetWare's configuration. This is easy enough to fix by looking at the **Startup.ncf** file. If the line **SET ENABLE IPX CHECKSUMS=2** is present, then change the 2 to 0. This is because NetWare uses checksums, but Windows does not. A value of 2 tells the client that checksums should be enabled. A value of 0 disables them.

As with most other troubleshooting tasks, the logon process provides a number of places in which problems can be found. For the most part, start your search simply—is the CAPS LOCK key pressed? Is the keyboard unplugged? These sound like insultingly simple places to check, but you'd be surprised at how often they are the problem. Problems also mount in environments in which mixed systems are present. No matter what your network configuration, troubleshooting logon problems is a matter of double-checking your settings and making sure nothing is out of whack.

Further Study

SAMBA: **http://samba.anu.edu.au/samba/**
Novell: **www.novell.com**
Microsoft: **www.microsoft.com**
Linux: **www.linux.org**, **www.linux.com**, **www.linuxjournal.com**

NETWORK PERFORMANCE AND BASELINING

One of the most difficult aspects of networking is discerning the difference between correct and incorrect network behavior. Networks are often complex and convoluted environments where it is virtually impossible to predict the demands of each workstation (or determine how the network will respond under every possible circumstance). Consequently, network troubleshooting often relies on the comparison of current operating performance against a known-good performance standard (or *baseline*). This identifies what's "normal" for your particular network. If a network's performance falls below established baselines, an administrator or technician can quantify the difference and investigate—and even use that data to make a case for network upgrades.

The trick is establishing the baseline and keeping it current. Often, networks are implemented without a sound baseline. Even worse, baselines are not updated as the network grows and changes. When trouble occurs (such as poor performance due to excessive traffic), technicians are then hard-pressed to define the problem in tangible terms. This chapter explains the importance of a network baseline and outlines a variety of baselining techniques using Observer Suite protocol analyzer software, along with System Monitor found in Windows 2000 Server (you can often find similar applications for UNIX/Linux).

Protocol Analysis

Whether you're building a new network from scratch or taking over from another administrator, it's important to create a good baseline of your network at the earliest opportunity. A baseline establishes the network's performance characteristics and tells you what the network looks like when it's running normally. When trouble strikes, a simple comparison of current performance against baseline performance can help you to isolate potential problem areas quickly. If you're contemplating a network upgrade, be sure to take a baseline before *and* after the upgrade is performed—this can provide you with an excellent picture of any resulting performance changes.

For example, you can't expect to look at network performance during your busiest time of the day (or week) and get "normal" values. Nor can you take several days worth of data and consider it to be gospel. Instead, you need to take at least a week's worth of data at a time of year when it's "business as usual"—if you can take a larger sample (several weeks or a month), that's even better. You can print out the data in text and graphic formats and keep it with your network documentation.

When trouble strikes, you take the same measurements and see which statistics meet your baseline, and which do *not*. Suppose that your network utilization on segment 2 never exceeds 20 percent, and never has an error rate of more than 2 percent when things are normal. If you discover that its utilization has unexpectedly jumped to 65 percent with an error rate of 12 percent, you would probably investigate that segment some more. As you might imagine, this kind of information pays real dividends when it's time to troubleshoot. Alternately, if you find that the traffic on that segment has gradually increased as more users have been added, you'll have the information needed to recommend a network upgrade in order to handle the increase in use.

NETWORK MONITORING TOOLS

Of course, once you realize the value of a network baseline, the next obvious problem is deciding just what statistics you'll need to baseline. Analytical tools like protocol analyzers are capable of capturing and recording vast amounts of information, so it's handy to consider some of the more useful baseline statistics.

Utilization

Simply stated, *utilization* is a percentage of the number of bits that travel across the network divided by the total number of bits that network can convey. The numerator is generally referred to as *throughput* and the denominator is generally referred to as the *bandwidth* of a network. The formula would be

```
Utilization = (Throughput / Bandwidth) x 100%
```

For example, if your network supports a bandwidth of 100 Mbps, and you're experiencing a throughput of 50 Mbps, the network's utilization is 50 percent (50/100 × 100%). You can then say that 50 percent of the bandwidth is being utilized. This may be acceptable in a token ring network, but may be pushing the performance of an Ethernet network (additional utilization may reduce performance due to excessive collisions).

Utilization information is critical for a network administrator. If more data is put onto the wire than the wire can handle, saturation occurs and data can be corrupted. For example, one workstation sending broadcast messages can consume the entire bandwidth and prevent other users from transmitting or receiving data. Utilization is usually presented in the form of minimum, maximum, and average values. It's helpful to know that you have peaks when your network activity is high, but on average the utilization should fall within a value that's appropriate for your network architecture. Critical utilization percentages are different for Ethernet networks and token ring networks. For example, at an average utilization of 30 percent, it is usually time to segment an Ethernet network, but a token ring network can often support up to 65–75-percent utilization before segmenting the token ring. Keep in mind that these are only guidelines. Some well-mannered client/server environments with a limited number of stations have been known to support up to 90-percent utilization—it's often a large number of stations that cause the collisions that limit utilization.

> Some protocol analyzers let you further subdivide utilization by protocols, so you can see if one protocol is hogging your network's bandwidth.

Checking Utilization   Tools like Observer Suite provide a one-button solution for utilization tracking. Simply click the Utilization History (UH) button, and the Utilization History dialog box will appear (see Figure 27-1). The display is updated about every 30 seconds. According to the figure, the maximum (peak) utilization during our brief testing was 10 percent, while the average utilization was just 0.2 percent. The Utilization History display can be cleared using the Clear button, or you can save Utilization History data to a comma-delimited file by choosing File, "Save Mode in Comma Delimited Format" from Observer's main menu.

Checking Efficiency   The Efficiency History test in Observer Suite provides a snapshot of your LAN's current efficiency. A common use for this tool is to judge the effectiveness (or lack of effectiveness) of changes and alterations to your network setup or configuration. Many administrators use this tool as a gauge prior to a network change, and then after the change is complete. If the efficiency goes down, you know that the change has impaired your LAN's ability to carry data. If the number goes up, the change improved your LAN's ability to carry data. Simply click the Efficiency History (EH) button, and the Efficiency History dialog box will appear (see Figure 27-2). According to the figure, LAN efficiency is roughly 97 percent (9.7 Mbps on a 10-Mbps segment).

When the Efficiency History tool is active, the test is run every 10 seconds. The test consists of Observer bursting 70 packets for Ethernet and Fast Ethernet (or 30 packets for token ring) onto the LAN. The packets are measured for the LAN's ability to let data flow. Results are displayed in Mbps. Efficiency History generates a small amount of network traffic, and will have no significant effect on overall network performance.

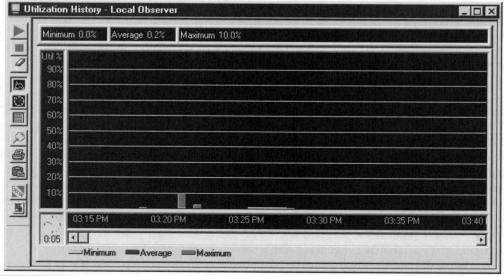

FIGURE   27-1   Utilization tells you how much of the network's available bandwidth is being used.

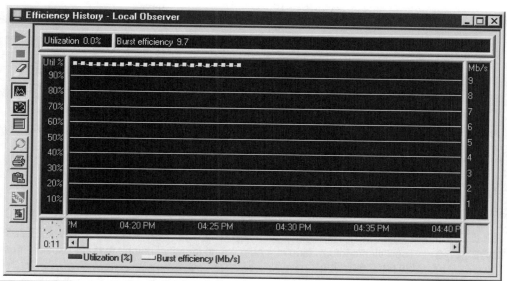

FIGURE 27-2   Efficiency indicates the LAN's ability to carry data, and can help you gauge the effectiveness of network upgrades or reconfiguration.

Traffic Patterns

Analyzing the traffic patterns on a network can provide more key information to the administrator—revealing segments (and specific workstations) that are producing excessive traffic and causing poor performance. For example, if two nodes are jamming the segment with traffic, it might be necessary for an administrator to separate those two nodes by placing them on separate network segments.

Analyze network traffic by examining the number of frames and their average lengths to determine what kind of traffic is traversing the network. Shorter frames could indicate lots of database queries, while larger frames might indicate file transfers. Knowing what kind of traffic is moving (and when peak periods occur) can prove helpful in scheduling times for performing certain activities. For example, if a user transfers files to another node on a daily basis in the morning, perhaps these transfers should be rescheduled at night when the network is less busy.

Top Talkers   Utilities like Observer Suite will list the top talkers on your network. Top Talkers shows all the stations on your LAN, along with the Broadcast/Multicast statistics. This information provides detailed traffic flow statistics that can show a runaway station, a broadcast/multicast storm, or unbalanced switch. Simply click the Top Talker (TT) button and the Top Talkers Statistics dialog box will appear (see Figure 27-3). The display can show stations by either MAC (hard network) address or IP address. Selecting the MAC or IP button from the selection bar will select which view is displayed. For example, you can see that station **192.168.168.6** is the busiest station on the segment, followed by broadcast traffic from **255.255.255.255**.

If you're considering implementing a switch, Top Talker information can help divide stations effectively. Once you have implemented a switch, use the switched version of this mode to verify balanced port loads.

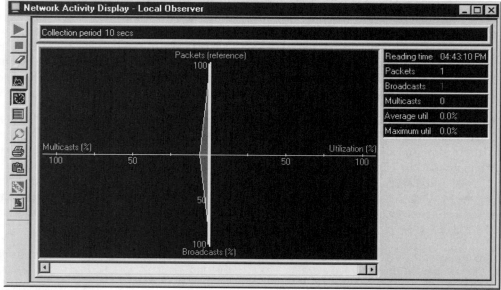

Top Talkers Statistics - Local Observer

Stations 11	Packets 237	Bytes 71342	Filter Not using filters

DNS Name	IP address	Packets in	Bytes in	Packets out	Bytes out	Packets total	Bytes total
	192.168.168.6	0	0	156	61868	156	61868
Broadcast	255.255.255.255	127	55544	0	0	127	55544
Multicast	192.168.168.255	87	14535	0	0	87	14535
MA007F13	192.168.168.7	0	0	26	3366	26	3366
AUTHOR1	192.168.168.3	15	849	13	1131	28	1980
	192.168.168.5	0	0	13	1413	13	1413
	192.168.168.2	0	0	9	1163	9	1163
berp-ba04.dial.aol....	152.163.6.14	7	343	14	665	21	1008
SC410234	192.168.168.8	0	0	4	976	4	976
	192.168.168.1	0	0	1	576	1	576
SERV1-Oxford-MA...	24.216.218.9	1	71	1	184	2	255

FIGURE 27-3   Top Talkers information can help you to identify stations that are causing most of the segment's traffic.

Checking Network Activity   The Network Activity Display (NAD) is available in tools like Observer Suite, and shows critical network utilization and broadcast information graphed against a packet traffic reference line. This display can show you the health of a LAN and can warn of impending slow-downs due to broadcast or multicast storms at a glance. Simply click the Network Activity Display (NAD) button, and the Network Activity Display dialog box will appear (see Figure 27-4). The display illustrates multicasts, packets, utilization, and broadcasts in four quadrants.

Network Activity Display - Local Observer

Collection period 10 secs

Packets (reference) 100

Multicasts (%) 100   50

Utilization (%) 50   100

50

100
Broadcasts (%)

Reading time	04:43:10 PM
Packets	1
Broadcasts	1
Multicasts	0
Average util	0.0%
Maximum util	0.0%

FIGURE 27-4   Network Activity Display illustrates the number of packets versus multicasts, broadcasts, and utilization.

The indicator lines change color for easy viewing of specific network conditions. If an indicator line is yellow, the NAD is showing a network condition that is essentially idle (total network utilization is under 5 percent). In this case, the percentage of broadcast or multicasts may be high compared to actual traffic. However, since the traffic is so low, this condition is not statistically important. If an indicator line segment is green, the NAD is displaying a normal network condition. If an indicator line segment displays red, the NAD is letting you know that a load condition exists—this is not necessarily a problem, but indicates that you should be aware of this condition.

Load conditions can mean different things depending on where the various lines appear. Typically, a red line means that a threshold has been overcome. Blue lines display on the side where the threshold may be an indication of trouble. Red lines will appear if broadcast or multicasts are representing more than 10 percent of total network utilization (or if utilization goes over 35 percent) by default. NAD information can be saved to a comma-delimited file by choosing File and "Save Mode in Comma Delimited Format".

Packet Size Distribution   The Packet Size Distribution Statistics display breaks down the traffic composition on every station of your LAN and highlights each station's traffic patterns (broken down by the size of the packet). This information can help to quickly pinpoint network flow problems and identify stations or routers that are sending mostly small packets, as opposed to larger packets. Simply click the Packet Size Distribution Statistics (SDS) button, and the Packet Size Distribution Statistics dialog box appears (see Figure 27-5). For each station, you can see the number of packets, the percentage of traffic, and the percentage of packets in each size range:

- 64 bytes or less
- 65–84 bytes
- 85–128 bytes
- 129–512 bytes
- 513–1,024 bytes
- 1,025 bytes and larger

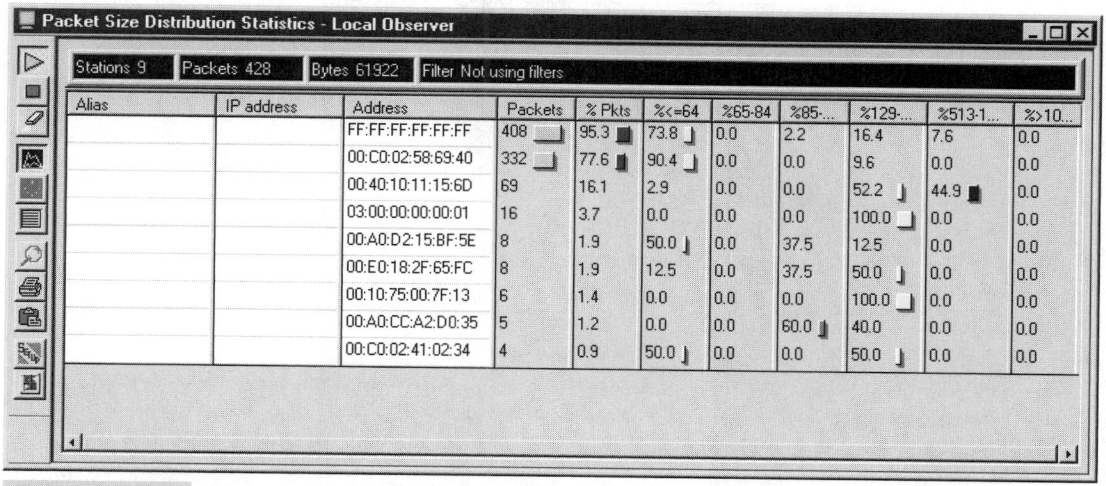

Packet Size Distribution Statistics - Local Observer

Stations: 9   Packets: 428   Bytes: 61922   Filter: Not using filters

Alias	IP address	Address	Packets	% Pkts	%<=64	%65-84	%85-...	%129-...	%513-1...	%>10...
		FF:FF:FF:FF:FF:FF	408	95.3	73.8	0.0	2.2	16.4	7.6	0.0
		00:C0:02:58:69:40	332	77.6	90.4	0.0	0.0	9.6	0.0	0.0
		00:40:10:11:15:6D	69	16.1	2.9	0.0	0.0	52.2	44.9	0.0
		03:00:00:00:00:01	16	3.7	0.0	0.0	0.0	100.0	0.0	0.0
		00:A0:D2:15:BF:5E	8	1.9	50.0	0.0	37.5	12.5	0.0	0.0
		00:E0:18:2F:65:FC	8	1.9	12.5	0.0	37.5	50.0	0.0	0.0
		00:10:75:00:7F:13	6	1.4	0.0	0.0	0.0	100.0	0.0	0.0
		00:A0:CC:A2:D0:35	5	1.2	0.0	0.0	60.0	40.0	0.0	0.0
		00:C0:02:41:02:34	4	0.9	50.0	0.0	0.0	50.0	0.0	0.0

FIGURE 27-5   Packet size distribution can help you to identify traffic characteristics for each station on the LAN.

Error Rates

The ability to measure and analyze errors on a network is also crucial. A node sending a frame that produces an error must retransmit that packet. A faulty node retransmitting packets could generate a lot of unnecessary traffic on a network. Increasing error rates on individual segments or stations should always be investigated, since they are often the first indicator of impending equipment failure (hubs, concentrators, NICs, and so on). A protocol analyzer can quickly display common errors that may alert you to network problems (see Chapter 30 for detailed troubleshooting with a protocol analyzer).

Checking Packets   Analyzers such as Observer Suite can easily capture and display packet statistics for you. Simply click the Packet Capture (PC) button, and the Packet Capture dialog box will appear. A graph displays by default, but switch to List display to review the results in a tabular format (such as Figure 27-6). In addition to basic traffic information, you'll also see a listing of dropped packets, and other errors such as CRC, Alignment, and Too small frames. When such errors become significant, you will need to take action. For example, a growing number of dropped packets across a network segment may indicate excessive traffic, and serve as an early indication that an upgrade is required. Of course, you may also need to troubleshoot such issues when they occur suddenly or sporadically.

Checking Vital Signs   The Network Vital Signs mode in Observer Suite shows the current LAN activity mapped with current error conditions on your LAN. This display has been designed to give you a complete snapshot of error conditions (and of the importance of those error conditions versus your current LAN activity). Simply click the Network Vital Signs button and the Ethernet Vital Signs and Collision Expert dialog box opens (see Figure 27-7). The display informs you as to the error condition and its severity with respect to traffic conditions by combining graphical shapes with specific color codes.

As with the Network Activity Display, the following colors have specific meanings. A yellow line anywhere in the display represents an idle condition. In other words, no matter what your display is telling you, activity is so low that the errors are not statistically important. A green line shows normal network activity and error counts. A red line indicates error counts out of "normal" range. When a red line condition is

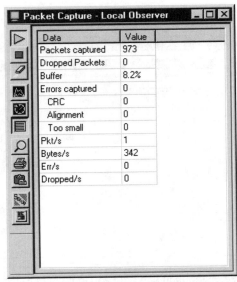

FIGURE 27-6   You can use a protocol analyzer to quickly measure common traffic errors.

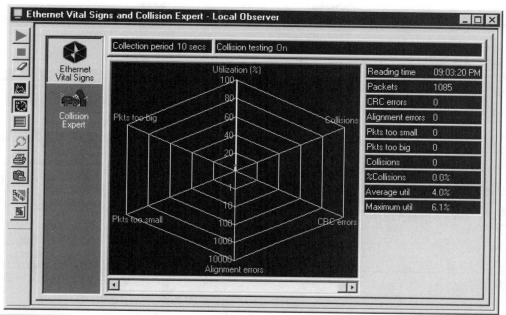

FIGURE 27-7 Some analyzers can display network utilization versus common errors to help you quickly measure the severity of network errors.

displayed, a blue line will connect the error condition with possible related or affected parts of the display. A red line will be displayed when the following default error counts are encountered:

- Utilization goes over 35 percent.
- CRC and packets too small represent more than 25 percent of the total traffic.
- Packets too big represent over 1 percent of total traffic.

Network Trending

To manage LANs efficiently, it is often important to view the trends of network traffic over days, weeks, and even months. Rather than collect and review current network statistics, Observer Suite's *Network Trending* mode (together with the Network Trending Viewer) allows administrators to automatically collect, store, view, and analyze the network traffic statistics over long periods—this is the main baselining feature of Observer Suite. Statistical data is stored in a format that can be easily compressed and viewed on any site that has an Observer network trending viewer installed. Once the data is collected, you can display it in either a chart or list format for the network as a whole, or for each station present on the network for any point in time during the collection period. Network trending can also create text reports about network conditions over specified periods.

Gathering Information

It takes time to establish a network baseline, and longer collection periods provide better baselines. When Observer Suite starts, the network trending dashboard is started automatically (see Figure 27-8). The dashboard display supplies a continuous heads-up display of the general network trends, Internet

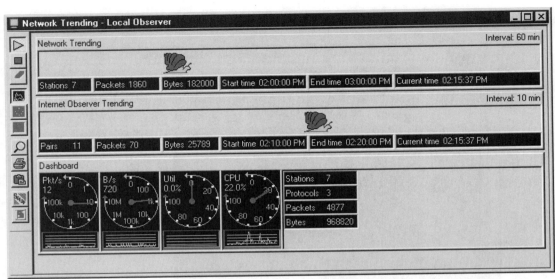

FIGURE 27-8 Network trending lets you track LAN behavior over time for further study and analysis.

networking trends, and CPU conditions on the segment being monitored. There are two progress markers (snails). One displays the progress of network trending and the other displays Internet observer trending. For example, if the collection interval is set for one hour, the snail will take one hour to progress from the left side of the progress track to the right side—this allows you to see the state of your data collection at a glance. The Network Trending pane contains the following items:

- **Interval** The block of time in which data will be collected.
- **Stations** The number of stations on the network that have sent traffic during the present interval.
- **Packets** The number of packets sent on the network during the present interval.
- **Bytes** The number of bytes sent on the network during the present interval.
- **Start Time** The start time of the present interval.
- **End Time** The end time of the present interval.
- **Current Time** The current time.

The Internet Observer Trending pane contains the following items:

- **Pairs** The number of station pairs on the network that have exchanged IP traffic during the present interval.
- **Packets** The number of IP packets sent on the network during the present interval.
- **Bytes** The number of bytes sent in IP packets on the network during the present interval.
- **Start Time** The start time of the present interval.
- **End Time** The end time of the present interval.
- **Current Time** The current time.

There are also four dial displays:

■ **Packets per second (Pkt/s)**   This displays the packets-per-second rate in dial and history (the graph below the dial) format.

■ **Bytes per second (B/s)**   This displays the bytes-per-second rate in dial and history (the graph below the dial) format.

■ **Bandwidth Utilization (Util)**   This displays the currently monitored segment's bandwidth utilization in dial and history (the graph below the dial) format.

■ **Processor Utilization (CPU)**   This displays the local (or *probe*) PC's current processor utilization in dial and history (the graph below the dial) format.

Finally, there are four additional items to the right of the dial displays:

■ **Stations**   The number of stations on the network that have sent traffic during the time that network trending has been running during the current session.

■ **Protocols**   The number of protocols used on the network during the time that network trending has been running during the current session.

■ **Packets**   The number of packets sent on the network during the time that network trending has been running during the current session.

■ **Bytes**   The number of bytes sent on the network during the current network trending session.

Observer allows you to customize network trending behavior by adding or editing IP subprotocols (to be included in the analysis), alter the days and times that trending is performed, and set collection intervals.

Viewing Results

Once you've collected your baseline data, you'll need to process and analyze the data to form conclusions and document the network. Observer Suite uses the Network Trending Viewer to present trending data. The Network Trending Viewer can display statistical data that has been collected in a chart or list format, and presented for the network as a whole, or for every individual station present on the network at any moment of time. Simply click the Load Network Trending Viewer button, and the Network Trending Viewer dialog box will appear (see Figure 27-9).

The Viewer tree on the left presents a list of available trending data for analysis. In the figure, data is available for Wednesday, January 9, 2002. Branches with a root entry ending with "Observer" or "Probe" contain network trending data. Branches with a root entry ending with "(Internet)" contain Internet Observer data. Branches ending with "(Switch)" contain switch trending data. The icons along the left side of the workspace are the available statistics that you can choose from, including

■ **Station activity time**   This displays when each station was first seen on the LAN, and when it was last seen on the LAN.

■ **Top talkers**   This lists each station's total packets in and out, and each station's total bytes in and out (see Figure 27-9).

■ **Packet size distribution**   This option displays the packet size distribution.

■ **Bandwidth utilization**   This option shows you the bandwidth utilization (maximum, average, and minimum) for the selected day (or days).

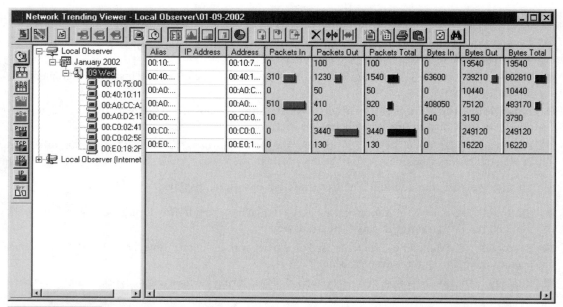

FIGURE 27-9   After trending, you can review results (such as Top Talkers) for specific dates.

■ **Router bandwidth utilization**   This displays router bandwidth utilization in total packet or percentage format. Remember that you must have a router and a router speed selected in Observer's Router Observer mode to see statistics in this dialog box and you must have the router selected in the list.

■ **Protocols**   This displays the protocols seen on the LAN. Available types are TCP/IP, IPX/SPX, NetBIOS (including NetBEUI), AppleTalk, DECNET, SNA, and Other.

■ **TCP/IP subprotocols**   This displays the subprotocols of TCP/IP seen on the LAN by type—this includes ARP, RARP, IP, TCP, UDP, ICMP, and Other.

■ **IPX Subprotocols**   This option displays the subprotocols of IPX/SPX seen on the LAN broken out by type. Available types are: SPX, IPX, SAP, NCP, RIP, NetBIOS, Diagn (Diagnostic), WatchDog, Serializ (Serialization), and Other.

■ **IP Applications**   This displays configurable (port-based) IP applications. These are configurable in the Network Trending Setup dialog boxes.

■ **Errors**   This display will be dependent on the topology of the trending data (such as token ring, Ethernet, or FDDI frame errors).

Selecting particular statistics lets you identify stations that are demanding unusually large amounts of network time, sending unusually large (or small) packets, using unexpected protocols, experiencing errors, and so on. For example, by selecting a specific station in the left pane (00:10:75:00:7F:13), choosing Packet Size Distribution (SDS), and then selecting the Alternate Columns Graph mode (see Figure 27-10), you can easily see that the station mainly used packets that were 129–512 bytes long.

Finally, the line of icons along the top of the workspace represents the available options, and these generally allow you to select presentation options (such as graph, dial, or list) to manage the way trending statistics are displayed, create reports, print reports, and so on.

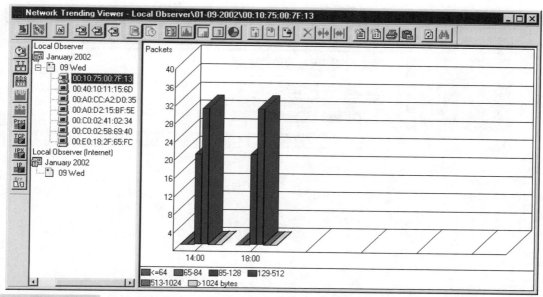

FIGURE 27-10   Graphing tools let you easily compare trending data for the LAN.

ADDITIONAL STATISTICS

While statistics like traffic and error measurement can help you establish a solid baseline for your network, there are many other attributes of your network's performance that can be measured and baselined. Tools like Observer Suite allow you to measure the performance of your network routers, Web, and Internet, so let's look at those features briefly.

Router Performance

Observer Suite provides the Router Observer mode, which allows you to look at a router (or group of routers) in real time to gauge their utilization rate. You can quickly find out if a router is acting as a bottleneck and whether the source of the packets clogging the router is incoming or outgoing (or both). By examining historical information, you can tell whether this is a chronic problem that might indicate the need for a faster connection, or an acute problem that might indicate a failure of some sort. Observer makes passive measurements, so the analyzer doesn't adversely affect router performance. To start Router Observer, simply select the Router Observer feature from Observer's toolbar, and the Router Observer dialog box will open. The dialog will report packets/sec, bytes/s, and the utilization percentage of the selected router IP address.

Web Observer

This mode was designed to view a Web server from the standpoint of traffic flow into and out of the server. In this mode, Observer focuses on all port 80 traffic (the default for Web traffic) or all port traffic going in and out of the specified device. To start Web Observer, simply click the Web Observer button and the Web Observer dialog box will open (see Figure 27-11). The main display shows the Web server address

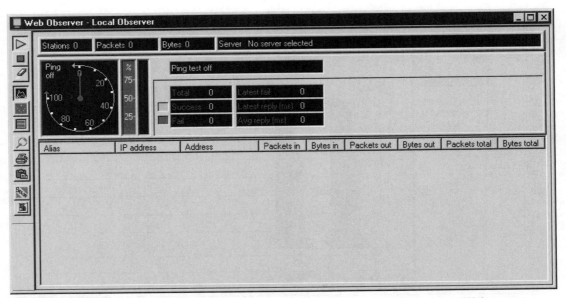

FIGURE 27-11   Tools like Web Observer let you baseline the operation of your Web server.

and the response time dial for the ICMP Ping test. Should the server go down, the dial display turns into a broken connection display. Click the Setup button and make the necessary selections:

■ You may "Select a Web server from the list" to select the server's IP address—including alias and comment.

■ You may use the "Remove inactive IP addresses after (min)" text box to set how long to keep IP addresses on the table before assuming they are inactive.

Web Observer displays the following items:

■ **Stations**   The number of stations that have exchanged traffic with the selected server during the time that Web Observer has been running, minus those stations whose IP addresses have been removed from the table.

■ **Packets**   The total number of packets transmitted and received by the selected server during the time that Web Observer has been running.

■ **Bytes**   The total number of bytes transmitted and received by the station during the time that Web Observer has been running.

■ **Server**   This displays the name, IP address, and MAC address of the specified Web server.

■ **Overall average packets per second**   This displays the average packets per second handled by the Web server.

■ **Overall average bytes per second**   This displays the average bytes per second handled by the Web server.

■ **Overall average utilization**   This displays the average utilization of the selected Web server.

On the bottom pane display, Observer lists the current IP addresses that are communicating with the specified Web server with the following information:

- **Alias**   This displays the name given to the listed station in Discover Network Names mode.
- **IP Address**   The IP address of the listed station.
- **Address**   The MAC address of the listed station.
- **In packets**   This displays the number of packets sent *to* the listed station *from* the specified Web server.
- **In bytes**   This displays the number of bytes sent *to* the listed station *from* the specified Web server.
- **Out packets**   This displays the number of bytes sent *to* the listed station *from* the specified Web server.
- **Out bytes**   This displays the number of bytes sent *from* the listed station *to* the specified Web server.
- **Total packets**   This displays the total number of packets sent between the listed station and the specified Web server.
- **Total bytes**   This displays the total number of bytes sent between the listed station and the specified Web server.
- **In % util**   The total utilization percentage received between the listed station from the specified Web server.
- **Out % util**   The total utilization transmitted to the listed station from the specified Web server.

Internet Observer

Internet Observer mode permits you to examine Internet traffic on your LAN. This can be used to monitor overall Internet usage, and to focus on a specific station or stations. It's also possible to break down Internet usage by subprotocols (for example, to see what proportion of Internet traffic involves the WWW or POP mail). Internet usage can be tracked by Internet Patrol, IP Pairs (Matrix), and IP SubProtocols. To start Internet Observer, simply click the Internet Observer button from the main toolbar, and the Internet Observer dialog box will open.

The *Internet Patrol* view displays MAC address to layer 3 IP address traffic. If the MAC address has an alias assigned, this text will be displayed instead of the true MAC address. Additionally, the IP addresses of the destination sites will be resolved using DNS. This view of your Internet traffic is most appropriate for local network traffic to and from the Internet, and for sites that use DHCP. Since DHCP changes IP addresses frequently, source IP addresses are not useful on DHCP site for identification. The *IP to IP Pairs (Matrix)* view displays true layer 3 IP address to true layer 3 IP address traffic. This view of your Internet traffic is appropriate for local segments talking to the Internet, and for backbone traffic flow. On a local network, this view will show all Internet usage *if* the IP addresses are static. If you're using DHCP on your local network, you should view your Internet traffic using the Internet Patrol mode. The *IP Subprotocols* view can display layer 3 IP address traffic flow broken down by subprotocol. Subprotocols are defined in the setup dialog box. Twelve user-defined subprotocols can be created ("other" indicates a protocol that did not match the criteria of the 12 user-defined protocols).

CONSIDER YOUR SECURITY

Security is another issue that should be addressed whenever you're using a protocol analyzer. Remember that a protocol analyzer can collect packets of information traveling all over the network, and it's possible that confidential information may wind up being copied to your system or department. If you send captured information to an outside firm for analysis, the security threat may be even more severe. All information captured with a protocol analyzer should be considered confidential—just like the corporate e-mail, salary data, and accounting records that typically flow through your network. Network administrators review security procedures with their legal departments to make sure that they are complying with all of their organization's binding nondisclosure or confidentiality requirements before sending any such information to outsiders.

 For additional security, prevent unauthorized users from accessing your protocol analyzer.

System Monitor

While tools like Observer Suite may be excellent for establishing communication baselines across your network, you may also need to check or document the hardware-oriented performance of your various network servers. Establishing a baseline for memory, processor, and disk utilization can help you to identify unusual server loads later—and indicate the need for upgrades such as additional RAM or a second processor. This part of the chapter shows you how to analyze your server with System Monitor (included with Windows 2000 Server).

BOTTLENECKS AND TUNING

A *bottleneck* occurs when one or more of your server resources are stretched to the point where the server's performance is impaired. For example, there may not be enough memory to run the number of applications necessary on a server. This causes additional disk access (to a swap file), and reduces server performance. As another example, excessive network traffic may be occurring at one NIC port, even though there is more than one NIC port on the server. In this case, it may be necessary to balance the network traffic in order to utilize all NIC ports more evenly. A bottleneck may occur for the following reasons:

- Resources are insufficient (i.e., insufficient RAM) and additional or upgraded components are required.
- Resources are not sharing workloads evenly and need to be balanced.
- A resource is malfunctioning and needs to be replaced (i.e., a NIC port fails, forcing additional traffic to remaining ports).
- A program is monopolizing a particular resource. This may require using another program, having a developer rewrite the program, adding or upgrading resources, or running the program during periods of low demand.
- A resource is incorrectly configured and configuration settings should be changed.

Once you identify a bottleneck and hypothesize a solution, you'll need to implement your solution—tuning the server to ease the bottleneck and improve performance. Regardless of the problem, make only *one* change at a time. In some cases, a problem that appears to relate to a single component may be the result of bottlenecks involving multiple components. For this reason, it is important to proceed with care. Making multiple changes simultaneously may make it impossible to assess the impact of each individual change.

Also, be sure to repeat monitoring after *every* change. This lets you understand the effect of the change, and determine whether additional changes are required. For example, if you feel that system memory is a bottleneck, you would add more memory, then measure performance again to verify that the additional memory has actually resolved the bottleneck. Remember that a change can also affect other resources, so it's important to establish a completely new set of baselines whenever any change is made. For example, that extra memory you just installed may have reduced the server's dependence on the disk subsystem (the swap file), so it's possible that the memory upgrade may improve the apparent performance of the disk subsystem as well. By rerunning a complete set of baselines, you can get a new picture of the server's performance.

Be sure to review event logs, because some performance problems generate output you can display in Event Viewer.

CHOOSING THE COMPUTER

When monitoring computers remotely, you have several options for collecting data. For example, you could run performance logging on the administrator's computer—drawing data continuously from each remote computer. In another case, you could have each computer running the service to collect data and use a batch program (at regular intervals) to transfer the data to the administrator's computer for analysis and archiving.

Centralized data collection (collection on a local computer from remote computers that you are monitoring) is simple to implement because only one logging service is running. You can collect data from multiple systems into a single log file. However, it causes additional network traffic, and may be restricted by available memory on the administrator's computer. Use the Add Counters dialog box to select a remote computer while running System Monitor on your local computer. *Distributed* data collection (data collection that occurs on the remote computers you are monitoring) does not incur the memory and network traffic problems of centralized collection. However, it does result in delayed availability of the data—requiring that the collected data be transferred to the administrator's computer for review. For distributed data collection, use computer management on a local computer to select a remote computer on which to collect data.

When monitoring remote computers, the remote computer will only allow access to user accounts that have permission to access it. To monitor remote systems from your computer, you must start the Performance Logs and Alerts service using an account that has permission to access the remote computers you want to monitor. By default, the service is started under the local computer's "system" account, which generally has permission only to access services and resources on the local computer. To start this under a different account, use Services under Computer Management and update the properties of the Performance Logs and Alerts service.

MEMORY PERFORMANCE

Let's start your server baseline by measuring memory performance. Processor and memory resources have such a significant influence on the operation of your server, it's important to understand how programs use these resources. Use System Monitor to observer key processor and memory items. Start System Monitor and Add the Process\ **% Processor Time** and Process\ **Working Set** counters to the graph (see Figure 27-12). % Processor Time is the percentage of elapsed time that a processor is busy executing all threads for a particular process (this is usually high for the Idle process when the system is not busy). Working Set is the current number of physical memory bytes used by a process. This value can be larger than the minimum number of bytes actually needed by the process. It may reflect physical bytes that are shared by multiple processes.

When a program starts, the Process\ **% Processor Time** values climb sharply for each program, decrease, and then level off. It's important to be aware that processor usage spikes at program startup—you

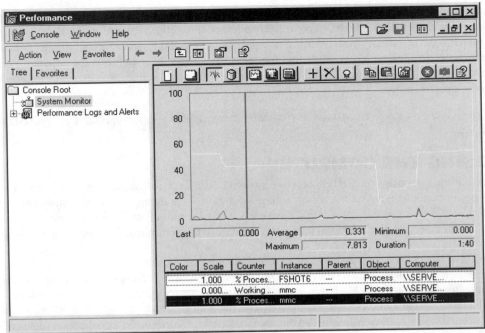

FIGURE 27-12   Use System Monitor to baseline memory performance and justify server memory upgrades.

may want to omit temporarily high startup values from your monitoring data to obtain a more accurate picture of typical processor usage by your programs. After startup, the graph should show increases in processor activity as the programs perform some activity (for example, as System Monitor reads a new set of counter values). You can observe this by changing the update interval for System Monitor. Notice that if System Monitor is configured with a short update interval, it will read data more frequently and generate more processor activity by System Monitor. A longer update interval will generate less processor activity.

For every program running on a computer, the operating system allocates a portion of physical memory (this is called the *working set*). Even if the program is not generating any activity, the operating system allocates memory for the program's working set. The working set value is of interest when the Memory\ Available Bytes counter falls below a certain threshold. Windows 2000 meets the memory requirements of programs by using free memory. As free memory falls into short supply, the operating system begins to take memory from the working sets of less active programs. Consequently, you'll see the values for one program's working set increase while the values for other programs decrease. If there isn't sufficient memory on the system to satisfy the requirements of all active programs, paging occurs and program performance suffers.

Low Memory

To monitor for a low-memory condition, use System Monitor and track Memory\Available Bytes and Memory\Pages/sec. Available Bytes indicates how many bytes of memory are currently available for use by processes. Low values for Available Bytes (4MB or less) may indicate there is an overall shortage of memory on your computer (or that a program is not releasing memory). Pages/sec provides the number of pages that were either retrieved from disk due to hard page faults or written to disk to free space in the working set due to page faults. If the value of Pages/sec is 20 or more, you should research the paging activity further. A high rate for Pages/sec may not indicate a memory problem but may instead be the result of running a program that uses a memory-mapped file.

If you suspect a *memory leak* (a program that is not releasing memory), monitor Memory\Available Bytes and Memory\Committed Bytes to observe memory behavior, and monitor Process\Private Bytes, Process\Working Set, and Process\Handle Count for processes you think may be leaking memory. Also monitor Memory\Pool Non-paged Bytes, Memory\Pool Non-paged Allocs, and Process <process_name>\ Pool Non-paged Bytes if you suspect that a kernel-mode process is causing the leak. If a particular program is causing a memory leak, you should contact the software maker for a patch or update (or use another similar program instead).

Excessive Paging

Excessive paging can make substantial use of the hard disk, and it is possible to confuse a memory shortage that causes paging with a disk bottleneck that results in paging. As a result, when you investigate the causes of paging (where a memory shortage is not apparent), make sure to track disk usage counters such as Physical Disk\% Disk Time and Physical Disk\Avg. Disk Queue Length along with memory counters.

For example, include Page Reads/sec with % Disk Time and Avg. Disk Queue Length. If a low rate of page-read operations occurs with high values for % Disk Time and Avg. Disk Queue Length, there could be a disk bottleneck. However, if an increase in queue length is not accompanied by a decrease in the pages-read rate, then a memory shortage exists. To determine the impact of excessive paging on disk activity, multiply the values of the Physical Disk\Avg. Disk sec/Transfer and Memory\Pages/sec counters. If the product of these counters exceeds 0.1, paging is taking more than 10 percent of disk access time. If this occurs over a long period, you probably need more memory.

Next, check for excessive paging due to programs that are running. If possible, stop the program with the highest Working Set value and see whether that dramatically changes the paging rate. If you suspect excessive paging, check the Memory\Pages/sec counter. This shows the number of pages that needed to be read from disk because they were not in physical memory. Again, a high paging rate may indicate the need for more memory.

Paging Files

If you conclude that paging is affecting server performance, you have some options for how to manage your paging file for better performance. For example, you can place a paging file on other disk drives. When you have multiple hard disks available, splitting up the paging file between disks can speed up the access time. If you have two hard disks and you split the paging file, both hard disks can be accessing information simultaneously, greatly increasing the throughput. However, if you have two hard disks and one hard disk is faster than the other, it may be more effective to store the paging file only on the faster hard disk. You may need to experiment to discover the best configuration for your system.

You can also increase the size of the paging file. When you start Windows 2000, it automatically creates a paging file (*pagefile.sys*) on the disk where you installed the operating system. Windows 2000 uses the paging file to provide virtual memory. The recommended size for the paging file is equivalent to 1.5 times the amount of RAM available on your system. However, the size of the file also depends on the amount of free space available on your hard disk when the file is created. You can find out how large your system's paging file is by looking at the file size shown for *pagefile.sys* in Windows Explorer. If your users tend to run several programs simultaneously, they might find that increasing the size of the paging file will enable some programs to start faster.

Although you can reset both the initial and the maximum sizes for the paging file, it is typically more efficient to expand initial paging file size, rather than force the operating system to allocate more paging file space as programs start (which fragments the disk). If the paging file reaches its maximum size, a warning is displayed and the system may halt. To see whether your paging file is approaching its upper limit before it reaches the upper limit, check the actual file size and compare it to the maximum paging file size setting in the System utility in Control Panel (see Figure 27-13). If these two numbers are close in value, consider increasing initial paging file size or running fewer programs.

Paging file counters offer another way to see whether the size of the *pagefile.sys* file is appropriate. Start System Monitor and track the Paging File\% Usage and Paging File\% Usage Peak (bytes) statistics. If the % Usage Peak value approaches the maximum paging file setting (or if % Usage nears 100 percent), consider increasing the initial file size. If multiple paging files are spread across multiple disk drives, the path name of each file appears as an instance of the Paging File object type. You can either add a counter for each paging file or select the _Total instance to look at combined usage data for all your paging files.

DISK PERFORMANCE

It's also important to monitor disk activity. Disk-usage statistics help you balance the workload of network servers. System Monitor provides a series of physical disk counters for troubleshooting, for capacity planning, and for measuring activity on a given physical volume. At a minimum, you should monitor the following counters (see Figure 27-14):

- Physical Disk\Disk Reads/sec and Disk Writes/sec
- Physical Disk\Current Disk Queue Length
- Physical Disk\% Disk Time
- LogicalDisk\% Free Space
- Additional counters may include Physical Disk\Avg. Disk sec/Transfer, Avg. Disk Bytes/Transfer, and Disk Bytes/sec.

When testing disk performance, try logging performance data to another disk (or computer) so that it does not interfere with the disk you are testing.

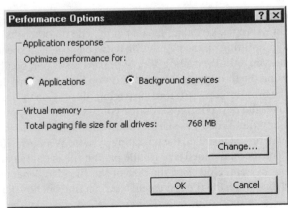

FIGURE 27-13   Performance Options indicates the maximum paging file size.

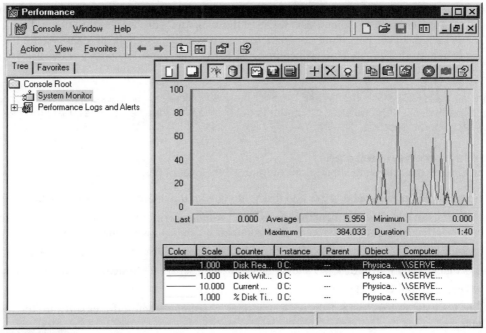

FIGURE 27-14   Use System Monitor to baseline disk subsystem performance and justify disk load balancing and upgrades.

The Avg. Disk sec/Transfer counter indicates how much time a disk takes to fulfill requests. A high value might indicate that the disk controller is continually retrying the disk because of failures. These misses will increase the average disk transfer time. For most disks, high average disk transfer times correspond to values greater than 0.3 seconds. You can also check the value of Avg. Disk Bytes/Transfer. A value greater than 20KB indicates that the disk drive is generally performing well—low values result if an application is accessing a disk inefficiently. For example, applications that access a disk randomly will raise Avg. Disk sec/Transfer times because random transfers require increased seek time. The Disk Bytes/sec counter gives you the throughput rate of your disk system.

Logical disk data is not collected by the operating system by default. You must type **diskperf -yv** at the command prompt. This causes the disk performance statistics driver used for collecting disk performance data to report data for logical drives or storage volumes.

Balancing Workload

A balanced drive workload helps the server achieve best efficiency. To balance the disk activity load on network servers, you'll need to know how busy the server disk drives are. Use the Physical Disk\% Disk Time counter to report the percentage of time a drive is active. If % Disk Time is high (over 90 percent), check the Physical Disk\Current Disk Queue Length counter to see how many system requests are waiting for disk access. The number of waiting I/O requests should be sustained at no more than 1.5 to 2 times the number of spindles making up the physical disk. Most disks have one spindle (though RAID devices usually have more). A hardware RAID device appears as one physical disk in System Monitor, but software RAID devices appear as multiple drives (instances).

You can either monitor the Physical Disk counters for each physical drive (other than RAID), or you can use the _Total instance to monitor data for all of the computer's drives. Use the values of the Current Disk Queue Length and % Disk Time counters to detect bottlenecks with the disk subsystem. If Current Disk Queue Length and % Disk Time values are consistently high, consider upgrading the disk drive(s) or moving some files to an additional disk or server.

When using a RAID device, the % Disk Time counter can indicate a value greater than 100 percent. If so, use the Avg. Disk Queue Length counter to determine how many system requests (on average) are waiting for disk access.

Disk Recommendations

You can employ the following suggestions to improve the overall performance of your disk system:

- Upgrade to a higher-speed disk (or add disks) along with the disk controller and the bus.
- On servers, use Disk Management to create striped volumes on multiple physical disks. This solution increases effective throughput because I/O commands can be issued concurrently.
- Distribute programs among servers. The distributed file system (DFS) can be used to balance workload.
- Tasks that heavily utilize disk I/O should be isolated on separate physical disks or disk controllers.
- Use Disk Defragmenter (Defrag) to optimize disk space.
- To improve the efficiency of disk access, consider installing the latest driver software for your host adapters.

PROCESSOR PERFORMANCE

Each application and program that runs on the server demands a certain amount of processor time. Monitoring the Processor and System object counters provides valuable information about the utilization of your processors and helps you determine whether or not a processing bottleneck exists on your server. You will want to include Processor\% Processor Time for processor usage. This counter shows the percentage of elapsed time that a processor is busy executing a nonidle thread. Also check Processor\% User Time and % Privileged Time for more detail. Finally, you can check System\Processor Queue Length for bottleneck detection (see Figure 27-15).

When you examine processor usage, consider the role of the computer and the type of work being performed. Depending on what the computer is doing, high processor values could mean that the system is efficiently handling a heavy workload, or that it's struggling to keep up. For example, if you're monitoring a computer used for computation, the computational program might easily use 100 percent of the processor's time—even if the performance of other applications on that computer seems to suffer. This can be addressed by changing workload. On the other hand, values around 100 percent on a server that processes client requests may indicate that processes are queuing up (waiting for processor time) and causing a bottleneck. Such a high level of sustained processor use is unacceptable for a server.

Processor Bottlenecks

A processor bottleneck develops when the threads of a process require more processor cycles than are available. Long processor queues can build up, and system response suffers. The two most common causes of processor bottlenecks are CPU-bound programs and drivers or subsystem components (usually disk or network components) that generate excessive interrupts.

To check processor bottleneck due to excessive demand for processor time, check the value of the System\Processor Queue Length counter. A queue of two or more items indicates a bottleneck. If more

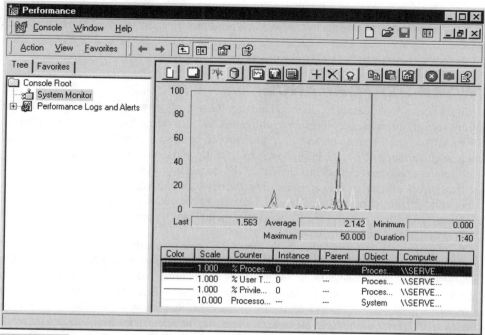

FIGURE 27-15 Use System Monitor to baseline processor performance and justify additional processors or processor speed upgrades.

than a few program processes are contending for most of the processor's time, installing a faster processor will improve throughput. An additional processor can help if you are running multithreaded processes, but remember that adding processors may have limited benefits. In addition, the Server Work Queues\Queue Length counter tracks the current length of the server work queue, and can reveal processor bottlenecks. A sustained queue length greater than 4 indicates possible processor congestion.

To see if interrupt activity is causing a bottleneck, watch the values of the Processor\Interrupts/sec counter to measure the rate of service requests from I/O devices. If this counter value increases dramatically without a corresponding increase in system activity, it can indicate a hardware problem. You can also monitor Processor\% Interrupt Time for an indirect indicator of disk drivers, network adapters, and other devices that generate interrupts. Finally, watch the values of System\File Control Bytes/second to look for hardware problems that may affect processor performance (such as IRQ conflicts).

Multiprocessor Efficiency

You can use System Monitor to observe the efficiency of a multiprocessor computer. The Process\% Processor Time counter reports the sum of processor time on each processor for all threads of the process. The Processor (_Total)\% Processor Time measures the processor activity for all processors in the computer. This sums the average nonidle time of all processors during the sample interval and divides it by the number of processors. For example, if all processors are busy for half of the sample interval (on average), it displays 50%. It also displays 50% if half of the processors are busy for the entire interval and the others are idle. Finally, use the Thread\% Processor Time counter to track the amount of processor time for a thread.

To assign a particular process or program to a single processor to improve its performance (at the expense of other processes), open the Task Manager and click Set Affinity. This option is available only on multiprocessor systems. Setting processor affinity can improve performance by reducing the number of processor cache flushes as threads move from one processor to another—this might be a good option for dedicated file servers. However, dedicating a program to a particular processor may not allow other program threads to migrate to the least busy processor.

NETWORK PERFORMANCE

System Monitor can also be used to baseline and monitor the server's network activity. Network monitoring typically consists of observing server resource utilization and measuring overall network traffic. The Network Segment\Broadcast frames received/sec statistic can be used to establish a baseline if monitored over time. Large variations from the baseline can be investigated to determine the cause of the problem. Since each computer processes every broadcast, high broadcast levels mean lower performance. Network Segment\% Network utilization indicates how close the network is to full capacity. The threshold depends on your network infrastructure and topology. If the value of the counter is above 30 to 40 percent, collisions can cause problems. Finally, the Network Segment\Total frames received/sec counter indicates when bridges and routers might be flooded.

Investigating network performance includes monitoring activity at different network layers. At the data link layer (including the NIC), use the Network Interface object with Bytes total/sec, Bytes sent/sec, and Bytes received/sec. At the network layer, use the IP object counters such as Datagrams Forwarded/sec, Datagrams Received/sec, Datagrams/sec, and Datagrams Sent/sec. When working at the transport layer, use TCP object counters such as Segments Received/sec, Segments Retransmitted/sec, Segments/sec, and Segments Sent/sec. If the retransmission rate is high, there may be a hardware problem. If you're using the NetBEUI protocol, employ the NetBEUI counters like Frame Bytes Received/sec, Frames Received/sec, Frames Rejected/sec, and NetBEUI Resource\Times Exhausted.

Consider Resources

Abnormal network counter values often indicate problems with a server's memory, processor, or disks. For that reason, the best approach to monitoring a server is to watch network counters in conjunction with Processor\% Processor Time, PhysicalDisk\% Disk Time, and Memory\Pages/sec. For example, if a dramatic increase in Pages/sec is accompanied by a decrease in Bytes Total/sec handled by a server, the computer is probably running short of physical memory for network operations. Most network resources (including network adapters and protocol software) use nonpaged memory. If a computer is paging excessively, most of its physical memory may have been allocated to network activities—leaving a small amount of memory for processes that use paged memory. To check this, review the computer's system event log for entries indicating that it has run out of paged or nonpaged memory.

When working at the presentation/program layer, use the Server object counters if you're monitoring a server, or the Redirector object counters if you're monitoring a user's client computer. The Redirector object counters collect data about requests transmitted by the Workstation service, and the Server object counters collect data about requests received and interpreted by the Server service. At a minimum, include the Bytes Total/sec counter for both the Redirector object (for client computers that you monitor) and the Server object (for server computers). Each of these objects provides several other counters you may want to monitor if you suspect problems with either the Workstation or Server services:

- Redirector\Current Commands
- Redirector\Network Errors/sec
- Redirector\Reads Denied/sec

- Redirector\Writes Denied/sec
- Redirector\Server Sessions Hung
- Server\Sessions Errored Out
- Server\Work Item Shortages
- Server\Pool Paged Peak
- Server\Nonpaged Pool Failures

Network Recommendations

You can employ the following suggestions to improve the overall network performance of your server:

- Configure your network so that systems shared by the same group of people are on the same subnet.
- Unbind infrequently used network adapters.
- If you're using more than one protocol, set the order in which the workstation and NetBIOS software bind to each protocol. If the protocol you use most frequently is first in the binding list, average connection time decreases. Also, some protocols are faster than others for certain network topologies. If you're optimizing a client computer, putting the faster protocol first in the bindings list improves performance.
- Install a high-performance NIC in the server. If your server uses a 16-bit adapter, you can significantly increase performance by replacing it with a high-performance 32-bit adapter.
- Use multiple network adapters. For example, Windows 2000 supports multiple adapters for a given protocol, and multiple protocols for a given adapter. Although this configuration can create distinct networks that cannot communicate with one another, it is a way to increase file-sharing throughput.

Further Study

Network Instruments: **www.networkinstruments.com**
Agilent: **www.agilent.com**
Hewlett-Packard: **www.hp.com**

28

NETWORK MANAGEMENT

Any pro can tell you that network administration is a difficult and time-consuming pursuit. Keeping track of the many users, servers, and system resources on even a small network can tax the patience of even the sharpest mind. Each year, organizations invest a tremendous amount of technical resources gathering information on network operation and devices. For example, just imagine the time required to inventory 150 workstations in order to check the video BIOS version, measure available hard drive space, and check proper fan or CPU voltage levels or other attributes.

The idea of *network management* has evolved to help administrators and technicians establish a level of control over a network's devices. In many cases, network management tools allow an administrator to inventory each station's hardware and software without ever looking at the individual PC. In addition, management tools often allow basic computer maintenance tasks (such as defragmenting a hard drive or updating a driver) to be handled remotely from a central "management console"—and even automating certain problem reports (such as low disk space or cooling fan failures) directly to the administrator.

Today, major PC manufacturers now provide powerful management tools such as HP's OpenView software, Compaq's Insight Manager 7, Dell's OpenManage, or Gateway's ManageX event manager. These tools can be installed on both servers and workstations, and report the detailed status of each managed device to the management console. This chapter illustrates the underlying technologies involved in network management, and highlights the capabilities of modern management tools.

Management Concepts

Network administration and maintenance can place tremendous demands on IT resources. To appreciate the importance of network management, you should understand some of the basic tasks that an administrator must perform at one time or another:

- New workstations and servers must be installed and configured.
- Existing workstations and servers must be upgraded.
- Operating systems and drivers must be upgraded.
- Applications (such as anti-virus tools) must be installed, patched, and upgraded.
- Devices like hubs, switches, and routers must be installed and configured.
- New wiring must be installed (and damaged wiring replaced).
- Backups must be performed and verified.
- Assets must be tracked (such as the configuration and repair records for each PC or server).
- Documentation must be updated to reflect changes and upgrades.
- Alarms and alerts must be reported, logged, and dealt with.
- Network performance must be quantified and tracked over time.

Of course, this is just an abbreviated list. Traditionally, each task had to be performed by an administrator or technician—often at each individual system location. For example, installing anti-virus client software typically meant long nights going from PC to PC and performing manual installations. As networks grew larger and more complex, the time and talent required to handle these types of tasks quickly became significant. This wasn't such a problem in the 1990s, when IT departments commanded large budgets and ample staffing. But today's corporate downsizing and budget restraints often leave IT departments struggling to meet the needs of network users.

NEED FOR MANAGEMENT

Network management allows for streamlined network monitoring, troubleshooting, and maintenance. Consider a midsized office network with 50 users, several servers, and assorted hubs and switches. Suppose that an administrator contemplated an operating system upgrade. Any good administrator will first check the PC hardware against the HCL to verify that the existing systems can handle the upgrade (or which systems may require an upgrade). However, this usually means checking each PC individually, and recording their hardware inventory by hand. With network management tools in place, an administrator can inventory "managed PCs" automatically, and generate a detailed report of each system's hardware and software configuration—this alone can save days of labor.

Let's look at another example. Suppose that your company institutes an antipiracy policy that prohibits software "sharing" in the workplace. In actual practice, there's no way for an administrator to enforce that kind of policy without going from PC to PC and manually checking each one to compare installed software against original installation CDs (or multiple installation licenses). A management platform can inventory installed software, and generate reports that the administrator can use immediately.

A management platform can also check the "health" of PCs by tracking key hardware attributes like power supply voltages, temperatures, cooling fan speeds, free disk space, and so on. A serious failure (i.e. a cooling fan stops) would generate an e-mail or page summoning a technician immediately. Minor failures (such as a slowing fan or elevated system temperatures) would trigger a routine visit, allowing a level of proactive support—stopping problems before they become serious.

But management isn't just for PCs. A management platform can be used to manage the setup and configuration of devices (such as routers) that are compliant with the particular management scheme. This allows an administrator to work through a standard management console rather than using proprietary management software with the device. In addition to setup and configuration, the management platform can also receive status and error messages from the device—generating an e-mail (or even a pager message) when errors occur.

MANAGEMENT AREAS

Network management is often defined as the process of controlling a complex network to maximize efficiency and productivity of the network and the IT staff responsible for it. Of course, this is a very broad definition, and is limited only by the management platform in use and the degree to which the platform is implemented in your organization. For example, installing instrumentation to monitor the hardware on only a few PCs would be a terrible underutilization of your management tools. Similarly, instrumenting all of the network's PCs has limited effect if you're not generating regular inventory reports or system alarms. Network management is typically broken up into five areas.

Network Problems

This involves solving problems and troubleshooting issues that occur across network stations (including workstations or servers), resources (like NAS servers and printers), interconnecting devices (such as hubs and switches), and wiring. As you'll see in Chapter 29, fault management involves several essential steps:

- Define the problem.
- Identify and isolate the problem's source.
- Repair the problem or replace the defective item(s).
- Retest the network.

The key to successful problem management is problem detection—recognizing that a problem exists (or may be likely to occur). Normally, problem management (or *troubleshooting*) starts when a user reports a problem, and must be performed manually using tools such as cable testers, multimeters, protocol analyzers, and so on. With some network management platforms, an administrator and technician can handle a wider range of problems with greater effectiveness. Management platforms can query network elements "on demand" or on a regular basis in order to monitor their proper operation. When a network device stops operating properly, the management platform can detect the event (often involving failure or impairment of network capabilities), prioritize the alert, take corrective action (if possible), and queue a technician to address or follow up on the trouble. For example, problem management tools can report system-specific issues like voltage or temperature problems—automatically generating an alarm and summoning a technician even before a system breaks down. Many common faults (such as low disk space or excessive fragmentation) can be addressed automatically without any human intervention at all.

There is a difference between an alarm and an alert. An *alarm* is a serious problem that demands immediate attention. An *alert* is a warning that should be investigated as soon as possible.

Network Setup and Configuration

As you've seen in previous chapters, device setup and configuration will have a profound impact on the operation of each device—and on the network as a whole. The problem for technicians and administrators is keeping track of such configuration information, and the time and effort needed to check or update the configuration of each device. Network management tools often allow you to gather and summarize the configuration of managed devices, with special emphasis on their hardware and software setup. When changes need to be made in the network, a technician can simply use management software to access and reconfigure the necessary managed devices (though some physical reconfiguration of cables and connections may also be needed to complete the process). It is also possible to review and compare the setup and configuration of multiple devices while planning network upgrades and maintenance activities.

This may sound simple, but it can present a very complex task. Setup and configuration management actually involves keeping detailed records of the software versions and hardware installations on most (if not all) devices on the network. For example, assume that all of the users on a network require the installation of a particular program, which requires the Windows 2000 Service Pack 2 updates (or later) released by Microsoft. Without a network management platform, you'd need to inventory each PC manually to determine the version of Windows on each system. However, the configuration management features of network management tools allow you to automatically inventory the connected PCs on demand. As another example, you may see that a new firmware version is available for an important switch. Rather than locating the switch and looking for a current firmware version marked "on the box," configuration management can let you query the switch and locate its current firmware version, along with other make and model information needed to select the correct firmware update file from the manufacturer.

Network Security

Management software can also help to secure your network resources. This normally involves keeping track of your network users and their activities. For example, you can use network security features to determine which users have been accessing sensitive files (such as payroll), and whether any unauthorized activities have taken place. Of course, most network operating systems today support detailed security logging that will provide you with much of the same information. Still, integrated security reporting means that the administrator doesn't need to go from server to server checking security logs to look for trouble. Failed logons and other unauthorized activity can be reported directly to the administrator's management console for further investigation.

Network Operations

An administrator must quantify network operation and performance, and many management platforms include the tools necessary to measure performance. Administrators can monitor a wide range of operational characteristics that will help to establish a viable network baseline, and identify any deviations from that baseline as potential network problems or encroaching bottlenecks as traffic levels increase. In addition, tracking such measurements over time will allow growth patterns to be anticipated and implemented before shortages develop (such as low storage space) or serious performance bottlenecks occur. See Chapter 27 for more information on network performance and baselining.

Network Cost Analysis

It costs money to operate a network, and a given network can only provide a finite amount of resources to an individual or group. An administrator must often account for the way in which a network is used. It is often difficult (even impossible) to make such determinations manually, but management platforms often include cost analysis tools that allow an administrator to monitor the network as if it were a consumable resource, and apply a financial dimension to network users. Once an administrator can quantify users and their activities, it becomes possible to associate costs with those users. In some cases, the cost analysis features of network management software can even allow an organization to change for network access.

Financial issues aside, accounting management must identify those users and groups that access given network resources (including servers, applications, printers, routers, or other elements of the network). By identifying clear patterns of use (and possibly comparing use against issues such as performance problems), an administrator can often plan effective upgrades or take corrective actions to streamline the network's operation. For example, suppose that a certain group within your organization made extensive use of a particular server, limiting the server's performance for users from other groups. You could make upgrade decisions based on that utilization data and give that group their own server. This would free up the existing server for all other users.

Introduction to SNMP

In order to implement network management, you'll need a standard protocol that's able to support a vast array of diverse network devices (regardless of their underlying architecture). The *Simple Network Management Protocol* (or SNMP) was proposed in 1988 as a set of Requests for Comments (RFCs). These RFCs defined the basic principles and implementation for a protocol that would establish a standard for Internet monitoring and management. This protocol could then serve as a single "universal" replacement for the myriad of vendor-specific network management solutions available at the time. Since then, SNMP has gained considerable popularity with network administrators. Although there are other management protocols available, SNMP has become widely accepted as the standard for network management. Most operating systems (including UNIX/Linux systems, NetWare servers, Windows 98/Me, and Windows NT/2000/XP) implement SNMP agents in their architecture, and most major computer hardware manufacturers now offer lines of networking products that support SNMP (including network cards, hubs, bridges, routers, switches, CSU/DSUs, and printers).

Subsequent RFCs for SNMP have corrected problems and supplemented the original standard database called the *Management Information Base* (or MIB). The standard MIB (defined by RFC1066 and later in RFC1213) defines network objects in ten groups: system, interfaces, address translation, IP, ICMP, TCP, UDP, EGP, transmission, and SNMP. However, manufacturers are constantly adding capabilities and features to their products, and the standard MIB objects and groups do not cover some features. To control additional features under SNMP, software and hardware vendors have developed proprietary MIBs.

Adding an SNMP agent to network hardware often increases the price of the product, so manufacturers usually offer versions with and without SNMP support.

In early 1990, the original SNMP specifications were revised and updated. New MIB groups were added, and some old MIB objects became obsolete. In general, the new MIB specification, called MIB II (or MIB-2) is compatible with the original MIB, now called MIB I (or MIB-1).

By the end of 1991, the standard SNMP MIB specification was extended through the *Remote Network Monitoring MIB* (called RMON). RMON provides a set of SNMP objects related to network analysis and monitoring. Information provided by RMON is somewhat different in scope from the typical SNMP information provided by network devices. Usually, an SNMP device collects information about the device itself (regarding the device's operation or its relationship to the network). By comparison, an RMON agent attempts to collect information about network traffic to and from other devices on the network (aside from the agent device). This information includes network statistics, history, information about hosts on the network, connections, and events. An RMON agent can set filters and capture traffic to and from specific devices on the network.

Security concerns with SNMP eventually prompted development of a secure SNMP called S-SNMP, and the first S-SNMP RFCs appeared in mid-1992. S-SNMP adds security enhancements to the original SNMP protocol, but does not offer any additional functionality. However, S-SNMP is *not* compatible with the original SNMP. About the same time, a considerable design effort focused on enhancing the SNMP protocol, incorporating the security features provided by S-SNMP and adding new MIB functions. The result of this effort is SNMP Version 2 (or SNMPv2). SMNPv2 was not well received by many software and hardware vendors—many of whom had devoted considerable effort to the development of SNMP MIB I and MIB II agents (and security was often not important for users). Even today, many agents currently provided by vendors are compliant with SNMP MIB II (not SNMPv2).

Keep in mind that SNMP MIB II and SNMPv2 are **not** the same thing.

By early 1999, the IETF had approved the draft standard for SNMPv3. The SNMPv3 specifications are built on the SNMPv2 draft standard protocol operations and transport mappings (RFC 1905-1907), and add security and remote configuration capabilities to SNMP. Still, SNMP MIB II is frequently encountered. For example, Compaq Insight Manager 7 only supports original v1-compliant agents and MIBs. So when compiling third-party MIBs in Compaq Insight Manager 7, be sure to obtain an SNMP v1-compliant version.

You can learn more about the features of SNMP versions with RFC2570 at **ftp://ftp.isi.edu/in-notes/rfc2570.txt**.

SNMP STATIONS AND AGENTS

The two main elements of any SNMP scheme are the *manager* (or *management station*) and the *agents* (often called *managed agents*). A management station is where a network administrator can view, analyze, and even manage local network devices. In actual practice, a management station can be a dedicated computer or workstation, or software running on a general-purpose workstation (like a PC running SNMP Extension on Windows 98/Me/NT/2000/XP). An SNMP agent is basically a program that runs on the managed device (such as bridges, routers, hubs, and workstations), and the program collects information about a device's operation. For example, if the object is a TCP/IP router, the agent can collect information about network traffic passing through the router and information about the behavior of the router itself under different load conditions.

Each SNMP agent maintains a database called the Management Information Base (MIB). The agent then uses the MIB to track and systematically update data. Information in a MIB is organized into a tree structure where each piece of data can be considered a leaf on various branches of the tree. Individual pieces of data are called data objects. When the management station needs information from an SNMP agent, it sends an SNMP request (SNMP specifications allow the station to ask for more than one MIB object in a single request).

When the SNMP agent receives the request from an SNMP management station, the agent searches its local MIB, finds the current values of the requested data, forms a response packet, and sends the response packet back to the management station. The management station receives the response packet, decodes it, and then displays the information as a list or a graphical format that allows the network manager to view, analyze, and modify the information. Applications designed to manage SNMP agents can vary widely in complexity and usefulness. Some applications are simple—only performing queries on certain devices and generating basic reports for the administrator. More sophisticated applications can map the network's topology, monitor network traffic, and trap selected events (producing alarms when those events occur). The best management console software can even produce trend analysis reports for capacity planning, which can help administrators plan upgrades and alterations to the network.

SNMP Messages

As you've seen, SNMP works by exchanging SNMP requests between a management station and SNMP agents throughout the network. Requests are usually transferred as a data portion of an IP (UDP) packet, although implementations of SNMP exist for TCP, IPX/SPX, and other protocols. For UDP, the SNMP management station sends requests to the agent over the network to UDP port number 161. The SNMP request message consists of two parts:

- The SNMP header, which includes the SNMP version number, request size information, and a password (called a *community name*).

- The block of one or more requested objects combined in the response packet.

Management software and device agents communicate using a limited set of operations referred to as *primitives*. These primitives are used to make requests and send information between the manager and agents. The following primitives are initiated by the management software:

- **GetRequest**   A management station uses the GetRequest primitive to retrieve the values of one or more objects from an agent. These values are usually singular—not columnar (like a table). When an agent receives a GetRequest order, it checks the packet for errors, finds the MIB values corresponding to the request packets, and sends a GetResponse packet back to the management station.

■ **GetResponse** Once the required data has been found in an agent's MIB, the agent sends a GetResponse packet back to the management station. If the error in the request packet occurs, the GetResponse packet returns an error message instead of the requested data. Any errors will be reported to the management station.

■ **GetNextRequest** The management station uses the GetNextRequest packet to retrieve one or more objects and their values from an agent. Usually these objects are multiple objects residing inside a table. To retrieve all lines of the table, the management station starts at the beginning of a table and sends GetNextRequest packets until all entries in the table are read. If no error occurs, the agent returns GetResponse packets after each of the GetNextRequest packets.

■ **SetRequest** The SetRequest packet is used by the management station to modify the value of an object on the SNMP agent. If no error occurs, the agent sets a new value for the specified object and returns a GetResponse packet as a confirmation of the successful operation.

■ **Traps** Agents send SNMP traps to the management station as notification when a predefined event occurs. The trap packet has a different format than the other four SNMP messages. With UDP, traps are sent to port 160 on the management station. Since trap messages can be sent from many different agents, the header of the trap packet includes an enterprise OID and agent address followed by the generic and specific trap types, timestamp, and the variable bindings field. There are seven generic trap types:

■ **ColdStart** The SNMP agent device is reinitializing in a way that allows the device or agent to be reconfigured.

■ **WarmStart** The SNMP agent device is reinitializing in the way that does not allow the device or agent to be reconfigured.

■ **LinkDown** The SNMP agent detected a failure in the connection link.

■ **LinkUp** The connection link came up.

■ **AuthenticationFailure** The SNMP management station did not properly authenticate with the agent.

■ **EGPNeighborLoss** An EGP peer of the SNMP agent is down.

■ **EnterpriseSpecific trap** The SNMP agent is notifying the management station about an event defined by the vendor for the device. The specific trap type provides more information.

Network Objects and MIBs

The primitives that support operations between managed SNMP objects would be pointless unless there were data to define the object and its status (or other contents). Management platforms store object information in the MIB (or MIB-II) database located on each agent device in the network. In some cases, a device may support numerous MIBs. Not only does the MIB hold details about the specific agent, but any pertinent information collected by the agent is also stored in its MIB. For example, a managed switch might include information that details the make, model, and firmware level, then track statistical details like incoming traffic, damaged traffic, destination addresses, and so on. When the management station makes a query using Get statements, that managed device (the agent) can return the requested details—or list corresponding errors. That information is then stored and displayed at the management station (often in a powerful database management system). Conversely, the management station can use Set statements to make configuration changes on the managed device as needed.

SNMP objects accommodate many different types of data in the tree structure, including numbers, text, addresses, bit-field assigned descriptions, and object IDs. Two specifications are used to describe the MIB objects: Abstract Syntax Notation One (ASN.1) and Basic Encoding Rules (BER).

Abstract Syntax Notation   *Abstract Syntax Notation One* (ASN.1) describes objects in textual MIB descriptions. It provides rules for writing consistent and compilable MIBs (both standard and proprietary). ASN.1 includes basic types (such as integer, octet string, object identifier, null, network address, and so on). For example, Figure 28-1 shows a sample of the ASN.1 object sysDescr from the MIB II System Group.

A singular SNMP object (such as Figure 28-1) is expressed as an OID appended by the ".0" address (OID.0). For example, the object sysDescr in the MIB System Group can be expressed as *1.3.6.1.2.1.1.1.0*, signifying that the object has only one instance. The SNMP Extension OID notation always uses the ".0" extension for singular objects in order to distinguish more clearly between singular and columnar objects.

In addition to singular objects, ASN.1 also describes the columnar objects such as tables or sequences of objects. A singular SNMP object represents only one value. In the situations where many data entries exist for a similar type (such as an IP routing table), it can be difficult or impossible to combine these values as singular values (particularly when the number of the entries is variable). In these situations, data is better represented by list-like structures or sequences called *tables*. Each line in a table represents one expression of the set of objects included in the table. Figure 28-2 illustrates a MIB II IP address table.

Basic Encoding Rules   *Basic Encoding Rules* (BERs) describe how to convert the values of MIB objects into a format that allows them to be transferred through a network. The BER specification provides a way to express all ASN.1 objects in binary format. BER rules are used for object types, object values, and object IDs. The usual format of a BER-encoded value includes the type field (1 byte), variable

```
-—the System group
sysDescr OBJECT-TYPE
SYNTAX OCTET STRING
ACCESS read-only
STATUS mandatory
DESCRIPTION
"A textual description of the entity. This value should include the full
name and version identification of the system's hardware type, software
operating-system, and networking software. It is mandatory that this only
contain printable ASCII characters."
::= { system 1 }
```

FIGURE 28-1   An example of an ASN.1 description of the MIB II object "sysDescr"

```
ipAddrTable OBJECT-TYPE
SYNTAX SEQUENCE OF IpAddrEntry
ACCESS not-accessible
STATUS mandatory
DESCRIPTION
"The table of addressing information relevant to this entity's IP addresses."
::= { ip 20 }
ipAddrEntry OBJECT-TYPE
SYNTAX IpAddrEntry
ACCESS not-accessible
STATUS mandatory
DESCRIPTION
"The addressing information for one of this entity's IP addresses."
INDEX { ipAdEntAddr }
::= { ipAddrTable 1 }
IpAddrEntry ::=
SEQUENCE {
ipAdEntAddr
IpAddress,
ipAdEntIfIndex
INTEGER,
ipAdEntNetMask
IpAddress,
ipAdEntBcastAddr
INTEGER
}
```

FIGURE 28-2   An example of an MIB II IP address table using SNMP

length, and data fields. The consistent format allows multiple objects to be placed in a single response packet on the transmitting side and decoded on the receiving side.

MIB Object Identifiers   Since each branch on the MIB tree is identified with a number, MIB objects are each defined by a unique address (called an *object identifier*) that traces the number of each branch up the tree. For example, the ISO8824 specification defines the lower branches of the SNMP MIB tree as *1.3.6.1*, where

■ 1 = iso

■ 3 = org

■ 6 = dod

■ 1 = Internet

But there are many other branches to consider. The SNMP tree resides under the Internet subtree, and four branches after the Internet subtree can be used by SNMP, such as

■ The *directory* subtree (1) is reserved for future use by OSI.

- The *mgmt* subtree (2) includes standard SNMP MIBs I or II (RFC1156 and RFC1213).

- The *experimental* subtree (3) is reserved for Internet experiments.

- The *private* subtree (4) provides space for vendor-specific MIBs.

All private MIBs are located under a further *enterprises* (1) branch. So, as an example, any private object ID (OID) should *begin* from the base MIB address of *1.3.6.1.4.1* (read "iso.org.dod.internet.private.enterprises"). As another example, the address *1.3.6.1.2.1* (read "iso.org.dod.internet.mgmt.mib") represents the address of a standard SNMP MIB I or II on the ISO tree (see Figure 28-3). Inside the *mib* branch, standard SNMP objects are organized beneath higher-level branches called *MIB groups*. Since there is a huge number of objects (the standard MIB II includes almost two hundred), MIB groups have been created to simplify addressing. Groups consist of related objects such as ICMP, TCP, EGP, and so on. The object address (the object's *instance*) is the path from the MIB's root to an object. For example, the object *sysDescr* in the MIB System Group (1.1) has the address *1.3.6.1.2.1.1.1*. There are numerous standard MIB groups in SNMP:

- **system**   This group identifies system hardware and software details.

- **interfaces**   This group identifies interface characteristics and limitations.

- **at**   This group provides information needed for address translation.

- **ip**   This group provides statistical information needed when using the Internet Protocol (IP).

- **icmp**   This group provides statistical information needed by the Internet Control Management Protocol (ICMP).

- **tcp**   This group provides connection information needed when using the Transmission Control Protocol (TCP).

- **udp**   This group provides statistical information needed when using the User Datagram Protocol (UDP).

- **egp**   This group provides component and status information when using the Exterior Gateway Protocol (EGP).

- **transmission**   This group provides information needed by objects that use particular transmission media.

- **snmp**   This group handles the objects used to collect information from across the network.

RMON

The SNMP approach uses a client/server scheme where the management platform acts as the server, and the various managed objects on the network act as clients. This technique works well but can sometimes cause excess traffic, as agents are systematically queried by the management station. Designers sought to overcome this potential pitfall by developing *Remote Network Monitoring* (or RMON). With RMON, this client/server relationship is reversed—each agent (or *RMON probe*) acts independently as its own "server" and does all of the active processing, and the management station serves as their "client." The management station no longer needs to poll its managed objects in order to collect updated data. Instead, the RMON probes do the work, only sending a trap to the management station and passing relevant information when certain events take place. This reduces the traffic overhead imposed by SNMP.

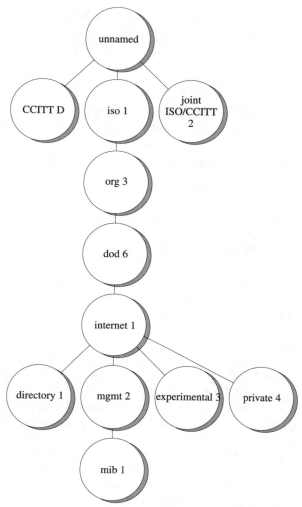

FIGURE 28-3   An example of an MIB object identifier tree (courtesy of Cisco Systems)

RMON Objects   Since RMON agents often have more "intelligence" than standard SNMP objects, the groupings are significantly different. For example, where SNMP objects generally start at address *1.3.6.1*, RMON MIB objects for Ethernet and token ring networks start at address *1.3.6.1.2.1.16*. The major objects for RMON fall into the following MIB groups:

- **statistics**   This group provides detailed information about network interfaces and is similar to the SNMP "interfaces" group.

- **history**   This group controls the way that data is collected on the network (such as sampling rate).

- **alarm**   This group manages the alarms used to signal selected events.
- **hosts**   This group monitors the MAC address of managed hosts discovered on the network.
- **hostTopN**   This group monitors statistical information regarding the managed hosts discovered on the network.
- **matrix**   This group monitors statistical information about the traffic between hosts on the network.
- **filter**   This group is used to select specific packets for capture.
- **capture**   This group uses the settings in the filter group to actually manage the capture of selected packets.
- **event**   This group manages the settings used to generate events to the management platform.

Modern RMON implementations also include many additional groups, such as the following:

TokenRing	protocolDir	protocolDist	addressMap
NlHost	nlMatrix	alHost	alMatrix
usrHistory	probeConfig	rmonConformance	

Ultimately, the many RMON groups and objects available provide a great deal of functionality to SNMP. RMON allows for the collection of statistical data from all levels of the OSI reference model—including applications at the highest level.

Non-SNMP Protocols

While SNMP (and RMON) is clearly a major management protocol, it is not the only protocol available. There are several other protocols that you should be aware of when planning or implementing network management: DMI, HTTP, and WEBM.

The *Desktop Management Task Force* (DMTF) was formed in 1992 and comprised of leading PC industry vendors and corporations. They established a common, platform-independent process for managing desktop hardware and software components. The DMTF defined the task force's two pieces of technology: the *Desktop Management Interface* (DMI) software and the *Management Information Format* (MIF) language. The DMI software serves as the liaison between desktop-resident management programs, manageable hardware, and software components on a computer.

Within the DMI framework, manageable devices contain a software component called a service layer. The service layer (and its extensions) monitors the various subsystems of the managed device, and provides this information to systems management consoles. DMI v2 delivers new functionality, including a standard method for communicating DMI information over the network and a method for handling alert notifications. Management software (such as Compaq Insight Manager 7) has the ability to accept DMI information, which is translated to traps in the management software, and is associated with the device sending the indication.

Some management software also takes advantage of the industry-standard HTTP protocol (the protocol used to transfer information over the Web) for transportation of management information. Major management developers base this effort on the *Web-based Enterprise Management* (WBEM) initiative. WBEM is an initiative supported by Compaq, Microsoft, Intel, BMC, Cisco, and 120 other platform, operating system, and application software suppliers.

When evaluating any management scheme, device compatibility is a key consideration. Avoid the use of management tools with limited or proprietary protocols that will not support your current or future network devices.

Dell OpenManage

Network management allows administrators to inventory, maintain, and upgrade software and drivers, and even troubleshoot client and server systems on a network—all from a centralized management station. Now that you've learned some of the basics involved in network management, let's look at one practical management platform, such as Dell's OpenManage. Unlike ordinary applications, management software is typically not implemented as a single universal program that is installed on all network devices. Instead, management platforms are generally divided up into a series of functional modules intended to provide specific features on a client, server, or other device.

Management tools can vary dramatically between manufacturers like HP, Compaq, Gateway, and others. This part of the chapter uses Dell's OpenManage tools as an example.

CLIENT ADMINISTRATION

Network management is only useful if the administrator is able to access and manage various workstations on the network. Each workstation must contain instrumentation—software that is able to check hardware conditions and software setups. In addition, there must also be a management console available to examine and report data collected from each workstation. Dell's OpenManage platform includes a variety of features for workstation management:

■ **OpenManage Client Instrumentation (OMCI)**   OMCI is an application intended to operate on Dell OptiPlex, Precision, and Latitude systems. OMCI is based on industry-standard management protocols such as DMI and CIM, and has support for SNMP. OMCI allows a DMI-, CIM-, or SNMP-compliant management console (a separate application) to collect inventory and configuration information and receive proactive notification of potential fault conditions. OMCI monitors the system hardware and sends an alert when a chassis has been compromised or a potential problem has been detected. Used in conjunction with tools like Dell's IT Assistant, OMCI allows an administrator to remotely perform remote BIOS updates and modify CMOS settings on a single system or a group of systems.

■ **OpenManage Image Management**   When you're deploying workstations with standard suites of software, it is often easier to install predefined disk images that can simply be transferred to a new station (rather than installing operating systems and applications manually). Dell's OpenManage image management is delivered through software provided by StorageSoft Corporation. The StorageSoft ImageCast IC3 product can help make the initial deployment of your corporate image much easier. Disk images can be deployed and updated on Dell clients for 30 days at no cost. ImageCast IC3 is a low-cost, rapid deployment tool that supports the multicasting of images over the network wire.

■ **OpenManage IT Assistant**   Dell's OpenManage IT Assistant is a workgroup management solution for managing clients and servers. It is not required to manage Dell client systems, but it is an easy to use, browser-based management console that allows an administrator to monitor system health at a glance. It has a discovery engine that will identify systems, place them in the appropriate group (such as desktop, portable, workstation, or server), and provide extensive detail on the configuration, OS, and hardware makeup of those systems.

■ **OpenManage Software Management**   Dell's OpenManage software management (such as the installation or upgrade of particular programs on network PCs) is delivered through software from ON Technology. ON Command CCM provides ongoing software and configuration management for enterprise customers that need more than the capabilities provided by traditional ghosting utilities. ON Command Special Edition assists with the initial setup and standardization of Dell clients for the first 30 days after purchase, at no charge, and can then be upgraded to the full ON Command CCM solution for ongoing software management.

■ **OpenManage Data/Personality Migration**   When a PC must be replaced (as a repair or upgrade), transferring the existing software, data, and user settings to the new system can be a time-consuming exercise. Personality Migration allows an existing PC to be transferred to another PC. OpenManage incorporates Miramar's Desktop DNA product as the system migration tool. Desktop DNA allows PC desktop users to selectively choose, save, and move customized system and application settings, applications, and files from one Windows PC to another, or to multiple PCs, locally or enterprise-wide. The result is reduced IT workloads and migration risks.

 There are additional OpenManage facilities available for array and cluster management support.

SERVER ADMINISTRATION

The OpenManage platform also includes Server Administrator software. This is a secure Web tool for managing individual servers like the Dell PowerEdge series. Server Administrator allows an administrator with an Internet/intranet connection to manage the server from any location using an ordinary Web browser. In addition to simply obtaining status information, an administrator can also troubleshoot, configure, and update the server (see Figure 28-4). In a typical scenario, the management console detects an event on a server that requires attention and sends an e-mail or page notification to an administrator (or technician). The administrator usually works at a central console to troubleshoot the problem. If diagnostics or system updates are required, a technician is often dispatched to the server itself.

Server Administrator runs on each managed network server. An administrator can access an operational server (which has not lost power or locked up). They can view system hardware and configuration information, run diagnostics, configure BIOS and system settings, view an audit log that records all hardware events, alerts, and commands that have occurred on the server, and perform system updates. If the administrator determines that other servers require the same update, an alternate command-line interface can be used to run automated scripts on groups of servers. Administrators can perform the following systems management functions from the Web interface or the command-line interface:

■ Run online diagnostics to troubleshoot problems.

■ Update firmware and BIOS.

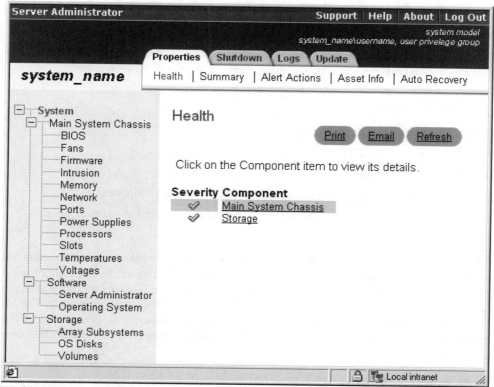

FIGURE 28-4 Managing network servers using the Dell OpenManage Server Administrator utility (courtesy of Dell Computer Corporation)

■ Maintain an audit trail of changes made to the server.

■ Monitor and report the status of the server.

■ Provide asset and array information.

■ Remote shutdown and restart.

Online Diagnostics

Administrators can run diagnostics on various components of the server (including the RAID and SCSI controllers, CPU, hard drive, memory, NIC, and PCI bus). Diagnostics that do not require administrator interaction can be scheduled for a later time and the results e-mailed to specific e-mail accounts. For example, the results could be e-mailed to the administrator or other technical staff that can use the information to provide better support.

Firmware and BIOS Updates

This feature allows system administrators to update the server's BIOS and firmware (including the Embedded Server Management 2, or ESM2, firmware found in Dell servers). Support for driver updates should be present in future versions of Server Administrator software. The updates can be performed on a single system from the Server Administrator Web interface, or on multiple systems through the command-line interface. An administrator can use the BIOS update feature to

- View a version report that includes the current versions for BIOS, firmware, and operating system.
- Select a BIOS or firmware update package.
- Validate the selected update package.
- Apply the update to the BIOS or firmware.
- Print BIOS and firmware information displayed on the home page.
- Send e-mail containing a report of the update to specified e-mail addresses.
- There is also a validation mechanism to ensure that the selected update package is valid.

Audit Trails

Server Administrator maintains a complete log of all hardware events, alerts, and commands that have occurred on the server, and this log can be presented through the Web interface. The location and size of the log file can be specified. The file is circular—when it reaches a specified size, the oldest information is written over by new information. This audit trail is useful when troubleshooting a problem. The administrator can refer to the log to identify commands executed on the server during the period in which the problem developed. The log can be exported as an ASCII file that can be gathered by automated scripts for archiving or analysis.

Monitor System Status

Server Administrator monitors the health of the system and provides rapid access to detailed fault and performance information gathered by system instrumentation agents. The reporting and viewing features let an administrator check the overall status for each of the server chassis that comprise the system. At the subsystem level, there is information about the voltages, temperatures, current fan RPM, and memory functioning at key points in the system. An account of cost-of-ownership information is available in summary view. Administrators can configure Server Administrator to generate alerts when specific conditions exist (such as a CPU temperature or voltage level that falls outside a normal range). Based on the type of alert, the software can be configured to respond in various ways, including sending a Simple Network Management Protocol (SNMP) trap to a central console, broadcasting a message to anyone logged onto the server, or launching an application.

Asset Information

A system summary screen provides basic system information such as the location of the server, its service tag, asset tag, processor information, inventory of slots available, and hard drive capacity. These asset reports can be exported for use in other software packages (such as Excel) for financial or inventory reporting systems.

Remote Shutdown and Restart

When a server is operational, it can be shut down and restarted from Server Administrator without requiring a remote access card (a remote access card is required to restart or diagnose problems on a server that is powered down).

Web and Command-Line Interfaces

Industry-standard systems management agents installed on the server gather detailed configuration, fault, and performance information. This information is reported via a standard set of system information reports available through the Web interface. The Web interface is portable (will work through various standard browsers, and allow remote access from systems outside of your LAN) and provides excellent performance. In addition to these reporting capabilities, online diagnostics and system update utilities enable actual management tasks using the tool.

By contrast, a command-line interface is available for environments in which system administrators perform most tasks using scripts that run on groups of servers. Using the Server Administrator command-line interface, an administrator could write a configuration script that specifies warning thresholds for each major system component and the actions required when a threshold is exceeded. For critical components, the script can specify that the system be powered down to prevent damage. The script can then be distributed to and executed on a group of systems. This scripting capability allows administrators to easily configure new systems or implement new system-administration policies on many existing systems.

In many cases, the command-line interface allows a user with a well-defined task to rapidly retrieve information about the system. The interface can be used to review a comprehensive summary of all system components, and save that summary information to a file for comparison with later system states. Administrators can also write batch programs or scripts to execute at specific times to capture reports on specific components (for example, fan RPMs during periods of high and low system usage). The formatted results can be routed to a file for later analysis. The primary Server Administrator commands are as follows:

- **omdiag**   Runs diagnostic tests on system hardware and software to isolate problems.

- **omupdate**   Updates BIOS and firmware versions.

- **omreport**   Displays summary information about components that pertain to the entire system.

- **omconfig**   Sets governing values for configurable system components (threshold values, actions required when threshold values are exceeded, asset information, and so on).

OS Support

When selecting management tools, it is also important to consider their compatibility with the operating systems on your network servers. For example, the full set of Server Administrator features is available under Windows NT Server 4 (Service Pack 5 or higher) and the Windows 2000 Server family (including Windows 2000 Server, Windows 2000 Advanced Server, Windows 2000 Terminal Services, and

Windows Small Business Server 2000). Dell's Server Administrator also runs on Red Hat Linux, version 7.1 or later. Server Administrator also runs with a limited feature set under Novell NetWare 5.1 (Service Pack 3), 6.0, or later. Under Novell, the online diagnostics and firmware/BIOS update features are not available.

Management Techniques and Troubleshooting

Dell OpenManage is just one suite of tools available for network management, but there are numerous management platforms available today (including tools from Compaq, HP, Gateway, and more). With such a variety of tools, it's often difficult to determine the best techniques for using those tools. This part of the chapter offers some insightful management suggestions.

READ THE DOCUMENTATION

Network management tools are usually composed of several powerful modules, so you should always make it a point to review the capabilities (and limitations) of your particular management platform. Understand how to initiate a first discovery and identification of your network devices, and know how to add additional devices to the management system. You may be able to use a configuration wizard (such as the Initial Configuration Wizard used with Compaq Insight Manager 7) to automate the discovery and identification of network devices.

UNDERSTAND SECURITY

Security is an important issue for network management, and administrators should take every possible precaution to prevent unauthorized users from accessing management information (especially through Web-based tools like Dell's OpenManage Server Administrator). Even when network data isn't vulnerable, the ability to use a network management platform to alter device parameters (and thus interrupt important network services) makes such platforms a handy target for malicious users. Familiarize yourself with the security features available in your particular management platform, and implement those features consistently.

REVIEW THE DISCOVERED DEVICES

It's important for an administrator to use their management platform to locate various devices and query their status. Once your management platform has discovered and identified the network devices, you should take some time to review the results. Use your management software to browse the servers, workstations, and other devices identified on the network, and practice creating queries so that you're comfortable locating specific items. For example, you can usually create a query to display the most important devices on your network.

The Compaq Insight Manager provides a device page that shows the most detailed information about discovered devices (see Figure 28-5). You can browse from the home page to the Compaq Insight Manager 7 Device page, and down to the various device agents. Then simply click the device links to learn details returned by a specific agent. For example, if you're viewing a cluster node, you can learn more about the cluster and its members by clicking on Compaq Intelligent Cluster Administrator device link. If you have finished browsing, and are ready to move on to other features, return to the Devices page and select appropriate links. Click on the Devices icon in the toolbar and select Overview to see a summary of the current device status and device events.

CONFIGURE DISCOVERY SCHEDULES

Management platforms often default to a preset schedule of network device rediscovery. However, you may wish to change the scheduling to a more convenient time, add or subtract subnets, and choose the

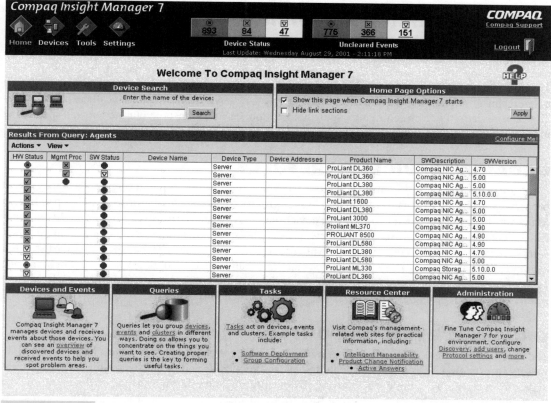

FIGURE 28-5 Managing networks with the Compaq Insight Manager 7 (courtesy of Compaq Computer Corporation)

way(s) that devices are discovered. If your network bandwidth is at a premium, you can optimize the SNMP and Ping settings to reduce traffic. This is also a good time to add new management console accounts, if necessary.

CUSTOMIZE IMPORTANT POLLING

Management platforms generally poll devices continually by launching a group of default scheduled tasks. However, you can create polling tasks that monitor a specific group of devices on their own schedule. For example, you might keep historical data on a certain type of device for later analysis and forecasting purposes. Generally, no recurring data collection (historical or single instance) is configured. You must create a task that is appropriate for your network. Keep in mind that data collection can create continuous traffic on your network, so design your tasks so that the devices you are most interested in are polled more frequently, and other devices are polled less often.

CONFIGURE ERROR NOTIFICATION

You must be notified when a problem occurs. The management console continually updates to inform you of the latest critical, major, or minor events. However, if you're away from the console, you can set up e-mail or paging notification (or set up your own notification method with an "launch application" task). The application can be as simple as sounding an audible alert on management consoles or as sophisticated as launching an application that communicates directly to a device (such as automatically restarting a service on a device). If you're setting up paging notification, be sure to install your modem and specify the modem settings as required by the manufacturer.

ORGANIZE DEVICES CAREFULLY

If you are managing several subnets, you might have hundreds of devices to interrogate. To manage them properly, you'll need to organize them into logical groups. Management platforms like Compaq Insight Manager 7 begin the sorting for you with the device queries it provides. However, you can modify the queries, delete those you don't use, and add new queries (and query categories) that complement your network management needs. You can specify which devices to interrogate and when to interrogate them. For example, you can create a query to interrogate an organizational group of devices, which might include servers, desktops, and printers. Alternately, you can interrogate a logical group of devices (such as all the printers in the purchasing group).

ORGANIZE EVENT REPORTING

A network of hundreds of devices can potentially generate thousands of messages. Some of these are merely informational. You can eliminate the excessive messages and make sure the important messages are received by using event filtering. Event filtering sorts through the messages to choose the more important ones. You can use event forwarding to specify console destinations where you know they will be acknowledged. Management platforms typically provide generic event querying and reporting, but you can modify these queries for your network environment, or you can create new queries for specific devices and events. For example, you can eliminate unneeded informational messages, or create an event query that checks the status of events on any servers that you don't want degrading (such as Web servers).

IDENTIFY UNKNOWN DEVICES

There's no guarantee that a management system will adequately identify every device on your network. Fortunately, many management systems allow you to create your own identification rules. For example, you could create a rule to identify unknown devices like printers. Most network-ready printers have Web-based configuration software. The management system discovers the Web-based software and adds links on the management console. From there, you can browse to the Web software to manage your printer. In addition, you can register MIBs from other companies, allowing you to discover, identify, and receive SNMP traps on those devices. For example, you can register MIBs to provide information about routers. You can also modify the SNMP trap messages to be more meaningful.

ADD NEW DEVICES

You can add one or more devices to an existing managed network without using automatic discovery. For example, if a new group is joining your management environment, add the group simultaneously using an IP address range, adding one device at a time, or by importing a hosts file. Using manual discovery conserves network resources. For example, you can export a file of device names and IP addresses and import it into the management system. On the next discovery cycle, the management system collects additional identification information to add to the database, but the process of discovering and identification has been automated for you.

CORRECTIVE ACTIONS

Given the proliferation of management components that are now available, it is extremely difficult to troubleshoot management platforms without referring to specific instructions from the manufacturer. However, the following tips offer a series of basic issues that you should be familiar with:

■ **TCP/IP problems**   The network administrator's TCP/IP address is missing or configured incorrectly in the management client administrator software (such as Dell OpenManage Client Administrator). Check the TCP/IP installation and setup in your operating system.

■ **Physical connection problems**   The computer (or other device) is not connected to the network. Check the network connection (cabling, NIC, and hub/switch).

■ **Logical connection problems**   The connection to the specified client is not valid. Try to reconnect to the client (i.e. DMI or SNMP) you want to manage, or reboot the offending client and try reconnecting again.

■ **Administration software disabled**   Client administrator software (such as Dell OpenManage Client Administrator) has been disabled on the local system. You must restart the computer to access the client administrator software again.

■ **BIOS update doesn't match**   Client administrator software cannot update the remote flash BIOS (firmware) because the BIOS update does not match the BIOS for the selected system(s). The new BIOS file is inappropriate for the system(s) you're trying to update. Download the correct BIOS file and try the update again.

■ **BIOS update times out**   A selected remote system has been turned off during the remote flash BIOS update process, and the client administrator software cannot update the BIOS for the selected remote system. Ensure that the remote system is connected to power and is turned on. Repeat the remote flash BIOS procedure for the remote system.

■ **BIOS update warnings**   When performing a remote flash BIOS (firmware) update, the remote system(s) being updated will need to be rebooted. Administrators should be sure that any systems being updated are not being used, or send a broadcast message to the affected station(s) allowing the users ample time to save their work and log off before the flash update begins. This is also a good policy before updating any applications remotely.

■ **Software connection problems**   The client administrator software cannot connect to a remote system in a client network. The remote system is turned off. Ensure that the remote system is connected to power and is turned on. If the remote system is a portable computer, check the battery status or ac adapter and ensure that the computer is turned on. The remote system is not configured for a DMI/SNMP client network. Configure the remote system for an appropriate client network protocol. The remote system does not have the client software (such as Dell OpenManage Client) installed. Ensure that the remote system has the proper client software installed.

■ **Device name changed**   The local system name has been updated or changed. The management client does not detect the updated system name until the local system is rebooted. Reboot the local system.

■ **Improper password**   The setup password cannot be set because the new password and old password do not match. Reenter the old password and new password as prompted.

■ **Shutdown warnings**   For example, a message indicates that the system will shut down in 60 seconds. This occurs when the client administrator software detects a noncritical, critical, or nonrecoverable event for the local system, which will cause the system to shut down. This is a normal precaution. To prevent data loss, save and exit all files, then restart the offending system.

Further Study

Compaq: **www.compaq.com**
Computer Associates: **www.ca.com**
Dell: **support.dell.com**
Gateway: **www.gateway.com**
HP: **www.hp.com**
MIBs: **www.cisco.com/univercd/cc/td/doc/product/software/ios112/mbook/mover.htm**
SNMPv3: **www.ibr.cs.tu-bs.de/projects/snmpv3/**
Tivoli: **www.tivoli.com**
Veritas: **www.veritas.com**

BASIC NETWORK TROUBLESHOOTING

Troubleshooting is a strange pursuit—something between an art and a science. Networks are great tools when everything is working properly, but they can be monstrously frustrating when problems strike. Any administrator or technician tasked with maintaining and troubleshooting computer networks will not only need to understand important network concepts and operations, but will also need to understand essential troubleshooting rules and practices. This is especially important when working through the many guidelines and symptoms presented throughout the book. This chapter is intended to provide entry-level technicians with a background in basic diagnostic practices, and outline several of the most popular utilities available for network troubleshooting. Even experienced technicians may find this chapter to be a handy reference.

Troubleshooting Guidelines

As a professional network technician, you must understand one basic rule of business—*time is money*. Whether you're the boss or work for someone else, the ability to identify and isolate a fault quickly and decisively is a critical element to your success. It requires a keen eye, some common sense, and a little bit of intuition. It also requires an understanding of the troubleshooting process, and a reliable plan of action.

You see, even though the number of network configurations and setups are virtually unlimited, the *methodology* used to approach each problem is always about the same. This part of the chapter is intended to illustrate the concepts of basic troubleshooting, and show you how to apply a suite of cause-and-effect relationships that will help you narrow the problem down *before* you even open a wiring closet. By applying a consistent technique, you can shave precious time from every repair.

THE UNIVERSAL TROUBLESHOOTING PROCEDURE

Regardless of how complex your particular computer or network may be, a dependable troubleshooting procedure can be broken down into four basic steps. These steps are illustrated in Figure 29-1: define your symptoms, identify and isolate the potential source (or location) of your problem, replace the suspected subassembly, and retest the system thoroughly to be sure that you have solved the problem. If you have *not* solved the problem, start again from Step #1. This is a "universal" procedure that you can apply to *any* sort of troubleshooting—not just for personal computer equipment or networks.

Define Your Symptoms

When a network breaks down, the cause may be as simple as a loose wire or connector, or as complicated as a chip or subassembly failure. Before you open your toolbox, you *must* have a firm understanding of *all* the symptoms. Think about the symptoms carefully—for example:

- Can other workstations access a server or router?
- Can you Ping one side of a router or network, but not the other?
- Is the Power or Activity LED lit?
- Does this problem occur only when the computer is tapped or moved?

By recognizing and understanding your symptoms, it can be much easier to trace a problem to the appropriate assembly or component. Take the time to write down as many symptoms as you can. This note taking may seem tedious now, but once you have begun your repair a written record of symptoms and

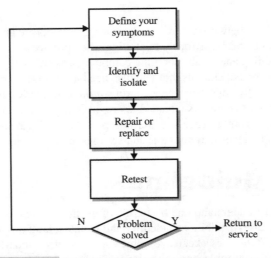

FIGURE 29-1 The universal troubleshooting process

circumstances will help to keep you focused on the task at hand. It will also help to jog your memory if you must explain the symptoms to someone else later. As a professional troubleshooter, you must often log problems or otherwise document your activities anyway.

Identify and Isolate

Before you try to isolate a problem within a network or hardware device, first be sure that it is the equipment itself that is *causing* the problem. In many circumstances, this will be obvious, but there may be situations that appear ambiguous (i.e., there is no power, no DOS prompt, and so on). Always remember that a network operates because of an intimate mingling of hardware and software. A faulty or improperly configured piece of software can cause confusing system errors just as effectively as a defective hardware device. When you have identified a potential problem area, you can begin the actual repair process and swap the suspect subassembly or reconfigure suspect software.

Replace

Since networks are designed as collections of subassemblies, it is usually easier to replace a subassembly outright rather than attempt to troubleshoot the subassembly to its component level. Modern networks are often critical for normal business productivity, so swapping a defective part (i.e., a failed NIC or hub) is often the most cost-effective way to get the network back up and running again. Manufacturers and their distributors often stock a selection of subassemblies and supplies. Keep in mind that you may need to know the manufacturer's part number for the subassembly in order to obtain a new one.

Another problem with the fast technological progress we enjoy is that parts rarely stay on the shelf long. That 16-port hub you bought last year is no longer available, is it? How about that CD-ROM jukebox you installed some time back? Today there's something newer and faster in its place. When a computer fails and you need to replace a broken device, chances are that you'll *need* to upgrade simply because you cannot obtain an identical replacement device. From this standpoint, *upgrading* is often a proxy of troubleshooting and repair.

Retest

When a repair is finally complete, the network devices must be reassembled carefully before testing. All guards, housings, cables, and shields *must* be replaced before final testing. If symptoms persist, you will have to reevaluate the symptoms and narrow the problem to another part of the network. If normal operation is restored (or greatly improved), test the network's various functions. When you can verify that your symptoms have stopped during actual operation, the equipment may be returned to service. As a general rule, it is wise to let the system run for at least 24 hours in order to ensure that a replacement subassembly will not fail prematurely. This is known as letting the system *burn-in*.

Do not be discouraged if the network still malfunctions. Perhaps you missed a connection. Maybe software settings and device drivers must be updated to accommodate the replacement subassembly. If you get stuck, simply walk away, clear your head, and start again by defining your current symptoms. Don't hesitate to ask for help—even the most experienced troubleshooters get overwhelmed from time to time. You should also realize that there may be more than one problem to deal with. Remember that a network is just a collection of assemblies, and each assembly is a collection of parts. Normally, everything works together, but when one assembly fails, it may cause one or more interconnected assemblies to fail as well.

Document the Fix

Documentation is another important practice that is frequently overlooked. When you perform a successful repair, you should take some time to record your findings and solutions on paper. This habit takes time and discipline to develop, but it's well worth the trouble. You can refer back to your notes for future repairs (possibly saving hours of trial and error). Notes can also be invaluable assets to other technicians faced with problems that you have already learned to resolve.

Give Feedback

Feedback is another important step that is often overlooked by busy administrators and technicians. All too often, calls for help are addressed with little (if any) information returned to the user. In many cases, a terse message simply tells the user to "try again." In other cases, the problem just mysteriously disappears. While it's certainly not necessary for you to communicate the details of your corrective action, it *is* important to acknowledge the user's inquiry, report that the problem has been fixed, and provide a brief explanation of the cause(s)—nothing fancy, a few sentences should be fine.

IDENTIFY CHANGES

When trouble strikes a network, one of the first issues to consider is *change*—what has changed between the time the network was last working and now? Changes occur to a PC when hardware is installed or upgraded, but changes may also occur when new software is installed or the system's configuration is altered. For example, installing an incorrect NIC driver may prevent the workstation's NIC from operating— effectively preventing the PC from accessing the network at all. As a technician, the troubleshooting process often starts by looking for change in PCs, cabling, protocol stacks, software, or other network devices.

Check with Users

Even well-meaning users can be a network's worst enemy. They often have a tendency to tinker, and sometimes make (unauthorized) changes in the system configuration, resulting in all manner of errors and performance problems. Sometimes those problems can affect the entire network. Suppose that one of your users installs a new browser, decides they don't like it, then forgets to delete it—only to find that they have trouble accessing the company's intranet the next day. Unless the user tells you of the new browser instal- lation, you may waste hours trying to determine the problem. When a problem surfaces, always take a moment to see if any users have made changes to their system.

To reduce the frequency of accidental changes by end users, you should actively discourage users from making changes such as hardware and software upgrades. Each system should have a stan- dard well-documented configuration, and only authorized technicians should actually perform main- tenance and upgrades.

Verify Your Own Changes

As a technician, you'll undoubtedly make occasional changes to system configurations (such as fixing servers and routers). This may be necessary to offer new services or fix problems. For example, you may find that the startup file for your IntraNetWare server does not automatically make a certain volume available, and you fix this by editing the startup file. The next day, you find that Windows NT users are complaining that their time is off by five hours. While this may not seem like a server issue, it may be that the server configura- tion file you edited to provide the volume may have been entered incorrectly. Instead of reading

```
SET TIME ZONE--EST5EDT
```

the line was accidentally edited to read

```
\SET TIME ZONE--EST5EDT
```

When the edited file was saved, the server suddenly had no idea what time zone it was in because it didn't understand the incorrect \SET command.

The idea is that *recent* changes (even if they seem unrelated to the symptom) can have an impact on the network. Once again, this is a case where good documentation can be important. If you can compare the date when the problem started to the dates of changes entered in your activity log, potential problem areas can leap out at you. If you share network responsibilities with others, be sure that *everyone* documents their activities thoroughly.

In general, you should always restart a device after a change has been made to it.

Outside Influence

Although you have control over your own internal LAN or other network configuration, many networks also rely on the communication services of a local phone company and Internet Service Provider (ISP). If nothing has changed internally, but communication services are no longer functioning as expected, it's worth a call to your ISP and local phone company—you may find that one of your outside vendors has made changes that are impairing your network's ability to communicate. These kinds of problems often materialize on Monday mornings since most changes are made over the weekend when utilization is traditionally lower.

Manage Your Rollouts

Eventually, it'll be time to upgrade your network with a new operating system or application—this is generally known as *rolling out* the upgrade, and is a huge source of change for any network. The problem is that new software often comes with its share of bugs. Very few network administrators want to beta test a software vendor's new product, so it's a good idea to wait six months or so to allow the manufacturer to work out the bugs in their new product. This also provides precious time for the manufacturer to develop patches and build a foundation of expertise supporting the new version (just look at all of the Service Packs for Windows NT and 2000).

Once the product has been refined, release the rollout in phases (if possible) starting with small groups of users. This way, you can observe the behavior of an upgrade in a relatively controlled environment. If the upgrade proves to be stable and reliable, you can implement the upgrade in subsequent phases. Of course, if there are serious problems, only a limited number of users are affected (so it's easier to recover if necessary).

DIVIDE AND CONQUER

As with PCs, networks are a combination of hardware devices and software configurations. When a problem occurs, splitting the problem area into smaller, more manageable pieces can usually isolate the trouble. For example, suppose a PC cannot access its hard drive. The trouble may be in the drive itself, the drive controller, cabling between the drive and controller, or the host computer's CMOS Setup routine. Once you've verified the CMOS Setup and checked the cabling (since these are easy and obvious things to check), you can isolate the fault by replacing the controller and then replacing the drive. You can easily apply this concept to entire networks.

Suppose a network problem occurs. You can use the divide-and-conquer concept to quickly narrow the trouble from the entire network to a single workstation or other device. Determine whether there's only a problem with one person (a local problem) or with a large group of people (a system problem). If you determine that it's just one person, you're *done* with the system-wide divide-and-conquer approach, and can now proceed to workstation-level troubleshooting. This may require additional divide-and-conquer troubleshooting at the PC level, or outright replacement of the defective workstation. If more than one person on the network is affected, it's time to gather more information.

Once you determine which functional group of users is affected, haul out that documentation and see what areas are experiencing the problem. Take a look at where these users are on your functional maps, and see what they have in common (or where they connect through). When you do this, it will probably become painfully obvious where the problem is. If two departments are saying that they're down, it might be that the server they use is down. If you see from your functional map that all the groups that go through a particular router are down, it's time to check that router. If users from just one segment are calling, it's most likely a problem with the physical network segment. In all cases, the idea is to simplify your troubleshooting tasks by narrowing down the potential problem area—this is even more critical when you're dealing with large networks involving many users.

Software Solutions

The divide-and-conquer approach also works with software and resolving software conflicts. When a PC experiences performance problems with no hardware cause, many technicians will "boot clean." This reduces the number of programs loading into memory at start time and eliminates many possible conflicts between various uncooperative programs. It's then often a matter of restoring one program at a time until a culprit appears. The same idea works with networks. For example, everybody in the office starts having problems shutting down. They all get stuck at the "Please wait while your computer shuts down" screen. Nobody has changed anything recently, and nothing has been upgraded. On the surface, this may not even seem like a network problem. If your office runs Windows NT or 2000, many of the programs that run at startup are in the Startup menu. You get rid of everything in the Startup menu and reboot. All of a sudden, you can shut down again. You systematically return the programs to the Startup folder and keep restarting until you find the source of the problem.

Suppose that the culprit turns out to be your e-mail notification program, but when you start with just that program running, you shut down fine. This means you've got a conflict between two programs. Fortunately, the divide-and-conquer technique works here also, so run the suspect program with each of your remaining programs in turn until you discover the other program that is causing the conflict. As an example, you may find that the trouble occurs when the e-mail notification program and virus protection utility are running together. If the network had been working with these two programs in the past, further investigation may lead you to discover that the virus utility had been updated automatically over the Internet, and that update precipitated the problem. In fact, a quick search of the vendor's Web sites may reveal a patch for the e-mail client (or the virus protection program), and the problem is fixed.

MAKING COMPARISONS

Another popular troubleshooting approach for PCs and networks is to compare the performance of a malfunctioning device against the operation of two or more identical devices that are functioning properly. The difference(s) between devices will usually help to identify the problem. For example, if you can't get a printer to work on a parallel port, but another printer does work on the parallel port, you know that the problem is with the first printer rather than the parallel port or cable. The same principle applies to misbehaving network devices. If you find an identical item that happens to be working, changing the problem item's configuration to match the one that is working can sometimes fix the problem, or at least suggest a defective device that can be replaced. This process also works for software (such as comparing login scripts or file versions), and is often referred to as the "ruling out" method.

Keep in mind that device comparisons work great at a low level (such as hubs), but get a bit problematic with critical network devices such as servers and routers. The problem is that there are often very few such high-level devices on a network, and even when there are multiple devices, they are rarely identical—this makes direct comparisons difficult.

CALLING FOR HELP

No matter how experienced you are, you may eventually encounter problems that you cannot resolve with the available time, tools, and other resources. When this happens, you can easily draw from the wealth of information and experience compiled by the many product manufacturers, discussion forums, and independent support organizations with networking know-how (much of which is free). With someone else's perspective available, you can sometimes collect observations or facts that you may have missed. And when you explain the problem to someone else, you may be coaxed into diagramming the flow of the problem, emphasizing important points and considering avenues that may have gone ignored.

Take advantage of the manufacturer's Web sites (especially their support site). Well-developed support sites will usually offer online documentation, user and setup guides, FAQs that already answer the most common questions, and lists of known compatibility issues and problems with other devices or software. In most cases, you'll also find updated device drivers, patches, diagnostic utilities, and other upgrades that may resolve your network problems. If you're really stuck, pick up the telephone and call the vendor. This may cost you (per minute or per incident), but when network downtime equates to real money, the cost of telephone support is often worthwhile.

Public forums and Usenet newsgroups are often an excellent source of real-world experience with a manufacturer's products (though you may need to skip through a pile of shocking expletives before you find useful information). You can locate newsgroups using a search engine such as Google (**http://groups.google.com/**). Vendors with comprehensive technical support may also include live forums on their Web sites—these can be particularly handy because the manufacturer's technical support staff monitors them.

Troubleshooting Basics

No matter how much you read about troubleshooting, the one question that comes up time and again is "Where do I start?" Successful troubleshooting requires you to isolate the problem as quickly as possible. Once the problem is identified, you can take steps to correct it—otherwise, you're just shooting from the hip, and will usually waste a lot of time and energy. This part of the chapter is intended to provide a novice troubleshooter with a practical guide that can help to isolate potential problems more quickly.

GETTING STARTED

The best way to start troubleshooting is to quantify the problem—to understand the problem that's occurring. You may not immediately know why the problem is occurring, but a good sense of what is happening and when can help you to reproduce the problem yourself, and select the next appropriate step. In most cases, your knowledge of the problem will come from users themselves (usually in the form of a phone at your desk). For example, a panicked user may tell you that they cannot logon to the server when they come into work at 7:30 A.M. This is also a great chance to learn about any particular circumstances that surround the user, their account, or their hardware. You should also reference any logical or physical maps of the network (such as Figure 29-2) to familiarize yourself with any local cabling, hubs/switches, and adjacent workstations.

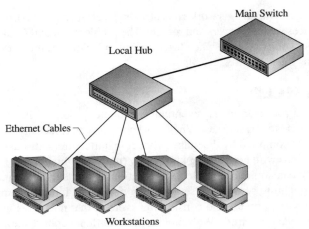

Main Switch

Local Hub

Ethernet Cables

Workstations

FIGURE 29-2   A portion of a hierarchical star network map listing several local workstations

Single PC Problem

When a problem strikes one workstation, but other workstations, servers, and other resources are operating normally, it's a good chance that the fault is in that particular PC, it's nearest connection to the network, or its software configuration. Here are the points to check when a single PC is affected:

■ *Check the power.* This may sound like a painfully obvious issue, but you'd be surprised at how many users come in to work and expect their PC to be on—never imagining that it may have been turned off. When the user reports that the system is off or won't start, be sure to check that the PC and monitor are plugged in and turned on. If the system is on but won't recover from a standby mode, try rebooting the system. Often, incompatible hardware or outdated drivers can impair proper recovery from power-saving modes. If the system is on but is failing to boot, you'll need to replace the PC so that the user can resume working, then troubleshoot the offending system separately on your workbench.

■ *Check for viruses.* This is a standard troubleshooting step that should be taken whenever network problems arise. Run an updated virus checker to verify that the PC is clean (and is not replicating infected files or macros to the rest of the network). If you do find a virus on the station, be sure to run a complete virus check on the entire network. See Chapter 19 for more virus information.

■ *Check the connection.* Take a look at the cable between the workstation and its corresponding hub/switch port (you may need to refer to a physical map for this connection information). Make sure that the Link LED is on. If not, the cable is disconnected or damaged, and you may need to trouble-shoot the physical cabling to restore a good connection. See Chapter 8 for more cabling information.

■ *Check the account.* Problems logging on to a network (especially on certain days or hours) may indi-cate an account issue. Perhaps logon hours have been restricted, or perhaps the account has been locked out due to excessive logon errors (maybe someone even tried an unauthorized logon). See that the account is set up properly, and check the server's security logs for any suspicious activity. You can also have the user try logging on from another authorized workstation. See Chapter 26 for logon trou-bleshooting details.

■ *Ping the station.* Use a tool like Ping to test the IP address of the troublesome station. If the station fails to respond, there may be a problem with the cabling, hub/switch port, or NIC that you can investigate further. If the station responds to a Ping (and can Ping out to other stations as well), but is otherwise behaving improperly on the network, chances are that the connection and NIC hardware are working but a software issue is causing the problem. Recheck the system's setup (like DNS setup, WINS setup, autoexec.bat file, *Hosts* file, *config.sys* file, or the Windows Registry error) and correct any oversights. There is more on Ping later in this chapter.

■ *Check the hub/switch port.* If your station is connected to a "managed" hub or switch, it's possible that the port has been disabled. Start the management utility and check the status of the station's corresponding port. If the port has been disabled, try reenabling it. If the port cannot be reenabled (or is shown as defective or not available), try reconnecting the station to another free port (or replace the hub/switch entirely). If the hub/port is not "managed," it may be worth rebooting the hub/switch or trying another available port to verify that the port is not at fault.

Segment Problem

Suppose that a problem affects several stations on the network. Logic dictates that the problem is an issue that is *common* to all of the affected stations. In most cases, this involves a fault in cabling or the hub/switch. For example, consider four stations in one part of the office that are connected to a hub—the hub is then connected to a switch that supports the server and other small groups connected to local hubs throughout the office (such as in Figure 29-2).

■ *Check the local hub power.* Verify that the small hub connecting your four remote workstations is receiving power. You can try rebooting the hub by disconnecting power for several seconds, then reconnecting power and allowing the hub to perform its self-checks. Also, verify that the Link LED is lit for each workstation attached to the local hub. If the Link LEDs are out, the local hub may have failed and should be replaced.

■ *Check for activity and collisions.* Unusually high activity levels and excessive collisions can impair the performance of stations on a segment. Examine the Activity and Collision LEDs for the stations. An Ethernet station with unusually high activity levels may be causing excessive collisions. If the offending station is not intentionally transmitting, the NIC may be jabbering and require replacement. Valid traffic that is causing excessive collisions may demand more bandwidth (i.e., upgrading 10BaseT to 100BaseT), or reconfiguring the segment (i.e., moving a busy station to another hub elsewhere).

■ *Check the backbone cable.* Take a look at the cable between the local and its corresponding switch port (you may need to refer to a physical map for this connection information). Make sure that the Link LED is on. If not, the cable is disconnected or damaged, and you may need to troubleshoot the physical cabling to restore a good connection. See Chapter 8 for more cabling information.

■ *Ping local stations.* Use the Ping utility to check the communication between the local stations. If you cannot Ping from one local station to another, the hub is defective and should be replaced.

■ *Ping remote stations.* If the local stations can Ping each other through the hub, try to Ping the switch, server, or other station(s) outside of the switch. If you cannot Ping from any of the local stations through the switch, the switch port may be defective or disabled. Try connecting to another available switch port. If the switch is "managed," use the management utility to check the port status and reenable the port if possible. Otherwise, replace the switch outright.

Network-Wide Problems

The most pressing and serious types of problems involve the entire network. For example, no users may be able to log on to the domain server, or no one can access the Internet, or the network printer is unavailable. While these may seem like sophisticated problems that require high-end equipment and years of experience to tackle, your most effective tool is a knowledge of the network's layout, and the understanding of cause-and-effect relationships—what is the common thread, or what doesn't belong.

For example, suppose that only *one* user is unable to log on to your Windows 2000 domain server, and all of your other users are working along normally. With only one station affected, the natural logic is to focus your troubleshooting on that one station (starting with a good network connection and appropriate account setup). On the other hand, suppose that *none* of your users can log on to the domain server. You can easily determine that the stations are all communicating (i.e., by sharing files and folders on other servers or PCs). In this case, the common thread is the domain server itself. It may be turned off or misconfigured, or there may be some hardware issue that requires configuration or repair.

As another example, suppose that none of your users can access the Internet through a simple Internet router. Since the Internet router and CSU/DSU (i.e., cable modem or other communications resource) are common to all Internet access, it makes sense to start by investigating those devices. You may find that the router or CSU/DSU hardware has been turned off or disconnected. A few quick Pings tell you that the router is responding, but there is no Activity LED on the CSU/DSU. This may suggest the need to reboot the CSU/DSU (and perhaps the router), or call for service to check or replace the CSU/DSU. In other cases, you may find that there is activity, but the router has been configured improperly.

The bottom line is that a little common sense goes a long way in network troubleshooting. A technician with adequate documentation and a rudimentary knowledge of networking can usually narrow down most problems to a workstation/server, cable, hub/switch, or other network device in just a few minutes with little (if any) fancy test equipment. Of course, it will take additional effort to locate and correct the exact problem (i.e., finding a cable break or configuring TCP/IP), but at least you can make the problem manageable.

Troubleshooting Tools

The troubleshooting concepts and guidelines you've learned about so far in this chapter give you a foundation in troubleshooting practices. Fortunately, troubleshooting isn't all systematic isolation—there are many diagnostic tools available to you that can identify network operation and performance issues. Numerous tools are available free with your operating system. This part of the chapter highlights a selection of tools that you can use to aid your troubleshooting efforts.

LOG FILES

Servers maintain several different log files that are used to track errors and other important operational conditions. Logs typically include a running list of all errors and notices, the date and time each event occurred, and other relevant information such as the related user or process involved. When trouble strikes, a log can tell you precisely what happened, when it happened, and which (if any) users were involved. A technician should know how to access the log files from operating systems like NetWare 5, Linux/UNIX, and Windows NT/2000.

 Not only are log files important diagnostic tools, they may also be used as legal evidence in the prosecution of unauthorized intrusion or other malicious activities.

NetWare Logs

Novell NetWare 5.x maintains three log files that can help you diagnose problems on a NetWare server:

- **The console.log file**   The console log file (*console.log*) keeps a history of all errors and information that have been displayed on the server's console. It is located in the *sys:\etc* directory on the server, and is created and maintained by the **conlog.nlm** utility that comes with NetWare versions 3.12 and later. You must load this utility manually (or place the load command in the *autoexec.ncf* file so that it starts automatically upon server startup) by typing *load conlog* at the console prompt. Once this utility is loaded, it erases the old *console.log* file and starts logging to the new file. For example, the log may indicate that someone edited the *autoexec.ncf* file and then restarted the server—this indicates a major change on the server. If we were trying to troubleshoot a server that started exhibiting strange problems after a recent reboot, this might be an issue to check.

■ **The abend.log File** An *abend* is an error condition that can halt the proper operation of the NetWare server, and this log file registers all abends on a NetWare server. Abends can be serious enough to lock the server, or they can simply force an NLM to shut down. You can see that an abend has occurred when an error message containing the word abend appears on the console. Additionally, the server command prompt will include a number in angle brackets (such as <1>) that indicates the number of times the server has abended since it was brought online. NetWare versions 4.11 and later include a routine to capture the output of the abend both to the console and to the *abend.log* file (located in the *sys:system* directory on the server). For example, the words "Page Fault" or "Stack" in the log may suggest that the abend occurred because of something to do with memory—a program or process tried to take memory that didn't belong to it. When NetWare detects this, it shuts down the offending process and issues an abend.

■ **The sys$log.err File** The general Server Log file, found in the *SYS:SYSTEM* directory, lists any errors that occur on the server, including abends and NDS errors and the time and date of their occurrence. An error in the *sys$log.err* file might look something like this:

```
1-07-2002        11:51:10 am:        DS-7.9-17
Severity = 1   Locus = 17   Class = 19
Directory Services: Could not open local database, error: - 723
```

Severity indicates the seriousness of the problem. *Locus* indicates which system component is affected by the error (for example, memory, disk, or NICs). *Class* indicates the type of error. The actual numbers for severity, locus, and class can be rather cryptic, so refer to your NetWare documentation for specific code listings. For the example above, a Severity of 1 indicates a warning (the problem isn't serious), a Locus of 17 indicates that the error relates to the operating system (which would make sense because this is a Directory Services error), and the Class of 19 indicates the problem is with a domain. This means the problem is defined by the operating system, but is not an operating system problem.

Windows Log Files

Windows NT/2000 employs a comprehensive set of error and information logs. Rather than using a separate log for each program or process, Microsoft uses the Event Viewer utility to track all notable events on a particular Windows NT/2000 computer. You should know how to access the Event Viewer and open the major logs available under Windows. Use the following steps to start Event Viewer under Windows NT:

1. Click Start | Programs | Administrative Tools. The Select Computer dialog box will open.

2. Enter the name of the computer that you want to view logs for (or double-click the computer's name in the list of available systems), then click OK.

 If you're connecting over a slow link such as a dial-up modem, click the Low Speed Connection box before clicking OK.

3. To view a log file, select a file from the list. To view a log for a different computer, click Log | Select Computer.

Use the following steps to start Event Viewer under Windows 2000:

1. Click Start | Programs | Administrative Tools | Computer Management.

2. Expand the System Tools and Event Viewer entries to see the list of available logs.

3. Select the desired log file to view it.

Log Types   There are three principle types of logs provided by Windows NT/2000: application logs, system logs, and security logs. The *application log* contains events logged by applications or programs. For example, a database program might record a file error in the application log. As a rule, the program developer decides which events to record. For example, administrators and technicians may find this log helpful when users report trouble with services like SQL Server. The *system log* contains events logged by the Windows NT/2000 system components (see Figure 29-3). For example, the failure of a driver or other system component to load during startup is recorded in the system log (the event types logged by system components are predetermined by Windows). Finally, the *security log* (as you saw in Chapter 26) can record security events such as valid and invalid logon attempts as well as events related to resource use such as creating, opening, or deleting files. An administrator can specify what events are recorded in the security log. For example, if you have enabled logon auditing, attempts to log on to the system are recorded in the security log.

You will need to enable logging under the Event Viewer.

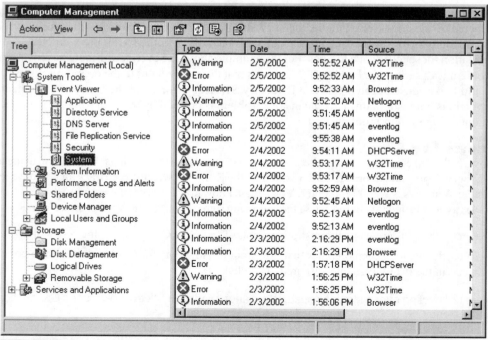

FIGURE 29-3   The system log can reveal important events causing system performance or stability problems.

Event Types   The Event Viewer utility will display five different types of events. You should understand the meaning and relative importance of each event so that you're able to prioritize corrective actions:

- **Error**   This is a significant system problem—such as loss of data or loss of functionality. For example, an error will be logged if a service fails to load during startup. Errors may require immediate attention and corrective action.

- **Warning**   This is an event that is not necessarily significant, but may indicate a possible future problem. For example, a warning will be logged when disk space is low. Warnings may not demand immediate attention, but should be checked and addressed in a timely fashion.

- **Information**   This event describes the successful operation of an application, driver, or service. For example, an information event will be logged when a network driver loads successfully. Most information events require no action, but may report unexpected (or unwanted) conditions.

- **Success audit**   This event reports an "audited" security access attempt that succeeds. For example, a user's successful attempt to log on to the system will be logged as a success audit event.

- **Failure audit**   This event reports an "audited" security access attempt that fails. For example, if a user tries to access a network drive and fails, the attempt will be logged as a failure audit event.

Event logging starts automatically when you start Windows. All users can view application and system logs, but only administrators can access security logs.

PING

The *Packet Internet Groper* (or Ping) is the quintessential troubleshooting tool for LAN and Internet connectivity between devices. Ping operates on a TCP/IP network by sending Internet Control Message Protocol (ICMP) Echo messages to a destination node. When the network and all its elements are properly configured, the destination node receives the ICMP Echo messages, then replies with an Echo Response message for each incoming Echo it receives. The Echo Response also echoes back any data that the sender supplied in the outgoing Echo—32, 56, or 64 bytes of data are typically included with each Ping operation. If the node that originated the Ping receives the responses within a predefined period, the connection is good—all of the IP network devices between the end node and the Pinging station are properly configured to carry IP traffic. Ping is available as a part of all TCP/IP kernels, including an IP-configured workstation (such as Windows 9x/Me/2000/XP), a Windows NT/2000 server, a Linux server, and from a NetWare server. Ping can provide an essential assortment of information:

- Ping places a unique sequence number on each packet it transmits, and reports the sequence numbers that it receives back. So you can determine if packets have been dropped, duplicated, or reordered.

- Ping verifies (checksums) each packet it exchanges, so you can detect some forms of damaged packets.

- Ping places a time stamp in each packet, which is echoed back and can easily be used to compute how long each packet exchange took—the round trip time (RTT).

- Ping reports other ICMP messages that might otherwise get buried in the system software. It reports, for example, if a router is declaring the target host unreachable.

However, Ping has its limitations, and there are some things that Ping cannot tell you:

- Some routers discard undeliverable packets, and others may believe a packet has been transmitted successfully when it has not been. So Ping may not always provide reasons why packets go unanswered.

■ Ping cannot tell you why a packet was damaged, delayed, or duplicated. It also cannot tell you where this happened—though you may be able to deduce it.

■ Ping cannot give you a detailed analysis of every host that handles a packet.

Using Ping

Ping uses a command line to launch the utility, specify options, and list the destination IP address. In its simplest form, Ping is simply shown with its destination IP address (and default options), such as

```
>ping 192.168.1.1
```

As an example, this command may Ping your network's Internet router. Ping will respond with any replies (see Figure 29-4), indicating the number of bytes sent and the time for the round trip. When the test is finished, Ping displays statistics indicating the amount of data lost (if any), along with minimum, maximum, and average timing. A properly configured network should have close to a 100-percent response rate for all Ping packets sent. Less than 90 percent may indicate problems such as high network congestion or a large number of hops (routers) between the Ping sender and its target address.

However, the exact syntax used for Ping will depend on your operating system. The precise syntax under Linux is

```
ping [-R] [-c number] [-d] [-I seconds] host
```

where the options are

■ **-R**   This option records the route taken by the packet.

■ **-c**   This is the number of ICMP echo_requests that are sent.

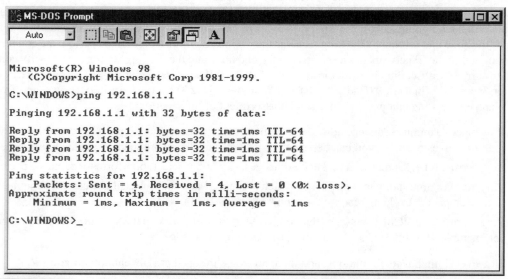

FIGURE 29-4   A typical Ping display will report connection timing and any data loss between two stations on the network.

■ **-d** This causes Ping to send packets as fast as they are echoed back from the destination system (up to 100 times per second). This can generate a high volume of network traffic.

■ **-I** This option specifies the number of seconds between each packet. The default is 1 second.

■ **host** This is the destination hostname or IP address.

The syntax under Red Hat Linux 7.x is a bit different:

```
ping [-LRUbdfnqrvV] [-c count] [-i interval] [-w wait] [-p pattern]
[-s packetsize] [-t ttl] [-I interface address] [ -T timestamp option ]
[ -Q tos ] host
```

Here is the syntax under BSD/OS 4.x:

```
ping [-dfnqRrv] [-a family] [-S security request] [-c count] [-i wait]
[-l preload] [-p pattern] [-s packetsize] host
```

The syntax under Windows is much different:

```
ping [-t] [-a] [-n count] [-l size] [-f] [-i TTL] [-v TOS] [-r count]
[-s count] [[-j host list] | [-k host list]] [-w timeout] destination list
```

where the options are

■ **-t** Continue to Ping until explicitly stopped by CTRL-C. Statistics are displayed after you stop the command.

■ **-a** This option resolves addresses to hostnames.

■ **-n count** This option specifies the number of ICMP echo_request packets to send.

■ **-l size** This option sends the buffer size.

■ **-f** This sets the "don't fragment" flag in the packet, and is particularly useful to determine whether a device is changing the packet size between nodes.

■ **-i TTL** This sets the "Time to Live" value for the packets.

■ **-v TOS** This sets the "Type of Service."

■ **-r count** This option displays route for count hops.

■ **-s count** This displays a time stamp for each hop.

■ **-j host list** This is a loose source route along the host list.

■ **-k host-list** This is a strict source route along the host list.

■ **-w timeout** This sets the timeout value to wait for each reply (in milliseconds).

■ **destination list** This is the destination host or IP address.

To run Ping from your NetWare server console prompt, type the following command:

```
load ping ip_address
```

With NetWare, the IP_address parameter is optional—you can use this parameter to specify which address you wish to Ping, or you can enter the address manually in the utility. If you're using a NetWare

4.x product such as NetWare NFS or Novell UNIX and Print Services, and have configured it for DNS name resolution, you can use the DNS hostname for the end node in place of the IP address. If the Ping utility is loaded without parameters, you will see the New Target screen. The New Target screen allows you to enter the IP address or DNS hostname of the node that you want to Ping. You can also adjust the number of seconds between Pings and the size of the IP packet (in bytes), though the default values of one second between Pings and a 40-byte IP packet work well in most situations. Press ESC to begin Pinging. The Ping screen in NetWare displays statistics for each node you are Pinging, such as

- **Node**   The node address of the Ping target.
- **Sent**   The number of Ping packets sent.
- **Received**   The number of Ping packets received.
- **High**   The highest round-trip time for a packet.
- **Low**   The lowest round-trip time for a packet.
- **Last**   The round-trip time for the last Ping.
- **Average**   The average round-trip time for Ping packets.
- **Trend**   The current trend of round-trip times.

Troubleshooting Configurations with Ping

Beyond the obvious cabling issues, you will not receive Ping responses if the devices on the network have not been properly configured. This may indicate that the end node does not have IP set up on it, or your server may not be configured properly. Another possibility is that there's a configuration problem with a router located between the two end nodes—either in the IP configuration on the router or with the routing protocol.

If you're attempting to Ping an address and receive no responses, you'll need to troubleshoot the IP setup. If your server has been installed on a network that is already running TCP/IP, make sure you have configured the TCP/IP parameters on the servers to be compatible with the existing setup. Confirm that you're using the same routing protocol as the rest of the network and that the IP addresses you have used for the network interfaces on the server are valid for the network. Check the frame type as well. If your network has not previously been configured for TCP/IP, make sure all of the devices on a single network segment contain the same IP network address and subnet mask, and no two devices on the segment have the same IP address. If the node you're attempting to Ping is on another segment, check the routing devices between your station and the destination node. All of the routers should be using the same routing protocol.

Once you've confirmed that all the devices between your server and the destination have been configured properly (and are on the same network segment), try the Ping again. If the server and destination are not on the same segment, first try to Ping the router that shares the segment with your server. If the Ping is successful, continue to Ping each of the routers that are between you and the destination node. If the Ping is not successful to the first router, check the frame types on the server and the router. If the Ping is successful to the first router, but not the second or any subsequent routers, check the routing protocol configuration on the routers and on your server to make sure they're compatible. This method of dividing one Ping into several smaller Pings will help you to discover exactly where the problem lies in your network configuration. Once you have identified the culprit, you can begin to take steps to resolve the problem.

If you can Ping a PC that is on the same segment as your workstation, but you can't Ping it from a different segment, check its subnet mask to make sure it is appropriate for the segment where the workstation is located.

TRACERT

As a technician, you may need to check the route taken by a packet between its source and destination. **tracert** (also called **traceroute** in operating systems like Linux) tracks and reports the hops taken by a packet. This can be particularly important when a sluggish response and slow Pings suggest excessive delays (which are often caused by an excessive number of hops). This is also handy in finding the last successful hop before the network fails (and a packet is lost). **tracert** accomplishes this by setting the TTL (time to live) value in the packet, hoping to receive an ICMP time_exceeded message from each hop the data packet takes on its path. The TTL value is the allowable number of hops a packet can take before it is discarded. So, by increasing this value (starting with one and incrementing by one for each pass), **tracert** can get the time_exceeded message from each router or other device through which the packet must pass.

Remember that common implementations of **tracert** and **traceroute** are different. **traceroute** is ICMP-based, and **tracert** uses a combination of UDP and ICMP.

Using tracert

tracert and **traceroute** use a command line to launch the utility, define options, and select the destination. The syntax for using **tracert** in Windows NT/2000 is

```
tracert [-d] [-h max hops] [-j host list] [-w timeout] destination
```

where the options include

- **-d**   Return only the IP address of each hop—do not resolve hostnames to addresses.
- **-h max hops**   This sets the maximum number of hops to search for destination node.
- **-j host list**   This is the loose source route along the host list.
- **-w timeout**   This sets the number of milliseconds to wait for a timeout.
- **destination**   The IP address or name of the target node.

Here is the **traceroute** syntax under Red Hat Linux 7.x:

```
traceroute [-dFInrvx] [-g gateway] [-i iface] [-f first_ttl] [-m max_ttl]
[ -p port] [-q nqueries] [-s src_addr] [-t tos] [-w waittime] host [packetlen]
```

For example, suppose that you wanted to examine the behavior of your Web server being handled by a Web hosting service. You can use **tracert** to investigate the hostname, such as

```
>tracert dlspubs.com
```

Or we can limit the number of hops to 10, such as

```
>tracert -h 10 dlspubs.com
```

tracert will generate a report such as that in Figure 29-5. The first column represents the hop count. The second three columns detail the round-trip time of each test (in milliseconds). The fifth column shows the IP address (and/or DNS name) of the router or node. Unusually long delays or timeouts may suggest excessive traffic at some point between your source and destination.

```
MS-DOS Prompt                                                    _ □ ✕
 Auto      ▼   ⬚  ⬚ ⬚  ⬚   ⬚ ⬚  A

Microsoft(R) Windows 98
   (C)Copyright Microsoft Corp 1981-1999.

C:\WINDOWS>tracert -h 10 dlspubs.com

Tracing route to dlspubs.com [216.71.48.253]
over a maximum of 10 hops:

    1     9 ms     8 ms     9 ms  10.80.32.1
    2    11 ms    22 ms    11 ms  065-0-189-66.wo.cpe.charter-ne.com [66.189.0.65]

    3    11 ms    11 ms    12 ms  002-0-189-66.wo.cpe.charter-ne.com [66.189.0.2]

    4    11 ms    15 ms    11 ms  230-0-189-66.wo.cpe.charter-ne.com [66.189.0.230
]
    5    13 ms    16 ms    14 ms  12.125.39.13
    6    14 ms    13 ms    12 ms  gbr1-p70.cb1ma.ip.att.net [12.123.40.98]
    7    20 ms    12 ms    11 ms  gbr3-p70.cb1ma.ip.att.net [12.122.5.53]
    8    17 ms    16 ms    16 ms  gbr4-p80.n54ny.ip.att.net [12.122.2.190]
    9    18 ms    16 ms    16 ms  ggr1-p370.n54ny.ip.att.net [12.123.1.125]
   10    16 ms    18 ms    17 ms  POS5-1.BR1.NYC9.ALTER.NET [204.255.169.93]

Trace complete.

C:\WINDOWS>_
```

FIGURE 29-5   tracert reports the path taken by your packets, and can reveal the point at which traffic is impaired or lost.

Troubleshooting with tracert

You can use **tracert** to determine the route taken by a packet. In the example below, a packet must travel through two routers (**10.0.0.1** and **192.168.0.1**) to get to host **172.16.0.99**. The default gateway of the host is **10.0.0.1** and the IP address of the router on the **192.168.0.0** network is **192.168.0.1**:

```
>tracert 172.16.0.99 -d
Tracing route to 172.16.0.99 over a maximum of 30 hops
1     2 ms     3 ms     2 ms  10.0.0.1
2    75 ms    83 ms    88 ms  192.168.0.1
3    73 ms    79 ms    93 ms  172.16.0.99
Trace complete.
```

You can also use the **tracert** command to determine where a packet stopped on the network. In the following example, the default gateway has determined that there is not a valid path for the host on **192.168.10.99**. There is probably a router configuration problem, or the **192.168.10.0** network node does not exist (i.e., a bad IP address).

```
>tracert 192.168.10.99
Tracing route to 192.168.10.99 over a maximum of 30 hops
1 10.0.0.1 reports: Destination net unreachable.
Trace complete.
```

PATHPING

The Windows 2000 **pathping** command is a route-tracing tool that combines features of the **ping** and **tracert** commands with additional information that neither of those tools provides. The **pathping** command sends packets to each router on the way to a final destination over a period of time, and then generates results based on the packets returned from each hop. Since the command shows the degree of packet loss at any given router or link, it is easy to determine which routers or links might be causing network problems.

Using pathping

pathping is launched from the command line, which includes the command, options, and destination, such as

```
>pathping dlspubs.com
```

but the full syntax under Windows 2000 is shown as

```
pathping [-n] [-h max hops] [-g host list] [-p period] [-q queries] [-w timeout]
[-T tag] [-R]
```

where the options are

- **-n** Return only the IP address of each hop—do not resolve addresses to hostnames.
- **-h max hops** The maximum number of hops to search for target.
- **-g host list** The loose source route along the host list.
- **-p period** The number of milliseconds to wait between Pings.
- **-q queries** The number of queries per hop.
- **-w timeout** The amount of time to wait (in milliseconds) for each reply.
- **-To tag** Attaches a layer-2 priority tag (for example, for IEEE 802.1p) to the packets and sends it to each of the network devices in the path. This helps in identifying the network devices that do not have layer 2 priority configured properly. The **-T** switch is used to test for Quality of Service (QoS) connectivity.
- **-R** The RSVP test checks to determine whether each router in the path supports the Resource Reservation Protocol (RSVP), which allows the host computer to reserve a certain amount of bandwidth for a data stream. The **-R** switch is used to test for Quality of Service (QoS) connectivity.

Troubleshooting with pathping

A typical **pathping** report is shown in Figure 29-6. When **pathping** is run, you first see the results for the route as it is tested for problems—this appears very similar to the display produced by **tracert**. However, **pathping** then displays a busy message for about two minutes (this time varies by the hop count). During this time, **pathping** gathers information from all the routers previously listed and from the links between them. At the end of this period, it displays the test results. The This Node/Link, Lost/Sent=Pct, and Address columns contain the most useful information. As you can see in Figure 29-6, the link between **10.80.32.1** (hop 1) and **66.189.0.65** (hop 2) is dropping 13 percent of the packets. All other links are working normally. The routers at hops 2 and 4 also drop packets addressed to them, but this loss does not affect their forwarding path.

```
>pathping -n aol.com
Tracing route to aol.com [64.12.187.25] over a maximum of 30 hops:
  0   192.168.168.5
  1   10.80.32.1
  2   66.189.0.65
  3   66.189.0.2
  4   66.189.0.230
  5   12.125.39.13
  6   12.123.40.98
  7   12.122.5.53
  8   12.122.2.13
  9   12.123.1.125
 10   144.232.18.225
 11   144.232.9.226
 12   144.232.14.174
 13   144.232.20.3
 14   144.223.246.130
 15   66.185.139.193
 16   66.185.152.114
 17   204.148.98.70
 18   204.148.101.206
 19   204.148.102.182
 20   64.12.129.18
Computing statistics for 525 seconds...
                 Source to Here    This Node/Link
Hop   RTT     Lost/Sent = Pct    Lost/Sent = Pct   Address
  0                                                 192.168.168.5
                                  0/ 100 =  0%    |
  1   2ms     0/ 100 =  0%        0/ 100 =  0%    10.80.32.1
                                  0/ 100 =  0%    |
  2   0ms    13/ 100 = 13%        0/ 100 =  0%    66.189.0.65
                                  0/ 100 =  0%    |
  3   0ms     0/ 100 =  0%        0/ 100 =  0%    66.189.0.2
                                  0/ 100 =  0%    |
  4   1ms     0/ 100 =  0%        0/ 100 =  0%    66.189.0.230
                                  0/ 100 =  0%    |
  5   1ms     0/ 100 =  0%        0/ 100 =  0%    12.125.39.13
                                  0/ 100 =  0%    |
  6   0ms     0/ 100 =  0%        0/ 100 =  0%    12.123.40.98
                                  0/ 100 =  0%    |
  7   1ms     0/ 100 =  0%        0/ 100 =  0%    12.122.5.53
                                  0/ 100 =  0%    |
  8   15ms    0/ 100 =  0%        0/ 100 =  0%    12.122.2.13
                                  0/ 100 =  0%    |
```

FIGURE 29-6   pathping combines the features of Ping and tracert to provide detailed reports on the performance of packets between two stations.

```
 9    15ms      0/ 100 =   0%     0/ 100 =   0%   12.123.1.125
                                  0/ 100 =   0%   |
10    15ms      0/ 100 =   0%     0/ 100 =   0%   144.232.18.225
                                  0/ 100 =   0%   |
11    16ms      0/ 100 =   0%     0/ 100 =   0%   144.232.9.226
                                  0/ 100 =   0%   |
12    16ms      0/ 100 =   0%     0/ 100 =   0%   144.232.14.174
                                  0/ 100 =   0%   |
13    16ms      0/ 100 =   0%     0/ 100 =   0%   144.232.20.3
                                  0/ 100 =   0%   |
14    ---     100/ 100 =100%    100/ 100 =100%   144.223.246.130
                                  0/ 100 =   0%   |
15    16ms      0/ 100 =   0%     0/ 100 =   0%   66.185.139.193
                                  0/ 100 =   0%   |
16    16ms      0/ 100 =   0%     0/ 100 =   0%   66.185.152.114
                                  0/ 100 =   0%   |
17    17ms      0/ 100 =   0%     0/ 100 =   0%   204.148.98.70
                                  0/ 100 =   0%   |
18    16ms      0/ 100 =   0%     0/ 100 =   0%   204.148.101.206
                                  0/ 100 =   0%   |
19    16ms      0/ 100 =   0%     0/ 100 =   0%   204.148.102.182
                                  0/ 100 =   0%   |
20    18ms      0/ 100 =   0%     0/ 100 =   0%   64.12.129.18
                                100/ 100 =100%   |
21    ---     100/ 100 =100%     0/ 100 =   0%   0.0.0.0
Trace complete.
```

FIGURE 29-6   pathping combines the features of Ping and tracert to provide detailed reports on the performance of packets between two stations. *(continued)*

The loss rates displayed for the links (marked as a "|") indicate losses of packets being forwarded along the path—this loss suggests link congestion. The loss rates displayed for routers (indicated by their IP addresses in the rightmost column) indicate that the CPUs in those routers might be overworked. For example, hops 14 and 21 appear to timeout. Such congested routers might also be a factor in end-to-end problems (especially if packets are forwarded by software routers).

NETSTAT

Netstat provides technicians with a powerful tool that can display a comprehensive set of protocol statistics and current TCP/IP connections. The full syntax for **netstat** is

```
netstat [-a] [-e] [-n] [-s] [-p protocol] [-r] [interval]
```

where the options are

■   **-a**   Shows all connections and listening ports.

■   **-e**   Shows all Ethernet statistics.

■ **-n**   Shows all addresses and port numbers in numeric form, and will not resolve DNS names.

■ **-s**   Shows statistics for each of the following protocols: TCP, IP, UDP, ICMP.

■ **-p protocol**   Shows connections for the specified protocol.

■ **-r**   Shows the contents of the routing table.

■ **interval**   Redisplays statistics according to the specified interval (in seconds).

For example, the **netstat -a** command displays all connections, and **netstat -r** displays the route table plus active connections. The **netstat -e** command displays Ethernet statistics, and **netstat -s** displays per-protocol statistics. If you use **netstat -n**, addresses and port numbers are not converted to names. Figure 29-7 shows sample output for Netstat.

```
>netstat -a -e -s
Interface Statistics
                            Received            Sent
Bytes                        6381673         4608428
Unicast packets                20025           19780
Non-unicast packets             3339             238
Discards                           0               0
Errors                             0               0
Unknown protocols               9780
IP Statistics
  Packets Received                     = 23121
  Received Header Errors               = 0
  Received Address Errors              = 1
  Datagrams Forwarded                  = 0
  Unknown Protocols Received           = 0
  Received Packets Discarded           = 0
  Received Packets Delivered           = 23120
  Output Requests                      = 19951
  Routing Discards                     = 0
  Discarded Output Packets             = 0
  Output Packet No Route               = 0
  Reassembly Required                  = 0
  Reassembly Successful                = 0
  Reassembly Failures                  = 0
  Datagrams Successfully Fragmented    = 0
  Datagrams Failing Fragmentation      = 0
  Fragments Created                    = 0
ICMP Statistics
                            Received    Sent
  Messages                     3389     3507
  Errors                          0        0
  Destination Unreachable         0        8
```

FIGURE 29-7   Netstat provides a detailed report of the station's TCP/IP connections and status.

```
Time Exceeded              40              0
Parameter Problems          0              0
Source Quenches             0              0
Redirects                   0              0
Echos                     688           2811
Echo Replies             2661            688
Timestamps                  0              0
Timestamp Replies           0              0
Address Masks               0              0
Address Mask Replies        0              0
TCP Statistics
  Active Opens                     =   489
  Passive Opens                    =   487
  Failed Connection Attempts       =     0
  Reset Connections                =     3
  Current Connections              =    20
  Segments Received                = 15921
  Segments Sent                    = 15658
  Segments Retransmitted           =    12
UDP Statistics
  Datagrams Received   =  1556
  No Ports             =  4955
  Receive Errors       =     0
  Datagrams Sent       =   774
```

FIGURE 29-7   Netstat provides a detailed report of the station's TCP/IP
connections and status. *(continued)*

IPCONFIG

The **ipconfig** utility is a handy tool that can investigate the TCP/IP configuration of a Windows NT/2000 system (UNIX/Linux systems use the **ifconfig** utility). Use **ipconfig** to display network configuration information about each network adapter on a particular system—this information includes

- IP address
- Subnet mask
- Default gateway
- DNS server(s)
- Domain identification

For Windows 9x clients, use the **winipcfg** command instead of **ipconfig**.

Using ipconfig

When you use the **ipconfig** command with the */all* option, a detailed configuration report is produced for all interfaces—including any configured serial ports. You can also use this output to confirm the TCP/IP configuration of each computer on the network, or to further investigate TCP/IP network problems. For example, if a computer is configured with an IP address that is a duplicate of an existing IP address, the subnet mask appears as *0.0.0.0*. The example in Figure 29-8 shows the output of the **ipconfig /all** command on a Windows 2000 domain server.

> If no problems appear in the TCP/IP configuration, the next step is testing the ability to connect to other host computers on the TCP/IP network using a tool like Ping.

Release/Renew

When you troubleshoot a TCP/IP networking problem, begin by checking the TCP/IP configuration on the computer that is experiencing the problem. If the computer is DHCP-enabled (and is using a DHCP server to obtain configuration), you can use the **ipconfig /release** command to immediately release the current DHCP configuration for a host, then initiate a refresh of the lease by using the **ipconfig /renew** command. When you use **ipconfig /renew**, all network adapters on the computer that use DHCP (except

```
>ipconfig /all
Windows 2000 IP Configuration
     Host Name . . . . . . . . . . . . : SERVER01
     Primary DNS Suffix  . . . . . . . : admintration.dls.com
     Node Type . . . . . . . . . . . . : Broadcast
     IP Routing Enabled. . . . . . . . : No
     WINS Proxy Enabled. . . . . . . . : No
     DNS Suffix Search List. . . . . . : admintration.dls.com
                                         dls.com
Ethernet adapter Local Area Connection:
     Connection-specific DNS Suffix  . :
     Description . . . . . . . . . . . : 82559 Fast Ethernet
     Physical Address. . . . . . . . . : 00-E0-18-2F-65-FC
     DHCP Enabled. . . . . . . . . . . : Yes
     Autoconfiguration Enabled . . . . : Yes
     IP Address. . . . . . . . . . . . : 192.168.168.5
     Subnet Mask . . . . . . . . . . . : 255.255.255.0
     Default Gateway . . . . . . . . . : 192.168.168.1
     DHCP Server . . . . . . . . . . . : 192.168.168.1
     DNS Servers . . . . . . . . . . . : 24.216.218.9
                                         24.216.218.25
                                         24.216.218.41
     Lease Obtained. . . . . . . . . . : Tuesday, February 05, 2002
     Lease Expires . . . . . . . . . . : Wednesday, February 06, 2002
```

FIGURE 29-8   ipconfig allows technicians to check and adjust a station's NIC and logical network configuration.

those that are manually configured) try to contact a DHCP server and renew their existing configuration or obtain a new configuration.

Other IPCONFIG Options

The **ipconfig /flushdns** command provides you with a means to flush and reset the contents of the Windows 2000 DNS client cache on demand. During DNS troubleshooting, you can use this command (if necessary) to discard negative cache entries from the cache, as well as any other dynamically added entries. Remember that resetting the cache does not eliminate entries that are preloaded from the local hosts file.

The **ipconfig /registerdns** command under Windows 2000 provides you with a means to manually initiate dynamic registration for the DNS names and IP addresses configured at a computer. This option can assist in troubleshooting a failed DNS name registration or in resolving a dynamic update problem between a client and the DNS server without requiring a client reboot. By default, the **ipconfig /registerdns** command refreshes all DHCP address leases and registers all related DNS names configured and used by the client computer. To find the names of adapters that you can specify with this command, type the **ipconfig** command by itself (do not specify any additional parameters). The command output displays all adapters by name that are available for use at the computer. Then you may use the command **ipconfig /registerdns [adapter]**. If you're troubleshooting a failed DNS dynamic registration for a client computer and its DNS names, it might help to verify that the cause is not related to one of the commonly known causes for such failures:

- The zone where the client requires update or registration is not able to accept dynamic updates.

- The DNS servers that the client is configured to use do not support or recognize the DNS dynamic update protocol.

- The primary (or directory-integrated) DNS server for the zone refused the update request. This can most likely occur because the client is not permitted the access rights to update its own name.

- The server or zone is not available because of other problems, such as a network or server failure.

To show DHCP class ID information at a Windows 2000 client computer, use the **ipconfig /showclassid** command to show the DHCP class ID that the client uses when obtaining its lease from the DHCP server. The example in Figure 29-9 uses the default adapter name "Local Area Connection", and shows an ASCII string ("MyNewClassId") that is currently set as the DHCP class ID for the local area network connection at the client computer.

Finally, you can set the DHCP class ID for a network adapter on a Windows 2000 client using the **ipconfig /setclassid** command, which should include the name of the network adapter, along with the new ASCII string to be used as the class name. For example, the command

```
>ipconfig /setclassid "Local Area Connection" MyNewClassId
```

will set the ASCII string ("MyNewClassId") as the DHCP class ID string for the local area network connection in use at the client computer.

ifconfig

UNIX/Linux systems employ the **ifconfig** command. It not only displays IP configuration information, but also makes changes to the configuration. The **ifconfig** command is used during the boot sequence to

```
>ipconfig /showclassid "Local Area Connection"
Windows 2000 IP Configuration
DHCP Class ID for Adapter "Local Area Connection":
    DHCP ClassID Name . . . . . . . . : Default BOOTP Class
    DHCP ClassID Description  . . . . : User class for BOOTP clients
    DHCP ClassID Name . . . . . . . . : Default Remote Access Class
    DHCP ClassID Description  . . . . : User class for remote access clients
    Host Name . . . . . . . . . . . . : SERVER01
    Primary DNS Suffix  . . . . . . . : admintration.dlspubs.com
    Node Type . . . . . . . . . . . . : Hybrid
    IP Routing Enabled. . . . . . . . : No
    WINS Proxy Enabled. . . . . . . . : No
Ethernet adapter Local Area Connection:
    Connection-specific DNS Suffix  . :
    Description . . . . . . . . . . . : Combo PCMCIA EthernetCard
    Physical Address. . . . . . . . . : 00-00-00-00-7C-DC
    DHCP Enabled. . . . . . . . . . . : Yes
    Autoconfiguration Enabled . . . . : Yes
    IP Address. . . . . . . . . . . . : 192.168.1.51
    Subnet Mask . . . . . . . . . . . : 255.255.255.0
    Default Gateway . . . . . . . . . : 10.0.0.1
    DHCP Class ID . . . . . . . . . . : MyNewClassId
    DNS servers . . . . . . . . . . . : 10.0.0.3
    Primary WINS server . . . . . . . : 10.0.0.5
```

FIGURE 29-9   ipconfig can also be used to check and set the station's DHCP configuration.

perform the initial configuration for network adapters that are attached to the system. After the system is up and running, only the **superuser** can use this command to change the configuration. For UNIX/Linux troubleshooting, **ifconfig** is a quick way to determine if the system was properly configured. To simply display the current configuration information, you can execute the **ifconfig** command with no parameters. For the **superuser**, the following commands can be used to modify the configuration:

■ **ifconfig arp**   This enables the Address Resolution Protocol (ARP). Use the **ifconfig -arp** command to disable ARP.

■ **ifconfig dhcp**   Use DHCP to acquire an address for the network adapter. Try the **ifconfig auto-dhcp** command as an alternate.

■ **ifconfig down**   This command indicates that the interface is down, effectively shutting down network communications using this adapter.

■ **ifconfig metric [value]**   This command changes the routing metric for this interface.

■ **ifconfig netmask [mask]**   This command sets the subnet mask for this network adapter.

Further Study

ifconfig: **www.linuxdoc.org/LDP/nag2/x-087-2-iface.ifconfig.html**
ipconfig: **www.computerhope.com/ipconfig.htm**
netstat: **support.morehouse.edu/winipcfg.html**
pathping: **www.ece.villanova.edu/~kpreddy/Pathping.html**
ping: **www.ping127001.com/pingpage.htm**
tracert: **www.tracert.com**
winipcfg: **support.microsoft.com/directory/article.asp?ID=KB;EN-US;Q141698**

TROUBLESHOOTING WITH A PROTOCOL ANALYZER

As you've seen, networks have become an important asset for all sizes of business. By providing shared resources, accounting, e-mail, and Internet access, computer networks have reduced costs, streamlined processes, and facilitated the sharing of information. However, networks are often complex and convoluted assortments of hardware and software, and network problems can impact the productivity of dozens (even hundreds) of users. It's important for a technician to find the cause of the problem and correct it as quickly as possible. Without the means to display and interpret the network's traffic, a technician is limited to time-consuming trial-and-error troubleshooting methods. *Protocol analyzers* offer technicians a powerful and versatile tool to analyze the operations of a network and locate trouble spots. For example, a protocol analyzer can help a technician to identify a station that's sending excessive traffic, or experiencing errors—information that's virtually impossible to discern by trial and error. This chapter examines a suite of network troubleshooting techniques using protocol analyzer software on a networked PC.

 Although dedicated hardware-based protocol analyzers are available, this chapter assumes that you're using a software-based protocol analyzer on a local PC such as a networked laptop or other diagnostic PC platform.

Protocol Analyzer Basics

The protocol analyzer provides technicians with a powerful tool for monitoring network traffic, then analyzing that network traffic to develop real-time or trending information that can help to efficiently pinpoint up to 85 percent of all network problems. They can even simulate traffic and other network conditions. For example, a protocol analyzer can

- Identify problem stations on the network.
- Filter and save data based on a range of criteria.
- Identify the source and destination of selected network traffic.
- Measure network utilization and efficiency.
- Raise alarms when preselected settings are exceeded.

Without the type of information yielded by a protocol analyzer, there's no practical way to know what's going on "inside the network wiring," and network problems could go undetected and uncorrected until a hardware failure occurs. This can cost an organization dearly in lost productivity of an impaired network, or in countless hours of frustrating trial-and-error troubleshooting. Current network analyzers can decode and process captured information to determine what events are causing specific error conditions, and then provide information as to the possible causes of the events.

However, protocol analyzers demand a certain amount of knowledge on the part of the technician or administrator using the tool. Since protocol analyzers basically capture frames, a good working knowledge of protocols (down to the frame level) is necessary to interpret captured information. Knowledge of access methods in Ethernet and token ring is also important to fully understanding the impact of captured information. For example, a technician needs to understand CSMA/CD in order to appreciate the importance of excessive collisions in an Ethernet segment, and know Ethernet frame lengths to realize the trouble caused by jabber frames.

In addition to diagnosis, a protocol analyzer can help to quantify your needs for network expansion, and can be used to simulate network traffic loads and operating conditions. An analyzer can capture network trends to provide long-term performance information for the network administrator, and is an invaluable aid in forecasting growth needs. An analyzer can even generate traffic on a network in order to evaluate potential "what-if" scenarios before upgrades are implemented (see Chapter 27, "Network Performance and Baselining").

HARDWARE VS. SOFTWARE ANALYZERS

Protocol analyzers typically involve some combination of hardware and software, and have come a long way in the last few years. Early analyzers were typically large unwieldy cases that provided relatively simple hardware-based capture and reporting. With a minimum of postprocessing and interpretive features, these analyzers provided raw data that only technical wizards could understand. Such analyzers were also pricey (in the $30,000 range), and limited to the very largest of organizations.

Software-Based Analyzers

As PC processing power increased, it didn't take long for software-based protocol analysis to emerge. By using analysis software on a PC, its NIC could be made to grab all packets passing by on the network medium, no matter what their address. Many NIC models are capable of gathering all packets—a feature often termed *promiscuous mode*. Thus, it became possible to capture, record, process, and display network data on an ordinary PC rather than a specialized hardware device (for a price far lower than hardware-based devices). Software-based protocol analyzers typically include a data-collection component that gathers information about the data flowing on a LAN segment. The data-collection element sends the data (through the host PC's operating system) to an analysis component that decodes, processes, and displays the analyzed data in one of several forms. The shift to software-based analysis reduced the cost of analyzers greatly, but this approach was still not very portable (the PC would typically need to be carted from segment to segment). Today, laptop PCs offer the processing power needed for high-end protocol analysis software, and the portability needed to operate anywhere in the company.

 Remember that merely adding analysis software on just any PC might result in dropped frames (if the NIC buffers get overloaded).

Alternatively, current software-based protocol analyzers (such as Network Instruments Observer or Network General Sniffer) can run on any Windows 98/Me/NT/2000/XP workstation connected to the computer network. To enable the protocol analyzer to collect data from other parts of a LAN or WAN (in addition to the local LAN segment), external software components (called *probes*) are added to workstations on other network segments—this is called a *distributed environment*. The remote probes collect data exactly as the local probe does, and send that data to the protocol analyzer's console for analysis and analysis. The use of probes makes it possible to troubleshoot multiple segments from a single workstation.

New Life for Hardware

Still, hardware-based analyzers have improved dramatically with the addition of postprocessing and interpretive software, and they continue to be an option for high-end networks. Hardware-based protocol analyzers can provide functionality in a critical situation that cannot be obtained with a software-based product. A hardware instrument will usually be better capable of coping with a high-speed network environment (such as 100/1000BaseT) than a software application that relies on an ordinary NIC to get traffic from the network medium. Hardware analyzers contain special circuitry that is used to perform many functions much faster than can be accomplished through software—they are usually more reliable as well.

Remember that a PC-based analyzer may be limited by the NIC. For example, some ordinary adapter cards have a function (built into their firmware) that automatically discards certain kinds of packets that contain errors. So if you're trying to detect certain errors that are causing problems on your network, a software product running on a PC might not be able to help you. Also, while a NIC can literally see every packet on the network as it passes, there's no guarantee that they can capture the data and pass it up to higher-level protocols. When a NIC captures all frames and passes them up the protocol stack, it is operating in *promiscuous mode*. Some NICs (especially older ones) are not capable of promiscuous mode, so be sure to check the documentation that comes with the NIC you might want to use on a workstation intended to host protocol analyzer software.

A hybrid type of protocol analyzer combines the best of the hardware and software products. Hybrid analyzers implement the capturing and filtering functions in a dedicated hardware component that attaches to a workstation (or laptop)—the PC portion then provides the processing, display, and storage functions. The hardware component has dedicated circuitry and processing power to capture data from the wire, while a software application on the PC is used to filter, manipulate, and display the data. This type of analyzer is more expensive than a software-only solution, but can handle analysis at much higher data rates, and can prove very useful in high-bandwidth environments (like optical fiber networks).

BASIC FUNCTIONS

In simplest terms, a protocol analyzer's purpose is to capture and display data on the network wire. An analyzer basically connects to the network as a recording device, monitoring traffic but generating little (if any) additional traffic of its own. Every frame of data that goes through the wire is saved to the analyzer's memory buffer (though filters can be set to eliminate certain types of traffic from capture). Let's look at the basic functions of a protocol analyzer.

Capture Data

A protocol analyzer captures data packets as they travel through a network segment, and applies a timestamp to every packet. Many analyzers are used to capture traces (a set of frames) over a preselected time, or in a response to a specific event (see Figure 30-1). The analyzer receives data through its buffer, and usually offers options to save the buffer contents to a file on a floppy or hard drive for later analysis or comparison.

An analyzer captures data to a limited-size buffer, so when the buffer space is filled, the analyzer will start writing over data captured in the beginning of the buffer. For example, leaving an analyzer connected to the network all day might cause data collected early in the day to be lost, because it may be overwritten by data collected later in the day. Consequently, it's advisable to configure a larger capture buffer (for software-based analyzers), or buy as much memory and hard disk space as you can afford (for hardware-based analyzers). The more space available to store your captures, the more data you'll have available for later analysis.

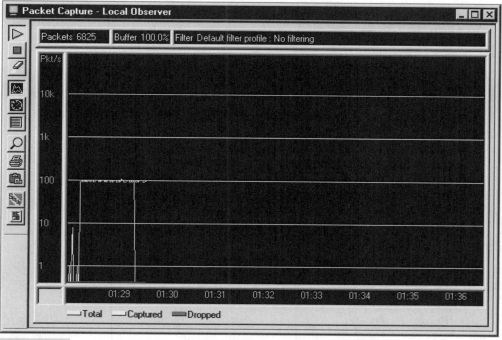

FIGURE 30-1   Use the analyzer's packet capture to record network traffic for later analysis.

Filter Data

Capturing every single packet of data across a network could easily provide more information than you really need to troubleshoot a particular problem (and fill even the largest buffer). Virtually all types of protocol analyzers provide a series of capture *filters* that can be set that eliminate all but desired type(s) of traffic (see Figure 30-2). Filtering can be selected by node, server, protocol, destination class, or network event. For example, if you know that a given problem is IPX-based, then you can set a protocol filter to capture only IPX packets—eliminating all other protocols and reducing the data captured to the buffer. Alternately, if you know that there's a problem with a particular node, you can set the capture filter to examine all packets going to and from that particular node. Filtering can be done during capture or display. For example, you may want to capture all of the frames during a particular time frame, but you may want to view only certain frames for troubleshooting purposes.

Decode Data

Once packets have been captured, they can be decoded by the protocol analyzer using a protocol interpreter. Some protocol analyzers decode only one type of protocol, while others have multiple protocol interpreters that can be purchased separately (or may come as an add-on package when the product is purchased). The decoding process involves breaking down each captured packet in sequence, then decoding the various protocol layers in the captured frames. This information is usually displayed in a summary presented in plain English (see Figure 30-3). This is what you'd read to actually "see inside" of a particular frame.

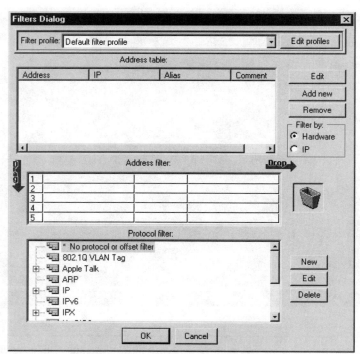

FIGURE 30-2   Capture filters let you focus on capturing just the packets that you're interested in, allowing longer captures with less memory.

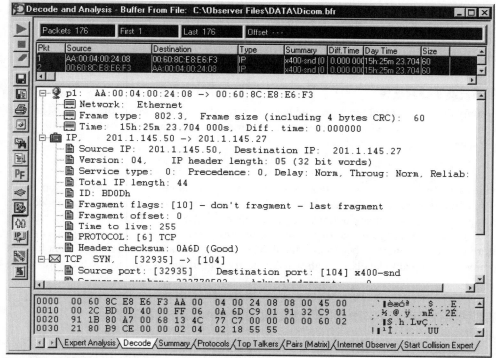

FIGURE 30-3   After data is captured, you can decode individual packets to check for damage or other problems.

As a rule, protocol analyzers do not decode packets and compare them to the OSI model on a layer-to-layer basis. In practice, the analyzer often combines layers. For example, the upper three layers of the OSI model (application, presentation, and session) are often combined into one decoding layer called the *application layer*—usually because only a small number of protocols (like NetBIOS) operate at the session or presentation layers. At this level, the analyzer is mainly concerned with the way two nodes in a connection are set up by an application, and how those two end nodes communicate with each other through an application. Items like slow file transfers can be detected.

Analyzers often refer to the OSI transport layer as the *connection layer*, and analyze the efficiency of end-to-end communication and error recovery. The OSI network layer is called the *network station layer* by some analyzers, and this is concerned with network addresses and routing issues. Duplicate network addresses are detected at this decoding layer. At the OSI data link and physical layers (called the *DLC station layer* by some analyzers), the analyzer works with the actual transmission of data and the physical errors that occur along the way. Throughput, broadcast frames, and CRC errors are decoded at this level.

Display Data

Of course, a protocol analyzer would be useless unless it displayed the decoded information for an administrator. This display can be presented as a separate step from the capture (capture first, then review the data file), or concurrently while the capture is active. The concurrent method is often more helpful—it permits the administrator to toggle back and forth between screens to analyze what is happening in real time. Most analyzers provide graphical displays for items like network utilization, protocol utilization, and more. Once a frame makes it past the display filter, it can be displayed in summary mode, detail mode, hex with ASCII mode, and so on. Some analyzers permit all three types of display to appear on the screen at once (though that can be confusing).

OTHER FEATURES

There are certainly many additional functions and features offered by modern protocol analyzers, and the following features can usually be found in modern analyzer software such as Observer. Consider these features when selecting your own analyzer.

Alarms

Alarms provide a network administrator with a proactive approach to monitoring the network. Some analyzers allow an administrator to set thresholds on the analyzer that produce alarms when exceeded. For example, setting a 25-percent utilization threshold on an Ethernet network could provide a valuable alert before the network becomes congested, allowing an administrator to start planning for an upgrade or optimization before a network condition becomes critical. Most analyzers come with default thresholds that are set to commonly acceptable levels, though you can easily set thresholds yourself (see Figure 30-4).

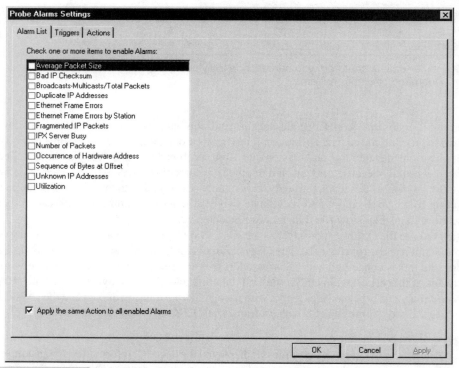

FIGURE 30-4   Alarms can be used to flag potential problems before they become serious enough to impair the network.

Triggers and Actions

An administrator can easily configure the analyzer to recognize a specific network event, and take one or more particular actions. For example, when the analyzer detects the trigger event (such as a duplicate network address), it begins recording or capturing to disk, and can optionally stop capturing after the event occurs. This feature is extremely useful in situations where you know *what* events you want to capture, but not *when* they might occur. Rather than haphazard capturing and time-consuming reviews—hoping to catch the event—the analyzer can be programmed to capture when the event occurs.

Let's look at an example using a software-based analyzer like Observer. Suppose that you want to set the analyzer to take action on Ethernet frame errors. You'd start by opening the Alarm List tab (as in Figure 30-4 earlier) and checking the Ethernet Frame Errors box. Click the Triggers tab to configure the trigger for the alarm (see Figure 30-5). In this case, there is only one trigger available, but you may set the trigger for the percentage of frames with errors, the minimum number of packets, and the averaging period. After you apply your trigger settings, select the Actions tab (see Figure 30-6) to determine how the analyzer will respond. Check the desired boxes corresponding to the desired action(s), and apply those selections as well. You can see how this provides precise, unattended monitoring of network conditions.

Baselining

Some protocol analyzers like Observer provide the ability to track network activity and performance during normal operation in order to learn the "normal" levels of network activity. This information is then used as a baseline for comparison if problems occur on the network later. In some cases, a capture can be

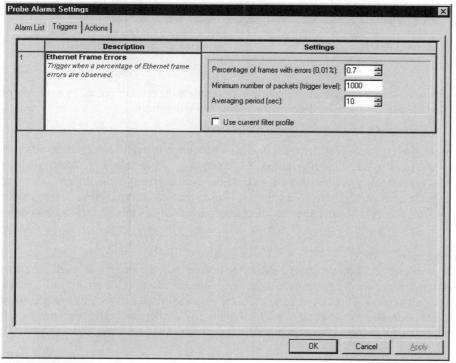

FIGURE 30-5   Configure your alarms by setting the trigger characteristics.

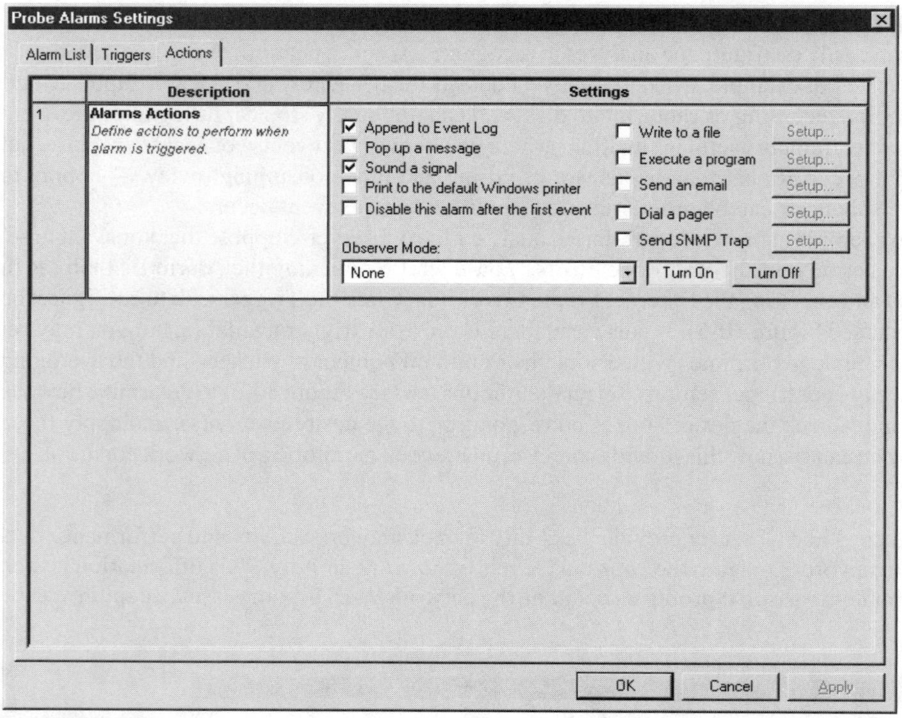

FIGURE 30-6 Once alarms are set, you can select actions for the analyzer to take automatically.

stored that may later be used to reproduce a particular error, or simulate the error on a healthy network for research purposes. See Chapter 27 for more information on network baselining.

Aliases

One issue with protocol analysis is that results are sometimes difficult to match to a particular station or user. For example, it's easy to see that IP address *192.168.1.4* is a top talker, or MAC address *03:FD:3E:44:A5:50* is experiencing an excessive number of Ethernet errors, but it's another matter to see that it's John's workstation or the R&D server. Many protocol analyzers maintain a table of addresses that correspond to users (called aliases). The analyzer may do this automatically, or allow you to load a predefined listing of aliases.

Traffic Generation

Protocol analyzers (like Observer) include a traffic generator feature that supports a variety of protocols (see Figure 30-7)—sometimes called a *simulator*. A traffic generator can provide packets of specific sizes, rates, quantities, and headers. This can be very useful for an administrator that wants to experiment with "what-if" scenarios between particular stations. Simulations give the network administrator a look at how the network will behave if subjected to certain traffic conditions.

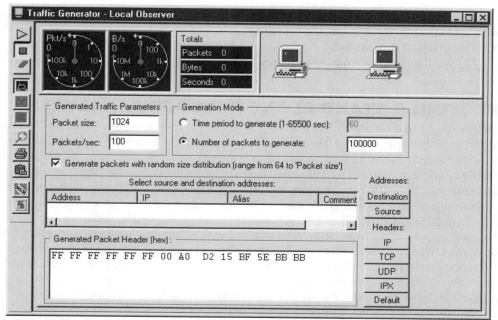

FIGURE 30-7   A traffic generator feature can simulate a wide range of traffic conditions on the network for stress-testing and "what-if" scenarios.

Analyzing Network Hardware

Although most of the analyzer's usefulness comes from examining the packets sent over the network, some analyzers (like Observer) can get a more direct look at some of the network hardware and make determinations of the hardware's operation:

- Features like Router Observer let you look at a router (or group of routers) in real-time to see their utilization rate. You can quickly find out if a router is acting as a bottleneck, and determine if the source of the packets clogging the router is incoming or outgoing (or both). By examining historical information, you can tell whether this is a chronic problem (which might indicate the need for a faster connection) or an acute problem, which might indicate a failure of some sort.

- You can track network errors by station if Observer is running on a workstation with a supported NIC and the Network Instruments' ErrorTrak driver for that NIC. This mode allows you to pinpoint errors by the sending station and the type of error. You can also gauge the severity of the error stream from a given station by viewing the error rates. This kind of data has traditionally required expensive hardware-based analyzers. But this type of PC-based analysis demands particular NIC models and drivers, so implementing this feature may limit your PC platform options.

- Analyzers can help you correctly configure a new switch for optimal throughput by showing how your network load is distributed between devices. Tools like Observer can also help you determine why you are not getting acceptable performance out of an existing switch.

- An efficiency history mode can show when a change or reconfiguration of the network has negatively impacted network throughput by grading the segment's ability to carry data. This is a handy tool to use both before and after an upgrade.

- An analyzer can help isolate a failing hub or NIC by identifying stations on the network with excessive retransmissions.

CONNECTING A STAND-ALONE PROTOCOL ANALYZER

The first step in using a portable protocol analyzer is to physically connect it to the network you intend to test and to configure it correctly for that connection. The analyzer can be connected as a node on the network, or it can be connected such that it monitors traffic between nodes. The connection and configuration that you choose is influenced not only by the kinds of tests you intend to run, but also the physical environment (hubs versus switches). A hub transmits any packet that arrives at one port to all the other ports of the hub. This means that all nodes connected to a hub are able to listen to all other nodes. By comparison, switches can learn the position of nodes in the network by mapping the physical addresses of the nodes localized in each segment of the network and then forwarding or filtering the packets, depending on the destination address. When a packet reaches a switch, the switch compares the physical source and destination addresses of the conversation and isolates this conversation from the rest of the ports of the switch.

Consequently, switch management and monitoring are often an issue. One of the biggest challenges when testing in a switched network is the dynamic change in traffic patterns—the switch will open and close ports depending on the traffic. When connecting the analyzer to a network, you must take this into account. For example, if you connect and configure the analyzer as a node in a switched environment, you will not see all the traffic you might otherwise hope to see. Since no other network element will know about the existence of the analyzer, no traffic will be sent to the analyzer specifically, and the switch will block the physical port to which the analyzer is connected. The only traffic that the analyzer will capture is broadcast traffic.

Before connecting the analyzer, determine whether you're connecting in a switched or hub environment. When connecting in a switched environment, you will want to connect and configure the analyzer as a *monitor* so that the analyzer sees all traffic between a specific switch and server/workstation. When connecting in a hub environment, you'll want to connect and configure the analyzer as a *node* so that the analyzer sees all the traffic destined for all the ports on the hub.

Connecting a Node

A *node connection* (sometimes referred to as a *point-to-point connection*) simply attaches a port on the analyzer to an available port on the hub or switch, and is used primarily in a hub environment. This connection allows the analyzer to serve as a node—an independent point on the network. The analyzer will see all the traffic that passes through the hub in the same way that any other Ethernet node would. With this connection, the analyzer is attached directly to an available hub port using a RJ-45 100BaseT cable (with a maximum length of 100 meters). The analyzer can monitor traffic from all the stations having the same collision domain as the hub port where the analyzer is connected. This setup also allows the analyzer to generate traffic onto the network. Node connections let the analyzer operate in a half-duplex or full-duplex mode. Half duplex is typically used in 10-Mbps Ethernet environments where the analyzer node transmits and receives at different times. Full duplex is commonly used in Fast Ethernet environments in which both transmit and receive lines transmit simultaneously, resulting in up to 200-Mbps throughput.

Connecting a Monitor

The *monitor mode* (sometimes called the *inline* or *through* mode) is usually used in a switched environment where the analyzer is placed inline between a switch port and a server (or server segment). In actual practice, the switch is normally connected directly to the server through a crossover cable. To connect the analyzer between the server and the switch, disconnect the cable from the server and connect the cable to the node port of the analyzer. Then connect a crossover cable from the switch to the switch port of the analyzer. This mode can be used for both 10-Mbps Ethernet and 100-Mbps Fast Ethernet. Remember the following limitations when using an analyzer in monitor mode:

- The monitor mode typically does not allow traffic generation by the analyzer.

- The monitor mode allows for full-duplex monitoring where switch-to-server and server-to-switch traffic will be captured.

- Always use the existing cable that is connected between the server and the switch. The cable can be either a crossover or a straight-through cable, depending on the specific equipment used. In addition to using the existing cable, the second cable should always be a straight-through cable so signals are not accidentally inverted.

- When using the monitor mode, the signal is not regenerated in the analyzer, so the combined length of *both* cables should not exceed 100 meters.

- If the analyzer's power is turned off, the connection between the switch and the server is usually maintained.

In a switched fiber environment, the switch is normally connected directly to the server through a fiber cable. However, you will still need to insert the analyzer inline between the switch and server. As with RJ-45 cables, disconnect the fiber cable from the server and connect the cable to the node port of the analyzer. You may encounter devices with ST or SC type connectors, so be sure that your protocol analyzer's module can accommodate the cable.

Using the Analyzer

Now that you've learned a bit about what protocol analyzers are and how they work, it's time to look at the actual use of a protocol analyzer, and see how it's applied in basic troubleshooting situations. For this chapter, we'll be working with the very capable Observer Suite from Network Instruments. Remember that protocol analyzers can vary dramatically in their features and performance, so always refer to your analyzer's documentation for additional details and uses.

REAL-TIME DIAGNOSTICS

Of course, you can jump right into packet capture and analysis, but most protocol analyzers provide a suite of tools that can be applied in real time to test and diagnose network problems. It's often helpful to start with these tools in order to understand the full effects of a problem, then use packet capture and analysis when necessary to discern specific problems from bits of traffic.

Discover Network Names

The Discover Network Names mode captures all network addresses on the segment, stores them in the filter table, and assigns them aliases. This feature lets you see just what stations are on your network, and can be helpful when a particular station becomes inaccessible, or when you're testing to see if a newly connected station is responding. You can assign a name to a network address or use the IP address, DNS name, NetWare login name, or Microsoft network login name. After storing the network names, you can use the stored names in all your queries. Knowing the network names often makes it easier for a technician to identify problem workstations or other network devices. If you cannot directly discover a group of network names, Observer also allows you to import an address list into the address table. Simply click the Discover Network Names icon in Observer's tool bar, and the dialog box will open (see Figure 30-8). Start the discovery process, and let it run. You'll see the table fill in as the cycle continues. Once Discover Network Names completes its active discovery, Observer will passively "listen" to your LAN and record all of the network addresses seen.

Discover Network Names will auto-alias network addresses that it finds in three possible ways: IP, IPX, or Microsoft (Msft). The default mode is IP. In this mode, Observer will first try to ARP all of the addresses in the IP address (that you can specify) twice, and then listen for any additional hard addresses that may show up over time. In the IPX mode, Observer queries any local NetWare servers and asks the server for a NetWare login name for each hard address found on the local segment. This is done by creating IPX packets and logging into the server as administrator. You will be prompted for a NetWare administrator password before Observer begins to poll the server. In Microsoft (Msft) mode, Observer is passively listening to packets in this mode and will only find the NetBIOS/NetBEUI names as they are broadcast on the LAN. To alias all of the names on a LAN this way may take anywhere from five minutes to many hours.

Bandwidth Utilization

If you'd like to measure the amount of bandwidth being utilized by your network segment, use the Bandwidth Utilization feature. Unexpected bandwidth demands may indicate excess traffic (requiring an upgrade), or trouble with a NIC's retransmissions. Bandwidth utilization is calculated by recording the number of bytes seen by Observer (or a probe station) over a 1-second interval. This value is then adjusted by adding to the appropriate MAC header and footer data size information. Then the amount of data is compared to the maximum theoretical throughput that your NIC driver reports (such as 10/100/1000 Mbps, or whatever your NIC card is reporting) and a percentage statistic is displayed as a graph.

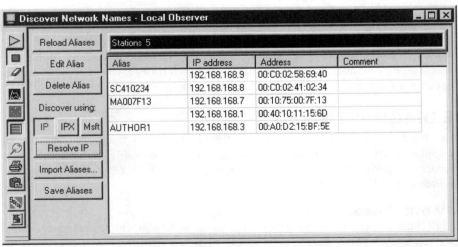

FIGURE 30-8   Discover network names to find the stations on your network, along with their IP, MAC, and alias designations.

To measure bandwidth utilization, click the Bandwidth Utilization (BU) button in Observer's toolbar. The Bandwidth Utilization dialog box will appear (see Figure 30-9). The graph shows the current bandwidth utilization, along with maximum, average, and latest utilization values.

Network Activity

The Network Activity Display shows critical network utilization and broadcast information displayed as a graph against traffic (packets/sec) and utilization percentage. This type of display can illustrate the overall health of a LAN, and can warn of impending slowdowns due to broadcast or multicast storms. To check network activity, click the Network Activity Display (NAD) button on the Observer toolbar, and the Network Activity Display dialog box will appear (see Figure 30-10). The graph tracks broadcast, multicast, average utilization, and maximum utilization. Excessive broadcasts may indicate trouble with a station's NIC.

Network Vital Signs

Observer's Network Vital Signs mode shows the current LAN activity (packets/sec and utilization percentage) mapped against current error conditions such as CRC, alignment, small frames, big frames, collisions, average utilization, and maximum utilization. To start the Network Vital Signs (NVS) mode, click the icon on Observer's toolbar, and the vital signs graph appears (see Figure 30-11). This display gives you a complete snapshot of error conditions, and the level of those error conditions versus the current LAN activity. The level of the error condition is important in determining the severity of a particular error. For example, a 50-percent CRC packet error level is not a problem if the sample size (total activity) is only two packets. On the other hand, a 10-percent CRC packet error level during a busy traffic period represents a critical problem.

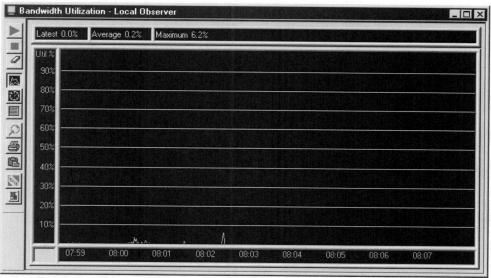

FIGURE 30-9   Bandwidth utilization can report excessive traffic, and provide early warning of network problems or upgrade needs.

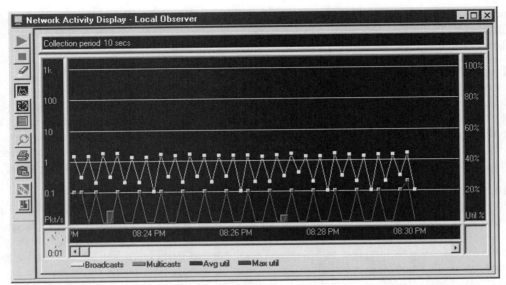

FIGURE 30-10   Network activity can quickly report utilization and broadcast/multicast activity across the network.

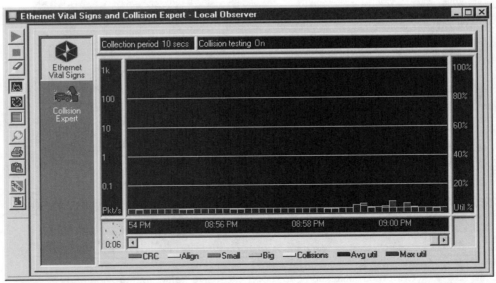

FIGURE 30-11   Network Vital Signs can quickly display common error conditions in your network traffic.

Network Errors by Station

If Network Vital Signs indicate the presence of errors, use the Network Errors by Station mode to identify and display Ethernet error packets that are broken down by the source (station) of the error along with the type of error packet. You can check for network errors by clicking the Network Errors by Station (NES) icon, and the Network Errors by Station dialog box appears (see the troubleshooting section later in this chapter for help on correcting each error type). The dialog box reports a suite of detailed information for each offending station, including

- Alias
- IP Address
- Address
- Errors
- CRC
- Alignment
- Too Small
- Packets
- % Errors
- Errors/sec
- CRCs/sec
- Alignment/sec
- Too Small/sec
- Packets/sec

Observer's ability to track Ethernet errors by station requires the use of a Network Instruments ErrorTrak driver and a certified network adapter card. Other protocol analyzers may impose other limitations.

Protocol Distribution

The Protocol Distribution mode shows how your LAN's data is being distributed based on particular protocols, and can present a breakdown of protocols in list or chart format. Inspecting protocols can give you a picture of the various servers and applications that are being used, and show you if there are any unknown or misconfigured protocols on your LAN. To review protocol distribution, click the Protocol Distribution (PD) icon in Observer's toolbar, and the Protocol Distribution dialog box will appear (see Figure 30-12). In All mode, the dialog box will display all available protocols traversing the network, but you can also select IP or IPX protocols only.

Packet Size Distribution

Packet Size Distribution Statistics will show each station's traffic patterns on your LAN broken down by the size of the packet. This type of information can help pinpoint network flow problems. For example, you can easily identify stations or routers that are sending mostly small packets as opposed to larger packets. By default, the stations listed are all the stations on your LAN (this is the unfiltered traffic), but filters can be employed to help isolate packet sizes for source or destination stations. Open the statistics dialog box

Protocol Distribution Statistics - Local Observer
All
IP
IPX
Protocols 3
Packets 1791
Protocol
Total
Total %
IP
1626
90.787
IPX
156
8.710
NetBIOS
9
0.503

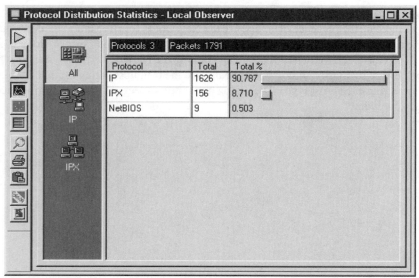

FIGURE 30-12 Protocol distribution can quickly tell you if stations are improperly configured (using the wrong protocol).

by clicking the Packet Size Distribution Statistics (SDS) icon in Observer's toolbar (see Figure 30-13). The display shows the percentage of packets in each size range as a list or graph. In the first entry, the station with MAC address **00:40:10:11:15:6D** sent 1626 packets, 48.7 percent of those packets were under 64 bytes, but 49.4 percent of those frames were between 512 and 1,024 bytes.

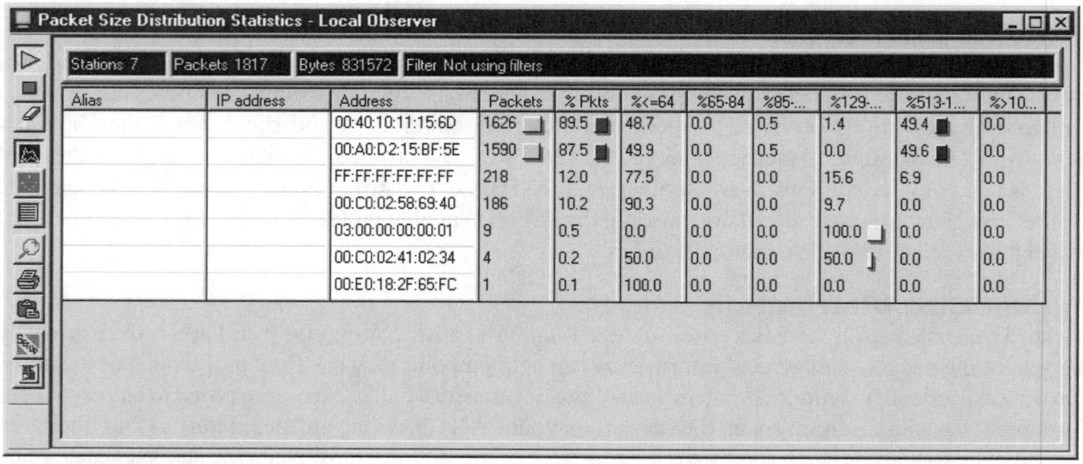

Packet Size Distribution Statistics - Local Observer
Stations 7
Packets 1817
Bytes 831572
Filter Not using filters
Alias
IP address
Address
Packets
% Pkts
%<=64
%65-84
%85-...
%129-...
%513-1...
%>10...
00:40:10:11:15:6D 1626 89.5 48.7 0.0 0.5 1.4 49.4 0.0
00:A0:D2:15:BF:5E 1590 87.5 49.9 0.0 0.5 0.0 49.6 0.0
FF:FF:FF:FF:FF:FF 218 12.0 77.5 0.0 0.0 15.6 6.9 0.0
00:C0:02:58:69:40 186 10.2 90.3 0.0 0.0 9.7 0.0 0.0
03:00:00:00:00:01 9 0.5 0.0 0.0 0.0 100.0 0.0 0.0
00:C0:02:41:02:34 4 0.2 50.0 0.0 0.0 50.0 0.0 0.0
00:E0:18:2F:65:FC 1 0.1 100.0 0.0 0.0 0.0 0.0 0.0

FIGURE 30-13 Packet size distribution can quickly tell you when stations are generating packets of improper size.

PACKET CAPTURE AND ANALYSIS

Now that you've seen some common diagnostic tools available in an analyzer, it's time to review the main feature of a protocol analyzer—packet capture and analysis. The Packet Capture mode captures LAN traffic and stores the data for later viewing in a decode window. Packet capture can also be used to view specific packets during a network conversation (be sure to understand the security implications of checking specific data packets). After examining the information being sent and the specific reply, you can often get a clear view of a problem or an incorrect communication.

Once the packets are captured, they can be viewed and analyzed in list and graph formats. Analysis features are available for live captures (captures in real time where Observer captures and saves traffic on the local segment, or uses a probe to capture and save traffic on a remote segment). Analysis is also available for analysis of saved buffer files (where the local copy of Observer can be used to examine and analyze packets captured by any copy of Observer). To access packet capture and analysis, click the Packet Capture (PC) icon in Observer's toolbar. The Packet Capture dialog box will appear. Use the Setup feature to configure the capture parameters (such as the buffer size and other options), then start the capture such as in Figure 30-1 above. The dialog box will list the number of packets captured and the amount of buffer space consumed. The graph will also track the number of total, captured, and dropped packets. The capture will stop when the buffer is filled—though you can stop the capture manually.

 Remember that dropped packets are an error condition. If you're seeing dropped packets, you should begin to check your network hardware for problems, or verify that the host PC's processing power meets the minimum requirements of the protocol analyzer.

The Decode and Analysis portion of Packet Capture mode is where the captured buffer is decoded and the packet conversations can be examined and analyzed in detail. Observer allows you to analyze the capture buffer by protocols, top talkers, pair conversations, and so on. A Collision Expert is also available, enabling you to view an Ethernet network's vital signs and test for collisions that may be caused by a malfunctioning NIC card somewhere on the network. To start the analysis, click the View icon in the Capture dialog box, and the analysis window will open.

Troubleshooting with Expert Analysis

One of the limitations with older protocol analyzers is that raw data was typically presented with little (if any) interpretation. However, modern protocol analyzers like Network Instruments' Observer provide a summary of error analysis and reporting. Click the Expert Analysis tab, and a listing of errors (if any) will appear. This part of the chapter explains the common errors listed by a protocol analyzer and offers some suggestions for corrective action.

Alignment Errors   Alignment errors (sometimes called Ethernet alignment errors) are detected when a packet is not aligned on a transmission's phase boundary. For timing purposes, the NIC assembles and sends a preamble for Ethernet packets. Timers on both the sending and receiving Ethernet adapters synchronize phase timing and calculate a phase position to begin the actual packet. This phase position is used so that the receiving adapter can know when the packet begins, and how the packet should correspond to the actual signal.

Alignment errors can be caused by a number of factors. Typically, they are caused by a previous collision resulting in an alignment error. If the collision occurs during a transmission (after the preamble), the position of the resulting signal relative to the phase of the signal is incorrect—the receiving NIC acknowledges this, and the packet is discarded. Alignment errors can also be caused by bad cabling between the station and a hub/switch, a cable that is too long (or electrical interference on the cable), or a bad Ethernet NIC or router connection.

Bad IP Checksum   Checksums and cyclic redundancy checks (CRCs) are methods used to verify the integrity of data by computing some extra bits and transmitting them along with the data. The receiver applies the same algorithm to regenerate the extra information and verify that it is correct. A bad IP checksum occurs when the packet generated by the NIC appears to be correct, but the protocol section of the packet is corrupt. While a MAC layer checksum would result in the packet being discarded, a bad IP checksum would be processed by the stack and passed up to the associated IP application. Bad IP checksums can occur because of a failing NIC at the transmission source, a failing cable or connector along the transmission route, or by bad TCP/IP drivers or protocol processing software at the source. Take the offending station offline, check the cabling and NIC, replace the defective NIC if necessary, and reinstall the protocol drivers or software.

Broadcast Storm/Multicast Storm   A *broadcast storm* (or *data storm*) is excessive transmission of broadcast traffic in a network. This happens when a broadcast across a network results in even more responses, and each response results in still more responses—causing a snowball effect. If network traffic reaches near 100 percent of the available bandwidth, all network traffic can be blocked. Broadcast storms are often caused by a defective NIC or defective cabling, where the card or cable floods the network with packets. For example, if a NIC card repeats the same ARP request at a rate of several hundred times a second, the requests may be propagated around the network by other devices. This can be fixed quickly by identifying and disconnecting the offending computer from the network and then replacing the Ethernet card, or by checking the network cable for any breaks, kinks, or loosened connectors, and then making repairs as needed. Broadcast storms can also be caused by misconfigured NetBIOS/NetBEUI servers or devices. A broadcast storm can also occur between routers when a broadcast packet is forwarded more times than it should be. The broadcast will eventually drop when the hop count reaches zero, but may saturate WAN links in the meantime.

Collisions   Ethernet networks operate using the Carrier Sense Multiple Access with Collision Detection (CSMA/CD) principle, so a station listens to the wire for any other traffic before sending. If no other stations are sending, that station may send its packet. Otherwise, it must wait and repeat the carrier sensing later. During periods of heavy traffic, several stations may be waiting to send data. If two (or more) of these stations carrier sense at the same time, both may decide to send. If this occurs, a *collision* will result (this may also cause an alignment error, CRC error, or both—depending on the timing).

At relatively low levels (usually about 5 percent of network traffic), collisions are a natural and acceptable part of any Ethernet network. The busier the network, the more collisions you may experience, but excessive collisions can bring your network to a standstill. Collisions are frequently caused by a faulty network adapter or a congested network segment. Take the offending station(s) offline and test their NIC. Any faulty NICs must be replaced. When the NIC is working properly, upgrading to higher-capacity NICs (i.e., moving from 10BaseT to 100BaseT NICs) or network segmentation is usually the best option.

Duplicate IP Address   This error event appears when two device IP addresses are identical, but seen from different hardware devices (MAC addresses) on your network. Duplicate IP addresses are common when there is a mixture of static IP addresses and DHCP being used without limiting the scope of the DHCP server's address table. For example, a user assigns their own IP address without contacting an administrator. In this case, one of the offending stations will need to be reconfigured to an available IP address (or use DHCP). In other cases, a new device has been put on the LAN without being properly configured, and that device will need to be configured properly.

Ethernet CRC Errors   There are two types of Ethernet CRC errors that you should be aware of: MAC frame CRC errors, and internal protocol CRC errors. MAC frame CRC errors are the most common, and are what most devices and analyzers refer to when they report a CRC error. Ethernet packets are encapsulated in a MAC frame that contains a preamble and a post-envelope CRC check. The Ethernet NIC on the sending station is responsible for creation of the preamble, the insertion of the packet data (addressing, protocol, data, and so on), then calculating a CRC checksum and inserting this at the end of the packet. The receiving station uses the checksum to determine if the packet was received intact. If the checksum is not correct, the packet is probably damaged and is discarded.

MAC frame CRC errors can be caused by a number of factors. Typically, they are caused by faulty cabling, or as the result of a collision. If the cabling connecting an Ethernet NIC or hub is faulty, the electrical connection may flutter on and off many times during a transmission—this "fluttering" can interrupt parts of a transmission and damage the signal. If a collision occurs during packet transmission, the signal for the specific packet will be interrupted, and the resulting received packet will be damaged. If the signal is partially interrupted during transmission, the CRC checksum calculated by the NIC will not be valid, and the packet will be flagged with a CRC error and discarded. Remember that CRC errors are common on a busy network, and a small percentage does not reflect a network problem. If the percentage is large, or when a single station shows a notably higher number of CRC errors, there is probably a cabling, NIC, or hub/switch port problem that needs to be addressed.

Internal protocol CRC checksums are another problem to be considered. Some protocols (such as TCP/IP) have a second checksum for data integrity purposes (in addition to the MAC frame CRC checksum). This second checksum is calculated on only a portion of the internal data in each packet, and can provide a second independent check on the packet's integrity. The protocol analyzer calculates this checksum independently and displays the results in the protocol analysis display. Such CRC errors are very rare, and can be caused by malfunctioning software or protocol drivers.

ICMP Destination Unreachable   If the network specified in the Internet destination field of a datagram is unreachable based on the information in a router or gateway's routing tables (i.e., the distance to the network is infinity), the router or gateway may send a "destination unreachable" message to the Internet source of the datagram. The router or gateway in some networks may be able to determine if the Internet destination is unreachable, and routers or gateways in these networks may send "destination unreachable" messages to the source when the destination host is unreachable. Also, when the IP module in the destination cannot deliver the datagram because the indicated protocol module (or process port) is not active, the destination host may send a "destination unreachable" message to the source host. Another case may occur when a datagram must be fragmented to be forwarded by a gateway, yet the Don't Fragment flag is set. In this case, the gateway must discard the datagram, and may return a "destination unreachable" message.

These errors can occur when the router's routing tables are misconfigured, the destination just doesn't exist, the destination has been excluded as a possible valid address (i.e., disallowed), or the service requested is not available on the destination system. Verify that the destination exists and is allowed as a valid address, then check or update the routing tables as necessary.

ICMP Parameter Problem   If the router, gateway, or host processing a datagram finds a problem with the header parameters (and it cannot finish processing the datagram), it must discard the datagram. This often occurs when there are incorrect arguments in an option, and the router, gateway, or host may notify the source using the "parameter problem" message—this message is only sent if the error caused the datagram to be discarded. This error can also occur if the sending station's TCP stack is failing, has a bad NIC, or a bad network connection. This error can also be traced to a failing router or gateway network connection (or one whose TCP stack is failing).

ICMP Time to Live Exceeded   If a router or gateway processing a datagram finds the TTL field is zero, it must discard the datagram. The router or gateway may also notify the source using the "TTL exceeded" message. If a host reassembling a fragmented datagram cannot complete the reassembly due to missing fragments within a time limit, it also discards the datagram and may send a "TTL exceeded" message. This error often occurs when a routing problem exists—the route tables have identified a route that is either incorrect, or beyond the number of hops the host considers the maximum. This error can also be attributed to a packet that was lost due to a malfunctioning router, busy network, or failing NIC card on host or router.

Local Routing Problem   Local routing problems are usually triggered when a nonrouter station is using an incorrect IP network mask and sending local traffic to the default router to be routed. In this case, you will need to apply the correct IP network mask at the nonrouter station. In other cases, two stations (nonrouters) may have the same IP address, or a nonrouter station is configured with an incorrect default gateway.

Maximum Utilization Exceeded   This error may or may not indicate a network problem—it may be a simple case of normal (but high) network utilization. If your response times are lower than expected, and a high utilization rate is discovered, try to determine the source of the high network load. Sources typically include

- A station that is resending error packets, or is stuck in a continuous sending loop
- A router or bridge that is incorrectly sending data repeatedly
- Too many stations located on one collision domain
- A station or group of stations that are transferring a large amount of data

Packets Too Small/Too Big   The Ethernet specification requires that all packets be at least 64 bytes long, and no larger than 1,518 bytes (including checksum). Any packet on the wire that is less than 64 bytes is considered to be "too small," and any packet larger than 1,518 bytes is flagged as an error and discarded—these packets are sometimes called jabber frames. In both cases, packet size problems are usually caused by faulty hardware. The NIC in a station showing a high rate of packet problems should be tested and replaced.

Routing Problem   Routing problems normally occur when a nonrouter station (the IP address indicated in the error) is configured with an incorrect default gateway. Check and reconfigure the offending station as necessary.

TCP/UDP Excessive Retransmissions   This error occurs when a TCP sequence number is either identical to a previous sequence number or is less than a previous sequence number. This indicates that the packet is a duplicate of one previously sent. For example, the sending station did not receive an acknowledgment, or the packet was lost, dropped, or otherwise damaged. TCP retransmissions can occur because the receiving station was too busy to respond to the sending station, or network traffic was so high that the original packet was lost (or the acknowledge was never received due to high network utilization). In other cases, a router dropped the packet (or was unable to forward the packet), possibly because the router is too busy or malfunctioning. Finally, you may find that bad cabling or a failing switch/hub is causing an intermittent network failure, resulting in excessive retransmissions.

TCP Excessive Zero Windows   When a TCP station communicates with another station, a "window value" is sent to indicate the amount of data the sending station is willing to take for the next packet.

If the sending station advertises a *zero window*, it means the station is unable to process any additional data at `the moment. Zero windows may occur when the system (reporting the zero window) is too busy to process any more data. There may also be a serious mismatch between the processing ability of sending and receiving stations (i.e., a busy 100BaseT station trying to feed a 10BaseT station). In other cases, an application is so slow that it cannot keep up with the data stream from the network, or is waiting for another event to occur. Check any network applications for updates or patches that may improve performance.

TCP Slow Establishing Connection/TCP Slow Response   A slow connection or response may be caused by a high network load. In other cases, the system that is being connected to is too busy or overloaded, or the connection is being made over an overloaded link (i.e., the router is slow to forward packets).

Decode

The Decode page (see Figure 30-14) allows you to step through the capture buffer and "look inside" each packet. Observer's Decode window is divided into three main areas: the header area, the decode area, and the raw data area. The header area lists each packet with source, destination, packet type, summary, timestamp information, and size. You can quickly scroll up and down this lengthy list of captured packets and select one that you're interested in. For example, select packet 4 and the desired packet shows up in the Decode window. The selected packet's raw data is presented in the bottom window. The Decode window

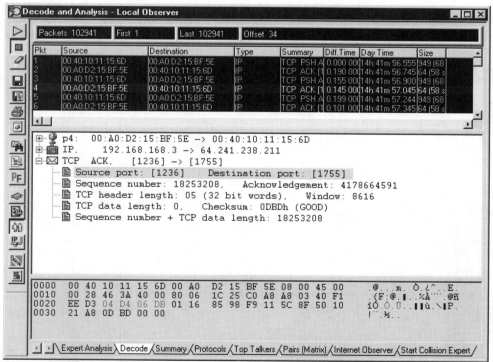

FIGURE 30-14   The Decode page provides a detailed look inside each selected packet in the capture buffer.

interprets the packet and presents its contents in "human readable" form. For the example of packet 4, you can see the preamble, IP level, and TCP-level entries—expand the entry that you want to see (such as TCP), and scroll down to see the entire contents interpreted. This offers you a means to examine each packet and look for potential problems between stations or other network devices. For our figure, you can see that the TCP checksum 0DBDh is good, so you know that the frame arrived intact.

Collision Expert

Collisions can be analyzed using the Collision Expert mode (see Figure 30-15). This examines all stations that were active immediately prior, during, and just after a collision occurs. Offending stations (stations that are consistently present or resending at the time of the collision) are flagged and tracked. This shows the top ten colliders on your network, the number of packets and collisions that were observed, and the percent of collisions caused by each of the top ten colliders. When one or more stations show consistently high retransmissions around collisions, the station(s) logic will show collision events, and statistically summarize those stations that show unusually high collision rates. The summary area will make recommendations regarding what station(s) should be checked for failing hardware. Replacing the NIC on the offending station(s) helps to resolve collisions, but checking cabling is another option.

Connection Dynamics

The Connection Dynamics page (see Figure 30-16) shows a selected conversation graphically illustrating the interpacket delay (shown as a spacing between packets). Packet-to-packet delay times are shown graphically, allowing instant identification of long latency and response times. The packet display can contain either a brief or detailed view of each packet's contents, and retransmissions and lost packets are flagged in red for quick identification. To access the Connection Dynamics page, right-click on a conversation in either the TCP Events or the UDP Events dialog box and select Connection Dynamics from the

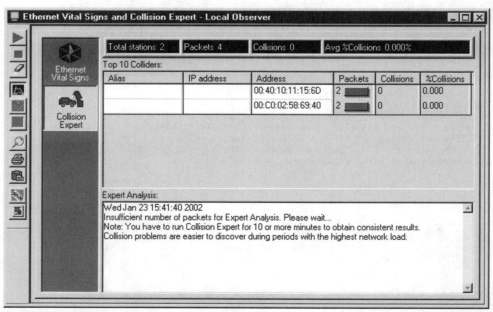

FIGURE 30-15 Observer's Collision Expert can help you to identify the source of excess collisions on the network.

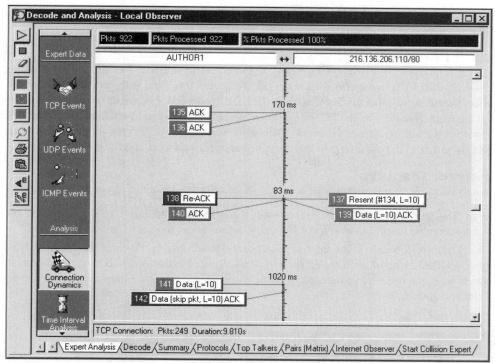

FIGURE 30-16   Connection dynamics reveal an entire conversation based on time and packet condition.

menu. The selected conversation is then displayed in the Connection Dynamics page—scroll up and down to see the entire conversation.

The display can provide a great deal of information depending on how you use your mouse. When no packet is under the mouse, the status bar displays the type of conversation in the display (TCP or UDP), the conversation's duration (in seconds), and packet count. In Observer, the packet under the mouse cursor will turn blue. When a packet is not under the mouse cursor, the color of the packet frame gives information about the packet. Packets will be colored accordingly:

- **Gray**   This is a normal response time—there is no problem with this packet.

- **Purple**   There is a possible problem. There is not necessarily a problem with this connection, but it should be examined further to see if there might be a more serious problem—particularly if there are several purple-coded packets.

- **Red**   There is a definite problem with the packet (such as response time, CRC error, skipped packets, excessive retransmission, or other issue). The protocol analyzer has determined that there is a problem with this packet, and the administrator should investigate to determine if the problem is temporary and transient, or indicates a more serious problem on the network.

In the example of Figure 30-16, you can see that packet 137 (red) is a resend of packet 134. If you decode packet 134, you'd find that the packet's checksum turned out bad. However, the Expert Analysis summary does not report any significant error conditions, so we can assume that the bad frame is a normal part of the Ethernet network's performance.

Time Interval Analysis

The Time Interval Analysis feature displays TCP or UDP Event conversations in a table format—showing the conversation divided by a user-defined time period. To access the Time Interval Analysis display, right-click on a conversation in either the TCP Events or the UDP Events dialog box, then select Time Interval Analysis from the menu (see Figure 30-17). Time periods can be defined by right-clicking the display and selecting Properties. Columns include Network Utilization and Network Packets/sec (along with the number of packets and delay conditions) to help determine the overall network conditions and any errors.

Other Analyzer Displays

Observer's Analysis mode provides you with access to other information about the captured data:

- **Summary**   The Summary page gives you an overview of capture attributes, packet statistics, and errors. It may often be helpful to check the summary before searching for troublesome packets.

- **Protocols**   The Protocols page is similar in appearance and function to the Protocol Distribution statistics feature explained earlier. You'll see a listing of protocols used in the capture buffer, the number of those packets sent, and the relative percentage of their use. This lets you see unexpected or improper protocol use at a glance.

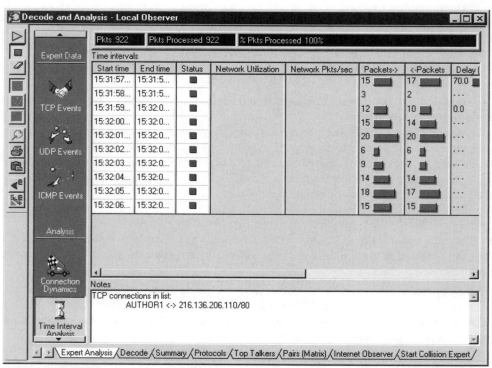

FIGURE 30-17   Time interval analysis lets you see the time-related statistics for a particular conversation in the packet capture buffer.

- **Top Talkers**   The Top Talkers page is similar in appearance and function to the Top Talkers feature explained earlier. Top Talkers in the capture buffer are displayed with their traffic statistics listed. This makes it easy for you to identify stations demanding more than their share of network bandwidth.

- **Pairs**   The Pairs (Matrix) page shows you how stations on the network are communicating with one another. The dial display shows a matrix of all conversations, with line thickness representing the relative amount of data flowing between each pair. This feature graphically illustrates stations that may be sharing unusually high amounts of traffic, or stations that are not communicating well (if at all)4 with other PCs on the network.

- **Internet Observer**   The Internet Observer page permits you to examine captured Internet traffic on your LAN. This can be used to monitor overall Internet usage and to focus on a specific station or stations. It's also possible to break down Internet usage by subprotocols (for example, to see what proportion of Internet traffic involves Web access versus POPmail). This tool can help to reveal unauthorized Web use, or indicate the need for additional communications bandwidth.

Troubleshooting with the Analyzer

A network's infrastructure includes cables, connectors, and network interface cards. Equally important is the protocol layer that provides the interface between the physical layer and upper layer applications—the data link layer. Most network problems (80 to 90 percent) are caused at the physical layer, at the interface between the physical and data link layers, or at the data link layer itself. Many of the network inefficiencies caused by problems at layers 1 and 2 are masked by the large bandwidth available in most modern Ethernet networks (100/1,000 Mbps). Inefficiencies may not seriously affect the network's performance, but as the network grows or new services are added, these inefficiencies can begin to cause problems. It is best to recognize and address problems before they turn into network failure and downtime. This part of the chapter offers some guidelines for troubleshooting with a protocol analyzer.

COMMON ETHERNET PROBLEMS

If you've established a baseline of network performance, spotting problem conditions can be much easier because you have a "normal" range to compare against your current testing. However, errors don't always jump right out at you. There are several common issues to look for when reviewing capture and trending data:

- Look for unusual traffic patterns (like FTPs with an average packet size of 100 bytes). When a node sends a file using the File Transfer Protocol (FTP), it is more efficient to do it in large packets instead of small ones. The largest Ethernet packet is 1,518 bytes—much larger than 100 bytes. This may indicate a misconfigured station.

- Look for sustained utilization. Levels greater than 35 percent indicates a congested network. While you can expect utilization to occasionally burst to 80 or 90 percent, this should not be a sustained condition. When the utilization is constantly high, the probability of collisions in the network increases, resulting in undesirable retransmissions.

- Collision rates should not be greater than 5 percent of packet rate. For example, if the network is transmitting 100 packets per second, collisions should not occur more than five times per second. Collisions are part of the CSMA/CD access method. They are necessary, but a large number of collisions indicates problems.

■ Check the error rate. It's normal to have a small number of errors, but the error rate should not be greater than 5 percent of the packet rate.

■ Check your physical LAN segments. Individual Ethernet segments should not contain more than 200 active stations—network demand will probably be high and the physical limits of the network can easily be exceeded.

■ Broadcast and multicast traffic levels greater than about 20 pps (packets per second) are also a problem because a broadcast creates an interruption in the node CPU. This slows the performance of the desktops in the network.

■ Top talkers should normally be routers and servers. Any other device in the network with high levels of utilization deserves a close look.

■ Response time should vary less than 10 percent over time. If the response time varies more than this, there could be new users or applications affecting the network. There could also be some physical (cable/NIC) problems or an error in protocols.

■ The protocol distribution should be in accordance with programmed protocols. If you have a Novell network, which primarily uses IPX, and IP appears to be the most used protocol, encapsulation problems or improper configurations could be the problem.

TESTING THE PHYSICAL LAYER

Most network troubleshooting begins by attempting to isolate possible physical problems such as false contacts, loose cables, and defective NICs. Verifying that the network's cabling and interface cards are working properly is an essential step in verifying proper network operation. Problems at the physical layer will most often manifest themselves in a variety of symptoms, so use your protocol analyzer to measure and display statistics for

■ Unreasonably high utilization

■ Excessive collisions

■ Bad frame check sequences (FCSs)

■ Alignment errors

■ Runts (small frames)

■ Jabbers (large frames)

■ Broadcast/multicast conditions

 Protocol analyzers like Observer offer a summary page in the packet capture and analysis that conveniently lists a range of packet errors found in the capture buffer.

Utilization

One of the first things to examine is utilization levels. Note the maximum utilization, and the length of time that maximum utilization has occurred. A healthy Ethernet network should have a maximum of 34- to 40-percent constant utilization. If utilization levels are consistently higher than this, response time slows, the number of collisions increases, and overall performance is degraded.

Collisions

Another important physical layer parameter is collisions. Collisions are a normal part of Ethernet network operations, but an excessive number of collisions severely reduces a network's throughput—and suggests physical layer problems. If the collision (or error) rate is very high in a coaxial network, immediately suspect a cable problem such as a bad or missing terminator, a loose barrel or T-connector, or a crushed cable.

In order to isolate the causes of excessive collisions, you must determine if they are normal or late collisions. *Late collisions* occur after the normal collision window of 512 bits into a frame (8 bytes of preamble plus 56 frame bytes). Late collisions are caused by excessively long node-to-node propagation time (the total time for the signal to travel through all cable segments and repeaters/hubs). Network cards whose carrier sense circuitry is not functioning properly can also cause them. Since many Ethernet networks tend to grow a bit at a time, an extra length of cable or new repeater can cause propagation time to exceed Ethernet design specifications. In most cases, this is remedied by reconfiguring the topology of the network. Excessive "*normal collisions*" can be caused by factors such as

■ Impedance mismatches such as bad terminators, loose barrel or T-connectors, too many connectors in a segment, cable kinks, and segments of other than 50-ohm coaxial cable (i.e., video cable).

■ Improper grounding often causes noise on the cable. To prevent ground loops, the network should only be grounded in one location.

■ Poor or intermittent connections.

Remote late collisions occur when a fragment is received that is likely to be the result of a late collision on another segment of the network. To be identified as a remote late collision, the fragment must be longer than 64 bytes, have a bad FCS, and contain the jam pattern of alternating 1s and 0s. On 10BaseT networks, virtually all late collisions appear as remote late collisions. On coax-based networks, these collisions will be common if the network involves heavy traffic and repeaters.

Remote late collisions should occur only rarely on a normal network, and infrequent remote late collisions cause little damage. A consistent occurrence of remote late collisions indicates a network that is physically too long, has too much delay from repeaters and bridges, or is very susceptible to noise interruptions. If remote late collisions are appearing consistently on coax-based networks, try moving the analyzer to different segments to determine which segment has the local late collisions, and investigate from there. When you have few collisions but a relatively large number of errors, excessive cable noise (or perhaps a bad NIC) might be the cause.

Errors

Other indications of collisions or physical layer failure are errors such as runts (frames shorter than 64 bytes), jabbers (frames longer than 1,518 bytes), and bad FCSs. These common error conditions are explained below:

■ A *runt* is most often a frame fragment resulting from two collided frames. This is a normal network condition, and in small coaxial-based networks runts will be almost nonexistent because the actual collision occurs within the frame preamble. You are more likely to see runts in a larger, or 10/100BaseT, network. In larger networks, the longer end-to-end propagation time causes collisions to occur within the transmitted frame. In a 10/100BaseT network, collisions occur inside the hub. The associated hub delays cause many frame fragments (i.e., runts) to be propagated throughout the network.

■ Bad *frame check sequences* can come from many sources: collisions, cable noise, bad network interface cards, and poor connections. It is important to systematically identify the source of these errors. If they are a result of collisions, and the collision rate is not too high, then it need not be a concern.

■ *Jabbers* are not a normal network condition and generally are a serious problem. Jabbers (sometimes called *giant frames*) are frames that are longer than 1,518 bytes, and are usually caused by a node generating frames outside Ethernet specifications or a faulty transceiver on the network. Other possible sources of jabbers include ground loops, or malfunctioning NICs or MAUs.

TESTING THE DATA LINK LAYER

Once physical layer checks have been performed, proceed to a data link layer (protocol layer) analysis and study the composition of your protocols and packets. Obviously, evaluating data link layer integrity is more difficult and complex than the physical infrastructure because there are many more variables to consider. A few of the most important things to consider are the function of the segment in question (i.e., backbone), the types of nodes attached, and the location of spanning devices (including repeaters, brides, routers, and switches). These factors influence the utilization, broadcast traffic, and protocol mix. Here are some general guidelines to consider:

■ When working with a bridge/router, you should expect a higher percentage of broadcast and multicast packets (broadcast and multicast packets are propagated throughout bridged networks because they are always forwarded). Additionally, average frame sizes will be smaller.

■ Pay particular attention to the amount of broadcast traffic. Ideally, it should be less than 20 packets per second. All nodes, regardless of the protocol stack being used, are required to process broadcast traffic. Broadcast traffic affects the performance of all nodes on the network.

■ Link utilization is highly dependent upon the applications being used (i.e., file transfers vs. interactive processes).

Let's look at an example. Suppose that network users begin to complain that their access to shared network devices has slowed. When a series of diagnostic tests are run on the network, you discover that the collision rate seems excessive. Often, a divide-and-conquer approach is used to solve this kind of problem on a network by progressively dividing the network in half physically until the segment creating the problem is found by a process of elimination. The process moves then to the segment itself in a similar fashion, continually dividing the segment in half physically until the station creating the problem has been found. While effective, this process is slow and inefficient. With a protocol analyzer, this process is simplified considerably, and an analysis of your packet capture buffer reveals that the network is experiencing excessive collisions.

In an Ethernet network, you normally allow a collision rate of 5 percent of the average network utilization (measured in frames per second). Collision statistics that exceed the threshold limit are usually shown as errors when decoded. Once you know the kind of problem, you then need to find the source of the problem. Examine captured traffic until you find a frame with an error indicated. You'll note that frames involved in collisions have FF, 55, AA, A5, or 5A hexadecimal notations in the address entries.

Now that you have identified the frames that have been involved in collisions, you need to identify where they're coming from. Typically, the frame immediately *following* the damaged frame will be from one of the two stations causing the collision. To verify this, look at the timestamp. If the time difference between the bad frame and the next frame is less than about 150 milliseconds (depending upon the location of the station on the network and the length of the segment), it probably is one of the frames that collided. If traffic levels are high on the network, another station could have sent a frame prior to the offending station sending its frame. You will also want to check the frames following several other bad frames. If the collision rate is high, there should be a large number of errors. One of the stations causing the collisions should keep reappearing after the bad frame. Having discovered the offending station, you can take corrective action. You can then repeat the network tests to check that the collision rate is once more in an acceptable range.

 Tools like Observer provide a Collision Expert feature designed to help identify the sources of collisions automatically.

Duplicate IP Addresses

An IP (Internet Protocol) duplicate address is a conflict between logical addresses that occurs when two physical MAC addresses erroneously share the same logical IP address. Sometimes when changes are made in a network, or when the network administrator does not have strict control of assigned IP addresses, errors in configuration can occur and result in this type of duplication. Symptoms of duplicated IP addresses can include users complaining of erratic TCP connection losses or ICMP warning messages from routers in the network.

The easiest way to corroborate a duplicate IP address is to use ARP to see if more than one MAC station on your network is using the suspect IP address. Typically, this can be done by Pinging the suspected IP address using Ping commands on a network workstation or by using the analyzer's Ping utility. Duplicate IP addresses are typically reported when the capture buffer is analyzed (such as in Observer's Expert Analysis page). Report information may include the IP network address, the conflicting MAC addresses, and the frame numbers (as assigned by the analyzer) of the two captured frames. When the analyzer identifies routers, these routers are excluded from the duplicate IP reporting. However, an erroneous duplicate IP address may be reported for a short time span if a router has not yet been identified. Router MAC addresses are ignored as sources of duplicates.

TOKEN RING TROUBLESHOOTING

Protocol analyzers like Observer can also help you to troubleshoot token ring MAC errors. Token ring errors are generally classified as either soft or hard errors. *Hard errors* usually bring down the whole token ring network, and are very difficult to troubleshoot with protocol analyzers—for a protocol analyzer to be useful in troubleshooting, a network needs to function at least partially. Hard errors include the following:

- **Streaming errors**   These are usually associated with a faulty adapter that starts out of sequence and overwrites (or destroys) the frames and tokens. In the extreme case (called frame streaming), an adapter can continuously transmit frames, tokens, and noise.

- **Frequency errors**   These can occur if the signal frequency of the incoming frames is out of standard range by more than 0.6 percent. Fortunately, the design of the modern token ring devices makes this error quite rare.

- **Signal loss errors**   These are usually associated with faulty (or out of specification) wiring, and sometimes with bad adapters, MAUs, or repeaters. In most cases, it is a hardware problem—not a software or driver error.

- **Internal errors**   These are errors of the adapter hardware that are serious enough to cause an adapter (already established on the ring) to remove itself from the network.

■ **Hardware incompatibility errors**   These are caused by a hardware conflict between the adapter and another piece of hardware installed on the local station (i.e., an interrupt or DMA conflict). In most of these cases, the adapter simply does not join the ring.

There are four types of soft errors to consider. Type 1 errors are simple noncritical errors that generally do not require recovery. Type 2 errors are a bit more important, and will need a ring purge. Type 3 errors are even more serious, and will require monitor contention. The final type of soft error is a beacon (a beacon frame). Type 1 soft errors fall into the following classifications:

■ **Line errors**   This is the token ring equivalent of Ethernet CRC errors. Every station performs a CRC check on incoming frames. When the station finds an inconsistency between the frame checksum number and the checksum itself, it reports this error. Line errors are often present on a busy network. However, if a station continuously reports line errors, it usually indicates a bad NIC in the upstream neighbor.

■ **Internal errors**   This happens when a station discovers a recoverable hardware error. If an adapter consistently reports internal errors, it may indicate that it is beginning to fail. Recheck all connections before replacing the NIC.

■ **ARI/FCI set error**   This error is reported when a station detects two "standby monitor present" frames with the ARI/FCI bit set to zero (without the intervention of the active monitor) during a ring poll process. This error is rare.

■ **Receive congestion errors**   This is reported by a station with insufficient buffer space to copy the packets addressed to it. If an adapter consistently reports receive congestion errors, this can be an indication of either a hardware or software problem on the reporting station, or a defective (noisy) connection to the MAU upstream of the station (this can overfill the receiving circuitry of the adapter).

■ **Frame copied errors**   These errors are reported when an ARI/FCI bit is already set in the frame addressed to the station. This indicates the presence of two network cards with the same address on the network. This can happen on bridged multiring networks with locally assigned token ring addresses.

There are a variety of Type 2 soft errors, which require a bit more consideration while troubleshooting:

■ **Burst errors**   These are reported when a station detects a signal loss for at least five half-byte cycles. Burst errors are encountered quite often during token ring operation, and usually occur when a station joins or leaves the ring. If this error persists, it may indicate a hardware problem on an upstream neighbor of the reporting adapter (or its MAU relays). Burst errors are usually accompanied by line errors, lost frame errors, or token errors.

■ **Abort delimiter transmitted error**   This error is reported when a station transmits an abort delimiter for any reason. The active monitor in this case detects the interruption in the token protocol and purges the ring.

■ **Lost frame errors**   When a station transmits a frame trailer, it sets a timer that specifies how much time to wait for the frame trailer to return from upstream. When the frame returns, the station strips it from the network and takes an appropriate action, depending on whether the FCI bit is set or not. If the station does not receive the same frame trailer before the timer expires, it considers the frame lost and increases the lost frames count.

■ **Token errors**   These are reported by the active monitor when it detects a corrupted token or frame, a lost token, a circulating frame, or a priority token.

Type 3 errors are some of the most serious errors, and should receive immediate attention on the part of a technician:

■ **Lost monitor errors**   These errors occur when an active monitor leaves the ring or becomes inoperative. The error is reported by the standby monitor that discovered the active monitor to be missing. Remaining standby monitors then begin the monitor contention process to elect a new active monitor station.

■ **Frequency errors**   These errors are the result of a bad active monitor clock. This error is usually resolved by monitor contention, during which a different standby monitor becomes the active monitor.

Finally, you should understand how to handle *beacons*. A NIC transmits beacon frames when it detects silence on the cable (no tokens or data frames from the upstream neighbor). The adapter sends beacons downstream to alert all other devices. If the upstream neighbor receives a beacon from its downstream neighbor (and the beaconing condition was caused by a temporary hardware fault), the downstream neighbor will eventually hear a signal from upstream. Otherwise, these two adapters remove themselves from the ring and try to reattach. In the case of a cable or hardware problem, the defective station will fail to reattach and the network will resume operation (this is called "resolved beaconing condition"). If the beaconing condition fails to resolve itself, it may require direct intervention from the technician.

Further Study

Network Instruments: **www.networkinstruments.com**
Agilent: **www.agilent.com**
Hewlett-Packard: **www.hp.com**
Protocol.com: **www.protocols.com**

ADDITIONAL WEB RESOURCES

Although there are numerous Web sources listed at the end of each chapter, there are broader resources that are available to technicians with Internet access. Some resources listed here are provided by specific manufacturers, while other resources are maintained by independent groups or organizations.

Web Sites

3Com Knowledgebase: **knowledgebase.3com.com**
3Com Support: **support.3com.com**
ANSI: **www.ansi.org**
ATM Forum: **www.atmforum.com**
Cabling Installation/Maintenance: **cim.pennnet.com/home.cfm**
Cisco Troubleshooting: **www.cisco.com/public/technotes/serv_tips.shtml**
Compaq Manuals: **www.compaq.com/support/techpubs/maintenance_guides/index.html**
Dell Support: **support.dell.com/us/en/home.asp**
DUN Troubleshooting: **www.webcom.com/~llarrow/trouble.html**
Ethernet Guide: **wwwhost.ots.utexas.edu/ethernet/ethernet.html**
Frame Relay Forum: **www.frforum.com**
Global Engineering Documents: **www.global.ihs.com**
HP Support: **www.hp.com/cposupport/eschome.html**
IBM Networking Support: **www.networking.ibm.com/netsupt.html**
IEEE (802.3): **grouper.ieee.org/groups/802/3/index.html**
IEEE (802.5): **www.8025.org**
IEEE Unique Identifiers: **standards.ieee.org/regauth/oui/tutorials/lanman.html**
InterNIC: **www.internic.net**
ITU: **www.itu.int/home/index.html**
Microsoft Support: **support.microsoft.com**
Network Computing: **www.networkcomputing.com/netdesign/troubleintro.html**
Network Troubleshooting: **www.k12.hi.us/~network/1999/41200nettrbleshoot/**
Network Troubleshooting: **www.networktroubleshooting.com**
Network Troubleshooting: **www2.ucsc.edu/cats/sc/tools/network-troubleshoot/index.shtml**
North American ISDN Users Forum: **www.niuf.nist.gov/**
Novell Support: **support.novell.com**
Sun Knowledge Base: **www.sun.com/service/support/**
Telcordia: **www.telcordia.com/pssindex.html**
TroubleTree: **www.troubletree.com/**
Wireless Repair: **www.practicallynetworked.com/support/troubleshoot_wireless.htm**

Newsgroups

comp.dcom.cabling
comp.dcom.lans.ethernet
comp.dcom.lans.fddi
comp.dcom.lans.misc
comp.dcom.lans.token-ring
comp.dcom.moderns.cable
comp.dcom.sys.cisco
comp.dcom.xdsl
comp.dcorn.modems
comp.os.linux.networking
comp.os.linux.setup
comp.os.ms-windows.networking.misc
comp.os.ms-windows.networking.tcp-ip
comp.os.ms-windows.networking.win95
comp.os.ms-windows.nt.admin.misc
comp.os.ms-windows.nt.admin.networking
comp.os.ms-windows.nt.misc
comp.protocols.tcp-ip
comp.sys.mac.misc
comp.unix.solaris
han.cornp.os.linux
han.cornp.os.winnt
microsoft.public.win95.networking
microsoft.public.win98.networking
microsoft.public.win98.performance
microsoft.public.win98.setup
microsoft.public.windowsnt.protocol.tcpip

UNDERSTANDING NET+ AND SERVER+

Whether you're starting a new career, planning a change, or hoping for an important promotion, the most difficult thing to show a prospective employer is *qualification*—how "qualified" you are for a given role in the company. One of the easiest ways to demonstrate your qualifications is to hold a suitable certification in a corresponding technology. A certification that has been accepted by the industry will indicate that you've completed the educational background and have the base of knowledge required to perform at a specified level. Today, virtually every technology professional can benefit by pursuing a well-chosen certification. Being certified can increase your salary, enhance your skills, and make your job more satisfying.

There are many different certifications in the computer industry, and most manufacturers offer proprietary certifications for their own products. However, some of the most popular and well-respected certifications are "industry neutral" (such as A+, Network+, and Server+ sponsored by CompTIA and administered by Prometric and VUE). That is, the certification covers popular practices and commonly used equipment. Certification offers many compelling advantages that should be seriously considered by employees and employers alike:

- **Objective recruiting**   Requiring an appropriate industry-neutral certification assures a minimum knowledge level for all prospective applicants. This makes it easier to screen applicants, and promote only applicants that are qualified.

- **Broader knowledge**   While manufacturer-specific certifications are certainly helpful, industry-neutral certifications generally support a broader range of knowledge and equipment, resulting in better-rounded individuals. This flexibility is a substantial advantage in the fast-changing technology marketplace.

- **Greater prestige and credibility**   Certification provides a competitive advantage in today's busy technology marketplaces. Both the certificate holder and the hiring company enjoy the advantage of this credibility.

- **Better job opportunities**   By incorporating certifications into company structures, it's easier to define the role(s) that a certified employer may perform, and identify new/alternative certifications needed to improve the company's skills base. This makes more job and educational opportunities available to employees.

- **Better career enhancement**   Since certifications also highlight skills, it is possible to create objective pay levels based on the level of an employee's certification(s).

To learn more about the certifications offered by CompTIA, check the CompTIA Web site at **www.comptia.com**. You can schedule and pay for exams through Prometric (**www.2test.com/index.jsp**) and VUE (**www.vue.com/comptia**).

Server+

The "Server Hardware Specialist" (or Server+) exam is a relatively new CompTIA certification intended to deal with advanced PC hardware issues such as RAID, SCSI, multiple CPUs, and so on. The Server Hardware Specialist focuses on the activities and complex problems involved in server configuration, maintenance, and repair. A Server+ specialist is expected to have an in-depth understanding of the planning, installation, and maintenance of servers—including knowledge of server-level hardware, data storage, data recovery, and I/O subsystems. A server technician should know the behavior of all parts of the server system, and understand the ramifications of their actions. The Server+ specialist usually works independently, solves complex problems, and may seek assistance from systems support for particularly challenging issues. The recommended experience for this certification includes the following:

- At least 18 to 24 months of experience in the server technologies (networking) industry
- Direct experience installing, configuring, diagnosing, and troubleshooting server hardware and NOS issues
- At least one other IT certification such as CompTIA A+, Compaq ACT, Novell CNA, Microsoft MCP, HP STAR, SCO, or Banyan
- An ability to communicate and document effectively

SERVER+ EXAM AREAS

For the initial release of the Server+ exam, candidates are expected to know the following topic areas, and each area is detailed next:

Installation	17 percent
Configuration	18 percent
Upgrading	12 percent
Preventive Maintenance	9 percent
Environmental Issues	5 percent
Troubleshooting	27 percent
Disaster Recovery	12 percent

This list outlines the standard Server+ exam blueprint.

Installation

- Conduct preinstallation planning activities.
  - Plan the installation.
  - Verify the installation plan.
  - Verify hardware compatibility with operating system.
  - Verify power sources, space, and UPS and network availability.
  - Verify that all correct components and cables have been delivered.

■ Install hardware (i.e., boards, drives, processors, memory, internal cable, etc.).

   ■ Mount a rack installation.

   ■ Cut and crimp network cabling.

   ■ Install a UPS.

   ■ Verify SCSI ID configuration and termination.

   ■ Install external devices (i.e., keyboards, monitors, subsystems, modem rack, etc.).

   ■ Verify the power-on via power-on sequence.

Configuration

■ Check and upgrade BIOS/firmware levels (i.e., system board, RAID, controller, hard drive, etc.).

■ Configure RAID.

■ Install a NOS:

   ■ Configure network.

   ■ Verify network connectivity.

■ Configure external peripherals (i.e., UPS, external drive subsystems, etc.).

■ Install NOS updates.

■ Update manufacturer's drivers.

■ Install service tools (i.e., backup software, system monitoring agents, event logs, etc.).

■ Perform a server baseline.

■ Document the configuration.

Upgrading

■ Perform backup/restore operations:

   ■ Verify backup.

■ Add processors:

   ■ On single processor upgrade, verify compatibility.

   ■ Verify N 1 stepping.

   ■ Verify speed and cache matching.

   ■ Perform BIOS upgrade.

   ■ Perform OS upgrade to support multiprocessors.

   ■ Locate/obtain latest test drivers, OS updates, software.

■ Add hard drives:

   ■ Verify that drives are the appropriate type.

   ■ Confirm termination and cabling.

   ■ For ATA/IDE drives, confirm cabling, and master/slave and potential cross-brand compatibility.

   ■ Upgrade mass storage devices.

- Add drives to a RAID array.
- Replace existing drives.
- Integrate drives into a storage solution and make it available to the operating system.
- Increase memory:
  - Verify hardware and OS support for capacity increase.
  - Verify memory is on hardware/vendor compatibility list.
  - Verify memory compatibility.
  - Verify that the server and OS recognize the added memory.
  - Perform server optimization to make use of additional RAM.
- Upgrade BIOS/firmware.
- Upgrade important adapters (i.e., NICs, SCSI cards, RAID, etc.).
- Upgrade internal and external peripheral devices:
  - Verify appropriate system resources (i.e., expansion slots, IRQ, DMA, etc.).
- Upgrade system monitoring agents.
- Upgrade service tools (i.e., diagnostic tools, diagnostic partition, SSU, etc.).
- Upgrade UPS.

Preventive Maintenance

- Perform regular backup.
- Create baseline and compare performance.
- Set SNMP thresholds.
- Perform physical housekeeping.
- Perform hardware verification.
- Establish remote notification.

Environmental Issues

- Recognize and report on physical security issues:
  - Limit access to server room and backup tapes.
  - Ensure physical locks exist on doors.
  - Establish anti-theft devices for hardware (lock server racks).
- Recognize and report on server room environmental issues.

Troubleshooting

- Perform problem determination:
  - Learn how to handle problem determination.
  - Identify contact(s) responsible for problem resolution.
  - Use senses to observe problem.

■ Use diagnostic hardware and software tools and utilities:
   ■ Identify common diagnostic tools.
   ■ Perform OS shutdowns.
   ■ Select the appropriate tool.
   ■ Use the selected tool effectively.
   ■ Replace defective hardware components as appropriate.
   ■ Identify defective devices and replace with correct part.
   ■ Interpret error logs, operating system errors, health logs, and critical events.
   ■ Use documentation from a previous technician successfully.
   ■ Gather resources to get problem solved.
   ■ Describe how to perform remote troubleshooting for a wake-on-LAN.
   ■ Describe how to perform remote troubleshooting for a remote alert.
■ Identify bottlenecks (i.e., processor, bus transfer, I/O, disk I/O, network I/O, memory).
■ Identify and correct configuration problems and/or upgrades.
■ Determine if problem is hardware, software, or virus related.

Disaster Recovery

■ Plan for disaster recovery:
   ■ Plan for redundancy (i.e. hard drives, power supplies, fans, NICs, processors, UPS).
   ■ Use the technique of hot swap, warm swap, and hot spare to ensure availability.
   ■ Use the concepts of fault tolerance/fault recovery to create a disaster recovery plan.
   ■ Develop disaster recovery plan.
   ■ Identify types of backup hardware.
   ■ Identify types of backup and restoration schemes.
   ■ Confirm and use off-site storage for backup.
   ■ Document and test the disaster recovery plan regularly, and update as needed.
■ Restoring:
   ■ Identify hardware replacements.
   ■ Identify hot and cold sites.
   ■ Implement disaster recovery plan.

Network+

The "Network Specialist" (or Network+) exam is a well-established CompTIA certification intended to deal with network administration and support issues that reflect 18–24 months of experience in the IT industry. The Network+ exam has been revised for 2002, and will certify that the successful candidates know the layers of the OSI model, can describe the features and functions of network components, and have skills needed to install, configure, and troubleshoot basic networking hardware peripherals and protocols. A typical candidate should have A+ certification or equivalent knowledge, but A+ certification is not required. In addition to A+ certification level knowledge, candidates are encouraged to have at least nine months of experience in network support or administration.

The 2002 update of Network+ also expands on new technologies such as wireless networking and gigabit Ethernet. The scope of networking systems is broadened with an increased emphasis on Linux/UNIX, Windows 9x, Windows NT, Windows 2000, and including AppleTalk as a network protocol. There is additional emphasis on hands-on experience knowledge needed in the areas of network implementation and network support, including troubleshooting scenarios.

NETWORK+ EXAM AREAS

For the 2002 revised version of the Network+ exam, candidates are expected to know the following topic areas, and each area is detailed next:

Media and Topologies	20 percent
Protocols and Standards	25 percent
Network Implementation	23 percent
Network Support	32 percent

Media and Topologies

- Recognize logical and physical network topologies given a schematic diagram or description.
- Specify the main features of 802.2 (LLC), 802.3 (Ethernet), 802.5 (token ring), 802.11b (wireless), and FDDI networking technologies.
- Specify the characteristics (such as speed, length, topology, cable type, etc.) of 802.3 (Ethernet) standards.
- Recognize common media connectors and/or describe their uses.
- Choose the appropriate media type and connectors to add a client to an existing network.
- Identify the purpose, features, and functions of common network components, such as hubs, switches, bridges, routers, gateways, CSU/DSUs, NICs, WAPs, and so on.

Protocols and Standards

- Identify a MAC address.
- Identify the seven layers of the OSI model and their functions.
- Differentiate between common network protocols in terms of routing, addressing schemes, interoperability, and naming conventions.
- Identify the OSI layers at which common network components operate.
- Define the purpose, function, and/or use of common protocols within TCP/IP.
- Define the function of TCP/UDP ports, and identify well-known ports.
- Identify the purpose of network services such as DHCP/Bootp, DNS, NAT/ICS, WINS, and SNMP.
- Identify IP addresses (IPv4, IPv6) and their default subnet masks.
- Identify the purpose of subnetting and default gateways.
- Identify the differences between public and private networks.

- Identify the basic characteristics (such as speed, capacity, media) of important WAN technologies.
- Define the function of remote access protocols and services.
- Identify important security protocols and describe their purpose and function.

Network Implementation

- Identify the basic capabilities (such as client support, interoperability, authentication, file and print services, application support, and security) of server operating systems.
- Identify the basic capabilities of client workstations (such as client connectivity, local security mechanisms, and authentication).
- Identify the main characteristics of VLANs.
- Identify the main characteristics of network attached storage.
- Identify the purpose and characteristics of fault tolerance.
- Identify the purpose and characteristics of disaster recovery.
- Given a remote connectivity scenario (such as IP, IPX, dial-up, PPPoE, authentication, physical connectivity, etc.), configure the connection.
- Identify the purpose, benefits, and characteristics of using a firewall.
- Identify the purpose, benefits, and characteristics of using a proxy.
- Given a scenario, predict the impact of a particular security implementation on network functionality (such as blocking port numbers, encryption, and so on).
- Given a network configuration, select the appropriate NIC and network configuration settings (DHCP, DNS, WINS, protocols, NETBIOS/host name, and so on).

Network Support

- Given a troubleshooting scenario, select the appropriate TCP/IP utility such as Tracert, Ping, Arp, Netstat, Nbtstat, Ipconfig/Ifconfig, Winipcfg, Nslookup, and so on.
- Given a troubleshooting scenario involving a small office/home office network failure (such as DSL, cable, home satellite, wireless, POTS), identify the cause of the failure.
- Given a troubleshooting scenario involving a remote connectivity problem (such as authentication failure, protocol configuration, physical connectivity), identify the problem.
- Given specific parameters, configure a client to connect to servers such as UNIX/Linux, NetWare, Windows, or Macintosh.
- Given a wiring task, select the appropriate tool (such as a wire crimper, media tester/checker, punch down tool, tone generator, optical tester, and so on).
- Given a network scenario, interpret visual indicators (such as Link or Collision LEDs) to determine the nature of the problem.
- Given output from a diagnostic utility (such as Tracert, Ping, Ipconfig, and so on), identify the utility and interpret the output.
- Given a scenario, predict the impact of modifying, adding, or removing network services (such as DHCP, DNS, WINS, etc.) on network resources and users.

- Given a network problem scenario, select an appropriate course of action based on a general trouble-shooting strategy.

- Given a troubleshooting scenario involving a network with a particular physical topology (such as bus, star/hierarchical, mesh, ring, and wireless), identify the network area affected and the cause of the problem.

- Given a network troubleshooting scenario involving a client connectivity problem (such as incorrect protocol, wrong client software, improper authentication configuration, or insufficient rights/ permission), identify the cause of the problem.

- Given a network troubleshooting scenario involving a wiring/infrastructure problem, identify the cause of the problem (such as bad media, interference, network hardware, or other issues).

THE DLS NETWORK TECHNICIAN'S CERTIFICATE EXAM

The certification of technical knowledge serves several important goals. It gives the individuals being certified an opportunity to review and tie together all of the important ideas they have learned during their studies. Successful certification also demonstrates proficiency in the subject area to employers and customers. There are many different approaches to education and certification in the computer industry. Most involve off-site testing or training to one extent or another, although many firms provide very good private-study networking courses.

Understanding the Exam

The problem with most network-related courses is that they are terribly expensive for the starting administrator or entry-level technician. This book has been designed to serve as both a practical reference text and a learning tool. The 200-question DLS Network Technician's Certificate exam allows you to test your understanding of the topics covered in this edition of the book, and provides you with a printed certificate upon successful completion of this "final" examination.

WHY BOTHER WITH A CERTIFICATE?

The big complaint about certificates is that they are "just pieces of paper"—frame them, hang them on a wall, dust them off from time to time—`big deal. Fortunately, there are some *very real* incentives to shoot for the DLS Network Technician's Certificate. First, the certificate offers something for everyone—novices have an inexpensive means to enhance their knowledge (and perhaps build a bridge to that new career). Veteran troubleshooters can use this test to check their knowledge and keep important skills up-to-date. Any professional will tell you that up-to-date skills are a key to long-term employability. Also, the exam may also aid you in preparing for the industry-recognized Net+ and Server+ exams.

WHAT IT COSTS

There is a one-time test processing fee of $50 (US) to offset the administrative cost of grading, printing, and mailing. If you pass the test, you will receive a Certificate of Completion (suitable for framing). If you should fail the test for any reason, you will be informed of your grade in writing, and a new set of information/answer sheets will be sent to you. You may then take the test again, as often as you like *at no additional cost.*

Dynamic Learning Systems observes a "global pricing policy" for this exam, so the fee is only $50 (US) regardless of where you are. However, the exam fee must be paid in US dollars or by credit card.

BUT I'M NO GOOD AT TESTS

Fair enough. That happens to a lot of people—there's no reason to feel bad. But before you say, "I can't do that" and close this appendix, you should know that completing the DLS Network Technician's Certificate exam could be surprisingly painless. Go ahead and give it a try. Just consider some of the following points:

- *There is no pressure.* Work at your own pace. You're not being timed here, so you're free to take the exam on your own schedule when *you* are ready.

- *There are no time limits.* You can take as long as you need to finish the exam. Spread it out over a weekend or several weeks—even several months—whatever your time permits.

- *You don't have to cram.* The exam is open-book. Purists might criticize this as an unfair advantage, but how many professionals out there know everything there is without having to refer to a book or magazine at one time or another?

- *You can't lose money.* Since there is only a one-time fee, you can retake the test as many times as you need to in order to pass with *no* additional fee.

TEST INSTRUCTIONS

Taking the exam is very easy. Just follow the steps outlined here and you should have no problems at all:

1. Carefully tear out and/or photocopy the Information Cover Sheet and all pages of the Answer Sheet.

2. Photocopy the Information and Answer Sheets, and use the photocopied pages to complete the test (keep the original pages tucked away).

3. Open the book and start the test at Question #1 below.

4. Fill in your answers by *carefully* circling or blacking-in the desired letter using a #2 pencil. Although you can use marker or pen as well, pencil is *strongly* recommended because it can be erased completely.

Answers with more than one letter circled or blacked out must be marked *incorrect*.

5. Answer *all* 200 questions. You can answer them in any order, but you should remember to answer them *all*. Unanswered questions *must* be marked incorrect. Be sure to double-check your answers before submitting the exam.

6. When all questions have been completed, and you're satisfied with the answers, fill out the Information Cover Sheet. The information must be filled out entirely so that you receive your credit.

7. Send the completed Information Cover Sheet and Answer Sheets with payment to Dynamic Learning Systems. Do *not* submit the actual question pages from the book.

Submitting the Exam

If you're paying by check, mail the forms and check or money order to:

Dynamic Learning Systems
PO Box 402
Leicester, MA 01524-0402

If you are paying by credit card, you can mail the forms, or fax them to:

508-892-1482

Your exam will be promptly graded, and you will receive a reply within four weeks. If you have questions or trouble understanding the instructions listed above, contact Customer Service at 508-892-1475. Best of luck to you!

MAKING THE GRADE

So, how do you pass? You need a 70 percent or higher score to *pass* the exam. With 200 questions, you will need to answer 140 questions correctly. The official grade is strictly "pass or fail"—there will be no letter grade assigned (though we usually note a letter equivalent for your personal reference).

Exam Questions

The 200 questions comprising the DLS Network Technician's Certificate exam are presented below. Please mark your answers on the Answer Sheets only—there is no need for you to mark up or submit these question pages in the book.

 Do not mark up and return these question pages—only submit the Answer and Information Sheets.

1. A networked computer that provides resources is called a:

   a. client

   b. server

   c. disk array

   d. cluster

2. Networks that are typically less than 5km in size are referred to as:

   a. local area networks (LANs)

   b. metropolitan area networks (MANs)

   c. wide area networks (WANs)

   d. intranets

3. HTML can be provided over the Internet by implementing a:

   a. file server

   b. print server

   c. news server

   d. Web server

4. Which of the following is *not* an advantage of client/server networks?

   a. Security

   b. Fault tolerance

   c. User management

   d. Superior bandwidth

5. The ability to pull out a failed component and plug in a new one while the power is still on and the system is operating is known as:

   a. failover

   b. hot swapping

   c. RAID

   d. high availability

6. The combination of two or more server PCs that appear as a single server to the network is called a:

   a. file server

   b. backup server

   c. server cluster

   d. reliable server

7. The cable that connects each station in a bus topology is called a:

   a. trunk

   b. segment

   c. BNC

   d. vampire tap

8. A bus topology network can experience problems when:

   a. a break occurs in one of the cable segments

   b. a terminator is removed or failed

   c. a cable is disconnected

   d. any of the above

9. Stations in a star topology can be connected through a:

   a. MAU

   b. hub/switch

   c. firewall

   d. server

10. The key packet that is circulated through a ring topology is called a:

    a. token

    b. frame

    c. icon

    d. preamble

11. The resistance of a coaxial cable is roughly:

    a. 25 ohms

    b. 40 ohms

    c. 50 ohms

    d. 75 ohms

12. The category of UTP cable for high-speed data transmissions up to 100 Mbps is:

   a. Category 3

   b. Category 4

   c. Category 5

   d. Category 6

13. Rather than exchanging entire files at one time, data is broken down into much smaller chunks called:

   a. frames

   b. CRCs

   c. preambles

   d. trailers

14. Ethernet stations access the wire using a technique called:

   a. retention

   b. contention

   c. recession

   d. continuance

15. An Ethernet collision on the local segment during the first 64 bytes of a frame is known as:

   a. early collision

   b. late frame

   c. impaired collision

   d. jabber frame

16. Ethernet collisions can be caused by:

   a. poor network topology

   b. defective network hardware

   c. excessive network traffic

   d. all of the above

17. The first thing to check for when you experience reduced Ethernet performance is:

   a. excessive distance between stations

   b. noise or electrical interference on the network cable

   c. the installation or configuration of the NIC

   d. a defective or improperly configured router

18. Intermittent Ethernet connections with jabber frames should first be checked by:

   a. disconnecting the affected network segment from the hub/switch

   b. finding cable problems (such as current loops) caused by more than one ground location in the cabling

   c. rebooting the offending station (or all stations on the segment)

   d. none of the above

19. Token ring networks use which physical topology?

   a. Tree

   b. Star

   c. Ring

   d. Mesh

20. Where Ethernet frames are up to 1,518 bytes, a token ring frame is typically up to:

   a. 1 or 2KB

   b. 2 or 3KB

   c. 4 or 6KB

   d. 4 or 8KB

21. The station that starts the first token frame through the ring when the network is started is called the:

   a. diagnostic station

   b. management console

   c. active monitor

   d. network server

22. A station receives a frame that is destined for it, but does not have enough buffer space to copy the frame. This is reported as a:

   a. receive congestion error

   b. token error

   c. abort delimiter transmitted error

   d. line error

23. The set of specifications that describes a network architecture for connecting dissimilar devices is called the:

   a. Open Systems Interconnection (OSI) model

   b. Cyclical Redundancy Check (CRC) test

   c. File Transfer Protocol (FTP) check

   d. none of the above

24. The layer that describes the format used to exchange data among networked computers is called:

   a. layer 7

   b. layer 6

   c. layer 5

   d. layer 4

25. A request forwarded from the client to the network is a process known as:

   a. coherence

   b. contention

   c. redirection

   d. none of the above

26. The IEEE Ethernet standard is generally termed as:

    a. 802.1

    b. 802.2

    c. 803.3

    d. 802.4

27. A combination of protocols is known as a:

    a. protocol stack

    b. frame

    c. packet

    d. cell

28. The physical address of a NIC is known as a:

    a. primary address

    b. LCC address

    c. network address

    d. MAC address

29. An IP address of 193.134.23.123 would be classified as a:

    a. class A address

    b. class B address

    c. class C address

    d. class D address

30. An IP address range can be portioned using:

    a. DCHP server

    b. name resolution

    c. subnet masks

    d. none of the above

31. What type of multitasking allows the operating system to take control of the processor without the task's cooperation?

    a. Preemptive multitasking

    b. Nonpreemptive multitasking

    c. Cooperative multitasking

    d. none of the above

32. The assignment of a letter or name to a resource so that the operating system or network server can locate it is called:

    a. name assignment

    b. drive mapping

    c. resource allocation

    d. user accounting

33. The ability of computer operating systems to function and access resources in different network environments is called:

   a. clustering

   b. high availability

   c. compatibility

   d. interoperability

34. The network equivalent of a phone book is:

   a. directory services

   b. DCHP services

   c. DNS services

   d. IIS Web services

35. Which of the following is not a directory service?

   a. Active Directory

   b. X.400

   c. NDS

   d. LDAP

36. Naming services (like DNS) allow IP addresses to be translated to:

   a. MAC addresses

   b. lookup tables

   c. human-readable names

   d. network maps

37. A network should have a minimum of how many DNS servers?

   a. 10

   b. 7

   c. 4

   d. 2

38. Which utility lets users find the IP address associated with a name?

   a. nslookup

   b. ipconfig

   c. tracert

   d. ping

39. IP addresses can be automatically assigned to network devices using:

   a. DNS

   b. NetBIOS

   c. DHCP

   d. LDAP

40. Automatic IP assignments can wind up being duplicated when:

    a. new stations are added to the network

    b. static (fixed) IP addresses are assigned

    c. leases expire (or are released)

    d. a local name server fails

41. The ISM band used for wireless networking devices is:

    a. 310 to 520MHz

    b. 434MHz to 1.23GHz

    c. 521MHz to 2.44GHz

    d. 902MHz to 5.85GHz

42. Wireless devices can communicate with a wired LAN by interfacing through a wireless:

    a. entry device

    b. access point

    c. docking station

    d. network interface card

43. Wireless devices typically employ which access method?

    a. CSMA/CA (collision avoidance)

    b. CSMA/CD (collision detection)

    c. CSMA/MM (multimodulation)

    d. CSMA/AP (access point)

44. Which of the following will *not* help to optimize the range of wireless devices?

    a. locate the AP at a central point between wireless devices

    b. get a clear line of site to all wireless devices

    c. keep wireless devices away from large metal objects

    d. orient wireless antennas horizontally

45. When a wireless device must access other devices in a wired LAN, it should operate in:

    a. ad-hoc mode

    b. infrastructure mode

    c. roaming mode

    d. any of the above

46. When a wireless NIC isn't recognized by a host PC, you should first check to see that:

    a. the wireless NIC is properly and fully inserted into the PC.

    b. the wireless NIC is properly powered.

    c. the wireless NIC is using the proper drivers.

    d. the wireless NIC is compatible with the operating system.

47. A real static path from one point to another across a WAN is established by a:

   a. timing-switched network

   b. circuit-switched network

   c. packet-switched network

   d. router-switched network

48. The WAN transmission type designed to squeeze the maximum throughput from available bandwidth is called:

   a. cell relay

   b. dial-up access

   c. framing

   d. none of the above

49. VPNs use what technique to carry their private network data over the public network?

   a. timing

   b. treading

   c. talking

   d. tunneling

50. IPSec authentication is handled with:

   a. tickets

   b. certificates

   c. requests

   d. smart cards

51. Frame relay and X.25 packet switching protocols are mainly differentiated by:

   a. the additional error control information in X.25 packets

   b. the lack of error checking in X.25 packets

   c. the larger packets used in frame relay

   d. none of the above

52. The unprotected area "in front" of a LAN's firewall is called the:

   a. demilitarized zone

   b. demarcation zone

   c. deliberation zone

   d. exposed zone

53. Attenuation across a length of cable is measured in:

   a. ohms (Ω)

   b. millivolts (mV)

   c. megahertz (MHz)

   d. decibels (dB)

54. Thicknet connections to workstations are made by using a:

   a. serial connector

   b. USB connector

   c. vampire tab

   d. BNC connector

55. A correct resistance test of a coaxial cable installation should be about:

   a. 10 ohms

   b. 25 ohms

   c. 50 ohms

   d. 105 ohms

56. Which of the following is not a common cause of twisted-pair cabling trouble?

   a. An excessively loose bend ratio

   b. Excessive cable length

   c. Poor wire quality

   d. Incorrectly attached RJ-45 connectors

57. Broken or intermittent cabling can often be spotted with a:

   a. timing test

   b. continuity test

   c. voltage measurement

   d. all of the above

58. The interference that occurs when signals on one wire pair interfere with the signals on another pair is known as:

   a. far-end crosstalk

   b. midrange crosstalk

   c. near-end crosstalk

   d. ground loop crosstalk

59. In a token ring network, "lobe cables" serve which purpose?

   a. They connect individual workstations to the central MAU.

   b. They connect multiple MAUs.

   c. They connect the MAU to a bridge or router.

   d. none of the above.

60. If you need an optical fiber connection over several miles, which cable would you use?

   a. multimode fiber

   b. multiplex fiber

   c. simplex fiber

   d. single-mode fiber

61. How many pins are included on a standard ATX power connector?

    a. 3 pins

    b. 10 pins

    c. 20 pins

    d. 38 pins

62. A motherboard's management controller monitors system events and logs their occurrence in nonvolatile memory called the:

    a. Windows 2000 Security Log

    b. System Event Log

    c. PC security record

    d. chassis violation record

63. A server's emergency management port allows a technician to:

    a. check the server from a remote location

    b. power the server on or off, and reset the server

    c. examine the contents of your SEL and SDR

    d. all of the above

64. Socket-type processors are secured to a motherboard using a:

    a. ZIF lever

    b. retention mechanism

    c. lag bolt

    d. thermal grease

65. To protect the BIOS, a motherboard's BIOS Write Enable jumper should be:

    a. reset

    b. removed

    c. set

    d. stationary

66. The BIOS sequence that tests the motherboard's hardware at boot time is called the:

    a. CMOS

    b. POST

    c. SSU

    d. DIMM

67. What is a common term used to designate a processor's engineering revision level?

    a. sequence number

    b. S-spec number

    c. stand digit

    d. all of the above

68. Processor cooling is often monitored with a:

    a.   infrared probe

    b.   fan tachometer signal

    c.   voltage regulator

    d.   heat sink

69. Which operating mode allows the processor full access to all of the system's memory?

    a.   real mode

    b.   virtual mode

    c.   protected mode

    d.   system mode

70. A 4M × 32-bit DIMM would provide how much memory to the PC?

    a.   16MB

    b.   32MB

    c.   64MB

    d.   128MB

71. In Table 9-5, a sensor event of 02h/04h means:

    a.   the processor voltage is low or incorrect.

    b.   the secondary processor has failed (or is not responding).

    c.   the primary processor fan has failed.

    d.   drive slot 2 is experiencing a fault.

72. Which of the following are *not* typical causes of parity errors?

    a.   One or more memory bits are intermittent or have failed entirely.

    b.   Poor connections between the memory module and socket.

    c.   Too many wait states entered in BIOS.

    d.   An intermittent failure or other fault has occurred in the power supply.

73. A server that encounters a power-on failure in the standby mode is best addressed by:

    a.   replacing the motherboard

    b.   replacing the processor(s)

    c.   resetting the CMOS Setup to BIOS default settings

    d.   replacing the power supply

74. Which of the following would be a MAC address?

    a.   192.168.1.1

    b.   00:04:5A:D1:9D:25

    c.   36g47-a

    d.   none of the above

75. What role does failover play in a NIC

    a. redundancy

    b. performance improvement

    c. upgrade potential

    d. all of the above

76. Which of the following attributes can improve NIC performance?

    a. select a NIC that supports direct memory access (DMA).

    b. select a NIC that supports shared adapter memory.

    c. select a NIC with shared system memory.

    d. all of the above.

77. What Windows 2000 utility is particularly useful for checking NIC performance?

    a. Event Viewer

    b. Performance Monitor

    c. System Event Log

    d. Security Log

78. If a NIC passes its internal diagnostics but cannot establish a network connection, you should first check:

    a. the NIC firmware version

    b. the NIC driver version

    c. the cable connection(s)

    d. the local hub or switch

79. When traffic passes across a NIC, you expect to see the:

    a. Activity LED blink

    b. Link LED blink

    c. Collision LED light solid

    d. Link LED light solid

80. What benefit can a RAID system provide to the server (and network):

    a. Data striping for improved R/W performance

    b. Disk spanning for larger logical drive spaces

    c. Disk mirroring for data redundancy

    d. all of the above

81. An extra (unused) disk drive that is part of the RAID disk subsystem is called a:

    a. backup disk

    b. hot spare

    c. D: drive

    d. logical drive

82. For basic disk mirroring, you'd use:

   a. RAID 0

   b. RAID 1

   c. RAID 2

   d. RAID 3

83. RAID controllers often cache their write and read operations in a large block of onboard RAM called a:

   a. RAID calibrator

   b. disk spanner

   c. battery backup

   d. array accelerator

84. A drive failure in a RAID array can usually be detected when:

   a. the operating system (or network console) indicates a logical drive failure.

   b. an LED illuminates on a failed drive in a hot-pluggable drive tray.

   c. the server's POST message lists failed drives.

   d. any of the above.

85. The inability to partition or format a RAID drive successfully may require you to:

   a. remove the drive's reserved sector.

   b. reinstall the network operating system.

   c. replace the server's RAID controller.

   d. inspect the drive signal cables.

86. In Table 11-2, a POST error of 1793 means that:

   a. the RAID controller card has failed.

   b. data in the array accelerator was lost.

   c. the RAID controller's firmware is corrupt.

   d. the array accelerator is loose or connected improperly.

87. Ultra3 SCSI can handle data transfers up to:

   a. 40 MB/s

   b. 80 MB/s

   c. 160 MB/s

   d. 320 MB/s

88. The fastest SCSI signaling uses:

   a. low-voltage differential signaling

   b. single-ended signaling

   c. differential signaling

   d. balanced low-voltage signaling

89. Intermittent SCSI signal problems are often caused by:

   a. improper termination

   b. faulty SCSI device(s)

   c. loose SCSI drive(s)

   d. none of the above

90. SCSI devices that do not appear to the operating system often:

   a. share an ID with another SCSI device

   b. are defective or improperly powered

   c. are incompatible with the host PC

   d. require a firmware upgrade

91. A SCSI error such as "start unit request failed" often means that:

   a. a timeout occurred while attempting to communicate with a SCSI device.

   b. the SCSI BIOS was unable to initiate a command to an installed SCSI device.

   c. the computer received no answer when requesting data from a SCSI device.

   d. the SCSI cable termination is missing or configured improperly.

92. A hub operates at which layer of the OSI model?

   a. application layer

   b. transport layer

   c. data link layer

   d. physical layer

93. Hubs with a "store-and-forward" capability can:

   a. look for damaged frames and make simple corrections.

   b. restrict retransmission to only desired network segments.

   c. improve network speed.

   d. all of the above.

94. Hubs can often be connected to one another using an:

   a. expansion port

   b. uplink port

   c. crosslink port

   d. regeneration port

95. An Ethernet cable must be less than:

   a. 100 ft

   b. 225 ft

   c. 328 ft

   d. 430 ft

96. Phantom addresses (jam bits) sent by a workstation generally mean that:

   a. the hub is defective.

   b. the cable between the hub and workstation is defective.

   c. the workstation's NIC is defective.

   d. the hub is not configured properly (or has locked up and requires a reboot).

97. Short interframe gaps may be caused by:

   a. NICs that transmit too soon after a collision

   b. NICs that do not maintain the proper spacing (9.6/0.96μs)

   c. packet fragments

   d. all of the above

98. The sporadic or continuous occurrence of beacon frames in a token ring network may indicate:

   a. a trunk concentrator unit (TCU) fault

   b. an intermittent workstation

   c. a faulty token ring NIC

   d. an extremely long lobe cable

99. A bridge that operates in a "learning mode" is also said to be operating in:

   a. bridge mode

   b. store-and-forward mode

   c. transparent bridging mode

   d. recall mode

100. You can use a bridge to:

   a. improve network security

   b. increase the length of the network

   c. reduce network congestion

   d. all of the above

101. A switch is used to forward an incoming frame:

   a. directly to the router or firewall for optimum network security

   b. directly to the network segment with the destination station

   c. directly to the nearest server

   d. all of the above

102. A switch that sends and receives data simultaneously on all its ports is in:

   a. full-duplex mode

   b. half-duplex mode

   c. switched-duplex mode

   d. omni-duplex mode

103. The "store-and-forward" switching technique:

    a. forwards each incoming frame as soon as it receives the header information

    b. does not make the forwarding decision until it has received the entire frame

    c. withholds a forwarding decision until the first 64 bytes of a packet are received

    d. forwards based on the number of runts and defective packets received at that port

104. A switch can be applied to:

    a. mix 10-Mbps and 100-Mbps Ethernet networks

    b. speed up a 10-Mbps network

    c. reduce traffic congestion on a network segment

    d. all of the above

105. The spanning tree algorithm can be used to:

    a. detect and disable network loops, and to provide backup links

    b. enable multiple bridges and routers for additional data handling capacity

    c. connect LAN segments located within the same geographic location

    d. none of the above

106. Switches that support "class of service" (CoS) features can:

    a. prioritize certain workstations over others

    b. buffer RAID data sent to certain network segments

    c. provide independent priorities for various types of data

    d. all of the above

107. The technique of "port trunking" allows:

    a. switch ports to be aggregated for higher data throughput

    b. additional network segments to be supported by the switch

    c. one or more switch ports to be disabled or slowed to handle low-priority segments

    d. all of the above

108. When there is no connection between segments linked by a switch, you should first:

    a. check the switch's configuration.

    b. replace the NIC on each affected workstation.

    c. update the switch's firmware.

    d. check the switch power and connections.

109. Distance vector and link state protocols are used in:

    a. data packet formation

    b. switching

    c. routing

    d. workstations

110. Routers operate at which layer of the OSI model?

   a. Layer 1

   b. Layer 2

   c. Layer 3

   d. Layer 4

111. A hacking tactic where a source address is made to look like it came from within your network is called:

   a. MAC address creation

   b. domain camouflage

   c. IP address spoofing

   d. OSI layer inversion

112. A stateful inspection device can:

   a. examine the source addresses of every packet

   b. examine the destination addresses of every packet

   c. track each request (and response) to be sure that they match

   d. all of the above

113. Well-known ports include ports:

   a. 1 to 1,023

   b. 512 to 2,048

   c. 1,024 to 49,151

   d. above 49,152

114. A "dictionary attack" is a hacker's attempt to discover your:

   a. IP address

   b. MAC address

   c. domain name

   d. password

115. Your first response to an attempted system attack should be to:

   a. prosecute the attacker with extreme prejudice.

   b. configure the firewall to block the attacker.

   c. upgrade the operating system.

   d. identify the attacker using the Whois database.

116. A parallel port printer can be interfaced to a network using a:

   a. print server

   b. print queue

   c. NIC adapter

   d. printer driver

117. Network path names for printers under Microsoft OS versions usually appear like:

    a. \\computer name\printer name

    b. //computer name/printer alias

    c. \\printer name\computer name

    d. \\computer alias\printer model

118. Printing with the lpd protocol is usually available under:

    a. Windows

    b. UNIX

    c. NetWare

    d. OS/2

119. A Status LED continuously lit on a print server often means that:

    a. the printer has crashed.

    b. the printer cable has been disconnected.

    c. the printer driver is corrupt.

    d. the print server has crashed.

120. In standby mode, your computer's current state is saved:

    a. to RAM

    b. to disk

    c. to another PC on the network

    d. none of the above

121. The current specification used to define power management behavior is called:

    a. APC

    b. AIM

    c. ACPI

    d. DHCP

122. You may not be able to use power conservation schemes with your monitor if:

    a. the monitor is less than one year old.

    b. the video driver doesn't fully support power conservation standards.

    c. the video adapter is defective or using an older version of DirectX.

    d. all of the above.

123. A UPS that only operates a load (provides battery power) when ac is lost is called an:

    a. online UPS

    b. quick-response UPS

    c. offline UPS

    d. light-load UPS

124. In order to ensure that PCs don't reboot before a UPS kicks in, select a UPS with a fast:

   a. current discharge curve

   b. transfer time

   c. surge suppressor

   d. protective fuse

125. The running time of a UPS depends on:

   a. the battery capacity and attached load

   b. the ac voltage level powering the UPS

   c. the number of days that the UPS has charged

   d. all of the above

126. A UPS "overload" alarm usually means:

   a. the battery pack is failing and must be replaced.

   b. the UPS control circuit has failed.

   c. the ac voltage charging the UPS is too high.

   d. the attached load is too high.

127. An NAS passthrough mode will:

   a. take user and group information from a primary domain controller

   b. automatically assign IP addresses to stations on the network

   c. allow the network to operate even when the NAS is turned off

   d. automatically send network queries to subsequent NAS units

128. When you cannot administer a NAS unit, you should first:

   a. check power and network connections.

   b. try a different port on the hub or switch.

   c. connect the cable directly to your PC.

   d. reboot the NAS and see if the trouble clears.

129. A high number of NAS drive errors may indicate:

   a. excessive traffic on the network segment

   b. an incorrect IP address assignment

   c. a serious problem with one or more NAS drives

   d. none of the above

130. A destructive program concealed as a useful, run-of-the-mill program is usually called a:

   a. software bug

   b. Trojan horse

   c. logic bomb

   d. worm

131. Anti-virus tools must be kept up-to-date by:

    a. periodically uninstalling and reinstalling them

    b. running more than one anti-virus program

    c. executing an infected file to see if the anti-virus tool catches it

    d. updating the virus signature file used by the anti-virus software

132. You're more likely to see false detections if:

    a. you do not keep the anti-virus tools up-to-date.

    b. you have anti-virus software from more than one vendor installed.

    c. you frequently download compressed files from the Internet.

    d. all of the above.

133. You can typically deal with a virus by:

    a. attempting a repair

    b. quarantining the infected file(s)

    c. deleting the infected file(s)

    d. all of the above

134. If you cannot remove a memory-resident anti-virus tool, you should first:

    a. check for a conflicting TSR or background application running in the system.

    b. check for disk problems or excessive file fragmentation.

    c. check for Link LEDs and other signs of adequate network connections.

    d. check for updates or patches for the anti-virus tool.

135. For the most complete backup, you'd use:

    a. an incremental backup

    b. a full backup

    c. a differential backup

    d. a sequential backup

136. The best insurance that a backup is valid would be:

    a. to store a backup off-site

    b. to rotate tapes regularly

    c. to leave the tape in a drive

    d. to verify the backup

137. Automatic Data Protection (ADP) would be used:

    a. to edit the contents of a tape

    b. to schedule regular (and unattended) backups

    c. to back up the setup files of each network router or bridge

    d. none of the above

138. Superior backup results can be achieved when:

   a. backups are performed regularly and consistently.

   b. backups are properly labeled and stored.

   c. adequate testing and maintenance are performed.

   d. all of the above.

139. Dropouts, media errors, and read/write errors are often attributed to:

   a. improper tape type in the drive

   b. inadequate head cleaning

   c. user errors in planning a backup

   d. tape drive failures

140. A BOT/EOT error is usually caused by:

   a. improperly installed or configured backup software

   b. anti-virus software conflicting with the backup software

   c. a defective (despooled) tape cartridge

   d. inadequate tape drive power

141. Backups that take an unusually long time to complete may be caused by:

   a. inadequate RAM in the PC performing the backup

   b. conflicting programs in the Startup folder

   c. one or more local disks running in DOS Compatibility Mode

   d. all of the above

142. The most difficult and frustrating part of network planning is often:

   a. choosing the vendors

   b. selecting subcontractors

   c. setting clear objectives

   d. running cable in the building

143. Network resources that need to be restricted through a common security scheme typically demand:

   a. a client/server network scheme

   b. a peer-to-peer network scheme

   c. a powerful server to provide enhanced security

   d. additional training for network users

144. Ethernet networks are often selected for their:

   a. high collision rates

   b. ease of troubleshooting

   c. self-monitoring ability

   d. time-critical performance

145. Total immunity from EMI/RFI will require the use of:

    a. UTP cable

    b. STP cable

    c. FO cable

    d. coaxial cable

146. Network computers intended for high mobility will benefit from:

    a. wireless connections

    b. UTP connections

    c. FO connections

    d. BNC connections

147. Routing tables often include information such as:

    a. all known network addresses

    b. instructions for connection to other networks

    c. the possible paths between routers

    d. all of the above

148. User accounts are normally organized into sets, more commonly known as:

    a. packages

    b. hierarchies

    c. groups

    d. pages

149. Proper server maintenance involves regularly:

    a. checking for viruses

    b. checking and tuning drives

    c. performing backup operations

    d. all of the above

150. A bus topology suffering from frequent network crashes or downtime due to cabling issues might benefit from an upgrade to a:

    a. larger type of coaxial cable

    b. star or ring topology

    c. a hub with additional ports

    d. new network segment to hold some additional stations

151. One of the most important issues of network upgrades is:

    a. hardware compatibility

    b. backup reliability

    c. traffic throughput

    d. user satisfaction

152. Before you attempt a BIOS upgrade, you must first:

   a. determine the age of the PC.

   b. remove the NIC.

   c. determine the current BIOS version.

   d. determine the current OS version.

153. The BIOS "boot block" feature allows you to:

   a. recover the original BIOS from a file on diskette.

   b. automatically download and install new BIOS versions.

   c. use BIOS versions from other PCs.

   d. none of the above.

154. When upgrading a NIC, you should first:

   a. install the new NIC drivers.

   b. remove the old NIC drivers.

   c. update the OS to its latest version or Service Pack.

   d. run diagnostics to verify the old NIC.

155. What should you *not* do when replacing a hot-pluggable drive?

   a. never remove more than one drive at a time.

   b. never remove a working drive when another drive has failed.

   c. never remove a drive while another drive is being rebuilt.

   d. all of the above.

156. Heat spreaders are typically found on which memory module(s)?

   a. SIMMs

   b. DIMMs

   c. RIMMs

   d. all of the above

157. When installing more than one CPU, verify that each processor:

   a. is using the same voltage

   b. is using the same bus multiplier

   c. is matched with the same revision level

   d. is using the same heat sink type

158. A markup language defines document appearance with:

   a. codes called "tags"

   b. VisualBasic script

   c. meta-labels

   d. hypertext links

159. Customizable Web pages are often provided through:

 a. HTML

 b. DHTML

 c. ASP

 d. none of the above

160. Content expiration allows site developers to:

 a. restrict objectionable or inappropriate site content.

 b. disable old or outdated site content.

 c. reuse content in other Web sites.

 d. none of the above.

161. A server that only allows as many connections as there are installed licenses is termed:

 a. per-seat licensing

 b. per-site licensing

 c. per-server licensing

 d. per-network licensing

162. If you need to check and debug scripts written in VBScript and Jscript, you should install:

 a. MS Script Debugger

 b. Message Queuing Services

 c. Networking Services

 d. Active Directory

163. An administrative grouping of computers on a Windows 2000 network that allows the network's resources to be administered from a single point is referred to as a:

 a. workgroup

 b. DNS

 c. domain

 d. certificate

164. Every network user must be established with:

 a. a user account

 b. a share

 c. a domain

 d. a disk drive

165. Every user in Windows 2000 Server domain is assigned a special number called a:

 a. password

 b. MAC address

 c. security ID

 d. switch port

166. Ideal passwords contain:

    a. more than eight characters

    b. letters and numbers

    c. special characters

    d. all of the above

167. The most common type of Windows 2000 group is a:

    a. distribution group

    b. security group

    c. universal group

    d. built-in group

168. Under Linux, drive partitions are treated as:

    a. master boot records

    b. directories

    c. physical disks

    d. applications

169. Where are Linux configuration files kept?

    a. /etc

    b. /home

    c. /usr

    d. /var

170. When installing Linux over a previous OS (and you no longer need the old OS), you should:

    a. remove all partitions on the system.

    b. remove all Linux partitions on the system.

    c. keep existing partitions and use free space.

    d. none of the above.

171. What purpose does GRUB serve under Linux?

    a. disk defragmenter

    b. file integrity checker

    c. boot loader

    d. desktop environment

172. What purpose does KDE serve under Linux?

    a. disk defragmenter

    b. file integrity checker

    c. boot loader

    d. desktop environment

173. The Linux root password is generally used by the:

   a. department head

   b. sales manager

   c. administrator

   d. research assistant

174. When faced with a logon issue, you should first:

   a. verify that the user's account exists.

   b. verify the user's logon credentials.

   c. verify that the account is not impaired.

   d. verify the user's logon hours.

175. How can you discourage users from changing back and forth between a set of common passwords?

   a. set a maximum password age.

   b. set a minimum password age.

   c. enforce password history.

   d. all of the above.

176. You can make passwords easier to remember by:

   a. reducing the minimum password length policy

   b. disabling password complexity requirements

   c. not requiring users to change their password

   d. all of the above

177. You might reduce the Account Lockout Threshold policy when:

   a. remote users are faced with poor connection speeds.

   b. users are frequently entering bad passwords.

   c. users are planning a vacation.

   d. users leave the company or change departments.

178. Routine logon tasks can be automated with:

   a. administrative rights

   b. Kerberos policies

   c. logon scripts

   d. event logs

179. Which tactic(s) can help to relieve logon problems?

   a. enforce reasonable password policies.

   b. place a backup domain controller (BDC) on every physical subnet.

   c. keep track of user accounts.

   d. all of the above.

180. You can detect failed logon attempts by checking the:

   a.   application log

   b.   security log

   c.   system log

   d.   file replication service log

181. Normal network performance can often be quantified by:

   a.   establishing a baseline

   b.   formatting the disk system

   c.   updating the RAID level

   d.   adding users to a new network segment

182. If your network supports a bandwidth of 100 Mbps and you're experiencing a throughput of 30 Mbps, the network's utilization is:

   a.   10 percent

   b.   20 percent

   c.   30 percent

   d.   40 percent

183. The effectiveness of a network upgrade can often be gauged by checking:

   a.   top talkers

   b.   protocol distribution

   c.   efficiency history

   d.   maximum throughput

184. Stations causing broadcast storms can often be identified by checking:

   a.   top talkers

   b.   protocol distribution

   c.   efficiency history

   d.   maximum throughput

185. With memory, the current number of physical memory bytes used by a process is termed:

   a.   % Processor Time

   b.   Working Set

   c.   Available Bytes

   d.   Avg. Disk sec/Transfer

186. The time a disk takes to fulfill requests is termed:

   a.   % Processor Time

   b.   Working Set

   c.   Available Bytes

   d.   Avg. Disk sec/Transfer

187. The fault management features of good management platforms allow you to:

    a. gather comprehensive information about hardware devices.

    b. list software and drivers installed on network systems.

    c. solve problems and troubleshoot network devices.

    d. all of the above.

188. Physical devices on the managed network are normally represented as:

    a. managed disk drives

    b. managed folders

    c. managed icons

    d. managed objects

189. Devices in a network are defined in the:

    a. SNMP

    b. CIM

    c. MIB

    d. SMART

190. Logical connection problems with a managed device can often be fixed by:

    a. rebooting the local hub or switch

    b. rebooting the suspect managed device

    c. rebooting the management console PC

    d. rebooting the network's router

191. Which of the following is not part of the universal troubleshooting procedure?

    a. report the findings to the customer.

    b. identify and isolate.

    c. replace the defective device.

    d. retest the system.

192. Introducing new devices or software in phases is generally known as a:

    a. rollout

    b. beta

    c. alpha

    d. transfer

193. When a single PC fails to respond, but the system powers up normally, you should next:

    a. check the user's account.

    b. check the station's connection.

    c. check for viruses.

    d. check the hub or switch.

194. A problem that affects an entire segment (or group) can often be traced to:

    a. the local hub or switch power

    b. the cable (backbone) to a higher hub or switch

    c. the local hub or switch configuration

    d. all of the above

195. Which utility can be used to check the connection between two stations?

    a. Netstat

    b. Ping

    c. Ipconfig

    d. Tracert

196. Which utility can be used to check the route between two stations?

    a. Netstat

    b. Ping

    c. Ipconfig

    d. Tracert

197. What feature(s) does a protocol analyzer offer?

    a. Locate nodes generating excessive errors.

    b. Filter packets for viewing (by protocol or type of packet).

    c. Analyze network utilization and efficiency.

    d. all of the above.

198. The "monitor" or "through" connection for a protocol analyzer usually involves:

    a. placing the analyzer inline between a switch port and a server

    b. placing the analyzer in any available hub or switch port

    c. installing the analyzer in place of the nearest network server

    d. none of the above

199. Alignment errors (sometimes called Ethernet alignment errors) are detected when:

    a. a network cable is damaged or disconnected.

    b. a hub port is configured improperly.

    c. a packet is not aligned on a transmission's phase boundary.

    d. the protocol analyzer is not installed properly.

200. When the packet generated by the NIC appears to be correct, but the protocol section of the packet is corrupt, this is normally seen as:

    a. an alignment error

    b. a bad IP checksum

    c. a jabber frame

    d. a jumbo frame

Congratulations! This completes the DLS Network Technician's Certificate examination. Before sending in the exam, be sure to take some time and check your answers, make sure that only *one* answer is marked for each question, verify that you have answered *every* question, and see that your contact/billing information on the cover sheet is correct and complete.

DLS Network Technician's Certificate Exam 1.0

Information Cover Sheet

Please print clearly

Name: _____

Address: _____

_____

City: _____

State: _ _   Zip or Postal Code: _____

Country (other than USA): _____

Telephone: _____

E-mail: _____

♦   the above information is required for proper grading, and to receive proper credit. Tests with incomplete information **cannot** be processed.

Method of Payment

Please Check One

___ Personal or Business *check* for **$50** (US)‡

___ MasterCard *charge* of $50 (US).   Card: _____

___ VISA *charge* of $50 (US).   Exp: __/__/__   Sig: _____

Mail to: **Dynamic Learning Systems, P.O. Box 402, Leicester, MA 01524 USA**

Fax to: **508-892-1482**   (24 hrs/day, 7 days/week)

‡ mail *only* - tests without payment cannot be processed. No Purchase Orders accepted.

DLS Network Technician's Certificate 1.0

Answer Sheet 1 of 2

Please Circle Only One Letter Corresponding to Each Answer

1 A B C D	26 A B C D	51 A B C D	76 A B C D
2 A B C D	27 A B C D	52 A B C D	77 A B C D
3 A B C D	28 A B C D	53 A B C D	78 A B C D
4 A B C D	29 A B C D	54 A B C D	79 A B C D
5 A B C D	30 A B C D	55 A B C D	80 A B C D
6 A B C D	31 A B C D	56 A B C D	81 A B C D
7 A B C D	32 A B C D	57 A B C D	82 A B C D
8 A B C D	33 A B C D	58 A B C D	83 A B C D
9 A B C D	34 A B C D	59 A B C D	84 A B C D
10 A B C D	35 A B C D	60 A B C D	85 A B C D
11 A B C D	36 A B C D	61 A B C D	86 A B C D
12 A B C D	37 A B C D	62 A B C D	87 A B C D
13 A B C D	38 A B C D	63 A B C D	88 A B C D
14 A B C D	39 A B C D	64 A B C D	89 A B C D
15 A B C D	40 A B C D	65 A B C D	90 A B C D
16 A B C D	41 A B C D	66 A B C D	91 A B C D
17 A B C D	42 A B C D	67 A B C D	92 A B C D
18 A B C D	43 A B C D	68 A B C D	93 A B C D
19 A B C D	44 A B C D	69 A B C D	94 A B C D
20 A B C D	45 A B C D	70 A B C D	95 A B C D
21 A B C D	46 A B C D	71 A B C D	96 A B C D
22 A B C D	47 A B C D	72 A B C D	97 A B C D
23 A B C D	48 A B C D	73 A B C D	98 A B C D
24 A B C D	49 A B C D	74 A B C D	99 A B C D
25 A B C D	50 A B C D	75 A B C D	100 A B C D

DLS Network Technician's Certificate 1.0

Answer Sheet 2 of 2

Please Circle Only One Letter Corresponding to Each Answer

101 A B C D	126 A B C D	151 A B C D	176 A B C D
102 A B C D	127 A B C D	152 A B C D	177 A B C D
103 A B C D	128 A B C D	153 A B C D	178 A B C D
104 A B C D	129 A B C D	154 A B C D	179 A B C D
105 A B C D	130 A B C D	155 A B C D	180 A B C D
106 A B C D	131 A B C D	156 A B C D	181 A B C D
107 A B C D	132 A B C D	157 A B C D	182 A B C D
108 A B C D	133 A B C D	158 A B C D	183 A B C D
109 A B C D	134 A B C D	159 A B C D	184 A B C D
110 A B C D	135 A B C D	160 A B C D	185 A B C D
111 A B C D	136 A B C D	161 A B C D	186 A B C D
112 A B C D	137 A B C D	162 A B C D	187 A B C D
113 A B C D	138 A B C D	163 A B C D	188 A B C D
114 A B C D	139 A B C D	164 A B C D	189 A B C D
115 A B C D	140 A B C D	165 A B C D	190 A B C D
116 A B C D	141 A B C D	166 A B C D	191 A B C D
117 A B C D	142 A B C D	167 A B C D	192 A B C D
118 A B C D	143 A B C D	168 A B C D	193 A B C D
119 A B C D	144 A B C D	169 A B C D	194 A B C D
120 A B C D	145 A B C D	170 A B C D	195 A B C D
121 A B C D	146 A B C D	171 A B C D	196 A B C D
122 A B C D	147 A B C D	172 A B C D	197 A B C D
123 A B C D	148 A B C D	173 A B C D	198 A B C D
124 A B C D	149 A B C D	174 A B C D	199 A B C D
125 A B C D	150 A B C D	175 A B C D	200 A B C D

INDEX

INTERNATIONAL CONTACT INFORMATION

AUSTRALIA
McGraw-Hill Book Company Australia Pty. Ltd.
TEL +61-2-9415-9899
FAX +61-2-9415-5687
http://www.mcgraw-hill.com.au
books-it_sydney@mcgraw-hill.com

CANADA
McGraw-Hill Ryerson Ltd.
TEL +905-430-5000
FAX +905-430-5020
http://www.mcgrawhill.ca

GREECE, MIDDLE EAST,
NORTHERN AFRICA
McGraw-Hill Hellas
TEL +30-1-656-0990-3-4
FAX +30-1-654-5525

MEXICO (Also serving Latin America)
McGraw-Hill Interamericana Editores S.A. de C.V.
TEL +525-117-1583
FAX +525-117-1589
http://www.mcgraw-hill.com.mx
fernando_castellanos@mcgraw-hill.com

SINGAPORE (Serving Asia)
McGraw-Hill Book Company
TEL +65-863-1580
FAX +65-862-3354
http://www.mcgraw-hill.com.sg
mghasia@mcgraw-hill.com

SOUTH AFRICA
McGraw-Hill South Africa
TEL +27-11-622-7512
FAX +27-11-622-9045
robyn_swanepoel@mcgraw-hill.com

UNITED KINGDOM & EUROPE
(Excluding Southern Europe)
McGraw-Hill Education Europe
TEL +44-1-628-502500
FAX +44-1-628-770224
http://www.mcgraw-hill.co.uk
computing_neurope@mcgraw-hill.com

ALL OTHER INQUIRIES Contact:
Osborne/McGraw-Hill
TEL +1-510-549-6600
FAX +1-510-883-7600
http://www.osborne.com
omg_international@mcgraw-hill.com